2015/16

THE GUIDE TO

UK COMPANY GIVING

TENTH EDITION

Denise Lillya, Jennifer Reynolds and Gabriele Zagnojute

Additional research by:
Ian Pembridge, Tom Traynor and Emma Weston

dsc
directory of social change

Published by the Directory of Social Change (Registered Charity no. 800517 in England and Wales)

Head office: Resource for London, 352 Holloway Rd, London N7 6PA

Northern office: Suite 103, 1 Old Hall Street, Liverpool L3 9HG

Tel: 08450 77 77 07

Visit www.dsc.org.uk to find out more about our books, subscription funding websites and training events. You can also sign up for e-newsletters so that you're always the first to hear about what's new.

The publisher welcomes suggestions and comments that will help to inform and improve future versions of this and all of our titles. Please give us your feedback by emailing publications@dsc.org.uk.

First published 1998
Second edition 1999
Third edition 2000
Fourth edition 2002
Fifth edition 2004
Sixth edition 2007
Seventh edition 2009
Eighth edition 2011
Ninth edition 2013
Tenth edition 2015

ISBN 978 1 906294 99 1

British Library Cataloguing in Publication Data
A catalogue record for this book is available from the British Library

Cover and text design by Kate Bass
Typeset by Marlinzo Services, Frome
Printed and bound by Page Bros, Norwich

MIX
Paper from responsible sources
FSC® C023114
FSC
www.fsc.org

Contents

Foreword

Today, perhaps more than ever, CSR is considered an integral, strategic competitive activity rather than an important if marginalised add-on.

What's more, as we continue through this period of austerity, a flexible and agile approach to CSR, and those that recognise how and when to change, will allow the most progressive businesses to gain the greatest competitive advantage and to drive added value.

In such periods of rapid change, guides like *The Guide to UK Company Giving* can be part of the armoury to aid businesses and charities alike to identify emerging trends in company giving and adapt accordingly.

At The Co-operative we have continuously sought to respond to the changing commercial and societal environment in which we operate and with a history as long as ours (we were formed in 1844) we have been well placed to respond to some of the defining issues of our time. One hundred years ago we campaigned for universal suffrage; more than two decades ago we were one of the first businesses to recognise and respond to climate change; and throughout our history our commitment to ethical trade (and latterly Fairtrade) has seen us respond to matters of inequality and human rights.

We continue to take a bottom up approach, engaging our members in their communities to help identify the issues that are most relevant to them today, issues of national significance with a local impact and where we could look to make a real difference, whether that be responding to the challenges faced by young people, building stronger, more resilient communities or improving the sustainability of our food, for example reducing food waste.

We need to see a move away from the more established company giving activity built primarily on raising money for charitable causes, to the formation of partnerships that seek to deliver campaign aims and to bring about tangible, measureable changes in society.

In this way businesses and charity partners can focus increasingly on the long-term, systemic change that they can bring about. Such partnerships need to be increasingly about the solution as about the fundraising, in which businesses can mobilise their assets, not least their employee volunteers, to build a lasting legacy.

The Guide to UK Company Giving is an invaluable resource to connect businesses, charities, community groups and voluntary organisations with shared interests to help develop this exciting evolution in company giving activity.

Barry Clavin
Ethical Policies and Sustainability Reporting Manager, The Co-operative Group

Introduction

Welcome to the tenth edition of *The Guide to UK Company Giving* which continues to provide relevant, updated policy information and commentary on the current state of corporate community involvement in the UK.

This edition features 400 companies, and for the first time, full details of 114 associated corporate charities, which together gave around £658 million (ninth edition: £598.5 million) in community support, including £369 million in cash donations (ninth edition: £470.1 million), mostly in the financial years 2013 or 2013/14.

There appears to be a significant reduction in the total amount given in cash donations from the previous edition and this may be for a number of reasons, rather than one overriding cause.

First, when undertaking the research for this edition of the guide we came across a high number of companies which had chosen not to declare their charitable donations in their annual report and accounts. This is now a choice for companies following the reforms to the Companies Act 2006 brought in by the Department for Business, Innovation and Skills in 2013 (which came into force for periods ending on or after 30 September 2013). However, where possible, we have estimated a figure based on previous research and so this may not have affected the actual cash total substantially.

Added to this we found during our research that some companies have ceased to exist, been taken over by other companies, or have suspended their charitable giving, perhaps sometimes due to a merger or because of decreasing profits. Where no evidence of potential cash donations or significant community contributions could be found, those companies have been omitted.

There are also fewer entries in this edition as we have focused our research on those companies that give more substantial amounts. However, again, we do not think that this affects the total in any significant way as those companies that have been omitted are known to give under £5,000 a year.

Finally, and significantly, the top UK 25 cash contributors gave £69.7 million less than in the ninth edition. This is the equivalent to the value of each position in the table decreasing on average by £2.8 million.

The new corporate charities section on page 387 is a review of information on 114 corporate charities established by and/or closely associated with a company listed in the guide, and acting as a channel for its charitable giving. We look into the topic in more detail on page xi. We trust that this will be of real use to our readers when looking for charitable funding given by companies.

Each of the 400 company entries provides essential information for accessing funding and other resources. Throughout our research we look at thousands of pages of annual reports, accounts and corporate social responsibility (CSR) reports as well as the companies' own websites, with the aim of providing a comprehensive overview of the community-related activities by a particular business. The entries primarily look at the direct financial support provided by the company; however, we are also interested in other types of support, such as in-kind donations, and make a note of commercially led, yet community-related initiatives, or other community-orientated contributions by the company.

Most of the guide consists of individual company entries, but it contains additional sections offering advice and information for fundraisers, voluntary organisations, community groups, companies and individuals.

Company information

Our basic criteria for inclusion are that the company has made either: cash donations; gifts in kind such as equipment, volunteering, mentoring or secondment of its staff; and/or provided sponsorship or established partnerships in support of the community.

Wherever possible, we have quoted the UK charitable donations figure declared by the company in its annual report and accounts, as this provides a tangible and unambiguous indicator of its commitment to the community. Failing this, and where appropriate, we quote the worldwide donations figure, while making it clear that this is the case.

Where companies have made the (in our view regressive and short-sighted) choice not to declare their charitable donations following the government reforms just mentioned, we have estimated the company's donation based on case studies, information on its activities taken from its website and previous DSC research. In most cases we have taken an average of the last three years' cash UK totals from our database and used this as these companies' 2013/14 UK cash donation.

We do acknowledge that cash donations are not the only way in which companies provide support for charities and community groups. In many instances, and increasingly, the support given by companies in resources far outweighs their cash donations.

Since CSR reporting does not follow an agreed format, there is a range of ways in which companies choose to outline their contributions to society. Some corporate bodies now choose to refer to the support given as 'community/social investment' or 'community/social contributions', which often comprise all types of assistance available: cash, in-kind gifts, employee and customer fundraising, volunteering time, commercially led initiatives and management costs to the company.

Unfortunately, a breakdown of the overall amount is not always given and companies do not show separate details of the cost of the different types of support, rather just the total cost to the company. This is not so useful for our purposes where we want to show our readers what is available both in cash and in in-kind gifts and services.

These blanket terms of 'social investment/community contributions' are often misleading and can relate to payments, activities or services which should be part of the company's good practice rather than regarded as a philanthropic benefit to the community. For example, there are companies where, although the company provides charitable contributions, part of its overall community or social 'investment' is directly related to amending the adverse impact of its own business activities, or a company might state that its community investment includes creating employment. Occasionally CSR reviews will claim recognition for what are clearly mandatory operating standards, such as the payment of tax.

The means of measuring the value of 'social investment' contributions, and even what should be included under this heading, are open to debate. In our view, the term should cover a company's charitable donations and the value of gifts in kind, such as equipment, pro bono work, secondments and employee volunteering during company time. In light of that, where possible, we have deducted management costs, employee- or customer-raised donations and similar amounts from the total sum, making it clear that this is the case. We believe this allows a clearer picture of the scale of contributions made available by the company to the community and is what our readers are interested in.

Where applicable, we also specify details of any existing or previous charity partnerships. Quite often these will be in a form of a Charity of the Year programme, whereby the company will support and/or staff members will fundraise/volunteer for (usually) employee-chosen causes. See a helpful overview of such partnerships on page xv.

Various partnerships between the private and voluntary sectors have been a popular way for companies to engage with communities as well as enhancing their brand reputation. It appears to be a general rule that most companies will choose to support partners that are closely associated with the nature of their business activities and/or in the area where the company has a presence.

Many businesses view their responsibilities in the communities where they operate to be essential to their 'licence to operate' – a notion that featured in a number of CSR reports. Royal Mail plc for instance states:

> *Many local community groups have suffered significant cuts to their funding following the economic downturn. The role that Royal Mail people and their fundraising efforts play in supporting these groups is therefore all the more important. Many of these organisations are key support mechanisms, providing services to vulnerable people and strengthening the health and wellbeing of the community. We consider it a natural extension of our presence within local communities to support them in their work.*
>
> **Royal Mail 2014**

The company may be more likely to support causes related to its business activities as it will often have a good indication of particular issues affecting its target audience. For instance, Simmons & Simmons LLP, a legal firm, noted that in response to the legal aid cuts made in England and Wales from April 2013, which affect the most vulnerable in the community, the firm has increased its commitment and support provided to both individuals and community groups via LawWorks, the legal pro bono charity for solicitors, in-house counsel, mediators and students which 'identifies need, brokers casework and connects volunteer lawyers with communities nationwide' (Simmons & Simmons 2014).

During our research we found that companies are also often more inclined to support causes that are important to their employees or shareholders. This way a variety of support can be delivered – financial, employee-led and other support. Perhaps unsurprisingly companies favour initiatives that bring some benefit to the business, for example, many recognise the staff development opportunities emerging from volunteering activities and are willing to support such employee involvement.

Furthermore, education and employment-related initiatives while benefiting the community also neatly fit in with the diversity agenda. We know that a number of male-dominated markets are increasingly working in partnership with educational and voluntary organisations to target female students to choose a particular career path, with the aim of eventually increasing female participation in a particular industry. A number of companies, particularly those concerned with industrial markets or science and technology, also have various educational and training schemes for young people and co-operate with educational establishments and non-profit organisations to invest financial resources or in-kind product donations as well as provide services such as career guidance and employability skills development sessions delivered by the staff. We can clearly see that these arrangements are mutually beneficial.

Whilst we often see the largest companies partnering with the well-known national charities, there is no reason similar principles would not apply on a more regional level, providing help to smaller, more community-based organisations. Nevertheless, for many charities, direct grants will remain the most desirable and the most suitable form of support and for the businesses the most practical and effective way of giving.

We specify in-kind contributions, employee involvement and commercially led activities separately and give useful examples of the types of initiatives undertaken. The term 'gifts in kind' can be misleading – it can include anything from the 'gift' of an old computer or a group of willing but unfocused volunteers with little to offer practically, to the really worthwhile contribution of pro bono legal or accountancy work provided by some private, professional firms, or the secondment of a key member of staff to achieve a significant target or the restructure a charity.

The term would have originally referred to goods, pieces of furniture or items of equipment (nearly always second-hand), whereas now, with CSR high on the agenda for many companies, they are increasingly offering staff time and skills as gifts in kind, which can be a very valuable asset for a charity and equally provide valuable new skills and experience for staff development. However, the term is often used in relation to physical items alone without reference to professional or support services, and this can cause confusion.

Throughout the entries we note the presence of payroll giving and matched funding schemes as well as other employee involvement initiatives, for example, a lottery for the company's employees with the proportion of income being available for charitable donations.

Finally, we include examples of any cause-related marketing initiatives that a company may have undertaken; however, we do not include this in the total community contributions figure for the year because the motivation and first priority of such giving is the company's profits and is not driven by philanthropy. Such examples, although of secondary focus here, include some interesting initiatives; for example, following legal changes in Wales requiring all retailers to charge for single use carrier bags, a number of businesses chose to donate all or part of the proceeds to good causes, thus significantly increasing the funds available for the Welsh voluntary sector.

Entry layout

The layouts used for the entries in this guide are described in the breakdown of the fictional company entry, 'Fictitious Productions plc', on page xxxvi. We hope that this example will help users in accessing the information they require on the various types of support that each company offers.

Geographical and activity indexes

Most companies state that a link between the company and the charity must exist for any appeal to be considered. The most obvious links are geographical, business activity or employee involvement. To help you prepare a preliminary list of companies to look at further, we have included a registered/head office location index (see page 457) and a company activity listing (see page 464). Although the office address index is geographically biased towards London, it provides a useful starting point.

Comprehensive search facilities are available at DSC's subscription-based website: www.companygiving.org.uk.

Company listings

There are companies which, by virtue of membership of one or more specific organisations, have declared an interest in supporting the community. So, even though the companies concerned do not necessarily have an entry in this guide (because they do not meet our criteria), we have listed all current corporate members of Business in the Community (BITC), Scottish Business in the Community and LBG (London Benchmarking Group). We have also listed those companies which have achieved BITC's Community Mark status which recognises companies that take an active and more holistic approach to community investment.

Details of ProHelp are also included as potentially a very useful source of support for charities. ProHelp is made up of a group of professional practices (including surveyors, architects, accountants and solicitors), each of which has offered to provide their professional services free of charge (or at minimal cost) to voluntary and community groups in their area. See further details on page 455.

Company comparisons

The level of giving by companies in this guide varies greatly and covers a range of channels. Contributions can range from staff volunteering days with minimal or no cash donations given by the company, to tens of millions of pounds from funds contributed through customer fundraising schemes matched by the company, to considerable amounts channelled solely through a corporate charity. Although the 'big giver' is often equated with 'most generous', this could be misleading. Whilst very large companies may give large amounts in cash, smaller companies that give a few hundred thousand pounds may actually be contributing a far greater proportion of their profits to charity. Moreover, measuring social or community impact does not rely solely on money given for good causes and, as can be seen in the examples throughout the book, will often include mutually beneficial partnerships between charities and businesses, where financial assistance will only form part of the contribution.

Some companies' donation levels remain fairly constant year on year, while others' fluctuate significantly, and this often depends on the company's economic position. There are fluctuations for a variety of reasons – a poor year for the company in terms of profits, a change in its community giving policy, cutting down on cash donations and giving gifts in kind instead, or simply because in one year the company decided to substantially boost the free reserves of its associated charity, thereby skewing its giving figures in that particular year.

The entries in this guide list both the latest published figures available at the time of writing and, where obtainable, the amounts contributed in the previous year so that readers can see the company's giving patterns. Predicting and analysing company trends and making comparisons year on year can be a difficult task with so many variables to take into account. This has been further exacerbated by the unwillingness of many companies to declare UK-specific donations and recently any charitable donations at all.

Many companies are choosing neither to provide any sort of breakdown of the overall global figure in terms of each country where they give nor to specify what has been given in real terms, and an increased number no longer declare any figure. The reluctance of the majority of companies to be truly transparent leads to confusion over not only who gave most but also what they gave and what it is that applicants should be realistically applying for.

Where available, the entries in this book specify details of the company's CSR policy, reporting and governance, and it is clear that *most* of the companies in this guide invest significant amounts of time and resources to prepare an overview of their community investment. Nevertheless, even the most elaborate sustainability sections within the annual report and the thickest CSR reports can fail to include any conclusive figures on the money given, volunteering hours provided, equipment or products gifted, and so on. If companies state that funding or support is part of their commitment to their communities and they reap the benefits that this brings, then it is not unreasonable to ask what the breakdown of the contribution was, where it went, what good it did and how the successful applicants were selected.

Facts and figures

How much do companies give?

While the new legislation introduced (the recent changes to the Companies Act 2006 referred to earlier) has increased levels of reporting on environmental issues, employees, and social, community and human rights, since its introduction, obtaining figures for corporate charitable donations has become much more difficult.

From our research of 400 companies we found that 165 (41.25%) did not declare charitable donations in their last year's reporting. This figure relates to companies which historically have declared their charitable donations. This does not take into account the companies whose accounts were published before the date of the legislation coming into force and so, the actual proportion of companies that no longer declare charitable donations may be higher.

With companies no longer having a legal obligation to declare charitable donations, the area surrounding company giving is becoming increasingly opaque. Obtaining figures for companies' giving is becoming dependent on their own commitment to transparency and, as a result, we have been hindered in our efforts to depict a truly accurate picture of financial support which may be available from the corporate sector.

Even for those companies from whose accounts we were able to gather a figure for charitable donations, figures for total community contributions often remain difficult to obtain.

Some companies (the global figure is more than 300) are members of LBG and, using its model, make available a clear breakdown of their community giving. LBG companies work together to measure corporate community investment. The LBG model provides a comprehensive and consistent set of measures against which companies can determine their contribution to the community, including cash, time and in-kind donations, and management costs. The model also captures the outputs and longer-term impact of the company's community investment projects on society and the business itself, and is widely regarded as the international standard for measuring such investment.

Unfortunately, the adoption of this methodology by companies is the exception rather than the rule, and the absence of any sort of breakdown by most companies makes comparisons and analysis of total community contributions all the more difficult.

Furthermore, in trying to provide an accurate picture of the level of company support in the UK, we have been hindered by a significant number of the biggest givers failing to provide UK-specific figures.

Total UK cash donations made by the 400 companies in this guide is estimated to be around £369 million, a decrease of 21.5% on the previous edition of this guide. Total UK community contributions amounted to £658 million.

Charitable donations

Table 1 shows that 67.6% of UK cash contributions came from the top 25 companies. The threshold for admittance into the top 25 is £3.3 million, compared with £4.3 million in the last edition.

Table 1: the top 25 companies (UK cash donations)

No.	Name	UK cash donations
1	Lloyds Banking Group	£53.7 million
2	Tesco plc	£25.4 million
3	Goldman Sachs International	£22.1 million
4	Santander UK plc	£17 million
5	HSBC Holdings plc	£14.5 million
6	Shell (UK Ltd)	£11.8 million
7	FIL Holdings (UK) Ltd (formerly Fidelity Investment Management Ltd)	£10.2 million
8	Barclays plc	£9.1 million
9	Berkeley Group plc	£9 million
10	Marks and Spencer Group plc	£8.4 million
11	John Lewis Partnership plc	£6.8 million
12	BAE Systems plc	£5.5 million
13	Ecclesiastical Insurance Group plc	£5.5 million
14	Virgin Atlantic Two Ltd (formerly Virgin Atlantic Ltd)	£5.5 million
15	Dyson Ltd	£5 million
16	WPP plc	£4.9 million
17	Prudential plc	£4.7 million
18	Scottish and Southern Energy plc (SSE)	£4.5 million
19	Asda Stores Ltd	£4.3 million
20	Thomson Reuters (Reuters Ltd)	£4 million
21	ICAP plc	£3.8 million
22	GlaxoSmithKline plc	£3.6 million
23	EDF Energy plc	£3.5 million
24	ScottishPower UK plc	£3.3 million
25	William Hill plc	£3.3 million
	Total	£249.3 million

Community contributions

Table 2 shows that the top 25 companies' UK community contributions represented 71.4% of the total. The minimum entry figure for the top 25 is £5.5 million, up by £300,000 from the previous edition.

Table 2: the Top 25 Companies (UK community contributions)

No.	Name	UK contributions
1	Redrow Group plc	£113 million
2	Lloyds Banking Group	£85 million
3	Microsoft Ltd	£25.4 million
4	Tesco plc	£25.4 million
5	Goldman Sachs International	£22.1 million
6	Santander UK plc	£21.6 million
7	HSBC Holdings plc	£15.25 million
8	British Sky Broadcasting Group plc	£14.5 million
9	Marks and Spencer Group plc	£14.2 million
10	Barclays plc	£12.1 million
11	Shell (UK Ltd)	£11.8 million
12	FIL Holdings (UK) Ltd (formerly Fidelity Investment Management Ltd)	£10.2 million
13	John Lewis Partnership plc	£9.8 million
14	Royal Mail plc	£9.4 million
15	Berkeley Group	£9 million
16	BP plc	£8.5 million
17	Co-operative Group Ltd	£8.2 million
18	Impetus – The Private Equity Foundation	£8.2 million
19	Deutsche Bank	£8.1 million
20	British Airways plc	£7.5 million
21	PricewaterhouseCoopers LLP	£7.1 million
22	ScottishPower UK plc	£6.5 million
23	Virgin Atlantic Two Ltd (formerly Virgin Atlantic Ltd)	£6 million
24	Ecclesiastical Insurance Group plc	£5.6 million
25	BAE Systems plc	£5.5 million
	Total	£469.9 million

Corporate social responsibility

Corporate social responsibility (CSR), also known as corporate responsibility, corporate citizenship or sustainable responsible business (SRB), is a much-used term which seeks to define what an increasing number of people and groups believe the wider role of business in society should be.

Ideally, a CSR model should provide for the self-regulation of a company's impact on society and how to address that with measurable targets where possible. It should include the monitoring and review of its ethical policies and procedures, its environmental policy, its health and safety procedures, its employees' welfare, and the effect the company's business has on its customers, suppliers, communities and stakeholders.

During our research for this tenth edition of *The Guide to UK Company Giving*, we have noted that again, as with the research undertaken for the ninth edition, the recording of CSR initiatives and their successes is increasing, providing the public with more information from which to assess companies' contribution to their communities and society in general. Out of 400 companies researched, 338 reported on CSR or sustainability, some to a great extent, others less so.

Many companies, depending on the nature of their business, quite naturally focus on the environmental impact they are having and what measures they are taking to try to redress this. These programmes are often under the heading of sustainability as opposed to CSR.

For our purposes, for the benefit of our readers, we focus our research on companies' contributions to UK voluntary organisations, both in cash and in kind. Where a company gives abroad and provides information, we will record this but it is the small and medium-sized charity working with beneficiaries in the UK that we hope to assist most.

From our research we know that companies which establish partnerships or close links with the charities they support are appreciative of those charities, their staff and the needs which they meet. This is probably more so for those that have a link to the nature of the company's business; for example, a sports clothing retailer has a very direct link with the beneficiaries of a voluntary group supporting young people. As a bonus, the beneficiaries of the voluntary organisation are often the company's customers or potential customers – a 'win–win' situation as one CSR spokesperson said.

Companies are also realising that there are substantial benefits to be gained in supporting such voluntary groups. These benefits include:

- Getting good publicity and building brand awareness through association with an organisation or cause
- Gaining a deeper understanding of their own customer base
- In the case of staff volunteering (for example, mentoring or providing pro bono work), reaping a real staff development benefit with opportunities for skills and leadership development and even the improvement of financial performance (BITC 2008)

Clearly, working in partnership can be of mutual benefit – companies bring their core business skills, including financial or logistical expertise, and access to supply chains and high-level contacts. Charities can provide their own professional skills and a real knowledge of what is needed on the ground and what approaches will be most effective. We know that companies continue to set up corporate charities through which to channel their community/charitable contributions, realising that the skills present in the voluntary sector are exactly those required to carry out the company's CSR related charitable objectives.

Gender diversity in CSR

For the last edition of this guide we started recording the ratio of women to men on corporate boards; this year we are able to make some simple comparisons based on the figures we collated. This research could potentially form the basis for more detailed analysis of what we found, for example, whether companies where the majority of the board members are women affects the companies' charitable giving/support in any respect.

Throughout our research we were also noting how companies approach diversity within the workforce and recorded a number of initiatives aimed at supporting women into leadership.

Research findings

Ninth edition

In the ninth edition of the guide we were able to determine the ratio of women and men on the boards of 413 companies. It could be seen that the overall percentage of women on boards was around 13%, while men on boards represented almost 87%. Out of the 413 businesses researched, 33% had no female board members at all. For 16% of boards, at least one-quarter of its members were female and under 2% of all 413 boards had either equal numbers of women and men or were female-led.

Tenth edition

Preparing the tenth edition of the guide we looked at 400 UK companies and were able to determine the ratio of women and men on boards of 317 companies. The overall percentage of women on boards was 19% and men represented 81%. A higher proportion than before, about 29%, of the 317 companies had 25% or more female members on their boards. The percentage of boards where the numbers of female and male members were equal or where the board is led by women has remained about the same and did not reach more than 2% of the overall number of companies.

Similar to our research for the ninth edition, we found that female-led companies were extremely rare. The few examples we did find included a co-operative and a charitable company.

The gender balance in the corporate world was brought into the spotlight with Lord Davies' report, *Women on Boards* (Davies 2011). Since then a number of UK companies have been increasing the number of females on their boards of directors in order to reach the 25% rate of women on boards expected in 2015. Our research indicates a slight increase in the numbers of women on boards and also more attention being paid to programmes aimed at increasing the numbers of women in businesses both at a senior level and throughout the workforce where historically the workforce has been predominantly male, for instance in mining or engineering. Even though the increasing female 'presence' sends a positive message, it is yet to be seen if this can prove a meaningful change in the male-dominated corporate world and whether the figures will be maintained and indeed improved on.

Gender focus

Following the recent changes to the Companies Act 2006, which came into force in October 2013, the strategic report of a company must include information on gender balance throughout its workforce as well as on the executive level (The Companies Act 2006 (Strategic Report and Directors' Report) Regulations 2013, Ch. 4A, s. 414C, subs. 8(c)). While some companies provide a standard diversity compliance statement, we could also find some proactive internal and external measures to increase the female presence within the business.

There are claims suggesting that women are less likely to be on boards because a particular sector does not have many women in the business at all. This is usually referred to as a 'sector challenge' in science, industrial, technology and IT businesses.

Some maintain that they 'do not have diversity targets or quotas and do not focus exclusively on one group of employees over and above any other group of employees' but rather 'aim to provide all [their] employees with a supportive work environment' (Shire 2014). Others have chosen to address this by approaching the issue from the very grassroots and seek to 'attract, develop and engage women at all levels to 'grow [their] own female leaders from new graduates up to senior management level' (WH Smith 2014) or aim for a 50/50 gender split for graduate recruitment (Barclays 2015). Developing the talent pipeline within a company has been one of the recommendations made by Lord Davies and seems to have been taken on by a number of businesses.

We could see initiatives emerging to invite more girls into science education through related educational programmes, particularly STEM (science, technology, engineering, mathematics) initiatives, and work experience opportunities. Initiatives such as these are long-term investments, but are nevertheless positive ones. It should be noted that the problem of low numbers of women within business hardly applies in the wide range of other industries where women not only form a substantial part or majority of the workforce but also are the target audience.

The recommendations by Lord Davies chose to avoid any statutory provisions to control the board ratio of women and men and relied on the corporate world to make the change voluntarily (while a different, perhaps more efficient, route of introducing compulsory quotas for the number of women and men on boards has been taken in some other European countries such as Norway, Finland and, more recently, Germany). While the overall picture shows some improvements, the corporate world in the UK appears to be slow in embracing a change in its practices.

The Business in the Community campaign Opportunity Now has produced an interesting case for corporate bodies to embrace a more balanced board diversity claiming clear-cut performance benefits for the business. The campaign stresses flexible working as being 'a key enabler towards women's participation in the labour market'. Notably employers are recognising this aspect and we found some examples of programmes aimed at better supporting work–life balance or enhancing the maternity/paternity leave provisions.

There are a number of schemes undertaken by some companies, various networking events and leadership sessions both within an organisation and in partnership with others institutions. For instance, WPP Group states that 'through our support for the Women on Boards not-for-profit organisation, we give senior women in our business opportunities to attend workshops and seminars and build their careers by taking on non-executive directorships' (WPP 2014).

WH Smith also mentions holding 'meetings with women and those from other underrepresented groups within the organisation to gain feedback on their experience of WH Smith as an employer and any other ideas they may have around what could be done differently to support them' (WH Smith 2010).

Less attention in the CSR overviews has been paid on iterating possibilities of employing more women from an existing pool of competent female professionals or addressing other barriers faced by women, such as the gender pay gap. Some interesting projects have been reported by Thales global group on activities in France, for instance, 'a specific budget to rectify unwarranted discrepancies in compensation between men and women' in order to address the pay gap (Thales 2014). Some more proactive companies have also mentioned making commitments to 'work closely with external recruitment partners' to appoint more women to the board (Yorkshire Building Society 2014).

We look forward to undertaking this research for the next edition of the guide when further comparisons can be made, and we hope to find new initiatives that positively address diversity in the workplace, including the ratio of women and men on boards.

Our new corporate charities section

New to this edition is our section on corporate grant-making charities, which provides a comprehensive analysis of companies' charitable and community contributions by detailing how much they donate, as well as to which organisations and the locations where they focus their giving. The 114 charities listed have an association, either historically or currently, with a company and each entry includes full details of the charity, its purposes and contact details.

To be deemed a corporate charity in line with DSC's criteria and consequently to have a place in this guide, charities, generally speaking, must be run by directors or employees of the company, or have members on the trustee body and usually have their support costs and overheads covered by the associated company. Typically, corporate charities are based on company premises. These charities should also receive all, or a substantial amount of their income from a connected company through an annual donation from company profits or in the form of income derived from an initial endowment of company shares.

Corporate charities can be an excellent vehicle for corporate giving. They:

- Provide a professional, structured and effective channel for charitable donations with trustees acting in the best interest of the charity (and not the company)
- Often employ skilled, motivated staff
- Apply the Charities SORP, which provides the openness and transparency often lacking in companies' reporting
- Are often a way for companies to focus their charitable giving while demonstrating long-term support for their communities through the voluntary sector

Corporate organisations can contribute to the communities in which they operate through the charity's activities while also seeing an indirect benefit to their business. For example, a finance company might want to fund debt advice agencies and can do so through the corporate charity, provided this falls within the charity's objects.

In this edition there are corporate charities listed that give nationally and internationally as well as those that give only in the areas in which they have a local presence. As well as the traditional method of receiving donations directly from the yearly profits of the company, corporate charities can also receive income from other sources, for example from staff/customer fundraising or perhaps dividends from a previously donated portfolio of company shares. All income streams contribute towards grant-making unless they have a pre-determined restriction which prevents this. From our research for this edition of the guide, the total amount given in grants through corporate charities totalled around £202 million. This figure was derived from the combined grant totals of each of the corporate charities listed and does not represent what was given by the companies themselves in that financial year.

The inclusion of corporate charities to this edition adds another valuable component to DSC's examination of UK companies' charitable giving. It is a traditional and straightforward way of giving but, nevertheless, an important and worthwhile avenue for charities to consider when searching for funding.

Measuring corporate support

The methods we use to gather information on companies' charitable support are relatively straightforward. Basic financial details of the company's performance and the level of cash donations for a particular year are obtained, when available, from published annual reports and accounts, information lodged at Companies House or the company's website.

For other support in addition to cash donations, (gifts in kind such as pro bono work, employee volunteering and so on), and the specifics of a company's charitable support policy, we have referred to the company's CSR report and/ or its website. Such information is increasingly to be found on websites, which can sometimes be very helpful and informative, and often gives advice on how to apply for funding, the company's criteria, what good causes they favour and also case studies of beneficiaries.

The inclusion of 'policy' details within a company entry, such as any eligibility criteria, is an important aspect of our work: this provides fundraisers with the information necessary to make an informed decision about which companies to target. We do not recommend the scattershot approach, believing this to be not particularly successful, a waste of time for the parties concerned and potentially damaging to other, more qualified applicants.

For those without the necessary matching profile or fundraising resources, this guide, with its focus on cash donations and resources, provides straightforward evidence of the level of corporate community support for any of our listed companies and points the way for small and medium-sized organisations to make informed decisions about which companies to approach.

Transparency

DSC has always maintained that it is in the public and the voluntary sector's interest to know about individual company policies and contributions so that a clearer picture of what support is available, where and for what purposes may be seen.

Companies, unlike grant-making charities, are clearly not primarily established to support good causes and they consequently don't have the same practices and policies in place as grant-making charities, nor perhaps, the inclination to sort through many applications looking for the most appropriate or worthwhile. For this reason it is important for the company to make clear and publicise its criteria for giving and, likewise, for the potential applicants to ensure that they have a match or link, in order to save time and other resources for both parties.

We know from our research for this guide that some companies are gradually recognising and acting on the moral requirement to publish their policies on community/charitable giving, their targets, performance and the delivery of those targets, and also who they have benefitted in a particular financial year. However, a glossy brochure or section in the annual report with a myriad of statistics is not always transparent in a way that is useful to potential applicants. Very often the information given is emotive rather than substantive, avoids actual money spent, and/or concentrates on its employees' contributions, not distinguishing between the efforts of staff (and sometimes customers/clients) and the actual resources donated by the company itself in cash or in kind.

Our research shows that companies are improving in their publication of programmes and activities that are beneficial to their communities and society at large and this is why the removal of the requirement to declare charitable donations is a backward and regrettable step. It is a contradictory practice to profess openness and transparency in one statement and to choose not to declare funding to the communities served by the company in the directors' annual report.

Caution – please note

We are told that companies continue to receive many unsolicited or inappropriate appeals for support. Whilst many bring this upon themselves due to a lack of clear guidelines for potential applicants, this should not be seen as an excuse to conduct blanket mailings. It is vitally important for success to do your research thoroughly and only apply to those companies which are likely to consider your application or request.

Further information on how to approach businesses for support successfully is given in the 'Applying to companies' section on page xxii. In general, however, before approaching any company in this guide, its entry should be read carefully. As we have stated previously, unless there is some clear link with a company, or your project is clearly within its defined areas of support, you are unlikely to be successful.

We also recommend that you download a copy of *Charities Working with Business Code of Fundraising Practice*, published by the Institute of Fundraising. This gives a good overview of the issues involved in undertaking a relationship with a company and is available at: www.institute-of-fundraising.org.uk.

DSC campaigns and the current environment

DSC's Great Giving campaign aims to achieve better funding relationships between charities and their funders. We want to support and help develop good funding practice among those organisations which give to charities and other voluntary organisations. The current focus of the Great Giving campaign is on giving from companies.

We use research to develop recommendations and practical tools for funders and fundraisers to positively change behaviour and practice. Our first *UK Company Giving Almanac* mapped company giving to UK charitable causes and raised some fundamental questions.

Companies provide only 2% of the UK voluntary sector's income. The amount given has been static for at least a decade but our research shows signs of a recent decline. Shockingly, understanding this has become even more difficult following the recent changes we've outlined to company reporting requirements which make company giving less transparent.

The lack of transparency apparent when companies or their financial advisers have chosen not to declare charitable donations has resulted in fundraisers and others having no information available to them of that particular company's giving and as a consequence whether they should spend resources making an application or bid. It also affects the conclusions of research carried out to map company giving either geographically, by cause or by any other criterion.

The economic crisis has simultaneously made it harder for many charities to raise funds while also increasing demand for their charitable services. The economy has also been difficult for business too, but we believe there is still huge potential for companies to give more, for more companies to give, and for companies to be better givers.

Conclusion

At this juncture we would normally comment on whether the companies listed in this guide have given more or less than in our last edition, providing useful information on any change in the companies' funding landscape. During our research for this edition, however, we found that this is proving a more difficult task because, as we have noted at various points in this introduction, the new narrative reporting requirements for UK companies has meant that charitable donations no longer need to be declared in the companies' directors' reports. As outlined in the 'Facts and figures' section, our research shows that 41% of companies that had declared charitable donations featured in the last edition of this publication failed to do so this time around.

In our view, companies have a moral responsibility to be open and transparent in their actions. We have seen, over many years of research, disingenuous companies using slick marketing to claim to do more than they actually are doing for their communities and society in general. It is not only in the public interest but also in the interest of the individual companies and the private sector as a whole to make their giving transparent. Importantly, those companies which are genuinely concerned with community and charitable issues should adopt good practice as an example, and continue to declare the amount of cash they are giving in their directors' reports. There does not seem to be any good reason not to do so.

What we would say on a positive note is that companies appear to be more open with regard to their programmes, initiatives and activities. There is also an increase in the publication of case studies, which are useful because they provide fundraisers with an illustration of the work being carried out by charities that have received funding or assistance, and give a good indication of whether an applicant's project/organisation/event might fit well with the company's giving priorities. This increase is also an indication that companies are monitoring and evaluating the contributions they make to their communities and taking this work seriously.

Our research for this edition suggests that companies are increasingly aware of the advantages of adopting and publicising clearer social responsibility policies: transparency in this area saves time and resources for all concerned. A company with clear guidelines and stated criteria for community giving will attract those charities that fit the bill, thereby reducing the number of ineligible applications made to them. In turn, charities will target those companies that are most likely to contribute to their cause.

Fundraisers should dedicate time when applying to companies, as they do in their applications to other funders. Companies' contributions, whether cash or in kind can be significant and, in the case of sponsorships or cause-related marketing, long lasting.

The aim of this guide is to provide the knowledge necessary to obtain company support through the provision of profile information on individual companies, identifying the kind of support available and how to access this effectively. We hope the use of it will help charities to secure company backing for the good causes they champion and support.

Acknowledgements

We would like to thank all the companies that have helped to compile this guide: both those which we have contacted directly and those which have made their annual reports and accounts and/or their websites informative and accessible. Notwithstanding this, any mistakes within the guide remain ours rather than theirs.

We would also like to thank Barry Clavin for writing the foreword to this edition. Barry leads the ethical policies and sustainability reporting function for The Co-operative Group, the UK's largest co-operative. He also leads on ethical matters at The Co-operative including the delivery of the Co-operative Bank Ethical Policy, providing stakeholder consultation and policy implementation. For over a decade Barry has produced and authored the annual *Ethical Consumerism Report.*

Last, but not least, we are indebted to Del Redvers and Belinda Hunt for their very helpful articles on 'Charity of the Year and smaller organisations' and 'Matched funding', respectively.

References

Barclays (2015), 'Diversity and inclusion' [web page], www.barclays.com, accessed 8 April 2015

BITC (2008), *The Value of Corporate Governance: The positive return of responsible business*, Business in the Community, available on www.bitc.org.uk

Davies, Evan Mervyn (2011), *Women on Boards*, Department for Business, Innovation & Skills, available on www.gov.uk

Royal Mail (2014), *Corporate Responsibility Report 2013/14*, Royal Mail Group, available on www.royalmailgroup.com

Shire (2014), *Annual Report 2014: Our journey forward*, Shire plc, available on www.shire.com

Simmons & Simmons (2014), *Corporate Responsibility 2013/14 Annual Review*, Simmons & Simmons LLP, available on www.simmons-simmons.com

Thales (2014), *2013 Report: Corporate Responsibility*, Thales Group, available on www.thalesgroup.com

WH Smith (2010), 'Diversity' [web page], www.whsmithplc.co.uk, accessed 8 April 2015

WH Smith (2014), *Corporate Responsibility Report 2014*, WH Smith plc, available on www.whsmithplc.co.uk

WPP (2014), *Sustainability Report 2013/2014*, WPP Group, available on www.wpp.com

Yorkshire Building Society (2014), *Report and Accounts 2013*, available on www.ybs.co.uk

And finally . . .

If you have any comments about the guide, positive or negative, please get in touch with us at the Research Department, Directory of Social Change, Suite 103, 1 Old Hall Street, Liverpool L3 9HG; tel: 0151 708 0136; email: research@dsc.org.uk

About the Directory of Social Change

DSC has a vision of an independent voluntary sector at the heart of social change. The activities of independent charities, voluntary organisations and community groups are fundamental to achieve social change. We exist to help these organisations and the people who support them to achieve their goals.

We do this by:

- Providing practical tools that organisations and activists need, including online and printed publications, training courses, and conferences on a huge range of topics
- Acting as a 'concerned citizen' in public policy debates, often on behalf of smaller charities, voluntary organisations and community groups
- Leading campaigns and stimulating debate on key policy issues that affect those groups
- Carrying out research and providing information to influence policymakers

DSC is the leading provider of information and training for the voluntary sector and publishes an extensive range of guides and handbooks covering subjects such as fundraising, management, communication, finance and law. We have a range of subscription-based websites containing a wealth of information on funding from trusts, companies and government sources. We run more than 300 training courses each year, including bespoke in-house training provided at the client's location. DSC conferences, many of which run on an annual basis, include the Charity Management Conference, the Charity Accountants' Conference and the Charity Law Conference. DSC's major annual event is Charityfair, which provides low-cost training on a wide variety of subjects.

For details of all our activities, and to order publications and book courses, go to www.dsc.org.uk, call 08450 777707 or email publications@dsc.org.uk.

Charity of the Year and smaller organisations

Del Redvers

This article was included in the last four editions of this guide; subsequently Business Community Connections has ceased operating. Nevertheless, we think the content of the article will still be of interest and use to many of our readers.

Del Redvers writes:

Charity of the Year is a label increasingly applied to all manner of partnerships, but what does it really mean? Business Community Connections (BCConnections) researched how different charities and businesses use the Charity of the Year concept and in doing so identified several critical factors for success.

There are many forms of Charity of the Year partnership but with certain common themes. Most obviously and significantly they are time limited relationships although certainly not always one year in duration. The most widespread understanding of the term is a partnership in which the staff from a business undertake a range of activities to raise money for the identified charity. At the end of the year businesses often feel the need to replace the charity they support in order to prevent fundraising fatigue, and to ensure wider appeal to staff and customers, as no one charity will be relevant to all stakeholders. This also gives the business the opportunity to support another charity.

Increasingly, however, other elements are added to the staff fundraising concept, such as cash donations, employee volunteering or other in-kind donations, sponsorship, cause related marketing or lobbying and campaigning. Sometimes these partnerships involve very little or no staff fundraising at all. Many businesses involved in these other types of Charity of the Year relationship would not be able to support a staff fundraising partnership, perhaps because they have smaller numbers of higher paid staff with less free time. Similarly, it makes sense for companies with relevant goods or services to donate them in kind to the charity as part of their contribution. The term Charity of the Year is used to brand a relationship, because although it can be misleading, it is a widely understood and accepted term.

For smaller organisations

Traditionally Charity of the Year relationships have been the preserve of large charities, frequently those able to offer national exposure to large corporate partners. There is, however, evidence to suggest a growing trend in the number of smaller charities seeking and successfully establishing Charity of the Year partnerships. The BCConnections research shows no reason why Charity of the Year should be out of bounds to small or medium sized charities and by the same token to Small and Medium Enterprises (SMEs). There are however a number of risks which can offset the many benefits available to both charities and businesses and which need to be weighed very carefully irrespective of the size of the organisation.

The advantages . . .

The research suggests that in general Charity of the Year partnerships do work for both partners. On the whole charities tend to put a financial value on the relationship of six or seven times the cost of establishing and managing the partnership. Whilst larger charities frequently net income in excess of £100,000 through these relationships, smaller charities also tend to consider them worthwhile activities even if they are very unlikely to achieve a six-figure financial contribution. A Charity of the Year partnership can . . .

1 Provide a reasonably predictable and often large income stream over a fixed period of time.

2 Provide an excellent opportunity to significantly increase the profile and reputation of the charity.

3 Create a track record of working with the corporate sector.
4 Lever support from other businesses and customers.
5 Increase fundraising activity from existing supporters.
6 Educate the workforce and customers of the business about the charity or its cause.
7 Offer access to employees as a new market of potential supporters.
8 Last longer than one year. There is a growing trend towards the 'Charity of 2 or 3 years' giving the security of a longer-term income stream.
9 Generate unrestricted income, although there is a developing trend towards restricted funds in these relationships.
10 Increase the morale at the charity, especially amongst the fundraising team.

And pitfalls . . .

There are many issues for a charity to consider before deciding whether or not to pursue a Charity of the Year relationship.

These partnerships can be resource intensive to manage, most significantly in terms of staff time. The cost benefit analysis section of the BCConnections research reveals that managing a small Charity of the Year partnership often takes at least 10% of one person's time. A large partnership can occupy from one to three employees on a full-time basis. There may also be costs associated with legal agreements for joint promotions, licencing and sponsorship arrangements.

Pitching for major Charity of the Year partnerships can be a significant undertaking in itself, requiring the investment of resources at an early stage, with no promise of a return. Once a partnership is agreed there is often a lengthy planning period before it is launched. Consequently, there exists a time lag between investing resources to develop the partnership and receiving the support. This can create a cashflow problem, particularly for smaller charities but also where a charity is expected to cover early costs such as producing badges and promotional material. Despite what can amount to considerable set-up costs, these partnerships will always be time limited and therefore, for most charities, cannot be considered a sustainable source of income.

Frequently, businesses use voting schemes to engage staff in selecting the Charity of the Year. This often results in the exclusion of many types of charities from the selection process as in an unrestricted ballot, staff have a tendency to vote for charities such as children, cancer and other health related charities with poignant issues.

There is always an element of risk on both sides in any corporate community relationship as a link is forged between the reputations of the two partners. With Charity of the Year this link is likely to be well publicised and consequently the relationship can backfire if it is considered to be unethical.

Getting a Charity of the Year partnership

If your organisation is seeking a Charity of the Year partnership, there are some things you should bear in mind . . .

1 Be strategic in your approach. Focus on the good fit between your charity and your target companies. Start building relationships with these businesses and try to grow the company contacts you already have. Think ahead and plan which business may adopt you next year or the year after that.
2 Decide on the cost benefit ratio you are prepared to accept. This is usually not just a financial exercise as it may involve judgements about intangible benefits and the potential worth of a partnership with the company in the longer term.
3 Be prepared to walk away. One of the most important messages to come out of the research is that charities need to assess at an early stage the potential value of the partnership, and then negotiate and decide whether or not it is worthwhile pursuing.
4 Consider approaching new businesses not previously involved in Charity of the Year partnerships.
5 Consider the benefits and drawbacks of a Charity of the Year partnership from the business point of view. Try to gain an understanding of why your target business might want a Charity of the Year partnership and more specifically with your organisation. This can help you to value your charity's worth and feel more confident about negotiating with the business.
6 If possible seek advice from a previous Charity of the Year of your target business. This should increase your understanding of the company, how they work and what they may want out of the partnership. This should be supplemented by in-depth research on the company from published sources.
7 Ask the business for a meeting at an early stage. This will give you more guidance about what they want from the partnership, before you invest significant resources. It will also help start to develop a relationship.
8 Be flexible about including other types of involvement for the partnership, apart from staff fundraising.
9 Consider at the outset how you could monitor the impact of your proposed Charity of the Year partnership on the wider community.

The pitch

When pitching for a Charity of the Year partnership, a key consideration is how the charity will be selected. If it is a management decision, there needs to be a focus on benefits to the business whilst for a staff ballot the proposal should be more emotive.

Where possible engage the beneficiaries of the charity in the process.

Proposals should be tailored specifically to the business you are approaching and stick to any brief given. Should the pitch fail, always ask for feedback and if appropriate a contribution; it is worth asking if the business can compensate you in any way for the time and resources invested. However, always be mindful of possible future relationships with that business.

For smaller Charity of the Year partnerships there is often no formal pitch process. Businesses that already engage in small scale Charity of the Year partnerships are more likely to use existing contacts or staff recommendations to identify future partners. Smaller businesses that have never had a Charity of the Year may need some guidance from the charity to help them appreciate the potential of the relationship.

Setting up the partnership

Planning

The importance of development time prior to publicising the partnership cannot be underestimated. In the BCConnections research over a quarter of the organisations did not plan the partnerships. Many larger businesses now select their Charity of the Year six months to one year before the publicised partnership year begins. For smaller partnerships, however, one or two months can provide ample planning time.

Agreement

A written agreement outlining the parameters of the relationships (objectives, targets, timeframes and budgets) plays an important role in managing the expectations of your partner. Clearly allocate responsibility for tasks and costs.

Seek to maximise the mutual benefit of the partnership. The greater the benefit for your business partner, the more seriously they will take the relationship and the greater the likelihood they will invest in Charity of the Year partnerships in the future.

Develop a plan of events, and a process for regular communication and review. Use the expertise of charity fundraisers to generate ideas for activities. Most charities find it easier to have a phased programme of fundraising events rather than doing everything at once.

Financial return

Consider whether there should be a minimum guaranteed return to the charity from the partnership. Some charities recommended including minimum guarantees in any documentation to protect against risk such as a minimum amount of cash to be raised. In addition agree what percentage of money raised will be restricted. Some charities will ask for a percentage of funding to be unrestricted to cover the costs of running the partnership. Also establish the timings of payments to the charity throughout the year and consider the impact on cashflow.

Whilst a single large cheque handed over at the end of the year may look impressive, it is often not a practical option, particularly for smaller charities.

Communications

Establish who will be responsible for the overall publicity of the partnership. If a logo is to be designed for the new partnership who will pay for it? Ensure that use of logos is agreed in advance.

There is also the issue of internal communication with the company's employees. Several charities have commented that it takes time to motivate and inspire staff to get involved in a programme of fundraising or other activities and the timetable should allow for this. The appointment of charity champions amongst the staff of the business can help to co-ordinate activity and provides a communication channel, particularly for multi-site operations.

Thinking ahead

Discuss the sustainability of the partnership and develop an exit strategy early on in the relationship. During review meetings consider whether it is beneficial to both partners to keep the relationship going beyond the year. Even if the charity is not designated Charity of the Year going forward, it may be possible to maintain and develop specific elements of the relationship, such as relationships with suppliers and payroll giving.

Measuring and monitoring

There has been an increasing emphasis on measuring the impact and benefits of Charity of the Year partnerships as with all other aspects of corporate community involvement. Like other types of relationship, there need to be mechanisms for measuring the social impact, benefits to the business and benefits to the charity. Significantly, Charity of the Year partnerships require careful measurement of the relationship itself as it is often more involved than other types of corporate community partnership.

Critically both parties need to know if there was a positive benefit compared with the cost of their involvement. Effective measurement of the partnership enables both parties to decide whether to undertake similar ventures in the future and identifies areas for improvement. Knowing what you want to measure at the outset allows for the correct accounting procedures to be put in place. For instance, without prior planning it may be easy for a company to breakdown staff fundraising by office or team but not by individual activities. This would make it impossible to measure the effectiveness of each activity.

The following represent some of the measures used by the businesses and charities we interviewed during the course of the research to assess the success of the partnership.

- Targets met or exceeded in planning and preparation
- Financial target met or exceeded
- % of company branches involved

- Outcome of the partnership for charity beneficiaries; e.g. number of individuals helped as a result, or number of pieces of equipment purchased, amount of research time enabled etc.
- Positive PR; e.g. the number of articles/column cms or amount of television time
- Number of contacts the charity has developed
- Staff and customer surveys; e.g. awareness and perceptions of business and charity
- Feel good factor; e.g. for business – number of letters, comments received in chat room, etc.
- Number of charity champions that come forward in the business

Conclusions

Charity of the Year relationships are a popular and highly visible way for charities and businesses to work together for mutual benefit and to target the social impact of corporate support for the voluntary sector. Whilst there are no hard and fast rules about establishing and managing Charity of the Year partnerships, a considered and strategic approach will help to maximise the many advantages offered by this type of relationship while minimising the risk.

Smaller charities should be encouraged to consider how they can adapt the models developed by larger organisations. Although there is definitely the opportunity for charities of all sizes to benefit from Charity of the Year relationships, they are not necessarily appropriate for all organisations and represent just one of several types of relationship that can form between the voluntary and corporate sector.

Del Redvers, Head of Sustainability for BMT Group Ltd. Del's role involves advising BMT's companies and customers on sustainability issues and co-ordinating the group's corporate sustainability strategy. He is also responsible for BMT Giveback, the group-wide philanthropic initiative.

Matched funding

Belinda Hunt

CSR is no longer perceived as just making financial contributions to charities. Many companies now have seen the benefits of adopting a positive CSR or community-giving plan for themselves, and of their staff being proactive in the communities in which the company operates, or in society at large. At its best CSR includes companies looking at their resources and their employees' core skills, and working out how they can contribute to society in a more sustainable way.

The growing trend towards larger companies becoming more proactive in their community giving, for example, choosing partnerships which complement their business, and being more focused in their approach, does not bode well for most voluntary organisations. This is particularly true for smaller voluntary organisations, which cannot give the same publicity to a company's contribution as the larger ones, or the less popular, such as those charities supporting ex-offenders or people dealing with drug addiction.

One way in which this can be balanced is by encouraging companies to adopt matched funding schemes whereby they match the funds of those raised by their employees. This allows staff to choose causes for which they have an affinity, without considering what fits in with the company's particular business, or what the charity can give in return.

Our research for the tenth edition records 155 companies that provide staff with matched funding schemes, out of a total of 400. There is an opportunity here for fundraisers to approach both those companies with an existing scheme with a request to address staff on behalf of their own charity, or those companies which do not at present have a scheme in place.

The following article by Belinda Hunt of TrustCSR, details the positive aspects of matched funding and encourages fundraisers to approach companies with this potential resource in mind.

TrustCSR, which is part of The Trust Partnership, specialises in CSR consultancy and the delivery of employee engagement and community investment programmes. Within employee engagement, the main areas of expertise are the design, implementation, reporting and day-to-day management of programmes for a range of large corporate organisations.

The following information relates to TrustCSR's experience, its clients' views and statistics relating to their matched funding programmes and is not necessarily indicative of the entire market place. However, we consider that the information provided will be both informative and useful for our readers.

Belinda Hunt writes:

What is matched funding?

Matched Funding, Matched Giving, Charity Top Up, or Booster Funding – no matter what name the scheme goes by, they all have the same fundamental goal for the corporate organisations offering them – to increase employee engagement amongst their workforce, build motivation and commitment, and develop their corporate reputation, both as a good employer, and also in the communities in which they work. These simple mechanisms, which allow employees to raise funds for their chosen charities and gain support from their employer, can be a powerful fundraising tool.

How does matched funding work?

In the majority of cases, the schemes are open to employees at every level of the organisation providing they actively participate in fundraising events or volunteering activities. A few companies will consider matching giving applications where the fundraising has taken place during working hours but the majority see matched giving as a way of encouraging their employees to become actively engaged in the community during their own time. Some organisations will consider personal donations for matched funding and some will make a financial contribution towards their employees' volunteering hours.

What varies considerably from company to company is the amount they will donate per employee per year.

Schemes start from £250 and go up to £5,000 per employee per financial year. Some organisations will allow their employees to apply as many times as they like, up to the stipulated limits, while others will only allow their employees to apply once per financial year, whether they apply for their total annual allocation, or not.

Many companies also structure their matched funding programme around their Community Investment strategy, giving higher annual limits if employees choose to support charities those objects fit within their own focus areas. For example, if their focus is on medicine and health, then charities falling within that arena may receive up to 100% of what the employee has raised, but if the charity's objects fall outside medicine and health, they may receive as little as 25%.

What's been happening recently?

With CSR moving up the corporate agenda, companies are concentrating their efforts on aligning their charitable giving more closely with their operations and development strategies. Rather than making ad hoc donations and responding to unsolicited funding requests, they are actively seeking ways to increase the impact their donations have on the wider community and the success of their operations.

At TrustCSR we stress the importance of employee involvement in the overall success a company has in achieving its CSR goals, encouraging them to refine their employee engagement programmes to encompass as diverse a range of people as possible. We recognise that not everyone is inclined or able to scale mountains or run marathons but most people are involved in some sort of fundraising activity on a regular basis. Matched giving programmes recognise and reward the effort employees put into any fundraising activity or volunteering commitment.

By running schemes which are easily accessible, have clear and concise guidelines and are actively promoted within the organisation, our corporate clients have all seen an increase in employee participation in recent years.

Overall, our clients' matched giving donations equated to just over 60% of the value of their employees' fundraising totals in 2012. Although these donations decreased slightly to 59% in 2014, the positive impact of matched giving programmes on charities funds is still clearly evident.

In addition, the amounts raised by our clients' employees decreased by 6% in 2013. Whilst there was a small increase of 3% during 2014, the amounts being raised in recent years has not returned to the levels we saw during 2012.

Which types of charities are benefitting most?

In 2012 8.36% of all fundraising was done for smaller community charities such as Scout and Guide units, PTAs, sports clubs and village halls. By the end of 2014 this figure had decreased to only 3.35%.

Although these organisations and other small charities (with an income of less than £250,000) are getting local support, it is becoming increasingly difficult for them to compete with the large household names which have national campaigns and provide fundraisers with considerable support.

Another factor influencing these statistics is the decision by many corporates to put more emphasis on their charity partnerships, encouraging and indeed organising in-house fundraising events to support their charity partnerships.

What can charities do to maximise the benefits of matched funding?

As the success of these matching schemes strengthens and companies increase the budgets dedicated to them, it is likely that fewer corporate organisations will want to make ad hoc donations at their current level. The implication of building close relationships with individual donors and making them aware of matching schemes and other support their employers might offer will become increasingly important to fundraising strategies.

Tell your fundraisers about matched funding

Something as simple as reminding donors to ask their employer about matched funding could significantly boost a charity's annual income. Gift Aid information is included in most fundraising packs so why not matched funding information too?

Smaller organisations can use notice boards, circulars and newsletters to communicate the information.

Fundraise at any opportunity

Scout and Guide units, PTAs and sports clubs which have to rely on the generosity of their members, both in terms of time and hard cash, could benefit from holding frequent, small fundraising events out in the community, increasing local awareness. Bake sales, carwashes and jumble sales are a great opportunity to get your charity known in the local community. If you know your employer runs a matched giving programme, utilise this information to maximise the amount the public give.

Receipting

Every corporate organisation requires some form of proof of funds raised, whether this is a link to an online giving page, a formal receipt from the charity, or a letter of acknowledgement of the amount raised. Make it easy for your fundraiser to obtain this information in the format they require, publicise contact details and respond to requests for information.

Acknowledge corporate payments

Acknowledging the corporate donation, either through the employee or directly to the company helps to build better relationships and increases your charity's profile within the organisation. Many clients we speak to are frustrated by how few charities thank them for their matched funding and donations. As soon as you've cashed that corporate cheque, a letter of thanks, possibly including some detail about the community impacts achieved (or even photographs), makes it more likely that the company will run a story in an internal publication, in turn inspiring more employees to fundraise for that organisation and using their matched funding. It really is worth the effort.

Make corporate support easy

TrustCSR carries out due diligence checks on the majority of charities being supported by their client's employees. This includes money laundering, anti-terrorism and bank account verification checks.

By responding quickly and efficiently to requests for verification documents, your charity will be added to 'approved lists', receive prompt payment and develop a good reputation.

What about non-registered charities?

Some companies will support non-registered charitable organisations, but will often require a copy of their constitution. Make sure your fundraisers have access to a signed, up-to-date copy which they can supply upon request.

What is the future of matched funding?

With the increase in participation, higher budgets and stronger focus on employee engagement, matching funding is likely to become increasingly important as a source of funding for charities, particularly the small community groups.

Companies are investing more time, strategic thought and money in making their schemes more user friendly. The majority of our clients are in the process of adopting electronic platforms from which to run their matched funding, Give As You Earn and volunteering schemes, giving their employees greater power to choose which charities are supported and how.

Some companies are now rolling their matched funding schemes out across their global operations, giving each of their employees the same experience no matter where in world they are based. The impact of this is that more charities will be included in approved lists, making competition for this type of funding fiercer.

It is important therefore that, no matter what size your charity is, you take every opportunity to get your fundraisers to participate in their employers' schemes and show how you value the contribution corporate organisations make through this channel.

TrustCSR is part of The Trust Partnership

tel: 01285 841 900
email: info@TheTrustPartnership.com
website: www.TrustCSR.com

TRUST CSR
PART OF THE TRUST PARTNERSHIP LTD

TrustCSR
6 Trull Farm Buildings
Tetbury
Gloucestershire
GL8 8SQ

Applying to companies

This section gives basic information on identifying potential companies to approach, how to establish contact with them and how to put together a proposal for them to consider.

Corporate social responsibility

This guide deals with one aspect of CSR which, broadly speaking, is the philanthropic, usually referred to as its charitable or community investment. Despite the increasing use of CSR policies and programmes adopted by companies, it should be remembered that company giving is way below that of the general public and, to a lesser extent, grant-making charities. Nevertheless, companies remain an important target for local, regional and national fundraisers.

Why apply to companies?

Company boards are ultimately responsible to their shareholders and answer to them as to how they use their profits. They will not be motivated primarily by philanthropy or by a desire to see new and pioneering voluntary activity. In many cases, companies will be looking to improve their image and their economic position in relation to their competitors, whether at a local, regional or national level.

There is, however, among some businesses, a desire to be seen to be giving something back to their community or society in general, and it is important for charities to have a strategy for applying to such companies. It must be kept in mind that they are a different animal to grant-making charities and require a different approach.

An increasing number of companies have now set up their own charities which, whilst having close ties to and receiving assets from the company, are separate legal entities. Whether they are truly independent of the company in their giving is a matter of debate but they are nominally self-governing and set up for charitable purposes for the benefit of the public. In this respect, they should be applied to in the same way that you would make an application to any other grant-making charity.

The relationship you have with any company which donates to your cause, whether by cash, gifts in kind, staff time or other resources, is a two-way association. While you will be pleased to receive funding, the company will also benefit from the good publicity, awareness of local issues which they may not have previously had and a boost in morale for their staff. As with any relationship, your organisation needs to be selective about who it approaches: you need to be comfortable with the association you are about to establish. Research the company's website, or any other information, with this in mind.

Why companies give

To make an effective appeal to industry you must have a basic understanding of why firms give. This will enable you to put forward good reasons why they should support your work. Many companies, especially the larger, higher profile ones, receive hundreds, if not thousands, of requests for support from charities, voluntary sector organisations and local community groups each year. For your appeal to be successful it needs to be more than a general plea to 'put something back into the community'.

You can help a company justify its charitable support to its shareholders by telling them not just why you want the money, but why giving you support will be of interest to them. You can also tell them about any benefits they will receive in return for their money and about the impact their donation will have on your work. At the very least you should be able to demonstrate a clear link with the company through a geographical, product, or employee contact or some other relevant connection.

Most companies give out of enlightened self-interest rather than for pure altruistic or philanthropic reasons, and see their giving in terms of 'community involvement' or 'community investment'. The main reasons why companies give are:

- To create goodwill. Companies like to be seen as good citizens in the communities in which they operate and as caring companies by their employees and society at large.

- To be associated with causes that relate to their business. Financial companies often like to support debt advice charities for example.
- To build good relations with employees. Support for employee volunteering is a growing area of company giving, creating a 'feel good factor' among employees and a sense of loyalty to their socially responsible employer. It can also be an excellent staff-development resource. Increasingly some preference is given to those charities for which staff are raising money or doing volunteer work. Funds raised may be matched (usually up to a set limit) and/or employees given time off work in which to volunteer.
- Because they are asked or it is expected of them.
- They don't want to be seen as mean in relation to other rival companies in their particular business sector. They are concerned that the quantity and quality of their giving is appropriate to their status as a company.
- Because the chair/senior directors are interested in a particular cause (and perhaps support it personally).
- Because they have always given. Some companies never review their donations policy. They see donations more as an annual subscription to a list of charities they wish to support each year. Your aim should be to get your charity's name on to such a list, where it exists.
- Because the charity persists in its approach to the company and the company does not want to keep refusing a worthwhile cause. Persistence can pay, although if you are turned down you should consider whether you can improve your application, ask through another method, or ask for something else.
- For tax reasons. Giving to a charity can be done tax effectively. This will be an added benefit for the company (but seldom a determining factor).

It is worth pointing out that there is relatively little consistency in company giving. For privately owned or family-controlled companies their giving is often little different from personal giving. For public companies, where it is the shareholders' funds that are being given away, there is more likely to be a structure in place and some well-defined criteria. Where the company publishes its guidelines and criteria, please respect them. Dealing with a mass of clearly inappropriate applications is time-wasting for the corporate giver, and has caused some to consider winding-up their charitable support programme altogether.

What companies give

There are a variety of ways in which companies can support charities:

- A cash donation (usually a one-off grant)
- Pro bono (without charge) professional or technical work
- Sponsorship of an event or activity
- Sponsorship of promotional and educational materials
- Sponsorship of an award scheme
- Running a cause-related marketing campaign where the company contributes a donation to the charity in return for each product sold (in order to encourage sales)
- Donating physical items such as company products or surplus office equipment; making company facilities available, including meeting rooms, printing or design facilities; help with mailings
- Secondment of a member of staff to work with the charity, where a member of the company's staff helps on an agreed basis while remaining employed (and paid) by the company
- Offering internships or work experience to a charity beneficiary or student at an educational establishment
- Offering a senior member of staff to the charity's management board
- Providing expertise and advice or training
- Encouraging and making it easy for employees to volunteer
- Organising a fundraising campaign amongst employees, including encouraging employees to give through payroll giving
- Advertising in charity brochures and publications

Companies will always receive more applications than they will have the budget to meet. Community involvement budgets have not expanded in line with demands for support, and many companies now focus their grant-making quite narrowly.

Some larger companies set up small grants schemes in regions or towns where they have a major factory or business presence. Others have matching schemes, where they match money collected or donated by employees. Some develop special grants programmes, while others have a Charity of the Year for their major donation and as a focus for encouraging staff involvement.

Cash donations

This is the most obvious way that a company can be asked to support your organisation and is probably the help you would most like to receive. Many cash donations from companies are small although some companies will match their employees' fundraising which results in much larger total sums. You are more likely to be successful if you offer a 'shopping list' detailing the cost of specific items, rather than a vague request for general support.

In the entries at the end of this section we try to give an idea of the range of grants available from the large companies and what they like to support. This varies greatly from company to company. Some will have well-defined policies which work in a similar way to grant-making charities and will be clear about the causes they want to assist.

Some companies – especially the smaller ones – will have an informal approach. Here, any applications will be looked at by anyone from the personnel officer to the managing director, or their PA. They will not necessarily have any special insight into the voluntary sector and they will be doing the community support task on top of their work, and so often may have to fit it into the odd Friday afternoon once a month. It is most unlikely that they have the time to work through piles of paper or attend lengthy meetings to get to know the issues you are facing and the work you are doing.

A good number of companies will operate on the basis of the chair's six favourite charities and if you are not on the list you will have to find a way in, as the company giving policy will already be fixed. If you are successful with this sort of company, you may be successful with others, as part of company giving works on recommendation.

You might stand more chance of success if you can tie your application in with an event or celebration. For example, anniversaries are useful and you may be able to find a company to tie in with your 50th year (or theirs), or your 500th member. It will be particularly attractive if you have a time limit to your fundraising – this gives those working in the supporting company a definite target to work towards.

Gifts in kind

Giving items or services rather than money can often be easier for a company. The value of the gift to the charity may be much more than the cost to the company. Companies might give:

- Products for use by the charity
- Pro bono professional and technical advice
- Staff time
- Products as prizes or as lots to be auctioned
- Old stock and ends of lines for resale in charity shops
- Facilities such as meeting rooms, conference facilities or training

If a company donates items that it makes or sells in the course of its trade, or that it has used in its trade (such as computers and furniture), then this can be treated as a tax-deductible business expense. The 'book value' of donated items (value as given in the accounts) is written off before the donation is made (unsaleable or damaged stock, ends of lines, etc.) and attracts full tax relief. There are organisations which act as clearing houses for gifts in kind, such as In Kind Direct (formerly Gifts in Kind UK).

What kind of gift is a gift in kind?

Gifts in kind are donations of items or services, rather than the money to buy them. You might consider approaching specific companies for one of the following gifts, preferably one which has a link with the company's business, making it less expensive for them and more easily obtained:

- Secondment of staff with key skills to train or mentor your trustees, employees or volunteers
- Donation of coach, train, airline or ferry tickets
- Advertising on company websites
- Use of surplus storage or sports facilities
- Donation of hotel accommodation
- Use of telephones for helplines
- Design and printing of leaflets or posters
- Donation of surplus food or drinks
- Access to information on customer demography, attitudes or preferences
- Vacant sites for recreation projects
- Free loan of equipment, scaffolding, marquees, Portaloos, etc.
- Free advertising space on temporarily unused sites
- Insertion of a charity leaflet or appeal in a regular business or customer mailshot
- Free servicing of vehicles

Here are some practical tips on how to set about getting support in kind:

1. Make a list of everything you need – a 'wish list'. This can include services as well as products (such as the design for a leaflet you plan to produce).
2. Go through the list and try to identify companies that might have what you require. Personal knowledge is useful but you might also want to use business directories as well to widen your choice.
3. Make contact. Writing a letter can act as an introduction but you will probably need to follow it up with a phone call or personal visit. State your request, saying that it is for a charity, indicating how well used it will be or what impact it will make and how important it is to your organisation's future. If the company does not want to donate, it might be able to give you a discount.
4. Be positive and enthusiastic. It can be very difficult for the company to refuse if it knows what you want and how important it is for you and the local community. It will always cost the company far less to donate the item than it would cost you to purchase it.
5. Say thank you. Report back subsequently on the difference the donation has made. Send them your annual report and later, perhaps try to recruit the company as a cash donor.

Employee volunteering/secondments/pro bono work

A major resource that companies can offer is their staff time and this can be provided in a number of ways:

- **Employee volunteering:** many of the large companies encourage their staff to volunteer, in or out of office hours, on the basis that this enhances the skills of their employees and promotes good community relations. Some companies match the amount an employee has raised for a chosen project.
- **Professional skills:** banks, law firms, accountants, advertising and PR companies can all encourage staff to give their professional skills free of charge or to become trustees.
- **Secondment:** this is where the company loans you a member of staff full time for an extended period. There needs to be a good reason why the company would do this, as it is an expensive form of support.

Employee volunteering is not only valuable in itself, it is also strategically important since you will be building a relationship with a member of staff who can then act as an intermediary in asking the company for other forms of support at a later date, including cash donations.

Advertising

Companies will sometimes pay for an advertisement in a publication. Possibilities include:

- Your annual report
- Programmes produced specifically for fundraising events
- Conference folders, pads and pens
- Leaflets aimed at your service users and others
- Posters, including educational wall charts

However, you do need to think through whether you actually want an advertisement or company logo to appear prominently on your materials.

Advertising can be broken down into two categories:

- **Goodwill advertising:** where the primary purpose of the advertiser is to support a charity and to be seen supporting a good cause; this creates goodwill for the company rather than selling its products
- **Commercial advertising:** where the advertiser wishes to reach the audience that the charity's publication goes to, and the decision is made for purely financial considerations

What are you offering to advertisers?

Before trying to sell the advertising, you need to recognise what you are offering. If it is goodwill advertising, then the prestige of the event, the nature of the audience, the location and any celebrities who will be present will be major incentives. Price is less of an issue than the work of the charity, although the advertiser will want to know the circulation and readership of the publication, any special characteristics of that readership and any particular connection between it and their product. If it is commercial advertising, these details become much more significant.

Pricing the advertising

The first consideration when pricing the advertising is the format of the publication. A lavish souvenir brochure is different from an annual report, and this in turn is very different from a single colour newsletter produced on your computer. There are two factors to consider when deciding the cost of the advertising.

1 How much do you want to raise? Divide this target by the number of pages of advertising to get a page rate.

2 How much are advertisers prepared to pay? For commercial advertising this is especially important. Try to define the value of your audience to them.

Once you have decided a page rate, then you can then set prices for smaller spaces that are slightly higher than pro rata. For example, if the page rate is £250, then a half page might be priced at £150, a quarter page at £85, and eighth page at £50. You can ask for higher sums for special positions, such as the back cover, the inside front cover and facing the contents page. For a regular publication, you could offer a series discount for taking space in several issues.

You might consider producing a rate card which contains all the information that the advertiser needs to know, including:

- A deadline for agreeing to take space
- A deadline for receipt of artwork and an address where it is to be sent
- Publication size
- Print run
- Use of colour on cover and inside pages
- Page rates, including special positions, size of advertising space, and whether VAT is chargeable
- Payment details

A simple brochure or covering letter which sets out the reasons for advertising is useful, but posting copies out ad hoc will generate little response. The way to sell advertising is on the telephone, where you make a call to follow up a letter you have sent. For larger advertisers, you might try to arrange a personal visit. The majority of people you approach might say 'no' but your job is to persuade a significant proportion to buy a space.

Business sponsorship

Sponsorship needs to be carefully defined. It is not a donation and the fact that your organisation is a charity is largely irrelevant: it is a business arrangement. The charity is looking to raise funds for its work and the company wants to improve its image, promote and sell its products or entertain its customers.

The sponsor's contribution is usually money, although it could be a gift of goods such as football kits, services such as free transport, professional expertise such as promotion or marketing consultancy, the use of buildings such as an exhibition centre, or free promotion such as media coverage in a newspaper.

Many companies will provide much more in sponsorship than they would as a donation, but only so long as the commercial benefits warrant it. Developing links with major national and local corporate sponsors could be an investment in your future that is well worth making now.

Most sponsors are commercial companies. There are four main options for sponsorship:

1 Businesses wanting to promote themselves, to create a better image or generate awareness in the local communities where they operate. This includes those companies with an 'image problem' – for example, mining and extraction companies associated with damaging the environment that want to project a cleaner image by being associated with a conservationist cause.

2 Businesses wanting to introduce or promote a product or service. This could include a new brand of trainers or shampoo, or a supermarket opening in the area. Public awareness is important if a product or service is to get accepted, so companies may be open to proposals that give a product or service more exposure.

3 Companies looking for entertainment opportunities to influence customers, suppliers, regulators, the media and other opinion formers. They may be interested in sponsoring a concert, a theatrical event, an art exhibition or a sporting event which would provide them with an appropriate entertainment opportunity and the opportunity to meet and mingle.

4 Companies that are committed supporters of your organisation. You may be able to offer them a particular project or event that they feel an affinity with and would like to sponsor, even if it is not strictly for business but partly for philanthropic reasons.

What are companies looking for?

Voluntary organisations looking for sponsorship should be able to offer at least some of the following things:

- A respectable partner (with the right image).
- A real partnership. What involvement is the sponsor looking for and how well does this opportunity meet its needs?
- A proven track record (preferably in securing and delivering sponsorships) and a professional approach. Has the applicant approached the process of getting sponsorship in a professional way, and can they demonstrate a similar level of professionalism in the running of their organisation?
- An interesting project (at least to the company management team and possibly also company staff) and a new initiative. Does the sponsorship represent something that would not happen without the company's support? Is it interesting and lively?
- Continuity. Is there scope for a continuing relationship (over the next few years), or is the activity or event just a one-off?
- Genuine value for money. What are the benefits and how much money is the voluntary organisation asking for? How does this compare with other possible sponsorships that the company might consider? The relationship of cost to return and the importance of the return to the company are the dominant factors affecting the decision to sponsor.
- Visibility. How 'visible' will the event be, and what specific publicity and PR benefits will accrue to the sponsor? Will the company name be given a high profile?
- Appropriateness. Is the activity or event appropriate to the sponsor? (Are you approaching the right company that has an interest in what you are doing?)
- A targeted audience. (Could the activity or event lead to a direct marketing opportunity, such as providing the company's fair trade coffee at a reception for young entrepreneurs?)
- Other tangible benefits. (For example, could the activity or event offer good publicity, media coverage, a link with brand advertising, entertainment opportunities for company directors and staff, access to VIPs, involvement of company employees or retirees, training or experience for employees, etc.?)

Why companies like sponsorship

- It helps them get their message across
- It can enhance or change their image
- It can reach a target audience very precisely
- It can be a very cost-effective form of advertising or product promotion
- Further marketing opportunities may develop from the sponsorship
- It generates good publicity for the sponsor, often of a kind that money can't buy
- It generates an awareness of the company within the local community in which the company operates and from where it draws its workforce and customers
- Sponsors can entertain important clients at the events they sponsor

What can be sponsored?

There is an extremely wide range of things that can be sponsored, including:

- Cultural and sporting events
- Mass-participation fundraising events, such as a marathon or fun run
- The publication of a report or a book, with an attendant launch
- The production of fundraising materials, leaflets and posters, or the sponsorship of a complete fundraising campaign
- Conferences and seminars, especially to specialist audiences (such as doctors) where promotional material can be displayed
- Vehicles, where the acknowledgement can be painted on the side
- Equipment such as cars or computers produced by the company
- Competitions, awards and prizes
- Scholarships, bursaries and travel grants

The bulk of corporate sponsorship money goes to sport, with motor racing, golf, tennis, athletics, football and cricket all receiving huge amounts. These offer extensive media coverage, good opportunities for corporate entertainment and an association with a popular activity. The arts is another big recipient of company sponsorship when corporates can publicise their more cultural leanings or reach a new audience. Social sponsorship is much smaller by comparison, however; the 'market' is less crowded and there are all sorts of imaginative ways in which companies can sponsor events and activities run by charities.

Getting sponsorship: 10 practical tips

1 Before you begin, think about an ethical code. Are there some companies you wouldn't wish to be associated with?

2 Identify the right person in the company to contact. You need their name and job title. This will often be the marketing manager.

3 Stress the benefits of the sponsorship to the potential sponsor. This should be done often and as clearly as possible and backed up with statistics or other supporting information.

4 The size of the payment will be dependent upon the value of the sponsorship to the sponsor, not the cost of the work for you.

5 Help companies use their own resources to make the sponsorship work. Suggest, for instance, that they might like a picture story in their house magazine or in the trade press. Most are very keen to impress their colleagues and their rivals, but may not think of this without prompting.

6 Sponsorship, especially long-term deals, is all about working together. Promise only what you know you can deliver, and always try to deliver a little bit more than you promised.

7 Remember that most sponsorship money for small and medium-sized charities comes in sums of under £10,000 and it is a local event you are planning, not Live Aid.

8 Get into the habit of reading adverts. Look particularly at local papers and trade press. Who has got money to spend on promotion? What kind of image are they trying to promote? Who are they trying to reach? How can you help them?

9 Mention another company that supports you. One satisfied sponsor can help you to get another.

10 Keep trying. It is hard work but sponsorships can be really valuable.

There may be an advertising agency or marketing consultant that can introduce sponsorship opportunities to sponsors. They will sometimes charge you a fee; more usually they will receive a commission from the sponsor. It depends who retains them, and in whose interests they are acting.

Your sponsorship package

It is not enough to offer a company a potential target audience if, for example, they sponsor your event. You need to say who that target audience will be and how the company might benefit from their attendance at the event.

Think of each group that you reach in one way or another, say young people. Estimate an annual number for each group. The more you can define your different groups and find a link with them to the sponsor, the more likely the corporate is to support your event.

Contractual issues

Sponsorship involves giving something in return for the money you are receiving, so you need to agree terms through a contract. This can be set out in a legal agreement (for larger sponsorships) or in the form of a letter. You need to be clear about the following:

- How long the arrangement will run. Is it for one year, which would require you to find a new sponsor next year, or can you get a commitment for several years? What happens at the end of this period – does the sponsor have a first refusal on the following year's event? Most successful sponsorships last for several years, and the benefit builds up over the sponsorship period. However, some companies don't like being tied to sponsoring something indefinitely – their sponsorship programme might begin to look stale.
- The fee to be paid, and when the instalments are due. What benefits are to be delivered in return for the fee? These should be specified as clearly as possible, so that you know precisely what you are contracted to deliver.
- Whether VAT is chargeable. This will depend on whether your organisation is registered for VAT and the extent of the benefits offered to the sponsor. If VAT is chargeable, this should be discussed at the outset, and the fee agreed should be exclusive of VAT.
- Who will pay for what costs? Who pays for insurance (there may be more than one type needed) and the additional publicity the sponsor requires? Such items can be forgotten but are important and need to be agreed in writing. There needs to be a clear agreement as to who is responsible for what, so you can ensure that everything is covered and there are no misunderstandings later on.
- Who is responsible for doing what? You will need to clarify who will do the public relations, who will handle the bookings, who will invite the guests, whose staff will receive the guests and so on.
- Any termination arrangements in the event of the activity having to be cancelled.
- Who is responsible for managing the sponsorship?
- You will need a named person on both sides.
- Whether the sponsor is a 'commercial participator', as defined by current legislation, where legal requirements will apply.

If everything is written down and agreed, there will be fewer problems later and it ensures that everything has been properly thought through at the outset.

Note: This list is not exhaustive and you should contact the Charity Commission for further information or advice: see www.charitycommission.gov.uk

Joint promotions and cause-related marketing

Many larger charities are involved in promotional activity to help market a commercial product – this is often known as cause-related marketing. This can bring in large amounts of money and expose the name of the charity (and sponsor) to literally millions of people. The same idea on a smaller scale can also be adapted for use by local charities through local promotions.

Commercial promotions can include on-pack and licensing promotional deals, affinity credit cards, competitions and awards, the use of phone lines, etc. What they have in common is that they present an opportunity to raise money for your cause and to project your charity to new audiences, but they require that you work with the company and on its terms to achieve this.

This arrangement benefits both the charity and the commercial partner. It differs from sponsorship in that you are promoting the company's product or service (in return for a payment) as the primary purpose of the arrangement. But as with sponsorship, you will need to make a business case for it.

Getting started with promotions

Joint promotions are quite difficult to arrange and you must first talk about the possibility of your developing promotional links with companies with someone who has experience of this or with a marketing or advertising agency (but these can be costly).

You need to decide whether your charity is the type which can expect a commercial link of this sort. It has been generally accepted that national household-name charities and those addressing popular causes (such as helping children) are more likely to benefit from this area of fundraising than the less well-known charities or those addressing less 'popular' causes.

You should take the initiative yourself by contacting companies that might be interested in your work. You can also contact promotion agencies (that are not retained by you) to make them aware of the opportunities you are offering which they could include when appropriate in their sales pitch to companies.

If you are approached by a promotional agency pitching for business, this does not mean that anything is certain. It may be working independently, hoping that a good idea that involves your charity can then be sold to a company. Often these ideas come to nothing, and you may find you have put in considerable effort without getting any return.

Issues with sponsorships and joint promotions

Sponsorship involves a close working relationship with a company. Therefore you will need to be sure when you enter into any sponsorship agreement that this relationship will benefit your organisation and will not damage your charity's reputation. With commercial promotions the relationship is even closer. The charity is actively promoting the products of the company, so it is important that the product you are associated with is good value and good quality. With both arrangements it is important that you have no ethical problems in associating with that company. You should develop an ethical donations policy before you apply for any sponsorship or suggest a joint promotion – agreeing in advance which types of company you are happy to work with and which you are not. (See 'Ethical issues' on page xxxi)

There is also the question of who will benefit most from the arrangement. How much you should expect to receive from a sponsorship or commercial promotion is also a difficult question. It may be worth a great deal to them to be linked with you. Any negotiation should start from what you think the association is worth to them. Your need for money should not dim the value of your commercial worth.

Finally, there are important legal issues arising from current charity legislation which needs to be addressed when engaging in commercial ventures (for more information, see IoF's Code of Fundraising Practice L9.0 Commercial Participators.)

The Charity Commission suggests that trustees should consider the following points before allowing the charity's name to be associated with a particular business or product:

- The relationship is appropriate and will not damage the particular charity or the good name of charity as a whole
- The proposed fundraising venture is a more effective way of raising money than others that might be considered, and that the terms of the arrangement are generally advantageous to the charity
- The arrangement is set out in some detail and kept under review, such that the charity's name is not misused or improperly exploited, and the charity has the right to prevent future use of its name if the arrangement proves unsatisfactory; it may be worth taking legal advice in drawing up the terms of the arrangement

The types of companies that give

Multinational companies

Most multinational companies have global giving programmes, generally tied to areas where they have or are developing business interests. Some multinational companies have an international structure for managing their giving, with budgets set for each area and a common policy regarding what they wish to support. With others, community investment remains at the discretion of local company management in the country concerned.

Geographically speaking, the further out from the centre (i.e. the company's headquarters or operational sites) you are, the less you can expect to get. In general most money is spent in the home country of the giving company and often in the headquarters' town or region or its areas of operation.

Leading national companies

These are most likely to support large national charities, have their own sponsorship schemes and make smaller donations to local charities in the area in which they are headquartered or have a major business presence. Numerous national companies make grants through regional offices, while retail stores such as B&Q might use the local store manager to give advice on a local application. Such stores may also provide the manager with a small budget to spend at their discretion.

Larger local companies

In any city or region there are large companies which are important to the local economy. They will often feel a responsibility to support voluntary action and community initiatives in those areas, and value the good publicity this provides.

There are also companies with a regional remit. The water, electricity and independent television companies all have a specific geographical area within which they operate, even if they are part of a multinational company.

Smaller local companies

There are a myriad of companies that make up the local business community. Referred to as small and medium enterprises (SMEs), they are often overlooked in the rush to target the large companies on which good information is generally available. However, from manufacturers on trading estates to accountants and solicitors in the high street, the majority of SMEs claim to be involved with their local community. Many of these companies are privately owned, so the best approach will often be through the managing director or senior partner.

The best sources of information on what companies exist in your area are:

- The local Chamber of Commerce, where most of the more prominent local companies will be members
- The Kompass directory of companies, which is regionally organised and can be searched online (gb.kompass.com)
- The local council: the business department might produce a list of major business ratepayers; the economic development section may have a list of major employers
- The local newspaper, which will carry stories from time to time that mention local companies, and may provide information on new companies planning to set up in the area
- You – by keeping your eyes open you can often identify local companies that it could just be worth approaching

It is likely that most of the smaller companies you approach will not have a donations policy in place (if they give at all), and may well make their decisions on the basis of the personal interests of their managing director or senior partners. Some may never have made a charitable donation before and may not know about the related tax advantages available to them, so be prepared to tell them about these opportunities.

Some of these companies may prefer to give in kind – for example, a prize for a raffle or advertising in a souvenir brochure for a fundraising event. It might be easier to approach these companies for this sort of support in the first instance, and later on, once they have given something, see if they would like to make a cash donation.

Small and medium-sized businesses will react quickly to economic conditions. When business is falling, their concerns will be for their staff, and not giving money to charities.

Staff time is also at a premium as numbers are small and people are usually stretched with their workload. Staff volunteering schemes are therefore unlikely to be entered into.

Charitable giving is far more likely to be led by the enthusiasms of the partners or directors, but is also likely to be responsive to causes where staff are involved. One local business gives the following advice:

- Match your request to what the business can afford. If a project is too large and the business can only give a small donation they will see their contribution as being swallowed up and not making any difference at all.
- Lengthy letters take up too much time to consider. It's much better if they're simple, succinct and concise.
- Letters should be typed rather than hand-written.
- A good track record gives the appeal credence.
- Corporate giving is not just about money – partners tend to give their time and skills through involvement, more so than cash.
- Telephone to make things happen. If this is daunting, either delegate the contact work to someone else (perhaps someone on your management committee who already has links with business people) or try to increase your confidence in some way.

Who to approach

Key factors in approaching companies

Research

Research is very important, not only into companies but also into personal contacts. When planning an appeal, an important first step is to find which of the people associated with your charity have influence or know people who have. If you can find a link between one of your supporters/volunteers/staff/trustees and a particular company – use it.

You should try to find out as much as you can about the companies you have identified as potential donors. But, remember:

- Companies generally have less well-defined policies than grant-making charities, although you can often determine a pattern in their giving.
- The chance of an application made 'out of the blue' getting substantial support is low.
- Appeals made towards the end of a company's financial year are less likely to succeed.
- Companies are more conservative in their giving and are less likely to support innovative projects (at least until they are established) or anything that is risky or controversial.
- Companies' policies change more frequently than those of grant-makers, because of mergers, takeovers, or a fall or rise in profits, so ensure your research is up to date. Consulting a copy of the company's latest annual report and accounts is not necessarily enough; they may have been taken over since then. Check the company's website, the financial press on a regular basis, or make a quick telephone call to see if anything has changed such as company name, address or your contact.

The company

The firms to approach will depend on the nature of your organisation. If you are a national organisation then an appeal to the country's leading companies is appropriate. Local groups should approach local firms and local branches of national companies which have a presence in their area. Organisations can approach companies in allied fields: for example, theatres can appeal to fabric companies. Be imaginative when looking for a connection.

As outlined in the 'Smaller local companies' section on p. xxix, most local companies have no donations policy and you may have to explain the advantages to giving and approach them for in-kind support in the first instance.

Larger companies might have a manager who is responsible for dealing with charitable appeals, although a donations committee (which often includes senior management) may have the final say. The largest companies might also employ specialist staff to assess the applications and make recommendations.

You need to be selective when you decide on which companies to approach and then find out who you should contact within the company. The choice of company will depend upon what connection you have with them.

First, identify and match possible companies with various aspects of your work. In particular, try to find any local companies that are known for their generosity or might want to support your particular beneficiary group.

Second, contact BITC to find out about its membership or to help you identify local companies through its regional network.

Next, consider the following questions:

- Has the company supported you before?
- Does it have a stated interest in your project such as the environmental initiative that you are promoting?
- Is the company local to your community?
- Are you consumers of its service or product?
- Does the company need better publicity in the community and could you offer that with a link?
- Do your activities contribute to improving the business environment?
- Is the company a large employer in the area with an interest in the current and future workforce?

Lastly, one big problem you may face involves the ownership of seemingly independent companies. Many companies are in fact part of much larger concerns. In recent years there has been a substantial number of mergers and takeovers, plus the buying and selling of business between corporations. A useful, although expensive, source of information is the directory *Who Owns Whom* (published by Gap Books), which has a subsidiary index listing most subsidiaries of companies included in this guide. Check your main library to see if they have a copy.

You can also use company annual reports, which (for most companies) can be obtained from their website or on request. These reports provide good background information on the company concerned, and occasionally information on its charitable support programme. Some private (and occasionally public) companies will not send out annual reports except to shareholders; in such cases you can go to Companies House to get hold of a copy. Offices are situated in Cardiff, Edinburgh, Belfast and London and the website address is: www.companieshouse.gov.uk

The person

Once you have decided on the company, you will need to find out how it is organised and who makes any decisions about charitable giving. Where a company has a number of branches or operating units throughout the country these may have some autonomy in grant decisions. There is usually a maximum amount that they can decide, over which the application will be passed to the next level: regional or national. If you can find this out beforehand it will save time in the long run.

You need to tailor your request to the level at which you are asking and to which budget it might come from; it may not necessarily be from the company's charitable giving budget but possibly marketing or personnel. Once you have established the budget source and level, you will then need to find the right person to talk and write to. Here are a few tips:

1 Find out what, if any, previous contact you or your group has had with companies: any previous fundraising approaches that have been made, and with what success.

2 Find out whether any of your management committee, volunteers or supporters have any personal contact with the companies you plan to approach – and whether they know people who have credibility in the business world who can help you do the asking. It may be appropriate for one of these contacts to sign the appeal letter.

3 Look into whether one of your volunteers or supporters is an employee of the company.

4 Find out if any of your clients or users work for the company.

5 Alternatively, you might be able to tie your appeal in to a known personal interest of a director.

6 Enlist a senior business leader to assist you with your fundraising. This can be someone to serve as chair of a development or fundraising committee, or just to contact a few colleagues and sign a few letters.

Generally an appeal through a personal contact will work best. But if you don't have a contact and can see no way of developing one, then you will have to come up with another link.

As a first step you might contact the company to find out:

- Who is responsible for dealing with charitable appeals and their name and job title
- What information they can send regarding their company
- Any procedure or timetable for submitting applications
- Whether they might be interested in coming to see your organisation at work; visits are useful when discussing bigger donations with the larger companies, but are difficult to arrange for anything small

Unfortunately, there is no short cut if you have no inside knowledge of the company. Be prepared to spend time on the company's website or the telephone, particularly if the company has no decided policy on giving.

Almost certainly your appeal will be in the form of a letter. Make this as personal as you can. Circular letters are likely to end up in the bin and many companies will not consider them as a point of policy. Make the letter professional but motivating, and short and to the point.

Be specific in your approach

Rather than sending out a circular mailing to 100 or 1,000 companies, you will be more successful if you select a few companies you believe will be particularly interested in your project, and target your application to them and their policy.

Find a good reason why you believe the company should support you and include this prominently in your letter. You may be able to relate what you are doing as a charity to companies which have some relevance to your work: for example, a children's charity might appeal to companies making children's products; a housing charity to construction companies, building societies, etc. Any relationship, however tenuous, creates a point of contact on which you can build a good case for obtaining the company's support. If you can find no relationship, should you be approaching that company at all?

There may be occasions when a charity will not want to accept money from a company in a related industry (see the environmental/youth group examples in 'Ethical issues' below). Similarly, a local charity might not want money from a company that has made people in the area redundant. Each charity has to judge where it draws the line and ultimately what is in the best interests of the charity.

Be clear about why you need the money

You must be clear about the objectives of the work for which you are raising money, particularly its timescale and how it relates to your overall programme of work. Try to think in project terms rather than seeking money to cover basic administration costs. You need to develop projects out of your current activities to present to potential donors. You can build a percentage of administration costs into the costs of a project. If you relate what you are doing to a specific timescale, this again makes what you are applying for a project rather than a contribution to your year-on-year core costs.

Be persistent

Do not underestimate the persistence factor. If you do not receive a donation in the first year, do not assume that the company will never support you. Go back a second and even a third time.

If you are going back, mention the fact that you have applied to the company previously, perhaps saying that you are now presenting something different which may be (you hope) of more interest.

If the company gives you reasons for refusing support, use these to help you put in more appropriate applications in the future. If the response is that the company does not give to your particular type of activity, then you know that it is no use you going back. If the company said its funds were fully committed, you can try to find out when would be a better time to apply.

Note the response to your appeal and use any information you can glean to improve your chances the next time.

Ethical issues

Receiving support from companies can be problematic if the business values or practice of the company conflict with what your organisation stands for. There are two approaches:

1 Some organisations will accept money from anyone, on the basis that the money can be used to do good.

2 Others define certain types of company that they will not accept support from. Tobacco, alcohol, gambling, armaments, mining/oil industries, polluters and companies operating overseas that underpay their workforce are all areas of business activity that can cause problems.

An ethical stance is of particular importance where the work of the charity is directly connected with the issue.

Decide your ethical policy before approaching companies. It should be agreed by the trustees, perhaps in consultation with staff if they think that necessary, and recorded.

Sometimes the issues are clear cut. It is relatively easy, for example, for an environmental group to decide whether to accept money from a nuclear power company, or a youth charity from a tobacco or alcohol company. The product relationship with the cause is clear, and all the charity has to do is agree a position on the issue in its ethical policy.

Three organisations that chart the ethical behaviour of companies and which can provide you with the information you need to formulate an ethical donations policy:

1 EIRIS (Ethical Investment Research Services) researches companies on the FT All-Share Index. Its main aim is to advise on socially responsible investment. A charge is made for its services.

2 Ethical Consumer Research Association produces *Corporate Critic*, which rates more than 25,000 companies on their ethical performance at: www.corporatecritic.org.

3 Ethical Corporation provides 'business intelligence for sustainability', mainly aimed at big business but it also provides information which charities may find useful. It is a subscription service, although some free information is available: www.ethicalcorp.com.

Writing an appeal letter

Put yourself in the position of the company. Why should they want to give their shareholders' funds to you? Why should they choose your charity's appeal ahead of any others they might receive? Think about the benefits they will get from supporting you and mention these in your letter (for sponsorship proposals these benefits will be central to your success or failure). Then consider the following important points:

- Think of a project or aspect of your work that the business sector might like to support. Generally, do not appeal for administration costs or a contribution to an endowment fund. Recognise that companies are likely to be interested in some ideas and not others. For example, a charity supporting people with drug misuse problems might be more likely to get money for education than rehabilitation. An appreciation of the kind of projects that a particular company would like to support will be very helpful to you.
- Your letter should be clear and concise. Try to get it all on one side of A4. You can always supply other information as attachments. It should be written clearly and be free from jargon. Someone not familiar with what you are doing should be able to read and understand it and be persuaded to act on it. Give your letter in draft to someone outside your charity to read and comment on before finalising it and sending it out.
- State why you need the money and exactly how it will be spent. The letter itself should be straightforward. It should include the following information: why you think the company might be interested in supporting you; what your organisation does and some brief background on how it was set up; who the organisation serves; why the organisation needs funds; and how the donation would be spent if it were to be forthcoming.
- Attempt to communicate the urgency of your appeal. Fundraising is an intensively competitive business; there is a limited amount of money to give away, and you have to ensure that some of it comes your way. If it appears that although you would like the money now it would not matter terribly much if you got it next year, this might encourage company staff to consider more pressing applications. But don't give the impression you are fundraising at the last minute. Show them you are professional and you have carefully planned your fundraising appeal. You should also try to show that your charity is well-run, efficient and cost-effective in how it operates.
- You should mention why you think the company should support your cause. This could range from specific advantages such as improved customer relations and the good publicity the company will get from supporting your cause to more generalised notions of corporate responsibility and the creation of goodwill in the local community. If the firm's generosity is to be made public, for example through advertising or any publicity arising from the gift, then emphasise the goodwill which will accrue to the company.
- Ask for something specific. Many companies, having been persuaded to give, are not sure how much to give. You can ask a firm to give a donation of a specific amount (matched to what you believe its ability to contribute to be), or to contribute the cost of a particular item. You can suggest a figure by mentioning what other companies are giving. You can mention a total and say how many donations you will need to achieve this. Don't be unreasonable in your expectations. Just because a company is large and rich, this doesn't mean that it makes big grants.
- If you can demonstrate some form of 'leverage' this will be an added attraction. Company donations on the whole are quite modest, but companies like to feel they are having a substantial impact with the money they spend. If you can show that a small amount of money will enable a much larger project to go ahead, or will release further funds, say, on a matching basis from another source, this will definitely be an advantage.
- Having written a short appeal letter, you can append some background support literature. This should not be a 50-page treatise outlining your latest policies but, like your letter, should be concise and to the point: a record of your achievements, your latest annual report, press cuttings, or even a specially produced brochure to accompany your appeal.
- Make sure that the letter is addressed to the correct person at the correct address. It pays to do this background research. Keep all the information on file as it will make your job much easier next time.
- Don't assume that every company will give. Make parallel approaches to a number of companies.
- Consider who might be the best person to make the approach or sign the letter. It may not be you but could be a senior business executive from another company which has already supported your organisation. Their endorsement of your work can provide reassurance to other companies.

After the application

If you're unsuccessful in obtaining funding, check if the company is registered for payroll giving and, if it is, ask if you can promote your cause to its employees. In addition, you could try asking again next year (unless the company says that it is not its policy to support your type of organisation or to give to charity at all). Persistence can sometimes pay.

If you are successful, remember to say thank you; this is an elementary courtesy which is too often forgotten. If the company gives you any substantial amount of money, then you should try to keep it in touch with the achievements related to its donation (such as a brief progress report or copies of your annual report or latest publications).

If you have already received a donation, go back again next year. The company has demonstrated that it is interested in what you are doing and in supporting you. It may well do it again next year, especially if you have thanked it for the donation and kept it in touch with how the project developed.

How companies reply to you

Sadly, many companies will not even reply to your appeal. A few may acknowledge receipt of your letter, and occasionally you will get thanked for your request and be told that it is being considered and you will only hear the outcome if you are successful. Larger companies have a system for dealing with charity mail, and most will see it as good PR to send a reply.

Smaller companies which do not give much charitable support will not have the time or the resources to do anything but scan the mail and only consider those which stand out.

What sort of reply should you expect? If you do an extensive appeal, you will inevitably get a lot of refusals. These will normally be generic letters apologising and saying that they can't support you; occasionally you may get a letter sent to you personally. You might also receive a cheque.

Good luck!

Alphabetical listing of companies

This section gives information on 400 companies from all sectors of industry, gathered from a combination of annual reports and company websites, and supplemented by our own research.

Types of company

A company may be: a public limited company (designated plc), normally a company with shares quoted on the stock exchange; a privately owned company; or a subsidiary company. If it is a subsidiary it may have retained its own identity for charitable donations and we would include an entry in this guide. Other subsidiaries included are British-based subsidiaries of an overseas-based company.

Where a company has been recently acquired it may not yet have decided whether it will continue to manage its own charitable donations budget.

Through acquisitions and mergers, companies may now be owned by a holding company, a conglomerate, or a transnational company. You may have to do your own research to link local companies and plants with the head office that may have ultimate control over their donations. The company annual report, usually available free online or on request, lists subsidiary and associate (less than 50% owned) companies and reports on the activity of the company during the year. We have included a selection of subsidiaries of each company within the entry. However, for many companies this is taken from the latest annual report, which can be several months out of date. The *Who Owns Whom* directory (published by GAP Books) also lists subsidiaries of UK companies, and more up-to-date information can often be found on company websites.

Interpreting financial information

The charitable donations figure given is that published by the company in the 'Director's Report' section of its annual report and accounts. This should relate only to cash donations. However, companies are increasingly including the value of secondments, gifts in kind, advertising or sponsorship which, customarily, are included in the total contributions figure. Furthermore, a company's present level of donations does not necessarily indicate future commitments. Sending an appeal to less generous companies may actually persuade them to increase their donations. Certainly if they never receive appeals there will be no outside pressure on them to change their policy, although in general if a company is only giving a little your chances of success are reduced.

Because a significant number (165) of our 400 listed companies chose in this last year's reporting not to declare their charitable donations, we have had to rely on previously researched information and estimate the UK cash contribution made. This is in an attempt to give our readers at least an indication of what the company might have given and has given historically.

Normally a coordinated company donor will budget a certain sum for its charitable donations and stick within this amount. Some allocate their entire budget at an annual meeting; others spread donations throughout the year. Some give to causes they wish to support until the budget is used up and then stop; others continue to give even after the budget is spent if an appeal takes their fancy. If they reply to your appeal, many will write and say that their budget is 'fully committed'.

The year end is important in that if you get your appeal in soon afterwards, the company will not have spent its charitable budget for the coming year. However, if a company allocates its budget evenly throughout the year and receives a flood of applications at the start of its new financial year, some which would have been supported later in the year now miss out. There is no fail-safe answer to this problem. However, your chances of success are usually improved by sending the application earlier rather than later in the company's financial year.

How to interpret the donations policy

There are certain standard phrases that appear in the policy of the company entries.

No response to circular appeals

This means that 'Dear Sir/Madam' letters, whether they are hand-signed or use photocopied signatures, are probably not even read, let alone replied to.

Preference for local charities in areas of company presence/Preference for appeals relevant to company business/Preference for charities where a member of staff is involved

These are self-explanatory. Local charities should check whether appeals can be made locally or must be sent to head office. Any link with the company should be highlighted.

Preferred areas of support are . . .

This information is taken from our research and is subject to change.

Exclusions (no grants are given for . . .)

As above.

How to use this guide

Below is a typical company entry, showing the format we have used to present the information obtained from each of the companies. Remember to always check the company's website for information before making an application. You should submit your request in writing, but may wish to ask for details of the grants procedure, check the contact for charitable donations or request a copy of the latest annual report. The latter, along with community support information, may also be obtained via the quoted website address.

Fictitious Productions plc

The full name of the company is given with the companies listed in alphabetical order.

Spin

Correspondent: A Grant, CSR Manager, 68 Nowhere Street, Anytown AN6 2LM (tel: 01510 000000; fax: 01511 000000; website: www.fictprod.co.uk)

Only the large corporate givers have specialist staff dealing with appeals (a direct line number may be given in such instances). However, the company secretary, public relations or marketing departments will deal with appeals to many companies. Unless otherwise stated, the address is for the head office, to which appeals should be sent.

Directors: Terence Story, Chair; Shelley Yarn, Chief Executive; Luther Tale (women: 1; men: 2)

We give all available names of the directors and include the ratio of women to men on the board, where known.

Year end	31/03/2014
Turnover	£837,300,000
Pre-tax profit	£292,000,000

Financial statistics: The year end, turnover and pre-tax profit (a figure in brackets denotes a loss). Most relate to 2014. The figures give an indication of the scale of the company's giving relative to its size.

Nature of business: The company is involved in the production of fictitious information.

The main area of company activity. This can be useful if you are looking for a product link.

Company registration number: 116565

The registration number at Companies House, or in the case of a financial institution such as a Building Society, its FSA number, is also included.

Subsidiaries include: Cashflow Industries, False Publications, Sundry Matters, and Wage Packet Co.

A sample of the company's subsidiaries is listed here. Full details are usually given within the company's annual accounts.

Brands include: Storytime; Truth Ltd; Dizzy Media; and Blank Page.

A sample of the company's brands is given here. Full details are available on company websites.

Main locations: Grimsby, Liverpool, Bristol, Perth

The main locations are useful if you are looking for a geographical link.

UK employees: 3,872

Total employees: 7,689

The number of total employees and UK employees, where information is available.

Focus of giving: general charitable purposes.

We list the companies' charitable preferences.

Membership: BITC, LBG

Indicates whether the company is a member of Business in the Community and LBG.

Charity of the Year ✓
Overseas giving ✓

Any additional relevant information.

Charitable donations

Cash UK (latest available):	2014	£420,000
	2013	£400,000
	2012	£350,000
	2011	£225,000
	2010	£184,000
	2009	£243,000
Total UK (cash and in kind):	2014	£575,000
Cash worldwide:	2014	£1,234,000
Total worldwide (cash and in kind):	2014	£7,868,000

Figures for the last five years available are given. Also, figures for total UK and total worldwide contributions are given and these include the value of in-kind giving, good-cause sponsorship, secondments, etc., where available.

Community involvement

The company supports local enterprise agencies and considers secondment of employees to local economic development initiatives.

This provides an overview of the company's community support, detailing preferred causes and any geographical areas that are favoured.

Corporate giving

The company's community contributions totalled £575,000 in 2014. This included in-kind giving, the cost of secondments and arts sponsorship, and charitable donations of £420,000. National grants range from £250 to £5,000. Local grants range from £25 to £500.

Major grant recipients in 2014 included Any Town LGBT Network (for information leaflets), Perth Parent & Toddler Association (towards play equipment) and the local wildlife trust.

Quotes total cash donations made and, if available, total community contributions.

Examples of grants and their size, where known, are listed. Large grants are often a good indicator of the company's priorities.

In-kind support

The company donates surplus or used furniture/equipment to local causes.

Some companies give gifts in kind, which can be anything from used stock to valuable pro bono work.

Employee-led support

A charity is selected each year to benefit from employee fundraising, with the company making a contribution by way of matched funding.

Payroll giving: A scheme is operated by the company.

Many company employees give time and money to local causes, including fundraising and expertise. If a payroll giving scheme is operated, we state so.

Commercially led support

Sponsorship: The arts – The typical sponsorship range is from £1,000 to £25,000. It sponsors Southport Sinfonietta and supported music festivals in Grimsby and Perth.

Covers good-cause sponsorship, if undertaken, and will include a contact, if different from the main correspondent. Provides information on cause-related marketing promotions, if applicable.

Corporate social responsibility

CSR committee: The company has a separate CSR committee.

CSR information: All charitable contributions are made through the Fictitious Productions Foundation, which is funded by donations of bonuses from employees and matched funding by the company.

CSR report: A CSR report is available on the company's website.

Here we give details of the structure of any designated CSR committee and when it meets; the company's CSR policy (if one exists and is published), with details of its approach to community giving if known; and information on if and when a CSR/sustainability report is published and where it is available.

Exclusions

No response is given to circular appeals. No grants are given for fundraising events, purely denominational religious appeals, local appeals not in areas of company presence, large national appeals, overseas projects, political activities or individuals. Non-commercial advertising is not supported. It does not sponsor individuals or travel.

Lists any areas, subjects or types of grants the company will not consider. **Check here first.**

Applications

In writing to the correspondent. Applications are considered by a donations committee which meets three times a year.

Includes how to apply and when to submit an application. We also state whether there is further information available from the company.

3i Group plc

Financial services

Correspondent: Kathryn van der Kroft, Communications Director, 16 Palace Street, London SW1E 5JD (tel: 020 7975 3021; email: kathryn.vanderkroft@3i.com; website: www.3i.com)

Directors: Sir Adrian Montague, Chair; Simon Borrows, Chief Executive; Julia Wilson, Group Finance Director; Jonathan Asquith; Alistair Cox; Caroline Banszky; David Hutchison; Martine Verluyten (women: 3; men: 5)

Year end	31/03/2014

Nature of business: 3i is an international investor, with almost £13 billion of assets under management focusing on private equity, infrastructure and debt management.

Company registration number: 1142830

Subsidiary undertakings include: Action; Element Materials Technology; Inspecta; Mémora; Refresco. There is a detailed explanation of what is termed a 'subsidiary' in the annual report and accounts.

Main locations: London, UK

Total employees: 266

Focus of giving: General charitable purposes, education, heritage, housing, homelessness, arts, culture, poverty and social exclusion, children, young people, community/social welfare.

FTSE 100	✓
Matched funding	✓
Payroll giving	✓

Charitable donations

Cash UK (latest available):	2014	£250,000
	2013	£198,000
	2012	£410,000
	2011	£408,600
	2010	£407,490
Total UK (cash and in kind):	2014	£250,000
Cash worldwide:	2014	£250,000
Total worldwide (cash and in kind):	2014	£250,000

Community involvement

Beneficiaries of the group's corporate support include the following UK charities: Community Links; Enterprise Education Trust; Historic Royal Palaces; National Youth Orchestra and The Passage.

Case study – taken from the 2013/14 annual report:

> 3i has supported Community Links for 14 years and is currently supporting the Play, Sow and Grow community hub in east London. Play, Sow and Grow is a purpose built community space in Stratford, Newham, a borough that is ranked as the third most deprived in the UK, where 50% of children live in poverty and household income for most of these families is below the poverty line. Play, Sow and Grow uses the natural environment to deliver educational play schemes where children and young people are encouraged to spend time outdoors. The garden contains growing fruit and vegetables, roaming hens and a tree house, sand pit and other play equipment. During the year 2013/14 Play, Sow and Grow delivered activities including open access play for children including those with disabilities, youth workshops, summer schools, DIY gardening and summer schools.

Corporate giving

The group focuses its charitable activities on the disadvantaged, young people and education. Charities are supported on the basis of their effectiveness and impact. In 2013/14 charitable giving totalled £250,000 which would appear to have been given in cash.

In-kind support

3i has a policy of matching the amount raised by UK staff through sponsorship by family and friends of their fundraising efforts for UK-registered charities. 3i contributed £16,000 in the year to 31 March 2014. It is not clear if this amount has been included in the total contribution figure of £250,000.

Employee-led support

Staff contributed £40,000 in the year to 31 March 2014 by way of the Give As You Earn scheme, administered by the Charities Aid Foundation. Fundraising events by staff achieved £16,000 in the year which was matched by the group.

Corporate social responsibility

CSR committee: The Brand and Values committee assists the board in its oversight of the group's brand, corporate values, reputation, ethical approach and behaviours, together with its approach to corporate responsibility and makes recommendations and advice as it thinks fit.

CSR information: The group has policies and procedures in place for its CSR programme which include its environmental, ethical and social policies. Policies are available to view on the group's website.

CSR report: There is a helpful and concise CSR report which would appear to be published annually. There is also a CSR webpage on the group's website.

Exclusions

No support is given for political appeals or individuals.

Applications

In writing to the correspondent referenced 'Community support'.

3M United Kingdom plc

Chemicals and plastics

Correspondent: Communities Team, 3M Community, 3M United Kingdom plc, 3M Centre, Cain Road, Bracknell RG12 8HT (tel: 0870 536 0036; website: www.3M.com/uk)

Directors: Paul Keel, Managing Director; Donald Gray, General Manager, Finance; Paul Williams; Stella Heggarty (women: 1; men: 3)

Year end	31/12/2013
Turnover	£574,352,000
Pre-tax profit	£50,190,000

Nature of business: 3M is fundamentally a science-based company. Products manufactured in the UK include coated abrasives, personal safety equipment, adhesive tapes, industrial microbiology products, drug delivery systems, high performance coatings, secure documents, passport readers and imaging systems. There are 88,000 employees globally.

Company registration number: 1123045

Subsidiary undertakings include: 3M United Kingdom plc is a wholly owned subsidiary of 3M Company, a company incorporated in the United States, as the ultimate parent company and controlling party.

Brands include: Post-it; Scotch; Scotch-Brite; Scotchgard.

Main locations: Bangor, Bedford, Aycliffe, Atherstone, Bracknell, Manchester, Clitheroe, Hillington, Gorseinon, Bridgend, Runcorn, Northallerton

UK employees: 2,000

Total employees: 2,000

Focus of giving: General charitable purposes, education, environment, poverty and social exclusion, community/social welfare.

Membership: BITC, LBG

Gifts in kind	✓
Matched funding	✓

Charitable donations

Cash UK (latest available):	2013	£237,000
	2012	£274,000
	2010	£239,000
	2008	£423,000
	2007	£412,000
Total UK (cash and in kind):	2013	£237,000
Cash worldwide:	2013	£237,000
Total worldwide (cash and in kind):	2013	£237,000

Community involvement

The company believes that commercial success and corporate responsibility are inextricably linked and therefore its contribution is towards communities in which it has operations. It should be noted that the community programme is structured and not about responding to general requests. The website states that the company will 'support organisations that help communities help themselves'.

National programme

As a technology company, a large number of 3M's employees hold qualifications in STEM (science, technology, engineering and maths) subjects. It is recognised that too few pupils – in particular female students – are staying with these subjects beyond GCSE. 3M hopes to redress that in some way by working with educational specialists in order to provide free online educational resources that help make these subjects real and relevant to pupils.

This programme involves partnering with schools local to its major sites; the donation of in-kind gifts of 3M products and services; visits to (and the use of) 3M facilities; encouragement of employee volunteering – particularly STEM Ambassadors; matching employees' fundraising achievements, and creating free online teaching resources that can be used by schools throughout the UK and Ireland.

Local programmes

The local programmes are focused on three areas:

- Education: aiming to bridge the gap between classroom and work place, the company establishes links with local schools through activities relevant to the academic curriculum. 3M is particularly keen to support the science and technology curriculum
- Environment: the company has a commitment to promoting healthier, safer and more environmentally aware communities
- Relief of suffering: the company will support: health-related charities, welfare groups for the elderly, groups for people with disabilities and volunteer centres

In order to be considered for support, projects must fall within one or more of these topic areas and relate to a community in which 3M has a site presence.

Proposals must also fulfil one or more of the following criteria:

- Be a registered UK charitable concern (no individuals/teams/third party fundraisers or requests for funds for overseas can be considered)
- Address a specific identified local community need
- Involve 3M volunteers
- On completion, be able to demonstrate measurable results

Corporate giving

In 2013 the amount contributed in charitable donations by the UK company was £237,000. Research shows that significant in-kind contributions were made but figures for the cost of this have not been published.

In-kind support

3M's community support is inseparable from its commercial success and targets future potential employees by working with educational specialists in order to provide free online educational resources that help make STEM (science, technology, engineering and maths) subjects relevant. Online services include:

3M Streetwise – (aimed at 7–11) to help schools teach road safety through scientific principles.

3M Worldlywise – (aimed at 11–16) to help young people learn about sustainability and the environment as part of maths, science and geography. According to www.bitc.org.uk:

> This project has not only provided free online resources it has also enabled 3M to partner with schools and start work on a programme of research that will aim to show the impact of its activities on pupils' attitudes to STEM subjects and careers – information that the company plans to share with wider industry.

Employee-led support

There is a volunteer programme which should be utilised when applying for contributions under the local programme. See 'Community involvement' section.

Commercially led support

STEM Ambassadors go into schools to demonstrate that a wide range of interesting and rewarding careers are open to people with STEM qualifications. Through them, the company aims to engage and motivate students to choose science, technology, engineering and maths as their subject choices.

3M is a signatory to the UK Government's 'Your Life' campaign to encourage greater participation among women in STEM careers.

The NHS Innovation Challenge Prizes

This programme recognises and rewards proven innovations with potential for adoption across the NHS. Open only to NHS organisations in England, a £650,000 prize fund is available to disseminate and embed winning projects which are new to the NHS or applied in a novel way. Innovations should deliver more efficient models of care, better value for money or improved patient outcomes.

The programme's substantial funding is enhanced by professional support from industry partners. 3M, founder of the One Together collaborative programme to reduce the incidence of healthcare associated infections, has set the *Infection Control Challenge* – a prize of £50,000. 'Focused on minimising infection in care homes, community intravenous therapy or perioperative care, the challenge encourages new approaches to reducing avoidable harm and improving efficiencies across the whole patient journey.'

The prize is for the winner's NHS organisation. In addition the winner will benefit from a 3M professional mentor and attend leadership training and best practice sharing at 3M's global centre for healthcare innovation in St Paul, USA.

Corporate social responsibility

CSR committee: There is no evidence of a CSR committee.

CSR information: Extract from 3M's Vision taken from its global website:

> 3M's commitment is to actively contribute to sustainable development through environmental protection, social responsibility and economic progress. To us, that means meeting the needs of society today, while respecting the ability of future generations to meet their needs.

CSR report: There is no evidence of a separate CSR report.

Exclusions

No support is given for appeals from individuals, third party fundraisers, local appeals not in areas of company presence, large national appeals or overseas projects.

Applications

For more information, use the online facility at 'Contact Us' and reference 'Community'.

Abbott Mead Vickers – BBDO Ltd

Advertising/marketing

Correspondent: Company Secretary, 151 Marylebone Road, London NW1 5QE (tel: 020 7616 3500; fax: 020 7616 3600; website: www.amvbbdo.com)

Directors: Colin Fleming; Priscilla Snowball; Ian Pearman (women: 1; men: 2)

Year end	31/12/2013
Turnover	£137,359,000
Pre-tax profit	£13,755,000

Nature of business: AMV BBDO is an advertising agency that works with over 92 brands. AMV campaigns may incorporate digital, social, experiential, print or broadcast media. AMV is part of the BBDO network, the third largest agency network in the world, with 288 offices across 80 countries. BBDO is part of the Omnicom Group. AMV is also part of the AMV Group of communications companies, which includes specialists in customer relationship management, public relations, and contract publishing.

Company registration number: 1935786

Subsidiary undertakings include: The company is a subsidiary undertaking of Omnicom Group Inc., incorporated in the USA.

Main locations: London, UK

Total employees: 364

Focus of giving: General charitable purposes, enterprise/training, environment, heritage, housing, homelessness, individuals, arts, culture, poverty and social exclusion.

Payroll giving	✓

Charitable donations

Cash UK (latest available):	2013	£94,000
	2012	£104,000
	2011	£67,000
	2009	£62,000
	2008	£69,000
Total UK (cash and in kind):	2013	£94,000
Cash worldwide:	2013	£94,000
Total worldwide (cash and in kind):	2013	£94,000

Community involvement

Unfortunately we could not find any useful, relevant information regarding this company's charitable giving apart from its award winning payroll giving scheme.

Corporate giving

In 2013 the company made charitable donations of £94,000.

Employee-led support

Payroll giving

The company has received a platinum award for its payroll giving scheme which is administered by the Charities Aid Foundation.

Corporate social responsibility

CSR committee: No information available.

CSR information: There was no information available on CSR.

CSR report: No information available.

Applications

In writing to the correspondent referenced 'Charitable donations'.

Aberdeen Asset Management plc

Financial services

Correspondent: Corporate Social Responsibility Committee, 4th Floor, Union Plaza, 1 Union Wynd, Aberdeen AB10 1DQ (tel: 01224 631999; fax: 01224 647010; website: www.aberdeen-asset.co.uk)

Directors: Roger Cornick, Chair; Martin Gilbert, Chief Executive; Andrew Laing; Bill Rattray; Anne Richards; Hugh Young; Anita Frew; Julie Chakraverty; Jim Pettigrew; Simon Troughton; Akira Suzuki; Rod MacRae; Richard Mully; Jutta af Rosenborg (women: 4; men: 7)

Year end	30/09/2013
Turnover	£1,314,800,000
Pre-tax profit	£390,300,000

Nature of business: Aberdeen Asset Management plc is a global investment management group, managing assets for both institutional and retail clients from some 33 offices in 26 countries.

Company registration number: 82015

Subsidiary undertakings include: Aberdeen Asset Management Asia Ltd; Aberdeen Asset Managers Ltd; Aberdeen Asset Management Inc.; Aberdeen Global Services SA; Aberdeen International Fund Managers Ltd; Aberdeen Asset Management Life and Pensions Ltd; Aberdeen Fund Managers Ltd; Aberdeen Investments Jersey Ltd Fund; Aberdeen SVG Private Equity Managers Ltd.

Main locations: Aberdeen

UK employees: 384

Total employees: 2,200

Focus of giving: General charitable purposes, health, ill health, older people, overseas projects, children, young people, community/social welfare.

Membership: BITC

FTSE 100	✓
Gifts in kind	✓
Matched funding	✓
Overseas giving	✓
Payroll giving	✓
Sponsorship	✓

Charitable donations

Cash UK (latest available):	2013	£757,000
	2009	£202,000
	2008	£172,000
Total UK (cash and in kind):	2013	£757,000
Cash worldwide:	2013	£757,000
Total worldwide (cash and in kind):	2013	£1,300,000

Community involvement

Aberdeen Asset Management Charitable Foundation

Most of the company's charitable cash giving appears to be channelled through its corporate charity Aberdeen Asset Management Charitable Foundation (OSCR number SC042597).

In 2012/13 the trustees of the foundation made donations to more than 100 charities in 22 of the countries in which the group is located, with all donations made in line with the global guidelines.

The foundation has two core focuses – emerging markets and local communities, reflecting the group's ambition to give back to those areas which are a key strategic focus of the business and to the communities in which Aberdeen employees live and work.

Local communities

The foundation's board decided that, since the group's local offices have different cultures and charitable priorities, each office would have the authority to select projects they would like to support, along the general theme of making a positive impact on the surrounding community.

Employees have the opportunity to take volunteering leave to provide additional support, in time and expertise, to the locally elected charities. For example, in Aberdeen, the local committee made a donation to the Powis Gateway Community Centre to enable it to continue operating its daily breakfast club for disabled and disadvantaged young people throughout the north-east of Scotland. Unlike other breakfast clubs, the children's parents are encouraged to attend and enjoy breakfast with them. This family ethos means parents take responsibility for getting their children to attend school as well as establishing a morning routine for their mutual benefit.

Corporate giving

In 2012/13 the company's charitable contribution was declared as £1.25 million with the qualification that 'this includes donations made by the foundation (Aberdeen Asset Management Charitable Foundation), Aberdeen plc and Give As You Earn employer contributions, but excludes unspent contributions made by the plc to the foundation.'

Research shows that the foundation received £557,000 from the group and we have taken this amount, together with what the company donated by way of matched Give As You Earn employer's contributions of £200,000, making the UK cash donations £757,000.

See the corporate charity entry on p. 387 for more information.

In-kind support

Support is given by the company to charities and good causes by the provision of volunteers, staff receiving time off work for this purpose.

Employee-led support

At a local level, committees in the group's global offices supported a wide range of charities, all of which were selected for the positive impact they have on the areas where employees live and work. In addition to providing monetary support, staff used their time and expertise to volunteer and in 2012/13 more than 15% volunteered.

The company operates Give As You Earn (GAYE) scheme, for which it won a gold award, and in 2012/13 the company contributed £200,000 by way of matched contributions. We have included this cash amount in the UK cash contributions total.

Commercially led support

Aberdeen's sponsorship

The group sponsors a variety of activities from sporting fixtures to cultural events to demonstrate it supports the community and encourages excellence. Further information can be found on the group's website. Sponsorship includes that for: Aberdeen Asset Management Cowes Week; Aberdeen Dad Vail Regatta, Philadelphia; Aberdeen Asset Management Scottish Open; Aberdeen Asset Management Ladies Scottish Open; Paul Di Resta; Golf Ambassadors; Australian Farr 40 National Sailing Series; Extreme Sailing Series Singapore; and Swiss Ski Schools.

For any major sponsorship event, the company states it sees 'supporting an associated charity and considering the environmental implications of the event as part of our obligation to encourage responsible business practices'. At the Aberdeen Scottish Open at Castle Stuart, the company partnered with Connecting Carers, a local charity working across the Highlands to provide information and support to users of health and community care services and carers. At Cowes Week, the company completed the last year of its three year support for Toe in the Water. This is a tri-service initiative which uses competitive sailing to re-inspire injured service personnel to see beyond their injuries, and perform to their limits regardless of their physical condition.

Corporate social responsibility

CSR committee: The company's CR programme is driven by its board of directors. The company believes that this senior level commitment helps make CR a focal point for the business.

CSR information: In 2013 the group's approach was reviewed choosing to focus on three key areas which have a material impact on business operations:

Investing in the group's people

- Recruitment and selection
- Learning, development and talent management
- Equality and diversity
- Health, safety and well-being
- Human rights

Investing responsibly

- Corporate governance
- Responsible Investing
- Taking responsibility for Aberdeen's own environmental impact

Engaging with stakeholders

- The Aberdeen Asset Management Charitable Foundation
- Anti-bribery and corruption
- Whistleblowing
- Suppliers
- Public Policy

CSR report: There is an annual CSR report which can be downloaded from: aberdeen-asset.com and information can also be found in the annual report.

Corporate charity: Aberdeen Asset Management Charitable Foundation (OSCR number SC042597).

Applications

In writing to the correspondent.

Accenture UK Ltd

Accountants, information management and communication, professional support services

Correspondent: Corporate Citizenship Team, 1 Plantation Place, 30 Fenchurch Street, London EC3M 3BD (tel: 020 7844 4000; fax: 020 7844 4444; email: corporatecitizenship@accenture.com; website: www.accenture.com)

Directors: O. Benzecry, Chair and Managing Director; G. Bryant; A. Chapple; T. Fetherston-Dilke; J. Oates; P. Rowe; S. Whitehouse

Year end	31/08/2013
Turnover	£2,135,885,000
Pre-tax profit	£145,094,000

Nature of business: Accenture provides management consulting, technology and outsourcing services, with more than 305,000 employees; offices and operations in more than 200 cities in 56 countries. Accenture (UK) Ltd is a wholly owned subsidiary of the Accenture group and the main trading entity for Accenture in the United Kingdom.

Company registration number: 4757301

Subsidiary undertakings include: Accenture HR Services (Jersey) Ltd; Accenture Azerbaijan Ltd; Taleris Global LLP.

Main locations: Newcastle upon Tyne, Manchester, London, Aberdeen, Edinburgh

UK employees: 8,499

Total employees: 305,000

Focus of giving: Education, enterprise/ training, arts, culture, children, young people, community/social welfare.

Membership: BITC, LBG

Charity of the Year	✓
Humanitarian aid: overseas	✓
Overseas giving	✓
Sponsorship	✓

Charitable donations

Cash UK (latest available):	2013	£794,000
	2012	£118,250
	2009	£733,000
	2008	£182,000
	2007	£433,000
Total UK (cash and in kind):	2013	£794,000
Cash worldwide:	2013	£8,720,000
Total worldwide (cash and in kind):	2013	£29,543,000

Community involvement

Skills to Succeed

Accenture have developed this corporate citizenship initiative which focuses on building skills that enable people around the world to participate in and contribute to the economy. The website states:

> Skills to succeed helps address the global need for skills that open doors to employment and economic opportunity. It does this by drawing on two of Accenture's unique capabilities: training talent and convening powerful partnerships to develop collaborative solutions.

The company states that together with its strategic partners, it has equipped more than half a million people with the skills to get a job or build a business. The new target is that by 2015 a total of 700,000 people worldwide will be equipped with workplace and entrepreneurial skills.

Staff volunteering and pro bono consulting opportunities also help to 'create measurable impact that is greater than the sum of its parts'.

The Accenture Foundation (Charity Commission no: 1057696)

The foundation is funded by Accenture (UK) Ltd and certain Accenture employees. The foundation makes grants to registered or exempt charities working for educational, medical, community, cultural and charitable causes. The company provides all administrative resources for the management of the foundation.

It should be noted that the foundation runs a focused programme of long-term grants funded by the company. Through the establishment of long-term strategic partnerships the foundation states that it continues to make a real difference to its chosen charities (which include those listed at 'Community contributions').

Corporate giving

The company: In 2012/13 the company spent £29.5 million in cash donations, volunteer time, sponsorship and in-kind donations to charitable causes worldwide. In the UK company's accounts a cash donation to registered charities was declared at £794,000 and as no figure was given for the UK in community contributions, we have used this figure as both cash donations and community contributions although we realise both may be substantially more. Accenture does give a detailed breakdown of its giving but the UK figures are included in the geographical area of Europe, Middle East and Africa and we were not able to extract the UK-only figures.

Accenture Foundation: In 2012/13 the foundation had an income of over £208,000 and made grants totalling almost £1.8 million. Its assets stood at £6.6 million.

Beneficiaries included: Prince of Wales Youth Business International (£592,000); Leonard Cheshire Disability (£486,000); VSO (£312,000); Save the Children (£165,000); and Onside Northwest Ltd (£99,000). Smaller grants were also made totalling £53,000.

See the corporate charity entry on p. 388 for more information.

In-kind support

Accenture actively seeks opportunities that will allow it to best utilise its key skills and so have the most beneficial impact on society and its people. It does this through enabling its employees to engage in pro bono programmes, voluntary service overseas placements, projects conducted with Accenture Development Partnerships, three day community allowance and secondments.

Employee-led support

Payroll giving: *Give As You Earn* – Employees are able to sign up to donate to charities of their choice through tax effective payroll giving.

Commercially led support

Sponsorship: Accenture has sponsored numerous high profile community events and institutions over the past few years. The company claims that these associations help promote its business, while allowing it to enjoy the benefits of supporting worthwhile organisations that a make a positive impact on local culture and community. Accenture is the High Performance Business Partner of the world-renowned Royal Shakespeare Company (RSC).

Corporate social responsibility

CSR committee: We assume that there must be a corporate citizenship committee but could find no information on how it is constituted or who is a representative of it.

CSR information: The following statement is taken from the company's website:

> Accenture's Corporate Citizenship commitments are anchored in our core values, our Code of Business Ethics and, ultimately, reflected in the actions of our people. From **Skills to Succeed** to the environment, Accenture and our people work to make a sustainable, measurable difference to the communities in which we work and live.

We were unable to determine the ratio of women to men on the board of Accenture UK Ltd. On the global company's board there are four women and nine men.

CSR report: A Corporate Citizenship Report is available on the company's website.

Corporate charity: The Accenture Foundation (Charity Commission no. 1057696).

Exclusions

No support is given for political appeals or religious appeals.

Applications

For applications to the company itself apply in writing to the correspondent.

Accenture Foundation (Charity Commission no. 1057696)

Proposals are generally invited by the trustees or initiated at their request. Unsolicited applications are discouraged and are unlikely to be successful, even if they fall within the areas in which the trustees are interested.

The trustees have agreed criteria under the overarching theme of 'Building Skills for Better Futures'. This covers registered charities working within the areas of employability and enterprise.

Addleshaw Goddard LLP

Legal

Correspondent: Karen Sinclair, Milton Gate, 60 Chiswell Street, London EC1Y 4AG (tel: 020 7606 8855/020 7788 5504; fax: 020 7606 4390; email: karen.sinclair@addleshawgoddard.com; website: www.addleshawgoddard.com)

Directors: Paul Devitt; Monica Burch; Adam Bennett; Adrian Collins; John Joyce; Simon Kamstra; Michael Leftley; Richard Papworth (women: 1; men: 7)

Year end	30/04/2013
Turnover	£164,380,000
Pre-tax profit	£53,303,000

Nature of business: The provision of legal services.

Company registration number: OC318149

Main locations: London

UK employees: 978

Total employees: 978

Focus of giving: Education, health, ill health, housing, homelessness, poverty and social exclusion, community/social welfare.

Membership: BITC

Gifts in kind	✓
Matched funding	✓
Payroll giving	✓

Charitable donations

Cash UK (latest available):	2013	£220,700
	2009	£150,000
	2008	£150,000
	2007	£75,000
	2006	£66,000
Total UK (cash and in kind):	2013	£57,000
Cash worldwide:	2013	£57,000
Total worldwide (cash and in kind):	2013	£57,000

Community involvement

Money is raised through the efforts of staff social committees and charity committees. The following criteria are applied:

1. There are Charities of the Year, chosen by the people in each office, that are the main focus for fundraising activity
2. Charities of the Year usually rotate every 18 to 24 months
3. In order for a charity to be considered, an AG partner or employee must put the charity forward and be willing to act as the relationship manager, set up a charity committee and lead the fundraising efforts. Charities without an AG sponsor cannot be considered
4. Staff continue to fundraise and make collections for a limited number of charitable causes, where there is a history of providing support (for example, Children in Need/Red Nose Day)
5. The firm's charity trustees are willing to consider donating matched sponsorship money to AG people undertaking charitable activities that fall outside the criteria above (rules apply)
6. Unfortunately, any other good causes seeking funding, or support from staff, cannot usually be accommodated.

The 2013–2015 Charities of the Year are:

- Martin House Children's Hospice (Leeds office)
- St Joseph's Hospice, Hackney (London office)
- Bleakholt Animal Sanctuary (Manchester office)

According to the website:

> The company focuses on developing schemes and helping with programmes near to its offices. Its award winning Charity of the Year programme has created cash donations, since it was set up in November 2007, of over £350,000 in addition to the huge number of hours people have given to support these worthwhile causes. Whilst we can bring skills and enthusiasm to making a difference, we are also keen to work alongside others to learn from their experiences and many of our clients have participated in our community involvement. The company's charitable

contribution is based around the themes of education, social inclusion and access to justice.

The Addleshaw Goddard Charitable Trust (Charity Commission no. 286887) was established since 1983, and since 2003 it has made donations of over £350,000. The trust is funded entirely by the partners of the firm, who each make an annual contribution.

Corporate giving

In 2012/13 the company donated £50,000 to its corporate charity which included £2,300 of funding matched through staff fundraising.

See the corporate charity entry on p. 389 for more information.

Employee-led support

The following information was obtained from the firm's website:

Education and social inclusion

As a provider of legal advice, our firm is only as good as the people who work for it. Therefore, we have an interest in all aspects of the education process in the UK, from primary school reading projects, to senior school mentoring and on to higher education. We are especially interested in growing a future capability within the legal community and take an active role in supporting the education process where we can.

We are also mindful of the issues surrounding professional services and social mobility and seek to be supportive of people who may not have had the educational opportunities that are available to others.

Access to Justice

Our lawyers feel passionately about this subject and many share their skills and give time to help others who have fewer advantages in life by offering pro bono legal advice through a wide range of projects. We are members of the charity LawWorks which helps us to match willing individuals with charities or individuals who would benefit from their legal skills.

Examples of current initiatives include:

Hillside Legal Advice Service (HLAS)

HLAS is a drop in centre offering free legal advice. This is run in conjunction with two other law firms and our sessions run every fourth Wednesday at Hillside Centre in Beeston. The topics covered are varied and we offer free advice, write letters, contact third parties etc and keep an ongoing file which can be picked up by the other law firms.

Literacy Programme

We have been working with Learning Partnerships Volunteer Literacy Programme for the last 12 years. The literacy programme aims to rise standards and attainment in literacy and reduce the risk of children falling behind age related literacy levels. Currently, 23 staff give an hour a week and support over 90 children across 7 inner-city primary schools.

Lawyers in Schools

This programme, run with the Citizenship Foundation, involves groups of lawyers running sessions at a school in Leeds over the course of a term. It forms part of the school's Citizenship module for 14–16 year olds and involves six sessions (of one hour each) including interactive lessons on Youth Justice, Human Rights, Employment and Police Powers.

Our relationship with Workplace Giving, as our provider of 'give as you earn', encourages easy and tax efficient charitable giving.

Payroll giving originated in 1987 and since then over £700M has been donated in the UK. We operate our payroll giving scheme through Workplace Giving. After six months into the scheme the firm had achieved the Silver Standard for Payroll Giving, which we have retained.

To give a donation to your charity of choice couldn't be simpler and as it is a tax efficient way of giving, the benefit to the charity is greater than your contribution. For example: a £5 per month donation actually only costs £3 for a higher tax payer, but the charity gets the full amount.

All employees are given at least one day off a year to participate in CSR activities. This can be increased if agreed with management. The firm's lawyers undertake pro bono (free) legal work as a part of its community programme and this time counts towards the lawyers' chargeable hours targets.

Corporate social responsibility

CSR committee: Each UK office has a CSR partner. In London this is Michael Carter, in Leeds it is Sally Butt and in Manchester it is Phil McDonnell. The CSR partners lead their office's CSR efforts at a local level, while co-ordinating matters of firm-wide strategy or policy.

CSR information: The company states on its CSR community page that it now has a balanced portfolio, ranging from pure charity work, for example, collecting money on Red Nose Day, through to sophisticated programmes that have an impact on many people in the company's local communities and further afield.

In 2014, the company was listed in The Times Top 50 Employers for Women.

CSR report: The CSR report was available from the company's website.

Corporate charity: The Addleshaw Goddard Charitable Trust (Charity Commission no. 286887).

Exclusions

No support is given for general or circular appeals, local appeals not in the areas of company presence, animal welfare, individuals or political/religious appeals.

Applications

In writing to the correspondent.

adidas (UK) Ltd

Sports clothing

Correspondent: Jonathan Collinge, Internal Communications Manager, The adidas Centre, Pepper Road, Hazel Grove, Stockport SK7 5SD (tel: 01614 192500; fax: 01614 192603; email: jonathancollinge@adidas-group.com; website: www.adidas.com/home/uk)

Directors: G. A. C. R. Steyaert; A. R. Hackett; A. J. Richter; P. G. Thomson

Year end	31/12/2013
Turnover	£434,034,000
Pre-tax profit	£16,705,000

Nature of business: The distribution and retail of sports goods to the sports trade in the UK.

Company registration number: 1075951

Subsidiary undertakings include: Larasport (UK) Ltd; Sarragan (UK) Ltd; Three Stripes Ltd (all dormant). The immediate parent company is Reebok International Ltd, incorporated in the UK. The ultimate parent company is adidas AG, incorporated in Germany.

Main locations: Stockport, Bolton, Basingstoke, Chelmsford, UK

UK employees: 1,078

Total employees: 50,728

Focus of giving: Education, health, ill health, sport, recreation, children, young people, community/social welfare, disasters.

Cash donations undeclared	✓
Charity of the Year	✓
Gifts in kind	✓
Humanitarian aid: overseas	✓
Matched funding	✓
Overseas giving	✓
Sponsorship	✓

Charitable donations

Cash UK (latest available):	2013	£36,000
	2011	£36,500
	2010	£18,600
	2009	£43,000
	2008	£54,000
Total UK (cash and in kind):	2013	£36,000
Cash worldwide:	2013	£36,000
Total worldwide (cash and in kind):	2013	£36,000

Community involvement

The UK limited company gives a small amount in cash donations each year. This is distributed amongst UK-registered charities.

Charity partner

Save the Children has been adidas's charity partner since 2008.

Corporate giving

In 2013 the report and accounts for this company did not declare any charitable donations. We have taken an average of the last three years' information available and estimate the figure to be around £36,000. Previous beneficiaries have included: Operation Breakthrough; Right to Play; and Score.

The adidas group produces performance data for its community affairs activities within its Sustainability Progress Report 'Fair Play' and we know from this that a substantial amount is given by adidas globally both in cash, staff fundraising and in-kind contributions. However, separate figures are not available for the UK. Also, cash donations, global or otherwise are not declared and in-kind giving, (including volunteer hours and units of products donated) is not costed. We neither have figures for any commercially led activity.

In-kind support

The adidas group provides financial aid and donates products to international aid organisations to support victims affected by natural disasters, such as the tsunami in Japan and the floods in Thailand and Australia in 2011. The group has also been supporting Save the Children in emergencies since 2008, when the cyclone Nargis hit Myanmar.

Matched funding is provided but we do not know the rules surrounding this.

Employee-led support

The website tells us that after donating for relief work in India and Pakistan, the group asked international staff for donations to help children affected by the earthquake and the tsunami that hit Japan in 2011.

Matched funding

The group then matched all employee donations. With this funding, Save the Children provided direct support to children and their families, and also worked with community groups closest to affected communities.

The group designated 2013 as 'The Year of Running' and employees responded by organising a range of activities including a 'Run around the Globe'. This worldwide run involved 36 offices the staff from which raised funds for charity.

Commercially led support

There are sponsorship opportunities but we do not have details of these.

Corporate social responsibility

CSR committee: There is no CSR committee for the UK company. The group's Social and Environmental Affairs team was set up in the late 1990s to help select and govern projects.

CSR information: This information was obtained from the company's website:

'To help select projects that respond to local needs we have set up an efficient network made up of local businesses to exchange best practice and ensure mutual support.'

We were unable to determine the ratio of women to men on the board.

CSR report: There is a Sustainability Progress Report – 'Fair Play' published on the group's website. This does not cover the UK specifically.

Applications

Applications are accepted and reviewed throughout the year in the order in which they are received. Requests must be submitted in writing. Address to the correspondent and reference 'UK Charitable Giving'.

Admiral Group plc

Insurance

Correspondent: David Stevens, Chief Operating Officer, Capital Towers, Greyfriars Road, Cardiff CF10 3AZ (tel: 08718828282; website: www.admiralgroup.co.uk)

Directors: Alistair Lyons, Chair; Henry Engelhardt, Chief Executive Officer; David Stevens; Manfred Aldag; Martin Jackson; Annette Court; John Sussens; Kevin Chidwick, Chief Financial Officer; Lucy Kellaway; Margaret Johnson; Colin Holmes; Roger Abravanel; Jean Park (women: 4; men: 9)

Year end	31/12/2013
Turnover	£2,030,000,000
Pre-tax profit	£370,200,000

Nature of business: The group's core business is selling and underwriting private car insurance in the UK through four brands – Admiral, Bell, Diamond and elephant.co.uk.

Company registration number: 3849958

Subsidiary undertakings include: Admiral Insurance Company Ltd; Admiral Insurance (Gibraltar) Ltd; Able Insurance Services Ltd; Diamond Motor Insurance Services Ltd; Elephant Insurance Company; Elephant Insurance Services, LLC; EUI Ltd; Inspop Technologies Private Ltd; Inspop.com (France) Ltd; Inspop (Italy) Ltd; Rastreator.com Ltd.

Brands include: Admiral, Bell, Diamond, elephant.co.uk, Gladiator Commercial, Confused.com.

Main locations: Swansea, Cardiff, UK

Total employees: 7,000

Focus of giving: General charitable purposes, animal welfare, arts, culture, sport, recreation.

Membership: BITC

FTSE 100	✓
Gifts in kind	✓
Matched funding	✓
Payroll giving	✓
Sponsorship	✓

Charitable donations

Cash UK (latest available):	2013	£182,000
	2012	£141,000
	2011	£178,000
	2009	£100,000
	2008	£106,000
Total UK (cash and in kind):	2013	£413,000
Cash worldwide:	2013	£413,000
Total worldwide (cash and in kind):	2013	£413,000

Community involvement

This group would appear to have a very practical approach to giving. It draws its selection of beneficiary organisations by consulting with its staff members and taking the initiative for their and their families fundraising efforts. Its sponsorship deals benefit staff in a very personal way, see 'Commercially led support', as well as marketing the company. Admiral Group states that it sponsors many different events in the South Wales area for a number of reasons:

- To support the community of South Wales of which it is a part
- To support events that staff might have an interest in
- To reflect Admiral's vibrancy and fun culture
- To raise its profile as a good employer with the community

Corporate giving

In 2013 Admiral Group donated £182,000 to various local and national charities and £231,000 to support local events and organisations. We have taken these figures to be cash rather than in-kind costings.

In-kind support

Matched funding

In 1998, CEO Henry Engelhardt set up Admiral Community Chest to help staff and their families who are involved with local charities, clubs and organisations. Employees' fundraising endeavours are matched by the group from this community fund.

Employee-led support

Staff volunteering

Over the past six years the group has supported the Neath Port Talbot Festival of Sport both financially and by offering staff volunteering. The Festival of Sport is a week-long outdoor event with children of varying physical abilities participating in the outdoor activities. Admiral encourages staff volunteering and all staff involved receive specialist training to ensure that they have the skills required to take part.

Commercially led support

The group's sponsorship includes that for the Welsh Rugby Union who display the Admiral logo on their national team jersey. The group are able to secure some staff benefits through this sponsorship such as free rugby tickets, kit discounts and opportunities to attend training sessions and meet players.

The group also sponsors Chapter Arts Centre and NoFit State Circus both based in Cardiff. Again, staff members can benefit from discounts and visits.

The group have established The Admiral Young Driver Academy which aims to develop better-trained, safer young drivers in the UK. Although this is a commercial initiative, it has a focus on safety in the community.

Corporate social responsibility

CSR committee: We could not find reference to a specific CR committee but in view of Admiral's contribution and its publication of an annual CR report we consider it likely that there is a structure in place. The board representative for CR is David Stevens, Chief Operating Officer.

CSR information: CR strategy is centred on four of the group's significant stakeholders: customers, people, the community and the environment.

CSR report: In 2013, Admiral integrated its significant CR disclosures throughout the annual report to reflect how its role as a responsible business aligns with its business aims. The full CR report is intended to supplement this information. The CR report will continue to be published annually online.

Exclusions

No support is given for local appeals not in the areas of company presence or for political appeals.

Applications

In writing to the correspondent referenced 'CR/Community'. Note, however, that local support tends to be directed towards organisations involved with Admiral employees or their immediate family.

Adnams plc

Hotels, brewers/distillers

Correspondent: Rebecca Abrahall, Charity Administrator, Sole Bay Brewery, Southwold, Suffolk IP18 6JW (tel: 01502 727200; fax: 01502 727201; email: charity@adnams.co.uk; website: www.adnams.co.uk)

Directors: Jonathan Adnams, Chair; Andy Wood, Chief Executive; Stephen Pugh, Finance Director; Simon Loftus, Finance Director; Nicky Dulieu; Steven Sharp; Bridget McIntyre (women: 2; men: 5)

Year end	31/12/2013
Turnover	£60,500,000
Pre-tax profit	£4,128,000

Nature of business: The principal activities of the company are brewing, retailing and wholesaling beer, wines, spirits and minerals, property ownership and hotel management.

Company registration number: 31114

Subsidiary undertakings include: Adnams Bio Energy Ltd.

Main locations: Suffolk, UK

UK employees: 428

Total employees: 428

Focus of giving: Education, environment, health, ill health, arts, culture, sport, recreation, bricks and mortar appeals, children, young people, community/social welfare.

Membership: BITC

Charitable donations

Cash UK (latest available):	2013	£34,000
	2012	£32,000
	2010	£32,000
	2009	£34,000
	2008	£15,000
Total UK (cash and in kind):	2013	£34,000
Cash worldwide:	2013	£34,000
Total worldwide (cash and in kind):	2013	£34,000

Community involvement

The Adnams Charity (Charity Commission no. 1000203)

The company's charitable giving is channelled through this, its associated charity.

Corporate giving

Adnams is committed to giving not less than 1% of its annual profits to charitable causes. Donations to the Adnams Charity during the year amounted to £34,000 (2012: £32,000).

See the corporate charity entry on p. 389 for more information.

Employee-led support

Pennies – The electronic charity box

The company's 2013 annual report gives an example of a new facility it has introduced to encourage customer giving. The scheme, which was rolled out to all Cellar and Kitchen stores at the beginning of the year, is best described as an electronic charity box. When customers pay by card, they are given the opportunity to 'round up' to the nearest pound.

The company's chosen charity for the first year was Prostate Cancer UK and through the donation of small change, customers raised over £30,000.

Corporate social responsibility

CSR committee: There is no evidence of a CSR committee.

CSR information: The Adnams Charity was founded in 1990 to celebrate Adnams centenary as a public company. It is funded by a percentage of Adnams annual profits (not less than 1%), mandated dividends, donations and legacies.

The charity awards grants to worthy causes within 25 miles of Southwold or, in the case of national charities, exclusively for the benefit of those living within 25 miles of Southwold. Grants normally range from £100 to £2,500. The trustees expect to see the results of their donations within one year.

CSR report: A separate CSR report is available from the company's website.

Corporate charity: The Adnams Charity (Charity Commission no. 1000203).

Exclusions

The Adnams Charity does not normally make grants to religious organisations or private clubs unless these can demonstrate that the purpose of the grant is for something of clear public benefit, accessible to all. No grants to individuals, although public bodies and charities may apply on behalf of individuals.

Applications

An application form is available from the charity administrator by emailing: charity@adnams.co.uk, telephoning 01502 727200 or writing to the charity administrator, Rebecca Abrahall at the address given at 'Correspondent'.

The applicant organisation will be asked to provide information on:

- What the grant is for
- Who will benefit
- How much the item(s) will cost – provide a detailed quotation
- Other fundraising activities being undertaken and amount raised so far
- To whom cheques should be made payable in the event of a grant being made

In addition, where possible, the most recent set of audited accounts should be enclosed with the application. A copy of your 'reserves policy' if you are applying from a registered charity is also required. The trustees meet quarterly, normally in January, April, July and October. Applications should be submitted early to ensure they are placed on the review list.

Aegon (Scottish Equitable plc)

Insurance

Correspondent: James K. MacKenzie, Company Secretary, Edinburgh Park, Edinburgh EH12 9SE (tel: 08706000 337; website: www.aegonse.co.uk)

Directors: Adrian Grace, Chief Executive; Tommy Young, Chief Operating Officer; Clare Bousfield, Chief Financial Officer; Duncan Jarrett; Jim Ewing; Angela Seymour-Jackson; David Macmillan (women: 2; men: 5)

Year end	31/12/2013

Nature of business: The transaction of life assurance, pensions and other long-term insurance business in the UK. Aegon companies globally employ around 27,500 people.

Company registration number: 3679296

Subsidiary undertakings include: Aegon UK Services Ltd; Momentum Group Ltd; Origen Ltd. Scottish Equitable plc. The ultimate parent company is Aegon incorporated in the Netherlands.

Main locations: Lytham St Annes, Edinburgh

UK employees: 3,000

Focus of giving: Environment, children, young people, community/social welfare.

Cash donations undeclared	✓
Gifts in kind	✓
Overseas giving	✓
Sponsorship	✓

Charitable donations

Cash UK (latest available):	2013	£150,000
	2011	£153,000
Total UK (cash and in kind):	2013	£150,000
Cash worldwide:	2013	£150,000
Total worldwide (cash and in kind):	2013	£150,000

Community involvement

The company's website provides the following information:

In the UK corporate responsibility initiatives impact on the local environment, a range of charities, schoolchildren and improving access to tennis. Recent corporate social responsibility highlights include:

- 2,000 breakfasts served to schoolchildren
- Almost £150,000 donated to the company's charity partners and good causes last year
- Over two million schoolchildren reached through the Aegon Schools Tennis programme
- Over 200 parks offering communities improved access to tennis

Corporate giving

In 2013 the UK company donated £150,000 to its charity partners and good causes. We do not have costings for its in-kind giving. The group gives globally £4.6 million in donations and costs its employee volunteering at £460,000.

Note: changes in the company's accounting policy made it difficult to determine its revenue and pre-tax profit.

Commercially led support

Aegon is the Lead Partner of British Tennis and the sport's biggest UK sponsor. Its sponsorship helps to develop Britain's top young talent, backs UK national teams, and supports amateur competitions to world-class events like the Aegon Championships at The Queen's Club.

Corporate social responsibility

CSR committee: There were no details of a specific committee found for the UK company.

CSR information: CSR information taken from Ageon's website: 'in the UK, our corporate responsibility initiatives impact on the local environment, a range of charities, school children and improving access to tennis.'

The group has a 'Charitable Donations Policy' booklet downloadable from its website.

CSR report: CSR information is available on the website.

Applications

In writing to the correspondent referenced: 'Community Support UK'.

Ageas (UK) Ltd

Insurance

Correspondent: Rosemary Smith, Company Secretary, Ageas House, Hampshire Corporate Park, Templars Way, Eastleigh, Hampshire SO53 3YA (tel: 02380 644455; website: www.ageas.co.uk)

Directors: Andrew Watson, Chief Executive; Francois-Xavier Boisseau; Fernley Dyson; Mark Cliff; Robert Bright; Stephen Broughton; Bridget McIntyre; Guy de Selliers de Moranville; Bart De Smet; Barry Smith; Michael Urmston; Mark Wilmlow; Jan Zegering Hadders (women: 1; men: 12)

Year end	31/12/2013
Pre-tax profit	£98,834,000

Nature of business: Ageas UK Ltd is a holding company and part of Ageas Group, an international insurance business of significant scale.

Company registration number: 1093301

Subsidiary undertakings include: Ageas Insurance Ltd; Ageas 50 Ltd; Kwik-Fit Insurance Services Ltd; UKAIS Ltd.

Main locations: Eastleigh, Gloucester

UK employees: 6,000

Focus of giving: General charitable purposes, arts, culture, safety and crime prevention, sport, recreation, community/social welfare.

Cash donations undeclared	✓
Gifts in kind	✓
Market-led giving	✓
Matched funding	✓

Charitable donations

Cash UK (latest available):	2013	£28,000
	2010	£9,000
	2009	£35,000
	2008	£40,000
	2007	£48,000
Total UK (cash and in kind):	2013	£28,000
Cash worldwide:	2013	£28,000
Total worldwide (cash and in kind):	2013	£28,000

Community involvement

Ageas states that it strongly supports both national and local charities, all voted for by employees, and that there is support for employee involvement through volunteer days; support for national fundraising such as Comic Relief, Sports Relief and Children in Need; and a Charity of the Year nominated and voted for by employees.

Corporate giving

Ageas did not declare its charitable contributions in 2013, cash or otherwise. Taking the last three years for which we have figures we have estimated an average of around £28,000 in cash donations in the UK.

Employee-led support

Staff undertake community and charitable work including volunteering and fundraising.

Charity of the Year

We could not find the name of the current Charity of the Year.

Commercially led support

The Ageas Bowl

In February 2012, Ageas announced its partnership with the home of Hampshire Cricket. The partnership involved rebranding the stadium as 'The Ageas Bowl', as part of an 11 year deal.

Ageas Salisbury International Arts Festival

In December 2011, Ageas announced its partnership with the Salisbury International Arts Festival which is now known as the Ageas Salisbury International Arts Festival.

Road Safety

Since 2012, the group has sponsored the Road Safety Foundation's EuroRAP report, research that provides insight into the safety of road infrastructure. Ageas has also commissioned the Road Safety Foundation to produce 'Making Road Safety Pay', an analytical piece of research taking a comprehensive view of road safety.

Corporate social responsibility

CSR committee: There was no evidence of a separate CSR Committee.

CSR information: There was no CSR policy published.

CSR report: There was no evidence of a separate CSR report.

Applications

In writing to the correspondent.

Aggregate Industries Ltd

Building materials, quarrying

Correspondent: Local Community Liaison Group, Bardon Hall, Copt Oak Road, Markfield, Leicestershire LE67 9PJ (tel: 01530 816600; fax: 01530 816666; website: www.aggregate.com)

Directors: Roland Köhler; Alain Bourguignon; John Bowater; Bernard Terver (women: 0; men: 4)

Year end	31/12/2013
Turnover	£292,413,000
Pre-tax profit	£262,375,000

Nature of business: Aggregate Industries and its subsidiaries are engaged in the exploitation of land and mineral reserves principally for the supply of heavy building materials for construction activities. Operating at locations across the UK, Channel Islands, Norway and Northern Europe it employs over 3,500 people.

Aggregate Industries Ltd itself is a holding company with no employees. In 2005 it became part of the Holcim Group which is incorporated in Switzerland.

Company registration number: 5655952

Subsidiary undertakings include: Aggregate Industries UK Ltd; Evered Ltd; International Aggregates Ltd; London and Northern Group Ltd.

Main locations: Markfield

Focus of giving: General charitable purposes, education, environment, heritage, safety and crime prevention, sport, recreation, community/social welfare, disability.

Cash donations undeclared	✓
Gifts in kind	✓

Charitable donations

Cash UK (latest available):	2013	£76,000
	2012	£32,000
	2011	£141,000
	2010	£294,700
	2009	£138,500
Total UK (cash and in kind):	2013	£109,000
Cash worldwide:	2013	£76,000
Total worldwide (cash and in kind):	2013	£109,000

Community involvement

Although the company continues to provide cash donations to groups local to its sites, in line with its community plan, efforts are becoming more targeted towards in-kind donations; volunteer hours, skills and expertise.

Community Engagement Case Studies

The following information is taken from the company's website:

> *Lodmor Nature Reserve*: The RSPB's Lodmor Nature Reserve near Weymouth in Dorset has one of the south-west's largest common tern colonies. In September 2014 20 tonnes of clean gravel was donated from the company's Warmwell Quarry and this has been put to good use creating future breeding habitat for these delightful silver-grey and white birds.
>
> *Bere Regis School Crossing:* In 2011 Dorset County Council took the decision to stop funding the school crossing patrol site at Bere Regis First School. Vehicles delivering sand from the company's Warmwell Quarry regularly pass the school and the ongoing safety of children is a priority for the business. Aggregate Industries decided to step in and along with three other local aggregates companies have funded the school crossing patrol since 2012.
>
> *Upper Warren boardwalk restoration:* Upton Warren – also known as the Christopher Cadbury Wetland Reserve is the premier bird watching site in the region. As part of the annual improvement works, a new boardwalk, new hides and scrub management are being undertaken. In order to try and reduce the cost of the works, Worcestershire Wildlife Trust approached Aggregate Industries to ask if a donation of materials could be found to help. Haughmond Hill quarry provided 20 tonnes of 40mm – dust which will be used as sub-base for the boardwalk. The site provides an important landscape link between the Droitwich Canal wetlands, the Birmingham and Worcester Canal and the Rivers Salwarpe and Severn. It has hosted nesting bittern but also a wide array of other species including Cetti's warbler, otter, whimbrel and even a Mediterranean gull. Aggregate Industries' relationship with the Wildlife Trusts nationally is an important part of our CSR programme and many of our sites across the UK are corporate members – supporting environmental work in their local counties.

Corporate giving

In 2013 the group declared (on its website) cash donations totalling £141,000 and estimated value of materials given at over £32,000. Volunteer hours spent on community projects were recorded previously but figures were not given for 2013. The company also states that not all community donations are recorded. Previous beneficiaries include: Lismore Heritage Centre; Oban Lifeboat Fund; Oban Sea Cadets; and Riding for the Disabled Association.

In-kind support

In-kind support is given in various ways. In 2013 materials donated were costed at over £32,000; however, we could not find costings for the 1,473 hours volunteered by colleagues.

Employee-led support

There is an agreement with all UK colleagues that every year they can spend a day volunteering in company time.

Commercially led support

Millom Rock Park

Funded from a number of sources including Aggregate Industries and the Aggregate Levy Sustainability Funds of Cumbria County Council and Natural England, this project was completed by a committee comprising other members of the local community. The official opening saw one of the world's leading volcano experts, Professor Peter Kokelaar from the University of Liverpool speak about the role of geology in shaping the landscape and industrial heritage of the area.

Corporate social responsibility

CSR committee: There were no specific details found. There are, however, community liaison groups at most of the company's sites.

CSR information: The following is taken from the sustainability section on the company's website:

> People play a valuable part in sustainable construction. The people who live and work around us influence what we do and how we do it; they are fundamental to the maintenance of our licence to operate. Our community plan was developed as a result of numerous conversations with our neighbours over many years. Our expectation is that this plan will provide a simple framework to improve our support for those around us which in turn will allow us to build stronger connections with our communities.

CSR report: There is a sustainability section on the group's website and a Sustainability Report is produced annually. A Community Plan document is also available.

Exclusions

No support is given for political or religious appeals.

Applications

In writing to your local site addressed 'Community Liaison Group' and referenced 'Community Giving'.

Aggreko plc

Engineering, services

Correspondent: Peter Kennerley, Company Secretary, 8th Floor, 120 Bothwell Street, Glasgow G2 7JS (tel: 01412 255900; fax: 01412 255949; email: investors@aggreko.com; website: www.aggreko.co.uk)

Directors: Ken Hanna, Chair; Rupert Soames, Chief Executive; Angus Cockburn, Chief Financial Officer; Asterios Satrazemis; David Taylor-Smith; Ian Marchant; David Hamill; Robert MacLeod; Russell King; Debajit Das; Diana Leyfield; Rebecca McDonald (women: 2; men: 10)

Year end	31/12/2013
Turnover	£1,573,000,000
Pre-tax profit	£333,000,000

Nature of business: Specialist energy solutions.

Company registration number: SC177553

Subsidiary undertakings include: Aggreko Argentina SRL; Aggreko Generator Rentals Pry Ltd; Aggreko Barbados Ltd; Aggreko Belgium HV; Aggreko Energia Locacao de Geradores Ltd; Aggreko Canada Inc; Aggreko Financial Holdings Ltd. A full list is available in the company accounts.

Main locations: Greater London, Plymouth CC, Bristol CC, Great Yarmouth BC, Bedford BC, Manchester City MD, Doncaster MD, Neath Port Talbot County – Sir Castell-nedd Port Talbot, East Dunbartonshire UC

Total employees: 5,749

Focus of giving: Education, community/ social welfare, disasters.

Cash donations undeclared	✓
Charity of the Year	✓
FTSE 100	✓
Gifts in kind	✓
Humanitarian aid: overseas	✓
Humanitarian aid: UK	✓
Overseas giving	✓

Charitable donations

Cash UK (latest available):	2013	£56,000
	2011	£43,400
	2009	£49,000
	2008	£76,000
Total UK (cash and in kind):	2013	£56,000
Cash worldwide:	2013	£56,000
Total worldwide (cash and in kind):	2013	£56,000

Community involvement

Aggreko states it has a policy of encouraging local teams to engage with the communities in which they work. The company also makes cash donations to UK charities and supports in particular Book Aid International which distributes books in Cameroon, Kenya, Namibia, Tanzania and Uganda.

Charity partner

Although perhaps not officially a charity partner, Aggreko has been supporting Book Aid International for the past seven years.

Corporate giving

The 2013 annual report states that during 2013, the group 'contributed to a range of charitable, community and disaster relief organisations'. Unfortunately the group does not give a breakdown of what it gave, where and in what form. We have estimated the 2013 UK cash donations by taking an average of the last three years for which we have figures available and suggest that the total amount is around £56,000. The largest single donation goes to Book Aid International, a charity promoting literacy in various countries in Africa.

In-kind support

There is a suggestion that staff can, in company time, volunteer within their local communities to raise funds.

Employee-led support

Local teams are encouraged to engage with the communities in which they work, raising funds to help disadvantaged people or those affected by natural disasters.

Corporate social responsibility

CSR committee: The CSR Committee is partnered with the Ethics Committee.

CSR information: This information was obtained from the company's annual report:

> Aggreko has a policy of encouraging local teams to engage with the communities in which they work, and each year they undertake innumerable initiatives to help the disadvantaged or those affected by natural disasters.
>
> We have a policy of giving little donations to many organisations which are involved with the communities in which we work, rather than giving a lot of money to a few.

CSR report: The CSR report is published within the annual report; there is very little information given around charitable giving.

Applications

In writing to the correspondent.

Air Products Group Ltd

Oil and gas/fuel

Correspondent: Company Secretary, Hersham Place Technology Park, Molesey Road, Walton-on-Thames, Surrey KT12 4RZ (tel: 01932 249200; fax: 01932 258565; website: www.airproducts.co.uk)

Directors: P. M. Neligan; T. Hammons; C. Lloyd; W. Morrison-Bell; E. J. Pescod; M. J. Sambrook; D. Leney

Year end	30/09/2013
Turnover	£520,263,000
Pre-tax profit	£98,187,000

Nature of business: The manufacture and sale of industrial gases, the design and construction of equipment for the production and use of industrial gases, and the manufacture and sale of speciality chemicals.

Company registration number: 3101747

Subsidiary undertakings include: The company is a subsidiary undertaking of Air Products and Chemicals Inc., which is the ultimate parent company incorporated in Delaware USA.

Main locations: Crewe, Walton-on-Thames, UK

UK employees: 1,793

Total employees: 21,600

Focus of giving: Education, environment, health, ill health, arts, culture, sport, recreation, community/ social welfare.

Charitable donations

Cash UK (latest available):	2013	£14,000
	2012	£44,000
	2011	£65,500
	2009	£110,000
	2008	£110,000
Total UK (cash and in kind):	2013	£14,000
Cash worldwide:	2013	£1,407,600
Total worldwide (cash and in kind):	2013	£3,509,000

Community involvement

The UK company which is a subsidiary of Air Products and Chemicals Inc., seems to give very little in the way of cash contributions (£14,000) and we could find no real evidence of in-kind contributions such as staff volunteering. However, the parent company gives some £3.5 million in worldwide contributions which includes £1.4 million in cash. It is likely that some donations/contributions come to the UK from the American parent company but there is no geographical breakdown given and so we are not able to determine how much, if any, comes here, and if it does, what organisations or types of organisation benefit.

Corporate giving

During the year the company's donations to UK charities totalled £14,000. We have no details of beneficiaries but previous projects/ organisations supported by the company include: Rydens School, Surrey – Young Apprentice competition; London Schools Hydrogen Challenge; Wildlife Aid – Surrey; Manchester Camerata; The Police Community Clubs of Great Britain; Overton Rugby Festival; and Elmbridge Sports Awards.

Corporate social responsibility

CSR information: There was no CSR information available.

We were unable to determine the ratio of women to men on the board of the UK company.

The parent company states in its Sustainability Report for 2013:

> We are committed to our social responsibility as an employer and productive community member. This year, we contributed more than $5.6 million in cash, volunteer hours and in-kind donations to not-for-profit organisations. Our leadership and investment in employee development was recognized by E-Learning naming us one of 2012's top learning organisations. Stories such as our work with the SkillsUSA program demonstrate how our commitment to development extends beyond company walls.

Applications

In writing to the correspondent referenced 'Charitable donations – UK'. To apply to the American parent company, address any application to the Environmental, Safety and Public Policy Committee, Air Products and Chemicals, Inc., 7201 Hamilton Boulevard, Allentown, PA 18195–1501.

Alliance Boots Holdings Ltd

Healthcare, pharmaceuticals

Correspondent: Celene Rechnic, Assistant CSR Manager, D90 Building West G14, Nottingham NG90 1BS (tel: 01159 687242; email: celene.rechnic@ boots.co.uk; website: www.boots-uk. com/csr)

Directors: A. Clare; M. Delve; F. Standish

Year end	31/03/2014
Turnover	£864,000,000
Pre-tax profit	£852,000,000

Nature of business: Alliance Boots Holdings Ltd is a holding company. Boots UK is part of the Retail Pharmacy International Division of Walgreens Boots Alliance, Inc., the first global pharmacy-led, health and well-being enterprise. Boots became a subsidiary of the new company, Walgreens Boots Alliance, on 31 December 2014.

Accounts for the new company were not available at the time of writing (February 2014) and we have used turnover and profit before tax figures from the holding company Alliance Boots Holdings Ltd.

Company registration number: 4452715

Subsidiary undertakings include: Boots UK Ltd; Boots Opticians; Boots Norge A.S.; Boots Retail (Ireland) Ltd; Alliance Apotheek B.V.; Boots Retail (Thailand) Ltd.

Brands include: Almus, Alvita, Boots Pharmaceuticals, Boots Laboratories, Botanics, No7, Serum7, Solei SP, Soltan.

Main locations: Nottinghamshire

Focus of giving: Education, health, ill health, poverty and social exclusion, safety and crime prevention, community/social welfare.

Membership: BITC, LBG

Charity of the Year	✓
Gifts in kind	✓
Humanitarian aid: overseas	✓
Humanitarian aid: UK	✓
Market-led giving	✓
Matched funding	✓
Overseas giving	✓
Payroll giving	✓
Sponsorship	✓

Charitable donations

Cash UK (latest available):	2014	£800,000
	2013	£800,000
	2011	£1,360,000
	2010	£1,300,000
	2009	£1,500,000
Total UK (cash and in kind):	2014	£3,600,000
Cash worldwide:	2014	£800,000
Total worldwide (cash and in kind):	2014	£3,900,000

Community involvement

Note: All of the information contained herein refers to Boots UK.

The company's priority is to contribute positively to the communities that it serves. Community health is at the centre of this activity and the focus is on building active partnerships that will produce projects and initiatives with real health benefits.

Charity partners

In the UK Boots is working with two key charity partners – Macmillan Cancer Support and BBC Children in Need (which it has supported for a number of years). In addition, it works with other charities including Action for Blind People. The UK wholesale business has a number of charity partners including The Prostate Cancer Charity, Leonard Cheshire Disability and CLIC Sargent.

The Boots Charitable Trust is an independent grant-making trust established in the 1970's and wholly funded by the company. Currently the trust's giving is focused in the county of Nottinghamshire, in recognition of Boots' long history with the area.

The trust gives to charities and voluntary organisations that benefit Nottingham and Nottinghamshire. The trust's website states that grants are given in the following areas:

- **Health:** both community healthcare such as homecare or support for sufferers of medical conditions as well as health education and prevention
- **Lifelong learning:** for example literacy and numeracy projects
- **Community development:** such as supporting councils in providing voluntary services
- **Social care:** be it personal, social or community activities or schemes

Boots Benevolent Fund (Charity Commission no. 1046559)

The Boots Benevolent Fund is a registered charity which provides financial help and support to serving and retired colleagues who are unexpectedly experiencing financial hardship. The fund is open to all Boots' colleagues in the UK. It aims to help when unexpected events happen and staff are faced with homelessness, debts involving bailiffs, large utility bill arrears or essential living requirements where they are facing financial hardship. It annually supports about 600–800 people with grants and loans.

Corporate giving

In 2013/14 the company's UK contributions were £3.6 million through charitable donations, gifts in kind, management costs and employee time. The worldwide community contributions totalled (including the UK contribution) £3.9 million.

We have been able to give figures, provided by Boots in its annual CSR report 2013/14, which exclude management costs from its community contributions in the UK (which is our policy). However, we have not been able to extricate these costs from *where* the money was given. Consequently, the total UK and worldwide figures include the management costs.

A large proportion of the contributions made are to healthcare related projects reflecting the company's focus on pharmacy. Donations are usually made either at a national or a local level within the countries that Boots operates.

Purpose	£millions
Health	2.3
Education	0.7
Social welfare	0.5
Other	0.4

The Boots Charitable Trust

During the year to March 2013/14 the company donated £250,000 to the trust. It gave 40 grants totalling £250,000 in the following categories: health, social care, lifelong learning and community development.

Beneficiaries included: Groundwork Greater Nottingham (£15,000); Base 51 and Newark, Notts Child Bereavement and Loss Centre and Survivors Helping Each Other (£10,000 each); Home Start Newark (£8,200); Age UK Nottinghamshire and Pintsize Theatre Ltd (£7,000 each); Bassetlaw CVS (£6,300); and Malt Cross Trust Company, St Ann's Allotments, and Spring Nottingham (£5,000 each).

Grants under £5,000 totalled £29,000.

The Boots Benevolent Fund: In 2013/14 the fund made 728 grants and one loan to individuals facing hardship, which amounted to £230,000. For more information contact the fund via email: bbf@boots.co.uk or phone: 01159 591285.

See the corporate charity entry on p. 396 for more information.

In-kind support

Products

Unwanted products such as damaged or end of line stock have been donated to charities as gifts in kind. As well as being of benefit to the voluntary sector this reduces the amount of waste sent to landfill. National and international charities providing humanitarian aid and medical assistance are supported in this way.

Inspiring Young Talent

Boots UK continues to support youth employability with a variety of programmes, including work experience and apprenticeships. 'Inspiring Young Talent', supported over 3,000 young people with valuable work experience opportunities in 2013/14.

EORTC Charitable Trust

The company has a pan-European partnership with the European Organisation for Research and Treatment of Cancer (EORTC) Charitable Trust. Together they aim to support the creation and funding of a 'biobank' for colorectal cancer and later a platform for blood sampling to enable genetic profiling. This directly complements the ongoing partnership with Macmillan Cancer Support in the UK.

Matched funding

Through the Boots UK Make the Difference Fund employees are supported with matched funding up to £500. Typically, around 500 awards are granted each year providing additional funding to benefit the charities that are personally important to colleagues.

Employee-led support

Fundraising for charity partners

In 2014 Boots UK customers and employees raised £920,000 for BBC Children in Need and in the 11 years they have been supporting the charity have raised a total of £7.5 million. Since the start of supporting Macmillan Cancer Support customers, employees and suppliers have raised £9 million.

Macmillan in Every Community

A volunteer-led scheme that offers practical support to people affected by cancer, Macmillan in Every Community helps those affected by cancer get access to the services they need and to maintain independence and control over their lives. In June 2012 the company's Boots Macmillan in Every Community volunteer group was recognised for their work when they received the Macmillan Cancer Support Deborah Hutton Award. This award is given to volunteers who provide practical support and care to people affected by cancer.

Cancer Voices

Macmillan set up its Cancer Voices network so that people affected by cancer can use their experience in a range of positive ways. They share their experiences to help shape cancer services and improve cancer care.

Payroll giving

The company offers the Give As You Earn payroll giving facility. At the end of 2013/14, there were 3,000 colleagues giving regularly to a charity of their choice in this way.

Matched funding

Employees are encouraged to share their expertise to help people lead healthier lifestyles and are provided with opportunities to devote their time and energy to supporting causes that matter. Employees' fundraising efforts are also supported and the company provides a matched giving scheme to staff, enabling them to claim up to £500 to match their own funds raised.

Commercially led support

The **Boots Learning Store** website, provides educational support for children, teachers and parents. This is an interactive educational resource for all ages addressing issues of health, science and well-being. It includes a comprehensive set of teachers' notes which are available to download. The site also has a dedicated parents' section providing health advice and links to other health related sites. See www.bootslearningstore.com

Boots UK supports **Cares for Kids** – a partnership of businesses, schools and volunteers that is changing children's lives and raising their aspirations. Business funding, volunteers, parents and teachers have come together to create breakfast clubs which give children the best start to the day.

Boots UK continued to support the national **Eisteddfod of Wales**, one of Europe's largest and oldest annual cultural festivals, which attracts over 150,000 visitors a year.

Corporate social responsibility

CSR committee: Issues that make up Boots' CSR are regularly reviewed to make sure they reflect current thinking, meet the needs of stakeholders and are fully in line with the business strategy, as well as ensuring efforts meet Alliance Boots' overall priorities. Finally, progress is reported to the Boots UK executive team and to the Alliance Boots Social Responsibilities Committee.

CSR information: The following information is taken from the 2013/14 CSR report:

> *Our CSR mission and purpose*
> To be the UK's most socially responsible pharmacy-led health and beauty retailer. We'll do this by improving the health of our customers and their communities, protecting the environment, and leading the development of sustainable products, placing our customers and colleagues at the heart of our business.

We were unable to determine the ratio of women to men on the board for this particular Boots' company.

CSR report: A CSR report is published annually.

Corporate charity: Boots Charitable Trust (Charity Commission no. 1045927).

Exclusions

Boots Charitable Trust will not support the following:

- Projects benefiting people outside Nottinghamshire
- Individuals
- Organisations which are not registered charities and which have income or expenditure of more than £5,000 per year
- Charities seeking funds to redistribute to other charities
- Projects for which there is a legal statutory obligation or which replace statutory funding

Applications

Boots Charitable Trust

Applications to the trust are only accepted on the official application form which must be accompanied by your latest annual report and detailed accounts.

The application form can be downloaded as a Word document, or it can be posted out to you by the correspondent, to whom it should be returned once completed.

For amounts under £2,000 there is no deadline for applications and the decision period is one to two months.

For amounts over £2,000 the trustee meetings are held bi-monthly in January, March, May, July, September and November. The deadline for receipt of applications is the 7th of the month preceding the meeting i.e. 7 February for the March meeting, 7 April for the May meeting and so on. The decision period is two to four months.

Contact: Julie Lawrence, Boots Charitable Trust. Email: Julie.Lawrence@boots.co.uk

Boots Benevolent Fund

Applications are processed under delegated powers which permit donations and interest free loans to be made up to £1,500.

Email: bbf@boots.co.uk. Telephone: 01159 591285.

Alliance Trust plc

Financial services

Correspondent: Jack Willis, Secretary to the Staff Foundation Committee, 8 West Marketgait, Dundee DD1 1QN (tel: 01382 321000; fax: 01382 321185; email: jack.willis@alliancetrust.co.uk; website: www.alliancetrust.co.uk)

Directors: Karen Forseke, Chair; Allan Trotter, Chief Financial Officer; John Hylands; Alastair Kerr; Susan Noble; Win Robbins; Gregor Stewart; Katherine Garret-Cox (women: 4; men: 4)

Year end	31/12/2013
Turnover	£116,295,000
Pre-tax profit	£461,802,000

Company registration number: SC1731

Main locations: Dundee

UK employees: 225

Total employees: 225

Focus of giving: General charitable purposes.

Cash donations undeclared	✓
Gifts in kind	✓
Market-led giving	✓
Matched funding	✓
Sponsorship	✓

Charitable donations

Cash UK (latest available):	2013	£52,000
Total UK (cash and in kind):	2013	£52,000
Cash worldwide:	2013	£52,000
Total worldwide (cash and in kind):	2013	£52,000

Community involvement

The Alliance Trust Staff Foundation (OSCR no. SC044113)

Charitable giving is made by the company by way of matching employees' fundraising. This is donated to the foundation which was formed with the purpose of building partnerships between Alliance Trust and its local communities in Dundee, Edinburgh and London.

Corporate giving

For the year 2013 this company did not declare charitable donations; however, we know that its charitable contribution is made by matching employees' fundraising and are given via the Alliance Trust Staff Foundation. Unfortunately there were no accounts available for the foundation (it was registered in 2013) and so we have been unable to see what its income was and from where. We know from the foundation's 2014 annual newsletter that the company's sponsorship of the Cateran Yomp raised £104,000 and we have taken it that 50% of this was matched by the company. Total UK cash charitable contributions have therefore been estimated at £52,000; however, it is quite probable that the company gave more. There were no costings for gifts in kind such as staff volunteering hours.

See the corporate charity entry on p. 390 for more information.

In-kind support

Staff are encouraged to volunteer and events happen throughout the year.

Employee-led support

Staff fundraising through various events is what sustains the Alliance Trust Staff Foundation, together with matched funding from the company. The foundation has supported numerous local charities operating within Dundee, Edinburgh and London.

Volunteering

Staff support Pilotlight, which places business professionals onto the boards of charities, and some of the company's senior team members are now working directly with local charitable organisations.

In collaboration with FutureReach two workshops were run in local Dundee schools, helping to equip students with the necessary skills to secure employment in the future.

Two volunteering days per staff member are allocated each year in order to encourage participation with local projects and communities.

Commercially led support

Sponsorship

2014 marked the 4th Alliance Trust Cateran Yomp with 18 Alliance Trust teams and over 570 registered participants. In 2015 £69,400 will go to support ABF Soldiers' Charity and £34,700 to support the company's Alliance Trust Staff Foundation which will enable the foundation to make donations to a number of local charitable organisations next year.

Corporate social responsibility

CSR information: There was no evidence of a CSR policy although the sustainability section of the 2013 annual report stated:

> The Alliance Trust sustainability strategy is called Investing for Generations. This strategy is focused on building our business for the long-term. While we have been investing for 125 years we realise that to continue for the next 125 years, we need to remain as relevant to our shareholders, clients, and customers as we have always been.
>
> *Community*
>
> Our goal is to support the communities in which we operate. We established the Alliance Trust Staff Foundation and have supported local charities operating within Dundee, Edinburgh and London.

Corporate charity: Alliance Trust Staff Foundation (OSCR number SC044113).

Exclusions

None known.

Applications

In writing to the correspondent.

Allianz Insurance plc

Insurance

Correspondent: Sian Glennane, Senior Communications Officer, 57 Ladymead, Guildford, Surrey GU1 1DB (tel: 01483 568161; fax: 01483 300952; email: sian.glennane@allianz.co.uk; website: www.allianzcornhill.co.uk)

Directors: C. B. Booth, Chair; Baron C. von Bechtolsheim; B. Bovermann; D. Kingston; M. J. Churchlow; J. M. Dye; R. O. Hudson; R. M. Murison

Year end	31/12/2013
Turnover	£1,842,300,000
Pre-tax profit	£146,000,000

Nature of business: The group undertakes all classes of insurance business.

Company registration number: 84638

Group undertakings include: Allianz Properties Ltd; British Reserve Insurance Company Ltd; Pet Plan Ltd; Trafalgar Insurance Public Ltd Company.

Main locations: Brentford, Liphook, Guildford, Tunbridge Wells, UK

Total employees: 147,627

Focus of giving: Education, environment, equal opportunities, animal welfare, health, ill health, sport, recreation, community/social welfare.

Membership: BITC, LBG

Charity of the Year	✓
Gifts in kind	✓
Humanitarian aid: overseas	✓
Matched funding	✓

Payroll giving ✓

Charitable donations

Cash UK (latest available):	2010	£221,300
	2009	£367,452
	2008	£238,618
	2007	£146,095
	2006	£132,048
Cash worldwide:	2013	£14,900,000
Total worldwide (cash and in kind):	2013	£14,900,000

Community involvement

The company's website gives details of its community programme's aims:

Community Programme

The company aims to:

- Support charities and voluntary initiatives in the community that are relevant to its business objectives and brand values
- Increase financial contributions through company donations, employee fundraising and payroll giving
- Maximise contribution delivered through non-financial means, such as employee volunteering
- Create lasting value for community partners and employees through training and skills development
- Maximise the value of partnerships by measuring key performance indicators

The company's 2013 sustainability report states:

> In 2013, our corporate giving totalled €18.6 million (2012: €20.4 million) comprising corporate donations and charitable memberships, as well as grants made by our 13 foundations. While the total corporate giving in monetary form has decreased, we are increasingly providing in-kind support such as soft-skills, time and expertise of our employees through our 'employee volunteering programs' to support a positive impact on society. We are also actively engaged in 'partnerships' and sponsoring activities, which are not accounted for under corporate giving. We are currently focusing on improving the transparency and reporting beyond corporate giving.

Disaster response

One of the focus areas for donations is disaster response. In November 2013, following the devastation of Typhoon Haiyan in the Philippines, a group-wide employee donation appeal was launched. The funds were almost exclusively used to support the humanitarian work of the International Federation of Red Cross and Red Crescent Societies, Allianz's global partner for disaster response since 2011, in and around the most affected city, Tacloban.

Allianz foundations

There is an international network of 13 Allianz affiliated corporate foundations.

Charity partners

Help the Hospices

This partnership is structured so that the company's support can benefit the work of Help the Hospices nationally, as well as supporting 25 hospices that are local to its offices around the UK. Money that is raised in local branches may be donated to a local hospice; while money donated by the company (e.g. for matching employee fundraising) goes to Help the Hospices.

In the first 3.5 years of the partnership, Allianz Insurance plc and its employees have donated £560,000 to support the work of Help the Hospices nationwide.

The Prince's Trust

The Prince's Trust gives practical and financial support to 14- to 30-year-olds who have struggled at school, have been in care, are long-term unemployed or have been in trouble with the law and helps them to develop key workplace skills.

The company has supported the Prince's Trust since 2005 and aims to utilise the skills of its employees through volunteering with the trust to help young people enjoy a better future. The company employees are offered volunteering opportunities to deliver workshops as part of the Trust's Team programme: Work Placement workshops; and CV and Interview Skills. By delivering the workshops, employees will not only help the young people on the programmes, but also develop their own skills – including communication, leadership and management, presenting, adaptability, problem-solving, team work, and project management.

Corporate giving

In 2013 the group donated €18.6 million (£14.9 million) to support local communities. There did not appear to be any figure declared for UK cash donations/community contributions in any of the published documents or on the group's website.

In-kind support

Staff throughout the group are encouraged to get involved and volunteer with their local communities. Employees in the UK have volunteered for their local hospices and the company has also provided training and development courses for Help the Hospices staff and management. An international example is 'My Finance Coach' which fosters financial literacy among youth and reached more than 150,000 students in Germany alone in 2013.

A matched funding programme is available.

Employee-led support

Care International

In the event of a natural disaster that prompts an appeal by the Disaster Emergency Committee (DEC), Allianz responds by offering an immediate one-off payroll giving facility through which employees can make a tax-efficient donation to the disaster appeal. This donation will be channelled through Care International, the chosen international emergency partner for employee donations in the UK. The company also enables employees to support charities of their choice, in a tax-efficient way, by regularly donating through payroll giving – the company matching 10%.

Commercially led support

Sponsorship

Allianz is the first International Partner of the Paralympic Movement and supports athletes all over the world on their way to the Paralympics.

In July 2012, Allianz and Saracens Rugby Club entered into a long-term partnership agreement. Allianz is the main club sponsor and the innovative north London club's new home ground in Hendon will be named Allianz Park. The sponsorship deal with Saracens involves the following Allianz Group companies based in the UK: Allianz Insurance, Allianz Global Corporate and Specialty, Mondial Assistance (shortly becoming Allianz Global Assistance), Allianz Global Investors and Euler Hermes.

Allianz has been involved in Formula One motor racing since 2000 and the company stepped up a gear in 2007 to become Global Partner of Formula1. For the world's largest car insurer F1 is an excellent platform to reach millions of motor fans throughout the season with the Drive Safely message. Allianz is the first company to have branded the Safety and Medical Car in F1.

Corporate social responsibility

CSR committee: We could find no information on the membership or structure of any CSR committee.

CSR information: The company's approach to CSR is available on its website:

> Our social responsibility strategy aligns with our business mission to be the outstanding competitor in our chosen markets by addressing the four major priorities, which we believe will make a positive difference to our customers, our employees, the environment and the communities in which we operate:
>
> *Supporting our communities*
>
> By working with the right organisations to challenge the environmental and social issues that impact our business we aim to

bring about positive changes for the communities in which we operate.

We were unable to determine the ratio of women to men on the board.

CSR report: The annual CSR report is interactive and can be viewed at the company's website.

Exclusions

No support is given for political appeals or organisations whose activities are not aligned with the themes of the company.

Applications

For further details contact the correspondent.

Amec Foster Wheeler plc (formerly Amec plc)

Building/construction, consulting engineers, engineering, oil and gas/fuel, property

Correspondent: See 'Applications', Old Change House, 128 Queen Victoria Street, London EC4V 4BJ (tel: 020 7429 7525; email: frances.fay@amecfw.com; website: www.amecfw.com)

Directors: John Connolly, Chair; Samir Brikho, Chief Executive; Ian McHoul, Chief Financial Officer; Linda Adamany; Neil Carson; Stephanie Newby; Colin Day; Simon Thompson (women: 2; men: 6)

Year end	31/12/2013
Turnover	£3,974,000,000
Pre-tax profit	£255,000,000

Nature of business: Amec's £1.9 million deal to buy Foster Wheeler was completed on 13 November 2014. Amec Foster Wheeler designs, delivers and maintains strategic and complex infrastructure assets across a range of markets. It has a strong presence across the onshore and offshore oil and gas value chain – from production, through processing, gas monetisation, midstream, oil refining and chemicals. Amec Foster Wheeler is also in the mining, clean energy, power generation, environment and infrastructure markets. In addition, the company is a leading designer, fabricator and supplier of advanced boiler systems for the power generation and industrial markets.

Company registration number: 1675285

Subsidiary undertakings include: Amec Americas Ltd (Canada); Amec Nuclear UK Ltd; Atlantic Services Ltd (Bermuda); Incheon Bridge Co. Ltd (Korea); Nuclear Management Partners Ltd (UK); Paragon Angola Engenharia E Serviços, Limitada (Angola); Petersbogen Immobilengesellschaft GmbH and Co. KG (Germany); PT AMEC Berca Indonesia; Road Management (A13) Holdings Ltd (UK); Shanghai Zone Petrochemical Engineering Co. Ltd.

Main locations: Aberdeen, Ashford, London, Birchwood, Birmingham, Manchester

UK employees: 11,000

Total employees: 28,700

Focus of giving: General charitable purposes, education, enterprise/training, environment, health, ill health, overseas projects, children, young people, disasters.

Membership: BITC

Cash donations undeclared	✓
Charity of the Year	✓
Gifts in kind	✓
Humanitarian aid: overseas	✓
Matched funding	✓
Overseas giving	✓

Charitable donations

Cash UK (latest available):	2010	£295,000
	2009	£549,000
	2007	£188,000
	2006	£186,000
	2005	£108,000
Cash worldwide:	2013	£403,000
Total worldwide (cash and in kind):	2013	£1,200,000

Community involvement

The 2013 Sustainability Report provides information on the company's charitable donations and community contributions. It states that cash donations made by the company are concentrated on social development and health, with emergency relief efforts in 2013 going to both the natural disaster in the Philippines and the ongoing crisis in Syria. Education and young people dominate the giving, with 60% of the volunteer hours spent on these purposes. The company states that this is a result of the efforts to support STEM activities and its long-term strategic recruitment activity and that for Amec, 'education has a much longer lasting benefit than just providing charitable donations. Amec continues to form community and educational partnerships with local institutions; each designed to draw on the talents of our employees with the objective of building skills'. These partnerships are often long-term relationships and activities can include:

- Work experience days
- Supporting national events
- Tutoring/lecturing
- Supporting schools with STEM projects

Overseas

Example: In 2014, staff will be raising money for a water project in the SOS village in Peru where children and families need a new water pipe installed. This will improve their quality of life and save money as they will not have to fetch water or pay for its transportation. If more is raised than the costs of the water pipe, remaining funds will go into educational projects in SOS Children Villages in Azerbaijan and the Philippines.

Charity partner

SOS Children is the company's global strategic charity.

Corporate giving

In 2013 the company donated £403,000 to good causes and charities worldwide, including matched employee fundraising. Total worldwide contributions were £1.2 million, which included employee and other contributions, in-kind donations and volunteer hours in work time. Unfortunately, we could find no figure for UK cash donations or community contributions relating solely to the UK. The company appears to have stopped declaring these separately.

Note that most of the details for this company (bar its name, nature and directors) are taken from Amec's annual report and accounts for 2013, before the acquisition of Foster Wheeler.

In-kind support

The company provided expertise to IFRC (International Federation of Red Cross and Red Crescent Societies), designing transitional shelters to be used in disaster situations.

2,274 hours were volunteered globally by employees (in company time). The company also matches all staff fundraising.

Employee-led support

It is employees, as recognised in the annual report, who drive the company's charitable and community giving. In addition to the contributions made by Amec via matched funding and other activities, a further £613,000 was raised by employees through the year. Employees also volunteered an additional 6,045 hours of their own time to raise money or to support their local communities.

Overseas employee giving

Example: Save the Children in Baku supports refugees and their children from Iran, Afghanistan, Chechnya and Pakistan who have requested asylum in Azerbaijan. In order to help the children get the aid and education they need, employees from the company's office in Baku provided school uniforms and a supply of materials for 112 children at the refugee clinic in order for them to attend school.

Corporate social responsibility

CSR committee: There is a Sustainability Department.

CSR information: This information was obtained from the company's annual report for 2013: 'People, safety and integrity, together with environment, provide the foundations to our sustainability strategy.'

CSR report: There is currently a Sustainability Report which can be obtained from the company's website and is produced annually. This includes information on the company's charitable giving although there was no information in the 2013 report specifically on giving in the UK, most of which appears to be matched funding at a local level.

Applications

The company supports, with matched funding, charity and community events that its employees/local offices support and for this reason, applications for support should be made to the company's local offices. See www.amecfw.com/aboutus/offices for those local to your organisation.

If applying to the company for information on its policies in this area, or for information about its global strategic charity partner, SOS Children, or the company's overseas and humanitarian aid, write to the Head of Sustainability, Frances Fay, at the Old Change House address given, or email frances.fay@amecfw.com.

Amey UK plc

Miscellaneous

Correspondent: Social Responsibility Department, Sherard Building, Edmund Halley Road, Oxford OX4 4DQ (tel: 01865 713100; website: www.amey.co.uk)

Directors: Richard Mottram, Chair; Santiago Olivares, Vice Chair; Mel Ewell; Andrew Nelson, Chief Financial Officer; Jaime Aguirre; Nicolas Villen; Alfredo Garcia; Iñigo Jodra (women: 0; men: 8)

Year end	31/12/2013
Turnover	£1,761,540,000
Pre-tax profit	£78,709,000

Nature of business: A provider of support services in the UK, ranging from transportation and education, to defence and health. In April 2013 Enterprise was acquired and integrated into Amey. The acquisition added a number of new sectors to Amey's portfolio including utilities, waste collection and social housing.

Company registration number: 4736639

Subsidiary undertakings include: AHL Holdings (Manchester) Ltd; ALC (FMC) Ltd; Amey Birmingham Highways Holdings Ltd; Amey FMP Belfast; Amey Hallam Highways Holdings Ltd; AmeyCespa (MK) Holding Co. Limited; Carillion Enterprise Ltd; EduAction (Waltham Forest) Ltd; GEO Amey PECS Ltd; Integrated Bradford PSP Ltd; Modern Housing Solutions (Prime) Ltd; RSP (Holdings) Ltd; Services Support (Avon and Somerset) Holdings.

Main locations: Birmingham, Belfast, Preston, Manchester, Newport, Glasgow, Edinburgh, Bristol

UK employees: 21,000

Focus of giving: Enterprise/training, overseas projects, safety and crime prevention, sport, recreation, children, young people, community/social welfare.

Membership: BITC, LBG

Charity of the Year	✓
Gifts in kind	✓
Matched funding	✓

Charitable donations

Cash UK (latest available):	2013	£465,000
	2010	£74,000
	2009	£96,468
	2008	£96,468
	2007	£60,783
Total UK (cash and in kind):	2013	£465,000
Cash worldwide:	2013	£2,664,000
Total worldwide (cash and in kind):	2013	£2,664,000

Community involvement

In supporting employment, education and skills, the company conducts targeted employment, skills and training programmes aimed at disadvantaged people, including the unemployed, young people, ex-offenders and ex-military personnel.

Partnerships

Amey has supported youth charity The Duke of Edinburgh's Award for over ten years and in 2014, the company began a new initiative to help young people from disadvantaged backgrounds across the UK take part in the scheme. The programme identifies underserved communities and expands local DofE provision to help improve the life chances and employability of young people.

Through local community partnerships, Amey works with over 300 ex-offenders, homeless and disadvantaged young people to provide them with skills and support to find employment. The company's partnership with the Ministry of Justice enables it to recruit ex-offenders in highways maintenance as part of a scheme designed specifically to reduce reoffending rates.

In 2013 the group signed the Armed Forces Corporate Covenant employment across its UK-wide network of contracts. The Corporate Covenant is a voluntary pledge from businesses, public sector organisations and charities, wishing to demonstrate their support for the armed forces community. Amey recruited over 25 service leavers across the year into the business in a variety of roles.

Corporate giving

In the parent company's 2013 Integrated Annual Report it lists its 'voluntary contributions' in the UK as £465,000 and the total worldwide as £2.6 million.

Employee-led support

The Amey Foundation (not a registered charity, it appears to be a fund held by the company) supports employee charity fundraising activities in their local communities. Any employee taking part in an event to raise money for charity can apply for additional fundraising from the foundation which will match their efforts up to a total of £500.

The company provides one paid day a year for employees to participate in charities and community projects of their choice. With 21,000 employees, this is the equivalent of over 160,000 hours of community volunteering.

Corporate social responsibility

CSR committee: We could find no evidence of how the Social Responsibility Committee is constituted.

CSR information: This information was obtained from the company's website:

> Our ultimate aim is to create sustainable communities. We will create positive social change by working with our customers, partners and suppliers to maximise long-term benefits for the wider community.
>
> This year [2014], we pledged to reinvest profits back into supporting communities and people.
>
> Delivering vital services across almost every area of the UK means we have a huge impact on the communities we serve. We look to maximise positive outcomes by delivering services with the following aims:
>
> - Supporting the local economy
> - Supporting employment, education and skills
> - Protecting and conserving the environment
> - Being an active member of the community

CSR report: In Amey's annual report and accounts the 'community engagement' pages are contained within the strategic review. The parent company, Ferrovial, is a member of LBG España and provides an integrated annual report with 'social commitment' content giving a breakdown of giving.

Exclusions

No provision for funding or other support to political organisations of any sort, and only exceptionally to provide funding or support to religious organisations as part of an initiative to the general benefit of a community. No funding or support will be given to individuals outside the business.

Applications

In writing to the correspondent referenced 'Community Engagement'.

Amlin plc

Insurance

Correspondent: Charities and Community Panel, St Helen's, 1 Undershaft, London EC3A 8ND (tel: 020 7746 1000; fax: 020 7746 1696; website: www.amlin.co.uk)

Directors: Sir Richard Davey, Chair; Charles Philipps; Julie Chakraverty; Marty Feinstein; Brian Carpenter; Simon Beale; Richard Hextall; Sir Mark Wrightson; Shonaid Jemmett-Page; Sir Alan Collins (women: 2; men: 8)

Year end	31/12/2013
Turnover	£2,440,600,000
Pre-tax profit	£325,700,000

Nature of business: Amlin is an independent insurer specialising in providing insurance cover to commercial enterprises and reinsurance protection to other insurance companies around the world.

Company registration number: 2854310

Subsidiary undertakings include: Amlin Investments Ltd; Amlin Corporate Member Ltd; Amlin Underwriting Services Ltd, Delian (A-L) Ltd Companies; St Margaret's Insurance Services Ltd; Syndicate 2001.

Main locations: East London, Chelmsford BC

UK employees: 1,123

Total employees: 1,886

Focus of giving: Health, ill health, overseas projects, community/social welfare, disability.

Charity of the Year	✓
Gifts in kind	✓
Matched funding	✓
Overseas giving	✓
Payroll giving	✓

Charitable donations

Cash UK (latest available):	2013	£274,000
	2010	£147,300
	2009	£134,000
	2008	£81,000
Total UK (cash and in kind):	2013	£274,000
Cash worldwide:	2013	£274,000
Total worldwide (cash and in kind):	2013	£274,000

Community involvement

Support is given in the communities in which Amlin does business and for the education and development of young people, and charities which are relevant for employees. In the UK, charitable giving is co-ordinated through a Community and Charities Panel chaired by a senior underwriter.

Amlin also supports scholarship programmes to support young people. In the UK, Amlin funds vocational training for ten candidates selected by UK Youth.

Partner charities

Little Haven's Hospice; Lloyd's Community Programme; Macmillan Cancer Support; The Outward Bound Trust; and UK Youth.

Corporate giving

In 2013, Amlin Group's charitable donations were declared at £274,000 and it would appear that this was the group's UK donation. Five main UK charity partners were supported during the year and cash donations were given to: Macmillan Cancer Support (£20,000); UK Youth (£19,000); and The Outward Bound Trust (£10,000). Little Haven's Hospice, Chelmsford and Lloyd's Community Programme were also supported by UK offices but no amounts were given.

In-kind support

During 2013, Amlin supported 83 employees involved in community activities and charity fundraising, with funding of up to £750 per event. Amlin's annual sponsored go-karting event raised £22,000, split between Richard House Children's Hospice and Macmillan Cancer Support, one of Amlin's charity partners. Additionally, 15 Amlin staff members participated in the International Community Action Learning programme in Namibia.

Employee-led support

Amlin employees are encouraged to volunteer for community activities and payroll giving is promoted.

Commercially led support

Sponsorship

Since 2009, Amlin has sponsored Art for Youth London, (an affordable art sale held each October at the Royal College of Art). Proceeds from this event support UK Youth programmes across the country and now, in its 26th year, the event has raised in excess of £1 million. Amlin also sponsors the Amlin Platinum programme whereby ten young people achieve the highest qualification available through the charity.

Corporate social responsibility

CSR committee: The charities budget in the UK is managed by a Community and Charities Panel chaired by a senior underwriter. Non-UK subsidiaries' community and charities budgets are managed locally under the direction of their boards.

CSR information: This information was obtained from the company's website:

> Amlin is committed to building a sustainable business through the consistent application of our values in relationships with our shareholders, employees, clients and other stakeholders. We aim to make a positive contribution to the communities in which we operate, placing integrity and professional excellence at the heart of our business practice.

CSR report: There is an annual CSR report.

Applications

In writing to the correspondent.

Anglian Water

Water

Correspondent: Sustainable Development Department, Lancaster House, Lancaster Way, Ermine Business Park, Huntingdon, Cambridgeshire PE29 6YJ (tel: 03457919155; website: www.awg.com)

Directors: Andre Bourbonnais; Philip White; Andrew Cox; Werner Kerschl; Niall Mills; Christian Seymour; Adrian Montague, Chair; Peter Simpson, Managing Director, Anglian Water Services; Scott Longhurst, Managing Director, Finance and Non Reg. Business; Dr Timothy Stone; Mark Rogers; Dr Timothy Stone (women: 1; men: 11)

Year end	31/03/2014
Turnover	£1,270,500,000
Pre-tax profit	£7,300,000

Nature of business: Water supply and distribution, waste water collection and treatment, providing social housing repairs and property development. The group is registered under the Companies (Jersey) Law 1991.

Company registration number: 2366656

Subsidiary undertakings include: Alpheus Environmental Ltd; Anglian Water (Osprey) Financing plc; AWG Parent Co. Limited; AWG Group Ltd; AWG Holdings Ltd; AWG UK Holdings Ltd; Osprey Acquisitions Ltd; Osprey Holdco Ltd; Rutland Insurance Ltd. A full list of subsidiaries is lodged with Companies House.

Main locations: Peterborough, Huntingdon

UK employees: 4,300

Total employees: 4,300

Focus of giving: Education, environment, heritage, overseas projects, children, young people, community/ social welfare.

Membership: BITC

Charity of the Year	✓
Gifts in kind	✓
Matched funding	✓
Payroll giving	✓
Sponsorship	✓

Charitable donations

Cash UK (latest available):	2014	£40,000
	2011	£790,000
	2010	£790,000
	2009	£790,000
	2008	£1,040,000
Total UK (cash and in kind):	2014	£40,000
Cash worldwide:	2014	£40,000
Total worldwide (cash and in kind):	2014	£40,000

Community involvement

The company is understandably engaged mainly in environmental work around the sites from which it operates. It supports its communities in various ways including:

- Providing a stimulating and hands-on experience of the industry, linked to the national curriculum, through its education programme delivered at dedicated centres or through school visits
- Raising community awareness of the value of water and encouraging everyone to do their bit
- Promoting Drop 20 and Keep it Clear campaigns through open days at its local sites and community presentations
- Supporting local communities through the employee volunteering scheme – Love to Help
- Involvement in charitable giving through the company's Give As You Earn scheme
- Working in partnership with regional and national bodies to add to the sustainability of the local environment, for example RiverCare

The company's website states: 'Due to the high numbers of requests, we are unable to give sponsorship to local events/charities. However support can be given through volunteering under Love to Help.'

The Anglian Water Assistance Fund (AWAF)

This fund has been set up to support customers in financial hardship. The fund is administered by Charis Grants Ltd on behalf of Anglian Water and the aims are:

- To administer a grants programme aimed at reducing water and sewerage debt for customers experiencing poverty and hardship throughout the region
- To make awards that will help people recover from the burden of debt and become financially more stable
- To make a positive long-term difference to an applicant's financial situation

Eligibility

The fund can consider helping you if you are in debt with your water and/or sewerage charges to Anglian or Hartlepool Water and you are a current domestic account holder of Anglian or Hartlepool Water.

The fund may be able to help you to clear arrears of domestic water and sewerage charges by offering a number of solutions.

How to apply for help

If you would like to apply for help you can download an application form from the website which should then be printed and completed. Alternatively you can call Charis Grants on 01733 421060 to request an application form. You will also need to send in proof with your completed application of the amount of income you have and where it comes from e.g. wages, benefits, etc. For more details visit: www.anglianwater.co.uk/household/your-bill/problems-paying/assistance.aspx

Charity partner

Anglian Water formally recognises WaterAid as its nominated charity and as such it does not offer charitable donations or sponsorship to other charities and bodies.

Corporate giving

During the year, the group donated £40,000 to WaterAid. With the support of employee volunteers, partners and suppliers across the business, the company's WaterAid Volunteers' Committee fundraised an extra £507,000 for WaterAid which was the highest amount ever raised by this committee.

No figure was available with regard to the company's in-kind support. We could neither find any figures for the amount the company has used, through the Assistance Fund, to help those struggling with their bills.

In-kind support

On occasion the company, due to upgrades on IT systems, has redundant computer hardware which its staff are no longer able to use. In support of its re-use/recycle ethos it can usually offer this equipment to charity/community organisations in the vicinity of its local offices. Equally, in some cases where office upgrades are necessary, some furniture (e.g. desks, chairs, filing cabinets) become surplus to requirement and are offered to the local community rather than simply being disposed of. To find out if there is a current recycling programme running in your area, contact the sustainable development department. Volunteering is encouraged by the company, see the Employee-led support section.

Employee-led support

Love To Help

The company's volunteering programme supports local good causes are supported by staff and the company then pledges to match up to 30 hours per year of work time to help staff do more volunteering. Volunteers can choose from the following three initiatives:

River Care

This is a company-driven initiative run in conjunction with the charity Keep Britain Tidy. The project supports volunteers in improving their local river environment by helping them with the removal of litter, fly-tipped debris and non-native species. This is the company's industry charity and Anglian Water is a supporter and fundraiser. Employees volunteer to help at regional or national events.

WaterAid

Volunteers can choose to support the company's charity partner.

Personal choice

Many employees give active support to good causes in the community which can range from volunteering with local scouts, through to being a school governor.

Payroll giving: The company operates the Give As You Earn scheme through the Charities Aid Foundation. Anglian Water pays the administration charges to enable chosen charities to receive 100% of the employee donation.

Commercially led support

Education centres

These purpose-built centres at water recycling sites offer tours at no charge to schools/organisations. The centres cater for groups from year 2 upwards. Special needs groups are welcome at all centres with disability access available. Secondary and further education groups are also welcome with specific sessions catering for GCSE, AS and A-level, BTEC and Young Apprentices.

The education centres can be found at Chelmsford in Essex and Leighton Linslade in Bedfordshire. Corby Education Centre in Northamptonshire is temporarily closed.

The website states that: **Love Every Drop** is the company's strategy to 'put water at the heart of a whole new way of living. Taken together, the ten ambitious business goals we've set ourselves and the commitments and measures that underpin them form our sustainability roadmap'.

Sponsorship: WaterAid

The group sponsors, undertakes fundraising activities, offers payroll giving and volunteer company time to support this charity's international aid work.

Corporate social responsibility

CSR committee: There is a Sustainable Development department.

CSR information: The website states:

> AWG believes that corporate responsibility (CR) is about supporting and actively encouraging strategies and behaviours that demonstrate our commitment to the long-term viability of the business.
>
> This reinforces our belief that business decisions should take into account social and environmental issues, as well as economic ones. It is about making sure that we manage the key elements of our day-to-day business and long-term planning in ways that are sustainable.

The company's key issue is sustainability through improving water quality, the environment, climate change and reducing waste.

There are community pages on the website but this again involves in the main protecting and improving the environment.

CSR report: There is a CSR section on the company's website.

Exclusions

No support is given for advertising in charity brochures, appeals from individuals, political appeals or sport (unless at educational level), animal welfare, medical research or religious appeals.

Applications

In writing to the correspondent. **Note:** The group's 2010/11 annual report states: 'Individual requests for sponsorship were declined on the basis that the company's policy is to encourage community involvement rather than charitable donations.' This would appear still to be the case and the company has stated that it only supports WaterAid financially.

Anglo American plc

Mining

Correspondent: Hermione Botes, Principal Analyst: Engagement and Alignment, 20 Carlton House Terrace, London SW1Y 5AN (tel: 020 7968 8888; email: Hermien.botes@angloamerican.com; website: www.angloamerican.co.uk)

Directors: David Challen; Sir C. K. Chow; Rene Medori, Finance Director; Phuthuma Nhleko; Jack Thompson; Sir Philip Hampton; Ray O'Rourke; John Parker, Chair; Mark Cutifani, Chief Executive; Byron Grote; Judy Dlamini; Mphu Ramatlapeng; Jim Rutherford; Anne Stevens (women: 2; men: 12)

Year end	31/12/2013
Turnover	£18,385,698,000
Pre-tax profit	£3,844,191,000

Nature of business: Mining. The employee figure excludes certain employees such as contractors.

Company registration number: 3564138

Subsidiary undertakings include: Anglo American Metallurgical Coal H; De Beers Société Anonyme; De Beers Consolidated Mines; Peace River Coal Inc.; Sishen Iron Ore Company.

Brands include: Forevermark.

Main locations: London

Total employees: 98

Focus of giving: Education, health, ill health, overseas projects, community/ social welfare.

Membership: BITC

FTSE 100	✓
Gifts in kind	✓
Matched funding	✓
Overseas giving	✓

Charitable donations

Cash UK (latest available):	2013	£1,400,000
	2011	£1,430,000
	2009	£1,608,000
	2007	£1,545,000
	2005	£824,402
Total UK (cash and in kind):	2013	£1,400,000
Cash worldwide:	2013	£1,400,000
Total worldwide (cash and in kind):	2013	£1,400,000

Community involvement

The company's charitable donations in the UK are primarily made through the **Anglo American Foundation** (Charity Commission no. 1111719). The foundation welcomes applications from organisations involved with the following areas: education; international development; health/HIV; environment; and London-based community development. The foundation seeks to develop continuing relationships with a small number of charitable organisations which contribute to its priority objectives. These will then be augmented from time to time by applications which come within the foundation's priorities and relate to those parts of the world where the group has operations.

Resources are also allocated by way of matching funds raised for charities by employees who work in the Anglo American London and Luxembourg offices.

Corporate giving

The following statement is taken from the group's annual report for 2013:

> During the year, Anglo American, its subsidiaries and the Anglo American Group Foundation made donations for charitable purposes or wider social investments amounting to $127.5 million (2.2% of profit before tax from subsidiaries and joint operations, before special items and remeasurements).
>
> Charitable donations of $0.8 million were made in the UK, of which the main categories were: education and training (47.7%) and health and welfare (41.5%). These figures were compiled with reference to the London Benchmarking Group model for defining and measuring social investment spending.

Note: CSI (Corporate Social Investment) spending is defined in the group's annual accounts as: 'CSI spend is the sum of donations for charitable purposes and community investment (which includes cash and in-kind donations and staff time) as well as investments in commercial initiatives with public benefit (such as enterprise development).'

Because this figure includes monies which we do not consider to have been spent on charitable purposes, we have been unable to determine the group's worldwide charitable donations or contributions.

A fuller analysis of the group's social investment activities can be found in the Sustainable Development Report 2013.

Anglo American Group Foundation

The foundation's 2013 annual accounts state that 'donations of £1.4 million were received from Anglo American Services (UK) Ltd (2012: £1.98 million). With the exception of A C Bromfield the trustees are employed by Anglo American Services(UK) Ltd which is a subsidiary of Anglo American plc.

We are taking this figure of £1.4 million as the UK cash donation total, as despite some of the money being sent for charitable activities abroad, it was received and is distributed by the foundation, a UK-registered charity.

See the corporate charity entry on p. 391 for more information.

In-kind support

The company may, from time to time, provide additional support through gifts in kind.

Partners

Partners include: CARE International; Fauna and Flora International; Natural History Museum; and Women in Mining.

Employee-led support

The company has an employee volunteering scheme and allows company time off for community support activities to take place. Employee fundraising is matched by the company up to a maximum of £500 per employee.

Payroll giving: A scheme is operated by the company on behalf of its employees.

Commercially led support

Sponsorship: Arts and good-cause sponsorship has been undertaken.

Corporate social responsibility

CSR committee: No details were found for the structure or membership of a specific CSR committee.

CSR information: Taken from the sustainability section on the group's website:

> As with any part of our business, we tackle community engagement with a focus on delivery. Applying our industry-leading Socio-Economic Assessment Toolbox (SEAT) shows us how our operations affect each community. We can then engage more effectively, accountably and transparently.

The UK version of the SEAT document has 247 pages.

CSR report: An annual Sustainable Development Report is published and available from the website.

Corporate charity: Anglo American Group Foundation (Charity Commission no. 1111719).

Exclusions

The company does not support appeals from individuals, medical research, political appeals, religious appeals or sport.

The foundation only funds registered charities and does not support:

- Animal charities
- Armed forces charities
- Community interest companies
- Educational fees
- Expeditions overseas
- General health charities
- Hospital trusts
- Individuals
- Music festivals and choirs
- Political or quasi-political bodies
- Religious organisations (other than community outreach)
- Trade unions

Applications

Applications to the company should be made to the correspondent referenced 'CSI – Communities'; and to the foundation to: Erica Shinnie, Anglo American Group Foundation, 20 Carlton House Terrace, London SW1Y 5AN; email: aagf@angloamerican.com; telephone: 020 7968 8727.

Apax Partners LLP

Financial services

Correspondent: David Marks, Trustee, The Apax Foundation, 33 Jermyn Street, London SW1Y 6DN (tel: 020 7872 6300; fax: 020 7666 6441; email: foundation@apax.com; website: www.apax.com)

Directors: Andrew Sillitoe, Co. Chief Executive; Mitch Truwit, Co. Chief Executive (women: 0; men: 2)

Year end	31/03/2014
Turnover	£189,246,000
Pre-tax profit	£119,132,000

Nature of business: Apax Partners is an independent global private equity advisory firm. Its website states:

> From 2013, to fulfil our commitment to Sir David Walker's Guidelines for Disclosure and Transparency in Private Equity, Apax Partners chose its corporate website as the primary platform for disclosing information on its activities publicly and regularly. The firm no longer publishes a separate Annual Report.

Company registration number: OC303117

Main locations: London

Total employees: 243

Focus of giving: General charitable purposes, economic generation, education, enterprise/training, poverty and social exclusion.

Gifts in kind	✓
Matched funding	✓

Charitable donations

Cash UK (latest available):	2014	£558,000
	2013	£1,359,000
	2011	£3,453,800
	2008	£2,800,000
Total UK (cash and in kind):	2014	£566,000
Cash worldwide:	2014	£558,000
Total worldwide (cash and in kind):	2014	£566,000

Community involvement

Established in 2006, **The Apax Foundation** (Charity Commission no. 1112845) is the formal channel for Apax Partners' corporate giving and community engagement globally and receives a percentage of the firm's profits and carried interest through its (the foundation's), subsidiary undertaking, Apax E Member Ltd.

The foundation concentrates its major grant-giving on the area of social entrepreneurship. This is a natural fit with what Apax does commercially and also an area where colleagues, including some of the foundation's trustees, have significant experience.

In order to encourage the personal charitable and philanthropic activities of the firm's employees, the foundation also commits to projects in which Apax staff take an active role.

Corporate giving

The foundation's wholly owned subsidiary, Apax E Member Ltd, received a profit share of £558,000 from Apax Partners LLP during the year (2013: £1.36 million) which was subsequently transferred to the foundation for distribution. £7,500 was received for in-kind purposes (the staff costs of the foundation).

See the corporate charity entry on p. 391 for more information.

In-kind support

The staff costs of the foundation are paid for by the firm.

Employee-led support

Matched funding

This matching scheme is designed to encourage and support colleagues' personal involvement with charities. The company makes a matching donation of at least £5,000 to any charity which benefits from the 'significant, active, ongoing involvement' of any member of a team in any of the company's regions.

Since the scheme's inception in 2007, the company has made donations of more than £1.4 million in support of the time and skills given by employees to a range of charities worldwide.

Corporate social responsibility

CSR committee: Sustainability is co-ordinated through the firm's operations by a dedicated sustainability committee drawn from senior members of the firm. This committee manages all aspects of the implementation of the Apax sustainability effort and provides regular feedback to the executive committee with regard to key projects. The committee is led by Seth Brody and meets on a monthly basis to cover a wide variety of projects, both with regard to internal matters and portfolio company monitoring.

CSR information: The following statements are taken from the firm's website:

> Apax Funds do not invest in companies involved in firearms, pornography or that derive significant revenues from the production or sale of tobacco.
>
> **Community**: Act with respect and consideration for the communities in which we operate.
>
> Apax is committed to engaging constructively with the communities in which its funds invest. It has policies in place for corporate giving and encouraging individual employees in their personal charitable endeavours.

CSR report: There is an annual sustainability report.

Corporate charity: The Apax Foundation (Charity Commission no. 1112845).

Applications

In writing to the correspondent – a trustee of the firm's foundation.

Archant

Media

Correspondent: John Ellison, Company Secretary, Prospect House, Rouen Road, Norwich NR1 1RE (tel: 01603 772772; email: john.ellison@archant.co.uk; website: www.archant.co.uk)

Directors: Richard Jewson, Chair; Adrian Jeakings, Chief Executive; Brian McCarthy; Simon Copeman; Johnny Hustler; Sonita Alleyne; Mike Walsh; John Ellison; Peter Troughton (women: 1; men: 9)

Year end	31/12/2013
Turnover	£126,623,000
Pre-tax profit	(£759,000)

Nature of business: Archant is a privately owned media company serving geographical and specialist interest communities across a wide range of media and employing around 1,600 members of staff. It has titles in East Anglia, London, Kent and the South West.

Company registration number: 4126997

Main locations: Barnstaple, Ilford, Dereham, Diss, Exeter, Ely, Felixstowe, Harlow, Hitchin, Huntingdon, Ipswich, Sudbury, Weston-super-Mare, Welwyn Garden City, Bury St Edmunds, Colchester, Cheltenham, Cromer, Maidstone, Lowestoft, London, Norwich, Wimbledon, Preston, Reigate, St Albans, Southampton

UK employees: 1,600

Total employees: 1,600

Focus of giving: General charitable purposes, poverty and social exclusion, children, young people, community/ social welfare, disability, disasters.

Membership: BITC

Gifts in kind	✓
Humanitarian aid: overseas	✓
Humanitarian aid: UK	✓
Matched funding	✓
Overseas giving	✓
Payroll giving	✓

Charitable donations

Cash UK (latest available):	2013	£55,000
	2012	£64,000
	2010	£73,000
	2009	£81,000
	2007	£102,000
Total UK (cash and in kind):	2013	£55,000
Cash worldwide:	2013	£55,000
Total worldwide (cash and in kind):	2013	£55,000

Community involvement

The group states in its 2013 annual report that it targets its corporate charitable donations towards charities local to its areas of publication and locally targeted appeals of national charities.

In addition to making direct contributions to charities, the company aims through its own publications to react quickly to local needs, enabling its readership to support local and national causes, and substantial sums have been raised in this way. Examples in 2013 include: the Eastern Daily Press raising in excess of £200,000 in just eight weeks to support those affected by the December 2013 tidal surge in the UK, and the annual Newham Recorder and Community Links Christmas Toy Appeal for disadvantaged children.

Corporate giving

In 2013 a total of £55,000 (2012: £64,000) was given by the group to charitable causes through corporate giving and matching both employees' fundraising activities and sums donated through their payroll giving.

Employee-led support

Employees are encouraged to volunteer and be involved with their local communities and the group supports them with matched funding of both payroll giving and fundraising activities.

Corporate social responsibility

CSR committee: There were no details published.

CSR information: Statement taken from the 2013 annual report: 'Our corporate social responsibilities are integral to our business activities and values.'

CSR report: Reporting of CSR is contained within the annual report.

Exclusions

No support is given for: advertising in charity brochures; appeals from individuals; fundraising events; overseas projects; political appeals; or religious appeals.

Applications

In writing to the correspondent, or to your local Archant office.

Arla Foods Ltd

Food manufacture

Correspondent: The Community Challenge Team, Arla House, 4 Savannah Way, Leeds Valley Park, Leeds LS10 1AB (tel: 01133 827000; fax: 01133 827030; email: arla@arlafoods.com; website: www.arlafoodsuk.com)

Directors: S. D. Stevens; J. E. Pederson; L. E. Dalsgaard Hoff; P. Lauritzen; A. Amirahmadi; P. Gioertz-Carlsen; A. Barber; T. Soar

Year end	31/12/2013
Turnover	£2,412,365,000
Pre-tax profit	(£18,787,000)

Nature of business: Arla Foods UK plc., through its subsidiary companies, is a supplier of milk and dairy products in the UK market. The group supplies liquid milk, cream, butter, spreads, cheeses, fresh dairy products, yoghurts and desserts to the major supermarkets.

Company registration number: 2143253

Subsidiary undertakings include: Associated Dairies Ltd; Craven Dairies Ltd; and The Free Range Butter Co. Limited.

Main locations: Manchester, Naim, Northallerton, Newcastle, Oakthorpe, Ruislip, Sheffield, Settle, Hatfield Peverel, Leeds, Ashby-de-la-Zouch

Focus of giving: General charitable purposes, environment, health, ill health, children, young people, community/ social welfare.

Charity of the Year	✓
Gifts in kind	✓
Matched funding	✓
Overseas giving	✓
Sponsorship	✓

Charitable donations

Cash UK (latest available):	2013	£117,000
	2012	£111,000
	2011	£46,000
	2009	£33,000
	2008	£36,000
Total UK (cash and in kind):	2013	£117,000
Cash worldwide:	2013	£117,000
Total worldwide (cash and in kind):	2013	£117,000

Community involvement

The following extract is taken from the Responsibility pages of the company's website:

> We have developed an initiative called Community Challenge which gives colleagues a say in how we utilise our community involvement budget. There are two ways Community Challenge will help local communities, either by match funding money colleagues raise for causes close to their heart or by providing Community Challenge funding to causes at which colleagues volunteer.

Charity partner

In the UK, Arla is a corporate partner to Marie Curie Cancer Care, which sees support to branches of the charity local to Arla's sites.

Corporate giving

In 2013 the company made donations to UK charitable organisations of £117,000. A list of beneficiaries was not available.

In-kind support

Matched funding is available to employees who volunteer for charitable/ community causes.

Employee-led support

Employees throughout the group volunteer for local charities and good causes.

Commercially led support

Sponsorship

In the UK, Arla is sponsoring a rugby organisation in the UK which works to stimulate an interest in sport among children and young people.

Denmark's Arla Foundation

In late 2012, in Denmark, Arla launched a long-term initiative called the Arla Foundation. The foundation will actively support children aged 10 to 14 to learn more about cooking, natural produce and outdoor physical activities in the countryside. The goal is to inspire this generation to adopt a healthy and sustainable lifestyle. We understand that beneficiaries must be Danish.

Corporate social responsibility

CSR committee: There is a CSR committee with the CEO as chair.

CSR information: The following statement is taken from the 2013 CSR report:

> Health will continue to be important to us, as will continuing our environmental work, particularly further improvements in sustainable dairy farming. We also have plans to develop a global initiative for community involvement that the whole of Arla can collectively embrace. Furthermore, we will, in the coming year, assess our global performance against the United Nations' Guiding principles for Human Rights.
>
> In all areas of responsibility, we want to be as open and transparent as possible. On-going dialogue with all our stakeholders is important, and we will strive to communicate with ever more clarity what we are doing and how and whether we are delivering on the commitments we have made.

It was not possible to determine the ratio of women to men on the board.

CSR report: A CSR report is published annually and is available online from the company's website.

Applications

In writing to the correspondent.

Arriva plc

Motors and accessories

Correspondent: Community Relations Support, Group Communications Department, 1 Admiral Way, Doxford International Business Park, Sunderland SR3 3XP (tel: 01915 204000; fax: 01915 204001; email: corporateresponsibility@arriva.co.uk; website: www.arriva.co.uk)

Directors: David Martin, Chief Executive; Martin Hibbert; T. Schein; Mike Cooper; U. Homburg; R. Lutz; N. Klumpt

Year end	31/12/2013
Turnover	-£23,143,000
Pre-tax profit	(£16,833,000)

Nature of business: The principal activities of the group are a holding company and the provider of central support services for its subsidiary companies which provide bus and train services in the UK and mainland Europe. Arriva plc was acquired by Deutsche Bahn on 27 August 2010.

Company registration number: 347103

Subsidiary undertakings include: Arriva Passenger Services Ltd; MTL Services Ltd; TGM Holdings Ltd; Zeta Automotive Ltd.

Focus of giving: General charitable purposes, education, environment, older people, arts, culture, sport, recreation, children, young people, disability.

Cash donations undeclared	✓
Gifts in kind	✓
Matched funding	✓
Overseas giving	✓

Charitable donations

Cash UK (latest available):	2013	£60,000
	2010	£17,250
	2009	£66,000
	2008	£97,000
	2007	£112,000
Total UK (cash and in kind):	2013	£60,000
Cash worldwide:	2013	£60,000
Total worldwide (cash and in kind):	2013	£60,000

Community involvement

Development and working in partnership

Partnership working with suitable organisations is a feature of Arriva's community relations programme. Its aim is to build long-term relationships with community partners and sees this as a mutual benefit both to the organisation/ charity and the company itself. Support may be financial or practical, and sometimes involves the direct support of its employees.

The company's website provides the following helpful information for applicants for support:

> Arriva seeks to build sustainable community relationships that are relevant to the group's activities across its operating areas. The aim is to deliver value for the communities it serves whilst reinforcing their relationship with the group.
>
> Our community relations activities aim to reflect and embrace the brand values of the group. Community relations practices vary in different countries according to local custom and we believe that decisions are best taken locally within the operating business on the appropriate level of involvement.
>
> As well as providing financial help, where practical and appropriate, Arriva uses its areas of expertise and resources to support its community partners and to help develop sustainable relationships. As a people business we value, encourage and celebrate the contribution our employees and others make to the communities we serve.
>
> Arriva provides support to charities and projects that make a direct contribution to the communities we serve.
>
> Examples of areas that are likely to meet this objective are listed below:
>
> - Assisting people with disabilities to make a positive contribution to their communities
> - Supporting the elderly
> - Encouraging the young to be involved in the community, including education projects improving the environment

Corporate giving

In 2013 Arriva plc did not declare its charitable donations. We have therefore taken an average from the last three years' figures we have available and estimate the UK cash donation to be £60,000. There is no total, or breakdown of the costs to the company of its in-kind giving.

In-kind support

Arriva Community Action Awards

This initiative recognises and rewards the volunteering activities of its staff. Each year the company provides a range of charities, groups and schools with free transport and travel advice.

Schools

Building positive relations with schools is an important part of the company's work. Across its operations it hosts visits with vehicles often becoming mobile classrooms for the day. Employees help with school projects, offer safety advice and explain the environmental benefits of public transport.

Sport

Grass-roots sport is supported by providing funding for equipment for clubs and teams across Europe.

Employee-led support

Employees are encouraged to volunteer in their local communities where the company provides services. For example, Arriva North West hosts an annual golf day organised and attended by employees which has raised more than £100,000 for a local baby hospice.

Aviva plc in the UK runs community action awards – see 'In-kind support' section.

Corporate social responsibility

CSR committee: There are no details of a separate CSR Committee for Arriva plc.

CSR information: Much of Arriva's charitable giving is in-kind donations. Arriva's corporate responsibility is concerned with minimising its impact on the environment, providing safe places to work and travel for employees and customers, and playing an active role in the communities in which it operates. The main areas of the company's corporate responsibility policy are: safety, environment, employees and community.

We were unable to determine the ratio of women to men on the board.

CSR report: There is a corporate responsibility section on Aviva's website.

Exclusions

No support is given for any activity in support of political parties or religious movements.

Applications

The company's website states: 'Unfortunately we cannot support all the requests for support that we receive. If you are a charitable organisation or community group who would like our support, read our community relations policy before contacting us'. If you have not been contacted within 28 days, you can assume your application has been unsuccessful.

Requests for support for community partnerships should be sent to corporateresponsibility@arriva.co.uk or in writing to the correspondent.

Arup Group Ltd

Consulting engineers

Correspondent: See 'Applications', 13 Fitzroy Street, London W1T 4BQ (tel: 020 7636 1531; fax: 020 7580 3924; email: london@arup.com; website: www.arup.com)

Directors: Ngaire Woods; Michael Bear; Alan Belfield; Tristram Carfrae; Michael Kwok; Gregory Hodkinson; L. M. Lui; Mahadev Raman; David Whittleton; Peter Bailey; Dervilla Mitchell; Peter Chamley (women: 1; men: 11)

Year end	31/03/2014
Turnover	£1,048,276,000
Pre-tax profit	£40,430,000

Nature of business: Arup is an independent firm of planners, designers, engineers and consultants working across the built environment. It is a wholly independent organisation, and is owned in trust for the benefit of its employees and their dependents. Each of Arup's employees receives a share of the firm's operating profit each year.

Company registration number: 1312454

Subsidiary undertakings include: Arup Americas Inc.; Arup Muhendislik ve Musavirlik; Fitzroy Insurance Services Ltd; Ove Arup Holdings Ltd; Ove Arup and Partners Poland. For a full list of subsidiaries see the group's accounts.

Main locations: Edinburgh, Dundee, Southampton, Glasgow, Bristol, Cardiff, Cambridge, Newcastle upon Tyne, Liverpool, London, Manchester, Nottingham, Leeds, Solihull, Sheffield, Wrexham, Winchester, Belfast

Total employees: 11,355

Focus of giving: General charitable purposes, education, environment, health, ill health, heritage, STEM (science, technology, engineering and mathematics), overseas projects, poverty and social exclusion, community/social welfare, disasters.

Membership: BITC

Charity of the Year	✓
Gifts in kind	✓
Humanitarian aid: overseas	✓
Humanitarian aid: UK	✓
Matched funding	✓
Overseas giving	✓

Charitable donations

Cash UK (latest available):	2014	£363,000
	2011	£219,000
	2009	£551,000
	2008	£281,000
	2007	£66,000
Total UK (cash and in kind):	2014	£481,000
Cash worldwide:	2014	£730,000
Total worldwide (cash and in kind):	2014	£1,258,000

Community involvement

The annual report for 2013/14 states:

> There are many advantages to operating as a trust-owned firm, including the independence to focus on the quality of the work rather than growth and short-term shareholder returns. In practice, this means the firm invests in research and development, charitable causes and staff members who benefit from a global profit share plan.

The Ove Arup Partnership Charitable Trust

The trust (Charity Commission no. 1038737) was established in 1978 by a Deed of Settlement. Its income is received through gifts from Arup Group Ltd and its objects are general charitable purposes. The beneficiaries would appear to be UK-registered charities.

The Ove Arup Foundation

Established to commemorate the life of the late Sir Ove Arup, The Ove Arup Foundation (Charity Commission no. 328138) is an educational trust supporting initiatives related to the built environment. Endowed by the partnership for the first seven years of its existence (1989–1995) through an annual gift, the trustees decided in 2000 to provide further funding over the next five years and to increase the scope of the foundation internationally.

Arup Education Trust, South Africa

The Arup Education Trust (AET) provides financial assistance to eligible beneficiaries in tertiary and secondary education. AET places qualified students into the corporate environment, eliminating the gap between study and employment.

Charity partners

Refer to the 'In-kind support' section.

Corporate giving

The annual report states that in 2013/14 the firm channelled £730,000 of profits to various charitable organisations. This is in keeping with a longstanding corporate commitment to donate directly to charitable causes. We believe this figure to be cash worldwide and the UK cash figure to be the total of those amounts donated to both the charitable foundation and the charitable trust. Although money spent in the UK could easily be more, we could find no further geographical breakdown.

Volunteering costs, which again we believe to be worldwide, are declared at £528,000 and we have divided this amount by the five regions of the company, giving the UK a further £106,000 in in-kind contributions, plus £12,000 in-kind, 'donated' to the foundation for services and expenses.

See the corporate charity entry on p. 392 for more information.

In-kind support

The sustainability and resilience section of the group's 2013/14 annual report states:

> At the corporate level, there is a formal framework for donating a proportion of the firm's profits directly into charities including the Ove Arup Foundation. In addition, Community Engagement committees in each of the firm's five regions encourage and support a wide range of other activities. Underpinning this approach is the principle that where possible staff members should work with external partners to build the capacity of local communities around the world to achieve their own development goals.

Following the devastation of Typhoon Haiyan, the firm provided emergency donations, matched funding and sought opportunities to provide pro bono technical assistance to aid the relief work.

In addition to direct giving, the firm supports the provision of professional services to help key partners and in 2013/14 pro bono engagement totalled 6,134 hours, equating to around £528,000 in equivalent professional fees.

Charity partnerships

There are a number of strategic partnerships where the firm has established relationships with charities including Habitat for Humanity, Engineers Without Borders, Bridges to Prosperity, The Smith Family, WaterAid, the Engineering Development Trust and RedR.

The annual report states: 'The firm is keen to work with partners to raise awareness of the many challenges communities face around the globe, while helping to build their capacity to create stronger, more resilient communities.'

Employee-led support

Staff members around the world carry out fundraising activities for a range of causes that they choose in the communities the firm serves. In this financial year, staff members responded generously in the wake of Typhoon Haiyan, which hit the Philippines to such devastating effect during November. Each region gave support through direct donations and salary sacrifice initiatives, volunteering and pro bono work.

Corporate social responsibility

CSR committee: There is a Community Engagement committee in each of the group's five regions.

CSR information: The website notes:

> Arup influences many people's lives through its projects. Shaping a sustainable future – particularly through the urban environment – will be one of the greatest challenges in the 21st century. Arup is rising to the challenge: investing in research, innovating and creating better solutions for its clients and the wider world.
>
> '. . . our lives are inextricably mixed up with those of our fellow human beings, and that there can be no real happiness in isolation . . . ' Ove Arup, 1970.

CSR report: There is a sustainability and resilience section within the annual report of the group.

Corporate charity: The Ove Arup Foundation (Charity Commission no. 328138).

Applications

For applications to the foundation, download and complete the application form from the website and address to John Ward – email: ovarfound@arup.com; for applications to the charitable trust, address to Stephanie Wilde – email: stephanie.wilde@arup.com. For applications to the group address correspondence to the Community Engagement Committee (UK). All are administered from the group's address at 13 Fitzroy Street.

Asda Stores Ltd

Retail – supermarkets

Correspondent: Julie Ward, The Asda Foundation Administrator, Asda House, Southbank, Great Wilson Street, Leeds LS11 5AD (tel: 01132 435435; fax: 01132 418666; website: www.asda.com)

Directors: A. Clarke; A. Moore; H. Tatum; S. Smith; M. Ibbotson; B. Williams; A. Russo

Year end	31/12/2013
Turnover	£23,299,400,000
Pre-tax profit	£605,100,000

Nature of business: The retail of food, clothing, general merchandise and services throughout the UK and online. In 1999 Asda became part of Wal-Mart Stores Inc., based in Arkansas.

Company registration number: 464777

Subsidiary undertakings include: Asda Storage Ltd; Asda Supermarkets Ltd; Ever 1295 Ltd; Netto Foodstores Ltd.

Brands include: George; Smart Price; Extra Special; Good for You!; Asda Brand; Asda Organics; Asda Great Stuff.

UK employees: 176,637

Total employees: 176,637

Focus of giving: General charitable purposes, education, health, ill health, sport, recreation, women's issues, children, young people, community/ social welfare.

Membership: BITC

Charity of the Year	✓
Gifts in kind	✓
Humanitarian aid: overseas	✓
Humanitarian aid: UK	✓

Charitable donations

Cash UK (latest available):	2013	£4,300,000
	2011	£2,200,000
	2009	£1,600,000
	2008	£600,000
	2007	£600,000
Total UK (cash and in kind):	2013	£4,300,000
Cash worldwide:	2013	£4,300,000
Total worldwide (cash and in kind):	2013	£4,300,000

Community involvement

Asda's charitable giving appears to be made mainly through its charity, **The Asda Foundation** (Charity Commission no. 1124268) where the trustees will distribute the funds to charities nominated by store colleagues. The foundation supplements the good causes that colleagues support locally, as well as a number of bigger ad-hoc projects.

You can find information for your local area on community initiatives, your local community champion and the opportunity to nominate an organisation by visiting the 'Find your nearest Asda' facility on the community webpage.

Corporate giving

Asda Stores Ltd channels most of its charitable giving through The Asda Foundation (see section on community involvement). Some of Asda's profits made on the sales of the mid-week National Lottery are donated by the group to the foundation for distribution to charitable causes and sustainable projects.

In the company's 2013 accounts it declares: 'cash donations to charitable organisations and other community projects totalled £20.8 million (2012: £16.9 million)'. Unfortunately there is no breakdown between cash raised by customers and staff and cash donated by the company from its profits.

The statement of financial activities for the year 2013 for the foundation, states that Asda Stores Ltd donated £4.3 million, with other sources such as the income from partner charities (with such income being restricted) totalling £4.1 million, and investment and sundry income bringing in £124,000. We have taken the donation by Asda Stores Ltd to represent money from profits and consider this to be the company's cash donation. There is no record of the cost of in-kind giving and because of this, we consider the community contribution to be £4.3 million (the cash figure).

See the corporate charity entry on p. 392 for more information.

In-kind support

In 2014 Asda stores teamed up with the British Heart Foundation (BHF) to put defibrillators in every store, office and depot by 2015. The defibrillators are available for any member of the public to use in an emergency and Asda has also partnered with local ambulance trusts to deliver training for all colleagues in how to use the life-saving equipment. Asda Stores funds admin expenses for the foundation.

Employee-led support

Employee and customer fundraising

Asda colleagues can choose a charity (or charities) to which they and their team wish to donate their fundraising monies. If there is no preference as to the good cause, the money will be donated to one of Asda's national charities:

- Breast Cancer Campaign and Breast Cancer Care
- Children in Need
- Fields in Trust
- Orchid
- Pedal Power
- Sporting Chance
- Text Santa
- Tommy's

In 2013, Asda staff and customers raised £4.1 million in total for the company's national charities and disaster relief.

Details of all Asda's national charities and examples of staff fundraising activities and achievements can be found at: your.asda.com/community

Corporate social responsibility

CSR information: There was no CSR information found. We were unable to determine the ratio of women to men on the board.

Corporate charity: The Asda Foundation (Charity Commission no. 1124268).

Applications

If you would like to apply to the foundation contact your local Asda and speak to the Community Life Champion who will be able to advise if the foundation would be able to support your project/organisation.

Ashmore Group plc

Business services

Correspondent: The Secretary to the Trustees, The Ashmore Foundation, 5th Floor, 61 Aldwych, London WC2B 4AE (tel: 020 3077 6000/020 3077 6153; email: foundation@ashmoregroup.com; website: www.ashmoregroup.com)

Directors: Michael Benson, Chair; Mark Coombs, Chief Executive Officer; Graeme Dell; Nick Land; Charles Outhwaite; Melda Donnelly; Tom Shippey, Group Finance Director; Anne Pringle (women: 1; men: 5)

Year end	30/06/2014
Turnover	£294,100,000
Pre-tax profit	£170,300,000

Nature of business: Ashmore Group is a specialist emerging markets fund manager across six core investment themes: external debt, local currency, special situations, equity, corporate high yield and multi-strategy.

Company registration number: 3675683

Subsidiary undertakings include: Ashmore Investments (UK) Ltd.

Main locations: London

Total employees: 290

Focus of giving: General charitable purposes, education, health, ill health, overseas projects, disability.

Humanitarian aid: overseas	✓
Matched funding	✓
Overseas giving	✓

Charitable donations

Cash UK (latest available):	2014	£100,000
	2013	£100,000
	2011	£177,500
	2010	£175,000
	2009	£139,000
Total UK (cash and in kind):	2014	£100,000
Cash worldwide:	2014	£100,000
Total worldwide (cash and in kind):	2014	£100,000

Community involvement

The group's charitable giving is channelled through **The Ashmore Foundation** (Charity Commission no. 1122351).

Taken from the CSR report: 'The Ashmore Foundation currently has seven priority countries (Brazil, Colombia, Mexico, India, Indonesia, Philippines and Turkey) based on the location of Ashmore offices and significant investments, as well as the existence of a strong civil sector and clear social needs on which the Ashmore Foundation can focus.'

Corporate giving

During the year, the group made charitable donations of £100,000 through its corporate charity, the Ashmore Foundation.

See the corporate charity entry on p. 392 for more information.

In-kind support

Ashmore also supports the foundation's charitable activities through the provision of pro bono office space, administrative support and a matched funding commitment for employee donations to the Ashmore Foundation.

Employee-led support

The Ashmore Foundation is supported solely by Ashmore and its employees globally. Crucially, this support from employees extends beyond financial aid through to active engagement in fundraising – such as the Ashmore Three Peaks Challenge which raised over £53,000 for two grantees – and a network of support which includes mentoring and helping NGOs expand their network of contacts.

Corporate social responsibility

CSR committee: We could not determine how the CSR committee was structured or who its members were.

CSR information: The group's website states the following about CSR:

> Ashmore (Ashmore Group plc and its affiliated companies in and outside the UK) recognises the importance of Corporate & Social Responsibility (CSR) incorporating transparency, fairness, accountability and integrity and believes that these principles are fundamental to the Group's operations. Ashmore Group plc has been listed on the London Stock Exchange since October 2006 and sees CSR as a continually evolving process. Ashmore is a signatory of the UN Principles for Responsible Investment (UNPRI).

All charitable contributions are currently made through The Ashmore Foundation set up in 2008 and funded by 'bonus sacrifices' from employees and matched funding by the company.

CSR report: A CSR report is available on the group's website.

Corporate charity: The Ashmore Foundation (Charity Commission no. 1122351).

Applications

The Ashmore Foundation does not accept unsolicited applications. They source new partners through recommendations from experts, existing partners, suggestions from Ashmore staff and detailed research by the Foundation team.

Associated British Ports Holdings Ltd and Subsidiaries

Transport and shipping services

Correspondent: Corporate Communications Manager, Aldwych House, 71–91 Aldwych, London WC2B 4HN (tel: 020 7430 1177; fax: 020 7430 1384; email: csr@abports.co.uk; website: www.abports.co.uk)

Directors: Sebastian Bull, Chief Financial Officer; Phillipe Busslinger; James Cooper, Chief Executive; Phillipe Camu; George Kay; Peter Lyneham; John McManus; Robert Walvis, Chair; Ed Clarke; David Kerr; John Morea; Stewart Hicks (women: 0; men: 12)

Year end	31/12/2013
Turnover	£503,800,000
Pre-tax profit	£312,900,000

Nature of business: This company is an intermediate holding company within the group of companies owned by ABP (Jersey) Ltd. The annual report and accounts cover the group activities, strategy, performance and operations of the company and its subsidiaries (the group).

The principal activities of the group comprise the provision of port facilities and related services to users of seaports in the UK. The group also provides other transport facilities and related services including the Hams Hall rail freight terminal in the Midlands.

Company registration number: 1612178

Subsidiary undertakings include: Associated British Ports; ABP Marine Environmental Research Ltd; The Teignmouth Quay Company Ltd.

Main locations: Southampton CC and Eastleigh BC, Plymouth CC, Teignbridge DC, Kings Lynn and West Norfolk BC, Waveney DC, Ipswich BC, Merseyside, Blackpool BC and Fylde BC and Wyre BC, Allerdale BC, Barrow-in-Furness BC, The Humber, Swansea City and County – Sir Abertawe, Neath Port Talbot County – Sir Castell-nedd Port Talbot, Vale of Glamorgan – Sir Bro Morgannwg, Cardiff City and County – Sir Caerdydd, Newport County – Sir Casnewydd, South Ayrshire UC

UK employees: 1,980

Total employees: 1,980

Focus of giving: General charitable purposes, advertising in charity brochures, education, enterprise/ training, environment, fundraising events, animal welfare, health, ill health, heritage, individuals, medical research, older people, arts, culture, sport, recreation, children, young people, community/social welfare, disability.

Charitable donations

Cash UK (latest available):	2011	£100,300
	2009	£90,000
	2008	£140,000
	2007	£91,000
	2006	£40,000
Total UK (cash and in kind):	2013	£316,000
Total worldwide (cash and in kind):	2013	£316,000

Community involvement

The group states in its 2013 report and accounts that its social and community initiatives are focused on education, charities, arts sponsorship, engagement with civic organisations and the provision of free access to its facilities where practical and appropriate.

ABP Southampton Sailing Academy
In 2014 ABP launched the ABP Southampton Sailing Academy. The Academy has been established with a contribution of £10,000 to Southampton Water Activities Centre (SWAC), managed by the sport and exercise charity Active Nation, and will mean that hundreds of young people from inner-city Southampton will experience 'life on the water'. ABP will provide sailing taster sessions for 8- to 16-year-olds from schools in the city and it is expected that in its first year some 160 children will benefit. Those children who want to go on and develop their skills will be invited to join the new ABP Southampton Sailing Academy and experience a variety of boating and water sports.

Corporate giving

In 2013 the group's total cash and in-kind contributions were £316,000. No detail was available as to what was raised by the employees and what was given by the group.

In-kind support

In-kind support includes staff volunteering and the provision of free access to the group's facilities.

Employee-led support

Employees are very involved in fundraising within their local communities. In June 2014 staff scaled six mountains in one weekend, raising £23,000 in the process, by taking part in various 'Three Peaks' challenges. A team from ABP Southampton tackled Ben Nevis, Scafell Pike, and Snowdon in aid of their local Charity of the Year, Countess Mountbatten Hospice.

Staff from ABP's four Humber ports, along with teams from Drax Power Ltd and ABP's head office, tackled the Yorkshire Three Peaks, taking in Pen-y-Ghent, Whernside, and Ingleborough, raising funds to help Hull's Marfleet Primary School build a new classroom.

Also in 2014 a group of employees from Humber have given up a few hours each week to help children in Grimsby and Immingham improve their reading skills. Each of the volunteers has been trained by Beanstalk and provided with appropriate books and literacy materials. Normally schools are asked for a donation, but ABP has covered these costs meaning the programme is free to the schools that use ABP employees.

Give As You Earn (GAYE): Through the scheme ABP continues to match employee donations and meet the administration costs.

Commercially led support

The group has sponsored the Welsh National Opera (WNO) continuously for over 25 years.

Corporate social responsibility

CSR committee: We could not find information on how any CSR committee was structured although it is clearly a part of the group's activities and ultimately the responsibility of the board.

CSR information: With regard to community and charitable contributions the group states that its ports are rooted in their communities and that it works hard to support causes employees hold dear on a local, regional, and national level.

CSR report: CSR information is contained within the 'ABP Annual Review'.

Exclusions

There are no definite exclusions; instead the company will consider all appeals individually.

Applications

In writing to the correspondent. Applications are sorted and likely candidates referred to the group chief executive.

AstraZeneca

Pharmaceuticals

Correspondent: Charitable Appeals Department, 15 Stanhope Gate, London W1K 1LN (tel: 020 7304 5000; fax: 020 7304 5151; website: www.astrazeneca.com)

Directors: Leif Johansson, Chair; Pascal Soriot, Chief Executive; Marc Dunoyer; Bruce Burlington; Jean-Philippe Courtois; Rudy Markham; Dame Nancy Rothwell; Shriti Vadera; John Varley; Marcus Wallenberg; Geneviève Berger; Graham Chipchase (women: 3; men: 9)

Year end	31/12/2013
Turnover	£16,110,513,296
Pre-tax profit	£3,267,000,000

Nature of business: The group's principal activities are the research, development and marketing of medicines for serious health conditions.

Company registration number: 2723534

Subsidiary undertakings include: AstraZeneca do Brasil Limitada; AstraZeneca Farmaceutica Spain; AstraZeneca Treasury Ltd; AstraZeneca UK Ltd; AstraZeneca Pharmaceuticals Co. Ltd.

Brands include: Crestor, Seroquel and Symbicort.

Main locations: Alderley Edge, Cambridge, Macclesfield, Loughborough, Luton, London, Stonehouse, Tytherington, Wilmslow, Chorlton-cum-Hardy, Brixham, Bristol, Edinburgh

UK employees: 7,200

Total employees: 51,600

Focus of giving: Education, health, ill health, housing, homelessness, medical research, science technology, children, young people, community/social welfare.

Membership: LBG

Cash donations undeclared	✓
FTSE 100	✓
Gifts in kind	✓
Humanitarian aid: overseas	✓
Humanitarian aid: UK	✓
Overseas giving	✓

Charitable donations

Cash UK (latest available):	2013	£52,000
	2011	£333,000
	2009	£100,000
Total UK (cash and in kind):	2013	£52,000
Cash worldwide:	2013	£52,000
Total worldwide (cash and in kind):	2013	£701,800,000

Community involvement

In the UK, Germany and the Netherlands the group's focus is on the health issues of homeless adolescents. Its global community investment strategy focuses on two key areas – healthcare in the community and science in education.

Youth Health Programme
The group's website states:

> One fifth of the world's population is aged between 10 and 19 years old and many of these young people don't get the support they need to deal with the health challenges that can significantly impact their lives.
>
> The AstraZeneca Young Health Programme (YHP) aims to positively impact the health of adolescents in marginalised communities worldwide through research, advocacy and on-the-ground programmes which are now focused on NCD [non-communicable diseases] prevention. Adolescent health remains an underserved part of the healthcare care agenda and this is a long-

> term investment programme that aims to make a measurable and sustainable difference, helping to improve a generation's health.

In 2013, the group continued with its Young Health Programme (YHP) and has 18 programmes under way around the world. Over 480,000 young people have been directly reached with the skills and information they need to improve their health. This includes young people in communities across five continents. Over 4,500 of these young people have been trained to share this health information with their peers and with the community, and over 9,000 frontline health providers have completed training programmes in adolescent health. It is hoped to reach 500,000 young people by the end of 2015.

AstraZeneca Science Teaching Trust
The AstraZeneca Science Teaching Trust (Charity Commission no. 1064864), an independent charity with a total trust fund of around £21 million provided by the company, supports a programme of projects designed to help build the knowledge, skills and understanding required to lead and teach science effectively and confidently in primary schools.

Employees are encouraged to become involved in community-based charitable activities through a matched funding scheme, whereby individuals' efforts in fundraising may be matched by a company donation.

The company's website states that 'We focus our support in the UK on charitable and not-for-profit organisations based near, or operating close to, AstraZeneca's key sites'. These sites are Alderley Park, Avlon, Brixham, London, Luton, and Macclesfield.

The group supports the work of The Brightside Trust (Charity Commission no. 1080243), a charity that aims to help underprivileged young people to enter the medical and healthcare professions.

Partnership
Support for science education in the community takes a number of forms. For example, in 2011, a three-year partnership was entered into with Career Academies UK to support increased participation by 16- to 19-year-olds in science, technology, engineering and maths (STEM) subjects. The target that one-third of Career Academies have a STEM theme by the 2014/2015 academic year, was exceeded in the 2013/2014 academic year, with 54 Career Academies (35%) having a STEM theme.

Charity partner
The British Red Cross continues to be the group's global disaster relief partner, with the majority of disaster relief donations channelled through it. In response to the typhoon in the Philippines in November 2013, the group donated $390,000 (£244,000) via the British Red Cross to the Philippines Disaster Appeal. Product donations with a wholesale average cost value of over $350,000 (£219,000) were also made to support the victims of the disaster.

Corporate giving

According to Astra Zeneca's annual report, in 2013 it spent $1.12 billion – £701.8 million (2012: $1.18 billion – £739.39 million) on community investment sponsorships, partnerships and charitable donations, including product donation and patient assistance programmes which make its medicines available free of charge or at reduced prices. Through the three patient assistance programmes in the US, the group donated products valued at an average wholesale price of more than $1.05 billion – £658 million (2012: $1.12 billion – £701.8 million). The group also donated products worth over $18 million (£11.3 million) valued at average wholesale prices, to charitable organisations AmeriCares and Direct Relief International.

In 2013 the group's charitable trust had an income of £19,000 and a total expenditure of £952,000.

Support for The Brightside Trust (Charity Commission no. 1080243) included an ongoing contribution in cash (around £100,000 over three years). We have used this figure plus the £19,000 to the Astra Zeneca Science Teaching Trust as the company's UK cash contribution. Clearly the group gave more but we have no other UK-only figures to work with.

In-kind support

Secondments and volunteering hours are offered by the group.

Employee-led support

Employee involvement has been facilitated by the introduction of a global volunteering allowance for all employees.

Corporate social responsibility

CSR committee: There is a Charitable Appeals department. We could not find any information on the structure or membership of a specific CSR committee.

CSR information: This information was obtained from the company's annual report:

> *Community investment*
> Making a positive contribution to our local communities around the world, through community support programmes consistent with improving health and promoting science.

There is a dedicated community support database that gathers global information centrally, enabling the sharing of information across the organisation, encouraging best practice and supporting accurate financial reporting of overall spend in community investment. The database is also another means of ensuring that the group's efforts are aligned with its commitment to bring benefit mainly through healthcare and science education initiatives.

CSR report: There was no evidence of a CSR report; however, the website states:

> AstraZeneca is a member of the London Benchmarking Group (LBG), a group of over 120 companies worldwide working together to measure community investment. Our membership of LBG provides the platform for improving how we capture our total community contribution, and will enable us to assign a tangible monetary value to the time and services of our employees where they are involved in community activities.

Exclusions

No support is given for circulars, advertising in charity brochures, individuals, older people, fundraising events, political/discriminatory groups, religious appeals, sport, anything contrary to the company's business, or capital projects or building appeals.

Applications

In writing to the Charitable Appeals Department at the head office address.

Avant Homes Group Ltd (formerly Gladedale Group Holdings Ltd)

Building/construction, property

Correspondent: David Scott, Group CR Director, Regency House, Crossgates Road, Halbeath, Dunfermline KY11 7EG (website: www.avanthomes.co.uk/sustainability)

Directors: Colin Lewis, Chief Executive; Jon Mortimore, Chief Finance Officer; Gerard Loftus; Paul Bridges, Chair; Giles Sharp; Barry Miller; Mike Smith; Joanne Massey (women: 1; men: 7)

Year end	31/12/2013

Nature of business: The company is residential and commercial property developer and is a wholly owned subsidiary of Avant Homes Holdings Ltd.

Company registration number: 6986776

Subsidiary undertakings include: Avant Homes Ltd; Gladedale Commercial Group Ltd

Main locations: UK

Focus of giving: General charitable purposes, community/social welfare.

Cash donations undeclared	✓
Sponsorship	✓

Charitable donations

Cash UK (latest available):	2013	£29,000
	2010	£29,000
	2009	£0
	2008	£0
	2006	£100,000
Total UK (cash and in kind):	2013	£29,000
Cash worldwide:	2013	£29,000
Total worldwide (cash and in kind):	2013	£29,000

Community involvement

We were unable to determine details of the company's community activities in 2013. It would appear that information on the website relating to community involvement has not been updated since research was conducted for the last edition of this publication. In previous years, charitable and community groups have benefitted from donations and sponsorship.

Corporate giving

A total for charitable donations was not declared in the annual report and accounts for 2013. In the most recent year for which we have a total, the company made contributions of £29,000. We have taken this as an estimate for charitable donations in 2013. The revenue and pre-tax profit for this company could not be found for this financial year.

Previous beneficiaries have included: Robert Burns World Federation Schools Festivals (2011).

Corporate social responsibility

CSR committee: There is a Corporate Responsibility Steering Group which meets at least twice a year.

CSR information: The following information was taken from the company's website:

> As a leading residential and commercial developer, we recognise that it is our duty to act as a responsible business and a good neighbour in the communities in which we work.
>
> We endeavour to conduct our business with integrity and openness, delivering optimum economic value and ensuring the observance of environmental and community issues.
>
> We embrace our responsibilities towards our employees, investors, customers, clients, stakeholders and the wider communities in which we work.

CSR report: There was no evidence of a separate CSR report but there is a section dedicated to CSR on the website.

Applications

In writing to the correspondent.

Aveva Group plc

Information technology

Correspondent: Corporate Responsibility Team, High Cross, Madingley Road, Cambridge CB3 0HB (tel: 01223 556655; fax: 01223 556666; website: www.aveva.com)

Directors: Philip Aiken, Chair; Richard Longdon, Chief Executive; Philip Dayer; Jonathan Brooks; Jennifer Allerton; James Kidd, Chief Financial Officer (women: 1; men: 5)

Year end	31/03/2014
Turnover	£237,336,000
Pre-tax profit	£68,989,000

Nature of business: The principal activities of the group are the marketing and development of computer software and services for engineering and related solutions. The company is a holding company.

Company registration number: 2937296

Subsidiary undertakings include: Aveva Solutions Ltd; Aveva East Asia Ltd; Aveva Pty Ltd; Aveva SA.

Main locations: Cambridge

UK employees: 473

Total employees: 1,491

Focus of giving: General charitable purposes, education, health, ill health, children, young people.

Cash donations undeclared	✓
Gifts in kind	✓
Market-led giving	✓
Matched funding	✓
Overseas giving	✓

Charitable donations

Cash UK (latest available):	2014	£36,000
	2011	£36,000
	2010	£36,000
Total UK (cash and in kind):	2014	£36,000
Cash worldwide:	2014	£36,000
Total worldwide (cash and in kind):	2014	£36,000

Community involvement

The group in their annual report for 2013/14 state that it is 'committed to the development of our global and local communities, and continually extend our involvement in educational partnerships and charitable giving'.

Corporate giving

In 2013/14 the group did not declare a charitable donations figure either for the UK or globally. The annual report and accounts state: 'As an organisation, we continue to sponsor a range of charities by giving corporate donations. Organisations we have supported over the last year include the Villiers Park Educational Trust, the Outward Bound Trust, MAGPAS and Macmillan Cancer Support.' We have based the group's cash donation of £36,000 on previous research.

In-kind support

Staff continue to work with Young Enterprise, a business and enterprise educational charity. Colleagues volunteer to be business advisors to students studying for a range of qualifications, providing insight into the commercial world for those young people.

Employee-led support

Previous research tells us that the staff enjoy a matched funding scheme.

Commercially led support

Education partnerships: The AVEVA Academic Initiative is a strategic investment that provides benefits to AVEVA, universities, and the broader engineering discipline. The three key objectives for the AVEVA Academic Initiative are:

- Work with universities to promote the use of AVEVA products during undergraduate and postgraduate studies by providing both software and training support
- Work with government agencies to re-skill engineers for employment in other disciplines by providing free training courses
- Work with engineering bodies to encourage graduates to pursue careers in engineering

Corporate social responsibility

CSR committee: The Chief Executive has board responsibilities for matters relating to the group's culture and ethical policies, environmental matters and customer and employee issues.

CSR information: This information was obtained from the company's 2013/14 annual report and accounts: Last year the group introduced a four-module approach to Corporate Social Responsibility (CSR). This covered its relationship with both internal and external stakeholders, as well as a focus on the environment and the local and global community.

CSR report: There was no evidence of a separate CSR report; however, information on CSR was available from the company's annual report and accounts.

Applications

In writing to the correspondent.

Aviva plc

Insurance

Correspondent: Corporate Responsibility Specialists Team, St Helen's, 1 Undershaft, London EC3P 3DQ (tel: 020 7283 2000; fax: 020 7662 8182; email: cr.team@aviva.com; website: www.aviva.com)

Directors: Patrick Regan, Chief Financial Officer; John McFarlane, Chair; Glyn Barker; Gay Huey Evans; Michael Hawker; Mark Wilson, Group Chief Executive Officer; Sir Adrian Montague; Patricia Cross; Michael Mire; Bob Stein; Scott Wheway (women: 1; men: 11)

Year end	31/12/2013
Turnover	£22,035,000,000
Pre-tax profit	£1,472,000,000

Nature of business: The company transacts life assurance and long-term savings business, fund management, and all classes of general insurance through its subsidiaries, associates and branches in the UK, Continental Europe, North America, Asia, Australia and other countries throughout the world.

Company registration number: 2468686

Subsidiary undertakings include: Aviva Annuity UK Ltd; Aviva Canada Inc. and its principal subsidiaries; Aviva Central Services UK Ltd; Aviva Consumer Products UK Ltd; Aviva France SA and its principal subsidiaries; Aviva Health UK Ltd; Aviva Insurance Ltd; Aviva Insurance Services UK Ltd; Aviva International Insurance Ltd; Aviva Life Insurance Company Ltd; Victoria Reinsurance Company Ltd.

Main locations: Croydon, Bristol, Cheadle, Eastleigh, Exeter, Glasgow, York, Southampton, Sheffield, Romford, Stevenage, Norwich, Newcastle

Total employees: 27,718

Focus of giving: Environment, health, ill health, heritage, safety and crime prevention, children, young people, community/social welfare.

Membership: BITC, LBG

Cash donations undeclared	✓
FTSE 100	✓
Humanitarian aid: overseas	✓
Humanitarian aid: UK	✓
Market-led giving	✓
Matched funding	✓
Overseas giving	✓
Sponsorship	✓

Charitable donations

Cash UK (latest available):	2011	£2,800,000
	2009	£1,300,000
	2008	£2,200,000
	2007	£1,400,000
	2006	£1,400,000
Cash worldwide:	2013	£536,000
Total worldwide (cash and in kind):	2013	£6,200,000

Community involvement

Through community programmes and long-term partnerships, the group aims to make a positive difference to the lives of many around the world. The Street to School programme has now helped over 800,000 street connected children and is an important part of the group's global community contribution.

Street to School

In 2009, Aviva launched Street to School, a five-year global charitable initiative, which aims to get children and young people off the street and into education. Working with leading charities and experts, and supported by employees and customers, the company aims to champion the needs of street children in the communities in which it has a presence. The Street to School programme will gradually be adopted in every country in which Aviva operates.

The programme around the world recognises that every child living or working on the street should have the opportunity to fulfil their potential. The UK's partner is Railway Children, a charity which fights for vulnerable children who are alone and at risk on the streets. During 2013 the group worked with its partners to develop more sustainable, lasting outcomes, and find new ways of helping more people to work together on behalf of street children. Focusing on advocacy is an important part of the initiative as well as raising awareness of the fact that in the UK one child runs away from home every five minutes. The group is also working with Plan UK in Indonesia and the Indonesian Government to help support a change in policy that increases access to birth registration.

The group held a round-table event in South East Asia involving the UN, governments, NGOs, businesses and academics. The key focus of the conversation was how we can act together to protect and promote the rights of children living and/or working on the street. The group are looking to 'create a global community in support of the cause'.

In Indonesia the group has teamed up with Plan – a global children's charity – to help some of the 4,300 street children in Jakarta to obtain their birth certificates. This small act is known to dramatically improve these children's access to school and healthcare.

In China

The group also supports a project called Twinkling Stars which helps children in rural China who have been left behind when other family members have moved to the city in search of work. Since 2010, more than 20 caring rooms have been built in more than ten provinces in China, over 600 volunteers have participated (including Aviva-Cofco staff and clients), and almost 60,000 left-behind children have received spiritual and psychological care through the well-prepared courses and various outdoor activities.

Oxfam 365

Aviva began supporting Oxfam 365, the agency's emergency fund in 2006. Since then the group has contributed over £1 million helping Oxfam to mount disaster-relief operations and support over half a million people in the wake of natural disasters like the earthquake in Haiti and Typhoon Haiyan in the Philippines.

In 2013 the group states that it continued to work with a diverse range of partners, including NGOs, businesses, public sector bodies and international organisations, 'using these connections to bring together different skills and points of view, so that we can start to develop new ways of tackling a range of issues all over the world'. In the UK, a lot of Aviva's efforts are geared towards helping parents and young people.

Railway Children

Work with the charity Railway Children revolves around raising awareness of the issue and young runaways. In 2013 over £437,000 was donated through donations and fundraising.

Sport

In the UK the group is partnering with the Norwich City Community Sports Foundation to help deliver Classroom Champions, a range of activities for local primary schoolchildren. And also in 2013 the group began supporting the Community Sports Fund Sporting Light Appeal, which encourages more people with disabilities to get involved in sports.

Men's health is also on Aviva's agenda through its sporting partnerships and it has teamed up with rugby union clubs in the Aviva Premiership to raise awareness of issues such as prostate and testicular cancer.

Charity partners: Organisations the group works with include:

- Office of the High Commissioner for Human Rights
- Oxfam – a partner since 2006 providing immediate help to international communities suffering life trauma
- Save the Children and the Consortium for Street Children – the major Street to School partners
- CSR Asia's Community Investment Roundtable and Qi Global – encouraging community investment in Asia Pacific
- Railway Children, Barnardo's, CRY (Child Rights and You), Covenant House, China Youth Federation,

- SHÇEK and HOPE Worldwide – a few of the Street to School partners from around the world
- Schools Business Partnership, Business in the Community, Free the Children, UK Athletics, Citizenship Foundation – some of the partners the group are working with to support education and financial literacy

Corporate giving

In 2013, the group made total community contributions of £6.2 million (2012: £11 million) into the community including cash, in-kind donations and skills-based volunteering. This decrease from the previous year in community investment is due to the completion of the group's UK Athletics sponsorship, which represented over 33% of total KPI (Key Performance Indicators) in 2012. Additionally, this year's reporting does not include the US business (sold in 2013) which contributed over 10% to this KPI in 2012.

We were unable to discover the UK-only figures or a breakdown of cash/in-kind contributions; however, we know that staff contributed £536,000 through payroll giving and that the group will match this. We have therefore used this as the cash donation although clearly the total cash giving is significantly more.

In-kind support

Employees are encouraged to take up to three days' volunteering leave a year. In 2013 the number of employee hours spent volunteering was 41,223. 41% of employees are directly involved in CR activities in the UK. Helping LILT's fight against cancer Aviva in Italy, together with LILT, an Italian association that fights against cancer, have joined forces to promote preventive medicine among Aviva employees. The company organised a week of prevention activities where employees could book appointments for skin tests and oral examinations with visiting oncologists and dermatologists.

The UK Life Retention Planning Manager, worked with Citizens Advice to create a brochure helping people manage their money over the festive season. Also, the Ireland Target Operating Model Lead, visits primary schools to educate children about the dangers of running away.

Employee-led support

Staff are encouraged to take part in community-related projects through various initiatives, such as staff volunteering, mentoring and fundraising activities, which the company matches. This is seen by the company as part of staff's personal development and employees can apply for up to three paid volunteering days per year. In 2013 a total of 27% of employees contributed their time, up by 9% from 2012.

Payroll giving: The Give As You Earn scheme is in operation and in 2013 employees donated over £536,000 through this.

Commercially led support

Sponsorship: Aviva sponsors Aviva Premiership Rugby, Norwich City Football Club and The Stonewall Equality Annual Dinner. In 2013, the group also supported the Mumsnet website, sponsoring a section of the site that provides information and advice to parents about runaway children, and the warning signs to look out for.

Grass-roots sports

Through sponsorship of Premiership Rugby, UK Athletics and Norwich City Football Club Aviva in the UK aims to:

- Make a difference beyond elite sport and direct a significant proportion of investment at grass-roots level
- Help children get active and play a role in positively impacting the trend for childhood obesity
- Help children build self-esteem through participation in sport
- Leave a legacy by growing the sport for the children of the future
- Allow employees to feel the benefits of the sponsorship programmes, for example by the participation of their children, parents getting involved in coaching and this positively impacting on how staff feel about working for Aviva

Corporate social responsibility

CSR committee: The board-level governance committee reviews and directs CR strategy and policy, receives market and functional reports four times a year and approves the group CR report. The committee comprises non-executive directors Scott Wheway (Chair), Michael Mire and Sir Adrian Montague, with Aviva chair John McFarlane and group CEO also invited to attend. The CSR report states: 'Reporting to the governance committee, the CR leadership team works to adopt, refine and implement our CR strategy, assess progress, identify actions and embed programmes in different parts of the business.'

CSR information: The following statement is taken from the 'Our Wider Impact' report:

> In 2013 we continued to work with a diverse range of partners, including NGOs, businesses, public sector bodies and international organisations. We use these connections to bring together different skills and points of view, so that we can start to develop new ways of tackling a range of issues all over the world.

CSR report: A new report is now published entitled 'Our Wider Impact' which covers material people and corporate responsibility information. There are also regular updates and a document detailing the reporting criteria for corporate responsibility key performance indicators for the year on the corporate website. There is also a section on corporate responsibility within the pages of the annual report.

Exclusions

At group level, Aviva will not normally consider supporting:

- Individuals looking for sponsorship or charity fundraising donations either on their own behalf or that of a charity (staff excluded)
- Political organisations
- Extreme 'high risk' or 'free sports'
- Organisations or issues already supported by Norwich Union in the UK
- Charities already receiving long-term support around the world, either from Norwich Union or an Aviva company
- A staff Charity of the Year (on a separate basis)
- Paid advertisements in charity brochures or events programmes

Applications

In writing to the correspondent.

Avon Cosmetics Ltd

Health/beauty products

Correspondent: Charitable Donations Department, Nunn Mills Road, Northampton NN1 5PA (tel: 01604 232425; fax: 01604 232444; website: www.avon.uk.com)

Directors: A. Gallagher; S. Hutchison; M. Parczuk; A. Slater

Year end	31/12/2013
Turnover	£274,801,683
Pre-tax profit	£7,531,439

Nature of business: The principal activities of the company are the distribution and sale of beauty, gift and decorative products.

Company registration number: 592235

Main locations: Northampton, County Durham

Total employees: 1,641

Focus of giving: Environment, health, ill health, safety and crime prevention, women's issues, disasters.

Charity of the Year	✓
Gifts in kind	✓
Humanitarian aid: overseas	✓
Market-led giving	✓
Matched funding	✓
Overseas giving	✓

Charitable donations

Cash UK (latest available):	2013	£694,000
	2010	£643,000
	2009	£53,300
Total UK (cash and in kind):	2013	£694,000
Cash worldwide:	2013	£10,268,000
Total worldwide (cash and in kind):	2013	£10,268,000

Community involvement

The UK website states: 'For more than 125 years, Avon has been passionate about empowering women. As a dedicated supporter of women's causes, we truly believe that by streamlining our efforts we can make a real difference to the lives of women.'

Avon in the UK will support fundraising efforts by offering products or donations through its charity partners. Avon states that it has made a commitment to the two causes that matter most to women: breast cancer and domestic violence. If you are fundraising, spreading awareness and/or care to benefit one of its charity partners (Breakthrough Breast Cancer, Crazy Hats, Breast Cancer Appeal, Refuge or Women's Aid), the company will donate a £50 product hamper to support your fundraising efforts.

The corporate report states: 'We are proud to be the leading corporate supporter of the breast cancer cause globally through the Avon Breast Cancer Crusade and a leading corporate supporter of ending violence against women through the Speak Out Against Domestic Violence initiative.'

The Avon Foundation (USA)
In 1955 the company formalised its philanthropic efforts with the creation of the Avon Foundation, which advances the mission to improve the lives of women and their families.

The foundation's main efforts are today focused on the critical issues of breast cancer and domestic violence and Avon global philanthropy is advancing these causes in more than 50 countries. Avon and the Avon Foundation also support emergency and disaster relief, while a scholarship programme for Avon associates and sales representatives maintains the tradition of supporting education. Examples of funding in 2013 were grants of £500,000 each to: See Signs and Speak Out; Avon Regional Domestic Violence grants programme; and the Jeanne Geiger Crisis Center.

The latest annual report for the foundation and details on mission programs, grants, educational materials and financial reports can be found on the Avon Foundation website – www.avonfoundation.org

Corporate giving

In 2013 the company made charitable donations amounting to £587,000 supporting the breast cancer cause and the fight to end violence against women. The company spent an additional £107,000 on campaigns and other charitable activities.

Beneficiaries included: Breakthrough, Crazy Hats, Kettering General Centenary Wing, Kids'n'Cancer, Look Good Feel Better, Refuge and Women's Aid.

We could find no breakdown of figures between UK and global giving and cash and in-kind donations and many of the totals quoted in the group's reports are since the beginning of a programme or an initiative rather than for a particular year. We have therefore used the amount donated to the Avon Foundation in 2013 which was $15.27 million: (£9.57 million) as the worldwide cash contribution.

It is clear that Avon gave much more in cash and in-kind, globally and in the UK but we have estimated on the figures we have available to us.

The global company Avon Inc. registered in the USA states in its annual report:

> Our 2013 philanthropic efforts made a difference in the lives of women and their families around the world. Since 1955 through the end of 2013, we raised more than $957 million (£600 million) through programs in over 50 countries for two of the causes most important to women: breast cancer and domestic violence.

It aims to reach a total donation of $1 billion (£626.6 million) by 2015.

In-kind support

Avon in the UK has a specific product donations initiative – see 'community involvement' section.

Employee-led support

Support is given to employees' volunteering/charitable activities through financial help, matching employee fundraising and giving, and allowing company time off to volunteer.

Payroll giving: Avon operates the Give As You Earn scheme.

Commercially led support

Cause-related marketing:
Representatives around the world sell specially designed 'pink ribbon' products that provide the opportunity for anyone to participate in the fight against breast cancer. Avon and the Avon Foundation award a portion of the proceeds to organisations and institutions to help eradicate breast cancer, with grants made within the country in which the funds are raised. Through 2013, global sales of Avon Breast Cancer Crusade pink ribbon fundraising products have totalled $321 million (£201.1 million).

Corporate social responsibility

CSR committee: There was no evidence of a separate CSR committee.

CSR information: This information was obtained from the company's website:

> In 1886, Avon Founder David H. McConnell committed his company 'to meet fully the obligations of corporate citizenship by contributing to the well-being of society and the environment in which it functions.' Today, these words are still central to our business and our success at Avon Products, Inc.
>
> Avon is passionate about supporting women's causes and we believe that by making a concentrated effort, we can help to make a real difference to women's lives. We have made a commitment to the two causes that matter most to women: breast cancer and domestic violence.

We were unable to determine the ratio of women to men on the board of the UK company.

CSR report: There was no evidence of a separate CSR report.

Exclusions

No support is given for advertising in charity brochures, animal welfare charities, appeals from individuals, the arts, political appeals, religious appeals, science/technology or sport.

Applications

In writing to the correspondent or contact your nearest Avon representative.

To apply for a product hamper to support your fundraising activities, make contact as follows:

Breast cancer cause – email avon@breakthrough.org.uk if you would like to request a product donation for activities supporting Breakthrough Breast Cancer or Crazy Hats Breast Cancer Appeal.

Domestic violence cause – email avon@womensaid.org.uk if you are raising funds or awareness for this charity. Email fundraising@refuge.org.uk if you are raising funds or awareness for Refuge.

Make sure you include:

- The name of the charity you are supporting
- The date of your fundraising event
- How you will use the product hamper to raise funds or awareness
- Your delivery address

AXA UK plc

Healthcare, insurance

Correspondent: J. P. Small, Company Secretary, 5 Old Broad Street, London EC2N 1AD (website: www.axa.co.uk)

Directors: I. Brimecome, Chair; P. J. Evans, Chief Executive; A. J. Blanc; H. de Castries; R. G. Dench; D. Duverne; K. G. Gibbs; P. Hazell; M. J. Kellard; Y. Masson; J. O'Neill; B. Poupart-Lafarge; R. S. Wilton

Year end	31/12/2013
Pre-tax profit	£199,000,000

Nature of business: This company acts as a holding company for AXA's wealth, general insurance, health insurance and distribution operations in the UK and the Republic of Ireland (the AXA UK group).

Company registration number: 2937724

Subsidiary undertakings include: Architas Multi-Manager Ltd; AXA Insurance plc; AXA Services Ltd; plc; AXA Sunlife Direct Ltd; Guardian Royal Exchange.

Main locations: London

Focus of giving: Education, health, ill health, medical research, poverty and social exclusion, sport, recreation, disasters.

Membership: LBG

Cash donations undeclared	✓
Charity of the Year	✓
Gifts in kind	✓
Humanitarian aid: overseas	✓
Overseas giving	✓

Charitable donations

Cash UK (latest available):	2013	£329,000
	2010	£702,300
	2009	£149,000
	2008	£137,000
Total UK (cash and in kind):	2013	£329,000
Cash worldwide:	2013	£329,000
Total worldwide (cash and in kind):	2013	£329,000

Community involvement

Community activities

We could not see current activities undertaken by the company or its group. Previously community activities across the UK and Ireland included:

- Support for the Junior Achievers programme – empowering youth and preparing them for a financially independent life
- Providing a contact centre of 100 lines for the Children in Need telethon appeal
- Supporting students in a Bolton school with CV writing, work experience and careers advice
- Raising money for Macmillan Cancer Support
- Raising money for the East Africa Crisis Appeal

In 2008, AXA established the **AXA Research Fund** to support scientific research that would contribute to understanding and preventing environmental, life and socio-economic risks. The purpose of the fund is to:

- Contribute to scientific breakthroughs
- Help reframe public debate on global risk-related issues
- Develop the group's expertise in cutting-edge science

In the UK the group has supported over 60 projects.

The group also supports CARE, a global humanitarian organisation which aims to address the underlying causes of poverty and move towards sustainable development. Most of its programmes are based on microfinance, education, AIDS relief, food security and drinking water.

Corporate giving

In 2013, the AXA UK company did not declare charitable donations. We have therefore taken an average based on our last three years' available figures and estimate the total for this accounting year to be around £329,000. Previous beneficiaries include: French Education Trust (£350,000); and Mesothelioma research (£175,000).

In-kind support

In addition to local and employee-specific fundraising campaigns, the company supports national campaigns with employee fundraising and in-kind donations.

Employee-led support

The following information has been on the group's website since 2011 and, at the time of writing, does not appear to have been updated:

> We want to be a good neighbour in the communities where we operate. So we work with community groups to address specific local needs and provide our people with personal development opportunities.
>
> We do this through the *Hearts in Action* volunteering scheme, fundraising for local charities and emergency relief. In 2011 we launched The AXA Ambition awards. The awards support talented young people in our local communities to fulfil their dreams and ambitions in the fields of science, community, sports and the arts.
>
> Hearts in Action is AXA's global community partnership programme. It provides volunteer and charity fundraising opportunities for employees and is designed to build links between our business, our people and our local communities. It acts as a guideline for community involvement but allows local offices to develop programmes that are suitable for their employees and local community needs.

Corporate social responsibility

CSR committee: There was no evidence of a separate CSR committee.

CSR information: AXA UK's corporate responsibility strategy is organised around four areas: marketplace, workplace, community and environment.

We were unable to determine the ratio of women to men on the board.

CSR report: There was no evidence of a CSR report. Information on the website about community giving appeared not to have been updated since 2011. The company has stopped declaring its charitable donations in its annual report and accounts.

Applications

In writing to the correspondent.

Babcock International Group plc

Consulting engineers, marine, transportation

Correspondent: Communications Team, Email via website (tel: 020 7355 5300; fax: 020 7355 5360; website: www.babcock.co.uk)

Directors: Mike Turner, Chair; Peter Rogers, Chief Executive; Franco Martinelli, Group Finance Director; Archie Bethel; Kevin Thomas; David Omand; Ian Duncan; Kate Swann; Bill Tame; John Davies; Anna Stewart; Jeff Randall (women: 2; men: 10)

Year end	31/03/2014
Turnover	£3,547,600,000
Pre-tax profit	£218,800,000

Nature of business: Babcock is a UK engineering support services organisation.

Defence, energy, telecommunications, transport and education are all sectors where Babcock is present, delivering critical support. Services are underpinned by three core capabilities:

- Managing assets and infrastructure
- Delivering projects and programmes
- Integrating engineering expertise

Company registration number: 2342138

Joint ventures include: Airwork Ltd; Ascent Flight Training; Greenwich BSF SPV Ltd; Holdfast Training Services Ltd; Lewisham Schools for the Future LEP Ltd.

Main locations: Bournemouth, Chichester, Bordon, Watford, Portsmouth, Reading, Southampton, London, Hove, Leatherhead

Total employees: 28,385

Focus of giving: Education, health, ill health, sport, recreation, children, young people.

Cash donations undeclared	✓
Charity of the Year	✓
FTSE 100	✓
Gifts in kind	✓
Matched funding	✓
Overseas giving	✓
Payroll giving	✓
Sponsorship	✓

Charitable donations

Cash UK (latest available):	2014	£263,000
	2012	£272,000
	2011	£236,000
	2009	£281,000
	2008	£212,000
Total UK (cash and in kind):	2014	£263,000
Cash worldwide:	2014	£263,000
Total worldwide (cash and in kind):	2014	£263,000

Community involvement

Babcock engages with communities around its areas of operation and seeks to provide opportunities for employees to assist with local initiatives and support local charities that are important to them.

Babcock supports the British armed forces and reservists. The company states that it is committed to the 'Total Support Force' and has signed the 'Corporate Covenant'. It actively recruits service leavers and reservists. It also supports employees, including providing paid time off for training, through its SaBRE recognised Reserve Forces Policy.

Corporate giving

In 2013/14 Babcock did not declare its charitable donations either in the UK or abroad. We have therefore estimated an average of the last three figures we have available and calculate the total in the UK to be around £263,000.

In-kind support

Previous research showed that the company also provides community support by way of employee volunteering, fundraising, mentoring and pro bono work as well as Give As You Earn and matched giving.

Overseas support

The Babcock International Group's Africa division supports a programme that provides high school education for underprivileged children. Currently, Babcock is sponsoring 20 children through various levels of high school with financial support while at the same time providing mentoring assistance and further bursaries for the children who go on to universities to study in the fields of science, technology, engineering and mathematics.

Commercially led support

Sponsorship

At group level, there is corporate sponsorship for the Soldiers, Sailors, Airmen and Families Association (SSAFA), the forces charity providing support to service families in times of need.

Corporate social responsibility

CSR committee: There were no details found on the structure of a specific committee.

CSR information: The following information is taken from the group's annual report and accounts:

> There are group-wide guidelines setting out [the group's] approach to charitable donations, its commitment to the communities in which it operates and the broader interests of customers.

CSR report: There was no report available. There is a sustainability section in the annual report and accounts which mentions community giving. This information can be found in the 'Community involvement' and 'Corporate giving' sections of this entry.

Exclusions

No support is given for advertising in charity brochures, animal welfare, appeals from individuals, the arts, environment/heritage or political appeals.

Applications

In writing to the correspondent. There is an email facility on the group's website.

BAE Systems plc

Defence, aerospace

Correspondent: The Company Giving Committee, 6 Carlton Gardens, London SW1Y 5AD (tel: 01252 373232; email: community@baesystems.com; website: www.baesystems.com)

Directors: Roger Carr, Chair; Ian King, Chief Executive Officer; Peter Lynas, Group Finance Director; Jerry Demuro; Paul Anderson; Harriet Green; Chris Grigg; Nick Rose; Paula Rosput Reynolds; Carl Symon; Ian Tyler (women: 2; men: 9)

Year end	31/12/2013
Turnover	£16,864,000,000
Pre-tax profit	£422,000,000

Nature of business: The main activity of the group is defence – comprising the design and manufacture of civil and military aircraft, surface ships, submarines, space systems, radar, avionics, communications, electronics and guided weapon systems. BAE operates in Australia, India, Saudi Arabia, UK and US.

The website states that in the UK there are about 34,800 employees (at the end of 2012).

Company registration number: 1470151

Subsidiary undertakings include: BAE Systems Controls Inc.; BAE Systems Information and Electronic Systems Integration Inc.; BAE Systems Land and Armaments LP; BAE Systems (Operations) Ltd; and BAE Systems Surface Ships Ltd. A full list of subsidiary undertakings can be obtained from Companies House.

Main locations: Strathclyde, Prestwick, Somerset, London, Northamptonshire, Wiltshire, Yorkshire, Surrey, Cumbria, Cwymbran, County Durham, Cheshire, Buckinghamshire, Bristol, Cambridgeshire, Bridgend, Lancashire, Leicestershire, Kent, Isle of Wight, Hertfordshire, Hampshire, Greater Manchester, Gloucestershire, Glascoed, Glasgow, Essex, Edinburgh, Dunfermline, Dorset

Total employees: 78,000

Focus of giving: Education, enterprise/training, environment, health, ill health, heritage, STEM (science, technology, engineering and mathematics), armed forces personnel, overseas projects, science technology, community/social welfare.

Membership: LBG

FTSE 100	✓
Gifts in kind	✓
Market-led giving	✓
Matched funding	✓
Overseas giving	✓
Payroll giving	✓
Sponsorship	✓

Charitable donations

Cash UK (latest available):	2013	£5,500,000
	2011	£1,400,000
	2009	£1,600,000
	2008	£3,400,000
	2007	£1,400,000
Total UK (cash and in kind):	2013	£5,500,000
Cash worldwide:	2013	£10,000,000
Total worldwide (cash and in kind):	2013	£10,000,000

Community involvement

The group focuses on issues connected to its business and primary focus areas include: the customers' needs; the armed forces and their families; education and skills, particularly science, technology, engineering and mathematics (STEM) education; and heritage. BAE 'works with local and national organisations with an objective to make a difference in the communities in which the group operates' by providing financial support and through volunteering.

Each regional market around the world also has its own strategy, which is relevant to specific local issues, charitable needs and culture and supports the Global Community Investment Strategy.

The group states that as well as one-off support it undertakes longer projects that help charities plan their work further in advance. This includes BAE's Relationship Charity Awards (in the UK)

that fund specific projects for up to five years.

Armed forces

Generally the largest proportion of support is given to armed forces causes. The group's website states:

> We focus on projects and organisations that support serving members of the armed forces and their families, as well as injured servicemen and women who need continued support. In the UK, we contribute to the work of The Royal British Legion which supports current and former members of the armed forces and their dependents, and our employees get involved in the Poppy Appeal, which raises funds for the Legion's work and highlights the contribution of the armed forces past and present. We also sponsor the British Forces Foundation which stages morale boosting concerts and events for servicemen and women and UK4U – a charity which gives Christmas gift boxes to UK forces serving away from home.

Education

The group supports various educational projects and has a BAE Systems Education Programme which organises a range of activities to promote engineering and science. Examples include Schools Roadshow and the Schools Challenge. Another part of the programme is various employability schemes – see 'Commercially led support'.

Prince's Trust

The trust's website states that BAE 'donates over [£111,0000] a year to support the trust's Team Programme in five local communities'. We are unsure whether the figure given on the website stands for £111,000 or £1.1 million.

Corporate giving

In 2013 the group and its employees contributed more than £10 million through the BAE's Community Investment programme. A total of £4.5 million was given to armed forces charities, £2.5 million to education charities and programmes and £1 million to the UK Defence and National Rehabilitation Centre. We found no information regarding the remaining £2 million. It appears that the armed forces support is mainly focused in the UK, therefore we estimate that at least £5.5 million was given in cash in the UK, although the figure might be higher.

Beneficiaries included: UK Defence and National Rehabilitation Centre (£1 million); FIRST (Foundation for Inspiration and Recognition of Science and Technology) in Australia; the National Math and Science Initiative in the US; Prince's Trust; the Queen Elizabeth Prize for Engineering; the Royal Navy and Royal Marines Charity; SSAFA; and United Service organisations (USO).

In-kind support

Employee time, knowledge and skills.

Employee-led support

The website states:

> Where possible, volunteering is integrated into formal career development programmes. Examples include running a careers advice session at a local school or providing health and safety training for a local charity. Employees are also regularly involved in a range of individual or team volunteering projects such as helping out in local schools and packing Christmas boxes for injured armed forces personnel and their families.

A number of staff support local community programmes involving education and training (such as job shadowing/work experience and mentoring schemes), and the development of local business enterprise initiatives. Staff are also seconded to charities and enterprise projects, through the individual business units rather than head office.

Matched funding

In the US employee fundraising is encouraged through the Matching Gift Plan 'that matches employee contributions dollar for dollar up to $10,000 per year, per employee'. Our research suggests that there is a matching scheme for hours spent by employees volunteering (up to an allocated amount).

Payroll giving

Various payroll deduction schemes are operated in some parts of the business.

Commercially led support

Sponsorship

Sponsorship is undertaken. For further details contact the community team.

Education and training

There are various apprenticeship, internship and graduate schemes operating. Bursaries and sponsorships are available.

Corporate social responsibility

CSR committee: There is a Corporate Responsibility Committee, chaired by Paul Anderson. The CSR report states that it 'monitors the group's performance in managing the group's significant non-financial risks, including those arising in respect of business conduct, health and safety, and the environment, and reports its findings to the board on a regular basis'.

The Company Giving Committee oversees the charitable giving activities.

CSR information: The following statements are taken from the group's website:

> Charities, schools and not-for-profit organisations make a hugely valuable contribution to society. We support their work through donations and sponsorships, by encouraging employees to share their time and expertise as volunteers and by supporting employee fundraising.
>
> We believe it is vital to help and encourage more young people to consider a career in science and engineering. We support education and skills development in schools and colleges across the global business.

The group's CSR activities seek to incorporate: responsible business operation; ethical conduct; employee well-being and development; environmental sustainability; working with suppliers; supporting communities and investing in education.

The annual report and accounts state: 'BAE Systems is committed to effecting change. This commitment is demonstrated through work with local and national organisations with an objective to make a difference in the communities in which the group operates.'

CSR report: A CSR report is published within the annual report and accounts.

Exclusions

Support is not given for:

- Third-party fundraisers
- Appeals directly from individuals
- Activities that place or appear to place existing customers, potential customers, suppliers or government officials under any obligations

Applications

Enquiries or requests for charity partnership should be made by completing an online form, referring to one of the following subjects:

- Donation
- Employee engagement opportunities including fundraising
- Sponsorship
- Education
- Community general

Further questions can also be directed to the correspondent. The Corporate Responsibility Committee meets five times a year. Local appeals are handled by the regional site managers.

According to the website, BAE 'proactively seeks organisations to support to enable [it] to have the greatest impact on local communities'.

Balfour Beatty plc

Business services

Correspondent: Paul Toyne, Sustainability Director, 130 Wilton Road, London SW1V 1LQ (tel: 020 7216 6800/020 7216 6800; fax: 020 7216 6950; email: sustainability@balfourbeatty.com; website: www.balfourbeatty.com)

Directors: Steve Marshall, Chair; Robert Amin; Bill Thomas; Duncan McGrath,

Chief Financial Officer; Andrew McNaughton, Chief Executive; Peter Zinkin; Ian Ferguson; Maureen Kempston Darkes; Belinda Richards; Graham Roberts (women: 2; men: 8)

Year end	31/12/2013
Turnover	£8,745,000,000
Pre-tax profit	£32,000,000

Nature of business: Balfour Beatty is an international infrastructure group that delivers services essential to the development, creation and care of infrastructure assets; from finance and development, through design and project management to construction and maintenance; either alone or in partnership and by integrating local supply chains.

Company registration number: 2818602

Subsidiary undertakings include: Refer to the company's accounts for details of the subsidiaries and joint ventures.

Total employees: 49,785

Focus of giving: General charitable purposes, education, enterprise/training, overseas projects, children, young people.

Cash donations undeclared	✓
Gifts in kind	✓
Matched funding	✓
Overseas giving	✓
Sponsorship	✓

Charitable donations

Cash UK (latest available):	2013	£210,000
	2011	£500,000
	2009	£2,500,000
Total UK (cash and in kind):	2013	£215,000
Cash worldwide:	2013	£210,000
Total worldwide (cash and in kind):	2013	£215,000

Community involvement

The company supports local communities by taking part in and supporting organisations and activities that aim to improve social cohesion and inclusion and through contributing to charitable causes.

The company channels much of its giving through the **Balfour Beatty Charitable Trust** (Charity Commission no. 1127453) which was established in the company's centenary year 2009, to advance in life and relieve the needs of young people suffering from disadvantage by assisting with the provision of advice, training and education and other activities. The trust can also support general charitable purposes. The trust was founded by Balfour Beatty to support the company's corporate and social responsibility provision and to act as a focus for employee fundraising as well as to develop into a significant grant funder.

Balfour Beatty plc matches donations which have been raised by employees through fundraising activities for the trust and has indicated that there will be continuing financial support of the trust's aims. However, there is no formal link between the trust and Balfour Beatty plc.

Through the trust and the community engagement programme branded 'Building Better Futures', the company has worked principally in partnership with Action for Children, The Prince's Trust and more recently Corum and Barnardo's, to deliver a series of programmes aimed at helping disadvantaged young people.

Building Better Futures is focused on three themes:

- Young people's employability and employment
- Helping the most disadvantaged young people in society
- Health, sport and well-being

Other charitable initiatives include 'Our Parklife' which provides training and work experience to disadvantaged young people in the five London Olympic Boroughs, in association with the company's long-term contract to manage the Olympic Park.

Corporate giving

In 2013 the company did not declare its charitable cash donations. We have taken the cash donation figure from the income received by the associated charitable trust which is £179,000 from generated funds, plus £31,000 matched funding by the company which totals over £210,000. For the total contribution we have added the £5,000 costs spent on the trust (see 'In-kind support').

See the corporate charity entry on p. 393 for more information.

In-kind support

In addition to grant income and matched funding of employee fundraising, Balfour Beatty also incurred certain costs on behalf of the Balfour Beatty Charitable Trust that would be considered as costs of generating voluntary income by the trust. These costs include the provision of 'Charity Champion' meetings (venue and refreshments) and the regular provision of communications and publicity materials within the Balfour Beatty group. These costs have not been passed on to the trust and are accounted for as an additional donation from Balfour Beatty plc offset by an equal amount within costs of fundraising activities. These costs total £5,175 (2012: £5,030).

Employee-led support

Every year hundreds of employees and their families give their time to volunteer at the London Youth Games.

Commercially led support

Sponsorship: Balfour Beatty continues to sponsor the London Youth Games, Europe's largest youth sports programme. In May 2014, the company announced that it will be extending its sponsorship of the Balfour Beatty London Youth Games to 2016, bringing the total investment to over £4 million.

As of 2014, Balfour Beatty has assumed the sponsorship of the London Youth Games Volunteer team, GamesForce, which offers opportunities for those aged 14+ to gain qualifications in officiating media and events, take on leadership roles and develop key teamwork skills.

Corporate social responsibility

CSR committee: There is a sustainability committee at the company's London office.

CSR information: Taken from the annual report of 2013: 'We have set a clear path to embed sustainability into everything we do by 2020. We focus on our sustainability activities in three key areas; profitable markets, healthy communities and environmental limits.'

CSR report: Sustainability is reported on within the annual report.

Corporate charity: The Balfour Beatty Charitable Trust (Charity Commission no. 1127453).

Applications

In writing to the Corporate Communications department.

Bank of England

Banking

Correspondent: Linda Barnard, Community Relations Manager, Threadneedle Street, London EC2R 8AH (tel: 020 7601 4444/020 7601 4329; email: charity@bankofengland.co.uk; website: www.bankofengland.co.uk)

Directors: Andrew Bailey; Charlie Bean; Sir David Lees, Chair of Court; Sir Roger Carr, Deputy Chair; Lady Susan Rice; John Stewart; Michael Cohrs; Bradley Fried; Tim Frost; David Prentis; Mark Carney; Sir Jon Cunliffe (women: 1; men: 11)

Year end	28/02/2014
Turnover	£649,000,000
Pre-tax profit	£180,000,000

Nature of business: The Bank of England is the central bank of the United Kingdom. The bank is based in London and has agencies in Belfast, Birmingham, Bristol, Cambridge, Exeter, Glasgow, Leeds, Liverpool, Manchester, Newcastle, Nottingham, Southampton, and Greater London.

Royal Charter companies are not obliged to register documents with Companies House, the accounts were however available on the bank's website.

Company registration number: RC000042

Subsidiary undertakings include: Bank of England Asset Purchase Facility Fund Ltd; Bank of England Nominees Ltd; Houblon Nominees Ltd; Olive 863 Ltd; Prudential Regulation Authority Ltd; TBE Pension Fund Trustees Ltd.; The Securities Management Trust Ltd.

Main locations: Belfast, Birmingham, Leeds, Cardiff, Cambridge, Bristol, Exeter, Gloucester, Glasgow, Southampton, Newcastle upon Tyne, Loughton, Manchester, Liverpool, London, Nottingham

UK employees: 3,489

Total employees: 3,489

Focus of giving: Environment, health, ill health, heritage, medical research, older people, children, young people, community/social welfare, disability, disasters.

Gifts in kind	✓
Humanitarian aid: overseas	✓
Humanitarian aid: UK	✓
Matched funding	✓
Overseas giving	✓
Payroll giving	✓

Charitable donations

Cash UK (latest available):	2014	£485,000
	2013	£348,000
	2011	£352,000
	2010	£384,000
	2009	£331,000
Total UK (cash and in kind):	2014	£824,000
Cash worldwide:	2014	£485,000
Total worldwide (cash and in kind):	2014	£824,000

Community involvement

Much of the 2013 programme of initiatives was aimed at promoting social mobility amongst young people. The Community Relations team hosted a number of events in the bank for community organisations helping school students from disadvantaged communities raise their aspirations and understanding of the world of work via activities such as mock selection centres. 678 students, mainly from the London area, attended these events. Activities further afield include reading schemes in Essex and a mentoring scheme based near the Leeds Cash Centre.

Corporate giving

The bank in its annual report for 2013/14 stated that it contributed an estimated total of £824,000 in support of its community programme (2012/13: £615,000). The bank estimates the total value of non-cash community contribution, including time spent by staff on community involvement, travel costs for volunteers and the costs of hosting charitable events at the bank, to be £339,000 in 2013/14 (2012/13: £152,000), of which £179,000 was for staff time involved in volunteering and taking civic duties and volunteering leave.

Cash donations totalled £485,000 (2012/13: £348,000), including:

To community organisations via the Staff Volunteering Award Scheme	£120,000
Supporting academic research	£112,000
Partner charitable organisations donations and membership donations	£93,000
Charities supported by the bank's agencies	£60,000
Matched staff payroll giving	£40,000
Matched staff fundraising	£35,000
Bank of England Court Awards	£15,000
David Sharp School Governor Awards	£10,000

A summary combined income statement and balance sheet as at 28 February 2014, aggregating the Banking Department, Issue Department and the PRA, are the revenue and pre-tax profits figures we have used in this entry.

In-kind support

See the 'Community involvement' section.

Employee-led support

Approximately 50% of staff took part in some form of community activity on behalf of or supported by the bank in 2013. The bank can grant staff paid leave to perform voluntary duties in the community, or to undertake public and civic duties.

Corporate social responsibility

CSR committee: The Community Relations team runs a significant programme of activities that reflect the Bank's aims to be a socially responsible employer and encourage staff to be involved within the community. There is a Safety, Health and Environment (SHE) Committee which reports annually to Court and a Diversity and Inclusion Forum.

CSR information: We were unable to find CSR or sustainability policies.

CSR report: We could not find a CSR or sustainability report on the company's website. There is a diversity report for 2013/14.

Exclusions

No support is given towards: expeditions; holidays; orchestras; conferences; overseas work; organisations of a political nature; religious activities (unless they benefit the wider community); appeals from individuals; choirs; theatres; churches; animals; or third-party fundraising.

Applications

Donations can be made locally at the discretion of the branch agent and subject to a limited budget. Otherwise, appeals should be addressed to the correspondent.

Bank of Ireland UK (plc)

Financial services

Correspondent: Corporate Responsibility Officer, Corporate Responsibility Forum, Head Office GB, Bow Bells House, 1 Bread Street, London EC4M 9BE (tel: 0845 850 1234; email: corporate.responsibility@boi.com; website: www.bank-of-ireland.co.uk)

Directors: Des Crowley, Chief Executive Officer; John O'Donovan; Christopher Fisher, Chair; David McGowan; Stephen Matchett; Laurel Powers-Freeling; Peter Shaw; David Bennett; Senan Murphy; Patrick Haren (women: 1; men: 9)

Year end	31/12/2013
Turnover	£1,101,000,000
Pre-tax profit	£61,000,000

Nature of business: Bank of Ireland UK's principal activities are the provision of an extensive range of banking and other financial services in Great Britain and Northern Ireland.

Company registration number: 7022885

Subsidiary undertakings include: Bank of Ireland International Finance Ltd; New Ireland Assurance Company plc; Bank of Ireland Mortgage Bank; Bank of Ireland (UK) plc; First Rate Exchange Services Holdings Ltd; ICS Building Society.

Main locations: London, Manchester

UK employees: 405

Total employees: 405

Focus of giving: Education, children, young people.

Cash donations undeclared	✓
Gifts in kind	✓
Humanitarian aid: overseas	✓
Matched funding	✓
Overseas giving	✓
Payroll giving	✓

Charitable donations

Cash UK (latest available):	2013	£475,000
Total UK (cash and in kind):	2013	£475,000
Cash worldwide:	2013	£475,000
Total worldwide (cash and in kind):	2013	£475,000

Community involvement

Give Together

The company's main approach has been to channel community investment into encouraging, facilitating and supporting employee volunteering and fundraising activities through an initiative called Give Together. To this end, every Bank of Ireland employee is given a day each year to volunteer for the cause of their choice. As well as facilitating employee volunteering, employees can supplement their fundraising efforts by applying for matched funding when they are involved in fundraising for a community or charitable organisation. There is also funding available for team volunteering projects to buy materials and equipment to enable their volunteering project.

Corporate giving

In 2013 neither this company, nor Bank of Ireland group of companies declared charitable contributions. However, the annual report for Bank of Ireland Group states that during that year employees have been involved in raising more than €2.4 million (£1.9 million) for over 300 different causes. We understand that the staff fundraising is matched and that giving is both in the UK and overseas. We have estimated that charitable cash giving in the UK is around £475,000 and worldwide around the same. No costings were given for in-kind contributions such as equipment, materials and volunteering hours.

In-kind support

Over 2,300 volunteer days have been given by the company in support of charitable activities.

In partnership with Business in the Community Ireland, 232 representatives from 119 charity and community groups have participated in 22 different free one day courses during 2013 in the group's Learning Zone. These programmes are designed to develop the skills and capabilities of participants. 104 Bank of Ireland business volunteers delivered the Financial Education, Learn to Earn programme in 205 secondary school classes, across 125 schools throughout Ireland during the 2012/13 school year. In the same year in Northern Ireland, 61 Bank of Ireland business volunteers taught 256 sessions in 79 schools.

Matched funding

The company match funds employees' fundraising.

Employee-led support

To date, over 7,500 employees have taken part in Give Together, whether through volunteering or fundraising.

Give As You Earn

In addition, employees participate in payroll giving schemes which donate a further €800,000 (£641,000) each year to causes both in Ireland and the financially developing world.

Corporate social responsibility

CSR committee: The Corporate Responsibility Forum was established in January 2004 to provide guidance and set direction for the group's approach to corporate responsibility.

CSR information: Taken from the company's CSR pages on its website:

> Corporate Responsibility is about the contribution a business makes to its social and environmental concerns as well as its economic ones. At Bank of Ireland, these wider responsibilities have always been important to us, but never more so than today in what are extraordinarily difficult times for all our stakeholders – the stockholders who invest in us, the Irish Government which has provided essential supports to us, our customers who bank with us, our employees who work for us, the communities in which we do business and environment in which we live.

CSR report: There does not appear to be a published CSR report. The annual report of the Bank of Ireland Group contains information on aspects of CSR.

Exclusions

No support is given to appeals from individuals, general appeals, religious appeals, overseas travel, arts and sports projects with no community or charitable element, or medical research, equipment or treatment.

Applications

In writing to the correspondent. As part of the Give Together initiative, the bank is operating a database of organisations that are interested in making volunteering opportunities known to Bank of Ireland employees. If you would like opportunities for your organisation to be included, send the details by post to: The Give Together Initiative, Bank of Ireland Group, 5th Floor, Baggot Street, Dublin 2, or email to givetogether@boimail.com.

The Banks Group Ltd

Mining, property

Correspondent: James Eaglesham, The Banks Community Fund, PO Box 542, Durham DH1 9EH (tel: 01913 786342; fax: 01913 782409; email: james@bankscommunityfund.org.uk; website: www.hjbanks.com)

Directors: Harry Banks; Richard Dunkley; Gavin Styles; Christopher Gill (women: 0; men: 4)

Year end	30/09/2013
Turnover	£97,372,000
Pre-tax profit	£6,961,000

Nature of business: The company is involved in opencast coal mining, renewable energy and the development of interests in land. Respectively, the Banks Group's activities are undertaken under three operational divisions: Banks Mining; Banks Renewables; and Banks Property.

The group's annual report and accounts for 2012/13 say that Harry Banks 'is the controlling party by virtue of his controlling interest in the equity share capital of The Banks Group Ltd'.

Company registration number: 2267400

Subsidiary undertakings include: Crossco (281) Ltd; Banks Property Ltd; Banks Renewables Manor Farm House Ltd; Banks Renewables South Dale Wind Farm Ltd; and H J Banks and Company Ltd. A full list of subsidiaries can be obtained from Companies House.

Main locations: West Midlands region, East Midlands, Northwestern England, Yorkshire and the Humber, Scotland

UK employees: 409

Total employees: 409

Focus of giving: Education, environment, small groups, local groups, older people, playgroups, sport, recreation, bricks and mortar appeals, children, young people, community/social welfare, disability.

Cash donations undeclared ✓
Market-led giving ✓

Charitable donations

Cash UK (latest available):	2013	£19,100
	2011	£14,200
	2009	£21,000
	2007	£22,000
Total UK (cash and in kind):	2013	£19,100
Cash worldwide:	2013	£19,100
Total worldwide (cash and in kind):	2013	£19,100

Community involvement

The following information has been gathered from the group's website.

The Banks Community Fund – administered by County Durham Community Foundation (Charity Commission no. 1047625)

The fund was established in 1997 with the aim of providing:

> Support to community groups, voluntary organisations and environmental projects that are charitable, educational, philanthropic or benevolent in purpose and which are located within close proximity of a current or proposed Banks Group development and provide benefit to the local community.

The fund comes from a variety of sources and different funds are grouped into key categories depending on which development is closest to the community in question. These are: wind farm communities, surface coal mine communities and landfill communities.

The Wind Farm Community Fund

The fund was 'established to provide financial assistance to community groups, voluntary organisations and the local community in the area of a wind farm' (normally restricted to the community councils or parishes in close proximity to the wind farm). Some of the funds can provide support for local training and employment initiatives as well. Projects outside the catchment area may be eligible if it can be shown that they benefit local people from the area of a wind farm.

Surface Coal Mine Community Funds
Which were 'established to provide financial assistance to community groups, voluntary organisations and the local community in the area of Banks Surface Coal Mines' (normally restricted to the wards in which the site is located and to the official route adopted for transportation of goods to and from the site). Similarly to the above, projects from other neighbouring settlements may apply for grants provided it can be demonstrated that residents from the eligible area may also benefit. Examples of the funds include The Banks Rusha Surface Coal Mine Community Fund serving Fauldhouse and Breich Valley Ward; Brenkley Lane Surface Coal Mine Community Fund serving the community near Dinnington on the Newcastle and Northumberland border.

Banks Communities Fund
The fund was 'designed to support organisations that are situated within 10 miles of a proposed Banks operation where a specific fund is not yet in place'.

The funds are reviewed by a funding panel, including representatives of the local community. The Grants Committee normally meets quarterly. The funds can provide grants in two categories – below and above £1,000 (different application forms have to be used) with a maximum grant usually being £5,000 for up to one year. Funding can be awarded to projects that seek to:

- Bring land back into use
- Reduce or prevent pollution
- Provide information on sustainable waste management
- Build, improve or maintain public parks or amenities
- Build, improve or maintain community buildings or amenities
- Improve quality of life in a local environment
- Promote or conserve biological diversity through the provision, conservation, restoration or enhancement of a natural habitat or the maintenance or recovery of a species in its natural habitat

Note that 'The Banks Community Fund may decide to prioritise applications from a particular category each year' and 'geographical areas of interest may change without notice'.

The Banks Community Fund guidelines also note that 'if you are successful in being awarded a grant, you will be required to pay 10% of the amount awarded'. Grants will not be paid until this money is received. The 10% can be contributed by: 'a business that has no interest in the project (such as financial or reputational gain); local authority; applicant organisation (through fundraising activities only); or local resident who has no interest in the project'.

The County Durham Community Foundation's annual report and accounts for 2012/13 note that 'most of the projects [supported by The Banks Community Fund] improve or maintain community buildings or places of worship'. Because the majority of the funding comes from the landfill tax credit scheme it is subject to the regulations of ENTRUST.

The group's website states: 'Durham-based Banks have been involved with County Durham Community Foundation since it was set up in 1995, and is currently its largest corporate donor.'

Note: the website also states that 'The Landfill Communities Fund (LCF) is regulated by ENTRUST which has announced that all projects granted LCF funding in Scotland must be completed by the 31 March 2017.'

Some examples of support provided through the funds, given in the 'Working With Your Community' brochure for 2014, include: a £5,500 grant to the Tees Wheelyboat Club to purchase a wheelchair-accessible boat operating from the River Tees Water Sports Centre; and a £7,000 grant to residents of Haughton for development of a new memorial garden created by the village's residents association. Other organisations supported include scout and guide groups, sports teams, dance clubs, elderly people's clubs, schools and playgroups. Support has also been given to Northumberland Wildlife Trust towards its work with local people to enhance a number of environmental and biodiversity projects in the area, for example improvements to the boardwalk and pond-dipping platform at Choppington Community Woodland.

> ***Connect2Renewables***
> Connect2Renewables is an initiative between the local communities, Banks and South Lanarkshire Council which seeks to maximise the social and economic benefit of the development to the local area.

Corporate giving

The annual report and accounts for 2012/13 appear not to declare charitable donations. We were unable to find the figure of the group's contribution elsewhere, therefore we estimate that about £19,100 was given in charitable donations during the year (based on the figures from the three previous years known to us).

The group's website news (dated March 2014) notes that 'in total Banks has provided grants worth £2.6 million to community groups, environmental projects and other local good causes across the north of England and Scotland in the last 19 years'.

According to the same announcement, The Banks Group's 'relationship with County Durham Community Foundation began with a small donor-advised fund to which the company still contributes today, and has since grown to encompass 17 funds, including an endowment fund that has reached the £1 million landmark'.

Commercially led support

Warmer Schemes

The group states on its website that part of its 'development with care approach' it seeks to help communities to tackle poor energy efficiency and lower energy bills. This is done through undertaking energy audits, evaluating required developments and identifying funding to enable necessary work to be done (this may include the Banks Community Fund). 'In addition many of our developments have site specific community development funds available to communities to fund projects in the area if the project is successful in gaining planning permission.'

Education and training

Work has been undertaken with a local college near Cramlington in Northumberland 'to develop a bespoke training programme to train apprentice mechanics and welders'.

Northumbria University
Over 200 students of the university were challenged to come up with ideas for a redevelopment scheme for the group's site in Newcastle's Ouseburn Valley and had an opportunity to work with industry professionals gaining hands-on experience.

Coquet Youth Group
Over a six month period 'representatives from the [youth group] were invited to visit [the] Shotton surface mine to gain a better understanding of how [the group] operates, and to see how some of [its] technologies ... work'.

Corporate social responsibility

CSR committee: According to the website:

> The Banks Group has a dedicated community team working within the communities closest to [its] sites providing information to local people, encouraging a two way dialogue between local people and the specific project team and identifying community projects that may benefit from The Banks Community Fund.

CSR information: The following statements are taken from the group's website and mainly refer to liaison with the community over the group's property development proposals:

Development with care' is central to the aims and objectives of our business. The phrase ideally describes how we interact with people inside and outside our company and it is the guiding principle of the way we carry out our business at all times.

Our 'development with care' approach ensures that we conduct our activities in a responsible manner with consideration for the environment, for local communities in which we operate and for our customers, employees and suppliers.

We recognise that our developments provide an opportunity to make significant changes to the environment and to society and that it is our responsibility to optimise the positive environmental, social and economic benefits and minimise any adverse impacts associated with our business.

The group seeks to:

- Inform the local community or its representatives of [its] intentions to ensure they have an opportunity to respond to [the] proposals
- For [its] schemes to provide tangible benefits to local people, maximising both community and environmental benefits
- To encourage open channels of communication with the community throughout the life of the scheme
- To be transparent with regard to environmental and planning issues
- To involve the community in the design stages of [its] proposals where possible

CSR report: We could not find a separate CSR report, although some information regarding The Banks Community Fund is given on the website and a 'Working With Your Community' brochure is published.

Exclusions

Our research suggests that support is generally not given for: 'animal welfare; general contributions to large appeals (except specific items); medical research and equipment; grants for more than one year; freehold or leasehold land rights; minibuses or other vehicles; overseas travel; legal or redundancy fees'.

According to the guidance notes for applicants, funding will not be given for:

Profit-making companies; projects that are part of the planning process; statutory responsibilities; sponsored events; national or regional charities with no independent office in the area the project is being delivered in; improvements to land that is not open to the general public at convenient hours; projects promoting political or religious activities; deficit or retrospective funding; faith groups promoting religious, non-community based activities (although this does not exclude funding for church restoration); part of a project cost that is VAT recoverable.

Only projects which fit the guiding criteria, are open to general public, community based and have necessary permissions can be supported.

Applications

Application forms for the Banks Community Fund, alongside further guidelines, are available on the group's website. It is asked that applicants 'do not contact The Banks Group or any member of its staff to discuss [the] application'.

Any queries or questions about the application *process* can be directed to the correspondent. Further information is available at: www.bankscommunityfund.org.uk.

Barclays plc

Banking

Correspondent: Barclays Community Affairs, 1 Churchill Place, Canary Wharf, London E14 5HP (tel: 020 7116 4451; email: ukcommunity@barclays.com; website: www.barclays.com)

Directors: David Walker, Chair; Antony Jenkins, Group Chief Executive Officer; Mike Ashley; Tim Breedon; Crawford Gillies; Ruben Jeffery III; Wendy Lucas-Bull; John McFarlane; Tushar Morzaria, Group Finance Director; Dambisa Moyo; Frits van Paasschen; Michael Rake; Diane de Saint Victor; John Sunderland; Stephen Thieke (women: 3; men: 12)

Year end	31/12/2013
Turnover	£18,315,000,000
Pre-tax profit	£2,868,000,000

Nature of business: Barclays plc is a UK-based financial services group engaged primarily in the banking and investment banking businesses. In terms of assets employed, Barclays is one of the biggest financial service groups in the UK. The group also operates in many other countries around the world.

Company registration number: 48839

Subsidiary undertakings include: Barclays Bank Delaware; Barclays Bank of Kenya Ltd; Barclays Capital Securities Ltd; and Barclays Private Clients International Ltd. A full list of subsidiaries can be found in the group's accounts.

Brands include: Barclaycard, FirstPlus, Woolwich

Main locations: London, UK

Total employees: 32,900

Focus of giving: Education, environment, heritage, financial education, armed forces personnel, arts, culture, poverty and social exclusion, sponsorship, sport, recreation, children, young people, disability.

Membership: BITC, LBG

Cash donations undeclared	✓
FTSE 100	✓
Gifts in kind	✓
Market-led giving	✓
Matched funding	✓
Overseas giving	✓
Payroll giving	✓
Sponsorship	✓

Charitable donations

Cash UK (latest available):	2013	£9,075,000
	2011	£22,600,000
	2009	£19,300,000
	2008	£19,600,000
	2007	£30,400,000
Total UK (cash and in kind):	2013	£12,100,000
Cash worldwide:	2013	£66,240,000
Total worldwide (cash and in kind):	2013	£72,000,000

Community involvement

Barclays 'works in partnership with NGOs and experts to develop high-performing programmes and volunteering opportunities that harness the skills and passion of Barclays' employees'. The group has decided to collaborate with a small number of organisations in order 'to have fewer and deeper relationship and ultimately ... have the greatest impact on the communities in which [it] operates'. The website states – 'for this reason, we are unable to provide funding to many of the individual requests we receive'.

Support to the communities is provided through 'investing money, time and skills in partnerships with respected and relevant non-governmental organisations, charities and social enterprises' as well as 'enabling colleagues to use their professional skills and expertise in a range of activities, including volunteering and fundraising'. In 2013 a total of £72 million was invested in community programmes globally.

5 million Young Futures

The strategy runs from 2012 to 2015. Barclays says - '5 million Young Futures is our commitment to invest £250 million and to help five million young achievers build a better future for themselves.' To do that the group is 'leveraging [its] resources and employees' time and expertise to provide the next generation with the skills they need to build a better future for themselves and their families'.

The key areas of focus are:

- Enterprise skills to help a new generation of entrepreneurs start their own businesses or start-ups
- Employability skills to empower young people with financial literacy and financial management proficiency
- Financial skills to give young people in-depth training and employment opportunities to help them support themselves and their families

Barclays Spaces for Sports

The scheme is a global programme bringing sports sites and projects to disadvantaged communities. It focuses on regeneration and sports, creating sustainable sports sites for people to engage in sport and physical activities in areas without such facilities. In the UK there are 200 community sports sites created.

Community investment in the UK

Barclays' assistance has been given to the following projects:

Bikeworks

Since 2011 the group has partnered with this social enterprise 'that uses cycling as a tool to address community issues' and 'offers young people professional-level training in cycle mechanics and customer service, as well as work experience in an authentic business environment'. Barclays' people provide an ongoing support to the organisation through regular CV and interview workshops.

Music Potential

The scheme is aimed at 16- to 25-year-old NEETs and seeks to help them 'develop talent and enhance employability skills to ultimately enable them to build a career in the music and creative industries'. The website states that 'young people are also connected with opportunities to gain work and performance experience as part of Barclaycard's network of music and entertainment-related partnerships'.

Street League

The partnership with this organisation forms a part of the Barclays Spaces for Sports programme and 'aims to help young people gain the skills they need to find employment'. The structured employability and football curriculum particularly targets those who have dropped out of school or have limited opportunities for training and education. Barclays' employees 'support participants with personal development and confidence-building to help raise aspirations and enhance job prospects'.

The Armed Forces Transition Employment and Resettlement programme (AFTER)

AFTER was launched in partnership with the Ministry of Defence and a number of service charities to provide 'work placements, employment opportunities, CV and interview training and money management sessions, as well as funding for education and vocational courses'. Since its inception of the scheme in 2010 'Barclays has invested in and reached in excess of 2,800 ex-service men and women ... with more than 70 veterans having been hired into full-time positions in Barclays since 2013.'

In addition the reach of the programme has been extended to include wider military community 'by providing specialised reviews for mortgage and loan applications and making calls to Barclays free for serving members of the military, helping them preserve phone credits while on tour'.

Barclays Money Skills

The financial capability programme, launched in 2010, has seen Barclays invest 'almost £20 million in partnership with experienced charities to deliver industry-leading programmes and relevant, interactive sessions to help the next generation improve money-management skills, knowledge and confidence'. Partner organisations have included: Action for Children; the National Skills Academy for Financial Services; and the National Youth Agency. The initiative offers practical guidance on financial matters to 16- to 25-year-olds 'and other vulnerable groups'.

Barclays has an excellent website where its community programmes are described giving detailed information regarding its charitable giving and staff contributions. Details of worldwide projects are also given online, categorised by regions.

Holiday E-card

The annual report and accounts for 2013 note: 'This year, Barclays launched its first ever multicultural holiday e-card, which was available to send to all clients and customers, and donated £10 million to UNICEF along with additional donations for every e-card sent.'

Armed forces

It is also noted in the annual report and accounts that Barclays helps Royal British Legion London Poppy Day, 'supporting poppy sales with [the] colleagues and contactless terminals'.

LGBT

Barclays states: 'We continue to support Pride events and awareness campaigns around the world, including World AIDS Day and other fundraising events which take place across Barclays.'

Corporate giving

In 2013 Barclays group provided £72 million (2012: £64.5 million) in total community investment and 'invested £12.1 million in UK community programmes focused on developing the enterprise, employability and financial skills of the next generation'. According to the website, more than 700,000 young people benefited.

The annual report and accounts of the group also states the following:

> We would like to take this opportunity to thank our shareholders for helping us to make two fantastic donations to charity. Firstly, thank you to all of our Barclays Dividend Re-investment Plan (DRIP) participants (which was withdrawn in June 2013) who chose to donate their DRIP cash residue to our chosen charity, ABF The Soldier's Charity. As at the end of January 2014, we had raised over £40,000. Secondly, following the close of the Rights Issue in October 2013, shareholders who let some or all of their Rights lapse received a cheque for their share of the net premium provided that it was £3.00 or more. Any amounts due to shareholders that were less than £3.00 were donated to UNICEF. We are delighted to tell you that Barclays' shareholders have donated over £89,000 to UNICEF.

We have not included the two above donations in the overall figure of Barclays contributions, as these were made by shareholders. It is known that a donation of £10 million was made to UNICEF 'along with additional donations for every [multicultural holiday] e-card sent'. We could not find a further breakdown of the 'total community investment'; we estimate that about £66.2 million was given in cash worldwide and over £9 million in cash in the UK, based on the proportions of giving in the previous year known to us.

Beneficiaries have included: Barclays Money Skills; Bikeworks; Music Potential; Street League; The Armed Forces Transition Employment and Resettlement programme (AFTER); and UNICEF.

In-kind support

Employee volunteering time and expert skills.

In the past Community Placements scheme has operated which introduced former Barclays' employees (who have recently left the bank either through retirement or a redundancy package) to voluntary organisations which would benefit from the individual's financial skills and knowledge, and which fit the bank's community programme's focus. We found details of the scheme presently operating.

Employee-led support

Because of the wide range of organisations (national and local) Barclay's employees want to support, traditionally the group's approach has been not to limit help to a single 'adopted' charity but rather support employees in their choices in a variety of ways.

According to the website, 'Barclays employees are given time during working hours, as well as grants, to support the volunteering activities that are important to them throughout the year.' Our research indicates that staff have a two-day volunteering allowance and those who gather a group of volunteers can also receive a grant of up to £500 towards materials and expenses for their project. Employee volunteering activities include mentoring, employability skills workshops, advising young entrepreneurs and teaching money management classes. In 2013 a total of 71,000 staff members donated 447,000 hours to local communities.

Make a Difference Day
The annual volunteering campaign (October each year) 'encourages employees to give time and skills – not money – to support the communities'. Charities or community groups which think they would benefit from Barclays volunteer support through the Make a Difference Day are encouraged to email the bank's local community team. The initiative is organised by Community Service Volunteers.

Matched funding
Barclays matches employees fundraising for their favourite charities and community organisations. We have found indications that employee donations are matched pound to pound. In 2013 (with Barclays matching) 22,000 employees raised £35 million (2012: £30.3 million) across the group.

Payroll giving
Regular contributions to charitable causes can be made and in 2013 a total of 26,000 employees donated through:

- *Payroll Giving (Give As You Earn)* – Barclays matches contributions by up to £750 per employee each year (in the past up to three times per year)
- *Pennies from Heaven* – allows UK employees to donate from their salary each month to nominated charities

There are also the Barclays Citizenship Awards that recognise those who have made an outstanding contribution to their communities.

Commercially led support

Sponsorships
The following information has been gathered from the website.

Barclays 'looks for sponsorships that will help form positive associations with [its] brand'. Areas sponsored are:

- Arts and Culture – including popular culture and entertainment
- Sport – from global to local properties
- Thought Leadership – we are at the forefront of a changing banking industry and we want to be associated with like-minded properties and organisations that will help create distinction from our competitors

Our research notes that arts and good-cause sponsorship is *only* undertaken at regional level.

Sports

- Barclays has been a corporate sponsor of Barclays Premier League since 2001. The current sponsorship runs until the end of the 2015–2016 season. In addition to that sponsorship is provided to key football bodies in the UK, such as the Football Writers' Association and the League Managers Association
- In South Africa Absa (a financial services institution majority-owned by Barclays) is a major supporter of sport in South Africa and sponsors the Absa Premiership domestic football competition
- The group is also a supporter of the Barclays ATP World Tour Finals. According to the website, 'held at The O2 Arena in London, it is now the largest indoor tennis tournament in the world'
- Through Absa support is given to rugby activities. The company sponsors Springbok Sevens team, the SA under-20s and the Springbok Women's team. Absa has also been a long-term sponsor of the Currie Cup
- Sponsorship is provided to golf events in the US, the Barclays Kenya Open, the European Challenge Tour and golfer Phil Mickelson
- Since 2010 sponsorship of London's Barclays Cycle Hire and Barclays Cycle Superhighways schemes has been undertaken

Arts and Culture
Sponsorships include: Barclaycard British Summertime; Barclays Center ('a state-of-the-art sports and entertainment venue in New York City'); Barclaycard Mercury Prize (recognises the UK Albums of the Year); Klein Karoo Nasionale Kunstefees (Asba supported arts festival); National Indoor Arena in Birmingham; Noot vir Noot (Absa-supported musical game show); The O2 indoor arena; and The Donmar Warehouse (a subsidised theatre in London's West End).

Apprenticeships
There is an apprenticeship scheme operating, delivered as part of the citizenship agenda and 'supporting the most disadvantaged people into work'.

Corporate social responsibility

CSR committee: The following information has been gathered from the group's website.

The remit of Board Citizenship Committee was broadened in 2013 to include reputation and operational risk and the way Barclays conducts its business. It is now called the Board Conduct, Reputation and Operational Risk Committee and retains responsibility for oversight of the citizenship strategy.

The Executive Committee is responsible for managing the delivery of the citizenship agenda and is supported by the Citizenship Leadership Council (CLC), comprised of senior leaders from every business and function.

There are Steering Committees implementing specific business or regional citizenship strategies as well as a network of experts throughout the organisation to support, monitor and ensure the delivery of the citizenship objectives in specific areas.

CSR information: The website notes:

> Citizenship is a fundamental part of how Barclays is changing to become the 'Go-To' bank for all our stakeholders, and one of the ways in which we live and embed our purpose and values. It means taking into account the needs of all our stakeholders and making decisions which, in the short and long-term, are positive for our customers and clients, shareholders, colleagues and the communities in which we operate.
>
> Barclays plays a broader role in the communities in which we live and work beyond what we deliver through our core business activities. We do this through community investment programmes, and the direct efforts of our employees.

CSR report: There is an annual Citizenship Report published within the annual report and accounts.

Exclusions

According to the website, Barclays cannot fund:

- Political parties or political bodies
- The promotion of religious beliefs (we do consider projects led by religious organisations that provide benefits to the whole community)
- The sponsorship of individuals
- Rotary, Lions Clubs and other third-party giving organisations
- Hospital costs
- Medical charities including medical treatment and research
- Capital appeals (for example, for buildings)
- Educational institutions (unless the donation provides direct support to a disadvantaged group)
- The arts (unless the donation provides direct support to a disadvantaged group)
- Microfinance loan fund capital (donations can be used to support the establishment and operation of community-motivated microfinance programmes, but cannot be used as capital for direct on-lending to clients)

The website also states:

> As a global brand, we attract a huge amount of **sponsorship** requests. In order to meet our sponsorship objectives, it is Barclays' policy not to sponsor the following categories:
>
> - Political or religious associations
> - Sponsorship properties which already have given significant brand exposure for our competitors in banking
> - Sponsorship properties that are perceived to have or encompass a violent or dangerous nature (such as boxing)
> - Sponsorships where Barclays or its colleagues may have – or be perceived to have – a conflict of interest
> - Sponsorship of teams (by exception only)
> - Sponsorship of individuals (by exception only)

- An event which is due to commence within the next 2 months

Barclays does not normally give any money for political purposes in the UK or the rest of the EU.

Applications

Community support enquiries/appeals should be addressed to the correspondent.

Sponsorships: Applications should be made at sponsorshipenquiries@barclays.com (check the 'Applying for sponsorship section' on the website for the details required for any application before submitting your details).

The group states:

> Our aim is to review EVERY proposal received, however, we are only able to reply to those opportunities that we feel fit with existing marketing and business objectives and require further investigation, although we will ensure that all enquiries sent to us are logged and held on file for future consideration should our focus and position change.

A. G. Barr plc

Drinks manufacture

Correspondent: Marie Holcroft, Charity, Good Cause and Community Team, 2nd Floor, Mansell House, Aspinall Close, Middlebrook, Horwich, Bolton BL6 6QQ (tel: 01236 852400; email: marieholcroft@agbarr.co.uk; website: www.agbarr.co.uk)

Directors: Ronald G. Hanna, Chair; Roger A. White, Chief Executive; Martin Griffiths; Andrew Memmott; Jonathan Kemp; W. Robin G. Barr; Jonathan Warburton; John R. Nicholson; Pamela Powell (women: 1; men: 8)

Year end	31/01/2014
Turnover	£254,085,000
Pre-tax profit	£34,294,000

Nature of business: The group trades principally as a manufacturer, distributor and seller of soft drinks.

Company registration number: SC005653

Subsidiary undertakings include: Findlays Ltd; Rubicon Drinks Ltd.

Brands include: IRN-BRU; KA; Orangina; Rubicon; Strathmore Water; Tizer.

Main locations: Cumbernauld, Moston, Pitcox, Bolton, Mansfield, Newcastle, Wembley, Tredegar, Sheffield, Forfar, Walthamstow, Wednesbury

UK employees: 1,000

Total employees: 1,000

Focus of giving: General charitable purposes, children, young people, community/social welfare.

Gifts in kind ✓

Market-led giving ✓

Charitable donations

Cash UK (latest available):	2014	£284,000
	2013	£254,000
	2011	£225,850
	2010	£170,000
	2009	£113,000
Total UK (cash and in kind):	2014	£284,000
Cash worldwide:	2014	£284,000
Total worldwide (cash and in kind):	2014	£284,000

Community involvement

1% of after-tax profits is used in supporting charities, good causes and community groups each year. This comprises a mixture of cash, product and merchandise donations and employees' time. This investment is spread across a broad spectrum of activities, including contributions to national charities like The Prince's Trust and The Big Issue Scotland, and international charities like The British Asian Trust. The company also supports many small and medium sized charities and community groups throughout the UK

Areas of charitable and community focuses are: active lifestyle; education; sport; health; people who are disadvantaged.

Organisations benefiting from the company's support during 2013/14 were: Bluebellwood Children's Hospice (Sheffield) C4WS Homeless Project (Walthamstow), Hamilton Thai Boxing Club, Henshaws Society for the Blind, Make A Difference (Milton Keynes), Motor Neurone Disease Association, Royal Mencap Homes Foundation, Tredegar Orpheus Male Voice Choir, St Luke's Hospice Harrow, Thornham Cricket Club, Whitehills Hospital Forfar, Watch Us Grow Cumbernauld and Willowbrook Hospice, Prescott.

Corporate giving

There appears to be no record of the total amount in donations given in 2013/14 to charitable causes. However, the company has stated in its annual report that it gives 1% of after-tax profit to charitable causes. With this in mind, we can estimate that the company made donations of around £284,000 in this financial year.

Beneficiaries: An annual donation of £40,000 is made to The Prince's Trust.

In-kind support

The A.G. Barr Site Community Fund provides support for charities and community organisations near the company's 12 UK sites. Through the fund, employees volunteer their time for causes that are important to them as individuals. Over the years thousands of community groups, charities and good causes have been assisted with donations of Barr Soft drinks products and merchandise in order to help them raise funds. Glasgow Hospice is one such charity to benefit. Free products are given to its shop and cafe which the hospice can then sell on to visitors, with proceeds going towards the work the hospice carries out for terminally ill people and their families.

If you would like to approach the company for a product or merchandise (subject to availability) donation then send your request in writing detailing some background information on your group, what event or activity you would like A. G. Barr to support, when the event or activity is happening and exactly what level of support you are looking for. Due to the high number of requests, allow two to four weeks for a response on whether or not you will be assisted. Either write by post or email the correspondent.

Employee-led support

Employees take part in initiatives throughout the year to help local groups and charities, for example, raising funds for The Prince's Trust, helping the charity to deliver its team programme education courses in Scotland and supporting its XL club programme in England.

Commercially led support

The company's Strathmore brand carries The Prince's Trust logo, together with details of the company's support and how consumers can find out more about the work of the charity, on over 57 million bottles each year distributed throughout the UK

Corporate social responsibility

CSR committee: The CSR committee's 'board sponsor' is the operations director of the company and the steering group consists of representatives from marketing, customer management, quality, HR and the supply chain. The programmes cover environment, consumers, employees and the community.

CSR information: The following information is taken from the CSR section of the website:

> Corporate responsibility at Barr is neither a new thing nor a separate programme of activity – it is part of what we believe makes good business sense.
>
> Corporate responsibility is an integral part of our overall business and remains one of the 7 core areas of our strategic focus, sponsored by Andrew Memmott our Operations Director.
>
> Our corporate responsibility strategy comprises a programme encouraging all our employees to 'do the right thing' and has been aligned within 4 key areas:
>
> - Environment
> - Our Consumers

- Our People
- Community

CSR report: There was no evidence of a separate CSR report.

Applications

In writing to the correspondent for both cash donations and in-kind support. See the 'In-kind support' section of this entry for further details.

Barratt Developments plc

Building/construction

Correspondent: See 'Applications', Kent House, 1st Floor, 14–17 Market Place, London W1W 8AJ (tel: 020 7299 4898; fax: 020 7299 4851; email: cr@barrattplc.co.uk; website: www.barrattdevelopments.co.uk)

Directors: John Allan, Chair; Mark Clare, Group Chief Executive; Robert Davies; Tessa Bamford; David Thomas, Group Finance Director; Steven Boyes; Clive Fenton; Roderick MacEachrane; Mark Rolfe; Richard Akers; Tessa Bamford; Tom Keevil; Nina Bibby (women: 2; men: 7)

Year end	30/06/2014
Turnover	£3,157,000,000
Pre-tax profit	£390,600,000

Nature of business: The group's principal activities comprise house building and commercial development.

Company registration number: 5688068

Subsidiary undertakings include: BDW Trading Ltd

UK employees: 5,755

Total employees: 5,755

Focus of giving: Education, enterprise/training, women's issues, children, young people, community/social welfare, disability.

Gifts in kind ✓
Market-led giving ✓

Charitable donations

Cash UK (latest available):	2014	£116,000
	2013	£40,000
	2012	£30,000
	2011	£45,700
	2010	£36,100
Total UK (cash and in kind):	2014	£219,000
Cash worldwide:	2014	£116,000
Total worldwide (cash and in kind):	2014	£219,000

Community involvement

The group is engaged in 'scoping out' a national charity to support. Although not officially a charity partner, the group has supported 'KidsOut' for around five years.

Corporate giving

During the financial year 2013/14 the group made charitable donations of £116,000. A further £62,000 was raised by staff. Total declared charitable contributions were £219,000. The charity KidsOut was one beneficiary but we have no further information of others who might have benefited.

Employee-led support

The group supports a wide range of charitable giving and community volunteering initiatives which are widely promoted at a divisional level and within communities. In 2013/14 employees raised £68,000 by way of fundraising.

Commercially led support

The 2014 Sustainability Report states:

> As part of our commitment to improve the image of house building amongst young people, we will be encouraging our employees to go into their local school or college to talk about working in the house building sector, as part of the 'Inspiring the Future' initiative. Learn more at www.inspiringthefuture.org.

Corporate social responsibility

CSR committee: There was no evidence of a separate CSR Committee.

CSR information: The company states in its Sustainability Report for 2014 that it has formalised its approach to community involvement and charitable giving in a new policy.

CSR report: The group now has an annual Sustainability Report which includes community initiatives and charitable giving information.

Applications

Local charities should contact the nearest regional office.

BASF plc

Chemicals and plastics

Correspondent: Company Secretary, PO Box 4, Earl Road, Cheadle Hulme, Cheshire SK8 6QG (tel: 01614 856222; fax: 01614 860891; website: www.basf.de/uk)

Directors: T. B. Jensen; S. Hatton; G. A. Thomson; G. W. Mackey; T. Urwin; H. D. Michels

Year end	31/12/2013
Turnover	£362,787,000
Pre-tax profit	£35,331,000

Nature of business: BASF is a leading chemical company. BASF plc is concerned with the production of Hexamethylenediamine at Seal Sands, the import and distribution of chemicals mainly to the agriculture markets and construction industry, and agency sales of chemicals on behalf of BASF Societas Europaea, its ultimate parent company.

Company registration number: 667980

Subsidiary undertakings include: BASF Construction Chemicals Ltd; Sorex Holdings Ltd.

Main locations: Wantage, Cheadle, Deeside, Manchester, Woolpit, Middlesbrough, Ruddington, Cinderford, London, Nottingham, Alfreton

UK employees: 384

Focus of giving: Education, science technology, children, young people, community/social welfare.

Cash donations undeclared ✓
Gifts in kind ✓

Charitable donations

Cash UK (latest available):	2013	£362,500
	2011	£220,500
	2009	£51,000
	2008	£91,000
Total UK (cash and in kind):	2013	£362,500
Cash worldwide:	2013	£362,500
Total worldwide (cash and in kind):	2013	£362,500

Community involvement

We could find no information regarding the UK company's community involvement either in its accounts or website apart from information given on the following:

Kids' Lab

At the site in Bradford groups from local primary schools can experience hands-on experiments in a laboratory developed just for them.

Corporate giving

In BASF plc's 2013 company report and accounts there were no charitable donations declared. We therefore had to take an average of the UK charitable cash donations based on the previous years' amounts we have available. This is estimated at £362,500.

Note: In the 2013 group Sustainability Report, it was stated that €49.2 million (£39.4 million) was donated in group donations, sponsorship and own projects. Of this amount, the report states that 'we donated 27%' [which is £10.6 million]. It would seem from this wording that £10.6 million was given by the group in cash worldwide. As to the £39.4 million worldwide we are unable to determine how much of this was raised by staff or were in-kind contributions by the group.

In-kind support

See 'Community involvement' section – Kids' Lab.

Corporate social responsibility

CSR information: There was no UK information available regarding CSR for this company. The group's corporate purpose is to 'create chemistry for a sustainable future'. The group's chair, Dr Kurt Bock states on the group's website:

'For us, sustainability means aligning economic success with environmental and social responsibility. This will ensure our long-term business success.'

We were unable to determine the ratio of women to men on the board of the UK company.

CSR report: There is an annual Sustainability Report for the group but this focuses on worldwide giving and not company activities/giving in the UK.

Applications

In writing to the correspondent for national appeals referenced 'Charitable Donations'. For local appeals contact the nearest relevant site.

Baxter Healthcare Ltd

Healthcare

Correspondent: The Company Secretary, Wallington, Compton, Newbury, Berkshire RG20 7QW (tel: 01635 206000; fax: 01635 206115; website: www.baxterhealthcare.co.uk)

Directors: G. E. Braham; J. S. Kim

Year end	31/12/2013
Turnover	£196,423,000
Pre-tax profit	£29,576,000

Nature of business: Technologies related to the blood and circulatory system.

The company is a wholly owned subsidiary of Baxter Healthcare (Holdings) Ltd which in turn is ultimately owned and controlled by Baxter International Inc.

Company registration number: 461365

Subsidiary undertakings include: Baxter Healthcare Pension Plan Trustees Ltd; Baxter (Hellas) EPE – incorporated and operating in Greece; and Willow Healthcare Services Ltd.

Main locations: Thetford, Stockport, Liverpool, Northampton, Newbury, Oxford

Total employees: 1,140

Focus of giving: Education, health, ill health, older people, children, young people.

Cash donations undeclared ✓

Charitable donations

Cash UK (latest available):	2013	£20,000
	2010	£16,000
	2009	£15,000
	2008	£29,000
Total UK (cash and in kind):	2013	£20,000
Cash worldwide:	2013	£20,000
Total worldwide (cash and in kind):	2013	£20,000

Community involvement

Previous research shows that support is only given to registered charities; these are sometimes nominated by a Baxter employee, especially if they operate in an area where there is a Baxter facility, or where a large number of Baxter employees live. In the UK, assistance is only given in the areas where the company operates. Currently, these are Liverpool, Newbury, Northampton, Oxford, Stockport and Thetford.

There is an international corporate foundation (Baxter International Foundation) which is open to charities in the UK.

The website states:

> Grants awarded in 2013 fulfilled local needs to increase access to dental care, mental health, and other healthcare services for children, the uninsured, veterans, and the elderly. Recipient organisations included the following:
>
> - **United Kingdom** – National Society for the Prevention of Cruelty to Children (NSPCC), in London, to help expand the FEDUP program into the West London area by hiring of a full-time Child Services Practitioner. FEDUP is an innovative and comprehensive program that works with children and young people who are affected by parental substance misuse
> - **India** – Sightsavers International, in Delhi, to support year two of Vision Delhi – an initiative to strengthen primary eye care services in Delhi slums
> - **USA** – Catalyst Schools/Circle Rock Charter School in Chicago, IL to support the salary for the school's first full-time Mental Health Counsellor, who will focus on reducing bullying behaviour
> - **Colombia** – To Love Is To Give Ministries Inc. (TLTG), in Cali, to add a nurse practitioner to the staff and contribute to the early childhood development of 390 children

For further information visit Baxter's website (www.baxter.com/about_baxter/sustainability/international_foundation)

Corporate giving

In 2013 the UK company unusually did not declare its charitable donations in the annual report and accounts. We have averaged the donations for the three most recent years for which we have figures and estimate the amount available to be around £20,000.

Corporate social responsibility

CSR committee: Not known.

CSR information: Taken from the Baxter International Inc. website: 'We define sustainability as a long-term approach to including our social, economic and environmental responsibilities among our business priorities. Baxter's efforts in this area align with and support our mission of saving and sustaining lives.'

The ratio of women to men on the board is not known.

CSR report: We found none for this UK company.

Applications

To be considered for support from the foundation, registered charities must be nominated by a Baxter employee, not via unsolicited applications, and be eligible under the foundation's guidelines. Details of the latter can be found at www.baxter.com.

Baxters Food Group Ltd

Food manufacture

Correspondent: Peter McLuckie, Company Secretary, Highfield House, Fochabers, Moray, Scotland IV32 7LD (tel: 01343 820393; email: info@baxters.co.uk; website: www.baxters.com)

Directors: Audrey Baxter, Executive Chair; William King, Chief Executive; Andrew Baxter; Nicholas Wheater (women: 1; men: 3)

Year end	01/06/2013
Turnover	£156,993,000
Pre-tax profit	£1,785,000

Nature of business: The manufacture of food including chilled, tinned and frozen products, supplying retail, food manufacturers and foodservice customers in the UK and key overseas markets. The immediate and ultimate parent undertaking is W A Baxter and Sons (Holdings) Ltd, a company registered in Scotland.

Company registration number: SC23572

Subsidiary undertakings include: Baxters Canada; Baxters Polska sp. z o.o; Jensen's Choice Foods Pty Ltd; Moray Microbiological Ltd.

Brands include: Baxters.

Main locations: Moray

Total employees: 994

Focus of giving: General charitable purposes, education, health, ill health, heritage, older people, arts, culture, poverty and social exclusion, science technology, sport, recreation, children, young people, community/social welfare, disability.

Sponsorship ✓

Charitable donations

Cash UK (latest available):	2013	£4,000
	2012	£17,000
	2011	£15,000
	2009	£6,000
	2007	£128,000
Total UK (cash and in kind):	2013	£4,000
Cash worldwide:	2013	£4,000
Total worldwide (cash and in kind):	2013	£4,000

Community involvement

Baxters has UK foundation based at the company's address in Scotland (OSCR no. 033432). The foundation's interests are the relief of poverty, health, education, citizenship, community, development, the arts, heritage, culture, science, sports and recreation and the environment. The foundation benefits children and young people, older people, and people with disabilities or health problems.

It is not clear whether the UK foundation is still operational as it has not had any charitable expenditure since 2010 (according to the records of the Office of the Scottish Charity Regulator) although it did in that year have an income of over £50,000 and so holds those funds at least.

Corporate giving

In 2012/13 Baxters Food Group Ltd declared £4,000 to 'local charities'. We understand this to mean local to the company's offices in Moray in Scotland. No further information was available.

Commercially led support

Sponsorship: Baxters sponsors the Baxters Loch Ness Marathon and Festival of Running which is a notable fixture on the running calendar.

Corporate social responsibility

CSR committee: There was no evidence of a separate CSR Committee.

CSR information: No information regarding CSR was available from the company's website.

CSR report: There was no evidence of a separate CSR report.

Applications

Applications to the foundation should be made to the secretary to the trustees at the company's address referenced 'Baxters Foundation'.

Bayer plc

Chemicals and plastics

Correspondent: CSR Committee, Bayer House, Strawberry Hill, Newbury, Berkshire RG14 1JA (fax: 01635 563513; email: communications.ukireland@bayer.com; website: www.bayer.co.uk)

Directors: A. Moscho; I. Paterson

Year end	31/12/2013
Turnover	£410,044,000
Pre-tax profit	£22,449,000

Nature of business: Bayer in the UK/Ireland region is part of the global concern Bayer AG, based in Leverkusen, Germany. In Europe, where 44% of the company's turnover resides, the UK/Ireland region is placed fifth, has around 1,000 employees and three main operating companies, whose activities mirror Bayer's operations globally.

In the UK/Ireland, HealthCare represents 51% of sales, CropScience 24% and MaterialScience 25%.

Company registration number: 935048

Subsidiary undertakings include: Bayer Agriculture Ltd; Bayer CropScience Ltd; PBI Home and Garden Ltd.

Main locations: East Staffordshire BC, Babergh DC, South Cambridgeshire DC, Broxbourne BC, Sheffield MD, Bridgend County – Sir Pen-y-bont ar Ogwr

UK employees: 691

Focus of giving: Education, environment, arts, culture, community/social welfare.

Charitable donations

Cash UK (latest available):	2013	£348,000
	2009	£11,000
Total UK (cash and in kind):	2013	£348,000
Cash worldwide:	2013	£348,000
Total worldwide (cash and in kind):	2013	£348,000

Community involvement

It is fairly unusual for a company to acknowledge the following, taken from Bayer's website: 'Our communities are our hosts, they provide us with our working environment, our employees and our licence to operate.'

The activities and support that make up Bayer's Corporate Social Responsibility programme complement its mission and values.

The company supports activities that are local to its operations and are also:

- Linked to employees' own community activities
- Linked to one of Bayer's products or services
- Specifically benefiting from Bayer's involvement
- Beneficial to numbers or groups of people

Support is given for activities which enhance local quality of life through:

- The environment
- Community care
- Culture and the arts
- Education
- Projects in line with the company's Mission Statement
- Projects benefiting groups and not individuals

While activities meeting the above criteria will be considered, they do not automatically qualify for support, as other factors (such as budget already committed) are taken into account.

Bayer UK and Ireland has been involved in social, community and environmental programmes across the region for a number of years. It supports numerous social responsibility programs, often in partnership with other organisations.

Global community support is given through the Bayer Foundations which donate primarily to healthcare related organisations. The Foundation's headquarters is in Leverkusen, Germany.

Partners – Science Museum

Bayer continues its partnership with London's Science Museum. This partnership has included support of the climate science 'atmosphere' gallery – a fresh and exciting way to make sense of the climate. It aims to deepen public understanding of the science behind climate change, and to be the main UK destination for clear, accurate and up-to-date climate science information.

Corporate giving

In 2013 the company spent £348,000 on various corporate social responsibility programmes. We were unable to determine whether the company had costed in-kind giving and included this in the figure and so with no information to the contrary, we have taken the cash donations to be the total amount.

Employee-led support

During its 150th anniversary year (2013), Bayer worked closely with the Volunteer Centre, West Berkshire, to develop a number of volunteering projects for colleagues. These included team challenges at local charities Growing2Gether, Headley, and the Five a Day market garden at Englefield. Wanting to create a lasting legacy, there was also the planting of indigenous trees and shrubs at Goldwell Park, Newbury.

Commercially led support

Sponsorships

The Henley Festival is run by a charitable organisation, dedicated to promoting the arts and encouraging young artists in many disciplines. It is the only arts festival that does not require assistance from the public purse to meet its charitable aims, instead relying on income from its hugely successful Festival Week and on donations from corporate supporters, such as Bayer.

Bayer Newbury 10K

Staged in and around Newbury, the Bayer Newbury 10K is a regular fixture in the Newbury sporting calendar. The multi-terrain route welcomes runners from across the UK, Ireland and Europe and due to its popularity, has grown in size from year to year.

Bayer works in partnership with the Newbury Athletic Club (NAC) in organising the event and a local charity is chosen to benefit from the entrance fees each year.

Corporate social responsibility

CSR committee: This information was obtained from the company's UK/Ireland website:

> Our community support programme is overseen by a committee which aims to be professional, sympathetic, impartial and systematic. That must include a firm and clear statement of what we can and cannot support, subject to available funds

> and the balance of our existing community work.

CSR information: This information was obtained from the company's UK/ Ireland website:

> Bayer has many responsibilities – one of which is to generate benefits for the communities in which we operate. This may happen through support at a national or international level, usually business linked and often driven by the needs of the community itself. Here in the UK/ Ireland, we also believe in the importance of local community support.

We were unable to determine the ratio of women to men on the UK company's board.

CSR report: There was no evidence of a CSR report; however, very helpful information was available from the company's website.

Exclusions

Bayer is unable to support:

- Individuals rather than group activities
- Religious, political or racially aligned movements
- Projects or activities bridging a gap in government or local authority funding
- Sporting or recreational activities unless closely associated to Bayer
- Entries in log books, year books or support advertising
- Projects of a local nature which are outside key locations of Newbury, Cambridge, Norwich and Dublin
- Conferences, lectures, trips, respite breaks or holidays

Applications

Given that you meet Bayer's criteria, you will then need to complete the 'CSR Request Form' (available from the website). The information you provide will supply Bayer with the key details required to make an informed decision regarding your proposal.

Post your completed CSR Request Form and supporting materials to: CSR Committee, Bayer plc, Bayer House, Strawberry Hill, Newbury, Berkshire RG14 1JA.

Alternatively, you can send it by email: corporate.communications@bayer.co.uk or by fax: 01635 563513. Note that Bayer only accepts postal, email or faxed requests and is unable to take phone calls to discuss individual requests.

Bayer's committee reviews applications received on a monthly basis throughout the year. Bayer will contact you by email or letter to let you know if they are able to support you or not.

BBA Aviation plc

Engineering, transport and communications

Correspondent: Community Involvement and Charitable Giving, 105 Wigmore Street, London W1U 1QY (tel: 020 7514 3999; fax: 020 7408 2318; email: info@bbaaviation.com; website: www.bbaaviation.com)

Directors: Sir Nigel Rudd, Chair; Simon Pryce, Chief Executive; Nick Land; Peter Ratcliffe; Mike Powell, Group Finance Director; Susan Kilsby; Wayne Edmunds (women: 1; men: 6)

Nature of business: An international group of aviation services and materials technology businesses.

Year end	31/12/2013
Turnover	£1,390,174,820
Pre-tax profit	£90,982,323

Company registration number: 53688

Subsidiary undertakings include: Signature Flight Support Paris SA; APPH Ltd; APPH Aviation Services Ltd; ASIG Ltd; Balderton Aviation Holdings Ltd; H+S Aviation Ltd; Signature Flight Support London Luton Ltd; Signature Flight Support Heathrow Ltd; Signature Flight Support UK Regions Ltd; Aircraft Service International Group Incorporated; APPH Wichita Incorporated; APPH Houston Incorporated; Barrett Turbine Engine Company; Dallas Airmotive Incorporated; Executive Beechcraft Incorporated; International Governor Services; Ontic Engineering and Manufacturing Incorporated; Signature Flight Support Corporation.

UK employees: 2,691

Total employees: 10,873

Focus of giving: Education, children, young people, community/social welfare.

Cash donations undeclared	✓
Gifts in kind	✓
Overseas giving	✓

Charitable donations

Cash UK (latest available):	2013	£43,000
	2010	£76,000
	2009	£30,000
	2008	£26,000
Total UK (cash and in kind):	2013	£43,000
Cash worldwide:	2013	£276,000
Total worldwide (cash and in kind):	2013	£276,000

Community involvement

Established in 2010, BBA Aviation's group-wide Community Involvement and Charitable Giving Framework sets out the approach the company's sites should take to projects, volunteering and fundraising in their local communities. Having this framework has led to a more structured way of working and has encouraged businesses and employees to focus on fewer, more ambitious activities, enabling teams to make a bigger contribution to the causes that they care about and fostering longer-term relationships with those organisations.

The CSR report for 2013 states:

> In 2013 BBA Aviation will continue to encourage its businesses to identify opportunities to benefit their local communities and assist organisations by building stronger links. Priorities include:
>
> - encouraging all locations to build deeper relationships in and with their local communities
> - communicating news of community activities in and throughout the group to inspire sites and employees to set up and pursue their own projects.

Corporate giving

In 2012/13 group donations to charities worldwide were $440,000 (£276,000) when twenty donations were made to organisations with strong local connections to BBA Aviation sites and to organisations in the aviation, engineering or education sectors. No UK cash charitable donations were declared in the annual report and we have estimated this amount by calculating the average of the last three annual cash UK figures we have available.

Beneficiaries include: The Rachel Madocks Special School in Hampshire which is a co-educational school for pupils aged 2–19 years with multiple learning difficulties and complex medical needs. The school has been supported by H+S Aviation since 2011, with many H+S employees involved in fundraising and volunteering activities.

In-kind support

In 2013 a total of 74 employees from Dallas Airmotive's Heritage Park facility volunteered for the GRACE (Grapevine Relief and Community Exchange) Feed Our Kids programme at which 1,515 lunches were served to local children over the course of a week. Volunteers cooked and served meals every day and co-ordinated travel to and from the venue to ensure the safety of those attending. Members of the team also used the event as an opportunity to talk to the children about safety.

Employee-led support

Employees are encouraged to fundraise and get involved with local community and charitable groups, for example ten health and safety Aviation employees completed the ascent and descent of the highest peaks in England, Scotland and Wales in 24 hours, raising £5,000. Volunteer hours recorded for the year 2012/13 were up by more than 40% on the previous year as employees got involved in events from blood drives to career fairs to the regular American Cancer Society 24 hour Relay for Life.

Corporate social responsibility

CSR committee: There is a Community Involvement and Charitable Giving Committee.

CSR information: This information was obtained from the company's website:

> Corporate Social Responsibility is embedded in BBA Aviation's vision, mission and values. It is a fundamental part of our business model and a driver of success. Every day our people put our values into action with pride, performing services for customers and working in their communities safely, responsibly and with integrity.

CSR report: There is a separate CSR report, information on the company's website and some also within the company's annual accounts.

Applications

In writing to the correspondent. Under the BBA Aviation charitable giving programme employees or sites can, on behalf of a charity or not-for-profit organisation, apply to the BBA Aviation Charitable Giving Committee for a donation. Priority is given to organisations with a strong local connection to sites and/or those connected with aviation, engineering or education.

BC Partners Ltd

Financial services

Correspondent: Secretary, BCP Foundation, 40 Portman Square, London W1H 6DA (tel: 020 7009 4800/020 7009 4800; fax: 020 7009 4899; email: bcpfoundation@bcpartners.com; website: www.bcpartners.com)

Directors: S. Quadrio Curzio, Chair; R. Svider; M. A. Twinning; F. Loredon

Year end	31/12/2013
Turnover	£109,382,156
Pre-tax profit	£17,722,406

Nature of business: Investment advisers to the managers of offshore funds for investment in principally unquoted companies.

Company registration number: 2020410

Subsidiary undertakings include: BC Partners SarL; BC Partners GmbH; BC Partners Inc.

UK employees: 106

Focus of giving: General appeals.

Membership: BITC

Gifts in kind	✓
Matched funding	✓

Charitable donations

Cash UK (latest available):	2013	£242,000
	2012	£32,000
	2010	£138,000
	2009	£136,000
	2008	£132,250
Total UK (cash and in kind):	2013	£242,000
Cash worldwide:	2013	£242,000
Total worldwide (cash and in kind):	2013	£242,000

Community involvement

Donations from BC Partners Ltd is channelled through the firm's charitable foundation – BC Partners Foundation, a charity registered in the UK since 2010 (Charity Commission no. 1136596).

A sister charity, the BC Partners Foundation (US), Inc. has been established as a 501(c)(3) organisation in the US in 2012 to coordinate giving in the US.

Neither foundation accepts unsolicited grant requests.

Corporate giving

In 2013 BC Partners Ltd donated £242,000 (2012: £32,000) for charitable purposes. Donations are channelled through the company's foundation.

See the corporate charity entry on p. 393 for more information.

In-kind support

The BC Partners Foundation is primarily funded by BC Partners Ltd. The foundation co-ordinates charitable giving by staff, as well as the charitable activities of BC Partners worldwide.

Employee-led support

The foundation's main charitable activity focuses on providing employee matching grants and supporting charities proposed by the employees of BC Partners or trustees of the BC Partners Foundation.

Corporate social responsibility

CSR committee: There was no evidence of a CSR Committee.

CSR information: There was no information available regarding a CSR policy. We were unable to determine the ratio of women to men on the board.

CSR report: There was no evidence of a CSR report.

Corporate charity: BC Partners Foundation (Charity Commission no. 1136956).

Applications

In writing to the correspondent at the company's foundation.

Beazley plc

Insurance

Correspondent: UK Charity Committee, Plantation Place South, 60 Great Tower Street, London EC3R 5AD (tel: 020 7667 0623; fax: 020 7674 7100; email: info@beazley.ie; website: www.beazley.com)

Directors: Andrew Horton, Chief Executive; Martin Bride, Finance Director; Adrian Cox; Neil Maidment; Clive Washbourn; George Blunden; Padraic O'Connor; Vincent Sheridan; Ken Sroka; Dennis Holt, Chair; Rolf Albert Wilhelm Tolle; Angela Doreen Crawford-Ingle (women: 1; men: 11)

Year end	31/12/2014
Turnover	£1,266,859,934
Pre-tax profit	£164,106,547

Company registration number: 102680

Subsidiary undertakings include: Beazley Group Ltd; Beazley Management Ltd; Beazley Staff Underwriting Ltd; First State Management Group Inc.; Swift No. 1 Ltd; Swift No. 2 Ltd.

Focus of giving: General charitable purposes.

Charity of the Year	✓
Gifts in kind	✓
Humanitarian aid: overseas	✓
Humanitarian aid: UK	✓
Market-led giving	✓
Matched funding	✓
Overseas giving	✓
Payroll giving	✓
Sponsorship	✓

Charitable donations

Cash UK (latest available):	2014	£100,090
	2011	£57,500
	2010	£56,265
	2009	£53,000
	2008	£67,000
Total UK (cash and in kind):	2014	£100,090
Cash worldwide:	2014	£100,090
Total worldwide (cash and in kind):	2014	£100,090

Community involvement

This information was obtained from the company's website:

> Our responsible business committee, chaired by Clive Washbourn, sets the global strategy for corporate social responsibility, which at Beazley is focused on:
>
> - Charity
> - Community
> - Sustainability
> - Marketplace
> - Health, well-being and safety
> - Diversity and inclusion

Charity partners

Feeding America, Rwanda Aid, ShelterBox, The Conservation Fund and World Child Cancer.

Corporate giving

In 2014, the group made charitable donations in the UK and the US of £200,000. The group supports three chosen charities to which the committee donates an annual payment. We were unable to discover how the money was split between the UK and the US and we have estimated 50/50. The company also supports staff in fundraising for their chosen charities. Unfortunately there were no costings of volunteer hours that were spent.

Employee-led support

The group encourages employee involvement in a range of community programmes across the group and each employee can take up to two days per year to participate in charitable and local community initiatives. In 2014, 280 Beazley employees volunteered for 23 community projects in 11 cities around the world, ranging from schools in east London to food banks in San Francisco.

Payroll giving: The group runs a payroll giving scheme in the UK in association with the Charities Aid Foundation.

Matched funding: The company matches employees fundraising.

Corporate social responsibility

CSR committee: The charity committees in the UK and US are made up of employees across the business whose remit is to: encourage and support Beazley people to participate in charitable and community activities; manage Beazley's corporate charitable partnerships; and oversee Beazley's response to large scale disasters.

CSR information: The group states on its website: 'We take our social and environmental responsibilities seriously. But this aspect of our work and of our lives is more than a responsibility. We support causes our employees feel passionate about – causes to which we can contribute not only money but also our time and expertise.'

Applications

In writing to the correspondent.

Bellway plc

Building/construction

Correspondent: G. Kevin Wrightson, Company Secretary, Seaton Burn House, Dudley Lane, Seaton Burn, Newcastle upon Tyne NE13 6BE (tel: 01912 170717; fax: 01912 366230; email: kevin.wrightson@bellway.co.uk; website: www.bellway.co.uk)

Directors: John K. Watson, Chair; Kevin Wrightson; John Cuthbert; Edward (Ted) F. Ayres, Chief Executive; Peter M. Johnson; Mike R. Toms; Keith Adey, Finance Director; Paul Hampden Smith; Denise Jagger (women: 1; men: 8)

Year end	31/07/2013
Turnover	£1,110,676,000
Pre-tax profit	£140,927,000

Nature of business: The company's main activity is house building.

Company registration number: 1372603

Subsidiary undertakings include: Litrose Investments Ltd; Bellway Financial Services Ltd; Bellway Housing Trust Ltd; The Victoria Dock Company Ltd.

Main locations: Bedworth, Altrincham, Wetherby, Tamworth, Uxbridge, Wakefield, Ringwood, Merstham, Newcastle upon Tyne, Glasgow, Eastcote, Chadderton, Chelmsford, Cardiff

UK employees: 2,000

Total employees: 2,000

Focus of giving: General charitable purposes, children, young people, community/social welfare.

Charitable donations

Cash UK (latest available):	2013	£78,000
	2012	£46,000
	2011	£20,700
	2009	£11,300
	2008	£22,000
Total UK (cash and in kind):	2013	£78,000
Cash worldwide:	2013	£78,000
Total worldwide (cash and in kind):	2013	£78,000

Community involvement

There is very little information on charitable giving within the communities in which the group operates or society in general.

Corporate giving

In 2013 the group gave a total cash donation of £78,000 which has been distributed amongst UK-registered charities including: Alzheimer's Society, British Heart Foundation, Cancer Research UK, Centrepoint, Groundwork, Help for Heroes, NSPCC, Prince's Trust, RSPB and Shelter and Woodland Trust.

Employee-led support

Employees involve themselves in local charitable projects.

Corporate social responsibility

CSR committee: The chief executive is responsible for this policy and reports to the board and external stakeholders on performance in relation to all corporate responsibility matters. There is a Corporate Responsibility Group which includes senior employees who are responsible for the development and review of this policy. They in turn delegate to managers within each of the divisions who are responsible for implementation.

CSR information: The group's vision statement taken from its website is:

> Through sustainable building we aim to create new communities and life-supporting environments for people now and in the future. Using our skills, and in consultation with our partners, we aim to enhance the environment in which we are working and secure the advantages that this offers to the Bellway Group, its shareholders, employees and customers.

All policies are available on the Bellway website www.bellway.co.uk and are reviewed annually.

CSR report: The group states that it is committed to reporting annually on its 'approach' to corporate responsibility and has established key performance indicators.

There is very little information on charitable giving within the communities in which the group operates or society in general and the group's community initiatives focus mainly on sustainability.

Exclusions

No support is given for advertising in charity brochures, appeals from individuals, animal welfare, fundraising events, overseas projects, political appeals, or religious appeals.

Applications

In writing to the correspondent.

Berkeley Group plc

Building/construction, property

Correspondent: Charmaine Young, Trustee of The Berkeley Foundation, Berkeley House, 19 Portsmouth Road, Cobham, Surrey KT11 1JG (tel: 020 7720 2600; website: www.berkeleygroup.com)

Directors: Tony Pidgley, Chair; Rob Perrins, Managing Director; Nick Simpkin, Group Finance Director; Karl Whiteman; Sean Ellis; David Howell; Greg Fry; Sir John Armitt; Glyn Barber; Adrian Li; Alison Nimmo; Veronica Wadley; Andy Myers; Diana Brightmore (women: 3; men: 11)

Year end	30/04/2014
Turnover	£1,372,600,000
Pre-tax profit	£270,700,000

Nature of business: Berkeley is a developer of residential-led, mixed-use schemes building homes and neighbourhoods in its core markets of London and the South of England.

Company registration number: 1454064

Subsidiary undertakings include: Berkeley Commercial Developments Ltd; Berkeley First Ltd; Berkeley Homes (Capital) plc; Berkeley Partnership Homes Ltd; Berkeley Homes (Carmelite) Ltd; Berkeley Ryewood Ltd; Berkeley Homes (Central London) Ltd; Berkeley Homes (Oxford and Chiltern) Ltd; St George West London Ltd; Berkeley Homes (PCL) Ltd St James (Grosvenor

Dock) Ltd; Berkeley Homes (South East London) Ltd; Berkeley Homes (Urban Renaissance) Ltd; The Tower, One St George Wharf Ltd.

Main locations: Edgbaston, Twickenham, Cobham, Potters Bar, Portsmouth

UK employees: 1,868

Total employees: 1,868

Focus of giving: General charitable purposes, environment, health, ill health, heritage, housing, homelessness, children, young people, community/ social welfare, disability.

Charity of the Year	✓
Gifts in kind	✓
Matched funding	✓
Payroll giving	✓

Charitable donations

Cash UK (latest available):	2014	£9,000,000
	2012	£800,000
	2011	£800,000
	2009	£127,599
	2008	£268,286
Total UK (cash and in kind):	2014	£9,000,000
Cash worldwide:	2014	£9,000,000
Total worldwide (cash and in kind):	2014	£9,000,000

Community involvement

The group channels its charitable and community giving through its registered charity, The Berkeley Foundation (Charity Commission no. 1152596) which was established by the Berkeley Group in March 2011. Over the past three years, it has supported young people and their families in the communities in which it operates. The group has adopted a new five-year strategic plan which will see the charity through to 2019. It includes the foundation's mission statement, vision, values, levels of investment and targets, along with milestones for the charity's future.

Through strategic partnerships, designated charities chosen by Berkeley staff and one-off grants, donations and sponsorship through a community investment fund, the foundation focuses on helping people in four key areas: developing their skills, helping them secure a job, ensuring they have access to housing advice and offering care to those with life-limiting illness, physical or mental disability or learning difficulties.

Funding for the foundation comes from a variety of sources. Group staff raise money through sponsorship, Give As You Earn and by donating their time and skills. The group matches any monies raised, as well as providing the foundation's core funding, paying the overheads and covering the cost of specific events. In 2013/14 the foundation also received direct donations from individuals and other companies who support its work.

Charities of the year/strategic partnerships are: Bexley Snap; Chyps; Crisis; Daisy's Dream; Demelza; Helen and Douglas House; Kids Company; Longridge; Mayor's Fund for London; Muscular Dystrophy; North London Hospice; No Second Night Out; QEF; Rainbow Trust; Richard House; Shelter; Spear; Street Elite; The Lord's Taverner's; Thrive; Toyhouse; Trinity Hospice; and Vauxhall City Farm.

Corporate giving

In 2013 the group donated £900,000 to its foundation. Since it was established in 2011, the Berkeley Foundation has committed £2.8 million to more than 40 charities and worthy causes according to the foundation's annual review for 2013. These range from partnerships with major national charities to small local charities chosen by staff. The money comes from two sources: staff from the Berkeley group have raised £550,000 so far from friends, family, colleagues and other companies; the rest is given to the foundation by the Berkeley group itself. We do not have a figure for in-kind giving.

See the corporate charity entry on p. 394 for more information.

In-kind support

Staff are encouraged to volunteer both for the foundation and for local charities and the group matches funds.

Matched funding: is given to encourage staff fundraising.

Employee-led support

In 2013, 66% of staff surveyed across the Berkeley Group were involved in the group's foundation directly, whether by fundraising, volunteering or payroll giving.

Payroll giving: there is a scheme in place.

Corporate social responsibility

CSR committee: The website states in its sustainability pages that the Berkeley Group has clearly defined governance structures and management processes in place.

CSR information: The group's sustainability ethic centres on the communities where it builds. The report commissioned by the group – 'Social Sustainability' – is about people's quality of life, now and in the future. It describes the extent to which a neighbourhood supports individual and collective well-being. 'Social sustainability combines design of the physical environment with a focus on how the people who live in and use a space relate to each other and function as a community. It is enhanced by development which provides the right infrastructure to support a strong social and cultural life, opportunities for people to get involved, and scope for the place and the community to evolve.'

In 2010, the group set up the Berkeley Charitable Foundation. The foundation is designed to capture, coordinate and drive forward the group's corporate social responsibility activities.

CSR report: There was no evidence of a separate CSR report; however, information regarding donations and the establishment of The Berkeley Foundation are available both on the website and in the annual report. There are also sustainability reports/ information documents on the website.

Corporate charity: The Berkeley Foundation (Charity Commission no. 1152596).

Exclusions

No support is given for political appeals.

Applications

In writing to the correspondent for an application to the foundation.

Bestway (Holdings) Ltd

Cash 'n' Carry

Correspondent: Mohhamed Younus Sheikh, Secretary to the Foundation, 2 Abbey Road, Park Royal, London NW10 7BW (tel: 020 8453 1234; fax: 020 8965 0359; email: zulfikaur.wajid-hasan@bestway.co.uk; website: www.bestway.co.uk)

Directors: Sir M. A. Pervez, Chair; Z. M. Choudrey; M. Y. Sheikh; A. K. Bhatu; A. K. Choudhary; A. M. Choudhary; R. Pervez; D. Pervez

Year end	30/06/2013
Turnover	£1,957,186,000
Pre-tax profit	£164,346,000

Nature of business: An independent food wholesale group in the UK with 63 Bestway and Batleys branches across England, Scotland and Wales.

Company registration number: 1392861

Subsidiary undertakings include: Bestway Cash and Carry Ltd; Bestway Cement Ltd; Bestway Direct Ltd; Batleys Properties Ltd; UBL Insurers Ltd.

Brands include: Bestpets; Best-One.

Main locations: Bolton, Birmingham, Oldbury, Luton, London, Liverpool, Manchester, Northampton, Newcastle-under-Lyme, Peterborough, Plymouth, Romford, Swansea, Croydon, Bristol, Cardiff, Gateshead, Exeter, Leicester, Leeds

Total employees: 5,664

Focus of giving: Education, environment, health, ill health, medical research, older people, overseas projects, poverty and social exclusion, children, young people, disability, disasters.

Charity of the Year ✓
Gifts in kind ✓
Humanitarian aid: overseas ✓
Overseas giving ✓

Charitable donations

Cash UK (latest available):	2013	£450,000
	2011	£723,000
	2009	£869,000
	2007	£680,000
	2006	£787,000
Total UK (cash and in kind):	2013	£450,000
Cash worldwide:	2013	£739,000
Total worldwide (cash and in kind):	2013	£739,000

Community involvement

The company donates 2.5% of its yearly profits to charitable causes, almost all of which is channelled through the group's charities, the Bestway Foundation (Charity Commission no. 297178) and the Bestway Foundation Pakistan. The UK registered foundation provides scholarships/grants to university students of South Asian origin, both in the UK and overseas. The foundation also relieves sickness and preserves good health, both in the UK and South Asia, by giving grants to organisations including hospitals and medical research establishments. The foundation also supports UK charities that provide relief in suffering of people with disabilities, elderly people and those in need.

In order to further enhance the grant-giving mechanism, a sister organisation was established in Pakistan in 1997 and Zameer Choudrey was appointed Chair of Bestway Foundation Pakistan.

The group's mission statement encompasses its purposes and activities around charitable giving:

> The advancement of education for public benefit in both the UK and overseas by providing assistance through promotion of local schools; provision of scholarships to university students; supporting education initiatives and endowing universities. The relief of sickness and the preservation of health for public benefit in both the UK and overseas by way of grants and endowments to existing hospitals, clinics, medical research establishments; and by establishing new health facilities. The provision of financial and material support to victims of natural disasters. To have a significant impact on poverty reduction in Pakistan through strategic investments in affordable financial and social services catering to the poor. The development of technical skills within the local communities in which we operate through structured apprenticeship and training programmes.

The Bestway Foundation regularly donates towards relief and rehabilitation works in the aftermath of natural disasters, such as the Sri Lankan Tsunami and the Gujarat earthquake. Since 1997 The Bestway Foundation has invested over £500,000 in 35 schools, in support of the Government's Specialist Schools and Academies programme. The object of the programme is to give practical support to transforming education by building and enabling a world-class network of innovative, high-performing schools and academies in partnership with business and the wider community.

Corporate giving

The group's 2014 CSR report states that each year it contributes approximately 2.5% of its profit to the foundation for various charitable activities. These are focused on the health and education sectors with preference given to local communities in which the group operates. In 2012/13 the group donated £439,000 to the foundation with a further £289,000 donated by Bestway Cement to its sister charity in Pakistan. Donations of £11,000 were made to 'other charities'.

See the corporate charity entry on p. 394 for more information.

In-kind support

The Bestway Group has been associated with GroceryAid, formerly known as Caravan, since 1987, donating in excess of £80,000 to the initiative over the years. In March 2010 Bestway Group Chief Executive, Zameer Choudary became a trustee of the charity.

In November 2013, Bestway hosted a special lunch to boost awareness of GroceryAid's 24/7 freephone welfare helpline.

Commercially led support

Sponsorship

Royal Ascot Charity Race Day
Bestway has been staging this annual charity event for 17 years – each year selecting a charity to which the proceeds are donated. To date the event has raised more than £1 million for a wide variety of worthy causes, including: Barnardo's, Crimestoppers, Great Ormond Street Hospital Charity, Imran Khan Cancer Appeal, National Hospital Development Fund, President of Pakistan Earthquake Relief Fund, Save the Children and Sports Aid.

Charity of the Year

In 2014, this event raised £60,000 for the Royal Marsden Hospital Charity.

Corporate social responsibility

CSR committee: The board appears to be responsible for CSR policies and initiatives. The trustees are responsible for the activities of the group's foundations.

CSR information: The following is taken from the CSR report for 2014:

> We are determined to contribute to the communities in which we operate, and we aim to build long-term relationships with local community and interest groups. We are equally committed to our policy of reducing our carbon footprint and promoting sustainability. In summary, our CSR policies reflect senior management's overall commitment to high standards of integrity and ethical conduct.

We were unable to determine the ratio of women to men on the board.

CSR report: An annual CSR report is published on the group's website.

Corporate charity: The Bestway Foundation (Charity Commission no. 297178).

Applications

In writing to the correspondent, enclosing an sae.

Betfair Group Ltd

Gaming

Correspondent: Corporate Social Responsibility Team, Waterfront, Hammersmith Embankment, Chancellors Road (access on Winslow Road), London W6 9HP (tel: 020 8834 8000; email: corporate@betfair.com; website: corporate.betfair.com)

Directors: Gerald Corbett, Chair; Breon Corcoran, Chief Executive Officer; Alex Garsh, Chief Financial Officer; Zillah Byng-Maddick; Ian Dyson; Leo Quinn; Peter Rigby; Peter Jackson (women: 1; men: 7)

Year end	30/04/2014
Turnover	£393,600,000
Pre-tax profit	£61,100,000

Nature of business: The provision of betting services and online gaming products.

Company registration number: 6489716

Subsidiary undertakings include: Betfair Casino Ltd; Betfair International plc; London Multi Asset Exchange (Holdings) Ltd; The Sporting Exchange Ltd; Winslow Four.

Main locations: Hammersmith, Stevenage

Total employees: 1,739

Focus of giving: Animal welfare, sport, recreation, children, young people.

Cash donations undeclared ✓
Gifts in kind ✓
Payroll giving ✓

Charitable donations

Cash UK (latest available):	2014	£380,000
	2011	£560,000
	2009	£250,000
	2008	£331,000
	2007	£290,000
Total UK (cash and in kind):	2014	£380,000
Cash worldwide:	2014	£380,000
Total worldwide (cash and in kind):	2014	£380,000

Community involvement

Each office around the world makes a CR investment with employees actively engaged in deciding what organisations and charities Betfair should support at each location. For example, at Betfair's Hammersmith HQ, staff volunteered to tidy up and maintain the grounds at Maggie's Cancer Centre based at Charing Cross and the company also made a financial donation.

The company's community investment programme encourages employees to get actively engaged with the communities where they live and work, and provides investment in grass-roots sport.

Cash 4 Clubs is Betfair's own programme which enables community sports clubs to apply for a grant to improve facilities, buy new equipment, improve coaching and nurture young talent. Grants of up to £1,000 are available. More details can be found at www.cash-4-clubs.com.

Corporate giving

In 2013/14 the company did not declare its cash donations to charity. We have taken an average figure based on the three totals we have available for previous years and estimate this year's figure to be around £380,000. There were no costings given for in-kind giving and we have been unable to estimate this figure.

In-kind support

Staff are encouraged to volunteer with local charities/organisations.

Employee-led support

Betfair supports community working offering every employee up to two days' paid leave per year for volunteer work.

Give As You Earn There is a scheme in operation giving employees the opportunity to make charitable donations directly from their salary through payroll.

Commercially led support

Funding the research, education and treatment of problem gambling. In the UK Betfair makes annual voluntary contributions to the Responsible Gambling Trust. Major operators, like Betfair, donate on the understanding that a minimum target, currently set at £6 million, will be reached with other operators, each year.

Corporate social responsibility

CSR committee: The 2014 annual report states that Gerald Corbett was appointed as the chair of the Corporate Responsibility Committee on 31 March 2014. The other committee members include the group operations director, the HR director, the company secretary and the group financial controller. The committee meets four times during the year and was established to define, support and monitor the execution of Betfair's corporate responsibility strategy.

CSR information: The following statement is taken from the CSR pages in the 2013/14 annual report:

> ***Engagement with local communities and charities***
> Betfair believes in being a good corporate citizen. We seek to support and be part of the local community wherever we have an office. We continue to innovate within key industry areas including integrity and consumer protection.

CSR report: There is a separate section in the company's annual report for 2013/14 detailing CSR initiatives and activities.

Applications

In writing to the correspondent or to your local Betfair operator.

BHP Billiton

Mining

Correspondent: (see 'Applications'), Neathouse Place, London SW1V 1BH (tel: 020 7802 4000; fax: 020 7802 4111; website: www.bhpbilliton.com)

Directors: Carlos Cordeiro; Jacques Nasser, Chair; Keith Rumble; Dr John Schubert; Sir John Buchanan; Wayne Murdy; Malcolm Broomhead; Carolyn Hewson; Lindsay Maxsted; Baroness Shriti Vadera; Andrew Mackenzie; Malcolm Brinded; Pat Davies (women: 2; men: 11)

Year end	30/06/2014
Turnover	£42,111,281,420
Pre-tax profit	£13,933,078,202

Nature of business: The principal activities of the group are the discovery, acquisition, development and marketing of natural resources. The website states: 'Our strategy is to own and operate large, long-life, low-cost, expandable, upstream assets diversified by commodity, geography and market.'

Company registration number: 3196209

Subsidiary undertakings include: BHP Billiton Aluminium Australia Pty Ltd; BHP Billiton Aluminium (RAA) Pty Ltd; BHP Billiton Aluminium (Worsley) Pty Ltd; BHP Billiton Canada Inc.; BHP Billiton Direct Reduced Iron Pty Ltd; BHP Billiton Energy Coal South Africa Proprietary Ltd.

Main locations: London

Total employees: 123,803

Focus of giving: Education, environment, overseas projects, community/social welfare, disasters.

Membership: BITC

FTSE 100	✓
Gifts in kind	✓
Humanitarian aid: overseas	✓
Matched funding	✓
Overseas giving	✓
Payroll giving	✓

Charitable donations

Cash UK (latest available):	2013	£0
	2011	£19,290,000
	2009	£39,000,000
	2008	£723,000
	2007	£375,000
Cash worldwide:	2014	£62,600,000
Total worldwide (cash and in kind):	2014	£151,400,000

Community involvement

This group gives generously worldwide in areas where it has operational sites. It no longer has this in the UK, since the Liverpool Bay operation was divested in 2014, but the registered office is still in London and in-kind giving may be available from there. It is thought that the UK charity will continue for at least the next five years. It is not clear if UK charities can still benefit from grants during that time but even if that were the case, most grant-giving has in the past been overseas.

The origins of BHP Billiton go back to the mid-19th century when the two original mining companies, Broken Hill Proprietary and Billiton, were established in Australia and Indonesia respectively. Following the merger of these companies in 2001, BHP Billiton is now 'one of the world's largest diversified resources companies and producers of major commodities, including aluminium, coal, copper, iron ore, manganese, nickel, silver and uranium' and has 'substantial interests in oil and gas. The company is registered in the UK and headquartered in London, although the BHP Billiton Group is based in Melbourne, Australia.

BHP Billiton Sustainable Communities (Charity Commission no. 1131006) and the BHP Billiton Foundation are independent charities established by BHP Billiton to contribute to improving the quality of life of people living in regions and countries where BHP Billiton has a business interest.

The website states: 'The corporate charities provide grants to organisations to deliver long-term social projects that have a footprint that extends beyond the operations of our business.'

The charities do not accept unsolicited proposals, but work proactively to identify significant social issues in the region of interest, and then work collaboratively with non-government organisations that have a strong track record in the issue, to design an appropriate project. 'In assessing potential partner organisations, important criteria include the capacity to effectively deliver a large scale project, compliance with due diligence and anti-corruption criteria and experience operating in the country and region interest.'

The corporate charities aim to complement the local community development work undertaken by BHP Billiton's businesses. When developing projects, care is taken not to duplicate or displace existing agencies and services, but rather to strengthen and support local capacity development.

Projects are generally selected from three broad areas – health, education and governance.

In the UK, the company's support for these communities has been notionally channelled through BHP Billiton Sustainable Communities, although this charity supports projects and causes worldwide; during 2012/13 there were no discernible grants made to organisations or projects in the UK. The charity's latest accounts, for the financial year 2012/13, show that it received an income of £456,000 from investments. This income is derived from significant donations made by the company to the charity in previous years (£41.8 million in 2011/12), although no such donation was made in 2012/13. During the latest financial year the charity spent around £10.7 million on charitable activities, all of which was given to projects and organisations outside the UK which have a connection to the company's areas of operation and expertise. These included: PATH Windows of Opportunity project (£1.5 million); and Engineers Without Boarders (£246,500). The charity also spent around £5 million on the company's Matched Giving Program, which 'double matches' employees' financial contributions to charity around the world. No geographical breakdown of these contributions is given so it is not possible to determine whether any of this funding made its way to organisations in the UK.

During 2013, BHP Billiton undertook a review of the long-term sustainability of the future funding for its corporate UK charity, BHP Billiton Sustainable Communities. It was concluded that the United Kingdom would be unable to fund the charity in the longer term (the objects of the charity would appear to preclude it as the charity can only give to communities around operational sites). BHP Billiton United States activities were considered to be better prospects for ongoing funding of a charitable entity and as such, the BHP Billiton Foundation was incorporated as a not-for-profit corporation in the state of Texas on the 30 of May 2013. A BHP Billiton entity in the United States deposited $106 million to the foundation during the year ended 30 June 2013 and considered the foundation to be a more sustainable project. The trustees will continue to identify and consider new opportunities for funding in the short term; however they will also review the future of the charity in light of the establishment of the foundation.

Corporate giving

The company gives annually 1% of pre-tax profits invested in community programmes, including cash, in-kind support and administration, calculated on the average of the previous three years' pre-tax profit. In 2014 community investment totalled US$241.7 million (£151.4 million) invested in community programmes and comprising US$141.7 million (£88.8 million) of cash, in-kind support and administrative costs and a US$100 million (£62.6 million) contribution to the BHP Billiton Foundation (A charity based in the US).

The annual report states:

> The cash component of the 2014 community investment is an aggregate of the total funds invested across the group and includes:
>
> - Direct voluntary funding provided as one-off donations and to support medium to longer-term community projects
> - Contributions made at the local operational level to charitable foundations (excluding the BHP Billiton Foundation and the BHP Billiton Sustainable Communities)
> - Funds used to deliver the Enterprise Development and Socio-economic Development components of our Broad-Based Black Economic Empowerment programs in South Africa
>
> Excluding the contribution to the BHP Billiton Foundation, 46 per cent of the cash component of our expenditure was invested in local communities, 44 per cent was invested regionally, and the remaining 10 per cent was invested in national or international programs in countries where we operate. This has been added to the figure we give for worldwide cash contributions.

See the corporate charity entry on p. 394 for more information.

In-kind support

International relief

The company supports the work of international aid agencies, such as the Red Cross, has helped deliver emergency food, shelter, water, security and medical aid to people in need and to assist in the recovery process following natural disasters. It also contributes to the long-term recovery of communities devastated by natural disasters. This includes contributing to the rebuilding of essential health, education, transport and public infrastructure.

Employees

Employees have also generously contributed to relief efforts in the aftermath of natural disasters through donations and volunteering. Where an event has occurred in a region where the group operates, they have volunteered their help including supplying equipment to clear debris, providing transport and logistics expertise, and volunteering in clean-up activities. All donations and volunteering hours are matched through the BHP Billiton matched giving programme.

Employees are also encouraged to support their local communities and the group in turn provides support for them. See matched giving in 'Employee-led support' section.

Employee-led support

Matched giving

BHP Billiton has established a matched giving programme through which the company will match the community contributions made by employees. Every employee (including full- and part-time) is entitled each year to match their contributions to not-for-profit organisations that benefit the community. These contributions can be employee volunteering, fundraising or cash donations (including payroll donations). In 2014, more than 8,700 of employees worldwide participated in the scheme volunteering approximately 66,500 hours of their personal time to community activities. Employee contributions benefited more than 1,894 not-for-profit organisations.

Give As You Earn

There is a system in place.

Corporate social responsibility

CSR committee: There is a Forum on Corporate Responsibility which meets regularly.

CSR information: According to the website, sustainability for the group is: 'Putting health and safety first, being environmentally responsible and supporting our communities.'

CSR report: There is a very detailed and informative annual Sustainability Report – 'Resourcing the Future.'

Corporate charity: BHP Billiton Sustainable Communities (Charity Commission no. 1131066).

Applications

Applications to the registered charity BHP Billiton Sustainable Communities (Charity Commission no. 1131066) should be made in writing to the correspondent after checking the website for information regarding grants from the charity.

Write to: BHP Billiton Sustainable Communities, 1 Neathouse Place,

Westminster, London SW1V 1BH; tel: 020 7802 4000; email: hsec@bhpbilliton.com.

Birmingham International Airport Ltd

Airport operators

Correspondent: The Trust Fund Administrator, Diamond House, Birmingham Airport, Birmingham B26 3QJ (tel: 01217 677448/01217 677448; fax: 01217 677065; email: community@birmirminghamairport.co.uk; website: www.bhx.co.uk)

Directors: T. Ali; H. Banger; H. Bills; M. Bird; A. Bore; D. Calaca; P. Dransfield; J. McNicholas; M. Morsillo; R. Piper; G. Richards; D. Stanton; C. Thomazi; P. Tilsley; M. Toms

Year end	31/03/2014
Turnover	£113,754,000
Pre-tax profit	£18,774,000

Nature of business: The principal activity is the operation and management of Birmingham International Airport and the provision of associated facilities and services.

Company registration number: 3312673

Subsidiary undertakings include: Euro-Hub (Birmingham) Ltd; First Castle Developments Ltd; BHX Fire and Rescue Ltd.

Main locations: Birmingham

UK employees: 586

Total employees: 586

Focus of giving: General charitable purposes, environment, heritage, older people, sport, recreation, community/social welfare.

Charity of the Year	✓
Gifts in kind	✓

Charitable donations

Cash UK (latest available):	2014	£75,000
	2012	£75,000
	2011	£50,000
	2008	£52,000
	2007	£52,000
Total UK (cash and in kind):	2014	£75,000
Cash worldwide:	2014	£75,000
Total worldwide (cash and in kind):	2014	£75,000

Community involvement

The company's main charitable giving is channelled through **The Birmingham International Airport Community Trust Fund** (Charity Commission no. 1071176).

The company set up this trust to fund a wide range of community-based projects which will benefit the community and environment around Birmingham Airport.

Corporate giving

Each year the company donates £75,000 to its corporate charity and this is topped up by any penalties imposed on airlines that breach the strict Night Flying Policy. In 2013/14 the total donation was £75,250.

See the corporate charity entry on p. 395 for more information.

Employee-led support

The airport's nominated charity is Acorns Children's Hospice Trust. Acorns provides care and support for children and young people who have life-limiting or life-threatening conditions. They support children and families, including those who are bereaved. Their specialist nursing and support services provide a vital lifeline for these families who would face a much tougher challenge coping alone. Since the partnership with Acorns began, staff have raised over £22,500.

On the last Friday of each month, non-uniformed staff take advantage of 'Dress Down Friday' where, for a small donation, they are able to wear casual clothes to work. The proceeds are donated to a different local charity each month, nominated by the staff themselves.

Corporate social responsibility

CSR committee: There was no evidence of a separate CSR committee.

CSR information: Some information was available from the company's website.

We were unable to determine the ratio of women to men on the board.

CSR report: There was no evidence of a separate CSR report; however information was available from the company's website.

Corporate charity: Birmingham International Airport Community Trust (Charity Commission no. 1071176).

Applications

You can find out if your community project may be eligible for an award from the company's foundation by downloading the Community Trust Fund Guidelines on the company's website.

To apply, you should contact the trust fund administrator on 01217 677448, or at community@birminghamairport.co.uk to receive an application form. This allows the foundation to discuss with you whether or not your proposal meets the trust fund criteria and how to maximise your chances of making a successful application. The trustees meet twice a year in April and October and there are deadlines in February and August respectively for the receipt of completed applications. Late applications cannot be considered.

Biwater Holdings Ltd

Engineering, waste management, water

Correspondent: J. S. Lamb, Company Secretary, Biwater House, Station Approach, Dorking RH4 1TZ (tel: 01306 740740; fax: 01306 885233; website: www.biwater.com)

Directors: A. E. White, Chair; C. A. White; D. F. W. White; J. J. Jones

Year end	31/03/2013
Turnover	£62,900,000
Pre-tax profit	£3,100,000

Nature of business: Principal activities: contracting, manufacturing and the provision of services to the water industry worldwide.

Company registration number: 929686

Subsidiary undertakings include: BWS Finance Ltd; Bournemouth and West Hampshire Water plc; Cascal Services Ltd; and Biwater Capital plc.

Main locations: Dorking, Heywood, Bournemouth

UK employees: 53

Total employees: 817

Focus of giving: Education, health, ill health, community/social welfare.

Charitable donations

Cash UK (latest available):	2013	£380
	2012	£650
	2011	£25,600
	2008	£79,000
	2007	£55,000
Total UK (cash and in kind):	2013	£380
Cash worldwide:	2013	£2,700
Total worldwide (cash and in kind):	2013	£2,700

Community involvement

Previous research suggested that the company supports mainly Dorking charities.

Corporate giving

In 2012/13 the company and its subsidiary undertakings made donations for charitable purposes of just £2,700 of which £380 was in the UK and £2,360 abroad mainly for education, community support and medical purposes. Charitable cash giving both at home and overseas has taken a drastic cut over the last two years, (although at least the company is declaring a figure). In 2008 the company gave £79,000 in the UK.

Corporate social responsibility

CSR committee: There is no dedicated CSR committee.

CSR information: Taken from the company's website:

> At Biwater we take our corporate and social responsibilities very seriously. This code is a fundamental element of our business practice. With it, we are fully engaged with our employees, our customers, our suppliers, and investors and government agencies with whom we inter relate both in the UK and abroad. We employ this code in the workplaces where Biwater is operating, in protecting the environment around us, and in supporting the communities in which we live and work.
>
> [In communities with:]
> - Interaction with local populations, respecting established customs and priorities
> - Sponsorship and charitable support for communal activity
> - Social and sports commitments to the wider society.

It is not clear from the annual report and accounts what the ratio of women to men is on the board.

CSR report: There is no CSR report published.

Applications

In writing to the correspondent.

BlackRock Investment Management (UK) Ltd

Financial services

Correspondent: Miss Agnieszka Caban, Charity Correspondent, Blackrock (UK) Charitable Trust, 12 Throgmorton Avenue LondonEC2N 2DL (tel: 020 7743 3000; fax: 020 7743 1000; website: www.blackrock.co.uk/index.htm)

Directors: J. Charrington, Chair; J. DesMarais; E. Fishwick; N. Hall; M. Naylor; C. Prideaux; B. Sklar; C. Thomson; R. Webb; T. Webb

Year end	31/12/2013
Turnover	£873,550,000
Pre-tax profit	£198,607,000

Nature of business: BlackRock is a provider of global investment management, risk management and advisory services to institutional and retail clients around the world.

Company registration number: 2020394

Main locations: London

Total employees: 2,331

Focus of giving: General charitable purposes, education, health, ill health, sport, recreation, children, young people, community/social welfare.

Charitable donations

Cash UK (latest available):	2013	£1,200
	2012	£2,000
	2011	£34,000
	2010	£118,000
	2009	£146,500
Total UK (cash and in kind):	2013	£1,200
Cash worldwide:	2013	£1,200
Total worldwide (cash and in kind):	2013	£1,200

Community involvement

The BlackRock (UK) Charitable Trust (Charity Commission no. 1065447)

The company is wholly owned subsidiary of BlackRock Group Ltd (formerly Merrill Lynch Investment Managers Ltd) and directs its community support through the BlackRock (UK) Charitable Trust.

It would seem that currently BlackRock Investment Management (UK) Ltd is not making UK charitable donations and although it has a corporate charity, the income for this has been decreasing over the last five years and is now less than £2,000 per annum. Attempts to speak to the correspondent of the trust were unsuccessful. We have retained the entry while the trust remains active and on the Central Register of Charities hoping that donations might increase to their previous levels.

Corporate giving

In 2013 the company donated £1,200 to its associated charitable trust. Previous beneficiaries have included: The Prostate Cancer Charity (£31,000); BlackRock Community Action Team (£26,000); The Burnaby Blue Foundation and Ovarian Cancer Action (£7,000 each).

See the corporate charity entry on p. 395 for more information.

Corporate social responsibility

CSR information: There was no evidence of any CSR activity or publications for this company. The firm donates to its charitable trust which then distributes the money accordingly.

We were unable to determine the ratio of women to men on the board.

Corporate charity: The BlackRock (UK) Charitable Trust (Charity Commission no. 1065447).

Applications

The trustees invite staff, clients and business associates of the firm to submit applications on behalf of a registered charity of their choice.

Bloomsbury Publishing plc

Media

Correspondent: Michael Daykin, Company Secretary, 36 Soho Square, London W1D 3QY (tel: 020 7494 2111; fax: 020 7434 0151; email: csm@bloomsbury.com; website: www.bloomsbury.com)

Directors: Nigel Newton, Chief Executive; Wendy Pallot, Finance Director; Richard Charkin; Ian Cormack; Jill Jones; Sir Anthony Salz; Stephen Page (women: 2; men: 5)

Year end	28/02/2014
Turnover	£109,496,000
Pre-tax profit	£9,479,000

Nature of business: Bloomsbury Publishing plc is an independent worldwide publisher listed on the London stock exchange with publishing offices in London, New York and Sydney.

Company registration number: 1984336

Subsidiary undertakings include: A.& C. Black plc; Bloomsbury Publishing Inc.; Featherstone Education Ltd; Christopher Helm (Publishers) Ltd; Herbert Press Ltd; Reed's Almanac Ltd; John Wisden (Holdings) Ltd; John Wisden and Co. Limited.

Main locations: London

Total employees: 524

Focus of giving: General charitable purposes, education, housing, homelessness, overseas projects, children, young people.

Gifts in kind	✓
Market-led giving	✓
Overseas giving	✓

Charitable donations

Cash UK (latest available):	2014	£6,200
	2013	£0
	2011	£10,000
	2009	£100
	2008	£3,500
Total UK (cash and in kind):	2014	£6,200
Cash worldwide:	2014	£6,200
Total worldwide (cash and in kind):	2014	£6,200

Community involvement

Bloomsbury states in its annual report that it 'actively support numerous organisations worldwide including schools, universities, libraries and other good causes and charities'. A small number of 'targeted minor cash donations' are made each year to not-for-profit organisations that support literature, literacy and education.

Corporate giving

In 2013/14 the company declared cash donations of £6,200 of which £5,000 was awarded to The Charleston Trust. In

2013 the company donated no cash for charities. Previous beneficiary organisations have included donations to BookAid International, the Churchill Centre and the Independent Publishers Guild.

In-kind support

The UK, US and Australia offices donate, or provide at a nominal cost, a substantial quantity of books each year which includes donations of mainstream titles to schools and libraries. Book donations have been made to good causes such as Barnardo's, Oxfam, Red Cross and smaller organisations local to the Bloomsbury office. The Bloomsbury Institute (the events function of Bloomsbury) has organised charitable fundraising events such as for Book Aid and for Womankind to celebrate International Women's Day.

Employee-led support

Staff volunteer in their own time for good causes sometimes, either directly or indirectly assisted by the business. For example: employees, both privately and through a Bloomsbury co-ordinator, are involved in formal volunteer reading schemes and regularly attend state schools and organise reading groups in libraries. These provide supervised reading support to young readers who are often from disadvantaged backgrounds where their opportunities to develop reading skills may be hindered. In one Bloomsbury office the employees take turns to volunteer each week at a local charity for homeless people.

Commercially led support

In 2013/14 the company invited a student of fashion studies to review its existing measures as an academic visual arts publisher and to suggest improvements to cater for students with visual or learning disabilities, especially for those with dyslexia or dyspraxia, for Bloomsbury's books and online resources.

Sponsorship: Bloomsbury is a sponsor and partner of World Book Day which was established by UNESCO to promote reading amongst children and adults.

Corporate social responsibility

CSR committee: There was no evidence of a separate CSR Committee.

CSR report: There was no evidence of a separate CSR report and information on community contributions is limited in the annual report.

Exclusions

No support is given for individuals, or for religious or political appeals.

Applications

In writing to the correspondent.

BMW UK Ltd

Motors and accessories

Correspondent: G. Woolley, Company Secretary, Ellesfield Avenue, Bracknell, Berkshire RG12 8TA (tel: 01344 426565; fax: 01344 480203; website: www.bmw.co.uk)

Directors: T. Abbott; T. Ferreira; N. Peter

Year end	31/12/2013
Turnover	£4,164,873,000
Pre-tax profit	£179,186,000

Nature of business: The principal activity is the importation, storage and distribution of BMW products in the UK.

Company registration number: 1378137

Subsidiary undertakings include: BMW (P&A) Ltd; Park Lane Ltd; BMW Drivers Club Ltd; BMW Car Club Ltd; BMW (GB) Ltd.

Main locations: Birmingham, Swindon, Hook, Thorne, Coleshill, Oxford, Goodwood, Bracknell

Focus of giving: Education, health, ill health, children, young people, community/social welfare.

Charitable donations

Cash UK (latest available):	2013	£189,000
	2012	£131,000
	2010	£121,000
	2009	£25,000
	2006	£25,000
Total UK (cash and in kind):	2013	£189,000
Cash worldwide:	2013	£189,000
Total worldwide (cash and in kind):	2013	£189,000

Community involvement

This company gives to charities in its operating areas and the giving is in cash which allows the recipient charities to decide where it is best spent.

Corporate giving

During the year the company made charitable donations of £189,000. Donations over £2,000 were as follows: BEN – Motor and Allied Trades Benevolent Fund (£137,000); and Cancer Research UK (£40,000).

Corporate social responsibility

CSR committee: There was no evidence of a separate CSR Committee.

CSR information: The company's CSR focuses mainly on environmental issues such as climate change and greenhouse gas emissions. The Managing Director was appointed President of The Society of Motor Manufacturers and Traders (SMMT). This exists to support and promote the interests of the UK automotive industry at home and abroad. The company quotes the Managing Director's presence on a number of SMMT's working groups as part of its CSR. The company did usefully declare its UK charitable cash contributions.

We were unable to determine the ratio of women to men on the board.

CSR report: There was no evidence of a current CSR report.

Exclusions

No response to circular appeals.

Applications

Contact your local dealership for information.

The Body Shop International plc

Retail – miscellaneous

Correspondent: Lisa Jackson, Chief Executive – The Body Shop Foundation, Watersmead, Littlehampton, West Sussex BN17 6LS (tel: 01903 844039 (foundation) or 0800 092 9090; email: foundationenquiries@thebodyshop.com; website: www.thebodyshopfoundation.org)

Directors: Jeremy Schwartz, Chief Executive Officer; Christian Mulliez; Geoff Skingsley (women: 0; men: 3)

Year end	28/12/2013
Turnover	£435,700,000
Pre-tax profit	£57,000,000

Nature of business: The Body Shop is a multi-local, values-led, global retailer of personal care products sold through its own shops and franchised outlets.

The Body Shop is a wholly owned subsidiary of the L'Oréal SA Group which de-listed from the London Stock Exchange on 12 July 2006. The website states: 'It retains its unique identity and values and continues to be based in the United Kingdom. It operates independently within the L'Oréal Group and is led by the current management team of The Body Shop reporting directly to the CEO of L'Oréal.'

Company registration number: 1284170

Subsidiary undertakings include: Body Store SA; Dibel SA; Skin and Hair Preparations Inc.; The Body Shop Queenslie Ltd; The Body Shop Svenska AV; and The Body Shop Worldwide Ltd. A full list of subsidiary undertakings can be obtained from Companies House.

Total employees: 2,997

Focus of giving: Human rights, education, environment, animal welfare, heritage, unpopular causes, overseas projects, women's issues, community/social welfare.

Membership: BITC

Cash donations undeclared ✓
Gifts in kind ✓
Humanitarian aid: overseas ✓

Humanitarian aid: UK ✓
Overseas giving ✓

Charitable donations

Cash UK (latest available):	2013	£664,000
	2011	£700,000
	2009	£1,900,000
	2008	£1,500,000
	2007	£1,700,000
Total UK (cash and in kind):	2013	£684,000
Cash worldwide:	2013	£1,400,000
Total worldwide (cash and in kind):	2013	£1,400,000

Community involvement

Founder of The Body Shop, Dame Anita Roddick, stated: 'The business of business should not just be about money, it should be about responsibility. It should be about public good, not private greed.'

The majority of the company's corporate donations are made through its charitable arm – the corporate foundation.

The Body Shop Foundation (Charity Commission no. 802757)

The foundation is funded by annual donations from the company, sale of special range products and through various fundraising initiatives. The foundation's approach to funding is to actively seek out groups working towards social and environmental change, particularly charities and projects focusing on unconventional issues who might not otherwise attract funding. The Values Report states that since its inception in 1989 the foundation has awarded more than £21 million around the world. It is further specified that 'every year the board of trustees agree the foundation's funding remit and groups who work within the specific remits are invited to apply'. The foundation's website states:

> Although we'd love to fund everyone's wonderful projects, unfortunately we can't. To this end, and to ensure a wide global reach, we rely on staff from markets of The Body Shop making recommendations and highlighting community projects local to them.

The foundation mainly supports the areas of: human and civil rights, and environmental and animal protection.

Global funding focus for 2014 was: 'prevent and campaign against the commercial exploitation of animals; address issues around land and marine pollution; and realise every child's basic right to a childhood'.

UK and US Head Office Community Grants Programme

The programme forms part of the foundation's giving and in the UK distributes grants to projects in London and West Sussex area, chosen by the employees through an email voting system.

Charity partnership

In 2013 the company partnered with Teenage Cancer Trust and raised funds through various initiatives to help young people. The relationship extends beyond fundraising with the company providing a range of activities for young people with cancer, such as beauty care workshops in the charity's specialist cancer units and work experience in the stores.

Fair Trade

In 2013, the Body Shop was voted International Responsible Business of the Year by Business in the Community for its pioneering Community Fair Trade programme, launched in 1987, which 'supports several hundred thousand people in some twenty countries through the direct sourcing of the finest ingredients from local communities'.

Corporate giving

We could not identify the amount given in charitable contributions in 2012/13 as the company stopped declaring charitable and community contributions in the annual report and accounts. Based on the figures from the three previous years known to us, we estimate that total charitable contributions reached about £1.4 million. The foundation's annual report for 2012/13 notes that a total of £664,000 of its income came from corporate donors, which we attribute to the company. Further £19,500 was donated through in-kind support. The information for 2013/14 notes the foundation receiving £748,000 from corporate donors and £19,500 worth of in-kind support. We take the grant to the foundation to represent the company's cash contributions in the UK.

Beneficiaries include: The Body Shop Foundation (£664,000).

See the corporate charity entry on p. 395 for more information.

In-kind support

Fundraising initiatives, including charity shops and product sales, are carried out by the company's foundation and form part of its income. The company employees donate their time and efforts for good causes.

The foundation's annual report and accounts for 2013/14 note that 'The Body Shop not only gives donated product, it also offers other 'in kind' services – including office space, warehouse facilities, furniture, telephone costs, postage costs, legal advice, insurance and IT support.' The value of in-kind support to the foundation was at £19,500 during the year.

Employee-led support

Employees are encouraged to take an active role in their local communities. Our research indicates that at the UK global head office employees are entitled to six days of volunteer time, supporting local projects and causes as individuals and as business teams. The Values Report notes that in 2012/13 the foundation received a total of 3,470 hours of volunteering by company and external volunteers.

Commercially led support

Campaigning

The Body Shop has a long history of campaigning including issues fundamental to its values, such as being actively against animal testing and sponsoring posters for Greenpeace. Recently the company campaigned to stop sex trafficking of children and young people.

In-store fundraising

The company has fundraising initiatives whereby during a promotional period all customers can vote for their favourite charity. The group with the most votes wins the majority of the profits from the in-store product (currently Dragon Fruit Lip Butter), while the groups with the second and third votes receive a sliding scale of profits.

Corporate social responsibility

CSR committee: There were no details found.

CSR information: There is no specific CSR information given for the company. However, the website gives full details of the company's core values, campaigns, ethics and fair trading initiatives.

The annual Values Report for 2014 states the following:

> At The Body Shop our five core values have guided us for the past three decades; the principles of Activate Self Esteem, Against Animal Testing, Support Community Fair Trade, Defend Human Rights and Protect The Planet, remain the foundations which guide our business across the world.

CSR report: There is an annual Values Report published available from the company's website.

Corporate charity: The Body Shop Foundation (Charity Commission no. 802757).

Exclusions

Our research indicates that support is not given to:

- Sponsor individuals
- Fund sporting activities or the arts
- Sponsor or support fundraising events, receptions or conferences

Donations are not made to promote religious causes or political campaign causes, although the foundation may work with religious or political organisations on partnership projects and fundraise with organisations that have a political or religious foundation for causes that support its values and principles.

No donations can be made to, nor funds raised for organisations linked to animal testing, organisations advocating violence or discrimination or in other ways promoting behaviour not in keeping with the foundation's principles.

Applications

Our research suggests that The Body Shop International and The Body Shop Foundation no longer accept unsolicited applications for funding. However, in exceptional circumstances, the company may respond to a humanitarian emergency and make a special donation to a public appeal, but such a donation must have the approval of the CEO.

Bodycote plc

Engineering

Correspondent: Ute Ball, Company Secretary, Springwood Court, Springwood Close, Tytherington Business Park, Macclesfield, Cheshire SK10 2XF (tel: 01625 505300; fax: 01625 505313; email: info@bodycote.com; website: www.bodycote.com)

Directors: Alan Thomson, Chair; Stephen Harris, Chief Executive; David Landless, Finance Director; Eva Lindqvist; John Biles; Raj Rajagopal; Ute Ball (women: 2; men: 5)

Year end	31/12/2013
Turnover	£619,600,000
Pre-tax profit	£98,400,000

Nature of business: Global provider of subcontract thermal processing services

Company registration number: 519057

Subsidiary undertakings include: Bodycote (Ningbo) Heat Treatment Co. Limited; Bodycote Singapore Pte Ltd; Bodycote Surface Technology Ltd.

Total employees: 5,808

Focus of giving: General charitable purposes.

Cash donations undeclared ✓
Staff fundraising only ✓

Charitable donations

Cash UK (latest available):	2013	£5,000
	2011	£9,000
	2010	£3,000
	2009	£3,000
	2008	£11,000
Total UK (cash and in kind):	2013	£5,000
Cash worldwide:	2013	£5,000
Total worldwide (cash and in kind):	2013	£5,000

Community involvement

There is no information in the 2013 annual report and accounts regarding this group's charitable contribution to society except for its staff's endeavours.

Corporate giving

In 2013 this company/group did not declare any charitable donations. We have taken an average of the past three years' donations and estimated the group's cash donation in the UK to be around £5,000. However, it is not clear if the group gave at all.

Employee-led support

Taken from the website: 'Many of Bodycote's facilities around the world contribute to local communities through charitable acts. Much of this charitable activity is organised by the company's staff through personal endeavour or as teams.'

Corporate social responsibility

CSR committee: We could not find evidence of a separate CSR committee.

CSR information: The group has policies in place for sustainability and these focus mainly on the group itself and the environment. Policies include:

- Ethical standards
- Compliance with laws
- Competition
- Conflicts of interest
- Politics
- Safety and health
- Environment

CSR report: There appeared to be no evidence of a CSR report; however, information was available from the company's website but very little about its contribution to 'society'.

Applications

In writing to the correspondent.

Boodle & Dunthorne Ltd

Retail – miscellaneous

Correspondent: N. A. Wainwright, Trustee, The Boodle & Dunthorne Charitable Trust, Boodles House, Lord Street, Liverpool L2 9SQ (tel: 01512 240580/01512 240580; website: www.boodles.co.uk)

Directors: N. A. Wainwright, Chair; F. J. Wainwright; M. J. Wainwright, Managing Director; E. A. Wainwright; J. A. Wainwright; J. B. Amos

Year end	28/02/2014
Turnover	£61,744,000
Pre-tax profit	£8,529,000

Nature of business: Designer jewellers and silversmiths.

Company registration number: 472968

UK employees: 94

Total employees: 94

Focus of giving: General charitable purposes, health, ill health, unpopular causes, overseas projects, children, young people.

Overseas giving ✓

Charitable donations

Cash UK (latest available):	2014	£345,000
	2013	£317,000
	2011	£142,300
	2009	£112,600
	2008	£184,000
Total UK (cash and in kind):	2014	£345,000
Cash worldwide:	2014	£345,000
Total worldwide (cash and in kind):	2014	£345,000

Community involvement

Charitable giving is channelled through the company's associated charity, The Boodle Charitable Foundation (Charity Commission no. 1077748) which is established for general charitable purposes and looks to benefit mainly young people. The trustees do not fundraise and the foundation's only income is derived from its investments and by donations received from Boodle & Dunthorne Ltd.

Corporate giving

In 2013/14 Boodle & Dunthorne declared in its accounts cash donations of £345,000 (2012/13: £317,000) to charities in the UK. We know that previous beneficiaries of the company's charitable foundation in 2012/13 included: Shining Faces – a UK-registered charity providing aid to a Christian orphanage in southern India (£50,000); Rainbow Trust (£14,000); Great Ormond Street Children's Charity and The Household Cavalry (£10,000 each); The Outward Bound Trust (£5,000); Emmanuel Baptist Church (£2,500); and CRY (£250).

See the corporate charity entry on p. 396 for more information.

Corporate social responsibility

CSR committee: There is no evidence of a separate CSR committee.

CSR information: Boodle & Dunthorne has a specific interest in UK-based charities, especially those that work with young people and children. We could not find any reference to a CSR policy or statement.

We were unable to determine the ratio of women to men on the board.

CSR report: There is no evidence of a separate CSR report.

Corporate charity: The Boodle & Dunthorne Charitable Trust (Charity Commission no. 1077748).

Exclusions

Not known.

Applications

In writing to the correspondent.

Booker Group plc

Cash 'n' Carry, wholesale

Correspondent: Mark Chilton, Company Secretary, Equity House, Irthlingborough Road, Wellingborough, Northamptonshire NN8 1LT (tel: 01933 371000; fax: 01933 371010; email: info@bookergroup.com; website: www.bookergroup.com)

Directors: Richard Rose, Chair; Charles Wilson, Chief Executive; Jonathan Prentis, Group Finance Director; Mark Aylwin; Guy Farrant; Bryn Satherley; Lord Bilimoria; Andrew Cripps; Stewart Gilliland; Karen Jones; Helena Andreas (women: 2; men: 9)

Year end	28/03/2014
Turnover	£4,681,600,000
Pre-tax profit	£122,100,000

Nature of business: Booker Group is the UK's leading food wholesaler. It supplies caterers, retailers and small businesses via the internet, delivery and cash and carry.

Company registration number: 5145685

Subsidiary undertakings include: Booker Ltd; Makro Holding Ltd; Makro Self Service Wholesalers Ltd; and Makro Properties Ltd.

Brands include: The group now comprises Booker Wholesale, Makro, Booker Direct, Classic Drinks, Ritter Courivaud, Chef Direct and Booker India.

Total employees: 12,859

Focus of giving: General charitable purposes.

Cash donations undeclared	✓
Gifts in kind	✓
Humanitarian aid: UK	✓
Payroll giving	✓

Charitable donations

Cash UK (latest available):	2014	£350,000
	2011	£22,000
	2010	£20,000
Total UK (cash and in kind):	2014	£350,000
Cash worldwide:	2014	£350,000
Total worldwide (cash and in kind):	2014	£350,000

Community involvement

The group's CSR focuses mainly on environmental and sustainability issues and states that it 'builds sustainable relationships primarily through improving its products and services, supplied to its customers, who are often independent businesses at the heart of their communities'.

In 2013/14 additional support provided has included:

- Each business centre, distribution centre and support centre has nominated a local charity to support. Colleagues raised £86,000 for these charities
- Throughout the year the group donated surplus food to local homelessness charities from Booker business centres and distribution centres. The equivalent of 200,000 meals were donated to charities across the UK, with an additional 30 tonnes of food reprocessed for animal feed
- Floods and storms caused disruption throughout the winter of 2013/14 and many of Booker's customers' businesses were affected. Booker colleagues maintained deliveries and support customers during this time. In addition, the group established a fund of £350,000 to enable branches in the worst affected areas to support customers recovering from the damage

Corporate giving

In the group's 2013/14 annual report and accounts, no charitable cash donations were declared other than £350,000 which was set up to assist flood victims in the UK. There was also no breakdown of cash and in-kind costings. We have therefore used the £350,000 as the group's UK and worldwide contributions.

In-kind support

A scheme introduced by the Welsh government which provides for companies to charge for plastic bags produced a surplus which the company donated to Keep Britain Tidy. Surplus food is distributed to local charities.

Employee-led support

Previous research showed that a **Give As You Earn** scheme was in operation.

Corporate social responsibility

CSR committee: There was no evidence of a separate CSR Committee.

CSR information: The following statement is taken from the group's website:

> The group recognises that it has social and environmental responsibilities arising from its operations and is committed to responsible business practices. These improve the welfare of colleagues and the communities in which we operate, and reduce our impact on the environment.

CSR report: There was no evidence of a separate CSR report.

Applications

Contact the local outlet or the correspondent.

Bournemouth International Airport Ltd

Airport operators

Correspondent: Community Fund Administrator, Bournemouth Airport, Christchurch, Dorset BH23 6SE (email: community@bournemouthairport.com; website: www.bournemouthairport.com)

Year end	31/03/2014

Nature of business: Airport operator. Bournemouth airport is now owned by M.A.G plc. This entry concentrates on the subsidiary company Bournemouth International Airport.

The Manchester Airports Group plc (M.A.G) is the country's largest UK-owned airport operator. M.A.G owns and operates Manchester, Stansted, East Midlands and Bournemouth airports. Its property and facilities management arm, M.A.G Developments, is responsible for the group's estate and also the development of Manchester's Airport City.

M.A.G is privately managed on behalf of its shareholders: Council of the City of Manchester (35.5%), Industry Funds Management (35.5%) and the nine remaining Greater Manchester local authorities (29%).

Focus of giving: General charitable purposes, environment, sport, recreation, community/social welfare.

Sponsorship	✓

Community involvement

The Bournemouth Airport Community Fund is a completely separate fund that is managed independently by the Community Fund Management Committee. It is open to community, social, recreational and environmental groups operating within the Borough of Christchurch. The money in the fund comes from a substantial annual donation from Bournemouth Airport, which was agreed following negotiations with Christchurch borough council as a result of the redevelopment of the new terminal building.

Fund objectives

The Community Fund objectives are outlined below. In order for a project to receive a grant from the fund it must meet at least one of the following:

- To bring the community closer together through facilities for sport, recreation and other leisure time activities
- Offer environmental improvement and/or heritage conservation

- Improve awareness of environmental issues through environmental education
- Encourage and/or protect wildlife

Corporate giving

The information in this entry is limited as Bournemouth airport is now owned by M.A.G plc. Figures relating to charitable giving and information on the company's activities relate to the Bournemouth airport site. M.A.G plc also owns the airports at Bristol, East Midlands, Manchester and Stansted – see separate entries. We have not recorded the amount spent by the Community Fund as this would have meant recording the group's figures twice.

Commercially led support

Bournemouth Airport is committed to investing in the arts, enriching the arts and culture in the regions in which it operates. The website states that the company believes 'that a thriving theatre and arts scene help support inbound tourism and inward investment'.

Applications for arts sponsorship should be submitted using the online sponsorship request form. The sponsorship section of the website also gives deadline dates.

Applications

In writing to the correspondent using the community fund's application pack which is available online.

BP plc

Oil and gas/fuel

Correspondent: The UK Social and Community Affairs Team, International Headquarters, 1 St James's Square, London SW1Y 4PD (tel: 020 7496 4000; fax: 020 7496 4630; website: www.bp.com)

Directors: Carl-Henric Svanberg, Chair; Bob Dudley, Group hief Executive Officer; Professor Ann Dowling; Frank Bowman; Brendan Nelson; Phuthuma Nhleko; Iain Conn; Dr Brian Gilvary; George David; Paul Anderson; Andrew Shilston; Ian Davis; Antony Burgmans; Cynthia Carroll (women: 2; men: 12)

Year end	31/12/2013
Turnover	£236,429,211,914
Pre-tax profit	£18,845,815,784

Nature of business: The group's principal activities comprise exploration and production of crude oil and natural gas, refining, marketing, supply and transportation and the manufacturing and marketing of petrochemicals. BP has major operations in Europe, North and South America, Asia, Australasia and parts of Africa.

Company registration number: 102498

Subsidiary undertakings include: Atlantic Richfield Company; BP Capital Markets; BP Exploration Operating Company; BP Company North America; BP Oil International; Burmah Castrol; and Standard Oil Company. A full list of subsidiary undertakings can be obtained from Companies House.

Main locations: London

Total employees: 83,900

Focus of giving: Education, enterprise/training, environment, STEM (science, technology, engineering and mathematics), arts, culture, science technology, children, young people.

Membership: BITC

Cash donations undeclared	✓
FTSE 100	✓
Gifts in kind	✓
Humanitarian aid: overseas	✓
Market-led giving	✓
Matched funding	✓
Overseas giving	✓
Sponsorship	✓

Charitable donations

Cash UK (latest available):	2013	£2,700,000
	2011	£4,500,000
	2009	£850,000
Total UK (cash and in kind):	2013	£8,500,000
Total worldwide (cash and in kind):	2013	£49,100,000

Community involvement

The BP website states: 'We passionately believe in supporting activities that strengthen the skills and abilities of people and community groups to take effective action in the development of their communities.'

Enterprise and training

In partnership with Business in the Community BP supports the 'arc' initiative, which helps social enterprises to grow and create jobs.

Young Leaders Programme

In partnership with Inspiring Scotland and the Dame Kelly Holmes Trust BP supports Glasgow 2014 Young Leaders Programme and is providing 'mentoring and development of 50 young people aged between 17–21 to help give them the chance to develop skills that will help make them more employable'. This programme was set to finish in early 2015.

Education programme

Since 1968 BP has had a nationwide education programme for young people between 5 and 19 years of age which has now developed into a comprehensive programme contributing to every area of education in the UK (early stage, primary, secondary, tertiary and vocational). There are three main strands to the group's educational support:

- BP Educational Service (BPES) – providing resources to support STEM education
- Schools Link – 'linking with local schools, mentoring pupils, enabling employees to act as school governors and providing work experience placements'
- ENTHUSE – BP is a founder partner in 'a joint initiative with the Government and The Wellcome Trust to deliver continuing professional development for science teachers in maintained schools'
- Enterprising Science – the initiative was re-launched in 2013 as a major partnership with the Science Museum and King's College London to engage more young people into engineering and science career
- Science Museum – in addition to the Enterprise Science initiative, the partnership with the museum has seen exhibitions and website resources and support to the Talk Science programme
- Engineering Development Trust and Engineering Development Trust Scotland – support is given for the Go4SET programme and Engineering Education Scheme aimed at 13- to 19-year-olds providing experience and inspiring them to further explore science
- CREST Awards – BP supports the British Science Association's CREST (CREativity in Science and Technology) awards for young people
- Royal Academy of Engineering and the Queen Elizabeth Prize for Engineering – BP has helped launching Engineering Further Education programme supporting teaching and learning in further education colleges and developing a e-mentoring programme 'Bright Links Engineering' as well as supporting the global engineering prize

Environment

BP has a long-standing investment in the Scottish Forest Alliance and has 'supported local people by planning new woodlands and planting trees'.

The annual report and accounts state that BP welcomes comments and feedback on its reporting. For every survey completed the group will make a £2 donation to the British Paralympic Association.

Currently the group has set up a special committee and maintains an ongoing restoration commitment to repairing the damage done by the Deepwater Horizon accident in 2010 in the Gulf of Mexico; large amounts of funding are directed for reparation purposes.

BP Foundation

There is a global BP foundation, based in the US. It is funded entirely by contributions from the BP group and gives worldwide. In the UK the foundation has supported TeachFirst. Humanitarian aid is also provided through the foundation – in 2013 about $1.4 million (£873,000) was given in 2013 to locally-based relief organisations in Canada, Germany, India, Mexico, the Philippines, and the US.

Corporate giving

The Sustainability Review for 2013 notes that a total of $78.8 million (£49.1 million) (2012: $90.6/ £56.4 million) was 'spent on community investment'. Out of this sum, $13.7 million (£8.5 million) was contributed in the UK. No further breakdown of the figures could be found. The group states that its community investment falls into several categories, which include: enterprise development; education; access to energy; infrastructure and health; and direct spending on communities. Confusingly, the Sustainability Review states that BP's 'direct spending on community programmes including disaster relief in 2013 was $78.8 million' – the sum referred to as 'social investment' in the annual report and accounts. We take the figures provided by the company to represent its total contributions, not the cash donations. Based on the figures from the two previous years known to us we estimate that about £2.7 million was given in cash in the UK.

Note: In the annual report and accounts financial figures are given in US dollars. We have used the exchange rates applicable at the time of writing.

In-kind support

Employee time and skills. BP says that it supports 'a range of mentoring and coaching programmes to enhance the skills and confidence of people in our local communities'.

Employee-led support

Employees get involved in volunteering and fundraising activities. A past example includes the London 2012 Young Leaders Programme supported by BP, staff volunteers and working in partnership with charities the programme helped disadvantaged young people to learn new skills and develop their personalities. BP employees were coaching young people from communities around the UK, helping them organise community programmes, take a high-profile role in the Games and build skills they will need to be the leaders in their communities after the Games have ended.

Matched funding

The website states: 'Through the BP Foundation, our employees are able to access matching funds for time spent on charitable activities and for donations and gifts to good causes.'

This information applied to the UK; however, note that the BP Foundation is an American based organisation.

The global website states that in 2013, 'employees gave around $7.1 million [£4.4 million], volunteered their time and raised funds to benefit charitable organisations worldwide. The BP Foundation matched these activities with grants of approximately $10.1 million [£6.3 million]'.

Commercially led support

Arts and culture

BP is a Principal member of Arts & Business.

According to the website, 'BP's support for arts and culture in the UK goes back over 35 years [and] today it is focused on long-term partnerships with the British Museum, National Portrait Gallery, Royal Opera House and Tate Britain.' The group made a £10 million investment in extending these relationships until 2017. Programmes undertaken with the partners are also becoming international.

In 2013 BP supported the Royal Shakespeare Company's £5 ticket scheme to enable 16- to 25-year-olds afford live theatrical performances.

As part of the Education Programme BP supports engineering and science awards – also see the 'Community involvement' section.

Corporate social responsibility

CSR committee: There is a Safety, Ethics and Environment Assurance Committee. CSR matters are implemented throughout the group's specialist management systems.

CSR information: The annual report and accounts for 2013 notes:

> BP's social investments, the contributions we make to social and community programmes in locations where we operate, support development activities that aim for a meaningful and sustainable impact. We look for social investment opportunities that are relevant to local needs, aligned with BP's business, and offer partnerships with local organisations.

The website states:

> BP's community investments aim to create meaningful and sustainable impacts. Community engagement, impact assessments and specific challenges, such as health and safety issues or skills shortages, shape our approach to community investment. We work with local authorities, community groups and specialists to deliver the programmes.

A great part of the group's overall sustainability focus is on environment, often related to the impact of the business activities.

CSR report: There is a Sustainability Review available.

Applications

In writing to the correspondent. UK community investment and sponsorship enquiries can be made via an online form under the 'Contact BP in the UK' section on the company's website.

BP Educational Services (BPES): The scheme can be contacted by writing to: PO Box 105, Rochester, Kent ME2 4BE (tel: 08714723020; email: bpes@bp.com).

Bradford & Bingley plc

Building society

Correspondent: Company Secretary, PO Box 88, Croft Road, Crossflatts, Bingley BD16 2UA (tel: 01274 555555; website: www.bbg.co.uk)

Directors: Richard Pym, Chair; Kent Atkinson; Richard Banks; Michael Buckley; Sue Langley; Keith Morgan; Louise Patten; John Tattershall; Christopher Fox (women: 2; men: 7)

Year end	31/03/2014
Turnover	£511,900,000
Pre-tax profit	£363,700,000

Nature of business: On 29 September 2008, all of B&B's retail branches and its savings accounts were transferred to Abbey. These were rebranded Santander in January 2010. The remainder of the business, including the mortgage books of B&B and specialist lending arm Mortgage Express were nationalised and taken into public ownership by the Government. B&B is permanently closed to new lending, but continues to provide services to existing borrowers.

UK Asset Resolution Ltd (UKAR) is the holding company established on 1 October 2010 to bring together the government-owned businesses of Bradford & Bingley plc (B&B) and Northern Rock (Asset Management) plc (NRAM). The management and control of B&B was integrated with NRAM under UKAR on 1 October 2010.

For company information about Bradford & Bingley and Mortgage Express, or for information supporting customers and mortgage intermediaries visit the Bradford & Bingley website.

Company registration number: 2269202

UK employees: 2,248

Total employees: 2,248

Focus of giving: General charitable purposes, housing, homelessness.

Matched funding ✓

Charitable donations

Cash UK (latest available):	2014	£31,000
	2013	£27,500
	2011	£13,150
	2009	£1,000,000
	2008	£1,400,000
Total UK (cash and in kind):	2014	£31,000
Cash worldwide:	2014	£31,000
Total worldwide (cash and in kind):	2014	£31,000

Community involvement

Bradford & Bingley no longer lends but supports its existing mortgage holders. It is now part of UK Asset Resolution (for which there is a separate entry). Bradford & Bingley's charitable contribution appears to be simply supporting the fundraising activities of its staff by matching the first £250 of funds raised per employee and by matching employee donations through a payroll giving programme.

Corporate giving

During the 15 months of these financial accounts, the company matched employee fundraising to the total of £17,000 (2012: £14,000) and payroll giving totalled £14,000 (2012: £13,500).

Corporate social responsibility

CSR committee: There were no details found.

CSR information: It appears that there is no longer a CSR policy for this company. See UKAR's website: www.ukar.co.uk

CSR report: None found.

Applications

In writing to the correspondent, although in view of the circumstances of Bradford & Bingley, it may be that charitable donations are simply going to be those matched by the company with staff donations and fundraising, as opposed to the company making charitable contributions to organisations itself.

Bristol Airport Ltd

Airport operators

Correspondent: Bristol Airport Local Community Fund Administrator, Bristol Airport, Bristol BS48 3DY (tel: 01275 473615; email: communityfund@bristolairport.com)

Year end	31/03/2014

Nature of business: Airport operator. Bristol airport is now owned by M.A.G plc. This entry concentrates on the subsidiary company Bristol International Airport.

The Manchester Airports Group plc (M.A.G) is the country's largest UK-owned airport operator. M.A.G owns and operates Manchester, Bournemouth, Bristol, Stansted and East Midlands airports. Its property and facilities management arm, M.A.G Developments, is responsible for the group's estate and also the development of Manchester's Airport City.

M.A.G is privately managed on behalf of its shareholders: Council of the City of Manchester (35.5%), Industry Funds Management (35.5%) and the nine remaining Greater Manchester local authorities (29%).

Company registration number: 2078692

Focus of giving: General charitable purposes, environment, health, ill health, community/social welfare.

Charity of the Year	✓
Humanitarian aid: overseas	✓

Community involvement

The airport's charitable giving is through its **Local Community Fund (formally, Airport Environmental Improvement Fund)**. Each year Bristol Airport contributes £100,000 to the fund, (which has been donated to Bristol Airport from the group M.A.G plc). The fund's management committee includes representatives from both the airport and North Somerset Council and is independently chaired. The website states that the fund's purpose is to 'help mitigate the impact of the airport's operations and to give something back to surrounding communities who are situated in close proximity to the site'.

Projects which could be eligible for support include initiatives to mitigate the impact of aircraft and ground noise, improvements to transport infrastructure, measures to reduce community severance, nature conservation, educational projects and local sustainability initiatives. The fund's area of benefit includes the parishes of Winford, Wrington, Backwell, Brockley, Cleeve and Barrow Gurney. The committee meets quarterly; refer to the website for current application deadlines and for further information contact the Bristol Airport Local Community Fund Administrator on 01275 473615 or email communityfund@bristolairport.com.

Charity of the Year: Macmillan Cancer Support

In recent years Bristol airport's staff, business partners and customers have raised in excess of £220,000 for a variety of charities, which includes: Children in Need, Children's Hospice South West, The Cots for Tots Appeal, The Jessie May Trust, NSPCC (Bristol Teacher Training project), Royal British Legion Poppy Appeal, Springboard Opportunity Group, Phuket Special School and Phuket Primary School (following the tsunami), and Weston Hospicecare.

Corporate giving

In 2013 a total of 26 projects received contributions from the Local Community Fund ranging from £400 to £11,000. Local initiatives supported include an improved pedestrian crossing on the A38 at Cowslip Green in Wrington; a community art programme at Backwell School; improved road safety signage on the A370 at Cleeve; courses for small businesses based in North Somerset; outdoor play equipment in Flax Bourton; and a Countryside Day aimed at teaching local children about food production.

The information in this entry is limited as Bristol airport is now owned by M.A.G plc. Figures relating to charitable giving and information on the company's activities in this entry, relate to the Bristol airport site. M.A.G plc also owns airports at Bournemouth, East Midlands, Manchester and Stansted – see separate entries. We have not recorded the amount spent by the Community Fund as this would have meant recording the group's figures twice.

Applications

In writing to the correspondent at the company's address.

British Airways plc

Aviation

Correspondent: Community Relations, HBBG, Waterside, Harmondsworth, Middlesex UB7 0GB (tel: 0870 850 9850; email: community.branch@britishairways.com; website: www.ba.com)

Directors: Keith Williams, Chair; Alison Reed; Nick Swift, Chief Financial Officer; Andrew Crawley; Frank van der Post; Ken Smart; Gavin Patterson; Garrett Copeland; Julia Simpson (women: 2; men: 7)

Year end	31/12/2013
Turnover	£11,421,000,000
Pre-tax profit	£300,000,000

Nature of business: Principal activities: the operation of international and domestic scheduled and charter air services for the carriage of passengers, freight and mail and the provision of ancillary airline and travel services.

Company registration number: 1777777

Subsidiary undertakings include: The Mileage Company; OpenSkies; and BA European Ltd.

Main locations: Harmondsworth

UK employees: 36,453

Total employees: 41,857

Focus of giving: Education, environment, heritage, sport, recreation, children, young people, community/ social welfare.

Membership: BITC, LBG

Cash donations undeclared	✓
Charity of the Year	✓
Gifts in kind	✓
Payroll giving	✓

Charitable donations

Cash UK (latest available):	2013	£53,000
	2011	£170,000
	2010	£190,000
	2009	£444,000
	2008	£398,000
Total UK (cash and in kind):	2013	£7,500,000
Cash worldwide:	2013	£53,000
Total worldwide (cash and in kind):	2013	£7,500,000

Community involvement

Sustainable Communities

The company's community work focuses on four specific areas:

- Flying Start – the partnership with Comic Relief
- Colleague volunteering
- The British Airways Community and Conservation programme (BACC)
- The Community Learning Centre which provides airline specific activities for schools and colleagues across the Heathrow community

The company stated in its latest sustainability booklet that in 2014 it aimed to:

- Raise over £2 million for Flying Start as well as launch a new 'call to action' for the partnership in April
- Launch Flying Start in America in May
- Launch Gift Aid on ba.com to make it easier for customers to donate to the Flying Start partnership
- Formally launch the volunteering programme and build it into ASCEND, the company's new learning platform
- Build on the Community and Conservation programme and use it as an engagement tool for colleagues
- Showcase the work of community partners by building more strategic relationships which make a real impact on the communities served
- Look to take the carbon fund overseas and help one of the African communities near Mombasa as well as schools and communities across the UK
- Grow the work experience programme by engaging new departments across the airline and increase the number of young people participating
- Develop a talent pipeline through work related programmes at the Community Learning Centre and increase the chances for young people to access development opportunities through the company's apprenticeship scheme

Charity Partner: Comic Relief and others

Corporate giving

Total direct and in-kind donations to charity for 2013 amounted to £7.5 million, £53,000 of which was direct charitable donations and although not stated, we think this cash was given in the UK.

In-kind support

British Airways' Community and Conservation Programme

BA has 40 community and conservation partners all of which are UK-registered charities, based in communities across its worldwide network. The main focus is on education, youth development and conservation. The company provides flight bursaries, excess baggage and cargo to support these partners in their work.

Disaster appeals

British Airways continues to provide assistance to official disaster emergency appeals. In November 2013, it funded an IAG Cargo freighter flight to Cebu. Space was given to Oxfam, Save the Children, UNICEF and the Reina Sofia Foundation of Spain carrying supplies that would provide necessary water and sanitation equipment, medical supplies and other necessary equipment to support the relief effort. In total 95 tonnes of supplies were carried at an estimated value of £294,000, which included the cost of the aircraft and the value of the supplies.

Employee-led support

Flying Start

In 2010, BA launched Flying Start, a charity partnership with Comic Relief. The aim was to raise £6 million and 'change the lives of children worldwide'. In 2013, the £6 million was exceeded by £0.75 million, thanks to the generosity of customers and the efforts of colleagues across the airline who have taken part in fundraising events.

Volunteering

In July 2013 the volunteering programme was formalised which means employees can now volunteer both in the UK and overseas 'within a structured framework contributing to their own development'. Over 800 employees took part in the volunteering programme in 2013.

BA Fun Run

In 2013 the BA Fun Run, in aid of Cancer Research UK, raised £23,000 making the total raised in excess of £953,000 since British Airways began the partnership in 1993

Payroll giving

Over 3,000 current and retired colleagues donate to charity through the company's payroll giving scheme, raising over £632,000 for their chosen charities.

Commercially led support

The British Airways Community Learning Centre

Opened in 1999, the centre provides learning opportunities for young people from schools and colleges across the Heathrow community and further afield. The team of specialist trainers provide insights into the world of work and the airline industry. In this financial year, 9,167 young learners and teachers benefited from education sessions at the Community Learning Centre, or in-house at their schools. To date 91,000 young people have benefited from this initiative.

Apprentices and work placement positions

Since 2009 BA has taken on over 850 students for placements of five days in 21 departments. A number of former work experience students are now BA employees, having successfully secured places on apprenticeship programmes. Currently there are over 400 individuals on apprenticeship programmes in various areas of the business around the Heathrow base.

Corporate social responsibility

CSR committee: There is a corporate responsibility team.

CSR information: Statement taken from the company's sustainability booklet:

> At British Airways we recognise that we need to ensure that all aspects of our business operation are carried out responsibly and that we positively influence those people and communities with who we interact. The three statements shown below articulate the areas around which we, and our stakeholders believe our sustainability efforts should be concentrated:
>
> - Mitigate our environmental impact
> - Be a responsible business and employer
> - Enrich livelihoods and communities

CSR report: Published annually and entitled: 'Responsible Flying for Everyone'.

Exclusions

No support is given for appeals from individuals, political appeals or religious appeals. Advertising in charity brochures is rarely undertaken.

Applications

All requests must be made in writing and sent on charity headed paper to the correspondent by fax to 020 8738 9848 or by post.

British American Tobacco plc

Tobacco

Correspondent: UK Social Reporting Mananger, Globe House, 4 Temple Place, London WC2R 2PG (tel: 020 7845 1000; fax: 020 7240 0555; website: www.bat.com)

Directors: Christine Morin-Postel; Karen de Segundo; Dr Gerard Murphy; Richard Burrows, Chair; Nicandro Durante, Chief Executive; Ben Stevens, Finance Director and Chief Information Officer; Ann Godbehere; Kieran Poynter; Sue Farr; Savio Kwan; Dr Pedro Malan; Dr Richard Tubb; Dimitri Panayotopoulos (women: 4; men: 9)

Year end	31/12/2013
Turnover	£46,185,000,000
Pre-tax profit	£5,799,000,000

Nature of business: Principal activities: the manufacture, market and sale of cigarettes and other tobacco products.

Company registration number: 3407696

Subsidiary undertakings include: British American Tobacco (1998) Ltd; B.A.T. International Finance plc; B.A.T Capital Corporation and BATMark Ltd.

Brands include: Benson and Hedges, Dunhill, Lucky Strike, Rothmans.

Main locations: London, Southampton, Aylesbury

Total employees: 89,820

Focus of giving: General charitable purposes, education, environment, heritage, arts, culture.

Membership: BITC, LBG

Cash donations undeclared	✓
FTSE 100	✓
Gifts in kind	✓
Overseas giving	✓

Charitable donations

Cash UK (latest available):	2013	£1,970,000
	2011	£1,900,000
	2009	£2,000,000
	2008	£2,000,000
	2007	£2,200,000
Total UK (cash and in kind):	2013	£1,970,000
Cash worldwide:	2013	£1,970,000
Total worldwide (cash and in kind):	2013	£8,700,000

Community involvement

The group's approach to corporate social investment (CSI) is 'to regard it as a means of maintaining good relationships with local communities, rather than as a means of promotion'. Guidance on selecting, managing and evaluating major CSI activities is provided to group companies. However, it is recognised that local community needs are diverse. As a result, within the parameters of this guidance and guidelines on focus of spend, CSI is managed locally to ensure the most appropriate projects are supported.

Charity partners

At group level, the major activities supported by the company are the British American Tobacco Biodiversity Partnership and the Eliminating Child Labour in Tobacco Growing Foundation.

Corporate giving

In 2013 global corporate social investment expenditure was £8.7 million (2012: £11.5 million) 'as defined by the London Benchmarking Group's criteria for charitable donations'.

We could find no information regarding the UK cash or in-kind contributions although in the past the company has declared this information. We have therefore taken an estimate based on averaging the last three years' totals of UK cash donations which is around £1.97 million. We do not know how any of the monies were distributed either in the UK or globally. The Sustainability Report for 2013 states that reporting on community programmes is not given as it is considered that this information is more relevant locally and therefore global data is not collected.

Corporate social responsibility

CSR committee: The group's corporate social responsibility (CSR) performance is monitored through a Board CSR Committee and at regional and local levels through combined audit and CSR committees. This structure supports the embedding of CSR and sustainability principles across the group and allows performance against those principles to be monitored.

CSR information: The CSR committee reviews CSR and makes recommendations to the board as regards the company's management of its CSR and the conduct of business in accordance with the Statement of Business Principles; monitors and reviews the effectiveness of social, environmental and reputational issues, the group's plans for and progress of business sustainability; and the effectiveness of the CSR governance process.

CSR report: There is an annual Sustainability Report. The report does not contain information on community programmes as it is considered that this information is more relevant locally and global data is not collected.

Exclusions

No support is given for causes outside the company's areas of focus.

Applications

In writing to the correspondent.

The British Land Company plc

Financial services, property

Correspondent: Joanne Hammond, Charity and Volunteering Executive, York House, 45 Seymour Street, London W1H 7LX (tel: 020 7467 3452; fax: 020 7935 5552; email: joanne.hammond@britishland.com; website: www.britishland.com)

Directors: Chris Grigg, Chief Executive Officer; John Gildersleeve, Chair; Lucinda Bell, Finance Director; Tim Roberts; Charles Maudsley; Lord Turnbull; Aubrey Adams; Simon Borrows; William Jackson; Tim Score; Victoria Penrice, Company Secretary (women: 2; men: 9)

Year end	31/03/2014
Turnover	£384,000,000
Pre-tax profit	£1,110,000,000

Nature of business: British Land deals with property investment and development, finance and investment services.

Company registration number: 621920

Subsidiary undertakings include: BL European Fund Management LLP; BL D Property Holdings Ltd; British Land Property Management Ltd; Linestair Ltd; Stockton Retail Park Ltd; The British Land Corporation Ltd; and York House W1 Ltd. A full list of subsidiary undertakings can be obtained from Companies House.

Main locations: London

UK employees: 556

Total employees: 556

Focus of giving: Economic generation, education, enterprise/training, environment, children, young people, community/social welfare.

Membership: BITC, LBG

FTSE 100	✓
Gifts in kind	✓
Market-led giving	✓
Matched funding	✓
Payroll giving	✓
Sponsorship	✓

Charitable donations

Cash UK (latest available):	2014	£1,100,000
	2013	£1,000,000
	2011	£38,590
	2009	£92,400
	2008	£36,000
Total UK (cash and in kind):	2014	£1,100,000
Cash worldwide:	2014	£1,100,000
Total worldwide (cash and in kind):	2014	£1,100,000

Community involvement

The following information has been obtained from the website. The group provides funding to national, regional and local community causes in the areas where it operates. Particular focus is placed on young people, education, employment and training, and local regeneration of community infrastructure and facilities. Projects which 'address specific local issues in communities where the major properties and developments are located, present opportunities for local teams to become engaged and actively involved, deliver best value in terms of meaningful, measurable impacts in the local community and offer long-term opportunities for partnership' are favoured. Note that before committing to an ongoing funding British Land may pilot the proposed initiative for a year. While the majority of organisations applying are registered charities this is not an exclusive requirement and the group is 'always interested to consider requests for funding'.

Some of the schemes supported by the group include:

The Prince's Trust

British Land has been supporting the trust's Get into Retail course since 2007. According to the group's website, in 2013/14 more than £140,000 has been invested:

> in retail and hospitality training programmes at [its] properties around the UK, working with The Prince's Trust, retailers and local partners.
>
> *Pathways to Property*
>
> Over the last two years, almost 140 sixth formers from state schools and colleges have taken part in the Pathways to Property summer school, delivered by the Reading Real Estate Foundation. The programme is free for students and runs in partnership with British Land, other real estate firms and social mobility foundation The Sutton Trust.

Westminster Academy

The group funded the Design Engineer Construct! course to reach a younger group of learners. Children were given a chance to develop their skills, helped identify the A-level subjects needed to pursue engineering opportunities, and could spend time with professionals from British Land and its partners.

National Literacy Trust

The partnership with the trust has been established since 2004 and is currently delivering a five-year programme to encourage a love for reading amongst children, often from disadvantaged communities. British Land is providing £736,000 of funding and support. In 2014 the Young Readers Programme was run at 18 sites, providing fun literacy events for children and support to schools through training and tools to embed reading for enjoyment.

Pursuing Independent Paths (PIP)

British Land provided practical help and expertise to the charity helping people with learning disabilities.

Create

A relationship with the arts charity Create has been developed since 2007. Lately supporting the art:space programme for young carers in the London Boroughs of Camden, Hackney, Southwark and Westminster. British Land's staff and local teams have also become increasingly involved, volunteering at creative sessions.

Capital Kids Cricket League

The group sponsors UK's largest children's cricket competition. In 2013, together with Capital Kids Cricket an inclusive league project was piloted to encourage team sports participation amongst children with special educational needs. A total of £50,000 of funding is committed to Capital Kids Cricket each year.

Construction Youth Trust

Staff volunteers and project teams help students gain insights into career opportunities in the built environment through the Budding Brunels programme. In 2013 a total of £19,800 was given to the trust.

The Source Skills Academy

The retail training centre was set up by British Land in partnership with Sheffield City Council in 2003. In 2013 a total of £64,000 was provided to The Source to support apprenticeships.

LandAid

British Land is one of this property industry charity's Foundation Partners. The charity helps disadvantaged young people around the UK achieve their potential and has been supported by £60,000 of funding over the three years as well as further £53,000 raised by staff and property teams in London.

Further examples of the causes supported are available on the group's website.

Corporate giving

In 2013/14 the group contributed a total of £1.1 million (2012/13: over £1 million). The CR Report for 2014 maintains that during the year 19,800 people, including apprentices, jobseekers and schoolchildren, benefited from the group's £1.4 million community programme (including cash, time and gifts in kind). We take the figure of £1.1 million, given in the accounts, to represent the group's charitable giving.

Beneficiaries include: Construction Youth Trust; LandAid; National Literacy Trust; Pursuing Independent Paths (PIP); The Prince's Trust; and The Sutton Trust.

In-kind support

In-kind support is available, which includes staff volunteering efforts and expert advice.

Employee-led support

The group employees participate in community involvement initiatives. The annual report and accounts for 2013/14 state that 77% of the staff members are volunteering. For example, according to the website, British Land 'volunteers and project teams have helped more than 130 students to gain insights into career opportunities in the built environment, many of whom have gained a nationally recognised qualification through charity Construction Youth Trust's Budding Brunels programme'.

Payroll giving

There is a payroll giving scheme operating which provides 50% matched funding by the group (up to £5,000 per person each year).

Matched funding

British Land matches up to two fundraising initiatives per year at each of its retail properties around the UK, up to £750 per project per year.

Commercially led support

Work experience

The group is interested in raising interest in construction, engineering, facilities management and similar fields and provides apprenticeships and internships on its own sites and through industry partners. According to the website, over the last two years a total of £112,000 has been invested in apprenticeships, alongside matched funding from suppliers, occupiers and local authorities.

Sponsorship

The group sponsors the Capital Kids Cricket League.

Corporate social responsibility

CSR committee: There is a CR Committee, chaired by Lucinda Bell, Finance Director. It reports to the board on a quarterly basis and annually reviews the CR strategy. According to the annual report, it:

> Assesses emerging social, environmental and ethical issues to determine whether a response is required and considers social, environmental and governance risks, and the mitigating actions that are in place. . . . Any proposed changes in CR strategy are presented to the Executive Committee for approval.

CSR information: The group's CR policy states:

> Our corporate responsibility strategy is core to our corporate aim of building the best Real Estate Investment Trust (REIT) in Europe. It helps ensure that we do the right thing (as individuals and as a company), and that we manage physical,

fiscal and regulatory risks, care for our reputation, and enhance and create asset value. We go beyond compliance with relevant legal and other minimum requirements, seeking continuous performance improvement by setting long-term targets that we report against annually. We also publish audited, comprehensive performance data annually, with regular updates throughout the year. We take our responsibilities seriously throughout the property life cycle, and work in partnership with our occupiers, suppliers and staff to be the best in the four areas we believe are the most important to us and our stakeholders:

- Managing buildings efficiently
- Supporting communities
- Developing sustainable buildings
- Engaging staff

We are committed to an ethical approach to business and demand the same standards throughout our supply chain, actively working with our suppliers to address environmental and social issues. We treat our staff and suppliers with fairness, dignity and respect, and we are committed to equal opportunities. We actively work to prohibit corruption and bribery, prevent pollution, and support the protection of internationally recognised human rights. All our employees are responsible for the implementation of this policy.

The CR strategy currently encompasses social and environmental targets. The CR Report for 2013/14, however, states: 'Our long-term targets will conclude in March 2015. In view of this, we are reviewing how corporate responsibility supports the business and will publish a revised strategy and targets in 2015.'

CSR report: A full CSR report is available from the company's website.

Exclusions

The company does not provide support for political purposes and will not normally:

- Fund programmes outside the regions in which it operates
- Subsidise government funding
- Provide commercial sponsorship
- Support religious causes

Applications

Applications can be made either by getting in touch with the Building Manager at a local British Land shopping centre, retail park or office estate, or by contacting the correspondent.

The Charity and Community Committee, meets quarterly and votes on the funding proposals.

British Sky Broadcasting Group plc

Media

Correspondent: The Bigger Picture Team, Grant Way, Isleworth, Middlesex TW7 5QD (tel: 03331000333; fax: 03331000444; email: biggerpicture@bskyb.com; website: corporate.sky.com)

Directors: Nick Fergusson, Chair; Jeremy Darroch, Chief Executive Officer; Andrew Griffith, Chief Financial Officer; Chase Carey; Tracy Clarke; David DeVoe; Martin Gilbert; Adine Grate; Andy Higginson; Dave Lewis; Mathieu Pigasse; Danny Rimer; Arthur Siskind; Andrew Sukawaty; James Murdoch (women: 2; men: 13)

Year end	30/06/2014
Turnover	£7,632,000,000
Pre-tax profit	£1,082,000,000

Nature of business: Sky is Europe-wide entertainment company. In the UK and Ireland the group provides paid television, broadband and streaming services. BSkyB launched its digital television services in the UK on 1 October 1998.

Company registration number: 2247735

Subsidiary undertakings include: Bonne Terre Ltd; British Sky Broadcasting Ltd; BSkyB Finance UK plc; Hestview Ltd; NGC Network International LLC; and Sky In-Home Service Ltd. A full list of subsidiaries can be found in the group's annual report and accounts.

Main locations: Leeds, Manchester, Harrogate, Livingstone, Dunfermline, Isleworth, Hounslow

Total employees: 20,841

Focus of giving: Environment, arts, culture, sponsorship, sport, recreation, children, young people, community/ social welfare.

Membership: BITC, LBG

FTSE 100	✓
Gifts in kind	✓
Market-led giving	✓
Matched funding	✓
Payroll giving	✓
Sponsorship	✓

Charitable donations

Cash UK (latest available):	2014	£513,000
	2011	£9,119,000
	2010	£9,160,000
	2008	£5,195,000
	2006	£3,825,000
Total UK (cash and in kind):	2014	£14,475,000
Cash worldwide:	2014	£513,000
Total worldwide (cash and in kind):	2014	£14,475,000

Community involvement

The Bigger Picture

This is the group's community programme focusing on the arts, education, environment, sport, health and taking social responsibility for its activities. Sky continues to align its community investment to the wider goals of the business and its customers and utilises its brand, platform and technology in community investment.

Current initiatives undertaken under the Bigger Picture Programme include: Sky Academy; Cycling; and Sky Rainforest Rescue.

Sky Academy

The programme was launched in 2013. The website states:

> Headquartered in our new Believe in Better building at the heart of our West London campus, Sky Academy is comprised of five initiatives:
>
> Sky Sports Living for Sport, Sky Academy Skills Studios, Sky Academy Careers Lab, Sky Academy Starting Out and Sky Academy Scholarships.

The following information summarises these intiatives (see the corporate.sky.com website for more details):

- Sky Sports Living for Sport – a sports initiative run in partnership with the Youth Sport Trust (see 'Commercially led support')
- Sky Academy Skills Studios – 'an interactive learning experience that takes schools behind the scenes at Sky'
- Sky Academy Careers Lab – 'a full-day careers experience for 16–19 year olds helping them to build employability skills and discover career opportunities in media, business and technology'
- Sky Academy Starting Out – aimed at people starting out in their career the initiative offers work experience as well as placement, apprenticeship and graduate programmes
- Sky Academy Scholarships – a bursary scheme to support emerging talent in the worlds of sport and the arts through financial support and mentoring from Sky's staff and other experts

Cycling

In an ongoing partnership with British Cycling Sky aims to transform cycling at all levels, from the grass roots through to the elite. Through the Sky Ride initiative the group is providing ways for people to get involved in cycling, for instance, by opening up the streets of major cities across the country encouraging people to ride around traffic-free streets. Another example includes Ride Social which helps people find like-minded cyclists in their area, allowing them to connect and arrange rides online.

For a more detailed description of the programmes and most recent updates see an informative Sky's website.

Sky Rainforest Rescue
Delivered in partnership with WWF the initiative seeks to help save around 3 million hectares of forest from deforestation in Brazil. During the year a total of £4 million was fundraised which Sky has matched to reach a total of over £8 million to support the project. The group raises awareness of the issue through its media platforms.

Corporate giving

The group values its 'community contribution' (based on London Benchmarking Group model) at £17.1 million. A further breakdown is given on the group's website which details the following information:

Cash	81%	£13.9 million
Management	15%	£2.5 million
In-kind	2%	£293,000
Time	2%	£282,000

The following areas were supported:

Education and young people	44%
Health	25%
Environment	16%
Social welfare	6%
Arts and culture	4%
Other	3%
Economic development	2%

The 'community contribution' consisted of:

Community investment	76%
Commercial initiative	21%
Charitable gifts	3%

We have calculated 'charitable gifts' to amount to about £513,000. Since the figure is specified separately we use this to represent the group's total cash donations. We take it that total contributions were of £14.4 million (excluding the management costs).

In-kind support

Sky Sports Living for Sport
As part of the initiative Sky provides teachers, who submit their plans for a bespoke project online, a starter pack and sports kit for all young people to help get the project underway. As each school project progresses, a mentoring visit is arranged from a member of Sky's team of past and present sports stars, to offer inspiration and motivation to the group.

Sky Sports ECB Coach Education
The programme has trained over 23,000 grass-roots coaches, helping the ECB (England and Wales Cricket Board) to provide more coaching courses and deliver better quality coaching resources. The programme offers training at four levels, beginning with 14- to 18-year-olds who want to get involved in leading cricket activities at school or a club. It goes right through to training at Head Coach level, equipping coaches with the skills to enable the development of players' technical, tactical, mental, physical and lifestyle requirements, at club, district or county level.

Employee-led support

Volunteering
About 10% of Sky employees engage in volunteering activities, particularly participating in the Sky's Bigger Picture programmes, such as Sky Academy. We know that in the past Sky employees were entitled to two days of paid time off annually.

Payroll giving
Our research suggests that employees can participate in a Give As You Earn scheme. Our research suggests that the group has been providing an extra 50p for every £1 given. The CSR report notes that about 5% of employees have signed up for the scheme.

Matched funding
The group matches employee fundraising efforts pound to pound (previously up to £300 if fundraising as an individual, or £1,000 if fundraising as part of a team of two or more Sky people). An example is matched funding provided in support of Sky Rainforest Rescue. According to the CSR report, 2% of staff apply to the scheme.

Commercially led support

Sponsorship

The arts
The CSR report for 2013/14 says: 'We also continued to contribute to the arts through our dedicated Sky Arts channels and by collaborating with leading arts organisations to produce two brand new works.'

A £2.6 million investment saw Sky working with over 150 production companies in the previous year 'providing a platform for their creativity and helping them grow their own businesses'. Arts activities of the group included:

- *Sky Arts Ignition: Memory Palace* – the project collaborated with six arts organisations over three years to create new works. For each chosen project, Sky Arts provided cash investment of up to £200,000 and worked with the arts partners to bring their projects to a wider audience on screen and on the ground as well as providing other marketing and publicity support
- *Sky Arts Ignition: The Rise and Fall of the City of Mahagonny* – in Ireland a digital project and on-air programming accompanied Rough Magic and Opera theatre companies' production

The group also supports arts festivals and events. In the past Sky has worked with projects, including Isle of Wight, Latitude and the Cambridge Folk Festival.

Sports
Over the past 20 years Sky has contributed more than £10 billion to British and Irish sports organisations, covering a wide range of sports, such as cycling, rugby, golf and cricket. Cycling is one of the main group's sponsorships with the collaboration with British Cycling, the Sky Ride campaign and support of elite cycling through Team Sky, a professional British road racing team.

Sky Sports Living for Sport
The sports initiative run in partnership with the Youth Sport Trust is aimed to students from primary and secondary schools across Britain and Ireland. The programme aims to support teachers working with young people between the ages of 11 and 16 who may be finding school life difficult for one reason or another. At the heart of the scheme is a team of world-class athlete mentors who go into schools and use sports skills to help build young people's confidence and life skills, regardless of their athletic abilities. The group also hosts Sky Sports Living for Sport Community Games events for primary schoolchildren throughout the UK.

Corporate social responsibility

CSR committee: There is a Bigger Picture Committee as well as Bigger Picture Team and Steering Groups. The committee provides strategic leadership for the Bigger Picture initiatives and is chaired by James Murdoch. It meets at least twice a year.

CSR information: The CSR report says:

> Seeing the bigger picture is our approach to sustainability at Sky. Our strategy – our contribution, responsible business and inspiring action – is also informed by the views of our stakeholders, our assessment of the material risks to our business, and the opportunities we identify to make a positive difference to a more sustainable society.

The website states:

> As a broadcaster and communications provider in 11.5 million homes across Britain and Ireland, we are reaching beyond our business to inspire action in three ways. Our Sky Academy initiatives create opportunities for young people to build skills for a changing world. Our partnership with British Cycling inspires people to get on their bikes. And our Sky Rainforest Rescue campaign with WWF inspires customers to join with us in helping to protect one billion trees in the Amazon.

CSR report: There is the Bigger Picture Review – a comprehensive annual report on the company's CSR activities.

Exclusions

Our research suggests that support is not generally given for animal welfare charities, appeals from individuals, elderly people, heritage, medical research, overseas projects and political or religious appeals.

Applications

In writing to the correspondent.

British Sugar plc

Sugar refiners

Correspondent: R. S. Schofield, Company Secretary, Sugar Way, Peterborough PE2 9AY (tel: 01733 563171; fax: 01733 563068; website: www.britishsugar.co.uk)

Directors: M. I. Carr; M. Rowlands; S. D. Moon; R. N. Pike; G. Rhodes

Year end	14/09/2013
Turnover	£1,043,200,000
Pre-tax profit	£296,800,000

Nature of business: British Sugar plc's principal activities are the processing of sugar beet and the manufacture and sale of sugar, animal feeds, bio-ethanol and other co-products of the sugar manufacturing process. It is a wholly owned subsidiary of international food, ingredients and retail group, Associated British Foods plc (ABF) for which there is a separate listing.

Company registration number: 315158

Subsidiary undertakings include: BBRO; The Billington Food Group Ltd; Broomco (2704) Ltd; Sukpak; Wereham Gravel Company Ltd.

Main locations: Wissington, Newark, Peterborough, Bury St Edmunds, Cantley

UK employees: 2,036

Total employees: 2,036

Focus of giving: Education, enterprise/ training, environment, health, ill health.

Matched funding ✓

Charitable donations

Cash UK (latest available):	2013	£90,000
	2012	£38,000
	2011	£33,000
	2009	£48,000
	2008	£34,000
Total UK (cash and in kind):	2013	£90,000
Cash worldwide:	2013	£90,000
Total worldwide (cash and in kind):	2013	£90,000

Community involvement

British Sugar has particular interests in projects in the areas of health and healthcare, education, environment and enterprise, with employee inspired community projects receiving special attention.

All of British Sugar's sponsorship and charitable funds are allocated to its employee fundraising activities through a 'Supporting YOU to support others' programme. According to the website: 'This programme demonstrates British Sugar's commitment and support to our employees' charitable organisations or causes close to their hearts.'

Charitable donations used to be made through the company's charity, British Sugar Foundation. At a board meeting on 24 January 2008 the trustees resolved to wind up the charity and it was removed from the Central Register of Charities in November 2010.

Corporate giving

In 2012/13 donations amounted to £90,000 (2011/12: £38,000).

In-kind support

British Sugar encourages its sites to play an active role in local communities through media visits, schools activities, agricultural and environmental events.

Employee-led support

Funding from the company is given through a matched funding initiative.

Corporate social responsibility

CSR committee: There was no evidence of a separate CSR Committee.

CSR information: There was no evidence of a CSR policy.

We were unable to determine the ratio of women to men on the board.

CSR report: There was no separate CSR report; however, a little information was available from the company's website.

Exclusions

No support is given for individuals or political purposes.

Applications

In writing to the correspondent.

Britvic Soft Drinks plc

Drinks manufacture

Correspondent: Sustainable Business Committee, Breakspear Park, Breakspear Way, Hemel Hempstead HP2 4TZ (tel: 01217 111102; email: info@britvic.co.uk; website: www.britvic.co.uk)

Directors: Gerald Corbett, Chair; Simon Litherland, Chief Executive; John Gibney, Chief Financial Officer; Ben Gordon; Joanne Averiss; Michael Shallow; Bob Ivell; Clare Thomas (women: 2; men: 6)

Year end	29/09/2013
Turnover	£1,321,900,000
Pre-tax profit	£82,600,000

Nature of business: Britvic is one of the leading soft drinks companies in Europe, with operations in Great Britain (GB), Ireland and France. Britvic is the largest supplier of branded still soft drinks and the number two supplier of branded carbonated soft drinks in GB, and it is an industry leader in Ireland and France. Through franchising, export and licensing, Britvic has also been growing its reach into other territories, particularly the United States. Britvic is listed on the London Stock Exchange under the code BVIC.

Company registration number: 5604923

Subsidiary undertakings include: Britannia Soft Drinks Ltd; Britvic Finance No. 2 Ltd; Britvic International Ltd; Britvic Property Partnership; Britvic Worldwide Brands Ltd; Fruité Entreprises SA; and Teisseire SAS.

Brands include: J20; Pepsi; Red Devil; Robinsons.

Main locations: Ballygowan, Beckton, Huddersfield, Leeds, Norwich, Rugby, Widford

Total employees: 3,276

Focus of giving: Education, environment, health, ill health, community/social welfare.

Membership: BITC, LBG

Cash donations undeclared	✓
Charity of the Year	✓
Gifts in kind	✓
Market-led giving	✓
Overseas giving	✓
Payroll giving	✓

Charitable donations

Cash UK (latest available):	2011	£581,300
	2009	£242,000
	2008	£83,000
Total worldwide (cash and in kind):	2013	£700,000

Community involvement

The company's support for communities ranges from global projects via charity partners in countries from which it sources materials, to local initiatives via its community foundation funds. As part of their overall policy on corporate responsibility and long-term corporate vision of supporting local communities, Britvic established the **Britvic Community Fund** administered by the Essex Community Foundation (Charity Commission no. 1052061). The fund focuses on supporting charities and voluntary groups in Essex, initially with a particular focus on those working with families in the Chelmsford area. Grass-roots projects, such as local breakfast clubs and local charities, also receive funding.

Charity partner

Britvic's main charity partner appears to be Street League. The website lists Cancer Research UK as its 'corporate partner'. It also has a number of other partners and a full list is available from its website, they include: HIS Food, Street League and WRAP.

Corporate giving

During 2013, the group and its subsidiaries donated £0.7 million for charitable purposes (2012: £1.6 million).

This included cash and product donations directly to charitable organisations and other investment in support of community programmes including employee volunteering.

In-kind support

Learning Zones

In 2009 Britvic's first Learning Zone in Beckton was launched to provide a dedicated space in which to help teachers connect classroom learning with an understanding of business. Since then, Learning Zones have been opened across the company's manufacturing sites and its head office in Hemel Hempstead. The company continues to run its enterprise learning module in partnership with The British Soft Drinks Association (BSDA), as well as its new 'Young People Employability' workshops. An online educational toolkit has also been updated and is available at: www.britviclearningzone.co.uk

Employee-led support

Learning for Life

A long-term community investment strategy has been launched – 'Learning for Life'. Community investment and volunteering policies underpin the programme and these policies encourage employees to play their part in the community and support their chosen charities. Britvic employees are given two paid days a year to use for volunteering opportunities – either individually or as part of a team.

Corporate social responsibility

CSR committee: We could not find the members or structure of a CSR committee.

CSR information: Statement taken from the company's website:

> At Britvic we believe our sustainable business programme, aimed at ensuring we are trusted and respected within our communities, is critical to our business success. Our strategy focuses around three core principles - People, Planet and Profit and ensures we play our part in the key areas of public health, creating a great place to work, supporting the most disadvantaged young people and responsibly using natural resources such as water, materials and energy.
>
> The programme incorporates both long- and short-term economic, environmental and social considerations within our decision making and everyday activities and each of our business units are responsible for embedding our sustainability principles and delivering our goals.

CSR report: There is a Sustainable Business Report and also policy documents relating to CSR available on the company's website.

Applications

In writing to the correspondent referenced 'Charitable giving, UK' or 'Community contributions, UK'.

Broadland Properties Ltd

Property

Correspondent: B. P. Swiers, Company Secretary, 137 Scalby Road, Scarborough, North Yorkshire YO12 6TB (tel: 01723 373461; fax: 01723 500021)

Directors: J. Guthrie, Chair; P. J. Guthrie; R. Guthrie; M. Robson; R. G. Urquhart; J. M. Hill

Year end	30/09/2013
Turnover	£33,837,000
Pre-tax profit	£1,101,000

Nature of business: The company is a holding company with increasing interests in farming and renewable energy generation as well as leisure and forestry enterprises. Subsidiaries include a stately home open to the public, overseas farming, renewable energy generation and both trading and investment companies engaged in the development and letting of commercial, industrial and residential property.

Company registration number: 483844

Subsidiary undertakings include: Baltic UK Ltd; County Properties Group Ltd; Hever Castle Ltd; Marshall Estates Ltd; Nevis Property Co. Ltd; New Cavendish Estates Ltd; The Oak Brewery Co. Ltd; Pavilion Square (Scarborough) Ltd; Pluspure plc; Rothley Temple Estates Ltd; York and District Investment Company Ltd.

Main locations: Scarborough

Total employees: 309

Focus of giving: General charitable purposes, arts, culture, sport, recreation, community/social welfare.

Cash donations undeclared ✓

Charitable donations

Cash UK (latest available):	2013	£60,000
	2011	£49,300
	2009	£10,700
	2008	£684,500
	2007	£288,500
Total UK (cash and in kind):	2013	£60,000
Cash worldwide:	2013	£60,000
Total worldwide (cash and in kind):	2013	£60,000

Community involvement

Previously the company has declared its charitable donations and we have records showing which groups the company gave to and where. In 2012/13 no donations were declared. Support seems to concentrate on the Scarborough area with sport, music and community groups benefiting. We were unable to find a website address for this company.

Corporate giving

Charitable donations were not declared in the company's annual report and accounts. We have taken the last two years for which we have amounts available and estimate its cash contribution in 2013 in the UK to be around £60,000. Previous beneficiaries have included: Scarborough Cricket Club (£8,000); Scarborough Rugby Union Football Club (£7,500); Scarborough Symphony Orchestra (£2,500) and Spifox (£1,950).

Corporate social responsibility

CSR information: There was no information regarding CSR.

We were unable to determine the ratio of women to men on the board.

Exclusions

No support is given for advertising in charity brochures, animal welfare, appeals from individuals, overseas projects, political appeals, religious appeals or, generally, groups operating in areas outside Scarborough.

Applications

In writing to the correspondent. The company's UK giving, in the main supports groups with a Scarborough postcode, although there have been exceptions.

N Brown Group plc

Retail – miscellaneous

Correspondent: CSR Team, Griffin House, 40 Lever Street, Manchester M60 6ES (tel: 01612 368256; fax: 01612 382662; email: enquiries@nbrown.co.uk; website: www.nbrown.co.uk/acting_responsibly)

Directors: Andrew Higginson, Chair; Angela Spindler, Chief Executive; Lord Alliance of Manchester; Dean Moore, Group Finance Director; Ivan Fallon; Ron Macmillan; Fiona Laird; Simon Patterson; Philip Harland (women: 2; men: 7)

Year end	01/03/2014
Turnover	£834,900,000
Pre-tax profit	£97,300,000

Nature of business: Provider of internet and catalogue shopping, specialising in clothing, footwear, household and electrical goods.

Company registration number: 814103

Subsidiary undertakings include: J D Williams and Co. Limited; J D W Finance Ltd; Oxendale and Co. Limited; N B Insurance Guernsey Ltd; Gray and Osbourn Ltd; Speciality Home Shopping (US) Ltd.

Brands include: Ambrose Wilson; Home Shopping Direct; Jacamo; J D Williams; Marisota; Simply Be

Main locations: Manchester

Total employees: 3,432

Focus of giving: Health, ill health, small groups, local groups, older people, children, young people, community/social welfare.

Matched funding ✓
Sponsorship ✓

Charitable donations

Cash UK (latest available):	2014	£49,000
	2013	£40,000
	2012	£71,000
	2011	£71,000
	2010	£70,569
Total UK (cash and in kind):	2014	£49,000
Cash worldwide:	2014	£49,000
Total worldwide (cash and in kind):	2014	£49,000

Community involvement

N Brown Group 'takes great pride in its links with local communities and actively supports the communities in which it operates'. It maintains close links with the Christie Hospital in Manchester and the Retail Trust. Employee fundraising activities are encouraged and the group operates a matched funding scheme.

There was no information concerning 2013/14 beneficiaries.

Corporate giving

In 2013/14 the group made charitable donations totalling £49,000.

Employee-led support

The group encourages its employees in their fundraising activities and operates a matched funding scheme to double the amounts raised. The logistics division provides Christmas gifts and Easter eggs for children in local hospitals, sponsors local bonfire night celebrations and Christmas lights displays, makes donations to schools and fundraises for charities in the local area.

Corporate social responsibility

CSR committee: A CSR committee was established in December 2013 and is currently chaired by Fiona Laird.

CSR information: The group actively supports the communities in which it operates.

CSR report: CSR reporting is contained within the annual report and accounts and there is a section dedicated to CSR on the group's website.

Exclusions

No support is given for political appeals.

Applications

In writing to the correspondent.

Bruntwood Group Ltd

Property

Correspondent: Sally Hill, Trustee of The Bruntwood Charity, City Tower, Piccadilly Plaza, Manchester, Greater Manchester M1 4BT (tel: 01612 361647; email: info@bruntwood.co.uk; website: www.bruntwood.co.uk)

Directors: Michael Oglesby, Chair; Chris Oglesby, Chief Executive; Rowena Burns; Kate Vokes; Kevin Crotty, Chief Financial Officer; Andrew Butterworth; Peter Crowther; Chris Roberts; John Marland; Colin Sinclair; Craig Burrow; Richard Burgess (women: 2; men: 10)

Year end	30/09/2013
Turnover	£106,306,000
Pre-tax profit	£12,377,000

Nature of business: Bruntwood is a family-owned and run property investment, development and management group with over 110 properties in four UK cities and provides office space, serviced and virtual offices and meeting rooms and retail premises to companies across a range of different business sectors.

Company registration number: 2825044

Subsidiary undertakings include: Afflecks Ltd; Bruntwood Ltd; Bruntwood Alpha plc; Bruntwood Investments plc; Bruntwood Estates Ltd; Cobco 907 Ltd; Langleycourt Ltd.

Main locations: Manchester, UK

UK employees: 464

Total employees: 464

Focus of giving: Education, environment, health, ill health, heritage, inner cities, medical research, arts, culture, children, young people, community/social welfare.

Gifts in kind ✓

Charitable donations

Cash UK (latest available):	2013	£1,609,000
	2011	£1,200,000
	2009	£690,000
	2007	£500,000
Total UK (cash and in kind):	2013	£1,609,000
Cash worldwide:	2013	£1,609,000
Total worldwide (cash and in kind):	2013	£1,609,000

Community involvement

The Oglesby Charitable Trust (Charity Commission no.1026669)

The trustees support a variety of charitable causes including artistic development, both at an individual and a group level, educational grants and building projects, environmental improvement projects, medical aid and research and improving the lives and welfare of the underprivileged, where possible, by the encouragement of self-help. Their policy is primarily, but not exclusively, to support local charities in the Greater Manchester Area and the North West of England. They have recently widened their geographical support to make donations to charities involved in projects of which the trustees have become aware in East Africa and Northern India.

Acorn Fund (smaller donations)

The Oglesby Charitable Trust has a fund set aside each year for smaller donations and these range between £200 and £1,000. This fund is now administered in conjunction with Forever Manchester (formerly the Community Foundation). For applications refer to its website: www.forevermanchester.com

The Bruntwood Charity (Charity Commission no. 1135777)

Through the Bruntwood Charity four nominated charitable causes are supported across the regions the group operates in. Charities are selected on the basis of the real difference they can make to the lives of people in these communities. Staff devise their own ways of raising money to reach fundraising targets. The website states: 'It means they get to have fun together, build team relationships and meet other people in the business that they may not otherwise work with.'

Charity partners: Claire House; Gemma's Hospice; Onside; The Factory Youth Zone; and Whizz-Kidz.

Corporate giving

In excess of 10% of the company's profit is given to charities and good causes annually. In 2012/13 this figure amounted to £1.6 million, £1.2 million of which was donated to The Oglesby Charitable Trust.

See the corporate charity entry on p. 397 for more information.

In-kind support

In-kind support is given by way of employee volunteering and fundraising. Every year staff raise an average of £120,000 for their four nominated charities and donate over 900 volunteering hours to the group's local communities.

Employee-led support

Employee fundraising and their in-kind support is given through The Bruntwood Trust (see 'Community involvement' section for details).

Through the trust charities are supported in four areas:

Manchester: Here support is focused on partners Onside and The Factory Youth Zone. Youth Zones give young people top quality, purpose built, safe and affordable places to go in their leisure time.

Leeds: St Gemma's Hospice, which is the largest hospice in Yorkshire and one of the largest in England. St Gemma's Hospice provides specialist medical and nursing care for people with life threatening illnesses, predominantly cancer, along with support for their families.

Liverpool: Claire House Children's Hospice cares for children and young adults and in addition looks after the needs of the whole family, providing bereavement support and other support for as long as it is needed.

Birmingham: Whizz-Kidz is employees' preferred charity in Birmingham. Whizz-Kidz provides children and young people with disabilities with vital mobility equipment, opportunities to meet and have fun, and training to help them gain skills and look forward to a bright future.

Commercially led support

Sponsorship

The group's sponsorship programme invests in organisations and events that help to 'add to the vibrancy of the cities we operate in'. The group currently provides a platform to showcase creative talent from encouraging writers, through The Bruntwood Prize for Playwriting.

Manchester International Festival (MIF), which features works from across the spectrum of performing arts, music, visual arts and popular culture, has quickly established itself on the international arts calendar as well as being a major contributor to the culture of the city. Bruntwood was one of the first companies to sign up as sponsors to the inaugural MIF in 2007.

Previous sponsorship activity includes:

- 2004 Cow Parade
- The Bruntwood Awards for Arts and Business
- The Royal Exchange Theatre
- The 2004 Commonwealth Games
- Birmingham Repertory Theatre
- Superlambanana
- West Yorkshire Playhouse
- Manchester Art Gallery
- The Lowry Theatre
- The Birmingham Hippodrome

See more at: www.bruntwood.co.uk/makingadifference

Corporate social responsibility

CSR committee: There was no evidence of a separate CSR Committee.

CSR information: This information was obtained from the company's 'Making a difference' report:

> Bruntwood's work in its communities covers a very broad canvas, from working to take care of the environment to improving people's quality of life through charitable and cultural support. We are committed to spend 10% of our annual profits on charitable activity, as well as the additional contributions made by our staff in volunteering and fundraising and the personal contribution of the family through the Oglesby Charitable Trust.

CSR report: The interesting and detailed 'Making a difference' report is available on the company's website.

Corporate charity: The Bruntwood Charity (Charity Commission no. 1135777).

Exclusions

A list of eligibility criteria and exclusions for the trust can be found on: www.oglesbycharitabletrust.co.uk/eligibility.

Applications

For the Bruntwood Charity and the Oglesby Charitable Trust applications should be made in writing to the correspondent. Although the website of the Oglesby Charitable Trust states: 'Note that this form should only be used when requested by trustees and any unsolicited requests will not be acknowledged and are unlikely to be read.'

Enquiries regarding the staff's chosen charities (see employee-led support section) should be addressed to the correspondent, although again, the website for the charity states that the trustees do not accept unsolicited applications.

BT Group plc

Telecommunications

Correspondent: Better Future team, 81 Newgate Street, London EC1A 7AJ (tel: 020 7356 5000; website: www.btplc.com/Betterfuture)

Directors: Michael Rake, Chair; Gavin Patterson, Chief Executive; Tony Chanmugam, Group Finance Director; Dan Fitz; Tony Ball; Iain Conn; Warren East; Phil Hodkinson; Isabel Hudson; Karen Richardson; Nick Rose; Jasmine Whitbread (women: 3; men: 9)

Year end	31/03/2014
Turnover	£18,287,000,000
Pre-tax profit	£2,827,000,000

Nature of business: The provision of fixed lines, broadband, mobile and TV products and services and networked IT services.

Company registration number: 4190816

Main locations: London

Total employees: 87,700

Focus of giving: General charitable purposes, education, environment, heritage, overseas projects, poverty and social exclusion, children, young people.

Membership: BITC, LBG

Charity of the Year	✓
FTSE 100	✓
Gifts in kind	✓
Humanitarian aid: overseas	✓
Overseas giving	✓
Payroll giving	✓

Charitable donations

Cash UK (latest available):	2010	£2,500,000
	2009	£2,500,000
	2008	£2,500,000
	2007	£3,000,000
	2006	£2,500,000
Total worldwide (cash and in kind):	2014	£27,200,000

Community involvement

BT looks to support communities in the UK and overseas by sharing skills, supporting fundraising and providing technology to achieve its responsible business goals. These include Improving Lives, which aims to use BT's skills and technology to raise more than £1bn for good causes around the world, and Connected Society, which helps to contribute to society by promoting digital connections.

Charity partner: UNICEF UK

Corporate giving

The Better Future performance update for 2013/14 states that the group made cash, time and in-kind contributions worth £27.2 million. This meant that the group met its target to invest 1% of its profit before tax in 'responsible and sustainable business activities'. We were unable to determine the value of UK-only cash and in-kind donations.

The website states that in 2013/14: 'We used our skills and technology to help generate £85.53m for good causes.'

MyDonate

The Better Future Report 2014 states: 'Our MyDonate technology, raised over £57m for thousands of good causes in 2013/14. Our MyDonate for Fundraising service has seen the number of charities, and the number of donations, grow 60% year on year.' Through the platform, it would appear, £41 million was raised for Children in Need and DEC's Philippines appeals, as well as £16.4 million for other good causes.

Charity partners

BT has longstanding partnerships with a number of national and international charities who receive assistance with fundraising through the provision of communications technology, time and skills.

BBC Children in Need – BT helped to raise £11.6 million for the annual appeal.

Comic Relief – In partnership with Comic Relief, BT has helped to raise more than £2 million for The Supporters Club, an initiative that aims to make a positive difference for young people in the UK and internationally through sport.

ChildLine – BT's website describes: 'Our support ranges from staff and customer fundraising to offering mentoring and sharing technological expertise.' During the year, more than £265,000 was raised for the charity.

Disasters Emergency Committee (DEC) – BT's MyDonate for Telethons and Appeals and other technology helped to raise £24 million for DEC's work responding to Typhoon Haiyan and the crisis in Syria.

Through powering a telethon fundraising appeal and a celebrity sporting challenge, BT also helped to raise £9 million for Sport Relief.

In-kind support

Staff time and pro bono

Through the volunteering scheme, BT employees can spend three working days volunteering for charity. During 2013/14 more than 46,000 days were volunteered.

BT's employees assist charities by contributing their skills and expertise. For example, through BT Troubleshooter, charities can utilise a small team of volunteers with the appropriate skills and experience free of charge for one or half a day.

Connected Society

As part of the Connected Society element of its Better Future programme, BT runs Get IT Together programmes in conjunction with the charity Citizens Online. The regional programmes help to develop people's computer literacy and confidence. Through BT Digital Champions young people are encouraged to share their online knowledge with people in their community.

Around the world BT works with charities helping to improve IT education through local initiatives.

The group has entered into a three-year partnership with the charity to support the provision of face-to-face online safety training to parents, children and teachers. The partnership, which will run until 2017, will see workshops being run in 600 schools across the UK.

Gifts in kind

One of the ways in which BT contributes in-kind support is by providing communication infrastructure for fundraising appeals, for example.

Employee-led support

Payroll giving

Employees are able to donate to charities through the Give As You Earn (GAYE) scheme.

Employee volunteering

In 2013/14 13,600 BT employees volunteered and 1,300 charities benefitted. Employees contributed their time in a number of ways including: using skills; through sport; in community roles; through fundraising; by helping to get people online; by helping people with skills development and workplace experience.

The BT People Awards celebrates employees around the world who have contributed to improving their communities through volunteering.

Corporate social responsibility

CSR committee: The following information was taken from the website:

> Chaired by BT's Chairman Sir Michael Rake, the Board Committee for Sustainable and Responsible Business (CSRB) develops the Better Future programme with recommendations from executive management globally. It also oversees the implementation of the programme, and of our broader social and environmental activities.
>
> The CSRB is supported by our Sustainable Business Leadership Team (SBLT), which comprises senior executives from across our business units. The SBLT is charged with delivering the Better Future programme and embedding it throughout BT.

CSR information: The group conducts its responsibility and sustainability involvement through the Better Future programme. Three clear 'visions' have been set with goals the group aims to achieve by 2020. These visions are: Connected Society; Improving Lives; and Net Good.

CSR report: The Better Future Report is published annually and covers progress against BT's goal to be a responsible and sustainable business leader.

Exclusions

No response to circular appeals or generic applications. No denominational appeals, political appeals, appeals from individuals or brochure advertising.

Applications

BT states that it is proactive in its charitable giving and gives significant support to various programmes which are BT-led. It is also involved with specific charity partners and encourages employees worldwide to donate time, skills and expertise to charitable/good causes.

MyDonate

For more details of the MyDonate service, visit the website: www.btplc.com/mydonate.

BTG plc

Pharmaceuticals

Correspondent: Corporate Responsibility Department, 5 Fleet Place, London EC4M 7RD (tel: 020 7575 0000; fax: 020 7575 0010; email: info@btgplc.com; website: www.btgplc.com)

Directors: Garry Watts, Chair; Louise Makin, Chief Executive; Rolf Soderstrom, Chief Financial Officer; Giles Kerr; Richard Wohanka; Ian F. R. Much; Jim O'Shea (women: 1; men: 6)

Year end	31/03/2014
Turnover	£290,500,000
Pre-tax profit	£33,300,000

Nature of business: BTG is an international specialty pharmaceuticals company that develops and commercialises products targeting critical care, cancer, neurological and other disorders.

Company registration number: 2670500

Subsidiary undertakings include: BTG International Ltd; EKOS Corporation; Protherics UK Ltd.

Main locations: Ceredigion

Total employees: 776

Focus of giving: Health, ill health, overseas projects, science technology, children, young people, disability.

Gifts in kind	✓
Matched funding	✓
Overseas giving	✓
Payroll giving	✓

Charitable donations

Cash UK (latest available):	2014	£23,000
	2013	£137,000
	2011	£12,900
	2010	£6,200
	2009	£6,000
Total UK (cash and in kind):	2014	£23,000
Cash worldwide:	2014	£23,000
Total worldwide (cash and in kind):	2014	£23,000

Community involvement

The company states that it believes in making close ties with the communities in which it has operations and undertakes activities in order to raise its profile and drive recruitment. It periodically organises open days for friends and family of employees at its manufacturing facility in Wales, as well as educational open days for local schoolchildren.

Corporate giving

During 2013/14 charitable donations totalling £23,000 were made to a number of charities including: The Brain Tumour Charity; Breakthrough Breast Cancer; Pancreatic Cancer Action; and Wales Air Ambulance.

In 2012/13 in addition to the charitable contributions made by the group, BTG made a one-off donation of £125,000 to establish the BTG Junior Research Fellowship in the Biosciences at Lincoln College, Oxford, a registered charity. This position, which runs in perpetuity, recognises the long-standing relationship between BTG and the Sir William Dunn School of Pathology, Lincoln College, including the contribution made by the 'Factor IX protein' patent originally filed by inventors at the School in 1985 and licensed by BTG. This led to the commercial production of BeneFIX, a Factor IX protein free of contamination by viruses such a HIV or Hepatitis C virus for treatment of Haemophilia B patients.

In-kind support

Matched funding

Employees fundraising efforts are matched by the company up to a maximum of £250.

Employee-led support

In May 2013, 13 riders from each of the three UK sites raised over £11,000 for Leukaemia and Lymphoma Research by completing the BTG Cycle Challenge, a 270 mile journey from the company's site in West Wales to another site in Farnham, finishing at the headquarters in London. In June 2014, colleagues participated in the Trekfest Challenge a 29 or 54 mile hike in the Brecon Beacons in Wales and raised approximately £10,000 for Cancer Research UK.

The company operates a Give As You Earn scheme in the UK. This enables employees to efficiently donate so money that would normally be given in tax goes to their chosen charity instead.

Corporate social responsibility

CSR committee: The Corporate Responsibility Committee comprises individuals from across the business and meets quarterly to discuss new trends, set targets and monitor progress. The committee reports to Rolf Soderstrom, the chief financial officer and the board member with responsibility for this area of the business.

CSR information: This information was obtained from the company's annual report:

> We principally give to charities which either support diseases or conditions in which we are therapeutically focused or that benefit the local communities in which we operate. We encourage employees to support charitable events to raise money for their chosen charities and in most locations we match individual donations up to a designed cap.

CSR report: A CSR report was available from the company's website.

Applications

In writing to the correspondent referenced: 'UK Charitable Giving'.

Bunzl plc

Distribution, print/paper/ packaging

Correspondent: Julia Battyll, Bunzl Communities Co-ordinator, York House, 45 Seymour Street, London W1H 7JT (tel: 020 7725 5000; fax: 020 7725 5001; email: julia@edenwoodpr.demon.co.uk; website: www.bunzl.com)

Directors: Philip Rogerson, Chair; Michael Roney, Chief Executive; Vanda Murray; Patrick Larmon; David Sleath; Brian May; Peter Johnson; Eugenia Ulasewicz; Jean-Charles Pauze; Meinie Oldersma (women: 2; men: 8)

Year end	31/12/2013
Turnover	£6,097,700,000
Pre-tax profit	£289,900,000

Nature of business: Providing outsourcing solutions and customer service orientated distribution and light manufacture, primarily of plastic and paper based products.

Company registration number: 358948

Subsidiary undertakings include: Bunzl Australia Holdings Pty Ltd; Bunzl Finance plc; Bunzl Holding Danmark A/S; Bunzl Holdings France SNC; Bunzl Outsourcing Services BV; Bunzl UK Ltd; Bunzl USA Holdings LLC.

Main locations: London

UK employees: 3,456

Total employees: 13,675

Focus of giving: Education, environment, health, ill health, disability.

Cash donations undeclared	✓
FTSE 100	✓
Gifts in kind	✓
Overseas giving	✓

Charitable donations

Cash UK (latest available):	2013	£580,000
	2012	£480,000
	2011	£220,000
	2009	£210,000
	2007	£200,000
Cash worldwide:	2013	£580,000
Total worldwide (cash and in kind):	2013	£580,000

Community involvement

The following is taken from the group's website:

> Although Bunzl's operations are international, our strength is in the local nature of our businesses. In keeping with this ethos, we particularly support the fund raising activities championed by our employees locally. This is supplemented by donations made at group level to charities predominantly in the fields of healthcare, disability and the environment as well as benevolent societies to support projects in communities where our operations are based.

The group also continued to support projects with high environmental impact in the communities in which it operates, for example RHS Millennium Seed Bank which safeguards seeds in deep-freeze storage to conserve plant biodiversity in the face of multiple environmental threats.

Support was also continued with the development of a new weather station at the Eden Project in Cornwall. Other donations included a project with the Wildlife Trusts aimed at upgrading the current facilities at an EcoPark near Birmingham, to increase the provision of environmental education and accessibility for the community.

Corporate giving

Group wide, Bunzl donated a total of £580,000 (2012: £480,000) to charities in 2013. This does not include in-kind donations or employee fundraising. No UK cash donations or community contributions figures were declared separately.

In-kind support

In-kind support by way of volunteering hours and employee fundraising is given. In 2013 companies across the group continued to support local charity initiatives, often devising creative ways to raise funds for good causes. In North America employees participated in the 'Run for the Warriors' 5k fun run organized by the Walter Reed Society, to support soldiers who had sustained injuries in overseas conflicts. Similarly a team of employees from across the UK and Ireland took part in the Blenheim Triathlon to raise money for a range of charities including the Alzheimer's Society. In Australia, for every pair of Jane work boots sold, Bunzl Industrial and Safety donated $25 to the Jane McGrath Foundation. This money was put towards placing McGrath Breast Cancer Care nurses into communities across Australia.

Employee-led support

Local volunteering is encouraged by the group.

Corporate social responsibility

CSR committee: The board is ultimately responsible for CR governance. The Bunzl Risk Committee and the Bunzl Executive Committee support the board in overseeing and implementing the CR strategy. Within each business area there are people responsible for each element of the company's CR strategy 'and for working with the businesses to address social and environmental impacts'.

CSR information: This information was obtained from the company's CSR report: 'We are fully engaged in our wider responsibilities, including reducing environmental impact, a commitment to social well-being and supporting our people to develop their skills to benefit community initiatives.'

CSR report: An up-to-date CSR report is available from the company's website.

Exclusions

No support is given for political and religious appeals.

Applications

In writing to the correspondent.

Bupa Ltd

Healthcare, insurance

Correspondent: Lauren Young, UK Sustainability Manager, Bupa House, 15–19 Bloomsbury Way, London WC1A 2BA (tel: 0800 600 500; website: www.bupa.co.uk)

Directors: Stuart Fletcher, Chief Executive Officer; Evelyn Bourke, Chief Financial Officer; Lawrenece Churchill; Rita Clifton; Martin Houston; John Lorimer; Prof. Sir John Tooke; Julian Sanders, Company Secretary; Lord Leitch, Chair (women: 2; men: 7)

Year end	31/12/2014
Turnover	£9,800,000,000
Pre-tax profit	£637,800,000

Nature of business: Bupa is an international healthcare group offering health insurance and medical subscription products. It runs care homes, retirement villages, hospitals, primary care and diagnostic centres and dental clinics. Bupa also provides workplace health services, home healthcare, health assessments and long-term condition management services. Bupa has 29 million customers in 190 countries. With no shareholders, Bupa reinvests its profits to provide more and better healthcare and fulfil its purpose. Bupa employs 79,000 people, principally in the UK, Australia, Spain, Poland, New Zealand and Chile, as well as Saudi Arabia, Hong Kong, India, Thailand, and the USA.

Company registration number: 2306135

Subsidiaries include: Bupa Insurance Ltd; Sanitas, SA de Seguros (99% holding); Bupa Australia Pty Ltd; Australia Bupa Care Homes (BNH) Ltd; Bupa Asia Pacific Pty Ltd; Bupa (Asia) Ltd; Bupa Investments Overseas Ltd Bupa Occupational Health Ltd; Grupo Bupa Sanitas SL; UK Care No. 1 Ltd.

Total employees: 79,000

Focus of giving: Health, ill health, medical research, older people, children, young people.

Membership: BITC

Charitable donations

Cash worldwide:	2014	£1,000,000
Total worldwide (cash and in kind):	2014	£1,000,000

Community involvement

Charity partners

The following information was received from the Director of Government Affairs and Sustainability in March 2015:

> Bupa is committed to helping people live longer, healthier and happier lives. To support this they partner with three charities, Age UK, Diabetes UK and the Youth Sports Trust.
>
> Age UK is Bupa's strategic charity partner for 2015 and 2016. The partnership hopes to raise £1 million to support thousands of older people across the UK.
>
> Bupa works with Diabetes UK to provide support for people living with diabetes and raise awareness for those at risk of developing the condition.
>
> Their work with the Youth Sport Trust supports primary school teachers to inspire children to make healthy choices and stay active throughout their lives.

Corporate giving

The Bupa Foundation, the main channel of Bupa UK's giving, (though by no means its only channel), has ceased to exist and was removed from the Central Register of Charities in November 2014. We have been in correspondence with Bupa who have helpfully informed us that the group is reviewing its method of charitable giving and it is its intention to have a corporate charity for each country in which it operates. We understand that the new UK charity is in the process of being established and then registered.

For the years 2013 and 2014 the group does not appear to have declared any charitable contributions in its annual report and accounts; however, the following statement has been issued by the company in the UK which states:

> Bupa is establishing a new charitable foundation for the UK. The Bupa UK Foundation will provide funding for practical projects and initiatives that aim to tackle critical challenges in health and social care and improve people's health and well-being.
>
> The Bupa UK Foundation will be entirely funded by Bupa UK. In 2015, £1 million will be made available for grantmaking. This figure will be reviewed annually.
>
> More detailed information on the Bupa UK Foundation's funding focus for 2015 will be available from April.

We would advise readers to check the group's website for up-to-date information before contacting the correspondent.

Employee-led support

Employee fundraising and volunteering is carried out in support of Bupa's strategic charity partner, Age UK.

Matched funding: In the UK, Bupa matches up to £250 per employee, when they fundraise for health and/or adult social care charities.

Payroll giving: The company operates the Give As You Earn Scheme.

Commercially led support

Sponsorship:

Bupa previously sponsored the Bupa Great Run series. This relationship came to an end in 2014 after 22 years. Bupa will shortly be announcing a new brand communications platform to replace the series.

Corporate social responsibility

CSR committee: There is a Director of Government Affairs and Sustainability for the UK and a Sustainability Manager, Lauren Young, who is the correspondent listed here.

CSR information: The following statement is taken from the company's website where further information can be found:

> At Bupa, we recognise that the health of society is directly tied to the health of the planet. We are committed to engaging millions of people around the world in their health and well-being, and to having a minimal impact on the environment. This will see us maximise the delivery of our purpose in the wider world by using our healthcare expertise in a way that is good for our business, society and the environment – delivering our purpose of longer, healthier, happier lives.

CSR report: Sustainability goals are detailed in the group's annual report.

Exclusions

The company does not support appeals from individuals, political appeals or religious appeals.

Applications

On request from Bupa only. Contact the correspondent after checking the group's website for current information – see 'General' section in this entry.

bwin.party

Gaming

Correspondent: Martin Weigold, Chief Financial Officer, Suite 6, Atlantic Suites, Europort Avenue, Gibraltar (tel: 0035020078700; website: www.bwinparty.com)

Directors: Philip Yea, Chair; Norbert Teufelberger, Group Chief Executive Officer; Martin Weigold, Chief Financial Officer; Rod Perry; Per Afrell; Helmut

Kern; Daniel Silvers; Georg Riedl; Sylivia Coleman (women: 1; men: 8)

Year end	31/12/2013
Turnover	£488,174,465
Pre-tax profit	£35,968,220

Nature of business: Digital gaming. Following the merger of bwin and PartyGaming in March 2011, bwin.party is listed on the London Stock Exchange under the ticker: BPTY and is a member of the FTSE250 Index. This is a global online gaming business regulated and licensed in multiple territories including Gibraltar, Alderney, Belgium, France, Denmark, Italy, Spain and Schleswig-Holstein in Germany.

Subsidiary undertakings include: Bay Management Ltd, Cashcade Ltd, ElectraGames Ltd, ElectraWorks (Alderney) Ltd, EZE International Ltd, iGlobalMedia Entertainment Ltd, Paytech International Ltd, PGB Ltd, PKR Services Ltd, WPT Enterprises Inc.

Total employees: 2,770

Focus of giving: General appeals, environment, health, ill health, housing, homelessness, community/social welfare.

Cash donations undeclared	✓
Gifts in kind	✓
Humanitarian aid: overseas	✓
Overseas giving	✓

Charitable donations

Cash UK (latest available):	2013	£288,000
	2011	£145,000
	2009	£187,600
	2008	£101,700
Cash worldwide:	2013	£288,000
Total worldwide (cash and in kind):	2013	£288,000

Community involvement

The company's 2013 annual report states that:

> Helping to protect the environment and provide support to our local communities are important elements of our overall approach to responsibility. We fund a variety of responsible gaming organisations and more general charities and also run a pro bono scheme that allows employees to give their time to good causes. Helping to protect the environment and provide support to our local communities are important elements of our overall approach to responsibility. We fund a variety of responsible gaming organisations and more general charities and also run a pro bono scheme that allows employees to give their time to good causes.

Corporate giving

In 2013 the company donated more than £288,000 to gaming organisations in Europe including: FEJAR, Gambling Therapy, Jogo Responsável, The Responsible Gambling Trust, SOS Joueurs, Spielsuchthilfe, Spielerambulanz der TU Dresden, and the University Clinic Aarhus. Other beneficiaries have included: Children's Cancer Aid; Children's Cancer Research; Disaster Relief Fund of Red Cross; Great Ormond Street Hospital; and the Pioneers for Change course for social entrepreneurs. We have no information regarding the breakdown of the donations geographically or separately. We have therefore used this figure of £288,000 as the UK and worldwide cash and community contributions figures.

Employee-led support

Volunteering

Employees are encouraged to spend between four to eight hours on charitable, community or environmental projects every year. 'This allows them to enhance their personal development and broaden their perspective while returning something to their local communities.' In 2013, employees contributed over 1,350 working hours to good causes across the company's communities.

Employees from offices in India, Israel, Europe and the United States have participated in a variety of schemes over the years. Projects have included constructing a school in India, raising funds for cancer research, helping out at centres for elderly and homeless people, supporting children's charities and environmental projects including tree planting and helping to maintain and improve facilities at a big cat sanctuary in the UK.

Corporate social responsibility

CSR committee: Martin Weigold, Chief Financial Officer, has executive responsibility for corporate responsibility matters, a role he has held since 2005. The overall process is overseen by the Audit and Risk Committee comprising four independent non-executive directors – Helmut Kern, Rod Perry, Per Afrell and Sylvia Coleman. The committee oversees bwin.party's corporate social responsibility policies and procedures that have been adopted to manage relationships with stakeholders including customers, the wider community and the environment, regulators, suppliers and providers of capital.

CSR information: CSR information taken from the group's website:

> We took a view several years ago that we would only succeed over the long-term if we adopted a structured, integrated and evidence-based approach to responsibility, one which fosters innovation and goes beyond regulatory requirements. To us, responsibility means doing more than what is required: it is about doing what is right. This means understanding real needs of consumers; innovating and evaluating our gaming environment; developing best practices for safe and secure e-commerce; striving for a transparent and engaging dialogue with relevant stakeholders; and finally proving that we are doing all this – for real.

CSR report: There is a 'Focus on Responsibility' section published within the annual report and accounts.

Applications

In writing to the correspondent referencing: CSR/UK.

Cadogan Group Ltd

Furniture manufacture, property

Correspondent: Paul Loutit, Company Secretary, Correspondent to the Trustees, 18 Cadogan Gardens, London SW3 2RP (tel: 020 7730 4567; fax: 020 7881 2300; website: www.cadogan.co.uk)

Directors: Viscount Chelsea, Chair; J. H. M. Bruce; H. R. Seaborn, Chief Executive; R. J. Grant, Finance Director; C. V. Ellingworth; J. D. Gordon; J. A. de Havilland; F. W. Salway

Year end	31/12/2013
Turnover	£128,040,000
Pre-tax profit	£73,839,000

Nature of business: The principal activity of the group is property investment. Cadogan Group Ltd is the holding company for the UK property investment business of the family of Earl Cadogan. The company is ultimately owned by a number of charitable and family trusts.

Company registration number: 2997357

Subsidiary undertakings include: Cadogan Estates Ltd; Chelsea Land Ltd.

Main locations: London

UK employees: 180

Total employees: 180

Focus of giving: Education, environment, animal welfare, medical research, community/social welfare.

Charitable donations

Cash UK (latest available):	2013	£1,434,000
	2011	£1,380,220
	2008	£821,000
	2007	£178,000
	2006	£88,000
Total UK (cash and in kind):	2013	£1,434,000
Cash worldwide:	2013	£1,434,000
Total worldwide (cash and in kind):	2013	£1,434,000

Community involvement

The group makes most of its charitable donations through The Cadogan Charity (Charity Commission no: 247773).

The charity supports organisations involved in: community/social welfare; medical research; education; the environment; animal welfare; and military charities. Particular preference is given to those based, or operating in, London and Scotland.

The following is taken from the company's website and although most of its commitments are possibly commercially led, it demonstrates Cadogan Estate's pledge to its community including to charities and good causes:

> We have a long-standing commitment to stakeholders in the local community as well as those stakeholders outside the immediate bounds of the Estate. Cadogan has a significant history of working to enhance our community, supporting local charities and community projects, and lending our weight and influence in support of relevant community issues and concerns.
>
> Over the years the Cadogan family have also donated land and buildings around Chelsea for charitable and community purposes including schools, social housing and churches. We are committed to maintaining our position as a business which contributes positively and have made the following formal commitments to our community stakeholders:
>
> *Community Commitments*
>
> - To actively engage with local communities whenever works are being carried out that will impact them, taking their opinions into consideration wherever possible
> - To continue to engage actively with neighbourhood forums and residents associations to ensure that we positively contribute to, and are able to act on, their feedback wherever possible
> - To continue Cadogan's long-established practice of providing resources to local charitable organisations to positively contribute to our wider community
> - To continue to strive to make the estate a great place to work, shop and live through funding relevant activities which benefit the community

Corporate giving

In 2013 the company declared £43,000 in charitable donations, together with a donation to The Cadogan Charity which received £1.4 million (2012 – £2.3 million) from the annual dividend received from Cadogan Group Ltd. The charity received other income but this was not derived from the company's shares.

See the corporate charity entry on p. 397 for more information.

Commercially led support

Sponsorship

Significant recent contributions have included:

- Sponsor of Team GB at 2012 Olympics
- Sponsor of the Thames Diamond Jubilee Foundation
- Sponsor of the Royal Philharmonic Orchestra, based at Cadogan Hall
- Lead sponsor of the Princes Foundation for Children and the Arts Carol Concert
- Sponsor of Chelsea Gardens Exhibition by the Chelsea Society
- Organising and running Chelsea in Bloom, in alliance with the RHS, held during Chelsea Flower Show
- Sponsor of Chelsea Festival of Music
- Funding and erecting of the Christmas lights in and around the Estate
- Support for several local churches
- Financial support to the National Army Museum
- Ongoing financial support to the Royal Court Theatre on Sloane Square

Corporate social responsibility

CSR information: There was no CSR information available. The following statement regarding the community can be found on the company's website:

> Our business does not operate in isolation; we form part of a wider community which includes local residents, businesses, community groups, the local authority and all those who work and shop in the area. As a major land owner and developer we recognise our responsibility to play an active role in issues impacting our community.

We were unable to determine the ratio of women to men on the board.

Corporate charity: The Cadogan Charity (Charity Commission no. 247773).

Exclusions

No grants to individuals.

Applications

In writing to the correspondent. However, note that we have received information stating that the trust's funds are fully committed until 2016.

Caledonia Investments

Accountants, financial services, leisure, property

Correspondent: Graeme Denison, Company Secretary, Cayzer House, 30 Buckingham Gate, London SW1E 6NN (tel: 020 7802 8080; fax: 020 7802 8090; email: enquiries@caledonia.com; website: www.caledonia.com)

Directors: Will Wyatt; Stephen King; Jamie Cayzer-Colvin; Charles Allen-Jones; Charles Gregson; Rod Kent; Stuart Bridges; Charles Cayzer; Harold Boël; Robert Woods (women: 0; men: 10)

Year end	31/03/2014
Turnover	£193,100,000
Pre-tax profit	£180,800,000

Nature of business: Caledonia is a self-managed investment trust listed on the London Stock Exchange. Acquired by the Cayzer family in 1951 as a holding company for their various shipping interests, Caledonia came into its own as an investment company in 1987. It still has the backing of the Cayzer family, who collectively own some 48.5% of the share capital.

Company registration number: 3142560

Subsidiary undertakings include: Amber 2010 Ltd; Buckingham Gate Ltd; Edinmore Holdings Ltd; and Sloane Club Properties Ltd.

Main locations: London

UK employees: 45

Total employees: 45

Focus of giving: Education, enterprise/training, environment, heritage, arts, culture.

Cash donations undeclared ✓

Charitable donations

Cash UK (latest available):	2014	£85,000
	2011	£60,800
	2008	£110,000
Total UK (cash and in kind):	2014	£85,000
Cash worldwide:	2014	£85,000
Total worldwide (cash and in kind):	2014	£85,000

Community involvement

The company's website states that each year it makes small donations to charities with a connection to its historic interests or portfolio companies. We have no other information regarding the company's charitable or community giving. There was a note in the accounts however, stating that:

> During the year, certain artworks and memorabilia relating to the Cayzer family and its historic shipping interests were sold by the group for £0.3m to The Cayzer Family Archive, a charitable foundation established to preserve an historical archive of the Cayzer family and its heritage in shipping. The items sold represented only part of a larger collection of artefacts (not all relating to shipping) originally acquired from British & Commonwealth Holdings plc, which had been valued at some £0.5m. The Cayzer Family Archive has granted a licence to the group to continue to display the items sold at its premises at no cost other than maintenance and insurance obligations.

We include this for interest only.

Corporate giving

In 2013/14 the company did not declare its charitable donations. We have therefore used the last two figures we have available for UK cash giving and used the average (£85,000) as this financial year's contributions.

Employee-led support

The company's website states that it encourages employees to support local voluntary organisations and charitable causes; however, we do not know if employees do this in their own or company time.

Corporate social responsibility

CSR committee: There was no evidence of a separate CSR Committee. The board of directors is responsible for charitable and political donations.

CSR information: This information was obtained from the company's website: 'As an investment company with strong family values, we believe in the highest standards of integrity and take our environmental and social responsibilities very seriously.'

CSR report: There was no evidence of a separate CSR report. The company's website has a 'Social Responsibility' section and the annual report has a 'Sustainability' section. We could not find much information about charitable or community giving.

Applications

In writing to the correspondent.

Calor Gas Ltd

Oil and gas/fuel

Correspondent: Sustainability Team (Community), Athena House, Athena Drive, Tachbrook Park, Warwick CV34 6RL (tel: 01926 330088; email: sustainability@calor.co.uk; website: www.calor.co.uk)

Directors: S. Rennie; T. Collins; A. Thompson

Year end	28/12/2013
Turnover	£533,300,000
Pre-tax profit	£61,500,000

Nature of business: The principal activity of the company is the processing, marketing and distribution of liquefied petroleum gas in the UK.

Company registration number: 303703

Main locations: Warwick

UK employees: 1,298

Total employees: 1,298

Focus of giving: General charitable purposes, education, environment, health, ill health, children, young people.

Membership: BITC

Cash donations undeclared	✓
Charity of the Year	✓
Gifts in kind	✓
Market-led giving	✓

Charitable donations

Cash UK (latest available):	2013	£26,000
	2010	£34,000
	2009	£14,000
	2008	£29,000
Total UK (cash and in kind):	2013	£26,000
Cash worldwide:	2013	£26,000
Total worldwide (cash and in kind):	2013	£26,000

Community involvement

Charity Partner/Charity of the Year

The company states on its website that it has found it more valuable and effective to focus support on the work of one charity as a means of engaging staff around a central cause. A national charity is chosen by an all-staff voting process, typically for a three-year duration, for which the majority of corporate fundraising efforts are undertaken. Following a successful partnership with Make-A-Wish Foundation UK, the new corporate charity is Alzheimer's Society. It is hoped that £100,000 will be raised through staff fundraising and company donations.

Corporate giving

In 2013, the company did not declare its charitable donations and only the cash donations raised by staff were detailed on the website. We have therefore taken an average of the last three figures we have available and estimate the total UK cash giving by the company was £26,000. We do not know the costings of in-kind giving as no information was provided as to the financial aspect of this.

In-kind support

In 2011 the company created the Calor Wood at its Stoney Stanton site in Leicestershire. Around 400 people including local schoolchildren, Calor staff and their families planted 2,500 saplings on two hectares of unused scrubland in support of the Woodland Trust's MOREwoods scheme.

A partnership has also been struck with Warwickshire's Myton School to increase students' knowledge of the workplace and improve their employability skills. As part of Calor's involvement in the Confederation of British Industry (CBI) 'Business in the Classroom' initiative, the company offered students from years 7, 8, 9 and 12 the opportunity to obtain a better understanding of business by spending a day in the workplace and undertaking a long-term real life business project. In November 2013, 18 students from Myton School spent the day in Calor's head office where they received presentations from a range of Calor staff from different positions and business functions. The 18 students will work across the year groups to launch an environmental engagement campaign in the school during 2014.

Employee-led support

Calor actively encourages all permanent staff to give something back to local communities. Start From the Heart is a scheme which gives employees one day's paid leave each year to do something which can make a difference to their community. Employees can either choose to participate in an event co-ordinated by Calor or they are free to choose their own Start From the Heart activity, as long as they meet the criteria of education and sustainability; 'this involves from picking up litter from our local woods to re-decorating a local school'. In 2013 there were 226 staff involved in this initiative.

In 2013 employees raised £63,000 for the company's Charity of the Year.

Commercially led support

The company has a 'Gift of the Gas' scheme whereby it pledges to donate £5 (subject to terms and conditions) to its partner charity for every disused Calor cylinder returned to an approved Calor outlet.

Corporate social responsibility

CSR committee: There were no details available, although there is a yearly sustainability report and it is very likely that there is a sustainability team.

CSR information: Taken from the company's website:

> Our vision is 'To become the sustainable energy company of choice in rural Britain'. We want to lead the way in tackling the biggest environmental and social issues facing our industry; we want sustainability to be incorporated into the daily fibre of our business. But we recognise that this means doing a lot more than simply managing our carbon footprint, so we are investing in a sustainable future across five key areas of the business: environment, innovation, community, workplace and marketplace.

We were unable to determine the ratio of women to men on the board.

CSR report: Each year a sustainability report is compiled detailing the company's performance in key areas; this is published online.

Applications

In writing to the correspondent.

Camelot UK Lotteries Ltd

Gaming

Correspondent: Corporate Responsibility Board, Magdalen House, Tolpits Lane, Watford, Herts WD18 9RN (tel: 01923 425000; fax: 01923 425050; website: www.camelotgroup.co.uk)

Directors: Wayne Kozun; Lee Sienna, Chair; Sir Patrick Brown; Tony Illesley; Sir Gerald Archer; Andy Duncan, Chief Executive Officer; Jane Rowe; David Kelly (women: 1; men: 7)

Year end	31/03/2014
Turnover	£6,730,900,000
Pre-tax profit	£76,800,000

Nature of business: Camelot is the operator of The UK National Lottery and has a licence to run it up to 2023.

The company changed its status during 2011, from a public limited company to a private limited company.

Company registration number: 2822203

Subsidiary undertakings include: Camelot Lotteries Ltd; CISL Ltd; National Lottery Enterprises Ltd.

UK employees: 628

Total employees: 628

Focus of giving: Enterprise/training, poverty and social exclusion, community/social welfare.

Membership: BITC

Cash donations undeclared	✓
Charity of the Year	✓
Gifts in kind	✓
Matched funding	✓
Payroll giving	✓
Sponsorship	✓

Charitable donations

Cash UK (latest available):	2014	£500,000
	2011	£300,000
	2009	£900,000
	2008	£1,900,000
	2007	£3,100,000
Total UK (cash and in kind):	2014	£500,000
Cash worldwide:	2014	£500,000
Total worldwide (cash and in kind):	2014	£500,000

Community involvement

The company gives cash donations to registered charities and encourages staff to volunteer for charitable activities both locally and nationally.

Organisations that Camelot has worked with include: Media Trust, Common Purpose, Education Extra and GamCare.

Charity of the Year: The Prince's Trust.

Corporate giving

The company did not declare its charitable donations for this accounting year. We have used the last three annual figures that we have available and estimate the total for 2013/14 to be around £500,000. Camelot's contribution has dropped considerably over the years, in 1998 the company gave £3.5 million and in 2007 the contribution to registered charities was £3.1 million.

In-kind support

Support is provided through gifts in kind and staff secondments. The company provides channels for community organisations to promote their activities within Camelot in order to encourage fundraising and volunteering by staff. The company's recycling collection point has facilities for collecting foreign coins, stamps, ink cartridges, toners and mobile phones.

Employee-led support

Recycling for charity

The company's facilities team raised over £28,000 by selling disused furniture and donated this to Marie Curie Cancer Care.

Volunteering days

All permanent employees can use four working hours per month, which is the equivalent to three consecutive or six non-consecutive working days a year (this is pro-rated for employees who work part-time), as volunteering time to work within a community group.

Team days

Employees take part in team-building days when they get the opportunity to use their skills within their community.

Matched funding

There is a matched funding programme in place where money raised by Camelot employees for registered charities will be matched up to £750 per individual per financial year.

Give As You Earn (GAYE)

Employees can donate to a charity tax-free directly through the company's payroll. The company covers all administration costs.

Commercially led support

Sponsorship

Watford Football Club has been at the heart of Watford's community for many years and the Watford FC's Community Sports and Education Trust delivers a diverse range of high quality programmes in the local area. As a registered charity the trust uses the power of sport and education to make a positive impact in local communities.

Corporate social responsibility

CSR committee: Membership consists of directors and senior managers from across the business. The Corporate Responsibility Board (CRB) assesses group-wide business strategy and performance from a CR perspective, and develops and decides future direction. The CRB consults and is advised by the independent advisory panel for corporate responsibility.

CSR information: This statement is taken from the company's website:

> At Camelot, we understand the importance of our local community, and the influence that we have upon it. That is why we are continually committed to ensuring we affect our local areas in a positive manner. We are also committed to helping employees invest in the causes they feel are important within these communities, drawing on their wealth of local knowledge which, in turn, helps us to invest wisely. Although we primarily support programmes that are aligned to our business impacts, we realise that many people already have their own local causes that they are involved with and we want to support them in this. We provide employees with the chance to support local initiatives through various fundraising and volunteering channels.

CSR report: The company's CR report is called 'Playing Our Part, Camelot's Corporate Responsibility' and can be downloaded from the website.

Exclusions

Activity outside the community involvement policy; overseas appeals/ sponsorship; individuals; advertisements in charity brochures/programmes; general appeals.

Applications

In writing to the correspondent.

Canary Wharf Group plc

Property

Correspondent: John Garwood, Secretary, The Corporate Responsibility Group, One Canada Square, Canary Wharf, London E14 5AB (tel: 020 7418 2000; fax: 020 7418 2222; email: info@canarywharf.com; website: group.canarywharf.com)

Directors: Peter Anderson II; George Iacobescu, Chair and Chief Executive Officer; Kahled Al-Rabban; Cai Zhiwei; Olivier de Poulpiquet; Sam Levinson; Alex Midgen; Brian Niles (women: 0; men: 8)

Year end	31/12/2013
Turnover	£364,300,000
Pre-tax profit	£6,700,000

Nature of business: The group is involved in property development, investment, and management.

Company registration number: 4191122

Subsidiary undertakings include: Canary Wharf Developments Ltd; Canary Wharf Estate Ltd; Canary Wharf Management Ltd; Heron Quays Properties Ltd; and South Quay Properties Ltd. A full list of subsidiaries is available from Companies House.

Main locations: London

UK employees: 972

Total employees: 972

Focus of giving: Economic generation, education, health, ill health, local groups, arts, culture, religion, sponsorship, sport, recreation, children, young people, community/social welfare.

Membership: BITC

Gifts in kind	✓
Market-led giving	✓
Matched funding	✓
Payroll giving	✓
Sponsorship	✓

Charitable donations

Cash UK (latest available):	2013	£626,000
	2010	£550,000
	2009	£687,000
	2008	£1,000,000
	2007	£394,500
Total UK (cash and in kind):	2013	£2,100,000
Cash worldwide:	2013	£626,000
Total worldwide (cash and in kind):	2013	£2,100,000

Community involvement

The group's community work covers nine main areas of activity:

- Representation and corporate leadership
- Corporate charitable support
- Employment and training
- Employee volunteering
- Community engagement and support
- Educational engagement and research
- Economic development – support for local businesses
- Sports sponsorship
- Arts and events

The primary areas of support are local community initiatives in and around the East Docklands and Tower Hamlets areas and since 2013 it seeks to engage with communities in the South Bank.

Demelza Hospice Care for Children

An example of community engagement includes help to Demelza Hospice Care for Children to create a Garden of Tranquility where it donated the design, project management, construction equipment, materials, trees and shrubs. Volunteers provided weekend labour to make the garden a reality. In addition to that more than £500,000 was fundraised in cash and in-kind donations from suppliers and their sub-contractors.

Spotlight

In 2013 the group made a joint donation of £30,000 with British Land and Land Aid (totalling £90,000) to fund a studio, a media suite and two classrooms for the charity. Through the partnership Canary Wharf group assists the charities activities in providing free tuition and coaching in activities, including drama, dance, broadcasting, fashion, styling and boxing.

SPLASH

The group has been supporting the local charity SPLASH 'with enough funding to employ an outreach worker to contact local young people and provide advice and engagement'.

Local community

The group states: 'We have also been active in community programmes that focus on the other segments of the local community.'

Examples include: Cubitt Town Bangladeshi Cultural Association; The Globe Town Pensioners; and The Stifford Centre (run by the Bangladeshi community).

Annually the group sponsors Christmas parties for local groups of pensioners and residents associations across the Isle of Dogs and neighbouring areas. It also organises tea dances, sponsors trips to the seaside and invites groups of local pensioners into the building to see the view and to have tea and cakes.

Various community events have been extended into the local Muslim community. The group provided funding for Eid parties in both the Bangladeshi and Somali communities and hosted a large iftar (breaking of the fast) gathering for all the local Muslim elders. Work has been undertaken with the Somali community in Tower Hamlets 'on a programme to improve the educational achievement of young people, and we work extensively with the many Bangladeshi community groups across Tower Hamlets on various projects ranging from after school clubs to support for growing social enterprises'.

Other charitable and community partners include CM Sounds, the BFI, London College of Fashion, the National Theatre and Whitechapel Gallery.

East End Community Foundation (EECF)

The group supports the foundation which is a merger of the Isle of Dogs CF and the St Katherine and Shadwell Trust. In 2013/14 a total of £20,000 was given to the organisation.

Canary Wharf Film Fund

Instead of charging a location fee for professional filming and photography in the Canary Wharf locations, the group asks crews to make a donation, half of which goes to the Canary Wharf Film Fund (CWFF), and the other half to local charities. The fund 'fosters film making and media in the local community, investing in equipment, training and projects that encourage young people to acquire the passion and skills that may eventually see them employed in the growing media sector in Canary Wharf and East London'. Projects recently funded by CWFF include digital video equipment for local schools and a summer training programme to introduce young people to film-making.

Education

The Tower Hamlets and Canary Wharf Further Education Trust (Charity Commission no. 1002772)

The trust began in 1990 as a of £2.5 million endowment 'to fund grants for local people to access further and higher education' and is now jointly administered by representatives of Canary Wharf Group and the London Borough of Tower Hamlets, It provides approximately £250,000 each year to local people who need additional support to access college, university or professional courses.

The Canary Wharf Achievement Fund

The Fund of £50,000 a year was set up in 1997 'to support a series of initiatives designed to improve local educational results through innovative programmes'. Some of the projects carried out through this programme have included: After School Clubs; Getting Ready for Reading and Talking Time; CommTAP.org; and Singing Playgrounds.

The group has also supported a number of organisations and projects on an ad-hoc basis. These included: Bygrove Primary School; Careers Academies UK; Culloden Primary School; George Green's School Café Vert; London Enterprise Challenge; Manorfield Primary School; Teach First; University of East London Art School Travel Bursaries.

Corporate giving

According to the Sustainability Report for 2013, during the year the group spent a total of £2.1 million (2012: £1.4 million) in 'community investment. The following breakdown is given:

Staff focused on community engagement	£1.1 million
Cash donations	£626,000
In-kind, including use of space	£281,000

Political donations: The annual report and accounts note that political donations, including gifts in kind made by the group 'during 2013 comprised £28,000 to the Labour Party, £24,000 to the Conservative Party and £31,000 to the Liberal Democrat Party (2012 – £22,000 to the Labour Party, £15,400 to the Conservative Party and £18,000 to the Liberal Democrat Party)'.

In-kind support

The group provides free office space for charities (such as Article 25, Medicins du Monde and Teach First), as well as other in-kind donations, as required.

Equipment on Loan Scheme

Through the scheme local grass-roots football teams are loaned proper training equipment.

Employee-led support

Volunteering

The Employee Volunteering Policy 2014 document notes that 'the group actively encourages its employees to develop their skills within the context of their personal development plans and to harness their skills to add value to the many voluntary and community organisations who rely on volunteers to achieve their objectives'. Each member of staff is entitled to two working days of paid work time per year for community volunteering (subject to operational need and the Line Manager's approval), generally to registered charities. 'The Group hopes that the employee would match that commitment by contributing their own time also.' In addition to its own staff volunteering the group encourages engagement of volunteers from tenant and occupier firms. It also have participated in BITC's 'Give and Gain Day' – a national day of corporate volunteering.

In 2013 the group facilitated six volunteering activities, including: time spent on the East End Community Foundation's Christmas Bag Appeal for Elders (see below); assisting the Cubitt Town Library Community Garden; and helping the Spitalfields City Farm. During the year at work a total of 40 staff members volunteered to supervise and mentor work placement participants.

Canary Wharf Group sponsors 'a Christmas Gift bag collection and delivery to hundreds of single, less well-off local pensioners' through a project run with EECF. It involves people who work on the Wharf buying £10 worth of Christmas food and gifts and volunteers delivering bags door to door.

An example of employee engagement, given in the Sustainability Report, also includes a regeneration of a derelict garden on Bate Street together with local community. 'Volunteers from the group, the LBTH Green Team and Spitalfields Farm tidied up the area and planted a rose garden with bushes provided by the group.'

Payroll giving

A scheme operates to allow regular donations from employees' salaries.

Matched funding

A scheme operates.

Commercially led support

Sponsorships

Good causes sponsorship is available.

Sports

Sponsorship has been provided to a range of local sports groups. Examples have included: Bethnal Green United Football Club; Tower Hamlets Schools Gymnastics and Dance Display Team; Millwall Albion Football Club Bethnal Green Sharks Swimming Club; Middlesex County Championships; Annual Summer Sports Programme; ONE Ball. ONE Game. ONE Community; and East London Summer Football League. See the group's website for further details.

British Heart Foundation Canary Wharf Jog

The annual event involves more than 1,000 fun-runners, raising over £100,000 for the charity.

Arts and culture

The group has assisted a number of events and programmes for the national youth charity UK Youth, the London Festival of Architecture, the National Youth Theatre, and the Jewish Association of Business Ethics. It has been involved in a five-year programme helping Heritage of London Trust's work to restore and protect historic structures and provides an ongoing support to the Museum of London Docklands.

Education and training

In partnership with the University of East London's Royal Docks Business School Canary Wharf Group enabled the graduates 'to prepare and position themselves for jobs with Canary Wharf's major financial and professional services firms'. To assist the programme the group donated office space and held guest tutorials from leading London executives, policy makers and regulators as well as provided job training sessions and networking opportunities.

Corporate social responsibility

CSR committee: There was no evidence of a separate CSR committee. The board retains overall responsibility for the monitoring and implementation of the group's sustainability, environmental and social policies and activities. There is a Corporate Responsibility Group (CRG) which assists the board and regularly provides additional focus on a range of issues, including the community.

CSR information: The Community Policy Statement 2014 says:

> Canary Wharf Group plc's Community Policy is based on two simple principles of corporate responsibility.
>
> First of all, our developments should open the widest possible economic opportunity to people living in the surrounding areas. This may take the form of direct employment, either during construction phases or on completed developments, indirect employment through our supply chain or that of our tenants, or business opportunities for local small companies and social enterprises.
>
> Secondly, our developments should benefit those who, for whatever reason, are unable to, or do not wish to access the resultant economic opportunities. Instead we seek to be a good neighbour, keeping local people and stakeholders consulted and informed about our plans and activities and supporting activities which help make our communities great places to live.

The annual report and accounts note:

> The objective of the group's Community, Social and Economic Development strategy is to maintain and enhance the relationship with the surrounding community. The aim is to support employment opportunities and enhance skills, as well as investing in young people. The Group also has a strong commitment to the local business environment, while understanding the vision for the future. Improving the transition from education to employment; securing opportunities for local job seekers; maximising supply chains and community led development is a priority for the group especially as it diversifies and evolves.

The main focus of Canary Wharf Group is engagement with the communities. The group states – 'in contrast to traditional developers, we stay involved in our sites long after construction is complete'.

CSR report: A Sustainability Report was available from the group's website.

Exclusions

Our research suggests that support is not generally given for advertising in charity brochures, animal welfare, appeals from individuals, local appeals not in areas of company presence or potential Charity of the Year partners.

Applications

The company: In writing to the correspondent. The CRG meets six times a year.

The trust: The formal contact for the trust is David Stone (tel: 020 7364 4888; email: david.stone@towerhamlets.gov.uk) at London Borough of Tower Hamlets, Mulberry Place, 5 Clove Crescent, London E14 2BG.

Caparo Group Ltd

Manufacturing

Correspondent: Company Secretary, Caparo House, 103 Baker Street, London W1U 6LN (tel: 020 7486 1417; fax: 020 7224 4109; website: www.caparo.co.uk)

Directors: Hon Lord Paul of Marylebone, Chair; Hon Anjili Paul; Hon Akash Paul; Hon Angad Paul

Year end	31/12/2013
Turnover	£375,800,000
Pre-tax profit	(£200,000)

Nature of business: Specialists in the manufacture and supply of steel and engineering products. The directors are jointly and indirectly interested in the whole of the issued share capital of Caparo Group Ltd through shareholdings registered in the name of Aparo International Corporation, a company registered in the British Virgin Islands. Caparo International Corporation ultimately holds the issued share capital of Caparo Group Ltd on behalf of a series of family trusts.

Company registration number: 1387694

Subsidiary undertakings include: Caparo plc; Caparo Industries plc.

Main locations: London

Total employees: 2,354

Focus of giving: Education, medical research, science technology, children, young people.

Charitable donations

Cash UK (latest available):	2013	£338,000
	2012	£220,000
	2010	£213,000
	2008	£500,000
	2007	£1,042,510

Community involvement

Lord Paul came to Britain in 1966 for medical treatment for his daughter, Ambika. He remained in England after her tragic death in 1968 and sees all he has created in the Caparo Group as a dedication to her memory. In 1994 Lord Paul took the opportunity to commemorate the rebuilding of London's Children's Zoo in her name. Whilst receiving treatment in London, the Zoo became Ambika's favourite destination.

The Ambika Paul Foundation (Charity Number: 276127) focuses its charitable contributions on education/training, medical/health/sickness, overseas famine relief and arts and culture. It specifically wishes to benefit children/young people and people of a particular nationality.

Caparo Industries is a diversified manufacturer of engineered and steel products with multiple sites across the West Midlands. The business has long standing relationships with a number of educational and charitable organisations in the region (such as the University of Wolverhampton and the RSA Academy in Tipton) and has always aimed to support causes, which further children's health, education and welfare. Consequently, when locally based branch of charity KIDS, the Orchard Centre, contacted Caparo in October with a request for support with a garden improvement project, the company responded with a donation and help with the project's management.

Corporate giving

During 2013 Caparo declared £338,000 (2012: £220,000) in charitable donations. Previously we know that donations have been made to the Ambika Paul Foundation.

See the corporate charity entry on p. 422 for more information.

In-kind support

Project management support was provided for support of a garden improvement project in Stourbridge.

Corporate social responsibility

CSR committee: There is no evidence of a separate CSR committee.

CSR information: This information was obtained from the company's website:

> At Caparo, Corporate Social Responsibility and concern for environment, health and safety are the intrinsic elements of the company's long-term strategy. Caparo's CSR commitment is a manifestation of its determination to improve quality of life not only for its employees, but the society at large.

CSR report: There is no evidence of a separate CSR report; however, CSR information was available on the company's website.

Corporate charity: Ambika Paul Foundation (Charity Commission no. 276127).

Exclusions

The organisation will not offer support for political appeals or fundraising events.

Applications

In writing to: Trustees of The Ambika Paul Foundation, 103 Baker Street, London W1U 6LN.

Capital One (Europe) plc

Financial services

Correspondent: UK Community Relations Team, Trent House, Station Street, Nottingham NG2 3HX (website: www.capitalone.co.uk)

Directors: Chris Newkirk, Head of International; Victoria Mitchell, UK. Vice President and UK. Chief Operating Officer; Rob Harding, UK. Vice President and Chief Information Officer; Neil Herbert, International Chief Financial Officer; Jaidev Janardana (women: 1; men: 4)

Year end	31/12/2013
Turnover	£526,009,000
Pre-tax profit	£139,977,000

Nature of business: The company provides a range of financial services in the UK primarily comprising credit card lending.

Company registration number: 3879023

Investments in subsidiary undertakings include: Capital One Homeowner Loans Ltd; Capital One Loans (UK) Ltd; Capital One Mortgages Ltd; Castle Credit Card Securitisation Funding Ltd; Tenby Castle Funding Group Ltd; Sherwood Castle Holdings Ltd.

Main locations: Nottingham, London

UK employees: 1,200

Focus of giving: Education, local groups, sport, recreation, children, young people, community/social welfare, disability.

Membership: BITC, LBG

Gifts in kind	✓
Market-led giving	✓
Matched funding	✓
Payroll giving	✓

Charitable donations

Cash UK (latest available):	2013	£1,200,000
	2012	£1,100,000
	2010	£330,200
	2009	£430,550
	2008	£335,300
Total UK (cash and in kind):	2013	£1,200,000
Cash worldwide:	2013	£1,200,000
Total worldwide (cash and in kind):	2013	£1,200,000

Community involvement

The Capital One website states that the company wants to:

> Help young people, regardless of where they live, develop behaviours and skills that will help them become more employable, access a wider range of job opportunities and achieve their potential. By learning to be proactive, building resilience, being confident with their finances and developing the broader skills needed to be successful in the world of work, young people will become more confident and more employable.

In the 16 years that the company has been in the UK it has supported projects like the Nottingham Forest Football Club Community programme, been flagship supporters of the Nottingham Ice Centre's youth skating programme, and has 'raised millions of pounds for local and national charities'.

It is the company's intention at the time of writing (2014) to start focusing more on employability and financial capability programmes.

Partners include: Capital One continues to financially support the Money Advice Trust each year to support its valuable work of free, independent financial advice for those with debt problems.

Corporate giving

During the year 2013 the company made charitable contributions of £1.2 million directly benefitting around 105,000 individuals from 247 charitable organisations. We are taking this statement taken from the company's accounts, to refer to cash donations. We do not know the worldwide figure.

In-kind support

The company has several donation schemes for employees:

- A 'Pound for Pound' scheme whereby the company matches 100% of the money raised for charity
- A volunteer grant is available for employees who work on a regular basis for a local community group
- A 'Pennies From Heaven' scheme helps employees automatically donate the odd pence in their salaries to Macmillan Cancer Support
- The Give As You Earn programme gives employees a tax efficient way of donating to their favourite charity straight from their salary

Cheese Matters

This programme, developed and run in partnership with two other businesses and Businesses in the Community (BITC), brings secondary school pupils closer to the reality of financial management. It follows the story of a young man who has got himself into debt, explores the consequences and then lets the students make decisions about what the outcome should be. The programme has been delivered to over 1,000 local students, and the aim is to cover every school in Nottingham by July 2014.

Employee-led support

Employees are encouraged to take at least one day a year – or the equivalent in hours – to get involved with the company's community activities. They use their skills to benefit local charitable organisations for example assisting with business plans, websites, databases and providing financial consultancy.

81% of employees took part in some form of community activity in 2013.

Commercially led support

The company has been supporting local schools Bulwell Academy and Big Wood School, in Nottingham for many years. It focuses its contribution on delivering employability workshops and financial capability sessions through Cheese Matters. Work experience is available for students at partner schools, which teaches students about the company, the world of credit and what it takes to be successful in the world of work.

Additionally, tours are available under the company's AWE (Aspirational Work Experience) initiative to local primary schools. These are one-day experiences which cover the basics of financial management, an introduction to the world of work and a fun insight into what the company does. The sessions are facilitated by volunteer employees.

Corporate social responsibility

CSR committee: There were no specific details of a CSR Committee published on the UK website.

CSR information: The following is taken from the company's website: 'We're committed to doing everything we can to support our communities, the environment and our employees. We have an award-winning community programme, helping young people in particular try new things and reach their full potential.'

CSR report: No CSR report is published on the website.

Applications

In writing to the correspondent. We were unable to find a telephone number which related to applications for charitable/community giving, nor an appropriate email address.

Cargill plc

Commodity traders, distribution, food services, shipping

Correspondent: See 'Applications', Knowle Hill Park, Fairmile Lane, Cobham, Surrey KT11 2PD (tel: 01932 861000; website: www.cargill.co.uk/en/corporate-responsibility/index.jsp)

Directors: Peter de Braal; Martin Douglas; Christopher Oliver; Melanie Pollard; Robin Thurston (women: 1; men: 4)

Year end	31/05/2014
Turnover	£1,222,630,000
Pre-tax profit	£42,513,000

Nature of business: The company trades commodities and processes and distributes foodstuffs.

Company registration number: 1387437

Main locations: London, Wolverhampton, York, Worksop, Manchester, Liverpool, Hereford, Hull, Cobham, Within St Hughes

Total employees: 719

Focus of giving: Education, environment, health, ill health, STEM (science, technology, engineering and mathematics), poverty and social exclusion, science technology, children, young people.

Gifts in kind ✓

Charitable donations

Cash UK (latest available):	2014	£227,000
	2013	£163,000
	2011	£231,500
	2009	£39,800
	2008	£115,500
Total UK (cash and in kind):	2014	£227,000
Cash worldwide:	2014	£227,000
Total worldwide (cash and in kind):	2014	£227,000

Community involvement

Cargill's five UK Cares Councils support initiatives and projects in the areas of health, education and environmental stewardship. Corporate support is complemented by employee volunteering.

Corporate giving

The company's annual report for 2013/14 declared charitable contributions of £227,000.

We were unable to determine a value for the in-kind support given by the company.

Charity partner

Cargill began supporting FareShare in 2009 with a two year commitment to help establish FareShare Merseyside. The company is now part of the way into a new three year £225,000 commitment to support FareShare North West and FareShare Merseyside, helping to support people suffering from food poverty. Cargill employees have also volunteered at FareShare's Liverpool and Manchester depots.

Beneficiaries include: FareShare

Employee-led support

Employee volunteering

Employees volunteer with activities to support projects in the areas of health, education and environmental stewardship. These have included: employees helping to establish a vegetable garden at a homeless shelter in Manchester; volunteers providing one-to-one reading sessions with local schoolchildren; and employees from the Cobham, London, Manchester and Liverpool sites spending two days helping the conservation work of the Wildfowl and Wetlands Trust.

Commercially led support

Cargill supports programmes that provide training and schooling in science, technology and engineering.

Corporate social responsibility

CSR committee: In the UK, there are five Cares Councils who support a number of initiatives and projects across the UK.

CSR information: The following is taken from the company's UK website:

> As we expand around the globe, we are creating strong relationships with our customers, employees and communities. We recognize our continued success depends on the growth and health of our communities and partners, as well as the vitality and conservation of our natural resources.
>
> We support programmes that focus on improving nutrition and health, education and environmental stewardship.

CSR report: A report on global corporate responsibility actions is published annually.

Exclusions

Our research indicates that grants are not given to/for the following:

- Organisations that do not serve communities where Cargill has a business presence
- Individuals or groups seeking support for research, planning, personal needs or travel
- Public service or political campaigns
- Lobbying, political or fraternal activities
- Benefit dinners, fundraising events or tickets to the same
- Fundraising campaigns, walk-a-thons, or promotions to eliminate or control specific diseases
- Athletic scholarships

- Advertising sponsorships
- Religious groups for religious purposes
- Publications, audio-visual productions or special broadcasts
- Lobbying, political or fraternal activities
- Medical equipment (ambulances, defibrillators)

Applications

Cargill businesses and facilities and their employees give through 350 employee-led, worldwide Cargill Cares Councils. The councils provide support for local charitable and civic organisations and programmes such as food relief agencies, schools and youth programs, and local environmental projects.

The following information was taken from the Cargill Inc. website: 'If your program or project is in a Cargill community contact the Cargill manager or Cargill Cares Council. They are typically responsible for reviewing local grant requests and making funding decisions.'

Carillion plc

Building/construction

Correspondent: Sustainability Dept., 84 Salop Street, Wolverhampton WV3 0SR (tel: 01902 318766.; email: sustainability@carillionplc.com; website: www.carillionplc.com/sustainability)

Directors: Philip Green, Chair; Richard Howson, Group Chief Executive; Richard Adam, Group Finance Director; Andrew Dougal; Steve Mogford; Alison Horner; Ceri Powell (women: 2; men: 5)

Year end	31/12/2013
Turnover	£3,332,600,000
Pre-tax profit	£110,600,000

Nature of business: Providing expertise in commercial and industrial building, refurbishment, civil engineering, road and rail construction and maintenance, mechanical and electrical services, facilities management and PFI Solutions

Company registration number: 3782379

Subsidiary undertakings include: Carillion (AMBS) Ltd; Carillion (Aspire Construction) Holdings No. 2 Ltd; Carillion (Aspire Services) Holdings No. 2 Ltd; Carillion Alawi LLC (Oman) 49%; Carillion Canada Inc (Canada); Carillion CR Ltd

Main locations: Wolverhampton, Leeds, Manchester, Liverpool, London, Bristol, Brentford, Glasgow

UK employees: 16,149

Total employees: 25,915

Focus of giving: Economic generation, education, enterprise/training, environment, housing, homelessness, poverty and social exclusion, children, young people, community/social welfare.

Membership: BITC, LBG

Gifts in kind	✓
Overseas giving	✓
Payroll giving	✓

Charitable donations

Cash UK (latest available):	2013	£200,000
	2012	£200,000
	2010	£200,000
	2009	£200,000
	2008	£129,000
Total UK (cash and in kind):	2013	£1,580,000
Cash worldwide:	2013	£200,000
Total worldwide (cash and in kind):	2013	£1,820,000

Community involvement

Carillion plc supports the communities in which it has a presence by contributing to local causes the equivalent of 1% of its pre-tax profits in cash and in-kind (staff time) donations. Numerous charities around the world are supported, including those in the areas of: food, health and nutrition campaigns; biodiversity projects; education; and assisting underprivileged people. Through the Armed Forces Corporate Covenant, the group has also pledged its support of the UK armed forces community.

Corporate giving

The annual report and accounts of 2013 declared payments for charitable purposes of £200,000. The report also stated: 'The Carillion Group also contributes the equivalent of one per cent of profits per annum in cash or in-kind (staff time on community projects) to community activities.' In 2013 these cash and in-kind (staff time) contributions totalled more than £1.8 million, including management costs.

A performance data page on the website offered a breakdown of contributions made during the year by business region:

UK	£1.4 million
Group	£237,000
Canada	£118,000
MENA	£83,000

We were unable to determine the proportion of these donations given in cash/in-kind; however, we believe that the £237,000 stated for group donations includes the £200,000 declared in charitable payments in the annual report and accounts. The primary beneficiaries appear to have been UK-registered charities and so, we have taken this as our figure for UK cash donations. As we could not determine a total for cash donations worldwide, we have also taken this as our global figure.

Beneficiaries included: Barnardo's (£20,000); Business in the Community; CRASH; Walking With the Wounded; The Wildlife Trust

Carillion Charities Fund

The fund gives money to charities nominated by Carillion employees worldwide. In 2013, from more than 260 nominations, £40,000 was donated to 80 charities, with each receiving £500.

Beneficiaries included: Alzheimer's Research UK; Camsley Grange Riding for the Disabled Group; Leeds Mencap; Mind; The Haven Wolverhampton; The Seashell Trust

Charity partner

Barnardo's – Carillion made an initial donation of £20,000 to the charity, which will also benefit from sponsorship, fundraising events, volunteering, mentoring and skills training.

In-kind support

Staff time

Carillion's Special Leave Policy allows employees six days leave per year to be spent volunteering in their local communities.

Employee-led support

Employee volunteering

Globally, 12% of Carillion employees volunteer in their communities. UK employees can register on a national database to volunteer in local schools through Inspiring the Future, which encourages young people to further their careers aspirations, and can also volunteer as mentors on the 'Ready for Work' scheme.

Payroll giving

UK staff are able to donate to charities through the payroll giving scheme.

Commercially led support

Employment and education

Carillion helps to engage marginalised groups such as long-term unemployed and homeless people, ex-offenders and wounded service personnel through the work of the Carillion Academy.

Building relationships with schools

The group supported Business in the Community's Business Class programme, engaging with local schools to help open the eyes of young people to the world of business and encourage them to study STEM subjects. Schools in Manchester, Nottingham and Wolverhampton were involved. Carillion is also in a ten year contract with Oxfordshire County Council, in partnership with STEMNET and Science Oxford. This sees volunteer employees promoting the study of STEM subjects and inspiring the next generation of engineers and architects.

Helping the unemployed into stable employment

As part of its Business Action on Homelessness partnership, Carillion has supported BITC's Ready to Work programme. Two-week work placements were offered to 140 people who had been affected by homelessness, who were then coached for six months by employee volunteers.

Corporate social responsibility

CSR committee: The board is responsible for driving the group's commitment to sustainability, evaluating performances and approving new sustainability initiatives. It receives a monthly report about sustainability and meets three times a year with external advisors. The Group Chief Executive, Richard Howson, has board-level responsibility for sustainability and the Chief Sustainability Officer, David Picton, has overall accountability for sustainability across the group

CSR information: Carillion's 2020 Sustainability Strategy is based on six 'positive outcomes'. These are:

- Enabling low-carbon economies
- Protecting the environment
- Supporting sustainable communities
- Providing better prospects for employees
- Leading the way in the sector
- Building a successful business

CSR report: There is an annual sustainability report published online.

Applications

In writing to the correspondent.

CEF Holdings Ltd

Electronics/computers

Correspondent: M. S. Jacobs, Company Secretary, 141 Farmer Ward Road, Kenilworth, Warwickshire CV8 2SU (tel: 01926 514380; website: www.cef.co.uk)

Directors: R. H. Thorn; T. B. Yallop; A. Jackson; M. S. Jacobs; K. A. D. Barnett; G. L. Hartland; T. A. Hartland Mackie; J. A. Mackie; C. H. Beddows

Year end	30/04/2013
Turnover	£437,300,000
Pre-tax profit	£19,710,000

Nature of business: Principal activity: electrical wholesalers and manufacturers.

Company registration number: 316018

Subsidiaries not listed in this company's accounts.

UK employees: 2,895

Total employees: 2,895

Focus of giving: Education, health, ill health, medical research, children, young people, disability.

Cash donations undeclared ✓

Charitable donations

Cash UK (latest available):	2013	£470,000
	2011	£454,000
	2009	£467,000
	2008	£490,000
	2007	£438,000
Total UK (cash and in kind):	2013	£470,000
Cash worldwide:	2013	£470,000
Total worldwide (cash and in kind):	2013	£470,000

Community involvement

Unfortunately, there was no information available regarding this company's charitable giving. Previous research has shown that historically, the Janet Nash Charitable Trust (Charity Commission no. 326880) is a recurring beneficiary and applications for donations are unlikely to be successful.

Corporate giving

In 2012/13 the company did not declare its charitable donations in its annual report and accounts. We have therefore averaged its UK charitable donations based on the last three figures available to us and estimated the total to be £470,000.

In-kind support

Not known.

Employee-led support

Not known.

Corporate social responsibility

CSR information: No CSR details published. We were unable to determine the ratio of women to men on the board.

Exclusions

Previous research determined that there was no support for advertising, animal welfare, appeals from individuals, fundraising events, overseas projects, political appeals, religious appeals or local appeals not in areas of company presence.

Applications

The company has an historic association with one charity and therefore unsolicited applications are unlikely to be responded to.

Celtic Energy Ltd

Mining

Correspondent: Community Relations, 9 Beddau Way, Castlegate Business Park, Caerphilly CF83 2AX (tel: 02920 760990; email: email: enquiries@coal.com; website: www.coal.com)

Directors: R. Morris; DHM. Consultancy Ltd; W. Watson; R. Thompson

Year end	31/03/2013
Turnover	£94,795,000
Pre-tax profit	£14,474,000

Nature of business: Celtic Mining Group Ltd (CMGL) was formed in 2004 by Richard Walters as a vehicle for acquiring the entire share capital of Celtic Group Holdings Ltd, which in turn owns Celtic Energy Ltd, the principal operating company of the group. Celtic Energy Ltd is the successor in South Wales to the former British Coal Corporation that was privatised by the Government in 1994 and was responsible for all of British Coal's surface coal mining activities in South Wales.

Owner Richard Walters is a member of the Walters family which owns the Walters Group of companies that include a major civil engineering and plant hire company operating out of South Wales.

Company registration number: 2997376

Subsidiary undertakings include: Not known.

Main locations: Caerphilly

UK employees: 343

Total employees: 343

Focus of giving: Education, children, young people, community/social welfare.

Charitable donations

Cash UK (latest available):	2013	£19,000
	2012	£81,000
	2011	£73,000
	2009	£28,000
	2008	£17,000
Total UK (cash and in kind):	2013	£19,000
Cash worldwide:	2013	£19,000
Total worldwide (cash and in kind):	2013	£19,000

Community involvement

Probably because of the nature of the business, the company is particularly keen to have good relations with its communities. To promote this, each site has a community liaison committee which comprises local councillors and residents. Meeting on a regular basis, the committee is kept fully up to date on the site's progress, and each member has the opportunity to air their views.

The company states it is committed to supporting local good causes for the long-term benefit of residents of South Wales.

Corporate giving

In 2012/13 the company declared £19,000 in charitable cash donations, significantly less than in the previous year which was £81,000. In view of what the company says on its website about its community involvement, we consider the amount may be much more than this; however, further research did not reveal any more detailed financial information. The website states that the community liaison committee is also responsible for administering a 'significant community donations budget' throughout the life of the site. This is in addition to the community benefit package provided by the company. Schools, charities, sporting groups and local organisations throughout South Wales have benefited from donations from Celtic Energy.

In-kind support

Visitors are welcome to visit any of Celtic Energy's operating sites and see for themselves the work that is undertaken on site and the work that goes on in the community. Occasionally, the sites hold open days to encourage local residents and visitors to South Wales to view and discuss the operations of a surface coal mine. The company considers that this is particularly important for the education of children who are also encouraged to accompany their parents.

Prospective visitors are advised to contact their local Mine Manager or the Head Office at Caerphilly if they would like to arrange a visit.

Corporate social responsibility

CSR committee: Each site has a community liaison committee which comprises local councillors and residents.

CSR information: There were no CSR details published. The company's community contribution appears to focus mainly on good customer relations.

Unable to determine the ratio of women to men on the board.

Exclusions

No support is given for political or religious appeals or for local appeals not in areas of company presence.

Applications

In writing to the correspondent address.

To discuss site visits or concerns with regard to operations in your area telephone 0845678943 or email: enquiries@coal.com.

CEMEX UK Operations Ltd

Building/construction

Correspondent: Secretary to The Cemex Foundation, CEMEX House, Coldharbour Lane, Thorpe, Egham, Surrey TW20 8TD (tel: 01932 568833; fax: 01932 568933; website: www.cemex.co.uk)

Directors: L. H. Russell; C. A. Leese; L. Zea; I. Madridejos; J. Gonzalez; D. M. J. O'Donnell; C. Uruchurtu; J. A. Smalley

Year end	31/12/2013
Turnover	£733,126,000
Pre-tax profit	(£10,553,000)

Nature of business: Cemex is a global building materials company with a presence in more than 50 countries. Cemex UK Operations Ltd is the principal Cemex trading company in the UK.

Company registration number: 658390

'Agents of the company' include: Cemex UK Cement Ltd; Cemex UK Marine Ltd; Cemex Paving Solutions Ltd; Rombus Leasing Ltd; RMC Logistics Scotland Ltd.

Main locations: Rugby, Barrington, South Ferriby, Rochester, Egham

UK employees: 2,873

Total employees: 44,000

Focus of giving: Education, environment, community/social welfare.

Charity of the Year	✓
Gifts in kind	✓
Humanitarian aid: overseas	✓
Matched funding	✓

Charitable donations

Cash UK (latest available):	2013	£59,000
	2012	£53,000
	2010	£27,000
	2009	£72,309
	2008	£130,614
Total UK (cash and in kind):	2013	£59,000
Cash worldwide:	2013	£164,000
Total worldwide (cash and in kind):	2013	£164,000

Community involvement

CEMEX UK Foundation

The company channels its charitable contributions through the CEMEX UK Foundation (which is not a registered charity). The foundation has been created to provide a single point of focus for all the company's charitable, community support and employee engagement activities. The company states that this focus will enable financial and in-kind support to be more effectively used for the benefit of those individuals and organisations applying for support.

Cemex Community Fund

Created to administer a proportion of the landfill tax receipts paid to government by the company in support of environmental and community projects, this fund has supported over 170 projects to the value of £10 million since its inception.

Since the disposal of the company's principal landfill activities, this fund now has a more modest income than previously and likes to fund individual projects of around £15,000 each.

Partnerships

The company works with Groundwork UK to improve communities where the company operates.

Charity of the Year: Butterfly Conservation – there is a long-standing and continuing relationship with this charity. The company not only supports it in cash terms but works with it to improve wildlife habitats where it has an operational presence.

Corporate giving

During 2013, the company made charitable donations totalling £59,000 (2012: £53,000). We have no information regarding the value of the company's global giving except for its matched funding which we estimate to be around £105,000. We have taken this to be the worldwide cash donations and added the £59,000 that we know to have been given in the UK making £164,000.

In-kind support

Matched funding: Employees involved in raising money for charities and their communities have their efforts matched by the company by up to a maximum of £250.

The 2013 annual report for Cemex states that US$500,000 was raised from its worldwide employees' donations and the company's two-to-one matching contributions to help families impacted by Typhoon Haiyan in the Philippines. Although likely to be more, we have used a percentage of this figure as the company's worldwide cash donation and worldwide contributions.

Employee-led support

In the UK, volunteers from local CEMEX UK sites and offices spent time helping to plant over 400 trees at the RSPB nature reserve, Baron's Haugh, as part of the company's volunteering scheme, Lendahand. The company's employees globally raise funds for humanitarian relief.

Corporate social responsibility

CSR committee: There is an advisory panel for sustainability globally.

CSR information: The company channels its charitable contribution through the CEMEX UK Foundation but there appears to be no written policy published with regard to its charitable and community giving.

We could not determine the ratio of women to men on the board.

CSR report: The global company produces a Sustainability Report annually.

Exclusions

No support is given for political appeals.

Applications

In writing to the correspondent. Applicants wishing to establish if they meet the company's proximity criteria can now visit: www.cemexlocations.co.uk.

Center Parcs Ltd

Leisure

Correspondent: Corporate Social Responsibility Team, One Edison Rise, New Ollerton, Newark, Nottinghamshire NG22 9DP (website: www.centerparcs.co.uk)

Directors: Don Camilleri; Martin Dalby, Chief Executive Officer; Paul Kent; Judi Leavor; Colin Whaley; Graham White; Paul Inglett, Finance Director; Andrea Valeri; Peter Stoll; Michael Pegler; Farhad Karim; Tania Daguere-Lindback (women: 3; men: 9)

Year end	24/04/2014
Turnover	£314,600,000
Pre-tax profit	£20,600,000

Nature of business: Managing the development of the UK Center Parcs villages. The business is ultimately owned by investment funds advised by the Blackstone Group.

The Center Parcs business is managed in the UK by the board of directors which comprises representatives of its principal shareholder, the Blackstone Group, together with three executive members. Listed as 'contacts' are the members of the operating board who have the responsibility of day to day management.

All financial information given in this entry relates to the original four villages and excludes the Woburn Forest Village which opened in 2014.

Company registration number: 1908230

Subsidiary undertakings include: Center Parcs Energy Services Ltd, Center Parcs Card Services Ltd, Center Parcs (Nominees) Ltd, and Centrepark Ltd.

Main locations: Penrith, Newark, Brandon, Warminster

UK employees: 6,000

Total employees: 6,000

Focus of giving: Environment, health, ill health, children, young people.

Cash donations undeclared	✓
Charity of the Year	✓
Gifts in kind	✓
Matched funding	✓
Payroll giving	✓

Charitable donations

Cash UK (latest available):	2014	£50,000
	2012	£52,000
	2011	£90,000
	2009	£15,000
Total UK (cash and in kind):	2014	£50,000
Cash worldwide:	2014	£52,000
Total worldwide (cash and in kind):	2014	£50,000

Community involvement

At each village and at its head office there are employee representative committees known as 'councils' where staff donated in total over £9,000 in this financial year. The group also supports charities local to its operations by staff fundraising and volunteering, cash donations and in-kind products.

Charity partnerships

Every few years the group makes a commitment to a long-term charitable partnership or partnerships. For 2014 and 2015 these will be ChildLine and The Wildlife Trusts. Guests will be invited to make donations which the group will match.

Corporate giving

In 2013/14 cash donations were not specified in the group's annual accounts and report and we have taken an average of the last two years figures (that we have available) and estimated the cash donation to be around £50,000. In 2013/14 the group donated short breaks to the charities listed at 'In-kind support'. Unfortunately we do not know the cost to the group of these donations.

In-kind support

In-kind support is given in the form of holiday breaks to disadvantaged families going through difficult times including those whose children are seriously ill. Charities to benefit include: Make-A-Wish Foundation UK, The Lily Foundation, Nicola's Fund and the Rainbow Trust.

The group will match donations made by staff for its partnership charities, ChildLine and The Woodlands Trusts.

Employee-led support

The group encourages staff to volunteer at local community projects by giving them a day a year for this purpose. Staff volunteer at schools, community groups and nature projects.

Payroll giving raised £4,000 for local charities.

Corporate social responsibility

CSR committee: There was no information available on the constitution of the CSR team.

CSR information: The group's 2013/14 annual report states that as a sustainable business it seeks to benefit the communities in which it operates. It sources local services and produce wherever possible and works with employees, local suppliers, communities and charities across the UK to improve the way it operates.

CSR report: The group's CSR report is given in its annual review which covers: people, nature and biodiversity, sustainability and charity.

Applications

In writing to the correspondent referenced 'Charitable giving' or write to the 'Employee Representative Council' at your nearest Center Parcs.

Central England Co-operative

Retail – department and variety stores, retail – miscellaneous, retail – supermarkets

Correspondent: Community Dividend Selection Committee, Central House, Hermes Road, Lichfield, Staffordshire WS13 6RH (tel: 01543 414140; website: www.centralengland.coop)

Directors: Richard Bickle; Elaine Dean, Vice-President; Paul Singh; Dave Ellgood; Robin Farrell; Marta Mayhew; Graeme Watkins; Sue Rushton; Max Hunt; Stuart Unwin; Maria Lee, President; Sean Clothier (women: 4; men: 8)

Year end	25/01/2014
Turnover	£717,845,000
Pre-tax profit	£10,988,000

Nature of business: The society's principal business activities are food, petrol filling stations and funeral services.

On 19 September 2013, it was announced that the boards of Anglia Regional Co-operative Society and Midlands Co-operative Society had agreed merger terms. Approved by members on 4 and 18 November, legal completion of the merger took place on 1 December, with the Anglia Society transferring engagements to Midlands Co-operative. On 15 January 2014, members of the merged society approved a change of name to Central England Co-operative effective from 25 January 2014. Central England Co-operative is one of the largest independent retailers in the UK, with over 400 trading outlets, around 8,600 colleagues and more than 330,000 regular trading members. Independent from The Co-operative Group, it is part of the wider co-operative movement, working together to provide all sorts of benefits for our members and customers. Central England Co-operative trades across 16 counties from the Midlands to the East Coast.

Company registration number: IP10143R

Subsidiary undertakings include: Advantage Motor Group Ltd; Anglia Co-operative (Food) Ltd; Anglia Co-operative Properties Ltd; Leicester Carriage Builders 2002 Ltd; Midlands Co-op Scottish Ltd Partnership; Oakwell Stores Society Ltd; Shaws Petroleum Ltd; Westgate Optical Ltd; Yaxley Farm Ltd.

Main locations: Peterborough

UK employees: 8,700

Total employees: 8,700

Focus of giving: General charitable purposes, advertising in charity brochures, education, fundraising events, medical research, older people, children, young people.

Membership: BITC

Charity of the Year	✓
Gifts in kind	✓

Charitable donations

Cash UK (latest available):	2014	£514,000
	2011	£27,000
	2009	£30,000
	2008	£30,000
	2007	£67,000
Total UK (cash and in kind):	2014	£514,000
Cash worldwide:	2014	£514,000
Total worldwide (cash and in kind):	2014	£514,000

Community involvement

The Making a Difference Community Dividend scheme distributes 1% of trading profits to the local communities served by the society. The dividend will be allocated by the board's Community Dividend Selection Committee to a wide range of community groups and good causes across the society's trading area. This will bring the total amount granted since the inception of the scheme to £2.2 million. A full review of the society's funding approach to support community activities, local charities and good causes will be undertaken during 2014. This will take full account of the existing arrangements in respect of the Midlands 'Making a Difference Community Dividend' scheme and the Anglia Co-operative Community Fund (ACCF). Both schemes will continue to be supported in the interim period.

Charity partners

Newlife Foundation (Charity Commission no. 1001817) a national charity that funds a range of specialist equipment designed to meet the needs of children with disabilities, was chosen by colleagues as the society's charity partner in 2012. Since then, colleagues have raised over £449,000 for the charity, 'with every pound raised going towards helping children within the society's trading area'.

A partnership with the **Salvation Army** (Charity Commission no. 214779) to site their clothing banks at 72 retail stores has also provided an income of over £138,000 which has been equally shared between the Salvation Army and Newlife Foundation.

Information relating to community involvement was obtained from the society's 2013/14 annual report and accounts.

Corporate giving

In 2013/14 the company declared £225,000 in community dividend charitable donations in the UK. The performance indicator in the annual report and accounts details a further £289,000 for its corporate charity, Newlife Foundation.

In-kind support

Selly Oak Trust School – Business Class

In 2013 the society entered into a partnership with Selly Oak Trust School in Birmingham as part of a Business in the Community (BITC) initiative called Business Class. This three year commitment will help to provide quality work experience opportunities and master classes to raise the aspirations of students with learning difficulties.

Journey to a Job

Also, in 2013 the society developed the Journey to a Job programme to work in conjunction with Job Centre Plus to support the Institute of Grocery Distribution's (IGD) Feeding Britain's Future, a month-long campaign in September 2013 that focused on addressing growing unemployment and the lack of training opportunities for young people between the ages of 16 and 24. Its primary focus is to give young unemployed people a helping hand in their search for a job. The programme allowed 57 unemployed young people from the society's trading area to take part in a series of workshops organised by the society which aimed to give young people the chance to gain important skills which would help them find, get and keep a job. Some were inspired to apply for positions with the society and three months after attending the workshop ten young people had secured permanent employment.

Food bank policy

The society is also committed to helping to address the issue of food poverty by working with local food banks across its trading areas to provide emergency food and support to individuals and families in crisis and has developed a food bank policy which is currently being implemented across many of its food stores.

Employee-led support

Employees are involved in fundraising for local charities and good causes and in selecting and raising funds for the society's charity partners.

Corporate social responsibility

CSR committee: A 'Corporate Responsibility Delivery Framework' has been put in place with a CR steering group chaired by the deputy chief executive and four work groups. The four work groups have been established to 'drive forward initiatives under each of the four key pillars' and a number of projects have already commenced making a real impact on vulnerable people in local communities.

There is at present also a Community Dividend Selection Committee – see the 'Community involvement' section.

CSR information: Taken from the 2013/14 annual report and accounts: 'In 2013 the society built on the launch of its corporate responsibility policy in the previous year with the permanent appointment of a corporate responsibility manager and the development of a new CR strategy which incorporates four key pillars: 'Workplace', 'Marketplace', 'Environment' and 'Community'.'

Community: The society aims to work with its communities to 'help them to improve their sustainability and well-being'.

The society has a separate fund for community giving. See 'Community involvement' section for interim information following the merger.

CSR report: CR is reported in the society's annual report and accounts.

Applications

In writing to the correspondent.

Channel 4 Television Corporation

Telecommunications

Correspondent: Corporate Responsibility Team, 124 Horseferry Road, London SW1P 2TX (email: CRin4@channel4.co.uk; website: www.channel4.com)

Directors: Lord Burns, Chair; David Abraham, Chief Executive; Mark Price, Deputy Chair (women: 0; men: 3)

Year end	31/12/2013
Turnover	£908,000,000
Pre-tax profit	(£15,000,000)

Nature of business: Channel 4 is a publicly-owned, commercially-funded public service broadcaster. It does not receive any public funding and has a remit to be innovative, experimental and distinctive. Channel 4 works across television, film and digital media to deliver its public service remit, as outlined in the 2003 Communications

Act and most recently the 2010 Digital Economy Act.

Company registration number: 1533774

Subsidiary undertakings include: Channel 4 Radio Ltd; Channel 4 Radio Services Ltd; FilmFour Ltd; Life One Broadcasting Ltd; Life Two Broadcasting Ltd; Life Showcase Ltd.

Main locations: Belfast, Glasgow, Edinburgh, Manchester

Total employees: 746

Focus of giving: Education, enterprise/ training.

Cash donations undeclared	✓
Gifts in kind	✓
Market-led giving	✓
Matched funding	✓
Payroll giving	✓

Charitable donations

Cash UK (latest available):	2013	£1,200,000
	2011	£1,500,000
	2009	£1,000,000
	2008	£1,100,000
Total UK (cash and in kind):	2013	£1,200,000
Cash worldwide:	2013	£1,200,000
Total worldwide (cash and in kind):	2013	£1,200,000

Community involvement

We know that previously donations have been made to charitable organisations to pay for training and that volunteering, matched funding and payroll giving has also been in place. The amount paid to charities in 2011 was a substantial £1.5 million. Unfortunately, the organisation, or its accountants, have not declared its charitable cash giving in 2013. However, the 2013 annual report states that during that year the in-house campaigns were reviewed and the company created a framework of quarterly employee engagement activities aimed at raising awareness of issues surrounding the environment and sustainability, as well as focusing on specific campaigns such as volunteering and charitable giving. As this review initiative is ongoing, we hope there will be more information available in next available annual report and accounts.

Channel 4 is a member of the Media CSR Forum (mediacsrforum.org), Business in the Community (bitc.org.uk) and the Corporate Responsibility Group (crguk.org).

Corporate giving

During 2013, the group did not declare charitable donations. We do not know what the company gave either directly or from matched funding. We neither know who benefited from employee volunteering nor staff fundraising. We have taken an average of the last three totals we have recorded and estimate that cash UK giving was around £1.2 million.

In-kind support

Disaster Emergency Committee

Channel 4, working in partnership with the Independent Television Network (ITN), is a broadcast partner for the DEC. When a large-scale international crisis strikes, Channel 4 broadcasts a two to three-minute national television appeal, to publicise the situation and raise funds.

Room space and equipment

Channel 4 has formed links with several local charities and community groups and provides support in terms of meeting room space, building tours and donations of surplus office furniture and technical equipment. Office supplies such as toners and ink cartridges are donated to charity for recycling and cooking oil is donated as green fuel.

Employee-led support

Volunteering: Channel 4 recognises that volunteering can have a meaningful, positive impact on both staff and community, and this is supported by its volunteering policy and volunteering open day. Opportunities are identified to support the community, to identify opportunities and promote them as part of staff personal development.

Matched Funding: The company matches funding pound-for-pound up to £2,500 if teams of two or more staff team up to support a good cause.

Payroll Giving: There is a scheme in operation.

Commercially led support

Big4 art project: The Big 4 is a 50-foot-high metal '4' outside the company's London headquarters. Since its inception in 2007, a variety of artists, both internationally renowned and emerging talent, have created 'skins' for the 4. The project has evolved into a regular competition for art and design students and recent graduates, with the winning design chosen by a panel of art and design experts.

Open House: For the fourth year running, the company supported Open-City's Architecture in Schools programme by giving years 3 and 4 students a tour of the headquarters building along with a question and answer session. In addition, the company participated in Open-City's Open House in September and received 1,500 visitors over a two-day period.

Corporate social responsibility

CSR committee: The CSR section on the company's website states:

> Our board and executive team have committed to promoting the highest standards of responsible corporate behaviour and are ultimately accountable for this. In support of this, we have a corporate code of conduct and a suite of other policies and procedures providing a framework for accountability.
>
> To ensure we continue to develop our CR Strategy in an enlightened and informed manner, we are members of Business in the Community, the Media CSR Forum, and the Corporate Responsibility Group. Membership of these groups and forums enables us to share good practice and methods in order to overcome common obstacles.

CSR information: The following statement is taken from the company's website:

> *Corporate Responsibility*
> Channel 4's role goes beyond creating powerful television. Our operating model has always required us to strike a balance between public service and commercial content.
>
> The aim of our Corporate Responsibility (CR) strategy is to fulfil our public service remit in a responsible manner.
>
> To this end, our mission is to promote social, environmental and personal change.
>
> In order to achieve our mission, we continue to develop our strategy around the following 5 impact areas:
>
> *Accountability*
> We aim to promote responsible behaviour.
>
> *Community*
> We aim to continue to play a responsible role in the community.
>
> *Environment*
> We are committed to minimising any adverse effects of our operations on the natural environment and finite resources.
>
> *People*
> Our belief is that diversity contributes to the fulfilment of our public service remit and to being the best that we can creatively be. We aim to nurture and develop talent within our business and across the media industry in order to work with the most diverse range of people across the UK.
>
> *Suppliers*
> Where applicable, we aim to promote responsible behaviour in the supply chain.

CSR report: CSR is reported in the annual reports and accounts with a small section given over to community. The CSR section of the website appears to have been written in 2011 and not updated since.

Applications

In writing to the correspondent.

CIBC World Markets plc

Banking

Correspondent: Angus Scott, Trustee, The CIBC World Markets Children's Foundation, Canadian Imperial Bank of Commerce, 150 Cheapside, London EC2V 6ET (tel: 020 7234 6000/020 7234 6000; fax: 020 7234 6691; email: ukchildrensmiracle@cibc.co.uk; website: www.cibcwm.com)

Directors: K. Li; J. Miller; L. Hourigan; N. Wickes; M. Bailey; C. Gerber; T. Kelly; L. Mason; K. Patterson

Year end	31/10/2014
Turnover	£3,299,238
Pre-tax profit	£7,747,438

Nature of business: CIBC World Markets plc is a wholly owned subsidiary of Canadian Imperial Bank of Commerce and is engaged in wholesale banking. The information in this entry relates for the most part to the subsidiary – CIBC World Markets plc.

Company registration number: 2733036

Main locations: London

UK employees: 17

Total employees: 17

Focus of giving: Health, ill health, children, young people, community/ social welfare.

Cash donations undeclared	✓
Gifts in kind	✓
Matched funding	✓
Staff fundraising only	✓

Charitable donations

Cash UK (latest available):	2014	£5,000
	2011	£102,000
	2009	£36,000
	2008	£216,600
	2007	£125,000
	2006	£213,000
Total UK (cash and in kind):	2014	£8,000

Community involvement

CIBC World Markets Children's Miracle Foundation: The company's charitable fundraising is mainly focused on Miracle Day, which occurs on the first Wednesday of December each year. All commission generated on that day is donated to children's charities via the CIBC World Markets Children's Miracle Foundations (the UK charity is registered under Charity Commission no. 1105094). Further funds are raised at a number of events hosted by CIBC World Markets for clients and staff.

The key objectives of Miracle Day include:

- To raise the quality of life for children in the communities served by CIBC World Markets
- To demonstrate CIBC's dedication in helping to prepare children for future success
- To encourage volunteerism and foster community involvement on the part of employees

To be eligible to apply for UK funds groups must be UK/European registered charities which are well-administered, with a record of achievement and the potential for success which will bring a tangible benefit to children in the communities where they live within Europe. The foundation supports both UK registered and recognised European charities that are dedicated to the health, welfare and education of children. Examples include children's hospitals, counselling and special programmes for at-risk children.

A committee of CIBC staff coordinates the day to day activities of the charity, working with the trustees to fulfil the foundation's objectives. Four of the trustees regularly sit on the committee and ensure that the decisions which are made fully comply with the overall aims and objectives set out in the foundation's governing document.

There are similar foundations in Canada, the USA and Hong Kong (covering Asia and Pacific).

Corporate giving

In 2013/14 the company did not declare its charitable donations and we looked to the foundation (see the 'Community involvement' section), to see what the company had donated through this channel. The primary source of voluntary income of the foundation was from the CIBC donation on Miracle Day of £95,000 (2012: £80,000). This figure comprises fees and commissions for that day from the trading activities of CIBC staff of £90,000, and an additional fundraising matching donation from CIBC of £5,000. As the £90,000 was donated by the staff of the company, we have estimated the UK cash donation of the UK company itself to be the £5,000 only. This is in line with our usual practice. A further £3,000 was given for administration expenses by the company.

The latest accounts for the UK foundation were from 2013/14 and show £851,000 in grants to registered children's charities. Beneficiaries under the large donation project were: CHICKS (£380,000); the PACE Centre (£250,000) and Honeypot (£28,000). The trustees also decided to support three 'Charities of the Year' which were: Haven House Children's Hospital; Rainbow Trust Children's Charity; and Rays of Sunshine; (£63,000 each).

We have marked this entry with 'staff fundraising only' because the vast majority of donations are raised by employees.

See the corporate charity entry on p. 398 for more information.

In-kind support

Staff are actively involved in volunteering, mentoring and pro bono work.

Employee-led support

CIBC Miracle Day

Launched in 1984 this is an employee-driven initiative that aims to improve the lives of children. Every year, on the first Wednesday in December, CIBC's wholesale banking employees and CIBC Wood Gundy Investment Advisors donate their fees and commissions to help disadvantaged children – see 'Community involvement' section.

Commercially led support

Sponsorship appears to be financed by the global company and for Canadian organisations only, for example it is the long-term partner of the Canadian Breast Cancer Foundation, CIBC Run for the Cure and regional sponsor for events like the Pink Tour and the Tour CIBC Charles-Bruneau.

Corporate social responsibility

CSR information: The global company has a CSR section in its annual report and the information focuses mainly on Canada. We could not find any information on CSR for the UK.

We were unable to determine the ratio of women to men on the board of the plc.

Corporate charity: The CIBC World Markets Children's Miracle Foundation (Charity Commission no. 1105094).

Applications

In writing to the correspondent.

Citroen UK Ltd

Motors and accessories

Correspondent: Human Resources Deptartment, Pinley House, 2 Sunbeam Way, Coventry CV3 1ND (tel: 0844 463 0010; website: www.citroen.co.uk)

Directors: B. Hassan; N. Willetts; M. Hamill; J. Tilestone; L. Jackson; P. de Rovira; D. Connell; A. Leclerc

Year end	31/12/2013
Turnover	£261,246,000
Pre-tax profit	£9,424,000

Nature of business: The main activity of the company is the importing and the sale of Citroën cars, vans and replacement parts.

Company registration number: 191579

Subsidiary undertakings include: Not disclosed in accounts.

Main locations: Coventry

UK employees: 464

Total employees: 464

Focus of giving: Poverty and social exclusion.

Charitable donations

Cash UK (latest available):	2013	£127,000
	2012	£49,000
	2010	£78,000
	2009	£44,000
	2008	£81,000
Total UK (cash and in kind):	2013	£127,000
Cash worldwide:	2013	£127,000
Total worldwide (cash and in kind):	2013	£127,000

Community involvement

The company's 2013 annual report states that its financial support is to aid BEN in its mission to provide care and support to retired automotive employees and their dependents in times of need. Previously we were advised that, as a general rule, it is better to apply for support through the individual dealerships.

Corporate giving

In 2013, the company made contributions for charitable purposes of £127,000 (2012: £49,000) to BEN, the motor trade benevolent fund.

Corporate social responsibility

CSR information: We could find no evidence of published CSR information. We were unable to determine the ratio of women to men on the board.

Exclusions

No support is given for individuals.

Applications

As the company does not seem to vary in its giving to BEN, applicants are advised to contact their local dealerships. If applying to the company's head office, then apply in writing to the correspondent referenced 'Charitable donations'.

Close Brothers Group plc

Financial services, banking

Correspondent: Corporate Social Responsibility Committee, 10 Crown Place, London EC2A 4FT (tel: 020 7655 3100; fax: 020 7655 8917; website: www.closebrothers.co.uk)

Directors: Strone Macpherson, Chair; Preben Prebensen, Chief Executive; Jonathan Howell, Finance Director; Bruce Carnegie-Brown; Elizabeth Lee; Lesley Jones (women: 2; men: 6)

Year end	31/07/2014
Turnover	£491,300,000
Pre-tax profit	£195,700,000

Nature of business: Close Brothers is the parent company of a group of companies involved in merchant banking.

Company registration number: 520241

Subsidiary undertakings include: Allenbridge Group plc; Cavanagh Group plc; Chartwell Group Ltd; Close Asset Finance Ltd Commercial; Close Asset Management Holdings Ltd; Close Brothers Holdings Ltd; Close Brothers Ltd; Winterflood Securities Ltd.

Main locations: London

Focus of giving: Health, ill health, medical research, community/social welfare, disasters.

Charity of the Year	✓
Gifts in kind	✓
Matched funding	✓
Payroll giving	✓

Charitable donations

Cash UK (latest available):	2014	£125,000
	2009	£154,000
	2008	£168,000
	2007	£186,000
	2006	£147,000
Total UK (cash and in kind):	2014	£125,000
Cash worldwide:	2014	£125,000
Total worldwide (cash and in kind):	2014	£125,000

Community involvement

Charity partner

Cancer Research UK (CRUK) continues to be the group's lead charitable partner, although a number of additional charities are also supported by its local businesses, including Macmillan Cancer Support, the Motor Neurone Disease charity and The Prince's Trust.

Corporate giving

In 2013/14 the group's UK cash charitable donations were £251,000 (2013: £228,000), raised through ongoing fundraising activities and company contributions through matched funding. The company's matched funding contribution was over £125,000.

In-kind support

The group provides matched funding support for funds raised by employees.

Employee-led support

Employees are actively encouraged to participate in a range of events held during the company's designated charity week, and throughout the year, including sponsored fitness initiatives, dress down days, baking competitions and quizzes.

Give As You Earn

Employees are also encouraged to donate to charities of their own choice through the Give As You Earn payroll giving scheme. The group maintained its Payroll Giving Quality Mark Gold Award for the fourth consecutive year in recognition of the ongoing strong participation rate of 11% (2013: 10%) in the scheme.

Corporate social responsibility

CSR committee: A CR committee was established in 2010 and is chaired by a member of the executive committee. The committee includes representatives from across the divisions and provides a forum for sharing ideas and raising awareness of the group's CR objectives.

CSR information: The following statement has been taken from the group's 20/1314 Sustainability Report contained within the annual report and accounts:

> At Close Brothers, we aim to provide our clients with a safe, trustworthy and capable financial partner through the economic cycle by maintaining the highest standards of practice in dealing with environmental, social and governance (ESG) issues. We achieve this not only by maintaining a strong financial position, but by investing in our employees, considering environmental and social practices in our business strategies and operating responsibly to protect natural resources. Our focus on developing sustainable business practices will ensure our future continuity and success, enabling us to continue to provide the support that smallbusinesses and individuals need.

CSR report: Information regarding CSR is published within the group's annual report and accounts.

Exclusions

No support is given for political appeals.

Applications

In writing to the correspondent referenced 'Charitable UK giving'.

Clydesdale Bank plc

Banking

Correspondent: Irene Swankie, CR and Community Affairs Manager, Ground Floor Mezzanine, 30 St Vincent Place, Glasgow G1 2HL (tel: 01412 487070; fax: 01412 040828; email: irene.swankie@nabgroup.com; website: www.cbonline.co.uk)

Directors: David Gillespie, UK. Executive; Richard Gregory; James Pettigrew, Chair; David Thorburn, UK. Chief Executive; David Allvey; David Browne; Barbara Ridpath; Teresa Robson-Capps; Alexander Shapland; Debbie Crosbie, UK. Executive; Ian Smith, UK. Chief Financial Officer; Eric Gunn, UK. Executive; James Peirson, UK. Executive; Lynn McManus, UK. Executive; Helen Page, UK. Executive; Kevin Page, UK. Executive; Paul Shephard, UK. Director; John Shovelin, UK. Director; Richard Sawers (women: 1; men: 8)

Year end	30/09/2014
Turnover	£1,135,000,000
Pre-tax profit	(£216,000,000)

Nature of business: The Clydesdale Bank plc together with its subsidiary undertakings (which together comprise the Group) is the United Kingdom arm of the National Australia Bank Ltd.

Company registration number: SC001111

Brands include: Yorkshire Bank; Clydesdale Bank.

Main locations: Glasgow, Edinburgh

Focus of giving: General charitable purposes, environment, health, ill health, heritage, older people, children, young people, community/social welfare, disability.

Membership: BITC

Gifts in kind	✓
Matched funding	✓
Payroll giving	✓
Sponsorship	✓

Charitable donations

Cash UK (latest available):	2014	£700,000
	2011	£808,000
	2010	£921,000
	2009	£842,000
	2008	£336,000
	2007	£280,000
Total UK (cash and in kind):	2014	£700,000
Cash worldwide:	2014	£700,000
Total worldwide (cash and in kind):	2014	£700,000

Community involvement

Community partnership

Through its Community Partnership programme, the bank works with a select number of groups to address shared issues of concern. Current priorities are education, employability and environment. One of its flagship programmes is Count Me In.

Count Me In 123

Count Me In 123 is a community programme which focuses on numeracy and is aimed at the under-five age group.

The programme uses books and accessories to animate the learning process and strengthen mathematical concepts through story and rhyme. Accessed through libraries in eight local authorities throughout Scotland (Aberdeen, Dundee, Falkirk, Glasgow, North Ayrshire, North Lanarkshire, South Lanarkshire and West Dunbartonshire), parents and carers can take advantage of Count Me In 123 learning bags which have been created for three specific age groups – under one-year-olds, two- to three-year-olds and four- to five-year-olds. The bags have also been developed in a number of languages including Hindi, Punjabi and Chinese.

Count Me In Primary

Count Me In Primary is an extension of Count Me In 123 and is aimed at children aged 5 to 11 years. It is currently operating through Glasgow City Council and can be accessed through public or school libraries. It consists of a series of learning bags specifically created for Primary school age children.

Partnerships

As well as proactively seeking suitable community partners, Clydesdale Bank also welcomes approaches from charities or not-for-profit organisations that can demonstrate their ability to manage a community project and evaluate its success objectively.

If your organisation satisfies these criteria and would like to consider a partnership simply send the correspondent, Irene Swankie a summary of your proposal.

Note that Clydesdale Bank receives a significant volume of partnership proposals and it is unable to accommodate them all. In view of the volume, staff are unable to discuss proposals by telephone or to meet with organisations prior to receiving a written proposal.

Yorkshire and Clydesdale Bank Foundation

In July 2008 Clydesdale Bank launched this foundation which is a charity registered with the Office of the Scottish Charity Regulator (OSCR No. SC039747) and which supports people and their local communities. The foundation provides funds to support registered charities, not-for-profit groups, community and other voluntary organisations. See separate section on corporate charities.

Corporate giving

The bank appears to channel its charitable donations, apart from matched funding, through the Yorkshire and Clydesdale Foundation, which was established in 2008 – see 'Community involvement'. We know that voluntary income of the foundation was declared at over £711,000 and that included 'total donations, fundraising and agencies'. Based on this we estimate the total donated by the bank to the foundation to be around £700,000.

See the corporate charity entry on p. 440 for more information.

In-kind support

Rental of office premises is provided to the Common Purpose and Home Start organisations in the UK.

Employee-led support

Charity partner

On 1 February 2008 Clydesdale and Yorkshire Banks joined forces to announce the launch of a new charity partnership with Hospice UK (formerly Help the Hospices). Hospice UK (Charity Commission no. 1014851) is the leading charity supporting hospice care throughout the UK. Hospices aim to provide the best possible care for people living with life-limiting or terminal illnesses. Hospice care is provided free of charge to patients and tailored to their individual needs. The majority of hospice care in the UK is provided by Hospice UK member hospices – local charities rooted in the communities they serve.

In almost seven years together, the bank has raised over £3.8 million for hospice care. Employees have raised almost £2 million and the banks have match funded this pound for pound. The money raised supports 97 local hospices throughout the UK.

Employees have also provided over 34,000 volunteering hours for their local hospices.

Volunteering

Over 17,000 hours were given by employees volunteering in 2013/14.

Employees also volunteer in their own time to support their local community. The bank's Employee Volunteer Grant Programme rewards and recognises the personal contribution of employees by providing grants to the charitable organisations which they work with in their own time. Grants of up to £500 are awarded quarterly

Payroll giving

This scheme allows employees to make voluntary donations every month direct from their salary to a variety of causes close to their hearts. To date over 20% of employees are donating to charities and the company has been awarded H M Gold Quality Mark for Payroll Giving. Employees who choose to donate to the bank's charity partner will have their donation matched pound for pound by the bank.

Commercially led support

Sponsorship

Current sponsorship properties include Scottish Exhibition and Conference Centre and Hydro arena.

Corporate social responsibility

CSR committee: There is a CR and Community Affairs Manager – see 'Applications'.

CSR information: In relation to its community commitments, the bank on its website states:

> We recognise that the strength of our business and our people is related to the health and well-being of those communities in which we operate. We want to play a positive role in the development of strong communities and that is why we continue to develop and grow our community activities. Through direct donations and partnership working arrangements with various organisations we endeavour to support local communities.

CSR report: Information regarding charitable giving is contained within the annual report and accounts. However, we could only find a cumulative total for giving and not an annual one.

Corporate charity: Yorkshire and Clydesdale Bank Foundation (OSCR number SC039747).

Applications

If you wish to apply for an award from the Yorkshire and Clydesdale Foundation, see the corporate charity entry on p. 440 for more information.

Community partnerships

As well as proactively seeking suitable community partners, Clydesdale Bank also welcomes approaches from charities or not-for-profit organisations that can demonstrate their ability to manage a community project and evaluate its success objectively. The bank does not normally support:

- Activities taking place outside Clydesdale Bank's operating area
- Individuals and individual fundraisers
- Capital projects
- Salary expenses
- Third party fundraising (i.e. advertising in charity programmes or gala fundraising events)
- Political or religious organisations

If your organisation satisfies these criteria and would like to consider a partnership there is no application form to complete. Send a summary of your proposal to the correspondent, Irene Swankie.

Note that in view of the volume of proposals received, the bank is unable to enter into discussion by telephone or to meet with organisations prior to receiving a written proposal.

Cobham plc

Aerospace, electronics/ computers

Correspondent: Daisy Campbell, Corporate Responsibility and Sustainability Officer, Brook Road, Wimborne, Dorset BH21 2BJ (tel: 01202 882020; fax: 01202 840523; email: crs@cobham.com; website: www.cobham.com)

Directors: J. Devaney, Chair; R. Murphy, Chief Executive Officer; S. Nicholls, Chief Financial Officer; M. Hagee; D. Flint; M. Wareing; M. Ronald; B. Nørgaard; A. Wood (women: 2; men: 7)

Year end	31/12/2010
Turnover	£1,789,700,000
Pre-tax profit	£126,600,000

Nature of business: Provides technologies and services to solve challenging problems across commercial, defence and security markets, 'from deep space to the depths of the ocean', such as air-to-air refuelling; aviation services; audio, video and data communications, including satellite communications; defence electronics; life support; and mission equipment.

Company registration number: 30470

Subsidiary undertakings include: Air Précision SA; Axell Wireless Ltd; Chelton Ltd; Cobham Defence Communications Ltd; Omnipless Manufacturing (Pty) Ltd; Sensor and Antenna Systems, Lansdale, Inc. A full list of the group's subsidiaries is given in the annual report and accounts.

Main locations: Almondbank, Bournemouth, Southampton, Wimbourne, Teesside, Kinloss

Total employees: 10,090

Focus of giving: Education, enterprise/ training, health, ill health, medical research, science technology, children, young people, disability.

Membership: BITC

Gifts in kind	✓
Humanitarian aid: overseas	✓
Humanitarian aid: UK	✓
Matched funding	✓
Overseas giving	✓

Charitable donations

Cash UK (latest available):	2014	£164,000
	2010	£84,000
	2009	£85,000
	2008	£85,000
	2007	£68,000
Total UK (cash and in kind):	2010	£164,000
Cash worldwide:	2010	£164,000
Total worldwide (cash and in kind):	2010	£164,000

Community involvement

The group states that it is 'committed to helping strengthen the communities where we operate by fundraising and donating our time, expertise and products. Investing in our communities helps us forge productive relationships with local people.'

A strategic review of Cobham's community investment activities took place in 2010. As a result, Cobham strengthened its community relationships and improved its reporting. A group-level community involvement strategy was developed and implemented in 2012 to further encourage employees to take part in community activities and align these efforts with the group's business strategy. The strategy reinforces its focus on support for science, technology, engineering and maths (STEM) education; ex-services personnel; causes in the communities surrounding group sites; and disaster relief appeals.

Corporate giving

During 2013, Cobham donated £164,000 to charitable causes representing 0.07% of the basic underlying profit before tax, compared with £154,000 (0.06% of underlying profit before tax) reported in 2012.

Previous beneficiaries have included: Air League Trust, Combat Stress, Cancer Research UK, Help for Heroes, Make-A-Wish Foundation and Red Cross Hurricane Sandy Appeal.

In-kind support

Disaster relief

On 15 January 2010, three days after a major earthquake hit the Caribbean island of Haiti, Cobham SATCOM in Orlando teamed up with IT Broadcasting and Haiti Satellite to form a communications response team. The team provided data communications and internet access to emergency responders, doctors and relief agencies. It also organised a chartered cargo flight which delivered 6,000lbs of equipment and 2,000lbs of medical supplies.

Matched funding

Fundraising by employees can be matched by the company.

Employee-led support

Employees raised £15,000 for the Red Cross and Mercy Corps, following an appeal for donations to support the emergency response following the Japanese earthquake. Employees were given a day of paid time to dedicate to fundraising. UK highlights included a martial arts display by Cobham Mission Equipment in Wimborne and a football tournament at Cobham Technical Services in Leatherhead. A fancy dress competition at Cobham Antenna

Systems charged people for both wearing red *and* not wearing red – ensuring everyone contributed.

The amount raised was matched by the company. Cobham North America, which raised an average of £25 (US$42) per person.

Corporate social responsibility

CSR committee: The CEO has overall responsibility for the group's approach. He is supported by the CR&S Committee, which he chairs, in ensuring that appropriate policies, monitoring and operational systems are in place to achieve the group's objectives. The CEO updates the board on CR&S matters. The board in turn assesses the significance of environmental, social and corporate governance risks and opportunities to the group's Strategic Plan.

CSR information: The group's website states:

> At Cobham we recognise that acting responsibly and sustainably creates value for our stakeholders. We are working to make this part of everything we do. We will achieve this through strong corporate governance, improving key stakeholder relationships, finding innovative uses of our technology for positive social and environmental impact, striving for the highest ethical standards, developing our people, pursuing a zero harm policy and engaging in our communities.

With regard to community involvement, the group states it is committed to helping strengthen the communities where it operates by fundraising and donating time, expertise and products. It believes that investing in communities helps forge productive relationships with local people.

CSR report: There is a separate section on the group's website detailing CSR including community investment.

Exclusions

No support is given for animal welfare, individuals, the arts, elderly people, environment/heritage, overseas projects, political appeals, religious appeals, social welfare or sport.

Applications

In writing to the correspondent.

Coca-Cola Holdings (United Kingdom) Ltd

Drinks manufacture

Correspondent: Corporate Responsibility and Sustainability Team, Cray Road, Sidcup, Kent DA14 5DF (tel: 0800 227 711; website: www.coca-cola.co.uk/citizenship)

Directors: J. Woods; S. Roche; D. Canham; D. Kearney; G. Rutz; S. Hutton

Year end	31/12/2013
Turnover	£161,173,033
Pre-tax profit	£43,940,282

Nature of business: Coca-Cola's business in the UK is made up of two separate companies with different roles. Together, these companies manufacture, distribute and market its range of drinks.

The companies are Coca-Cola Great Britain (CCGB), which is a wholly owned subsidiary of The Coca-Cola Company and Coca-Cola Enterprises Ltd (CCE), which is part of Coca-Cola Enterprises Inc. These two companies form the business in Great Britain. CCGB markets and develops new and existing brands. CCE manufactures and distributes soft drinks for both The Coca-Cola Company and other brand owners.

Company registration number: 1724995

Subsidiaries included: Coca-Cola International Sales Ltd and Beverage Services Ltd.

Brands include: Coca-Cola; Coke Zero; Diet Coke; Fanta; Powerade; Schweppes.

Main locations: East Kilbride, Aberdeen, Peterlee, Wakefield, Warrington, Nottingham, Coventry, Peterborough, Northampton, Milton Keynes, Bristol, Cardiff, Uxbridge, London

Focus of giving: Education, environment, health, ill health, overseas projects, sport, recreation, women's issues, children, young people, disasters.

Membership: BITC, LBG

FTSE 100	✓
Gifts in kind	✓
Humanitarian aid: overseas	✓
Humanitarian aid: UK	✓
Market-led giving	✓
Matched funding	✓
Overseas giving	✓

Charitable donations

Cash UK (latest available):	2010	£10,000
	2008	£151,000
Total UK (cash and in kind):	2013	£3,000,000
Total worldwide (cash and in kind):	2013	£89,600,000

Community involvement

Coca-Cola in the UK contributes to community projects and partnerships, particularly those that support the development of young people, protect the environment and encourage active healthy living.

Its education programme, **The Real Experience**, consists of five education centres based at operational sites and a recycling plant in Hemswell. Together the centres saw 13,000 visitors in 2013 and the education centre in East Kilbride celebrated its 30,000th visitor since it opened in 2002. In 2013, £850,000 was invested in the new entre in Milton Keynes, which will open later in 2015.

The Real Business Challenge is CCE's award-winning enterprise education competition, for which secondary school students form small 'companies' and complete business-relevant tasks for the opportunity of working alongside CCE volunteers on a live project. More than 560 schools competed and, at the regional finals, the teams were tasked with developing a campaign to promote the Special Olympics National Summer Games 2013. The 11 posters were displayed as bus-stop advertisements in their local area, and the winning students from Strathaven Academy, Lanarkshire, had the honour of presenting medals at the event in Bath.

5by20 is The Coca-Cola Company's global initiative to empower women economically across the world. In the UK the company teamed up with a social enterprise design company that makes bags, belts and home accessories from recycled materials. The company also helped them start an apprenticeship scheme for young women from disadvantaged communities to learn artisan skills. In 2013, the social enterprise employed its first apprentice and aims to help more over the next four years.

The Coca-Cola Foundation (US)

This is for information only as we could see no evidence of the foundation supporting projects/organisations in the UK.

In 1984, Roberto Goizueta, then Chair and CEO of The Coca-Cola Company, established The Coca-Cola Foundation. Over the past three decades, The foundation has grown from a local foundation into a global philanthropic organisation awarding $98 million (£61.4 million) in 2013 to impact approximately 134 million people in 122 countries.

Priority areas

- *Women:* economic empowerment and entrepreneurship
- *Water:* access to clean water, water conservation and recycling
- *Well-being:* active healthy living, education and youth development

In addition, the foundation supports many local community programs such as arts and culture, community and economic development programs in the United States, as well as HIV/AIDS prevention and awareness programs in Africa and Latin America.

Coca-Cola and its foundation also support natural disasters by responding with emergency relief.

Corporate giving

In 2013 the company Coca-Cola Holdings (United Kingdom) Ltd declared charitable contributions of £24,000 with awards made to communities in which the group operates. However, the Coca-Cola Great Britain website states that in 2013 Coca-Cola gave nearly £3 million to community projects and partnerships. We are taking that figure to be the company's total contribution in the UK in this financial year. We do not have a breakdown of cash and in-kind giving. We neither know in which set of accounts this amount (or the cash part of it) was declared, (if at all) and have continued to use Coca-Cola Holdings (UK) Ltd as the basis for this entry even though it in fact only declared £24,000 as that individual holding company's contribution.

The Coca-Cola Company is committed to giving back 1% of its prior year's operating income annually. This commitment is made through The Coca-Cola Foundation and company donations. The foundation's website states that in 2013, The Coca-Cola Company and The Coca-Cola Foundation invested more than $143 million (£89.6 million) in communities worldwide. While we do not know if this figure includes monies which we would not normally include in our totals, e.g. sponsorship, we consider it better to use this figure than record nothing. For more information visit: www.coca-colacompany.com/our-company/the-coca-cola-foundation.

In-kind support

See employee-led section.

Employee-led support

The company states in its corporate sustainability review that its community commitments are ongoing. Additionally, each year it organises a week to celebrate the contribution of employees and to encourage others to join in activities such as mentoring young people, fundraising and volunteering for local charities and organisations, including local Special Olympics clubs.

Commercially led support

Sponsorship

Coca-Cola is the new sponsor of the London Eye.

Corporate social responsibility

CSR committee: We could not find details of the members of a CSR committee or its structure but consider that there must be a team as there is an annual report published by Coca-Cola Great Britain.

CSR information: Statements taken from Coca-Cola Great Britain's website:

> ***Sustainability Framework***
>
> At Coca-Cola Enterprises, we have a plan – Deliver for Today: Inspire for Tomorrow – which sets out our sustainability goals. The Coca-Cola Company has a vision for sustainability called 'Live Positively' – our commitment to making a positive difference in the world.
>
> ***Community***
>
> We are a local business with strong regional presence, from Sidcup in Kent to East Kilbride in Scotland, and we support the communities in which we operate in a number of ways: direct investment in community programmes and partnerships; opportunities for our employees to volunteer their time; giving in kind.

We were unable to determine the ratio of women to men on the board.

CSR report: There is an annual Corporate Responsibility and Sustainability Review for Coca-Cola in Great Britain available from the website: www.coca-cola.co.uk/about-us/corporate-responsibility

Applications

In writing to the correspondent.

Colgate-Palmolive UK Ltd

Personal care products

Correspondent: Company Secretary, Guildford Business Park, Middleton Road, Guildford GU2 8JZ (tel: 01483 302222; website: www.colgate.co.uk)

Directors: C. Burniston; M. Poli; G. Malcolm

Year end	31/12/2013
Turnover	£254,901,000
Pre-tax profit	£44,676,000

Nature of business: This particular UK company's principal activity is the sale of household and personal care products and it sources all products from associated subsidiaries of its ultimate parent, Colgate-Palmolive Company. It operates as a limited risk distributor.

Company registration number: 178909

Subsidiary undertakings include: Colgate-Palmolive Operations (Ireland) Ltd; Colgate-Palmolive Investments (UK) Ltd.

Brands include: Ajax, Colgate, Palmolive, Softlan.

Main locations: Guildford

Focus of giving: General charitable purposes, health, ill health, children, young people.

Market-led giving	✓
Matched funding	✓
Overseas giving	✓
Sponsorship	✓

Charitable donations

Cash UK (latest available):	2013	£203,000
	2010	£32,000
	2008	£5,000
	2007	£6,000
Total UK (cash and in kind):	2013	£203,000
Cash worldwide:	2013	£15,800,000
Total worldwide (cash and in kind):	2013	£22,300,000

Community involvement

In the UK the company matches employee payments to charities. The company's own giving would appear to be around children and health.

The parent company in the United States supports children's causes across the world concerned with promoting the importance of oral health through education and prevention. The primary focus is to reach children in schools through videos, storybooks, songs, CD-ROMs and interactive activities.

Emergency financial aid has been provided to a number of natural disaster areas, including Germany, where there was severe flooding; the Philippines, where there were devastating fires; and the states of Colorado and California in the U.S., where there were wildfires.

Corporate giving

In 2013 this UK company gave £203,000 in cash charitable donations principally by way of the matched funding of money raised by employees. We have no details of beneficiaries. Worldwide cash and community contributions given in this entry were taken from the US parent company's website. For details visit: www.colgate.com and view the section on 'key performance indicators'.

In-kind support

There is significant in-kind support globally and this was costed by the US company at $10.38 million (£6.5 million).

Employee-led support

Colgate employees around the world volunteer their time to enhance the lives of those in their communities.

Commercially led support

The following information was taken from the Colgate UK website:

> Bright Smiles, Bright Futures reaches children around the world with free dental screenings and oral health education. The programme is among the most far-reaching, successful children's oral health initiatives in the world. With long-standing partnerships with governments, schools and communities, Colgate Bright Smiles, Bright Futures has reached more than half a billion children and their families across 80 countries with free dental screenings and oral health education.

Colgate Bright Smiles, Bright Futures educational curriculum is available in 30 languages and in many countries, has become a part of the permanent school curriculum.

Corporate social responsibility

CSR committee: There appears to be a sustainability committee in the US, responsible for the global programme.

CSR information: There was no CSR information was available for this company. The US company has a sustainability section on its website, for further information visit: www.colgate.com/app/Colgate/US/Corp/LivingOurValues/Sustainability

We were unable to determine the ratio of women to men on the board of the UK company or to find staff numbers.

CSR report: There is an annual sustainability report on the global website.

Applications

In writing to the correspondent referenced 'UK Community Programme'.

Computacenter plc

Information technology

Correspondent: The Charity Committee, Hatfield Avenue, Hatfield Business Park, Hatfield AL10 9TW (tel: 01707 631000; email: charity@computacenter.com; website: www.computacenter.com)

Directors: Mike Norris, Chief Executive; Tony Conophy, Chief Finance Officer; Greg Lock, Chair; Peter Ogden, Director; John Ormerod, Director; Brian McBride, Director; Philip Hulme, Director; Regine Stachelhaus; Minnow Powell (women: 1; men: 8)

Year end	31/12/2013
Turnover	£302,075,000
Pre-tax profit	£50,525,000

Nature of business: Computacenter is an independent provider of IT infrastructure services in Europe offering services and solutions at every stage of infrastructure investment.

Company registration number: 3110569

Subsidiary undertakings include: Computacenter (UK) Ltd; Computacenter France SA; Computacenter Holding GmbH; Computacenter GmbH; CC Managed Services GmbH; Computacenter NV/SA; Damax AG; Digica Group Holdings Ltd; HSD Consult GmbH; RD Trading Ltd; Top Info SAS.

Main locations: Hatfield, Belfast, Birmingham, Bristol, Cardiff, Edinburgh, Manchester, Milton Keynes, Nottingham, Reading

UK employees: 5,385

Total employees: 12,591

Focus of giving: General charitable purposes, health, ill health, children, young people.

Charity of the Year	✓
Gifts in kind	✓
Market-led giving	✓
Matched funding	✓
Payroll giving	✓
Sponsorship	✓

Charitable donations

Cash UK (latest available):	2013	£130,000
	2012	£73,000
	2011	£83,000
	2009	£100,000
	2008	£87,000
Total UK (cash and in kind):	2013	£130,000
Cash worldwide:	2013	£130,000
Total worldwide (cash and in kind):	2013	£130,000

Community involvement

The following information is taken from the 'Charity activities' section of company's website:

> *Charity Policy*
>
> Computacenter's charity policy is to support three corporate charities for a two-year period. At the end of that period, staff are asked to select alternatives from a shortlist that includes the current charity partners. The charities are approved by the Charity Committee and are registered within the UK. Each of the charities will receive considerable support from Computacenter in this period. Funds collected via fundraising activities within the programme are in most instances matched by Computacenter. In working with these charities, we hope to achieve three main aims:
>
> - To demonstrate our commitment to the wider community
> - To motivate staff across the company by encouraging teambuilding activities in a worthwhile cause
> - To communicate Computacenter's core values to customers, staff and other stake-holders.

Charity partners: Partners, which are selected by employees, are Teenage Cancer Trust, Alzheimer's Society and Prostate Cancer UK.

The UK business also supports Kidsafe, a schools initiative to teach children about road safety, the danger of drugs and bullying.

Corporate giving

In 2013 employees in the UK raised nearly £130,000 (2012: £73,000) for the chosen charity partners. The company's accounts do not declare a donation for charitable purposes from the company itself but the website states that staff fundraising is matched. We have therefore taken the cash donation from the company to be £130,000. Support for the Hertfordshire Fire and Rescue dogs continued, as well as support as a founding member of Herts 100, Kidsafe and the three charity partners. We could not discover the group's worldwide contribution.

Employee-led support

Employees 'demonstrate a wider sense of social responsibility by raising tens of thousands of pounds each year for Computacenter's charity partners'. Proceeds generated by employees for their three chosen charities are matched by the company.

Give As You Earn: A company-wide Give As You Earn (GAYE) scheme allows employees to make monthly contributions to any UK charity of their choice through automatic deduction from their salaries. This is tax deductible and attracts a 10% subsidy from HMRC. The full amount of the contribution goes to the charity because Computacenter handles all the administration at its own expense.

Commercially led support

Sponsorship: Computacenter is the official IT supplier to the RPA – a non-profit making trade union dedicated to the welfare of all professional rugby players. The company also sponsors Hertfordshire Fire and Rescue Service, the Fire Investigation Dog Programme.

Corporate social responsibility

CSR committee: The group's Corporate Sustainable Development Policy is annually reviewed by the Computacenter plc board of directors, and is implemented and monitored through the group's Corporate Sustainable Development Committee, constituted out of representatives from across the group as a whole.

Charity Committee Computacenter's charity programme is steered by the Charity Committee, which comprises a cross section of employees throughout the company. Any questions about the programme, fundraising activities or suggestions can be emailed to charity@computacenter.com.

CSR information: See the 'Community involvement' section for information on the group's charity policy.

CSR report: There was no report found but there is a specific section on the website which details the company's/staff charitable goals and achievements.

Applications

In writing to the correspondent. There is a specific enquiry email submission form for charity enquiries on the website. Visit: www.computacenter.com/who_we_are/contact_us/contact_charity.aspx.

Congregational & General Insurance plc

Insurance

Correspondent: Julie Porter, Trust Administrator, Currer HouseCurrer StreetBradfordBD1 5BA (tel: 01274 700700; fax: 01274 370754; email: trust@congregational.co.uk; website: www.congregational.co.uk)

Directors: Carlo Cavaliere, Chief Executive; Ian Campbell, Finance Director; Martin Scott; Harry Driver; Stephen Lockley; Barry Pollard; Penny Iversen; Edward Jenner; Robert Wade; Stuart Young (women: 1; men: 9)

Year end	31/12/2013
Turnover	£5,284,000
Pre-tax profit	£746,000

Nature of business: The transaction of general insurance business, in the form of the insurance for fire and other damage to property.

Company registration number: 93688

Subsidiary undertakings include: Iconica Business Services Ltd.

Main locations: Bradford

Focus of giving: General charitable purposes, education, religion, children, young people.

Charitable donations

Cash UK (latest available):	2013	£150,000
	2012	£150,000
	2011	£747,000
Total UK (cash and in kind):	2013	£150,000
Cash worldwide:	2013	£150,000
Total worldwide (cash and in kind):	2013	£150,000

Community involvement

This company is a wholly owned subsidiary of The Congregational & General Charitable Trust (Charity Commission no. 297013). The trust was established in 1956 to 'promote the Christian religion and in particular United Reformed Church and Congregational denominations and other churches which are of the Protestant tradition'. It supports a wide range of churches, educational establishments, charitable organisations and community projects. The trust receives annual gift aid payments from the company.

A council of management is responsible for the administration and management of the trust and the awarding of all grants.

Trust objectives

- To make grants for the overall care, upkeep and extension of churches
- To make grants towards the capital costs of church community projects
- To promote the Christian religion and, in particular, the United Reformed Church, Congregational Denominations and other churches which are of the Protestant tradition

Clear and helpful instructions on how to apply for a grant can be found on the company's website.

Corporate giving

Congregational & General Insurance plc pays annually to the charitable trust a proportion of its profits and in 2013 (a nine month accounting period due to a change of financial year by the group of companies), the company paid £150,000 (2012: £150,000). A council of members is responsible for the administration and management of the trust and all grants are made entirely on merit. A list of beneficiaries was not contained within the accounts. Any in-kind donations that the company makes do not appear to be publicised.

See the corporate charity entry on p. 398 for more information.

Corporate social responsibility

CSR information: There was no CSR information available.

Corporate charity: The Congregational & General Charitable Trust (Charity Commission no. 297013).

Applications

Applications to the associated charity should be made to the correspondent. When sending your application attach any supporting documentation – such as your church's or organisation's accounts, the project's accounts, appeal leaflets or project literature – along with your signed application form.

Grants are awarded by the Congregational & General Charitable Trust twice a year to churches and charitable causes. The closing dates for applications to be considered are 31 January and 31 July each year.

Note that as the trust does not have any full-time employees it is unable to take any queries or applications by telephone. If you wish to email do so at: trust@congregational.co.uk.

Co-operative Group Ltd

Insurance, legal, pharmaceuticals, retail – department and variety stores, banking, retail – supermarkets

Correspondent: The Community Fund Team, 1 Angel Square, Manchester M60 0AG (tel: 01618 341212; fax: 01618 331383; website: www.co-operative.coop/corporate)

Directors: Ursula Lidbetter, Chair; Michael Harriott; Frank Nelson; Eric Calderwood; Martyn Cheatle; Duncan Bowdler; Marc Bicknell; Richard Pennycook; Christopher Kelly; Simon Burke (women: 1; men: 9)

Year end	04/01/2014
Turnover	£10,534,000,000
Pre-tax profit	(£227,000,000)

Nature of business: The Co-operative Group is the UK's largest mutual business, owned not by private shareholders but by over six million consumers. The business areas of the group: food retail and convenience store operation; financial and legal services; funeral care; travel; property investment; electrical products; and banking.

Company registration number: 525R

Subsidiary undertakings include: Brompton Homes Ltd; Co-op Cruise Holidays Ltd; Co-operative Foodstores Ltd; Cumbria Group and Business Travel Ltd; Ekonsol Ltd; Fiesta Sun Ltd; Gilsland Spa Ltd; K G Orme Ltd; Mayflower Linen Services Ltd; Personal Travel Advisors Ltd; and Yorkshire Funeral Services Ltd. A full list of subsidiaries is available on the group's website.

Brands include: CIS Co-operative Insurance, Co-operative Bank, Co-op e-store, smile, Shoefayre, Travelcare, Somerfield, Britannia.

Main locations: Manchester

UK employees: 88,046

Total employees: 88,046

Focus of giving: General charitable purposes, education, environment, local groups, overseas projects, sponsorship, sport, recreation, children, young people, community/social welfare.

Membership: BITC, LBG

Charity of the Year	✓
Gifts in kind	✓
Market-led giving	✓
Matched funding	✓
Overseas giving	✓
Payroll giving	✓
Sponsorship	✓

Charitable donations

Cash UK (latest available):	2014	£1,500,000
	2011	£8,800,000
	2009	£7,000,000
	2007	£8,300,000
	2005	£4,400,000
Total UK (cash and in kind):	2014	£8,200,000
Cash worldwide:	2014	£1,500,000
Total worldwide (cash and in kind):	2014	£8,200,000

Community involvement

The Co-operative Community Investment Foundation (Charity Commission no. 1093028)

The foundation was established in 2000 as an independent charitable trust and operates both The Co-operative Membership Community Fund (The Community Fund) and Truth about Youth.

The Co-operative Membership Community Fund

The fund supports voluntary and self-help community organisations by awarding small grants of between £100 and £2,000. The fund is mainly funded through donations from members providing part or all of their share of profits each year and also the Sustainability Report notes that in 2013 there was a decrease in the total amount donated and the number of awards made but there was an increase in the average award value.

In 2013 the fund:

- Received 4,509 requests
- Awarded 2,270 grants
- Dispersed a total of £2.8 million
- Had an average award of £1,233

Note that currently applications are not accepted and the trustees are 'looking at the best way to develop the scheme and to continue to support local communities in the future'.

Truth about Youth

The grant-making scheme has been developed in 2009 through the foundation 'to challenge and change negative perceptions of young people'. Seven charities (one in each of Cooperative's democratic regions) have been working in partnership with the Foundation for five years. Each charity was given a grant of £140,000 per year, with a total of £5 million being spent on the programme.

Inspiring Young People

The programme was launched in 2010 'to help bring about a cultural shift in the way that young people are viewed and treated in the UK' and is supported by The Co-operative Community Investment Foundation. Co-operative invests in a range of projects aimed at young people. In 2013 the programme was benefiting 1.5 million people and saw cash investment of £1.6 million. The group states – 'as the Inspiring Young People programme has matured, our efforts have moved from establishing new projects, to a focus on maintaining and delivering core activities, as reflected in our capital investment'.

Co-operative Schools and Academies

In 2010 Co-operative committed £1 million to support the expansion of Co-operative Trust Schools and Co-operative academies and in 2013 a further £439,000 (2012: £318,000) was allocated to improve schools. The group provides both financial and in-kind support to the member-owned Schools Co-operative Society (SCS) 'which aims to raise the profile and capability of the Co-operative schools sector'. The Sustainability Report says:

> We work in partnership with local councils and educational institutions to provide an education programme based on co-operative values. Senior leaders from our businesses work closely with the academies to provide support and scrutiny and to champion good governance.

Co-operative British Youth Film Academy and Co-operative Film Festival

The initiatives are aimed young people (14–25 years of age) and seek to encourage their co-operation, creativity and self-expression. The website states – 'the Co-operative's £1.2 million, six-year partnership with The Co-operative British Youth Film Academy is working towards creating the UK's most accessible youth film making academy'.

Charity of the Year

The partnership runs on a biennial basis and enables a national charity, selected by colleagues and members, to benefit from employee fundraising for a dedicated 12-month period. In 2013 the group adopted the Carers Trust as its charity partner. During the year a total of £6 million was raised. The group states that the focus of the partnership 'was notsimply on fundraising, but on working alongside young carers to develop a programme of support to specifically meet their needs'.

StreetGames Young Volunteers

This programme operates in some of the most deprived areas in the UK and seeks to develop young people's sports coaching and community leadership skills. The scheme provides volunteers with training, support and resources. For many this experience leads to pursue vocational qualifications and further training.

Co-operative Enterprise Hub

The initiative was set up and is funded by The Co-operative Group. It aims to help the development and growth of co-operatives in the UK and delivers free of charge services by experienced co-operative development advisers.

'Chasing Ice'

The group is supporting the UK distribution of the Oscar-nominated film and offers free screenings across the country.

International support

Overseas the group supports co-operative and development projects. There is an ongoing partnership with The One Foundation. In 2013 a total of £750,000 was leveraged for the organisation through sales of Fairbourne Springs and One Eggs. The group also supports and funds Fairtrade projects. See the Sustainability Report for more detailed account of overseas contributions.

Corporate giving

According to the Sustainability Report for 2013 the group invested a total in £15.7 million (2012: £17.6 million) in UK communities. This figure included contributions by employees, customers, members and suppliers that Co-operative facilitated (shown as 'Leverage').

Community support for overseas projects and human rights initiatives is excluded from the above figure.

The report gives the following breakdown of support:

Leverage	£7 million
Cash	£6.6 million
Employee time	£1.3 million
Management costs	£500,000
Gifts in kind	£300,000

And outlines its top UK community programmes (investments over £1 million), which were:

Charity of the Year	£3.5 million
Inspiring Young People	£2.7 million
Co-operative Membership Community Fund	£2.6 million
Charitable donations to UK charities	£1.5 million
Co-operative Enterprise Hub	£1.2 million
Supporting local community events and activities (non-fundraising)	£1.31 million
Total contribution	£12.8 million

We have not included the amounts given for 'Leverage' or 'Management costs' into the total contributions figure and calculate it to be about £8.2 million. We take the figure of 'charitable donations to UK charities' as the group's cash contribution.

The annual report and accounts of The Co-operative Community Investment Foundation note the following: 'In November 2013 the Co-operative Group was unable to distribute a share of profits to its members and, recognising the impact this would have on the income of CCIF, made a donation of £800,000 to the Community Fund.'

See the corporate charity entry on p. 399 for more information.

In-kind support

The group can provide in-kind contributions, which generally total about £300,000 each year. Staff volunteering time and fundraising efforts are available.

Green Schools Revolution

Green Schools Revolution is a sustainability education programme which allows colleagues from Co-operative food stores to develop links with their local schools. There are also teaching resources available as well as a school visits programme offering 40 fully funded school visits to nine sustainability-themed venues across the country.

Grass-roots programme

The Co-operative Insurance runs an extensive programme of grass-roots initiatives throughout the UK, including football coaching and the provision of kits and equipment to junior teams. To date it has provided football kits to over 3,700 youth football teams and coaching for over 16,500 children.

Drinkaware

The group supports the campaign and raises awareness of the Drinkaware brand on its promotional material. The value of the in-kind support delivered for Drinkaware in 2013 was almost £381,000.

Employee-led support

Volunteering

The number of employees involved in community activity in work time during 2013 was 13,966 and the number of days invested in community activity in work time was 12,775 (95,810 hours), equating to a donation of time worth £1.3 million. Colleague volunteering included the Mencap Inspire Me programme. 'Through this programme, employees from across the UK became mentors for young people with learning disabilities, providing personal support, guidance, encouragement and inspiration.' According to the Sustainability Report 2013, in that year employees participated in Reading Partners, Number Partners and e-mentoring initiatives, acted as school governors and helped local communities through 103 team challenges benefiting schools and community organisations.

During 2013 Co-operative also created a Community Pioneer role in its stores – this allowed additional community hours and budget available to staff.

Fundraising

Employees raise funds for their chosen Charity of the Year. Alongside fundraising, local communities are also engaged in the charitable aims of the nominated charity, to raise awareness and influence change. In 2013 a total of over £5 million was raised by colleagues, members and customers.

Matched funding

The Co-operative Booster Fund offers one-off contributions to supplement employees' fundraising activities. In 2013 almost £51,000 was awarded to employee teams and individuals to support over 150 national and local charities. Fundraising efforts are topped-up by £100 for an individual and £400 for a team (subject to terms and conditions).

Payroll giving

Our research suggests that staff are able to contribute to their chosen charity through the provision of a payroll giving scheme.

Commercially led support

Cause-related marketing

The group has undertaken commercially led initiatives whereby donations were made based on the amount spent in store or upon a purchase of a specific product.

Charity Credit Cards

The bank offers a range of credit cards, each linked to one of charity partners. A donation is made to the chosen charity when an account is opened and additional donations are made in proportion to the amount spent using the card. Partners include: Amnesty International; Oxfam; RSPB; Save the Children; Tearfund; and Woodland.

Fairbourne Springs Water

For every bottle of water purchased money is donated to fund clean water projects in Africa.

Antibacterial Handwash

The Co-operative Pharmacy launched this affinity product with UNICEF in 2011. Donations collected through sales of the product helped to expand an existing sanitation project in Togo.

The Global Development Co-operative (GDC)

The initiative launched in 2011 aims to raise £20 million from organisations that support international development and extend the reach of the co-operative model. These funds will then be used to provide low-cost loans for capital and infrastructure projects around the world. The Co-operative Bank has developed the initiative as part the group's Ethical Plan and provides administrative support to the GDC.

CARE International UK

The group works with the organisation to support lendwithcare.org – 'a scheme whereby people in the UK can lend small sums of money to entrepreneurs in the developing world to help grow their business'.

Sponsorship

Sponsorship activities are focused 'on grassroots sport, providing opportunities for primary school age children to try various sports'. Currently partnerships include Rochdale, Stoke City and Bradford City Football Clubs.

Apprenticeship Academy

The academy seeks to address 'growing unemployment and lack of training opportunities for young people'.

Skills for Work

During 2013 the group ran skills workshops for 825 young people not in employment, education or training (NEET) on topics including behaviours in the workplace, interview skills and customer service. The workshops are run as part of a national Feeding Britain's Future campaign. In addition workplace opportunities are available through placements and internships.

Carrier Bags

The Sustainability Report says that in 2013 £200,000 was generated from a levy on carrier bags in Wales and was used to fund environmental projects in the region, chiefly through Wildlife Trust Wales.

Corporate social responsibility

CSR committee: There is a Community Fund Team.

CSR information: The group's website states:

> The Co-operative has always had a purpose beyond profit, and corporate social responsibility has been embedded in our approach to business since our formation over 150 years ago. We are guided by the long-established co-operative values of self-help, self-responsibility, democracy, equality, equity and solidarity.
>
> Concern for community is enshrined in our co-operative principles. As a retailer with a presence in every UK postal area, our community impact is extensive and is supported by our community activities. Like all co-operatives, we are committed to helping people work together and create sustainable enterprises to address challenges in their community.

The group's commitments encompass: UK community investment; international communities; employee community engagement; and Inspiring Young People programme.

CSR report: A comprehensive and informative Sustainability Report is published annually.

Corporate charity: Co-operative Community Investment Foundation (Charity Commission no. 1093028).

Exclusions

Our research suggests that The Co-operative Membership Community Fund generally excludes:

- Groups other than community, self-help and voluntary groups
- The core activities of auxiliary groups
- Non-charitable purposes (although a group does not have to be a registered charity)
- Overseas activities
- Grant or loan schemes
- Religious worship
- Core activities of statutory services
- Improvements to property not owned by the applicant
- Party political activity
- Individual sponsorship
- Cadets

Applications

The Community Fund: According to The Co-operative Community Investment Foundation's annual report and accounts, The Community Fund 'invites applications for funding of projects through advertising in the Co-operative Group retail outlets, via the Co-operative Group's website and through active promotion in areas in which the Co-operative Group trades'. Applicants are invited to submit a summary of their proposals in a specific format to be reviewed against specific criteria to be successful.

To be successful, a group must 'carry out positive work in the community' and a project must:

- Address a community issue
- Provide a good long-term benefit to the community
- Support co-operative values and principles
- Ideally be innovative in its approach

Note: Currently applications are not accepted – 'The charity's trustees are currently looking at the best way to develop the scheme and to continue to support local communities in the future.' Enquiries can be made via phone at 0844 262 4001 or email at community.fund@co-operative.coop.

The principal contact person for The Co-operative Community Investment Foundation is Clare Oakley at the company's address.

Costcutter Supermarkets Group Ltd

Retail – supermarkets

Correspondent: See 'Applications', Harvest Mills, Common Road, Dunnington, York YO19 5RY (tel: 01904 488663; website: www.costcutter.com)

Directors: D. M. Thompson; A. M. Barber; J. R. Davison; D. Willson-Rymer; K. R. Widdrington; R. Collins; R. G. Marshall; S. Potter; J. P. S. Ryrie; D. Quest; V. L. Reay

Year end	28/12/2013
Turnover	£775,724,000
Pre-tax profit	£48,000

Nature of business: The Costcutter Supermarkets Group is a franchise operation, with convenience stores throughout the UK.

Costcutter Supermarkets Group is a wholly owned subsidiary of Bibby Line Group and part of the Bibby Retail Services division. The 200-year-old family-owned business bought Costcutter Supermarket Group in 2011 and operated a diverse portfolio of business across sectors including distribution, financial services, off-shore, shipping and retail services.

In 2013 Costcutter Supermarkets Group announced a new partnership with leading delivered wholesaler Palmer and Harvey with a new supply chain launched in 2014. The BuyCo, a new joint venture buying group, was also created with the remit of negotiating the best prices for Costcutter Supermarkets Group's retailers.

Company registration number: 2059678

Subsidiary undertakings include: Ebor Foodmarkets Ltd; PDQ Ltd; Primex UK Ltd.

Brands include: Independent; Kwiksave; Mace; Supershop; Your Store.

UK employees: 238

Total employees: 238

Focus of giving: General charitable purposes, health, ill health, sport, recreation, community/social welfare.

Charitable donations

Cash UK (latest available):	2013	£4,500
	2012	£1,600
	2011	£2,600
	2009	£218,000
Total UK (cash and in kind):	2013	£4,500
Cash worldwide:	2013	£4,500
Total worldwide (cash and in kind):	2013	£4,500

Community involvement

The following information is taken from the company's website:

> Over the last few years Costcutter has helped raise over £700,000 through our previous charity initiative to help to make a real difference to the local communities that our stores serve. We are currently working on our new charity scheme to allow our customers and retailers raise even money for worthy causes.

Check back to the website for further updates.

Corporate giving

The company accounts state that in 2013 charitable donations of £4,500 were made mainly to sporting and medical charities.

Corporate social responsibility

CSR information: There was no CSR information available.

We were unable to determine the ratio of women to men on the board.

Applications

In writing to your local store. Enquiries regarding the charity, Making A Difference Locally Ltd., should be sent to the correspondent.

Coutts and Co

Banking

Correspondent: Kay Boland, The Coutts Charitable Trust, 440 Strand, London WC2R 0QS (tel: 020 7753 1000/020 7957 2822; fax: 020 7753 1028; email: kay.boland@coutts.com; website: www.coutts.com)

Directors: The Rt Hon Lord Waldegrave of North Hill, Chair; Francesca Barnes; Michael John Morley; Rory Tapner (women: 1; men: 3)

Year end	31/12/2013
Turnover	£570,511,000
Pre-tax profit	£84,293,000

Nature of business: Banking and allied financial services. Coutts is the private banking arm of the Royal Bank of Scotland Group. The bank's main location is London, but there are offices internationally.

Company registration number: 36695

Brands include: RBS; Coutts.

Main locations: Liverpool, Manchester, Newcastle upon Tyne, Oxford, Nottingham, Winchester, Tunbridge Wells, Bristol, Cardiff, Cambridge, Isle of Man, Jersey, Leeds, Eton, Guildford, Bath, Birmingham, Bournemouth, London

Total employees: 2,256

Focus of giving: General charitable purposes, education, health, ill health, housing, homelessness, medical research, marginalised people, older people, poverty and social exclusion, children, young people, community/social welfare, disability.

Gifts in kind	✓
Payroll giving	✓
Sponsorship	✓

Charitable donations

Cash UK (latest available):	2013	£642,000
	2011	£750,590
	2009	£1,267,500
	2006	£832,956
	2005	£522,088
Total UK (cash and in kind):	2013	£642,000
Cash worldwide:	2013	£642,000
Total worldwide (cash and in kind):	2013	£642,000

Community involvement

The Coutts Foundation (Charity Commission no. 1000135)

The mission of the foundation is:

> To support sustainable approaches to tackle the causes and consequences of poverty, focusing on the communities where Coutts has a presence.
>
> Thismission builds on the legacy of Angela Burdett-Coutts, the grand-daughter of Thomas Coutts, who was a progressive 19th century philanthropist who was concerned with breaking the

> cycles of poverty and the provision of basic human needs.

The foundation was set up in 1987 to formalise Coutts & Co.'s charitable giving and makes donations to a wide range of charities each year. Its main source of funding is derived from a fixed percentage of the bank's pre-tax profits, which is distributed to selected causes.

Grants are given by the foundation to UK organisations only and the trustees prefer to support organisations in areas where the bank has a presence, mainly London. Charities supported include those involved with helping the homeless, rehabilitation and teaching self-help (drug and alcohol misuse, young offenders), disadvantaged adults and children, youth organisations, the elderly, medical research, heritage, education and the relief of poverty.

> Many applications are supported by key clients and, in these circumstances, the criteria may be relaxed. Staff and pensioners of Coutts & Company, involved with charities in a personal capacity, are encouraged to apply to the trust and support is also given to members of staff who give their time voluntarily to raise funds for charities of their choice.

Corporate giving

The total amount given for charitable purposes, via the foundation, by the company and its subsidiary undertakings during the year 2013 was £642,000. The figure we have used for UK charitable cash contributions is that received by the Coutts Foundation for the period 2013/14.

See the corporate charity entry on p. 400 for more information.

In-kind support

In 2013 Coutts worked with The Connection, a London homelessness charity, giving time to raise funds and support their work. The bank provided over 600 hours of volunteering time and raised £55,000. 'Our efforts globally included a house-building programme in Batam, Indonesia, and a painting project to refurbish the facilities for vulnerable children.'

Employee-led support

Volunteering is encouraged by the firm, see example in the section 'In-kind support'.

Payroll giving: The Give As You Earn scheme is in operation.

Commercially led support

Sponsorship: Support has been given to the following: ABF The Soldiers' Charity for the charity's inaugural garden at 2014's RHS Chelsea Flower Show; Almeida Theatre; the Design Museum; the Grierson Awards; the National Portrait Gallery; and the Royal Opera House, amongst others.

Corporate social responsibility

CSR committee: With regard to charitable giving, the foundation's board, includes Coutts staff and other highly experienced individuals who strongly identify with the foundation's mission and approach. The board is supported by a team from Coutts to manage its governance and grant-making operations.

CSR information: We could not discover a CSR policy but we believe that most charitable giving is channelled through the company's charitable foundation. The company's website states the foundation's mission which is: 'To support sustainable approaches to tackle the causes and consequences of poverty, focusing on the communities where Coutts has a presence.'

Coutts also sponsors 'causes and organisations that share our values and tradition, and we celebrate success, nurture talent and champion events. Sponsorship plays an important role in building our brand profile and supporting our clients' passions'.

CSR report: There was at one time an annual review available online but we could not find a current publication at the time the research was carried out (February 2015).

Corporate charity: Coutts Charitable Foundation (Charity Commission no. 1150784).

Exclusions

No response to circular appeals. No support is given for appeals from individuals or overseas projects.

Applications

The following information is taken from the company's website:

> The Coutts Foundation takes a proactive approach to identifying its grantees. We prefer to fund organisations where our funding can be catalytic – either testing a new idea or helping scale a tested programme.
>
> The foundation does not accept unsolicited proposals for funding. However, we welcome information about organisations that fit our funding priorities and approach.

There is an information submission form on the website which can be emailed or posted to the foundation.

Coventry Building Society

Building society

Correspondent: Alison Readman, Correspondent, Coventry BS Charitable Foundation, Oakfield House, PO Box 600, Binley, Coventry CV3 9YR (tel: 0845 766 5522/02476 435231; email: alison.readman@thecoventry.co.uk; website: www.thecoventry.co.uk)

Directors: Bridget Blow; David Stewart, Chief Executive; John Lowe, Finance Director; Colin Franklin; Roger Burnell; Ian Geden; Ian Pickering, Chair; Glyn Smith; Peter Ayliffe; Janet Ashdown; Peter Frost; Feike Brouwers; Thomas Crane (women: 2; men: 11)

Year end	31/12/2013
Turnover	£790,200,000
Pre-tax profit	£53,800,000

Nature of business: Building Society

Company registration number: 5830727

Main locations: Coventry

Focus of giving: General charitable purposes, health, ill health, older people, poverty and social exclusion, children, young people, community/social welfare, disability.

Cash donations undeclared	✓
Charity of the Year	✓
Gifts in kind	✓
Market-led giving	✓

Charitable donations

Cash UK (latest available):	2013	£500,000
	2012	£2,000,000
	2011	£1,100,000
	2009	£100,000
	2008	£200,000
Total UK (cash and in kind):	2013	£500,000
Cash worldwide:	2013	£500,000
Total worldwide (cash and in kind):	2013	£500,000

Community involvement

Community programmes

The society's community programmes focus on specific areas, including the development of financial literacy, helping young people in education develop the skills to gain work and supporting national and local charities. It encourages volunteering amongst its employees to carry these activities out.

The society provides internships and apprentice schemes to provide work experience opportunities. A key part of this activity has taken place at a local level with many successful community partnerships now established between branches, head office teams and community groups.

Coventry Building Society Charitable Foundation (Charity Commission no. 1072244) was launched in 1998. It is entirely funded by Coventry Building

Society and is an independent entity with a board of trustees who determine the criteria by which grants are made.

Corporate giving

In 2013 the society 'provided for donations of £1.9 million (2012: £2.0 million) to charitable organisations'. This included a provision for £1.6 million (2012: £1.9 million) to The Royal British Legion's Poppy Appeal; £200,000 to Cancer Research UK; and £102,000 (2012: £60,000) to the Coventry Building Society Charitable Foundation. The society's annual report states that 'Through a combination of fundraising, volunteering and affinity activities, the total community investment supported by the society in 2013 was £2.3 million'. We know that £1.8 million came from market-led activity (see commercially-led support section), which it our practice not to include. This leaves a remaining amount of around £500,000 for which we do not have a breakdown of how much was cash donations and how much was in-kind giving. We have therefore set the UK and world community contribution at £500,000; the cash donations are unknown.

According to the foundation's 2013 accounts, the Coventry Building Society currently donates £60,000 per annum to the foundation. During the year, David Stewart, Chief Executive of Coventry Building Society, elected to waive his 2012 annual bonus. The society donated an additional amount equivalent to the remuneration waived (£46,800) to the foundation. (This appears to be included in the £102,000 mentioned above). Mr Stewart states in the 2013 annual report that during 2014, he expects total donations to the foundation to reach £1 million (since its inception).

See the corporate charity entry on p. 400 for more information.

In-kind support

The financial literacy activities supported by society volunteers range from basic reading and numeracy programmes to sessions explaining savings, spending and budgets. Volunteers also work with schools to help students prepare for job applications and interviews.

The society works with other service providers to deliver financial literacy activities. An example is the long-running partnership with Coventry Citizens Advice through which the society supports debt awareness and advice sessions for young and vulnerable adults.

Employee-led support

Community Partner programme

This initiative encourages employees to adopt a local charity or community group and support it through fundraising and volunteering. For example, in 2013, one head office partnership raised over £10,000 for a local hospice, and over 74 such partnerships are now in place across the society.

In addition to the funds raised directly, money raised by corporate events is made available via Community Partner Fund grants, and in 2013 over £14,000 was distributed to local charities through this route.

> The programme is an increasingly successful way of connecting the society and its staff to local communities. The local element, often supported by personal experience of the work of these organisations, has increased fundraising and volunteering and community activity continues to be a source of motivation and engagement for society staff.

Commercially led support

The society is a provider of charitable affinity accounts. In 2013, the society donated £1.6 million to the Poppy Appeal as a result of its successful Poppy savings portfolio and an inaugural 'Race for Life Bond' led to a donation of over £200,000 for Cancer Research UK.

Corporate social responsibility

CSR committee: There appears to be no designated committee and that apart from the society's foundation, responsibility lies with the board.

CSR information: The society's community programmes encourage the high engagement of staff.

CSR report: The CSR report is contained within the society's annual report.

Corporate charity: Coventry Building Society Charitable Foundation (Charity Commission no. 1072244).

Exclusions

No grants can be given outside the Midlands area. The following are not eligible for support:

- Large charities which enjoy national coverage
- Charities with no base within the branch area
- Charities with an annual donated income in excess of £250,000
- Charities with assets over £500,000
- Projects requiring an ongoing commitment
- Large capital projects
- Maintenance or building works for buildings, gardens or playgrounds
- Major fundraising
- Projects which are normally the responsibility of other organisations (such as the NHS, Education Department and local authorities)
- Sponsorship of individuals
- Requests from individuals
- Replacing funds that were the responsibility of another body
- Educational institutions unless for the relief of disadvantage
- Sporting clubs or organisations unless for the relief of disadvantage
- Medical research and equipment
- More than one donation for the same organisation in any one year – further applications will be considered after three years
- Animal welfare
- Promotion of religious political or military causes

Applications

Applications can be made online through your local community foundation. In order to do this choose the area closest to where your charity operates from the table at the bottom of the Coventry Building Society Charitable Foundation website and click on the relevant link. This will take you to go to the community foundation website for your area. From here, you will be able to find out more about your local community foundation and all of the information that you'll need to apply for a grant.

Cummins Ltd

Engineering

Correspondent: Community Involvement Team, 49–51 Gresham Road, Staines, Middlesex TW18 2BD (website: www.cummins.com)

Directors: A. J. Robinson; J. M. Barrowman; R. J. Eyres; H. S. Foden; M. R. Firth

Year end	31/12/2013
Turnover	£1,055,585,000
Pre-tax profit	£200,750,000

Nature of business: The principal activity is the manufacture, sale, distribution and servicing of diesel engines and components. The company is a subsidiary of Cummins Inc (US).

Company registration number: 573951

Subsidiary undertakings include:

Main locations: Ramsgate, Huddersfield, Daventry, Darlington, Stamford, Hinckley, Wellingborough, Cumbernauld, Stockton-on-Tees, Peterborough

Focus of giving: Human rights, education, environment, poverty and social exclusion, children, young people, community/social welfare.

Cash donations undeclared	✓
Gifts in kind	✓
Humanitarian aid: overseas	✓
Overseas giving	✓

Charitable donations

Cash UK (latest available):	2013	£39,000
	2010	£54,000
	2008	£43,000
	2007	£19,300
	2006	£49,900
Total UK (cash and in kind):	2013	£39,000
Cash worldwide:	2013	£4,200,000
Total worldwide (cash and in kind):	2013	£4,200,000

Community involvement

This company donates to a variety of registered charities in the UK. Previously, we were advised that within the UK, the company prefers to support projects local to its manufacturing plants and offices. Organisations concerned with youth, education, the environment, and disadvantaged people are favoured. There is also a global foundation but UK giving from that appears minimal.

The Cummins Foundation (US) was created in 1954 and was one of the early corporate foundations. It is part of the global giving arm of Cummins Inc. It makes grants primarily in Cummins' communities around the world and for projects that engage Cummins employees. Global support currently focuses on environment, education and social justice.

On looking through the 2012 tax return, it would seem that there is no substantial giving in the UK.

In addition, Cummins has two international foundations in India and Mexico: Asociación Filantrópica Cummins (AFIC), Mexico and Cummins India Foundation (CIF), India.

Corporate giving

In 2013 the company did not declare its charitable donations. We have therefore taken an average of the last three years for which we have totals available and estimate the UK cash contribution to be around £39,000. The company usually distributes to a variety of registered charities. We do not have a worldwide contributions figure and have taken the total cash given on the US Foundation's tax return (for 2012 – the latest available) of $6.7 million – over £4.2 million. We consider total cash contributions will be more, as will the company's in-kind contributions, for which we could find no figures.

In-kind support

Employee engagement is also evidenced with Community Impact Six Sigma (CISS), which helps to solve community problems through skills-based volunteerism by joining with partners around the globe to leverage our Six Sigma skills and training. CISS projects use data to drive sustainable improvement through the use of business tools and skills.

Employee-led support

Volunteering around the world

Employees engage through a network of more than 200 Community Involvement Teams (CIT) around the world. There are 219 such teams in 45 countries. CITs serve as liaisons to their communities and are the primary on-site co-ordinators for community involvement initiatives. Using such tools as a community needs assessment, CITs determine how to use employees' skills and talents to tackle the biggest problems facing their communities.

Every employee is given the opportunity to contribute at least four hours on company time to his or her community. Many employees, particularly those engaged in skills-based projects, contribute more hours than that each year; 62% of employees gave 222,000 hours in volunteering in their communities.

Matched funding: Employees' charitable contributions are matched by the US foundation through the North American United Way campaign and company-established global matching programmes. These programmes give Cummins' employees options to donate to local organisations and projects that are meaningful to them.

Corporate social responsibility

CSR committee: We could not find the members or structure of a specific CSR committee; however, there are Community Involvement teams in the company's offices around the world.

CSR information: There was no CSR information available for the UK company. The global company states on its website:

> Corporate Responsibility and The Cummins Foundation [U.S.} are investing resources in three global strategic initiatives: TEC: Technical Education for Communities, Power to Prosper and the Environmental Challenge. These programs hold the promise of driving immense change. They align with business goals and link to our employees' technical skills and passions.

We were unable to determine the ratio of women to men on the board of the UK company.

CSR report: Global information is published in a separate section on the global website.

Applications

In writing to the correspondent for UK company giving referenced 'UK Charitable Donations'.

For application to the US Foundation, write to: The Cummins Foundation, 500 Jackson Street, M.C. 60633, Columbus, IN 47201Fax: (812) 377–7897email: cummins.foundation@cummins.com.

P. Z. Cussons plc

Household, pharmaceuticals

Correspondent: CSR Team, 3500 Aviator Way, Manchester Business Park, Manchester M22 5TG (tel: 01614 351000; website: www.pzcussons.com/en_int/csr)

Directors: Alex Kanellis, Group Chief Executive; Chris Davis; Brandon Leigh, Chief Financial Officer; Richard Harvey, Chair; James Steel; Professor John Arnold; Ngozi Edozien; Helen Owers; Caroline Silver (women: 3; men: 6)

Year end	31/05/2014
Turnover	£861,400,000
Pre-tax profit	£123,700,000

Nature of business: Principal activities: manufacture and distribution of soaps, toiletries, cleaning agents, pharmaceuticals, refrigerators and air conditioners.

Company registration number: 19457

Subsidiary undertakings include: Seven Scent Ltd; PZ Cussons (Holdings) Ltd; PZ Cussons (International) Ltd; PZ Cussons (UK) Ltd.

Brands include: Carex, Charles Worthington, Original Source, Imperial Leather, Venus, Sanctuary Spa, St Tropez.

Main locations: Stockport

Total employees: 5,779

Focus of giving: Education, health, ill health, small groups, overseas projects, children, young people, community/social welfare, disability.

Membership: BITC

Charity of the Year	✓
Gifts in kind	✓
Overseas giving	✓

Charitable donations

Cash UK (latest available):	2014	£663,000
	2013	£474,000
	2012	£253,000
	2011	£50,000
	2009	£343,000
Total UK (cash and in kind):	2014	£663,000
Cash worldwide:	2014	£663,000
Total worldwide (cash and in kind):	2014	£663,000

Community involvement

PZ Cussons supports local communities and charities in the places where it operates, particularly through projects involving children and young people, social welfare, medical, education and people with disabilities. Most support is given through **The Zochonis Charitable Trust** (Charity Commission no. 274769), a shareholding trust. Contributions are also made through staff time and gifts in kind. The group's PZ Cussons Nigeria Foundation works to support its local communities in Nigeria to improve education and health.

The group also looks to support charitable causes through its various brands. During 2014, the Sanctuary Spa brand will work to generate funds and raise awareness for Wellbeing of Women, a charity celebrating its 50th birthday that is working to improve the health of women and babies. A product of this support will be the funding of a new research project. The Mum and Me brand is also working in partnership with the charity and the Royal College of Midwives to fund a new research fellowship which will enable a midwife to undertake PhD research.

Corporate giving

During the year charitable contributions made by the group in the UK totalled £663,000.

We were unable to determine a value for PZ Cussons' in-kind contributions, or for support given for overseas causes.

Beneficiaries included: Global Hand Washing Day; The Seashell Trust; Wellbeing of Women.

See the corporate charity entry on p. 441 for more information.

In-kind support

In-kind support forms an important part of PZ Cussons' charitable contributions.

Case study 1: The Seashell Trust
The group has had a long-term involvement with the Manchester-based The Seashell Trust, which works to support adults and children with severe learning disabilities, and has worked on a number of related projects. During the year, the group's head office in Manchester worked with the trust to offer a work experience placement to a student, helping to broaden their skills and work opportunities.

Case study 2: Carex
Each year, the team at the group's Carex brand host activities in support of Global Hand Washing Day. In the UK, the 'Hands Up for Hygiene' Education programme provides resources to complement the school curriculum.

Corporate social responsibility

CSR committee: The board is responsible for overseeing CSR within the group and is supported by a CSR Committee. Following each CSR Committee meeting, the CSR Committee's Chair 'reports to the board on the CSR Committee's proceedings relating to matters within the scope of its remit'.

CSR information: The following information is taken from the annual report:

> We are a business which recognises our social responsibilities, proactively working with the local communities and charities where we operate to make a real difference. We encourage our employees across the globe to get involved and to date they have demonstrated a continued commitment to helping us to deliver projects, raise funds and make life changing contributions to society.

CSR report: There is a CSR report included in the annual report and a section dedicated to CSR on the company's website.

Corporate charity: The Zochonis Charitable Trust (Charity Commission no. 274769).

Applications

In writing to the correspondent.

Dairy Crest Group plc

Dairy products

Correspondent: The CSR Committee, Claygate House, Littleworth Road, Esher, Surrey KT10 9PN (tel: 01372 472200; fax: 01372 472333; website: www.dairycrest.co.uk)

Directors: Mark Allen, Chief Executive Officer; Martyn Wilks; Stephen Alexander, Chair; Andrew Carr-Locke; Richard Macdonald; Sue Farr; Robin Miller, Company Secretray; Tom Atherton, Finance Director (women: 1; men: 7)

Year end	31/03/2014
Turnover	£1,391,000,000
Pre-tax profit	£54,200,000

Nature of business: Dairy Crest is a dairy company, processing and selling fresh milk and branded dairy products in the UK and Europe.

Note: In November 2014 Dairy Crest agreed to sell its dairies operations to Müller UK and Ireland Group. 'The sale is conditional on the approval of the relevant competition authorities' and 'on the approval of Dairy Crest's shareholders and employee consultation'. The process was expected to take several months during which the group's operations would continue as normal.

Company registration number: 3162897

Subsidiary undertakings include: Dairy Crest Ltd; FoodTec UK Ltd; Philpot Dairy Products Ltd; Morehands Ltd; and Wexford Creamery Ltd.

Brands include: Cathedral City; Clover; Country Life; Frijj; and Willow.

Main locations: Surrey

Total employees: 4,545

Focus of giving: General charitable purposes, economic generation, education, enterprise/training, environment, health, ill health, local groups, armed forces personnel, poverty and social exclusion, sponsorship, community/social welfare, disasters.

Membership: BITC

Cash donations undeclared	✓
Charity of the Year	✓
Gifts in kind	✓
Humanitarian aid: overseas	✓
Humanitarian aid: UK	✓
Market-led giving	✓
Sponsorship	✓

Charitable donations

Cash UK (latest available):	2014	£100,000
	2011	£100,000
	2010	£100,000
	2009	£100,000
Total UK (cash and in kind):	2014	£100,000
Cash worldwide:	2014	£100,000
Total worldwide (cash and in kind):	2014	£100,000

Community involvement

The Prince's Countryside Fund
According to the company's CR Report, Dairy Crest (together with other businesses and the Prince of Wales) contributed to setting up the fund to 'improve the sustainability of British farming and rural communities, target the areas of greatest need, reconnect consumers with the countryside and to support farming and rural crisis charities through a dedicated emergency funding stream'. Through the stream help was given to projects to help people affected by 2013/14 flooding in the UK, particularly Somerset. Furthermore, the CR report states:

> By working collaboratively through the fund, and with our Davidstow and Country Life brands, since 2010 all the companies involved have been able to donate £3.9 million in grants, support over 87 rural projects ranging from helping upland farmers through to supporting rural youth unemployment groups the UK. In total the fund has helped more than 64,000 people.

Pub is the Hub
The group is supporting the non-profit organisation:

> That encourages local authorities, local communities, licensees and pub owners to work together to support, retain and locate services [such as shops, school meals, post offices, community centres, community cafes, keep fit, library services, allotments, play areas, take away food, cinemas, theatre, community travel, community acquisition and computer training services] within rural pubs.

Dairy Crest has helped to fund rural community shops in pubs in the South West of England – 'facilities that provide isolated communities with access to locally produced food and household goods'.

Local communities
Engaging with local communities is the fourth strand of Dairy Crest's community strategy. The Local Community programme is owned and run by the staff. The group states:

> Through this programme any employee can put forward a good cause they would like the company to support either through money, a product donation or volunteering. Over the course of 2013/14 Dairy Crest staff supported over 110 good causes.

Local Community Committees are made up of five to six employees and each has responsibility for their own budget and for the decisions they make. Money allocations to the local community committees 'reflect the size of the workforce, the socio-economic challenges of the area and the maturity of the programme'.

Over the course of 2013/14 staff supported over 110 local good causes through volunteering work time, product donations or a direct financial donation.

As well as funding good causes through local community budgets, staff can also nominate good causes they wish to support through the money raised as a result of the company's staff lottery 'Quids In'. About £1,500 is donated to charitable causes each month through this scheme.

Support is given to:

- Local good causes that make a positive and direct contribution to the communities where [Dairy Crest's] workplaces are based
- Good causes that improve health, education, the environment or countryside

Charity partnership

In 2013/14 the group's staff charity partner was the Prince's Countryside Fund. The organisation benefited from employee fundraising efforts. The website notes that 'in addition to contributing £100,000 to the fund via [Country Life and Davidstow] brands, staff – including franchisee milkman – have set themselves the target of raising £50,000 for the charity by July 2016'.

Corporate giving

Unfortunately, Dairy Crest's annual report and accounts for 2013/14 did not appear to declare charitable donations. Since no figures could be found, we estimate that about £100,000 was given in cash in the UK, based on the figures form three previous years known to us. **Beneficiaries included**: Chipstead FC; Girlguides Cheam; Kingston Hospital Born Too Soon; Lady Brook Bug Garden; Philippines Flood; Romsey Fire Station; Royal British Legion; Prostate Cancer; Sacred Heart School; Weddington Allotment Association; and Wooden Tops Day Nursery.

A full list of beneficiaries can be found on the group's website.

In-kind support

Employee fundraising efforts and volunteering time as well as product donations are available.

The 'Volunteering Policy' document (created in 2010) states that 'where practical support to employee volunteers will include making Dairy Crest's facilities, including office space, telephones, computers and stationery, available to them to assist with their work'.

Employee-led support

The Local Community programme (also see' Community involvement' section) is the fourth strand of Dairy Crest's community strategy and is owned and run by the staff. Employees can nominate a cause for the group to support and during 2013/14 more than 110 local health, education and countryside related good causes were supported. The group provides one day off a year for volunteering purposes. Dairy Crest employees also fundraised for the charity partner – Prince's Countryside Fund.

The website also says:

> As well as funding good causes through our local community budgets, staff can also nominate good causes they wish to support through the money raised as a result of our staff lottery 'Quids In'. About £1,500 is donated to charitable causes each month through this scheme.

Elmbridge Council's Meals on Wheels

The group supported the programme with the staff members volunteering their time to deliver hot meals to vulnerable people in the local community.

Commercially led support

The Prince's Rural Action Programme and The Prince's Dairy Initiative

Through programme Dairy Crest 'is working with a diverse number of companies from banks to retailers to understand the impact businesses can have on improving rural communities and put these thoughts into action'. One of the projects was The Prince's Dairy Initiative through which businesses try to help 'the most vulnerable, non-aligned, dairy farmers become more economically viable'. The pilot with 74 dairy farms was run in 2012 and the group is expecting to help a further 300 farms by 2016.

Education and Training

Dairy Crest seeks to help young people into the career in food industry through a number of education programmes 'catering for GCSE, A-Level, undergraduate and postgraduate students' and by supporting the Institute of Grocers and Distributors (IGD) Feeding Britain's Future Programme.

Dairy Crest sponsors places for school pupils to attend summer schools at Nottingham and Reading Universities.

Feeding Britain's Future

In supporting the programme Dairy Crest sits on the steering group of the IGD Employability Group and in 2013 'supported over 400 young people in their quest to get a job'. Events have been held at the group's Davidstow Creamery and Nuneaton Distribution Centre as well as over 30 co-hosted sessions with Sainsbury's, Asda and Marks and Spencer. The annual report notes:

The group states: 'In September 2013 we set up a new employability steering group to ensure that going forward we continue to focus on the skills gaps needed for both Dairy Crest and food manufacturing as a whole.'

The Rural Action Award

The group sponsors of the Dairy Crest Rural Action Award, run by Business in the Community. The award 'recognises companies that are helping to address issues faced by rural communities in order to maintain a vibrant, sustainable rural economy'.

Corporate social responsibility

CSR committee: There is a CSR Committee the purpose of which is 'to ensure on behalf of the group board that corporate responsibility and sustainability are integral to the group's business, operations and culture'.

CSR information: The annual report and accounts for 2013/14 state that:

> Dairy Crest is a responsible business that demonstrates its commitment to corporate responsibility in many ways. ... It is a core principle of the business to hold high values in the safety and well-being of our people; to engage with our local communities; to reduce our environmental footprint; and to play our part in a healthy marketplace.

It is further specified that the group's community commitments include:

- Looking after the countryside and broader environment
- Promoting healthy living
- Supporting education and employability
- Engaging with local communities

CSR report: CSR reporting is contained within the group's annual report and accounts. The group's website provides a helpful overview of its CSR activities.

Exclusions

Political donations are not made.

Applications

In writing to your local site, referenced, 'Local Community Committee', or to the correspondent for corporate CSR enquiries.

DDB UK Ltd

Advertising/marketing

Correspondent: Head of Human Resources, 12 Bishops Bridge Road, London W2 6AA (tel: 020 7258 3979; fax: 020 7402 4871; website: www.ddblondon.com)

Directors: S. Watson; D. Nagy; J. B. P. Murphy

Year end	31/12/2013
Turnover	£113,388,361
Pre-tax profit	£9,512,986

Nature of business: The principal activity of the company is that of an advertising agency.

Company registration number: 933578

Main locations: London

Focus of giving: Human rights, advertising in charity brochures, enterprise/training, environment, fundraising events, groups not already known, animal welfare, health, ill health, heritage, medical research, older people, arts, culture, political appeals, religion, science technology, sport, recreation, children, young people, community/social welfare, disability.

Charitable donations

Cash UK (latest available):	2013	£46,000
	2012	£29,000
	2011	£36,000
	2009	£32,000
	2008	£23,000
Total UK (cash and in kind):	2013	£46,000
Cash worldwide:	2013	£46,000
Total worldwide (cash and in kind):	2013	£46,000

Community involvement

We were previously advised that the company supports national and international charities with direct donations. The preferred areas are: animal protection, the arts, children/youth, education, the elderly, enterprise/training, environment/heritage, fundraising events, health, medical research, political and religious appeals, science/technology, sickness/disability, social welfare, sport and advertising in charity brochures.

Charity of the Year

The company's Charity of the Year is chosen through staff nomination of a charity which is directly involved with any of the issues stated above.

Corporate giving

In 2013, cash donations to charity totalled £46,000 (2012: £29,000). We do not have details of beneficiaries but previous recipient organisations have included: Brain Tumour UK; History of Advertising Trust; NABS; and World Wildlife Fund.

Employee-led support

There is a volunteer scheme for employees.

Payroll giving: The Give As You Earn and NABS schemes are in operation.

Corporate social responsibility

CSR committee: There were no details.

CSR information: No CR details available.

We could not determine the ratio of women to men on the board.

CSR report: None published.

Applications

In writing to the correspondent.

Debenhams plc

Retail – department and variety stores

Correspondent: Ms Kate Thomas, Correspondent to the Trustees, Debenhams Foundation, 10 Brock Street, Regent's Place, London NW1 3FG (tel: 020 7408 4444/020 3549 6418; email: kate.thomas@debenhams.com; website: www.debenhamsplc.com)

Directors: Nigel Northridge, Chair; Michael Sharp, Chief Executive; Suzanne Harlow, Group Trading Director; Dennis Millard; Martina King; Peter Fitzgerald; Mark Rolfe; Sophie Turner Laing; Stephen Ingham (women: 3; men: 6)

Year end	30/08/2014
Turnover	£2,300,000,000
Pre-tax profit	£110,300,000

Nature of business: Debenhams is an international, multi-channel brand which trades out of 246 stores across 28 countries. It is available online in 70 countries.

Company registration number: 5448421

Subsidiary undertakings include: Debenhams Retail plc; Debenhams Group holdings Ltd; Debenhams Retail (Ireland) Ltd; Debenhams Properties Ltd; Aktieselskabet Th. Wessel and Vett Magasin du Nord.

Total employees: 28,233

Focus of giving: General charitable purposes, environment, health, ill health, community/social welfare, disability.

Cash donations undeclared	✓
Charity of the Year	✓
Gifts in kind	✓
Humanitarian aid: overseas	✓
Humanitarian aid: UK	✓
Market-led giving	✓
Payroll giving	✓

Charitable donations

Cash UK (latest available):	2014	£500,000
	2011	£1,100,000
	2009	£409,000
	2008	£293,000
Total UK (cash and in kind):	2014	£500,000
Cash worldwide:	2014	£500,000
Total worldwide (cash and in kind):	2014	£500,000

Community involvement

In 2011, following a charity audit by the company, the **Debenhams Foundation** (Charity Commission no. 1147682) was established through which all charitable giving is channelled. The objects of the foundation are to preserve and protect health and relieve financial hardship and for general charitable purposes. These objects will be achieved primarily through grant-making. The foundation operates worldwide and will also provide relief aid through the Disasters Emergency Committee (DEC). The foundation's trustees also manage the annual donation of funds from Debenhams plc to the Debenhams Retirement Association.

Many charities are supported by Debenhams at a local level including children's charities, schools, sports clubs, animal and wildlife charities, old people's homes, hospitals, hospices and medical charities. The food services division is a corporate member of the Anaphylaxis Campaign and fully supports the great work they do, helping people with severe allergens and persuading the food industry (including catering) of the need to provide detailed and accurate allergen information.

Charity partners: BBC Children in Need; Help for Heroes and Think Pink.

Corporate giving

In the financial year 2013/14 the group did not declare any charitable donations in its annual report and accounts. The Debenhams Foundation was launched in 2012 with the goal of giving clear visibility of the money raised for good causes' and to channel Debenhams' company, staff and customers' giving. The foundation's aim is to raise funds through store and head office's fundraising and through product sales. 'Think Pink' is a subsidiary of the foundation and its trading arm. Profits from Think Pink go directly to the foundation and this is then the group's charitable donation as it does not receive the profits from those sales. Accounts are not due from this newly formed (2013) subsidiary company and in the 2013/14 accounting period for the foundation, it appears that the group made a donation of £500,000 separately from the fundraising endeavours of staff and customers.

See the corporate charity entry on p. 401 for more information.

In-kind support

The group provides legal, accounting and marketing support to the foundation at no cost.

Employee-led support

Payroll giving

The silver award for payroll giving 2014 was received from the Charities Aid Foundation in recognition of the generosity of Debenhams' employees.

Commercially led support

Think Pink

October 2012 saw the launch of Debenhams' own breast cancer initiative Think Pink which raises money for three breast cancer charities: Breakthrough Breast Cancer, Breast Cancer Campaign and Pink Ribbon Foundation. A range of products including womenswear, home products and accessories were sold in store making donations to the cause. In addition, stores also fundraised in various ways including fancy dress, staff bake sales, cosmetics events, and team challenges.

Whilst commercially-led activities are not usually included in DSC's group's total giving figures, this is an exception as the company Think Pink was specifically set up to trade on behalf of the foundation and all its profits are covenanted over.

Corporate social responsibility

CSR information: The following statement is taken from the company's website:

> As a retail business, Debenhams' activities can impact the lives of millions of people: our customers, our employees, the communities in which we operate, those who work in our supply chain and their own communities. We have a responsibility to all these people and to our planet to try to have a positive impact upon them and to take their needs into account when we make decisions about the business.
>
> We believe the best way to live up to these responsibilities is to embed them into our everyday working practices. We do not therefore have a corporate responsibility or sustainability department. Instead, accountability and responsibility rests with those who best understand how and why we can make a difference as we execute the four pillars of our strategy to build a leading international, multi-channel brand.

CSR report: The principal method of communication for sustainability issues is online. Community issues are also recorded briefly in the annual report.

Corporate charity: Debenhams Foundation (Charity Commission no. 1147682).

Applications

In writing to the correspondent for grant-giving or to the local store for community projects, gifts in kind, etc. Most of the group's charitable giving is directed through its associated foundation – see 'Community involvement' section.

Deep Sea Leisure plc

Leisure

Correspondent: S. O. Evans, Company Secretary, Forthside Terrace, North Queensferry, Inverkeithing, Fife KY11 1JR (tel: 01383 411411; website: www.blueplanetaquarium.com)

Directors: S. J. Elaiho; A. Barrachina, Chair; J. Fernandes-Pinero; D. L. Soriano

Year end	31/10/2013
Turnover	£12,263,000
Pre-tax profit	£2,810,000

Nature of business: Owner and operator of public aquarium visitor attractions. Deep Sea Leisure plc is owned 99.58% by Aspro Parks S.L.U. in Spain who in turn are owned 100% by Leisure Resources International SA registered in Luxembourg.

We were unable to determine the ratio of women to men on the board.

Company registration number: SC135353

Subsidiary undertakings include: None listed in the accounts.

Main locations: Ellesmere Port

UK employees: 210

Total employees: 210

Focus of giving: General charitable purposes, environment, animal welfare, children, young people, disability.

Cash donations undeclared ✓

Charitable donations

Cash UK (latest available):	2013	£7,200
	2011	£3,000
	2008	£6,800
	2007	£11,918
	2006	£9,730
Total UK (cash and in kind):	2013	£7,200
Cash worldwide:	2013	£7,200
Total worldwide (cash and in kind):	2013	£7,200

Community involvement

Deep Sea Leisure provides small scale support to charities working with children, people with disabilities, animal welfare and the environment. There is some preference for Scottish-based organisations. We could not access any further information about the company's community involvement or giving.

Corporate giving

In 2012/13 charitable donations were not listed in the company's accounts. In previous years beneficiaries included the following: Anthony Nolan Trust (£550); Ellesmere Port Scouts and North West Air Ambulance (£500 each); Youth Federation (£140); and Shark Trust (£120). Taking an average of the last three years for which we have figures, we estimate the cash donation to be around £7,200.

Corporate social responsibility

CSR information: No CSR information available.

Applications

In writing to the correspondent. However, be aware that there is a limited budget and that some grant recipients are supported regularly.

Deutsche Bank

Banking

Correspondent: Sabira Rouf, Charities and Fundraising, Corporate Citizenship UK, Winchester House, 1 Great Winchester Street, London EC2N 2DB (tel: 020 7545 5194; email: sabira.rouf@db.com; website: www.db.com/unitedkingdom/responsibility.html)

Directors: Jürgen Fitschen, Co-Chief Executive; Anshu Jain, Co-Chief Executive; Stefan Krause, Chief Financial Officer; Stephan Leithner; Stuart Lewis; Rainer Neske; Henry Ritchotte; Christian Sewing

Year end	31/12/2013
Turnover	£23,612,000,000
Pre-tax profit	£1,077,000,000

Nature of business: Deutsche Bank is the holding company of a group providing international merchant banking and investment management services.

Company registration number: BR000005

Subsidiary undertakings include: Abbey Life Assurance Company Ltd; Autumn Leasing Ltd; B.T.I. Investments; Cardales UK Ltd; DAHOC (UK) Ltd; DB Equity Ltd

Main locations: Edinburgh, London

Total employees: 98,000

Focus of giving: Education, environment, heritage, housing, homelessness, financial education, STEM (science, technology, engineering and mathematics), arts, culture, science technology, sport, recreation, children, young people, community/social welfare.

Membership: BITC, LBG

Cash donations undeclared	✓
Charity of the Year	✓
Gifts in kind	✓
Humanitarian aid: overseas	✓
Matched funding	✓
Overseas giving	✓

Payroll giving	✓
Sponsorship	✓

Charitable donations

Cash UK (latest available):	2011	£6,842,000
	2009	£6,247,000
	2007	£4,800,000
	2006	£3,000,000
	2005	£4,500,000
Total UK (cash and in kind):	2013	£8,100,000
Total worldwide (cash and in kind):	2013	£57,800,000

Community involvement

The Deutsche Bank United Kingdom website states:

> In the UK, the bank's Corporate Citizenship team invest in the activities of around 20 different partner organisations and broker volunteering opportunities for over 2,100 employees. Our programmes support those most in need in the communities local to our offices. All of these activities are geared towards raising aspirations, developing skills, building confidence, creating opportunities and breaking down barriers for some of the most disadvantaged individuals.

Born to Be

Currently, the focus of Deutsche Bank's 'social finance strategy' is on youth unemployment, with the flagship Born to Be programme acting as the framework for its community investment. The programme encompasses various initiatives and partnerships and aims to reach 160,000 young people in the UK in the four years from 2013. Born to Be is based on six pillars:

- Equality of opportunity
- Work ready
- Enterprise skills
- Cultural learning
- Social initiatives
- Sports for development

Born to Be has a broad programme of initiatives. See the dedicated section of the Deutsche Bank UK website for an in depth description of the programme.

In line with its community focuses, the bank operates some smaller-scale funding streams in conjunction with its community partners:

The Deutsche Bank Small Grants Fund

The fund makes grants to grass-roots organisations in London, Birmingham, Liverpool, Edinburgh and Glasgow working to address issues important to the bank. From 2013, youth unemployment became the focus of the fund in line with the Born to Be programme. Employees sit on grants panels to help select beneficiaries.

Impact Investment Fund

In 2011, Deutsche Bank launched a £10 million impact investment fund which invests in intermediaries that provide funding for social enterprises in the UK. The Fund aims to focus on the following themes:

- Employment, Education and Training
- Community Sustainability
- Financial and Social Inclusion

Charities of the Year

Each year, Deutsche Bank champions two charities, voted for by employees and sharing its Born to Be mission to help young people fulfil their potential. In 2015 these charities are Sparks and World Child Cancer

Art Works

Art is also a key them of Deutsche Bank's global Corporate Citizenship programme. Through Art Works the bank offers employees, clients and the general public access to contemporary art through workplace collections, exhibitions and education programmes, for example. Deutsche Bank supports joint projects with museums, art fairs and other institutions to award and support upcoming talent. The Artist of the Year, for example, acts as a platform for contemporary artists.

Corporate giving

Deutsche Bank and its foundations invested a total of €78.2 million (approximately £57.8 million) in its corporate responsibility programmes in 2013. Of this amount, we know that €9.9 million (approx. £7.4 million) was the given by employees and the bank through matched funding schemes.

The regional split for total investment was as follows:

Germany	42%
Americas	20%
UK	14%
Asia Pacific (including Japan)	14%
Europe/Middle East/Africa	10%

By taking into account these percentages, we have estimated UK corporate responsibility investments to have been around £8.1 million.

StreetSmart partnership

In partnership with StreetSmart, the bank has helped to raise more than £4.5 million since 2006 by adding an optional £1 donation onto restaurant and hotel bills in sites nationwide. Deutsche Bank supports the campaign costs, meaning every penny is donated directed to UK-registered charities supporting the homeless.

In-kind support

Corporate volunteering initiatives

The annual report and accounts describe how, at a global level, the bank encourages employees' involvement by supporting teams of employee volunteers with donations, paid leave and the costs of necessary materials, and by providing pro bono support to schools, charities, microfinance institutions, social businesses or foundations.

All UK employees are able to dedicate two working days each year to volunteering, and there are numerous activities they can participate with through the Born to Be programme.

Employee-led support

Employee volunteering

In the UK, the bank's Corporate Citizenship team provides volunteer support to those individuals most in need in the communities local to the company's offices. All activities are geared towards raising aspirations, building confidence, creating opportunities and breaking down barriers for some of the most disadvantaged individuals. In 2013 2,160 volunteers from the UK contributed to the corporate volunteering programmes.

The global Volunteer Award was launched in 2013 to help recognise employees' volunteering beyond the bank's programmes. Employees nominated and voted on more than 200 projects from around the world, with the 18 regional winners each receiving a donation.

Employee fundraising

Employees raise funds for charity in a number of ways.

UK Charities of the Year – In 2014 more than £1.7 million was raised for the Charities of the Year (Malaria No More and the Rainbow Trust Children's Charity) through various activities such as sports events, raffles, appeals, challenges and quizzes.

One Day/Donate-a-Day – Employees in the UK and Singapore are encouraged to donate one day's pay to charitable causes. In 2013 around €818,000 (approximately £606,000) was raised.

Matched funding

The bank matches employee charitable donations through payroll giving or one-off donations like for like, (up to £3,000 per employee per year). Employees who undertake fundraising activities also have another £1,000 matched giving allowance which they can apply for, which they would have received from sponsorship.

Payroll giving

Our research indicates that the Give As You Earn scheme is in operation and that the bank automatically matches employee donations.

Commercially led support

Sponsorship

Sponsorship is undertaken; however, as a rule, unsolicited requests for sponsorship are not accepted. Enquiries relating to sponsorship should be directed to sponsorship.uk@db.com. The banks notes in its guidelines (which are available to download from the website) that 'Please note we receive a large number of requests for funding and sponsorship, as such it can take some time to respond.'

Corporate social responsibility

CSR committee: There is a UK Corporate Citizenship team.

CSR information: The following information was taken from the Deutsche Bank United Kingdom website:

> Deutsche Bank Corporate Citizenship UK promotes and coordinates socially responsible activities on behalf of the Bank and its employees in the UK. The Bank supports charities and community organisations within our key focus areas: our education projects realise potential, our social initiatives create opportunity and our art and music programmes foster creativity.

CSR report: There is an annual global CSR report.

Exclusions

The bank focuses its support on selected social issues in order to remain targeted and strategic in its corporate citizenship activities. It therefore does not support the following activities:

- Animal welfare projects
- Drugs related projects
- Emergency funding
- Heritage projects
- Medical, medical research
- Capital projects
- Individual sponsorship
- Sponsorship of events/tables for projects not associated with our core community development activities
- Charities or initiatives with religious/ political objectives

Applications

There is a helpful booklet Deutsche Bank Corporate Citizenship UK guide for charitable organisations available from the company's UK website. This includes all current contacts for the company's various UK initiatives.

Dhamecha Holdings Ltd

Cash 'n' Carry, property

Correspondent: Mr Pradip Dhamecha, Trustee of Laduma Dhamecha Charitable Trust, 2 Hathaway Close, Stanmore HA7 3NR (tel: 020 8903 8181/020 8903 8181; fax: 020 8902 4420; email: info@dhamecha.com; website: www.dhamecha.com)

Directors: K. R. Dhamecha; S. R. Dhamecha; J. Patel

Year end	31/03/2013
Turnover	£585,564,000
Pre-tax profit	£11,252,000

Nature of business: The principal activities are wholesale food cash and carry, property dealings and the manufacture and sale of paper disposable products.

Company registration number: 6519903

Main locations: Wembley, Barking, Croydon, Enfield, Watford

Focus of giving: General charitable purposes, education, medical research, arts, culture, poverty and social exclusion, community/social welfare.

Humanitarian aid: overseas ✓
Overseas giving ✓

Charitable donations

Cash UK (latest available):	2013	£301,000
	2012	£300,000
	2011	£200,000
	2009	£246,700
	2007	£225,000
Total UK (cash and in kind):	2013	£301,000
Cash worldwide:	2013	£301,000
Total worldwide (cash and in kind):	2013	£301,000

Community involvement

The company makes its charitable contributions through the Laduma Dhamecha Charitable Trust (Charity Commission no: 328678). Through this trust, the Dhamecha Group has supported a large number of long-term good causes on a local, a national and a global basis. In addition, they also donate to an array of charities.

Corporate giving

In 2012/13 the company declared £301,000 in cash donations. In line with company policy, the total amount was donated to the company's charitable trust.

See the corporate charity entry on p. 401 for more information.

Corporate social responsibility

CSR information: The following statement is taken from the company's website:

> Over the years, the Dhamecha Group have developed a reputation for looking after the welfare of its people.
>
> They work hard to create a safe working environment for their staff and – as a consequence – that of their customers, through regular, up-to-date Health and Safety training, encouraging a positive attitude towards their environment and taking practical, preventative precautions on a daily basis.
>
> They also enhance – in a range of ways – the economic development of the communities in which they operate. When K R, S R and J R Dhamecha started the business, they set up a charitable foundation in recognition of the important part that their mother, Laduma, had played in their personal development (their father died at an early age).
>
> Since that day, and through this trust, the Dhamecha Group have supported a large number of long-term good causes on a local, a national and a global basis. In addition, they also donate to an array of worthy charities.

There was no other CSR information available.

We were unable to determine the ratio of women to men on the board.

Corporate charity: The Laduma Dhamecha Charitable Trust (Charity Commission no. 328678).

Applications

Applications to the trust should be made in writing to the correspondent who is a trustee of the Laduma Dhamecha Charitable Trust.

Diageo plc

Food manufacture, brewers/ distillers

Correspondent: Sustainability and Responsibility Team, Lakeside Drive, Park Royal, London NW10 7HQ (tel: 020 8978 6000 (main switchboard); email: csr@diageo.com; website: www.diageo.com)

Directors: Dr Franz Humer, Chair; Ivan Menezes, Chief Executive Officer; Deirdre Mahlan; Peggy Bruzelius; Laurence Danon; Lord Davies of Abersoch; Betsy Holden; Ho Kwon Ping; Nicola Mendelsohn; Phillip Scott; Alan Stewart; Paul Tunnacliffe, Company Secretary (women: 5; men: 7)

Year end	30/06/2014
Turnover	£13,980,000,000
Pre-tax profit	£2,711,000,000

Nature of business: The group's principal activity is the manufacture and distribution of spirits, wines and beer. The group has presence in over 180 countries around the world.

Company registration number: 23307

Subsidiary undertakings include: Diageo Brands VB; Diageo Capital BV; Diageo Capital plc; Diageo Great Britain Ltd; Diageo Finance BV; Diageo Finance plc; Diageo Ireland; Diageo North America, Inc; Moët Hennessy, SNC (associate); and United Spirits Ltd (associate). A full list of subsidiary undertakings can be obtained from Companies House.

Brands include: Baileys; Bell's; Blossom Hill; Buchanan's; Captain Morgan; Ciroc; Crown Royal; Don Julio; Gordon's; Guinness; J&B; Johnnie Walker; Ketel One; Smirnoff; and Tanqueray. An extensive overview of all brands can be found on the group's website.

Main locations: London

Total employees: 27,355

Focus of giving: Education, enterprise/ training, environment, health, ill health, heritage, overseas projects, sponsorship, women's issues, children, young people, community/social welfare, disasters.

Membership: BITC, LBG

Cash donations undeclared	✓
FTSE 100	✓
Gifts in kind	✓
Market-led giving	✓
Matched funding	✓
Overseas giving	✓
Payroll giving	✓
Sponsorship	✓

Charitable donations

Cash UK (latest available):	2014	£1,000,000
	2011	£10,500,000
	2009	£11,200,000
	2008	£10,700,000
	2007	£10,600,000
	2006	£11,800,000
Total UK (cash and in kind):	2014	£1,000,000
Total worldwide (cash and in kind):	2014	£16,500,000

Community involvement

Diageo invests in a variety of programmes that aim to empower its stakeholders, which represent the group's longstanding commitment to investing in communities. These focus particularly on: alcohol in society; training and education; access to clean water; and on empowering women and farmers.

The group's website states:

> In recent years, we have made a meaningful assessment of the potential impact of our entire value chain on our local communities, and we are increasingly focusing our community programmes on empowering stakeholders ranging from small-scale farmers who grow our grains to the bartenders who sell our brands.

Water of Life

The programme aims to help provide access to water for local communities as well 'driving progress against targets for water efficiency, water wasted in waterstressed areas and water quality'. Through the programme Diageo invests in infrastructure and sanitation in local communities, primarily in Africa. According to the Performance Addendum, in 2013 a total of £467,000 was given for local projects.

Learning for Life

The programme provides education and vocational training in the hospitality, retail and alcohol industries to young unemployed people. According to the annual report and accounts, participants benefit from advice in areas, such as interview preparation, teamwork, communication, ongoing mentoring and assistance to guide them both during the training and the job application process. The programme is run in 30 countries, principally in Latin America and the Caribbean, and recently in Scotland, Germany and Ireland.

Plan W

The programme was launched in 2012 and is run in Asia Pacific 'to empower women to play a greater role in the economy by developing their hospitality and business enterprise skills'. Since its inception work has been undertaken with 57,295 women in 16 countries in partnership with 13 organisations. The group states – 'we also believe that educating men on issues that concern women ultimately can help empower women, and thus far 19,501 men have gone through the programme'.

National Organisation for Foetal Alcohol Syndrome (NOFAS UK)

Diageo provided funding for a face-to-face, online and distance training to 10,000 midwives to help them educate expectant mothers about the risks of alcohol to their unborn child.

The group also supports local charities, particularly through employee engagement, and helps in disaster relief in the form of emergency relief and supporting longer-term reparation projects, as well as helping through the Diageo Foundation.

The Diageo Foundation (Charity Commission no. 1014681)

The Diageo Foundation was established in 1992 with the aim to create positive, long-term change in the community. It focuses on areas of humanitarian need, primarily in financially developing countries in Africa, Latin America, Asia and Eastern Europe, where it can make the most difference. The foundation provides kick-start funding and expertise in establishing local projects, some of which are run in partnership with local businesses.

It is funded entirely by Diageo and makes charitable donations in support of projects or causes proposed by Diageo businesses and externally, matches employee fundraising in the UK and provides longer-term social investment in areas where it can make the most difference.

According to the website:

> Targeting developing countries in Africa, Latin America, Asia and Eastern Europe, as well as awarding grants, the foundation acts as a catalyst for:
> - Encouraging contributions from Diageo businesses and external sources
> - Engaging Diageo employees in fundraising, giving and volunteering
> - Developing partnerships with NGOs and other external bodies
> - Providing expertise and support for establishing and managing effective projects

There is normally a three-year limit to any funding commitment with the maximum funding available for any one project being £50,000. Projects which obtain additional funding from external sources are encouraged as this can lead to sustainability.

Eligible projects must fall within one of the four key focus areas (Skills for Life; Water of Life; Local Communities; or Disaster Relief) and also:

- Address a community/social need, in particular excluded and disadvantaged people who, with support, can help themselves to transform their own lives
- Build partnerships with community groups and NGOs
- Help build the skills-base of individuals or communities
- Maximise grants to make them as effective as possible
- Build the economic prosperity of a community
- Plan a clear exit strategy and appropriate mechanisms to ensure that the benefits derived from the project are sustainable
- Have clear, well-defined objectives in place, including planned outcomes, desired impact, measurement and evaluation
- Enhance the project, if appropriate, by working in partnership with a local Diageo business

Corporate giving

The annual report and accounts for 2013/14 say that during the year Diageo 'invested £16.5 million or 0.6% of operating profits to charitable projects that help serve critical local need'. It is further noted that the amount:

> Marks a decrease from the charitable giving reported last year, primarily because [the group] has chosen not to include [its] legacy commitment of £10.3 million to the Thalidomide Trust and the Thalidomide Foundation Ltd and instead focus [the] community investment reporting on [its] long-term, actively managed flagship programmes.

Note: The 'Performance Addendum' explains 'that 'community investment' includes contributions (in the form of cash, in-kind donations or employee time) from Diageo plc and the Diageo Foundation'. It consists of contributions 'to charitable entities, non-branded responsible drinking programmes that benefit charities, and management costs associated with the Diageo Foundation'. The group states it uses the principles of the London Benchmarking Group to estimate its community investment.

The annual report and accounts give the following breakdown of community investment by focus area:

Brand-led and local community spend*	31%
Community aspects of responsible drinking projects**	30%
Learning for Life	20%
Plan W	11%
Social Enterprise	5%
Water of Life	3%

*This includes cause-related brand campaigns, local market giving and disaster relief.

**This forms a sub-section of the total responsible drinking budget.

It is further stated that 'Western Europe and Global functions' account to 26% of the 'community investment'.

The foundation's annual report and accounts for 2013 state that during the year it received £991,000 (2012: 1.4 million) and gifts in kind totalling £34,000 (2012: £29,000) from Diageo plc. The foundation made 206 (2012: 528) grants totalling £1.2 million.

We could not distinguish between worldwide and UK charitable giving. It is clear that at least over £1 million was given to the UK registered Diageo Foundation and we use this figure as cash donations in the UK, which may potentially be higher. We take the figure of £16.5 million 'invested to charitable projects' to represent the group total worldwide contributions (even though we were unable to deduct management costs). We were unable to separate direct cash giving from other types of investment worldwide.

See the corporate charity entry on p. 402 for more information.

In-kind support

The group acknowledges that whilst financial contributions are important, the giving of time and skills by its staff or surplus products and other in-kind donations can often achieve more.

Staff members provide accounting and administration support to the foundation.

Employee-led support

Diageo's employees are involved in volunteering and fundraising activities for good causes.

Matched funding
Employee fundraising/giving receives matched funding.

Payroll giving
Our research suggests that the group operates a Give As You Earn scheme.

Commercially led support

Sponsorship
The group undertakes good cause sponsorship, including sport events, for example Ryder Cup and National Basketball Association (NBA).

Responsible drinking
Part of Diageo's focus is responsible drinking programmes and responsible marketing strategies (including mandatory standards) aimed at preventing and addressing the negative aspects of the business activity. The group states that it supports 373 responsible drinking programmes in 53 countries focusing on preventing drink driving, underage drinking and excessive drinking. In Western Europe Diageo focuses on 'promoting responsible drinking in every country through partnerships with government agencies, non-governmental organisations (NGOs), independent charities and large retail customers'. Further details on responsible drinking promotion can be found on Diageo's website.

Brand-led programmes
The group recognises that its 'world-famous brands provide a great opportunity to engage consumers in campaigns that champion social and environmental causes'. Examples include: the Arthur Guinness Fund (established in 2009) which supports social entrepreneurs; and Bell's campaign to raise money for Help for Heroes run since 2012.

Corporate social responsibility

CSR committee: The group's CEO and his Executive Committee 'are ultimately accountable for performance against sustainability and responsibility goals'. Much of the work takes place at the local/market level with regional presidents and general managers having front-line responsibility.

The Corporate Relations Director and Chief Marketing Officer both hold responsibilities regarding 'community empowerment' and 'alcohol in society' aspects of the CSR.

CSR information: The website states:

> Putting the principles of sustainability and responsibility into practice means accounting for our most material social and environmental impacts in every aspect of what we do – from sourcing raw materials, to running our manufacturing safely and efficiently, to influencing how our brands are sold and consumed.

The group's sustainability and responsibility strategy addresses six areas:

- Creating a positive role for alcohol in society
- Addressing global water and environmental challenges at [its] operations and in [the] local communities
- Empowering the communities in which [it] operates
- Creating a great place to work for [its] people
- Holding [the group] to the highest standards of governance and ethics
- Building partnerships along the value chain to ensure the sustainability of [its] business model

CSR report: There is a 'Sustainability and Responsibility Performance Addendum' and a 'Sustainability and Responsibility' review within the annual report and accounts.

Corporate charity: The Diageo Foundation (Charity Commission no. 1014681).

Exclusions

Political donations are not made in the UK or to EU political organisations or EU political expenditure.

The foundation will not normally fund the following areas:

- Organisations which are not registered charities
- Individuals
- Loans, business finance or endowment funds
- Medical charities or hospitals
- Promotion of religion
- Animal welfare
- Expeditions or overseas travel
- Political organisations
- Advertising
- Product donations
- Capital projects (such as buildings)

Applications

The company: In writing to the correspondent.

The Diageo Foundation: Applications to the foundation should be addressed to Lynne Smethurst (tel: 020 8978 6000; email: diageofoundation@diageo.com) at the company's address.

Applicants should provide details of the project, how it relates to the Diageo Foundation's focus areas and the amount of funding required (on no more than two sides of a sheet of paper). The foundation will contact you if further details are required. A written notification is normally provided within six to eight weeks, regardless of whether your application has been successful or not.

Domino Printing Sciences plc

Business services, print/paper/packaging

Correspondent: Richard Pryn, Company Secretary, Trafalgar Way, Bar Hill, Cambridge CB23 8TU (tel: 01954 781888; website: www.domino-printing.com)

Directors: Peter Byrom, Chair; Nigel Bond, Group Managing Director; Gary Havens; Andrew Herbert, Group Finance Director; Philip Ruffles; Mark Wrightson; David Brown; Christopher Brimsmead (women: 0; men: 8)

Year end	31/10/2013
Turnover	£335,673,000
Pre-tax profit	£17,673,000

Nature of business: A global provider of total coding and printing solutions.

Company registration number: 1363137

Subsidiary undertakings include: Alpha Dot Ltd; Domino UK Ltd; Labeljet SA; Purex North America Ltd; Squid Ltd; PotJet Systems Ltd.

Total employees: 2,316

Focus of giving: Enterprise/training, health, ill health, arts, culture.

Matched funding ✓

Charitable donations

Cash UK (latest available):	2013	£30,000
	2011	£24,000
	2009	£25,100
	2008	£35,600
Total UK (cash and in kind):	2013	£30,000
Cash worldwide:	2013	£30,000
Total worldwide (cash and in kind):	2013	£30,000

Community involvement

It is part of the group's ethics policy to make contributions to the local community. This is achieved by charitable donations, and through association with local schools and colleges, the provision of training and work experience including accommodating overseas students needing to use their English language skills in a business environment.

Corporate giving

In 2012/13 the group made charitable donations totalling £30,000. Staff raised £22,000. The annual report for this financial year states: 'Donations have been made to a broad range of organisations including Macmillan Cancer Support, Marie Curie Cancer Care and Guide Dogs for the Blind as well as local hospitals and youth organisations.'

We therefore assume that these donations have been made in the UK.

In-kind support

Staff are encouraged to become involved in charitable activities and fundraising by matching their funds (up to a pre-set limit), and allowing them to nominate which organisations the company supports.

Employee-led support

Staff are involved in fundraising events for charities. In 2013 in the UK, 40 staff took part in a London to Cambridge bike ride raising funds for a breast cancer charity.

Corporate social responsibility

CSR committee: We could not find any information on how a CSR committee is constituted.

CSR information: The following statement is taken from the company's website: 'Domino sponsors local philanthropic causes that promote science, technology, engineering, or mathematics (STEM) skills and STEM educational programmes operating near its facilities. It is company policy to make available work placement schemes for local students.'

CSR report: The CSR report is contained within the annual report but there is very little information on the community aspect.

Applications

In writing to the correspondent.

Doughty Hanson & Co. Managers Ltd

Financial services, information technology, property

Correspondent: Ms Julie Foreman, The Doughty Hanson Charitable Trust, PO Box 31064, LONDON SW1Y 5ZP (tel: 020 7663 9300; website: www.doughtyhanson.com)

Directors: Richard Hanson, Chair; Richard Lund; Stephen Marquardt; Graeme Stening (women: 0; men: 4)

Year end	31/12/2013
Turnover	£19,638,000
Pre-tax profit	(£7,152,000)

Nature of business: Doughty Hanson has three main businesses: Private Equity; Real Estate; and Technology Ventures. The ultimate parent undertaking and controlling party is DHC Ltd.

Company registration number: 3015047

UK employees: 78

Total employees: 78

Focus of giving: General charitable purposes, education, individuals, small groups, older people, arts, culture, religion, science technology, children, young people.

Humanitarian aid: overseas ✓
Market-led giving ✓
Matched funding ✓
Overseas giving ✓
Sponsorship ✓

Charitable donations

Cash UK (latest available):	2013	£287,000
	2012	£233,000
	2011	£244,200
	2009	£245,000
	2008	£428,000
Total UK (cash and in kind):	2013	£287,000
Cash worldwide:	2013	£287,000
Total worldwide (cash and in kind):	2013	£287,000

Community involvement

The Doughty Hanson Charitable Foundation

Most of the company's charitable giving is channelled through its charitable foundation, (Charity Commission no. 1080755) which was established in 2000 for the relief of poverty, distress and suffering, to promote, develop and maintain public education and appreciation of the arts and science and to further religious work and education in any part of the world, and any other charitable purposes. Since its inception the foundation has supported more than 260 different charities and causes with donations totalling over £2.2 million.

The company states that many of the charities it supports receive more than one donation or annual support.

For more information on the activities of the foundation, or to suggest a charity, contact: dhcf@doughtyhanson.com.

Corporate giving

In 2013 the company gave £287,000 in cash donations (2012: £233,000), of which £268,000 (2012: £232,000) was donated to the company's foundation.

See the corporate charity entry on p. 402 for more information.

In-kind support

Gifts in kind in the form of services provided by the company are given to the foundation. We have no specific details of what these are only that they are mentioned in the foundation's accounts.

Employee-led support

Match-funding

The foundation will match any amounts raised in sponsorship by an employee.

Commercially led support

Sponsorship

In 2012 and throughout 2013, Doughty Hanson funded an Assistant Curator position at the Scottish National Gallery of Modern Art, which is part of the National Galleries of Scotland.

In November 2011 Doughty Hanson published a report in partnership with the WWF highlighting the increased returns that private equity firms can generate from a more sustainable approach to investing.

Doughty Hanson supports the European Venture Philanthropy Association (EVPA), a registered non-profit association established in 2004. The EVPA is a network of philanthropic funds that applies venture capital business models to the non-profit and charitable sectors.

Corporate social responsibility

CSR committee: There were no details found on the structure or remit of any CSR committee/subcommittee. We do know that the company's foundation is run by the directors of the company with the support of a committee made up of seven members of staff who evaluate the causes and projects to be supported and oversee the disbursement of funds.

CSR information: The following is taken from the company's website:

> Within the spectrum of responsible investing activities, we distinguish between two different types of engagement:
>
> *Environmental, Social and Governance (ESG) Engagement*
> Working with our investee companies and our own dedicated Head of Sustainability, we undertake a range of ESG initiatives across the portfolio to improve energy efficiency, reduce waste, improve health and safety practices and introduce higher standards of labour practices and more ethical supply chain management.
>
> *Corporate Social Responsibility*
> Doughty Hanson and its portfolio companies are involved with a number of charities and social enterprises. Unlike our ESG initiatives, the work we do in the CSR arena is primarily driven by the social, community and philanthropic impact it generates rather than any commercial imperative. Wherever possible we seek to align some of our philanthropic activities with those undertaken within our portfolio.

CSR report: There is an annual sustainability report published and available online.

Corporate charity: The Doughty Hanson Charitable Foundation (Charity Commission no. 1080755).

Applications

Applications should be made to the correspondent.

Dow Chemical Company Ltd

Chemicals and plastics

Correspondent: Company Secretary, Diamond House, Lotus Park, Kingsbury Crescent, Staines, Middlesex TW18 3AG (tel: 020 3139 4000; fax: 020 3139 4004; website: www.dow.com)

Directors: J. West; N. Ephgrave (women: 2; men: 8)

Year end	31/12/2013
Turnover	£415,573,000
Pre-tax profit	£7,128,000

Nature of business: The company is a manufacturer and supplier of chemicals and performance products, plastics, hydrocarbons and energy, and consumer specialities including agricultural products, and consumer products.

Company registration number: 537161

Subsidiary undertakings include: Ascot Group Pension Trustees Ltd; Hyperlast Ltd; and Dow Chemco Pension Trust Ltd.

Main locations: King's Lynn, Wilton, Sandbach, Seal Sands, Staines, Middlesbrough, Mirfield, Nuneaton, Billingham

Total employees: 53,000

Focus of giving: Education, environment, animal welfare, health, ill health, heritage, medical research, older people, arts, culture, science technology, children, young people, community/ social welfare, disability.

Cash donations undeclared	✓
Gifts in kind	✓
Market-led giving	✓
Overseas giving	✓
Sponsorship	✓

Charitable donations

Cash UK (latest available):	2013	£29,000
	2010	£29,000
Total UK (cash and in kind):	2013	£29,000
Cash worldwide:	2013	£17,200,000
Total worldwide (cash and in kind):	2013	£22,600,000

Community involvement

The Dow Chemical Company Foundation (US)

Established in 1979, The Dow Chemical Company Foundation contributes to a more sustainable world by supporting charitable initiatives focused on community success, science education and environmental stewardship. The foundation is a separately governed, private foundation designed to carry out the charitable efforts of Dow, and is the primary funding source for Dow charitable donations.

Corporate giving

In 2013 the company did not appear to declare its charitable donations in the UK. For this reason we have calculated the cash donations amount from the information we have available and estimate it to be around £29,000. In 2013, contributions of The Dow Chemical Company Foundation (see Community involvement details), totalled $21.5 million dollars (£17.2 million) globally, as well as an additional $6 million (£4.8 million) granted in product donations.

In-kind support

Product donations are made but these are probably made globally and few will be given in the UK.

Commercially led support

Sponsorship

Dow sponsors a number of events 'to communicate the power of chemistry and encourage further collaboration and innovation; for example, Change the Equation and Dow Racing.

Corporate social responsibility

CSR information: The website states: 'Dow's established corporate citizenship program illustrates our commitments through preserving and investing in communities, creating products to advance human progress, and generating shared value through philanthropic efforts around the world.'

No CSR information available specifically applicable to the UK.

Applications

Previous research suggested that preferential consideration is given to requests for donations recommended by employees. Unsolicited applications/ blanket appeal letters will probably not be considered.

Dow Corning Ltd

Chemicals and plastics

Correspondent: Community Donations Co-ordinator, Community Donations Team, Barry Plant, Cardiff Road, Barry, Vale of Glamorgan CF63 2YL (tel: 01446 732350; fax: 01446 747944; website: www.dowcorning.com/barry)

Directors: S. Dore; P. Cartwright; S. Dopp; M. Matthews; K. Kaufman; I. Wilson; B. Tessin; H. Austin

Year end	31/12/2013
Turnover	£523,583,000
Pre-tax profit	£41,879,000

Nature of business: Manufacture and marketing of silicone and silicon-based products, technologies, and services.

Company registration number: 486170

Subsidiary undertakings include: None listed in accounts.

Main locations: Barry

UK employees: 599

Focus of giving: Education, environment, science technology, children, young people, community/ social welfare.

Charitable donations

Cash UK (latest available):	2013	£26,000
	2012	£27,000
	2010	£26,000
	2009	£17,000
	2008	£23,000
Total UK (cash and in kind):	2013	£23,000

Community involvement

Dow Corning targets investment in communities where its employees work and live. Its corporate giving programmes operate at major sites in Asia, Europe, and the Americas, with each site managing its own programme. In the UK the company operates from Barry, South Wales and has its own education centre on site. We have no figures for the Dow Corning Corporation's global giving.

Barry site Nature Centre

The following information is taken from the company's website:

> The Barry site has a fantastic 30 acre nature reserve with an education building suitable for school and group educational

> visits. This sits adjacent to our manufacturing areas showing that wildlife and industry can coexist side by side. The area offers some unique habitats for wildlife to flourish. Educational visits are encouraged and we can offer activities to support the sustainability curriculum that schools follow. The centre is built overlooking the large fishing ponds and can be used by schools and local groups for environmental studies, field trips and science projects. With a commitment to sustainability, Dow Corning used materials from sustainable resources wherever possible when designing and constructing the education centre. Environmental features were incorporated – for example ground source heating and solar panels provide heat and power for the centre; while rainwater is harvested and recycled to provide a water source.

Dow Corning continues to focus on advancing science, technology, engineering and maths education; community vitality and high tech employment opportunities. The group's website gives details of its programmes across its sites.

Regular communication with local people takes place through a number of channels, these include a monthly newsletter and a Community Advisory Panel consisting of representatives from the Barry area.

Guidelines for grants:
The following guidelines are taken from the company's website:

> A small team of employees, our community donations team, meets monthly to discuss all the requests. Priority is given to requests from local groups and the team tries to make sure that any donation we make helps as many people as possible and has a long-term benefit . . .
>
> We will consider requests that meet the following criteria:
>
> - Projects that are local to the Barry, South Wales site and benefit people locally with preference given to requests from Barry and Sully areas and then the Vale of Glamorgan
> - We prefer to make donations to properly established organizations rather than to an informal group
> - Donations must have a wide benefit ensuring a good number of people can be impacted by the funding
>
> If the above broad criteria can be met then requests must meet the following more specific criteria:
>
> - Activities that will help young people learn more about science, math and technology, or skills that they will need in their future careers, or to make them better citizens
> - Ideas that will help organizations or communities to improve safety or the local environment
> - Activities or projects that help improve the local community's health and wellbeing
> - Projects that help improve the local biodiversity (nature, wildlife, etc.)
> - Projects that promote good citizenship
> - Projects that can help the elderly

There is a Dow Corning Foundation detailed on the company's website; however, projects must benefit the US communities in which employees live and work.

Corporate giving

In 2013 the company gave £26,000 in charitable cash donations (2012: £27,000). This figure is not a reflection of the company's total contribution to its local community; however, we could find no figures for in-kind giving.

In-kind support

The company in Barry has an active volunteering programme and supports its staff in their involvement with local schools and organisations. For example, since 1997 Dow Corning has been involved in National Science and Engineering Week by inviting primary schoolchildren from local schools to visit the site for hands-on experiments. Experiments are linked to Dow Corning and its products so the children get to handle real silicone materials and they can see how science has an application to the wider world. Many Dow Corning employees help out during the week-long programme to guide students through their tasks. They work on a one-to-two ratio to allow all children to be on-task regardless of ability.

Employee-led support

Employees are encouraged to become involved in supporting their local communities through practical help. A major part of this is the active programme the company has in supporting students and teachers in local schools with science, maths and technology. Employee fundraising is matched by the company up to a maximum amount.

Corporate social responsibility

CSR committee: There is a group Corporate Responsibility Committee. There is a Community Donations Team at Barry, South Glamorgan for the support of UK charities.

CSR information: The following statement is taken from the group's website:

> Corporate social responsibility at Dow Corning is rooted in our commitment to sustainability. As citizens of the world, Dow Corning is committed to using our global resources and our knowledge of silicon-based chemistry to improve the lives of people, sustain the planet and generate prosperity.
>
> *In our local communities*
> We want the communities where our facilities are located to be great places to live, work, grow and play. So we reach out to our neighbours and work with local educators, civic groups, charities and community leaders to advance education and improve the quality of life for all.

We were unable to determine the ratio of women to men on the board.

CSR report: There is a group Sustainability Report published annually.

Exclusions

No support is given for raffle prizes, for individuals (such as sponsorship for overseas travel or individual fundraising), donations to central funds of charities, political or religious groups, one-off events such as fetes, parades, shows, tournaments, concerts, group travel expenses for excursions or overseas adventures, medical research, general fundraising appeals where Dow Corning funding is not used on specific projects or purchases, uniforms or sports strips for sports teams, national or international appeals, advertising, or requests that make Dow Corning a 'corporate sponsor'.

Applications

In writing to the correspondent. Only written appeals will be considered.

Drax Group plc

Electricity

Correspondent: Sponsorship Team, Drax Power Station, Selby, North Yorkshire YO8 8PH (tel: 01757 618381; email: enquiries@drax.com; website: www.draxgroup.plc.uk)

Directors: Charles Berry, Chair; Dorothy Thompson, Chief Executive; Tony Quinlan, Finance Director; Peter Emery; Tim Cobbold; Paul Taylor; Melanie Gee; David Lindsell; Tony Thorne (women: 2; men: 7)

Year end	31/12/2013
Turnover	£2,062,100,000
Pre-tax profit	£31,800,000

Nature of business: Drax Group has three principal activities: sourcing fuel (including sustainable biomass); electricity production; and electricity sales to the wholesale market and business customers.

Company registration number: 5562053

Subsidiary undertakings include: Drax Power Ltd; Haven Power Ltd; Morehouse BioEnergy LLC.

UK employees: 1,201

Total employees: 1,201

Focus of giving: Economic generation, environment, heritage, sport, recreation.

Membership: BITC

Charitable donations

Cash UK (latest available):	2013	£142,000
	2010	£87,400
	2009	£96,000
Total UK (cash and in kind):	2013	£142,000
Cash worldwide:	2013	£142,000
Total worldwide (cash and in kind):	2013	£142,000

Community involvement

The company's community involvement takes the form of sponsoring a variety of local charities and fundraising events, focusing on the three themes of youth sport, education and the environment, and maintaining open communication channels and good working relationships with the region's key opinion formers.

Corporate giving

During 2013, the group gave financial support of £200,000 (2012: £182,000) in total across a range of charitable and non-charitable community causes. Of that total, charitable donations amounted to £142,000 (2012: £127,000).

Employee-led support

Matched funding: Drax also operates a pound for pound and Give As You Earn matching scheme, under which we match any monies raised for, or donated to, charity by employees.

Commercially led support

A state-of-the-art visitor centre is open for people to explore the properties of electricity, discover how a power station works and consider the environmental issues related to electricity generation.

Another visitor opportunity exists at the company's nature reserve situated at its ash disposal site. Established as a sanctuary for over 100 species of wildlife, it is specially designed to help schoolchildren understand more about the natural habitat and ecology of the area.

Sponsorship

A variety of local events are sponsored. Campaigns such as Cricket in the Community, Art in the Community and the Community Pride Awards are now established in the company's annual calendar of community events.

Corporate social responsibility

CSR committee: Donations are considered by the Sponsorship Team.

CSR information: The following is taken from annual report and accounts 2013: 'We are committed to being a good neighbour to our local community and our caring for the community philosophy involves being part of local and regional communities.'

CSR report: Reporting on CSR is contained within the annual report and accounts.

Applications

In writing to the correspondent.

Duchy Originals Ltd

Food services

Correspondent: See 'Applications', Clarence House, St James's Palace, London SW1A 1BA

Directors: Andrew Wright; Michael Jary, Chair; Stephen Nelson; Craig Sams (women: 0; men: 4)

Year end	31/03/2014
Turnover	£2,956,719
Pre-tax profit	£2,828,361

Nature of business: The ownership of a range of premium organic food and drink products under the 'Duchy Originals' brand. The company's ultimate controlling party is The Prince of Wales's Charitable Foundation.

Company registration number: 2478770

Brands include: Duchy Originals

UK employees: 1

Total employees: 1

Focus of giving: General charitable purposes, education, enterprise/training, environment, animal welfare, health, ill health, heritage, armed forces personnel, arts, culture, women's issues, children, young people.

Humanitarian aid: overseas	✓
Humanitarian aid: UK	✓
Overseas giving	✓

Charitable donations

Cash UK (latest available):	2014	£2,805,000
	2012	£2,877,000
	2011	£625,000
	2009	£0
	2008	£0
Total UK (cash and in kind):	2014	£2,805,000
Cash worldwide:	2014	£2,805,000
Total worldwide (cash and in kind):	2014	£2,805,000

Community involvement

The Prince of Wales founded Duchy Originals in 1990 to promote sustainable produce and champion organic foods. Now managed by Waitrose, the brand has expanded to 230 products and has generated more than £11 million for charitable causes since its inception. The company no longer has its own website but now links directly to the Waitrose website and this is where the following information was obtained:

The Prince of Wales's Charitable Foundation (Charity Commission no. 1127255)

This charitable company is the ultimate controlling party of Duchy Originals Ltd. The brand Duchy Originals is marketed and sold by Waitrose. The foundation's website states that it 'provides a fair deal for the people who grow and make the food and generates funds for good causes'.

A royalty from the sale of Duchy from Waitrose products is given to The Prince of Wales's Charitable Foundation annually. Almost £3 million is raised annually in this way for distribution to charitable causes, of which £75,000 goes to The Prince's Countryside Fund. (Charity no 1136077). The supermarket states: 'We want the people who supply us to earn a fair return on the commitments they make to produce a superior product. Organic farming preserves hedgerow habitats and wildlife food sources by avoiding chemicals in the soil and ground water. This protects wildlife and promotes biodiversity.'

Donations are made to an extensive variety of causes working with environmental issues, health and hospices, community and welfare, education, heritage, the built environment and charities supporting servicemen and women.

Corporate giving

In 2012/13 a total of £2.8 million was donated to the company's ultimate controlling party, The Prince of Wales's Charitable Foundation.

Commercially led support

The company works in partnership with Waitrose who manage all Duchy Originals products.

Corporate social responsibility

CSR information: No specific policy, report or team given by the company – its only contribution is given directly to The Prince of Wales's Charitable Foundation.

Applications

In writing to: Yvonne Abba-Opoku, Secretary to the Trustees, The Prince of Wales's Charitable Foundation, Clarence House, St James's, London SW1A 1BA (Tel: 020 7930 4832).

Dunelm Group plc

Retail – clothing and footwear, retail – department and variety stores

Correspondent: Corporate Social Responsibility Team, Watermead Business Park, Syston, Leicestershire LE7 1AD (tel: 0845 165 6565; email: customerservices@dunelm-mill.co.uk; website: www.dunelm-mill.com)

Directors: Geoff Cooper, Chair; Will Adderley, Chief Executive; Marion Sears; David Stead, Finance Director; Simon Emeny (women: 1; men: 5)

Year end	28/06/2014
Turnover	£730,152,000
Pre-tax profit	£115,986,000

Nature of business: Specialist out-of-town homewares retailer providing a comprehensive range of products to a wide customer base, under the brand name Dunelm Mill.

Company registration number: 4708277

Subsidiary undertakings include: Dunelm (Soft Furnishings) Ltd, Dunelm Estates Ltd; Zoncolan Ltd.

UK employees: 4,859

Total employees: 4,859

Focus of giving: Health, ill health, children, young people.

Charity of the Year	✓
Gifts in kind	✓
Matched funding	✓

Charitable donations

Cash UK (latest available):	2014	£206,000
	2013	£80,000
	2011	£56,000
	2009	£49,000
	2008	£46,000
Total UK (cash and in kind):	2014	£206,000
Cash worldwide:	2014	£206,000
Total worldwide (cash and in kind):	2014	£206,000

Community involvement

The company adopts a Charity of the Year for which collections are made in-store, specific fundraising events are organised and the group makes its own donations. Colleagues are supported by matched funding.

Charity of the Year: Barnardo's is the 2013/14 choice with funds raised in a variety of ways. Barnardo's will continue as the company's Charity of the Year for the period 2014/15.

Corporate giving

The total value of donations made by the group in the year 2013/14 was £206,000. In addition, £146,000 was raised by staff. Full details of beneficiaries of the company's charitable giving were not listed but it may be that all cash donations go to its Charity of the Year.

In-kind support

Work experience opportunities are offered for long-term unemployed people. The company works with Job Centre Plus to facilitate this. The company provides one paid day a year off for colleagues to engage in volunteering.

Employee-led support

Staff are involved in fundraising events and activities and many take a day's paid leave to volunteer for local charities.

Corporate social responsibility

CSR committee: The board of directors has overall responsibility for CSR with the executive board having line responsibility for managing certain CSR topics. Chief Executive, Will Adderley, is responsible for reporting to the board on all CSR matters. Each month the board receives a 'score card' which includes CSR measures and there is a separate health and safety report.

The company's approach is to embed CSR into the responsibilities of members of the operating board who then report to the Chief Executive in respect of those matters.

The company reports its achievements to colleagues through the in-house magazine, the 'Gazette'.

CSR information: The following is taken from the company's website:

> Dunelm Group plc recognises its duty to behave responsibly to all parties affected by its business operations and to minimise its business related social, ethical and environmental impacts. As part of this commitment we have focused on reducing key impacts in many significant areas such as waste management, energy reduction and carbon emissions.
>
> The board places particular emphasis on maintaining good relationships with its customers, employees and suppliers; on health and safety and ethical sourcing; on environmental issues; and charitable contributions.
>
> The company has a commitment to nominate a Charity of the Year and to support it through collections in stores and various employee events throughout the year, matched by donations from the group.

CSR report: The CSR report is contained within the company's annual report and accounts.

Applications

In writing to the correspondent.

Dwr Cymru Welsh Water

Water

Correspondent: Richard Curtis, Company Secretary, Pentwyn Road, Nelson, Treharris CF46 6LY (tel: 01443 452300; fax: 01443 452323; website: www.dwrcymru.com)

Directors: Robert Ayling, Chair; Chris Jones, Chief Executive; Peter Perry; John Bryant; Graham Edwards; James Strachan; Stephen Palmer; Menna Richards; Anna Walker; John Warren (women: 2; men: 8)

Year end	31/03/2014
Turnover	£736,500,000
Pre-tax profit	£144,500,000

Nature of business: Provision of water services.

Company registration number: 2366777

Subsidiary undertakings include: Dwr Cymru Holdings Ltd; Dwr Cymru (Finance) Ltd.

Main locations: Treharris

UK employees: 2,954

Total employees: 2,954

Focus of giving: Community/social welfare.

Membership: BITC

Cash donations undeclared	✓
Humanitarian aid: UK	✓
Matched funding	✓

Charitable donations

Cash UK (latest available):	2014	£23,000
	2011	£8,000
	2009	£44,000
	2008	£18,500
	2007	£32,874
Total UK (cash and in kind):	2014	£23,000
Cash worldwide:	2014	£23,000
Total worldwide (cash and in kind):	2014	£23,000

Community involvement

The company states in its 2013/14 annual report that it does not engage in sponsorship but instead supports its staff in community schemes by providing their business/management expertise, mentoring or other skills. The company supports and provides resources for advancing education in conservation issues, particularly that of teaching schoolchildren the value of water and how to conserve it, and is also a supporter of the international charity WaterAid.

Corporate giving

In 2013/14 the company did not declare charitable donations in its annual report and accounts. Based on previous years' donations we have estimated the amount given in total cash donations in the UK to be around £23,000. Previous beneficiaries included: Wales Air Ambulance (£500); WaterAid (£750); Hope House Children's Hospice and Milford Haven Port Authority (£1,500 each).

In-kind support

The company supports its staff in community schemes by providing their business/management expertise, mentoring or other skills. The company may offer assistance to communities in its area of operations that are experiencing flooding.

Employee-led support

Staff fundraise for charities including WaterAid.

Commercially led support

Education continues to be one of the main areas of 'community support'. There is an ongoing outreach programme, combining both school visits and site visits to the company's education centres which demonstrate the importance of preserving water and protecting the environment. Since 1997, over 164,000 pupils have visited one of the four education centres. The available information which is developed with educational experts is linked to the national curriculum.

Examples of commitment to CSR from 2013/14 include the company's education centres, detailed above, RainScape and Stop the Block campaigns, also a wide range of ecological and biodiversity related projects such as work to regenerate upland peat bogs, and protect the quality of raw water sources.

Corporate social responsibility

CSR committee: No specific information published.

CSR information: Regarding corporate social responsibility the company states in its annual report that:

> We have a firm commitment to environmental responsibility and to being a good neighbour and a trusted partner in the communities we serve. To earn this trust we have to show that we behave fairly and responsibly in the interests of customers, that we use resources wisely, and that we make an appropriate contribution to community.

CSR report: There is an annual sustainability report. Brief information about charitable giving is contained within the annual report.

Applications

Note: As a not-for-profit company operating for the benefit of its customers, any donations that are made by Welsh Water are done so in support of employees fundraising efforts. Applications outside this are not, therefore, accepted or acknowledged.

Dyson Ltd

Domestic appliances, engineering

Correspondent: Kevin Walker, The James Dyson Foundation, Tetbury Hill, Malmesbury, Wiltshire NS16 0RP (tel: 01666 828416/01666 828416; email: jamesdysonfoundation@dyson.com; website: www.dyson.co.uk)

Directors: Max Conze; James Shipsey (women: 0; men: 2)

Year end	31/12/2013
Turnover	£246,500,000
Pre-tax profit	£2,800,000

Nature of business: Manufacturer of domestic appliances. The Dyson website states:

> In 1978, James Dyson became frustrated with his vacuum cleaner's diminishing performance. Taking it apart, he discovered that its bag was clogging with dust, causing suction to drop. He'd recently built an industrial cyclone tower for his factory that separated paint particles from the air using centrifugal force. But could the same principle work in a vacuum cleaner? Five years and 5,127 prototypes later, he had invented the world's first bagless vacuum cleaner.

Company registration number: 2627406

Subsidiary undertakings include: Dyson Appliances (Australia) Pty Ltd; Dyson BV; Dyson Canada Ltd; Dyson GmbH; Dyson KK; Dyson SAS.

Main locations: Malmesbury

UK employees: 863

Total employees: 4,545

Focus of giving: Education, arts, culture, science technology, community/social welfare.

Gifts in kind	✓
Market-led giving	✓

Charitable donations

Cash UK (latest available):	2013	£5,000,000
	2012	£100,000
	2011	£200,000
	2008	£3,092,000
	2007	£3,525,000
Total UK (cash and in kind):	2013	£5,000,000
Cash worldwide:	2013	£5,000,000
Total worldwide (cash and in kind):	2013	£5,000,000

Community involvement

Community involvement:

The company's support is channelled through the James Dyson Foundation (Charity Commission no. 1099709). Established in 2002, the foundation promotes charitable giving, especially to charities working in the fields of science, engineering, medicine, education and social and community welfare, particularly in the area of Malmesbury. With a committee to manage giving, and registered charity status, it is intended that the James Dyson Foundation will assist educational institutions working in the field of design, technology and engineering, as well as charities carrying out medical or scientific research. Locally, the foundation seeks to support charitable projects in or nearby Malmesbury, the town where Dyson is based.

Dyson's own employees also contribute to the foundation and are encouraged to take an active role in selecting projects and fundraising, especially for Dyson's charity partnerships (CLIC – Cancer and Leukaemia in Childhood, Meningitis Research Foundation and Breakthrough Breast Cancer).

Occasionally small grants are granted to charitable projects that fall within the foundation's criteria.

Corporate giving

Charitable donations are mainly (usually) channelled through the James Dyson Foundation and in 2013 the company declared £5 million in donations, with a further £200,000 pledged. Of the £5 million given in this accounting year, a donation of £1 million was made to the foundation with a further donation of £4 million to The Royal United Hospital.

See the corporate charity entry on p. 402 for more information.

In-kind support

In-kind support: Design engineers from Dyson host workshops at schools and universities throughout the country and the foundation provides free resources to Design and Technology teachers throughout the UK. The company provides an information pack for teachers and lecturers which can be used in conjunction with the Dyson Education Box and both are free of charge.

Each year, the company donates a number of Dyson vacuum cleaners to charitable causes within the James Dyson Foundation's objectives.

Employee-led support

Employee-led support: Dyson workers in Malmesbury, Wiltshire, also contribute to the foundation and are encouraged to take an active role in selecting projects and fundraising, especially for Dyson's charity partnerships.

Commercially led support

Market-led support: A special edition Dyson vacuum helped raise £1.7 million, funding the Dyson Microarray Laboratory at the Royal Marsden in London. This state-of-the-art facility helps scientists study thousands of genes at a time, identifying patterns relevant to breast cancer and its treatment. 'Having lost both his parents to cancer, the charity holds special relevance to James Dyson.'

The annual James Dyson Award inspires students from around the world to engineer a solution to an everyday problem and elevates their work on a global platform. Contenders have included folding plugs, sprinkler taps, emergency rescue devices, water purifiers and airless tyres. The international winner gets a £10,000 towards the development of their idea. A further £10,000 goes to their university department. Some of the winners have gone on to join the Dyson team.

Corporate social responsibility

CSR committee: There is no specific information given, although sustainability and issues around the environment are key to this company, so it would seem that there is a dedicated team reporting on these issues.

CSR information: The following information is taken from Dyson's CSR web pages:

> There will always be machines. But when they work better – more efficiently – then they needn't be at odds with sustainability. This lean mindset is what got me hooked on engineering – when I discovered the fatal flaw with vacuum bags and came up with something less wasteful and more efficient. That is the beauty of lean engineering – by its very nature, it does more with less.

CSR report: Charitable giving is detailed in the company's annual report and accounts.

Corporate charity: The James Dyson Foundation (Charity Commission no. 1099709).

Exclusions

The foundation does not provide support for political purposes and local appeals not in areas of company presence.

Applications

In writing to the correspondent at The James Dyson Foundation.

East Midlands Airport

Airport operators

Correspondent: Community Relations Team, Building 34, Nottingham East Midlands Airport, Castle Donnington, Derby DE74 2SA (tel: 01332 852801/ 01332 818414; fax: 01332 852959; email: community@eastmidlandsairport.com; website: www.eastmidlandsairport.com)

Year end	31/03/2014

Nature of business: Airport operator. East Midlands airport is now owned by M.A.G plc. This entry concentrates on the subsidiary company East Midlands Airport.

The Manchester Airports Group plc (M.A.G) is the country's largest UK-owned airport operator. M.A.G owns and operates Manchester, Stansted, East Midlands and Bournemouth airports. Its property and facilities management arm, M.A.G Developments, is responsible for the group's estate and also the development of Manchester's Airport City.

M.A.G is privately managed on behalf of its shareholders, the local authorities of Greater Manchester and Industry Funds Management. M.A.G is a private company, with shareholdings held by Council of the City of Manchester (35.5%), Industry Funds Management (35.5%) and the nine remaining Greater Manchester local authorities (29%).

Main locations: Derby

Focus of giving: General charitable purposes, education, environment, animal welfare, heritage, sport, recreation, community/social welfare.

Charity of the Year	✓
Gifts in kind	✓
Market-led giving	✓

Charitable donations

Cash UK (latest available):	2013	£50,000
	2012	£400,000
	2011	£100,000
	2009	£18,000
	2007	£50,000

Community involvement

East Midlands airport is now owned by M.A.G plc. Figures relating to charitable giving and information on the company's activities relate to the East Midlands Airport site. M.A.G plc also owns the airports at Bristol, Bournemouth, Manchester and Stansted – see separate entries.

The following information is taken from the company's (East Midlands Airport) website:

> East Midlands Airport supports a number of local charities and organisations through a variety of methods.
>
> *Community Fund*
>
> The East Midlands Airport Community Fund was established in April 2002 and since then over £750,000 has been awarded to 1,000 projects, to bring lasting benefit to the communities around the airport.
>
> The Community Fund is managed independently by a Community Fund Management Committee that meets six times a year, and is open to community groups within a defined 'area of benefit' that meet certain criteria.
>
> The Fund is currently supported by an annual donation of £50,000 from the airport and through the fines imposed when aircraft exceed our strict noise limits. The Community Fund awards grants to support eligible projects that have a long-lasting community and/or environmental benefit and can award a maximum of £2,000 per application.
>
> *Fund objectives*
>
> In order for an application to be successful it must meet at least one of the following objectives:
>
> - To bring the community closer together through facilities for sport, recreation and other leisure time activities
> - Offer environmental improvement and/ or heritage conservation
> - Improve awareness of environmental issues through environmental education
> - Encourage and/or protect wildlife

DepARTures

Now in its fifth year DepARTures remains a key feature in the airport terminal. The scheme is designed to offer local artists the opportunity to display their work to the millions of passengers that travel through the airport.

Charity partner

Every December the airport supports local charity When You Wish Upon A Star with their flight to Lapland for children with life limiting illness.

Corporate giving

During 2013/14 the committee awarded £40,000 from the community fund to 57 projects. The company recognises that some community projects may not fit the Community Fund criteria, so in addition it offers the opportunity for these groups to apply for a small amount of funding from the airport in order to ensure their continuation. During 2013/14 the company awarded £10,300 to 92 local groups. These included Aston on Trent Village Walk, Castle Donington Volunteers Centre, Melbourne Fete and Carnival and the North West Leicestershire Heritage Forum for their WW1 memorial book.

The information in this entry is limited as East Midlands airport is now owned by M.A.G plc. Figures relating to charitable giving and information on the company's activities in this entry relate to the Stansted airport site. M.A.G plc also owns the airports at Bristol, Bournemouth, Manchester and East Midlands – see separate entries. We have not recorded the amount spent by the East Midlands Community Fund in 'Cash donations' as that fund is ultimately funded by M.A.G. and this would have meant recording the group's giving figures twice.

In-kind support

During 2013/14 the company supported 63 groups/organisations with 71 colleagues spending 292 hours volunteering.

The company donated 75 books to the schools that staff visited on World Book Day for them to add to their library collection. It also donated 83 raffle prizes to support local fundraising.

Employee-led support

Coins for Causes – During 2013/14 colleagues voted for Hayward House Cancer Care Trust to be the recipient of money donated by passengers on their return to the airport. Hayward House is based in Nottingham and provides palliative care for people suffering with cancer. Coin collection boxes are located in the baggage reclaim area encouraging passengers to donate any left over foreign currency or simply make a donation. East Midlands Airport passengers gave £678 to Hayward House. Staff have decided that in 2014/15 Guide Dogs Derby will benefit from this initiative.

During the week of World Book Day airport colleagues spent time visiting five local primary schools to share books with the children. Colleagues visited a different school each day of the week and read with groups of children in an effort to support the schools and encourage children to read.

Commercially led support

Work experience students – The company received 94 applications for 14 one week placements from April until October. The aim of the programme is to ensure that the young people chosen to work at the airport have a positive and quality experience of the real world of work. The programme is split into two streams – travel and tourism and STEM (science, technology, engineering and maths).

Outreach events – A full programme of outreach events was held during 2013/14. Airport colleagues spent time at seven different outreach events across five villages including Castle Donington, Kegworth, East Leake, Aston on Trent and Diseworth. The events were held at local community venues and staff were on hand to answer any questions community members had. In addition, early in 2014 as part of the Sustainable Development Plan programme the company hosted a further six events to support the consultation process. After each event attendees are asked for feedback.

The Aerozone – is an on-site education centre, providing young people from foundation stage to university age, the opportunity to get a real insight into life at the airport. Since opening in 2010 staff have welcomed over 9,000 young people through organised visits and community events. The aim with those who visit, whatever their age, is that they learn as much as possible about the airport, how it operates and why.

The Community Flyer – is used for sharing information with the communities that surround the airport. The newsletter is designed to keep local people up to date with the latest community and environment activities as well as the latest airport developments. It is distributed to over 33,000 homes surrounding the airport. The latest version can also be seen on the company's website.

Corporate social responsibility

CSR information: Andy Cliffe, Managing Director of East Midlands Airport states in the company's Community Investment Report:

> Our community programme is key in ensuring we know what the local issues are and how we as a business can support the local area. Our ultimate aim is to be a responsible, sustainable and trusted local business whilst offering our passengers the best customer experience possible. We believe that these go hand in hand.

CSR report: There is a Community Investment Report for East Midlands Airport.

Exclusions

No support is given for local appeals not within ten miles of the airport boundary.

Applications

Guidance notes and an application form are downloadable from EMA's website. Completed applications should be returned to the correspondent.

Ecclesiastical Insurance Group plc

Insurance

Correspondent: Rachel Jane Hall, Company Secretary of the Allchurches Trust Ltd, Beaufort House, Brunswick Road, Gloucester GL1 1JZ (tel: 01452 873184; fax: 01452 423557; email: atl@allchurches.co.uk; website: www.ecclesiastical.co.uk)

Directors: The Venerable Christine Wilson; M. D. Couve; John Hylands; Tony Latham; Philip Mawer; Will Samuel, Chair; Mark Hews, Group Chief Executive; Denise Wilson; Tim Carroll; David Christie; Jacinta Whyte (women: 3; men: 9)

Year end	31/12/2013
Turnover	£399,345,000
Pre-tax profit	£66,937,000

Nature of business: Specialist financial services group established by Anglican churchmen in 1887 to provide protection to church properties, now provides financial services to selected markets. Allchurches Trust Ltd, a registered charity, owns the group.

Company registration number: 1718196

Subsidiary undertakings include: Ansvar Insurance Ltd; Ecclesiastical Life Ltd; Ecclesiastical Underwriting Management Ltd; South Essex Insurance Brokers Ltd.

Main locations: Gloucester

UK employees: 842

Total employees: 1,034

Focus of giving: General charitable purposes, heritage, arts, culture, poverty and social exclusion, religion, community/social welfare, disability.

Membership: BITC

Charity of the Year	✓
Gifts in kind	✓
Humanitarian aid: overseas	✓
Matched funding	✓
Overseas giving	✓
Payroll giving	✓

Charitable donations

Cash UK (latest available):	2013	£5,500,000
	2012	£5,700,000
	2011	£11,700,000
	2010	£10,000,000
	2009	£900,000
Total UK (cash and in kind):	2013	£5,582,000
Cash worldwide:	2013	£5,500,000
Total worldwide (cash and in kind):	2013	£5,582,000

Community involvement

Support for communities in 2013 was given through a range of initiatives, including cash donations to the Allchurches Trust (Charity Commission no. 263960), company matching for staff giving, the company's Helping Hands volunteering programme and grant-giving through the Ecclesiastical 125 Fund, set up in the group's 125th anniversary year in 2012.

The company is owned by the Allchurches Trust to which profits are donated. The object of the trust is to promote the Christian religion and to contribute to the funds of any charitable institutions, associations, funds or objects and to carry out any charitable purpose.

Applicants are advised to visit the website: www.allchurches.co.uk

The Ecclesiastical 125 Fund

Ecclesiastical's 125 Fund was set up with the Gloucestershire Community Foundation in 2012 and currently receives 100% government matched funding. It distributes small grants to Gloucestershire's local registered charities, social enterprises and voluntary or community groups that:

- Support people who care for others
- Work with vulnerable children and adults
- Focus on preserving our heritage

National charity partnerships

In 2012 Ecclesiastical chose the Carers Trust as the company's national charity to support in 2012/2013 because it has strong links with a number of the group's core business areas. In the first year, activity as part of the partnership included supporting the charity's first national network conference and financing the post of a care adviser. In the second year of our partnership we funded the charity's national research into dementia care in the UK, resulting in the first ever in-depth report into dementia care in the UK entitled 'A Road Less Rocky'.

Corporate giving

In 2013 charitable donations paid, and provided for, by the group in the year amounted to £5.5 million (2012: £5.7 million). A payment of £4 million was paid to the Allchurches Trust with a remaining £1.5 million of donations going to other charitable causes. It would appear from the Allchurches Trust's accounts for 2013 that the company also donated £82,000 in services. During the last ten years, a total of £95.3 million (2012: £94.3 million) has been provided by group companies for church and charitable purposes.

See the Allchurches Trust Ltd (Charity Commission no. 263960) entry on p. 390 for more information.

In-kind support

The group's staff volunteer and support local community-minded charities. In 2013, employee time donated (during normal working hours) was 1,600 hours.

BITC Business Class programme
The group's support to Gloucestershire-based Millbrook Academy through a number of mentoring and coaching activities marked the launch of the UK-wide BITC Business Class programme in Gloucestershire. As part of the initiative, local schools and businesses are grouped together to meet on a regular basis to share best practice and pool resources. Programme members are also able to share learning and ideas with other Business Class clusters nationwide.

Employee-led support

In 2013 a total of £40,000 was raised through payroll giving and the total employee fundraising for the group's charity partners was £78,000.

The group also donated £25,000 to the DEC Philippines Appeal and provided 100% matched funding of all staff donations.

Corporate social responsibility

CSR committee: Formal responsibility and accountability for the group's corporate responsibility is structured at all levels of the organisation. There is an Employee Community Panel, a Corporate Affairs Team and a Group Strategy and Corporate Affairs Director.

CSR information: Extract taken from the 2013 Corporate Responsibility Report:

> *Core Issues*
> Over the last few years our community investment programme has focused on issues that are important to our customers and the communities we operate in. We have used our understanding of our customers (charity, heritage, faith and education sectors) and the challenges they face to focus on three core issues, which all of our community investment projects aim to tackle in some way:
> - Protecting our heritage against crime and anti-social behaviour
> - Supporting vulnerable children and adults in our local communities
> - Supporting the sustainability of local charities that address the specific needs of our communities

CSR report: The CSR report is published within the annual report and accounts.

Corporate charity: Allchurches Trust Ltd (Charity Commission no. 263960).

Exclusions

The trustees do not make grants to charities with political associations. Support is not normally given for charities with a political association, national charities, individuals, appeals for running costs and salaries or more than one appeal from an organisation with a 24 month period.

Applications

Applications for grants are not considered by the company but by the trustees of the Allchurches Trust Ltd., which owns the group. We have taken the following information from the trust's helpful website:

> Applications should be submitted via our online tool. If you have difficulty in doing this, applications can be submitted in writing using the downloadable application form.
>
> Written applications should be sent to:
>
> The Relationship and Grants Manager, Allchurches Trust Ltd, Beaufort House, Brunswick Road, Gloucester GL1 1JZ.

See the Statement and Policy page on the trust's website for details about its policies and other guidelines before completing your application.

Economist Newspaper Ltd

Business services, media

Correspondent: Mathew Hanratty, Corporate Communications Manager, 25 St James's Street, London SW1A 1HG (tel: 020 7830 7000; fax: 020 7839 2968/9; email: mathewhanratty@economist.com; website: www.economist.com)

Directors: Chris Stibbs, Chief Executive; Rupert Pennant-Rea, Chair; Lynn Forester de Rothschild; Philip Hoffman; John Elkann; John Micklethwait; Chris Stibbs; Sir Simon Robertson; John Ridding; Dr Eric Schmidt; Luke Swanson (women: 1; men: 10)

Year end	31/03/2014
Turnover	£331,545,000
Pre-tax profit	£56,924,000

Nature of business: The publication of The Economist and specialist publications.

Company registration number: 236383

Subsidiary undertakings include: Capitol Advantage LLC; CQ-Roll Call, Inc.; Ryder Street Properties Ltd; TEG India Private Ltd; TEG New Jersey (LLC) USA.

Main locations: London

Total employees: 1,312

Focus of giving: Education, enterprise/training, overseas projects, disasters.

Gifts in kind	✓
Matched funding	✓
Payroll giving	✓
Sponsorship	✓

Charitable donations

Cash UK (latest available):	2014	£103,000
	2013	£124,000
	2011	£129,000
	2009	£132,000
	2008	£151,000
Total UK (cash and in kind):	2014	£103,000
Cash worldwide:	2014	£103,000
Total worldwide (cash and in kind):	2014	£103,000

Community involvement

Cash donations are largely made through The Economist Charitable Trust (Charity Commission no. 293709). The principal activity of the trust is the disbursement of monies received from The Economist Newspaper Ltd to various charities. 50–60% of the trust's donations go to charities in the fields of communication, education, literacy and retraining for individuals and groups who are disadvantaged in some way. Approximately 30–40% of funds are used to match donations made by employees of The Economist Group. Remaining funds are utilised to make small donations to small and local charities.

Corporate giving

In 2013/14 The Economist donated £103,000 to The Economist Charitable Trust.

See the corporate charity entry on p. 403 for more information.

In-kind support

Employee donations of time and money to charities are matched by the company.

Employee-led support

Employees are encouraged to participate in charitable and community activities for which they are given time off.

Payroll giving: The company operates the Give As You Earn scheme.

Commercially led support

Sponsorship: Arts sponsorship may be undertaken.

Corporate social responsibility

CSR information: There is no CSR information available.

Corporate charity: The Economist Charitable Trust (Charity Commission no. 293709).

Exclusions

The Economist Charitable Trust does not support appeals from non-registered charities, circular appeals, applications of a chain-letter type, gala charity events, advertising in charity brochures, appeals from individuals, larger national appeals, church restoration appeals, politically sensitive organisations, organisations of a religious or denominational nature, single service (among forces) charities, arts sponsorship or appeals from ordinary educational establishments (such as schools or university building funds). *Special schools or projects for students with disabilities are the exception to this rule.*

Animal welfare appeals are supported via staff matching only. Fundraising events are only supported by gifts in kind, and these are usually bought from other voluntary organisations. Sport appeals are only supported if for people with disabilities.

Applications

Applications to the trust should be addressed to: Mathew Hanratty, Correspondent, The Economist Charitable Trust at the company's address.

A simple letter plus latest report and accounts is preferred – a telephone call to clarify specific queries is welcomed (ring: 020 7576 8546). The Economist Charitable Trust is run by a small team of staff volunteers. Applications can be made at any time.

Advice to applicants: The company states that multiple approaches are wasteful and counter-productive, particularly when they are addressed to directors who retired some time ago, indicating use of out-of-date lists. A few applications each year are rejected simply because they are badly presented. Many more fail because their deadlines for events are far too close when they apply. Applicants are also advised that if they are asked for additional information, this is a sign of interest in the project and not the opposite.

Unsigned, circular appeals will not receive a response.

EDF Energy plc

Electricity

Correspondent: Community Investment Team, 40 Grosvenor Place, Victoria, London SW1X 7EN (tel: 020 7242 9050; email: corporate.responsibility@edfenergy.com; website: www.edfenergy.com)

Directors: Simone Rossi; Vincent de Rivaz, Chief Executive (women: 1; men: 1)

Year end	31/01/2014
Turnover	£5,628,800,000
Pre-tax profit	(£46,300,000)

Nature of business: EDF Energy (the group) is an integrated energy company with over 15,000 employees. It generates and supplies electricity and gas for the UK from a nuclear, coal, gas and renewable energy portfolio.

Company registration number: 2366852

Subsidiary undertakings include: British Energy Direct Ltd; Cheshire Cavity Storage Group Ltd; Deletepicnic Ltd; High Hedley Hope Wind Ltd; SEEBOARD Energy Gas Ltd; Sutton Bridge Financing Ltd.

Main locations: Sunderland, London

UK employees: 1,237

Total employees: 1,237

Focus of giving: Education, environment, heritage, STEM (science, technology, engineering and mathematics), poverty and social exclusion, sport, recreation, children, young people, community/social welfare, disability.

Membership: BITC

Charity of the Year	✓
Gifts in kind	✓
Market-led giving	✓
Matched funding	✓
Payroll giving	✓
Sponsorship	✓

Charitable donations

Cash UK (latest available):	2014	£3,470,000
	2010	£3,230,900
	2009	£3,386,000
	2008	£2,799,000
	2007	£2,724,824
Total UK (cash and in kind):	2014	£3,470,000
Cash worldwide:	2014	£3,470,000
Total worldwide (cash and in kind):	2014	£3,470,000

Community involvement

The company is interested in causes concerned with education, youth, community development, environment and sport. Support is given in the area the company operates which covers London, the south east and the south west of England, as well as around its customer services centre in Sunderland.

EDF Energy Trust (Charity Commission no. 1099446)

The company recognises the financial problems some customers face and helps those in need through the EDF Energy Trust which was the first energy trust to be established in the UK. Grants are awarded by the trust to vulnerable domestic customers of EDF Energy who are in debt with or struggling to pay their gas/electricity charges, and/or need help with other essential household debts or essential household items.

Receiving donations from EDF Energy since 2003, the trust is independent of its donor company and is governed by the usual board of trustees. However, the administration of the trust is undertaken by Charis Grants Ltd (Charis) on their behalf.

Charis exists to facilitate charitable and corporate giving by designing, developing and managing a range of services in support of vulnerable members of society. Grant management is undertaken by Charis awarding grants to its beneficiary group for utility debt and other essential household bills and costs.

The EDF Trust, through Charis, actively encourages applications from customers for grants. Contact: admin@charisgrants.com for further information.

The EDF Trust also provides occasional grants to organisations whose objectives are broadly charitable, for the provision of money management or fuel debt advice projects. The applicant organisation must operate, or serve potential beneficiaries, in the main regions of the charity's operations.

Charity Partner: Marie Curie Cancer Care – see 'Employee-led support' section.

Corporate giving

In 2013/14, the company made total cash donations in the UK of over £3.4 million, £3 million of which went to the EDF Energy Trust. (The accounts for EDF Energy plc 2013/14 declare various charitable donations totalling £470,000. However they do not make reference to the £3 million which was received by the EDF Energy Trust and shown as income in the trust's accounts as received from EDF Energy plc.)

See the corporate charity entry on p. 403 for more information.

In-kind support

A range of educational programmes supports the company's climate and social commitments:

The Pod – Programme for greener schools

The Pod is EDF's award-winning sustainable schools programme – it now reaches 50% of all schools (over 18,000 schools) in the UK. Established in September 2008, the Pod was founded on a concept of 'learn, act, inspire' to engage young people in energy, science and sustainability. It provides free curriculum-linked resources and runs campaigns to teach young people (aged 4 – 14) about these issues, empower them to act on their learning, and enable them inspire others with their achievements. The programme provides a wide range of resources for schools including lesson and assembly plans for different age groups, practical activity guides, films, games and resources linked to campaigns such as the Pod's Waste Week and Switch Off Fortnight. Pod campaigns are designed to help get the whole school, parents and the local community engaged in living more sustainable lifestyles.

Since September 2008, the Pod is estimated to have engaged over 10 million young people on energy, science and sustainability. It also now reaches 138 schools in 30 different countries. EDF works closely with a number of partners on the Pod including:

The British Science Association which champions access, engagement and ownership on science to people from all walks of life.

Eco-Schools: an international programme that guides schools on their sustainability journey by providing a framework to embed this into the heart of school life.

The Meteorological Office which is a world leader in climate science.

Wastebuster: an environmental education programme that supports teachers to creatively explore waste in the curriculum, and helps children work towards creating sustainable schools, homes and communities.

In addition to its annual Waste Week and Switch Off Fortnight campaigns in 2013, the Pod, Wastebuster and the British Science Association joined forces to launch a new campaign, 'Science in Schools'. The campaign combines environmental education about waste and climate science with a textile recycling programme. Schools and community groups can exchange unwanted clothing and textiles for free resources and equipment to get children excited about science and engineering. Schools book a collection and encourage everyone to donate unwanted textiles for recycling. These are collected, weighed and the school then receives points for the recycled textiles that can be exchanged for science equipment. In 2014, EDF expanded the programme to EDF Energy offices and other Pod partners.

In January 2014 an initiative was launched through the Pod to inspire over 100,000 children, their parents and teachers to participate in a series of mass participation experiments that tackle real scientific questions. The Great EDF Energy Experiment is a five-year programme run in partnership with the British Science Association.

Employee-led support

In 2013 a three-year partnership with Marie Curie Cancer Care was launched and employees raised over £100,000 six months ahead of schedule. The group's goal at the start of the partnership was for employees to raise £100,000 each year of the partnership which EDF Energy would match fund to a total of £300,000 over the three years.

Working with the charity, EDF is also using staff expertise to help improve the energy efficiency of their hospices, and raise awareness of the work and services it offers.

The company has a Helping Hands scheme which allows all employees to spend two days performing voluntary work on normal pay if they match these two days of work in their own time. By donating their time and energy, employees are encouraged to build relationships with charities, community groups and schools. A Company Makers scheme has been launched with around 300 employees taking part in the pilot programme.

Payroll giving: EDF Energy employees make regular charitable donations through a payroll giving scheme, supporting more than 156 charities.

Commercially led support

Along with the Institute of Physics, EDF arranged a 'Lab in a Lorry' visit to Bridgwater College Academy for 150 Year 9 students in September 2013. Students swapped their classroom for a lesson delivered from the mobile laboratory and had the opportunity to explore science though specially created interactive experiments.

Over 400 schoolchildren from across Kent were treated to a science and maths 'festive extravaganza' in December 2013 when the company helped the annual LabLive Lecture come to Romney Marsh. The event gave students the opportunity to experience 'spectacular science' and understand the benefits of studying STEM subjects at GCSE. 'The free LabLive shows have amazed around 1,000 Key Stage 3 pupils since it started in 2011.'

Sponsorship: EDF is the principal sponsor of the Cheltenham Science Festival and the Generation Science programme in Scotland. The company has supported The Times Cheltenham Science Festival for 11 years and is the principal sponsor of its Science for Schools programme, which offers 16 educational lectures and 37 interactive science workshops for student visitors.

Corporate social responsibility

CSR committee: There is a Community Investment Team.

CSR information: The group's CSR focuses on sustainability. The following is taken from the group's website:

> Driving progress for people – a successful and responsible long-term energy business, trusted by customers and powering a thriving society and a healthy environment.

CSR report: A Sustainability Commitments Performance Update is published annually in the Sustainability Report.

Corporate charity: EDF Energy Trust (EDFET) (Charity Commission no. 1099446).

Applications

Organisational grants from the trust: it is advisable to contact the foundation for further information on future grant programmes and deadlines.

Individual grants from the trust: the easiest way to apply for a grant is via the trust's online application form. Alternatively you can print an application form to complete by hand which can be sent to the trust's freepost address or request one from the trust. Forms may also be available from some advice centres such as the Citizens Advice Bureau.

Organisations wishing to apply to the company should apply in writing to the correspondent.

EE Ltd (formerly T-Mobile (UK) Ltd)

Telecommunications

Correspondent: Responsibility Team, Trident PlaceMosquito Way HatfieldHertfordshireAL10 9BW (tel: 01707 315000; fax: 01707 319001; email: responsibility@ee.co.uk; website: ee.co.uk/our-company/corporate-responsibility)

Directors: Olaf Swantee, Chief Executive Officer; Neal Milsom, Chief Financial Officer; Thomas Dannenfeldt; Gervais Pellissier, Chair; Benoit Scheen; Michael Tsamaz (women: 0; men: 6)

Year end	31/12/2013
Turnover	£6,482,000,000
Pre-tax profit	(£101,000,000)

Nature of business: UK mobile communications provider. The group, which operates exclusively in the UK, runs EE, Orange and T-Mobile and was formed in April 2010 when France Telecom S.A. and Deutsche Telekom A.G. combined their respective UK mobile businesses as a joint venture.

Company registration number: 2382161

Subsidiary undertakings include: EE (Group) Ltd; Orange Home UK Ltd; Orange Services India Private Ltd; Orange Personal Communications Services Ltd; EE Finance plc.

Brands include: EE, Orange, T Mobile.

Total employees: 12,849

Focus of giving: Enterprise/training, marginalised people, older people, science technology.

Membership: BITC

Cash donations undeclared	✓
Gifts in kind	✓
Humanitarian aid: overseas	✓

Charitable donations

Cash UK (latest available):	2013	£261,000
	2012	£13,300
	2011	£45,700
	2010	£147,000
	2009	£189,000
Total UK (cash and in kind):	2013	£530,000
Cash worldwide:	2013	£261,000
Total worldwide (cash and in kind):	2013	£530,000

Community involvement

Much of the charitable activity EE commits to has the aim of promoting digital inclusion. The group is a core founder partner of Go ON UK, a charity formed by eight organisations from the business, charity and public sectors with the aim of bringing 'the benefits of the Internet to every individual and every organisation in every community across the UK'.

Corporate giving

There is a downloadable 2013 GRI table on the website and it is from this that we have taken the following information. The group made total contributions of £650,000, of which, management costs amounted to £120,000. The value of cash, in-kind and time contributions totalled £530,000, and was distributed as follows:

Cash donations	£261,000
Time costs	£256,000
In-kind costs	£12,500

Through payroll giving and fundraising for causes such as the Philippines Typhoon appeal, employees and customers raised a further £1.6 million during the year though, as is our usual practice, we have not included this figure in the total for contributions from the group.

In-kind support

Through partnership with Age UK and Go ON UK, EE runs 'Techy Tea Parties' at its stores to help promote digital inclusion. Older people who need help understanding and using digital technology can get free advice from an EE Digital Champion – a specially trained EE employee – over a cup of tea. In 2013 68 Techy Tea Parties were held, with 565 EE employees volunteering to help improve the digital skills of 861 people.

Employee-led support

Employee fundraising

The group supports employees with set up and top up costs of fundraising activities. In 2013 employees, with EE's support, raised £350,000 for charitable causes.

Employee volunteering

Employees are able to contribute volunteering time. EE employees are able to spend two days per year volunteering, either for an activity of their choice or on one of the group's volunteering programmes such as EE Digital Champions.

Corporate social responsibility

CSR committee: There is a Responsibility Team. Strategy is signed off by the CEO and Head of Responsibility is Chief of Staff, Stephen Harris.

CSR information: The following information is taken from the group's website:

> *Responsibility*
>
> We developed our strategy through a detailed assessment of our business, our potential risks and our performance in the responsibility space.
>
> *External Advisory Board*
>
> In 2013 we established EE's External Advisory Board to help us develop and improve our responsibility activity. The board is composed of senior business leaders and sustainability specialists who meet twice a year to share their views. We invite the board to provide feedback on what we do well and the areas where we can improve. We're committed to integrating the views of the board into our activity and will also use the board as a forum where we can share our ideas for the future.

CSR report: Reports are published annually.

Applications

In writing to the correspondent.

Electrocomponents plc

Distribution

Correspondent: My Community Management Committee, International Management Centre, 8050 Oxford Business Park North, Oxford OX4 2HW (tel: 01865 204000; fax: 01865 207400; email: queries@electrocomponents.com; website: www.electrocomponents.com)

Directors: Ian Mason, Group Chief Executive; Peter Johnson, Chair; Simon Brodie, Group Finance Officer; Adrian Auer; Paul Hollingworth; Rupert Soames; Ian Haslegrave; Karen Guerra; John Pattullo (women: 1; men: 8)

Year end	31/03/2014
Turnover	£1,273,100,000
Pre-tax profit	£101,100,000

Nature of business: Founded in 1937, the company is a global distributor of electronics and maintenance products.

Company registration number: 647788

Subsidiary undertakings include: Allied Electronics (Canada) Inc.; Amidata SAu; Radionics Ltd; RS Components Pty Ltd; RS Components Handelsges.m.b.H; RS Componentes Electrónicos Limitada; RS Components BV; RS Components AS; RS Components (Shanghai) Company Ltd; RS Components Pte Ltd. A full list is contained within the company's annual accounts.

Brands include: RS Components and Allied Electronics.

Total employees: 43

Focus of giving: Education, community/social welfare, disasters.

Cash donations undeclared	✓
Gifts in kind	✓
Humanitarian aid: overseas	✓
Matched funding	✓
Overseas giving	✓

Charitable donations

Cash UK (latest available):	2014	£10,000
	2011	£10,000
	2010	£9,000
	2009	£172,000
Total UK (cash and in kind):	2014	£10,000
Cash worldwide:	2014	£10,000
Total worldwide (cash and in kind):	2014	£95,000

Community involvement

The company's website explains its UK community involvement which is the forum My Community, created in the UK to focus on employee-led community and volunteer activities.

My Community is inclusive and accessible to all employees and participation is on a voluntary basis.

The My Community management committee meets monthly to review and make decisions about community activities and charity requests. An annual budget is made available to support employee-led initiatives on a matched giving basis and to support local school initiatives.

A newsletter is published monthly and initiatives are promoted internally and communicated externally. Donations are generally made to local charities.

The company states it adopts a multi-level approach to community activities that includes:

- Provision of time and expertise
- Employee-led fundraising
- Direct donations
- Corporate matching of donations
- Donations of stock

In the UK, the company has been granted patron status of the children's charity, the NSPCC.

Corporate giving

In 2013/14 the company declared its total fundraising (£240,000), mainly led by employees, but did not declare its charitable cash donations from profits. We have taken the last two total amounts we have available for this and estimate that this year's cash giving by the company was around £10,000 in the UK.

We also have no figures for cash giving worldwide although we do know that to date, over £85,000 worth of end-of-line products, such as power tools, protective clothing, fire extinguishers, and batteries were sourced to help with the Philippines Typhoon disaster. We have therefore used this figure as the worldwide in-kind total, (although it is undoubtedly more), and with the £10,000 cash this totals £95,000 for worldwide contributions.

In-kind support

Humanitarian aid

This information is taken from the company's website:

> In response to [the Typhoon Haiyan] disaster, RS [a subsidiary] teams across the world collected end-of-line products to aid the rebuilding of the devastated areas of the Philippines. To date, RS has sourced over £85,000 worth of end-of-line products, such as power tools, protective clothing, fire extinguishers, and batteries. The items were gathered from across the world and our people helped to pick and pack the products.
>
> In addition, employees in Australia and Spain organised events to raise money for the Philippines relief. RS Italy donated 274 hours of their salary to raise money for CARITAS, a charity actively involved in providing aid to the affected people of the Philippines. Donated hours equated to 6,025 Euros; this was matched by the company resulting in a monetary donation of 12,050 Euros.
>
> In South East Asia, the RS team also worked together and raised money to donate to the Philippines relief efforts. Many employees were personally affected by the disaster and donated much of their time helping in many ways to rebuild the devastated areas across the Philippines.

Employee-led support

The company supports engagement with its local communities globally and employees are encouraged to be proactive in choosing which organisations/groups to be involved with.

Across the world employees invest their time and money to raise funds for valuable causes, from disaster and cancer charities to community youth projects. During 2014, global fundraising reached over £240,000. Some examples of these initiatives include:

- The UK business's call centre supporting the Comic Relief and Sport Relief charities as part of the donation network across the country
- The Allied business in the United States actively supporting United Way, an organisation dedicated to improving education, income and health in communities across the country
- The Asia Pacific team donating to those affected by Typhoon Haiyan in the Philippines
- The Italian business supporting a contemporary photography activity for high school students in Milan to help them develop their social and cognitive skills
- UK employees raising funds for the Lakelands Hospice in Corby, Northamptonshire

Corporate social responsibility

CSR committee: The Group Chief Executive is the director responsible for CR and the board monitors CR matters across the group's business operations.

CSR information: The following statement is taken from the company's 2013/14 annual report:

> Corporate responsibility (CR) is an integral part of our business and we strive to align our values and strategy with responsible and ethical business policies and practices. We embrace responsibility for the Company's actions and through our activities encourage a positive impact on our environment, consumers, employees, communities and other stakeholders.

CSR report: An annual CR report is contained within the annual report and accounts.

Applications

In writing to the correspondent.

Elementis plc

Chemicals and plastics

Correspondent: Wai Wong, Company Secretary, 10 Albemarle Street, London W1S 4HH (tel: 020 7408 9300; fax: 020 7493 2194; email: elementis.info@elementis.com; website: www.elementis.com)

Directors: David Dutro, Chief Executive Officer; Andrew Duff, Chair; Brian Taylorson, Finance Director; Andrew Christie; Nick Salmon; Steve Good; Anne Hyland (women: 1; men: 6)

Year end	31/12/2013
Turnover	£486,742,901
Pre-tax profit	£84,152,383

Nature of business: Elementis plc is a global specialty chemicals company with operations worldwide that serve customers in North and Latin America, Europe and Asia in a wide range of markets and sectors.

Company registration number: 3299608

Subsidiary undertakings include: Elementis Chromium LLP; Elementis UK Ltd trading as Elementis Specialties; Elementis Chromium LP; Elementis Specialties Inc; Elementis Specialities; Deuchem Co., Ltd.

Total employees: 1,365

Focus of giving: Education, health, ill health, medical research, arts, culture, overseas projects, sport, recreation, children, young people, disasters.

Cash donations undeclared	✓
Gifts in kind	✓
Humanitarian aid: overseas	✓
Humanitarian aid: UK	✓
Matched funding	✓
Overseas giving	✓
Payroll giving	✓

Charitable donations

Cash UK (latest available):	2013	£6,000
	2010	£8,230
	2009	£7,200
	2008	£2,200
Total UK (cash and in kind):	2013	£6,000
Cash worldwide:	2013	£6,000
Total worldwide (cash and in kind):	2013	£6,000

Community involvement

We understand that the company's preference is to support the areas and causes in which its employees participate.

Corporate giving

In 2013 Elementis plc did not declare charitable donations either worldwide or in the UK. We have taken the last three annual totals we have available for UK cash donations and estimated an average of £6,000 for the year. Previous beneficiaries have included the global Red Cross relief effort following the earthquake in Haiti, local youth and sports clubs, schools, arts groups, hospices, a drought relief and education initiative, and medical research and health-related charities.

Employee-led support

Examples of corporate support include: sponsoring an employee who participated in the London Marathon to raise funds for the Alzheimer's Society; matching donations raised by a group of employees from the Livingston plant, who participated in a fundraising walk to Ben Nevis, in order to help fund home care to a young girl who has a serious medical condition; and sponsoring a child from Belarus, organised by the UK-registered charity Friends of Chernobyl Children.

Matched funding

The company will match fund employees' fundraising but we could not find any criteria for this.

Payroll Giving:

The company operates a payroll giving programme in the UK.

Corporate social responsibility

CSR committee: The chief executive is responsible at board level for all CR matters.

CSR information: The following information is taken from the company's 2013 annual report:

> It is Elementis policy to actively promote the safety and well-being of the communities in which we operate and to ensure that we conduct our business in a

way that is open and transparent to our neighbours.

We seek to engage positively with our local communities. It is our policy to operate as a good neighbour and we encourage and facilitate employees volunteering or fund raising in support of local community organisations.

Elementis takes a decentralised approach to working with the communities in which we operate. The Company sets guidelines but does not dictate any specific areas or priority for corporate support, since we are aware that needs and priorities vary from community to community.

This bottom up approach is designed to encourage management and employees at individual sites to focus on local issues and to take full responsibility for implementation of local programmes.

CSR report: There is a CSR report contained within the annual report and accounts.

Applications

In writing to the correspondent.

ERM Group Holdings Ltd

Consultancy, business services

Correspondent: Shona King, ERM Foundation, 2nd Floor, Exchequer Court, 33 St Mary Axe, London EC3A 8AA (tel: 020 3206 5200; fax: 020 3206 5440; email: shona.king@erm.com; website: www.erm.com)

Directors: Andrew Silverbeck; Mark Pearson (women: 0; men: 2)

Year end	31/03/2014
Pre-tax profit	(£9,687,565)

Nature of business: The principal activities of the group are the provision of environmental, social, risk and health and safety consulting services. Environmental Resources Management (ERM) Group operates around the world has over 150 offices in 40 countries and territories employing more than 5,000 people.

The ERM Group Holdings Ltd has no employees and is a UK registered intermediate group holding company and a member of ERM Worldwide Ltd companies. Its immediate parent company is Emerald 3 Ltd.

The group's website notes that 'ERM has been in business in the UK since 1971 and now has seven offices in London, Oxford, Manchester, Edinburgh, Swansea, Bristol, and Aberdeen, employing over 300 people.'

Company registration number: 5593398

Subsidiary undertakings include: ERM Group Ltd.

Focus of giving: Education, environment, overseas projects.

Cash donations undeclared	✓
Gifts in kind	✓
Matched funding	✓
Overseas giving	✓

Charitable donations

Cash UK (latest available):	2014	£104,000
	2011	£62,600
	2008	£111,000
	2007	£138,000
Total UK (cash and in kind):	2014	£104,000
Total worldwide (cash and in kind):	2014	£873,000

Community involvement

The ERM Foundation (Charity Commission no. 1113415)

The foundation was established in 2006 with an objective of 'providing human resources and/or financial assistance to projects that contribute to the improvement of the Earth's environment, quality of life and sustainable development throughout the world through appropriate charitable, educational and scientific endeavours.' The foundation selects projects in one or more of the following areas: reducing carbon emissions; environmental education; biodiversity and conservation; and clean water and sanitation. It works with a wide range of partners, including the company itself and other not-for-profit, private and public sector organisations, both overseas and in the UK. Financial contributions are available as well as volunteering and pro bono services.

It is a practice of the foundation to fund organisations which ERM employees are involved with – the foundation is advised by a committee of specialists from ERM's current staff and alumni. The majority of its income comes from ERM employee donations and other donors through locally organised fundraising events. The company matches a portion of these contributions.

The foundation's key programme is The Low Carbon Enterprise Fund (LCEF) which supports enterprises in the developing world where the entrepreneurs are seeking to build a low carbon business by providing low interest loans and equity stakes as well as pro bono support.

During the year The ERM Foundation raised significant funds for its regional long-term flagship project (the Ruvuma Elephant Conservation project in Tanzania). The funds will be disbursed during the course of 2015. In addition technical support was provided for a UK wildlife trust to protect an endangered new species.

This seems to be the main channel of the company's charitable support.

Corporate giving

The annual report and accounts of the company did not declare any charitable donations. We estimate that about £104,000 was given in cash donations in the UK, based on the figures from three previous years known to us.

The ERM Foundation's annual report and accounts for 2013/14 note that:

> ERM Worldwide Ltd supported The ERM Foundation with pro-bono time and matching funds for monies raised by ERM Staff to support foundation projects. The cost of the audit was borne by ERM Europe Ltd who also provided management and administrative support. As the management support received by The ERM Foundation was so small it has been deemed immaterial and has therefore not been reflected in gift in kind.

During the year a total of $49,000 (£31,000) was given in grants to environmental charities from the foundation.

The *global* website states that 'in 2013/14 ERM contributed more than $1.4 million (£873,000) ... primarily through The ERM Foundation and its programs.'

Note: Figures given in the company's annual report and accounts for 2013/14 have been stated in US dollars; we have used the exchange rate applicable at the time of writing.

See the corporate charity entry on p. 403 for more information.

In-kind support

The foundation states that 'ERM has provided generous support through making available technical, administrative and management support on an as-needed basis.' As well as supporting The ERM Foundation, staff members get involved with a range of local causes through fundraising and volunteering.

Globally in 2013/14 more than 1,600 pro bono hours were contributed by 127 employees to support 47 projects in 22 countries. Additional volunteer hours and ongoing support to projects was further given by many staff members.

Employee-led support

The global website states: 'We encourage our employees to engage with the communities in which they live and work, and to play an active role in global initiatives.'

The group's employees provide professional and volunteering support to environmental initiatives (co-ordinated by the foundation) for the benefit of local communities. For instance, provision of ecology surveys for a wildlife trust in the UK, technical support for the foundation's elephant conservation project in Tanzania and developing environmental education materials for schoolchildren in the UK.

Volunteering initiatives are often aligned with global events, for example, Earth Day, World Environment Day and the annual International Coastal Clean-up.

In addition to the work of the Foundation ERM employees contribute to local projects and community activities. ERM supports these initiatives by providing basic supplies when needed.

Matched funding

The company provides matched funding for donations raised by employees specifically for charitable purposes – global website notes this being 75 cents for every dollar raised. An example of employee fundraising during 2013/14 includes employees raising funds for a cycle charity in Oxford.

Corporate social responsibility

CSR committee: The group's website states:

> Our regional committees, chaired by our regional CEOs and with employee representation, drive the work of the foundation across ERM. The foundation's global Pro Bono and Matching Funds Committees involve senior leadership, supported by employees from across the business.

CSR information: The website states:

> Sustainability at ERM is a commitment to supporting socioeconomic development that meets the needs of the present without compromising the ability of future generations to meet their own needs. This includes minimizing society's impact on the environment such that it can support those future needs while promoting social and economic development that allows all communities to enjoy these benefits going forward.

The key focus areas are: employees; health and safety; business conduct and ethics; environment; community; thought leadership; and customers.

CSR report: A group-wide CSR report is available online.

Corporate charity: The ERM Foundation (Charity Commission no. 1113415).

Applications

Applications to the foundation should be made in writing to the correspondent.

Esh Group

Building/construction

Correspondent: Added Value Team, Bowburn North Industrial Estate, Bowburn, Durham DH6 5PF (tel: 01913 774570; fax: 01913 774571; email: addedvalue@esh.uk.com; website: www.eshaddedvalue.co.uk)

Directors: Austin Donohoe, Chair; Brian Manning, Chief Executive; Andy Radcliffe, Finance Director and Company Secretary; John Davies; Michael Hogan; John Walker (women: 0; men: 6)

Year end	31/12/2013
Turnover	£192,457,000
Pre-tax profit	£3,228,000

Nature of business: The principal activities of the group during the year were building, construction, civil engineering and property refurbishment.

Company registration number: 3724890

Subsidiary undertakings include: Refer to the annual report and accounts for a full list of subsidiaries.

Brands include: Esh Border Construction, Esh Build, Esh Construction, Esh Facilities, Esh Property Services, Lumsden and Carroll Civil Engineering

Total employees: 880

Focus of giving: Education, enterprise/training, environment, health, ill health, small groups, local groups, unpopular causes, children, young people, community/social welfare.

Membership: BITC

Sponsorship ✓

Charitable donations

Cash UK (latest available):	2013	£130,000
	2010	£107,000
	2008	£215,000
	2007	£221,177
	2006	£201,660
Total UK (cash and in kind):	2013	£130,000
Cash worldwide:	2013	£130,000
Total worldwide (cash and in kind):	2013	£130,000

Community involvement

It would appear that Esh Group's cash support for charitable and community organisations are primarily made via the **Esh Foundation** (Charity Commission no. 1112040), referred to by the company as the Esh Charitable Trust. The foundation supports causes in five key areas – children and young people; vulnerable people; environmental community regeneration; education and skills development; and health – based in the North of England (the counties of North Yorkshire, County Durham, Northumberland and Cumbria.

Esh runs its CSR initiative through a series of programmes under the title 'Esh Added Value'. These programmes are:

Esh Employability – An employability skills programme, Building My Skills, helps to introduce young people (Key Stages 3 and 4) to the world of work through mentoring, guest workshops and interview experiences. The programme was developed in partnership with Ryder, Arup and Turner Townsend, and has involved a number of partner organisations. In 2013 the programme was expanded to include schools and colleges in Cumbria and Yorkshire, as well as in the North East.

Esh Communities – Launched in 2012, grants up to £1,000 are available through the programme for projects and services run by local groups and charities working to make a positive difference in areas where Esh operates.

Esh Connexts – A range of programmes designed to help local people through pre-employment training, work experience, placements, apprenticeships and other opportunities. The scheme was launched in 2010 in partnership with Connexions with the aim of supporting young men who were underachieving in their final years at school. The Chance for Change programme looks to support prisoners with their re-entry into society through a 15 week course of classroom based workshops.

For more details of these programmes, view the Esh Added Value website.

Corporate giving

In 2013 the group made community contributions of at least £130,000. This included a donation of £100,000 to the **Esh Foundation**. Though Esh Communities schemes 31 projects (Esh Communities Yorkshire, nine projects; Esh Communities North East, 12 projects; and Esh Communities Cumbria, ten projects) were awarded a total of £30,000 during the year.

See the corporate charity entry on p. 404 for more information.

Employee-led support

Employee fundraising

Esh Group staff have supported their communities and various charities with their fundraising efforts.

Commercially led support

Sponsorship

Esh Group is the main sponsor of the Newcastle Eagles basketball team and, together with fellow sponsors, is working with the club to develop its North East based community programmes for young people, disadvantaged groups and the wheelchair basketball team.

Corporate social responsibility

CSR committee: We found no evidence of there being a CSR committee.

CSR information: The group's website states:

> It has been identified that skill creation is important in local economic development and as such Esh Group has designed and implemented programmes in partnership with Local Authorities and representative agencies in an effort to influence training infrastructure.
>
> Esh Group realises the greater benefit of community engagement to our

organisation. Our community engagement programmes cover:

- Business & Enterprise
- Esh Employability
- Education Enrichment
- Hard To Reach Groups
- Social Enterprise
- Higher Education

CSR report: A CSR report is published within the annual report and accounts of the group.

Corporate charity: Esh Foundation (Charity Commission no. 1112040).

Exclusions

No support is given for political appeals.

Applications

Further details of how to apply to the charitable foundation, eligibility criteria and so on, are available at: www.eshcharitabletrust.org.uk

Further details on how to apply for an Esh Communities grant are available at: www.eshaddedvalue.co.uk.

Euro Packaging UK Ltd

Manufacturing

Correspondent: Nasir Awan, Trustee, Euro Charity Trust, 20 Brickfield Road, Yardley, Birmingham B25 8EH (email: info@eurocharity.org.uk; website: www.europackaging.co.uk)

Directors: S. Flaherty; M. Higson

Year end	31/12/2013
Turnover	£82,925,000
Pre-tax profit	(£577,000)

Nature of business: Euro Packaging UK Ltd is a manufacturer and distributor of paper and plastic packaging, allied products, disposable packaging products and consolidated logistics.

It would appear that the company was formerly known as Euro Packaging Ltd and now operates under the name of Euro Packaging UK Ltd, from whose accounts we have taken our company information. As a private limited company, wholly owned by the Majid family, it has been difficult to determine details of the company's current set-up. The ultimate parent company is Euro Packaging Jersey Ltd.

Company registration number: 7012425

Subsidiary undertakings include: See Companies House for details on related companies.

UK employees: 291

Total employees: 291

Focus of giving: General charitable purposes, economic generation, education, general appeals, overseas projects, poverty and social exclusion, community/social welfare.

Charitable donations

Cash UK (latest available):	2013	£1,000
	2012	£451,000
	2011	£3,200
	2010	£2,800,000
	2009	£122,000
Total UK (cash and in kind):	2013	£152,000
Cash worldwide:	2013	£152,000
Total worldwide (cash and in kind):	2013	£152,000

Community involvement

The company appears to make its charitable donations through the **Euro Charity Trust** (Charity Commission no. 1058460). The mission of the trust is: 'To assist the underprivileged to improve their lives, who in turn can assist their families and communities and live a healthy and dignified way of life'. This mission is met in the main by relieving poverty, providing education and forming partnerships to deliver and sustain projects.

Corporate giving

In 2013 the company donated £1,000, which we believe was received by Euro Charity Trust. However, charitable giving from the company appears to vary drastically by year; for example, 2010 (£2.8 million), 2011 (£3,200), 2012 (£451,000). The average of charitable donations in the three most recent years for which we have figures was £152,000 and we have taken this as an estimate for the company's contributions in 2013.

We have obtained this information from the Euro Packaging UK Ltd annual report and accounts as well as from those of the **Euro Charity Trust**.

See the 'Corporate charity' entry for more details.

See the corporate charity entry on p. 404 for more information.

Corporate social responsibility

CSR committee: We were unable to determine if there was a CSR committee present.

CSR information: The company appears to filter its charitable giving through **Euro Charity Trust**.

We were unable to determine the ratio of men to women on the board of directors.

CSR report: No published report.

Corporate charity: Euro Charity Trust (Charity Commission no. 1058460).

Applications

Applications to the trust should be made in writing to the correspondent.

Evans Property Group Ltd

Property

Correspondent: The Administrator, Millshaw, Ring Road, Beeston, Leeds LS11 8EG (tel: 01132 711888; fax: 01132 718487; website: www.evanspropertygroup.com)

Directors: James Pitt; Roderick Evans, Managing Director; Paul Millington, Financial Director; Alan Syers; Simon Bottomley (women: 0; men: 5)

Year end	31/03/2014
Pre-tax profit	£891,434

Nature of business: Property investment and development.

Company registration number: 4422612

Subsidiary undertakings include: Astra No. 1 Ltd; Astra No. 2 Ltd; Gemro Associates Ltd. The ultimate parent company is Drachs Investments No. 3 Ltd., a Jersey company owned by a trust for the benefit of the Evans family.

Focus of giving: General charitable purposes, health, ill health, small groups, local groups, children, young people, community/social welfare, disability.

Cash donations undeclared	✓
Gifts in kind	✓
Market-led giving	✓
Matched funding	✓
Sponsorship	✓

Charitable donations

Cash UK (latest available):	2009	£120,000

Community involvement

Evans Property Group supports both local and national charities and is one of the co-founding companies of ARISE (the Alliance to Reward Initiatives and Social Enterprise), which acts as a source of whole or part-funding for community-based initiatives and activities by groups and organisations in South Leeds.

Corporate giving

We could find no reference in the group's accounts to the amount given in charitable cash donations or other contributions in 2013/14; however, the following is stated on the website: 'Evans Property Group is proud to support a wide variety of local and national charities'

Beneficiaries include: Breast Cancer Haven, Outward Bound and Variety Club

Employee-led support

Our research indicates that the group also operates employee volunteering and matched funding schemes and that support is also given in the form of gifts in kind and joint promotions.

Commercially led support

Sponsorship

Our research tells us that the group also conducts 'arts and good cause' sponsorship.

Corporate social responsibility

CSR committee: We found no evidence of there being a CSR committee.

CSR information: The following information is taken from the company's website:

> Evans Property Group corporate responsibility encompasses the way we do business, our people, our clients, our community and charitable support; and the environment around us and sustainability issues.
>
> Evans Property Group is keenly aware of its responsibilities to the communities in which it operates and we strive to ensure that all of our operations and business practices are at all times conducted responsibly and ethically

CSR report: We found no evidence of there being a CSR report.

Exclusions

Our research tells us that no support is given for local appeals not in areas of company presence, appeals from individuals, animal welfare, overseas projects, and political or religious appeals.

Applications

In writing to the correspondent.

Further details about the ARISE initiative can be obtained from administrator Tim Flanagan c/o Polo Media Partnership, Tel. 01423 870134.

Family Assurance Friendly Society Ltd

Financial services

Correspondent: Community Programme Manager, 16–17 West Street, Brighton, East Sussex BN1 2RL (website: www.familyinvestments.co.uk/landing/in-the-community)

Directors: Norman Riddell, Chair; Ian Buckley; Peter Box; Veronica France; Simon Markey, Chief Executive; John Adams, Finance Director; Keith Meeres (women: 1; men: 6)

Year end	31/12/2013
Turnover	£186,672,000
Pre-tax profit	£4,909,000

Nature of business: Provision of financial services (life assurance, savings and protection schemes).

Company registration number: 110067

Subsidiary undertakings include: Family Enterprise Ltd; Family Equity Plan Ltd; Family Investment Management Ltd; Family PEP Managers Ltd; Governor Finance Ltd

Main locations: Brighton

Total employees: 400

Focus of giving: General charitable purposes, education, health, ill health, financial education, children, young people.

Membership: BITC

Cash donations undeclared	✓
Gifts in kind	✓
Matched funding	✓

Charitable donations

Cash UK (latest available):	2013	£20,000
	2011	£19,000
	2009	£13,000
	2007	£19,000
	2005	£7,000
Total UK (cash and in kind):	2013	£20,000
Cash worldwide:	2013	£20,000
Total worldwide (cash and in kind):	2013	£20,000

Community involvement

Through its community programme, 'Doing the Right Thing' Family Investments' staff take part in a number of community and education support activities, as well as charity fundraising events, in the area local to their Brighton base. Employees are supported in their fundraising efforts a charity matching scheme.

Supported charities: Chestnut Tree House; Children's Hospice Care; Family Support Work; Raystede; Rockinghorse; Sussex Deaf Association; Winston's Wish

The website states:

> Looking forward, we have ambitious plans to build on our local success by creating a programme with significant funding and a national footprint – the Family Foundation. The Family Foundation will provide us a genuine opportunity to play a bigger role in building a better society while, at the same time, allowing employees and customers to take an active role in their local community.

Corporate giving

The annual report and accounts for 2013 state that £20,000 was raised for 30 local and national charities through employee fundraising and the group's charity matched funding scheme. We were unable to determine the value of support given directly by the group in cash or in-kind donations and, though it is not our usual practice, we have taken £20,000 as our figure for contributions from the group for the year.

In-kind support

In the build-up to Christmas, Family Investments opened up its office to members of Age UK, who joined staff for a cup of tea. The 120 invitees were able to use the office phones to make calls to friends and family around the world and brought in their Christmas cards to be posted. More than 2,700 Christmas cards were posted for free and 140 phone calls were made.

Educational initiatives

Education became a key focus of the community programme in 2013. Family Investment's involvement included running maths lessons for Brighton primary school pupils and interview skills events for Sixth form students. The group also works with Magnified Learning to deliver their Money, Money, Money financial education programme, and has supported Albion in the Community's Want to Work programme, which assists people who are struggling to find employment.

Employee-led support

Employee volunteering

The website states that almost half of staff volunteered in the community, contributing a total of 223 working days. Activities included practical assistance for charities, such as garden maintenance or decorating, and taking part in the group's local educational initiatives.

Employee fundraising

Employees fundraise for a wide range of local and national causes. Staff have also donated clothes, toiletries and food to a day centre working to support people who are sleeping rough.

Matched funding

The group operates a charity matching scheme.

Corporate social responsibility

CSR committee: We found no details of a CSR committee.

CSR information: Family Investments' local Community Programme has been running for more than 20 years, and has encouraged employees to get involved in the Brighton community.

CSR report: There is CSR material contained within the annual report and accounts.

Exclusions

The society does not normally support advertising in charity brochures, appeals from individuals, enterprise/training, heritage, overseas projects, political/religious appeals, science/technology or social welfare.

Applications

In writing to the correspondent.

Fenner plc

Chemicals and plastics

Correspondent: Corporate Responsibility Team, Hesslewood Country Office Park, Ferriby Road, Hessle, East Yorkshire HU13 0PW (tel: 01482 626500; fax: 01482 626502; website: fenner.com/en/people_values/corporate_responsibility_report)

Directors: Mark Abrahams, Chair; Nicholas Hobson, Chief Executive Officer; Richard Perry, Group Finance Director; Vanda Murray; John Sheldrick; Alan Wood; Debra Bradbury (women: 2; men: 5)

Year end	31/08/2013
Turnover	£820,600,000
Pre-tax profit	£67,900,000

Nature of business: Manufacturer and distributor of conveyor belting and reinforced precision polymer products.

Company registration number: 329377

Subsidiary undertakings include: A full list is published in the annual report and accounts.

Total employees: 5,272

Focus of giving: General charitable purposes, education, general appeals, local groups, older people, overseas projects, poverty and social exclusion, sport, recreation, children, young people, community/social welfare.

Gifts in kind	✓
Humanitarian aid: overseas	✓
Matched funding	✓
Overseas giving	✓
Sponsorship	✓

Charitable donations

Cash UK (latest available):	2011	£151,000
	2009	£10,000
	2008	£10,000
Cash worldwide:	2013	£108,000
Total worldwide (cash and in kind):	2013	£108,000

Community involvement

Fenner plc operates its charitable giving on a local level through its operating units, which support employee community involvement through the application of the group's resources. The main beneficiaries of this charitable involvement appear to be community, education and health charities and projects in areas where the group's operating units are located worldwide.

Corporate giving

In 2012/13 group made donations of £108,000 to charitable, social and community related organisations. As this support is 'driven at a local, rather than a group level' through the group's operating units, which are based around the world, we have taken this figure as the total for worldwide donations.

During the year, donations from the group were split between the following charitable purposes: Community (44%); Education (44%); Health (12%).

In-kind support

Fenner operating units support their local communities through in-kind donations of various sorts. Examples include:

Fenner Dunlop Europe, Hull – provided on-site playing facilities for local rugby, football, cricket and bowls teams.

Fenner South Africa – provided support for a disadvantaged student at a tertiary institution, though it was not evident if this included financial support.

Employee-led support

Employee volunteering

Fenner employees take an active role in their communities. Examples of their efforts include:

Fenner Drives, Manheim, USA – through Junior Achievement USA, employees volunteered to teach classes at local schools to help promote education and life skills to students, whilst encouraging them to discover their potential.

Employee contributions

Fenner Dunlop, Drachten, Netherlands – Employees were given the option of donating the value of their customary Christmas hamper to charity, with the company doubling the amount of money raised. The money raised was split between the Imena Foundation, which supports projects in Africa, including improved education and the provision of clean drinking water and healthcare for the poorest people; the Salvation Army, to help furnish a local community kitchen; and 'A better Romanian world', which helps orphaned children, elderly and poor people.

Commercially led support

Sponsorship

During the year, Fenner Dunlop Europe in Hull sponsored local sports teams.

Corporate social responsibility

CSR committee: The following information was taken from the group's website:

> The board sets the strategy and has overall responsibility for the development and monitoring of the group's policies relating to corporate responsibility. The task of ensuring that these policies are communicated and applied at a divisional and operating unit level is delegated through the Chief Executive Officer to senior managing directors and on to each operating unit's senior management.

CSR information: The following information was obtained from the group's website:

> Fenner believes that good relations and long-term partnerships with the communities in which it works are fundamental to its success. Fenner always considers the potential social and environmental impacts that its business activities may have on those communities and such considerations are embedded within the group's decision making processes.
>
> Our support for the communities in which we operate is driven at a local, rather than group level, with operating units supporting and enhancing employee efforts in their communities through the application of the group's resources.

CSR report: A CSR report is published within the annual report and accounts.

Applications

In writing to the correspondent.

Fenwick Ltd

Retail – department and variety stores

Correspondent: The Company Secretary, Elswick Court, 39 Northumberland Street, Newcastle upon Tyne NE99 1AR (tel: 01912 325100; website: www.fenwick.co.uk)

Directors: M. A. Fenwick, Chair; N. A. H. Fenwick, Group Managing Director; J. F. Fenwick; J. A. Fenwick; H. M. Fenwick

Year end	31/01/2014
Turnover	£295,800,000
Pre-tax profit	£35,025,000

Nature of business: Department stores.

Company registration number: 52411

Subsidiary undertakings include: Bentalls plc; Williams and Griffin Ltd

Main locations: Canterbury, Brent Cross, Leicester, Kingston, Newcastle, London, York, Windsor, Tunbridge Wells

UK employees: 2,285

Total employees: 2,285

Focus of giving: General charitable purposes, education, environment, health, ill health, medical research, older people, arts, culture, children, young people, community/social welfare, disability.

Charitable donations

Cash UK (latest available):	2014	£151,000
	2013	£157,000
	2011	£106,000
	2009	£142,700
	2007	£116,000
Total UK (cash and in kind):	2014	£151,000
Cash worldwide:	2014	£151,000
Total worldwide (cash and in kind):	2014	£151,000

Community involvement

The group makes donations in support of causes local to its stores. At the time of writing, its stores are located in the following places: Bond Street; Bracknell; Brent Cross; Canterbury; Colchester; Kingston; Leicester; Newcastle; Tunbridge Wells; Windsor; and York.

Corporate giving

In 2013/14 the group made charitable donations of £151,000 to causes in the local areas of its stores. We have no information regarding beneficiary groups.

Corporate social responsibility

CSR information: There was no CSR information available. We were unable to determine the ratio of women to men on the board.

Exclusions

Our research suggests that no support is given for circular appeals, advertising in charity brochures, political appeals, overseas projects or small purely local appeals not in areas of company presence.

Applications

In writing to your local Fenwick's store, the details of which are available from the website. Our research tells us that local stores have an independent budget for appeals.

Fidessa Group plc

Business services

Correspondent: The Company Secretary, Dukes Court, Duke Street, Woking, Surrey GU21 5BH (tel: 01483 206300; fax: 01483 206301; email: eu.info@fidessa.com; website: www.fidessa.com/about-fidessa/corporate-responsibility)

Directors: John Hamer, Chair; Chris Aspinwall, Chief Executive; Andy Malpass, Finance Director; Ron Mackintosh; Elizabeth Lake; John Worby (women: 1; men: 5)

Year end	31/12/2013
Turnover	£279,000,000
Pre-tax profit	£43,100,000

Nature of business: Fidessa group is a supplier of multi-asset trading, portfolio analysis, decision support, compliance, market data and connectivity solutions for firms involved in trading the world's financial markets.

Company registration number: 3234176

Subsidiary undertakings include: Fidessa Buy-side Ltd; Fidessa Software Ltd; Fidessa Investments Ltd; Royalblue Financial Ltd, Royalblue Group Ltd.

Total employees: 1,671

Focus of giving: General charitable purposes, general appeals.

Cash donations undeclared	✓
Sponsorship	✓

Charitable donations

Cash UK (latest available):	2013	£32,000
	2012	£24,000
	2011	£44,000
	2010	£29,000
	2009	£27,000
Total UK (cash and in kind):	2013	£32,000
Cash worldwide:	2013	£32,000
Total worldwide (cash and in kind):	2013	£32,000

Community involvement

Fidessa Group plc employees nominate and actively raise funds for their chosen charities. The group sponsors charity events and employees' fundraising efforts.

Corporate giving

Fidessa Group's 2013 annual report included no information on charitable donations. Based on figures published in previous years' annual reports, however, charitable donations have averaged £32,000 each year. We have taken this as an estimate for charitable donations given in 2013.

Employee-led support

Employee fundraising

The following information is taken from the website:

> Employees are encouraged to nominate charities they would like to raise funds for and to participate actively in raising money for those charities through internal fundraising events, several of which are typically held each year. In addition, the group sponsors charity events, such as, for example, charity runs or bicycle rides, and also give sponsorship to individual staff who undertake activities for charity.

Corporate social responsibility

CSR committee: There was no evidence of there being a CSR committee.

CSR information: The following information is taken from the group's website:

> The board believes the group has a relatively low social impact but nevertheless sees the value that can be added through corporate social responsibility. Participation in activities with local communities where it carries out its business helps to integrate the group with local communities

CSR report: Although there is a CSR page on its website, the group appears to have very little by way of a programme regarding charitable activity.

Applications

In writing to the correspondent referenced 'Charitable donations'.

FIL Holdings (UK) Ltd (formerly Fidelity Investment Management Ltd)

Financial services

Correspondent: Corporate Citizenship Dept., Oakhill House, 130 Tonbridge Road, Hildenborough, Tonbridge Kent TN11 9DZ (website: www.fidelity.co.uk/investor/about/corporate-citizenship/default.page)

Directors: J. Burton; K. Isherwood; C. J. Rimmer; B. Weatherill; P. Shea; M. Webb

Year end	30/06/2014
Turnover	£814,698,000
Pre-tax profit	£31,537,000

Nature of business: Holding company for a group of companies whose principal business is the management and distribution of collective investment funds, the management of defined benefit pension funds, and the management and administration of defined contribution pension funds.

This entry formerly appeared as Fidelity Investment Management Ltd, which is a subsidiary of FIL Holdings (UK) Ltd.

Company registration number: 2349713

Subsidiary undertakings include: FIL Investment Advisors (UK) Ltd; FIL Investment Management Ltd; FIL Investments Services (UK) Ltd; FIL Investments International; FIL Pensions Management Ltd; Financial Administration Services Ltd.

Total employees: 2,492

Focus of giving: Education, health, ill health, arts, culture, community/social welfare.

Gifts in kind	✓
Matched funding	✓
Payroll giving	✓
Sponsorship	✓

Charitable donations

Cash UK (latest available):	2014	£10,200,000
	2013	£3,380,000
	2011	£10,161,205
	2009	£3,975,000
	2008	£5,942,000
Total UK (cash and in kind):	2014	£10,200,000
Cash worldwide:	2014	£10,200,000
Total worldwide (cash and in kind):	2014	£10,200,000

Community involvement

Fidelity directs its community support through two main channels:

Corporate Citizenship Programme

The programme supports local charities and employees in their efforts to contribute to their communities. Employees are encourage to lend their support to good causes through volunteering, fundraising and payroll giving. The group sponsors charity fundraising events and has a small budget from which grants are made to support local charities that are working to benefit the communities in areas where the group has a presence.

The Fidelity UK Foundation (Charity Commission no. 327899)
The foundation was established in 1988 to receive donations from FIL Ltd (FHL's parent company) and its UK subsidiaries. Operating as a grant-maker, the foundation supports UK-registered charities in areas where Fidelity has its corporate offices – London, Kent and Surrey – and applications are also considered from registered charities based and operating in Birmingham and Manchester. Grantmaking is directed towards the following sectors: arts and culture; community development; education; and health. Funding is typically directed towards projects in the following categories: capital improvements; information technology upgrades; organisational development; and planning initiatives.

Charity Partners have included: Age UK Hackney; Ataxia UK; Community Links; Create Arts; Help for Heroes; Mitchemp Trust.

Corporate giving

In 2013/14 FIL made donations of £10 million to **The Fidelity UK Foundation**. The group also made donations totalling £200,000 to a wide range of charities, including through the employee grant matching scheme. A 'substantial' number of individual donations were made to, for example, local children's charities, schools and hospitals.

We have taken our financial information from the annual report and accounts of FIL Holdings (UK) Ltd (FHL) and have taken our CSR information from the website of FIL Ltd, which is the ultimate parent undertaking and controlling party FHL, registered in Bermuda.

See the corporate charity entry on p. 405 for more information.

Employee-led support

Fidelity supports and encourages its employees to be active members of their communities. They do this through the schemes listed below.

Grant matching
Through the employee grant-matching programme, funds raised for charitable organisations are matched by the company.

Volunteering
Fidelity provides its employees with access to potential volunteering opportunities. Activities have included mentoring and reading with schoolchildren, and sharing business expertise with headteachers. Group of employees have also participated with woodland clearing, decorating and building projects.

Payroll giving
Through Give As You Earn, Fidelity facilitates regular giving by providing this scheme for employees paid under PAYE.

Commercially led support

Sponsorship
Fidelity sponsors charity fundraising events in the areas local to its offices.

Corporate social responsibility

CSR committee: There is a dedicated Global ESG (Environmental, Social and Governance) Specialist, who works with management teams, directors and heads of research around the world, and sits on the Corporate Governance group.

CSR information: The Corporate Citizenship Programme is focused on three key areas:

- **Employees** – supporting employees to be active members of their communities through direct cash support and provision of volunteering and fundraising opportunities
- **Communities** – supporting the communities local to offices by sponsoring charity fundraising events and providing small grants to local charities
- **Volunteering** – supporting a favourite charity or a Fidelity selected charity by giving up time

We were unable to determine the ratio of women to men on the board of directors.

CSR report: There was no published CSR report; however, there is an informative 'Corporate Citizenship' section on the website.

Corporate charity: The Fidelity UK Foundation (Charity Commission no. 327899).

Exclusions

Fundraising events sponsorship
Fidelity does not support the following:

- Religious, political and animal-support charities
- Individuals and individual schools
- Events for exclusive audiences such as black tie events
- High-risk activities, such as parachute jumps, motor racing and abseiling

Sports events, clubs and teams and advertisements in charity event programmes, diaries or directories are not usually supported.

The foundation – see the foundation entry for a full list of exclusions.

Applications

The Fidelity UK Foundation
In writing to the correspondent. Applicants should enclose a summary form (which can be downloaded from the foundation's website) as well as a separate document outlining:

- Organisation history and key achievements
- An overview of the organisations forward strategy and key objectives

You should also attach the following:

- A list of the directors and trustees with their backgrounds
- The most recently audited annual financial statements
- The most recent monthly management accounts

See the foundation website for further details: www.fidelityukfoundation.org

Contact the foundation at: Head of Foundations, Oakhill House, 130 Tonbridge Road, Hildenborough, Kent TN11 9DZ; Tel: 01732 777364

Note: Grants for projects outside the UK are awarded by the FIL Foundation, a separate organisations, whose main donor is Fidelity Worldwide Investment. More details are available from the Fidelity UK Foundation website.

Corporate sponsorship and donations
Fundraising events sponsorship: Organisations that fit the following criteria are favoured for sponsorship:

- Support communities within ten miles of any Fidelity office
- Have a good profile locally
- Provide co-branding at their event
- Link us to related press coverage
- Are registered charities or not-for-profit organisations
- Organise fundraising events that directly benefit their users
- Provide opportunities for employee involvement

The website notes that: 'Generally we like to be the sole sponsor of an event, and favour those that benefit the wider community rather than an exclusive audience.'

Small grants for local charities: 'We have a small dedicated budget to support local organisations who deliver services at a grass roots level. These funds must go to a project that directly benefits the local community.'

For more information on these programmes, contact Fidelity's Corporate Citizenship department: Corporate Citizenship, FIL Ltd, 25 Cannon Street EC4M 5TA; Email: corporate.citizenship@fil.com.

Filtronic plc

Electronics/computers

Correspondent: HR Manager, Filtronic House, 3 Airport West, Lancaster Way, Yeadon, West Yorkshire LS19 7ZA (tel: 01132 200000; website: www.filtronic.co.uk)

Directors: Howard Ford, Chair; Alan Needle, Chief Executive; Rob Smith, Chief Financial Officer; Graham Meek; Reg Gott; Dr Maura Moynihan; Michael Roller (women: 1; men: 6)

Year end	31/05/2014
Turnover	£32,900,000
Pre-tax profit	(£3,673,000)

Nature of business: The principal activity is the design and manufacture of RF, microwave and millimetre wave components and subsystems.

Company registration number: 2891064

Subsidiary undertakings include: Filtronic Broadband Ltd; Filtronic Holdings UK Ltd; Isotek (Holdings) Ltd.

Main locations: Newton Aycliffe, Shipley, East Kilbride, Wolverhampton

Total employees: 186

Focus of giving: General charitable purposes.

Gifts in kind	✓
Matched funding	✓
Sponsorship	✓

Charitable donations

Cash UK (latest available):	2014	£100
	2013	£0
	2012	£500
	2011	£450
	2009	£0
Total UK (cash and in kind):	2014	£100
Cash worldwide:	2014	£100
Total worldwide (cash and in kind):	2014	£100

Community involvement

Filtronic plc supports charities, it would appear, mainly through the sponsorship of employees for their chosen charity events.

Corporate giving

In 2013/14 the group donated £100 to 'various charities'. We were unable to determine a value for the in-kind donations given by the group.

In-kind support

Following the relocation of its broadband business to Sedgefield, County Durham, in 2014 the group also provided practical help. This was given in the form of PCs to a local primary school and office and lab equipment, received by educational establishments.

Employee-led support

Matched funding

The group matches sponsorship given by employees for charity events of their choice. Recent beneficiaries have included The Stroke Association, Mind and Mind the Gap.

Commercially led support

The group aims to support engineering and technology, which it does through developing partnerships with universities. Activities have included: sponsoring a PhD student; awarding a sponsored prize to an 'outstanding undergraduate student' in electronic communications; and supporting knowledge sharing events.

Corporate social responsibility

CSR committee: We were unable to find evidence of there being a CSR committee.

CSR information: The group's approach to CSR is detailed within the CSR section of the annual report and accounts.

CSR report: There is a CSR section within the annual report and accounts.

Exclusions

The company will not support any political purposes.

Applications

In writing to the correspondent.

Findel plc

Catalogue shopping

Correspondent: The Company Secretary, 2 Gregory Street, Hyde, Cheshire SK14 4TH (tel: 01613 033465; fax: 01613 672139; website: www.findel.co.uk/csr/overview)

Directors: D. A. Sugden, Chair; R. W. J. Siddle, Chief Executive; T. J. Kowalski, Finance Director; P. B. Maudsley; E. F. Tracey; F. Coumau; W. Grimsey; A. Kinney Pritchard (women: 1; men: 7)

Year end	28/03/2014
Turnover	£514,700,000
Pre-tax profit	£22,000,000

Nature of business: Findel plc is a general merchandise supplier to the home and education sectors.

Company registration number: 549034

Subsidiary undertakings include: Express Gifts Ltd; Kitbag Ltd; Kleeneze Ltd; Findel Education Ltd.

Brands include: Davies Sports; Health and Home Shopping; Kitbag; Kleeneze.

UK employees: 2,088

Focus of giving: General charitable purposes, education, children, young people.

Cash donations undeclared	✓
Gifts in kind	✓

Charitable donations

Cash UK (latest available):	2014	£25,000
	2013	£26,000
	2012	£24,000
	2011	£16,000
	2009	£75,000
Total UK (cash and in kind):	2014	£25,000
Cash worldwide:	2014	£25,000
Total worldwide (cash and in kind):	2014	£25,000

Community involvement

Findel supports 'a number of local and national charities, together with local communities and organisations close to our various bases of operation'.

Corporate giving

We were unable to locate a figure for charitable donations given by Findel plc during the 2013/14 financial year. However, in the two preceding financial years (2011/12 and 2012/13), charitable donations averaged £25,000 each year. We have, therefore, taken this figure as an estimate for the group's donations in 2013/14.

We were not able to find a value for in-kind donations given by the group.

In-kind support

As part of a Business in the Community initiative, two of Findel's subsidiary companies, Express Gifts and Findel Education, have partnered local schools to provide 'support and guidance to staff and students'. Findel Education, as well as serving as a trustee to Sale Grammar School, also helps primary schoolchildren through its participation with the Greggs Breakfast Club, which promotes the importance of 'health, well-being and development'.

Employee-led support

Employee fundraising

The managing director of Kitbag, one of Findel plc's subsidiary companies, acts as a patron for Mahdlo, a youth organisation in Oldham. During the year, employees took part in a number of fundraising events for the organisation, including a 360 km, three-day charity bike ride which helped raise over £8,000.

Corporate social responsibility

CSR committee: There does not appear to be a dedicated CSR committee.

CSR information: The following statement is taken from the group's website:

> The success of the group is firmly linked to its actions in respect of its corporate social responsibilities. As well as remaining fully compliant with all relevant legislation, the group is determined to continually evaluate and enhance its performance in this area.

CSR report: There is a CSR report contained within the annual report and accounts, which includes a small section on community support. There are also relevant pages on the website.

Applications

In writing to the correspondent referenced 'Charitable Donations'.

FirstGroup plc

Transport and communications

Correspondent: Charity and Sponsorship Committee, 395 King Street, Aberdeen AB24 5RP (tel: 01224 650100; fax: 01224 650140; website: www.firstgroupplc.com/responsibility.aspx)

Directors: John McFarlane, Chair; Tim O'Toole, Chief Executive; Chris Surch, Group Finance Director; Warwick Brady; Drummond Hall; Brian Wallace; Imelda Walsh; Jim Winestock; Mick Barker (women: 1; men: 8)

Year end	31/03/2014
Turnover	£6,717,400,000
Pre-tax profit	£58,500,000

Nature of business: The provision of passenger transport services primarily through the provision of local bus and coach services and passenger railways. The company operates in the UK and North America.

Company registration number: SC157176

Subsidiary undertakings include: First Aberdeen Ltd; First Beeline Buses Ltd; First Bristol Ltd; First Capital Connect Ltd; First Greater Western Ltd; First ScotRail Ltd

Main locations: London, Aberdeen

Total employees: 116,497

Focus of giving: General charitable purposes, economic generation, enterprise/training, environment, health, ill health, medical research, older people, sport, recreation, children, young people, community/social welfare, disability.

Membership: BITC, LBG

Cash donations undeclared	✓
Charity of the Year	✓
Gifts in kind	✓
Matched funding	✓
Overseas giving	✓
Payroll giving	✓
Sponsorship	✓

Charitable donations

Cash UK (latest available):	2013	£193,000
	2012	£254,000
	2011	£260,000
	2010	£64,000
	2009	£107,000
Cash worldwide:	2014	£949,000
Total worldwide (cash and in kind):	2014	£1,500,000

Community involvement

FirstGroup plc focuses the majority of its charitable involvement on promoting education, employability and skills (particularly in the areas of STEM), which it does, in the main, through donations of cash, in-kind support and staff volunteering time. Much of the group's community involvement, it would appear, is conducted at a local level 'at the heart of the communities' in which it operates. The group's website states that support is also focused 'in a number of other areas where strong, relevant partnerships with community organisations can provide mutual benefits for our business and our local communities'.

Charity of the Year: Macmillan Cancer Support

Other partnerships

Smallpiece Trust: The group works with the trust to deliver residential courses for young people to learn about specific areas of engineering. Nine of the group's graduate engineers from the UK Rail Division mentored school students attending the residential courses.

Forestry Commission England: Through a partnership with First TransPennine Express, grants from the Green Giants programme are made to projects contributing a 'long-term visible improvement' to the physical local environment, to the benefit of the local community. So far, 13 successful applicants have received £20,000 in grants.

As part of its efforts to 'keep people moving' on its services, the group also works alongside other charities, including those for people with disabilities or reduced mobility. These have included Guide Dogs for the Blind and RNIB, for example.

Corporate giving

In 2013/14 more than £1.5 million was contributed by the group. This included cash donations (£949,000), in-kind contributions (£395,000), and staff time (£172,000). Leverage, which includes funds raised by customers, and by employees through fundraising and payroll giving, amounted to an additional £387,000, though, as is our usual practice, we have not included this figure in the total for the group's community contributions.

We have no separate figure for cash donations in the UK. The average of these donations for the three most recent years for which we have figures was £193,000. We have taken this as an estimate for UK cash giving in 2013/14.

Charity partner: Macmillan Cancer Support

Since July 2012, the group has been in partnership with Macmillan, which has received support in the form of employee fundraising, as well as cash and in-kind corporate donations. Funds raised by FirstGroup go towards the charity's grant-making programme, which helps cancer patients suffering extreme financial hardship.

During the year, more than £303,000 was raised for Macmillan, of which the group contributed in-kind gifts, such as advertising space on buses, with a commercial value of £161,000, and gave £93,000 in corporate donations. Employees raised an additional £49,000. The partnership is on course to raise the target of £1 million by March 2015.

In-kind support

Gifts in kind

In-kind support given by the group includes donated travel tickets, advertising space and vehicle hire.

Staff time

The group's First Student service donated 271 hours of driver and vehicle time to schools and community groups during 2013/14.

Employee-led support

Payroll giving

The group operates a payroll giving scheme, through which 3.81% of its UK employees donate to charities.

Matched funding

The group operates a matched funding scheme.

Employee fundraising

During the year, FirstGroup employees took part in various charity fundraising activities for Macmillan Cancer Support. This included running marathons, baked bean baths and taking part in Macmillan's World's Biggest Coffee Morning, which raised £22,000.

Corporate social responsibility

CSR committee: There is a Charity and Sponsorship Committee.

CSR information: The following information was taken from the 2014 Corporate Responsibility Report:

> Our charitable programmes focus on those areas where we believe we can deploy our scale and expertise to achieve the greatest impact. Our programmes all link back to our vision – to provide solutions for an increasingly congested world, keeping people moving and communities prospering.
>
> Working at the heart of the communities we serve, our local teams are uniquely placed to drive this by:developing long-term partnerships with the charitable organisations most aligned with our businessmobilising our people to support these partnerships through our charity committees and charity champion programmes, and by encouraging personal commitments like fundraising and payroll giving.

CSR report: A CSR report is published annually and is available to download from the website.

Applications

At the time of writing, the group's charitable giving is currently under review. The annual report and accounts for 2013/14 state that after a 'robust' consultation to review the focus of its charitable giving programmes, the group 'will launch a fresh programme in 2014/15'.

Ford Motor Company Ltd

Motors and accessories

Correspondent: Director, Ford Britain Trust, Room 1/445, Eagle Way, Brentwood, Essex CM13 3BW (tel: 01277 252551; email: fbtrust@ford.com; website: www.ford.co.uk/fbtrust)

Directors: M. Ovenden, Chair; G. Hoare; M. Turner; S. Glanville; T. Holmes; M. Hallward; J. Skerry

Year end	31/12/2013
Turnover	£9,248,000,000
Pre-tax profit	£253,000,000

Nature of business: The Ford Motor Company Ltd is a wholly owned subsidiary of the Ford Motor Company of Dearborn, Michigan, USA.

The company's principal activity is the design, engineering and manufacture of low carbon technologies, commercial vehicles and automotive components and the sale of motor vehicles and automotive components.

The company and its subsidiaries operate principally in the UK and the Republic of Ireland. It is part of an integrated vehicle manufacturing group of Ford companies throughout Europe.

Company registration number: 235446

Subsidiary undertakings include: Ford Component Sales Ltd; Ford International Liquidity Management Ltd; Ford Retail Group Ltd; Henry Ford and Son Ltd

UK employees: 9,999

Total employees: 10,124

Focus of giving: Education, environment, health, ill health, local groups, older people, sport, recreation, children, young people, community/ social welfare, disability.

Membership: BITC

Cash donations undeclared ✓

Charitable donations

Cash UK (latest available):	2013	£167,000
	2011	£167,000
	2009	£313,000
	2008	£317,000
	2006	£828,000
Total UK (cash and in kind):	2013	£167,000
Cash worldwide:	2013	£167,000
Total worldwide (cash and in kind):	2013	£167,000

Community involvement

Ford Motor Company Ltd operates the **Ford Britain Trust** (registered charity: 269410), which makes grants for projects in communities close to Ford's locations, particularly those that focus on the areas of education, environment, children, disabled people, youth activities and projects working to benefit the community. The company also appears to support a small number of charities, including those in the areas of health and sports, some of which are supported on an ongoing basis. Employees are encouraged to contribute to their communities through volunteering efforts.

Corporate giving

The annual report and accounts for 2013 did not declare a figure for charitable donations during the year. In the last year for which we have a figure, these contributions totalled £167,000, and we have taken this as an estimate for charitable donations in 2013.

Beneficiaries included: BEN (Motor and Allied Trades Benevolent Fund); JDRF (Juvenile Diabetes Research Foundation) Lord's Taverners; Motorvations Projects Ltd; RJ Mitchell Primary School; Wooden Spoon.

See the corporate charity entry on p. 406 for more information.

Employee-led support

Employee volunteering

Ford employees are encouraged to contribute to their communities through volunteering their time and skills.

Corporate social responsibility

CSR committee: We found no evidence of a separate CSR Committee.

CSR information: The following information was obtained from the company's website:

> We define corporate social responsibility as being willing to help others, being environmentally conscious and socially tolerant. With those guiding principles in mind, we've designed a special programme to promote tolerance and equal opportunities, and actively support social and environmental protection programmes. Through our Ford Britain Trust, we provide grants to fund local education and other not-for-profit projects.

We were unable to determine the ratio of women to men on the board.

CSR report: There was a short CSR report included in the annual report and accounts.

Corporate charity: Ford Britain Trust (Charity Commission no. 269410).

Exclusions

Ford Britain Trust does not make grants for the following purposes:

- Major building works
- Sponsorship or advertising
- Research
- Overseas projects
- Travel
- Religious projects
- Political projects
- Purchase of second-hand vehicles
- Third party fundraising initiatives (exceptions may be made for fundraising initiatives by Ford Motor Company Ltd employees and retirees)

Applications

Ford Britain Trust

Applications can be made in three ways:

- Download the PDF version from the website to print out, complete and return by post to the correspondence address
- Save the Word version to your computer, complete it electronically and return it by email to fbtrust@ford.com
- Request a paper copy on 01277 252551 to complete and return by post to the correspondence address

Applications for large grants should include a copy of the organisation's most recent report and accounts.

Small grant applications are considered in March, June, September and November and should be submitted by the 1st of each month. Applications for large grants are considered in March and September.

Forth Ports plc

Marine

Correspondent: The Company Secretary, 1 Prince of Wales DockEdinburgh EH6 7DX (tel: 01315 558700; website: www.forthports.co.uk/about-us/CSR)

Directors: Charles Hammond; Perry Glading; Stuart Paterson; Simon Gray; Stuart Gray; Michael Seymour; Patrick Samson; Jean-Bastien Auger (Alternate); Russell Goodman; Graham Marr (women: 0; men: 10)

Year end	31/12/2013
Turnover	£217,200,000
Pre-tax profit	£69,400,000

Nature of business: Forth Ports plc (Forth Ports) provides handling and logistic-related services. Forth Ports owns and operates eight commercial ports on the Firth of Forth, the Firth of Tay and the Thames: Tilbury (London), Grangemouth, Dundee, Leith (Edinburgh), Rosyth, Methil, Burntisland, and Kirkcaldy.

Company registration number: SC134741

Subsidiary undertakings include: Forth Estuary Towage Ltd; Forth Ports Finance Ltd; Forth Properties Ltd; International Transport Ltd; Port of Dundee Ltd; Port of Tilbury London Ltd

Main locations: Tilbury, Leith, Dundee

UK employees: 1,140

Total employees: 1,140

Focus of giving: General charitable purposes, education, enterprise/training, health, ill health, disability.

Cash donations undeclared ✓
Gifts in kind ✓

Charitable donations

Cash UK (latest available):	2013	£21,000
	2010	£21,000
	2009	£20,000
Total UK (cash and in kind):	2013	£21,000
Cash worldwide:	2013	£21,000
Total worldwide (cash and in kind):	2013	£21,000

Community involvement

Forth Ports Ltd looks to engage with local communities, and particularly those impacted by its projects. Its charitable contributions extend from cash donations, to fundraising, to in-kind support in the form of services, time and support, and appear to be focused primarily on the areas of education and skills development. Amongst its charitable activities, the group's Tilbury port has assisted local schools and 'actively' supports Thurrock Council through the Thurrock Learning Partnership and the Thurrock Workforce Development Group. Forth Ports also funds two PhD students at the universities of Glasgow and Dundee.

Organisations working on projects related to the group's nature of business, for example, Seafarer's UK, have, in the past, benefitted from the fundraising activities of employees.

Corporate giving

We were unable to find a figure for community/charitable contributions in the 2013 annual report and accounts. The average of donations in the years for which we have figures was £21,000, and we have taken this as an estimate for 2013 charitable giving.

In-kind support

Forth Ports offers its land free of charge for certain public events and has previously donated land to The Merchant Navy Memorial Trust, upon which a monument was erected.

Pro bono

The group's website states that across a number of its ports, but especially Tilbury, it provides interview training for young people in schools, supports 'educational challenges' and offers work experience opportunities.

Employee-led support

Employee fundraising

Employees have taken part in fundraising activities, including white water rafting, to help raise funds for charitable causes.

Corporate social responsibility

CSR committee: We found no evidence of there being a CSR committee.

CSR information: The following information was obtained from the website: 'We believe that it is important to engage with local communities, particularly where projects we are progressing have an impact on them.'

CSR report: We found no evidence of there being a CSR report.

Applications

In writing to the correspondent, referenced 'Charitable donations'.

Freshfields Bruuckhaus Deringer LLP

Legal

Correspondent: Corporate Responsibility Dept., 65 Fleet Street, London EC4Y 1HS (tel: 020 7936 4000; fax: 020 7832 7001; website: www.freshfields.com)

Directors: William Lawes, Senior Partner; David Aitman, Managing Partner; Stephen Eilers, Executive Partner (women: 0; men: 3)

Year end	30/04/2014
Turnover	£1,277,800,000
Pre-tax profit	£514,800,000

Nature of business: The provision of legal services through a network of offices in Europe, Asia, the Middle East and the United States.

Company registration number: OC334789

Subsidiary undertakings include: A full list of the group's principal investments is given in the annual report and accounts.

Main locations: London

Total employees: 4,621

Focus of giving: Education, enterprise/training, health, ill health, housing, homelessness, children, young people, community/social welfare.

Membership: BITC, LBG

Charitable donations

Cash UK (latest available):	2008	£540,000
	2007	£490,447
	2006	£481,994
	2005	£245,949
Total worldwide (cash and in kind):	2014	£15,460,000

Community involvement

Social inclusion is the core theme of Freshfields Bruckhaus Deringer's global community investment programme. The firm's projects look to make a positive contribution to the communities in which it operates, focusing on education, raising aspirations and building employability skills. The firm's offices around the world work in partnership with various organisations to deliver on its community objectives.

Through its pro bono programme, the firm contributes its legal expertise 'for the public good' and focuses its work particularly on shaping the areas around the rule of law, access to justice, and work to support the Millennium Development Goals (eight international development goals established by the United Nations in 2000).

Corporate giving

The Responsible Business Update Report 2014 shows that £15.46 million was given in community contributions during the year. This figure includes management costs and we were unable to determine the amount given in cash and pro bono contributions in the UK.

Beneficiaries have included: Shelter

In-kind support

Pro bono

The Responsible Business Update Report 2014 states the following:

> The work our pro bono programme takes on ranges from one-off legal interventions on important areas of law, to supporting the legal needs of global NGOs tasked with assisting the world's most vulnerable people and hundreds of different matters in between.
>
> Over the past year we have seen our programme reach over 56,000 hours – the most pro bono hours we have ever recorded.

In 2013/14, across the firm, 39% of employees were involved in pro bono and community investment work, helping to contribute a total of more than 79,000 working hours.

Examples include:

Homelessness – The firm gives pro bono support as part of its efforts to help combat youth homelessness. From its London base, the firm staffs a housing law clinic in Tower Hamlets and has sent a trainee to their housing team on secondment). Through its involvement with Shelter, support has also been given with casework involving children and with strategic interventions at the Court of Appeal and Supreme Court.

Improving access to justice – In the UK, following cuts to legal aid and local government advice funding Freshfields' pitched 'CourtNav' to its pro bono client, the Royal Courts of Justice Advice Bureau.

The website states: 'CourtNav is an online tool helps people who can't afford a lawyer navigate the court system. As well as our legal input, Freshfields IT and PR professionals advised on the tool. The prototype secured funding from the Ministry of Justice to develop the first module.'

Employee-led support

Employee volunteering

Employees are encouraged to spend at least one business day a year volunteering with a team for a community challenge sponsored by the firm.

Payroll giving

Aside from their involvement with Freshfields' community investment and pro bono work, employees are also able to support charities through payroll giving. During the year, 5% of UK employees donated through the scheme.

Matched giving

Employees are support in their fundraising efforts through a matched giving scheme.

Commercially led support

Ready for Work programme

The firm's London office has worked on the work experience, training and job coaching programme run in conjunction with Business in the Community. The programme aims to 'break the cycle of homelessness'. Similar initiatives are carried out by the firm's offices based around the globe.

Corporate social responsibility

CSR information: The following information was obtained from the Responsible Business Update Report 2014: 'At Freshfields, the global theme of our community investment programme is social inclusion. Our projects focus on education, raising aspirations and building employability skills within the communities where we operate.'

CSR report: The firm publishes an annual CSR report. In 2014, this took the title of a 'Responsible Business Update'.

Applications

In writing to the correspondent.

Friends Life Group plc (formerly Friends Provident plc)

Insurance

Correspondent: Corporate Responsibility Manager, Pixham End, Dorking, Surrey RH4 1QA (tel: 0845 602 9189; fax: 01306 740150; website: www.friendslife.com/crreport)

Directors: Sir Malcolm Williamson, Chair; Andy Briggs, Group Chief Executive; Tim Tookey, Chief Financial Officer; David Allvey; Tim Wade; Nick Lyons; Karl Sternberg; Mel Carvill; Marian Glen; Peter Gibbs; Roger Perkin; Robert Phipps; Belinda Richards (women: 2; men: 11)

Year end	31/12/2013
Turnover	£10,989,000,000
Pre-tax profit	£369,000,000

Nature of business: Friends Life Group Ltd is a FTSE 100 listed company focused on providing financial security for over five million customers, with a heritage dating back over 200 years.

The following information was obtained from the website:

> Friends Life was created in 2011 following the amalgamation of Friends Provident plc, the majority of the AXA UK Life insurance business and Bupa Health Assurance, as part of the Resolution Group's UK Life Project. The businesses were brought together and rebranded to form Friends Life Group, providing pensions, investments and insurance and retirement income products, alongside a heritage business looking after legacy products and an International division.
>
> On 8 May 2014 following approval at its AGM, Resolution Ltd changed its listed brand name to Friends Life Group Ltd.

Company registration number: 4113107

Brands include: fpg AG, Friends Life, Friends Provident International, Sesame Bankhall Group

Main locations: Dorking, Exeter, Salisbury, Manchester

Total employees: 4

Focus of giving: General charitable purposes, education, health, ill health, medical research, sponsorship, sport, recreation, children, young people, disability.

Membership: BITC, LBG

Charity of the Year	✓
FTSE 100	✓
Gifts in kind	✓
Matched funding	✓
Overseas giving	✓
Payroll giving	✓
Sponsorship	✓

Charitable donations

Cash UK (latest available):	2009	£180,000
	2008	£55,000
	2007	£83,000
Cash worldwide:	2013	£1,538,000
Total worldwide (cash and in kind):	2013	£1,900,000

Community involvement

Friends Life supports the communities local to its offices through cash and donations of staff time and expertise. It supports its employees' charitable involvement through matched funding and Give As You Earn schemes, notably through its annual Challenge Fortnight.

Financial resilience

Much of the group's community investment in the UK is currently targeted towards promoting financial resilience for individuals and communities. It has recently invested financially to set up named endowments with community foundations near to its offices in the UK, funding from which will be directed towards 'money management and debt advice issues'. In 2014 its employees ran workshop sessions for groups from the Prince's Trust XL clubs to promote the benefits of saving instead of borrowing.

Corporate giving

In 2013 the group contributed a total of almost £1.9 million, of which £1.5 million was given in cash. Through its Challenge Fortnight, the group contributed employee time worth £133,000.

The group invested £45,000 in establishing named endowments with community foundations close to its UK offices.

During the year, employees contributed around £116,000 to charity through the payroll giving facility, with the group contributing a further £50,000 in administration costs and matched funding. Employees also raised more than £233,000 for charitable causes, including £33,000 for BBC Children in Need. Employees also raised funds for Friends Life partner charity, Macmillan Cancer Support. As is our usual practice, we have not included employee-raised funds in our total for company charitable contributions.

We were unable to determine a total amount for UK charitable contributions from the group.

Charity of the Year

Macmillan Cancer Support: The group entered into partnership with Macmillan in 2011 and, together with its employees, has helped to raise funds for specific Macmillan-led projects. These have included the development of a Welfare Benefits and Information Centre at UCL Hospital in London, and another similar centre at Lister Hospital in Stevenage.

For the latter project, £140,000 was raised through employee fundraising and company donations.

The information used in this entry was obtained from the group's CR report microsite.

In-kind support

Staff time

The group invested 7,309 hours of staff working time in 2013.

Employee-led support

Payroll giving

The group operates the Give As You Earn scheme. Figures state that, in 2013, 314 employees (11.2% of eligible UK colleagues) gave through the scheme.

Matched funding

In 2013 an annual budget of £25,000 was reintroduced for matched funding purposes for causes other than the group's official charity partner, Macmillan Cancer Support. The group's CR report microsite states that: 'This was in direct response to colleague demand, and is intended to refocus our community engagement to provide more direct support to local or national causes that Friends Life colleagues care about, usually for very personal reasons.'

Employee fundraising

The group's employee fundraising is led by a network of community ambassadors across its UK offices. In 2013 74 community ambassadors volunteered 1,776 hours of time which has been instrumental in making colleague fundraising the success it has been.

Employee volunteering

The annual Challenge Fortnight saw teams of employees contribute to community projects, which included ground clearance for a local hospice and creating a relaxation area for a disability charity. In 2013 more than 700 employees took part.

Employees in the groups various offices around the world also volunteered in aid of local causes. For example, Friends Provident International volunteered a combined total of more than 575 hours to 18 different charities local to offices in the Isle of Man, Hong Kong, Dubai and Singapore.

As part of the group's community engagement activities, the group looked to reward the volunteering efforts of its employees with the introduction of the annual Community and Environment Champion Awards. These awards recognise employees who have given their 'time and energy' in support of good causes 'both in work and in the wider community'.

Commercially led support

Sponsorship

In the Isle of Man, Friends Provident International sponsored the Heroes in the Community awards, which takes place at a ceremony which celebrates 'everyday heroes'.

For the third year running, Friends Life also sponsored the Business in the Community 'Seeing is Believing' alumni network.

Corporate social responsibility

CSR committee: There is a Corporate Responsibility Strategy Committee (CRSC). The following was stated in the group's annual report and accounts:

> Following the simplification of the governance structure, the composition of the Corporate Responsibility Strategy Committee (CRSC) changed. Until May 2013 it was chaired by Phil Hodkinson and on his resignation Andy Briggs, Group Chief Executive, took responsibility for chairing these meetings. The CRSC comprises all members of the Group Executive Committee and Marian Glen, an independent non-executive director. The CRSC's terms of reference are reviewed annually to ensure they clearly set out the purpose of the Committee and guidance on the parameters of the Group's activities. Each year the CRSC produce a report which summarises the Group's activities throughout the year.

CSR information: The following information was obtained from the annual report and accounts:

> During 2013 the CRSC identified four overarching areas: Workplace, Environment, Community and Marketplace, and within each of these four core areas identified 16 areas of activity. These were prioritised according to business need. Key initiatives prioritised during the year were actions within Workplace and Community that focused on driving up employee engagement, strengthening our partnership with Macmillan Cancer Support and generating momentum for Diversity and Wellbeing.

CSR report: A CSR report is published within the annual report and accounts. There is also an informative CSR microsite.

Exclusions

Our research suggests that the company does not support: individuals conducting their own fundraising for charity; political or religious organisations, including local churches; overseas trips and travel expenses; or applications for specialist school status or school building projects.

Applications

Our research indicates that enquiries regarding corporate support at a local level should be addressed to the appropriate person at the relevant site.

Fujitsu Services Holdings plc

Information technology

Correspondent: Head of Corporate Social Responsibility, 22 Baker Street, London W1U 3BW (tel: 08433547998; website: www.fujitsu.com/uk/about/local/corporate-responsibility)

Directors: Duncan Tait; Stephen Clayton; Ella Bennett; David Roberts; Akihisa Kamata; Yoshikazu Kudoh; Hidehiro Tsukano; Hidenori Furuta

Year end	31/03/2014
Turnover	£2,419,400,000
Pre-tax profit	£80,800,000

Nature of business: Holding company of an IT services group.

Company registration number: 142200

Subsidiary undertakings include: Fujitsu (Ireland) Ltd; Fujitsu Services Ltd; Fujitsu Services (Insurance Services) Ltd; Fujitsu Services Holding BV; Fujitsu Services Inc., Fujitsu Telecommunications Europe Ltd

Main locations: London

UK employees: 11,610

Total employees: 15,854

Focus of giving: General charitable purposes, education, enterprise/training, marginalised people, armed forces personnel, poverty and social exclusion, science technology, children, young people.

Membership: BITC

Charity of the Year	✓
Gifts in kind	✓
Matched funding	✓

Charitable donations

Cash UK (latest available):	2014	£133,000
	2013	£166,000
	2011	£149,500
	2009	£126,000
	2008	£107,000
Total UK (cash and in kind):	2014	£133,000
Cash worldwide:	2014	£133,000
Total worldwide (cash and in kind):	2014	£133,000

Community involvement

Fujitsu UK and Ireland looks to address issues affecting the communities in which it operates in three main ways: by forming relationships with charities and community groups; running a Charity Partner (Charity of the Year) scheme; and employee community involvement. Aside from its Charity of the Year partnership, which runs on a two year basis, Fujitsu has also partnered Business in the Community (BITC) and has supported Children in Need and The Prince's Trust, which have benefitted from support including employee fundraising and volunteering.

Five areas in which Fujitsu might make the biggest difference have been identified: youth unemployment; digital divide; social exclusion; disadvantaged children; and armed forces involvement.

Impact on Society (IOS) groups
Charitable involvement is conducted at a local level through regional Impact on Society groups. These groups are led by employees and manage requests for funding and sponsorship, as well as employee volunteering opportunities in their local area.

Corporate giving

The annual report and accounts 2013/14 state that, during the year, the group made donations of £133,000.

We were unable to determine a value for the in-kind contributions made by the group.

Charity of the Year
Shelter was Fujitsu UK and Ireland's Charity Partner for 2012–2014, during which time the charity benefitted from contributions of £353,000, of which £153,000 was in pro bono services and equipment. The charity will continue to receive support from the group on an ad-hoc basis. The 2014–2016 Charity of the Year, nominated by employees is Action for Children.

In-kind support

Staff time
Fujitsu employees are able to commit one day per year to sharing their time and skills with locally and company-led charitable and community causes.

Gifts in kind
Support has been given in the form of gifts in kind; for example, Fujitsu Telecommunications Europe Ltd (FTEL) provided facilities and equipment at a school for children with autism.

Employee-led support

'Impact on Society'
Employees are able to support their local communities through Impact on Society groups and also support Fujitsu's partner charities. IOS offers a variety of volunteering opportunities for employees and, where possible, provides financial support for staff fundraising and volunteering activities.

Commercially led support

One of the aims of the Impact on Society groups is to engage with schools and colleges to promote careers in ICT.

Corporate social responsibility

CSR committee: The following information was taken from the online Corporate Responsibility Report:

> Responsibility for Fujitsu's Corporate Social Responsibility (CSR) is held by Gavin Bounds, Chief Operating Officer, on behalf of Michael Keegan, Head of UK & Ireland, and Duncan Tait, Head of EMEIA.
>
> Gavin Bounds chairs both the EMEIA Responsible Business Board and the UK Responsible Business Board. These direct our CSR programme, oversee implementation and review performance against targets. Membership of the UK & Ireland Responsible Business Board (281 KB) includes all of our Executive Leadership Team, senior members of the CSR team and additional stakeholders.

CSR information: The Fujitsu approach to CSR is based around five pillars: environment; social action; inclusion; well-being; and safety.

The following information was obtained from the online CSR report:

> Our community engagement has grown strongly in recent times and we are committed to sustaining and improving on this over the coming year through effective charitable and community relationships and employee led activities. The work we do in the community is guided not only by the needs of communities, but by issues that are important to Fujitsu.

CSR report: Fujitsu UK and Ireland publishes a CSR report online.

Applications

In writing to the correspondent. The Fujitsu UK and Ireland online CSR report states the following: 'Each IOS region is allocated a budget to support or sponsor causes that fit the remit.' We would, therefore, suggest that local funding requests should be made in writing to the Impact on Society group at the relevant site.

Future plc

Media

Correspondent: Human Resources Dept, Quay House, The Ambury, Bath BA1 1UA (tel: 01225 442244; website: www.futureplc.com)

Directors: Peter Allen, Chair; Zillah Byng-Maddick, Chief Executive; Richard Haley, Chief Financial Officer and Company Secretary; Manjit Wolstenholm; Mark Whiteling; Mark Wood (women: 2; men: 4)

Year end	30/09/2013
Turnover	£112,300,000
Pre-tax profit	£5,800,000

Nature of business: Future plc produces magazines, websites, events and a range of multi-media services for commercial partners.

Company registration number: 3757874

Subsidiary undertakings include: Future Publishing Ltd; Future US, Inc.

Main locations: Bath

UK employees: 831

Total employees: 980

Focus of giving: Health, ill health, small groups, children, young people, community/social welfare, disability.

Cash donations undeclared ✓

Charitable donations

Cash UK (latest available):	2013	£29,000
	2012	£12,000
	2011	£37,000
	2010	£39,000
	2009	£55,000
Total UK (cash and in kind):	2013	£29,000
Cash worldwide:	2013	£29,000
Total worldwide (cash and in kind):	2013	£29,000

Community involvement

Future plc looks to engage in the communities where it has a presence. Since 2008 the group has a named revenue fund with the Bath-based Quartet Community Foundation, which administers grants to small local charities and voluntary groups on its behalf.

Corporate giving

The 2013 annual report did not include figures for charitable donations made by the group during the year. From the information that was available in previous years' annual reports, we can see that charitable donations from the group had decreased from £39,000 (2010) to £12,000 (2012). While we have estimated the 2013 total for charitable donations based on the average of figures available from the three previous years, there was no indication in the latest annual report of the group having continued its matched funding scheme. With these factors in mind, the amount given by the group during the 2013 may have varied significantly from our £29,000 estimate.

Recent beneficiaries have included: Bath Deaf Club; the Beechen Cliff Youth Project; and Positive Action on Cancer.

Employee-led support

Employee volunteering
The group's London-based Advertising and Sales Team have worked in partnership with the Apples and Pears playground in Hackney. Staff based overseas in the US helped to support a food bank in San Francisco and organised a 'goodwill clothing drive'.

Commercially led support

The group holds The Golden Joystick Awards, which recognises the best computer and video games in the market and, during the year, helped to raise money for GamesAid, a charity based in the UK which supports disabled and disadvantaged children.

Corporate social responsibility

CSR committee: There was no evidence of a separate CSR Committee.

CSR information: Future actively supports the communities in which it operates through charitable donations and by encouraging employees to get involved with community initiatives.

CSR report: There is a section dedicated to corporate responsibility in the annual report.

Applications

Donations are made on behalf of the group by Quartet Community Foundation. More details are available on the foundation's website (www.quartetcf.org.uk).

G4S plc

Transport and communications

Correspondent: CSR Dept., The Manor, Manor Royal, Crawley, West Sussex RH10 9UN (tel: 020 8770 7000; email: csr@g4s.com; website: www.g4s.com/en/Social%20Responsibility)

Directors: John Connolly, Chair; Mark Seligman, Deputy Chair; Ashley Almanza, Chief Executive; Adam Crozier; Mark Elliott; Grahame Gibson; Winnie Kin Wah Fok; Himanshu Raja, Chief Financial Officer; Paul Spence; Clare Spottiswoode; Tim Weller (women: 2; men: 9)

Year end	31/12/2013
Turnover	£7,428,000,000
Pre-tax profit	(£170,000,000)

Nature of business: G4S plc provides security services, cash services and justice services internationally.

Company registration number: 4992207

Subsidiary undertakings include: G4S Cash Solutions (UK) Ltd; G4S Integrated Services (UK) Ltd; G4S Risk Management Ltd; G4S Secure Solutions (UK) Ltd; G4S Security Services (UK) Ltd; G4S Utility and Outsourcing Service (UK) Ltd.

Main locations: Crawley

Total employees: 618,000

Focus of giving: General charitable purposes, education, health, ill health, children, young people, community/social welfare.

Membership: BITC

Cash donations undeclared	✓
FTSE 100	✓
Overseas giving	✓

Charitable donations

Cash UK (latest available):	2012	£2,600,000
	2011	£52,000
	2010	£63,000
	2009	£311,000
	2008	£313,000
Cash worldwide:	2013	£932,000
Total worldwide (cash and in kind):	2013	£1,300,000

Community involvement

G4S community involvement is operated on a 'decentralised' basis at a local level. The group predominantly supports the health, education and welfare of children and young people, 'with the wider aim of helping to raise aspirations and reduce crime in those communities' by working with community and charity partners. Support is given through cash donations, the provision of in-kind goods and services and contributions of staff time through employee volunteering activities. The group also looks to support sports organisations and people through sponsorship.

Crimestoppers partnership

G4S UK has entered into partnership with Crimestoppers, by which employees will be recruited and trained to deliver Fearless, a programme to 'help educate and empower young people with the knowledge and choices to enable them to make their community a safer place.

Corporate giving

In 2013 the group contributed cash donations and provided goods and services worth a total £1.3 million. More than 400 community programmes in 76 countries benefitted.

Of the total contributed, £932,000 was in the form of cash support. We believe this included matched funding of employee-raised funds to the value of £28,000, given in more than 70 payments for local community causes. Beneficiaries included a children's hospital ward, veterans' injury rehabilitation and equipment for schools.

Goods and services given amounted to £407,000

The group also facilitated employee and third party donations totalling £93,000, though, as is our usual practice, we have not included this in the figure for corporate contributions.

We were unable to determine a figure for cash or in-kind contributions given in the UK.

In-kind support

Gifts in kind

The group contributes in-kind donations to community programmes and charities through the provision of goods and services.

Staff time

During 2013, the group facilitated 26,000 hours worth of employee volunteering time.

Employee-led support

Employee volunteering

G4S employees are able to contribute to their local communities through volunteering.

Employee fundraising

In the UK, employees have fundraised by participating in charity bike rides, sponsored marathon runs, hill climbs and abseiling, for example.

Matched funding

The group operates its matched funding scheme, Match-it, by which it matches employee fundraising efforts up to the value of £500 per application.

Commercially led support

Sponsorship

The website states that sponsorship is one of the ways in which G4S 'supports many clubs and sports people'.

Corporate social responsibility

CSR committee: The CSR Committee has been a full board committee since 2011. The group website states:

> The CSR Committee is responsible for reviewing and monitoring the group's CSR strategy. This includes developing policies on various CSR-related matters for consideration by the board, reviewing the activities of the executives who are responsible for CSR matters and monitoring performance of the group against its policies and any associated targets. It also takes responsibility for the company's CSR report.

CSR information: G4S seeks to make a positive impact on local communities. The group encourages investment in community projects, whether directly through cash or through staff volunteering, and fundraising. The majority of the group's investment focuses on the health, education, welfare and support of children and young people.

CSR report: A CSR report was available from the company's website.

Applications

In writing to the correspondent.

Game Digital plc (formerly The Game Group plc)

Computer software

Correspondent: The Corporate Responsibility Committee, Unity House, Telford Road, Basingstoke, Hampshire RG21 6YJ (tel: 01256 784000; website: www.gamegroup.plc.uk)

Directors: David Hamid, Chair; Martyn Gibbs, Chief Executive Officer; Benedict Smith, Chied Financial Officer; John Jackson; Lesley Watkins; Caspar Wooley; Franck Tuil (women: 1; men: 6)

Year end	26/07/2014
Turnover	£861,800,000
Pre-tax profit	£7,300,000

Nature of business: The group is a video games retailer in the UK and Spain trading through stores, online and mobile channels.

Previously we have used the details of The Game Group plc which went into administration in 2012. The business was re-started through Game Digital plc.

Company registration number: 9040213

Subsidiary undertakings include: Capitex Holdings Ltd; Cherrilux Investments S.à.r.l;.Game Retail Ltd; and Game Stores Iberia SLU. Further details can be obtained from Companies House.

Total employees: 4,712

Focus of giving: General charitable purposes.

Cash donations undeclared	✓
Gifts in kind	✓
Market-led giving	✓
Staff fundraising only	✓

Charitable donations

Cash UK (latest available):	2011	£173,000
	2010	£160,000

Community involvement

It seems that currently support is mainly channelled through employees' involvement.

Corporate giving

The annual report and accounts did not seem to declare the amount given in charitable contributions. It appears that currently support is mainly given by employees. Previous the company has given about £167,000 a year on average (based on the figures from two previous years known to us).

In-kind support

The group can donate gaming items. We were unable to identify the cost to the company.

Employee-led support

National and local community projects

According to the annual report and accounts Game Digital seeks to make 'a positive impact on the local communities in which [it is] based and are proud to support [its] staff and even customers in their individual fundraising efforts for their charitable causes'. In 2012/13 the group 'raised funds, donated gaming items and provided support to over 300 individual charities across a wide range of community projects at both a local and national level'. Supported activities include cake sales, ice bucket challenges, and marathons or treks between GAME stores.

Furthermore, the accounts state:

> Over the coming year our teams will be focused on establishing a clearly defined community investment programme that fully leverages our community of gamers, our wider local communities and the group's strengths to maximise the positive difference we can achieve in our community.

Commercially led support

Protecting younger customers

The group works with industry bodies, including the Entertainment and Leisure Software Publishers Association (ELSPA), the Video Standards Council (VSC) and the Entertainment Retailers Association (ERA), 'to advise and share best practice across the industry' in order to ensure customers' safety.

Corporate social responsibility

CSR committee: It would appear that, unlike previously, there is no separate CSR committee. The board and the CEO are ultimately responsible for the CSR matters.

CSR information: The group's website states the following:

> We have a duty to maintain the trust of our colleagues, customers, owners, suppliers and other stakeholders by ensuring that we act with integrity at all times. Corporate and Social Responsibility is a core part of that commitment. We recognise that by acting in a responsible and considerate way with everyone who comes into contact with us, we will positively impact both the societies we operate in and the gaming communities that lie at the heart of our business, supporting the long-term value of the company.
>
> We are at the beginning of our CSR journey and are focused on developing a comprehensive, integrated and enduring CSR strategy that touches every part of the group, building on the foundations we have put in place to reduce our impact on the environment, ensuring we act as a responsible and fair employer and supporting the national and local community projects that our staff are involved in.

CSR report: CSR details are published within the annual report and accounts.

Applications

In writing to the correspondent.

GAP (UK Holdings) Ltd

Clothing manufacture, retail – clothing and footwear

Correspondent: The Company Secretary, Berkeley Square House, Berkeley Square, London, WIJ 6BS (website: www.gapinc.com/content/csr/html.html)

Directors: R. Chelemedos; N. Groom; D. Mireskandari (women: 3; men: 7)

Year end	01/02/2014
Turnover	£268,124,000
Pre-tax profit	£2,988,000

Nature of business: A regional merchandise purchasing company.

At 1 February 2014, the immediate parent company was Gap (RHC) B.V., a company registered in the Netherlands. The ultimate parent company and controlling entity was The Gap Inc., a company incorporated and registered in the United States of America.

Company registration number: 3720778

Subsidiary undertakings include: A list of subsidiary investments is included in the annual report and accounts.

Main locations: London, Coventry, Rugby

Focus of giving: Education, health, ill health, arts, culture, community/social welfare.

Charitable donations

Cash UK (latest available):	2014	£110,000
	2011	£110,000
	2009	£110,000
	2008	£110,000
	2007	£108,000
Total UK (cash and in kind):	2014	£110,000
Cash worldwide:	2014	£110,000
Total worldwide (cash and in kind):	2014	£110,000

Community involvement

Our research indicates that UK donations are given through the **Gap Foundation**. Whilst the company provides much information on its grant-making activities in the USA, little is available on its work in the UK. However, based on previous research, funding appears to come via the Gap Foundation, it can be assumed that the main areas of work supported here are as they are globally. These areas are: underserved youth in the developed world and women in the developing world. Based on previous research, it would appear that the geographical focus of its UK support is Warwickshire and the surrounding areas, with some support also given to charities based in London, where the company has an office.

Corporate giving

The annual report and accounts for 2013/14 did not include a figure for charitable donations. Our research indicates that UK giving through the Gap Foundation averages around £110,000, though the company's actual contribution may vary from this figure.

Previous beneficiaries have included: Prince's Trust (£45,000); NCH Children's Charity (£25,000); Centrepoint (£25,000); Coventry and Warwickshire YMCA (£8,000); and Bradby Club – Rugby (£6,000).

In-kind support

Gifts in kind

Gap partners with Gifts In Kind International (GIKI) to process all merchandise donations that become available.

Employee-led support

Matched funding

Our previous research indicates that the foundation matches funds raised by employees for qualifying charitable organisations.

Employee volunteering

It would appear that employees volunteer 'their time and talent' to community organisations in their local areas.

Corporate social responsibility

CSR information: We were unable to determine details of Social Responsibility policies specific to the UK. It would appear that Social Responsibility practices are managed and reported on at a global level by Gap Inc., the ultimate parent company.

Applications

Cash donations: Gap Foundation does not accept unsolicited proposals or requests for sponsorships.

In-kind donations: The following information was obtained from the Gap Inc. website:

> Gap Foundation typically does not make merchandise donations by request. We do, however, partner with Gifts In Kind International (GIKI) to process all merchandise donations that become available. Interested nonprofit organisations may sign up with GIKI to potentially receive donations from Gap Inc. and all of GIKI's other clients.

GE Healthcare Ltd

Healthcare

Correspondent: The Company Secretary, Pollard's Wood, Nightingale Lane, Chalfont St Giles, Buckinghamshire HP8 4SP (tel: 01494 544000; email: sustainability@ge.com; website: www.gesustainability.com)

Directors: Mr P. Grenouillet; Mr M. Murphy; Mr K. O'Neill; Mr R. A. Cornell, Jr (women: 0; men: 4)

Year end	31/12/2013
Turnover	£181,679,000
Pre-tax profit	(£8,101,000)

Nature of business: Principal activities are the development, manufacture and sale of specialised products for research-based biotechnology supply and for the diagnosis and treatment of disease. Major UK locations are Pollards Wood, Hatfield, Little Chalfont, Amersham and Belfast.

The company's immediate parent undertaking is GE Healthcare UK Ltd, a company incorporated in England and Wales. The ultimate parent undertaking is General Electric Company, a company incorporated in the United States of America.

Company registration number: 1002610

Subsidiary undertakings include: GE Healthcare SAS; Amersham Japan KK; Amersham NMP China Ltd; Imanet Holdings Ltd; Nihan Medi-Physics Co. Limited; GE Healthcare d.o.o.

Main locations: Amersham, Aberdeen, Cardiff, Chalfont St Giles, Little Chalfont, Gloucester

Total employees: 1,294

Focus of giving: General charitable purposes, education, health, ill health, community/social welfare.

Cash donations undeclared	✓
Gifts in kind	✓
Matched funding	✓
Overseas giving	✓

Charitable donations

Cash UK (latest available):	2013	£57,000
	2011	£57,000
	2009	£63,000
	2008	£90,000
	2006	£23,000
Total UK (cash and in kind):	2013	£57,000
Cash worldwide:	2013	£57,000
Total worldwide (cash and in kind):	2013	£57,000

Community involvement

Information on the community involvement of GE Healthcare in the UK appears to be limited. It would appear that charitable support from GE companies is filtered through **GE Foundation** (US charity), which develops and supports programmes in the communities in which GE has a presence. This can be in the form of financial support or employee volunteering.

Corporate giving

A figure for charitable contributions was not included in the company's annual report and accounts for 2013. In the most recent year for which we have a figure, the company made donations of £57,000, and we have taken this as an estimate for charitable donations in 2013.

Our research tells us that, in the UK, the **GE Foundation** has previously supported the following initiatives:

Sandfields School – GE is supporting a Neath Port Talbot Council project at Sandfields School, Port Talbot which aims to get at risk youngsters back into school

Bristol Education Action Zone – GE is supporting an innovative project to develop the skills and confidence of children in four of Bristol's inner city schools

SETNET – GE is a major supporter of SETNET – the Science, Engineering, Technology and Mathematics Network

Employee-led support

Matched funding

It would appear that funds raised by employee/retiree contributions are matched by contributions from GE Foundation.

Employee volunteering

GE employees are encouraged to volunteer in their communities through the GE Volunteers network. The following information was noted on the GE Sustainability website:

> GE Volunteers is a global network that includes employees, retirees, affinity groups, friends and family – good people doing great things – all supported by GE businesses and corporate resources. The global mission of GE Volunteers is to facilitate and support volunteering activities that improve life in the communities where GE people live and work. These are carried out through a wide range of projects in the areas of community-building, education, the environment and health.

Corporate social responsibility

CSR committee: We found no evidence of a separate UK CSR committee; however, there is a GE Citizenship Advisory Panel which 'supports, challenges and advises GE on its approach to sustainability'.

CSR information: The following information was obtained from the GE Sustainability website:

> Communities need to build resilient infrastructures in order to prosper, as well as access infrastructure such as transportation that moves people and products, power that energizes them, and healthcare to cure people. All of this requires innovation to reduce cost (including the environmental cost), improve quality, and provide access to the products, services and jobs needed for a better life. These needs closely align with GE's business strategy, and working to solve some of the world's biggest challenges inspires our thinking and drives our actions.

CSR report: We found no evidence of a separate report for CSR in the UK; however, there is a GE Sustainability website which focuses on the CSR activities of the GE family of companies across the globe.

Applications

Our research indicates that for local, small scale UK support, applications should be made in writing to the correspondent.

GE Foundation

The GE Foundation does not encourage unsolicited proposals. Through ongoing research in the field, the GE Foundation develops targeted initiatives and invites specific institutions and organisations to apply within those initiatives. Its capacity to review unsolicited proposals is extremely limited.

General Motors UK Ltd (Vauxhall Motors)

Motors and accessories

Correspondent: Cherie Denton, Community Relations Dept, Griffin House, Osborne Road, Luton LU1 3YT (tel: 01582 721122; fax: 01582 427400; email: cherie.denton@vauxhall.co.uk; website: www.vauxhall.co.uk/about-vauxhall/about-us/our-values.html)

Directors: P. Millward; A. R. Gilson; J. R. Fulcher; D. Borland; M. Wright; S. Fesser; T. Tozer

Year end	31/12/2013
Turnover	£3,677,900,000
Pre-tax profit	£151,500,000

Nature of business: The company manufactures, markets and services Vauxhall branded passenger cars and light vans and supplies vehicles to other General Motors companies, principally in Europe, which are sold under the Opel brand.

Vauxhall Motors is the trading name of General Motors UK Ltd.

Company registration number: 135767

Main locations: Ellesmere Port, Luton

Total employees: 2,493

Focus of giving: General charitable purposes, education, enterprise/training, health, ill health, STEM (science, technology, engineering and mathematics), children, young people, community/social welfare.

Cash donations undeclared	✓
Charity of the Year	✓
Gifts in kind	✓
Market-led giving	✓
Sponsorship	✓

Charitable donations

Cash UK (latest available):	2013	£190,000
	2011	£278,000
	2009	£101,000
	2007	£231,000
	2006	£218,000
Total UK (cash and in kind):	2013	£190,000
Cash worldwide:	2013	£190,000
Total worldwide (cash and in kind):	2013	£190,000

Community involvement

Vauxhall has a history of engaging with the community, especially in the areas surrounding its manufacturing site at Ellesmere Port and in Luton. It would appear that much of the company's community strategy is based around supporting young people in Britain, which it does through its community projects – Griffin's Den; Vans 'R' Us; and the Ellesmere Port Community Project – its youth football programme, as well as through its support of local youth initiatives. The company's employees fundraise for its partner charity, Help for Heroes. Vauxhall also supports national automotive charities.

Corporate giving

The annual report and accounts for 2013 did not include a figure for charitable donations made during the year. The average of such contributions in the two most recent years for which we have figures was £190,000, and we have taken this as an estimate for charitable donations in 2013.

We were unable to determine a value for the in-kind donations given by the company.

Beneficiaries included: LAMP (£2,000), Mitalee Youth Association, SOS Bus Luton, Tokko

Automotive charities

Vauxhall has lent its support to automotive charities, BEN and WOMAC (Women on the Move Against Cancer). BEN has benefitted since 1996 from donations from car and van sales and its welfare officer in Cheshire benefits from use of a loan vehicle.

Partner charity

Vauxhall has been in partnership with Help for Heroes since 2010. Through staff fundraising activities, more than £250,000 has been raised for the charity. As part of the partnership, Vauxhall also provides support vehicles in the form of three Astra Sports Tourers and a Movano van, and has helped to fund a number of specially adapted minibuses for the charity's Recovery Centres.

In-kind support

In association with the FA, Vauxhall has established the Vauxhall Youth Football Programme, which encourages young people between the ages of 12 and 18 to get back into football. Since its formation in 2012, more than 7,600 young people have taken part.

Gifts in kind

Through Business in the Community, Vauxhall has donated 15 VX 220s to schools and universities across the country, helping to encourage young people's development of practical and technical skills in engineering and design.

Since March 2010, Vauxhall has supported the SOS Bus Luton initiative through providing maintenance for two vehicles and contributing to their fuel cost.

Near to its Ellesmere Port site, the company has supported the Barnstondale Centre, which provides disadvantaged young people in the wider Merseyside area with affordable residential and non-residential breaks, with a loan vehicle.

Employee-led support

Employee fundraising

Vauxhall employees helped to raise £43,000 for the company's partner charity, Help for Heroes. Activities included a London to Paris bike ride, a superhero day, and a charity concert by the Vauxhall Male Voice Choir. Employees at Vauxhall's sites have also fundraised for causes in line with the company's CSR strategy of supporting Britain's Youth, amongst other local community initiatives. At the company's Luton base, for example, employees helped to raise funds for Keech Hospice's new community outreach programme – Complementary Therapist Callings.

Vauxhall Employees Charities Funds

Each Vauxhall site has its own fund, supported by employee donations, which support national and local charities. Through their fund, for example, Luton employees were able to help 26 charities having raised £6,550 in 2013. The IBC Charity Committee (registered charity: 800728) meets once a month to discuss local and national requests for support. The company matches employee donations to the charity.

Commercially led support

Career awareness

Through three youth community programmes, Griffin's Den, Vans 'R' Us and the Ellesmere Port Community Project, Vauxhall aims to improve students' awareness of STEM (Science, Engineering, Technology and Maths) subjects, helping to inspire them to take up a career in the STEM sector. In 2013, more than 30 schools were visited as part of the programmes.

Sponsorship

Vauxhall sponsors the football associations of all four home nations.

Product sales

Through its support of BEN, the automotive charity, between 1996 and 2013, more than £2.1 million was donated based on a contribution per car or van sold.

Corporate social responsibility

CSR committee: Matters relating to CSR are represented by board-level Directors. Strategy, performance, risks and achievements are discussed quarterly during the Chair's Strategy meeting. A committee in charge of leading the CSR strategy of Vauxhall was established and meets on a monthly basis to review progress and assess challenges.

CSR information: The following information was obtained from the website:

> At Vauxhall, we aim always to be a socially responsible company. We continuously look to improve our social

> responsibility performance through environmental management, effective engagement with our partners, being a responsible employer and playing a key role in the community.

We were unable to determine the ratio of women to men on the board.

CSR report: There is a CSR report available from the company's website.

Exclusions

Our research indicates that no grants are given for circular appeals, advertising in charity brochures, appeals from individuals, fundraising events, medical research, overseas projects, political appeals, religious appeals, or local appeals not in areas of company presence.

Applications

In writing to the correspondent.

Genting UK plc (formerly Genting Stanley plc)

Gaming

Correspondent: The Company Secretary, Genting Club Star City, Watson Road, Birmingham B7 5SA (website: www.gentingcasinos.co.uk/playitsafe)

Directors: Tan Sn Kok Thay Lim; P. M. Brooks; Lord K. W. Baker of Dorking; Dato' Sn Choong Yan Lee; Dato' Justin Ming Loong Leong

Year end	31/12/2013
Turnover	£324,400,000
Pre-tax profit	£25,600,000

Nature of business: The main activity of the company is that of casino operators.

Company registration number: 1519749

Subsidiary undertakings include: Genting Casinos UK Ltd; Genting International Investment Properties (UK) Ltd; Genting (Park Lane Mews Hotel) Ltd; Stanley Casinos Holdings Ltd; Stanley Interactive Ltd; Stanley Overseas Holdings Ltd;

Main locations: Birmingham

Total employees: 3,828

Focus of giving: Education, health, ill health, financial education, children, young people.

Charitable donations

Cash UK (latest available):	2013	£231,000
	2012	£210,000
	2011	£205,500
	2009	£122,000
	2008	£90,000
Total UK (cash and in kind):	2013	£231,000
Cash worldwide:	2013	£231,000
Total worldwide (cash and in kind):	2013	£231,000

Community involvement

Genting UK plc looks to make a positive contribution to the communities in areas in which it operates. Genting UK actively supports the promotion of responsible gambling in its casinos and distributes information on the matter through printed and online channels. The group states that it is 'committed to the development of awareness, prevention and counselling programmes for problem and underage gambling', both in its premises and in the wider community in which it operates. The group is an active supporter of the Responsible Gambling Trust, which funds education, research and treatment services and engages in research relating to gambling-related harm.

Corporate giving

In 2013 the group made a donation of £231,000 to the Responsible Gambling Trust.

In previous years, cash donations have also been made to various local charities, though we were unable to find details relating to this in the annual report and accounts for 2013.

Beneficiaries included: Responsible Gambling Trust (£231,000), GamCare

In-kind support

Genting UK promotes the services that Gamcare, a registered charity, offers for individuals with gambling problems.

Employee-led support

Employee fundraising

Genting UK employees help to raise funds for charitable causes in their local areas by completing fundraising activities and organising events. Examples include: two administrators from Genting Club Westcliff who helped to raise £700 for the Keyhole Cancer Charity by completing a charity abseil; and a Wirral-based team of employees who cycled from London to Paris, raising more than £7,000 for Clatterbridge Cancer Charity.

Commercially led support

Genting supports charitable fundraising events and activities, an example of which was the Masquerade Ball, which was held at a Genting club in Sheffield in aid of Weston Park Hospital Cancer Charity, and helped to raise more than £8,700. More than 270 guests enjoyed a three course dinner, gaming and entertainment.

Corporate social responsibility

CSR committee: We found no evidence of a separate CSR Committee.

CSR information: The website states:

> At Genting, community is very important. We strive to deliver both a first class gaming experience and at the same time ensure that we fulfil our commitment to responsible gambling. With this in mind we want to ensure that we're supporting key charities in their endeavour to deliver key services to those in need of fast and effective treatment and support.

We were unable to determine the ratio of women to men on the board.

CSR report: We found no evidence of a separate CSR report.

Exclusions

Our research indicates that no support is given for appeals from individuals; the arts; environment/heritage; fundraising events; overseas projects; political appeals; religious appeals; or science/technology.

Applications

In writing to the correspondent, referenced 'Charitable donations'.

GKN plc

Engineering

Correspondent: Corporate Responsibility Team, PO Box 55, Ipsley House, Ipsley Church Lane, Redditch, Worcestershire B98 0TL (tel: 01527 517715; fax: 01527 517700; email: cr@gkn.com; website: www.gkn.com/corporateresponsibility)

Directors: Michael Turner, Chair; Nigel Stein, Chief Executive; Marcus Bryson; Angus Cockburn; Tufan Erginbilgic; Shonaid Jemmett-Page; Richard Parry-Jones; Andrew Reynolds Smith; Adam Walker, Finance Director; Jos Sclater (women: 1; men: 9)

Year end	31/12/2013
Turnover	£7,136,000,000
Pre-tax profit	£484,000,000

Nature of business: An international engineering group involved in the automotive and aerospace industries.

Company registration number: 4191106

Subsidiary undertakings include: GKN Aerospace Services Ltd; GKN Aerospace North America, Inc; GKN Aerospace Sweden AB; GKN do Brasil Ltda; GKN Driveline Japan Ltd; GKN Driveline North America, Inc.

Main locations: Birmingham, London, Weston super Mare, West Bromwich, Sutton Coalfield, Walsall, Telford, Portsmouth, Redditch, Yeovil, Edgware, Eastleigh, Chesterfield, Lichfield, Leek, Isle of Wight

Total employees: 42,998

Focus of giving: Education, health, ill health, medical research, science technology, children, young people, community/social welfare.

FTSE 100	✓
Gifts in kind	✓
Humanitarian aid: overseas	✓
Overseas giving	✓

Charitable donations

Cash UK (latest available):	2013	£101,000
	2012	£58,600
	2011	£34,300
	2010	£77,000
	2009	£191,400
Total UK (cash and in kind):	2013	£101,000
Cash worldwide:	2013	£731,000
Total worldwide (cash and in kind):	2013	£731,000

Community involvement

GKN supports communities around the globe in which it operates. The group's companies and employees contribute to charitable work, fundraising and community projects, with a particular focus on: preparing young people for the world of work, particularly in relation to STEM (science, technology, engineering and maths) subjects; and improving local communities through social projects and charitable donations.

Corporate giving

In 2013 group companies made donations totalling £731,000, of which £101,000 was given to charities registered in the UK.

The group had its own charity, **GKN Millennium Trust** (Charity Commission no.: 1051266) which supported the Engineering Development Trust and Young Enterprise programmes, although this ceased to exist in January 2015. We believe its 2013 income of £6,900 may account for some of the £101,000 given in donations by the group during the year.

Costings for the in-kind donations given by the group were not included in the report.

In-kind support

Staff time

The group actively encourages its employees to engage in their local communities and offers paid volunteering time.

Employee-led support

Employee volunteering

GKN 'provides opportunities for its employees to volunteer and fundraise'. There are examples of employees' fundraising and volunteering activities in the group's overseas locations on its website. The GKN Hearts of Gold programme was established in 2008 to celebrate the contributions made by individuals and teams of employees who have undertaken projects and activities in their local areas.

Commercially led support

During 2013 the group took part in the government-backed See Inside Manufacturing programme, through which local schoolchildren were able to visit seven GKN Aerospace and GKN Driveline sites.

Corporate social responsibility

CSR committee: There was no evidence of a separate CSR Committee.

CSR information: The following information is taken from the group's website:

> Not only do we support projects and activities in the local areas, we also seek to minimise any negative impact on our communities, pride ourselves on promoting good business practice, create job opportunities and support the introduction of people into the world of work. At all times, we are sensitive to the cultural issues which play a major part in the life of the local communities and wider societies where our operations are located.
>
> We support charities and community organisations, as well as provide opportunities for employees to volunteer and fundraise, in a variety of ways, including:
>
> - Providing paid time off for employees involved in community activities
> - Fundraising for local causes
> - Operating a charitable giving scheme
> - Providing volunteer support for community projects
> - Building links with local education establishments
> - Offering work experience placements

CSR report: A sustainability report is included in the annual report and there is a detailed section on Corporate Responsibility on the group's website.

Exclusions

No support is given for political appeals.

Applications

In writing to the correspondent.

GlaxoSmithKline plc

Healthcare, pharmaceuticals

Correspondent: Global Community Partnerships, GSK House, 980 Great West Road, Brentford, Middlesex TW6 9GS (email: community.partnerships@gsk.com; website: www.gsk.com/en-gb/responsibility)

Directors: Simon Dingemans, Chief Financial Officer; Christopher Gent, Chair; Andrew Witty, Chief Executive; Professor Sir Roy Anderson; Dr Stephanie Burns; Stacey Cartwright; Lynn Elsenhans; Judy Lewent; Deryck Maughan; Dr Daniel Podolsky; Dr Moncef Slaoui; Tom de Swaan; Jing Ulrich; Hans Wijers; Philip Hampton; Urs Rohner (women: 5; men: 11)

Year end	31/12/2013
Turnover	£26,505,000,000
Pre-tax profit	£6,647,000,000

Nature of business: The group's principal activities are the creation and discovery, development, manufacture and marketing of pharmaceutical products, including vaccines, over-the-counter medicines and health-related consumer products.

Company registration number: 1047315

Subsidiary undertakings include: Glaxo Group Ltd; GlaxoSmithKline LLC; GlaxoSmithKline UK Ltd; Setfirst Ltd; Stiefel Laboratories Inc.; Wellcome Ltd

Brands include: Aquafresh, Beechams, Horlicks, Macleans, Nicorette, NiQuitin, Oilatum, Panadol, Pronamel, Sensodyne

Main locations: Stevenage, Hertfordshire, Stockley Park, Middlesex, Ulverston, Cumbria, Ware, Hertfordshire, Montrose, Tayside, Greenford, Middlesex, Dartford, Kent, Barnard Castle, County Durham, Beckenham, Kent

Total employees: 99,817

Focus of giving: Education, environment, health, ill health, medical research, STEM (science, technology, engineering and mathematics), overseas projects, science technology, children, young people.

Membership: BITC, LBG

Charity of the Year	✓
FTSE 100	✓
Gifts in kind	✓
Humanitarian aid: overseas	✓
Overseas giving	✓
Payroll giving	✓
Sponsorship	✓

Charitable donations

Cash UK (latest available):	2013	£3,600,000
	2011	£1,400,000
	2009	£5,600,000
	2007	£6,000,000
	2005	£4,000,000
Total UK (cash and in kind):	2013	£3,600,000
Cash worldwide:	2013	£54,000,000
Total worldwide (cash and in kind):	2013	£204,000,000

Community involvement

GlaxoSmithKline looks to improve the well-being of its communities by supporting programmes that improve healthcare infrastructure, promote science and health education, and assist with humanitarian relief. Cash and in-kind donations are made and employee time is contributed.

The GSK website states: 'We are transparent about our charitable giving with data being published in our Annual Report and Corporate Responsibility Report in March each year. We are further increasing transparency by publishing details of our individual charitable grants over £10,000 ($15,000).' Details of GSK's grants awarded can be found on the Responsibility section of the company's website.

Global Charity partner: Save the Children

Corporate giving

In 2013 in the UK, GlaxoSmithKline made donations of £10,000 or more directly to charitable organisations totalling £3.6 million, helping over 50 organisations in health, medical research, science education, the arts and the environment. The company also makes smaller grants, although these are as yet unreported, so the figure we quote here is likely to be higher. No figure was available for 2013 for in-kind support in the UK. Potential applicants should note that the company's website states that: 'GlaxoSmithKline supports community initiatives in both the developed and the developing world. Identifying the right projects is an important responsibility, and that's why the company takes a strategic, proactive approach and **does not generally support unsolicited requests for funding**'.

Beneficiaries of grants in the UK during 2013 included: Tres Cantos Open Lab Foundation (£750,000); Age UK (£300,000); British Lung Foundation (£107,000); Asthma Enterprises (£60,000); Global Leadership Foundation (£25,000); Hounslow Arts Trust (£10,000)

GlaxoSmithKline IMPACT Awards

The annual GlaxoSmithKline IMPACT Awards are run in partnership with the King's Fund to recognise and promote excellence in community healthcare. In the past 16 years, more than £8 million has been awarded to 450 winning healthcare charities in the UK and USA.

To be eligible for a GSK IMPACT Award, organisations must be registered, have an annual income of between £25,000 and £2 million, be working in a health-related field, and must have been operating in the UK for at least three years:

- Up to ten winners receive £30,000 plus the overall winner will receive an extra £10,000
- Up to ten runners-up receive £3,000
- Organisations do not need to present a new project, and winners decide how to spend the award money
- Winning organisations will be offered free development and training up to the value of £6,000

For further details, visit the King's Fund's website: www.kingsfund.org.uk.

The company works with charities, including Crisis, WellChild, Scope and Help for Heroes, to help to deliver healthcare-related programmes and services.

Global contributions

Global contributions during the year totalled £204 million, not including £17 million spent in management costs:

Product and in-kind	£146 million
Cash	£54 million
Time	£4 million

Support was allocated to programmes in the following areas: Health and well-being (66%); Education (23%); Other (19%).

In-kind support

GlaxoSmithKline makes in-kind contributions in the form of product donations and staff time. During the year, products were donated to GSK's partners AmeriCares, Direct Relief, IMA World Health, MAP International, and Project for Hope. Medicines were distributed in 87 countries in 2013 and included supplies of antibiotics and basic medicines to people affected by natural disasters and conflict in places, for example, such as Pakistan, the Philippines and tornado-affected areas of the USA.

Employee-led support

Employee volunteering

The company supports employees' charitable and community involvement through two main volunteering programmes.

PULSE Volunteer Partnership – The programme gives GSK employees the opportunity to work with a non-profit organisation full-time for three or six months. In 2013 PULSE saw 99 employees work with 47 organisations, including Save the Children, GSK's global charity partner, to help to develop their leadership skills whilst lending their skills and expertise to address global healthcare problems.

Orange Day volunteer programme – Through the Orange Day volunteer programme, employees are able to take one paid day's leave for volunteering purposes each year.

2013 marked the first time GSK employees in all 115 countries where it has a presence lent their support to a single cause. As part of Orange United Employee Engagement, a target was set to fundraise £1 million for the company's partner charity, Save the Children and in Orange Week alone close to £337,000 was raised towards the target.

Payroll giving

The company operates the Give As You Earn scheme

Commercially led support

Science education programmes

In the UK, GSK supports a range of programmes, activities and resources designed to make science more relevant to young people, including a website www.gskscienceeducation.com. The company's science education programme is based around three themes – Extraordinary beings; Body matters; and Tackling world health – each of which has a host of associated resources for teachers to access for free. As part of the programme, in 2013, GSK teamed up with Formula One's McLaren Group to help create the Fast Forward Challenge, which saw UK students investigate ways in which driver can improve their reaction times. A similar programme in 2014, Pit Stop Challenge, focused students on finding ways to improve the performance of F1 pit stop teams through science.

A central focus of the programme and its associated activities is the promotion of science, technology, engineering and maths (STEM) subjects to students, with the aim of raising awareness of careers in the science industry.

Sponsorship

GlaxoSmithKline sponsored a small number of UK events and organisations during 2013, including:

Association of Respiratory Nurse Specialists – GSK served as a sponsor of the association during the year.

Pharmaceutical Care Awards – The company sponsored the awards, which are run by the Royal Pharmaceutical Society.

Corporate social responsibility

CSR committee: There is a board level Corporate Responsibility Committee, the job of which it is to provide guidance and oversight to the board on matters relating to responsible business.

CSR information: The following information was obtained from the CSR report:

> We also create value by making direct and indirect economic and social contributions in the countries where we operate. These wider benefits to society include contributions through tax, employment and enhancing the well-being of our local communities through our global community initiatives.

CSR report: A detailed CSR report is available on the company's website, and there is a section related to CSR within the annual report and accounts.

Exclusions

Our research indicates that no support is given in response to appeals from individuals. The company is unable to provide support for individual students or Raleigh International applicants, for example. It does, however, support organisations which in turn provide financial assistance to medical students. Our research also indicates that no support is given for fundraising events, advertising in charity brochures, purely denominational (religious) appeals, political appeals or sport.

Applications

For more information on funding requests, contact the correspondent.

However, not the following from the website:

> GSK supports community initiatives in both the developed and the developing world. Identifying the right projects is an important responsibility, and that's why the company takes a strategic, proactive approach and **does not generally support unsolicited requests for funding**.

The Go Ahead Group plc

Transport and communications

Correspondent: Sarah Boundy, Group Corporate Communications Director, 4 Matthew Parker Street, Westminster, London SW1H 9NP (tel: 020 7799 8983; email: sarah.boundy@go-ahead.com; website: www.go-ahead.com)

Directors: Andrew Allner, Chair; Katherine Innes Ker; Nick Horler; David Brown, Group Chief Executive; Keith Down, Group Finance Director; Adrian Ewer (women: 1; men: 5)

Year end	28/06/2014
Turnover	£2,702,400,000
Pre-tax profit	£91,200,000

Nature of business: The principal activity of the group is the provision of rail and bus public transport services. Its subsidiaries provide transport solutions across London, the Home Counties, the North East and the South East of England.

Company registration number: 2100855

Subsidiary undertakings include: Anglian Bus Ltd; Brighton and Hove Bus and Coach Company Ltd; Go-Ahead Scotland Ltd; Go South Coast Ltd; Konectbus Ltd; Metrobus Ltd; and The City of Oxford Motor Services Ltd. A full list of subsidiary undertakings is available from the company's accounts.

Brands include: Chambers; Gatwick Express; London Midland; Southern; and Thames Travel.

Main locations: Brighton and Hove, Newcastle upon Tyne, London, North Eastern England, Oxford, Wiltshire, Dorset, Blackburn, Glasgow, Cardiff

UK employees: 23,792

Total employees: 23,792

Focus of giving: Education, enterprise/training, environment, health, ill health, older people, safety and crime prevention, children, young people, community/social welfare, disability.

Membership: LBG

Charity of the Year	✓
Gifts in kind	✓
Market-led giving	✓

Charitable donations

Cash UK (latest available):	2014	£251,000
	2011	£182,000
	2009	£270,000
	2008	£302,000
	2007	£100,000
Total UK (cash and in kind):	2014	£367,000
Cash worldwide:	2014	£251,000
Total worldwide (cash and in kind):	2014	£367,000

Community involvement

The group states that 'its businesses are part of the local communities in which they operate' and '[its] aim is to play a constructive role in the towns and cities [it] serves, working closely with local community groups.'

The Community Policy and Charitable Investment paper notes that support is given to smaller charities and to various community organisations and groups in the areas of the group's presence. The main focus areas are: education; children and young people; social inclusion; and health charities.

Go-Learn Education

The group operates an online educational programme to help young people develop skills and knowledge of independent travel. There are free downloadable teaching resources, mapped against the National Curriculum, which can be used to support literacy, numeracy, citizenship skills and help in delivering personal, social and health education. Many of the Go-Ahead companies also work with local schools.

Charity partnerships

In 2012 the group entered into three year partnerships with Transaid and Railway Children, aiming to raise over £100,000 to support the work of both organisations.

Corporate giving

The latest CSR report available at the time of writing was for 2012/13 which stated that a total of £270,000 was spent in supporting charities and the community. The sustainability datasheet for 2013/14 notes that community spend totalled about £367,000 across the group, which we take to represent the figure of total contributions by the group. We believe that this sum includes both direct cash contributions and other types of support. We were unable to distinguish the amount given in cash, therefore we estimate it to be around £251,000, based on the figures from the three previous years known to us.

In-kind support

The group's non-cash support includes free travel service provision to charities, advertising space, programmes on travel safety available to schoolchildren (see Go-Learn Education in the 'Community involvement' section in this entry), educational material, also staff time and efforts.

A good example of the group's in-kind support is Go North East's Buses in the Community scheme which provides transport for day trips, staff time to assist with various projects and raffle prizes for fundraising initiatives.

Employee-led support

Our research suggests that the group will assist employees volunteering and charitable activities through financial support.

Commercially led support

Access for All

The group seeks to accommodate every customer. For example, older people can use bus travel services for free and/or receive concessions. There are also initiatives to help passengers with disabilities. In partnership with the Royal National Institute of Blind People (RNIB) 'Maps for All' have been installed with information in braille and raised coloured plastic so that passengers can find their own way to the station facilities.

Employability

Apprenticeship schemes are operated across bus and rail divisions in customer service and engineering roles.

Corporate social responsibility

CSR committee: There was no evidence of a separate CSR Committee. The Executive Board has full responsibility for sustainability issues with the CEO having the overall overview of sustainability performance.

CSR information: The group's annual report for 2013/14 notes the following:

> Sustainability and corporate responsibility are integral to our strategy and the way we operate at every level of the business. . . . Our former five key sustainability areas of Safety, Environment, Passengers, Employees and Communities have now been aligned with our strategic priorities of *Society*, *Customers, Our People* and *Finance*.

The group's website states:

> We believe that a strong and growing public transport network is vital to the sustainable development of the UK. As a leading provider of public transport, we are committed to operating our bus and rail services in a safe, environmentally and socially responsible manner.

CSR report: A full CSR report is available from the company's website.

Exclusions

Our research suggests that support is not given for advertising in charity brochures, animal welfare, appeals from individuals, environment/heritage causes, overseas projects and political or religious appeals.

Applications

In writing to the correspondent.

Goldman Sachs International

Banking, securities/shares

Correspondent: Mike Housden, Correspondent to the Trustees, Peterborough Court, 133 Fleet Street, London EC4A 2BB (tel: 020 7774 1000; website: www.goldmansachs.com/citizenship/index.html)

Directors: P. D. Sutherland, Chair; R. J. Gnodde, Co-Chief Executive Officer; Lord Griffiths of Fforestfach; M. S. Sherwood, Co-Chief Executive Officer; C. Dahlback

Year end	31/12/2013
Turnover	£3,419,000,000
Pre-tax profit	£197,300,000

Nature of business: Provision of investment banking, trading, asset management and securities to corporations, financial institutions, governments and wealthy individuals.

Company registration number: 2263951

Subsidiary undertakings include: Goldman Sachs International Investments Ltd; Goldman Sachs (Cayman) Ltd

Main locations: London

Total employees: 5,462

Focus of giving: General charitable purposes, education, poverty and social exclusion, children, young people.

Membership: BITC

Gifts in kind	✓
Matched funding	✓
Overseas giving	✓
Sponsorship	✓

Charitable donations

Cash UK (latest available):	2013	£22,100,000
	2011	£40,100,000
	2009	£1,986,000
	2008	£16,904,300
	2007	£1,940,000
Total UK (cash and in kind):	2013	£22,100,000
Cash worldwide:	2013	£24,900,000
Total worldwide (cash and in kind):	2013	£24,900,000

Community involvement

At a global level, Goldman Sachs' philanthropy includes four major initiatives: Goldman Sachs Gives, a donor-advised fund with which former and current senior employees have an input; Community Teamworks, a worldwide employee volunteering initiative; 10,000 Women, which looks to boost local economies by supporting females entrepreneurs; and 10,000 Small Businesses, which looks to create jobs and economic growth by investing in business education, opportunities and support services for entrepreneurs.

In the UK Goldman Sachs has established two registered grant-making charities:

The Goldman Sachs Charitable Gift Fund (UK) – (Charity Commission no. 1120148) – set up for the advancement of education, the relief of poverty, the advancement of religion and any other purposes charitable in both English and American law; and

Goldman Sachs Gives (UK) – (Charity Commission no. 1123956) – established for the advancement of education, the relief of poverty, the advancement of religion and any other charitable purposes. The ongoing strategy of the fund is to make grants pursuant to its objects.

Corporate giving

The annual report and accounts for 2013 state that more than $37.5 million ($24.9 million) was donated to charity during the year. Of this amount, $33.3 million (£22.1 million) was donated to Goldman Sachs Gives (UK) for general charitable purposes in England and Wales.

We were unable to determine a figure for the in-kind support given by the company.

The figures used in this entry have been taken from the annual report and accounts of Goldman Sachs International. We have obtained our CSR information from the global website of Goldman Sachs Group, Inc., which is the ultimate controlling undertaking and the parent company, incorporated in the United States of America. Goldman Sachs Group Inc. made global charitable contributions totalling $155 million (£103 million) in 2013.

See the corporate charity entries on pp. 407 and 407 for more information.

In-kind support

Various initiatives are supported on a local basis in the communities in which Goldman Sachs has a presence and the firm contributes its 'ideas, people and resources'.

Employee-led support

Community TeamWorks

The volunteer programme is in operation for Goldman Sachs employees around the globe, who spend one day per year volunteering with non-profit organisations. The website states that:

> In 2014 52 Goldman Sachs offices partnered with nearly 900 non-profit organisations on over 1,580 projects worldwide. More than 25,000 Goldman Sachs people, family and friends joined together to contribute over 125,000 hours to the communities where we work and live.

The London office, for example, supported WellChild in transforming outdoor spaces for families in need.

Goldman Sachs Gives

Through the fund, current and retired senior employees can recommend eligible non-profit organisations to receive grants. The fund is donor-advised, and its income is derived from donations from individuals, as well as from Goldman Sachs subsidiaries. The program focuses on four areas: Increasing Educational Opportunities; Building and Stabilising Communities; Honouring Service and Veterans; and Creating Jobs and Economic Growth. In the UK funding, it would appear, is distributed through Goldman Sachs' two registered charities.

Matched funding

There is an employee gift matching programme in operation.

Commercially led support

Citizenship programmes

10,000 Women – The initiative was launched in 2008 by the Goldman Sachs Foundation to support 10,000 across 43 countries by providing business and management education, as well as mentoring and networking opportunities.

10,000 Small Businesses – Funded by Goldman Sachs and the Goldman Sachs Foundation, the initiative invests to assist entrepreneurs provide jobs and opportunities through providing greater access to education, capital and business support services. It is in operation in both the UK and the United States.

Sponsorship: The British Museum's 2013 Pompeii exhibition, titled Life and Death in Pompeii and Herculaneum, was sponsored by Goldman Sachs.

In Summer 2015 Goldman Sachs will sponsor the Serpentine Gallery Pavilion in London.

For a number of years, the firm has sponsored the London Evening Standard's Ladder for London campaign to help unemployed young people into apprenticeships.

Corporate social responsibility

CSR committee: Goldman Sachs has an Office of Corporate Engagement, which the global website describes as advancing 'the firm's objective to make a difference in its philanthropy by programming and coordinating charitable activities'.

CSR information: The following information was taken from the Goldman Sachs global website: 'Goldman Sachs' philanthropic efforts include the following four major initiatives, which advance the firm's objective of driving economic growth and making a difference.' These are: 10,000 Women; 10,000 Small Businesses;

Goldman Sachs Gives; and Community Teamworks.

We were unable to determine the ratio of women to men on the board.

CSR report: There is an annual global Environmental, Social and Governance Report published on the group's website.

Corporate charity: Goldman Sachs Gives (UK) (Charity Commission no. 1123956); Goldman Sachs Charitable Gift Fund (Charity Commission no. 1120148).

Exclusions

Our research indicates that grants will not be made to individuals; fraternal organisations; political causes, campaigns or candidates; or for fundraising events.

Applications

For company applications contact the Charitable Services Team at the company's address.

For both The Goldman Sachs Charitable Gift Fund (UK) and Goldman Sachs Gives (UK): Charities Aid Foundation (CAF) and CAF America, and Ayco Company L.P. review grant eligibility applications and other requests for grant funding on behalf of the directors. Subject to the express approval of each grant application by one of the directors on behalf of the directors, Ayco then distributes funds in furtherance of the fund's objects.

In the first instance, address applications to Mike Housden, a trustee of both charities.

Note that CAF's contact details are: Charities Aid Foundation, 25 Kings Hill Avenue, Kings Hill, West Malling Kent ME19 4TA. T: 03000 123 000, F: 03000 123 001, E: enquiries@cafonline.org.

Grainger plc

Property

Correspondent: Dave Butler, Director of Strategy and Change, No.1 London Bridge, 3rd Floor East, London SE1 9BG (tel: 020 7940 9500; fax: 07920 292309; email: dbutler@graingerplc.co.uk; website: www.graingerplc.co.uk/responsibility.aspx)

Directors: Robin Broadhurst, Chair; Andrew Cunningham, Chief Executive; Nick Jopling; Mark Greenwood, Finance Director; John Barnsley; Baroness Margaret Ford; Belinda Richards; Simon Davies; Tony Wray (women: 2; men: 7)

Year end	30/09/2013
Turnover	£283,200,000
Pre-tax profit	£64,300,000

Nature of business: The group owns, acquires and trades regulated and market-let tenanted properties.

Company registration number: 125575

Subsidiary undertakings include: Northumberland and Durham Property Trust Ltd; Grainger Residential Management Ltd; Grainger Asset Management Ltd; Grainger Unitholder No. 1 Ltd; West Waterlooville Developments Ltd.

Main locations: London

Total employees: 267

Focus of giving: Education, general appeals, housing, homelessness, children, young people, community/social welfare.

Gifts in kind	✓
Payroll giving	✓

Charitable donations

Cash UK (latest available):	2013	£19,400
	2012	£30,000
	2011	£17,500
	2010	£17,500
	2009	£12,600
Total UK (cash and in kind):	2013	£26,000
Cash worldwide:	2013	£19,400
Total worldwide (cash and in kind):	2013	£26,000

Community involvement

Grainger plc looks to improve the social, economic and environmental outlook for the communities in which it operates. Charities have been supported through cash donations and employee volunteering time.

Corporate giving

During 2012/13 the group made donations of £19,400 to charitable causes. In kind giving through staff volunteering time was costed at a further £6,900.

Beneficiaries: The group is a foundation partner of LandAid, the UK property industry charity, and its contributions have also benefitted the following charities: Breast Cancer Support; Great Ormond Street Hospital; Help for Heroes; Macmillan; Northern Counties Kidney Research Fund; and Shelter. Refer to the 'Responsibility' section of the group's website for a full list of beneficiary organisations.

In-kind support

Staff time

The amount of staff working time contributed towards charitable causes totalled 41 days.

Employee-led support

Employee fundraising

During the year, Grainger employees raised more than £14,000 for charitable causes through fundraising activities.

Payroll giving

Employees donated a further £11,200 through the payroll giving facility.

Corporate social responsibility

CSR committee: The group has a Sustainability Committee.

CSR information: The following information is taken from the Grainger plc website:

> Our commitment to corporate responsibility is based on a firm belief that this will help us to maintain commercial advantage, manage the risks associated with our operations, increase our efficiency and enhance our reputation. To this end we seek to align our CR strategy with over-arching business plans and decision-making processes and embed our principles into the way we operate on a daily basis. Corporate Responsibility is very much in line with our strategic objectives and our values.

CSR report: A CSR report is available from the group's website.

Applications

In writing to the correspondent.

Great Portland Estates plc

Property

Correspondent: Janine Cole, Head of Sustainability, 33 Cavendish Square, London W1G 0PW (tel: 020 7647 3000; fax: 020 7016 5500; email: janine.cole@gpe.co.uk; website: www.gpe.co.uk/responsibility.aspx)

Directors: Martin Scicluna, Chair; Toby Courtauld, Chief Executive; Neil Thompson; Nick Sanderson, Finance Director; Jonathan Nicholls; Jonathan Short; Charles Philipps; Elizabeth Holden (women: 1; men: 7)

Year end	31/03/2014
Turnover	£85,200,000
Pre-tax profit	£422,200,000

Nature of business: The main activity of the company is property development and investment.

Company registration number: 596137

Subsidiary undertakings include: B and H S Management Ltd; Collin Estates Ltd; Courtana Investments Ltd; G.P.E. (Bermondsey Street) Ltd; Great Portland Estates Capital (Jersey) Ltd; G.P.E (Marcol House) Ltd.

Main locations: London

Total employees: 86

Focus of giving: Health, ill health, housing, homelessness, older people, children, young people, disability.

Charity of the Year	✓
Gifts in kind	✓
Matched funding	✓

Charitable donations

Cash UK (latest available):	2014	£48,000
	2013	£49,000
	2012	£52,000
	2011	£48,000
	2010	£45,000
Total UK (cash and in kind):	2014	£48,000
Cash worldwide:	2014	£48,000
Total worldwide (cash and in kind):	2014	£48,000

Community involvement

Great Portland Estates plc actively participates in associations working to improve central London in various ways. Each financial year, the group's directors and employees nominate four charities, both local and national, to receive support.

Corporate giving

In 2014 the group made donations totalling £48,000 to charities. This total included an annual donation of £10,000 given to Land Aid.

We were unable to determine the value for the in-kind support given by the group.

Beneficiaries: Pancreatic Cancer UK; Shelter from the Storm; SWAN UK (Syndromes Without A Name), a project run by Genetic Alliance UK; and Teenage Cancer Trust.

In-kind support

Gifts in kind

The group encourages its building managers to work with tenants to identify local and national charities which it can support through its buildings. During the year this approach helped to support charities including: Bliss; Children in Need; Comic Relief; Great Ormond Street; Help for Heroes; and Macmillan Cancer Support. Space was also let at the company's developments at 90/92 Great Portland Street and 21/23 Riding House Street to Pump Aid and The Orchid Project respectively, though it is not clear whether this was at a commercial rate or otherwise.

Employee-led support

Employee fundraising

The group encourages its employees to participate with charitable activities.

Matched funding

Up to £250 for each fundraising event is given through the matched funding scheme.

Commercially led support

The group supported a number of London-based educational establishments through hosting a 'series of talks, tours and presentations' at some of its development sites. City of Westminster College, Kings Cross Construction Skills Centre, Lewisham and Southwark College and the University of Westminster all benefitted from the group's support. Its Head of Development also acts as a mentor for a student at Reading University.

Corporate social responsibility

CSR committee: The group has a Health and Safety, Environment and Corporate Responsibility Working Group.

CSR information: The group looks to improve the local environment for its tenants through: community partnerships; community initiatives; educational initiatives; Section 106 payments; repurposing vacant space; and supporting charities.

CSR report: There is a sustainability report included in the annual report and an informative section regarding corporate responsibility on the group's website.

Exclusions

No support is given for political appeals or appeals in an area where the company has no presence.

Applications

In writing to the correspondent.

Greene King plc

Brewers/distillers

Correspondent: Joanna Kreckler, Corporate Communications Manager, Westgate Brewery, Bury St Edmunds, Suffolk IP33 1QT (tel: 01284 714123; email: corporateresponsibility@greeneking.co.uk; website: www.greeneking.co.uk/index.asp?pageid=5)

Directors: Rooney Anand, Chief Executive; Tim Bridge, Chair; Mike Coupe; Ian Durant; Rob Rowley; Lynne Weedall; Kirk Davis, Chief Financial Officer (women: 1; men: 6)

Year end	04/05/2014
Turnover	£1,301,600,000
Pre-tax profit	£173,100,000

Nature of business: Greene King is a pub retailer and brewer, running pubs, restaurants and hotels.

Company registration number: 24511

Subsidiary undertakings include: Greene King Brewing and Retailing Ltd; Greene King Retailing Parent Ltd; Greene King Pubs Ltd; Greene King Investments Ltd; Greene King Retailing Ltd; Premium Dining Restaurants and Pubs Ltd.

Brands include: Greene King IPA; Hungry Horse; Loch Fyne Seafood and Grill; Old Speckled Hen.

UK employees: 23,541

Total employees: 23,541

Focus of giving: General charitable purposes, general appeals, unpopular causes, sport, recreation, community/social welfare.

Cash donations undeclared	✓
Charity of the Year	✓
Market-led giving	✓
Payroll giving	✓

Charitable donations

Cash UK (latest available):	2014	£15,000
	2013	£17,300
	2012	£29,000
	2011	£25,800
	2010	£18,400
Total UK (cash and in kind):	2014	£15,000
Cash worldwide:	2014	£15,000
Total worldwide (cash and in kind):	2014	£15,000

Community involvement

Greene King is currently working in partnership with two charities and also supports the local charities its employees 'most care about'. It makes product donations, supports employee volunteering and operates a payroll giving scheme. The group's employees, licensees and customers help to raise funds for local, national and international causes through a varied range of activities such as sports events, quizzes, raffles, auctions, and karaoke.

Corporate giving

In 2013/14 the group gave at least £15,000 to charitable causes. This was a donation to Pub is the Hub, a not-for-profit organisation which offers 'specialist advice on rural services diversification or community ownership on new pubs'. The funding given by Greene King contributed to the organisation's Community Services Fund which, during the year, helped to support 33,000 in village communities 'through investment or planned investment via the local pub'.

Charity partnerships

Macmillan Cancer Support: In 2012 the group launched its first charity partnership with Macmillan Cancer Support with the aim of raising £1 million over three years. So far, after only two years, employees and customers have raised £900,000. To help raise awareness of Macmillan's Not Alone campaign, 50,000 wristbands have been sold and funds raised through Macmillan's World's Biggest Coffee Morning amounted to £117,000.

Focus 12: In 2013/14 the group also continued its support of Focus 12, a charity based close to its Bury St Edmunds office, which provides treatment and support for people who are affected by alcohol and drugs dependency. The Greene King Charity Ball is hosted annually and raises around £20,000 for Focus 12 each year.

Employee-led support

Employee volunteering

The group supports employee volunteering. During the year, 162 Greene King employees took part in the Three Peaks Challenge to help raise more than £50,000 in support of partner charity, Macmillan Cancer Support. Fundraising activities also included running marathons, skydiving, swimming, bike riding and mountain climbing.

Payroll giving

Employees are able to donate to charities through a payroll giving scheme facilitated by the group.

Commercially led support

Product sales

During the year, the group raised £50,000 'by introducing donations on desserts across all divisions'.

Corporate social responsibility

CSR committee: There was no mention of a specific committee found.

CSR information: This information was taken from the CSR report:

> Pubs will always play a vital role in the community. They are a place where everyone comes together to relax and to discuss issues that affect their neighbourhood. We recognise the value of that role within the social fabric of our society and how, for everyone, maintaining the presence of a pub in a community is essential. We have developed a programme to support key organisations that address the inequalities in our society.

CSR report: A CSR report is published within the annual report and accounts.

Applications

In writing to the correspondent.

Greggs plc

Food manufacture, retail – miscellaneous

Correspondent: Social Responsibility Team, Fernwood House, Clayton Road, Jesmond, Newcastle upon Tyne NE2 1TL (tel: 01912 817721; website: corporate.greggs.co.uk/social-responsibility)

Directors: Ian Durant, Chair; Roger Whiteside, Chief Executive; Raymond Reynolds; Richard Hutton, Finance Director; Allison Kirkby; Helena Ganczakowski; Peter McPhillips; Sandra Turner; Jonathan Jowett (women: 3; men: 6)

Year end	28/12/2013
Turnover	£762,379,000
Pre-tax profit	£33,152,000

Nature of business: The principal activity of the group is the retailing of sandwiches, savouries and other bakery related products with a particular focus on takeaway food and catering. The majority of products sold are manufactured in house.

Company registration number: 502851

Main locations: Newcastle upon Tyne

UK employees: 20,179

Total employees: 20,179

Focus of giving: Education, health, ill health, marginalised people, unpopular causes, arts, culture, poverty and social exclusion, community/social welfare.

Membership: BITC

Gifts in kind	✓
Payroll giving	✓

Charitable donations

Cash UK (latest available):	2013	£650,000
	2010	£1,400,000
	2009	£300,000
	2007	£730,000
	2006	£548,000
Total UK (cash and in kind):	2013	£650,000
Cash worldwide:	2013	£659,000
Total worldwide (cash and in kind):	2013	£659,000

Community involvement

Greggs plc looks to focus its community involvement through in a number of ways, including through the **Greggs Foundation**, work inclusion programmes and employee involvement through volunteering and fundraising activities.

Greggs Foundation

Each year, Greggs plc donates at least 1% of its pre-tax profit through its charity, the **Greggs Foundation** (Charity Commission no. 296590). The foundation supports a number of community initiatives, including the Greggs Breakfast Club scheme, though its grant-making is predominantly focused in the north east of England.

BITC Business Connector

Greggs has supported Business in the Communitys Business Connector initiative since 2011, through which the company has undertaken long-term secondments. Working to build relationships between local businesses and charitable/community organisations, at the time of writing, five Business Connectors are currently on secondment at Greggs.

Corporate giving

In 2013 the company donated £650,000 to the Greggs Foundation, which also benefitted from donated services, in the form of free office space and the provision of management staff.

The Greggs Foundation's annual report and accounts for 2013 also states that employees donated £40,000 to the foundation through the Give As You Earn Scheme.

As is our usual practice, we have not included employee or customer-raised funds in our total. We were unable to determine the value of the in-kind support not given to the Greggs Foundation.

See the corporate charity entry on p. 407 for more information.

In-kind support

Staff time

The company runs a volunteering scheme for employees, through which 566 days were donated in 2013.

Donated services

The company assists the Greggs Foundation through the provision of free office space and management staff.

Employee-led support

Payroll giving

The company operates the Give As You Earn scheme, money from which is contributed to the Greggs Foundation.

Employee volunteering

Employees are able to volunteer in support of local groups and charities in their communities. During the year, workers took part in, for example, primary school breakfast clubs, food banks, a disabled riding school and the South East Wales Riding Club.

Employee fundraising

Employees helped to raise funds for a number of causes and, in the last three months of the year, supported BBC Children in Need, the Philippines Typhoon Appeal and Royal British Legion's Poppy Appeal.

Commercially led support

Work inclusion programmes

During the year, the company continued its involvement with employment initiatives focused on young people and marginalised groups. More than 250 people were helped to develop their employability skills through three programmes: Ready to Work (in conjunction with the prisons and probation trusts), which is designed to assist ex-offenders gain assessment and interview experience; A Taste of Greggs (in partnership with Job Centre Plus), which offers work experience and, if possible, employment opportunities to young people; and Work Programme (assisted by various work providers), which helps to provide people who have been unemployed over a longer term with work experience and, if possible, employment opportunities.

Corporate social responsibility

CSR committee: The following information was taken from the annual report and accounts:

> We take our social responsibilities very seriously, with the Chief Executive

> responsible for delivery, and the Board ultimately accountable for performance. Delivery is managed through a Steering Group, chaired by the Company Secretary, comprising the Chief Executive and four members of the Operating Board. An Operating Board Director champions each of the four key areas of focus for Greggs, ensuring top level commitment across the business.

CSR information: The website states:

> Whilst we do not have a formal community policy, we do have a long history of supporting the communities which have helped us to grow as a business over the years. This ethos is a key part of our culture and as a successful business we feel a particular responsibility to support those less fortunate than ourselves. The success of our Breakfast Clubs and volunteering programmes as well as our employability work is testament to the effectiveness of our achievements in this area.

CSR report: There are 'Social Responsibility' sections included both in the annual report and accounts and on the website.

Corporate charity: The Greggs Foundation (formerly Greggs Trust) (Charity Commission no. 296590).

Exclusions

Exclusions for grant programmes administered by the Greggs Foundation can be found on its website.

Applications

The company appears to direct its charitable donations through the Greggs Foundation (Charity Commission no. 296590), which administers a number of grant programmes. Each grant programme has its own criteria, guidelines and application process, all of which are available to view on the foundation's website: www.greggsfoundation.org.uk.

Grosvenor Group

Property

Correspondent: Virginia Parish, Senior Manager, Westminster Foundation, The Grosvenor Office, 70 Grosvenor Street, London W1K 3JP (tel: 020 7408 0988; email: virginia.parish@grosvenor.com; website: www.grosvenor.com)

Directors: Domenico Siniscalco; Mark Preston, Group Chief Executive; Nicholas Scarles, Group Finance Director; Jeffrey Weingarten; Christopher Pratt; Jeremy Newsum; Michael McLintock; Lesley Knox, Chair (women: 1; men: 7)

Year end	31/12/2013
Turnover	£204,200,000
Pre-tax profit	£175,100,000

Nature of business: The group's principal activities are property investment, financial services and general management in Britain and Ireland, North America, Continental Europe and Asia Pacific.

Company registration number: 3219943

Subsidiary undertakings include: Grosvenor Investments Ltd; Grosvenor Developments Ltd; Grosvenor Estate Management Ltd; Grosvenor Realty Investments Ltd; Victoria Properties (London) Ltd; Quarrydale Two Ltd.

Main locations: Liverpool, London

Focus of giving: General charitable purposes, education, enterprise/training, environment, health, ill health, poverty and social exclusion, children, young people, community/social welfare.

Gifts in kind	✓
Matched funding	✓
Overseas giving	✓
Payroll giving	✓

Charitable donations

Cash UK (latest available):	2013	£1,900,000
	2011	£1,500,000
	2009	£1,800,000
	2008	£1,700,000
	2007	£2,000,000
Total UK (cash and in kind):	2013	£1,900,000
Cash worldwide:	2013	£2,400,000
Total worldwide (cash and in kind):	2013	£2,400,000

Community involvement

Grosvenor's community support is, in the main, routed through the **Westminster Foundation** (Charity Commission no. 267618) which was established in 1974 as the Grosvenor family's charitable foundation and supports a wide range of charitable causes.

The group also established the Liverpool ONE Foundation in 2009, which is now managed by Community Foundation for Merseyside and awards funding for projects based around children and young people, education and employability in Merseyside, and particularly Liverpool.

The Living Cities Community Fund, which was founded by Grosvenor in 2014 and is managed by the London Community Foundation, supports community organisations primarily in the south of Westminster at grass-roots level.

Corporate giving

In 2013 the group donated a total of £2.4 million, 79% (approx. £1.9 million) of which went to the Westminster Foundation.

The group lets 22,000 sq ft of office space to over 30 charities in small office units in South Belgravia. Each charity receives a contribution from the Westminster Foundation towards its rent, 50% of which the group funds directly.

Previous research suggests that the group has, in the past, also donated to overseas causes.

This total does not include the value of the in-kind donations contributed by the group.

See the corporate charity entry on p. 438 for more information.

In-kind support

Though a description of the in-kind donations contributed by the group was not included in the accounts, previous research tells us that pro bono support is given by the group and its employees.

Employee-led support

Previous research tells us that staff are encouraged to undertake their own fundraising for charities by the active promotion of Give As You Earn within the UK, as well as by the matched funding of employees' charitable fundraising across the group's Operating Companies.

Corporate social responsibility

CSR committee: No specific CSR committee details found.

CSR information: The following information is taken from the 2013 annual report: 'we have incorporated environmental and social sustainability considerations further into our decisionmaking. Now all the Operating Companies' strategic plans explicitly address longterm sustainability to the year 2030'.

CSR report: There is a published environmental review. Currently focused on environmental issues, the report is available to download from the website.

Corporate charity: The Westminster Foundation (Charity Commission no. 267618).

Applications

Previous research suggests applications should be made in writing to the correspondent who will ensure that they are passed dealt with appropriately, i.e. passed to the relevant foundation.

Guardian Media Group plc

Media

Correspondent: The Company Secretary, Kings Place, 90 York Way, London N1 9GU (tel: 020 3353 2000; website: www.gmgplc.co.uk/gmg/responsibility)

Directors: Andrew Miller, Chief Executive; Neil Berkett, Chair; Alan Rusbridger; Nick Backhouse; Ronan Dunne; Judy Gibbons; Brent Hoberman; Jennifer Duvalier; Nigel Morris; John Paton; Darren Singer, Chief Financial

Officer; Philip Tranter (women: 2; men: 10)

Year end	30/03/2014
Turnover	£210,200,000
Pre-tax profit	(£26,100,000)

Nature of business: Newspaper and magazine publishing. The group has national newspapers as well as regional evening and weekly papers in the North West, Berkshire and Surrey.

Company registration number: 94531

Subsidiary undertakings include: GNM Australia Pty Ltd; Guardian News and Media Ltd; Guardian News and Media LLC

Main locations: Manchester, London

Total employees: 1,539

Focus of giving: Prepared to fund.

Cash donations undeclared	✓
Gifts in kind	✓
Overseas giving	✓

Charitable donations

Cash UK (latest available):	2014	£337,000
	2013	£441,000
	2012	£298,000
	2011	£370,000
	2010	£370,000
Total UK (cash and in kind):	2014	£337,000
Cash worldwide:	2014	£337,000
Total worldwide (cash and in kind):	2014	£337,000

Community involvement

Guardian Media Group makes donations to **The Scott Trust Foundation** (also known as the Guardian Foundation – Charity Commission no. 1027893) is the umbrella organisation for the charitable activities of the Scott Trust, which owns the group. The GMG website states that the foundation's remit 'reflects one of the trust's key objectives of 'promoting the causes of freedom of the press and liberal journalism both in Britain and elsewhere'.

The foundation operates through its three arms – the Guardian Foundation, the Newsroom visitor and archive centre and the Scott Trust Charitable Fund – and also funds internships and bursaries for budding journalists. Through the Scott Trust Charitable Fund, support is given to projects, both in the UK and overseas, associated with independent journalism, journalistic efforts, media literacy and journalistic training, although the charitable fund does not make grants directly to other organisations as such.

The community programme of the group's core business, Guardian News and Media, sees support given in the form of fundraising or pro bono work, for example, to organisations, schools and charities based locally to the group's offices.

Corporate giving

The annual report and accounts for 2013/14 did not declare a figure for charitable donations. They do, however, state that during the year the group paid £270,000 in charitable donations to The Scott Trust Foundation.

In previous years, donations have been made additionally to other national, as well as to local charities. We have taken the average of donations to each, based on the three most recent years for which we were able to obtain figures. During this time, the average of donations to national charities (other than The Scott Trust Foundation) was £32,000 and the average of donations to local charities was £35,000. We have taken these figures as estimates and have combined them with the figure stated for donations to the Scott Trust Foundation.

We estimate the total of charitable donations to The Scott Trust Foundation, national and local charities to be around £337,000.

In-kind support

Through Guardian News and Media's community programme, Guardian employees volunteered on 50 different projects with the group's community partners in 2013/14.

Employee-led support

Employee volunteering

In 2013/14 340 staff from Guardian News and Media, the group's core business, volunteered more than 3,000 hours through the volunteering programme, the annual volunteering week and at the GNM Education centre, which is funded by The Scott Trust Foundation (The Guardian Foundation).

Corporate social responsibility

CSR committee: A CSR steering committee has been created and is chaired by the Chief Executive.

CSR information: The following information was obtained from the company's website:

> At GMG an awareness of the wider responsibilities of business has always been at the heart of what we do. The Manchester Guardian was founded to promote liberal interest and the ethos of public service has long been part of the Group's DNA.
>
> The Scott Trust Foundation and GMG's subsidiaries are involved in a range of activities designed to support the wider community, manage environmental impacts and promote press freedom in the UK and abroad.

CSR report: The group's core business, Guardian News and Media has an online sustainability report titled Living our values.

Exclusions

Our research indicates that no support is given for political appeals.

Applications

In writing to the correspondent, referenced 'Charitable donations'. Our research indicates that appeals sent directly to individual papers are dealt with separately.

Halfords Group plc

Retail – miscellaneous

Correspondent: Community and CSR Manager, Icknield Street Drive, Washford West, Redditch, Worcestershire B98 0DE (tel: 01527 517601; website: www.halfordscompany.com/responsibility)

Directors: Dennis Millard, Chair; Matt Davies, Group Chief Executive; Helen Jones; Claudia Arney; Andrew Findlay, Chief Financial Officer; David Adams (women: 2; men: 4)

Year end	28/03/2014
Turnover	£939,700,000
Pre-tax profit	£72,800,000

Nature of business: The principal activity of the group is the retailing of auto, leisure and cycling products.

Company registration number: 4457314

Subsidiary undertakings include: Halfords Holdings (2006) Ltd; Halfords Holdings Ltd; Halfords Finance Ltd; Halfords Ltd.

Main locations: Manchester, Brighton, London, Glasgow, Berwick on Tweed, Workington

UK employees: 11,694

Total employees: 11,694

Focus of giving: Education, animal welfare, health, ill health, not prepared to fund, children, young people.

Membership: BITC

Cash donations undeclared	✓
Charity of the Year	✓
Gifts in kind	✓
Payroll giving	✓
Sponsorship	✓

Charitable donations

Cash UK (latest available):	2014	£50,000
	2013	£50,000
	2012	£50,000
	2011	£73,000
	2009	£26,000
Total UK (cash and in kind):	2014	£50,000
Cash worldwide:	2014	£50,000
Total worldwide (cash and in kind):	2014	£50,000

Community involvement

The following information is taken from Halfords' company website:

> As much as we'd like to help everyone who contacts us, we receive an average

> of five requests for support each day and it's just not possible to help all. So at Halfords we made the decision to make a big difference to one charity and we direct all of our focus there right now by supporting our 12,000 colleagues in fundraising activities for this charity.

Charity of the Year

In 2013 the group entered into a long-term partnership with Re-Cycle, a charity that donates unwanted bikes from the UK to Africa, and its automotive centres continued their partnership with BEN, a charity supporting individuals who have worked in the automotive industry with financial, practical and emotional support.

Corporate giving

We found no information regarding charitable donations in the 2014 annual report and accounts. The annual total of charitable donations has averaged £50,000 in recent years, and we have taken this figure as an estimate for contributions in 2014.

In-kind support

During the year, the group also joined forces with the Scouts Association to provide 'in-depth' in-store workshops for 2,200 cubs working towards their Cyclist Activity Badge.

Employee-led support

Employee fundraising

Halford employees take an active role in raising funds for the group's charitable partners. As part of the Re-Cycle partnership, for example, employees took part in a number of fundraising initiatives, to help cover the cost of sending bikes to Africa. During the year, 'cycle rides, fun days, Snowdon and Ben Nevis challenges, cake sales, raffles, continuous turbo trainer contests and car washes' were some of the ways employees contributed to the cause, raising more than £90,000.

Commercially led support

In partnership with the Ministry of Justice, the group is working to provide skills training and employment opportunities for ex-offenders from Onley Prison.

Corporate social responsibility

CSR committee: The Community and CSR Manager is responsible for 'developing and implementing community programmes' as part of the group's community strategy.

CSR information: This information was obtained from the company's sustainability report:

> Halfords has a clear group strategy for how we operate our business to benefit our customers and colleagues, and of course, to generate value for our shareholders. We recognise that to be successful in achieving our group strategy Halfords must contribute positively to the world in which we operate. Acting responsibly in all our operations, and towards our colleagues, customers and other stakeholders, supports the delivery of our group strategy and thereby benefits our business and our brand.

CSR report: A section of the annual report was devoted to CSR.

Applications

In writing to the correspondent.

Hammerson plc

Property

Correspondent: Community Manager, 10 Grosvenor Street, London W1K 4BJ (tel: 020 7887 1000; email: sustainability@hammerson.com; website: sustainability.hammerson.com)

Directors: David Tyler, Chair; David Atkins, Chief Executive; Peter Cole; Timon Drakesmith, Chief Financial Officer; Terry Duddy; Jacques Espinasse; Anthony Watson; Jean-Philippe Mouton; Judy Gibbons; Gwyn Burr (women: 2; men: 8)

Year end	31/12/2013
Turnover	£321,200,000
Pre-tax profit	£326,300,000

Nature of business: Owner-manager and developer of retail and office property in the UK and France.

Company registration number: 360632

Subsidiary undertakings include: Grantchester Holdings Ltd; Hammerson (Brent Cross) Ltd; Hammerson (Bristol Investments) Ltd; Hammerson International Holdings Ltd; Hammerson SAS; Hammerson UK Properties plc

Main locations: Aberdeen, Birmingham, Brent Cross, Bristol, Leicester, Peterborough, Reading, Southampton, London

UK employees: 300

Total employees: 415

Focus of giving: General charitable purposes, economic generation, education, enterprise/training, health, ill health, safety and crime prevention, children, young people, community/ social welfare.

Membership: BITC, LBG

Gifts in kind ✓

Charitable donations

Cash UK (latest available):	2012	£151,000
	2011	£145,000
	2010	£125,000
	2009	£135,000
	2008	£140,000
Cash worldwide:	2013	£250,000
Total worldwide (cash and in kind):	2013	£394,000

Community involvement

Hammerson looks to develop relationships in the communities in which it has a presence at a local and regional level. One of the ways in which it enforces its CR strategy is through the Positive Places framework, which is conducted on a local basis through Community Plans unique to each of its developments. The main themes of the Community Plans, in line with the business' focuses are: Health and Wellbeing; Regeneration; Skills and Employment for Young People; and Enterprise. See 'In-kind support' for examples of the plans in action.

Hammerson makes community contributions in cash, in kind and in the form of staff volunteering time and, in addition, runs the Hammerson Community Day, which in 2013 saw 214 employees supporting 15 different community organisations across the UK.

Corporate giving

The Hammerson Corporate Responsibility Report, Data and Disclosure 2013 states that the total value of direct contributions from the group to the community was £394,000. This included the following: cash contributions (£250,000); in-kind donations (£66,000); value of staff time (£58,000).

Indirect contributions to the community, generated from non-Hammerson sources (charity collections, charity sales, employee contributions, etc.) amounted to a further £363,000, though, as is our usual practice, we have not included this amount in our figure for corporate contributions.

Note: the Corporate Responsibility Report declares different figures for both direct (£432,000) and indirect contributions (£299,000) than those above. We have used the above figures as they include a breakdown of the specific types of contributions (cash, in kind, staff time).

In-kind support

Staff time

Hammerson's volunteering policy entitles staff to 15 hours volunteering time per year, which is equivalent to two paid working days. This is in addition to the annual Hammerson Community Day, with which all staff participate. In certain cases Hammerson can approve volunteering time for a longer project, for example the Haiti Hospital working visit.

Community plans

Hammerson's Positive Places strategy is conducted on a local basis through its assets and developments. This allows each plan to be altered according to geographical need. Each plan follows four main themes in line with the focus of the group: health and well-being; regeneration; skills and employment for young people; and enterprise. Examples include:

- Silverburn Shopping Centre which developed a long-term relationship with a local food bank, engaging retailers to give donations, worked with local Young Enterprise and made cash/in-kind contributions of £88,000
- Leeds (Victoria Gate) Development which: worked with a local social enterprise in collaboration with a local food bank to create a healthy recipe book; in celebration of the diversity of Leeds and the Tour de France partnered with Kirkgate Market to organise international-themed tours of the market for local schools
- Croydon Partnership Development which: supported Lives Not Knives, a scheme for young people based around educational workshops, code-club training and advice on employment and training; helped a local social enterprise with business planning and advice; engaged young people with Croydon's development plans in partnership with the Architecture Foundation and Croydon Urban Pioneers; worked in partnership with other businesses and developers in support of the Croydon community; sponsored the Croydon Heritage Festival

Employee-led support

Employee volunteering
Employees are able to select their own volunteering opportunities in line with the Hammerson Community Strategy and/or skills development framework.

Corporate social responsibility

CSR committee: Hammerson's CR Board is responsible for sustainability performance. The CR Board meets quarterly and is chaired by the Chief Executive, who reports to the Board of Directors.

CSR information: The following information was obtained from the Positive Places website:

> All sustainability activity at Hammerson is designed, delivered and reported on through our Positive Places framework.
>
> Positive Places is based on an ambitious sustainability vision; a strategy for delivery through the different areas of the business, supported by relevant targets that specifically address our material impacts; and fundamental building blocks like robust policies and frameworks.
>
> Our five key stakeholder groups, through which our development and asset management activity are delivered, are central to our success in delivering Positive Places. The framework allows us to ensure that at least one of these groups is engaged in all our sustainability activities and initiatives. This makes sure our activity remains relevant and focused on what really matters for our customers, investors, communities, suppliers and employees.

CSR report: There is an informative website entitled 'Positive Places', containing all details of the group's CSR reporting, including key data.

Exclusions

No support is given for political appeals.

Applications

In writing to the correspondent, referenced 'Charitable donations'. Our research indicates that each application is considered on its merits, but that around 95% of applications will be unsuccessful.

Hasbro UK Ltd

Toy manufacture and distribution

Correspondent: Community Affairs Dept., Hasbro in the Community, 4 The Square, Stockley Park, Uxbridge, Middlesex UB11 1ET (tel: 020 8569 1234; email: helen.dunlop@hasbro.co.uk; website: www.hasbro.com/en_GB/corporate/community)

Directors: D. Ferry; F. Pascoe; N. Hutton

Year end	29/12/2013
Turnover	£24,083,000
Pre-tax profit	£6,403,000

Nature of business: Toy and game manufacturer.

Company registration number: 1981543

Subsidiary undertakings include: 3D Licensing Ltd.

Brands include: Battleship, Furby, GI Joe, Monopoly, Mr Potato Head, My Little Pony, Play-Doh

Main locations: Uxbridge, Newport

UK employees: 165

Total employees: 165

Focus of giving: Education, children, young people, community/social welfare.

Gifts in kind	✓
Payroll giving	✓
Sponsorship	✓

Charitable donations

Cash UK (latest available):	2013	£15,100
	2012	£13,200
	2011	£47,200
	2010	£36,000
	2009	£34,000
Total UK (cash and in kind):	2013	£15,100
Cash worldwide:	2013	£15,100
Total worldwide (cash and in kind):	2013	£15,100

Community involvement

Hasbro UK gives in-kind support to community groups, schools and organisations, principally in the form of product donations. Priority is given to charitable and community organisations that work with children and families, and schools in the Hillingdon borough and close to the company's warehouse in Newport. In-kind support has also been given through the free use of Hasbro brands in charitable fundraising initiatives and via the 'Team Hasbro' scheme, through which Hasbro employees are able to volunteer in the communities local to their offices at Stockley Park, Hillingdon and Newport.

Note the following from the website: 'We usually only give cash donations/sponsorship to our nominated charities of the year.' Examples of this have included a donation made to children's cancer charity CLIC Sargent to support its London Home from Home project and sponsorship of Sunshine Magazine, a community magazine for the residents of Hillingdon.

At an international level, Hasbro is involved in 'many local, national and global programmes to support charities and groups'. More details on these global initiatives are available from the US website.

Corporate giving

In 2013 the company made charitable donations of £15,000.

We were unable to determine a value for the in-kind donations given by the company.

In-kind support

Gifts in kind
The company supports thousands of community groups, schools and organisations, particularly those in the vicinity of its offices at Hillingdon and Newport, through product donations.

Charities have also been permitted to use the Hasbro brand in their fundraising activities, free of charge. Shelter, for example, was allowed to use the Monopoly logo as part of its fundraiser recruitment drive ahead of the London Marathon.

Staff time
Hasbro UK employees are able to take time out of their working day to accommodate their volunteering activities.

Employee-led support

Payroll giving
Staff are able to donate from their salaries through a Give As You Earn scheme.

Employee volunteering

Employees are able to contribute to their local communities through the 'Team Hasbro' volunteering scheme.

Corporate social responsibility

CSR committee: We found no evidence of a separate CSR Committee.

CSR information: The company supports communities worldwide by partnering with charities, providing financial and product donations and encouraging employees to volunteer.

We were unable to determine the ratio of women to men on the board.

CSR report: A CSR report was available from the group website.

Exclusions

Donations are not given to individuals or organisations working with animals. Hasbro does not undertake any form of advertising in souvenir brochures, for example, for a charity dinner. Donated products must not be sold on for profit.

Applications

Product donations: To apply for a Lucky Dip Box, the online application form must be completed on Hasbro UK's website. Applications are accepted between 21 January and 12 November, and applicants may only apply once each year.

Brands: Organisations wishing to use a Hasbro brand for fundraising purposes must complete the Request Form, which is located on the Hasbro UK website.

'Team Hasbro' volunteering: To recommend a project located close to the Hasbro offices for 'Team Hasbro' to help out with, contact the correspondent with full details of the project and how you think the team could help.

We suggest that applicants refer to the website for more information regarding applications criteria and FAQs.

Heathrow Airport Holdings Ltd (formerly BAA Ltd)

Airport operators

Correspondent: Caroline Nicholls, Director BAA Communities Trust, The Compass Centre, Nelson Road, London Heathrow Airport, Hounslow TW6 2GW (tel: 07836 342495; email: communitiestrust@heathrow.com; website: www.heathrowairport.com/about-us/community-and-environment)

Directors: John Holland-Kaye, Chief Executive; Jose Leo, Chief Financial Officer; Akbar Al Baker; Stuart Baldwin; Chris Beale; Professor David Begg; Ali Bouzarif; Renaud Faucher; Jorge Gil; Rachel Lomax; Ernesto Lopez Mozo; Santiago Olivares; Qing Zhang; Carol Hui (women: 2; men: 12)

Year end	31/12/2013
Turnover	£2,652,000,000
Pre-tax profit	£324,000,000

Nature of business: A holding company for a group of companies that provide and manage airport facilities in the UK, including Heathrow, Stansted, Glasgow, Aberdeen International and Southampton International.

Company registration number: 1970855

Subsidiary undertakings include: For a list of subsidiaries, see the annual report and accounts.

Main locations: Heathrow, Gatwick, Edinburgh, Glasgow, Southampton, Stansted, Aberdeen

UK employees: 7,354

Total employees: 7,354

Focus of giving: Education, environment, children, young people, community/social welfare, disability.

Membership: BITC

FTSE 100	✓
Gifts in kind	✓
Matched funding	✓

Charitable donations

Cash UK (latest available):	2013	£2,000,000
	2012	£2,000,000
	2011	£1,000,000
	2009	£1,000,000
	2008	£1,300,000
Total UK (cash and in kind):	2013	£2,000,000
Cash worldwide:	2013	£2,000,000
Total worldwide (cash and in kind):	2013	£2,000,000

Community involvement

Heathrow Airport Holdings Ltd supports projects in its local communities through the **LHR Airport Communities Trust** (Charity Commission no. 1058617), which distributes funds through community funds at Heathrow, Glasgow, Aberdeen and Southampton airports. The trust's main focuses are: education opportunities for young people; employment/skills development; and the environment. Employees are supported in their volunteering and fundraising efforts through contributions from the trust.

Corporate giving

The group's annual report and accounts for 2013 state that charitable donations amounted to £2 million. This figure included a donation of £750,000 awarded to the group's own LHR Airport Communities Trust.

During the year an additional £5,000 was donated towards the funding of West London Jobs and Apprenticeships Fair 2013. This was classed as a political donation by the Electoral Commission.

We were unable to determine a value for the in-kind support given by the group.

Beneficiaries included: Hillingdon Communities Trust (£1 million); Communities Trust (£750,000); Whizz-Kidz (£96,000); The Groundwork South Trust (£15,000).

See the corporate charity entry on p. 412 for more information.

In-kind support

The group provides support in the form of resources such as the sharing of professional skills and expertise, or the use of equipment and premises.

Employee-led support

Matched funding

Airport staff are supported with grants to support their volunteering and fundraising activity. The company matches employee giving on a pound for pound basis, and employee fundraising to a maximum of £250.

Corporate social responsibility

CSR committee: There appear to be Community Relations teams located at the airports run by the group.

CSR information: The following information was obtained from the Heathrow Airport website: 'We have a strong commitment to the communities around our airport and aim to address issues of prime local concern.'

It would appear that each airport run by the group has its own information regarding its CSR policy.

CSR report: Each airport's website has a section providing information on local community involvement.

Corporate charity: LHR Airport Communities Trust (Charity Commission no. 1058617).

Exclusions

Our research indicates that no support is given to circular appeals, advertising in charity brochures, animal welfare, appeals from individuals, the arts, elderly people, fundraising events, heritage, medical research, overseas projects, political appeals, religious appeals, science/technology, sickness/disability, or sport.

Applications

Applicants are advised to contact the Community Relations Manager at their local airport. For more information on local community funds, visit the relevant airport's website.

H. J. Heinz Manufacturing UK Ltd (formerly H. J. Heinz Company Ltd)

Food manufacture

Correspondent: Kelly Barker, Trust Administrator, Hayes Park South Building, Hayes, Middlesex UB4 8AL (tel: 020 8848 2346; email: charitable.trust@uk.hjheinz.com; website: www.heinz.co.uk)

Directors: C. Page; M. Brown; S. Lawson; E. Vare

Year end	29/12/2013
Turnover	£113,400,000
Pre-tax profit	£1,316,000,000

Nature of business: The principal activity of the company is the manufacturing of processed food products.

The following information was obtained from the annual report and accounts:

> On 29 April 2013, the Heinz UK business implemented a reorganisation of its operations to align to a new Europe-wide centralised supply chain business model.
>
> As part of the above restructuring, the company's selling activities and related assets and liabilities were transferred to a new company, H J Heinz Foods UK Ltd.

Company registration number: 147624

Subsidiary undertakings include: H J Heinz Asset Leasing Ltd; H J Heinz Frozen and Chilled Food Ltd; Heinz Single Service Ltd

Main locations: Worcester, Hayes, Kitt Green, Leamington, Kendal, Grimsby, Westwick, Okehampton, Telford

Total employees: 1,362

Focus of giving: Education, environment, health, ill health, arts, culture, community/social welfare.

Cash donations undeclared ✓

Charitable donations

Cash UK (latest available):	2013	£85,000
	2011	£85,000
	2008	£85,500
	2007	£180,000
	2006	£136,000
Total UK (cash and in kind):	2013	£85,000
Cash worldwide:	2013	£85,000
Total worldwide (cash and in kind):	2013	£85,000

Community involvement

The company makes its charitable donations through **The H J Heinz Company Ltd Charitable Trust** (Charity Commission no. 326254), which looks to improve the quality of life of those living in the communities where Heinz has a presence. The Trust is overseen by a group of appointed trustees, drawn from all areas of the company. The HCT has guidelines that charities it supports should be from one of the following areas:

- *Nutrition* – Promoting improvements in and a better understanding of good nutrition, and contributing to the health and well-being of people and communities
- *Healthy Children and Families* – Improving the overall well-being of people by ensuring children and families have the resources and services necessary to help them live healthy and happy lives.

Based on this criteria, each Heinz site has a local Charity of the Year.

Corporate giving

The company's annual report and accounts for 2012/13 did not declare a figure for charitable donations made during the financial year.

In previous years, the majority of the company's charitable contributions have been made through the H J Heinz Company Ltd Charitable Trust. Though the trust's annual report and accounts (2012) stated that 'The trustees have no reason to believe that the financial support from H J Heinz Company Ltd will be withdrawn in the foreseeable future', in 2013, the trust's income was unusually low (£3,600). As a result, it was not required to submit its accounts to the Charity Commission. This, unfortunately, means that we were unable to determine how much of the trust's income was donated by the company.

In the most recent year for which we have a figure (2011) the company made donations of £85,000, and we have taken this as an estimate for charitable donations in 2012/13. It is, however, likely that the actual figure varies considerably from our estimate if the trust's income is taken as an indicator.

See the corporate charity entry on p. 408 for more information.

Employee-led support

Employee fundraising

Employees who wish to fundraise for their own chosen cause are supported by the HCT.

Corporate social responsibility

CSR committee: We found no evidence of a CSR committee.

CSR information: The following information was obtained from the company website: 'The Heinz Charitable Trust has long been committed to providing support to promote the quality of life among the communities in which we are present. The Trust is overseen by a group of appointed Trustees, drawn from all areas of our company.'

We were unable to determine the ratio of women to men on the board of directors.

CSR report: We found no evidence of a CSR report; however, the Heinz UK website has a section dedicated to sustainability.

Corporate charity: The H J Heinz Company Ltd Charitable Trust (Charity Commission no. 326254).

Exclusions

Our research indicates that the Heinz Charitable Trust does not:

- Support politically oriented causes in any way
- Consider religious appeals if the object is to promote denominational principles
- Take advertising space in charity programmes/brochures
- Support individuals undertaking educational/vocational studies
- Consider unsolicited research projects
- Directly support individuals or groups undertaking sponsored events
- Accept commercial sponsorship

Applications

Applications to the trust should be made in writing to the correspondent.

Note that, generally, only organisations registered as national charity organisations will be considered.

The trustees meet once a year to consider major appeals for donations. However, a subcommittee, which is authorised to make grants of up to £10,000, meets more frequently. This committee also selects applications to be considered by the trustees at their annual meeting.

Helical bar plc

Property

Correspondent: The Company Secretary, 5 Hanover Square, London W1S 1HQ (tel: 020 7629 0113; fax: 020 7408 1666; website: www.helical.co.uk)

Directors: Michael Slade, Chief Executive Officer; Matthew Bonning-Snook; Tim Murphy, Finance Director; Gerald Kaye; Jack Pitman; Duncan Walker; Nigel McNair Scott, Chair; Richard Gillingwater; Andrew Gulliford; Michael O'Donnell; Richard Grant (women: 0; men: 11)

Year end	31/03/2014
Turnover	£123,600,000
Pre-tax profit	£101,700,000

Nature of business: Helical Bar is a property development and investment company.

Company registration number: 156663

Subsidiary undertakings include: A list of subsidiaries is contained within the annual report and accounts.

UK employees: 50

Total employees: 50

Focus of giving: General charitable purposes, education, environment, general appeals, community/social welfare.

Gifts in kind	✓
Market-led giving	✓
Sponsorship	✓

Charitable donations

Cash UK (latest available):	2014	£17,400
	2011	£13,000
	2010	£13,000
Total UK (cash and in kind):	2014	£17,400
Cash worldwide:	2014	£17,400
Total worldwide (cash and in kind):	2014	£17,400

Community involvement

The group engages in community involvement in areas where it has a presence. These activities range from the free provision of commercial space, to partnerships with a local university, to sponsorship of local events. Clyde Shopping Centre, The Morgan Quarter in Cardiff and Idlewells Shopping Centre all participated in various community activities in their local areas during the year. More details of these activities are listed in the group's annual report.

Corporate giving

In the 2013/14 financial year Helical Bar made donations totalling £17,400 to a number of charities. We were unable to locate a value for in-kind donations given by the group.

Beneficiaries included: The Haven (Breast Cancer Charity); LandAid; Schools Around the World; and Walking With the Wounded.

In-kind support

See the 'Community involvement' section for more details.

Employee-led support

See the 'Community involvement' section for more details.

Commercially led support

See the 'Community involvement' section for more details.

Corporate social responsibility

CSR committee: The Board of Directors has responsibility for CSR.

CSR information: The following information is taken from the 2014 annual report:

> Helical Bar recognises that our business activities impact on the environment and the wider communities in which we operate. As our business involves working with joint venture partners and outsourcing partners, our direct impacts as a business are relatively small. However, we are aware of the influence we can exert through the implementation of responsible environmental and social practices via our partners, contractors and suppliers.

More information on the Helical Bar's CSR policy is detailed on its website and in its annual report.

CSR report: A CSR report is included in the group's annual report.

Applications

In writing to the correspondent referenced 'Charitable Donations'.

Henderson Group plc

Financial services

Correspondent: Director of Corporate Affairs, 201 Bishopsgate, London EC2M 3AE (tel: 020 7818 1818; fax: 020 7818 1820; website: www.henderson.com)

Directors: Richard Gillingwater, Chair; Andrew Formica, Chief Executive; Roger Thompson, Chief Financial Officer; Sarah Arkle; Kevin Dolan; Tim How; Robert Jeens; Angela Seymour-Jackson (women: 2; men: 6)

Year end	31/12/2013
Turnover	£578,200,000
Pre-tax profit	£107,300,000

Nature of business: The principal activity of the group is the provision of investment management services. The group has businesses in the UK, Europe, Australia, Asia and the US.

Company registration number: 2072534

Subsidiary undertakings include: Henderson Group Holdings Asset Management Ltd; Gartmore Investment Ltd; Henderson Administration Ltd; Henderson Alternative Investment Advisor Ltd; Henderson Fund Management Ltd; Henderson Global Investors Ltd

Total employees: 1,009

Focus of giving: General charitable purposes, environment, health, ill health, heritage, medical research, arts, culture, community/social welfare.

Gifts in kind	✓
Matched funding	✓
Payroll giving	✓
Sponsorship	✓

Charitable donations

Cash UK (latest available):	2013	£222,000
	2012	£162,000
	2011	£149,500
	2010	£36,000
	2009	£53,000
Total UK (cash and in kind):	2013	£222,000
Cash worldwide:	2013	£222,000
Total worldwide (cash and in kind):	2013	£222,000

Community involvement

Henderson Group plc looks to support communities in the area close to its London office. Aside from making charitable donations and sponsorships, the group also supports its employees in their charitable activities by operating matched funding and payroll giving schemes, and encouraging employee volunteering. In 2011 the group established the **Henderson Foundation** which continues to bring 'greater focus and clarity' towards its corporate responsibility objectives.

Corporate giving

In 2013 the group donated a total of £222,000 for community and charitable purposes, the majority of which was given through matching employee fundraising for more than 100 local, national and international causes.

The group's annual report and accounts state that the group continued its £50,000 'sponsorship of the Isaac Newton Institute, and £8,400 to Community Links, our preferred charity since 1987'. We have not discounted this from the total of donations as the group receives only a small mention (amongst other funders) on the institute's website and, in reports from previous years, these payments have been classed as donations.

In-kind support

Employee volunteering

The group offers time off for its employees to contribute to community and charitable activities.

Employee-led support

Matched funding

Henderson Group plc matches funds raised by employees.

Payroll giving

The group operates a Give As You Earn scheme, through which employees can donate from their pay packet to UK-registered charities.

Commercially led support

Sponsorship

During the year, the group continued its sponsorship of the Isaac Newton Institute, an international research institute for mathematical sciences.

Corporate social responsibility

CSR committee: We found no evidence of a CSR Committee.

CSR information: The following information was taken from the annual report: 'We foster positive relationships with communities near our London office, and continuously look to support and encourage our employees to engage in community and charitable activities.'

CSR report: A sustainability report is included in the annual report and accounts.

Exclusions

No response to circular appeals or to sponsorship requests for individuals. No support is given for: fundraising events; advertising in charity brochures; religious appeals; or overseas projects.

Applications

In writing to the correspondent.

HESCO Bastion Ltd

Defence

Correspondent: The Company Secretary, Unit 41, Knowsthorpe Way, Cross Green Ind. Est., Leeds LS9 0SW (tel: 01132 486633; email: info@hesco.com; website: www.hescobastion.com)

Directors: Michael Hughes; Kevin Lyons; Mandy Atkinson (women: 1; men: 2)

Year end	31/01/2014
Turnover	£19,937,935
Pre-tax profit	£4,482,380

Nature of business: The company designs and manufactures rapidly deployable barrier systems.

Company registration number: 2600319

Total employees: 96

Focus of giving: General charitable purposes, community/social welfare.

Cash donations undeclared ✓

Charitable donations

Cash UK (latest available):	2014	£44,000
	2013	£3,700
	2012	£85,000
	2011	£10,044,600
	2009	£3,050,000
Total UK (cash and in kind):	2014	£44,000
Cash worldwide:	2014	£44,000
Total worldwide (cash and in kind):	2014	£44,000

Community involvement

HESCO Bastion contributes to charities in the area local to where the company has a presence (mainly Leeds). We were unable to determine further details of the company's community involvement.

Corporate giving

The annual report and accounts for 2013/14 did not declare a figure for charitable donations made by the company during the year, and we were unable to gather further information from the company. Though we would typically take the average of the three most recent years for which we have figures, in one of these years, a one-off contribution of £10 million was made to Leeds Community Foundation to a fund established by Jim Heselden, HESCO Bastion's late founder (now called Jimbo's Fund). We have therefore taken the average of only the two most recent years for which we were able to obtain figures. This average was £44,000, and we have taken this amount as our estimate for charitable donations from the company in 2013/14.

Corporate social responsibility

CSR committee: We found no details of a CSR committee.

CSR information: The following information was obtained from the website:

> We believe in supporting the communities in which we operate as best as we can, with regard to the business environment in which we work. Where possible, we seek to use local resources and we contribute to local charities, as well as supporting national organisations.

CSR report: We found no CSR report.

Applications

In writing to the correspondent, referenced 'Charitable donations'.

Highland Group Holdings Ltd (entry formerly House of Fraser (Stores) Ltd)

Retail – department and variety stores

Correspondent: Peter Hearsey, Company Secretary, Granite House, 4th Floor, 31 Stockwell Street, Glasgow G1 4RZ (website: www.houseoffraser.co.uk/charities/charities,default,pg.html)

Directors: Don McCarthy, Chair; John King, Chief Executive; Mark Gifford, Chief Financial Officer; Mr S. Cassar; Mr V. Gupta; Ms S. Ingleson; Mr M. Pacitti; Mr S. Rose; Mr K. Stanford (women: 1; men: 8)

Year end	25/01/2014
Turnover	£731,700,000
Pre-tax profit	(£2,000,000)

Nature of business: The group is a multi-branded, multi-channel retailer in the UK and Ireland, trading principally through the House of Fraser brand name.

The entry for the group has previously existed on our database under the name House of Fraser (Stores) Ltd.

Company registration number: 5845860

Subsidiary undertakings include: House of Fraser Ltd; House of Fraser (Finance) Ltd; House of Fraser (Stores) Ltd; House of Fraser (Storecard) Ltd; James Beattie Ltd

Brands include: Biba, Episode, House of Fraser, Kenneth Cole New York, Linea

Main locations: Glasgow, Swindon

UK employees: 5,073

Total employees: 5,073

Focus of giving: General charitable purposes, education, enterprise/training, environment, heritage, medical research, arts, culture, children, young people, community/social welfare.

Charity of the Year ✓

Charitable donations

Cash UK (latest available):	2014	£0
	2013	£0
	2012	£83,000
	2011	£161,000
	2009	£245,000
Cash worldwide:	2014	£0

Community involvement

Highland Group Holdings Ltd supports its nominated charities and encourages its individual stores to raise money for local and national charities. The group's retail and support centre employees organise their own fundraising events for various charities. It would appear that, in recent years, fundraising has been the primary way in which the group has helped to support charities, notably through the annual House of Fraser Charity Golf Day.

Corporate giving

The annual report and accounts for 2013/14 state that no charitable donations were made by the group.

The annual House of Fraser Charity Golf Day helped to raise more than £235,000 for charitable causes though, as is our usual practice, we have not included this amount in our total figure for corporate cash donations.

The annual report and accounts state that: 'The group also supported various other charities throughout the period, including Walk the Walk and the Retail Trust, and a host of local charities throughout the country.' We were unable to determine a value for this support.

Beneficiaries included: Retail Trust; Walk the Walk

Employee-led support

Employee fundraising

Employees at House of Fraser stores are encouraged to raise funds through events and activities for charities in their local areas.

Commercially led support

Since 2004, House of Fraser has held a Charity Golf Day, helping to raise funds for numerous charities.

Corporate social responsibility

CSR committee: There was no evidence of a separate CSR Committee.

CSR information: This information was obtained from the company's website: 'We make charitable donations wherever possible and, along with our nominated charity of the year, the stores are encouraged to undertake their own fundraising events and activities for local charities.'

CSR report: There was no evidence of a separate CSR report; however, there is a section dedicated to social responsibility on the website.

Exclusions

Our research suggests that support is not generally given to circular appeals, appeals from individuals, purely denominational (religious or political) appeals, local appeals not in areas of company presence or overseas projects.

Applications

In writing to the correspondent, referenced 'Charitable donations'. Our research indicates that local charities are supported at the discretion of the store managers in their region. It would appear that the majority of initiatives supported by stores and support offices are suggested by staff.

Hikma Pharmaceuticals plc

Pharmaceuticals

Correspondent: CR Team, 13 Hanover Square, London W1S 1HL (tel: 020 7399 2760; fax: 020 7399 2761; website: www.hikma.com/en/corporate-responsibility.aspx)

Directors: Said Darwazah, Chair and Chief Executive; Mazen Darwazah; Ali Al-Husry; Robert Pickering; Michael Ashton; Breffni Byrne; Ronald Goode; Patrick Butler (women: 0; men: 8)

Year end	31/12/2013
Turnover	£868,656,000
Pre-tax profit	£189,655,000

Nature of business: The principal activities of the group are the development, manufacture and marketing of a broad range of generic and in-licensed pharmaceutical products in solid, semi-solid, liquid and injectable final dosage forms. The majority of Hikma's operations are in the MENA region, the United States and Europe.

Company registration number: 5557934

Subsidiary undertakings include: Hikma Pharma Ltd; Hikma Ltd; Hikma Acquisitions (UK) Ltd

Total employees: 7,067

Focus of giving: Education, health, ill health.

Gifts in kind	✓
Humanitarian aid: overseas	✓
Overseas giving	✓
Sponsorship	✓

Charitable donations

Cash UK (latest available):	2009	£689,700
	2008	£1,515,800
Cash worldwide:	2013	£3,245,000
Total worldwide (cash and in kind):	2013	£3,951,000

Community involvement

Hikma Pharmaceuticals plc looks to give to local causes in areas where the group operates, donate medicines to NGOs and to 'support communities in crisis'. It would appear that most of the group's charitable support is directed towards health and health education. Employees of the group are also encouraged to volunteer 'whenever possible'.

Corporate giving

During the year charitable contributions from the group totalled £3.95 million ($6.2 million), of which around £3.25 million ($5.1 million) was donated to local charities serving the communities in which the group operates. We have taken this amount to represent cash donations.

The remaining amount of around £704,000 ($1.1 million) was made up of in kind medical donations to NGOs.

We were unable to locate a figure for UK cash donations or details of beneficiaries in the UK.

Employee-led support

Employee volunteering

Each April, Hikma's Global Volunteering Day sees Hikma employees contribute to their local communities worldwide. Charitable activities include: 'donating blood, cleaning and painting hospitals, kindergartens and orphanages, spending time with children and patients, raising money for research, organising awareness campaigns'.

Corporate social responsibility

CSR committee: The group has a Compliance, Responsibility and Ethics Committee (CREC), which is supported by the CR committee. The following information is taken from the groups CR report:

> The Executive Vice Chairman champions Hikma's corporate responsibility programme within the Company and is Chairman of Hikma's Corporate Responsibility Committee. The VP of Communications is responsible for CR at an operational level.
>
> The CREC Chairman, Director of Communications, divisional and functional heads and Company Secretary are members of the CR Committee. The CR Committee reviews, supports and promotes Hikma's CR activities and reports directly to the CREC.
>
> The CR team, lead by the VP of Communications, regularly present developments to the CREC.

CSR information: This information was obtained from the company's website:

> Our five-year Corporate Responsibility (CR) plan, which takes us from 2010 to 2015, revolves around two broad themes, well-being and education, and four key platforms, our people, our community, our environment and global welfare and ethics. These platforms reflect Hikma's genuine commitment to its stakeholders and its dedication to fully integrate CR within its business strategy.

CSR report: A CSR report was available from the company's website.

Applications

In writing to the correspondent.

William Hill plc

Gaming, leisure

Correspondent: The Corporate Responsibility Committee, Greenside House, 50 Station Road, Wood Green, London N22 7TP (tel: 020 8918 3600; fax: 020 8918 3775; website: www.williamhillplc.co.uk)

Directors: Gareth Davis, Chair; James Henderson, Chief Executive Officer; Neil Cooper, Group Finance Director; Roy Gardner; Ashley Highfield; David Lowden; Georgina Harvey; Imelda Walsh; Luke Thomas, Company Secretary (women: 2; men: 7)

Year end	31/12/2013
Turnover	£1,486,500,000
Pre-tax profit	£257,000,000

Nature of business: The principal activities of the group include operation of licensed betting offices and the provision of telephone, online and interactive television betting and online casino and poker services. The group also operates greyhound stadia.

Company registration number: 4212563

Subsidiary undertakings include: Ad-gency Ltd; Leroy's Horse and Sports Place; Tom Waterhouse N.T. Pty Ltd; WHG Spain plc; William Hill Holdings Ltd; Will Hill Ltd; Willstan Ltd; and William Hill organisation Ltd. A full list of subsidiary undertakings is available from the group's accounts or Companies House.

Main locations: Haringey

Total employees: 17,089

Focus of giving: Education, animal welfare, individuals, unpopular causes, arts, culture, overseas projects, safety and crime prevention, sponsorship, community/social welfare.

Gifts in kind	✓
Humanitarian aid: overseas	✓
Market-led giving	✓
Matched funding	✓
Overseas giving	✓
Sponsorship	✓

Charitable donations

Cash UK (latest available):	2013	£3,300,000
	2011	£986,000
	2009	£920,000
	2008	£773,000
	2007	£581,000
Total UK (cash and in kind):	2013	£3,300,000
Cash worldwide:	2013	£3,300,000
Total worldwide (cash and in kind):	2013	£3,300,000

Community involvement

According to William Hill's charitable donations policy, outlined on the company's website, the company seeks to support the communities in which it operates through charitable donations and other relevant payments, generally 'to organisations involved in areas of greatest relevance to its business'. This can include:

> Promoting a responsible approach to gambling; undertaking research into problem gambling, and providing information, advice and help to those who are at risk or are experiencing difficulties with their gambling; greyhound and racehorse welfare; and supporting disadvantaged individuals in horse and greyhound racing.

The information quoted in this section is taken from the Corporate Responsibility Report 2014. The group's main annual charitable donation is given to the Responsible Gambling Trust 'to fund the research, education and treatment of problem gambling'. In 2013 £863,000 was donated.

Through its two greyhound stadia William Hill assists with greyhound welfare, for example, by funding 'an establishment that houses up to 25 dogs for up to three months with the intention of permanently re-homing them'.

The William Hill Foundation (Charity Commission no. 1146270)

The foundation was created in 2011 and registered with the Charity Commission in 2012. It was designed as a hardship fund to support colleagues but now also acts as an umbrella organisation for Project Africa. 'Four directors – all William Hill leaders – administer the £100,000 hardship fund and the donations received from colleagues for Project Africa. '

Disaster Relief

Following the Typhoon Haiyan in Philippines in 2013, William Hill 'donated £25,000 to the Disasters Emergency Committee and gave grants to colleagues affected by the typhoon to help them recover'. It appears from the annual report and accounts of the William Hill Foundation that this sum was channelled through the charity.

Examples of local initiatives worldwide are available from the CR Report.

Corporate giving

According to the annual report and accounts of the group, in 2013 charitable donations amounted to £963,000 (including £863,000 given to the Responsible Gambling Trust and £57,000 in matched funding).

The annual report and accounts of the William Hill Foundation state that during 2013 it received a total of £113,000 (2012: £92,000) from William Hill organisation Ltd (a subsidiary of William Hill plc) and further £137,000 was received in donations to support the Project Africa appeal. The charity made grants totalling £163,000, of which £47,000 supported 32 William Hill employees and their families, £30,000 was donated to other causes (including the Disasters Emergency Committee) and a further £86,000 supported the work on Project Africa.

The annual report and accounts state the following:

> We continue to support the horseracing industry, which receives funds from us both from the statutory levy (10.75% of Retail UK horseracing gross win) and for payments for TV pictures from the tracks [over £60 million was paid in content costs for pictures from the race tracks]. The Levy in 2013 was £17.5m. The four major LBOs operators reached a longterm deal with the horseracing industry in 2013, increasing the existing Levy yield by £4.5m per annum and providing a guaranteed underpin of £47m a year. We paid a voluntary donation of £2.4m to the British Greyhound Racing Fund for the upkeep of stadias and animal welfare.

We use the figure of £3.3 million as the group's total charitable contributions, even though a voluntary donation of £2.4 million to the British Greyhound Racing Fund, referred to in the annual report and accounts as well as the group's website, does not seem to be included in the charitable donations figure provided by the company.

Beneficiaries included: British Greyhound Racing Fund (£2.4 million); Responsible Gambling Trust (£863,000); and The William Hill Charitable Foundation.

In-kind support

The group continues its engagement with local communities to combat crime. Working with successful initiatives in the Metropolitan Police area, Northumbria, Strathclyde and Manchester, also Bristol and the West Midlands. In the past the partnership saw campaign literature being sent to postcode districts and posters displayed in William Hill shops and distributed by local Police Community Support Officers.

As part of the Project Africa initiative employee time and skills are donated.

Employee-led support

Staff members spend their time volunteering and contribute to good causes through their own fundraising efforts. For example, a UK team participated in a sponsored walk along the Ridgeway raising money for the Greatwood Foundation charity for retired racehorses (selected through the 2012 Different Perspectives event), and a team from the UK and Bulgaria participated in the Responsible Gambling Trust's Kilimanjaro fundraising expedition which raised more than £15,000 for the charity.

Different Perspectives

According to the company's webste, this initiative initially focused on developing female managers of the future but in 2012 changed its focus to:

> Encouraging managers to develop the balance in their lives between working, playing, giving and learning. An initial group of 50 managers are giving their time to a variety of charities, most with a personal or local connection to William Hill colleagues. The vision is to extend this initiative further to ensure more colleagues are developing themselves through charitable giving.

In 2013 work was undertaken with Catch 22 – a charity working with troubled and vulnerable young people, families and offenders. Activities undertaken by the volunteering staff include: assisting young people in getting ready for work; CV writing advice; help with job applications and interview practice; networking skills; and mentoring for women offenders based in London as part of a six-month programme with the London Probation Trust. Similar projects are undertaken in Northern Ireland, Tel Aviv, Bulgaria and the US.

Project Africa

According to the website, the group started initiatives in Kenyan community in 2012:

> Project Africa aims to improve the educational and medicinal facilities of the community, and ensure a clean water supply is available for all whilst developing and stretching William Hill people. ... It is supported by the William Hill Foundation and its patron Robbie Savage. To date, William Hill colleagues have raised over £200,000 to support the project.

In 2013 the library project was finished with the group spending 'thousands of pounds on stocking the library with a wide range of books' and 'employing and training two librarians who manage the library six days a week'. The main building project for 2013 was to establish better quality accommodation for the teachers – eight houses have been built.

The website also notes:

> Thanks to the fundraising efforts of our retail colleagues, we were able to supply every pupil with some essential kit in

> 2013: a pair of shoes, a school rucksack and a full set of stationery items. We are also now sponsoring four pupils a year to go on to secondary school education.

Part of the project is development of clean water access in the community – so far the group's activities have included digging reservoirs, building hands-free kits for children to wash their hands and placing water tanks to capture rainfall.

Future focus will also be placed on malnutrition, health care and teacher development, amongst others.

Matched funding

There is a proportion of the charitable donations budget match funds (up to a limit) raised by employees on local charitable initiatives. In 2013 matched donations totalled almost £57,000.

Payroll giving

Our research suggests that there has been a payroll giving scheme that allows employees to make donations directly to charities they choose.

Commercially led support

Sponsorship

The group's website notes that the group has 'significantly extended [its] sponsorship activities in recent times and supports sports as diverse as football, darts and snooker' in the UK and Australia. UK sponsorships include: All England Festival; Ayr Gold Cup; Grand Slam of Darts; Greyhound Derby; Kempton Winter Festival; and Lincoln Handicap. 'In Australia, Sportingbet's sponsorships include the Brisbane Broncos rugby league football club and a number of racetracks, including Moonee Valley and Darwin Turf Club.'

A sponsorship agreement has been made with The Football Association to sponsor the England football team and act as an 'Official Supporter' and 'Official Betting Partner' of the FA Cup. In Scotland the group is an 'Official Betting Partner' of the Scottish national football team, a sponsor of the William Hill Scottish Cup and an 'Official Betting Partner of the Scottish Premier League'.

Responsible gambling

The main focus of the group is addressing the negative impact of gambling activities. 'William Hill has established a responsible gambling website as an information resource for customers, those who are concerned about gambling by their friends or family members, and for anyone else interested in responsible gambling.'

Apprenticeships

The group is launching an apprenticeship scheme for 18- to 24-year-olds, recruiting up to 200 apprentices in the first instance in 2014.

Corporate social responsibility

CSR committee: There is a Corporate Responsibility Committee which:

> Sets the group's CR policies, ensures the business operates in a sustainable way and advises the board on environmental, social and ethical matters. The CR Committee's meetings are now regularly attended by relevant members of the executive committee and management team, and presentations are made by individuals responsible for key areas, such as HR, health and safety, security and compliance.

CSR information: The group's corporate responsibility activities are framed by the William Hill Commitment, which focuses on colleagues, customers and community (for detailed information see the Commitment document available online).

Information taken from the company's website states the following:

> Three important principles – keeping crime and disorder out of gambling, protecting children and the vulnerable, and keeping gambling fair – are embodied in the licensing objectives of the Gambling Commission under the UK's Gambling Act 2005. These underpin the overarching objectives of our Corporate Responsibility Committee. They are at the heart of our UK business and are the principles we adopt across our international operations as well.

Charitable donations policy paper, formulated in 2010, says:

> We are committed to being a responsible corporate citizen and we recognise our wider social responsibility by seeking to support the communities in which we operate through our charitable donations and through voluntary contributions to the British Greyhound Racing Fund.

CSR report: A CSR report is published annually.

Exclusions

William Hill does not make donations to political parties.

Applications

The group: In writing to the correspondent.

The foundation: The principal contact person is Heather Hamilton (tel: 020 8918 3600; email: williamhillfoundation@williamhill.co.uk) at the company's address. More details can also be found online, visiting www.thewilliamhillfoundation.org.

Honda of the UK Manufacturing Ltd

Motors and accessories

Correspondent: CSR Team, Highworth Road, South Marston, Swindon SN3 4TZ (tel: 01793 831183; fax: 01793 831177; website: www.hondamanufacturing.co.uk/responsibility-community)

Directors: T. Mikoshiba, Chair; S. Takizawa

Year end	31/03/2014
Turnover	£1,988,448,000
Pre-tax profit	£1,054,000

Nature of business: The principal activity of the company is the manufacture of motor vehicles, including the manufacture of motor engines and other vehicle parts.

Company registration number: 1887872

Main locations: Slough, Swindon

UK employees: 3,315

Total employees: 3,315

Focus of giving: General charitable purposes, education, environment, community/social welfare.

Gifts in kind ✓

Charitable donations

Cash UK (latest available):	2014	£12,600
	2013	£12,700
	2011	£29,000
	2009	£13,000
	2008	£110,000
Total UK (cash and in kind):	2014	£12,600
Cash worldwide:	2014	£12,600
Total worldwide (cash and in kind):	2014	£12,600

Community involvement

Honda of the UK Manufacturing Ltd predominantly supports charitable and community initiatives in the area local to its Swindon base. Its donations are managed by Community Foundation for Wiltshire and Swindon and are given to support projects within a 15-mile radius of the company's facility. Additionally, the company also supports initiatives including:

Safe Drive, Stay Alive

The company supports this road safety initiative for young drivers, which helps to fund a permanent education officer within the Wiltshire Fire Brigade.

The Junior Good Citizen Scheme

Honda UK supports this educational programme in conjunction with emergency services and local authorities. The programme aims to equip ten and eleven year old with life skills as they makes the transition from primary to secondary school, focusing on the promotion of safety and awareness across various areas, including fire, smoking and alcohol, antisocial behaviour, and the Internet.

Corporate giving

In 2013/14 the company made charitable donations of £12,600.

We were unable to determine a value for the in-kind donations given by the company.

In-kind support

Gifts in kind

Honda has supported BEN (The Automotive Industry Charity) through Honda UK, making donations in the form of cars, bikes and 'individual giving'.

Corporate social responsibility

CSR committee: The following information was taken from the Honda Worldwide CSR report:

> *CSR Management Framework*
>
> In fiscal 2014, cognizant of the growing global emphasis on evaluating business activity from a long-range perspective, Honda expanded the scope of the World Environment and Safety Committee to include matters under the heading Society and Governance, as well as Environment, thereby creating a framework for global deliberation, implementation, and communication of Honda's sustainability strategy. In addition, in April 2014 Honda transferred jurisdiction over CSR management functions from Business Support Operations to the newly established CSR Planning Office under the Corporate Planning Division, in recognition of the importance of CSR management. The new organisation strengthens Honda's central CSR planning capabilities and creates a framework in which the CSR Planning Office reports planning and progress on Honda's sustainability strategy directly to the World Environment and Safety Committee along with the Environment and Safety Planning Office, previously established under the Corporate Planning Division.

CSR information: The following information is taken from the website:

> As a company with a global viewpoint, we are dedicated to contributing to the well-being of local communities around the world through our products and technologies. As a good corporate citizen, we will deepen our commitment to all local communities where we do business. We will contribute to the nurturing of a society where caring and energetic individuals actively participate in socially responsible activities.

We were unable to determine the ratio of women to men on the board.

CSR report: Honda UK has a 'responsibility and community' section on its website. There is also a community section on the Honda Worldwide website and a downloadable CSR report, though these focus predominantly on the CSR activities of Honda overseas.

Applications

The company appears to direct its giving through Wiltshire Community Foundation (formerly Community Foundation for Wiltshire and Swindon), the application information for which can be found on the foundation's website (wiltshirecf.org.uk/apply-for-a-grant).

Hoover Ltd

Domestic appliances

Correspondent: Ms Susan Whetter, Hoover Foundation, Hoover Candy Group, Pentrebach, Merthyr Tydfil, Mid Glamorgan CF48 4TU (tel: 01685 725530; email: susan.whetter@hoovercandy.com; website: www.hoover.co.uk)

Directors: A. Bertali, Chair; R. B. Mudie; G. Palma; D. Meyerowitz; M. Osguthorpe; M. Severgnini; A. H. Bokhari; M. R. Given; A. P. Lane

Year end	31/12/2010
Turnover	£172,406,000
Pre-tax profit	(£771,000)

Nature of business: Manufacture of domestic laundry, refrigeration, and vacuuming appliances.

Company registration number: 2521528

UK employees: 479

Total employees: 479

Focus of giving: General charitable purposes, education, health, ill health, community/social welfare.

Cash donations undeclared ✓

Charitable donations

Cash UK (latest available):	2010	£6,200
	2009	£84,000

Community involvement

Hoover Ltd appears to direct its grant-giving through the **Hoover Foundation** (Registered charity: 200274) which supports registered charities in Wales, England and Scotland, particularly in the areas of Glasgow, South Wales and Bolton, although no money was received from the company be the foundation in 2012/13. The foundation primarily supports health, education and social welfare.

Corporate giving

Hoover Ltd appears to direct its charitable giving through the Hoover Foundation. In its accounts for 2012/13, the foundation had an income of £87,000, all of which it received through returns on investments.

See the corporate charity entry on p. 409 for more information.

Corporate social responsibility

CSR committee: We found no evidence of a separate CSR Committee.

CSR information: The company's website states the following:

> The business reference for any organisation today has moved beyond just return on investment criteria.
>
> By defining and putting into operation a policy not only linked to 'traditional' policies & procedures relating to aspects, such as Quality, Environment and Safety, Hoover (as part of the Hoover Candy Group) has been among the first big industrial groups within Europe to embrace the ethos of Sustainable Development as a fully integrated Corporate Social Responsibility (CSR) Policy.

The company directs it charitable involvement through the Hoover Foundation.

We were unable to determine the ratio of women to men on the board.

CSR report: There was no evidence of a separate CSR report.

Corporate charity: The Hoover Foundation (Charity Commission no. 200274).

Exclusions

No grants to individuals, including students.

Applications

In writing to the correspondent.

HP Enterprise Services UK Ltd

Information technology

Correspondent: Company Secretary, Amen Corner, Cain Road, Bracknell, Berkshire RG12 1HN (website: www.hp.com/hpinfo/globalcitizenship)

Directors: M. Birch; P. Bladen; S. Burr; A. Isherwood; T. Trower; C. Wilson

Year end	31/10/2013
Turnover	£2,373,225,000
Pre-tax profit	(£70,106,000)

Nature of business: HP Enterprise Services is a technology services company delivering a broad portfolio of information technology and business outsourcing services. The company is a subsidiary of Hewlett-Packard Company.

Company registration number: 53419

Subsidiary undertakings include: See the annual report and accounts.

Main locations: London, Luton, Uxbridge

UK employees: 10,785

Total employees: 10,785

Focus of giving: General charitable purposes, education, health, ill health, arts, culture.

Charitable donations

Cash UK (latest available):	2013	£29,000
	2012	£10,600
	2010	£9,400
	2009	£15,400
	2008	£61,700
Total UK (cash and in kind):	2013	£29,000
Cash worldwide:	2013	£29,000
Total worldwide (cash and in kind):	2013	£29,000

Community involvement

We were unable to determine specific details of HP Enterprise Services UK Ltd's community involvement. For information on 'HP Living Progress', the CSR initiative of Hewlett-Packard Company (parent company), see the website.

Corporate giving

In 2012/13 the company made charitable donations of £29,000. A list of beneficiaries was not available.

Corporate social responsibility

CSR information: We found no information regarding CSR specific to the UK.

We were unable to determine the ratio of men to women on the board.

CSR report: There is a CSR report on the parent company's website, which focuses on activities in the USA and at a global level.

Applications

In writing to the correspondent, referenced 'Charitable donations'.

HSBC Holdings plc

Financial services, banking

Correspondent: Sustainability Dept., Level 36, 8 Canada Square, London EC3R 6AE (tel: 020 7991 8888; email: sustainability@hsbc.com; website: www.hsbc.com/citizenship/sustainability)

Directors: Stuart Gulliver, Group Chief Executive; Douglas Flint, Group Chair; Safra Catz; Laura Cha; Rona Fairhead; Joachim Faber; John Lipsky; Sam Laidlaw; Rachel Lomax; Iain Mackay, Group Finance Director; Sir Simon Robertson; Kathleen Casey; Sir Jonathan Evans; Heidi Miller; Marc Moses; Jonathan Symonds; Ben Matthews (women: 6; men: 11)

Year end	31/12/2013
Turnover	£51,700,000,000
Pre-tax profit	£14,893,000,000

Nature of business: Retail banking and wealth management, commercial banking, global banking and markets, and global private banking.

Company registration number: 617987

Subsidiary undertakings include: HSBC Asset Finance (UK) Ltd; HSBC Bank A. S.; HSBC Bank plc; HSBC France; HSBC Private Banking Holdings (Suisse) SA; HSBC Trinkaus and Burkhardt AG.

Main locations: Leeds, London

UK employees: 46,000

Total employees: 263,000

Focus of giving: Education, environment, individuals, financial education, overseas projects, poverty and social exclusion, children, young people.

Membership: BITC

FTSE 100	✓
Gifts in kind	✓
Humanitarian aid: overseas	✓
Matched funding	✓
Overseas giving	✓
Payroll giving	✓
Sponsorship	✓

Charitable donations

Cash UK (latest available):	2013	£14,500,000
	2011	£10,600,000
	2009	£6,500,000
	2007	£18,400,000
	2006	£16,400,000
Total UK (cash and in kind):	2013	£15,250,000
Cash worldwide:	2013	£78,000,000
Total worldwide (cash and in kind):	2013	£82,000,000

Community involvement

HSBC's UK website states the following: 'At HSBC, we recognise the value of education and the life-changing opportunity it can bring. Education is also an essential building block to driving economic development, helping to create thriving communities and inspiring young people to achieve their potential.' Through the HSBC Young People's Programme, which is a group of 13 programmes, the bank invests in young people's education. These education programmes focus on six key areas: access to education (including scholarships and bursaries); emotional well-being; employability and entrepreneurship; cultural awareness; financial literacy; and life skills.

HSBC employees are supported in their volunteering efforts for the group's various national programmes, as well as for registered local projects. HSBC customers are able to make donations to six employee-nominated charities through ATMs and online banking. Globally, HSBC supports various educational and environmental initiatives, including the HSBC Water Programme, a five-year partnership with Earthwatch, WaterAid and WWF.

Corporate giving

The Sustainability Report 2013 states that every year, £14 million is donated to charities working on education, life skills and entrepreneurship through HSBC's UK Young People Programme. We have estimated the total community contributions to be £15.25 million, using the ratio of UK cash donations to worldwide cash donations.

The Opportunity Partnership – An example of a programme that has benefitted from these donations is The Opportunity Partnership, a £30 million programme through which HSBC works with four charities – Catch22; St Giles Trust; The Prince's Trust; and Tomorrow's People – to help improve the educational, training and employment opportunities of 25,000 of the most disadvantaged young people in the UK.

In 2013, more than 82 local projects were approved for additional funding through the employee grants scheme, receiving £500,000.

We have estimated the total community contributions to be £15.25 million, using the ratio of UK cash donations to worldwide cash donations.

Globally, minus management costs, the group contributed £82 million ($117 million) in community investment during the year. This figure includes employee time to the value of more than £4.6 million ($7.3 million).

The worldwide allocation of cash donations was distributed for the following purposes: Education (49%); Environment (39%); Other (21%).

ATM and online donations

HSBC customers are able to support charities through ATM and online donation facilities. Every two years, six national charities are nominated by employees to benefit through the scheme. In 2013, customers donated £190,000 to the six selected national charities, as well as a further £386,000 to the Disaster Emergency Committee (DEC) Philippines Typhoon Appeal. As is our usual practice, we have not included these figures in our figures for company cash or total contributions as they are not contributed by HSBC itself. The six nominated charities during the year were: Alzheimer's Society; British Heart Foundation; Cancer Research UK; Dogs Trust; Great Ormond Hospital; Macmillan Cancer Support.

In-kind support

Pro bono

HSBC employees are entitled to take one day's paid leave annually to volunteer with a UK-registered charity.

As part of its drive to promote financial literacy, HSBC partners JA Worldwide on a global financial programme to help educate young people about financial literacy. In the 2012/13 academic year, more than 900 staff volunteers took part.

Employee-led support

Employee volunteering

Employees are able to volunteer with the bank's national programmes, such as

Opportunity Partnership and the HSBC Water Programme, as well as with local projects. During 2013 1,175 UK employees volunteered more than 17,000 hours of their own time with projects such as building sensory gardens in schools, supporting city farms and other environmental projects, and helping with refurbishments in their communities. Globally, employees volunteered more than 250,000 hours of work time and over 400,000 hours of their own time. Employees can apply for funding to help their project.

Payroll giving

The bank operates the Give As You Earn scheme.

Commercially led support

Vocational training course pilot scheme

In 2014 a four week pilot training course was run for disadvantaged young people in the UK to help them develop experience and skills to access entry level job opportunities at HSBC.

Sponsorship

The website states the following: 'We know how important it is to understand the passions of our customers, which is why our sponsorships focus on developing key relationships, building loyalty, nurturing youth and embracing different cultures.' HSBC sponsors organisations in the areas of sport (mainly rugby and golf) and culture.

To apply for sponsorship, complete and submit the online form – www.hsbc.com/about-hsbc/sponsorship

Corporate social responsibility

CSR committee: There was formerly a group Corporate Sustainability Committee; however, note the following from the annual report and accounts: 'The Committee has been demised by resolution of the Board with effect from 31 December 2013. A Conduct & Values Committee has been established which undertakes much of what was previously done by the Corporate Sustainability Committee.'

CSR information: The HSBC UK website states the following: 'Our community investment programme focuses on education and the environment across three areas: supporting and enabling donations to charity; supporting access to education, life skills and entrepreneurship; cultural understanding and encouraging volunteering.'

CSR report: There is a comprehensive Sustainability Report published annually. The report also contains information about overseas and global CSR activities.

Exclusions

Our research indicates that no support is given for advertising in charity brochures, animal welfare, appeals from individuals, the arts, elderly people, fundraising events, political appeals, religious appeals, science/technology, sickness/disability, or sport.

Applications

In writing to the correspondent.

Alan Hudson Ltd

Agriculture

Correspondent: David Ball, Trustee, 1–3, York Row, Wisbech, Cambridgeshire PE13 1EA (tel: 01945 583087/01945 461456)

Directors: Stephen Hutchinson; Stephen Layton; David Ball, Chair; Edward Newling

Year end	31/07/2013
Turnover	£1,192,337

Nature of business: Fruit growers. The company is wholly owned by the Hudson Foundation (Charity Commission no.280332) and donates its taxable profits for the year to the charity by way of Gift Aid.

Company registration number: 613979

UK employees: 22

Total employees: 22

Focus of giving: General charitable purposes.

Cash donations undeclared ✓

Charitable donations

Cash UK (latest available):	2013	£97,000
	2012	£125,000
	2010	£21,000
	2008	£218,000
	2007	£141,000
Total UK (cash and in kind):	2013	£97,000
Cash worldwide:	2013	£97,000
Total worldwide (cash and in kind):	2013	£97,000

Community involvement

Giving is made through the Hudson Foundation (Charity Commission no. 280332).

Corporate giving

Alan Hudson Ltd is the principal subsidiary of the Hudson Foundation and donates its profits to the foundation by way of gift aid. For 2012/13 it was not clear from either set of accounts what amount was paid by the company to the foundation. We have taken the amount spent in charitable giving to organisations (see the foundation's accounts) as the figure for the cash donations made by the company.

See the corporate charity entry on p. 409 for more information.

Corporate social responsibility

CSR information: There was no information about CSR found in the company's or foundation's accounts. No website was available.

Corporate charity: The Hudson Foundation (Charity Commission no. 280332).

Applications

In writing to the correspondent at: The Hudson Foundation, 1–3 York Row, Wisbech, Cambridgeshire PE13 1EA.

IBM United Kingdom Ltd

Electronics/computers

Correspondent: UK Corporate Citizenship Team, PO Box 41, North Harbour, Portsmouth, Hampshire PO6 3AU (tel: 0239256 1000; email: CCRUK@uk.ibm.com; website: www.ibm.com/uk/en)

Directors: D. Stokes; N. Hill; T. Eagle; S. Leonard; S. Smith; S. Tickle

Year end	31/12/2013
Turnover	£3,954,300,000
Pre-tax profit	£279,700,000

Nature of business: IBM United Kingdom Ltd is the UK subsidiary of IBM Corporation. It is involved in the provision of information technology services and solutions, and the development, production and supply of advanced information technology products.

Company registration number: 741598

Subsidiary undertakings include: TeaLeaf Technology, UK Ltd; Varicent Software (UK) Ltd

Main locations: London, Portsmouth, Glasgow

UK employees: 15,762

Total employees: 15,930

Focus of giving: Education, environment, health, ill health, arts, culture, children, young people, community/social welfare.

Membership: BITC

Cash donations undeclared	✓
Gifts in kind	✓
Payroll giving	✓

Charitable donations

Cash UK (latest available):	2013	£200,000
	2011	£200,000
	2010	£200,000
	2008	£800,000
	2007	£800,000
Total UK (cash and in kind):	2013	£200,000
Cash worldwide:	2013	£200,000
Total worldwide (cash and in kind):	2013	£200,000

Community involvement

Globally, IBM looks to support charities and schools by making cash and in-kind donations and by contributing employees' time. Through its community programmes, IBM focuses on improving the quality of life for people living in the most disadvantaged communities, using Information Technology and business skills to make a difference.

IBM's employees play a central role in the company's community involvement through the IBM On Demand Community Programme. Through On Demand, employees and former employees can register to volunteer for organisations in their community and, in the UK, can apply for funding for eligible organisations through the IBM UK Community Grants Programme.

IBM United Kingdom Trust

The company also makes contributions to its associated charity, **IBM United Kingdom Trust** (Charity Commission no. 290462), which derives most of its income from the IBM International Foundation and IBM subsidiaries.

The trust's primary focuses are:

- To increase the scope, usage and understanding of information technology
- To enable disadvantaged people to acquire skills, particularly through the use of informationtechnology
- To provide aid in the form of technology and technical support for disaster relief

In the main, the trust meets these aims by supporting IBM's community programmes through grants of equipment, technical support and cash.

Corporate giving

The annual report and accounts for 2013 did not declare a figure for charitable donations. In the most recent years for which we have figures, the company made donations of £200,000, and we have taken this figure as an estimate for charitable contributions in 2013. In these years, grants were made to organisations where IBM employees volunteer. We understand that the majority of this is disbursed through the company's trust, **IBM United Kingdom Trust** (Charity Commission no. 290462).

See the corporate charity entry on p. 409 for more information.

Employee-led support

Employee volunteering

Through its On Demand Community initiative, IBM encourages and supports employees and retirees to undertake voluntary work, organising its community involvement policies to motivate people to volunteer. The company's intranet site has a database of volunteer opportunities which allows staff to find a good cause which matches their interests.

Payroll giving

The company operates the Give As You Earn scheme.

Corporate social responsibility

CSR information: The following information was taken from the website: 'IBM has a long-standing commitment to transforming and empowering local communities, and we encourage employees and retirees to continue making a difference, through their time and skills.'

We were unable to determine the ratio of women to men on the board.

Corporate charity: IBM United Kingdom Trust (Charity Commission no. 290462).

Exclusions

IBM states in its grant guidelines that it will not support organisations which:

> Advocate, support, or practice activities inconsistent with IBM's non-discrimination policies, whether based on race, colour, religion, gender, gender identity or expression, sexual orientation, national origin, disability or age. Documentation (in the form of an Equality of Opportunity statement) demonstrating that organisations comply with the above statement will be required . . .
>
> IBM reserves the right to determine which organisations are eligible for grants.

Applications

UK Community Grants Programme

All requests for funding need to be requested by the employee rather than the recipient organisation, as organisations without an IBM employee volunteering cannot be supported. It might, however, be worth charitable and community groups based around company sites advertising voluntary positions on the company's intranet site to open up this avenue of funding.

IBM United Kingdom Trust

The trust's approach to grant-making falls into three key areas:

- The provision of grants that advance both the aims of the trust and support IBM programmes
- The provision of small grants in support of charitable organisations in the communities surrounding IBM sites
- The provision of grants that support and encourage employee volunteering by IBM staff

Our research indicates that unsolicited applications from organisations are not considered by the trust.

ICAP plc

Financial services

Correspondent: The Charity Day Team, 2 Broadgate, London EC2M 7UR (tel: 020 7000 5000; email: charity.day@icap.com; website: www.icapcharityday.com)

Directors: John Nixon; John Sievwright; Charles Gregson, Chair; Michael Spencer, Group Chief Executive Officer; Diane Schueneman; Ivan Ritossa; Robert Standing (women: 1; men: 6)

Year end	31/03/2014
Turnover	£1,397,000,000
Pre-tax profit	£122,000,000

Nature of business: The company is the world's largest interdealer broker and is active in the wholesale markets for OTC derivatives, fixed income securities, money market products, foreign exchange, energy, credit and equity derivatives.

Company registration number: 3611426

Subsidiary undertakings include: Garban Group Holdings Ltd; ICAP Group Holdings plc; Intercapital Ltd

Main locations: London

Total employees: 4,934

Focus of giving: General charitable purposes, education, environment, health, ill health, heritage, medical research, older people, arts, culture, overseas projects, sport, recreation, children, young people, community/ social welfare, disability.

Matched funding	✓
Payroll giving	✓

Charitable donations

Cash UK (latest available):	2014	£3,800,000
	2012	£4,900,000
	2010	£5,000,000
	2009	£5,000,000
	2007	£9,200,000
Total UK (cash and in kind):	2014	£3,800,000
Cash worldwide:	2014	£8,000,000
Total worldwide (cash and in kind):	2014	£8,000,000

Community involvement

The company donates to charitable causes the money raised each year during its Charity Day, launched in 1993. On this day each year, the group donates its entire revenue, without any cost reductions, to various charities selected by local offices. This unique event includes the commission made by brokers as well as the company's revenue. The company recognises this as also having the benefit of motivating employees.

There is significant staff, customer, supplier and celebrity involvement in Charity Day and the charities are selected by ICAP's staff in each region in which it operates.

The revenue would otherwise contribute directly to the broker commission pool and, as such, staff also contribute directly in a personal financial way to the good causes supported.

The following statement is taken from the company's website:

> Charity Day has made such a big impact on the charities we support around the world because giving away one day's revenue and commissions every year has enabled us to fund entire projects – such as a badly-needed clinic in a remote part of Kenya, a science laboratory in a rural school in India or research into conditions such as cystic fibrosis which has progressed as far as clinical trials... over 1,800 projects worldwide.
>
> We have been following up on some of these projects and you can read about them in the 'Success Stories' section of the website.

Corporate giving

In 2014 ICAP raised £8 million for causes worldwide, bringing the total amount raised over Charity Day's 22 year history to £120 million. Approximately £3.8 million of this was distributed to charities in the UK.

Beneficiaries included: Action Against Hunger; Almeida Theatre; Cheryl's Trust; Down's Syndrome Association; Magic Bus; National Foundation for Youth Music; Prostate Cancer UK; Women for Women

Note that we have obtained the company's financial information (turnover, pre-tax profit) from its annual report and accounts for 2013/14. The most recent figures available for charitable donations, however, date from Charity Day in 2014 which took place in the following financial year, and these are the figures we have used.

Employee-led support

Our research tells us that the company operates both matched funding and payroll giving schemes.

Corporate social responsibility

CSR committee: There is a dedicated Charity Day Team.

CSR information: ICAP runs an annual Charity Day.

CSR report: A CSR report is published within the annual report and accounts. There is also a separate website dedicated to the Charity Day initiative.

Applications

Organisations with an interest in applying to become a potential beneficiary of ICAP Charity Day can complete an online application form, the link to which is available on the 'Contact us' section of the website: www.icapcharityday.com/contact-us.

Imagination Technologies Group plc

Manufacturing

Correspondent: HR Manager, Imagination House, Home Park Estate, Kings Langley, Hertfordshire WD4 8LZ (tel: 01923 260511; fax: 01923 268969; email: info@imgtec.com; website: www.imgtec.com/investors/corporate-responsibility.asp)

Directors: Geoff Shingles, Chair; Sir Hossein Yassaie, Chief Executive; Richard Smith, Chief Financial Officer; Andrew Heath; Gilles Delfassy; David Anderson; David Hurst-Brown; Ian Pearson (women: 0; men: 8)

Year end	30/04/2014
Turnover	£170,800,000
Pre-tax profit	(£300,000)

Nature of business: Imagination Technologies Group plc is an international semiconductor creation and licensing company, specialising in the development of PowerVR multimedia, MIPS processors and Ensigma communications.

Company registration number: 2920061

Subsidiary undertakings include: PowerVR Technologies Ltd; Metagence Technologies Ltd; Ensigma Technologies Ltd; VideoLogic Systems Ltd; Cross Products Ltd; and Pure Digital Ltd.

Total employees: 1,529

Focus of giving: General appeals.

Cash donations undeclared	✓
Gifts in kind	✓
Matched funding	✓
Sponsorship	✓

Charitable donations

Cash UK (latest available):	2014	£3,700
	2013	£3,600
	2012	£3,800
	2011	£1,200
	2010	£16,000
Total UK (cash and in kind):	2014	£3,700
Cash worldwide:	2014	£3,700
Total worldwide (cash and in kind):	2014	£3,700

Community involvement

Employees are consulted 'to ensure that donations given by the group represent all the interests and locations where employees are based'. The group invites its employees to vote on a list of selected charities to determine which will receive funding from the group's charitable donation pot.

Corporate giving

The group's accounts state that it 'gives charitable donations both locally and nationally', though we were unable to determine a figure for its charitable giving in 2013/14. In the two preceding financial years, however, charitable donations from the group averaged around £3,700. We have taken this figure as an estimate for charitable donations in 2013/14.

We were unable to find a value for the in-kind contributions made by the group.

In-kind support

Gifts in kind

In the past year, the group has recycled PCs in return for donations towards its nominated charities.

Employee-led support

Matched funding

The group operates a matched funding policy by which if employees raise funds for one of the nominated charities, the group will double the amount of money raised.

Commercially led support

Sponsorship

The group has formed links with universities in line with its 'intellectual property activities'. Its 2013/14 annual report states that it sponsors five PhDs at selected universities in areas of 'technical relevance to the group's activities' and that it has recently begun sponsoring and providing development kits to universities to assist with teaching. The group activities also include the sponsorship of electronic courses at local schools and the provision of scholarships for university students in order to promote future opportunities with the group. Over the next three years, the group has pledged to sponsor the government's Your Life Campaign, which aims to inspire more young people, and particularly women, to pursue education and careers in maths and sciences. The group will donate £25,000 each year to sponsor a mathematics/physics chair.

Corporate social responsibility

CSR committee: There was no evidence of a separate CSR Committee.

CSR information: The group's approach to CSR is detailed with the CSR section of its annual report and on its website.

CSR report: A CSR report is included in the group's annual report.

Applications

In writing to the correspondent.

IMI plc

Engineering

Correspondent: The Company Secretary, Lakeside, Solihull Parkway, Birmingham Business Park, Birmingham B37 7XZ (tel: 01217 173700; fax: 01217 173701; website: www.imiplc.com/responsible-business.aspx)

Directors: Roberto Quarta, Chair; Mark Selway, Chief Executive; Douglas Hurt, Finance Director; Roy Twite; Anita Frew; Bob Stack; Carl-Peter Forster; Phil Bentley; Birgit Nørgaard; Ross McInnes; John O'Shea; Geoff Tranfield; Daniel Shook (women: 2; men: 11)

Year end	31/12/2013
Turnover	£1,743,000,000
Pre-tax profit	£249,300,000

Nature of business: IMI is a diversified engineering group focused on the precise control and movement of fluids in critical applications, delivering engineering solutions to address global trends such as clean energy, energy efficiency, healthcare and increasing automation.

Company registration number: 714275

Subsidiary undertakings include: 3Wire Group Inc. USA; Control Components Inc. USA; Eley Ltd; IMI Cornelius (UK) Ltd; IMI Scott Ltd; IMI Webber Ltd

Main locations: Birmingham, Manchester, Liverpool, Yorkshire

UK employees: 2,143

Total employees: 15,639

Focus of giving: General charitable purposes, education, health, ill health, arts, culture, overseas projects, children, young people, community/social welfare.

Cash donations undeclared	✓
Gifts in kind	✓
Overseas giving	✓

Charitable donations

Cash UK (latest available):	2013	£201,000
	2012	£209,000
	2011	£214,000
	2010	£180,000
	2009	£233,000
Total UK (cash and in kind):	2013	£201,000
Cash worldwide:	2013	£201,000
Total worldwide (cash and in kind):	2013	£201,000

Community involvement

IMI plc contributes to the local communities, supporting charitable and educational programmes in the areas where its facilities are based. Through the annual 'IMI Way Day' employees spend an afternoon volunteering for local charities and community causes. Throughout the year, employees continue their support of charitable causes through fundraising and organising initiatives. It would appear that support is given to causes involving community, young people/children, health/ill health and education.

Corporate giving

The annual report and accounts for 2013 did not declare a figure for charitable donations from the group. The average of these contributions in the three most recent years for which we have figures was £201,000, and we have taken this as an estimate for charitable donations in 2013.

We were unable to determine a value for the in-kind support given by the group.

We were unable to determine details of community involvement specific to the UK.

In-kind support

Staff time

IMI Way Day – One afternoon each year sees group employees volunteering for local charitable and community causes in their area.

Employee-led support

Employee volunteering

On the IMI Way Day, employees volunteer to help good causes in their local communities. In 2013, examples included: the team at the group's Norgren facility in Louisville who held a bike-building competition for disadvantaged children from the charity Big Brothers, Big Sisters; and 300 employees at the group's manufacturing base in Brno, Czech Republic, who helped to renovate a day centre for children and adults with disabilities.

Employee fundraising

Throughout the year, employees also support their chosen charitable causes with various fundraising activities. Initiatives such as food and toy collections have also been organised.

Corporate social responsibility

CSR committee: The following information was taken from the website:

> A major ethics and compliance programme runs across the Group. Reports on compliance and The IMI Way programme are considered at every regular meeting of the Board and the Executive Committee.
>
> The Board takes account of the social, environmental and ethical impact of its decisions and The IMI Way Code of Responsible Business incorporates a series of corporate policies and standards for responsible business across the Group.
>
> At a Group level, responsible business activity is co-ordinated through a steering group and key issues of corporate social responsibility are identified, monitored and addressed through the Group's general business processes and risk management framework.

CSR information: The following information was obtained from the website:

> The communities where we operate are crucial to the success of IMI. We have a duty to be a responsible business citizen and to meet our commitments to these communities. Although our projects and facilities can bring benefits to local communities by creating jobs and investment in the surrounding area, they can also give rise to concerns.
>
> Consequently, IMI works to be a good neighbour and demonstrates high economic, social and environmental standards. We also remain respectful of human rights and assist our local communities through charitable activities and community volunteering.

CSR report: There was a report focused on matters relating to CSR titled 'How we do business: Our Approach' contained within the 2013 annual report, and there is a section dedicated to Responsible Business on the website.

Exclusions

Our research indicates that no support is given for political appeals.

Applications

In writing to the correspondent, referenced 'Charitable donations'. Local appeals should be sent to the relevant local plant or branch.

Imperial Tobacco Group plc

Tobacco

Correspondent: Kirsty Mann, Senior CR Engagement Manager, Winterstoke Road, Bristol BS3 2LL (tel: 01179 636636; email: cr@uk.imptob.com; website: www.imperial-tobacco.com/cr)

Directors: Ken Burnett; Michael Herlihy; Mark Williamson, Chair; Malcolm Wyman; Matthew Phillips; Alison Cooper, Chief Executive; Oliver Tant, Chief Financial Officer; David Haines; Karen Witts; John Downing (women: 2; men: 8)

Year end	30/09/2013
Turnover	£28,269,000,000
Pre-tax profit	£1,261,000,000

Nature of business: Tobacco manufacturer.

Company registration number: 3236483

Subsidiary undertakings include: Imperial Tobacco Holdings (2007) Ltd; Imperial Tobacco Ltd; Imperial Tobacco International Ltd; Imperial Tobacco Finance plc; Altadis SAU; Commonwealth Brands Inc.

Brands include: Davidoff, Golden Virginia, L and B, Parker and Simpson, Rizla, USA Gold

Main locations: Bristol, Nottingham

Total employees: 1,195

Focus of giving: Education, environment, health, ill health, older people, community/social welfare, disasters.

Membership: BITC

FTSE 100	✓
Gifts in kind	✓
Humanitarian aid: overseas	✓
Overseas giving	✓

Charitable donations

Cash UK (latest available):	2013	£2,000,000
	2011	£1,800,000
	2009	£1,900,000
	2007	£200,000
	2006	£700,000
Total UK (cash and in kind):	2013	£2,000,000
Cash worldwide:	2013	£3,200,000
Total worldwide (cash and in kind):	2013	£3,200,000

Community involvement

Imperial Tobacco Group looks to support community initiatives in markets where it has a presence and contributes funds centrally. Employees of the group also contribute through volunteering activities. The group runs Altadis Foundation, a charity registered with the Spanish Ministry of Culture, which works to improve livelihoods in areas where the group operates, as well as the Leaf Partnership Committee, which aims to supports tobacco farming communities. The majority of the group's charitable contributions appear to be given for overseas causes, either directly or through UK-registered charities.

The following information was published in the group's CSR review 2013:

> We have internal guidelines for donations and partnerships that apply throughout the group and are referenced in our Code of Conduct. We do not make political donations and give preference to officially recognised or registered not-for-profit organisations. In some instances we enable our community support through supplier partnerships. Where possible we give preference to charities, in which our employees are actively involved. We avoid projects which may result in criticism for either us or the charitable organisation concerned. We do not use community investment for advertising or the promotion of our products.
>
> We choose to have a community investment budget in consideration of the interests of our employees and the communities connected to our business footprint, with the greatest need. We work within the constraints of a well-considered central budget, whilst allowing local budget holders to make additional financial contributions as they deem appropriate. We also actively encourage volunteering which is enabled at a local level.
>
> We seek to support community livelihoods to help others improve their own financial security so that they can have more future choices. We direct our community investment towards employability, meeting basic needs and the elimination of child labour. Our support is prioritised towards the most disadvantaged in the communities around our factories, offices and tobacco sourcing activities.

Corporate giving

In 2012/13 £3.2 million was allocated to partnership and community investment. The following breakdown was included in the Directors' Governance Report for the year:

> From this figure, we have donated £0.2 million (2012: £0.2 million) to UK-registered charities operating in the UK, £0.2 million (2012: £0.3 million) to UK-registered charities operating abroad, £1.6 million (2012: £1.6 million) through the UK Charities Aid Foundation to charities based overseas and £0.2 million (2012: Nil) to charities registered and operating abroad.
>
> We have donated the remaining amount of £1.0 million (2012: Nil) to Leaf Partnership projects abroad. These partnerships have charitable aims under contract but are not registered charities.

In line with our usual practice, we have taken all donations to UK-registered charities as the UK cash contribution.

Employee-led support

Employee volunteering

The group supports employee volunteering as a way of engaging with local communities. During the year, employees contributed to causes including reforestation projects and helping homeless people.

Corporate social responsibility

CSR committee: The management of CR within the group is described on its website:

> CR issues are predominantly cross-functional and we have regular forums to discuss these issues. Several advisory groups and committees provide advice on responsible conduct to the board and Operating Executive.
>
> We also have functional and cross-functional networks of specialists, who deal with CR issues within their areas of specialism. These include our International Corporate Affairs Network, Occupation Health Safety & Environmental professionals, Human Resource managers, and market coordinators.
>
> The group's Company Secretary, a direct report to the Chief Executive, manages a small central team of CR specialists. The team supports the Code of Conduct across the Group and is a central point to help facilitate our CR approach.

CSR information: The group's website states:

> Operating responsibly is integral to all that we do and underpins our on-going commercial success. It's about operating in a way that is financially, socially and environmentally responsible and considers stakeholders expectations. For us, this is how we behave towards employees, suppliers, customers, consumers, governments, communities and the environment.

CSR report: A CSR review is published annually, a CR overview is included in the annual report, and there is an informative 'Responsibility' section on the website.

Exclusions

No support is given to individuals, or for research projects, expeditions or trips.

Applications

Note the following from the website: 'If you represent a charitable or not-for-profit organisation please note that we are not currently looking to fund new partners and we cannot support all appeals.'

Impetus – Private Equity Foundation

Financial services, professional support services

Correspondent: Courtney White, Investment Team Assistant, 183 Eversholt Street, London NW1 1BU (tel: 020 3474 1000; email: courtney.white@impetus-pef.org.uk; website: www.impetus-pef.org.uk)

Directors: Daniela Soares, Chief Executive Officer; Richard Lackman, Chief Financial Officer; Amelia Sussman; Barbara Storch; Chiku Bernardi; Elisabeth Paulson; Elly de Decker; Jenny North; Julia Grant; Kawika Solidum; Kevin Munday; Philip Rubenstein; Sarah Young; Sebastien Ergas; Erin Chase; Vanessa Morphet (women: 11; men: 5)

Year end	31/12/2013
Turnover	£15,539,456

Nature of business: Impetus – Private Equity Foundation (Impetus-PEF) is a venture philanthropy organisation which works with high-potential charities and social enterprises to empower young people from disadvantaged backgrounds to reach their full potential. Its investments packages address the NEET (young people not in education, employment or training) issue and include both financial contributions and pro bono expertise.

Company registration number: 8460519

Trading subsidiaries: PEF Trading Ltd; ThinkForward Social Impact.

Main locations: Shoreditch

Focus of giving: Education, enterprise/training, equal opportunities, poverty and social exclusion, children, young people.

Gifts in kind ✓

Charitable donations

Cash UK (latest available):	2013	£3,200,000
	2011	£3,860,000
	2009	£2,535,000
	2008	£3,900,000
	2007	£4,028,606
Total UK (cash and in kind):	2013	£8,200,000
Cash worldwide:	2013	£3,200,000
Total worldwide (cash and in kind):	2013	£8,200,000

Community involvement

The current organisation was created following a merger of the Private Equity Foundation (established in 2006) and Impetus (set up in 2002) in 2013. Impetus-PEF is both a private company limited by guarantee and a registered charity (Charity Commission no. 1116139). The organisation normally works with a charity or social enterprise for four to ten years and offers a 'venture philanthropy package' of unrestricted funding, management support and pro bono work to help build, develop and expand their activities. It has a network of over 400 individuals and over 60 companies offering pro bono help – in 2013 a total of 8,300 hours was donated to 200 projects.

Charity partnerships
Private Equity Foundation 1 Inc. is Impetus-PEF's independent non-profit sister organisation in the USA. PEF 1 shares the charitable goals and charitable investment approach of Impetus-PEF and supports its charity portfolio.

The Education Endowment Foundation (EEF), set up in 2011 and funded by a £125 million grant from the Department for Education, is overseen by Impetus-PEF and The Sutton Trust. During 2013 EEF was given £42,000 by the organisation for general capacity building.

Impetus-PEF co-operates with government bodies and worldwide partners – it is a member of the European Venture Philanthropy Association (EVPA), maintains relationships with the Asian Venture Philanthropy Network (AVPN) and is part of the 'best practice' alliance together with New Profit Inc., LIFT Philanthropy Partners and Social ventures Australia (SVA). It is funded through both individual/corporate donations or charities and government departments and agencies.

The annual report for 2013 also notes that during the year it was actively producing, sponsoring and publishing research into educational and employment issues. Research projects included collaboration with The Work Foundation, Trust for London and Barclays. The report states: 'we wish to work in partnership with other philanthropists, companies and foundations to embark on a unique and vital journey to really help children and young people living in economic disadvantage in the UK'.

Corporate giving

In 2013 the organisation spent a total of £8.2 million supporting charities, which included grants (£3.2 million), pro bono services (£2.6 million) and Investment Team support (£2.2 million). The annual report notes additional funds raised for the portfolio (£500,000) which is not included in the accounts. The annual report specifies that about 35% of charitable expenditure was given for strategic funding, about 30% each in pro bono services and management support, and about 5% amounted to additional funds raised for the organisation.

The organisation has a target for 2014 to invest £4.1 million in grants and £2.7 million in pro bono support. Its website states that currently 26 organisations are included in the investment portfolio.

Grant beneficiaries included: Place2Be (£516,000); Tomorrow's People (ThinkForward) (£418,000); WorkingRite (£240,000); Street League (£179,000); Into University (£100,000); Second Chance (£75,000); Unitas (£50,000); and Prisoners' Education Trust, Family Links and Kainos Community (£5,000 each).

Other organisations in the portfolio include: Big Brother Big Sister; Educational Endowment Foundation; Family Nurse Partnership; Resurgo Social Ventures; Sapere; Shannon Trust; Skills Force; Teens and Toddlers.

See the corporate charity entry on p. 410 for more information.

In-kind support

Pro bono work provided by external professionals to the charities in the organisation's portfolio, also other services, including management support.

Corporate social responsibility

CSR committee: The investment committee oversees the direction of the portfolio, scrutinises and recommends charities for investment.

CSR information: The organisation operates as both a registered and a company limited by guarantee. No specific CSR details found.

Corporate charity: Impetus – Private Equity Foundation (Impetus-PEF) (Charity Commission no. 1152262).

Applications

The organisation searches for promising charities and social enterprises. It has its own selection criteria and carefully scrutinises potential investments before making a decision. Referrals and expressions of interest are welcomed and should be addressed to the correspondent.

Inchcape plc

Motors and accessories

Correspondent: Marie Giannini, Group Communications Manager, 22a St James's Square, London SW1Y 5LP (tel: 020 7546 0022; email: contact@inchcape.com; website: www.inchcape.com/responsibility)

Directors: Ken Hanna, Chair; Andre Lacroix, Group Chief Executive; John McConnell, Group Finance Director; Alison Cooper; Nigel Northridge; Simon Borrows; John Langston; Vicky Bindra; Till Vestring; Coline McConville (women: 2; men: 8)

Year end	31/12/2013
Turnover	£6,524,900,000
Pre-tax profit	£266,100,000

Nature of business: Inchcape is a scale automotive retail group operating in Australia, Belgium, Hong Kong, Russia, Singapore and the UK. The group also has operations in a number of other global markets.

Company registration number: 609782

Subsidiary undertakings include: Inchcape Finance plc; Inchcape International Holdings Ltd

Main locations: London, Watford

UK employees: 4,994

Total employees: 14,402

Focus of giving: Health, ill health, overseas projects, children, young people, disability.

Cash donations undeclared ✓
Charity of the Year ✓
Sponsorship ✓

Charitable donations

Cash UK (latest available):	2009	£0
	2007	£100,000
	2006	£100,000
	2005	£100,000

Community involvement

Inchcape supports 'a number of charities around the world, with an emphasis on local charities that help local people'. Employees at its London head office annually nominate and vote for a Charity of the Year.

Charity of the Year 2013: Sense

Previous Charity of the Year beneficiaries include: Kids Company (2012); CHASE (2011); Havens Hospices (2010); Moorfields Eye Hospital (2008 and 2009)

Corporate giving

A figure for charitable donations was not included in the group's annual report for 2013; however, the group's website states the following:

> With our extensive international businesses, we firmly believe in supporting the many different communities and cultures within which we operate, often through sponsorship and support for local charities for local people. These inspirational activities are decided on and driven by our people, who are passionate about the causes and charities they support.

Employee-led support

Employee fundraising

Employees nominate and vote for a Charity of the Year which becomes the focus of fundraising activities during the year.

Corporate social responsibility

CSR committee: There is a CR committee.

CSR information: The following information was obtained from the group's website:

> With our extensive international businesses, we firmly believe in supporting the many different communities and cultures within which we operate, often through sponsorship and support for local charities for local people. These inspirational activities are decided on and driven by our people, who are passionate about the causes and charities they support.

CSR report: A CSR report is available to download from the 'Responsibility' section of the group's website.

Applications

In writing to the correspondent.

Informa plc

Business services, information management and communication

Correspondent: The CR Manager, Informa House, 30–32 Mortimer Street, London W1W 7RE (tel: 020 7017 5000; email: csr@informa.com; website: www.informa.com/Corporate-responsibility)

Directors: Derek Mapp, Chair; Stephen Carter, Group Chief Executive; John Davis; Dr Brendan O'Neill; Rupert Hopley; Gareth Wright, Group Finance Director; Cindy Rose; Geoffrey Cooper; Helen Owers; Gareth Bullock (women: 2; men: 8)

Year end	31/12/2013
Turnover	£1,132,400,000
Pre-tax profit	£115,700,000

Nature of business: Informa is an international provider of specialist information and services for the academic and scientific, professional and commercial business communities across 40 countries.

Company registration number: 3099067

Subsidiary undertakings include: BTS Feiras, Eventos e Editora Ltda; Informa Australia Pty Ltd; Informa Canada Inc,; Informa UK Ltd; Informa Global Markets (Europe) Ltd; Taylor and Francis Group LLC

Main locations: Tunbridge Wells, Colchester, Ashford, Richmond, Byfleet, Victoria, London

Total employees: 6,594

Focus of giving: General charitable purposes, education, enterprise/training, local groups, children, young people, community/social welfare.

Charity of the Year	✓
Gifts in kind	✓
Market-led giving	✓
Overseas giving	✓

Charitable donations

Cash UK (latest available):	2013	£357,000
	2011	£300,000
	2009	£200,000
	2008	£200,000
	2007	£208,464
Cash worldwide:	2013	£357,000
Total worldwide (cash and in kind):	2013	£630,000

Community involvement

Informa develops strategic relationships with community partners, both locally and internationally, by making cash and in-kind donations, and contributing skills and expertise through employee volunteering.

Charity partner: World Cancer Research Fund (WCRF)

Corporate giving

In 2013 community contributions from the group totalled £630,000. The CR report provided a breakdown of contributions.

Cash donations	£357,000
Gifts in kind	£190,000
Volunteer programme costs	£83,000

We have not included funds raised by employees or through the charity auction in our total figures.

We were unable to determine the proportion of these amounts distributed in the UK.

In-kind support

Community partnerships

Informa builds relationships with various community partners, using its resources to help deliver on their strategic objectives. 2013 examples include:

- **The Prince's Trust** – Informa employees helped to set up two mini enterprises, aiming to raise £10,000 for the Million Makers scheme. Students from the trust also experienced placements in the group's London offices
- **BookAid International** – Taylor and Francis partnered with the charity, providing books resources to promote lifelong education. More than 4,500 books were donated in the past year
- **AuthorAID** – Taylor and Francis also contributed time and skills towards mentoring academic authors from developing countries. In 2014 the partnership was extended to involve co-hosting writing workshops in Kenya and Ethiopia
- **Schools** – Euroforum entered into partnership with four German schools to share skills through a variety of activities, including economics lessons, CV and interview skills workshops and internships

Employee-led support

Employee volunteering

Employees are able to dedicate one working day a year for volunteering purposes through 'Stop! for the community'. During the year, 7% of Informa staff took part in various activities, including as part of the group's work with its charity partners.

Employee fundraising

Employees helped to raise more than £100,000 for good causes in 2013. Through the 'Go Bananas' worldwide fundraising event, which is held annually, £83,000 was raised through employee fundraising and corporate donations for the group's charity partner, World Cancer Research Fund (WCRF). As part of the event, the group's CEO in London wore a banana suit and employees were challenged to 'beat the banana'. Throughout the year, funds were also raised for numerous local causes.

Commercially led support

Charity auction

The group holds a biannual charity watch auction at the Monaco Yacht Show. More than £4.2 million was raised in 2013 for Duchenne Muscular Dystrophy.

Corporate social responsibility

CSR committee: The 2013 CR report states:

> Louder than Words is headed up by Emma Blaney, Group HR Director and Head of Corporate Responsibility, with support from a small dedicated CR team and external advisors. The CR team reports directly into the Chief Executive. Local ownership of 'Louder than Words' is located within a network of 21 CR leaders from across the group with whom the CR team engage regularly.

CSR information: Informa's CR strategy is titled 'Louder than Words' and focuses on four areas: People; Community; Environment and Content.

CSR report: There is an annual CSR report available to download from the group's website.

Exclusions

No support is given for political appeals.

Applications

In writing to the correspondent.

International Personal Finance

Financial services

Correspondent: Corporate Responsbility Department, Number Three, Leeds City Office Park, Meadow Lane, Leeds LS11 5BD (tel: 01132 856700; email: enquiries@ipfin.co.uk; website: www.ipfin.co.uk/sustainability.aspx)

Directors: Christopher Rodrigues, Chair; Gerard Ryan, Chief Executive; Adrian Gardner, Chief Financial Officer; Tony Hales; Edyta Kurek; Richard Moat; Nicholas Page; Cathryn Riley; David Broadbent (women: 2; men: 7)

Year end	31/12/2013
Turnover	£746,800,000
Pre-tax profit	£130,500,000

Nature of business: International Personal Finance is an international home credit business operating using the Provident brand in Poland, the Czech Republic, Slovakia, Hungary, Mexico, Romania, Lithuania and Bulgaria. One of its head offices is based in Leeds, UK.

Company registration number: 6018973

Subsidiary undertakings include: International Personal Finance Investments Ltd; IPF Financing Ltd; IPF Holdings Ltd; IPF International Ltd; Provident Mexico S.A. de C.V.; Provident Polska S.A.

Total employees: 9,841

Focus of giving: Economic generation, enterprise/training, local groups, financial education, poverty and social exclusion, community/social welfare.

Membership: LBG

Cash donations undeclared	✓
Gifts in kind	✓
Payroll giving	✓

Charitable donations

Cash UK (latest available):	2013	£66,000
	2012	£94,000
	2011	£56,000
	2010	£49,000
	2009	£750,000
Total worldwide (cash and in kind):	2013	£767,000

Community involvement

International Personal Finance supports charities and community organisation in areas local to where it has a presence. The group operates its community investment strategy via three strands: improving financial education; promoting social inclusion to those disadvantaged by 'poverty, lack of education or physical or mental impairment'; and employee volunteering.

International Personal Finance Fund

As part of its social inclusion initiative in the UK, the group has established the International Personal Finance Fund with Leeds Community Foundation, which helps to fund local educational projects and to 'help organisations to become self-sustainable'. Since 2007, 44 projects have benefitted from £96,000 in grants, for purposes such as financial education, money advice, or vocational training to support social inclusion and to promote family stability.

Corporate giving

In 2013 £767,000 was contributed to community investment across the group as a whole, which we believe includes cash donations, employee time, management costs and in-kind contributions.

A figure for UK cash contributions was not included in the annual report and accounts for the year, though a graph depicting a breakdown of community investment by market (country) can be viewed on the sustainability section of the website. The average amount of UK charitable donations in the three most recent years for which we have figures was £66,000 and we have taken this as an estimate for the group's UK cash contributions during the year.

In-kind support

Staff time

During the year, the group contributed 21,500 hours of staff time to a variety of community activities. This was an increase of 19% from the previous year.

The following information was obtained from the website:

> Through Business in the Community (BITC) we are part of the Business Class West Yorkshire Cluster focusing our volunteering efforts on the students of just one school: Swallow Hill Community college in Leeds, delivering world of work sessions, work experience, mentoring and direct support to improve educational performance.

Employee-led support

Employee volunteering

During the year, UK employees contributed 420 hours for volunteering purposes and were involved in projects such as a student mentoring programme and a sustainable business challenge. In the group's other countries of operation, employee volunteering formed a key part of its corporate responsibility programmes. In Mexico and Romania, for example, volunteer employees have contributed to external financial literacy programmes.

Payroll giving and employee fundraising

Although there was no mention of either payroll giving or employee fundraising included in the annual report and accounts for 2013, the group's website and our research suggest that its employees have supported charities through fundraising and payroll contributions.

Corporate social responsibility

CSR committee: For details of the group's sustainability governance, visit: www.ipfin.co.uk/sustainability/governance.aspx

CSR information: The following information was obtained from the group website:

> We set broad community-investment objectives for the group, but have a regional approach to the delivery of specific programmes to ensure specific needs are met. For this reason we have community investment specialists in all markets and wherever possible we work with external specialists from the charity, community and/or consumer protection sector.
>
> The key area of focus is financial education. This is because we want to empower consumers to make informed choices and create a market of well-informed consumers. Some of our local programmes have been the first of their kind and we have some great examples where our programmes are starting to mature.

CSR report: A CSR report (titled 'Working in partnership') is contained within the annual report and accounts.

Applications

In writing to the correspondent. For details on applying for funding from the International Personal Finance Fund, visit Leeds Community Foundation's website at www.leedscf.org.uk/international-personal-finance-fund.

intu Properties plc (formerly Capital Shopping Centres Group plc)

Financial services

Correspondent: Jennifer Sandars, Corporate Responsibility Manager, 40 Broadway, London SW1H 0BT (tel: 020 7887 4220; email: jennifer.sandars@intu.co.uk; website: www.capital-shopping-centres.co.uk)

Directors: Patrick Burgess, Chair; David Fischel, Chief Executive; Matthew Roberts, Chief Financial Officers; John Whittaker; Andrew Huntley; Adele Anderson; Richard Gordon; Louise Patten; Neil Sachdev; Andrew Strang (women: 2; men: 10)

Year end		31/12/2013
Turnover		£533,200,000
Pre-tax profit		£362,900,000

Nature of business: The principal activity is that of a property investment company. It is the leading company in the UK regional shopping centre industry. Formerly Liberty International plc, the company was renamed Capital Shopping Centres Group plc 2010 upon the demerger of its central London business into a separate listed company, Capital and Counties.

Company registration number: 1503621

Subsidiary undertakings include: intu Shopping Centres plc; intu debenture plc; Liberty International Holdings Ltd.

Main locations: London

Total employees: 1,280

Focus of giving: Education, environment, medical research, arts, culture, children, young people, community/social welfare, disasters.

Membership: BITC, LBG

FTSE 100	✓
Gifts in kind	✓
Humanitarian aid: overseas	✓

Charitable donations

Cash UK (latest available):	2013	£351,000
	2011	£332,000
	2009	£309,000
	2008	£290,000
	2007	£271,000
Total UK (cash and in kind):	2013	£1,951,000
Cash worldwide:	2013	£351,000
Total worldwide (cash and in kind):	2013	£1,951,000

Community involvement

Joint community projects

The group's annual report for 2013 provides the following information:

> Our shopping centres are integral to the communities they serve providing places for people to come together to meet, eat, drink and socialise. They support charities and community organisations that address fundamental issues in modern society which are important to the long-term success of our business.

Joint community projects focus on youth, education and the prevention of anti-social behaviour.

Working together in long-term community partnerships is a key feature of the group's community strategy. During 2013,the group worked with 12 community partners delivering 22 projects at its centres. The group states that these projects have directly reached almost 2,500 participants.

Retail Academy

In support of young people and acknowledging the high percentage of entrants to retail careers aged under 25, the group continues to fund projects which support retail education under the banner of 'Retail Academy'. In 2013 that included Retail Gold, a three-way partnership between intu, retailers and local education business partnerships to provide retail placements undertaken as a key part of their school/college course learning.

The group also supported West College Scotland to provide a retail training course at Kirklandneuk Community Centre.

Corporate giving

In 2013 the total donations of £1.9 million 'cash equivalent, including facilitated donations', supporting a variety of charities that represent young people and education, arts and culture, health, economic development, environment and emergency relief.

Corporate social responsibility

CSR committee: The board takes direct responsibility for determining policy and strategic direction on CR matters. There is a CR board committee and progress against operational objectives is delegated to the CR Management Committee.

CSR information: The following quotes are taken from the company's annual strategic report for 2013: 'Our centres cannot be developed or marketed without engagement with local stakeholders. Our CR initiatives work to bring partnerships together, including our employees, and foster relationships which contribute to achievement of our longer-term business objectives.'

CSR report: The company produces an annual CSR report.

Applications

In writing to the correspondent.

ITV plc

Media

Correspondent: Head of Corporate Responsibility, 104 Kirkstall Road, Leeds LS3 1JS (tel: 020 7157 3000; email: responsibility@itv.com; website: itvresponsibility.com)

Directors: Archie Norman, Chair; Adam Crozier, Chief Executive; Ian Griffiths, Group Finance Director; Andy Haste; John Ormerod; Roger Faxon; Peter Bazalgette; Mary Harris (women: 1; men: 7)

Year end		31/12/2013
Turnover		£2,389,000,000
Pre-tax profit		£435,000,000

Nature of business: Independent television company.

Company registration number: 4967001

Subsidiary undertakings include: 12 Yard (North) Productions Ltd; Broad Street Films Ltd; Carbon Media Ltd; Carlton Food Network Ltd; Cosgrove Hall Films Ltd; Juice Music UK Ltd

Main locations: Leeds

Total employees: 4,257

Focus of giving: Education, environment, health, ill health, arts, culture, science technology, community/social welfare.

Membership: BITC

Cash donations undeclared	✓
FTSE 100	✓
Gifts in kind	✓
Payroll giving	✓
Sponsorship	✓

Charitable donations

Cash UK (latest available):	2013	£1,600,000
	2012	£1,700,000
	2011	£1,500,000
	2010	£1,500,000
	2009	£1,710,000
Total UK (cash and in kind):	2013	£5,000,000
Cash worldwide:	2013	£1,600,000
Total worldwide (cash and in kind):	2013	£5,000,000

Community involvement

ITV's Responsibility website states the following:

> Our giving strategy reflects our position as a regional and UK broadcaster, where we aim to strike a balance between supporting a diverse range of national and local causes. By far, our largest contribution to society is through the use of our airtime to profile good causes and act as a catalyst for further contribution.

The company's strategy for giving is divided into a number of areas. The following information was obtained from the website:

ITV Appeals: Campaigns or causes that are defined at corporate level and aligned to ITV's key issues or priorities. The benefactors are 'determined through a selection process or generated through an editorial idea'. ITV rarely adopts causes pitched from outside the company, as its campaigns have very specific requirements from its partners.

ITV Social Action Campaigns: ITV supports its employees wherever possible and allows programmes and individuals to put forward proposals to work with national or local charities and causes. Within its policy guidelines, ITV looks to support activities where its campaign calendar allows and expectations can be fulfiled. Examples include People's Millions, Pride of Britain nominations and Take a Moment.

Individual requests for support or sponsorship: Whilst ITV does give ad hoc, this is in response to employee and team requests for charities or causes with which they have a connection. The Responsibility website notes: 'Unfortunately we do not have the additional resources to support general requests.'

Corporate giving

The annual report and accounts for 2013 did not declare a figure for charitable contributions from the company. However, ITV provided the following statement: 'In 2013, ITV contributed £5 million in cash and in-kind support that, along with viewer donations, helped raise over £15.5 million for charitable causes.' The average of cash donations in the three most recent years for which we were able to obtain figures was £1.6 million, and we have taken this as an estimate for 2013. We did not include viewer donations in our figure for total contributions.

In-kind support

Employee volunteering, mentoring, training opportunities, guest appearances, open days and access to our facilities are some of the ways in which ITV contributes to its communities.

Employee-led support

Employee volunteering

Employees are able to take one paid day's leave a year for volunteering purposes. As well as volunteering for their own chosen causes, employees are encouraged to help with ITV's own charitable initiatives, such as Text Santa or Soccer Aid.

Payroll giving

ITV promotes the Give As You Earn scheme to employees.

Commercially led support

Local communities

ITV looks to raise awareness of issues and to people making a difference in their local communities though its regional news teams and various other initiatives. These include:

People's Millions – Each year this annual competition, run in partnership with the Big Lottery Fund, awards grants of up to £50,000 to community groups working to improve the lives of people in their area.

Pride of Britain – The awards acknowledge people who have inspired and contributed to their community and celebrate them at an annual event. ITV champions and broadcasts the awards, which are run by the Daily Mirror.

Fixers – Through Fixers, young people are supported to make a difference with social issues by getting creative, making films, posters and websites, for example. ITV backs the initiative, which is run by the charity The Public Service Broadcasting Trust.

Partnerships

The company develops relationships with other broadcasters, local organisations and knowledge specialists to 'make the most impact within our communities'.

Corporate social responsibility

CSR committee: ITV's Governance Board has overall responsibility for the direction and delivery of its Corporate Responsibility strategy and includes members of the management board, divisional board teams and specialists from across the company. A list of board members is available on the Responsibility website.

The Head of Corporate Responsibility manages external and internal relationships around the company's CSR agenda, and with support from the team, co-ordinates activity with partners and colleagues to deliver agreed objectives. The Head of Corporate Responsibility reports to the Group HR Director, and for governance issues, the Group Legal Director.

More details of ITV's CSR governance is available from the Responsibility website.

CSR information: The following information came from the Responsibility website: 'It's our duty of care to ensure that we are responsible members of our local communities, contributing to the economic, social and environmental sustainability of each region.'

CSR report: There is a separate Responsibility website.

Exclusions

The company does not consider circular or general appeals.

Applications

There are extensive guidelines on ITV Appeals and Social Action Campaigns available to download from the Responsibility website. For general CSR enquiries, contact the correspondent.

Jaguar Land Rover Ltd

Motors and accessories

Correspondent: S. L. Pearson, Company Secretary, Abbey Road, Whitley, Coventry CV3 4LF (website: www.jaguar.co.uk/about-jaguar/responsibility/index.html)

Directors: W. K. Epple; K. D. M. Gregor; P. Hodgkinson; P. C. Popham; Dr R. D. Speth; M. D. Wright; W. Stadler

Year end	31/03/2014
Turnover	£15,693,600,000
Pre-tax profit	£1,736,600,000

Nature of business: The design, development, manufacture and marketing of high performance luxury saloons, specialist sports cars, four wheel drive off-road vehicles and related components.

In March 2008, the company was sold by Ford to the Indian company Tata. The 2013/14 annual report and accounts state: 'The immediate parent undertaking is Jaguar Land Rover Holdings Ltd and the ultimate parent and controlling party is Tata Motors Ltd, India.'

Company registration number: 1672070

Main locations: Birmingham, Halewood, Coventry, Gaydon

Total employees: 26,761

Focus of giving: Education, STEM (science, technology, engineering and mathematics), children, young people, community/social welfare, disability.

Membership: BITC, LBG

Gifts in kind	✓
Humanitarian aid: overseas	✓
Humanitarian aid: UK	✓
Market-led giving	✓
Overseas giving	✓
Sponsorship	✓

Charitable donations

Cash UK (latest available):	2014	£641,000
	2013	£570,000
	2012	£42,450
	2009	£34,000
	2006	£103,000
Total UK (cash and in kind):	2014	£641,000
Cash worldwide:	2014	£641,000
Total worldwide (cash and in kind):	2014	£641,000

Community involvement

Jaguar Land Rover's community involvement appears to focus on the support of educational, youth and environmental initiatives. A key part of the company's community programme in the UK is the promotion of STEM (science, technology, engineering and maths) and the development of the next generation of engineers and manufacturers. Employees contribute their time and skills for volunteering and fundraising activities in their communities.

Corporate giving

In 2013/14 the company made charitable donations of £641,000, 'principally to national charities'. The website states: 'In the UK, we focus our corporate charity programme on the National Society for the Prevention of Cruelty to Children and BEN, the automotive industry charity.'

We were unable to determine a value for the in-kind support given by the company.

Beneficiaries include: BEN, NSPCC

In-kind support

Pro bono

The company encourages its employees to contribute their time and skills to the benefit of their communities. Each employee is able to spend 16 hours per year volunteering for community programmes. Jaguar Land Rover graduates spend two days each year supporting community activities 'concentrating on education and promoting the STEM agenda, as part of their personal development'.

Employee-led support

Employee fundraising

Jaguar Land Rover employees help to support their communities and community initiatives through various fundraising projects.

Employee volunteering

Employees contribute time and skills to assisting with initiatives in the areas of education, young people and the environment. Activities have included work with disabled students, maintenance of ancient woodlands and becoming school governors.

Commercially led support

Inspiring Tomorrow's Engineers

A central part of the company's CSR programme involves the development of the next generation of engineers. One of the ways in which it does this is through the Inspiring Tomorrow's Engineers (IET) programme. In collaboration with schools and colleges, the programme promotes 'learning and engagement on STEM subjects', with the aim of inspiring young people to take up careers in engineering or manufacturing. Also in promotion of the government's STEM agenda, the company has worked with 'other automotive, engineering and academic organisations to develop national challenge projects for schools'.

Jaguar Land Rover also operates five Education Business Partnership Centres (EBPCs) in association with local education authorities and education charities. Through the EBPCs, young people benefit from classroom activities and plant visits.

Product sales

The sustainability report for 2012/13 tells us that, in support of BEN, Jaguar Land Rover donates 70p for every vehicle sold.

Corporate social responsibility

CSR committee: There is a Sustainability Steering Group which meets quarterly. The CEO and board of directors have ultimate responsibility for sustainability.

CSR information: The latest sustainability report available was dated 2012/13 and states:

> By 2020 we aim to have a positive impact for 12 million people worldwide through our global corporate social responsibility (CSR) programme.
>
> We will advance knowledge and skills by nurturing talent in our workforce and providing 2 million young people with inspiring learning experiences in science, engineering and technology.
>
> Our global CSR programme will also create opportunities for 10 million vulnerable people to make a positive change in their lives. We are achieving this by working with external partners and engaging our network of National Sales Companies across our markets to deliver projects that protect the environment, improve humanitarian and health issues, and promote education and talent development.

We were unable to determine the ratio of women to men on the board.

CSR report: There is a sustainability report which is available to download from the website.

Applications

In writing to the correspondent.

Jardine Lloyd Thompson Group plc

Insurance

Correspondent: Group Charity Committee, The St Botolph Building, 138 Houndsditch, London EC3A 7AW (tel: 020 7528 4444; website: www.jltgroup.com/about/csr)

Directors: Geoffrey Howe, Chair; Dominic Burke, Group Chief Executive; Mark Drummond Brady; Mike Reynolds, Finance Director; James Twining; Lord Leach of Fairford; Richard Harvey; Annette Court; Jonathan Dawson; Lord Sassoon; Nicholas Walsh (women: 1; men: 10)

Year end	31/12/2013
Turnover	£979,200,000
Pre-tax profit	£154,600,000

Nature of business: JLT is a provider of insurance, reinsurance and employee benefits-related advice, brokerage and associated services.

Company registration number: 1679424

Subsidiary undertakings include: Expacare Ltd; JLT Re Ltd; JLT Reinsurance Brokers Ltd; Lloyd and Partners Ltd; Profund Solutions Ltd; Thistle Insurance Services Ltd.

Main locations: London

UK employees: 3,627

Total employees: 8,295

Focus of giving: General charitable purposes, education, health, ill health, unpopular causes, community/social welfare.

Gifts in kind	✓
Matched funding	✓
Overseas giving	✓

Charitable donations

Cash UK (latest available):	2009	£106,000
	2007	£267,000
	2006	£389,000
	2005	£462,000
Cash worldwide:	2013	£651,000
Total worldwide (cash and in kind):	2013	£651,000

Community involvement

JLT Group looks to support organisations in areas local to where it operates mainly by matching funds raised by employees and supporting their volunteering activities. The group has a Charities Committee which makes donations to organisations, wherever possible, in conjunction with employees' fundraising activities. Each year, the group also supports a number of charitable projects.

Charities of the Year

Action on Addiction, UK: In 2012 the group entered into a three year agreement with Action on Addiction, which works to 'better understand the causes and treatment of addiction'. The group will help fund activities and will help support the organisation's development.

Lighthouse Club, UK: Through the group's CR programme the charity, which supports individuals or families who have been affected by construction-related injuries or death, has received £32,000 to date

Udaan Foundation, India: The foundation is based near the group's Mumbai office and works to encourage and support young people through education and into employment. JLT employees worldwide have raised funds for the foundation and the group has provided volunteers to teach English to students.

Westmead Children's Hospital, Australia: Money raised through JLT Australia's annual golf day helps to fund a part-time dietician for patients at the hospital's Cystic Fibrosis Clinic, annual learning and the JLT Fellowship for cystic fibrosis doctors.

Corporate giving

In 2013 the group contributed £651,000 to charitable causes worldwide, a significant proportion we believe was donated through matched funding. We were unable to determine how much of this amount was given in the UK.

In-kind support

Staff time

The group contributes one day of volunteering time per employee per year.

Employee-led support

Matched funding

In the UK the group matches employee-raised funds up to a value of £2,500 through its Charity Matching Scheme.

Employee volunteering
Employees are entitled to take off one day a year to spend volunteering.

Corporate social responsibility

CSR committee: A new CR Committee was formed in 2013.

CSR information: This information was obtained from the company's website:

> The JLT Group Charities Committee makes donations to organisations based on:
> - Organisational merit
> - Similarities to our own company vision and values
> - Alignment with our location
> - Employee interest and enthusiasm
>
> Organisations and employees can apply for support which we provide where possible in conjunction with the employee's own fundraising activities.

CSR report: A CR section is included in the annual report and accounts. The website states that the group does not product a separate CR or sustainability report.

Exclusions

No grants for fundraising events, advertising in charity brochures, appeals from individuals or large national appeals.

Applications

In writing to the correspondent.

JD Sports Fashion plc

Retail – clothing and footwear

Correspondent: The Company Secretary, Hollinsbrook Way, Pilsworth, Bury, Lancashire BL9 8RR (tel: 01617 671000; email: info@jdplc.com; website: www.jdplc.com/investor-relations/csr.aspx)

Directors: Peter Cowgill, Chair; Brian Small, Group Finance Director; Martin Davies; Andrew Leslie (women: 0; men: 4)

Year end	01/02/2014
Turnover	£1,330,578,000
Pre-tax profit	£57,850,000

Nature of business: JD Sports Fashion plc is a retailer of sports inspired fashion apparel and footwear. It has operations in the UK and Ireland, France, Spain, Holland and Germany.

Company registration number: 1888425

Subsidiary undertakings include: Athleisure Ltd; John David Sports Fashion (Ireland) Ltd; Kooga Rugby Ltd; Nicholas Deakins Ltd; Pink Soda Ltd; R.D. Scott Ltd.

Total employees: 17,015

Focus of giving: General charitable purposes, health, ill health, overseas projects, poverty and social exclusion, sport, recreation, children, young people, disability.

Cash donations undeclared	✓
Charity of the Year	✓
Gifts in kind	✓
Sponsorship	✓

Charitable donations

Cash UK (latest available):	2014	£49,000
	2013	£46,000
	2012	£61,000
	2011	£39,000
	2010	£17,000
Total UK (cash and in kind):	2014	£49,000
Cash worldwide:	2014	£49,000
Total worldwide (cash and in kind):	2014	£49,000

Community involvement

JD Sports Fashion plc appears to mainly support charities based in the North West by contributing from its resources and skills bases. In 2013/14 the group supported groups working in the areas of health (particularly cancer-related causes), community and sports.

Corporate giving

The 2013/14 annual report and accounts did not include a total for charitable donations from the group. The average amount given in donations in the three previous years was £49,000. We have, therefore, taken this figure as an estimate for charitable donations from the group in 2013/14.

Beneficiaries included: The Marina Dalglish Appeal (£3,900); Gloves Community Centre (£3,000); Manchester City Football Club in the Community (£2,500).

Partner organisation
In 2011, the group joined with Christie Hospital to help raise £500,000 for a teenage cancer unit. Through staff fundraising events and activities, including charity balls, this target was reached in 2014.

Employee-led support

Employee volunteering
Employees helped to raise funds for the group's partner, Christie Hospital. Activities included Team JD competing in the Bupa Great Manchester Run and organising charity balls.

Commercially led support

Sponsorship
The group sponsored the Once Upon A Smile celebrity football team with £10,000. The charity works to support families who have suffered the loss of a child or a parent (of young children) from a long-term or terminal illness.

Corporate social responsibility

CSR committee: There was no evidence of a separate CSR Committee.

CSR information: The following information is taken from the group's website:

> The group recognises that it has a responsibility to ensure its business is carried out in a way that ensures high standards of environmental and human behaviour. With the help and co-operation of all employees, the group endeavours to comply with all relevant laws in order to meet that duty and responsibility wherever it operates.

CSR report: A CSR report is published within the annual report and accounts.

Applications

In writing to the correspondent, referenced 'Charitable donations'.

S. C. Johnson Ltd

Household

Correspondent: Faye Gilbert, Trustee, Johnson Wax Ltd Charitable Trust, Frimley Green, Camberley, Surrey GU16 7AJ (tel: 01276 852000; fax: 01276 852412; email: givinguk@scj.com; website: www.scjohnson.co.uk)

Directors: J. M. Hayes; T. P. Howard (women: 0; men: 2)

Year end	28/06/2013
Turnover	£128,826,000
Pre-tax profit	£3,975,000

Nature of business: The company manufactures and markets waxes, polishes, air fresheners and cleaning products for the consumer and industrial markets.

The ultimate parent company of S. C. Johnson Ltd is S. C. Johnson and Son Inc, and the immediate parent company is Johnson Wax Ltd.

Company registration number: 4166155

Brands include: Autan; Brillo; Duck; Glade; Goddard's; Mr Muscle; Oust; Pledge; Raid; Shout.

Main locations: Frimley Green, Egham

UK employees: 41

Total employees: 41

Focus of giving: Education, environment, health, ill health, non-registered charities, arts, culture, sponsorship, sport, recreation, community/social welfare, disability.

Gifts in kind	✓
Market-led giving	✓
Matched funding	✓
Sponsorship	✓

Charitable donations

Cash UK (latest available):	2013	£132,000
	2011	£66,000
	2009	£228,000
	2008	£313,000
	2007	£317,000
Total UK (cash and in kind):	2013	£132,000
Cash worldwide:	2013	£132,000
Total worldwide (cash and in kind):	2013	£132,000

Community involvement

The Johnson Wax Charitable Trust (Charity Commission no. 200332)

The company channels its charitable support through its corporate foundation.

The company's website states:

> S. C. Johnson is dedicated to improving, protecting and sustaining the environment. The UK company gives time and funding for projects, such as rebuilding ponds in local woodlands, restoration work on the local canal and, employees volunteer to help in initiatives to improve the local environment. There are successful recycling programmes in place in the factory and offices and the company has made great progress with manufacturing waste reductions and has some challenging future objectives in this area. We're helping to make our local community a better place to be by giving time and funding to support the local NHS Trust, build partnerships with local schools, help those who need support in their everyday lives.

According to the Social Investment section of the website, the following areas and organisations have been supported in the past:

Health-related charities

- Frimley Park Hospital (Camberley) – update of the Family Room
- Heartline – money towards holiday activities for 24 children
- Multiple Sclerosis (Farnborough) – leisure activities and educational visits for local branch
- Cancer Research UK – donation towards Pace Network supplies
- Multiple Sclerosis Therapy Centre (Reading) – support packs for five newly diagnosed people

Education-related charities

S. C. Johnson supports local schools with the aim of providing resources that the schools cannot afford otherwise. Help provided includes:

- St Mark's Church of England Primary School (Farnborough) – Challenge Dance Competition
- Heather Ridge Infant School (Frimley) – donation towards swimming pool project
- Upland Primary School (Sandhurst) – donation towards new cookery room
- Children's Safety Education Foundation – child first aid training

Environment-related charities

The company aims to operate in environmentally responsible way. Globally the company has a number of environmental goals and in the UK support include sponsorships. Recent examples, according to the website, include:

> - Blackwater Valley Trust – Hawley Meadow Project
> - Provision of/and rejuvenation of existing hedgerows via the English Hedgerow Trust
> - Moor Green Lakes Group – local environmental group worked together to create a good quality path part of Blackwater Valley

Charities related to the local community

- Abbots Hospital (Guildford) – updating of alms houses for the elderly
- Basingstoke Dial A Ride – help towards a replacement vehicle
- Tongham Community Hall – support towards updating the building
- Homestart NE Hampshire – assistance towards supporting local families in need
- The Mayors or Surrey Heath and Runnymede – for their chosen charities
- Ravenscote School – support towards the local community fireworks night

Arts and sports for people with disabilities

Support is offered to both national organisations and to help smaller ones.

- Stopgap Dance Company (Farnham) – dance group of people with disabilities supported
- First Bagshot Scout Group (Bagshot) – money for new tables and benches
- CP Sport England and Wales – help to charity working with people with cerebral palsy to enable them fulfil their sporting potential
- Surrey Heath Arts Council – organisation of 'Surrey Heath Young Musician of the year'

Corporate giving

In 2012/13 the company donated a total of £132,000 (2012 – £66,000 to 23 local causes) to the Johnson Wax Charitable Trust. Each year about 2.5% of pre-tax profit from S. C. Johnson goes to the trust.

Beneficiaries have included: Abbots Hospital; Cancer Research UK; Johnson Wax Charitable Trust; Multiple Sclerosis; Tongham Community Hall; and Surrey Heath Arts Council.

See the corporate charity entry on p. 410 for more information.

Employee-led support

The company's website states:
'S. C. Johnson encourages its employees to volunteer their time and talents to charities and not-for-profit organisations. Over the years we have contributed tens of thousands of volunteer hours in local effort around the world to help make people's lives better.'

Employee involvement in the local Community

Local community
Activities undertaken by the staff include: refurbishment/repairs of family respite centre in Frimley; provision of computer equipment for an after school club for teenagers in Camberley; sponsorship of a Women's Aid Refuge; Christmas gifts for the elderly and families in need at Voluntary Services Surrey Heath; donation towards closure of road for a carnival; update of facilities at St Frances Church Hall in Frimley; donation to Ravenscote School towards the cost of fireworks; and sponsorship of mini bus for BPSA Blackwater Valley Group.

Community Day
One day a year in June the company gives its employees an opportunity to work on local community projects. Previously about 180 volunteers have worked at local schools to help create outdoor classrooms and improve outdoor and indoor areas for local children, including: Church Crookham Junior School; College Town Junior School; Parity for People with Multiple Disabilities; and Surrey Carers Ian Goodchild Centre.

Matched funding

Employee fundraising activities are matched pound-for-pound by the company up to £500 per individual, when they volunteer in their own time and help charities or non-profit organisations.

Pounds for Participating

An award of £300 is available to an organisation where a member of staff has donated their personal time for 25 hours or more.

Samuel C Johnson Community Service Awards

An award of £3,000 paid to an organisation where a member of staff 'has made a significant contribution through their voluntary work in community service'. Up to three further 'Specially Recognised' awards of £500 are available to an organisation where S. C. Johnson people have made noteworthy contributions.

Commercially led support

The company may provide sponsorships, including in the areas of environment, arts and sports, disability and health causes.

Corporate social responsibility

CSR committee: The company donates to its associated charitable trust and application should be made to the correspondent. No specific committee details found.

CSR information: The company's website states: 'The company's 'Giving

Back' programme is about giving something back to the communities where we operate and in the UK we focus on health, education, environment, local community, arts and sports for people with disabilities.'

CSR report: No UK report published.

Corporate charity: The Johnson Wax Ltd Charitable Trust (Charity Commission no. 200332).

Exclusions

Our research suggests that the following requests are not eligible for support:

- Ones that benefit a single individual
- From an individual raising money for a charity
- For another country
- For attendance at a charity dinner, conference and similar events
- For samples, gift bags or other marketing uses
- Payroll giving
- Ones that are in conflict with the interests of the company
- Duplicating the services of another organisation or project already existing in the community
- Duplicating a previous donation made within 12 months

The Johnson Wax Charitable Trust does not give to individuals and only gives grants to local organisations in which the company operates.

Applications

The Johnson Wax Charitable Trust: In writing to the correspondent

Sponsorship and company enquiries: can be addressed to the Company Secretary (J M Hayes).

Support is usually given to organisations operating close to the company's offices.

Johnson Matthey plc

Metals

Correspondent: Sustainability Team, 5th Floor, 25 Farringdon Street, London EC4A 4AB (tel: 020 7269 8400; email: sustainability@matthey.com; website: matthey.com/sustainability/community)

Directors: Tim Stevenson, Chair; Robert MacLeod, Chief Executive; Den Jones, Group Finance Director; Alan Ferguson; Odile Desforges; Colin Matthews; Dorothy Thompson; Larry Pentz; John Walker; Simon Farrant (women: 2; men: 8)

Year end	31/03/2014
Turnover	£11,155,200,000
Pre-tax profit	£406,600,000

Nature of business: Johnson Matthey plc is a speciality chemicals and sustainable technologies company that focuses on its core skills in catalysis, precious metals, fine chemicals and process technology.

Company registration number: 33774

Subsidiary undertakings include: Avocado Research Chemicals Ltd; Johnson Matthey and Brandenberger AG; Johnson Matthey AB; Johnson Matthey Davy Technologies Ltd; Macfarlan Smith Ltd; Tracerco Ltd

Main locations: Enfield, Fenton, Hanley, Clitheroe, Cambridge, Newcastle upon Tyne, London, Heysham, Wallsend, Swindon, Royston, Sheffield, Reading

Total employees: 11,331

Focus of giving: General charitable purposes, economic generation, education, enterprise/training, environment, health, ill health, medical research, arts, culture, overseas projects, science technology, children, young people, community/social welfare.

Membership: BITC, LBG

Cash donations undeclared	✓
Charity of the Year	✓
FTSE 100	✓
Gifts in kind	✓
Matched funding	✓
Overseas giving	✓
Payroll giving	✓

Charitable donations

Cash UK (latest available):	2014	£359,000
	2013	£379,000
	2012	£378,000
	2011	£320,000
	2010	£298,000
Total UK (cash and in kind):	2014	£359,000
Cash worldwide:	2014	£626,000
Total worldwide (cash and in kind):	2014	£626,000

Community involvement

Johnson Matthey sites around the world support charities, locally and nationally, in the form of cash and in-kind donations or by contributing employee time. Some of the charities assisted operate in areas close to the group's interests and others are chosen by employees. Many Johnson Matthey sites designate a budget for community investment activities. The group also has a corporate donations programme which focuses mainly on medical, health and social welfare programmes, and usually awards grants of £1,000. Support is also given to activities and programmes in the relation to science education. The group predominantly lends its support to charities working and/or operating in locations where it has a presence.

Charity of the Year

The group 'adopts' charities for 12 months or for a longer period of time to benefit from staff support and fundraising efforts.

2014–16 – Cancer Research UK

2012–14: CLIC Sargent, the children's cancer charity, was the group's chosen organisation in a two year partnership that came to an end in March 2014. Over the course of the partnership, employees and a company donation raised £75,000.

Other Charity of the Year beneficiaries have been: Alzheimer's Society; British Heart Foundation; EveryChild; The International Red Cross and Red Crescent Movement.

Corporate giving

In 2013/14 the group donated a total of £626,000 worldwide, at least £36,000 of which was contributed from central group funds through the matched funding scheme. A figure for UK charitable donations was not included in the annual report and accounts for the year. The average of UK donations in the three most recent years for which we have figures was £359,000 and we have taken this as the figure for charitable giving in 2013/14. However, if the rise in the group's worldwide giving is to be considered, the real figure for UK charitable donations may vary considerably from our estimate.

We were unable to determine a figure for the in-kind donations given by the group.

In-kind support

Employee time

The group's Community Investment Policy grants all employees two days annual leave for volunteering purposes, subject to their manager's approval.

In-kind donations

One of the ways through which Johnson Matthey sites support charities is by loaning company facilities.

Employee-led support

Employee volunteering

Johnson Matthey employees participate in charitable and community activities in their local areas.

Payroll giving

The group operates a payroll giving scheme.

Matched funding

Employees' fundraising efforts for registered charities may be matched with central group funds up to £1,000 per individual employee per year. Matched funding is capped at £50,000 per year across the group as a whole. During the year, 36 employees and 12 employee teams in three countries had their fundraising efforts matched to a value of £36,000.

Commercially led support

The group supports projects to advance science education and states on its website that 'encouraging the next generation of scientists is important to the sustainability of our industry'.

Corporate social responsibility

CSR committee: There is a CSR Compliance Committee.

CSR information: The following information was taken from the annual report and accounts:

> We have a strong tradition of getting involved with our communities and work hard to build good community relations, with our employees taking part in local programmes.
>
> This contributes powerfully to our goals for social sustainability. 'Social' is one of the five elements of our Sustainability 2017 strategy for building a sustainable business and we believe that investing in communities is an integral part of that social commitment.

CSR report: A sustainability report is contained within the annual report and accounts and there is an informative sustainability section on the group's website.

Exclusions

Our research tells us that no support is given for advertising in charity brochures, appeals from individuals, political appeals or religious appeals.

Applications

To request funding for a charitable project, download an application form from the website and return to group.charity@matthey.com.

Johnson Service Group plc

Miscellaneous

Correspondent: Tim Morris, Company Secretary, Johnson House, Abbots Park, Monks Way, Preston Brook, Cheshire WA7 3GH (tel: 01928 704600; fax: 01928 704620; email: enquiries@johnsonplc.com; website: www.jsg.com/corporate-responsibility)

Directors: Yvonne Monaghan, Chief Financial Officer; Chris Sander, Chief Executive; Michael Del Mar; William Shannon; Paul Moody, Chair; Tim Morris (women: 1; men: 5)

Year end	31/12/2013
Turnover	£193,600,000
Pre-tax profit	£12,200,000

Nature of business: The company is principally engaged in textile rental and dry cleaning services.

Company registration number: 523335

Subsidiary undertakings include: Johnsons Apparelmaster Ltd; Johnson Cleaners UK Ltd; Jeeves of Belgravia Ltd; Jeeves International Ltd; Johnson Group Properties plc; Johnson Investment Ltd; Semara Estates Ltd

UK employees: 4,588

Total employees: 4,588

Focus of giving: General charitable purposes, small groups, children, young people, community/social welfare.

Cash donations undeclared ✓
Charity of the Year ✓

Charitable donations

Cash UK (latest available):	2013	£30,000
	2012	£54,000
	2011	£19,900
	2010	£15,700
	2009	£31,000
Total UK (cash and in kind):	2013	£30,000
Cash worldwide:	2013	£30,000
Total worldwide (cash and in kind):	2013	£30,000

Community involvement

There is not a lot of information available on Johnson Service Group plc's charitable activities; however, its website states the following:

> The group and its individual operating companies seek to be good neighbours, and work in partnership with our people to help their local communities. Major ongoing charitable initiatives include Johnson Cleaners' partnership with Macmillan Cancer Relief to encourage the return and re-use of hangers, and the Johnson Group Cleaners Charity's support for a range of local registered charities dedicated to helping the underprivileged. Operating companies continue to develop links to their communities with simple but valued initiatives such as work experience placements to disadvantaged young adults.

Corporate giving

The group's annual report for 2013 did not include details on charitable donations made during the year. Based on figures obtained from previous years' reports, however, the group donates on average around £30,000 annually. We have therefore taken this as an estimate for charitable donations from the group for 2013.

Corporate social responsibility

CSR committee: We found no evidence of there being a separate CSR committee.

CSR information: This information was obtained from the group's website:

> The Johnson Service Group is acutely aware of its responsibilities to the communities in which it operates, and from which both its customers and employees are drawn. We are committed to progressively embedding Corporate Social Responsibility (CSR) best practice into every aspect of our operations. We endeavour to manage these in a responsible manner, believing that sound and demonstrable performance in relation to CSR policies and practices is a fundamental part of business success.
>
> The group is committed to continuous improvement in its CSR program and encourages its operating businesses and partners to strive for heightened performance.

CSR report: We found no evidence of there being a separate CSR report.

Applications

In writing to the correspondent referenced 'Charitable donations'.

Keepmoat Ltd

Building/construction

Correspondent: The Company Secretary, The Waterfront, Lakeside Boulevard, Doncaster DN4 5PL (tel: 01302 346620; website: www.keepmoat.com/about-us/social-responsibility)

Directors: Peter Warry, Chair; Dave Sheridan, Chief Executive; James Thomson, Chief Financial Officer; Aidan Birkett; Mike Paccitti (women: 0; men: 5)

Year end	31/03/2014
Turnover	£930,617,000
Pre-tax profit	£50,031,000

Nature of business: The Keepmoat group is principally engaged in the refurbishment and construction of residential dwellings.

Company registration number: 1998780

Subsidiary undertakings include: FWA West Ltd; Keepmoat Homes Ltd; Keepmoat Leeds (PFI) Ltd; Keepmoat Property Ltd; Keepmoat Property Services Ltd; Keepmoat Regeneration Ltd;

Main locations: Doncaster

Total employees: 2,921

Focus of giving: Children, young people, community/social welfare.

Cash donations undeclared ✓

Charitable donations

Cash UK (latest available):	2014	£76,000
	2013	£30,000
	2012	£114,000
	2011	£84,000
	2009	£106,000
Total UK (cash and in kind):	2014	£76,000
Cash worldwide:	2014	£76,000
Total worldwide (cash and in kind):	2014	£76,000

Community involvement

Keepmoat looks to support its local communities through the support of charitable causes whenever possible. Employees of the group are also encouraged to partake with charitable fundraising efforts.

Corporate giving

A figure for charitable donations was not included in the 2013/14 annual report and accounts. The average of these contributions in the three most recent years for which we have figures was £76,000. We have taken this as an estimate for charitable donations in 2013/14.

We were unable to determine details of beneficiaries.

Employee-led support

Employee fundraising

Keepmoat employees are encouraged to take part in charity fundraising events and activities.

Corporate social responsibility

CSR committee: There was no evidence of a separate CSR Committee.

CSR information: Keepmoat focuses its community responsibility on four central areas: environment; community; workplace; marketplace.

CSR report: There was no evidence of a separate CSR report; however, there is a section on social responsibility on the website.

Applications

In writing to the correspondent, referenced 'Charitable donations'.

Keysight Technologies UK Ltd (formerly Agilent Technologies UK Ltd)

Information technology

Correspondent: Company Secretary, 610 Wharfedale Road, Winnersh Triangle, Wokingham, Berkshire RG41 5TP (tel: 01314 520200; fax: 01314 520419; email: arlene_dickson@agilent.com; website: www.keysight.com)

Directors: Roy MacNaughton; Christopher Rennie; James Billett

Year end	31/10/2013
Turnover	£172,863,000
Pre-tax profit	(£4,184,000)

Nature of business: Keysight Technologies Inc. (NYSE: KEYS) sells to engineers and technicians across industry segments of communications; aerospace and defence; and industrial, computers, and semiconductors.

Keysight began operating as a wholly owned subsidiary of Agilent on 1 August, 2014 and is the Electronic Measurement Group for Agilent. Keysight has 9,500 employees, 12 R&D centres around the world, and serves customers in more than 100 countries.

The company Agilent Technologies UK Ltd changed its name on 1 August 2014 to Keysight Technologies UK Ltd. It retains the same company number.

Company registration number: 3809903

Subsidiary undertakings include: Agilent Finance Ltd; BT&D Technologies Ltd; Lab 901 Ltd; Libra (Syscom) Ltd.

Main locations: Wokingham

UK employees: 722

Focus of giving: Education, environment, science technology, women's issues, community/social welfare.

Cash donations undeclared	✓
Gifts in kind	✓
Matched funding	✓

Charitable donations

Cash UK (latest available):	2013	£26,000
	2011	£10,200
	2009	£23,000
	2008	£45,000
	2007	£54,000
Total UK (cash and in kind):	2013	£26,000
Cash worldwide:	2013	£26,000
Total worldwide (cash and in kind):	2013	£26,000

Community involvement

We have very little information on Keysight's charitable contribution to its communities/society. Most information is available on the global website where philanthropy is channelled through Agilent's foundation.

The Agilent Technologies Foundation (U.S.)

The following information is taken from The Agilent Foundation's website:

> We Agilent inherited a commitment to philanthropy from its parent company, Hewlett-Packard. The Agilent Technologies Foundation's roots go back to the founding of Agilent in 1999.
>
> As a global company, Agilent's objective is to be an economic, intellectual and social asset in the countries and communities in which it operates.
>
> Agilent's philanthropic efforts, through the Agilent Technologies Foundation, focus on education and development in life sciences, thus fostering innovation and advancement in children's education. The Foundation supports a range of pre-university-level science education programs aimed at helping students develop the critical thinking skills essential for tomorrow's jobs.
>
> In addition, the Foundation's match of employee giving strengthens a broad range of non-profit programs in communities where Agilent has a presence.

Corporate giving

The UK company supports science and mathematics in line with its overall objectives. In 2012/13 the company did not declare its charitable donations. We have taken the last three totals given for which we have details and estimate that charitable donations would be around £26,000. We have no information regarding the cost to the company of in-kind giving such as staff volunteering.

We have taken our figures from the UK company's accounts when it was still known as Agilent (2012/13). These were the latest available at Companies House.

In-kind support

In the US, the foundation matches employee giving dollar-for-dollar to a wide range of non-profit organisations. We do not know if the UK company adopts this practice.

Employee-led support

The Agilent Technologies Foundation's website states that every year, staff donate thousands of volunteer hours in support of the foundation's focus on improving science education.

Corporate social responsibility

CSR committee: No dedicated CSR committee for the UK.

CSR information: The Keysight Technologies global company states on its website that it: 'is committed to conducting its business in an ethical, environmentally sustainable and socially responsible manner. This commitment is consistent with our corporate objectives and is essential to continued business success'.

CSR report: There is a Corporate Citizenship Statement on the global website.

Applications

Local appeals should be made in writing to the correspondent.

For information about the Agilent Foundation (US philanthropic organisation) see the company's website.

Kier Group plc

Building/construction

Correspondent: Corporate Responsibility Dept., Tempsford Hall, Sandy, Bedfordshire SG19 2BD (tel: 01767 355000; fax: 01767 355633; website: www.kier.co.uk/corporate-responsibility.aspx)

Directors: Phil White, Chair; Haydn Mursell, Chief Executive; Beverley Dew, Finance Director; Steve Bowcott; Richard Bailey; Kirsty Bashforth; Amanda Mellor; Nick Winser; Hugh Raven (women: 2; men: 7)

Year end	30/06/2014
Turnover	£2,985,200,000
Pre-tax profit	£14,800,000

Nature of business: Activities span building, civil engineering, opencast mining, facilities management, residential and commercial property investment and PFI project investment.

Company registration number: 2708030

Subsidiary undertakings include: Kier Construction Ltd; Kier Energy Solutions Ltd; Kier Infrastructure and Overseas Ltd; Kier Plant Ltd; Kier Services Ltd; Pure Buildings Ltd;

UK employees: 14,318

Total employees: 15,335

Focus of giving: General charitable purposes, education, health, ill health, poverty and social exclusion, sport, recreation, children, young people, community/social welfare.

Membership: BITC

Cash donations undeclared	✓
Charity of the Year	✓
Gifts in kind	✓

Charitable donations

Cash UK (latest available):	2014	£81,000
	2013	£58,000
	2012	£122,000
	2011	£64,000
	2010	£97,000
Total UK (cash and in kind):	2014	£3,300,000
Cash worldwide:	2014	£81,000
Total worldwide (cash and in kind):	2014	£3,300,000

Community involvement

Kier Group looks to contribute to communities in the areas where the group has a presence. Group employees fundraise through **The Kier Foundation** (Charity Commission no. 1144803) and volunteer in their communities.

Corporate giving

The annual report and accounts for 2014 did not declare a figure for charitable donations made during the year. The average of such contributions in the three most recent years for which we have figures was £81,000, and we have taken this as an estimate for charitable donations in 2013/14. It would appear that in previous years, the majority of donations have been made to local charities in areas where the group has a presence.

The group's CSR report for 2014 states the following: 'We believe we have invested in cash terms within the communities we work in excess of £3.6m.' We believe that this figure includes the value of employee time (£2.9 million), as well as funds raised by employees (£299,000). As is our usual practice, we have deducted the latter figure from the total stated, and have taken the remaining £3.3 million as the amount for the group's total contributions.

It would appear that, whilst The Kier Foundation was established by an initial donation from the group in 2011, its income is now derived from funds raised by employees.

Charity of the Year

Over two years, employees helped to raise £250,000 for the group's charity partner, Barnardo's. Macmillan Cancer Support will be the group's new charity partner for the two years until June 2016.

In-kind support

Pro bono

On a voluntary basis, Kier companies have assisted their communities through helping to upgrade community facilities and providing training in constructions skills, for example. In 2013/14 almost 162,000 employee hours were spent on community initiatives.

Employee-led support

Employee fundraising

Kier Group employees fundraise for and are supported in their fundraising efforts by The Kier Foundation. Fundraising activities have included swimming, racing ferrets and even squeezing into small cars.

Employee volunteering

The Kier Group website states that employees contribute thousands of hours to community-related activities each year.

Commercially led support

The website states the following: 'the Kier Group gives thousands of people training, careers advice and workplace experience annually'. The group works with schools and colleges to promote industry-related training as part of the curriculum.

Corporate social responsibility

CSR committee: A central CR Team was established in 2014. There is also a Group CR Director, as well as a Group CR Steering Committee.

CSR information: The following information was obtained from the website:

> Kier strives to meet its pledge to 'deliver a brighter future for our communities' – by getting involved in the places we call home.
>
> Whether we are building new spaces or providing essential services, we are mindful of our role in communities throughout the UK. Wherever possible, we aim to make a positive difference to the people and places that welcome us.

CSR report: A CSR report is available from the website.

Applications

In writing to the correspondent.

KPMG LLP

Accountants

Correspondent: Corporate Responsibility Dept., Salisbury Square House, 8 Salisbury Square, London EC4Y 8BB (tel: 020 7311 1000; email: corporateresponsibility@kpmg.co.uk; website: www.kpmg.com/uk/en/about/whatmakesusdifferent/ourapproachtocorporateresponsibility/pages/default.aspx)

Directors: Simon Collins; Jim Marsh; David Matthews; Marianne Fallon; Tony Cates; Jane McCormick; Richard Fleming; Richard Gostling; Iain Moffatt; Bill Michael; Richard Reid; Kru Desai; Jonathan Hurst; Melanie Richards; David Sayer; Ian Starkey (women: 3; men: 13)

Year end	30/09/2014
Turnover	£1,909,000,000
Pre-tax profit	£414,000,000

Nature of business: The provision of professional services including audit, tax and advisory.

Company registration number: OC301540

Subsidiary undertakings include: KPMG Audit plc; KPMG Business Intelligence Ltd; KPMG Holdings Ltd; KPMG IT Advisory Ltd; KPMG UK Ltd; KPMG United Kingdom plc

Main locations: Birmingham, Bristol, Cardiff, Cambridge, Edinburgh, Gatwick, Glasgow, Ipswich, Leeds, Leicester, Milton Keynes, Newcastle upon Tyne, Liverpool, Manchester, Nottingham, Preston, Plymouth, Reading, St Albans, Southampton, Stoke-on-Trent, Watford, St Helens, St Asaph, Kings Norton, Aberdeen

Total employees: 11,929

Focus of giving: Education, enterprise/training, environment, poverty and social exclusion, children, young people.

Membership: BITC, LBG

Charity of the Year	✓
Gifts in kind	✓
Overseas giving	✓
Payroll giving	✓
Sponsorship	✓

Charitable donations

Cash UK (latest available):	2009	£12,275,000
	2007	£1,000,000
	2006	£813,000
Total worldwide (cash and in kind):	2014	£6,200,000

Community involvement

Social mobility is at the heart of KPMG's community strategy and promotes it in five key ways:

- Preparing young people for the world of work
- Increasing fair access to the profession
- Improving literacy for young people

- Increasing access to affordable and secure housing
- Tackling low pay through the Living Wage

The principal way in which the firm supports these objectives is through pro bono and volunteering work.

Support is also given through **The KPMG Foundation** (Charity Commission no. 1086518), a grant-making charity.

The website states:

> Over the next two to three years the foundation will particularly focus on projects which:
> - Unlock the potential of children and young people on the edge of care, in care or leaving care; and/or
> - Unlock the potential of children and young people in deprived families

The foundation does not accept unsolicited applications.

Corporate giving

Community data contained within the annual report and accounts shows that community contributions amounted to £6.2 million. This figure includes cash and in-kind donations as well as management costs, though we were unable to determine separate values for these amounts.

During the year, almost 12,300 individuals and 878 organisations were supported and an extra £945,000 was leveraged through the firm's activities to the benefit of the community.

National charities 2012–14: Action for Literacy and Shelter

The annual report and accounts state the following:

> This year we completed an award winning partnership with Shelter, National Literacy Trust and Dyslexia Action. KPMG volunteers over two years spent 900 hours volunteering on a wide range of projects including policy development, and the £1.2 million raised during the partnership is helping 2,700 families stay secure in their homes and helping over 8,000 young people improve their literacy skills.

In-kind support

Pro bono

KPMG's volunteering and pro bono policy allows staff to spend six days per year volunteering for charities that promote social mobility. In 2013/14 almost 48,000 working hours were spent volunteering.

Improving literacy for young people

As part of its partnership with Action for Literacy, a joint initiative between the National Literacy Trust (NLT) and Dyslexia Action, teams from KPMG worked pro bono on projects that included a review of NLT's information technology structure, helping to save the charity £10,000. Dyslexia Action was also advised on programme management set-up, data and information strategy, intellectual property strategy and client and customer engagement.

Employee-led support

Employee volunteering

KPMG employees play an active role in the group's community involvement, with more than 3,100 committing working time to community volunteering in 2013/14.

Payroll giving

Our research indicates that the Give As You Earn scheme is in operation nationally and is supported by the firm.

Commercially led support

Sponsorship

In line with its efforts to promote greater social mobility, KPMG sponsored Free the Children at the first UK 'We Day', which aims to inspire and educate young people to help make a difference in the world.

Preparing young people for the world of work

KPMG works with schools and colleges in disadvantaged communities to improve skills and increase academic attainment. The firm provides work placements, school leaver and internship opportunities, and in 2013/14 worked with more than 130 schools and colleges across the UK, helping to support more than 6,000 young people.

Corporate social responsibility

CSR committee: There is a Responsible Business Leadership Committee, which meets quarterly and is responsible for corporate responsibility strategy and performance.

CSR information: The following information was obtained from the website:

> We recognise that we have the scale, influence and business knowledge to make a significant and positive contribution to the issues that affect our communities and environments. We can do that in many different ways – through pro bono work, by using our convening power to influence policy, by sharing our professional and individual skills as volunteers and by demonstrating respect for the environment.

KPMG's corporate responsibility strategy focuses on four main areas: Social mobility; Young Leadership; Environment; and Sustainable Procurement.

CSR report: A CSR report is included within the annual report and accounts.

Exclusions

Our research indicates that assistance to private educational establishments, political parties, or primarily evangelical causes and campaigns is not given.

Applications

The KPMG Foundation

Note that the foundation is pro active in seeking projects to fund and regrets that it is not in a position to respond to unsolicited grant applications.

For more information on KPMG's approach to corporate responsibility, contact the correspondent.

Ladbrokes plc

Gaming, hotels, leisure

Correspondent: Ciaran O'Brien, Corporate and Government Affairs Director, Imperial House, Imperial Drive, Rayners Lane, Harrow, Middlesex HA2 7JW (tel: 020 8868 8899; email: ciaran.o'brien@ladbrokes.co.uk; website: www.ladbrokesplc.com/corporate-responsibility.aspx)

Directors: Peter Erskine, Chair; Richard Glynn, Chief Executive; Ian A. Bull, Chief Financial Officer; John M. Kelly; Sly Bailey; Darren Shapland; Christine M. Hodgson; Richard Moross; David R. Martin (women: 2; men: 7)

Year end	31/12/2013
Turnover	£1,117,700,000
Pre-tax profit	£67,000,000

Nature of business: The group's principal activity is the provision of a range of betting and gaming services.

Company registration number: 566221

Subsidiary undertakings include: Ladbrokes Betting and Gaming Ltd; Ladbrokes International plc; Ladbroke (Ireland) Ltd; Ladbrokes Leisure (Ireland) Ltd; Ladbrokes Sportsbook Ltd Partnership; Tierce Ladbroke SA

Main locations: Watford, Harlow

Total employees: 14,763

Focus of giving: Education, health, ill health, housing, homelessness, medical research, older people, poverty and social exclusion, sport, recreation, community/social welfare, disability.

Cash donations undeclared	✓
Charity of the Year	✓
Overseas giving	✓

Charitable donations

Cash UK (latest available):	2013	£674,000
	2012	£945,000
	2011	£932,000
	2010	£946,000
	2009	£700,000
Total UK (cash and in kind):	2013	£674,000
Cash worldwide:	2013	£674,000
Total worldwide (cash and in kind):	2013	£674,000

Community involvement

Ladbrokes supports communities through the **Ladbrokes Community Fund** (LCF), which makes grants to clubs and charities in areas where the group has a operates. Ladbrokes employees take an active role in supporting their communities, raising funds through the **Ladbrokes in the Community Charitable Trust** (Charity Commission no. 1101804). Support is focused principally on making grants to organisations working in the areas of: health (particularly research/treatment, hospice services and disability support); education/sports (particularly supporting the disabled/disadvantaged); and community (with a focus on homelessness, older people and social activity projects 'for those at risk').

The group is a member of the Responsible Gambling Trust (RGT), through which it supports a number of gambling charities. The group also supports a number of large healthcare charities and is a partner of Crimestoppers.

Charity partners included: the Bobby Moore Fund, Crimestoppers, Race for Life (Cancer Research)

Corporate giving

The annual report and accounts for 2013 stated that, during the year, the group donated £674,000 to the Responsible Gambling Trust. Unfortunately, a figure for total charitable donations was not declared in the annual report, though we know that financial support was given to charities through the Ladbrokes Community Fund and that, in previous years, a number of charitable causes, including those overseas, have received donations from the group. Though it is likely, based on this, that charitable donations from the group were far higher, we have taken £674,000 as the total for charitable donations during the year.

Beneficiaries included: Responsible Gambling Trust

See the corporate charity entry on p. 411 for more information.

Employee-led support

The group actively encourages employees to undertake fundraising activities, particularly in support of Ladbrokes in the Community Charitable Trust. Employees helped to raise more than £500,000 for the trust in 2013.

Corporate social responsibility

CSR committee: There is a CR committee. The following information was taken from the annual report and accounts for 2013: 'The social, environmental, ethical and human rights issues associated with the Ladbrokes core businesses, our joint ventures and major partnerships are reviewed by our CR Committee, our Risk Committee, and ultimately by the Board on a regular basis.'

CSR information: The following information was obtained from the group's website: 'Fair Play is built into the way we do business at Ladbrokes. Our CR goal is to be a leading responsible betting and gaming business within our sector. The success of our strategy rests on developing responsible relationships and running responsible operations.'

CSR report: There is a CSR section on the website and a CSR report available to download from the website.

Corporate charity: Ladbrokes in the Community Charitable Trust (Charity Commission no. 1101804).

Exclusions

Our research indicates that no support is given to appeals for advertising in charity brochures, the arts, appeals from individuals, circular appeals, fundraising events, overseas projects, political appeals, religious appeals, or small, purely local appeals not in an area of company presence.

Applications

For Ladbrokes in the Community Charitable Trust, the trustees meet each month to consider requests from 'shop and head office fundraisers and charities'. However, it would appear, based on our previous research, that the typical procedure is to secure the support of your local shop in raising funds on behalf of your cause.

Lafarge Aggregates Ltd

Quarrying

Correspondent: See applications, Portland House, Bickenhill Lane, Solihull, West Midlands B37 7RQ (website: www.lafargetarmac.com/sustainability)

Directors: G. F. Young; C. Ragoucy; P. Fleetham; M. Riley; J. M. Greenwood

Year end	31/12/2013
Turnover	£346,200,000
Pre-tax profit	(£110,500,000)

Nature of business: Supplier of asphalt, aggregate, readymix and contractor.

The annual report and accounts for 2013 state that: 'The company is a wholly owned subsidiary of its ultimate parent company, Lafarge Tarmac Holdings Ltd.'

Lafarge Tarmac Holdings Ltd:

> Acquired the entire issued share capitals of Lafarge Aggregates Ltd, Lafarge Tarmac Cement and Lime Ltd (formerly Lafarge Cement UK Ltd), Lafarge (UK) Services Ltd, Tarmac Industrial Minerals Holdings Ltd (formerly Anglo Industrial Mineral Holdings Ltd) and Tarmac Group Ltd.

As part of these arrangements, the company was contributed to Lafarge Tarmac on 7 January 2013.

Company registration number: 297905

Subsidiary undertakings include: Hertfordshire Road Maintenance Ltd; Lafarge Leasing Ltd; Redland Ltd; Redland Minerals Ltd; Redland Properties Ltd; Redland Property Holdings Ltd

Main locations: Leicester

UK employees: 981

Total employees: 981

Focus of giving: Education, environment, housing, homelessness, arts, culture, sport, recreation, community/social welfare.

Cash donations undeclared ✓
Gifts in kind ✓

Charitable donations

Cash UK (latest available):	2013	£22,000
	2011	£22,000
	2009	£38,000
	2008	£820,000
	2007	£820,000
Total UK (cash and in kind):	2013	£22,000
Cash worldwide:	2013	£22,000
Total worldwide (cash and in kind):	2013	£22,000

Community involvement

Lafarge Tarmac looks to make a 'positive contribution' to the communities in which it has a presence. One of the ways in which it does this is through its support of local community programmes and local projects, particularly in the areas of education, young people and the environment. The group's Sustainability Strategy states that by the end of 2014, its aim was to 'establish corporate engagement programmes with universities, schools and groups working with disadvantaged young people'.

Local community liaison

By the end of 2015 Lafarge Tarmac aims for all of its operational sites to have a framework in place for local community liaison.

Lafarge Tarmac Landfill Communities Fund

Derbyshire Environmental Trust (DET) has administered this fund since 2005 for projects near to Lafarge Tarmac quarry, asphalt plant, railhead, landfill or recycling sites in the UK.

Note: Whilst we have taken the financial information from the company accounts of Lafarge Aggregates Ltd, as sustainability policies are operated on a group level, we have taken the rest of our information from group sources.

Corporate giving

The annual report and accounts for 2013 did not included a figure for charitable contributions. In the most recent year for which we have a figure, donations amounted to around £22,000, and we have taken this as an estimate for charitable contributions in 2013.

We were unable to determine a value for the in-kind support contributed by the company.

In-kind support

Employee volunteering
It would appear that employee volunteering is a relatively new initiative. By 2020, Lafarge Tarmac aims to contribute one volunteering day per employee.

Corporate social responsibility

CSR committee: At a group level, an External Sustainability Panel has been established to provide 'expert advice and challenge about the group's sustainability strategy and performance'.

CSR information: The company's annual report and accounts for 2013 state: 'Sustainability is managed on a group-wide basis. The group believes sustainability is essential for the prosperity and well-being of society, our customers, the communities in which it operates as well as the long-term success of our business.' The group's four priority focuses are people; planet; performance; and solution.

We were unable to determine the ratio of women to men on the board.

CSR report: There is a Sustainability section on the group's website.

Exclusions

Local appeals not in areas of company presence.

Applications

Lafarge Tarmac Landfill Communities Fund grants
For grants from the Lafarge Tarmac Landfill Communities Fund, contact the Derbyshire Environmental Trust (DET) for more details and an application pack: Derbyshire Environmental Trust, County Hall, Matlock, Derbyshire DE4 3AG; Telephone: 01629 539182/538614; Email: det@derbyshire.gov.uk

Eligibility for grants from the fund is limited to projects within a seven-mile radius of a Lafarge Tarmac site. The project site must also be within a ten-mile radius of a licensed landfill site.

Leeds Building Society

Building society

Correspondent: The Secretary, Leeds Building Society Charitable Foundation, 105 Albion Street, Leeds LS1 5AS (tel: 01132 257508; website: www.leedsbuildingsociety.co.uk/your-society/about-us/charitable-foundation)

Directors: Robin Ashton, Chair; Peter Hill, Chief Executive; Philippa Brown; Susan Cooklin; David Fisher; Philip Jenks; Robin Litten, Finance Director; Les Platts; Abhai Rajguru; Kim Rebecchi; Ian Robertson; Karen Wint (women: 4; men: 8)

Year end	31/12/2013
Pre-tax profit	£70,900,000

Nature of business: The provision, to existing and prospective members, of residential mortgages and retail saving products.

FSA registration number: 164992

Subsidiary undertakings include: Headrow Commercial Property Services Ltd; Leeds Building Society Covered Bonds LLP; Leeds Financial Services Ltd; Leeds Mortgage Funding Ltd; Leeds Overseas (Isle of Man) Ltd; Mercantile Asset Management Ltd

Main locations: Leeds

UK employees: 1,054

Total employees: 1,054

Focus of giving: General charitable purposes, housing, homelessness, local groups, older people, poverty and social exclusion, children, young people, community/social welfare, disability.

Membership: BITC

Charity of the Year	✓
Gifts in kind	✓
Humanitarian aid: UK	✓
Market-led giving	✓
Matched funding	✓

Charitable donations

Cash UK (latest available):	2013	£110,000
	2011	£219,000
	2009	£180,000
	2007	£94,000
	2006	£80,000
Total UK (cash and in kind):	2013	£110,000
Cash worldwide:	2013	£110,000
Total worldwide (cash and in kind):	2013	£110,000

Community involvement

Leeds Building Society makes donations to registered charities in the areas near its branches, principally through **Leeds Building Society Charitable Foundation** (Charity Commission no. 1074429). It also runs the Lending a Hand employee volunteering scheme and employees are supported in their fundraising efforts through a matched funding scheme.

Partner charities: Age UK; Marie Curie Cancer Care; Variety, the Children's Charity

Corporate giving

The annual report and accounts for 2013 show that charitable donations amounted to £110,000 during the year. This includes a £90,000 donation to Leeds Building Society Charitable Foundation and other charitable donations amounting to £20,000. A further £26,000 was donated through the Caring Saver Account, though we have classed this as commercially led support and, as is our usual practice, we have not included this in our total figure for charitable donations from the group.

We were unable to determine the value of the in-kind support given by the group.

Beneficiaries: Leeds Building Society Charitable Foundation (£90,000)

See the corporate charity entry on p. 411 for more information.

In-kind support

Lending a Hand scheme
The scheme that was launched in 2013 entitles employees to one paid working day a year for volunteering purposes.

Employee-led support

Employee volunteering
Through the Lending a Hand scheme, employees have contributed their time to a number of volunteering activities for local causes including: tidying up gardens and helping to organise and run a school nativity play.

Employee fundraising
Employees raise funds for a number of charitable causes. Aside from supporting Children in Need and Comic Relief, Head of Departments have helped to organise fundraising activities for local charities, including for St Gemma's Hospice and Martin House Children's Hospice in Leeds and Tiny Lives Special Care Babies charity in Newcastle. In 2013 employees raised more than £27,000.

Matched funding
Employees are supported in their fundraising efforts through the matched funding scheme. In 2013 £9,200 was contributed through the scheme.

Commercially led support

Your Interest in Theirs scheme
The society's four charity partners benefit through the scheme, by which members give up to 99p of their interest each year.

Caring Saver accounts
Leeds Building Society makes an annual donation equivalent to 1% of the average balance held in all Caring Saver accounts.

Corporate social responsibility

CSR committee: We found no evidence of there being a CSR committee.

CSR information: The following information was obtained from the Corporate Responsibility report for 2013:

> As the UK's 5th largest buildingsociety, we have a national presence and our network of branches, and processing centres, play an important role in their local community. We have therefore developed our charity and community giving to provide a sustainable contribution to large national charities and local community causes.

CSR report: There is a Corporate Responsibility report published annually and available to download from the website.

Corporate charity: Leeds Building Society Charitable Foundation (Charity Commission no. 1074429).

Exclusions

The foundation is unlikely to support:

- The restoration or upgrading of building, including churches
- Environmental charities (unless there is a benefit to a disadvantaged community)
- Administration equipment such as IT equipment
- Projects with religious, political or military purposes
- Individuals, including sponsorship of individuals
- Animal welfare projects
- Medical research

Applications

Leeds Building Society Charitable Foundation

In writing to the correspondent, including the following information: the name of the organisation; the name of the project, and brief information about its work; a contact name, address and phone number; the registered charity number; details of what the donation would be used for; who would benefit from the donation; and the nearest Leeds Building Society branch.

Criteria is available to view on the website. The trustees meet four times a year in March, June, September and November. Following the meeting the foundation will write to each applicant to inform them as to whether their application has been successful.

The trust is unable to consider applications if support has been provided in the last two years.

The foundation operates independently of Leeds Building Society and so local branch staff are unable to answer questions about the foundation. Contact the foundation directly for further information.

Generally, applications for community based projects which aim to provide relief of suffering, hardship or poverty, or their direct consequences will be considered.

The foundation's website lists some of the areas it supports:

- Homeless people
- Adults and children with physical and mental disabilities
- Older people
- Underprivileged families
- Deaf, blind and partially sighted people
- Community projects benefiting local residents
- Victims of natural and civil disasters in the UK
- Scout, guide and play groups

The project must operate in the area of one of our 67 branches.

Donations are normally in the range of £250 to £1,000. The application must be for capital expenditure.

Lending a Hand scheme – volunteering opportunities

If you would like your charity to receive support through the employee volunteering scheme, email michaelward@leedsbuildingsociety.co.uk.

Legal & General plc

Financial services

Correspondent: Group Charity Committee, One Coleman Street, London EC2R 5AA (website: csr.legalandgeneralgroup.com/csr)

Directors: John Stewart, Chair; Nigel Wilson, Group Chief Executive; Rudy Markham; Mark Zinkula; John Pollock; Mark Gregory, Chief Financial Officer; Stuart Popham; Julia Wilson; Lindsay Tomlinson; Lizabeth Zlatkus; Olaf Swantee; Richard Meddings; Carolyn Bradley (women: 3; men: 10)

Year end	31/12/2013
Turnover	£6,162,000,000
Pre-tax profit	£1,315,000,000

Nature of business: The group's principal activities are: the provision of long-term insurance, investment management and general insurance.

Company registration number: 1417162

Subsidiary undertakings include: Legal & General Finance plc; Legal & General Resources Ltd

Main locations: London, Brighton, Cardiff, Birmingham

UK employees: 8,268

Total employees: 9,237

Focus of giving: General charitable purposes, enterprise/training, health, ill health, financial education, older people, poverty and social exclusion, safety and crime prevention, sport, recreation, children, young people.

Membership: BITC

FTSE 100	✓
Gifts in kind	✓
Matched funding	✓
Overseas giving	✓
Payroll giving	✓

Charitable donations

Cash UK (latest available):	2009	£2,800,000
	2008	£3,200,000
	2007	£1,860,000
	2006	£2,300,000
	2005	£2,279,000
Total UK (cash and in kind):	2013	£1,625,000
Total worldwide (cash and in kind):	2013	£1,625,000

Community involvement

Through its bases in the UK (Birmingham, Cardiff, Central London, Kingswood, Hove and Ipswich) and it locations overseas (Netherlands, France, and the USA), Legal & General plc looks to build relationships with schools, charities, community groups and local authorities in its communities.

Employees are involved in community initiatives at a local level through fundraising and volunteering activities. Legal & General does not have a Charity of the Year, with employees at each location nominating charities to support, though it does support a number of national charities in the areas of health, as well as Children in Need and Comic Relief. The group runs a number of community programmes in schools, key themes of which appear to be financial inclusion, young people, education and social mobility.

Corporate giving

In 2013 Legal & General and its employees contributed £4 million to non-profit organisations. We have taken this figure to include employee donated and raised funds in the UK (£1.8 million), overseas employee contributions (£812,000) and CSR management costs (£232,000), and, as is our usual practice, have not included these figures in the total for corporate contributions.

During the year the group contributed to the following purposes: Group campaign projects and gifts in kind (£816,000); Community projects (£431,000); Volunteering costs (£330,000); and School Governors (donations to schools where employees serve as governors, £48,000).

In-kind support

Pro bono

Legal & General's employee volunteering policy allows employees to commit one working day a year to community volunteering.

Community initiatives

The group takes part in a number of initiatives. These include:

Money, Money, Money – More than 90 employees participated in educating students on the financial demands in the 'real world' at schools in Ipswich, Cardiff, London, Leatherhead and Reigate.

Step up for Success – At its Cardiff, Kingswood and London locations, 30 students from three different schools were invited to receive mentoring and management for one week. A team of 12 employees at each site guide students through building confidence and understanding in the workplace.

Mentoring Scheme – In conjunction with Surrey Enterprise Business partnership (EBP), the group runs two schemes for years 10 and 11 at Beacon School in Banstead. During the year, 39 employees dedicated 518 hours to mentoring 110 young people.

Career Academies UK – Employees help to mentor students over a two year period, during which they experience advice, information and a workplace visit.

Employee-led support

Employees across the group contribute to building relationships with their local communities in the following ways:

Employee fundraising

Employees at each location nominate charities to benefit from fundraising activities.

Employee volunteering

During the year, more than 25% of employees contributed to their local communities through volunteering. One of the ways in which employees are able to contribute their time is through the School Governors scheme, by which employees with transferable skills are encourage to take up vacant posts on school boards. As part of the scheme, the group makes grants to schools where employees serve for use towards a specific maths programme.

Community Awards: Employees who contribute to charitable causes through volunteering and fundraising are celebrated at the annual Chair's Community Awards.

Payroll giving

Employees are able to donate to registered charities through the Give As You Earn scheme.

Matched funding

The group matches payroll giving up to £25, makes grants to schools where employees serve as governors and matches funds raised through 'dress down' days at its bases.

Corporate social responsibility

CSR committee: There is a GCRE (Group Corporate Responsibility and Ethics) Committee, which is chaired by the Group CEO and meets once a year to discuss matters relating to CRE policies and targets. There are a number of subcommittees including the Group Charity Committee. Each location has a Community Investment Committee.

CSR information: The following information was obtained from the group's website:

> We welcome third and not-for-profit sectors with their expertise and knowledge to help learn and improve the way we do business. We look at innovative approaches to training our employees, challenge our product designers or understanding a particular market that we may think differently about. Our relationships with our charities help us understand our customers and build upon the richness of our organisation.

CSR report: A CSR report is published annually. There is also an informative section regarding CSR on the group's website.

Exclusions

Legal & General does not support animal charities, overseas based charities or international projects, religious organisations (except where it can be proven that the project is undertaken on behalf of the community as a whole) or political organisations.

Applications

Information about national charities which meet the group's guidelines should be sent to the correspondent. Appropriate local appeals should be sent to the relevant local contact.

National decisions are made by the charity committee and approved by the group board on an annual basis; local appeals are considered by individual locations. Overseas grants are handled by the subsidiary company in each country.

John Lewis Partnership plc

Retail – department and variety stores, retail – supermarkets

Correspondent: Corporate Social Responsibility team, Partnership House, Carlisle Place, London SW1P 1BX (tel: 020 7828 1000; website: www.johnlewispartnership.co.uk/csr.html)

Directors: Charlie Mayfield, Chair; Mark Price; Kate Brewer; Jane Burgess; Steve Gardiner; Denis Hennequin; Baroness Hogg; Tracey Killen; Patrick Lewis; Kim Lowe; Kevin Payne; Dan Smith; Andy Street; Keith Williams; Loraine Woodhouse (women: 6; men: 9)

Year end	25/01/2014
Turnover	£9,027,800,000
Pre-tax profit	£329,100,000

Nature of business: The company trades under the name of John Lewis (full line department stores and smaller 'at home' stores) and Waitrose (food shops, including supermarkets and convenience stores).

The partnership is a retail business run on co-operative principles. All the ordinary share capital is held by a trustee – John Lewis Partnership Trust Ltd – on partners' (employees') behalf. Under irrevocable trusts the balance of profits is available to be shared among all partners after provision for prudent reserves and for interest on loans and fixed dividends on shares held outside. Management is accountable to the general body of partners, in particular through elected councils and through the partnership's journalism.

Company registration number: 238937

Subsidiaries: John Lewis plc

Subsidiaries of John Lewis plc include: Herbert Parkinson Ltd; JLP Insurance Ltd; John Lewis Car Finance Ltd; John Lewis Delivery Ltd; John Lewis Properties plc; Waitrose Ltd

Brands include: John Lewis, Waitrose.

Total employees: 86,600

Focus of giving: Education, environment, health, ill health, heritage, housing, homelessness, medical research, older people, arts, culture, children, young people, disability.

Membership: BITC, LBG

Cash donations undeclared	✓
Gifts in kind	✓
Humanitarian aid: overseas	✓
Market-led giving	✓
Overseas giving	✓
Payroll giving	✓
Sponsorship	✓

Charitable donations

Cash UK (latest available):	2014	£6,800,000
	2011	£5,654,000
	2010	£5,071,800
	2009	£4,009,490
	2008	£2,846,361
Total UK (cash and in kind):	2014	£9,800,000
Cash worldwide:	2014	£6,800,000
Total worldwide (cash and in kind):	2014	£9,800,000

Community involvement

John Lewis Partnership looks to build relationships with the communities in which it has a presence. One of the main ways in which this is conducted is by donating time to community initiatives. John Lewis and Waitrose partners are encouraged to fundraise and donate to good causes, and to strengthen local, regional and national community relationships by volunteering through the Partnership's **Golden Jubilee Trust (GJT)** (Charity Commission no. 1079195) secondment scheme.

The partnership makes cash and in-kind donations to charities in its local areas and to those with which its partners are personally involved. It prefers to help organisations working in the following areas: care for those who are sick or have disabilities; young people and children; care and housing for elderly people; medical research; and welfare and counselling services.

In addition to Golden Jubilee Trust, John Lewis Partnership has a number of associated charities:

The Waitrose and John Lewis Foundations were established in 2005 and 2010 respectively to help provide financial and practical support for a broad range of projects in the partnership's supplier communities. The Waitrose Foundation operates in South Africa, Kenya and Ghana, whilst the John Lewis Foundation has supported projects in India.

John Spedan Lewis Foundation (Charity Commission no. 240473) was established in 1964 to commemorate the life and interests of the partnership's founder. Applications for funding are considered for organisations in the following areas: horticulture; ornithology; entomology; environmental education; and conservation. Preference is given to small projects with educational content and grants typically range from around £500 to £7,000. A small number of specific PhD research projects are also funded.

John Spedan Lewis Trust for the Advancement of the Natural Sciences (Charity Commission no. 31335) is a small trust established in 1955. The trust manages nature reserves, supports the work of visiting experts and volunteers, and runs a programme of annual lectures.

Corporate giving

In 2013/14 the partnership contributed 4.33% of its pre-tax, pre-bonus profit to charitable and community causes. According to the London Benchmarking Group model, community contributions can be broken down into the following categories:

Cash contributions	£6.8 million
Time contributions	£2.4 million
In-kind contributions	£615,000

During the year, £2.9 million was donated to The Prince of Wales Charitable Foundation through royalties paid from the sale of Duchy Originals products from Waitrose, and £165,000 was raised for Save the Children through sales of the Bear and the Hare book and other merchandise. We have classed this support as having been commercially led. More than £1.3 million spent on management costs, and additional contributions from partners, customers and suppliers were leveraged to the value of £776,000. As is our usual practice, we have not included these amounts in our figures for total corporate contributions.

We were unable to determine the value or the type of support given overseas via the Waitrose and John Lewis Foundations, and this may be accounted for in the total stated above.

Community matters

Customers of John Lewis and Waitrose are able to vote on how much the partnership should donate to particular local charities, using a token at the end of their shop. Waitrose customers are also able to vote online. As a result in 2013/14 more than £4 million was donated to causes through the scheme. During the year, the scheme also took into account volunteering activity, which enabled time, as well as money, to be allocated.

In-kind support

Gifts in kind

In-kind support includes the donation of products, gift vouchers and resources such as meeting room space. In 2011 a number of John Lewis and Waitrose shops began providing space for charities and community groups to use free of charge.

Schools programmes

As part of its community investment, the partnership runs a number of programmes for primary school-aged children. These include:

Grow and Sell – A Waitrose-led initiative that encourages local 7- to 11-year-old to grow there own produce and sell it outside its stores. Partners help the children with information on planting, growing and selling their produce.

Bringing Skills to Life – An educational programme to help primary schoolchildren develop their practical skills and imagination. More than 1,500 schools are involved with the scheme, which provide teachers and parents with free resources, such as lesson plans and activity cards, based around three themes – Design and Make; Cook and Share; and Storytelling.

Employee-led support

Employee (partner) volunteering

The company sees a mutual benefit in encouraging its partners (staff) to get involved in community activities – it reinforces the company's commitment not just to its communities, but to staff as well. Partners develop their confidence, learn new skills, take on new responsibilities and become more motivated. The partnership's company-wide volunteering programme is the Golden Jubilee Trust (GJT), established as a charity in 2000. Through the GJT, any Partner can apply for a full- or part-time volunteering secondment with a UK-registered charity for up to six months. In 2013/14 more than 17,000 secondment hours were contributed by the trust and 45 charities were supported. Activities included the creation of a money management programme for young people by a partner, who is a Financial Assistance Specialist, volunteering with The Milton Keynes Money Lifeline.

Waitrose also took part in Business in the Community's Give and Gain global volunteering day, as part of which partners ran activities based around healthy food and eating in local primary schools.

Payroll giving

The partnership has an established Give As You Earn scheme with Sharing the Caring, the fundraising arm of the Charities Aid Foundation (CAF), to enable Partners to make tax-free charitable donations directly from their pay.

Commercially led support

Sponsorship

John Lewis sponsored the Glasgow 2014 Commonwealth Games, as part of which it supplied bedding and white goods for the Athlete's Village.

Market-led support

Waitrose sells Duchy Originals products in its stores, the royalties of which are donated to The Prince of Wales Charitable Foundation.

Through sales of the Bear and the Hare book and other merchandise, John Lewis raised money for Save the Children.

Corporate social responsibility

CSR committee: The website states that Director of Personnel, Tracey Killen, has principal responsibility for managing and co-ordinating sustainability in the Partnership. Operational management responsibility for sustainability is delegated from the Chair to the Managing Directors of John Lewis and Waitrose, who in turn impose responsibility on individual Board members.

CSR information: The following information was obtained from the website:

> Being a 'force for good' in the community has always been part of the Partnership's vision and our Partners offer their time to support local, regional and national initiatives that help to build more vibrant, economically sustainable communities.
>
> We like to get practically involved at a local level. The Partnership encourages close links between Partners, schools, institutions, charities and local authorities. We recognise that the benefits are mutual:

Partners are proud of helping to improve and support local communities, and community work also helps them to develop their own skills and experience.

CSR report: There is an annual published Sustainability Review and a dedicated CSR section on the website.

Exclusions

The company does not support: individuals; religious, ethnic or political groups; or third party fundraising activities.

Applications

As the Partnership's preference is now to support smaller, more local causes, qualifying applicants should contact the Community Liaison Coordinator at their nearest John Lewis shop, or the Waitrose champion for community giving at their nearest Waitrose.

The Partnership notes that it is contacted by so many organisations throughout the year, it may not be able to give a swift reply. However, if it feels it can help, a response will be given as soon as possible.

John Spedan Lewis Foundation (see 'Community involvement' for details)

Applications for funding should be made in writing to: Ms Bridget Chamberlain, The Secretary, Partnership House, Carlisle Place, London SW1P 1BX, *Email:* jslf@johnlewis.co.uk

Unsolicited applications for PhD funding from individuals, universities or research institutes are not considered.

Liverpool Victoria

Financial services, insurance

Correspondent: The Regional Community Committee, County Gates, Bournemouth, Dorset BH1 2NF (tel: 01202 292333; website: www.lv.com/about-us/lv-cares)

Directors: Mark Austen, Chair; Michael Rogers, Group Chief Executive; Richard Rowney; Philip Moore, Group Finance Director; John O'Roarke; John Edwards; Cath Keers; Caroline Burton; James Dean; David Neave (women: 2; men: 8)

Year end	31/12/2013
Turnover	£2,699,000,000
Pre-tax profit	£156,000,000

Nature of business: The society is an incorporated Friendly Society which carries on insurance and financial services business in the UK.

FSA registration number: 110035

Subsidiary undertakings include: Frizzell Financial Services Ltd; Liverpool Victoria Financial Advice Services Ltd; Liverpool Victoria Life Company Ltd; Liverpool Victoria Portfolio Managers Ltd; LV Capital plc; LV Life Services Ltd

UK employees: 5,800

Total employees: 5,800

Focus of giving: General charitable purposes, health, ill health, children, young people.

Gifts in kind	✓
Matched funding	✓
Payroll giving	✓
Sponsorship	✓

Charitable donations

Cash UK (latest available):	2013	£401,000
	2011	£212,000
	2009	£111,000
	2007	£70,000
	2005	£166,000
Total UK (cash and in kind):	2013	£613,000
Cash worldwide:	2013	£401,000
Total worldwide (cash and in kind):	2013	£613,000

Community involvement

Liverpool Victoria supports charities and communities in the locations in which it has a presence through donations, community sponsorship and by supporting its employees' fundraising and volunteering efforts. The group has also partnered national charities through sponsorship and fundraising support.

LV gives charitable support in various ways. These include:

Regional community committees

A network of employee-led committees based at the group's 17 offices decides where the company can contribute its support most effectively. During the year, more than 280 local charities, good causes and projects benefitted from contributions from these committees.

Member Community Fund

Four times a year a good cause, charity or individual nominated by a member of the group receives a donation of £10,000. Nominations are assessed by a small independent committee of members.

Member Support Fund

Established in 2001 to support members and their families 'who have fallen on hard times' by way of hardship grants.

Corporate giving

In 2013 the group 'raised, donated or invested' more than £1.1 million in UK communities, which was broken down into the following categories in its annual report: Community investment, £498,000; Community sponsorship, £229,000; Community fundraising, £390,000.

We have taken the figure for 'Community investment' to include both cash and in-kind donations. Our figure for cash contributions takes into account the following figures provided in the annual report and accounts: donations from 'regional community committees (£165,000); Member Support Fund (£61,000); Member Community Fund donations (£40,000); and a donation to The Rainbow Trust raised by AGM votes (£20,000). These figures were included in the total provided for 'Community investment', the remainder of which we have taken as the value of in-kind donations. Additionally, we have also included £78,000 given through the 'charity matching scheme' and a further £37,000, which was donated to community fundraising events such as Comic Relief, Movember and Children in Need. In the annual report, these two figures were included in the total for 'Community fundraising', the remainder of which we have taken as employee-raised funds.

As is our usual practice, we have not included the amount for 'Community sponsorship' in our figures for cash donations or total contributions.

Beneficiaries included: The Rainbow Trust (£20,000); Dogs for the Disabled (£10,000); BBC Children in Need; Comic Relief.

In-kind support

Gifts in kind

During the year, the group donated two minibuses to charities near its Brentwood and Ipswich offices.

Investing time and skills locally

More than 760 students were mentored in 'business, financial affairs' and with interview skills through the group's schools programme.

The group also matched more than 800 hours of employees' own time spent volunteering.

Employee-led support

Liverpool Victoria states in its annual report that: 'Getting behind causes that are close to our people is a major part of our community fundraising strategy.'

Matched funding

The group operates a charity matching scheme, which saw the funds raised by more than 370 employees topped up.

Volunteering

During 2013 the group matched more than 800 hours of employees' own time spent volunteering in the community. Hundreds of employees volunteered their evening to operate a call centre based in the group's offices for Children in Need.

Payroll giving

£128,000 was donated by employees to charities of their choice through the payroll giving scheme operated by the group.

Commercially led support

Community sponsorship

During the year, the group continued its support of:

LV=Streetwise, which saw 13,000 children visit an interactive safety centre which teaches about 'dangers in and outside the home'.

LV=KidZone, a beach safety scheme, helped 148 lost children find their families in Bournemouth during the summer months.

LV=SOS Kit Aid provided recycled sports kit and equipment for 35,000 underprivileged young people.

The group also sponsors the entrance pavilion at the Mary Rose Museum in Portsmouth, as well as supporting Fields in Trust in protecting outdoor recreational spaces, 12 of which have been secured near the group's larger offices.

Corporate social responsibility

CSR committee: There was no evidence of a separate CSR Committee.

CSR information: The following information is taken from the group's annual report: 'Our commitment to making a real difference within the communities where we live and work continued during 2013, and with the support of our employees we made a positive impact through our community fundraising, sponsorship and investment programmes.'

CSR report: A CSR report is included in the annual report and there is an 'LV= Cares' section on the website.

Applications

In writing to your nearest regional committee, locations and contact details of which are available from the website. Details of your project, charity or community initiative should be included, along with the type of support (funding or volunteering) you are looking for.

Lloyd's

Insurance

Correspondent: Corporate Social Responsibility Dept., One Lime Street, London EC3M 7HA (tel: 020 7327 1000; email: communityaffairs@lloyds.com; website: www.lloyds.com/lloyds/corporate-responsibility)

Directors: John Nelson, Chair; Inga Beale, Chief Executive Officer; Rupert Atkin; Andy Haste; Paul Jardine; Simon Beale; Henrique Meirelles; Robert Childs; Dominic Christian; Michael Deeny; Matthew Fosh; Christopher Harman; Lawrence Holder; Dr Fred Hu; Alan Lovell; David Manning; Michael Watson; Graham White (women: 1; men: 17)

Year end	31/12/2013
Turnover	£325,592,000
Pre-tax profit	£78,334,000

Nature of business: Insurance underwriting market.

Company registration number: 3189123

Principal subsidiary undertakings: Additional Securities Ltd; Centrewrite Ltd; Lloyd's Insurance Company (China) Ltd.

UK employees: 709

Total employees: 867

Focus of giving: Education, enterprise/training, environment, individuals, sport, recreation, children, young people, community/social welfare, disasters.

Membership: BITC

Gifts in kind	✓
Humanitarian aid: overseas	✓
Overseas giving	✓

Charitable donations

Cash UK (latest available):	2013	£1,132,000
	2012	£292,000
	2011	£618,000
	2010	£1,431,000
	2009	£352,000
Total UK (cash and in kind):	2013	£1,132,000
Cash worldwide:	2013	£1,132,000
Total worldwide (cash and in kind):	2013	£1,132,000

Community involvement

Lloyd's is committed to giving support through its four grant-making charities and supports the community in east London, where it is based, through the Lloyd's Community Programme.

Lloyd's Charities Trust (Charity Commission no. 207232) has supported local, national and international causes on Lloyd's behalf for more than 60 years. The Lloyd's website states that charitable giving from the trust is focused on the following areas:

- Making a great city greater: at home in London, we give to tackle disadvantage and foster opportunity.
- Responding to disasters and emergencies: around the world, we give to relieve suffering and rebuild lives.
- Preparing for the future: we give to equip individuals and communities with the resources and skills they need to meet the challenges of a rapidly changing world.

The trust supports Lloyd's partner charity, RedR, helping to support communities affected by natural disasters.

Lloyd's Patriotic Fund (Charity Commission no. 210173) provides support to a number of armed forces organisations with a particular focus on those working to help those in the military community who are disabled or face poverty, illness and hardship.

Lloyd's Benevolent Fund (Charity Commission no. 207231) financially and practically assists those who have worked in the Lloyd's community who are in need and, at the discretion of the trustees, their dependents. The fund can be contacted at the following address: Lloyd's Benevolent Fund, Lloyd's, One Lime Street, London EC3M 7HA.

Lloyd's Tercentenary Research Foundation (Charity Commission no: 298482)was established to mark the tercentenary of Lloyd's in 1988. the following information was taken from the website:

> Since then, it has funded over 100 years of academic research in the fields of engineering, science, medicine, business and the environment through the provision of post-doctoral fellowships and business scholarships.
>
> Today, through its partnership with the Insurance Intellectual Capital Initiative and UK Research Councils, Lloyd's Tercentenary Research Foundation continues its work of funding top flight academic research by supporting new programmes of research on insurance related issues.

For more information on the scholarships available, visit the Lloyd's website.

Corporate giving

In its annual report and accounts for 2013 the group declared charitable donations of more than £1.1 million.

We were unable to determine a value for the in-kind support given by Lloyd's.

Partner charity: RedR

See the corporate charity entry on p. 413 for more information.

Employee-led support

Lloyd's Community Programme

Through the programme, employees are able to contribute their time and skills to community projects in east London. More than 1,700 individuals from the Lloyd's market volunteered through the scheme in 2013. Participants can choose to volunteer with projects in one of the programme's four focus areas:

Words and Numbers – helping local primary schoolchildren to develop their literacy and numeracy skills.

Aiming Higher – encouraging young people from schools in Tower Hamlets in their employability development through mentoring or workshops.

Sporting Chances – helping to run sports events for young people in Tower Hamlets.

Helping Hands – teams of employees completing practical tasks for community organisations in east London, such as redecorating a centre or helping to cook breakfasts for homeless people.

The Lloyd's website also states that 'anyone who works in the Lloyd's market can apply for a donation to a charity or community organisation in which they are actively involved through the Lloyd's Market Charity Awards scheme'.

Lloyd's employees based internationally support their own local communities through volunteering and fundraising activities.

Corporate social responsibility

CSR committee: For useful CSR contacts visit: www.lloyds.com/lloyds/corporate-responsibility/contacts

CSR information: Lloyd's 2014–16 CSR strategy will focus partly on global social and environmental issues of relevance to insurance.

CSR report: There is an informative part of the Lloyd's website dedicated to CSR, as well as a section focusing on CSR in the annual report and accounts.

Corporate charity: Lloyd's Charities Trust (Charity Commission no. 207232).

Exclusions

No support is given for advertising in charity brochures, animal welfare, appeals from individuals, the arts, sponsorship, environment/heritage, fundraising events, medical research, political appeals, religious appeals, science/technology, sport or local appeals not in areas of company presence.

Applications

Lloyd's Charities Trust – Note the following from the website: 'Lloyd's Charities Trust will be supporting our partner charities for the next three years and are therefore not inviting new proposals for funding.'

Lloyd's Community Programme – For more information on the programme, contact Ana Svab, Relationship and Project Manager (Lloyd's Community Programme), Tel: 020 7655 0317, Fax: 020 7375 2323, Email: Ana.Svab@thebp.co.uk.

Lloyds Banking Group

Financial services, banking

Correspondent: Responsible Business Team, 25 Gresham Street, London EC2V 7HN (tel: 020 7626 1500; email: responsible.business@Lloydsbanking.com; website: www.lloydsbankinggroup.com/our-group/responsible-business)

Directors: Antonio Horta-Osario, Group Chief Executive; Juan Colombas; George Culmer, Chief Financial Officer; Lord Blackwell, Chair; Anita Frew; Alan Dickinson; Carolyn Fairbairn; Simon Henry; Dyfrig John; Nicholas Luff; Nick Prettejohn; Anthony Watson; Sara Weller (women: 3; men: 10)

Year end	31/12/2013
Turnover	£18,478,000,000
Pre-tax profit	£415,000,000

Nature of business: Lloyds Banking Group is one of the largest financial services companies in the UK, covering retail banking, commercial and corporate banking, mortgages, life assurance and pensions, general insurance, asset management, leasing, treasury and foreign exchange dealing. (Lloyds TSB Group plc was renamed Lloyds Banking Group on 19 January 2009, following the acquisition of HBOS plc.)

Company registration number: 2065

Subsidiary undertakings include: Bank of Scotland plc; HBOS plc; Lloyds Bank plc (formerly Lloyds TSB Bank plc); Scottish Widows plc; St Andrew's Insurance plc; TSB Bank plc (formerly Lloyds TSB Scotland plc).

Main locations: London

UK employees: 96,001

Total employees: 97,869

Focus of giving: Education, poverty and social exclusion, sponsorship, sport, recreation, community/social welfare, disability.

Membership: BITC

FTSE 100	✓
Gifts in kind	✓
Matched funding	✓
Sponsorship	✓

Charitable donations

Cash UK (latest available):	2013	£53,700,000
	2011	£43,800,000
	2009	£33,477,000
	2008	£29,603,000
	2007	£37,463,000
Total UK (cash and in kind):	2013	£85,000,000
Cash worldwide:	2013	£53,700,000
Total worldwide (cash and in kind):	2013	£85,000,000

Community involvement

Lloyds Banking Group runs one of the largest community programmes in the UK. Colleagues of the group volunteer and fundraise for organisations in their local areas. Through the Community Fund, employees can nominate local organisations to receive funding.

Charities are also supported through the group's associated foundations:

The Lloyds Bank, Lloyds TSB and Bank of Scotland Foundations

Lloyds Banking Group supports registered charities in England, Wales, Scotland, Northern Ireland and the Channel Islands through its foundations. The Responsible Business Report 2013 states the following:

> The Lloyds Bank Foundation for England and Wales has launched a new strategy that focuses on investing in charities that help people to break out of 'disadvantage' at critical points in their lives. With increased funding from the Group, the Bank of Scotland Foundation has launched two new grants programmes that will enable it to help a much wider range of charities than ever before.

The foundations support charities that enable people, especially disabled and disadvantaged people, to play a fuller role in society. Applications are only accepted from registered charities that fit the grant-giving criteria.

Corporate giving

In 2013 Lloyds Banking Group contributed a total of £85 million in community investment. The Responsible Business Report 2013 offers the following breakdown:

Cash donations	£53.7 million
Colleague time	£29.6 million
Gifts in kind	£1.3 million

Note that the total for 'Colleague time' includes management costs, the value of which we were unable to determine.

The Lloyds Bank, Lloyds TSB and Bank of Scotland Foundations

During the year, Lloyds Banking Group donated more than £29 million to the Lloyds Bank, Lloyds TSB and Bank of Scotland Foundations, enabling them to distribute grants to local, regional and national charities across the UK. Many beneficiary organisations are working with communities in economically deprived areas.

The Responsible Business Report states the following:

> This year, the Lloyds Bank Foundations for England and Wales, Northern Ireland and the Channel Islands and the Bank of Scotland Foundation have all agreed new funding arrangements with the Group, which will ensure that they can do even more to support those in need across Britain.

Giving Extra Awards

In 2013 the Halifax Giving Extra awards were launched to acknowledge people who give back to their local communities. 67 winners were awarded vouchers, ranging from £250 to £5,000, which were awarded to a cause of their choice.

Charity of the Year

The Charity of the Year for 2013/14 was the Alzheimer's Society and Alzheimer Scotland. Group colleagues helped to raise £2.5 million for the charities, which will help to fund the first UK-wide dementia carers' programme, the Live Well campaign.

See the corporate charity entries on pp. 413–416 for more information.

In-kind support

Examples of the in-kind support given by Lloyd's Banking Group include:

The Day to Make a Difference programme, which enables employees to spend one paid working day a year volunteering for a community or charity project of their choice.

Bank of Scotland has worked in partnership with the Scottish FA to run football matches for children across Scotland, with 60,000 12- to 16-year-olds taking part since 2003.

As part of its efforts to promote diversity and inclusion in its local communities, Lloyds supported the Stonewall Youth Volunteering Programme, helping to recruit 75 Youth Volunteers to partake with the charity's anti-homophobia campaigns.

Employee-led support

The Community Fund

In 2013 colleagues nominated more than 4,600 good causes to benefit through the Community Fund, which supports local organisations by making grants of either £300 or £3,000. Almost 1,600 organisations were shortlisted in 392 UK communities, and more than 2.7 million votes cast as to how funding would be distributed.

Employee volunteering

Colleagues volunteer with community projects in their local areas, as well as through the group's Day to Make a Difference scheme. Activities during the year have included employability skills training for young people, assisting schoolchildren with their development of literacy and numeracy; and providing business advice for charities.

Employee fundraising

Colleagues across LBG's various divisions raise funds for a range of national and local causes, including the group's Charity of the Year. During the year, for example, employees from the Insurance division helped to raise £3,000 for Macmillan's World's Biggest Coffee Morning and colleagues from the frontline agricultural teams raised funds for RABI (Royal Agricultural Benevolent Institution) and RSABI (Royal Scottish Agricultural Benevolent Institution).

Matched giving

The group's associated foundations increase funds raised by employees though a matched giving scheme. Each colleague can claim up to £1,000 through the scheme each year.

Commercially led support

Sponsorship

LBG sponsored the First Women Awards, celebrating women who have achieved in business and have opened doors for other women, as well as the 2013 and 2014 editions of Powerlist publication, which profiles the most influential black men and women in the Britain.

The group is one of the key sponsors of Business in the Community's Business Connectors programme.

Corporate social responsibility

CSR committee: There is a Responsible Business Committee (RBC) chaired by Anita Frew, a non-executive board member, which includes representatives from key business divisions and functions. As chairperson, Anita reports to the group Board. committee meets six times a year.

CSR information: The following information was obtained from the Responsible Business Report 2013: 'We invest in our local communities through a number of flagship community programmes and by encouraging colleagues to volunteer their time and expertise to help local organisations, including social enterprises and charities.'

CSR report: A detailed Responsible Business report is published annually. There is also an online

Corporate charity: Lloyds Bank Foundation for England and Wales (Charity Commission no. 327114); Lloyds Bank Foundation for Northern Ireland (NI charity no. XN72216); Lloyds Bank Foundation for the Channel Islands (Charity Commission no. 327113).

Exclusions

For foundations

The foundations do not fund the following types of organisations and work:

Organisations:

- Organisations that are **not** registered charities
- Second or third tier organisations (unless there is evidence of direct benefit to disadvantaged people)
- Charities that mainly work overseas
- Charities that mainly give funds to other charities, individuals or other organisations
- Hospitals, hospices or medical centres
- Rescue services
- Nurseries, pre-schools or playgroups
- Schools, colleges and universities
- Animal charities

Types of work:

- Medical care or medical research
- On-line or telephone advice service
- Events and short-term interventions this includes holidays, expeditions and trips
- Activities for which a statutory body is responsible
- Capital purchases or building work, including IT, building work, purchase of vehicles/equipment, etc.
- Environmental, arts based or sports activities
- The promotion of religion
- Loan repayments
- Sponsorship or funding towards an appeal
- Work that has already taken place
- Evaluation which is not related to the funded work
- Professional qualifications such as ACCA
- Professional fundraisers or bid writers
- Redundancy payments

Applications

For Lloyds TSB Foundations only: Lloyds Banking Group has devised an online eligibility test. This consists of a process which, if your application meets all the criteria, leads on to an online eligibility questionnaire.

Further details of grant-giving policies and guidelines can be obtained by contacting the appropriate Lloyds TSB Foundation for your locality.

- Lloyds Bank Foundation for England and Wales Pentagon House
  - 52–54 Southwark Street London SE1 1UN
  - 0870 411 1223; email: enquiries@lloydsbankfoundation.org.uk; website: www.lloydsbankfoundation.org.uk
- Lloyds TSB Foundation for Scotland
  - Riverside House, 502 Gorgie Road, Edinburgh EH11 3AF
  - 01314 444020; email: There is a contact form on the website; website: www.ltsbfoundationforscotland.org.uk
- Lloyds Bank Foundation for Northern Ireland
  - 2nd Floor, 14 Cromac Place, The Gasworks, Belfast BT7 2JB
  - 02890 323000; email: info@lloydstsbfoundationni.org; website: www.lloydstsbfoundationni.org
- Lloyds Bank Foundation for the Channel Islands
  - Lloyds TSB House, 25 New Street, St Helier, Jersey, Channel Islands JE4 8RG
  - 01534 845889; email: john.hutchins@Lloydstsbfoundations.org.uk; website: www.ltsbfoundationci.org
- Bank of Scotland Foundation
  - Lloyds Banking Group at The Mound, Edinburgh EH1 1YZ
  - Email: enquiries@bankofscotlandfoundation.org

Each of the foundations' websites provides detailed and very useful information on making an application for funding.

It should be noted that the foundations cannot fund all eligible applications, even if they are of a high quality, because each year the total amount requested by eligible charities exceeds budget. Other reasons for the foundations not being able to make a grant include:

- Charities' core work not being sufficiently focused on the foundations' mission
- Applications not falling within guidelines

- Applicants not filling in the application form properly
- Charities not having up-to-date annual returns or accounts filed with the Charity Commission or other relevant regulatory bodies

For Lloyds Banking Group plc only: Contact the correspondent.

Lofthouse of Fleetwood Ltd

Confectionery

Correspondent: Mrs D. W. Lofthouse, Trustee, The Lofthouse Foundation, Maritime Street, Fleetwood, Lancashire FY7 7LP (tel: 01253 872435; website: www.fishermansfriend.com/en-gb)

Directors: Mrs D. W. Lofthouse; J. A. Lofthouse; D. C. Lofthouse (women: 1; men: 2)

Year end	31/12/2013
Turnover	£43,354,161
Pre-tax profit	£1,916,744

Nature of business: Manufacturers of medicated confectionery.

Company registration number: 781277

Brands include: Fisherman's Friend

Main locations: Fleetwood

UK employees: 318

Total employees: 318

Focus of giving: Economic generation, community/social welfare.

Charitable donations

Cash UK (latest available):	2013	£0
	2012	£65,000
	2011	£65,000
	2010	£65,000
	2009	£65,500
Total UK (cash and in kind):	2013	£0
Cash worldwide:	2013	£0
Total worldwide (cash and in kind):	2013	£0

Community involvement

Lofthouse of Fleetwood Ltd appears to direct its charitable giving through **The Lofthouse Foundation** (Charity Commission no. 1038728). The foundation makes grants to assist with 'the provision of amenities and facilities for the benefit of the public' in Fleetwood and the surrounding area.

Corporate giving

In 2013 the company made no charitable donations to The Lofthouse Foundation.

Corporate social responsibility

CSR information: We found no details of CSR.

Applications

In writing to the correspondent.

Logica Ltd (formerly Logica plc)

Business services

Correspondent: CSR Dept., 250 Brook Drive, Green Park, Reading, Berkshire RG2 6UA (tel: 0845 070 7765; website: www.cgi.com/en/corporate-social-responsibility)

Directors: Faris M. K. Mohammed; Michael E. Roach; Timothy W. Gregory; Michael J. Whitchurch; Francois Boulanger (women: 0; men: 5)

Year end	30/09/2013
Pre-tax profit	£535,161,000

Nature of business: An intermediate holding company for the group headed by CGI Group Inc.

The annual report and accounts for 2013 state:

> On 20 August 2012 Logica plc, a company listed on the London Stock Exchange (LSE), was wholly acquired by CGI Group Inc., a public company registered in Canada and listed on the Toronto Stock Exchange and the New York Stock Exchange (NYSE). Subsequent to this transaction, Logica plc delisted from the LSE, re-registered as a private limited company and changed its name to Logica Ltd.

Company registration number: 1631639

Subsidiary undertakings include: CGI Finance (UK) Ltd; Logica Cosec Ltd; Logica Cymru Ltd; Logica Eurofin UK Ltd; Logica International Ltd

Focus of giving: Children, young people.

Cash donations undeclared	✓
Gifts in kind	✓
Payroll giving	✓

Charitable donations

Cash UK (latest available):	2013	£127,000
	2011	£191,000
	2009	£92,000
	2008	£97,100
Total UK (cash and in kind):	2013	£127,000
Cash worldwide:	2013	£127,000
Total worldwide (cash and in kind):	2013	£127,000

Community involvement

We were unable to determine details of community involvement we know to be specific to Logica Ltd. However, we know that CGI Group Inc., the parent company, contributes to causes serving the communities in which it has a presence through pro bono and volunteering work, as well as through 'financial investments'.

Corporate giving

Logica Ltd's annual report and accounts for 2013 did not state a figure for charitable donations during the year. In the three most recent years for which we have figures, the average of charitable donations was £127,000, and we have taken this as an estimate for such contributions in 2013.

In-kind support

Pro bono

CGI Group makes pro bono contributions to causes working to benefit the well-being of its local communities.

Employee-led support

Payroll giving

The payroll giving scheme is in operation.

Corporate social responsibility

CSR information: The CSR information we could find was for CGI Group Inc., the parent company of Logica Ltd. The CGI global website states:

> At CGI, we are passionate about the communities in which we live and work. We take the skills required to be a leading IT services companyproblem solving, creativity and dedicationand put them to work to make a positive difference. Through volunteer and pro-bono initiatives and financial investments, we are committed to contributing to those causes that benefit the well-being of our communities.

CSR report: CGI publishes an annual CSR report, though we were unable to determine if the UK-based initiatives mentioned refer to activities conducted by Logica Ltd.

Applications

We would advise organisations seeking pro bono assistance to write to their nearest CGI location, a list of which is available from the website: www.cgi-group.co.uk/offices.

Lush Cosmetics Ltd

Health/beauty products

Correspondent: Charity Pot team, 29 High Street, Poole, Dorset BH15 1AB (tel: 01202 641001; email: charitypot@lush.co.uk; website: www.lush.co.uk/tag/our-policies)

Directors: M. Constantine; Ms M. Constantine; Karl Bygrave (women: 1; men: 2)

Year end	30/06/2013
Turnover	£362,873,000
Pre-tax profit	£21,923,000

Nature of business: The production and retail of cosmetic products.

Company registration number: 4162033

Subsidiary undertakings include: Lush Dublin Ltd; Lush (Ireland) Ltd; Lush Ltd; Lush Manufacturing Ltd; Lush (New Zealand) Ltd; Lush Retail Ltd

Total employees: 6,659

Focus of giving: Human rights, environment, animal welfare, overseas projects.

Gifts in kind	✓
Humanitarian aid: overseas	✓
Humanitarian aid: UK	✓
Market-led giving	✓
Overseas giving	✓

Charitable donations

Cash UK (latest available):	2013	£898,000
	2011	£1,495,000
	2009	£836,000
	2008	£482,000
	2007	£160,000
Total UK (cash and in kind):	2013	£898,000
Cash worldwide:	2013	£3,100,000
Total worldwide (cash and in kind):	2013	£3,100,000

Community involvement

Lush Cosmetics focuses its charitable giving on supporting small, grass-roots organisations working in the areas of environment, human rights and animal protection. Lush looks to support less popular causes and organisations using education, campaigns and activism as a way to address global issues. Aside from supporting registered charities, Lush also supports non-violent campaign groups and other organisations not registered with the Charity Commission. Lush prefers to support projects looking to create a long-term change, which address the root causes of social issues. Funding is also given to projects that provide aid and support, such as an animal shelter or refugee support and advice groups.

The principal manner in which Lush supports charities and good causes is through sales of its Charity Pot product, though it also runs various other initiatives in line with its charitable interests, such as a self-imposed Carbon Tax and the Lush Prize for research against animal testing.

Corporate giving

During 2012/13 Lush partners worldwide donated £3.1 million to charities and other good causes, such as the Sustainable Lush Fund, Lush Prize and FunD. Of this amount, £2.9 million was from Lush Group or associate countries. In the UK, small charities, campaigns and organisations working in the areas of environment, animal protection and human rights received £898,000 during the year.

Charity Pot

The principal way in which Lush raises funds for the causes and charities it supports is through sales of Charity Pot. Except for VAT, all money raised from sales of the product is donated. In the UK and Ireland, more than £592,000 was raised from Charity Pot sales in 2013. Globally, more than £2.5 million was raised and distributed to 'frontline campaigns' for animals, human rights and the environment. Though it is our typical practice to not include product sales in our figures for charitable giving, funds raised through Charity Pot sales are substantial and account for a large portion of Lush's charitable giving. We were unable to determine the costs borne by Lush for the production of Charity Pot and so have included the total of funds raised through its sales in our overall figures for cash donations.

Carbon Tax

In the UK, Lush runs a Carbon Tax fund, through which money raised from a self-imposed tax on staff's international flights is donated to environmental groups. The tax is based on a rate of £50 per tonne of carbon dioxide emitted and, in 2013, raised more than £117,000.

Lush Prize

In 2013, as part of a new initiative, Lush donated a total of £250,000 in prizes to people working in the fields of research against animal testing.

Sustainable Lush Fund

Launched in 2010, £500,000 was set aside for fund in 2013, and £446,000 of this was donated, principally to permaculture farms and training conferences around the globe.

£20,000 Annual Awards

Lush distributes a total of £200,000 to ten groups it partners with or feels are making a significant social contribution.

2014 Annual Award beneficiaries: Animal Protection Agency; Campaign for Better Transport; Frack Off; Fuel Poverty Action; Global Exchange; Hunt Saboteurs Association; InterNICHE; Reprieve; Sea Shepherd UK; War on Want

Charity Pot beneficiaries included: Campaign Whale; Dignity Matters; Dog Rescue Federation; Liverpool Film Club; Robin Hood Solidarity Group; They Owe Us

In-kind support

Product donations

Individual Lush shops occasionally donate unwanted products to charities in their local areas.

Commercially led support

Product sales

FunD – For each bar of Fun soap sold, Lush gives 10p to the FunD, which makes grants to initiatives providing fun and recreation for children living in 'challenging environments'. So far, the FunD has supported projects based in areas of Japan affected by the Fukushima nuclear disaster.

Corporate social responsibility

CSR committee: We found no evidence of a dedicated CSR committee.

CSR information: The following information was taken from the website: 'We always wish to conduct our business so that all people who have contact with us, from our ingredients suppliers through to our staff and customers, benefit from their contact with Lush and have their lives enriched by it.'

CSR report: Information on Lush's charitable activities is given on its website.

Exclusions

Lush does not support any organisation that:

- Promotes or supports violence, aggression or oppression towards others (only non-violent action groups will be supported)
- Denies the human rights of others
- Is involved in cruelty or subjugation of animals, including testing on animals for research
- Forces or coerces others to change their religious beliefs
- Harbours racism, prejudice or judges others on anything other than their own actions
- Has not made every effort to be environmentally responsible

No funding is given to religious organisations, schools, councils, student expeditions or academic studies or for sponsored walks or other fundraising initiatives. Lush does not sponsor events.

Applications

Charity Pot grants

To apply for funding from the Charity Pot, a new application form must be completed. To obtain one, along with full guidelines, send an email to charitypot@lush.co.uk with the words 'Application Form Request' in the subject line. Emails should include a brief description (no more than a couple of paragraphs) about your organisation and the project for which the funding is needed.

Grants are made up to £10,000 per project, though the average grant is around £4,000. The majority of funding is directed towards small, grass-roots organisations with limited funding and almost all of the organisations supported have an income of less than £250,000. Lush looks to support less popular causes (charities in the areas of health, including medical research and hospices; social welfare; religious causes; children/ young people; and military-related causes are not a priority)

There are guidelines on the website: www.lush.co.uk/article/charity-pot-funding-guidelines. We recommend that these are read carefully before an application form is requested.

Product donations

Donations are only made for non-fundraising purposes for the service users of homeless shelters, hospices, women's refuges, children's groups and for overseas aid. Products are not given to other charitable organisations such as schools or religious groups.

Contact your local Lush shop to enquire if there is any available stock which may be donated.

Man Group plc

Financial services, agriculture

Correspondent: Man Group plc Charitable Trust, Riverbank House, 2 Swan Lane, London EC4R 3AD (tel: 020 7144 1000; email: charitable.trust@man.com; website: www.man.com/GB/corporate-responsibility)

Directors: Jon Aisbitt, Chair; Phillip Colebatch; Andrew Horton; Matthew Lester; Emmanuel Roman, Chief Executive; Dev Sanyal; Nina Shapiro; Jonathan Sorrell, Chief Financial Officer (women: 1; men: 7)

Year end	31/12/2013
Turnover	£773,800,000
Pre-tax profit	£37,400,000

Nature of business: The company is a global provider of alternative investment products and solutions.

Company registration number: 2921462

Subsidiary undertakings include: AHL Partners LLP; FRM (Americas) LLC; GLG Partners LP; Man Investments AG; Man Investments (CH) AG; Man Investments Ltd.

Main locations: London

Total employees: 1,163

Focus of giving: General charitable purposes, education, environment, health, ill health, housing, homelessness, medical research, small groups, local groups, older people, arts, culture, sport, recreation, children, young people, community/social welfare, disability, disasters.

Membership: LBG

Cash donations undeclared	✓
Charity of the Year	✓
FTSE 100	✓
Gifts in kind	✓
Matched funding	✓
Payroll giving	✓
Sponsorship	✓

Charitable donations

Cash UK (latest available):	2013	£0
	2011	£1,571,650
	2008	£5,500,000
	2007	£3,105,000
	2006	£2,455,000
Total UK (cash and in kind):	2013	£40,000
Cash worldwide:	2013	£0
Total worldwide (cash and in kind):	2013	£40,000

Community involvement

The majority of Man's community involvement is through its associated charity, **Man Group plc Charitable Trust** (Charity Commission no. 275386). The trust operates as a grant-maker and also supports the group's employees in their volunteering and fundraising efforts.

The trust tends to concentrate its support on smaller charities where its donations make a material difference and where it can work in partnership with charities that are less likely to obtain support from the general public. The Man Group website states the following: 'The trust likes to focus on activities that offer assistance directly to individuals, families and communities as well as those that increase the capacity of organisations and individuals.' Preference is given to charities working in deprived areas of London, and particularly organisations operating in Hackney, Lambeth, Lewisham, Peskham, Southwark and Tower Hamlets.

Charity of the Year

The employee-nominated charity for 2014/15 is Children's Cancer Recovery Project.

Corporate giving

The group's annual report and accounts for 2013 state: 'Man's charitable contribution is based on the financial performance of the business and as a result no donations were received by the trust in 2013.' In the UK the trust supported projects assisting, for example, disadvantaged and difficult-to-reach young people at risk of exclusion, the homeless and victims of human trafficking.

The trust's annual report and accounts for 2013 indicate that in-kind donations in the form of the administration and support of its donation programme were given by Man Group plc to the value of £40,000.

We were unable to determine a value for staff time given for volunteering purposes.

See the corporate charity entry on p. 417 for more information.

In-kind support

ManKind programme

The programme allows group employees two days paid leave to dedicate to volunteering.

Employee-led support

Employee volunteering

Employees are able to volunteer through the ManKind programme for their own chosen charity, or for one of those supported by the trust. Staff have taken part in many activities including serving breakfast to the homeless, facilitating employability workshops for disaffected youth and reading to primary schoolchildren.

Payroll giving

The Give As You Earn scheme is in operation.

Matched funding

The charitable trust matches funds raised by employees through its sponsorship matching programme (up to £1,000 per event) and the Give As You Earn scheme.

Commercially led support

Sponsorship

The arts – Man sponsors the Man Booker Prize for Fiction and the Man Booker International Prize.

Investment 2020 – Man is one of the sponsors of Investment 2020, a investment management-related training scheme helping to tackle youth unemployment.

Corporate social responsibility

CSR committee: We found no evidence of a dedicated CSR committee.

CSR information: The following statement is taken from the group's website:

> Our corporate responsibility strategy is to pursue high standards of behaviour, both corporate and individual, which underpin our reputation and maintain the trust and loyalty of all our key stakeholders. We focus on five key areas of corporate responsibility.
>
> - World class governance and risk management
> - Responsibilities to our marketplace and our clients
> - Attracting, motivating and developing the best people
> - Contributing to our communities
> - Protecting the environment

CSR report: A CSR report is published within the annual report and accounts and there is a section containing CSR information on the group's website.

Corporate charity: Man Group plc Charitable Trust (Charity Commission no. 275386).

Exclusions

The Man Group plc Charitable Trust does not generally support: large national charities; charities which use external fundraising agencies; animal charities; charities primarily devoted to promoting religious beliefs; endowment funds; requests that directly replace statutory funding; individual beneficiaries; successful applicants from the previous twelve months; general media campaigns or advocacy work to influence policy debates; work which has already been completed; capital projects and appeals; sponsorship or funding towards marketing appeals or fundraising events; organisations or projects whose primary purpose is political.

Applications

Grants

The Man Group website states that applications for grants from the charitable trust are made on 'an invitation to bid basis or through negotiated partnerships with selected charities'. The trust, unfortunately, cannot respond to unsolicited applications.

Volunteering

The website states that the trust is always interested to hear about volunteering opportunities.

Manchester Airport Group plc

Airport operators

Correspondent: Corporate Social Responsibility Team, M.A.G Sustainability, 6th Floor, Olympic House, Manchester Airport, Manchester M90 1AA (tel: 08712710711; fax: 01614 893813; email: sustainability@manairport.co.uk; website: www.manchesterairport.co.uk)

Directors: Mike Davies, Chair; Charlie Cornish, Chief Executive; Sir Richard Leese; Vanda Murray; David Partridge; Angela Spindler; James Wallace; Neil Thompson, Chief Financial Officer; Ken O'Toole (women: 2; men: 7)

Year end	31/03/2014
Turnover	£671,200,000
Pre-tax profit	£80,800,000

Nature of business: The second largest airport group in the UK. The Group (MAG) comprises Manchester – the largest UK airport outside London, East Midlands – a major regional base for low cost, charter and cargo airlines, together with regional airports at Humberside and Bournemouth. MAG also runs airport related businesses engaged in the management and development of property, car parking and retail activities. Owned by the ten Greater Manchester Councils comprising the Council of the City of Manchester (55%) and the nine neighbouring local authorities: Bolton, Bury, Oldham, Rochdale, Salford, Stockport, Tameside, Trafford and Wigan (5% each).

Company registration number: 4330721

Subsidiary undertakings include: Airport Advertising Ltd; Airport Petroleum Ltd; Bournemouth International Airport Ltd; East Midlands Airport; Derby Leicester Ltd; East Midlands International Airport Ltd; Humberside International Airport Ltd; Manchester Airport Aviation; Manchester Airport Ventures Ltd; Ringway Developments plc; Ringway Handling Services Ltd; Ringway Handling Ltd; Worknorth Ltd; Worknorth II Ltd.

UK employees: 4,231

Total employees: 4,231

Focus of giving: General charitable purposes, environment, overseas projects, community/social welfare.

Membership: BITC

Gifts in kind	✓
Market-led giving	✓
Overseas giving	✓
Sponsorship	✓

Charitable donations

Cash UK (latest available):	2014	£580,000
	2013	£300,000
	2011	£100,000
	2009	£150,000
	2008	£100,000
Total UK (cash and in kind):	2014	£695,000
Cash worldwide:	2014	£580,000
Total worldwide (cash and in kind):	2014	£695,000

Community involvement

All four airports now have community funds to which application can be made for grants. See 'Community contributions' for types of grant available where this is known. Generally, the funds support local community causes.

Corporate giving

Charitable donations made by the group and its subsidiaries during the year totalled £300,000 (2013: £300,000). No breakdown was given but we know from the individual airports' accounts that they received £100,000 each from the group. We have therefore recorded £300,000 plus the £280,000 given to the arts in sponsorship which we know was cash, as the group's total cash donation. For its contribution we have used the £300,000 and added the £395,000 given in arts and cultural initiatives which could include in-kind costings.

The following are details of the four airports charitable donations:

Manchester Airport's Community Fund is now in its seventeenth year and since its inception has awarded over £2.9 million to 1,208 different projects. In 2013/14 it donated £138,000 to 69 groups for community, environmental or social projects.

After 11 years in operation, the **East Midlands Airport Community Fund** has supported 146 different community organisations. In 2013/14 the airport donated £40,000 to 57 charities and groups.

Newly formed, the **London Stansted Airport's Community Fund** has donated £111,000 to local charities during this financial year. The number of beneficiaries was not published.

Bournemouth Airport has been supporting the local region through its Community Fund since 2008 and in that time has donated £52,000 to various regional organisations. No figures were given for 2013/14.

In-kind support

8,600 volunteering hours were volunteered by M.A.G colleagues in 2013/14 and this is a 27% increase on last year's figures. Manchester Airport was awarded the Business in the Community's 'North-West's Volunteering Company of the year' and all the airports in the group provide volunteers for local community groups and charities.

Employee-led support

All four of the group's airports involve significant fundraising by volunteers.

Commercially led support

Sponsorship

Investing in the Arts – 2014 marks 25 years of M.A.G giving to the Arts. Through its longstanding commitment in this area, it states it has 'become one of the UK's largest and best known arts sponsors'. In 2013/14 it invested £395,000 in arts and cultural initiatives. Examples of the arts and cultural initiatives supported in 2013/14 were: Manchester International Festival (£200,000); Hallé Orchestra (£70,000); and Library Theatre (£10,000).

Corporate social responsibility

CSR committee: There is a separate CSR committee which is a subcommittee of the board. To manage day-to-day CSR activities, each airport has dedicated teams which are embedded within the operations function at each airport.

CSR information: The group's CSR aim in relation to community issues is described as follows:

> Being a responsible neighbour is an integral part of our way of working. Our aim is to build long-lasting, collaborative relationships with our local communities, striving to understand the issues that are most important to them and seeking to contribute to local economic development.

CSR report: A CSR report was available from the company's website and contained within the annual report and accounts.

Applications

Apply to the specific airport community fund in your area. Referenced 'Community Fund'.

Manchester Airport plc

Airport operators

Correspondent: Wendy Sinfield, Community Relations Manager, Wythenshawe, Manchester M90 1QX (tel: 08712710711; fax: 01614 893813; email: community.relations@manairport.co.uk; website: www.manchesterairport.co.uk)

Directors: N. Thompson; K. O'Toole; C. Cornish

Year end	31/03/2014
Turnover	£353,826,000
Pre-tax profit	£75,359,000

Nature of business: International airport operation. Part of M.A.G plc.

Company registration number: 1960988

Main locations: Manchester

UK employees: 1,916

Total employees: 1,916

Focus of giving: General charitable purposes, advertising in charity brochures, education, enterprise/training, environment, animal welfare, heritage, older people, arts, culture, sport, recreation, children, young people, community/social welfare.

Membership: BITC

Cash donations undeclared	✓
Gifts in kind	✓

Charitable donations

Cash UK (latest available):	2014	£138,000
	2009	£100,000
	2008	£100,000
	2007	£189,000
	2006	£150,000

Community involvement

The following is taken from the airport's website:

> ***Working in our Community***
>
> At Manchester Airport, we have a long history of working in close and active partnership with our local communities to help share the benefits of our success. Over the years, we have worked with many local organisations to enable everyone to benefit from our expertise and resources. Today, we focus our community work on the areas closest to the airport and give priority to those with the greatest social and economic need. Our approach for working in the community in the next three years is set out in our Community Strategy 2012 to 2014. This is available from the company's website, together with Community Review 2013/14.
>
> We encourage our colleagues to participate in community initiatives, particularly where they have the opportunity to share skills and learn new ones. We believe that support in kind is often more important than money and do not offer direct financial support, other than through the Manchester Airport Community Trust Fund.
>
> Charities and schools in our community which do not qualify for funding from our Trust Fund may apply for prizes for fundraising.

Manchester Airport Community Trust Fund

The Manchester Airport Community Trust Fund (Charity Commission no. 1071703) is established to promote, enhance, improve and protect both the natural and built environment in the local community. The trustees award grants of a maximum of £3,000. See very helpful information on the Manchester Airport's website: www.manchesterairport.co.uk/manweb.nsf/Content/CommunityTrustFund.

Corporate giving

Each year Manchester Airports Group plc contributes £100,000 to each of three of its (recently four) airports' community funds. Any fines levied at aircraft that have breached noise limits are also paid in to each fund. These funds are then used to support neighbourhood and community projects throughout the particular airport's area. We have not recorded Manchester Airport's charitable donations separately, as these have already been credited to the group for its charitable donations (see separate entry for Manchester Airports Group plc) and the amount spent by the Manchester Airport Community Trust Fund of £138,000 was paid by the corporate charity, not the company.

See the corporate charity entry on p. 417 for more information.

In-kind support

Through a network of 'Community Champions' established right across its business, members of staff are encouraged to get involved in volunteering in local projects. Charities and schools in the community which do not qualify for funding from the trust fund may apply for prizes for fundraising.

Employee-led support

The company has an active employee volunteering scheme and allows employees company time off in which to volunteer.

Commercially led support

Sponsorship: *The arts* – New proposals should be relevant to at least one of the areas served by the group's airports, including the entire North West of England, Yorkshire, North Wales, Humberside, Bournemouth and the East Midlands. Arts organisations based in the group's operational areas generally (though not always) have priority over other applicants. However, consideration will also be given to applications from arts organisations based elsewhere in the UK for projects touring the areas served by the group's airports. Applications are particularly welcome from projects or organisations that encourage community-wide access to the arts or have outreach programmes.

All applications must be received by 31 December to be considered for sponsorship in the following year.

For sponsorship guidelines visit: www.manchesterairport.co.uk/manweb.nsf/Content/OurSponsorshipGuidelines

Contact: Sarah Brookes – Head of Public AffairsTel: +44 (0) 161 489 3719/2093Email: Sarah.Brookes@manairport.co.uk

Corporate social responsibility

CSR committee: For CSR details see entry for 'Manchester Airports Group plc'.

CSR information: We were unable to determine the number of women on the board of this company.

Corporate charity: Manchester Airport Community Trust Fund (Charity Commission no. 1071703).

Exclusions

No support is given for appeals from individuals, commercial organisations, organisations which have statutory responsibilities such as hospitals or schools (unless the project is clearly not a statutory responsibility), those working for profit, or for organisations outside the trust boundary.

Applications

Grant applications to the Manchester Airport Community Trust Fund should not be made without first reading the policy guidelines. These, along with an application form, are available on request from the Fund Administrator at the address given below. You can also get an application form and further information on-line from www.manchesterairport.co.uk

The AdministratorManchester Airport Community Trust FundCommunity RelationsManchester AirportManchesterM90 1QX

Tel: 01614 895281 (An answerphone is available for out-of-hours enquiries)Fax: 01614 893467email: trust.fund@manairport.co.uk

Trustees meeting dates are available on the company's website.

Charities and schools in communities in close proximity to Manchester airport which do not qualify for funding from the trust fund may apply for prizes for fundraising by contacting the correspondent.

Marks and Spencer Group plc

Financial services, retail – clothing and footwear

Correspondent: Mike Barry, Director of Sustainable Business (Plan A), Waterside House, 35 North Wharf Street, London W2 1NW (tel: 020 7935 4422; website: corporate.marksandspencer.com/plan-a)

Directors: Robert Swannell, Chair; Marc Bolland, Chief Executive; Patrick Bousquet-Chavanne; John Dixon; Steve Rowe; Laura Wade-Gery; Vindi Banga; Alison Brittain; Miranda Curtis; Andy Halford; Martha Lane Fox; Jan du Plessis; Amanda Mellor (women: 5; men: 8)

Year end	29/03/2014
Turnover	£10,309,700,000
Pre-tax profit	£580,400,000

Nature of business: The principal activities are retailing clothes, beauty products, home products, food and the provision of financial services.

Company registration number: 214436

Subsidiary undertakings include: Marks and Spencer plc; Marks and Spencer Czech Republic a.s.; Marks and Spencer (Ireland) Ltd; Marks and Spencer (Asia Pacific) Ltd; Marks and Spencer Simply Foods Ltd; Per Una Group Ltd

Brands include: Autograph, Blue Harbour, Per Una, Simply Food

Main locations: London, Chester

UK employees: 77,863

Total employees: 85,813

Focus of giving: Education, enterprise/training, environment, health, ill health, poverty and social exclusion, safety and crime prevention, community/social welfare.

Membership: BITC, LBG

FTSE 100	✓
Gifts in kind	✓
Market-led giving	✓
Matched funding	✓
Overseas giving	✓
Payroll giving	✓

Charitable donations

Cash UK (latest available):	2014	£8,400,000
	2012	£6,900,000
	2010	£5,200,000
	2009	£5,200,000
	2008	£5,400,000
Total UK (cash and in kind):	2014	£14,200,000
Cash worldwide:	2014	£8,400,000
Total worldwide (cash and in kind):	2014	£14,200,000

Community involvement

Marks and Spencer (M&S) supports charities in the areas local to its stores. Funds are raised through an annual Charity Challenge fundraising event, and each store has its own charity budget. These budgets are used to make small donations (up to £50) to local charities, including schools and hospitals. Employees are supported in their community involvement through a volunteering, payroll giving, matched funding and employee volunteer award schemes.

Charity partners

M&S has a number of national charities that it helps to raise funds for. Charities that fit in with the company's business are selected from the areas of environment, poverty and exclusion, and health and well-being. The current list of charity partners includes: Breakthrough Breast Cancer; Butterfly Conservation; Groundwork; Macmillan Cancer Support; Marie Keating Foundation; Oxfam; Prostate Cancer UK; Shelter; and WWE.

Charity partners of the company are also supported through in-kind donations.

Youth unemployment programmes

Youth employment initiatives, which can be divided into two categories – Youth employment at M&S and Youth employment outside M&S – make up a central part of the company's community involvement. Its flagship work experience programme, Marks and Start, which focuses on young unemployed people aged between 18 and 24, has been extended to include Make Your Mark, which aims to support more than 5,000 unemployed young people in the UK with 650,000 hours of training and work experience by 2016. The company has also established Movement to Work with suppliers, partners and other companies to create more than 100,000 vocational training and work experience placements over the next two years.

Corporate giving

In 2013/14 Marks and Spencer made community contributions totalling £14.2 million. These were distributed as follows:

Cash	£8.4 million
In-kind	£4.1 million
Time	£1.7 million

The Plan A report notes that there has been an increase in cash donations due to the extension of the company's youth employment programmes.

An additional £8.8 million was donated from leveraged funds. We have taken this to represent funds raised by employees, customers and suppliers, who took part in a number of activities and initiatives, raising £4.2 million. These included:

Shwopping – Customers donated more than 4 million garments through this clothes recycling initiative. Combined with matched funding from the government, the initiative helped to raise a total of £3.2 million for Oxfam.

In-kind support

Gifts in kind

M&S donates unsold clothing, food and unwanted equipment to a range of charity partners, including Newlife Foundation, Oxfam, Shelter and FareShare.

Employee-led support

Employee volunteering

Employees are encouraged to volunteer and fundraise for charities in their local communities and are given one day's paid time for volunteering purposes each year. At a national level, in 2013/14 more than 4,000 employees took part in The Big Beach Clean-Up and another 1,300 in the BIKE 24 cycle relay to help raise money for some of M&S's charity partners.

Matched funding

M&S matches funds raised by groups of employees (of five or more).

Payroll giving

The company operates a payroll giving facility.

Commercially led support

Product sales

Charities are selected from the company's existing list of partners to benefit from funds raised from charitable Christmas cards.

Corporate social responsibility

CSR committee: There is a 'How We Do Business' Committee, whose primary purpose is to oversee the implementation of Plan A. The committee meets monthly and reports to the board at least annually.

CSR information: Marks and Spencer's sustainability strategy is called 'Plan A'. The following information was obtained from the corporate website:

> We launched Plan A in January 2007, setting out 100 commitments to achieve in 5 years. We've now introduced Plan A 2020 which consists of 100 new, revised and existing commitments, with the

> ultimate goal of becoming the world's most sustainable major retailer.
>
> Through Plan A we are working with our suppliers and employees to inspire our customers, be in touch with the communities we depend on to succeed, innovate to improve things for the better and act with integrity.

A Global Community Programme has recently been launched, with the aim of increasing social, economic and environmental benefits for communities where M&S sources its products.

CSR report: The 'Plan A' report has a dedicated section on the corporate website as well as a downloadable report.

Exclusions

M&S stores are not able to support:

- Personal appeals on behalf of individual people, including overseas trips
- Advertising or goodwill messages
- Political parties
- Third party fundraising on behalf of a charity
- Religious bodies, except where the project provides non-denominational, non-sectarian support for the benefit of the general project
- Supplying clothing, other than in exceptional circumstances, as we already give clothes to Newlife and Shelter

Applications

To stand any chance of success, check that your organisation can help to address key areas of the company's policy before applying.

Marsh Ltd

Insurance

Correspondent: Zara Jeffrey, Head of CSR, Tower Place, Lower Thames Street, London EC3R 5BU (email: zara.jeffrey@marsh.com; website: uk.marsh.com/AboutUs/CorporateSocialResponsibility.aspx)

Directors: J. V. Barker, Chair; M. A. Weil, Chief Executive; P. J. Box; M. C. Chessher; G. E. Davies; N. C. Frankland; J. C. Grogan; J. R. Hirst; C. F. Kiddie (Alternate); C. J. Lay; J. J. Nicholson; D. Pigot; R. I. White

Year end	31/12/2013
Turnover	£730,900,000
Pre-tax profit	£173,200,000

Nature of business: The company provides risk management, insurance and reinsurance broking services.

The ultimate parent company and controlling entity is Marsh and McLennan Companies Inc., incorporated in the state of Delaware, USA.

Company registration number: 1507274

Subsidiary undertakings include: MMC Securities (Europe) Ltd.

Main locations: Liverpool, Birmingham, Edinburgh, Glasgow, Leeds, Bristol, Newcastle, London, Southampton

Focus of giving: General charitable purposes, education, enterprise/training, environment, health, ill health, marginalised people, arts, culture, community/social welfare.

Membership: BITC

Charity of the Year	✓
Gifts in kind	✓
Matched funding	✓
Payroll giving	✓

Charitable donations

Cash UK (latest available):	2013	£131,000
	2012	£173,000
	2011	£170,650
	2007	£319,000
	2006	£32,000
Total UK (cash and in kind):	2013	£131,000
Cash worldwide:	2013	£131,000
Total worldwide (cash and in kind):	2013	£131,000

Community involvement

Marsh UK contributes to the communities in which it has a presence through contributions of employee time and skills and by matching employee fundraising. The CSR programme also consists of the following initiatives:

Charity of the Year

Each year, employees of Marsh and other operating companies within the Marsh and McLennan companies nominate a Charity of the Year, which then benefits from the proceeds of a number of fundraising events.

Recent beneficiaries: British Red Cross

National charities

Note the following information from the website:

> Marsh's donation programme is administered centrally. Under the theme of Helping People and Communities at Risk, the Company has established an approval process, in which it works closely with the Charities Aid Foundation to select eight national UK charities, who when viewed in the aggregate, address a broad spectrum of human need. The Company establishes a multi-year partnership with those charities, agreeing with each at the outset of our association a particular project or activity which our donation will fund, and then working with the charity to ensure its achievement.

Corporate giving

In 2013 the company made charitable donations of £131,000. We believe this was received by the chosen national charities as well as through the matched funding schemes operated by the company.

We were unable to determine costings for the in-kind support given by the company.

National charity beneficiaries for 2013–16: Business in the Community; Centre for Social Justice Awards; Genetic Alliance; London Symphony Orchestra; The Maritime London Officer Cadet Sponsorship; Over the Wall; Special Olympics Great Britain; Trees for Cities.

In-kind support

Pro bono

Employees are entitled to contribute one day each year to a community programme through the employee volunteering scheme.

Employee-led support

Employee volunteering

Activities in which employees have taken part include 'Team Challenges' and one-to-one mentoring.

Matched funding

Through Marsh MAGIC (Matching and Giving for Involvement with Charities), Marsh matches employee fundraising efforts up to £300 per employee per year.

Marsh also contributes an additional 10% to donations made by employees through the Give As You Earn scheme.

Corporate social responsibility

CSR committee: The donations programme is administered centrally.

CSR information: The following information was taken from the Marsh UK website:

> We commit at all times to conducting business in a responsible way and demonstrate our Corporate Social Responsibility (CSR) through financial support and the time and skills of our employees to a wide variety of charities and community organisations in the cities and towns in which we operate, as well as an active environmental sustainability programme.

We were unable to determine the ratio of women to men on the board.

CSR report: There is a section dedicated to the CSR programme on the Marsh UK website.

A Corporate Citizenship is published by Marsh and McLennan annually.

Exclusions

Our research indicates that donations will not be made (other than in exceptional circumstances) to religious organisations or causes, political parties or causes, advertising in charity brochures, circular appeals, international crisis appeals, overseas causes, appeals for individuals' education, expeditions or recreation, animal welfare or sport.

Applications

For further information on Marsh's CSR programme contact the correspondent.

Marshall of Cambridge (Holdings) Ltd

Engineering

Correspondent: The Group Support Executive, The Airport, Cambridge CB5 8RX (tel: 01223 373737; website: www.marshall-group.co.uk)

Directors: Sir Michael Marshall, Chair; A. E. Cook; R. D. Marshall, Group Chief Executive; S. J. Moynihan; Sir Ralph Robins; A. J. F. Buxton; P. W. Johnson; J. D. Barker; W. C. M. Dastur, Group Financial Director; S. J. Fitz-Gerald; D. Gupta; S. J. Sillars; C. J. Sawyer; P. J. Harvey (women: 2; men: 12)

Year end	31/12/2013
Turnover	£1,292,522,000
Pre-tax profit	£18,105,000

Nature of business: The group conducts its activities through its four business sectors: aerospace and defence; motor retail and leasing; property; and fleet solutions.

Company registration number: 2051460

Subsidiary undertakings include: Marshall Fleet Solutions Ltd; Marshall of Cambridge Aerospace Ltd; Marshall Land Systems Ltd; Marshall of Cambridge (Airport Properties) Ltd; Marshall of Cambridge (Motor Holdings) Ltd; MGPH Ltd.

Main locations: Ipswich, Huntingdon, Cambridge, Croydon

Total employees: 4,498

Focus of giving: General charitable purposes, education, enterprise/training, local groups, STEM (science, technology, engineering and mathematics), overseas projects, community/social welfare.

Cash donations undeclared	✓
Payroll giving	✓

Charitable donations

Cash UK (latest available):	2013	£92,000
	2012	£101,000
	2011	£84,000
	2010	£91,000
	2009	£110,000
Total UK (cash and in kind):	2013	£92,000
Cash worldwide:	2013	£92,000
Total worldwide (cash and in kind):	2013	£92,000

Community involvement

Marshall of Cambridge (Holdings) Ltd 'selectively' supports organisations working to benefit communities in which the group operates or industries in which the group works. The group looks to support major community initiatives in areas where its businesses are based, both in the UK and overseas. Employees are encouraged to fundraise and to volunteer for a wide range of national and local charitable causes, rather than for one single Charity of the Year.

Through donations, payroll giving and fundraising events, the group and its employees actively support BEN, the automotive industry charity, for which one of its directors serves as a trustee.

It would appear that charitable giving from the group is filtered through the **D G Marshall of Cambridge Trust** (Charity Commission no. 286468), which supports charities local to the group's base in Cambridge.

Corporate giving

A figure for charitable donations was not included in the annual report and accounts for 2013. The average of these contributions in the three most recent years for which we have figures was £92,000, and we have taken this as an estimate for total charitable donations from the group in 2013.

However, information from the D G Marshall of Cambridge Trust's accounts for 2013/14 indicate that a donation of £150,000 was made by the group to the trust during 2013/14. 40 grants were made totalling £65,000.

These were broken down as follows:

Education	£17,000
Aviation	£17,000
Children's charities	£13,000
Disability, health and life threatening illnesses	£8,000
Hospitals and related organisations	£6,700
Local community	£2,700
Churches	£500

Beneficiaries included: SOS Children (£10,000); American Air Museum and Arthur Rank Hospice Charity (£5,000 each); Arkwright Scholarship Trust (£4,000); Battle of Britain Memorial Trust (£2,500); the Avenues Youth Project and Ely Cathedral Restoration Trust (£1,500 each); CLIC Sargent and East Anglian Children's Hospice (£1,000 each); Institute of Economic Affairs and Teversham Baptist Church (£500 each); and Rainbows Children's Hospice and Sheffield Children's Hospital (£250 each).

See the corporate charity entry on p. 418 for more information.

Employee-led support

Employee volunteering

Group employees are actively involved in community and charitable work. The annual report describes how activities have ranged from acting as special constables to reading assistants, from school governors to scout leaders and from sports team coaching to supporting a wide range of charitable activities.

Employee fundraising

Employees also support a wide range of charitable causes through fundraising activities and events, and are encouraged by the group to do so.

Payroll giving

Through the Give As You Earn scheme, employees are able to donate to charitable causes. The annual report and accounts state that this is one of the ways in which support was given to BEN, the automotive industry charity, an organisation the group actively supports.

Commercially led support

Promoting Careers in Engineering

The group participates in initiatives designed to encourage young people, and particularly young women, to take up careers in engineering. Apprentices and young engineers at the group support local schools and colleges with STEM (science, technology, engineering and mathematics) and students benefit from visits to the Cambridge site. The website states that 'a more comprehensive and co-ordinated programme' aimed at encouraging more young people in the Cambridge area to consider careers in engineering or engineering-related businesses will soon be launched.

Corporate social responsibility

CSR committee: We found no evidence of there being a CSR committee.

CSR information: The following information was obtained from the group's annual report and accounts:

> The group takes its responsibilities to its employees, customers and shareholders seriously, as well as its wider social responsibilities. The group has a policy of not making donations to political groups, parties or individuals, but has a positive policy of supporting, selectively, charities and organisations which benefit either the communities in which the group operates or the industries in which the group works.

CSR report: We found no evidence of a separate CSR report; however, the group's CSR practices are discussed in the Group Strategic Report section of the annual report.

Corporate charity: D G Marshall of Cambridge Trust (Charity Commission no. 286468).

Exclusions

The charity will consider all applications, providing they are consistent with the objectives of the charity.

Applications

Our research indicates that applications should be made in writing to the Group Support Executive.

Applications for the **D G Marshall of Cambridge Trust (Charity Commission no. 286468)** should be addressed to Sarah Moynihan, Company Secretary, at the trust c/o The Building, The Airport, Newmarket Road, Cambridge CB5 8RX.

Marston's plc

Brewers/distillers

Correspondent: Corporate Social Responsibilty (CSR) Committee, Marston's House, Brewery Road, Wolverhampton WV1 4JT (tel: 01902 711811; fax: 01902 429136; website: www.marstons.co.uk/responsibility)

Directors: Roger Devlin, Chair; Ralph Findlay, Chief Executive; Andrew Andrea, Chief Financial Officer; Peter Dalzell; Nick Backhouse; Carolyn Bradley; Rosalind Cuschieri; Neil Goulden; Robin Rowland; Anne-Marie Brennan (women: 3; men: 7)

Year end	04/10/2014
Turnover	£815,300,000
Pre-tax profit	(£59,200,000)

Nature of business: Brewers and pub management.

Company registration number: 31461

Subsidiary undertakings include: Bank's Brewery Insurance Ltd; Marston's Estates Ltd; Marston's Operating Ltd; Marston's Pubs Ltd; Marston's Property Developments Ltd; Marston's Trading Ltd

Brands include: Bank's, Boondoggle, Brakspear, Cumberland Ale, Hobgoblin, Pedigree

UK employees: 12,854

Total employees: 12,854

Focus of giving: General charitable purposes, general appeals, health, ill health, community/social welfare, disability.

Cash donations undeclared	✓
Gifts in kind	✓
Matched funding	✓

Charitable donations

Cash UK (latest available):	2014	£10,000
	2012	£10,244
	2009	£9,000
Total UK (cash and in kind):	2014	£10,000
Cash worldwide:	2014	£10,000
Total worldwide (cash and in kind):	2014	£10,000

Community involvement

Marston's staff and customers support good causes in their local areas various ways, mainly through fundraising. Marston's pubs assist by helping with collections, sponsored activities, the use of our rooms, and publicity. Employees are supported in their fundraising activities by matched funding from the **Marston's Inns and Taverns Charitable Trust** (not a registered charity).

Corporate giving

The annual report and accounts for 2013/14 did not declare a figure for total charitable donations. However, it did state that, during the year, the company made a donation of £10,000 to Pub is the Hub's Community Services Fund.

Marston's also supports an employee charity, which makes grants to various causes; however, we could not determine a value for the support contributed by the company in 2013/14.

Beneficiaries included: Pub is the Hub (Community Services Fund)

In-kind support

The CSR report states: 'Our pubs assist by helping with collections, sponsored activities, the use of our rooms and publicity.'

Employee-led support

Employee fundraising

Marston's staff fundraise for a variety of local causes. There is an employee charity, **Marston's Employee Charity Fund**, which is supported by the company and donated £18,000 to a range of causes in 2014.

Matched funding

Funds raised by Marston's employees are matched by the Marston's Inns and Taverns Charitable Trust. In 2014 contributions from the trust totalled £15,000.

Corporate social responsibility

CSR committee: There is a CSR committee.

CSR information: Marston's CSR strategy involves four 'pillars': Our People; Our Community; Our Environment; and Our Responsibilities.

CSR report: There is a CSR report published within the annual report and accounts.

Applications

In writing to the correspondent.

Mascolo Ltd

Health/beauty products, personal care products

Correspondent: Michela Lodovichi, 58–60 Stamford Street, London SE1 9LX (tel: oni; fax: 020 7921 9123; website: toniandguy.com/pages/category/charity/about-us)

Directors: Giuseppe Toni Mascolo; Sacha Mascolo-Tarbuck; C. F. Mascolo; P. R. Mascolo; R. Staal

Year end	31/08/2013
Turnover	£12,000,000
Pre-tax profit	(£5,447,000)

Nature of business: Hairdressing and other beauty treatments.

Company registration number: 770236

Subsidiary undertakings include: TONI&GUY Ltd.

Total employees: 283

Focus of giving: Health, ill health.

Gifts in kind	✓
Sponsorship	✓

Charitable donations

Cash UK (latest available):	2013	£19,100
	2012	£33,500
	2011	£28,500
	2009	£16,300
	2008	£143,000
Total UK (cash and in kind):	2013	£19,100
Cash worldwide:	2013	£54,000
Total worldwide (cash and in kind):	2013	£54,000

Community involvement

Mascolo Ltd is the parent company of the 200 or so TONI&GUY hair salons in the UK, some of which are franchised or partially-owned by the company. The company's charitable giving, both cash and in kind, appears to be directed through the **TONI&GUY Charitable Foundation** (Charity Commission no. 1095285).

Corporate giving

The TONI&GUY Charitable Foundation's accounts state that in 2012/13 £19,000 was given through 'donated services and facilities' by Mascolo Ltd, which we have taken to be the company's cash contributions for the year.

Mascolo Ltd's 2012/13 accounts state that a total of £54,000 was given in charitable contributions during the year. We believe this to include the donations stated above as well as in-kind contributions.

See 'corporate charity' entry for details of beneficiaries.

See the corporate charity entry on p. 434 for more information.

Employee-led support

Staff appear to be involved with the various initiatives led by the company's charitable foundation.

Corporate social responsibility

CSR committee: We found no evidence of there being a CSR committee.

CSR information: We found no information regarding the company's CSR policy.

It was not possible to determine the ratio of women to men on the board.

CSR report: We found no evidence of a published CSR report.

Corporate charity: TONI&GUY Charitable Foundation Ltd (Charity Commission no. 1095285).

Exclusions

The foundation does not make grants to individuals.

Applications

Those applying for grants to the TONI&GUY Charitable Foundation Ltd should write directly to Michela

Lodovichi, Charity and Fundraising Co-ordinator, via email: charitablefoundation@mascolo.co.uk.

Bernard Matthews Ltd

Food manufacture

Correspondent: David Reger, Company Secretary, Great Witchingham Hall, Norwich NR9 5QD (tel: 01603 872611; fax: 01603 871118; website: www.bernardmatthews.com)

Directors: David McCall; Noel Bartram (women: 0; men: 2)

Year end	03/07/2013
Turnover	£346,399,000
Pre-tax profit	(£18,089,000)

Nature of business: The principal activities of the group are the production and marketing of turkey and red meat products, oven-ready turkeys, day-old turkeys, fish products and other poultry products.

Company registration number: 625299

Main locations: Norwich

Focus of giving: Education, children, young people, community/social welfare.

Charitable donations

Cash UK (latest available):	2013	£37,000
	2012	£27,000
	2011	£85,000
	2009	£197,349
	2006	£197,349
Total UK (cash and in kind):	2013	£37,000
Cash worldwide:	2013	£37,000
Total worldwide (cash and in kind):	2013	£37,000

Community involvement

The Bernard Matthews Youth Awards have been set up to recognise and reward the success and achievements of young people aged between 11 and 18 years living in Norfolk and Suffolk. They are made up of eight categories: food and farming, sport, community, charity, arts, bravery and education. The winner of each of these seven categories receives £1,000 award money. There is also have a Hero category for adults that have made an impact with young people.

The company is a founder charter member of the Duke of Edinburgh Scheme, supporting this charity for over 17 years.

Corporate giving

During the year, the group made charitable contributions of £37,000 to a variety of national and local charities. The majority of these contributions were made to the Bernard Matthews Fund which is administered by the Norfolk Community Foundation which aims to support a wide range of charitable and community activities throughout Norfolk, North Suffolk and Lincolnshire.

Commercially led support

The Farm to Fork turkey education programme has reached over 40,000 UK schoolchildren. This is through a number of initiatives including educational stands at county shows, such as the Royal Norfolk Show and the development of Foodies, a web based curriculum pack and teaching resource for Key Stages 1 and 2.

Corporate social responsibility

CSR committee: There were no details found.

CSR information: No specific information found.

CSR report: There is a corporate responsibility document on the website dated June 2012.

Exclusions

No support is given for political appeals.

Applications

In writing to the correspondent.

Mazars LLP

Accountants

Correspondent: The Company Secretary, Tower Bridge House, St Katherine's Way, London E1W 1DD (tel: 020 7063 4000; fax: 020 7063 4001; website: www.mazars.co.uk/Home/About-us/Corporate-Responsibility)

Directors: David Herbinet; Glyn Williams; Tim Davies; Alistair Fraser; Nigel Grummitt; David Smithson; Phil Verity (women: 0; men: 7)

Year end	31/08/2013
Turnover	£120,572,000
Pre-tax profit	£22,182,000

Nature of business: Mazars specialises in audit, tax and advisory services.

Company registration number: OC308299

Subsidiary undertakings include: A full list of subsidiaries is available from the annual report and accounts.

Main locations: London

UK employees: 1,350

Total employees: 1,350

Focus of giving: General charitable purposes, poverty and social exclusion, community/social welfare.

Membership: BITC

Gifts in kind	✓
Matched funding	✓

Charitable donations

Cash UK (latest available):	2013	£525,000
	2011	£224,000
	2009	£270,719
	2007	£244,000
	2005	£165,866
Total UK (cash and in kind):	2013	£525,000
Cash worldwide:	2013	£525,000
Total worldwide (cash and in kind):	2013	£525,000

Community involvement

Mazars LLP donates 'a proportion' its annual profits to charities. It would appear that its charitable donations are made through **Mazars Charitable Trust** (Charity Commission no. 1150459). Mazars employees also volunteer in their communities, namely through 'Mazars Community Days' and take part in fundraising initiatives, which may be supported with a donation from the trust.

Corporate giving

The 2013/14 annual report and accounts for Mazars Charitable Trust state that the firm donated £525,000 to the trust during the year.

We were unable to determine a value for the in-kind support given by the group.

As the trust is the principal way in which the firm makes its charitable donations, we have used this figure as the firm's UK cash donation.

See the corporate charity entry on p. 418 for more information.

In-kind support

Mazars Community Days

Mazars offices organise 'Mazars Community Days' through which teams of employees participate in activities to the benefit of their local communities.

Employee-led support

Employee volunteering

Employees volunteer in their communities in 'Mazars Community Days'.

Employee fundraising

Individual Mazars employees raise funds through taking part in marathons, parachute jumps and swimathons, for example.

Matched funding

Employees who are fundraising may be eligible for a discretionary contribution from the Mazars Charitable Trust.

Corporate social responsibility

CSR committee: The following information was obtained from the website:

> Our Corporate Responsibility effort is led by Anthony Carey, a Partner in the business. Anthony has built a National Steering Group of people across the UK who have agreed to promote and manage CR activity at a regional level, and

contribute to the national effort by reporting and sharing initiatives and best practice.

There is also a national volunteer group which works with the Steering Group. The volunteer group efforts are co-ordinated by the individual Steering Group members.

CSR information: The website states:

> Mazars is committed to taking an active role in corporate responsibility issues as part of its commitment to providing fulfilling roles to members of the Mazars team and to making a contribution to the communities in which we operate. Our commitment is expressed in a number of ways.

These include employee volunteering and charitable giving initiatives.

CSR report: There is a section dedicated to CSR on the Mazars website.

Corporate charity: Mazars Charitable Trust (Charity Commission no. 1150459).

Applications

Charities cannot apply directly for funding but, rather, are nominated by Mazars partners and employees. Unsolicited applications will receive no response.

Sir Robert McAlpine Ltd

Building/construction, engineering

Correspondent: The Sustainability Team or Brian Arter, Charities Administrator, Eaton Court, Maylands Avenue, Hemel Hempstead, Hertfordshire HP2 7TR (tel: 01442 233444; fax: 01422 230024; email: sustainability@sir-robert-mcalpine.com; website: www.sir-robert-mcalpine.com)

Directors: Ian McAlpine; David McAlpine; Cullum McAlpine; Richard McAlpine; Andrew McAlpine; Edward McAlpine; Hector McAlpine; Anthony Aikenhead; Vince Corrigan; Boyd McFee; Miles Shelley (women: 0; men: 11)

Year end	31/10/2013
Turnover	£780,370,000
Pre-tax profit	£4,442,000

Nature of business: The principal activities of the company include provision of building construction, civil engineering, design and project development services, also renewable energy systems.

Company registration number: 566823

Subsidiary undertakings include: Bankside Electrical Contractors Ltd; British Contracts Company Ltd; Derby Joinery Ltd; McAlpine Properties Ltd; and Sir Robert McAlpine Management Contractors Ltd. The annual report and accounts state the following: 'The company is controlled by its immediate parent company Sir Robert McAlpine (Holdings) Ltd and its ultimate parent company Newarthill Ltd.'

Main locations: Hemel Hempstead

UK employees: 1,954

Total employees: 1,954

Focus of giving: Education, medical research, older people, children, young people, community/social welfare, disability.

Cash donations undeclared	✓
Sponsorship	✓

Charitable donations

Cash UK (latest available):	2013	£600,000
	2011	£400,000
	2009	£340,000
	2007	£666,000
Total UK (cash and in kind):	2013	£600,000
Cash worldwide:	2013	£600,000
Total worldwide (cash and in kind):	2013	£600,000

Community involvement

The sustainability report states that McAlpine 'aims to operate a socially responsible and inclusive business which makes a positive difference to those around it'. The company invests in the communities it operates in and seeks to establish links with local organisations, charities, schools, businesses and social enterprises. Some of the activities undertaken in 2013 include:

- Converting a house in Tyne and Wear for a retired couple (one of whom has a rare and debilitating neurological disorder), using staff volunteers and building materials, as part of the BBC show's project
- Provision of over 380 educational activities for about 12,000 students in the North East, including two-year educational sponsorship for 14 schools in Newcastle, Construction Week workshops, and Building Studies lessons
- Visiting 138 Schools and colleges, including St Barnabas and St Philip's Primary School pupils in Kensington, 'to enhance the curriculum for pupils, increase understanding of the industry and promote construction as a career'

Charity partnership projects

The company provided support to the Prince's Trust's Get Into Construction scheme aimed at 18- to 25-year-olds, offering work placements with the company.

The Robert McAlpine Foundation (Charity Commission no. 226646)

The foundation generally supports causes concerned with children with disabilities, older people, medical research and social welfare and charities with an income of less than £1 million. The annual report for 2012/13 states: 'The policy of the trustees [two of which are the directors of the company] is to make grants to charitable institutions of amounts from £2,500 upwards in the specific categories of objectives which they support.'

The McAlpine Educational Endowment (Charity Commission no. 313156)

This charity is aimed at 13- to 18-year-olds who have sound academic ability, show leadership potential and are facing financial hardship. The trustees (one of which is the company director) favours ten particular schools, with referrals coming from the headmasters.

Corporate giving

In 2013/14 **The Robert McAlpine Foundation** received a donation of £500,000 from the company and paid a total of £728,000 in charitable grants.

In 2012/13 **The McAlpine Educational Endowment** received a donation of £100,000 from McAlpine and spent £116,000 in grants. The annual report and accounts of the company made no reference to charitable contributions, therefore we take the figure of £600,000, donated to the two charities, to represent the company's giving.

Beneficiaries of the foundation included: Age Concern, Community Self Build Agency, DENS Action Against Homelessness, Downside Fisher Youth Club, Ewing Foundation, the Golden Oldies, Grateful Society, James Hopkins Trust, Merchants Academy Withywood, National Benevolent Fund for the Aged, National Eye Research Centre, Prostate UK, Royal Marsden NHS Trust, St Johns Youth Centre and the Towers School and 6th Form Centre.

See the corporate charity entry on p. 418 for more information.

Commercially led support

The company is a founding partner of the Supply Chain Sustainability School (SCSS) – a free online educational tool for the registered members (currently 350) of the company's supply chain. Part of the support is the supplier days, 'which allow suppliers and subcontractors to familiarise themselves with what it has to offer'.

Corporate social responsibility

CSR committee: There is a sustainability team dealing with corporate sustainability and responsibility matters. The Company Sustainability Manager is accountable for an annual review of the sustainability objectives, benchmarks and targets, and reporting to the Director Responsible for Sustainability. Throughout the company the staff have a responsibility for delivering sustainability through their daily operations.

CSR information: The company's sustainability policy states:

> Sir Robert McAlpine Ltd aims to deliver a resource efficient future through a strong management structure underpinned by a collaborative approach to business which forges and maintains enduring long-term relationships with our staff, clients, supply chain and the communities in which we work.

The sustainability report notes that McAlpine commitments cover four areas: resource management, community, working together, and natural environment.

The main charitable support is given through The Robert McAlpine Foundation and also The McAlpine Educational Endowment.

CSR report: There is an annual sustainability report available online.

Corporate charity: The Robert McAlpine Foundation (Charity Commission no. 226646).

Exclusions

Our research indicates that the company's support is not given for local appeals outside the areas of company's operation.

Applications

In writing to the correspondent.

Enquiries regarding the two charities should be addressed to Brian Arter only (email: b.arter@sir-robert-mcalpine.com; tel: 01442 233444).

McCain Foods (GB) Ltd

Food manufacture

Correspondent: Company Director, Marketing and Corporate Affairs, Havers Hill, Scarborough, North Yorkshire YO11 3BS (tel: 01723 584141; website: www.mccain.co.uk/about-mccain/our-community)

Directors: A. D. McCain; M. C. McCain; N. I. Vermont; W. A. Bartlett; G. Dent; R. A. Hunter; S. W. Herd; H. D. Snape; A. R. Bridges; H. J. Priestly; R. Smelt

Year end	30/06/2013
Turnover	£416,473,000
Pre-tax profit	£33,160,000

Nature of business: Manufacturer and supplier of frozen and ambient food products principally in the UK.

Company registration number: 733218

Main locations: Scarborough, Peterborough, Montrose, Wolverhampton, Teddington

UK employees: 1,503

Total employees: 1,503

Focus of giving: Economic generation, education, enterprise/training, environment, health, ill health, arts, culture, sport, recreation, children, young people, community/social welfare.

Membership: BITC

Gifts in kind	✓
Matched funding	✓
Sponsorship	✓

Charitable donations

Cash UK (latest available):	2013	£43,000
	2012	£16,000
	2011	£21,000
	2009	£36,000
	2008	£39,000
Total UK (cash and in kind):	2013	£43,000
Cash worldwide:	2013	£43,000
Total worldwide (cash and in kind):	2013	£43,000

Community involvement

McCain appears to support community causes in the areas near its facilities at Scarborough, Hull, Peterborough, Wombourne and Montrose, principally through the McCain Community Fund, its new community support programme. The fund focuses its resources around three key themes: educating the next generation; reducing food waste; and supporting sustainable wealth within its communities. Employees also play an active role in their communities through volunteering and fundraising supported by matched funding and grants from the company. At a national level, McCain partners and sponsors organisations that encourage prosperous communities, good health and better education.

Corporate giving

In 2012/13 the company made charitable donations of £43,000. We have no information regarding the beneficiaries but have been advised previously that support is only given to charities and organisations in the company's local area.

During the year, McCain supported FareShare, a national charity working to combat food poverty, as well as sponsoring UK Athletics.

The company has also supported PhunkyFoods, a classroom initiative that teaches primary schoolchildren about healthy eating and exercise.

In-kind support

Gifts in kind

Our research tells us that, in previous years, support has been given in the form of gifts in kind.

Employee-led support

Employee volunteering

Employees are encouraged to take an active role in their communities through volunteering.

McCain financially supports employee volunteering and fundraising efforts in a number of ways:

Matched funding

McCain matches funds raised by employees undertaking a physical challenge up to £250.

Employee grants

Employees volunteering locally can apply for a Community Grant, by which McCain matches time volunteered on a £ by hour basis, up to the value of £250 for the organisation involved.

Teams of employees involved with volunteering for a community project can apply for up to £250 in support of the project.

Employees whose children are talented in the areas of sports, arts or sciences can apply for a Bright Futures award up to £250 to help support their child's additional structured tuition, training and/or equipment.

Commercially led support

Sponsorship

Beginning in 2008 and lasting for five years, McCain was a principal partner of UK Athletics. As part of the sponsorship McCain was title sponsor for both the McCain Young Athlete League and the McCain Challenge Series, as well as engaging with the Track and Field Roadshow and a talent identification scheme.

Corporate social responsibility

CSR committee: The Marketing and Corporate Affairs directors are responsible for community activities.

CSR information: The following information was obtained from the company website:

> The interests of the local communities around our processing facilities and the broader communities we serve with our products are central to our operations. We rely on the goodwill of our communities, recruit our employees from them and supply our products to them. By supporting associations and charities at both local and national level, helping to address the issues surrounding healthy diet and lifestyle and by consulting and actively engaging with our communities on issues relating to our operations affecting them, we strive to build meaningful and lasting relationships of mutual benefit and trust.

We were unable to determine the ratio of women to men on the board of directors.

CSR report: There appeared to be no published CSR report.

Exclusions

Our research tells us that no support is given for: circular appeals; fundraising events; advertising in charity brochures; appeals from individuals; purely denominational (religious) appeals or local appeals not in areas of company presence.

Applications

In writing to the correspondent, referenced 'Charitable donations'.

McDonalds Restaurants Ltd

Retail – restaurants/fast food

Correspondent: Corporate Affairs Manager, 11–59 High Road, East Finchley, London N2 8AW (website: www.mcdonalds.co.uk/ukhome/Ourworld.html)

Directors: J. Tafani; P. Pomroy; G. McDonald; R. Forte; M. Hussain; D. Goare; M. Hicks; M. Flores

Year end	31/12/2013
Turnover	£1,497,573,000
Pre-tax profit	£244,885,000

Nature of business: The principal activity of the company is the franchising and operation of a chain of limited menu quick service restaurants.

Company registration number: 1002769

Main locations: London

Total employees: 37,796

Focus of giving: Education, environment, health, ill health, children, young people, disability.

Membership: BITC

Sponsorship ✓

Charitable donations

Cash UK (latest available):	2013	£569,000
	2012	£482,000
	2010	£380,000
	2008	£357,000
	2007	£367,000
Total UK (cash and in kind):	2013	£569,000
Cash worldwide:	2013	£569,000
Total worldwide (cash and in kind):	2013	£569,000

Community involvement

McDonald's appears to make its charitable contribution to its own charity, the **Ronald McDonald House Charities (UK)** (Charity Commission no. 802047), which provides free 'home away from home' accommodation for families of children in hospital and hospices across the UK. RMHC UK is one of a network of RMHC 'chapters' operating in countries throughout the world.

Corporate giving

The company's annual report and accounts for 2013 declared a charitable contribution of £569,000 to the Ronald McDonald House Charities (UK), though the charity's records account for only £415,000 of this.

The charity's website states: 'The biggest gift that McDonald's and their franchisees have ever given us is the opportunity to place our collection boxes in every one of their restaurants across the UK. These boxes provided Ronald McDonald House Charities with over £3.2 million in 2013.' As is our usual practice, we have not included this figure in our total for charitable contributions from the company.

Beneficiaries: Ronald McDonald House Charities (UK)

Commercially led support

Sponsorship

McDonald's supports community schemes run by home nations Football Associations including a club accreditation scheme and a kit scheme programme to support junior football teams with kits.

Corporate social responsibility

CSR information: There was little information regarding CSR in the UK; however, there is are pages on the UK website relating to environment and the Ronald McDonald House Charities. There is more information regarding CSR on the McDonalds corporate US website; however, this focuses principally on activities in the US and internationally.

We were unable to determine the ratio of women to men on the board.

Exclusions

No support is given for animal welfare charities, appeals from individuals, the arts, elderly people, medical research, overseas projects, political appeals, religious appeals, or science/technology.

Applications

It would appear that all of the company's charitable contributions are given to the RMHC.

Meggitt plc

Engineering

Correspondent: The Company Secretary, Atlantic House, Aviation Park West, Bournemouth International Airport, Christchurch, Dorset BH23 6EW (tel: 01202 597597; website: meggittinvestors.com/corporate-responsibility)

Directors: Sir Colin Terry, Chair; Stephen Young, Chief Executive; Guy Berruyer; Doug Webb, Chief Financial Officer; Philip Green; Paul Heiden; Brenda Reichelderfer; Philip Cox; Alison Goligher; David Williams (women: 2; men: 8)

Year end	31/12/2013
Turnover	£1,637,300,000
Pre-tax profit	£269,400,000

Nature of business: Meggitt plc is a global engineering group specialising in extreme environment components and sub-systems for aerospace, defence and energy markets

Company registration number: 432989

Subsidiary undertakings include: Meggitt Aerospace Ltd; Meggitt Aircraft Braking Systems Corporation; Meggitt Aircraft Braking Systems Kentucky Corporation; Meggitt Defence Systems Ltd; Meggitt Defense Systems Inc.; Meggitt Oregon Inc,.

UK employees: 2,797

Total employees: 10,715

Focus of giving: General charitable purposes, education, general appeals, local groups, STEM (science, technology, engineering and mathematics), community/social welfare.

Cash donations undeclared	✓
FTSE 100	✓
Gifts in kind	✓

Charitable donations

Cash UK (latest available):	2013	£151,000
	2012	£230,000
	2011	£115,000
	2010	£108,000
Total UK (cash and in kind):	2013	£151,000
Cash worldwide:	2013	£151,000
Total worldwide (cash and in kind):	2013	£151,000

Community involvement

Individual Meggitt facilities work with their local communities and support charities at their discretion. Meggitt's UK locations have supported Education Business partnerships and the government's STEM (Science, Technology, Education and Maths) initiatives on a local basis. Aside from cash donations, previous research indicates that support to the local community is also given through staff volunteering and fundraising efforts for a range of local and national causes.

The group also supports local community groups through **The Meggitt Fund**, which is administered by Community Foundation for Bournemouth, Dorset and Poole.

Corporate giving

The annual report and accounts for 2013 did not declare a figure for charitable donations made during the year. The average of these contributions in the three most recent years for which we have figures was £151,000, and we have taken this as an estimate for charitable contributions in 2013.

During the year, Meggitt's head office, based in Dorset, made contributions to the Arkwright Scholarship Trust, the Institute of Mechanical Engineers' Schools Aerospace Challenge, its local community foundation, and the Poole Hospital Staff Excellence Awards.

The Meggitt Fund

This fund is managed on behalf of Meggitt plc by the Community Foundation for Bournemouth, Dorset and Poole seeks to support small voluntary/community groups working to benefit local people and address community need in the Bournemouth, Poole and/or Dorset area. Grants of up to £250 are available.

The accounts of the community foundation show that, in its 2012/13 financial year, Meggitt made a contribution of £2,500 to the fund.

We were unable to determine a value for non-cash contributions given by the group.

Beneficiaries include: Arkwright Scholarship Trust; Community Foundation for Bournemouth, Dorset and Poole; the Institute of Mechanical Engineers

Employee-led support

Employee volunteering and fundraising

Employees at Meggitt facilities give time and money to a wide range of international and local causes.

Commercially led support

During the year, Education Business Partnerships and the UK government's STEM initiative were supported by individual Meggitt facilities.

Corporate social responsibility

CSR committee: The following information was obtained from the CSR report contained within the annual report and accounts:

> Health, safety and environment (HSE), ethics and business conduct and trade compliance are managed by a highly experienced team of functional specialists, under the leadership of the Corporate Affairs Director. Divisional presidents and site directors are responsible for implementing policies and programmes locally.The Board has approved policies on corporate responsibility, health and safety, environment, ethics and business conduct and trade compliance, and these are available on our website.The Board has an Ethics and Trade Compliance Committee, which meets quarterly to discuss these programmes in detail. HSE matters are reviewed and discussed at every Board meeting.

CSR information: The following information was taken from the CSR report:

> Meggitt is committed to:
> - Upholding sound corporate governance principles
> - Providing a supportive, rewarding and safe working environment
> - Conducting business relationships in an ethical manner
> - Minimising the environmental impact of products and processes
> - Acting as a responsible supplier and encouraging our contractors and suppliers to do the same
> - Supporting our local communities
> - Professional and comprehensive employee training programmes

CSR report: There is CSR report is contained within the annual report of the group.

Exclusions

The Meggitt Fund cannot support:

- Individuals
- Statutory organisations (such as schools)
- Trips abroad
- Mini buses
- Building costs or adaptations

Applications

In writing to the correspondent, referenced 'Charitable donations'.

The Meggitt Fund: Grants are made to small community groups working to benefit local people in the Bournemouth, Poole and/or Dorset areas. For more information on eligibility and applications for grants from the Meggitt Fund, visit www.dorsetcommunityfoundation.org/apply-for-a-grant/the-meggitt-fund.

John Menzies plc

Distribution, logistics

Correspondent: Charity Fund Administrator, 2 Lochside Avenue, Edinburgh Park EH12 9DJ (tel: 01312 258555; website: www.johnmenziesplc.com/responsibility.aspx)

Directors: Iain Napier, Chair; Jeremy Stafford, Chief Executive; Eric Born; Paula Bell, Group Finance Director; Ian Harley; Dermot Jenkinson; Silla Maizey; Octavia Morley; Craig Smyth; John Geddes (women: 3; men: 7)

Year end	31/12/2013
Turnover	£1,905,400,000
Pre-tax profit	£42,100,000

Nature of business: Logistics support services group.

Company registration number: SC34970

Subsidiary undertakings include: Menzies Distribution Ltd; Menzies Group Holdings Ltd; Princes Street (Jersey) Ltd; John Menzies Finance Ltd; Menzies Aviation plc; Menzies Aviation Holdings Ltd

Total employees: 23,623

Focus of giving: Advertising in charity brochures, environment, fundraising events, health, ill health, heritage, medical research, older people, arts, culture, overseas projects, sport, recreation, children, young people, community/social welfare, disability.

Gifts in kind	✓
Payroll giving	✓

Charitable donations

Cash UK (latest available):	2013	£90,000
	2012	£90,000
	2011	£80,000
	2010	£50,000
	2009	£57,000
Total UK (cash and in kind):	2013	£90,000
Cash worldwide:	2013	£90,000
Total worldwide (cash and in kind):	2013	£90,000

Community involvement

The group looks to contribute to communities particularly in places where it has a presence. Apart from contributing 'skills and expertise' in its local areas, the group also makes charitable donations through its two funds, the Charities Fund and the John M. Menzies Community Fund. The group actively supports its employees' fundraising and volunteering activities.

Corporate giving

In 2013 charitable donations from the group totalled £90,000.

Charities Fund

The group's Charities Fund supports a small number of charities which have been nominated by each operating division. In 2013, £70,000 was donated from this fund.

John M. Menzies Community Fund

The fund makes cash donations of up to £350 per individual or £700 per team for employees who are involved with a charity or community project. During the year almost £20,000 was donated through this fund.

2013 beneficiaries included: Alder Hey Children's Charity; Cerebral Palsy Care Kent; Children 1st; The Children's Hospital Charity; The Kiltwalk; NewstrAid

In-kind support

Pro bono

The group has contributed in-kind donations, for example, in the form of Menzies Aviation's Cross Cultural Team Challenge programme, which combines Senior Leadership Development with helping disadvantaged people. In India, the group worked alongside the Parikrma Foundation, which has links with its business there. In 2013, this involved the organising of an under-16s football tournament for schoolchildren at the Bangalore Stadium.

Employee-led support

Payroll giving

The group supports its employees in their charitable activities and operates a payroll giving scheme.

Employee fundraising

During the year, employees were involved with fundraising activities, including a seven day charity bike relay from Edinburgh to Kent, which was organised by Menzies Distribution and, with the help of more than 30 employees, helped to raise £30,000 for Children 1st and Anthony Nolan.

Corporate social responsibility

CSR committee: The group's website states:

> The two Divisional Managing Directors therefore have ultimate responsibility for CSR within their divisions and specifically includes Health and Safety and Employee welfare.
>
> Significant CSR issues arising in or affecting any of our businesses are raised and discussed at each Group Board meeting. The Group Board and the Divisional Operating Boards have systems in place, including access to adequate information, to identify and assess CSR risks, and to ensure that these risks, and exposure to them, are managed appropriately.

CSR information: This information was obtained from the group's 2013 annual report and accounts:

> John Menzies is aware that it has community obligations, particularly within the countries and localities where it does business. We have a positive duty to improve the well-being of individuals and to use our best endeavours to enhance community life. A positive approach to our community relations is in the best long-term interests of our Company and of those who work within it. We donate our skills and expertise to work in the communities in which we operate. Each year the group board sets a budget for its charitable activities and a charities committee allocates the expenditure.

CSR report: A full CSR report is published annually and is available from the group's website.

Exclusions

No support is given for animal welfare, appeals from individuals, enterprise/ training, overseas projects, political appeals, religious appeals, or science/ technology.

Applications

Unsolicited applications are not considered. Nominations are made by the group's divisions.

Merck Sharp & Dohme Ltd

Pharmaceuticals

Correspondent: The Grants Committee, Hertford Road, Hoddesdon, Hertfordshire EN11 9BU (email: grantscommittee@merck.com; website: www.msd-uk.com/responsibility/Pages/ home.aspx)

Directors: M. Nally; K. Bousfield; M. Leonard

Year end	31/12/2013
Turnover	£754,123,000
Pre-tax profit	£34,787,000

Nature of business: MSD is the UK subsidiary of Merck, a healthcare company that discovers, develops, manufactures and markets a wide range of innovative pharmaceutical products to improve human health.

The annual report and accounts for 2013 state: 'The immediate parent undertaking is Merck Sharp & Dohme (Holdings) Ltd. The ultimate parent undertaking and controlling party is Merck & Co., Inc, a company incorporate in the state of New Jersey, USA.'

Company registration number: 820771

Subsidiary undertakings include: See annual report and accounts

Main locations: Hoddesdon, Cramlington

UK employees: 1,337

Total employees: 1,337

Focus of giving: General charitable purposes, education, environment, health, ill health, community/social welfare.

Cash donations undeclared	✓
Gifts in kind	✓

Charitable donations

Cash UK (latest available):	2013	£109,000
	2010	£7,000
	2008	£0
	2006	£32,000
	2005	£51,000
Total UK (cash and in kind):	2013	£128,000
Cash worldwide:	2013	£109,000
Total worldwide (cash and in kind):	2013	£128,000

Community involvement

Merck Sharp & Dohme Ltd (MSD) supports academic, charitable and government organisations, predominantly through 'grants and donations', with the aim of 'bringing about better health outcomes for patients'. It has also supported local initiatives to help the communities in which it works.

Corporate giving

Unfortunately, the company's annual report and accounts for 2013 did not declare charitable donations. However, we were able to locate a PDF document on the website which provides a breakdown of 'grants, donations and payments' to patient groups and other institutions in the UK. We have taken these to have been given for charitable purposes.

The document shows that in 2013 MSD made grants totalling around £54,000 to patient organisations in the UK. Grants to 'other institutions' amounted to £55,000.

In-kind support from the company totalled around £19,000.

Beneficiaries included: British Society of Gastroenterology (£20,000); University of Liverpool (£20,000); National Ankylosing Spondylitis Society (NASS) (£10,000); Primary Care Women's Health Forum (£10,000); Ovarian Cancer Action (£10,000); The Hepatitis C Trust (£8,900)

For a complete list of grant recipients and projects supported by the company, view the document at www.msd-uk.com/ licensing/Pages/Patient-Groups.aspx

In-kind support

Pro bono

The company has provided a Patient Research Manager over periods of ten days to assist with research projects for Parkinson's UK, Patient Information Forum (PIF) and Positively UK, for example.

During the year, nine employees each spent 2.5 working hours volunteering for UK Sepsis Trust as part of the '365 Merck Days' employee volunteering programme.

Employee-led support

Employee volunteering

Our research suggests that employees are able to contribute time and skills through the '365 Merck Days' volunteering scheme.

Corporate social responsibility

CSR information: MSD's CSR framework focuses on four areas: access to health; environmental sustainability; employees; and ethics and transparency.

We were unable to determine the ratio of women to men on the board.

CSR report: A group CSR report can be found at www.merckresponsibility.com, through this appears to focus predominantly on activities in the US and overseas.

Applications

To apply for a grant, email your request with details of your project to the correspondent.

The Mersey Docks and Harbour Company Ltd

Marine, transport and communications

Correspondent: Caroline Gill, Company Secretary and Fund Administrator, Maritime Centre, Port of Liverpool, Liverpool L21 1LA (tel: 01519 496349; website: www.merseydocks.co.uk)

Directors: Thomas Allison; John Whittaker, Chair; Gary Hodgson; Steven Underwood; Dr Mark Whitworth, Group

Chief Executive Officer (women: 0; men: 5)

Year end		31/03/2014
Turnover		£147,100,000
Pre-tax profit		£57,800,000

Nature of business: The principal activities of the company are the operation and maintenance of port facilities on the Rivers Mersey and Medway, provision of cargo handling and marine related services as well as being the Statutory Authority for the Port of Liverpool.

The company is part of the Peel Group. Its immediate parent company is Peel Ports Investment Ltd and the ultimate holding company is Tokenhouse Ltd, incorporated in the Isle of Man. Tokenhouse Ltd is controlled by the Billown 1997 Settlement Trust, which is considered to be the ultimate controlling party. According to the website, 'the Peel Group is a privately owned conglomerate business with a wide range of interests from property to wind farms and hotels'.

Peel Ports Group is made up of Peel Ports Mersey, Clydeport in Scotland and Medway Ports in Kent.

Company registration number: 7438262

Subsidiary undertakings include: None listed in the annual report and accounts.

Main locations: Sheerness, Liverpool, Heysham, Birkenhead

UK employees: 409

Total employees: 409

Focus of giving: General charitable purposes, education, environment, health, ill health, medical research, small groups, local groups, older people, arts, culture, playgroups, sport, recreation, children, young people, community/ social welfare.

Market-led giving ✓

Charitable donations

Cash UK (latest available):	2014	£50,000
	2013	£41,000
	2011	£50,000
	2009	£152,594
	2008	£162,511
Total UK (cash and in kind):	2014	£50,000
Cash worldwide:	2014	£50,000
Total worldwide (cash and in kind):	2014	£50,000

Community involvement

The Mersey Docks and Harbour Board Charitable Fund (The Dock Charitable Fund) (Charity Commission no. 206913)

According to the fund's accounts, it was established with the following purposes:

- The reward of persons assisting in the preservation of the life of the crew of any ship wrecked in the port of Liverpool or in the preservation of the ship or cargo or in preserving or endeavouring to preserve persons from drowning
- The relief of sick, disabled or superannuated men in the dock service or the families of such men who were killed in service
- The benefit of charitable institutions in the town or port of Liverpool

The charity says that it 'seeks to maintain close links with many parts of the local community'.

Plaza Community Cinema

The Port of Liverpool contributed to the project in Crosby to save the facility for the benefit of the local community.

Peel Ports Mersey 500 Fund

The fund is ran by the Community Foundation for Merseyside and can provide 'a maximum of £500 to local charities based on a written submission against a set of criteria including, amount of people benefitting, sustainability of the group and track record'. The scheme has been in place since 2003 when it had an initial £15,000 contribution and since then has provided more than £102,000 to local groups, including scouts, clubs, poetry cafe, sea cadets and preschool groups.

The Seafarers Mission

The Peel Ports CSR Report for 2012/13 says 'the Seafarers Mission plays a valuable role in offering a warm welcome, the opportunity to contact relatives and a comfortable place to spend a few hours relaxing' for seafarers who visit the port and the city. Peel Ports Mersey supports the work of the project.

The Peel Group

Charity partnership

The Peel Group is working with a children's medical research charity Sparks, which operates throughout the North West.

Community Environment Fund (CEF)

The Peel Group's CSR Report for 2013 notes that as part of the Atlantic Gateway development, Peel has suggested a voluntary 1% contribution of a project's overall cost to form a fund to establish environmental projects to benefit the whole community.

Corporate giving

The company's annual report and accounts for 2013/14 state that a total of £50,000 (2012/13: £41,000) was given in charitable contributions. The Peel Ports' CSR Report for 2012/13 says that since 2006 over £750,000 has been donated to the charity partners by the ports group.

The Mersey Docks and Harbour Company Charitable Fund (Charity Commission no. 206913) annual report and accounts for 2013 (the latest available at the time of writing) note that a £40,000 donation was made by the company and the following beneficiaries of grants totalled the same figure: Community Foundation for Merseyside (£15,500); Liverpool Seafarer's Centre (formerly The Mersey Mission to Seafarers) (£10,500); Wirral Ark Project (£5,000); Plaza Community Cinema (£3,000); Farm Africa and North West Air Ambulance (£1,000 each); Brain Tumour Research (£500); DAPS (£200); and North West Cancer Research (£100).

See the corporate charity entry on p. 419 for more information.

Employee-led support

Group-wide activities undertaken by Peel Group's employees include donating their time to local organisations, acting as school governors and getting involved in various partnerships, for example, by sitting on the board or providing mentoring. Staff fundraising is also undertaken. We include this reference to the group assuming that the group policies would apply to the company as well.

Commercially led support

Apprenticeships

There is an apprenticeship scheme operating.

Corporate social responsibility

CSR committee: We found no indications of a separate CSR committee.

CSR information: Peel Ports Mersey CSR Report says that its:

> Programme of added value to communities and businesses in the North West ... is closely aligned to Peel Ports Mersey's 20 year Master Plan; detailing the companies long-term strategy for growth and regeneration, providing jobs, training and opportunities for local people, local suppliers and the business community. The main areas addressed are – communities, environment and people.

The Peel Group's CSR focuses on 'a pro-active approach to the principles of sustainable growth and development, working in partnership with all [its] stakeholders, and engaging with [local] communities'.

CSR report: There is a CSR report published online.

Corporate charity: The Mersey Docks and Harbour Company Charitable Fund (Charity Commission no. 206913).

Applications

In writing to the correspondent.

Michelin Tyre plc

Motors and accessories

Correspondent: Christine Reynolds, Campbell Road, Stoke-on-Trent ST4 4EY (website: www.michelinrespectforcommunities.com)

Directors: P. Berther; K. Shepherd; G. Alderman; M. Scovell; J. Reid; F. d'Avout d'Auerstaedt; W. Culbertson

Year end	31/12/2013
Turnover	£904,493,000
Pre-tax profit	£51,202,000

Nature of business: The manufacture and sale of tyres, tubes, wheels and accessories, maps and guides, and mobility support services.

Company registration number: 84559

Main locations: Ballymena, Stoke-on-Trent, Dundee

Total employees: 2,492

Focus of giving: General charitable purposes, enterprise/training, safety and crime prevention, children, young people, community/social welfare.

Membership: LBG

Cash donations undeclared	✓
Charity of the Year	✓
Gifts in kind	✓
Payroll giving	✓

Charitable donations

Cash UK (latest available):	2013	£84,000
	2011	£83,500
	2009	£125,000
	2007	£125,000
Total UK (cash and in kind):	2013	£84,000
Cash worldwide:	2013	£84,000
Total worldwide (cash and in kind):	2013	£84,000

Community involvement

Michelin looks to build relationships with organisations that work to benefit the local communities in which it operates. Support is given in the form of cash and in-kind donations, and employees play an important role in the company's community involvement. Priority is given to organisations in the company's key focus areas of education, mobility safety and environment.

The guidelines on the website state the following:

- Michelin Tyre PLC only provides support to charities, educational establishments and 'not-for-profit' entities. Support is generally awarded for specific activities, not general operating costs, however some operating costs may be allocated for the administration of a project.
- Michelin seeks to support worthwhile initiatives in the communities local to its manufacturing operations at Stoke-On-Trent, Dundee and Ballymena

Charities of the Year

Each year, Michelin selects a number of charities to receive Charity of the Year status, and to benefit from the fundraising efforts of the company and its employees.

Recent Charity of the Year partners include: Insight Counselling; The Peter Pan Nursery University Hospital; Tayside Children with Cancer and Leukaemia; University Hospital of North Staffordshire

Corporate giving

The annual report and accounts did not include a figure for charitable donations. In the most recent year for which we have a figure, these totalled around £84,000, and we have taken this as an estimate for charitable donations in 2013.

In-kind support

In-kind support given by the company in 2013 included, for example, the donation of nearly 200 cycling helmets to P6 students that had taken part in a Bikeability programme run by Dundee Active Schools and Dundee and Angus College. Another example of in-kind contributions has been the Michelin's running of a road safety simulation programme, which helped to educate students about dangers whilst driving.

Employee-led support

Employee fundraising

Michelin employees help to raise funds for the company's Charities of the Year.

Employee volunteering

Employees volunteer in the communities based around Michelin's UK operations at Ballymena, Stoke-on Trent and Dundee.

Payroll giving

Previous research suggests that the company operates the Give As You Earn scheme.

Commercially led support

Through its education programmes, local students were able to visit the Ballymena production plant, where they learned more about careers in manufacturing.

Corporate social responsibility

CSR committee: We found no evidence of there being a CSR committee.

CSR information: As part of its value 'respect for people', Michelin plays an active role in the communities local to its activities. The website states the following:

> Wherever we are, we have a role to play, a responsibility to accept by establishing 'good neighbour' relationships, by taking part in local life through training and development programmes, or through cultural and social exchanges.
>
> *Our Aim*
>
> - To enrich the quality of life in the communities where we live and work
> - To engage our employees in opportunities to positively contribute to the communities where we live and work
> - To enhance education, the environment and safety within our local communities

We were unable to determine the ratio of women to men on the board.

CSR report: We found no evidence of a separate CSR report; however, there is a section on the website dedicated to Michelin's community involvement.

Exclusions

Michelin Tyre plc's Community Involvement Programme does not support requests which relate to:

- Organisations that do not have tax-exempt status
- Individuals
- Political organisations, candidates or lobby organisations
- Organisations with a limited constituency or membership
- Travel costs for groups or individuals
- Advertising
- Organisations outside the United Kingdom
- Activities that are not in line with Michelin's corporate values and image

Applications

Application procedure

- All applications must be supported by a completed application form, which is available to download from the website
- Make sure you meet the above criteria before applying
- Add any supporting evidence and email to the relevant correspondent

Contacts

- Ballymena: Ballymena-PRM@uk.michelin.com
- Dundee: dawn.duncan@uk.michelin.com
- Stoke-on-Trent: michelin.requests@uk.michelin.com
- National: christine.reynolds@uk.michelin.com

Note: the 'National' contact should only be used for organisations that have a national presence or work on a national basis.

Micro Focus International plc

Business services

Correspondent: CSR Team/Charity Committee, The Lawn, 22–30 Old Bath Road, Newbury, Berkshire RG14 1QN (tel: 01635 565200; website: www.microfocus.com/about/responsibility/index.aspx)

Directors: Kevin Loosemore, Chair; Mike Phillips, Chief Financial Officer; David Maloney; Stephen Murdoch; Tom Skelton; Karen Slatford; Tom Virden; Richard Atkins (women: 1; men: 7)

Year end	30/04/2014
Turnover	£270,600,000
Pre-tax profit	£92,400,000

Nature of business: Micro Focus provides software that enables companies to develop, test, deploy, assess and modernize enterprise applications.

Company registration number: 5134647

Subsidiary undertakings include: Micro Focus Group Ltd; Micro Focus Holdings Ltd; Micro Focus Ltd; Micro Focus (US) Holdings; Borland Software Corporation; Borland (UK) Ltd.

Total employees: 1,237

Focus of giving: Education, children, young people, community/social welfare, disasters.

Cash donations undeclared	✓
Charity of the Year	✓
Gifts in kind	✓
Humanitarian aid: overseas	✓
Matched funding	✓
Overseas giving	✓
Payroll giving	✓

Charitable donations

Cash UK (latest available):	2011	£35,000
	2010	£46,900
	2009	£17,100
Cash worldwide:	2014	£47,000
Total worldwide (cash and in kind):	2014	£47,000

Community involvement

Micro Focus supports its employees' participation in charitable activities through a matched funding scheme and employee volunteering time. All initiatives supported follow the 'core themes of education and local community support'. The company's 2014 annual report states the following: 'A global charity was selected by the charity committee for the first half of the year, with the focus in the second six months turning to a number of local charities to achieve a balance between international and country level fundraising initiatives.'

The company has a local project grants initiative through which 12 charity or community organisations 'with wide geographic spread across Micro Focus operations worldwide' benefitted during the year.

Corporate giving

In 2013/14 more than $75,000 (£47,000) was raised and contributed by the company and its employees. $41,700 (£26,000) was given to local causes across seven countries, $22,400 (£14,000) was given to international causes, and $12,600 (£7,900 was donated to national causes in the UK, the USA and the Philippines. Employee-raised funds are not normally counted in our total figure for donations; however, a breakdown of corporate cash donations given in the UK was not included in the 2013/14 annual report.

Beneficiaries included: International Red Cross Philippines Typhoon Emergency Fund; Thames and Kennet Narrow Boat Trust (project grant); UNICEF (global charity).

In-kind support

A number of employee days are allocated each month so that teams or individuals can volunteer for a selected charity or a community initiative.

Employee-led support

Payroll giving

Payroll giving is available for employees and is matched by the company through its gift programme.

Employee fundraising

As an example, in June 2013 the Micro Focus board and management team helped to raise $2,000 (£1,200) for Make a Wish UK through participation in a sponsored carwash at the company's headquarters at Newbury.

Corporate social responsibility

CSR committee: CSR policies at Micro Focus are reviewed and monitored by the board on a twice yearly basis, with non-executive director, Karen Slatford, responsible for CSR at board level. During the year ended 30 April 2014 the CSR Committee met four times.

CSR information: The following information is taken from the company's annual report:

> The board is committed to running the company in accordance with best practice in corporate governance. This commitment includes recognition by the company of the importance of taking into account its corporate social responsibilities ('CSR') in operating the business. In this context, Micro Focus seeks to integrate CSR considerations relating particularly to social, ethical and health, safety and environment ('HS&E') issues in its day-to-day operations.

CSR report: A CSR report is included within the annual report.

Applications

In writing to the correspondent.

Microsoft Ltd

Computer software

Correspondent: UK Community Affairs Team, Microsoft Campus, Thames Valley Park, Reading RG6 1WG (website: www.microsoft.com/en-gb/about/charities-communities)

Directors: K. R. Dolliver; B. O. Orndorff; Michel Van der Bel

Year end	30/06/2013
Turnover	£860,174,000
Pre-tax profit	£69,839,000

Nature of business: Microsoft Ltd. is a subsidiary company of Microsoft Corporation – based in Redmond, Washington State – USA. It markets and supports systems, devices and applications software for business, professional and home use.

Company registration number: 1624297

Main locations: Edinburgh, London, Manchester, Reading

UK employees: 3,025

Total employees: 3,025

Focus of giving: Education, enterprise/training, safety and crime prevention, science technology, children, young people, community/social welfare, disability.

Charity of the Year	✓
Gifts in kind	✓
Matched funding	✓
Sponsorship	✓

Charitable donations

Cash UK (latest available):	2013	£411,000
	2012	£342,000
	2011	£312,000
	2009	£425,000
	2008	£286,000
Total UK (cash and in kind):	2013	£25,400,000
Cash worldwide:	2013	£411,000
Total worldwide (cash and in kind):	2013	£25,400,000

Community involvement

Microsoft, along with partners and employees, provides 'free or low-cost hardware, software services and support to charities'. With its community project and charity partners, the company uses technology to help improve lives in UK communities, supporting programmes based around computer literacy, online safety and young people.

Corporate giving

The annual report and accounts for 2012/13 declared charitable donations of £411,000.

The company website states the following: 'In our last financial year (FY13) we donated software with a total market value of £25m.' As we were unable to determine the 'cost' rather than the market value of these donated products, we have taken the figure given as the company's in-kind contributions.

We were unable to determine a value for the other in-kind support given by the company (staff time, etc.).

Charity partners include: AbilityNet; CEOP; UK Youth

In-kind support

Gifts in kind

Software donations – Since 2006, Microsoft has been one of the companies working with the Technology Trust to provide software donations to eligible UK charities. By the end of 2013, the company had donated software to the fair market value of £100 million.

Office 365 – Eligible UK charities may apply for Office 365 as a donation. A range of subscription plans are available, some of which donate the programme and others that offer the programme at a discounted price.

Staff time

Microsoft employees are able to take up to three days per year for volunteering purposes. In 2013 staff volunteered working 420 days.

Community programmes

Microsoft is involved in a number of community programmes based around IT including:

Microsoft Digital Literacy – A programme designed to teach and assess basic computer technology skills to people so that they can use them in day-to-day life and can develop new social and economic opportunities.

Online safety: *CEOP* – Microsoft has worked with the Child Exploitation and Online Protection Centre (CEOP), using technology to support efforts to keep children safe online and training CEOP staff to deliver resources to schoolchildren across the country.

Turning it off is not the answer – 100 employees have been trained to deliver a presentation to parents about the Internet, its risks and how to keep children safe.

Parenting in the Digital Age – In support of The Parent Zone, Microsoft has developed a training course for teachers, socials workers and others who work directly with parents, so that they can share online safety advice.

Microsoft IT Youth Hubs – In conjunction with its UK corporate charity partner, Microsoft has funded 30 youth clubs, through which young people are trained as IT champions and peer educate others in their communities.

Employee-led support

Employee volunteering

Employees are encouraged to volunteer in their communities through the employee volunteering policy operated by the company.

Employee fundraising

Microsoft employees fundraise for various good causes in their communities.

Matched funding

Microsoft will match funds raised for charity up to a value of £7,500 per employee.

Commercially led support

Sponsorship

Microsoft sponsors the Scouts' IT badge.

Young people

As part of its global commitment to young people, YoungSpark, Microsoft launched its Get On initiative in 2012 to help 300,000 British young people learn more about IT careers, opportunities to develop skills, and providing opportunities for new employment routes.

Corporate social responsibility

CSR committee: We found no evidence of a specific CSR committee.

CSR information: The following information was obtained from the company's website: 'Microsoft UK is working with technology industry leaders, charities, government and schools to drive Environmental sustainability, support charities and to address technology abuses.'

We were unable to determine the ratio of women to men on the board of directors.

CSR report: There is a section dedicated to Microsoft's UK involvement on the UK website. There is also a Citizenship Report available to download on the global website, which focuses on international activities.

Exclusions

Our research indicates that no support is given, in any form, for political, religious or racially motivated projects.

Applications

Software donations

Microsoft makes its software donations through Technology Trust. For more information see www.tt-exchange.org.

Office 365 options for charities

For more details of Office 365 donations or discounts see products.office.com/en-GB/nonprofit/office-365-nonprofit.

Low-cost hardware

Microsoft runs a PC refurbishment scheme through which charities and educational establishments are able to access low-cost Windows devices. For more information see www.microsoft.com/refurbishedpcs.

Microsoft Digital Literacy Curriculum

Instructor Resources to support the teaching of the Microsoft Digital Literacy Curriculum are free online or to download from www.microsoft.com/digitalliteracy.

Note that Microsoft is only able to donate cash to selected major charity projects.

The Midcounties Co-operative

Financial services, miscellaneous, retail – supermarkets

Correspondent: The Community Team, Co-operative House, Warwick Technology Park, Gallows Hill, Warwick CV34 6DA (tel: 01902 405700; email: community.team@midcounties.coop; website: www.midcounties.coop)

Directors: Patrick Gray; Helen Wiseman; Olivia Birch, Vice President; Isobel Burbidge, Vice President; Bernadette Connor; Ruth FitzJohn, President; Margaret Jarvis; Donald Morrison; Jean Nunn-Price; Vivian Woodell; Ellie Freeman; Hazel Gray; Matthew Lane; Louise Pevreal; Barbara Rainford; Judith Feeney (women: 12; men: 4)

Year end	25/01/2014
Turnover	£863,163,000
Pre-tax profit	£4,137,000

Nature of business: The Midcounties Co-operative is registered as an Industrial and Provident Society and has a number of diverse trading activities, including food, travel, property, childcare, energy and funeral services. Its heartlands are in Oxfordshire, Gloucestershire, Buckinghamshire, Shropshire, Staffordshire, the West Midlands, Wiltshire and Worcestershire, with a trading presence in the surrounding counties.

Company registration number: IP19025R

Subsidiary undertakings include: Britannia Cruise Club Ltd; Buffer Bear Ltd; Childcare Partners Ltd; Early Birds Nursery Ltd; GM Bailey (Hednesford) Ltd; Harry Tuffin Ltd; Kenmare Estates Ltd; Lichpharm Ltd; Midcounties Leasing Ltd; Petit Enfant Group Ltd; Places for Children Ltd; and West Midlands Co-operative Chemists Ltd. A full list of subsidiary undertakings can be obtained from the society's accounts.

Main locations: Gloucester, Oxford, Swindon

UK employees: 9,632

Total employees: 9,632

Focus of giving: Economic generation, children, young people, education, enterprise/training, environment, health, ill health, medical research, non-registered charities, local groups, poverty and social exclusion, women's issues, community/social welfare.

Membership: BITC

Gifts in kind	✓
Market-led giving	✓

Charitable donations

Cash UK (latest available):	2014	£302,000
	2012	£1,524,000
	2010	£260,000
	2008	£203,790
	2006	£150,000
Total UK (cash and in kind):	2014	£946,000
Cash worldwide:	2014	£302,000
Total worldwide (cash and in kind):	2014	£946,000

Community involvement

The society's website states:

> We work in partnership with community organisations to create focused projects on issues linked to our Board of Directors' social goals. The broad headings of our social goals are:
>
> - Developing young people
> - Supporting communities
> - Defending the environment
> - Developing co-operatives across the world
>
> Our project work combines funding and more focused volunteering. Our current project is based on working with young people and communities around the issues of underage drinking.

On a worldwide level support is given to various initiatives, which include fair trade, ethical sourcing and caring for the environment.

Charity partnerships

Women's Aid has been the company's charity partner for a number of years and fundraising efforts. The fundraising efforts are largely directed at supporting another charity partner – Teenage Cancer Trust.

Can You See Me?

Through the partnership with Women's Aid, the Midcounties Co-operative funded the 'Can You See Me?' educational resource on relationships and domestic abuse (produced by The Rural Media Company). It will be used to support the charity's work with young people and can be employed in schools and other educational settings.

The Outward Bound Trust

According to the society's Social Responsibility Report 2013/2014, a partnership has been established:

> To launch a new initiative to increase environmental awareness among young people at schools in [the society's] trading heartlands. ... The pilot scheme saw year nine students from Walsall Academy, one of our partner schools, spend three months learning about sustainable energy sources, developing leadership skills and designing an action plan for a greener, more sustainable lifestyle.

Community grants

Grants of up to £2,000 are available to members of The Midcounties Co-operative and whose group is working in a community where there is a Midcounties store. The website states: 'As a co-operative business we are working with ten of the UK's Community Foundations and welcome their support and local knowledge in helping us to fund even the smallest grass roots projects.'

The Oxford food bank

A grant of £10,000 was given to the food bank to enable it to purchase a second chiller.

Wyre Forest Nightstop

A grant of £5,000 was awarded for 'the continuation of the Volunteer for Success programme which is aimed at increasing the skills and confidence of unemployed young people aged 18 to 25'.

The CSR report for 2014 states that the overall amount of funding awarded through the community funding programme was planned to be lowered in 2014, including removing the enhanced grants element and supporting a new lower level grants programme to provide direct funding to local organisations that colleagues are also supporting through the volunteering programme.

Co-operative Futures

During the year the society worked with Co-operative Futures on various activities and provided £110,000 funding to support new co-operative enterprises.

Corporate giving

The society's annual report and accounts for 2013/14 state that during the year a total of over £644,000 was given to local communities through volunteering and colleagues have supplied over 44,000 volunteer hours (2012/13: £580,000 and 40,000 hours). The CSR report for 2013/14 notes that a total of £302,000 was distributed in grants from the community fund to support 196 grass-roots community organisations, including several enhanced grants (between £5,000 and £10,000).

Political donations: At the Annual General Meeting held on 11 May 2013, members approved a donation of £47,000 to the Co-operative Party. This included support at national level and grants to the Society's three local Co-operative Party Councils.

Beneficiaries have included: Prince's Trust; The Oxford Food Bank (£10,000); Teenage Cancer Trust; Women's Aid; and Wyre Forest Nightstop.

In-kind support

Raffle prizes

Community Cheque (subject to availability, speak to the manager) can be provided at local Midcounties stores to be used to buy chocolates or wine for a raffle or tombola.

The society also 'facilitates charity collections and information awareness days in a number of [its] larger supermarkets', thus providing a fundraising and information sharing platform for good causes. An example of this is The Post Office Group's Give at the Till event which launched the charity partnership with Teenage Cancer Trust and raised over £9,000.

Employee-led support

Colleague volunteering programme

Each colleague is entitled to up to three days a year to volunteer within their normal working hours. During 2013/14 more than 44,000 volunteer hours have been given. According to the website, 62% of all colleagues take part in the scheme participating in activities, such as painting a church hall, supporting employability events or one-to-one mentoring for young people from the Prince's Trust.

Colleagues' fundraising efforts generated over £273,000 to the charity partner Teenage Cancer Trust.

Note that the society's website states:

> From February 2014 the society's definition of volunteering will be changing. All society led volunteering will be defined as a colleague leaving their normal place of work or site to volunteer. This means that time spent fundraising in site will no longer be recorded as volunteering hours.

The society's members decide what percentage of the profits are returned to the members and to the local community and can also instruct to pay either 50% or 100% of their share of the profit to their your named charity/ies chosen from a published list.

Commercially led support

Work experience

Work experience and work placements are offered to young people and adults returning to the workplace across the society's businesses and trading area.

Information given in the CSR report for 2014 states:

> We have supported students at Swindon New College and Walsall College with employability and business studies, and will continue to develop this relationship through work experience opportunities.

Freshers' Fairs have been supported in 2014 at Oxford Brookes, Gloucester and Wolverhampton universities. Work is undertaken to co-operate with a number of other educational establishments:

> Including creating a programme of activity to support both the schools' ambitions and a programme of consistent support, such as fair trade workshops, work experience placements for 10 students from each school (70 in total), employability support to year nine and 10 students and DOES values workshops for staff and students.

Corporate social responsibility

CSR committee: The Social Responsibility Manager is Peter Westall. Separate members of the Executive and Board of Directors have named responsibilities with regards to CSR. The Co-operative Social Responsibility team helps to drive the CSR objectives and works together with colleagues to deliver the CSR agenda across the businesses.

CSR information: Information taken from the CSR report for 2014 states:

> At its heart a true co-operative organisation is socially responsible and effectively engaged with the communities it serves. Co-operatives have been operating for the good of their members, colleagues, communities and the environment since they came into being. It's just the way we do things. Social Responsibility is one of our four key DOES values and is central to everything we do as a society.
>
> *The values that shape our society*
>
> - Ensuring the views of our members are reflected in the way the Society is run
> - Being open, honest and fair in our dealings with everyone we come into contact with
> - Recognising the contribution that everyone can make to the development of the Society
> - Reflecting our responsibilities to the wider community in the way we conduct our business

The Midcounties Co-operative has a number of CSR goals grouped under four headings:

- Defending the environment
- Supporting our communities
- Developing young people
- Developing links with co-operatives across the world

The website states:

> At The Midcounties Co-operative we place a great importance on supporting the communities we serve, because it's something that matters to our members, our customers and our colleagues. Concern for the community is one of the co-operative principles on which we base our business and we look to give something back to our communities in a number of ways.
>
> From volunteering at schools and local charities to fundraising for our charity partner, and donating a share of our profits back to organisations that need our support, there are so many ways we are engaging with the people we serve.

CSR report: Published annually and available from the website.

Exclusions

Applications from outside the operating area of the Midcounties Co-operative Society, i.e. Oxfordshire, Gloucestershire, Buckinghamshire, Shropshire, Staffordshire, the West Midlands, Wiltshire and Worcestershire, and parts of surrounding counties.

Midcounties Co-operative is also unable to help with funding for individuals, businesses and funding for overseas projects.

Applications

Application forms for the Co-operative Community Funding, charity collection/ bag pack opportunities and awareness days in stores can be found online on the society's website. It is asked that applicants read the funding criteria to make sure they meet it. Further questions regarding the Community Funding can also be directed at: 01902 405700 or communityfund@ midcounties.coop.

The website also notes: 'If you need to email us about a query unrelated to our community programmes please contact our Customer Contact Centre by emailing: talktous@midcounties.coop.'

Miller Group Ltd

Building/construction, property

Correspondent: The Company Secretary, Miller House, 2 Lochside View, Edinburgh Park, Edinburgh EH12 9DH (tel: 0870 336 5000; website: www.miller.co.uk/cr.aspx)

Directors: Philip Bowman, Chair; Keith M. Miller, Group Chief Executive; Richard Hodsden, Group Finance Director; Michael Whitman; Tripp Smith; Michael Carruthers; Gordon Moore (women: 0; men: 7)

Year end	31/12/2013
Turnover	£817,300,000
Pre-tax profit	£10,400,000

Nature of business: Property business specialising in house building and commercial property.

Company registration number: SC018135

Subsidiary undertakings include: Miller Homes Holdings (UK) Ltd; Miller Homes Ltd; Miller Developments Holdings Ltd; Miller Holdings International Ltd; Miller Developments Ltd; Miller Corporate Holdings Ltd; Miller Construction (UK) Ltd.

Main locations: Glasgow

Total employees: 1,306

Focus of giving: Health, ill health, arts, culture, children, young people, community/social welfare.

Membership: BITC

Charity of the Year	✓
Gifts in kind	✓
Market-led giving	✓
Matched funding	✓
Sponsorship	✓

Charitable donations

Cash UK (latest available):	2013	£114,000
	2012	£84,000
	2011	£115,000
	2009	£88,000
	2007	£177,000
Total UK (cash and in kind):	2013	£114,000
Cash worldwide:	2013	£114,000
Total worldwide (cash and in kind):	2013	£114,000

Community involvement

The Miller Group has a charitable giving and sponsorship strategy that has lead charities supported directly by the business, employee nominated charities and a matched giving scheme. Through its charitable giving, the group looks to support: 'personal development for young people; to provide financial support for chosen health-based charities; and provide support for community-based organisations'. Through sponsorship, the group has the aim of supporting the arts, community-based organisations and sports.

Corporate giving

In 2013 the group made charitable donations of £114,000.

Costings for the in-kind donations given by the group were not included in this total.

During 2013 the group and its employees each nominated three charities to support:

2013 company nominated: Place2Be; Project Dream – Royal Lyceum Theatre; St Columba's Hospice.

2013 employee nominated: Camphill Communities; Royal Blind; UpRising.

In-kind support

The group shares 'time, knowledge and expertise' to the benefit of its chosen beneficiary organisations.

Employee-led support

Employee fundraising

Fundraising activities during the year included an abseil down the Forth Rail Bridge by Miller graduates in aid of the group's chosen charity, Place2Be.

Matched giving

A matched giving scheme is offered by the group to complement employee fundraising.

Commercially led support

Sponsorship

Though the Miller Group sponsors some larger organisations (in 2014, for example, its sponsorship includes National Museum of Scotland, Royal Zoological Society of Scotland, RSNO and SCO) its subsidiary companies have also given sponsorship on a more local basis. Examples include Miller Homes, which sponsors Currie Star, a community football club based in Edinburgh, with its kit, and Miller Construction, which sponsored Christmas lights at Newcastle Central Station.

Corporate social responsibility

CSR committee: The board is responsible for considering CR initiatives and strategy across the group.

CSR information: The following information is taken from the 2013 annual report and accounts.

> Our CR approach continues to be embedded across the business. During 2013, we achieved Silver accreditation in the Business in the Community CR Index.
>
> Our businesses do not exist in isolation and we understand that when we work in a location we have an opportunity or, as we see it, an obligation to be a good neighbour. We do this by both minimising our impact and by providing new opportunities for the local region.
>
> At a national level, we form strategic partnerships with charities giving not only financial support but sharing our time, knowledge and expertise to the benefit of both organisations.

CSR report: A CSR report is contained within the annual report and accounts.

Applications

In writing to the correspondent referenced 'Charitable donations'.

Mitchells & Butlers plc

Retail – restaurants/fast food

Correspondent: Sally Ellson, External Communications Manager, 27 Fleet Street, Birmingham B3 1JP (tel: 01214 984000; fax: 01212 332246; website: www.mbplc.com/responsibility)

Directors: Bob Ivell, Chair; Alistair Darby, Chief Executive; Tim Jones, Finance Director; Stewart Gilliland; Eddie Irwin; Douglas McMahon; Ron Robson; Colin Rutherford; Imelda Walsh (women: 1; men: 8)

Year end	28/09/2013
Turnover	£1,895,000,000
Pre-tax profit	£150,000,000

Nature of business: Operator of managed pubs and pub restaurants.

Company registration number: 4551498

Subsidiary undertakings include: Mitchells & Butlers Retail Ltd; Mitchells & Butlers Retail (No. 2) Ltd; Mitchells & Butlers (Property) Ltd; Mitchells & Butlers Leisure Retail Ltd; Mitchells & Butlers Finance plc; Mitchells & Butlers Germany GmbH.

Brands include: All Bar One, Browns, Crown Carveries, Harvester, Sizzling Pubs, Toby Carvery

Main locations: Birmingham

Total employees: 41,325

Focus of giving: General charitable purposes, education, health, ill health, local groups, children, young people, community/social welfare.

Charity of the Year	✓
Gifts in kind	✓
Market-led giving	✓

Charitable donations

Cash UK (latest available):	2013	£59,000
	2011	£65,000
	2009	£215,000
	2007	£215,000
	2006	£200,000
Total UK (cash and in kind):	2013	£59,000
Cash worldwide:	2013	£59,000
Total worldwide (cash and in kind):	2013	£59,000

Community involvement

Mitchells & Butlers looks to contribute to the local communities in which it operates, in the main, by supporting its employees in their fundraising for charities and good causes. The group and its brands have also supported charities through various initiatives including the sale of charity products, the organising of fundraising events, and through working in partnership with national charities, which in recent years have included the Prince's Trust and Marie Curie Cancer Care.

Corporate giving

In 2012/13 the group donated at least £59,000 to charitable causes. Aside from a donation of £15,000 to Prince's Trust, contributions were also made in the following ways:

Employee donations

Any Mitchells & Butlers employee can apply for a donation towards a charity event they are taking part in or organising. Through this scheme, £25,000 was donated by the group during the year.

Beneficiaries included: Air Ambulance; Birmingham Children's Hospital; Cancer Research UK

Good Cause Fund

Retail employees can apply for a donation towards a community or charity event they are taking part in. During the year, the group donated £19,000 to a number of local charities and groups.

Costings for the in-kind donations contributed by the group were not given.

Charity partner

Prince's Trust

Through its establishments, the group also lent support to The Marie Curie Daffodil Appeal, which helped to raise £26,000, and the Royal British Legion's Poppy Appeal.

In-kind support

As part of Armed Forces Day, Crown Carveries offered armed forces personnel and veterans a free breakfast or carvery meal and 6,967 meals were donated.

Fundraising events

During the year, O'Neills hosted a 'Join the Jig' fundraising event across the country, helping to raise more than £59,000 for a range of causes.

Employee-led support

Employee fundraising

Employees are supported in their various fundraising activities by the group through its employee donations programme and the Good Cause Fund. They have also helped to raise funds for the group's partner charity, Prince's Trust, through its Million Makers fundraising initiative. A team of Mitchells & Butlers employees, calling themselves 'Team Pride', helped to raise £75,000 through a variety of activities. Another team of employees helped to raise more than £6,000 for Birmingham Children's Hospital, Help for Heroes and LATCH, by completing the Tough Mudder 2013, a 12-mile long obstacle course.

For more details of fundraising efforts by the group's employees, see the 2013 Social Responsibility Report.

Commercially led support

Market-led giving

Harvester continued its support of Make a Wish and, along with fundraising activities, donated 10p from the sale of every charity sundae, raising £65,000.

Corporate social responsibility

CSR committee: We found no evidence of there being a CSR committee.

CSR information: The following statement is taken from the 2013 Social Responsibility Review: 'We take a simple approach to social responsibility which, for us, is all about how our business practices impact on: our people; our guests; the communities in which we operate; and the environment.'

CSR report: A Social Responsibility Review is published annually and is available to download from the website.

Exclusions

Our research tells us that the company will not support advertising space, political causes, sporting events, and religious appeals.

Applications

In writing to the correspondent.

MITIE Group plc

Business services

Correspondent: Sustainability Steering Group, 1 Harlequin Office Park, Fieldfare, Emersons Green, City of Bristol BS16 7FN (tel: 01179 708800; website: www.mitie.com/sustainability)

Directors: Roger Matthews, Chair; David Jenkins; Larry Hirst; Crawford Gillies; Jack Boyer; Ruby McGregor-Smith, Chief Executive; Suzanne Baxter, Group Finance Director; Bill Robson (women: 2; men: 6)

Year end	31/03/2014
Turnover	£2,221,100,000
Pre-tax profit	£68,400,000

Nature of business: The company provides facilities, property and asset management for public and private sector businesses.

Company registration number: SC 19230

Subsidiary undertakings include: Mitie Facilities Services Ltd; Mitie Cleaning and Environmental Services Ltd; Mitie Security Holdings Ltd; Mitie Technical Facilities Management Ltd; Mitie Property Services (UK) Ltd; Utilyx Ltd.

Total employees: 72,248

Focus of giving: Education, enterprise/training, health, ill health, children, young people.

Membership: BITC

Gifts in kind ✓

Charitable donations

Cash UK (latest available):	2014	£441,000
	2013	£154,000
	2012	£161,000
	2011	£191,000
	2010	£110,500
Total UK (cash and in kind):	2014	£834,000
Cash worldwide:	2014	£441,000
Total worldwide (cash and in kind):	2014	£834,000

Community involvement

Mitie Group supports charities and communities through donations, gifts in kind and employee volunteering time. The majority of the group's charitable involvement is through **The Mitie Foundation** (Charity Commission no. 1148858), which looks to 'create opportunities for people of all backgrounds to join the world of work'. However, the foundation informed us further that, 'whilst we are registered as a grant-maker, amongst other things, this will not be the primary activity of the charity and in fact it is unlikely to be making any grants in the foreseeable future'. The group is also active in the communities where it has social housing, conducting career activities in schools, work experience opportunities for young people, and social activities for residents.

Though a definitive list of beneficiaries was not given, we know that individuals, schools and further education colleges across the UK have benefitted from the group's contributions.

Corporate giving

In 2013/14 the group gave a total of £834,000 in charitable and community contributions, of which £441,000 was given in cash donations to charities. A considerable portion of this cash total was given to The Mitie Foundation.

Amongst its non-cash contributions, the group also gave gifts in kind worth £13,700 and contributed employee time, which was costed at £310,000.

In-kind support

In 2013/14 the group gave gifts in kind in the form of materials to its seven skills centres across the country. A total of 1,443 employee volunteering days were also contributed. The following information was stated on the website: 'Mitie's volunteering programme has been aligned with the foundation's focus areas and so the majority of employee volunteering now takes place within schools and FE colleges throughout the UK.'

Commercially led support

During the year, the social housing team gave career talks in local schools and work experience opportunities were provided for young talent in the area.

Corporate social responsibility

CSR committee: The group's website states that the Sustainability Steering Group is 'responsible for the development of Mitie's Sustainability policy, strategy and goals, as well as identifying, controlling and monitoring risks and opportunities associated with sustainability trends'.

CSR information: The following information is taken from the 2013/14 Sustainability Report:

> *Our sustainability targets for 2020*
> Last year we set ourselves aspirational targets to be achieved by 2020, supported by short-term milestones. Members of our Sustainability Steering Group are responsible for tracking progress on these targets and managing the milestones in their respective departments and operational businesses.

One of the targets set by the group is to 'dedicate 1% pre-tax profit to community investment, through the Mitie Foundation activities' by 2020.

CSR report: There is a sustainability review contained within the annual report and accounts, which is available to download separately from the informative 'Sustainability' section of the group's website.

Applications

It would appear that the group is increasingly making its charitable contributions through its foundation, **The Mitie Foundation**, which does not accept any unsolicited applications, but instead actively seeks 'like-minded' organisations. For more details on the foundation, its work and partner organisations, see the webpage (www.mitie.com/sustainability/the-mitie-foundation).

Mondelez UK Ltd (formerly Kraft Foods UK Ltd)

Food manufacture

Correspondent: Louise Ayling, Foundation Secretariat, Uxbridge Business Park, Sanderson Road, Uxbridge, Middlesex UB8 1DH (email: louise.ayling@mdlz.com; website: www.kraftfoods.co.uk)

Directors: A. Jennings; L. Stigant; J. Pipe; M. Brusadelli; M. Taylor; P. Greenhalgh; R. Hughes (women: 3; men: 9)

Year end	31/12/2013
Turnover	£1,832,722,000
Pre-tax profit	£51,204,000

Nature of business: The principal activity of the company is the manufacture of chocolate, chewing gum, sweets, coffee, cheese, biscuits and other food.

The annual report and accounts state:

> At 31 December 2013 the immediate parent company was Kraft Foods Schweiz GmbH, a company incorporated in Switzerland.
>
> At 31 December 2013 the company's ultimate parent company and controlling party was Mondelez International Inc., incorporated in the United States of America.

Company registration number: 203663

Subsidiary undertakings include: Kraft Foods UK Intellectual Property Ltd; Mondelez UK Biscuit Financing Ltd; Mondelez UK Production Ltd; Mondelez UK R&D Ltd

Brands include: Cadbury Dairy Milk, Kenco, Oreo

Main locations: Cheltenham, Banbury

UK employees: 868

Total employees: 868

Focus of giving: Education, environment, health, ill health, sport, recreation, children, young people, community/social welfare.

Cash donations undeclared ✓
Gifts in kind ✓
Matched funding ✓
Sponsorship ✓

Charitable donations

Cash UK (latest available):	2010	£750,000
	2008	£99,000
	2007	£94,000
	2006	£191,000
	2005	£97,500
Total UK (cash and in kind):	2013	£2,500,000

Community involvement

Mondelez supports the communities in which its sites are based through cash and in-kind contributions, and employee time. It also runs a number of programmes to target key social issues in these areas and is affiliated with the **Cadbury Foundation** (Charity Commission no. 1050482), which 'contributes to communities near the company's operations so that where possible donations can be backed up with employee volunteering work and gifts in kind'. The focus of grants falls on skills development; Olympic and Paralympic legacy; source projects; and 'employee passions'.

Corporate giving

We have taken our information from the website of Mondelez International, the ultimate parent company of Mondelez UK Ltd, which states: 'We invest more than £2.5 million each year in our UK and Ireland communities through cash, gifts in kind and employee time.' As we could not determine a breakdown between contributions in the UK and Ireland, we have taken the total of both.

See the corporate charity entry on p. 397 for more information.

In-kind support

Pro bono
Employees are supported in contributing their time and skills to charities local to Mondelez sites.

Employee-led support

Employee fundraising
The website states that employees have taken part in activities such as silent discos and skydives to raise funds for their favourite charities.

Matched funding
The company operates a 'cashmatch' programme.

Employee volunteering
Employees are able to volunteer with local charities and also play a part in supporting community programmes supported by Mondelez. An example of this is Health for Life, which is a five-year programme in south Birmingham, funded by the Mondelez International Foundation, with the aim of promoting healthy lifestyles for students in primary and secondary schools and to the wider community. The programme is delivered in conjunction with Life Education West Midlands and The Conservation Volunteers, and Mondelez International employees are regularly involved with its activities.

Commercially led support

Sponsorship
In the UK, Mondelez sponsors The British Paralympic Association in a commercial partnership that will run until March 2017.

Taste of Work
This is a community investment programme which operates in primary and secondary schools, as well as further education establishments. Employees of Mondelez share their business skills through the programme, which aims to support young people and disadvantaged adults who are at risk of becoming NEET (not in employment, education or training). The website states: 'The aim of the programme is to raise awareness and inspire young people about the food and drink industry and the career opportunities within our business.'

Corporate social responsibility

CSR committee: We found no evidence of there being a CSR committee.

CSR information: We were unable to determine the ratio of women to men on the board.

CSR report: We found no CSR report; however, there is a section on the website dedicated to Mondelez 'in the community'.

Corporate charity: The Cadbury Foundation (Charity Commission no. 1050482).

Applications

The Mondelez International website states of the Cadbury Foundation: 'Our approach is to actively seek out projects to support, which unfortunately means we cannot accept any unsolicited requests for funding.'

Moneysupermarket.com Group plc

Miscellaneous

Correspondent: Community Team, Moneysupermarket House, St David's Park, Ewloe, Chester CH5 3UZ (tel: 01244 665700; website: corporate.moneysupermarket.com/company/csr.aspx)

Directors: Bruce Carnegie-Brown, Chair; Peter Plumb, Chief Executive Officer; Simon Nixon; Matthew Price, Chief Financial Officer; Graham Donoghue; Michael Wemms; Rob Rowley; Sally James; Robin Klein; Andrew Fisher; Genevieve Shore; Darren Drabble (women: 2; men: 10)

Year end	31/12/2013
Turnover	£225,553,000
Pre-tax profit	£43,075,000

Nature of business: Price comparison websites.

Company registration number: 6160943

Subsidiary undertakings include: Moneysupermarket.com Financial Group Ltd; Moneysupermarket.com Ltd; MoneySavingExpert.com Ltd; Travelsupermarket.com Ltd; Insuresupermarket.com Ltd; Mortgage 2000 Ltd.

UK employees: 523

Total employees: 523

Focus of giving: General appeals, health, ill health, poverty and social exclusion, children, young people, community/social welfare, disability.

Cash donations undeclared ✓
Charity of the Year ✓
Gifts in kind ✓
Matched funding ✓

Charitable donations

Cash UK (latest available):	2013	£51,000
	2012	£37,000
	2011	£37,500
	2010	£30,000
	2009	£33,000
Total UK (cash and in kind):	2013	£51,000
Cash worldwide:	2013	£51,000
Total worldwide (cash and in kind):	2013	£51,000

Community involvement

Moneysupermarket.com plc and its employees supported more than 40 charities and community groups during 2013 through the.Community initiative and a staff volunteering scheme. The group and its employees also select a Charity of the Year to support on an annual basis.

Corporate giving

During 2013, the group made £2,000 available each month for its.Community initiative, which was 'channelled via the Charities Aid Foundation, enabling the group to make gross donations to registered charities'. A further £27,000 was donated by the group to its Charity of the Year, Mind. We, therefore, believe that the group made charitable donations totalling £51,000 during the year.

Costings for the in-kind donations given by the group were not included in the report.

Beneficiaries included: Bagillt Playgroup; Claire House; Daffodils Kingsley Cricket Club; Flintshire Citizens Advice; Royal British Legion

In-kind support

The group gives a total of 60 days a year through its staff volunteering scheme.

Employee-led support

Moneysupermarket.com employees play an active role in researching and finding local charitable causes for the group to help support. Each month, a volunteer group of employees meets to discuss requests for donations and to allocate funds in line with agreed guidelines.

Employee fundraising

During the year, employees helped to raise £27,000 for the group's Charity of the Year, Mind, and also took part in fundraising activities such as: answering telephones for Comic Relief; a sponsored bike ride; and a sponsored Three Peaks Challenge.

Charity of the Year

2013: Mind, which supports people affected by mental health problems, benefitted from corporate donations and employee fundraising worth a total of £54,000.

Corporate social responsibility

CSR committee: There was no evidence of a specific CSR committee.

CSR information: The following statement is taken from the company's annual report and accounts:

> The group's.Community initiative was launched in 2008 and has continued to develop during 2013. The initiative is focused on providing support to charities and community groups located within a few miles of the group's offices in Ewloe, so support is targeted primarily in Flintshire and Cheshire.

CSR report: The CSR report is contained within the annual report and is also available to download from the group's website.

Applications

In writing to the correspondent.

Morgan Advanced Materials plc

Manufacturing

Correspondent: Paul Bolton, Company Secretary and General Counsel, Quadrant, 55–57 High Street, Windsor, Berkshire SL4 1LP (tel: 01753 837000; fax: 01753 850872; email: company.secretariat@morganplc.com; website: www.morgancrucible.com)

Directors: Andrew Shilston, Chair; Mark Robertshaw, Chief Executive Officer; Kevin Dangerfield, Chief Financial Officer; Andrew Hosty; Douglas Caster; Andrew Given; Victoire de Margerie; Andrew Reynolds Smith; Rob Rowley; Peter Blausten; Simon Halliday; Keith Parker; Andrew Riley (women: 1; men: 12)

Year end	31/12/2013
Turnover	£957,800,000
Pre-tax profit	£64,000,000

Nature of business: The group is an international provider of materials and products for its target niches, including aerospace, defence and protection, power generation, medical, petrochemical and iron and steel markets.

Company registration number: 286773

Subsidiary undertakings include: Morgan Advanced Materials Canada Inc.; Morganite Crucible Inc.; Morgan Korea Company Ltd; NP Aerospace Ltd; Thermal Ceramics UK Ltd; and Wesgo Ceramics GmbH. A full list of subsidiary undertakings can be found within the group's accounts.

Total employees: 9,572

Focus of giving: Health, ill health, medical research, arts, culture, children, young people, community/social welfare, disability.

Gifts in kind ✓

Charitable donations

Cash UK (latest available):	2013	£125,000
	2011	£195,000
	2009	£90,000
	2008	£90,000
	2007	£87,000
Total UK (cash and in kind):	2013	£125,000
Cash worldwide:	2013	£125,000
Total worldwide (cash and in kind):	2013	£125,000

Community involvement

According to the group's website, 'the implementation of community-related policies and procedures is aligned with the management of the overall business and is focused at site level on engagement and initiatives which are relevant to the local community and to [the group's] business'. It has been stated that the group's focus is on supporting disadvantaged young people and helping local community projects which can also engage and involve employees.

We could not locate any specific examples in the annual report and accounts for 2013; however, past initiatives supported by the group have included: support to the Army Cadet Force Association (ACFA) Outreach Project (£60,000 over three-years); continued support to the joint Barnardo's/Outward Bound initiative which provides opportunities for young people to develop life skills at a centre in Ullswater; and helping British Heart Foundation and a number of sports and health-related charities and appeals.

Corporate giving

In 2013 a total of £125,000 (2012: £178,000) was given in charitable donations. We could not determine the distribution between the UK and the rest of the world nor the projects which have been supported – the correspondent informed us that this information is not available to third parties; based on the figures from the three previous years known to us, we estimate that this entire sum was given in cash in the UK.

In-kind support

Employee time and skills may be available.

Employee-led support

Our research suggests that the group employees donated their time and provide further funds to good causes.

Corporate social responsibility

CSR committee: There was no evidence of a separate CSR Committee. The board is ultimately responsible for CSR matters and receives regular reports on the group's performance.

CSR information: The group's annual report states:

> Corporate responsibility is integral to the Morgan Group; it means a commitment to behaving with integrity and having a positive impact on its employees, its stakeholders and the communities in which the group works.

The CSR strategy seeks to address: Human Rights issues; Environment and Health and Safety; Customers and Suppliers; and Community Engagement areas.

The group's website notes:

> Our practice is to engage with local communities in relation to matters of mutual interest and concern. . . .' 'We strive to be a valued member of the communities in which we have operations; to respect local culture and to be sensitive to local issues and aware of wider community and governmental issues.

CSR report: A CSR report is available within the group's annual report.

Exclusions

Support is not generally given for animal welfare causes, appeals from individuals, overseas projects, religious appeals, science/technology or sports. The group's policy is not to make 'donations to any political party, representative or candidate in any part of the world'.

Applications

In writing to the correspondent. Grant decisions are made by a donations committee which normally meets quarterly.

The group welcomes feedback on the community-related policies, systems, performance, reports and communications via email or post.

Morgan Stanley International Ltd

Financial services

Correspondent: Anish Shah, Morgan Stanley International Foundation, 20 Bank Street, London E14 4AD (tel: 020 7425 1302; email: communityaffairslondon@morganstanley.com; website: www.morganstanley.com/globalcitizen/community_affairs.html)

Directors: D. O. Cannon; E. J. W. Gieve; M. C. Phibbs; I. Plenderleith, Chair; R. P. Rooney; D. A. Russell; C. E. Woodman; T. C. Kelleher; Christopher Castello; Lee Guy

Year end	31/12/2013
Turnover	£3,647,000,000
Pre-tax profit	£203,000,000

Nature of business: The group's principal activity is the provision of financial services to corporations, governments and financial institutions.

Company registration number: 3584019

Subsidiary undertakings include: Morgan Stanley and Co. International plc; Morgan Stanley and Co. Ltd; Morgan Stanley Bank International Ltd; Morgan Stanley Group (Europe); Morgan Stanley Investment Management Ltd; Morgan Stanley Securities Ltd

Main locations: London

Total employees: 5,280

Focus of giving: Education, enterprise/training, health, ill health, housing, homelessness, medical research, arts, culture, children, young people, community/social welfare, disability.

Membership: BITC

Gifts in kind	✓
Matched funding	✓
Sponsorship	✓

Charitable donations

Cash UK (latest available):	2013	£900,000
	2011	£990,000
	2008	£3,300,000
	2007	£5,603,000
	2005	£2,610,000
Total UK (cash and in kind):	2013	£900,000
Cash worldwide:	2013	£1,850,000
Total worldwide (cash and in kind):	2013	£1,850,000

Community involvement

Morgan Stanley supports organisations in regions where it has a presence through the **Morgan Stanley International Foundation** (Charity Commission no. 1042671). This includes the boroughs of Tower Hamlets and Newham in London, Glasgow, as well as continental Europe, the Middle East and Africa. Grants are made to organisations focusing on children's health and education.

Morgan Stanley employees take an active role in their communities through volunteering and fundraising, and there are a number of schemes in place to support their efforts. Employees also nominate the Charity of the Year, which benefits from fundraising activities.

Corporate giving

The annual report and accounts for 2013 state that subsidiaries of the company made donations to various charities totalling $2.8 million (£1.85 million) of which $1.4 million was donated to the **Morgan Stanley International Foundation**, a charity registered in the UK. The foundation's accounts for 2013 state that it received a donation of £900,000 from Morgan Stanley and Co. International plc, a subsidiary company. We have taken this as our figure for UK cash contributions in 2013.

We were unable to determine a value for the in-kind support given by the company.

Beneficiaries included: Prince's Trust (£802,000); Kids Company (£116,000); Great Ormond Street Hospital (£78,000); Community Links and East End Community Foundation (£52,000 each); Action For Children (£40,000); UK Career Academy Foundation (£32,000); Pilotlight (£28,000); Tower Hamlets Summer University (£25,000); Gyermeketkeztetesi Alapitvany (£24,000); Tower Hamlets Education Business Partnership (£20,000); Reliable Cancer Therapies (£14,000); Movember Europe (£12,700); Envision (£10,000); Refuge (£4,000); and the Kiltwalk and Wildhearts (£2,500 each).

Charity of the Year

From February 2011 to 2013 Kids Company was the nominated Charity of the Year, with employees and the foundation raising more than £1.6 million (£115,000 of this was raised in 2013).

The Prince's Trust was nominated as Charity of the Year beginning in February 2013. Employees and the foundation are aiming to raise £500,000 over the course of the two year partnership.

See the corporate charity entry on p. 419 for more information.

In-kind support

Pro bono

Morgan Stanley's Global Volunteer Month: A worldwide service initiative that encourages employees to give back to their communities. Held each June, the campaign engages employees in teams and individually on local service projects, serving as a springboard for year-round volunteer engagement. The global website states the following: 'Annually, this effort involves more than 20,000 employees who contribute nearly 200,000 hours of volunteer work in more than 500 cities in 24 countries.'

Strategy Challenge: Through the annual challenge Morgan Stanley creates teams of high-performing employees who for eight weeks work with a non-profit organisation to help solve an important strategic issue for the organisation.

Employee-led support

The website states the following: 'Engagement in the community is a fundamental part of working at Morgan Stanley.' Aside from nominating the Charity of the Year, employees are also involved in the following ways:

Employee fundraising

Employees are encouraged to fundraise for charitable causes including their country Charity of the Year.

Employee volunteering

Employees are encouraged to volunteer in their communities and Morgan Stanley provides a number of incentives (see below).

Matched funding

Morgan Stanley's foundation matches funds raised by employees up to £500 each.

Volunteer Incentive Program (VIP)

Through the programme, Morgan Stanley's foundations offer grants up to £500 to organisations where its employees are volunteers.

Commercially led support

Sponsorships

The following information is taken from the global website:

> Morgan Stanley supports cultural institutions and events that enrich the lives of our communities. Wherever our people live and work around the world, we seek partners and opportunities that reflect our standards of excellence and complement the growth of our business.

Corporate social responsibility

CSR committee: There is a Community Affairs department in the London branch.

CSR information: The following information is taken from the global Morgan Stanley website: 'Morgan Stanley is dedicated to making a positive contribution to society through our focus on the environment, our communities, responsible business practices, strengthening the next generation of citizens, and our people.'

We were unable to determine the ratio of women to men on the board.

CSR report: There is a section dedicated to global citizenship on the Morgan Stanley global website. There is also a sustainability report available to download, though this contains little information on UK-specific CSR activities.

Corporate charity: Morgan Stanley International Foundation (Charity Commission no. 1042671).

Exclusions

The website states that:

> MSI foundation does not make contributions to organisations that fall within the following criteria:
>
> - Organisations which are not registered as a non-profit organisation with the appropriate regulatory agencies in their country (unless a state funded school)
> - National or international charities which do not operate in the regions we are located
> - Political or religious organisations, 'pressure groups' or individuals outside the firm who are seeking sponsorship either for themselves (e.g. to help pay for education) or for onward transmission to a charitable organisation
> - Programmes that do not include opportunities for employee volunteer engagement

Applications

Note the following from the website: 'Morgan Stanley International Foundation takes a proactive approach to grant making and therefore does not accept unsolicited proposals.' However, if you feel your organisation meets the criteria, send an email to correspondent to obtain guidelines. For more information on criteria, visit the website: www.morganstanley.com/globalcitizen/msif_guidelines.html.

T. J. Morris Ltd

Retail – department and variety stores

Correspondent: G. P. McLoughlin, Company Secretary, Axis Business Park, East Lancs Road, Gillmoss, Liverpool L11 0JA (tel: 01515 302920; website: www.homebargains.co.uk)

Directors: T. J. Morris; J. Morris (women: 0; men: 2)

Year end	30/06/2014
Turnover	£1,277,323,810
Pre-tax profit	£124,759,662

Nature of business: The principal activity of the company is wholesale distribution and retailing of toiletries, cosmetics and other household products.

The ultimate controlling party of the company is T. J. Morris which is the majority shareholder.

Company registration number: 1505036

Subsidiary undertakings include: Barbco 1330 limited; and Axis Business Park Liverpool Management Company limited

Brands include: Home Bargains

UK employees: 11,098

Total employees: 11,098

Focus of giving: Education, enterprise/training, health, ill health, arts, culture, sponsorship, children, young people, community/social welfare.

Market-led giving	✓
Sponsorship	✓

Charitable donations

Cash UK (latest available):	2014	£223,000
	2013	£155,000
	2011	£113,300
	2009	£350,483
	2008	£33,846
Total UK (cash and in kind):	2014	£223,000
Cash worldwide:	2014	£223,000
Total worldwide (cash and in kind):	2014	£223,000

Community involvement

The company's website provides some examples of projects supported in the past. These include:

Young Enterprise

The company is involved in assisting Young Enterprise programme in schools and universities across the North West and supported the running, preparation and coordination of 2014's North West Start Up Programme Final.

Alder Hey Children's Hospital

For the past six years the charity's Christmas cards have been sold in Home Bargains stores. An annual competition is organised for primary school children to submit their designs for the cards – all profit from the sales goes to the children's hospital and the winner of the competition receives a £50 Home Bargains voucher for their school.

Charity partnership

There is a ten year commitment with the National Society for the Prevention of Cruelty to Children (NSPCC). The company is supporting the annual NSPCC's Christmas 'Carols by Candlelight' concert, held in the Anglican Cathedral in Liverpool. In 2013 over £25,000 was raised for the society through the sale of Christmas cards.

Corporate giving

In 2013/14 charitable donations totalled almost £223,000 (2012/13: 155,000). We were unable to identify specific beneficiaries within the annual report and accounts but some examples of projects assisted are given on the company's website. See 'Community involvement' section in this entry for more details.

Recent beneficiaries included: Alzheimer's Society; Cystic Fibrosis; Knutsford Heritage Centre; Lord Mayors Appeal – Futures for kids worldwide; Macmillan Nurses; Marina Dalglish Appeal for cancer treatment; Merseyside Children's Holiday fund; St Andrew's Hospice; The Sheffield Children's Hospital Charity; and Variety Children's Charity.

Commercially led support

Sponsorship

Business on the move

The company sponsored this educational board game designed to introduce young people to business and the UK's supply chain. Home Bargains features in the game amongst other sponsors.

Tranmere Rovers sponsorship

Home Bargains will be the new shirt sponsor for Tranmere Rovers FC from next season onwards.

Corporate social responsibility

CSR committee: No indications of a CSR committee found.

CSR information: No specific CSR details found.

CSR report: None published. The website has details of the group's community involvement.

Exclusions

No support is given for political appeals.

Applications

In writing to the correspondent.

Wm Morrison Supermarkets plc

Retail – supermarkets

Correspondent: The Corporate Compliance and Responsibility Comm., Hillmore House, Gain Lane, Bradford BD3 7DL (tel: 0845 611 5000; website: www.morrisons.co.uk)

Directors: Ian Gibson, Chair; Dalton Philips, Chief Executive Officer; Richard Gillingwater; Philip Cox; Penny Hughes; Johanna Waterous; Trevor Strain, Chief Financial Officer (women: 2; men: 5)

Year end	02/02/2014
Turnover	£17,680,000,000
Pre-tax profit	(£176,000,000)

Nature of business: Manufacture and retail distribution of goods through nationwide network of supermarkets.

Company registration number: 358949

Subsidiary undertakings include: Farmers Boy Ltd; Kiddicare Ltd; Neerock Ltd; Optimisation Developments Ltd; Safeway Ltd; and Wm Morrison Produce Ltd. **Subsidiaries of other group companies include**: Safeway Stores Ltd. A full list of subsidiary undertakings of the group can be obtained from Companies House.

Main locations: Bradford

UK employees: 62,988

Total employees: 62,988

Focus of giving: Education, environment, health, ill health, housing, homelessness, non-registered charities, local groups, poverty and social exclusion, sponsorship, children, young people, community/social welfare.

Membership: BITC

Cash donations undeclared	✓
Charity of the Year	✓
FTSE 100	✓
Gifts in kind	✓
Market-led giving	✓
Sponsorship	✓

Charitable donations

Cash UK (latest available):	2014	£100,000
	2012	£100,000
	2009	£100,000
	2008	£100,000
	2007	£300,000
Total UK (cash and in kind):	2014	£100,000
Cash worldwide:	2014	£100,000
Total worldwide (cash and in kind):	2014	£100,000

Community involvement

Charity partnership – Raise a Smile

A new partnership has been established with Sue Ryder, as chosen by the staff. Funds raised by customers and employees will be used to help the charity to provide new community healthcare services, as well as offer online and personal support. Previous partner – Save the Children – received £7.1 million (since 2010) for its Eat Sleep Learn Play! and Families and Schools Together campaigns. The Morrisons' website reminds that the group is 'not currently looking for further sponsorship opportunities'.

Community champions

In 2013/14 the scheme had 478 people acting as community champions. They act as ambassadors linking each store with its local community and manage and build the relationships with local food banks. Each is provided with a development toolkit and allocated eight hours per week to engage with local charities, schools, organisations and community groups.

Community Shop

During 2013 Morrisons supported the UK's first social supermarket – Community Shop (a subsidiary of Company Shop), which allows people living in a specific postcode area and in receipt of welfare support, to access heavily discounted food and receive debt advice, cookery skills, home budgeting and CV writing advice. The group gives surplus products from its food online service to the Community Shop. Since the launch of the project around 1,000 products per week have been delivered.

Refresh

A two month trial has been undertaken with this Bristol based charity providing emergency food and support for the homeless in the local area. Morrisons, with the help from FareShare co-ordinating the initiative, provided surplus food from a local shop to the charity.

Love Food Hate Waste

Morrisons support this campaign (brought by a non-profit organisation WRAP) which aims to raises awareness about food waste and offers practical advice. The group hosts events held by the campaign at its stores.

The group plans to establish a new Morrisons Foundation for more coordinated charitable giving. It will 'provide match funding for [the] colleagues for the first time, along with support for national and local charities, and support Bradford initiatives'.

Corporate giving

We were unable to determine the amount donated to charitable causes as the group appears to have stopped declaring charitable contributions. The amount provided to Save the Children since 2010 is reported as £7.1 million; however, the company did not seem to provide any breakdown of this sum and it would appear to be that the sum was made up from customer and colleague donations. We could not find any specific figures relating to the money given by the company itself. Based on the figures from the three previous years known to us we can estimate that about £100,000 was given in cash in the UK.

Beneficiaries have included: Community Shop; Refresh; Save the Children; Sue Ryder; and WRAP.

In-kind support

Food banks

The group has worked with food poverty charities on a local level since 2007. In March 2014 there were over 150 store food bank collection points with 91 supporting food-poverty charities.

Morrisons' stores also arrange and support opportunities for groups and local charities to bag pack in stores, and welcome charity collections.

Let's Grow programme

As part of the programme, about £18 million worth of gardening equipment has been donated to schools across the UK, since the launch of the initiative. The scheme operates on a commercially-led basis (see 'Commercially-led support') and also offers online resources.

Employee-led support

Morrisons employees are 'encouraged to take part in charity partner fundraising through various events, collections and sponsored activities. Customers also give generously through our in-store collections raising money for appeals throughout the year'.

Matched funding

A matched funding scheme is planned to be operating through the Morrisons Foundation soon.

Commercially led support

Sponsorship

Morrisons was a sponsor of the 2013 National Special Olympics in Bath and Bristol. Together with joint sponsors DHL about 9,000 packed lunches were given to athletes, coaches and volunteers over three days.

Let's Grow programme

The programme has been run for about seven years and seeks 'to help schools capture the imagination of the nation's children by showing them where food comes from and inspiring them to grow their own fruit and veg in the school grounds'. According to the Corporate Responsibility Review for 2013/14, a total of 24,000 schools have registered to participate. Vouchers redeemable against any of the equipment in the Let's Grow catalogue can be received when shopping at Morrisons' stores. Further educational resources for teachers are provided on the website.

Carrier bags

The group provides a donation to charitable causes from the income of sales of carrier bags. In 2013 Save the Children received about £344,000 from the sales of bags in Wales. The partnership with the charity has now ended and the remaining money generated through the sales will be allocated to the Morrisons Foundation (which is being established). Following legal changes in charging for carrier bags in Scotland and England, similar procedures will operate to support charities in these two countries.

Education and training

During the Feeding Britain's Future Skills for Work Month 2013 Morrisons ran a programme holding two work placement weeks with some participants being offered employment opportunities.

Our Club

Morrisons ran its Our Club 'multi-employer led programme designed and proven to get young unemployed people back into work' with a number of people being employed at the end.

Corporate social responsibility

CSR committee: There is a Corporate Compliance and Responsibility Committee, chaired by Penny Hughes. It is accountable for 'development and implementation of policy on corporate compliance, and review and challenge of compliance with policies, procedures, ethical and governance standards'.

CSR information: The information obtained from the company's website states that Morrisons annually 'provides support to thousands of charities, fund-raisers and good causes, both nationally and in the communities which are home to [its] stores'.

The annual report and accounts for 2013/14 note: 'Our corporate responsibility (CR) programme ensures we work in a way that is right for our customers, colleagues, suppliers and communities, creating longer term sustainable growth.'

The information taken from the Corporate Responsibility Review for 2013/14 says:

> Contributing to community spirit is essential to Morrisons. We strive to be a good neighbour, creating a positive impact on the areas in which we operate. Where we are most effective is when we are at the heart of the local community and understand the issues that matter most to our customers and colleagues.

CSR report: The latest Corporate Responsibility Review is available from the website.

Exclusions

No response to circular appeals or support for the arts, overseas projects, or political appeals.

Applications

In writing to the correspondent. Note that the group has chosen a national charity and 'is not currently looking for further sponsorship opportunities'.

Enquiries regarding local support and in-kind contributions should be directed to the local store in the first instance.

Further requests for or enquiries about different types of support can be made using an online contact form available on the Morrison's website.

The website politely notes – 'on a daily basis Morrisons receives many requests from deserving causes and unfortunately we cannot offer help to them all'.

Mothercare plc

Catalogue shopping, retail – department and variety stores

Correspondent: Leanne Atkinson, Group Head of Corporate Social Responsibility, Mothercare plc, Cherry Tree Road, Watford, Hertfordshire WD24 6SH (tel: 01923 241000; email: CSR@mothercare.co.uk; website: www.mothercareplc.com/our-approach)

Directors: Alan Parker, Chair; Mark Newton-Jones, Chief Executive; Matthew Smith, Chief Financial Officer; Amanda Mackenzie; Angela Brav; Lee Ginsberg; Richard Rivers; Imelda Walsh; Nick Wharton (women: 3; men: 6)

Year end	29/03/2014
Turnover	£724,900,000
Pre-tax profit	(£26,300,000)

Nature of business: 'Mothercare is a specialist retailer of products for mothers-to-be, babies and children up to the age of eight.'

Company registration number: 1950509

Subsidiary undertakings include: Mothercare UK Ltd; Mothercare Procurement Ltd; Early Learning Centre Ltd.

Brands include: Mothercare, Early Learning Centre, Gurgle.com

UK employees: 5,628

Total employees: 5,809

Focus of giving: Education, health, ill health, medical research, women's issues, children, young people.

Charity of the Year	✓
Gifts in kind	✓
Sponsorship	✓
Staff fundraising only	✓

Charitable donations

Cash UK (latest available):	2014	£0
	2012	£32,000
	2011	£282,000
	2009	£125,000
	2008	£100,000
Total UK (cash and in kind):	2014	£0
Cash worldwide:	2014	£0
Total worldwide (cash and in kind):	2014	£0

Community involvement

Mothercare plc looks to carry out community and charitable work through three separate initiatives. These are: global charity partnership; the **Mothercare Group Foundation** (Charity Commission no. 1104386); and community events and activities. All of the group's charitable activities have the aim of helping parents and their children.

Corporate giving

In 2013/14 the group made no donations to the **Mothercare Group Foundation**. The foundation also made no donations.

Costings for the in-kind donations given by the group were not included in the annual report.

Global charity partnership

The Born to Care partnership saw Mothercare and the Early Learning Centre work together with Save the Children. Over the three year partnership, which began in 2010, the group had the aim of raising £1.75 million 'to reduce child mortality and to lift children out of poverty in the UK'.

See the corporate charity entry on p. 420 for more information.

In-kind support

The group recently opened 'Mumspace stores' in Romford, Edmonton, Leeds and Dudley which offer meeting spaces for parent and baby/child activities. Regular classes take place at these stores. Around 130 Mothercare stores host My Mothercare Events three times a year at which in-store experts give advice to parents in their baby's first year. Medical and first aid advice is also given through attending midwives, health visitors and assistance from the British Red Cross.

Employee-led support

The group's employees in its global locations have supported their local communities. The Responsible Sourcing Far East Team, for example, has supported local community projects by Save the Children, the donation of bookends to schools, and the donation of clothes and caps for children who suffered from the Gansu flood.

Commercially led support

Sponsorship

During the year, the group sponsored National Breastfeeding Week.

Corporate social responsibility

CSR committee: The strategic direction of the group's Corporate Responsibility programme is developed and agreed through the Corporate Responsibility Steering Committee, which is chaired by Louise Palmer as Group People Director. The committee, which is supported by the group's CSR Team, reports to the board through the Audit and Risk Committee.

CSR information: The following information is taken from the website:

> For Mothercare, our approach to Corporate Responsibility compliments our overall mission – to meet the needs and aspirations of parents and their children worldwide.
>
> There are four aspects to our approach which are shown graphically below. These four, linked together by Group policies, target setting, governance and reporting make up our overall CR programme.

The four aspects are: responsible sourcing; environment; community; our people.

CSR report: A CSR report is published within the annual report.

Corporate charity: Mothercare Group Foundation (Charity Commission no. 1104386).

Applications

At the time of writing (November 2014) the website stated the following: 'Regrettably, the foundation is not accepting funding applications at present, although this situation may change in the future.'

Müller UK and Ireland Group LLP (the entry formerly related to Robert Wiseman Dairies Ltd)

Dairy products

Correspondent: The CSR Team, Tern Valley Business Park, Shrewsbury Road, Market Drayton, Shropshire TF9 3SQ (tel: 01630 692000 (main switchboard); website: www.mullerdairy.co.uk)

Year end	31/12/2013
Turnover	£684,879,000
Pre-tax profit	(£55,251,000)

Nature of business: The processing and distribution of milk and associated products.

In 2012 Robert Wiseman Dairies (registered number SC146494) was acquired by Müller and is now part of the Müller UK and Ireland Group LLP. The information in this entry relates to the partnership (trading as Müller Dairy) which is a wholly owned subsidiary of TM Dairy Finance S.a.r.l., registered in Luxembourg. The ultimate controlling party is Herr Theo Müller.

Designated members of the partnership: Robert Wiseman and Sons Ltd; TM UK Production Ltd; and Müller Dairy (UK) Ltd. The annual report and accounts do not list the company's directors.

Company registration number: OC384928

Main locations: Glasgow

UK employees: 5,565

Total employees: 5,565

Focus of giving: Education, poverty and social exclusion, sponsorship, children, young people, community/social welfare.

Gifts in kind	✓
Market-led giving	✓
Sponsorship	✓

Charitable donations

Cash UK (latest available):	2013	£0
	2011	£28,000
	2009	£9,000
	2008	£12,000
	2007	£0
Total UK (cash and in kind):	2013	£0
Cash worldwide:	2013	£0
Total worldwide (cash and in kind):	2013	£0

Community involvement

The Müller Dairy website states: 'Throughout the year, we contribute to local life through events, fundraising, employee volunteering, farm visits for primary school children and educational support.'

Note that in the past most support has been concentrated in the Shropshire community and in Scotland. The examples of community involvement mainly relate to the years before the formation of the partnership, as the companies do not appear to have published more recent results.

The Prince's Dairy Initiative

Müller-Wiseman is one of the supporters of the initiative, which 'targets groups of local dairy farmers to engage in a bespoke programme of business support and advice'.

Country Trust

Müller Dairy has worked with the trust and farmers 'helping to fund farm visits for schools in disadvantaged inner city and urban areas'.

Mercy Ships

In the past Müller-Wiseman has supported the charity's Easter Breakfast 2010 campaign.

Corporate giving

The annual report and accounts of the partnership state that in 2013 there were no charitable donations made.

Note: We have used the figure defined as 'Loss for the period before discretionary division among members' as the partnership's financial loss for the year.

In-kind support

Wiseman Charity Month

Annually Müller Wiseman runs a Charity Month and gives opportunity for charities to use the space on production packaging to promote their activities and events. The latest example given on the Müller Wiseman website is for 2012, when packs featured Clic Sargent, Crimestoppers, RNLI and Send a Cow.

FareShare

The Müller-Wiseman website notes that the company is working with the charity to donate dairy products within their 'best before' dates that do not make it to retailers in time and would otherwise be considered waste.

Scottish National Milk Shake Day

In 2014 the project took place across schools in Scotland. The school meals service was selling milk shakes and panda cookies donating monies from the sales to the STV 2014 Appeal to help children in poverty in Scotland. Müller Wiseman Dairies donated vouchers for 100 bikes to be used as prizes in a competition run as part of the project.

Employee-led support

According to the annual report and accounts, 'Müller UK & Ireland Group LLP employees are able to volunteer time to support local community projects.'

Müller Dairy has 'an employee volunteering programme open to all of [its] employees, which supports educational, environmental and charitable projects around the county [Shropshire]'. The latest available CSR report from Müller Dairy dates to 2009 and states that staff members are entitled to one day per year to engage in local community volunteering initiatives. In the past about 1,600 hours of time had been donated by Müller Dairy employees to projects, such as re-decorating a local community centre, working with secondary school pupils on health and well-being topics, and repairing dry-stone walls.

Commercially led support

Royal Zoological Society of Scotland

Müller Wiseman Dairies and the Royal Zoological Society of Scotland run a partnership which allows children 'to discover both the benefits of drinking milk and the importance of the giant panda'.

Meet the Neighbours

Müller Dairy has been a participant in the Market Drayton Taste of the Town initiative which invited local residents to attend a tour of the Müller Dairy and sample yogurts.

Sponsorship

In the past Müller Dairy has sponsored the Shrewsbury Flower Show.

Corporate social responsibility

CSR committee: We found no indications of a CSR committee. The Müller Wiseman website states that:

> There are five 'Wiseman in the Community' groups, each centred on a dairy. The members of each group represent a cross section of all staff from the sites around the dairy. The groups are autonomous and are responsible for getting Wiseman involved in the local community.

CSR information: A great part of the CSR focus is on environmental sustainability issues, such as carbon/energy efficiency, packaging and waste to landfill.

Müller Dairy website states:

> At Müller Dairy we believe that our involvement with our local community is less of a 'project' and more of a philosophy. ... We are very proud of the role we play in the Shropshire community, so we are always looking to give something back.

Müller Wiseman website notes:

> As a company, we recognise the importance of being part of and supporting the communities we serve. With the growth of the company our community focus is becoming more and more national and as such we identified a need to overhaul our approach to

community involvement, and have established 'Wiseman in the Community.

CSR report: We found no CSR report relating to the current partnership. The latest available 'Mission Goodness' booklet from Müller Dairy is for 2009.

Exclusions

Local appeals not in areas of company presence and individual appeals are not generally supported. Political donations are not made.

Applications

In writing to the correspondent.

Muir Group plc

Property

Correspondent: The Company Secretary, Muir House, Belleknowes Industrial Estate, Inverkeithing, Fife KY11 1HY (tel: 01383 416191; website: www.muirgroup.co.uk)

Directors: J. W. Muir; C. Muir; R. W. Muir; J. S. H. Watt; A. C. Muir

Year end	02/02/2014
Turnover	£73,684,000
Pre-tax profit	£3,951,000

Nature of business: The principal activities of the group are building contracting, private house building, property development, manufactured joinery and owning and operating a golf and country club.

Company registration number: SC215392

Subsidiary undertakings include: JW Muir Group Ltd; Muir Construction Ltd; Muir Homes Ltd; Muir Leisure Ltd; Muir Timber Systems Ltd;

UK employees: 301

Total employees: 301

Focus of giving: General charitable purposes, education, environment, health, ill health, arts, culture, sport, recreation.

Charitable donations

Cash UK (latest available):	2014	£6,000
	2012	£3,000
	2011	£8,000
	2010	£46,000
	2009	£41,000
Total UK (cash and in kind):	2014	£6,000
Cash worldwide:	2014	£6,000
Total worldwide (cash and in kind):	2014	£6,000

Community involvement

We were unable to determine details of Muir Group plc's community involvement. However, our research in previous years identified that funding was spent on arts and sports, health, education and the environment.

Corporate giving

In 2013/14 the group made charitable donations of £6,000. We were unable to determine details of beneficiaries.

Corporate social responsibility

CSR information: We found no information on CSR.

We were unable to determine the ratio of women to men on the board.

Applications

In writing to the correspondent, referenced 'Charitable donations'.

National Express Group plc

Transport and communications

Correspondent: The Employee Charity Panel, National Express House, Mill Lane, Digbeth, Birmingham B5 6DD (tel: 0845 013 0130; website: www.nationalexpressgroup.com/our-way)

Directors: Sir John Armitt, Chair; Dean Finch, Group Chief Executive; Jez Maiden, Group Finance Director; Jackie Hunt; Joaquín Ayuso; Jorge Cosmen; Sir Andrew Foster; Jane Kingston; Chris Muntwyler; Lee Sander; Sandra Forbes (women: 3; men: 8)

Year end	31/12/2013
Turnover	£1,891,300,000
Pre-tax profit	£64,400,000

Nature of business: Principally the provision of passenger coach, bus and train services, operating in the UK, North America, Spain, Morocco and Germany.

Company registration number: 2590560

Subsidiary undertakings include: National Express Ltd; Euroline (UK) Ltd; Airlinks Airport Services Ltd; The Kings Ferry Ltd; West Midlands Travel Ltd; c2c Rail Ltd

Main locations: London

Total employees: 42,524

Focus of giving: Enterprise/training, environment, children, young people.

Gifts in kind	✓
Overseas giving	✓
Payroll giving	✓

Charitable donations

Cash UK (latest available):	2013	£17,000
	2012	£18,000
	2011	£228,000
	2009	£187,000
	2008	£386,000
Total UK (cash and in kind):	2013	£17,000
Cash worldwide:	2013	£356,000
Total worldwide (cash and in kind):	2013	£356,000

Community involvement

National Express Group looks to support charitable causes 'in areas aligned to its business and its employees'. Since 2011 it has been in partnership with Transaid, an international development charity, helping to improve safety and driving standards in Tanzania. **The National Express Foundation** (Charity Commission no. 1148231), which was launched in 2012, is a key part of the group's community support in the UK, making grants to charitable and community groups working to 'support young people and promote cross-community cohesion'. The group's companies also conduct their own community initiatives in their respective countries.

The group's employees play a central role in its community involvement though volunteering, fundraising activities and a payroll giving scheme. In 2009 the group launched the Employee Charity Panel, which meets quarterly to identify and allocate funds to charities in the UK.

Corporate giving

Whilst the £17,000 we have taken as the UK cash total for 2013 may seem like a significant drop in giving compared to the figures we have stated for previous years, the 2013 annual report and accounts for the group states the following: 'In the UK, the Employee Charity Panel made donations of almost £17,000 to 50 different charities and community groups.' Across the group as a whole, charitable donations amounted to £356,000 during the year. A comprehensive list of costings of the group's in-kind donations was not available.

The National Express Foundation, to which the group has pledged £500,000 in funding over the next five years, also continued to provide bursaries to individuals and grants to organisations.

Partner organisations: Transaid

2013 Employee Charity Panel beneficiaries: Birmingham Dogs Home; Cancer Research; Movember.

See the corporate charity entry on p. 420 for more information.

In-kind support

Case study: Transaid

As part of the group's partnership with Transaid, a UK-registered charity, two engineers visited the National Institute of Transport in Tanzania to assess the needs of local staff, and training inputs to develop the ability of local staff in delivering professional driver training were given by four of the group's Driver Trainers.

Employee-led support

Employee volunteering and fundraising

National Express Group actively encourages its employees to give charitably through 'volunteering and fundraising for local initiatives'. In the UK, employees can apply to the Employee Charity Panel for funding for charitable and community initiatives with which they are personally involved.

Payroll giving

The group operates a payroll giving initiative.

Corporate social responsibility

CSR information: The following information is taken from the 2013 annual report and accounts:

> Our Vision and Values were launched three years ago as a fundamental statement of who we are as a business and how we operate. They originate from the conviction of the Company that National Express wants to be. Rather than the potential 'gloss' of Corporate Social Responsibility, the way we act as a business embodies these Vision and Values. In National Express' view being a good and successful company should be – and are – synonymous.
>
> Underpinned by our Values of Safety, Customers, People and Community, the Vision and Values have guided how we operate as a business and prioritised what we have focused on.

CSR report: There is a section dedicated to 'Vision and Values' in both the annual report and on the website. There is also 'National Express in the Community', a downloadable review of the community activities, though it is not clear to which year it applies.

Corporate charity: The National Express Foundation (Charity Commission no. 1148231).

Exclusions

The following was also taken directly from the group's website:

> *What we don't support*
>
> The focus for our charitable support is in areas aligned to our business and our employees. We are therefore unable to support financial requests from individuals outside the business, political or denominational groups, arts or sports groups, medical and animal welfare organisations or building projects.
>
> We don't support requests for advertising or sponsorship unless they are part of a project we are already involved with.
>
> Because of the volume of requests we get, we are also unable to offer free travel for charity 'jailbreaks' and other external fundraising events

Though listed in these exclusions, we know that animal welfare and medical groups benefitted from donations approved by the Employee Charity Panel during the year. Contact the correspondent for clarification before spending time on an application.

Applications

We have taken the following information directly from the website.

> During 2009 we launched our Employee Charity Panel to encourage and support more staff to get involved with the community. Employees can apply for funding to support any charitable or community initiative they are personally involved with.
>
> These applications are reviewed by our Employee Charity Panel who meet quarterly to identify and allocate funds for those charities that they think will benefit most.

Also see 'Exclusions'

The National Express Foundation
(Charity Commission no. 1148231)

The foundation's website states that applicants are required to provide the following information:

- Background to the organisation, membership and funding
- Evidence of constitution and independent bank account
- Description of what the funding would be used for
- Explanation of how the proposed project would benefit the community
- Timescale and process for delivering the project
- Proposals for promoting the link with the foundation
- Plans to evaluate and quantify the benefits

> Applicants are asked to indicate what size of grant they are seeking, and explain what they could deliver for the level of grant applied for. The trustees plan to award more small grants (up to a maximum of £5,000) than large grants (up to maximum £10,000). The trustees may choose to support an organisation but offer a smaller amount than has been requested, so it would help if applicants can show what they would deliver for different levels of funding.

The National Farmers Union Mutual Insurance Society Ltd

Insurance

Correspondent: James Creechan, NFU Mutual Charitable Trust, Tiddington Road, Stratford-upon-Avon, Warwickshire CV37 7BJ (tel: 01789 204211 (main switchboard); email: nfu_mutual_charitable_trust@nfumutual.co.uk; website: www.nfumutual.co.uk)

Directors: Richard Percy, Chair; Kim Arif, Finance Director; Steve Bower; Brian Duffin; John Elliot; Sally-Ann Hibberd; Christine Kennedy; Eileen McCusker; Jim McLaren; Lindsay Sinclair, Group Chief Executive; Chris Stooke; Mark Tinsley; Nick Turner (women: 3; men: 10)

Year end	31/12/2013
Turnover	£1,288,000,000
Pre-tax profit	£775,000,000

Nature of business: National Farmers Union Mutual Insurance Society Ltd a mutual company providing insurance, pension and investment products and services.

Company registration number: 111982

Subsidiary undertakings include: Avon Insurance plc.; NFU Mutual Management Company Ltd; NFU Mutual Select Investments Ltd; NFU Mutual Risk Management Services Ltd; Reed Insurance Associates Ltd; Salmon Harvester Properties Ltd; and The Islands' Insurance Company Ltd. A full list of subsidiary undertakings can be found in the company's accounts.

UK employees: 3,833

Total employees: 3,833

Focus of giving: Economic generation, education, enterprise/training, environment, health, ill health, individuals, local groups, poverty and social exclusion, children, young people, community/social welfare.

Membership: BITC

Charity of the Year	✓
Gifts in kind	✓

Charitable donations

Cash UK (latest available):	2013	£279,000
	2011	£572,000
	2009	£256,000
	2008	£257,000
	2007	£262,000
Total UK (cash and in kind):	2013	£279,000
Cash worldwide:	2013	£279,000
Total worldwide (cash and in kind):	2013	£279,000

Community involvement

The group 'champions education and awareness campaigns on a number of key issues affecting those who live and work in rural communities'. NFU Mutual runs Farm Safety campaigns and makes financial contributions to support the farming industry as well as funding the work of the NFU Mutual Charitable Trust.

The NFU Mutual Charitable Trust (Charity Commission no. 1073064)

The trust was set up in 1998 with the aim of promoting and supporting charitable purposes, particularly in the areas of 'education of the public in relation to agriculture and insurance, research into agriculture, education of young people in rural areas, relief poverty in rural areas and advancement of social welfare in rural communities'. The group's website states - 'the trustees' continue to be to provide support through one-off donations and grants to charitable initiatives connected with agriculture, the countryside, farming education and the insurance industry'.

According to the group's annual report and accounts, in 2013 a total of over £333,000 was given by the trust of which £100,000 went to The Prince's Countryside Fund. Other recent beneficiaries have included: Agrifood Charities Partnership (AFCP); Farming Help Partnership; Farms for City Children; Nuffield Farming Scholarship Trust; Rural Support; The National Federation of Young Farmers' Clubs (NFYFC) and Wales YFC; and The Royal Highland Education Trust (RHET).

The NFU Mutual Charitable Trust Centenary Award

The award scheme was created in 2010 to celebrate the group's centenary. It 'helps identify rural leaders of the future and generate a legacy for the agricultural community' who are both 'excellent academic performers' and 'committed to the future of agriculture'. NFU Mutual donated £250,000 to fund the project, and since its inception 20 students have already benefited from the awards (3 postgraduate bursaries in 2013).

Community Giving Fund

This fund was set up in 2005 'to support local initiatives and charitable events within the communities in which NFU Mutual operates'. In 2013 the fund provided support totalling £10,400 to community groups, charities, local hospices, schools and sports clubs and in 2014 a total of £11,000 was given.

Country Crime Fighter Awards

The awards are in their second year and seek to reward individuals proactive and innovative in their approach to tackling crime in the countryside.

Charity partnership

In 2015 a new charity partner – Guide Dogs – was voted by employees with the target of £125,000 to be raised. Previously the group had a two-year partnership with Macmillan Cancer Support, raising over £295,000 to support Macmillan's Mobile Information Units and a three-year partnership with Make-A-Wish Foundation UK which resulted in over £605,000 being raised by the staff in support of the charity.

NFU Mutual also continues to provide financial support to the Farming Unions of England, Northern Ireland, Scotland and Wales. In 2013 such donations totalled £7 million.

Corporate giving

In 2013 the group made donations totalling over £279,000. Out of this sum £250,000 went to the NFUMutual Charitable Trust and £29,000 to the Community Giving Fund and Charity Matching Fund. According to the trust's annual report and accounts for 2013, the value of administration services provided by NFU Mutual totalled about £7,000.

Beneficiaries include: NFUMutual Charitable Trust (£250,000). The trust's beneficiaries have included: Agrifood Charities Partnership (AFCP); Farming Help Partnership; Farms for City Children; Nuffield Farming Scholarship Trust; Rural Support; The National Federation of Young Farmers' Clubs (NFYFC) and Wales YFC; The Prince's Countryside Fund; and The Royal Highland Education Trust (RHET).

Revenue: We have used the figure defined as 'Gross written premium before Mutual Bonus' in the accounts as the group's annual turnover.

See the corporate charity entry on p. 421 for more information.

In-kind support

Employee volunteering time and fundraising efforts.

Employee-led support

Employee volunteering programme

A new programme was launched in 2013, which 'provides teams in the business with development opportunities whilst promoting collaborative working'. Each member of staff is given one day a year to volunteer for either The National Trust or the official corporate charity partner – currently Guide Dogs.

Staff members fundraise in support of the charity partner and other charitable causes. In 2013 a total of almost £143,000 was raised to help Macmillan Cancer Support, including £11,000 from Macmillan's flagship fundraising event The World's Biggest Coffee Morning in September.

Corporate social responsibility

CSR committee: We found no indication of a CSR committee.

CSR information: The CSR report for 2013 states:

> NFU Mutual's Corporate Social Responsibility Programme (CSR) focuses on three distinct areas of activity: Community, Charity, and Environment. In each of these areas we examine the impact we have upon our members, the communities in which we operate and the wider environment. We aim to benefit all stakeholders in these areas.

CSR report: A CSR report is contained within the annual report and accounts.

Corporate charity: The NFU Mutual Charitable Trust (Charity Commission no. 1073064).

Applications

Applications for funding for projects and initiatives falling within the objects of the NFU Mutual Charitable Trust (Charity Commission no. 1073064) can be made in writing to the correspondent and should include details of:

- The project, initiative or organisation for which funding is sought
- An indication of the amount of the donation requested
- Any business plans
- Details of any other funding sought and or obtained
- Any recognition which would be given to the trust in recognition of its support
- Confirmation of whether or not the applicant is a registered charity

The website states:

> Following a recent strategic review, the trustees have indicated that in future, the trust will focus on providing funding to larger initiatives, which would have a significant impact on the rural community. The trustees are particularly interested in initiatives in the areas of education of young people in rural areas and relief of poverty within rural areas.

The trustees meet twice a year to consider applications, normally in June and December. Applications should be received by the end of May and November, respectively.

The Centenary Awards: Further details on applications for Centenary Awards (for individuals) can be found online.

National Grid plc

Electricity

Correspondent: See 'Applications', National Grid House, Warwick Technology Park, Gallows Hill, Warwick CV34 6DA (website: www2.nationalgrid.com/responsibility)

Directors: Sir Peter Gershon, Chair; Steve Holliday, Chief Executive; Philip Aiken; Andrew Bonfield, Finance Director; Nora Mead Brownell; Jonathan Dawson; Therese Esperdy; Paul Golby; Ruth Kelly; Tom King; John Pettigrew; Mark Williamson (women: 3; men: 8)

Year end	31/03/2014
Turnover	£14,809,000,000
Pre-tax profit	£2,748,000,000

Nature of business: The principal operations of the group are the ownership and operation of regulated electricity and gas infrastructure networks in the UK and the US.

Company registration number: 4031152

Subsidiary undertakings include: National Grid Electricity Transmission plc; National Grid Gas plc; National Grid Grain LNG Ltd; National Grid Holdings One plc; National Grid Metering Ltd; National Grid Property Holdings Ltd

Main locations: Warwick

Total employees: 23,909

Focus of giving: Education, enterprise/training, environment, community/social welfare.

Membership: BITC, LBG

Cash donations undeclared	✓
Charity of the Year	✓
FTSE 100	✓
Gifts in kind	✓
Overseas giving	✓
Sponsorship	✓

Charitable donations

Cash UK (latest available):	2011	£100,000
	2009	£1,100,000
	2008	£1,400,000
	2007	£2,900,000
	2005	£1,352,000
Cash worldwide:	2014	£11,200,000
Total worldwide (cash and in kind):	2014	£11,700,000

Community involvement

National Grid focuses a large part of its community involvement, both in the UK and the US, on education and skills development for young people in the form of cash donations, staff volunteering and sponsorship. Support is also directed towards environmental causes and community development

Aside from making donations, the group financially supports its own programmes centred around 'affordable warmth', education, university research, and young offenders.

Charity of the Year

During the year, the group embarked on its first ever charity partnership, with UK employees nominating Macmillan Cancer Support as the beneficiary partner.

The group has also entered into collaborations with TeachFirst and Step up to Serve.

Corporate giving

The National Grid website states:

> During 2013/14, approximately £11.7 million (2012/13: £15.0 million) was invested in support of community initiatives and relationships. The London Benchmarking Group model was again used to assess this overall community investment.
>
> In addition to our donations, financial support was provided for our affordable warmth programme, education programme, university research and our young offenders programme.

Of the total community investment, we believe that cash accounts for around £11.2 million.

We were unable to determine a figure for UK cash or in-kind contributions.

In-kind support

Pro bono

National grid employees shared their time and expertise, giving more than 18,000 hours in aid of community causes, including towards environmental initiatives and projects for young people to improve their STEM skills.

Employee-led support

Employee volunteering

In 2013/14 more than 2,730 employees contributed to their communities through volunteering. Beneficiaries included the group's partner organisations.

Employee fundraising

Employees partook in various fundraising activities during the year.

Commercially led support

Sponsorship

National Grid supported Special Olympics GB, acting as a sponsor for the National Summer Games.

Corporate social responsibility

CSR committee: The website states:

> With effect from the end of July 2012, our Board Risk & Responsibility Committee, created in 2002, was replaced by a new Safety, Environment & Health (SEH) Committee, chaired by Philip Aiken, focusing on safety, environmental and health matters.In relation to safety, environment and health, the committee reviews the strategies, policies, initiatives, risk exposure, targets and performance of the Company and, where appropriate, of its suppliers and contractors. It also monitors the resources we use for compliance and driving improvement in these areas.
>
> All other aspects of our non-financial performance, for example Talent & Skills, are overseen by our Executive Committee and reviewed, as appropriate, by our full board.

CSR information: The following information was obtained from the 'Connections that matter' summary report:

> The future will be shaped by what we all do now and the choices we make. By the technologies we develop and how we use them. Design engineering is critical, but our vision goes wider and deeper. We will play our part in building a more inclusive society, socially and economically.
>
> It will fall to coming generations to turn this vision into action. That's why we're active in education, sponsorship and volunteering work to engage young people in the challenges that lie in front of us, now and into the future.

CSR report: There is an online CR report.

Exclusions

Our research tells us that support is not given to circular appeals, advertising in charity brochures, appeals from individuals, overseas projects, political appeals, religious appeals, and local appeals not in areas of company presence.

Applications

For more information on community projects and volunteering, contact Kate Van Der Plank, Head of Community Investment (kate.vanderplank@nationalgrid.com).

For more information on corporate responsibility and sponsorships, contact Caroline Hooley, Corporate Responsibility and Sponsorships Manager (caroline.hooley@nationalgrid.com).

National Magazine Co. Ltd

Media

Correspondent: The Company Secretary, National Magazine House, 72 Broadwick Street, London W1F 9EP (tel: 020 7439 5000; website: www.natmags.co.uk)

Directors: F. A. Bennack Jr, Chair; J. D. Edwards; S. P. B. Horne; J. P. Loughlin; G. C. Maurer; M. Clinton; S. Swartz; D. F. Carey; Anna Jones, Chief Executive; Jimmy Weir, Chief Financial Officer

Year end	31/12/2013
Turnover	£312,116,000
Pre-tax profit	£12,698,000

Nature of business: The main activities are the publishing and distribution of magazines and periodicals. The National Magazine Co. Ltd is a wholly owned subsidiary of Hearst Holdings Inc. Hearst Magazines UK is the trading name of The National Magazine Co. Ltd.

Company registration number: 112955

Subsidiary undertakings include: Condé Nast and National Magazine Distributors Ltd; Distributors Ltd; Handbag.com Ltd; F.E.P (UK) Ltd; Hearst Dutch Trademarking Company BV; Hearst Magazines UK 2012–1 Ltd.

Brands include: Company, Cosmopolitan, Country Living, Digital Spy, Elle, Esquire

Main locations: London

Total employees: 1,134

Focus of giving: Health, ill health, women's issues, children, young people, community/social welfare.

Cash donations undeclared	✓
Charity of the Year	✓
Gifts in kind	✓

Charitable donations

Cash UK (latest available):	2010	£100
	2008	£2,600
	2007	£16,000
	2006	£12,000
	2005	£45,000

Community involvement

Hearst UK (trading name of National Magazine Company Ltd), through its various brands, supports charities, mainly in the areas of women, children and young people and health. The group runs Empowering Women (empowering.hearst.co.uk), a brand 'celebrating the lives, aspirations and achievements of British women', which is partnered by women and children's charity, Theirworld. Its brands also work alongside various charities such as: BEAT; Children in Crisis; Dementia Friends; Federation of City Friends and Community Gardens (Country Living magazine's Charity of the Year'; Prince's Trust; Women's Aid.

Corporate giving

There were no details of charitable contributions from the group included in its 2013 annual report.

Our research suggests that, in the past, the group has supported the work of groups near to its Soho office through making small donations and that it has previously supported employees' volunteering/charitable activities with financial contributions.

We were unable to determine if the charities supported by the group's brands received financial contributions during the year.

Corporate social responsibility

CSR committee: There was no evidence of a CSR committee.

CSR information: We were unable to find evidence of the group's CSR policy

We were unable to determine the ratio of women to men on the board.

CSR report: There was no evidence of a published CSR report.

Exclusions

Local appeals not in areas of company presence.

Applications

In writing to the correspondent referenced 'Charitable donations', or alternatively, in writing to one of Hearst UK's brands.

Nationwide Building Society

Building society

Correspondent: Citizenship Team, Nationwide House, Pipers Way, Swindon SN38 2SN (email: citizenship@nationwide.co.uk; website: your.nationwide.co.uk/your-news/articles/Pages/corporate-responsibility.aspx)

Directors: Geoffrey Howe, Chair; Graham Beale, Chief Executive; Chris Rhodes; Rita Clifton; Mitchel Lenson; Tony Prestedge; Lynne Peacock; Roger Perkin; Michael Jary; Mark Rennison, Group Finance Director; David Roberts (women: 2; men: 9)

Year end	04/04/2014
Turnover	£5,581,000,000
Pre-tax profit	£210,000,000

Nature of business: The group provides a comprehensive range of personal financial services.

FSA registration number: 106078

Subsidiary undertakings include: Derbyshire Home Loans Ltd; E-MEX Home Funding Ltd; Nationwide Syndications Ltd; The Mortgage Works (UK) plc; UBC Home Loans Corporation Ltd

Main locations: Swindon

UK employees: 17,268

Total employees: 17,268

Focus of giving: Economic generation, education, housing, homelessness, financial education, older people, poverty and social exclusion, community/social welfare.

Membership: BITC, LBG

Charity of the Year	✓
Gifts in kind	✓
Matched funding	✓
Payroll giving	✓
Sponsorship	✓

Charitable donations

Cash UK (latest available):	2014	£1,800,000
	2013	£1,500,000
	2011	£1,500,000
	2009	£4,474,000
	2008	£2,448,191
Total UK (cash and in kind):	2014	£3,200,000
Cash worldwide:	2014	£1,800,000
Total worldwide (cash and in kind):	2014	£3,200,000

Community involvement

Nationwide's community involvement is directed towards three areas in which it feels it can make the biggest impact – money management, housing and supporting its members' local communities (known respectively as 'Your money', 'Your home' and 'Your community').

Nationwide supports charities and community projects which have a 'tangible' impact on the communities close to its branches or admin centres. Support is given in the form of funding and in the form of pro bono work. Preference is given to projects focused on the areas of housing, financial education and money management, and particularly projects where Nationwide's support has the potential to help unlock further funding or its employees' skills and knowledge are useful.

Nationwide is the main benefactor of **The Nationwide Foundation** (Charity Commission no. 1065552) which makes grants and social investment to create decent affordable housing for people who are in need.

Charity partners: Macmillan Cancer Support, Shelter

Corporate giving

The annual report and accounts for 2013/14 state that charitable donations were made totalling £1.8 million, which included a donation of £608,000 to the **Nationwide Foundation**. Employee time worth more than £1.3 million was given through volunteering programmes.

Also stated in the annual report and accounts is the following: 'In 2013/14 our target was to channel £2.9 million into local communities. We actually achieved £3.9 million.' However, we believe this takes into account funds raised by employees and customers and we have taken the total of community contributions from Nationwide to be £3.2 million.

Member involvement

Nationwide's members can nominate charities for the group to support and each month vote for a different regional charity through the online Big Local scheme. Branch users can vote for one of three local causes, which have been nominated by members, to receive £500 through the branch Community Match scheme. In 2013/14 through Community Match and The Big Local, almost £338,000 was distributed to more than 1,000 charities.

At each AGM, members raise hundreds of thousands of pounds for charity, with a donation given for each vote received. As a result, Macmillan Cancer Support received a donation of more than £175,000 during the year.

Beneficiaries include: The Nationwide Foundation (£858,000); The Money Advice Trust (£85,000)

See the corporate charity entry on p. 421 for more information.

In-kind support

Pro bono

Employees are entitled to two days paid leave for volunteering purposes each year.

Nationwide Education website

The website holds resources which teachers can access to educate young people from the ages of 2–18+ about money, numeracy, careers, sustainability, and safety in the home and on the roads.

Numeracy programmes

Talking Numbers – Working alongside teachers and partner organisations, this new initiative was launched in February 2014 to help 200,000 young people improve their numeracy skills by 2017.

National Numeracy – A four year partnership that aims to improve the numeracy skills of more than one million adults.

Employee-led support

Employee volunteering

More than half of Nationwide employees are involved in volunteering initiatives in their communities, volunteering 74,000 hours in 2013/14.

Employee fundraising

Employees have taken part in various fundraising initiatives. For Nationwide's partner charity, Shelter, for example, employees raised £12,000 for the charity and delivered 632 shoeboxes for disadvantaged families. Fundraising activities were also run for local partner charities and for national appeals such as Comic Relief and Children in Need.

Matched funding

Nationwide matches employee fundraising up to £100 for an individual and up to £500 for a team.

Payroll giving

Give As You Earn – The Give As You Earn scheme is in operation.

Every Penny Helps – More than 4,000 employees take part in the Every Penny Helps scheme, which sees their monthly salary payment rounded down to the nearest pound, with the surplus pennies given to charity. Through the scheme, more than £25,000 was raised in support of Macmillan.

Commercially led support

Sponsorship

Nationwide sponsors the 'Your money' column in First News, a weekly newspaper for young people.

Corporate social responsibility

CSR committee: There is a Citizenship Committee, which is chaired by the CEO and meets quarterly.

CSR information: The following information was obtained from Nationwide's website:

> Our Citizenship is at the heart of our business. We want to do our best for our members, and a vital part of this is supporting the communities in which they live and work. In 2008, our members voted for at least 1% of our profits each year to be donated to good causes. This has allowed us to support thousands of charities and community projects across the UK.

In 2012 Nationwide launched a five year citizenship strategy called 'Living on your side', with focuses including 'Your community', which aims to strengthen local communities by investing or unlocking £15 million by 2017.

CSR report: There are sections dedicated to Citizenship on both the website and in the annual report and accounts.

Corporate charity: The Nationwide Foundation (Charity Commission no. 1065552).

Exclusions

No response to circular appeals. No support is given for advertising in charity brochures, animal welfare, appeals from individuals, medical research, overseas projects, political appeals, religious appeals, or for commercial (as opposed to community related) sponsorship.

The foundation will not consider funding for the following:

- Charities with 'unrestricted reserves' which exceed 50% of annual expenditure, as shown in their accounts
- Charities which are in significant debt as shown in their accounts
- Promotion of religion or politics
- Charities which have been declined by the foundation within the last 12 months
- Applications which do not comply with the foundation's funding criteria/guidelines

Applications

There are online forms through which charities can be nominated to receive funding or can request employee volunteers. They can be found on the 'Get involved' page on the 'Your Nationwide' section of the website: your.nationwide.co.uk/your-society/get-involved

For applications to the **Nationwide Foundation** (Charity Commission no. 1065552), further information can be obtained from the foundation's website (www.nationwidefoundation.org.uk). The foundation's website states that 'funding is only available for projects where alternative scalable models can provide more affordable homes, however there is not an open grant programme. If you think you have a project that might fit with our strategy, please contact us to discuss further'.

Nestlé Holdings (UK) plc

Drinks manufacture, food manufacture

Correspondent: Community Relations, 1 City Place, Gatwick, West Sussex RH6 0PA (tel: 020 8686 3333; email: community.relations@uk.nestle.com; website: www.nestle.co.uk/csv2013)

Directors: Fiona Kendrick, Chair and Chief Executive; M. Jones; E. Legge; P. Hagmann

Year end	31/12/2013
Pre-tax profit	£11,819,000

Nature of business: Holding company of some of the interests of Nestlé SA businesses operating in the UK. Nestlé manufactures and sells food products, pet food products and associated activities. In the UK, the principal operating companies are Nestlé UK Ltd and Nespresso UK Ltd.

Company registration number: 462438

Subsidiary undertakings include: Buxton Mineral Water Ltd; Nespresso UK Ltd; Nestlé UK Ltd; Nestlé Waters (UK) Holdings Ltd; Purlaw Company; Vitaflo International Holdings Ltd

Brands include: Aero, Dolce-Gusto, Milky Bar, Nestlé Cheerios, Purina Petcare, Smarties

Main locations: Hayes, Castleford, Croydon, Dalston, Fawdon, Girvan, Halifax, York, Tutbury

Focus of giving: Education, individuals, health, ill health, children, young people, community/social welfare.

Membership: BITC

Cash donations undeclared	✓
Charity of the Year	✓
Gifts in kind	✓

Charitable donations

Cash UK (latest available):	2013	£570,000
	2011	£570,000
	2009	£700,000
	2007	£1,005,954
	2006	£1,200,000
Total UK (cash and in kind):	2013	£570,000
Cash worldwide:	2013	£570,000
Total worldwide (cash and in kind):	2013	£570,000

Community involvement

Nestlé supports the communities in which its 22 sites in the UK and Ireland operate. The company works alongside community groups to promote healthier lifestyles and better education. It runs three principal initiatives: Nestlé Academy in the Community; Nestlé Healthy Kids global programme; and a Charity of the Year scheme (Charity of Choice).

Corporate giving

The annual report and accounts for 2013 did not declare a figure for charitable donations during the year. The most recent figure on our records dates from 2011, during which the company donated £570,000 to charities. We have taken this as an estimate for charitable donations in 2013, though the actual figure may vary from this considerably.

We were unable to determine a figure for the in-kind support given during the year.

Nestlé Healthy Kids global programme (& PhunkyFoods partnership)

Nestlé launched its global programme in 2009 and, in 2012, partnered the organisation PhunkyFoods in an initiative to help teach children about healthy eating. The website states that Nestlé has pledged to invest more than

£800,000 in the programme over three years to fund:

- The roll-out of the PhunkyFoods curriculum in local primary schools near our UK locations
- A team of nutritionists to help local schools to deliver the PhunkyFoods programme
- The development of a new PhunkyFoods website and online tools for parents
- A major research project by Leeds Metropolitan University to measure the impact of regular healthy lifestyle lessons on children's health

Charity of Choice

In 2012 the company launched a three year partnership with Action for Children, which was selected by employees.

In-kind support

Pro bono

As part of Nestlé Ireland's partnership with the Jack and Jill Foundation, relationship staff, in addition to fundraising, provided strategic advice for an advertising awareness campaign.

Nestlé is also involved in the community through a number of programmes:

Nestlé Academy in the Community

The Nestlé Academy was launched in 2012 to use its expertise to help young people in its communities. The programme has seen the company's involvement with a number of educational initiatives. Note that some of these initiatives appear to qualify also as being 'Commercially led':

Inspiring the Future – A programme Nestlé joined in 2013 which matches employees from local businesses with state schools to provide career insight talks and advice.

'Our Earth, Our Way' schools' green challenge – In conjunction with North Yorkshire Business and Education Partnership, Nestlé staff supported 700 pupils from York, Wakefield and Goole in a competition to find creative solutions to meet our energy needs to a panel of judges, which included Nestlé's Head of Sustainability.

Business Week and Global Entrepreneurship Week – As part of the event in York, Nestlé opened its doors to 23 students, who toured the York office and KIT KAT plant, taking part in an apprentice-style challenge to create a new brand of chocolates.

Gifts in kind: Research indicates that in previous years, Nestlé has given in-kind support, in the form of product, furniture and equipment donations to local good causes.

Employee-led support

Employee fundraising

During the year, employees raised funds for the company's Charity of Choice, Action for Children, through a variety of activities including running and baking cakes. On the first year anniversary of the partnership in July 2013, employees had helped to raise more than £250,000 for the charity.

Employee donations

The York site has their own employee charitable trust, which raises funds from employees and is donated in small grants to local organisations in which employees hold an interest. The trust is **The Nestlé Rowntree York Employees Community Fund Trust** (Registered charity: 516702).

Payroll giving: Previous research suggests that the company operates an internal payroll giving scheme, though we were unable to find more recent details.

Corporate social responsibility

CSR committee: There is a Creating Shared Value (CSV) Steering Group chaired by Fiona Kendrick, CEO.

CSR information: In the UK and Ireland, Nestlé conducts its CSR activities through the Creating Shared Value (CSV) Plan. The following information was obtained from the Nestlé UK website:

> At Nestlé we believe that, to succeed as a business in the long term and create value for our shareholders, we must also create value for society. Our aim is to provide safe, responsibly produced food and beverages of the highest quality. But we must do this in a way which protects natural resources for future generations and ensures the people and communities along our supply chain prosper.

We were unable to determine the ratio of women to men on the board.

CSR report: There is a 'Creating Shared Value' brochure available to download from the website.

Exclusions

Previous research indicates that no support is given towards student expeditions, individuals, political causes, third-party fundraising events or the purchase of advertising space in charity programmes.

Applications

Applications should be made to the nearest local site. Our research indicates that few national financial donations are given.

Network Rail Infrastructure Ltd

Engineering, transportation

Correspondent: Charities Panel, Network Rail, 1 Eversholt Street, London NW1 2DN (email: charitablegiving@networkrail.co.uk; website: www.networkrail.co.uk/charities)

Directors: Mark Carne, Chief Executive; Patrick Butcher, Group Finance Director; Chris Gibb; Robin Gisby; Paul Plummer; Richard Parry-Jones, Chair; Malcolm Brinded; Janis Kong; Bridget Rosewell; Michael O'Higgins; Sharon Flood (women: 3; men: 8)

Year end	31/03/2014
Turnover	£6,353,000,000
Pre-tax profit	£1,191,000,000

Nature of business: Network Rail owns, operates and maintains Britain's rail network.

Company registration number: 2904587

Subsidiary undertakings include: Network Rail (High Speed) Ltd; Network Rail (VY1) Ltd; Network Rail Certification Body Ltd; Network Rail Consulting Ltd; Network Rail Development Ltd; Network Rail Insurance Ltd

Total employees: 35,141

Focus of giving: Education, enterprise/training, environment, health, ill health, marginalised people, community/social welfare, disasters.

Membership: BITC

Cash donations undeclared	✓
Charity of the Year	✓
Gifts in kind	✓
Matched funding	✓
Payroll giving	✓

Charitable donations

Cash UK (latest available):	2014	£571,000
	2013	£490,000
	2012	£589,000
	2011	£635,000
	2010	£763,000
Total UK (cash and in kind):	2014	£2,600,000
Cash worldwide:	2014	£571,000
Total worldwide (cash and in kind):	2014	£2,600,000

Community involvement

Network Rail runs a Charity of Choice partnership and permits charity bucket collections in the stations it operates. This includes some of the busiest stations in Britain (Birmingham New Street, Cannon Street, Charing Cross, Edinburgh Waverley, Euston, Glasgow Central, King's Cross, Leeds City, Liverpool Lime Street, Liverpool Street, London Bridge, Manchester Piccadilly, Paddington, St Pancras, Victoria and Waterloo).

The company also supports charities on a local basis through its routes (Anglia, Kent, London North Eastern, East Midlands, London North Western, Scotland, Sussex, Wales, Wessex, Western) which have their own funding pots from which to make donations to local charities working in the areas of: education, employability and skills; emergency response; health and well-being; social inclusion; and transport and environment.

Network Rail also looks to form relationships with the communities in which it operates through its community schemes, by which voluntary groups can apply for support in transforming disused land in the areas surrounding railways in their area.

Corporate giving

The annual report and accounts for 2013/14 did not declare a figure for charitable donations during the year. The average of charitable donations in the three most recent years for which we have figures was £571,000, and we have taken this as an estimate for charitable donations in 2013/14.

The Sustainability update states that the central Charities Panel supported eight charities, in addition to the Charity of Choice, during the year. Network Rail's route charity panels supported 34 local charities.

Based on the ratio of cash to contributions in 2012/13 we have estimated total contributions for 2013/14 as £2.6 million. Note that this estimate is based on an average and, as a result, the actual of total contributions given by the company may vary considerably.

Charity of the Year

Network Rail's employee-nominated Charity of Choice for 2012/13 to 2013/14 was Action for Children. In 2013/14 the company and its employees raised more than £1.25 million for the charity in the form of gifts in kind, matched funding, workplace funding and other initiatives. In all, over the course of the two year partnership, more than £2 million was raised. CLIC Sargent became the two-year Charity of Choice in February 2014.

In-kind support

Charities are able to apply to run bucket collections at Network Rail's stations.

Network Rail works with Samaritans to address the issue of attempted suicide on its network.

Staff time

Through the employee volunteering scheme, Network Rail contributed more than 1,000 working days in 2013/14.

Employee-led support

Employee volunteering

In 2013/14 almost 800 employees spent time volunteering with, for example, helping students at Snowsfield Primary School with their reading and literacy skills for one hour a week through the Southwark Education Business Alliance.

Employee fundraising

During the year employees took part in various fundraising activities. These have included a team of 11 staff from signalling Scotland and North East who cycled from Morecambe to Scarborough, raising £4,800 for Macmillan Cancer Support.

Matched funding

Network Rail matches funds raised by its employees, with more than £200,000 contributed through the scheme in 2013/14.

Payroll giving

Employees are able to donate through payroll giving. In 2013/14 11% of employees took part in the scheme.

Corporate social responsibility

CSR committee: There is a Corporate Responsibility Group.

CSR information: The following information was taken from the Sustainability update 2013/14:

> Many people use and are impacted by the railways. We are committed to work in a conscientious way so that we maximise the wider social benefits of our network. We want to be a national example of best practice in community investment and to share the socio-economic opportunities created by the way we do business.

CSR report: A Sustainability Report is published annually on the website.

Exclusions

Our research indicates that no support is given for circulars, general appeals, individuals or political appeals.

Applications

In writing to the correspondent. The central Charities Panel meets around six times a year. More information is available from the website.

For local charities

To request more information on making a funding application to your local route, contact the appropriate person as listed on the Network Rail website.

Charity Collections

For registered charities wishing to host a bucket collection in a Network Rail-operated station, download and complete the appropriate forms from the Network Rail website and return to the correspondent.

Newcastle Building Society

Building society

Correspondent: Natalie Falkous, Head of Corporate Social Responsibility, Newcastle Building Society, FAO Corporate Social Responsibility, Portland House, New Bridge Street, Newcastle upon Tyne NE1 8AL (email: csr@newcastle.co.uk; website: csr.newcastle.co.uk)

Directors: Phil Moorhouse, Chair; Jim Willens, Chief Executive; Ron McCormick; Angela Russell, Finance Director; Patrick Ferguson; Andrew Haigh; John Morris; Richard Mayland; Catherine Vine-Lott; Ian Ward; David Buffham (women: 2; men: 9)

Year end	31/12/2013
Turnover	£95,200,000
Pre-tax profit	£2,200,000

Nature of business: Building Society.

FSA registration number: 156058

Subsidiary undertakings include: Kings Manor Properties Ltd; Newcastle Financial Services Ltd; Newcastle Mortgage Loans (Jersey) Ltd; Newcastle Portland House Ltd; Newcastle Strategic Solutions Ltd; Newton Facilities Management Ltd

UK employees: 944

Total employees: 944

Focus of giving: General charitable purposes, education, enterprise/training, older people, children, young people, community/social welfare.

Membership: BITC

Cash donations undeclared	✓
Charity of the Year	✓
Gifts in kind	✓
Market-led giving	✓
Overseas giving	✓

Charitable donations

Cash UK (latest available):	2013	£51,000
	2012	£43,000
	2011	£58,000
	2010	£2,200
	2009	£40,000
Total UK (cash and in kind):	2013	£51,000
Cash worldwide:	2013	£51,000
Total worldwide (cash and in kind):	2013	£51,000

Community involvement

Newcastle Building Society contributes to the communities local to its offices and branches, which it does partly through its Cornerstone in the Community community engagement initiative. This enables its locations to contribute to support good causes in their local area through employee fundraising, in-branch customer events and contributions of employee volunteering time. Part of the initiative involves the Cornerstone in the Community Awards, which recognise individuals and groups making a positive contribution to the Society's 'heartland area' (the North East). The society supports grass-roots causes in the North East through the **Newcastle Building Society Community Fund**, which is administered by Community Foundation serving Tyne and Wear and Northumberland (Charity Commission no. 700510). The Society runs a corporate Charity of the Year scheme, the beneficiary of which is voted for by employees.

Corporate giving

The annual report and accounts for 2013 did not declare a total for charitable donations. The average of such contributions in the two most recent years for which we have figures was £51,000, and we have taken this as an estimate for charitable donations in 2013.

We were unable to determine a value for the in-kind support given by the society. Based on research in previous years, however, we believe this has been considerable.

Note that we would typically take the average of the three most recent years for which we have figures; however, as contributions in 2010 were unusually low, we have chosen to use the figures from only the most recent two years.

Newcastle Building Community Fund

In 2013 the building society donated more than £8,000 to local grass-roots causes within the North East. Administered through Community Foundation serving Tyne and Wear and Northumberland, the fund focuses on supporting projects around 'education, nurturing new talent and improving the community'. Since being established in 1992, the society has donated more than £800,000 to more than 800 charities and causes, including community groups, children's support charities, adults with disabilities, kids' clubs, and emergency services, as well as individuals. During the year, the society decided to give higher amounts to fewer charities, so as to assist with larger projects.

Charity of the Year

The 2012/13 Charity of the Year was Help for Heroes, which received £24,000 from funds raised and in 2013/14 Alzheimer's Society received £14,400. Employees nominated Percy Hedley Foundation as its charity partner for a minimum time of two years.

It would appear that, as well as fundraising for Children in Need, Comic Relief and Macmillan Coffee Morning, individual branches of the society select their own charities of the year.

In-kind support

Staff time

A new volunteering policy was established in 2014 to allow staff the opportunity to take paid leave to volunteer their time and skills to groups in their communities.

Gifts in kind

Following a redesign of branch uniforms in 2013, 150 old uniforms were donated to Team Kenya, a charity working to support villages in Kenya.

Employee-led support

Employee volunteering

Employees at Newcastle Building Society's branches and offices volunteer in their local communities as part of the Cornerstone in the Community scheme. Examples include staff at the Hexham branch who visited a school as part of the Society's Boardroom Charity Challenge, a six-week curriculum-based financial education programme for children.

Employee fundraising

Employees fundraise for a range of local charitable causes, as well as for the Society's Charity of the Year. Fundraising activities during the year have included: senior staff at the Consett branch who took part in the Great North Run in aid of the branch's Charity of the Year, Willow Burn Hospice; and staff from head office and 19 of the Society's branches who took to their exercise bikes to cover the equivalent of the full distance of the Tour de France in the 'Tour de Branch' Challenge, raising £4,000.

Commercially led support

Sir Bobby Robson Foundation Accounts

In partnership with the Sir Bobby Robson Foundation, which supports projects within Newcastle upon Tyne Hospitals NHS Foundation Trust, the society offers its members The Sir Bobby Robson Foundation ISA and Saver (Issue 6). On its website, the society pledges to 'pay an additional 0.10% on all balances' held within these accounts to the Sir Bobby Robson Foundation. The website states that: 'So far, we've been able to donate an amount of just over £1.2 million' to the foundation.

Corporate social responsibility

CSR committee: The contact is head of CSR.

CSR information: The following information was taken from the Corporate Social Responsibility (CSR) website:

> As a mutual building society we aim to be a good social citizen. We are committed to supporting local causes within our Heartland and aim to assist grassroots charities with a special focus on social care and the elderly. These often include groups and associations proposed by both our customers and our staff.

CSR report: There is a dedicated corporate social responsibility website.

Exclusions

No grants for: sponsorship and fundraising events; small contributions to major appeals; large capital projects; endowments; political or religious groups; or work which should be funded by health and local authorities, or government grant aid.

Applications

For more details regarding the **Newcastle Building Society Community Fund**, visit Community Foundation serving Tyne and Wear and Northumberland's website: www.communityfoundation.org.uk.

We advise that local appeals for assistance should be directed to the relevant branch.

Next plc

Retail – clothing and footwear

Correspondent: Corporate Responsibility Manager, Legislation and Environment Department, Next plc, Desford Road, Enderby, Leicester LE19 4AT (tel: 03337774577; website: www.nextplc.co.uk/corporate-responsibility/community.aspx)

Directors: John Barton, Chair; Lord Wolfson of Aspley Guise, Chief Executive; David Keens, Group Finance Director; Michael Law; Jane Shields; Jonathan Dawson; Steve Barber; Francis Salway; Caroline Goodall (women: 2; men: 7)

Year end	25/01/2014
Turnover	£3,740,000,000
Pre-tax profit	£695,200,000

Nature of business: The principal activities of the group are high-street retailing, home shopping, customer services management and financial services.

Company registration number: 4521150

Subsidiary undertakings include: Next Group plc; Next Retail Ltd; Next Directory; Next Distribution Ltd; Lipsy Ltd; Next Sourcing Ltd; Next Manufacturing (Pvt) Ltd

Main locations: Bradford, Leeds, Leicester

UK employees: 25,000

Total employees: 29,000

Focus of giving: General charitable purposes, health, ill health, non-registered charities, children, young people, community/social welfare.

Membership: BITC

FTSE 100	✓
Gifts in kind	✓
Humanitarian aid: overseas	✓
Market-led giving	✓
Overseas giving	✓
Payroll giving	✓
Sponsorship	✓

Charitable donations

Cash UK (latest available):	2014	£1,060,000
	2011	£1,141,500
	2010	£996,623
	2008	£499,000
	2007	£383,000
Total UK (cash and in kind):	2014	£2,707,000
Cash worldwide:	2014	£1,060,000
Total worldwide (cash and in kind):	2014	£2,707,000

Community involvement

Rather than supporting one Charity of the Year, Next instead:

> Supports a wide range of registered charities and other groups and organisations without charitable status, providing donations of financial support or the offer of products which can be used to realise additional funding via charitable spend, gifts in kind and charity linked sales.

The group also sponsors a small number of organisations and its employees actively support charities through a GAYE scheme, donations and fundraising activities.

Corporate giving

During 2013/14, Next plc gave financial support to: registered charities amounting to £945,000; individual requests, local and national groups and organisations amounting to £115,000 and commercial support and sponsorship amounting to £120,000.

Financial support has been complemented with the following fundraising activities to generate additional funds for registered charities, individuals, groups or organisations: Next charity events £34,000; gifts in kind – donations of products £1.6 million; charity linked sales £363,000; employee fundraising £37,000.

The figures we use for the company's UK and worldwide contributions do not include commercial sponsorship, charity link sales and employee fundraising as is our usual practice; however, they are noted here to provide full information.

Beneficiaries included: Doncaster Refurnish; Oxfam; Rainbow Trust Children's Charity; ReusefulUK; Ty Hafan.

In-kind support

Next supports charities and community organisations through gifts in kind, mainly in the donation of products which are unsellable or no longer needed. During 2013, a number of national and local charities benefitted from these in-kind contributions.

Case study: Doncaster Refurnish

Next continued in its long-term partnership with Doncaster Refurnish, which collects and renovates donated furniture to resell to disadvantaged people at affordable prices, and is based near the group's warehouses in Doncaster. The group gives 'unsellable, damaged furniture and home accessories that the charity is able to use and repair'. Amongst its activities, the charity also runs a training and volunteering scheme to engage people who have disabilities, learning difficulties or have been unemployed long-term.

Next Charity Event

Next hosted a charity golf day, which helped to raise funds for the Rainbow Trust Children's Charity.

Employee-led support

Employee fundraising

Next employees have raised funds for a range of charities through activities such as 'running, cycling, sky diving, playing football, cake sales' and growing moustaches in support of Movember.

Payroll giving scheme

The group operates a payroll giving scheme, through which employees donated more than £25,000 in 2013/14.

Oxfam Collects at Work

Employees at Next Head Office are able to donate their unwanted goods, from which Oxfam is able to create value from. During 2013 more than £3,700 was raised through the scheme.

Commercially led support

Commercial sponsorship

Next offers commercial sponsorship to a small number of organisations. Local sporting teams are also supported and especially those with which an employee has a direct involvement.

Market-led giving

The group sells products in its stores, with royalties paid to charities 'based on an agreed percentage from the sale of the product'.

Since 2011 half of the fees charged for carrier bags from Next have been donated to Ty Hafan, South Wales' only children's hospice.

Corporate social responsibility

CSR committee: The following information is taken from the annual report and accounts:

> NEXT has a Corporate Responsibility (CR) forum of 15 senior managers and directors representing key areas of the business to develop and implement strategy. The forum identifies potential issues and opportunities and evaluates the success of NEXT's response. The CR Manager holds regular updates with the executive director responsible for CR.

CSR information: NEXT plc's website states:

> For NEXT, corporate responsibility (CR) means addressing key business-related social, ethical and environmental impacts in a way that aims to bring value to all our stakeholders, including our shareholders.
>
> *Community*
>
> With 541 stores in the United Kingdom and Ireland, we offer support to a wide range of charities and organisations of all sizes, by working to provide them with donations that are of most benefit to them and their particular cause, whether it be a financial donation, or the offer of products that can be used to realise additional funding. Our aim is to make a difference, so we do not support a single 'Charity of the Year', as we believe we are able to make a greater impact by working with a wider group of charities and organisations. In addition to supporting individual charity requests, we also agree to support some charities for an agreed number of years with a specified donation.

CSR report: A CR report is published annually. There is also a detailed CR section on the group's website.

Exclusions

No support is given to political causes.

Applications

In writing to the correspondent.

Northern Foods Ltd

Food manufacture

Correspondent: The Company Secretary, Trinity Park House, Fox Way, Wakefield WF2 8EE (website: www.2sfg.com)

Directors: R. S. Boparan; B. K. Boparan; K. Derry; S. Henderson; V. Patel; S. Amin; S. Wookey

Year end	27/07/2013
Turnover	£178,500,000
Pre-tax profit	£32,400,000

Nature of business: Northern Foods is a supplier of high-quality chilled foods under the own labels of the major multiple retailers, with strong brands of its own in premium quality biscuits, fresh chilled dairy products, frozen food and savoury pastry products.

Company registration number: 471864

Subsidiary undertakings include: In April 2011, BH Acquisitions Ltd (Boparan) announced that they had acquired or received valid acceptances representing 91.27% of the existing issued ordinary share capital of Northern Foods (excluding any treasury shares) and that they would be issuing compulsory acquisition notices setting out their intention to acquire compulsorily all remaining Northern

Foods shares. Shares of Northern Foods were delisted from the London Stock Exchange in May 2011 and Boparan became the sole shareholder of Northern Foods on 10 June 2011. Northern Foods is re-registered as a private limited company.

Main locations: Accrington, Bolton, Batley, Sheffield, Nottingham, Oldham, Market Drayton, Manchester, Worksop, Wakefield, Corby, Carlisle, Hull

Total employees: 248

Focus of giving: Education, enterprise/training, health, ill health, children, young people, community/social welfare.

Cash donations undeclared ✓
Payroll giving ✓

Charitable donations

Cash UK (latest available):	2013	£85,000
	2011	£100,000
	2009	£93,900
	2008	£60,000
	2007	£59,600
Total UK (cash and in kind):	2013	£85,000
Cash worldwide:	2013	£85,000
Total worldwide (cash and in kind):	2013	£85,000

Community involvement

Our research tells us that the company:

> Set up The Northern Foods Foundation for Science & Technology, (not a registered charity), which sponsors 30 new post A-Level students a year throughout their degree course at Leeds, Nottingham and Reading universities. The company supports students wishing to study food science by awarding grants of £1,000.

Corporate giving

A total for charitable donations was not included in the accounts for 2012/13. However, the average of charitable donations in the most recent three years for which we have figures was £85,000. Therefore, we have estimated this as the total for charitable donations in 2012/13. Details of beneficiaries were not available.

Employee-led support

Payroll giving

Our research indicates that the company also operates a Give As You Earn (GAYE) scheme for employees.

Corporate social responsibility

CSR information: No CSR information found.

We were unable to determine the ratio of women to men on the board.

Exclusions

No support is given for political or religious appeals.

Applications

In writing to the correspondent referenced 'Charitable donations'.

Northern Powergrid Holdings Company (formerly C. E. Electric UK Funding Company)

Electricity

Correspondent: The Company Secretary, Lloyds Court, 78 Grey Street, Newcastle upon Tyne NE1 6AF (website: www.northernpowergrid.com/about-us)

Directors: G. E. Abel, Chair; D. L. Anderson; R. Dixon; J. M. France; P. J. Goodman, Chief Financial Officer; P. A. Jones, Chief Executive; J. N. Reynolds

Year end	31/12/2013
Turnover	£722,015,000
Pre-tax profit	£280,554,000

Nature of business: Northern Powergrid Holdings Company (formerly C. E. Electric UK Funding Company) is responsible for delivering electricity to properties across the North East of England, Yorkshire and northern Lincolnshire.

Company registration number: 3476201

Subsidiary undertakings include: For a list of subsidiaries, see the annual report and accounts.

Focus of giving: Education, environment, poverty and social exclusion.

Membership: BITC

Cash donations undeclared ✓
Gifts in kind ✓

Charitable donations

Cash UK (latest available):	2013	£50,000
	2012	£42,000
	2011	£52,000
	2010	£56,800
	2009	£100,600
Total UK (cash and in kind):	2013	£50,000
Cash worldwide:	2013	£50,000
Total worldwide (cash and in kind):	2013	£50,000

Community involvement

Northern Powergrid looks to engage with the communities in which its customers live through its 'charity and sponsorship' programme.

Charity partnership programmes

A Priority Services Register is used to provide 'additional support' to customers from 'vulnerable areas' through the group's partnership programmes with the British Red Cross and the Trussell Trust. In 2012/13 500 priority service customers were visited by the British Red Cross and, in times of crisis, the Trussell Trust supports these customers by providing food boxes.

Corporate giving

A figure for charitable donations was not included in the 2013 annual report and accounts. In the three most recent years for which we have figures, charitable donations averaged £50,000. We have taken this figure as an estimate for charitable donations in 2013.

Though we could find no details of beneficiary organisations, we believe that donations were made principally to local charities serving in the communities in which the group operates.

In-kind support

In conjunction with National Energy Action, the group has promoted safety and awareness associated with electricity distribution. More than 40,000 children benefit each year from a booklet, 'Keep Warm and Stay Safe', and visits from the group's mascot, Vic Voltage, which give advice on electricity safety, saving money, keeping warm and staying healthy.

Corporate social responsibility

CSR committee: There was no evidence of a separate CSR committee.

CSR information: This information was obtained from the company website:

> We put our customers and their communities first.
>
> Our charity and sponsorship programme supports community engagement.

We were unable to determine the ratio of women to men on the board.

CSR report: There was no evidence of a separate CSR report.

Exclusions

Our research indicates that no support is given for circular appeals, advertising in national charity brochures, animal welfare, appeals from individuals, the arts, fundraising events, heritage, medical research, overseas projects, political or religious appeals, science/technology, sickness/disability, or a Charity of the Year.

Applications

In writing to the correspondent, referenced 'Charitable donations'.

Northern Shell & Media Group Ltd (entry formerly titled Northern & Shell Network Ltd)

Media

Correspondent: Robert Sanderson, Company Secretary, The Northern & Shell Building, Number 10 Lower Thames Street, London EC3R 6EN (tel: 020 8612 7000; website: www.northernandshell.co.uk/philanthropy)

Directors: Stan Myerson; Richard Desmond, Chair; Robert Sanderson; Martin Ellice; Dr Paul Ashford (women: 0; men: 5)

Year end	31/12/2013
Turnover	£610,878,000
Pre-tax profit	£36,769,000

Nature of business: The ultimate holding company in the Northern & Shell group of companies principally engaged in newspaper publishing and printing, magazine publishing, television broadcasting, lottery management services, property investment and the exploitation and further development of intellectual property.

Company registration number: 4086466

Subsidiary undertakings include: Northern & Shell Broadcasting Ltd; Northern & Shell Broadcasting (CI) Ltd; Northern & Shell Group Ltd; Northern & Shell Network Ltd; Northern & Shell Television Group Ltd; West Ferry Leasing Ltd

Brands include: Daily Express, Daily Star, Daily Star Sunday, OK!, Sunday Express, The Health Lottery

Total employees: 1,190

Focus of giving: General charitable purposes, health, ill health, older people, poverty and social exclusion, children, young people.

Gifts in kind	✓
Humanitarian aid: overseas	✓
Overseas giving	✓

Charitable donations

Cash UK (latest available):	2013	£103,000
	2012	£262,000
	2011	£518,000
	2008	£554,000
	2007	£547,000
Total UK (cash and in kind):	2013	£103,000
Cash worldwide:	2013	£103,000
Total worldwide (cash and in kind):	2013	£103,000

Community involvement

Northern & Shell Media Group Ltd supports charities through donations made via **The Desmond Foundation** (formerly known as The RD Crusaders Foundation, Charity Commission no. 1014352), though previous research suggests that a small number of donations have, in the past, been made to charities directly from the group. The Northern & Shell website describes that:

> In recent years the trust has focused its awards on children and young people's charities in the UK and has contributed extensively to further the well-being of disadvantaged sections of society; however, larger charities have also benefited extensively with donations to schools, hospitals, old people's homes, carer organisations, hospices and a wide range of medical support groups.

Though these areas remain the main focus of the foundation, other causes may also be considered by the trustees.

Corporate giving

The annual report and accounts for 2013 declared charitable donations of £103,000, the vast majority of which we believe was given to **The Desmond Foundation.** However, the foundation's accounts for 2013 state that £870,000 was donated by Richard Desmond, a trustee of the foundation and £15,000 was donated by ITN – a subsidiary of Northern & Shell Media Group Ltd.

In-kind donations of administrative services, accounting support and office space are given to the foundation by Northern & Shell plc, a subsidiary of the group. We could not determine a value for this support.

See the corporate charity entry on p. 401 for more information.

Commercially led support

The Health Lottery

Through The Health Lottery, Northern & Shell aims to generate funds for the country's most deprived and isolated community groups. Health Lottery support has helped more than a thousand local health charities since its creation. The Health Lottery's website states that '20p of every £1 played is donated to health-related good causes in Great Britain.' Donations are distributed through The People's Health Trust (PHT).

Corporate social responsibility

CSR committee: We found no evidence of a CSR committee.

CSR information: The following information was taken from the company's website:

> Charitable giving lies at the heart of Northern & Shell. As a responsible business we are constantly on the lookout for opportunities to support a diverse range of good causes in every possible way. As our Network has grown, so has our commitment to working in the community.

CSR report: We found no evidence of a CSR report.

Corporate charity: The Desmond Foundation (formerly known as the RD Crusaders Foundation) (Charity Commission no. 1014352).

Exclusions

No support is given for political appeals.

Applications

In writing to the correspondent, referenced 'Charitable donations'.

Applications to the Desmond Foundation (Charity Commission no. 1014352) should be made in writing to: Allison Racher, The Desmond Foundation, Northern & Shell Building, Number 10 Lower Thames Street, London EC3R 6EN. (Tel: 020 8612 7760; Email: allison.racher@express.co.uk).

Northumbrian Water Group Ltd (formerly Northumbrian Water Group plc)

Water

Correspondent: See 'Applications', Abbey Road, Pity Me, Durham DH1 5FJ (tel: 0870 608 4820; website: www.nwl.co.uk/your-home/community.aspx)

Directors: Andrew John Hunter, Chair; Heidi Mottram, Chief Executive; Loi Shun Chan; Frank Frame; Tak Chuen Edward Ip; Hing Lam Kam; Duncan Macrae; Wai Che Wendy Tong-Barnes; Martin Parker (women: 2; men: 6)

Year end	31/12/2013
Turnover	£826,800,000
Pre-tax profit	£120,200,000

Nature of business: Northumbrian Water Group contains Northumbrian Water Ltd (NWL), which provides water and sewerage services in the north east of England under the brand name Northumbrian Water and water services in the South East under the brand name Essex and Suffolk water.

The following information was taken from the Northumbrian Water Group website:

> Northumbrian Water Group was delisted from the London Stock Exchange on Friday 14th October 2011 following a cash acquisition by UK Water (2011) Ltd (a company indirectly wholly owned by a consortium comprising Cheung Kong Infrastructure Holdings Ltd, Cheung Kong (Holdings) Ltd and Li Ka Shing Foundation Ltd).

In October 2011, Northumbrian Water Group plc was reregistered as a private company and became Northumbrian Water Group Ltd.

Company registration number: 4760441

Subsidiary undertakings include: Ayr Environmental Services Ltd; Caledonian Environmental Services Ltd; Caledonian Levenmouth Treatment Services Ltd; Northumbrian Services Ltd; Northumbrian Water Finance plc; Northumbrian Water Ltd;

Brands include: Essex and Suffolk Water, Northumbrian Water

Main locations: Durham

UK employees: 3,138

Total employees: 3,138

Focus of giving: General charitable purposes, education, environment, health, ill health, heritage, older people, sport, recreation, children, young people, community/social welfare.

Membership: BITC

Cash donations undeclared	✓
Gifts in kind	✓
Matched funding	✓
Sponsorship	✓

Charitable donations

Cash UK (latest available):	2013	£155,000
	2012	£155,000
	2011	£152,000
	2010	£157,000
	2009	£134,000
Total UK (cash and in kind):	2013	£155,000
Cash worldwide:	2013	£155,000
Total worldwide (cash and in kind):	2013	£155,000

Community involvement

Northumbrian Water and Essex and Suffolk Water, support charities and communities in the areas in which they operate through cash and in-kind donations and employee time contributions through the 'Just an hour' volunteering scheme.

Community foundations

Community foundations serving the areas in which the group has a presence hold endowment funds which are used to support community and environmental initiatives. Grants decisions are based on criteria such as health, education, environment and community links and are made quarterly by employee committees. The community foundations are, in the North East, Tees Valley, County Durham, Tyne and Wear and Northumberland, and in Essex, Essex Community Foundation.

Environmental and health education

Northumbrian Water and Essex and Suffolk Water have formed a number of partnerships with organisations in the areas of environment, conservation and sports to support public education on these matters. Partners have included Northumberland Wildlife Trust (Kielder and Bakethin) and the Broads Authority. Contributions have included funding for project officers and providing expertise. Sports organisations have also been sponsored.

WaterAid

The group has supported WaterAid and, since 1997, employees and customers have raised more than £5 million.

Corporate giving

More than 160 organisations were supported with cash or in-kind support in 2013, though the group's annual report and accounts did not declare charitable donations made during the year. The latest figures for charitable donations available from the Northumbrian Water and the Essex and Suffolk Water websites appeared to date from 2011 to 2012. We have, therefore, taken an estimate based on the average of charitable donations in the three most recent years for which we have figures, which was £155,000.

In-kind support

Healthworks

Northumbrian Water has used one of its redundant buildings for a project to help tackle the long-term health issues of residents in Easington, County Durham, granting a 99 year lease to County Durham Primary Care Trust. The centre hosts the coming together of service providers and community groups.

Environmental and health education

As part of its efforts to educate the public about the environment, conservation and health, the group has developed a range on online educational resources which can be downloaded by teachers and children.

Employee-led support

Care for Safety scheme

The scheme, which encourages employees to reduce accidents and associated lost time in the workplace has helped to raise money for a number of health and emergency-related organisations.

Employee committees

Groups of employees meet quarterly with grants coordinators from the community foundations with which the group has funds to make decisions on grants applications.

Employee volunteering

Through the 'Just an hour' volunteering scheme, employees are encouraged to contribute their time, knowledge and skills in their local communities. Past activities have included organising charity balls, gardening, beach clean-ups and decorating challenges. In 2013 more than 700 organisations received a total of 16,000 hours of work-time through the scheme.

Employee fundraising

Employees are encouraged to fundraise for a wide range of good causes and can apply for sponsorship through the 'Cheque it out' scheme.

Commercially led support

Sponsorship

As part of its health campaign, Northumbrian Water works with sports and educational groups in the North East.

Castle View Enterprise Academy – Northumbrian Water is the lead sponsor of the academy, which is based in Sunderland.

Newcastle Eagles Hoops for Health – NWL has sponsored the Eagles' healthy living schools programme.

Essex and Suffolk Water also sponsors similar groups in its operational area, including:

Senior Daggers – A programme run in partnership with Dagenham and Redbridge FC, by which local residents can go to their football ground each week for social and well-being activities.

Corporate social responsibility

CSR committee: The CSR Committee consists of non-executive directors, NWL directors and senior managers who oversee all aspects of the company's CSR policy.

CSR information: The following information was taken from Northumbrian Water Ltd's website: 'We support the communities we serve in a number of different ways. We have been widely recognised as leaders in our support for projects that make the areas we serve better places in which to live, work or invest.'

CSR report: The group website states the following:

> In previous years we reported on corporate responsibility as a separate report. From 2011, in line with our vision and values, and reflecting the importance of sustainability to our business and how deeply it is embedded, we believe we should report sustainability issues alongside our core business activities. We have done this throughout our annual report with the sustainability text highlighted as green.

However, the most recent CSR information we were able to obtain at the time of writing dated to 2011.

Exclusions

No donations are given to individuals, exclusive religious projects, organisations outside its service area, or to cover wages.

Applications

The focus for both cash and in-kind support is on small, grass-roots organisations.

Essex and Suffolk Water

Essex and Suffolk Water supports organisations in the areas of Essex and Suffolk where it operates.

To request cash or in-kind support from Essex and Suffolk Water, note the following information from the website:

> If you represent an organisation seeking financial support or equipment for a project we would invite you to apply for a grant from our fund held with the Essex Community Foundation.
>
> Please apply on-line at www.essexcommunityfoundation.org.uk or call 01245 356018.
>
> An employees panel meets half yearly to consider applications in May and November. Your application will be presented to the next available panel meeting.

Essex and Suffolk Water also have a specific environmental fund 'Branch Out', which works in partnership to reconnect habitats for the benefit of people and wildlife. For more information or to apply please go to www.eswater.co.uk/your-home/environment/branch-out.aspx

If you are seeking sponsorship or support for a raffle or tombola prize, please send your request to partnerships@nwl.co.uk. Each request will be considered and responded to within six weeks.

'Just an hour' volunteering scheme

This scheme is designed to impact on education, the environment and the general well-being of the communities we work in and serve. One of the main goals is to add value to the community and to realise this, each of our employees has been given the opportunity to take a minimum of 15 working hours a year to support community initiatives. If you have a project or initiative that you feel we could support please visit the 'Just an hour' section of our website www.eswater.co.uk/your-home/how-to-get-involved.aspx for more information and details on how you can get involved.

Northumbrian Water

Northumbrian Water supports organisations in the areas of north east England where it operates.

To request cash or in-kind support from Northumbrian Water, note the following from the website:

> If you represent an organisation seeking financial support or equipment for a project we would invite you to apply for a grant through one of our community foundation funds.
>
> - If your organisation is based within County Durham please apply on-line at www.cdcf.org.uk or call 01913 786340
> - If your organisation is based within Tees Valley please apply on-line at www.teesvalleyfoundation.org or call 01642 260860
> - If your organisation is based within Tyne & Wear or Northumberland please apply on-line at www.communityfoundation.org.uk or call 01912 220945
>
> A panel of our employees meets quarterly, in May, August, November and February, to consider applications – Your application will be presented to the next available panel meeting.
>
> Northumbrian Water also has a specific environmental fund 'Branch Out', which works in partnership to reconnect habitats for the benefit of people and wildlife. For more information or to apply please go to www.nwl.co.uk/your-home/environment/branch-out.apsx.
>
> If you are seeking sponsorship or support for a raffle or tombola prize, please send your request to partnerships@nwl.co.uk. We will consider each request and respond to you within six weeks.
>
> ***'Just an hour' volunteering scheme***
>
> The scheme is designed to have a positive impact on education, the environment and the general well-being of the communities we work in and serve One of the main goals is to add value to the community and to realise this, each of our employees is given the opportunity to take a minimum of 15 working hours a year to support community initiatives. If you have a project or initiative that you feel we could support please visit the 'Just an hour' section of our website www.nwl.co.uk/your-home/community/how-to-get-involved.aspx for more information and details on how you can get involved.

Nottingham Building Society

Building society

Correspondent: Community Investment Team, Nottingham House, 3 Fulforth Street, Nottingham NG1 3DL (website: www.thenottingham.com/your-nottingham)

Directors: John Edwards, Chair; Keith Whitesides; David Marlow, Chief Executive; Simon Taylor; Jane Kibbey; Ashraf Piranie, Finance Director; Mary Phibbs; Andrew Neden (women: 2; men: 6)

Year end	31/12/2013
Turnover	£34,800,000
Pre-tax profit	£8,100,000

Nature of business: Independent building society offering a range of financial products and services.

FSA registration number: 200785

Main locations: Nottingham

UK employees: 599

Total employees: 599

Focus of giving: General charitable purposes, economic generation, education, enterprise/training, housing, homelessness, community/social welfare.

Charity of the Year	✓
Gifts in kind	✓
Sponsorship	✓

Charitable donations

Cash UK (latest available):	2013	£61,000
	2012	£61,000
	2011	£49,000
	2009	£0
	2007	£22,720
Total UK (cash and in kind):	2013	£61,000
Cash worldwide:	2013	£61,000
Total worldwide (cash and in kind):	2013	£61,000

Community involvement

Nottingham Building Society develops its community work through its Doing Good Together programme, which operates around three main elements – fundraising; community grants; and volunteering – predominantly focusing on the themes of homelessness, financial education and employability.

Cash for Your Community grants

In association with its media partners, each year the group gives grants to local causes.

Grants for Good

The group has worked with Nottinghamshire Community Foundation since 2011 to award grants to projects that support prosperous communities. The website states that 'previous grants have funded everything from employability courses to new home starter packs.

Doing Good in the Community

The group's website states the following:

> Our staff regularly volunteer their time and have supported a variety of initiatives including mobile phone collections, food and clothing collections, job clubs, marketing support and even helping out at Framework's Big Sleep Out!
>
> If you have a garden that needs some TLC, a room that needs a facelift or the advice of a business expert get in touch and we'll see what we can do to help.

Nominated charity

Framework, a Nottingham-based charity, which works to support and prevent homelessness and to assist with routes into employment, continued to benefit through its partnership with the group. In 2013, aside from fundraising activities, the partnership took on three major initiatives, which saw 'The Nottingham':

- Lend £800,000 on commercial terms to Framework to assist with building 14 units of 'move-on' accommodation
- Sign a five-year contact to lease the property of one of its former branches at a 'heavily discounted rate' to provide an emergency city centre service for homeless and vulnerable people
- Support Framework to launch its £10 million investment plan for homeless housing

For more details of the group's partnership with the charity, see the annual report.

Corporate giving

In 2013 charitable donations from the group totalled £61,000.

The following information is taken from the annual report and accounts:

> With the assistance from Nottinghamshire Community Foundation and East Midlands radio station Gem 106, the group gave community grants of £26,649 to several charitable groups in its heartland. In addition, in collaboration with The Nottingham Post £35,000 (of which The Nottingham contributed £25,000) was given to 140 worthy groups in the Nottinghamshire area.

We were unable to determine a value for the in-kind donations given by the group.

Beneficiaries: Nottinghamshire Fire and Rescue Prince's Trust Team Programme (£2,500)

In-kind support

The group's 'nominated charity', Framework has been leased a property by the group for five years at a 'heavily discounted rate'.

Employee-led support

Employee volunteering

Employees have spent time volunteering for the group's chosen charity, Framework. Activities have included decorating a day centre in Mansfield and renovating a room in a home for homeless people.

Employee fundraising

Employees from across the group have contributed to raising funds for charity, During the year activities included 29 employees taking part in a five day bike ride, raising £4,400 and one member of staff donating a day's wages.

Commercially led support

Sponsorship

As part of its support for SportsAid, the group has pledged to sponsor 13 young athletes who are involved in various sports and come from communities near to its branches.

Commercially led

As part of its support of Framework, the society launched a philanthropic savings bond with the charity, enabling investors to accept lower rates of interest on their savings in return for reduced interest rate payments on a loan made to Framework by the society to develop its follow-on accommodation.

Corporate social responsibility

CSR committee: There was no evidence of a separate CSR Committee.

CSR information: The group aims to help people with basic needs; education, housing, employment and personal finance management so that they can support themselves whilst also building strong, thriving communities.

CSR report: A CSR report is contained within the annual report and accounts.

Exclusions

Our research indicates that no support is given for: advertising in charity brochures; appeals from individuals; children/youth; education; elderly people enterprise/training; overseas projects; political appeals; part funding of a larger project; travel expenses; rent or property maintenance; staffing costs; or projects which are the responsibility of statutory organisations.

Applications

Our research tells us that application forms are available from the society or from local branches.

Novae Group plc

Insurance

Correspondent: Charities Committee, 71 Fenchurch Street, London EC3M 4HH (tel: 020 7903 7300; website: www.novae.com/about/corporate-responsibility)

Directors: Matthew Fosh, Chief Executive; Charles Fry, Chief Financial Officer; John Hastings-Bass, Chair; Jeremy Adams; Laurie Adams; Sir Bryan Carsberg; David Henderson; Mary Phibbs; David Pye; Teresa Furmston (women: 2; men: 8)

Year end	31/12/2013
Turnover	£513,800,000
Pre-tax profit	£42,800,000

Nature of business: Novae Group plc is the holding company of a group that writes both insurance and reinsurance in the property, casualty and marine, aviation and political risk markets. It has offices in London and Zurich.

Company registration number: 5673306

Subsidiary undertakings include: Novae Corporate Underwriting Ltd; Novae Holdings Ltd; Novae Management Ltd; Novae Syndicates Ltd; Novae Underwriting Ltd

Total employees: 263

Focus of giving: General charitable purposes, education, environment, health, ill health, children, young people.

Cash donations undeclared	✓
Gifts in kind	✓
Matched funding	✓
Overseas giving	✓
Sponsorship	✓

Charitable donations

Cash UK (latest available):	2013	£176,000
	2012	£194,000
	2011	£213,000
	2010	£121,000
	2009	£47,000
Total UK (cash and in kind):	2013	£176,000
Cash worldwide:	2013	£176,000
Total worldwide (cash and in kind):	2013	£176,000

Community involvement

Novae's community involvement is centred around the promotion of education. The two main ways in which it does this is through the Investing in the Next Generation programme and a partnership with The Prince's Trust, for which it serves as a patron.

The group also takes part in the Lloyd's Community Programme and has a charity committee through which staff are able to choose smaller charities to support.

Corporate giving

The 2013 annual report and accounts do not include a figure for charitable donations. The average amount given in the three most recent years for which we have figures was £176,000, and we have taken this as an estimate for charitable giving in 2013.

Beneficiaries included: Dan's Fund for Burns; Shackleton Foundation; Saint Francis Hospital; St John's Ambulance; Starlight Children's Foundation

In-kind support

In 2013, as part of the Investing in the Next Generation programme, which has the aim of improving the numeracy levels of young people, Novae distributed 4,500 'maths snap' games to 1,500 state junior schools.

As part of its partnership with The Prince's Trust, Novae offers two-week work experience placements for young people on the trust's The Team programme: a personal development course.

Pro bono

As part of its involvement in the Lloyd's Community Programme, Novae employees are involved with the Words and Numbers programme, which helps children attending schools in Tower Hamlets to improve their literacy and numeracy skills.

Employee-led support

Employee fundraising

During the year, group employees took part in various fundraising activities. This included three members of staff who took part in the Sierra Leone marathon in support of Street Child of Sierra Leone.

Matched funding

Novae matches funds raised by its staff for charitable causes, subject to a cap.

Commercially led support

Sponsorship

The group sponsors the Novae Educational Achiever of the Year award at The Prince's Trust awards.

Corporate social responsibility

CSR committee: There is a charity committee.

CSR information: The following information was obtained from the 2013 CSR report: 'Novae's Corporate Social Responsibility strategy centres around the importance of education and the belief that UK businesses have a significant role to play in society.'

CSR report: A CSR report is contained within the annual report and accounts.

Applications

In writing to the correspondent.

NRAM plc (formerly Northern Rock (Asset Management) plc)

Financial services

Correspondent: The Company Secretary, Croft Road, Crossflatts, Bingley, West Yorkshire BD16 2UA (website: www.ukar.com/csr.aspx)

Directors: Richard Pym, Chair; Richard Banks, Chief Executive; Kent Atkinson; Michael Buckley; Sue Langley; Keith Morgan; John Tattersall; David Lunn; Ian Hares, Finance and Investment Director (women: 1; men: 8)

Year end	31/03/2014
Turnover	£1,037,400,000
Pre-tax profit	£860,000,000

Nature of business: The following announcement was made by Northern Rock (Asset Management) plc (now NRAM plc): The legal and capital restructure of the former Northern Rock was successfully completed on 1 January 2010. This resulted in the creation of two separate entities: Northern Rock (Asset Management) plc, the existing company, and a new bank, Northern Rock plc.

- Northern Rock (Asset Management) plc, the existing company renamed, which held approximately £50 billion of residential mortgages and unsecured loans of £3.9 billion immediately post-restructure. Northern Rock (Asset Management) plc holds the government loan plus Northern Rock's non-deposit wholesale and secured funding instruments. Northern Rock (Asset Management) plc does not hold any retail deposits and does not offer any new mortgage lending
- Northern Rock plc, a savings and mortgage bank that holds and services all customer savings accounts and a mortgage book which includes approximately £10 billion of mortgages transferred from the former Northern Rock at the start of 2010. The new bank is regulated as a deposit taker and mortgage lender by the FSA. It offers new savings products and new mortgage lending to increase mortgage supply and help sustain a competitive market. Northern Rock plc also holds certain wholesale deposits

Note the following from the NRAM website:

In March 2010, the Government announced that it intended to integrate NRAM and Bradford & Bingley plc (B&B) under a single holding company. This new holding company – UK Asset Resolution Ltd (UKAR) – has now been established to facilitate the orderly management of the closed mortgage books of both NRAM and B&B and to maximise taxpayer value. Both companies remain as separate legal entities with their own balance sheets and Government support arrangements.

Company registration number: 3273685

Subsidiary undertakings include: A full list of subsidiaries is filed at Companies House.

Main locations: Newcastle upon Tyne

Total employees: 1,117

Focus of giving: General charitable purposes.

Market-led giving	✓
Payroll giving	✓

Charitable donations

Cash UK (latest available):	2014	£24,000
	2011	£11,640
	2010	£15,000,000
	2009	£15,000,000
	2008	£15,000,000
Total UK (cash and in kind):	2014	£24,000
Cash worldwide:	2014	£24,000
Total worldwide (cash and in kind):	2014	£24,000

Community involvement

It would appear that NRAM plc's charitable contributions are made primarily through matched funding of funds raised by employees and through payroll giving.

Its predecessor company had an associated registered charity:

The Northern Rock Foundation (Charity Commission no. 1063906)

The Northern Rock Foundation is an independent charity which aimed to tackle disadvantage and to improve the quality of life for communities in the North East and Cumbria.

In November 2011 it was announced that Virgin Money would become the new owners of Northern Rock plc, and this acquisition took place on 1 January 2012. As part of the sale, it was confirmed that Virgin Money would extend an existing commitment to provide 1% of pre-tax profits to the Northern Rock Foundation, in respect of the Northern Rock part of the business, until the end of 2013.

In April 2014, following discussions, Virgin Money announced that it would not commit further funding. However in May 2014 Virgin Money then offered the foundation £1 million per year for five years, on the condition that this was matched by the foundation raising £3 million per year from the private sector locally. Eventually it was concluded that, given the existing charitable commitments and links with other local funders of many other businesses in the region, this was not a viable option for the foundation.

In September 2014 the trustees announced that they must begin to prepare for the foundation's likely eventual closure.

Corporate giving

Financial information is taken from the annual report and accounts for 2014 of NRAM plc (formerly Northern Rock (Asset Management) plc).

The only charitable contributions we could determine from NRAM itself was in the form of support for staff, fundraising activities by way of matched funding and matching employee donations through a payroll giving programme. During the year, NRAM matched employee fundraising to the total of £18,600 and payroll giving totalled £5,300.

The company has, in the past, also given gifts in kind in the form of staff volunteering their skills, though we have no valuation for this contribution.

Employee-led support

Matched funding

NRAM supports fundraising activities by matching the first £250 of funds raised per employee during the year and by matching employee donations through the payroll giving programme.

Payroll giving

The Give As You Earn scheme is in operation.

Corporate social responsibility

CSR information: UKAR has devised a CSR strategy to cover its subsidiary businesses, including NRAM. The UKAR website states that it is committed to:

- Using the skills of the business to support education in our communities
- Building the skills of our colleagues through community engagement
- Supporting colleagues with their own community and charity initiatives

Applications

The foundation's remaining five grant programmes were closed at the end of 2014.

Ocado Group Ltd

Food services

Correspondent: Charity Committee, Titan Court, 3 Bishop Square, Hatfield Business Park, Hatfield, Hertfordshire AL10 9NE (tel: 01707 227800; website: www.ocadogroup.com/our-responsibilities.aspx)

Directors: Lord Rose, Chair; Tim Steiner, Chief Executive Officer; David Grigson; Duncan Tatton-Brown, Chief

Financial Officer; Neill Abrams; Mark Richardson; Ruth Anderson; Robert Gorrie; Jörn Rausing; Douglas McCallum; Alex Mahon (women: 2; men: 9)

Year end	01/12/2013
Turnover	£792,100,000
Pre-tax profit	(£12,500,000)

Nature of business: Online grocer operating home delivery.

Company registration number: 3875000

Subsidiary undertakings include: Jalapeno Partners Ltd; Last Mile Technology Ltd; Ocado Holdings Ltd; Ocado Information Technology Ltd; Ocado Ltd; Ocado Technology Ltd

Total employees: 5,742

Focus of giving: General charitable purposes, education, enterprise/training, environment, general appeals, health, ill health, children, young people.

Charity of the Year	✓
Gifts in kind	✓
Market-led giving	✓
Overseas giving	✓
Sponsorship	✓

Charitable donations

Cash UK (latest available):	2013	£50,000
	2009	£2,000
Total UK (cash and in kind):	2013	£50,000
Cash worldwide:	2013	£50,000
Total worldwide (cash and in kind):	2013	£50,000

Community involvement

Ocado appears to focus much of its community involvement on the three key areas of education and employment, environment and eating well. It has supported organisations in the form of cash and in-kind donations, sponsorship and product sales. Employees take an active role in the group's charitable initiatives, making up the Charity Committee which, during the year, helped to organise fundraising events in aid of the group's employee-elected Charity of the Year, Macmillan Cancer Support.

Corporate giving

In 2012/13 it would appear that the group made charitable donations of £50,000, £35,000 of which was given to 'various charities'. The remaining £15,000 was a donation made to Root Camp, an organisation working to provide camping cookery courses for teenagers, to support the attendance of underprivileged children on a residential course.

During the year, the group's charity committee organised a number of events, helping to raise more than £62,000 for Charity of the Year, Macmillan Cancer Support. Product sales amounted to £145,000 for the Prince of Wales's Charitable Foundation, and the group awarded sponsorship worth £52,000 to the Peace One Day Primary Education Resource. As is our usual practice, we have not included these amounts in our total figure for corporate donations.

We were unable to determine a value either for the in-kind support given by the group, nor for the donations received by Waitrose Foundation through the group's Sourcing Agreement with Waitrose.

Beneficiaries included: 'Various charities' (£35,000); Root Camp (£15,000)

Charity of the Year 2013: Macmillan Cancer Support

In-kind support

Gifts in kind

During the year, Ocado donated vouchers to approximately 700 registered charities. Food classed as 'waste', which is within its use-by-date is donated to charities.

Employee-led support

Employee involvement

The group's employee-nominated charity, Macmillan Cancer Support, benefitted from funds raised through events organised by the Charity Committee, which is made up of group employees.

Commercially led support

Sponsorship

During the year, Ocado continued its co-sponsorship of the Peace One Day Primary Education Resource which, through education, helps to raise awareness of 'peace day'. The group worked with the Peace One Day charity to launch a countrywide poetry competition to help encourage children to consider the theme and meaning of peace.

Product sales

Through sales of Duchy branded products, the group was able to make a donation to the Prince of Wales' Charitable Foundation, a group of 20 non-profit organisations working in the areas of environment, responsible business and enterprise, young people and education, and global sustainability.

Corporate social responsibility

CSR committee: In 2010 Ocado established a charity committee made up of eight employees, which increased to twelve employees in April 2011.

Following a review of its initiatives in 2012/13 the group appointed its first Head of Corporate Responsibility and established a group of CSR champions to follow up recommendations from the review.

CSR information: The CSR report states: 'Running our business in a responsible way is fundamental both to the way we operate and to delivering sustainable profits and longterm value for our shareholders.' Ocado looks to use its position and expertise as an opportunity for change and focuses on the areas of education and employment, environment and eating well.

CSR report: A CSR report is contained within the annual report and accounts.

Applications

In writing to the correspondent.

Organix Brands Ltd

Food manufacture, food services

Correspondent: The Company Secretary, The Greenhouse, 120–122 Commercial Road, Bournemouth, Dorset BH2 5LT (tel: 0800 393 511; website: www.organix.com/our-mission-you/our-values)

Directors: A. Rosier; R. Baenziger

Year end	31/12/2013
Turnover	£37,776,000
Pre-tax profit	£3,468,000

Nature of business: The supply of baby and children's organic food to retailers for sale to the public.

Company registration number: 2716145

Total employees: 50

Focus of giving: Health, ill health, medical research, children, young people.

Charitable donations

Cash UK (latest available):	2013	£0
	2012	£120,000
	2010	£120,000
	2009	£120,000
Total UK (cash and in kind):	2013	£0
Cash worldwide:	2013	£0
Total worldwide (cash and in kind):	2013	£0

Community involvement

We were unable to determine details of Organix Brands Ltd's community involvement. It would appear that Organix's sustainability strategy predominantly focuses on environmental issues.

Corporate giving

The annual report and accounts for 2013 state that the company made no donations during the year for charitable purposes and, in January 2014, the **Organix Foundation** was removed from the Charity Commission register.

We have retained this entry as it may be that charitable giving is under review by Organix and will continue via another channel.

Corporate social responsibility

CSR committee: We found no evidence of there being a CSR committee.

CSR information: Organix's sustainability policy focuses on the environment.

CSR report: We found no published CSR report.

Applications

In writing to the correspondent, referenced 'Charitable donations'.

Paragon Group of Companies plc

Property

Correspondent: Corporate Social Responsibility Team, 51 Homer Road, Solihull, West Midlands B91 3QJ (tel: 0845 849 4000; fax: 0845 849 4002; website: www.paragon-group.co.uk/About-us/Corporate-responsibility)

Directors: Bob Dench, Chair; Nigel Terrington, Chief Executive; Richard Woodman, Group Finance Director; John Heron; Edward Tilly; Alan Fletcher; Peter Hartill; Fiona Clutterbuck (women: 1; men: 7)

Year end	30/09/2013
Turnover	£177,900,000
Pre-tax profit	£105,400,000

Nature of business: Paragon is an independent UK buy-to-let specialist.

Company registration number: 2336032

Subsidiary undertakings include: Paragon Finance plc; Mortgage Trust Ltd; Paragon Mortgages Ltd; Paragon Mortgages (2010) Ltd; Paragon Car Finance Ltd; Idem Capital Holdings Ltd

Total employees: 1,046

Focus of giving: General charitable purposes, health, ill health, local groups, children, young people, disability.

Charity of the Year ✓

Charitable donations

Cash UK (latest available):	2013	£938,000
	2012	£371,000
	2011	£22,600
	2009	£51,000
	2008	£62,000
Total UK (cash and in kind):	2013	£938,000
Cash worldwide:	2013	£938,000
Total worldwide (cash and in kind):	2013	£938,000

Community involvement

The group looks to contribute to registered charities 'relating to financial services or serving the local communities in which it operates'. It has a particular focus on children's and local charities although, it states in its annual report, 'no charity request is overlooked'. The group also supports the employee-run Paragon's Charity Committee.

Employees vote yearly on which charities will benefit from the fundraising activities organised by the committee.

Corporate giving

In 2012/13 the group contributed £938,000 to charitable causes. Of this amount, £917,000 was donated in support of the Foundation for Credit Counselling, which operates StepChange Debt Charity. The group points out in its strategic report that: 'The increase in contributions from the previous year reflects the numbers of acquired customers making use of the charity's services.'

The remaining £21,000 was donated to other charitable causes, mainly children's and local charities.

Beneficiaries included: The Children's Heart Foundation; Disability Aid Trust; Rotary Club of St Alphege Solihull; Kids in Action; Butterflies Children's Charity; Brainwave.

Nominated charities (Charity of the Year)

2013: Almost £16,000 was raised for Macmillan Cancer Support and the RSPCA Birmingham Animal Centre and Hospital.

2014: Libby Mae's Little Angels and Wythall Animal Sanctuary.

Employee-led support

Employee fundraising

Paragon's Charity Committee is made up of volunteer employees who organise fundraising initiatives in aid of charities elected by the group's employees. Around £10,000 is raised for these nominated charitable causes each year.

Corporate social responsibility

CSR committee: We found no evidence of there being a separate CSR committee.

CSR information: Information taken from the company's 2013 annual report and accounts. 'The group believes that the long-term interests of shareholders, employees and customers are best served by acting in a socially responsible manner. As such, the group ensures that a high standard of corporate governance is maintained.'

CSR report: A CSR report is included in the annual report and accounts.

Applications

In writing to the correspondent.

Pennon Group plc

Water

Correspondent: Charitable Donations Committee, Peninsula House, Rydon Lane, Exeter EX2 7HR (tel: 01392 446688; website: www.pennon-group.co.uk/sustainability)

Directors: Kenneth Harvey, Chair; Ian McAulay, Chief Executive, Viridor; David Dupont, Group Director of Finance; Christopher Loughlin, Chief Executive, South West Water; Gerard Connell; Martin Angle; Gill Rider; Neil Cooper; Kenneth Woodier (women: 1; men: 8)

Year end	31/03/2014
Turnover	£1,321,200,000
Pre-tax profit	£158,700,000

Nature of business: Business is carried out through:

South West Water – the provider of water and sewerage services for Devon, Cornwall and parts of Dorset and Somerset.

Viridor Ltd – one of the leading UK recycling, renewable energy and waste management businesses.

Company registration number: 2366640

Subsidiary undertakings include: South West Water Ltd; Viridor Ltd

Main locations: Exeter

UK employees: 4,451

Total employees: 4,451

Focus of giving: Education, environment, fundraising events, STEM (science, technology, engineering and mathematics), older people, sport, recreation, children, young people, community/social welfare.

Cash donations undeclared ✓
Gifts in kind ✓
Matched funding ✓
Sponsorship ✓

Charitable donations

Cash UK (latest available):	2014	£79,000
	2013	£83,000
	2012	£74,000
	2011	£79,000
	2010	£132,000
Total UK (cash and in kind):	2014	£79,000
Cash worldwide:	2014	£79,000
Total worldwide (cash and in kind):	2014	£79,000

Community involvement

Pennon Group and its subsidiaries support communities and charities in the areas in which they operate.

Our research indicates that South West Water's support focuses on water, the environment and youth education in the South West, whilst Viridor's business is UK wide and its community support focuses on environmental and science education.

The group's financial involvement in the community is channelled through a number of initiatives:

- Community support, sponsorship and donations (South West Water and Viridor)
- Landfill Tax Credit Scheme (Viridor Waste)

Both South West Water and Viridor fundraise for their preferred charities: WaterAid; the Cystic Fibrosis Trust; and Trees for Cities.

Corporate giving

The annual report and accounts for 2013/14 did not declare a figure for charitable donations but did include combined figures for 'Community support, sponsorship and donations'. As we could not determine a separate figure for charitable donations, we have, therefore, taken the average of such donations from the three most recent years in which figures were declared. The average was £79,000, and we have taken this as an estimate for charitable donations made by the group in the 2013/14 financial year. Note that the actual figure of charitable donations from Pennon Group and its subsidiaries may vary significantly from our estimate.

In-kind support

Community programmes

During the year, South West Water continued its support of education by providing talks, resources, work experience placements and by giving lectures at regional universities.

Viridor operates or supports ten educational centres across the UK, which help to promote better understanding and practice of recycling and resource management. During the year, these centres had 14,000 visitors from schools, colleges and community groups.

Employee-led support

Employee fundraising

Employees help to raise funds for the companies' preferred charities.

Employee volunteering

South West Water employees took part in beach cleans and habitat management as part of the employee volunteering programme.

Matched funding

There is a matched funding scheme in operation.

Commercially led support

Sponsorship

Viridor's community sponsorship programme focuses on educational initiatives and particularly those in the areas of STEM (Science, Mathematics, Engineering and Science) and environment. This has included GO4SET, a Scottish flagship educational initiative with the Engineering Development Trust.

Corporate social responsibility

CSR committee: There is a Sustainability Committee.

CSR information: The following information was obtained from the Sustainability Report in the annual report and accounts for 2013:

> Pennon recognises it has a responsibility to contribute positively towards communities affected by our operations. In addition to investing in a high quality water and waste management service, we create local employment, use local supply chains, provide financial support to community projects and enhance the environment.

CSR report: There is an annual Sustainability Report published within the annual report and accounts.

Exclusions

No support is given for circular appeals, medical research, political appeals, religious appeals, local appeals not in areas of company presence or overseas projects.

Applications

In writing to the appropriate committee. Note that in October 2013 the Pennon Charitable Donations Committee was split into two committees, one operated by South West Water, the other by Viridor.

Persimmon plc

Building/construction

Correspondent: Corporate Responsibility Committee, Persimmon House, Fulford, York YO19 4FE (tel: 01904 642199; website: corporate.persimmonhomes.com/corporate-responsibility/policies)

Directors: Nicholas Wrigley, Chair; Jeff Fairburn, Group Chief Executive; Mike Killoran, Group Finance Director; Nigel Greenaway; David Jenkinson; Richard Pennycook; Jonathan Davie; Mark Preston; Marion Sears (women: 1; men: 8)

Year end	31/12/2013
Turnover	£2,090,000,000
Pre-tax profit	£329,600,000

Nature of business: Principal activities: residential building and development. Persimmon Homes is based in Anglia, Midlands, North East, North West, Scotland, South Coast, South East, South West, Thames Valley, Wales, Wessex, and Yorkshire.

Company registration number: 1818486

Subsidiary undertakings include: Persimmon Homes Ltd; Persimmon Holdings Ltd; Charles Church Developments Ltd; Persimmon Shared Equity Ltd; Persimmon Scottish Ltd Partnership.

Main locations: Leicester, Peterborough, Exeter, Fareham (Hampshire), Hamilton, York, Weybridge, Northampton, Llantrisant (Mid-Glamorgan), Lowestoft, Malmesbury (Wiltshire), Newcastle, Doncaster, Bristol, Lancaster, Leeds, Maidenhead, Warrington, Wolverhampton

UK employees: 2,791

Total employees: 2,791

Focus of giving: Education, environment, health, ill health, housing, homelessness, community/social welfare.

Charity of the Year	✓
FTSE 100	✓
Gifts in kind	✓
Sponsorship	✓

Charitable donations

Cash UK (latest available):	2013	£154,000
	2011	£94,000
	2009	£795,000
	2007	£210,000
	2006	£251,000
Total UK (cash and in kind):	2013	£154,000
Cash worldwide:	2013	£154,000
Total worldwide (cash and in kind):	2013	£154,000

Community involvement

Persimmon looks to contribute to the local communities in which it operates through its support of community projects, sponsorship and fundraising. During 2013 'Persimmon continued to support community initiatives where there has been an existing relationship, as well as getting involved in many more.'

Following a successful national charity competition in 2012 in which the winner, The Harley Staples Cancer Trust, won a new home, the group's North Midlands office named a new housing development in honour of the charity. For each home sold at Harley's Place in Bagworth, the charity will receive £100.

Corporate giving

The following information is taken from Persimmon's 2013 annual report: 'A combination of group donations and employee fundraising donated a total of £154,000 to charitable causes in 2013.'

The figures we give do not normally take into account funds raised by employees. In this instance, however, we were unable to locate a separate figure for donations given by the group. Note that a proportion of the total listed was raised by employees and, therefore, the amount given by the group may have been considerably lower than £154,000.

During the year, Persimmon continued in its support of the York Minster restoration campaign, donating £70,000 to help towards training schemes for apprentices required for specialist skills such as stonemasonry needed for the conservation and repair of the Minster. This was part of a ten year commitment which began in 2006.

In-kind support

An example given in the group's sustainability report was the visit paid to Persimmon Wessex's Westrop Park by primary schoolchildren as part of their Footprints from the Past project.

Employee-led support

Employee fundraising

Through fundraising activities, Persimmon employees raised some of the £154,000 which was donated to charitable causes during the year, though we were not able to locate a figure. Examples of fundraising efforts by employees are listed in the group's online sustainability report and include: 13 employees from Persimmon Anglia who completed the 'Three Peaks Challenge' to raise more than £13,000 for East Coast Hospice; and a team from Charles Church South Midlands who participated in the Stratford Big 10K run, helping to raise £7,500 for the Acorn's Children's Hospice.

Commercially led support

Sponsorship

An example given in the group's sustainability report was Persimmon South Midlands' sponsorship of Marston Green under 11s youth football squad.

Corporate social responsibility

CSR committee: There is a CSR committee.

CSR information: The following information is taken from the group's 2013 sustainability report:

> During 2013 we further developed the framework we use to manage sustainability within the business. The demands of society, the economy, resource constraints and legal regulations continuously change and so we must always adapt to ensure our approach remains relevant.
>
> The five key themes we use allow us to clearly explain our approach to our employees, shareholders and other stakeholders. These are: community; customers; resource efficiency; skills development; and health and safety.

More details of Persimmon's CSR policy is available from the website.

CSR report: A sustainability report is published each year.

Applications

In writing to the correspondent.

Personal Group Holdings plc

Insurance

Correspondent: Sarah Mace, Trustee PACT, John Ormond House, 899 Silbury Boulevard, Central Milton Keynes MK9 3XL (tel: 01908 605000; email: sarah.mace@personal-group.com; website: www.personal-group.com/About-Us/Corporate-Social-Responsibility)

Directors: C. J. Curling, Chair; M. W. Scanlon, Chief Executive; K. W. Rooney; M. I. Dugdale, Chief Financial Officer; H. H. Driver; M. Winlow (women: 0; men: 6)

Year end	31/12/2013
Turnover	£28,400,000
Pre-tax profit	£3,700,000

Nature of business: A provider of employee benefits and financial services.

Company registration number: 3194991

Subsidiary undertakings include: Berkeley Morgan Group Ltd; Berkeley Morgan Ltd; Universal Provident Ltd.

UK employees: 161

Total employees: 161

Focus of giving: General charitable purposes, health, ill health, community/social welfare.

Charity of the Year	✓
Overseas giving	✓

Charitable donations

Cash UK (latest available):	2013	£100,000
	2012	£100,000
	2011	£100,000
	2010	£80,000
	2009	£80,000
Total UK (cash and in kind):	2013	£100,000
Cash worldwide:	2013	£100,000
Total worldwide (cash and in kind):	2013	£100,000

Community involvement

The group looks to support 'a range of voluntary sector and community activities, primarily where its own employees or employees of host companies from whom the group derives its business are actively involved'.

Support is given to registered charities through the **Personal Assurance Charitable Trust** (Charity Commission no. 1023274) and, each year, Personal Group Holdings employees elect a Charity of the Year to benefit from fundraising and volunteering activities.

Charity of the Year 2012/13: Little Lives – a registered charity with the aim of raising money for children's health services in Scotland and overseas.

Charity of the Year 2013/14: Alzheimer's Society – works to improve the quality of life of people affected by dementia in England, Wales and Northern Ireland.

Corporate giving

In 2013 the group made charitable donations totalling £100,000 to the charitable trust.

See the corporate charity entry on p. 422 for more information.

Employee-led support

Employee fundraising

During the year, employees helped to fundraise for the group's Charity of the Year, Little Lives, raising £9,000 for specialised medical equipment.

Corporate social responsibility

CSR committee: There was no evidence of a separate CSR Committee.

CSR information: The following information was obtained from the company's website: 'We believe a good business is not only about profitability and growth, but also a responsible approach to the environment and our local communities.'

CSR report: A CSR report is included in the annual report and accounts.

Corporate charity: The Personal Assurance Charitable Trust (Charity Commission no. 1023274).

Applications

For Charity of the Year nominations, note the following from the website: 'When choosing a charity of the year we ask everyone in the company to nominate the charities they are interested in supporting. Once that list comes back we do some research and whittle it down to three charities which we then put forward to a public vote.'

For applications to the charitable trust, preference is given to recommendations made by policyholders of Personal Assurance plc and employees of Personal Group Holdings plc.

Pfizer Ltd

Chemicals and plastics, agriculture, healthcare

Correspondent: Corporate Responsibility team, Ramsgate Road, Sandwich, Kent CT13 9NJ (tel: 01304 616161; website: www.pfizer.co.uk/content/our-responsibility)

Directors: C. M. Seller; I. E. Franklin; R. A. Coles; R. M. McKernan; J. C. Emms; J. R. Smith; E. M. Greenfield; B. S. Phillips; B. J. Osborn; T. F. Dolan; P. Tully; D. Hughes

Year end	30/11/2013
Turnover	£1,359,501,000
Pre-tax profit	£84,736,000

Nature of business: The principal activities of the company are the discovery, development, manufacture, marketing and sale of pharmaceutical and animal health products.

Company registration number: 526209

Subsidiary undertakings include: None listed in accounts.

Main locations: Sandwich, Tadworth

Total employees: 2,357

Focus of giving: General charitable purposes, education, enterprise/training, environment, animal welfare, health, ill health, medical research, STEM (science, technology, engineering and mathematics), older people, science technology, sport, recreation, children, young people, community/social welfare, disability.

Gifts in kind	✓
Matched funding	✓
Sponsorship	✓

Charitable donations

Cash UK (latest available):	2013	£521,000
	2011	£1,000,000
	2009	£1,000,000
	2008	£1,000,000
	2007	£1,845,528
Cash worldwide:	2013	£521,000

Community involvement

Pfizer makes charitable contributions at both a corporate level, and through its sites at Sandwich in Kent, Walton Oaks in Surrey, Cambridge and Havant.

The company prefers to support activities and organisations that:

- Improve the quality and availability of healthcare, educate individuals and families about sound health practices in order to empower them to improve their health, and serve those most at risk of health problems
- Advance research and knowledge in medicine, healthcare and allied sciences and science education
- Advance public policy research and education about issues that affect the company's operating environment

Academic, community and cultural organisations in the areas where the company has a presence are also supported.

Support is given in the form of cash or in-kind donations, contributions of employee time and skills, and there is a matched funding scheme in operation.

Pfizer UK Foundation

Following a review, the decision has been made to no longer make grants to organisations through the Pfizer UK Foundation. The website states the following: 'Our new social investment programme will build on the legacy of the Foundation as Pfizer remains committed to tackling health inequalities in the UK.' Details of the new programme will be announced soon.

Corporate giving

In 2013 Pfizer Ltd invested more than £800,000 through donations and its support programmes.

Cash contributions were distributed as follows:

UK contributions via the Pfizer UK Foundation	£324,000
Matched funding (for employee fundraising and payroll giving)	£81,000
UK corporate donations (e.g. national charity appeals)	£50,000
Local support via site Local Community Funds	£50,000
Disaster appeal matching (Philippines Typhoon)	£16,000

Note that, as part of our usual practice, we would typically take the income of a foundation in whole or in part as the company's contribution during the year, rather than the amount distributed by the foundation in grants. However, as it was not a registered charity, we were unable to determine the amount contributed to the foundation by Pfizer during the year. As a result, the £324,000 referred to may have already been accounted for in figures we have stated in previous years. The foundation is no longer in operation.

We were unable to determine a specific value for the total in-kind support given during the year. This includes the costs of the 33,364 medicine packs donated for disaster relief in the Philippines and the value of more than 2,000 hours contributed in employee time. We have, however, determined the value of £2,000 for the in-kind support given through the company's local sites by deducting the £50,000 stated for local cash donations on the website, from the £52,000 given as the combined total for local cash and in-kind donations on the downloadable social investment table for 2013.

The company also made corporate sponsorships worth more than £300,000 and additional business-related donations of £122,000. We have not included these amounts in our totals for cash donations.

In-kind support

Gifts in kind include: the use of premises, use of equipment, e.g. use of projector and/or screens and photocopying; staff secondments; and, training schemes.

During the year, Pfizer supported humanitarian efforts in the Philippines following Typhoon Haiyan. This included donating 33,364 packs of medicines throughout the year to International Health Partners, which was working to support victims of the disaster.

Employee-led support

Employee volunteering

In 2013, employees donated more than 2,000 hours of their time to work with a range of community groups.

Employee fundraising

In 2013 employees raised funds for a number of good causes including Comic Relief and overseas disaster appeals, all of which was matched by the Pfizer.

Employees also donated food for the company's Christmas appeals for two local food banks. Colleagues at Walton Oaks headquarters also donated presents to charities working with disadvantaged children.

Payroll giving

The company operates a payroll giving scheme, where it matches employee individual donations to a maximum of £100 per calendar month.

Matched funding

The company supports individual fundraising activities, payroll giving and fundraising for the company's corporate campaigns through its matched funding scheme.

Commercially led support

Sponsorship

Pfizer provides sponsorship for events and academic institutions working to promote STEM (science, technology, engineering and mathematics) to young people, and those that link into the company's broader health and science agenda. Examples include the Cheltenham Science Festival and the Royal Society Awards.

Schools programme

In 2014 Pfizer launched a new programme to help to develop relationships with local schools and to promote the role of science in the company's work.

The pilot scheme sees Pfizer colleagues act as mentors for students at a secondary school close to Pfizer's headquarters in Tadworth, Surrey.

As part of the programme, which is a partnership with Surrey SATRO, employees provide ongoing support to pupils to help them develop the skills and experience for their personal and career success. Pfizer also supports a range of interactive business-related activities and challenges to help to develop pupils.

Corporate social responsibility

CSR committee: We found no details of a dedicated CSR committee.

CSR information: The following information was obtained from the company website:

> Here in the UK we are an active corporate citizen and make positive impacts through

> a range of social investment programmes which aim to improve the health and well-being of communities across the UK. At a more local level, we are committed to being a good neighbour and provide support to small organisations and projects that are making a difference in the communities close to our four UK sites.

We were unable to determine the ratio of women to men on the board.

CSR report: There is a section dedicated to CSR on the website entitled 'Our responsibility'.

Exclusions

Our research indicates that the company cannot support applications from organisations that:

- Are sectarian or political
- Are ex-service, fraternal, trade unions or professional societies
- Represent personal appeals by, or on behalf of, an individual
- Are seeking core funding i.e. building, equipment or ongoing staff costs
- Represent research projects

Applications

In writing to the correspondent.

For local appeals in areas of company presence, in writing to your local Pfizer site.

Philips Electronics UK Ltd

Electronics/computers

Correspondent: Martin Armstrong, Company Secretary, Philips Centre, Guildford Business Park, Guildford, Surrey GU2 8XH (tel: 0870 601 0101; website: www.philips.com/about/sustainability/index.page)

Directors: Callum Petrie; Peter Maskell, Chair and Managing Director; Hayden Vivash, Finance Director; Martin Armstrong; Joanna Rogers; Neil Mesher (women: 1; men: 5)

Year end	31/12/2013
Turnover	£788,000,000
Pre-tax profit	(£4,000,000)

Nature of business: The manufacture and supply of electrical and electronic equipment, supported by a research and development activity. The ultimate parent company is Koninklijke Philips NV, incorporated in the Netherlands.

Company registration number: 446897

Subsidiary undertakings include: Avent Holdings Ltd; Respironics Ltd; Respironics UK Holding Company Ltd; WRTL Exterior Lighting Ltd

Main locations: Guildford, Reigate, Redhill, Manchester, Colchester, Hamilton – Lanarkshire

UK employees: 1,893

Total employees: 1,893

Focus of giving: General charitable purposes, education, health, ill health, children, young people, community/social welfare.

Cash donations undeclared	✓
Humanitarian aid: overseas	✓
Overseas giving	✓

Charitable donations

Cash UK (latest available):	2013	£57,000
	2012	£140,000
	2011	£19,100
	2010	£13,000
	2008	£36,600
Total UK (cash and in kind):	2013	£57,000
Cash worldwide:	2013	£57,000
Total worldwide (cash and in kind):	2013	£57,000

Community involvement

There appears to be only limited information available on charitable and community activities conducted specifically by Philips Electronics UK Ltd. It would appear that information included in the global sustainability report focuses mainly on overseas involvement at a group level. The website states that the principal focuses of community investment are 'healthcare, access to light and healthy futures'.

At a group level, Philips is involved in social investment programmes such as:

SimplyHealthy@Schools – a programme which aims to educate children aged 8–12 about leading healthy lifestyles. In 2013 Philips employees visited 113 schools in 24 countries.

Philips Cares – in North America, the programme looks to create healthy and sustainable communities through employee participation. In 2013 more than 5,000 employees volunteered through partnerships with organisations such as American Heart Association, March of Dimes and Rebuilding Together.

WorldCoaches – In 2012 the group entered into a three year partnership with the Royal Dutch Football Association (KNVB), supporting its sports and community activities programme by installing more than 100 solar Light Centres in rural communities in Africa and South America.

The group also supports Breast Cancer Awareness Month, as part of which it funds international research and offers free testing and education to women in various locations around the globe.

Corporate giving

The annual report and accounts for 2013 did not declare a figure for charitable donations during the year. The average of contributions in the three most recent years for which we have figures was £57,000, and we have taken this as an estimate for donations in 2013. The actual figure may vary significantly from our estimate.

Corporate social responsibility

CSR committee: We found no evidence of there being a UK committee.

CSR information: The following information was taken from the group's website:

> Throughout 2014, Philips will roll out a new three pillar social investment strategy, comprising of a disaster relief program, a local community investment program and a signature social innovation program. The main focus will be on access to healthcare, access to light and healthy futures.

We were unable to determine the ratio of women to men on the board.

CSR report: There is a global sustainability report available from the group website.

Applications

In writing to the correspondent, referenced 'Charitable donations'.

Piranha Trading Ltd

Retail – DIY/furniture

Correspondent: Anthony Ponsford, Director, 71–75 Shelton Street, Covent Garden, London WC2H 9JQ (tel: 03300881693; email: info@piranhafurniture.com; website: piranhafurniture.com)

Director: Anthony Ponsford (women: 0; men: 1)

Year end	30/11/2013
Turnover	£2,130,900
Pre-tax profit	£209,619

Nature of business: Piranha Trading Ltd is the trading name for Piranha Furniture, a supplier of home/office furniture.

Company registration number: 6546159

Subsidiary undertakings include: No subsidiaries are listed in the company's accounts for 2012/13.

Focus of giving: General charitable purposes.

Charitable donations

Cash UK (latest available):	2013	£0
Total UK (cash and in kind):	2013	£0
Cash worldwide:	2013	£0
Total worldwide (cash and in kind):	2013	£0

Community involvement

This company was established in 2008 by Anthony Ponsford and has an unusually philanthropic business model. The website states: 'I strongly believe that people fortunate enough to have more than they need, should use that excess wealth to support charities and other good causes.'

In line with this ideal, the business will donate 25% of its pre-tax profits to UK-registered charities beginning in the financial year 2014/15.

The business model provides for the following: 25% of all profit made from sales on Piranha's website will go to charities nominated by customers (15%), employees (5%) and shareholders (5%).

Every time a customer buys an item from the website, s/he will be given the opportunity to nominate up to three UK-registered charities from a list provided. The customers' chosen charities will receive points, ultimately giving them a larger share of the 15% profit allocation.

Staff of the company and its shareholders will be able to nominate any UK-registered charity to receive a donation (up to 5% in total each of the company's pre-tax profit).

Corporate giving

In 2012/13 the company, which is new to charitable giving, did not declare any charitable donations. We understand from the director that 25% of pre-tax profits will be donated to UK-registered charities in the next financial year – 2014/15.

In-kind support

None known.

Employee-led support

None known.

Corporate social responsibility

CSR committee: There is no CSR committee.

CSR information: There is no written or published CSR policy.

CSR report: This is a company new to charitable giving. There is no CSR report written or published.

Exclusions

Exclusions include:

Applications

Address any queries to the correspondent and director, Anthony Ponsford who states:

> While 15% of our donations will be given to charities nominated by our customers, 5% will be decided by our shareholders and a further 5% by our employees. If you have a charitable cause that you feel would benefit from our support please get in touch with us and will make sure its passed on to our shareholders and employees.

PPL WW Holdings Ltd (Western Power Distribution)

Electricity

Correspondent: Tracy Carr, Community Liaison Officer, Avonbank, Feeder Road, Bristol BS2 0TB (tel: 01179 332376; fax: 01179 332001; email: info@westernpower.co.uk; website: www.westernpower.co.uk)

Directors: Robert Symons, Chief Executive Officer; Daniel Oosthuizen, Finance Director; Ricky Klingensmith; Philip Allen; Philip Swift; Vincent Sorgi; Alexander Torok; Mark Wilten (women: 0; men: 8)

Year end	31/03/2014
Turnover	£677,700,000
Pre-tax profit	£308,700,000

Nature of business: The distribution of electricity in the Midlands, South West and Wales.

WPD companies consist of: Western Power Distribution (East Midlands) plc (registered no. 2366923); Western Power Distribution (West Midlands) plc (registered no. 3600574); Western Power Distribution (South West) plc (registered no. 2366894); and Western Power Distribution (South Wales) plc (registered no. 2366985) – all registered at the company's address.

The immediate parent company of the four above entities is WPD Midlands Holdings Ltd and the smallest group in which the results of the companies are consolidated is headed by PPL WW Holdings Ltd (the accounts used for this entry). The ultimate parent undertaking of the group is PPL Corporation, incorporated in the US.

Company registration number: 4267536

Subsidiary undertakings include: South Western Helicopters Ltd; Western Power Generation Ltd; WPD Smart Metering Ltd; and WPD Property Investments Ltd. A full list of subsidiary undertakings can be found in the group's accounts.

Main locations: Bristol

UK employees: 2,579

Total employees: 2,579

Focus of giving: Education, environment, heritage, local groups, STEM (science, technology, engineering and mathematics), older people, arts, culture, safety and crime prevention, sponsorship, children, young people, community/social welfare.

Membership: BITC

Cash donations undeclared	✓
Gifts in kind	✓
Market-led giving	✓
Matched funding	✓
Sponsorship	✓

Charitable donations

Cash UK (latest available):	2014	£50,000
	2012	£15,000
	2009	£56,000
	2008	£154,000
	2006	£55,000
Total UK (cash and in kind):	2014	£50,000
Cash worldwide:	2014	£50,000
Total worldwide (cash and in kind):	2014	£50,000

Community involvement

Western Power Distribution (WPD) concentrates on three themes: education, safety and environment. In 2013 throughout the group more than 300 charitable and non-charitable organisations were supported. The CSR report within the 2013/14 accounts also says that while maintaining the core three themes, WPD have sought to establish and develop customer initiatives, such as the Community Chest partnership with the Centre for Sustainable Energy (CSE) to help 'fuel poor' customers reduce their energy consumption.

Community Chest

During the year more than 200 community groups and schools benefited from the campaigns delivered through newspaper groups in the Gloucester, Devon, Swansea, Llanelli and Carmarthen areas. The scheme, administered by CSE (Charity Commission no. 298740) awards grants of up to £1,000 to communities to reduce their energy use. Newspapers across South and Mid-Devon publish weekly coupons for charities to collect as many as they can to ensure a larger chunk of the pot. We know that in 2014 the third round of the scheme took place. Each time WPD donates a pot of £50,000 to be distributed to about 60 groups in WPD's area to help make energy saving improvements to village halls, scout huts and other similar community buildings. 2014 recipients included: Coastlands Family Church in Glamorgan; Hawkesbury Hospital Hall; Otterton Community Shop in Devon; and Passmore Edwards Institute.

Environment

There are tree planting partnerships with Silvarus Trust and Groundwork charities. In 2013 over 7,000 trees and shrubs were planted. The group also has links with various wildlife trusts across the region – through these partnerships about 4,000 children had environmentally-linked experience funded by WPD.

Keen To Be Green

The environmental initiative aims is to protect and enhance the communities served by WPD. It is suitable for a range of groups and organisations, including registered charities, schools and voluntary organisations which provide support to elderly or vulnerable people. Particular attention is given to those that are concerned with creation and protection of wildlife habitat, waste reduction or energy conservation.

Charity partnership

In 2015 WPD has become a corporate supported of Hope for Tomorrow cancer charity's Mobile Chemotherapy Unit refurbishment.

Some examples of support given by the group include:

- Arts Active Trust in Cardiff – WPD supported a partnership with the charity 'which encourages children to be environmentally aware'
- Derby Kids' Camp – according to the website, a donation of £500 was given to the organisation to fund a new PA system, radio microphones and CD player in 2013
- Three Ways School – the special needs academy in Bath received support from the group to fund a new poly tunnel in 2014

Corporate giving

The annual report and accounts, while providing an informative overview of the activities undertaken, did not seem to specify the amount given in charitable donations, which are made to both charitable and non-charitable organisations. We know that at least about £50,000 is donated for the Community Chest initiative. We use this figure to represent WPD's giving, as no other figures are available; however, the amount given could potentially be higher. The correspondent was unwilling to further discuss charitable activities undertaken, due to an influx of applications from outside the area of benefit, as a result of increased publicity.

In-kind support

During the year the company organised more than 200 safety/education events, including school visits. Staff time and expert skills may be available, usually through the group's organised programmes.

Employee-led support

Staff members take part in the safety and educational initiatives organised by WPD and also volunteer to support their local communities.

Matched funding

Our research suggests that employee fundraising efforts are matched by the group (in the past this has been pound to pound matched funding).

Commercially led support

Customer care

Working with CSE and Age UK, WPD 'distributed over 500 wireless energy monitors that help needy customers identify electrical items in their homes that are contributing to their fuel costs'. The group also states that 'links have been established with many organisations, such as the Royal Voluntary Service and British Red Cross to improve the understanding of the needs of vulnerable customers'. WPD's Priority Services Register is promoted with roadshows and events through radio stations and organisations, including Age UK, Wales Council for the Blind and Age Cymru. The Priority Services aim to ensure that vulnerable customers and those medically dependent on electricity are attended to during electricity supply interruptions.

Sponsorships

WPD has provided sponsorship to a number of events and initiatives including:

- The Gromit Unleashed public art exhibition across Bristol (the overall campaign helped secure £2.3 million for the Grand Appeal, the Bristol children's hospital charity)
- Age UK's Doorstep Crime (bogus callers) initiative across the Midlands (which involved a door sticker campaign), the door hanger advice schemes in South Wales, and a door safety chain campaign through Care And Repair in Neath and Port Talbot
- Major agricultural shows, such as Bath and West, Malvern and the Royal Welsh
- The Big Bang science events at Exeter, Church Village in South Wales and Malvern
- The Urdd Youth Eisteddfod's Action Song – Welsh language activity which was televised in Pembrokeshire
- The Pride of Stratford Customer Care Award at Worcester hosted by Touch FM, the Lifetime Achievement Award at the Northamptonshire Education Awards, the Inspire A Generation award at the Pride of Northamptonshire awards, the People's Choice Award at the Pride of Milton Keynes awards and the Community Achievement award at the Young Achievers Awards in Leicester

Education and safety

The group organises various initiatives aimed at children to educate about keeping safe with electricity and WPD infrastructure. This included a children's summer safety campaign with Carmarthenshire and Pembrokeshire radio stations or involving the safety character called Pylonman. In Northamptonshire a Look Up, Look Out competition was run with the local media 'to promote safety following an incident involving children playing near one of [WPD's] overhead lines'.

Apprenticeships

The group offers training through an apprenticeship scheme.

Corporate social responsibility

CSR committee: We found details of a separate CSR committee.

CSR information: CSR activities encompass environmental initiatives, community involvement and customer care. According to the website:

> It is the responsibility of large organisations like [WPD] to play a full and active role in the communities they serve.
>
> At Western Power Distribution we have an impressive track record of helping the community in a charitable sense and contributing in a practical and realistic way to its development and economic prosperity.

The group's annual report and accounts for 2013/14 state: 'The three themes of education, safety and the environment continue to form the bedrock of our support activity.'

CSR report: CSR review can be found within the annual report and accounts. Details are also given on the group's website.

Exclusions

Our research suggests that support is not generally given for local appeals not in areas of company presence, advertising in charity brochures, animal welfare, appeals from individuals, overseas appeals, religious and political appeals, or sports.

Applications

In writing to the correspondent. WPD has stressed that support can *only* be given in the areas where it operates and requests from outside the regions are not welcome. Make sure your organisation fits the criteria before applying.

Further details for specific area can be obtained via phone:

- South West – 01179 332005
- South Wales – 01633 628119
- Midlands – 01332 827172

Community Chest: Applications should be made through the Centre for Sustainable Energy (CSE).

Premier Farnell plc

Electronics/computers, engineering

Correspondent: Steven Webb, Company Secretary, 4th Floor, 55 The Strand, London WC2N 5LR (tel: 020 7851 4100; fax: 020 7851 4110; website: www.premierfarnell.com/sustainability)

Directors: Laurence Bain, Chief Executive; Mark Whiteling, Chief Financial Officer; Steven Webb; Val Gooding, Chair; Paul Withers; Dennis

Millard; Thomas Reddin; Andrew Dougal; Peter Ventress; Gary Hughes (women: 1; men: 9)

Year end		02/02/2014
Turnover		£968,000,000
Pre-tax profit		£74,800,000

Nature of business: Premier Farnell plc is engaged in the marketing and distribution of products and services in the electronics components distribution sector.

The group distributes its products and services throughout Europe, North America and Asia Pacific, supported by a global supply chain of suppliers.

Company registration number: 876412

Subsidiary undertakings include: Cadsoft Computer GmbH; element14 Ltd; element14 Pty Ltd; Farnell Danmark AS; Farnell GmbH; Premier Farnell UK Ltd;

Total employees: 4,537

Focus of giving: Education, enterprise/training, STEM (science, technology, engineering and mathematics), community/social welfare.

Cash donations undeclared	✓
Gifts in kind	✓
Overseas giving	✓

Charitable donations

Cash UK (latest available):	2014	£58,000
	2013	£56,000
	2012	£59,000
	2011	£59,000
	2010	£47,000
Total UK (cash and in kind):	2014	£58,000
Cash worldwide:	2014	£58,000
Total worldwide (cash and in kind):	2014	£58,000

Community involvement

Premier Farnell plc's community investment is focused on two main areas: STEM and Assistive Technologies. The group's website states: 'We focus on a partnership approach to community investment which emphasises our strengths as a business and the value that our skills and expertise can bring to community organisations that we partner with.'

Corporate giving

The annual report and accounts for 2013/14 did not state a figure for charitable donations during the year. The average of these contributions in the three most recent years for which we have figures was £58,000, and we have taken this as an estimate for charitable donations in 2013/14.

In-kind support

Pro bono

All employees are able to contribute their skills and expertise in their local communities during working hours.

Gifts in kind

Previous years' annual reports state that, in the US, the group has 'an ongoing policy of donating certain items of inventory to charitable organisations'.

Employee-led support

Employee volunteering

Employees of the group volunteer with community projects in their local areas.

Commercially led support

The 2013/14 Sustainability report states: 'We have taken the decision to focus our investment activities on two key areas: STEM education and Assistive Technologies; as this directly supports our business in the longer term, developing a pool of both potential employees and potential customers.' As part of its support in these areas, Premier Farnell has worked with the Make the Grade programme in the UK, which 'provides business support to local schools'. The group has provided science and engineering support to technology departments, as well as mentoring and workplace skills sessions for students at Swallow Hill Community College in Leeds.

Corporate social responsibility

CSR committee: The following information regarding CSR is taken from the website:

> While the CEO is responsible for the overall adherence of the Group to the policy, the global programme is managed at Group level by the Company Secretary and supported by the Corporate Social Responsibility Assistant. Functional Specialist support and business unit drive of the programme is provided by the senior leadership team, reporting directly to the CEO. Local projects are delivered by the appropriate individuals from the relevant business or function.

CSR information: The following information was taken from the group's website:

> Our vision is to become the world's most sustainable provider of products and services to Electronic Design Engineers by 2020
>
> Premier Farnell believes that the stakeholders for its approach to sustainability are:
> - The employees of the Premier Farnell Group
> - Potential future employees
> - Customers and suppliers of all Premier Farnell Group companies
> - Members of the local communities in which we operate
> - Premier Farnell plc shareholders and the investment community at large

CSR report: The board receives a full report on the group's sustainability performance at least every six months. Periodic updates will be provided on the www.premierfarnell.com website and a formal report appears each year in the company's annual report and accounts and a separate, online Sustainability Report. Quarterly reports focusing primarily on environmental affairs are presented to regional senior leadership, including a summary of other regional sustainability activity. The Premier Farnell Leadership Council of global senior leaders is updated twice annually on the programme as a part of the group's global strategy and engagement plans.

Applications

In writing to the correspondent, referenced 'Charitable donations'.

Our research indicates that individuals or groups with no direct connection to the company will only be considered at the discretion of the regional senior executive responsible for charitable giving.

Premier Foods plc

Food manufacture

Correspondent: See 'Applications', Premier House, Centrium Business Park, Griffiths Way, St Albans AL1 2RE (tel: 01727 815850; website: www.premierfoods.co.uk/sustainability)

Directors: Gavin Darby, Chief Executive; Alastair Murray, Chief Financial Officer; David Beever, Chair; Charles Miller Smith; Ian Krieger; Jennifer Laing; Pam Powell (women: 2; men: 5)

Year end		31/12/2013
Turnover		£856,200,000
Pre-tax profit		£4,400,000

Nature of business: Premier's principal products are bread, shelf stable groceries and chilled foods.

Company registration number: 5160050

Subsidiary undertakings include: Premier Foods Group Ltd; Premier Foods Group Services Ltd

Brands include: Brands: Ambrosia, Batchelors, Bisto, Loyd Grossman, Mr Kipling, Oxo, Sharwoods

Total employees: 4,283

Focus of giving: General charitable purposes, community/social welfare.

Cash donations undeclared	✓
Charity of the Year	✓

Charitable donations

Cash UK (latest available):	2013	£91,000
	2012	£60,000
	2011	£86,000
	2010	£167,000
	2009	£167,000
Total UK (cash and in kind):	2013	£91,000
Cash worldwide:	2013	£91,000
Total worldwide (cash and in kind):	2013	£91,000

Community involvement

Premier Foods plc supports community development projects and local charities across its sites. It also partners larger charities, which benefit from employee fundraising efforts.

Charity of the Year

Macmillan Cancer Support entered into a two year partnership with the group for 2013–14.

Corporate giving

The annual report and accounts for 2013 did not state details of charitable donations made by the group during the year. The average of donations for the most recent three years for which we have figures was £91,000, and we have taken this as an estimate for the group's charitable donations in 2013.

Employee-led support

Employee fundraising

During 2013, employees raised £195,000 for Macmillan Cancer Support, the group's charity partner, helping to fund more than 7,500 nursing hours.

Community and Charity Champions

Employees take an active role in all aspects of the group's community involvement. The website states:

> We have developed a network of Community & Charity Champions who identify local community opportunities for us to make a difference who talk on a bi-monthly basis. We have created a Community Involvement Fund that then supports the pursuit of such opportunities. Any site can apply for a grant from the fund in order to help fund a specific community project as long as the employees are directly involved in the work and we are making a tangible difference to the community through the work we do.

Corporate social responsibility

CSR committee: There is a Sustainability Steering Group which meets four times a year.

CSR information: The following information was obtained from the website:

> We strive to make a difference to the local communities in which we operate and our people are extremely passionate about charitable giving. We support community development projects and local charities across our sites, and have a corporate charity partnership that unites our business in their fundraising activities.

CSR report: There is a sustainability section on the website, with pages dedicated to community involvement.

Exclusions

Our research indicates that no support is given for local appeals not in areas of company presence or for political appeals.

Applications

Our research suggests that requests for donations should simply be addressed to the company as they will be passed to the appropriate person for consideration. It is advised to put '(Fundraising)' after the company name in the address.

Pricewaterhouse-Coopers LLP

Accountants, financial services

Correspondent: David Adair, Head of Community Affairs, 1 Embankment Place, London WC2N 6RH (tel: 020 7212 7140; website: www.pwc.co.uk)

Directors: Ian Powell, Chair; Gaenor Bagley; James Chalmers; John Dwyer; Kevin Ellis; Stephanie Hyde; Margaret Cole; Kevin Nicholson; Richard Oldfield; Warwick Hunt, Chief Financial Officer; Ashley Unwin; Dan Schwarzmann (women: 3; men: 9)

Year end	30/06/2014
Turnover	£2,814,000,000
Pre-tax profit	£793,000,000

Nature of business: Provider of assurance, tax and advisory services.

Company registration number: OC303525

Subsidiary undertakings include: PricewaterhouseCoopers Services Ltd; PricewaterhouseCoopers (Resources); PricewaterhouseCoopers (Middle East Group) Ltd; PricewaterhouseCoopers Overseas Ltd; GeoTraceability Ltd; PRPi Consulting Ltd; PricewaterhouseCoopers Legal LLP. More subsidiaries are available from the company's accounts and a full list is available from Companies House.

Main locations: Leeds, Bristol, Southampton, Manchester, London, Birmingham

Total employees: 18,096

Focus of giving: Economic generation, education, enterprise/training, health, ill health, medical research, non-registered charities, poverty and social exclusion, children, young people, disasters.

Membership: BITC, LBG

Cash donations undeclared	✓
Charity of the Year	✓
Gifts in kind	✓
Humanitarian aid: UK	✓
Market-led giving	✓
Matched funding	✓
Payroll giving	✓

Charitable donations

Cash UK (latest available):	2014	£1,600,000
	2010	£1,782,000
	2009	£1,738,000
	2006	£1,500,000
	2004	£1,107,914
Total UK (cash and in kind):	2014	£7,100,000
Cash worldwide:	2014	£1,600,000
Total worldwide (cash and in kind):	2014	£7,100,000

Community involvement

The company works with the communities in which it operates by providing employee expertise and financial contributions through charitable projects. PwC operates 'centres for social impact' in their offices and runs a Social Entrepreneurs' Club. The corporate sustainability report states that it is aimed to provide support to 250 social entrepreneurs by 2017. The company seeks to provide work experience and employment opportunities in its operational communities.

The company's website notes there being a Disaster Emergency Committee which will launch an appeal following a natural disaster. The executive board has an authority to consider contributions to appeals on a case by case basis.

The PwC Foundation (Charity Commission no. 1144124)

This foundation was established to develop social inclusion and sustainable development in the UK.

Note that PricewaterhouseCoopers has offices all around the world and contributes to local causes in overseas operating areas. The information in this entry relates to the UK sites' activities.

Corporate giving

In 2013 the value of community contributions was estimated at £7.1 million (2012: £7.2 million), which includes cash donations, in-kind support, time and 'other'. In-kind support accounts for the largest proportion of the total contribution closely followed by time, while cash donations appear to amount to less than one quarter of the overall estimated total. The corporate sustainability report notes that over 15,000 beneficiaries of the company's volunteering activities have been identified, schoolchildren constituting the largest proportion. It is mentioned that work with social enterprises is increasing. The company states that the volunteering 'aims to help improve the life chances of children in underperforming schools, and to solve social and environmental issues by supporting social enterprises'.

The company contributed about £200,000 through the Matched Giving Programme in 2013. We could not determine the amount awarded in UK cash donations, therefore we estimate the figure to be at about £1.6 million, based on the three previous years known to us.

The company also donated £985,000 to the PwC Foundation during 2012/13.

Previous beneficiaries have included: Alzheimer's Scotland; Alzheimer's Society; Beyond Food Foundation; Groundwork; National Literacy Trust; Prince's Trust; and Wellbeing of Women.

See the corporate charity entry on p. 423 for more information.

In-kind support

Non-cash donations include staff volunteering time and expertise, gifts of furniture and tickets to PwC Pantomime shows.

Employee-led support

The company staff and partners are given an opportunity to volunteer during working hours. In 2013 a total of 4,069 staff members gave over 45,000 hours of volunteering time. The company also provides Blueprint Volunteering Awards to recognise the volunteers. In 2013 a total of 145 of volunteering staff members were awarded and £46,000 was given to their charities. Four members achieved a further Blueprint Volunteering Excellence Award and £5,000 for their charity. PwC also runs a national One Firm One May volunteering initiative. In 2013 more than 1,800 staff members supported more than 160 social enterprises.

Part of the PwC Community programme is the PwC Pantomime. The initiative was created by 200 PwC staff and alumni who work on the productions in their spare time and is supported by the company's executive board and the fundraising efforts of the PwC Pantomime Production Team.

The PwC website states that:

> The PwC Pantomime aims to bring joy to children everywhere, particularly to children from inner-city schools and charities. The show also provides children from inner city schools and charities with the chance to see a theatrical production at a professional theatre and aspires to nurture a life-long love of the performing arts.
>
> During 2014's run of Cinderella, PwC gave away over 7,000 tickets to disadvantaged children from inner city schools and charities in addition to providing free transportation to the show and a goody bag, courtesy of our generous sponsors. Special performances were signed for hearing impaired children and described for visually impaired children respectively. The latter were also given a chance to interact with props, musical instruments and costumes before the show as part of our annual 'touch tour'. In addition, a performance was broadcast live to children in cinemas across the UK.
>
> In addition to meeting some of the firm's corporate sustainability objectives, the PwC Pantomime also provides PwC employees with a means of developing skills they can apply on the job such as teamwork, leadership, communication, planning and time management, and is a great example of the firm doing the right thing for our clients, our people and our communities.

Payroll giving

The employees are eligible to participate in the Give As You Earn scheme operated by the Charities Aid Foundation. All administration costs are covered by the company. The corporate sustainability report notes that 3.2% of staff are currently involved with annual donations of almost £500,000 in 2013.

Matched funding

Through the Matched Giving Programme the company increases employee donations to their chosen charities. The company's website specifies that in 2013 over 900 people participated in the scheme with about £200,000 being awarded by the company to 250 UK charities and voluntary organisations. It is further noted that almost half of the preferred causes are health-related.

Commercially led support

There is a scheme to offer subsidised support to smaller charities.

Corporate social responsibility

CSR committee: There is a Community Involvement department, informed by the Corporate Sustainability Strategy, and a Charities Group which offers audit, assurance, tax and advisory services 'in a way that's affordable to charities'.

CSR information: The Corporate Sustainability Report for 2013 notes that the company aims to make an impact through its Community Involvement strategy, which comprises staff volunteering, financial contributions, payroll giving scheme and in-kind contributions.

The policy seeks to 'make the biggest possible impact on behalf of our most significant community stakeholders, using the skills that are uniquely ours and which fit with our business aims' and encompasses:

- Tackling current UK issues
- Using their extensive networks for the mutual benefit of our community partners and our people
- Using their regional network and share our knowledge to amplify our impact
- Applying their unique impact measurement skills to our community work

The company aims to develop long-term relationships and make a lasting impact.

CSR report: An Annual Corporate Sustainability report is published and available from the firm's website. More details on the community involvement activities are available on the company's website.

Corporate charity: The PwC Foundation (Charity Commission no. 1144124).

Exclusions

The foundation will not fund political organisations, lobbying groups, animal rights groups or religious bodies.

Applications

Generally in writing to the correspondent, referenced 'Community Involvement Department'.

The PwC Foundation (Charity Commission no. 1144124) has stated on its website that 'the distribution of funds donated to the foundation are decided by the foundation trustees taking into account the voting preferences of our people'.

Principality Building Society

Building society, financial services

Correspondent: Pat Ashman, Sponsorship and Events Manager, PO Box 89, Principality Buildings, Queen Street, Cardiff CF10 1UA (tel: 02920 773318; email: pat.ashman@principality.co.uk; website: www.principality.co.uk)

Directors: Lawrence Adams, Chair; Nigel Annett; Natalie Elphicke; Gordon MacLean; Derek Howell; Steve Hughes, Group Finance Director; Robert Jones; Menna Richards; Joanne Kenrick; Graeme Yorston, Group Chief Executive (women: 3; men: 7)

Year end	31/12/2013
Turnover	£261,600,000
Pre-tax profit	£28,700,000

Nature of business: The provision of housing finance and a range of insurance and financial services.

FSA registration number: 155998

Subsidiaries: The company's website states that its one subsidiary business is Nemo Personal Finance; the annual report and accounts further notes that the society also holds 100% of the ordinary share capital of subsidiary undertakings which have not carried on business during the year, these include: Brokerpoint Ltd; Energy Assess Wales Ltd; Home Information Pack Wales Ltd; Principality Syndicated Loans Ltd; Roderick Price Ltd. A full list of subsidiaries can be obtained from the company's annual accounts.

Main locations: Cardiff

UK employees: 1,317

Total employees: 1,317

Focus of giving: Arts, culture, sport, recreation, children, young people, community/social welfare.

Membership: BITC

Cash donations undeclared	✓
Charity of the Year	✓
Gifts in kind	✓
Sponsorship	✓

Charitable donations

Cash UK (latest available):	2013	£37,000
	2011	£20,000
	2009	£45,000
	2008	£45,000
	2007	£25,000
Total UK (cash and in kind):	2013	£37,000
Cash worldwide:	2013	£37,000
Total worldwide (cash and in kind):	2013	£37,000

Community involvement

The company's annual report and accounts state that in 2013 it contributed to the community by 'supporting sustainable and affordable housing initiatives, funding and participating in events that celebrate the culture and heritage, raising money for the Charity of the Year, and giving time to support local schools and community projects'.

Charity of the Year

In the past supported charities have included: British Heart Foundation Cymru/Wales; Cancer Research Cymru/Wales; Wales Air Ambulance; NSPCC Cymru/Wales; Breast Cancer Care Cymru/Wales. In 2013 the charity of year was British Heart Foundation Cymru (awarded over £60,000) and in 2014 it is MS Society Cymru. Funds for the charity are raised by employees.

Corporate giving

We could not identify the total awarded in community contributions. We estimate the amount given in UK cash donations to be around £37,000, based on the figures from the three previous years known to us.

In-kind support

Non-cash support includes staff volunteering time.

Employee-led support

Staff volunteering efforts have involved painting and decorating, gardening, organising community groups to allow access to arts and music, supporting youth sports, elderly people companionship and so on.

Staff members choose a charity (see 'Charity of the Year') they would like to support through their fundraising. We found no evidence of the company match funding the amount raised by employees.

Commercially led support

There is a branch sponsorship scheme which aims to support sport, arts and culture. For more information on sponsorships you should contact the correspondent.

Beneficiaries of sponsorships have included: Royal Welsh Show; Wales Millennium Centre; Senior open Golf Championship; Principality Rugby Premiership. Principality continues to support The Mill development at Ely Bridge, Cardiff, work with Welsh housing associations, sponsor the NFU Cymru/Principality Welsh Rural Community Champion and the NFU Cymru/Principality Wales Woman Farmer of the Year awards.

Corporate social responsibility

CSR committee: There were no details found.

CSR information: 'Being close to our communities is at the very heart of our Society. That's why we like to get involved. Corporate responsibility focuses on the environment, employees and community.'

The company's website states:

> Supporting our communities and being part of them is inherent in our mutual ethos. It is one of our core values and one which will always remain at the forefront of our business.
>
> Principality is proud to be at the heart of the communities in which we live and work and we try to give back to them in a number of ways; from raising money for our charity of the year and supporting local sports clubs or major national events, to having branch staff out and giving their time to improve their local neighbourhoods.

CSR report: None published. A short update on CSR policies is contained within the annual report and accounts.

Exclusions

The company's website notes that it receives a high number of requests for sponsorships which are judged on an individual basis and support cannot be given for following:

- Political or religious causes
- Projects run on behalf of charities by companies for profit
- Outside the areas where the company has branches
- Development or running costs for projects
- Individuals

Applications

Sponsorships: In writing to the correspondent.

Community support: Local branch managers should be contacted to enquire about support for community events and projects.

Procter & Gamble UK

Health/beauty products, healthcare, household, personal care products

Correspondent: Janette Butler, UK and Ireland Community Matters Manager, The Heights, Brooklands, Weybridge, Surrey KT13 0XP (tel: 01932 896000 or 01912 975000; website: www.uk.pg.com)

Directors: Anthony Appleton; Brian Young (women: 0; men: 2)

Year end	30/06/2013
Pre-tax profit	(£276,000)

Nature of business: Procter & Gamble UK, operating in the UK and Ireland, is a wholly owned subsidiary of The Procter & Gamble Company, USA. The principal activities of the company and its subsidiaries are the manufacture and marketing of innovative consumer products, with associated research and development services.

We have used the accounts of Procter & Gamble Ltd, a UK registered holding company, which has no employees. The company's immediate parent company is Oral-B Laboratories and its ultimate parent company is The Procter & Gamble Company, both incorporated in the US.

Company registration number: 83758

Subsidiary undertakings include: Gillette Group UK Ltd; Oral-B Laboratories Ltd; Procter & Gamble (Enterprise Fund) Ltd; and Wella (UK) Holdings Ltd. A full list can be obtained from Companies House.

Brands include: Always; Ariel; Gillette; Head and Shoulders; Olay; Oral-B; Pampers; Pantene; Tide; Wella.

Main locations: Seaton Delaval, Skelmersdale, Weybridge, Manchester, Newcastle upon Tyne, West Thurrock, Egham, Harrogate, Bournemouth

Focus of giving: Education, enterprise/training, environment, health, ill health, heritage, older people, poverty and social exclusion, sponsorship, women's issues, children, young people, community/social welfare.

Membership: BITC, LBG

Cash donations undeclared	✓
Gifts in kind	✓
Humanitarian aid: overseas	✓
Market-led giving	✓
Overseas giving	✓
Sponsorship	✓

Charitable donations

Total UK (cash and in kind):	2013	£5,250,000

Community involvement

The website notes that the global P&G programme Live, Learn and Thrive aims to help children in need 'get off to a healthy start, receive access to education and build skills for life'. In the UK this cause is delivered through the P&G Community Matters scheme, by 'contributing funding, donating P&G product and providing a comprehensive employee volunteer programme'.

Part of the Live, Learn and Thrive programme is the Children's Safe Drinking Water (CSDW) Programme providing PUR packets – a water purifying technology, developed by P&G in its Innovation Centre in Newcastle in conjunction with the US Centers for Disease Control and Prevention. The CSDW programme works with more than 100 partners and responds to natural and biological emergencies.

Other aspects of the Live, Learn and Thrive programme include educational projects, children and youth support initiatives, and safe living practices.

The company's strategy is to 'support projects that will provide sustainable benefits to the communities in which [its people] live and work, so the programme is delivered from each of their sites across the UK & Ireland and serves that local community only'.

P&G also seeks to share its employees' expertise with local communities. An example of such giving is Business Skills Workshops for Charities, 'which gives charities an ideal opportunity to gain new perspectives on some of the everyday business and fundraising challenges that they face'. More details on the one day free course run at the company's headquarters can be requested from Bebe Hudd (hudd.b.1@pg.com).

P&G Fund and P&G Grassroots Funds

The Community Foundation for Tyne and Wear and Northumberland manages the above funds on behalf of Procter & Gamble to support the company's charitable giving. The foundation's website notes that the funding focus has recently been changed from following the Live, Learn and Thrive strategy to concentrating on two areas:

- Creating the experience of home: turning houses into homes and providing the comforts of home to the people without them or who have been displaced
- Everyday health and confidence: enabling healthy lives through everyday healthy behaviours and hygiene education that enable confidence and self-esteem

The funds are open to Tyne and Wear and Northumberland charities working with children in care, mental health, older people, other vulnerable/disadvantaged people, homelessness issues, people in palliative care and similar situations. Grants tend to be under £10,000 and applications should be made through the foundation.

Charity partnerships

The following information is taken from the company's website:

Teach First: P&G UK is a holder of Platinum partnership status with Teach First is an exclusive partner of the charity in their work in primary schools. The company has funded and supported one of the charity's projects – P&G Teaching Today for Brighter Tomorrows which aims to recognise the 'huge need to secure quality, primary head teachers, address the barriers identified and prepare Teach First graduates towards primary head teach roles'. P&G employees have volunteered on a range of projects (for example, coaching new teachers, assisting with communications strategy or advising on re-branding of the charity, and working with the students in marketing workshops).

In Kind Direct: Since 2002 over 2,500 different charities have received in-kind donations from the company through its partnership with In Kind Direct charity, totalling over £32 million in value of goods.

Look Good... Feel Better: The company has been supporting the LGFB (Bournemouth) since the beginning of this charity, which seeks to improve the self-esteem of people undergoing cancer treatment. Help is provided through in-kind donations of products and expert services (such as the P&G Max Factor team). About 220,000 products are donated annually to the charity.

Young Enterprise: This educational charity receives sponsorship for its Primary Programme and regional boards close to the company's operation sites are also supported. Help includes sponsorship, employees volunteering as advisers within schools, and retirees sharing their business expertise and experience on the charity's boards.

Disaster Relief

Globally P&G's disaster relief programmes provide daily essential products to victims of natural disasters as well as cash support. Help was given after Typhoon Haiyan in the Philippines, flooding in the Balkans, and tornadoes in the US.

Corporate giving

The annual report and accounts of P&G Ltd for 2012/13 (the latest available at the time of writing) say that no charitable contributions were made. We have used the information available from the global reports and its website, but could not find a figure for Procter & Gamble's UK charitable donations in 2013/14. Past examples of P&G charitable giving include donations in the UK supporting over 1,200 charities a year (over a third of which were organisations helping children and young people). The company's website also states that the total charitable return has been valued at £4.7 million and charitable contributions in the UK and Ireland have totalled £5.8 million. Based on the previous figures known to us, we estimate that about £5.2 million was given in UK total contributions.

The company is still a member of the London Benchmarking Group (LBG), therefore we are confident it still gives.

We could not determine the figure for the company's revenue/turnover.

In-kind support

Donations of company products (such as Fairy, Lenor, Wella, Pampers, Duracell and Gillette), staff volunteering time and expertise, business skills and resources. For example, since 2001 different charities have received in-kind donations from the company through its partnership with In Kind Direct charity, totalling over £40 million in value of goods in the UK.

Employee-led support

P&G employees volunteer their time and also work on various projects, including team-building, mentoring, teaching and so on. Part of the P&G and UNICEF co-operation has included offering P&G employees in Western Europe the opportunity to work with UNICEF while on a three-month sabbatical leave.

Commercially led support

For six years (since 2006) P&G (Pampers) has worked in partnership with UNICEF to deliver the vaccines for vulnerable women and their children. For every pack of Pampers bought the company would provide one vaccine for maternal and neonatal tetanus.

Corporate social responsibility

CSR committee: There was no evidence of a separate CSR Committee. Charitable support and community involvement are administered by the Community Matters Manager, in lines with the global sustainability policies.

CSR information: This information was obtained from the company's website: 'For more than 80 years, P&G brands and people have touched and improved consumers' lives. Our commitment extends to our social investments.'

The company aims to be 'closer to consumers from all walks of life and in touch with the needs of communities around the world' through its 'philanthropy, cause marketing, product donations, disaster relief, and employee engagement'. In addition, it states that 'P&G is committed to improving life for children in need throughout the world and each year improves life for more than 50 million children in need via our global cause, Live, Learn and Thrive.'

CSR report: There was no evidence of a separate CSR report for the UK. The annual CSR report relates to the group's worldwide activities. Some details on the UK community involvement are available on the company's website.

Exclusions

Our research indicates that no support is given to circular appeals, advertising in charity brochures, appeals from individuals, fundraising events, medical research, overseas projects, political or religious appeals, or local appeals not in areas of the company's presence.

Applications

Company: More information on community support in the UK and Ireland can be obtained by contacting one of the regional co-ordinators or the correspondent. Our research suggests that applications should be by letter only, addressed to the correspondent.

P&G Funds: For more information on financial grants in Tyne and Wear and Northumberland only, contact Su Legg (email: sl@communityfoundation.org.uk, tel: 01912 220945). Applications should be made on the standard foundation form.

Provident Financial plc

Financial services

Correspondent: The Corporate Responsibility Manager, No. 1 Godwin Street, Bradford BD1 2SU (tel: 01274 351135; fax: 01274 730606; email: corporateresponsibility@providentfinancial.com; website: www.providentfinancial.com)

Directors: Ken Mullen; Rob Anderson; Manjit Wolstenholme; Andrew Fisher, Finance Director; Peter Crook, Chief Executive; John van Kuffeler, Chair; Malcolm Le May; Stuart Sinclair; Alison Halsey (women: 2; men: 6)

Year end	31/12/2013
Turnover	£1,078,100,000
Pre-tax profit	£182,400,000

Nature of business: Personal credit products and services.

Company registration number: 668987

Subsidiary undertakings include: Greenwood Personal Credit; Provident Financial Management Services Ltd; Provident Investments plc; Vanquis Bank Ltd. Full list of subsidiaries is available in the accounts.

Brands include: Moneybarn; Provident Personal Credit; Tandem loans; Satsuma loans; Vanquis Bank.

Main locations: Bradford

Total employees: 3,833

Focus of giving: Education, sport, recreation, children, young people.

Membership: BITC, LBG

Gifts in kind	✓
Matched funding	✓
Overseas giving	✓

Charitable donations

Cash UK (latest available):	2013	£1,000,000
	2010	£1,237,000
	2009	£1,330,000
	2008	£507,000
	2007	£776,751
Total UK (cash and in kind):	2013	£1,000,000
Cash worldwide:	2013	£1,700,000
Total worldwide (cash and in kind):	2013	£2,000,000

Community involvement

The company's 2013 CR report notes that part of its community involvement strategy is Good Neighbourhood and The Vanquis Bank Active Community programmes.

Good Neighbour programme

The scheme was established in 2009 as a flagship community programme and supports local projects in the UK and Ireland offering volunteering and matched funding opportunities for the staff. The company seeks to address issues arising in the communities in which they operate, in particular to address social inclusion problems in deprived communities and through working with the money advice sector to improve financial education. At the end of 2013 there were 39 funding partnerships under the scheme and an estimated total of 79,347 people benefited directly.

Vanquis Bank Active Community Programme

This provides employee volunteering opportunities and supports local charities in London and Chatham as well as helping charities in Nairobi, Kenya through the Hatua charity (Charity Commission no. 1144452). There are plans to establish partnerships in Poland.

The company is a member of Associate Parliamentary Corporate Responsibility Group, Eco-Network, Business in the Community and Employer's Forum on Disability.

Corporate giving

The annual report and accounts for 2013 specify that community investment totalled £2 million through various community initiatives, support for the money advice sector and social research. The CR report and the accounts note that the group's cash contributions amounted to £1.7 million and employee volunteering time totalled £49,000. The CR report further notes that the company made charitable contributions totalling £1.3 million and the group invested £635,000 to support community programmes. We could not determine the amount given in cash in the UK. Based on the figures from the previous three years known to us, we estimate it was over £1 million.

Beneficiaries included: Harvey Girls, Burton-on-Trent; Immanuel Project in Bradford; Scottish Youth Hostel Association, Edinburgh; Young People Cornwall, Truro (Good Neighbourhood partnerships); Breaks for Kids programme; Glencoe Junior School (Vanquis Bank Active Community Programme). Further links are being developed with Kids Company, the Bradford Youth Development partnership, and the Outward Bound Trust.

In-kind support

Employee volunteering time.

Employee-led support

Staff members are encouraged to 'get involved in company-led volunteering initiatives, including one-to-one mentoring, Provident's Reading Partners scheme and team challenges'. Volunteer grants are also offered to organisations the staff volunteer for in their own time. During the year employees gave their time to One in a Million charitable school and raised money for their chosen causes, which included Comic Relief and Children in Need.

The website states:

> Through Good Neighbour and Vanquis' Active Community Programme, we encourage our employees to participate in their communities and offer them volunteering opportunities and matched funding. Employees are able to participate in team challenges which seek to address local community needs, a reading scheme to provide one-to-one support to children in need of additional reading assistance, and other volunteering initiatives in their community.

Matched funding

Employees can apply for funding to match fundraising activities they undertake outside work. The limit of funding is set at £500 per person for UK-registered charities.

Commercially led support

The group supports a number of money advice organisations. In 2013 these were: AdviceUK; Christians Against Poverty; Institute of Money Advisers; Money Advice Liaison Group (MALG); Money Advice Scotland (MAS); and Money Advice Trust (including National Debtline); also The Money Charity. It also provides assistance for research into the financial behaviour of people on low income, for example the Social Market Foundation research project.

Corporate social responsibility

CSR committee: The CR strategy is overseen by the Chief Executive Officer and regularly considered by the board. The executive committee is responsible for reviewing and approving the CR programme and budget. There is a number of groups designed to maintain daily running of the policies, these are:

- Corporate responsibility working group
- Environmental working groups within Vanquis Bank and CCD
- Vanquis Bank's Active Community Programme board
- Head office travel plan steering group

CSR information: The CR policy encompasses elements of customer care, environment, supply chain management, community involvement, health and safety practices, ethical standards, human rights and diversity issues, and is supported by various corporate policies.

The company's website notes that its CR strategy seeks to address six stakeholder groups: customers, communities, employees, suppliers, shareholders and regulators.

CSR report: A detailed CR report is published annually.

Exclusions

Our research indicates that support is not available for appeals from individuals, heritage, medical research, overseas projects, also political or religious appeals.

Applications

In writing to the correspondent.

Prudential plc

Financial services, insurance

Correspondent: Corporate Responsibility Team, Laurence Pountney Hill, London EC4R 0HH (tel: 020 7220 7588; email: responsibility@prudential.co.uk or community@prudential.co.uk; website: www.prudential.co.uk)

Directors: Paul Manduca, Chair; Tidjane Thiam, Ggroup Chief Executive; Nic Nicandrou, Chief Financial Officer; Pierre-Oliver Bouée; Jackie Hunt; Michael McLintock; Barry Stowe; Mike Wells; Phlip Remnant; Sir Howard Davies; Ann Godbehere; Alistair Johnston; Kai Nargolwala; Anthony Nightingale; Alice Schroeder; Lord Turnbull (women: 3; men: 13)

Year end	31/12/2013
Turnover	£30,502,000,000
Pre-tax profit	£2,082,000,000

Nature of business: Prudential plc provides retail financial services and insurance products in Europe, the US, Asia and, recently, Africa.

Company registration number: 1397169

Subsidiaries in the UK: Prudential Annuities Ltd; The Prudential Assurance Company Ltd; Prudential Retirement Income Ltd; M&G Investment Management Ltd. The annual accounts for 2013 state that 'details of all Prudential subsidiaries, joint ventures and associates will be annexed to the next Annual Returns of Prudential plc filed with the UK Registrar of Companies'.

Brands include: M&G; Jackson.

Main locations: Belfast, Chelmsford, Reading, Nottingham, London, Stirling

UK employees: 5,533

Total employees: 22,186

Focus of giving: Education, enterprise/training, equal opportunities, arts, culture, poverty and social exclusion, sport, recreation, women's issues, children, young people, community/social welfare.

Membership: BITC, LBG

Charity of the Year	✓
FTSE 100	✓
Gifts in kind	✓
Payroll giving	✓

Charitable donations

Cash UK (latest available):	2013	£4,700,000
	2012	£4,000,000
	2011	£2,800,000
	2009	£2,700,000
	2006	£3,150,000
Total UK (cash and in kind):	2013	£4,700,000
Cash worldwide:	2013	£15,900,000
Total worldwide (cash and in kind):	2013	£18,500,000

Community involvement

Community and Charity Policy

The UK Community and Charity Policy paper states:

> Our community investment activity is financed through a discretionary cash budget approved annually by the Prudential board. This is enhanced through support we also provide via the expertise of our people, and other in kind donations. We look for long-term strategic involvement with community partnerships to address local issues key to the interests of the communities we serve and to enhance our reputation as a responsible company. Many of our employees are actively involved in their local communities as volunteers and we have a volunteering policy in place to support them.

It is noted that any scheme must involve the company's employees with priority being given to projects that will make a positive difference to retirement. As stated by the policy paper the main areas of focus are:

- Education – raising levels of literacy and developing people to be the best they can be
- Employee Volunteering and personal development – encouraging our people to get involved in their local communities and at the same time developing their skills
- Making a Difference to retirement – focusing on volunteering schemes that make a difference to people's lives in retirement
- Giving to Charity – making it easy and tax efficient for employees to donate through our Payroll Giving scheme.

Financial education policy

Since April 2009 the Prudential Financial Education programme in the UK is managed by the UK business. The scheme aims to 'help address poor levels of financial capability across the UK, helping people become more informed about their financial needs and building the long-term capacity of community organisations to provide financial education'. To achieve this the company works with well-established organisations delivering front-line training to adults and children.

Education

The company runs a Business Class programme providing skilled volunteering opportunities. About 70 staff members are involved with partner schools in Reading, Stirling and Westminster. The website states that 'businesses partner with a school in the most deprived areas and work strategically for three years on an action plan driven by the school's needs, covering areas such as leadership, curriculum and achievement'.

In the UK Prudential offers apprenticeship opportunities for school leavers across sites in Stirling, Reading and London, together with a training partner, Capita. A commitment has been made to maintain a four-year annual scheme of 40 apprenticeships.

At M&G sponsorship of the 'Women in Investment Management' has been continued, and underprivileged students supported through the Social Mobility Foundation (in the way of mentoring and internships).

Well-being

The Prudential Ride London raised more than £7 million for charitable causes in 2013. A target of £12 million had been set in 2014 to support Bliss, and a Charity of the Year for 2015 event has been scheduled to be Scope.

Prudential has also been supporting SportsAid by providing grants to athletes to help cover the costs of training and equipment.

Disaster readiness and relief

There is a fund to support communities which have suffered from natural disasters. The website suggests that both financial and in-kind support is mainly offered in Asia, where natural catastrophes are most prone to happen.

Corporate giving

In 2013 a total of £18.5 million was spent in community investment (including cash and in-kind support). The value of community investment is calculated using the London Benchmarking Group (LBG) standards. It is further specified that cash donations totalled £15.9 million. About £11.2 was given from US and Asia operations and £4.7 from EU operations. The latter is broken down as follows: education (£1.8 million), social welfare and environment (£2.4 million), cultural (£226,000) and staff volunteering (£111,000). In-kind donations across the group totalled £2.6 million.

Beneficiaries have included: Bliss; Greenhouse; Scope; SportsAid; The British Museum; The National Gallery, The National Theatre; The Royal Opera House.

In-kind support

A range of in-kind support is offered to organisations on a local basis. This includes employees' volunteering time and skills, also office space, meeting rooms, computers and office furniture.

Employee-led support

Employees are encouraged to get involved in their communities through volunteering and fundraising efforts. There are also local fundraising teams organising all fundraising activities on site and donating the money to selected charities. In 2013 a total of 8,155 staff members across the group volunteered in their local communities, with 5,000 participating in Prudential's volunteering programme, the Chair's Challenge. Prudential donates £150 to charity partners for each employee who registers for the programme. The charities then use the money to seed-fund charitable projects for Prudential volunteers.

UK employees spent about 14,500 hours volunteering, including schoolchildren mentoring, supporting older people and skills-sharing with local charities. M&G employees spent over 1,000 hours working for community initiatives.

Payroll giving

The company operates the payroll giving scheme to allow making donations to local charities chosen by the staff.

Commercially led support

Prudential is a Principal Member of Arts & Business.

Corporate social responsibility

CSR committee: The group's CR policies and reports are regularly reviewed by the executive board. The group's Corporate Responsibility team collects data for internal and external reporting, publishes annual reports, oversees CR risks and manages group-wide strategies. National companies have their separate governance committees which decide policies and budget allocations.

The UK Community and Charity Policy paper states the Head of CR being 'accountable for delivering the community policy, managing internal and external relationships in the community and charity sector, and for the control of the budget'. The CR Committee is responsible for the decision making.

CSR information: The group's CR strategy places focus on three areas: education and life skills, well-being and protection, and disaster readiness and relief.

CSR report: CR reviews are published annually.

Exclusions

The UK Community and Charity Policy paper excludes the following from being eligible for support or sponsorship:

- Political parties or religious organisations
- Individuals
- Requests for sports equipment for employees taking part in local sports competitions on behalf of the organisation
- Requests for donations outside the Payroll Giving Scheme

Our research also indicates that fundraising events, advertising in charity brochures, circular appeals, local arts or drama groups, animal welfare, heritage and building projects, medical research, or science/technology are not generally supported.

Applications

Further information can be sought from the Corporate Responsibility Team at the address/telephone number given here.

Psion Holdings Ltd (Motorola Solutions)

Telecommunications

Correspondent: Group Communications, Jays Close, Viables Industrial Estate, Basingstoke, Hampshire RG22 4PD (tel: 01256 358211; website: www.motorolasolutions.com/XU-EN/Home)

Directors: Todd Naughton; Stephen Piercy (women: 0; men: 2)

Year end	31/12/2013
Pre-tax profit	(£61,696,000)

Nature of business: Psion was acquired by Motorola Solutions in 2012. The principal activity of the company (the accounts of which have been used) is holding of investments; no staff is employed.

The company's ultimate parent company and controlling party is Motorola Solutions Inc, incorporated in the US. The company's immediate parent company is Motorola Solutions International Holdings Ltd.

Motorola Solutions is an international provider of communication solutions for a range of industries, including safety, healthcare, national security, hospitality, logistics and so on.

Company registration number: 1520131

Subsidiary undertakings include: Psion Investments Canada; Psion NV; Psion SAS; Psion Services Ltd; Psion Teklogix KK; and Psion (UK) Ltd. A full list of subsidiary undertakings can be obtained from Companies House.

Main locations: Milton Keynes, London

Focus of giving: Education, environment, heritage, STEM (science, technology, engineering and mathematics), science technology.

Cash donations undeclared	✓
Gifts in kind	✓
Humanitarian aid: overseas	✓
Market-led giving	✓

Charitable donations

Cash UK (latest available):	2013	£0
	2011	£27,000
	2009	£22,000
	2008	£17,000
	2007	£18,000
Total UK (cash and in kind):	2013	£0
Cash worldwide:	2013	£0
Total worldwide (cash and in kind):	2013	£0

Community involvement

Motorola Solutions global website states that the group 'is committed to the communities where [it operates]' and applies 'talent and resources to make communities safer, students stronger, and to help communities rebuild after disaster'.

Donations in the UK so far have been limited to provision of employee time (see 'Employee-led support).

The group's 'charitable and philanthropic arm' is the global Motorola Solutions Foundation which focuses on public safety, disaster relief, employee programs and education, especially science, technology, engineering and maths programming. Most of the support from Motorola Solutions is given in North America. To learn more about extensive activities around the world delivered by Motorola Solutions, see the information on the group's website.

Corporate giving

The annual report and accounts of the company did not seem to declare charitable donations in 2013. It would appear from the information given on the Motorola Solutions website that in the UK charitable cash donations were not made. The figures from the past three years known to us show that (then)

Psion plc gave on average about £22,000 annually.

The global CSR report for 2013 says that in 2013 Motorola Solutions 'contributed $16.4 million [£10.2 million] from Motorola Solutions cash and in-kind product donations, Motorola Solutions Foundation grants, and employee giving', distributed between: Public Safety ($7.5/£4.6 million); Education ($5.8/£3.6 million); and Community and Disaster Relief ($3.1/£1.9 million). UK giving was not referred to separately. Grants in Europe, the Middle East and Africa amount to only about $900,000 (£561,000) of the overall amount given.

We were unable to determine the company's turnover/revenue for the year.

In-kind support

Employee volunteering time and expert skills.

Employee-led support

Motorola Solutions Service Corps Volunteering Program

Around the world the programme allows employees to contribute to local communities through volunteering. Activities include mentoring, serving as maths tutors, helping firefighters or acting as science fair judges. In 2013 a total of 71,000 volunteer hours were donated across the globe.

In the UK the group's employees have helped maintaining and restoring canals, wharfs and bridges throughout the country. So far the project saw work done between Melksham and Chippenham (this forms part of a 52-mile restoration project).

Commercially led support

STEM Education

The group's CSR report for 2013 notes UK STEM Educational Empowerment Team organising an event for 100 school students in collaboration with Engineering UK. The event allowed students to learn about the role the Motorola Solutions emergency services in public safety and create and present business plans 'to sharpen their innovation and communication skills'.

Corporate social responsibility

CSR committee: There were no details found relating to the company.

CSR information: Motorola Solutions website states: 'Corporate responsibility (CR) means operating ethically, protecting the environment – through our products, services, and operations – and supporting the communities where we do business.'

The community investment is focused in the areas where the group can have the greatest impact:

- Education - supporting programs that advance science, technology, engineering and math (STEM) in the United States and globally, preparing our next generation of innovators
- Public safety – making our communities safer by using our leadership in public safety innovation to provide resources to first responders and the communities they serve
- Disaster relief – partnering with humanitarian organisations to provide relief to disaster victims. Our donations provide vital support to emergency workers who are at the front lines of disaster relief
- Employee giving – supporting our employees who volunteer through matching programs in the United States and globally

CSR report: The group CSR report is available online.

Exclusions

Support will not normally be given for appeals from individuals or local appeals not in areas of company presence.

Applications

In writing to the correspondent.

Punch Taverns plc

Catering services, food services, retail – restaurants/ fast food

Correspondent: Jackie Burn, HR Director, Jubilee House, Second Avenue, Burton upon Trent, Staffordshire DE14 2WF (tel: 01283 501600; fax: 01283 501601; email: punchcommunitypromise@punchtaverns.com; website: www.punchtavernsplc.com)

Directors: Steve Dando, Chief Finance Officer; Stephen Billingham, Chair; Angus Porter; John Allkins; Ian Dyson (women: 0; men: 5)

Year end	17/08/2013
Turnover	£457,600,000
Pre-tax profit	£17,000,000

Nature of business: Punch Taverns is a leased pub group.

Company registration number: 3752645

Subsidiary undertakings include: Punch Partnerships (PGRP); Punch Partnerships (PTL); Punch Taverns (PRAF); Punch Taverns (Services) Ltd; Punch Taverns (Finco) Ltd. A full list of subsidiaries is available in the group's accounts.

UK employees: 451

Total employees: 451

Focus of giving: Health, ill health, community/social welfare.

Gifts in kind	✓
Sponsorship	✓

Charitable donations

Cash UK (latest available):	2013	£23,000
	2011	£18,000
	2009	£19,400
	2008	£12,000
Total UK (cash and in kind):	2013	£23,000
Cash worldwide:	2013	£23,000
Total worldwide (cash and in kind):	2013	£23,000

Community involvement

The Punch Community Promise

The initiative has been set up at the group's support centre in Burton. It operates by donating time and money to local charities or causes located within a 15-mile radius of the company's offices in Burton-on-Trent. Priority is given to requests from employees. Eligible projects must be:

- A local cause (national causes with a local focus may be considered)
- Not third party fundraising
- For capital costs, not running costs
- Not individual sponsorship

Application forms can be downloaded from the company's website.

The programme support has included help to local scout and football clubs, funding for a new minibus for PHAB charity and the Hawthorns Resource Centre League of Friends, one-to-one swimming lessons to visually impaired young people, and so on. An annual donation of £20,000 is made to Licensed Trade Support and Care (part of the Licensed Trade Charity), offering support to people who have worked in the licensed drinks trade and find themselves in crisis. The money is used by the charity to run a national Volunteer Visitor programme.

The website also notes that all the group's partners are encouraged to engage with their local communities. 'Many pubs, especially those in rural areas, have diversified to provide a wider community service, perhaps hosting the post office or local shop, providing web access and meeting spaces for local clubs and societies.' The group's partners are also fundraising to support PubAid. Punch Taverns is a supporter of the non-profit organisation Pub is the Hub and its senior members participate in the Regional Advisory Hubs.

Corporate giving

In 2013 the group donated a total of over £23,000 in charitable contributions, out of which £20,000 constituted trade volunteer sponsorships. We could not determine where the remaining money was awarded and through what means.

Beneficiaries include: Drinkaware; Hawthorns Resource Centre League of Friends; Licensed Trade Support and Care (part of the Licensed Trade Charity); PHAB.

In-kind support

Staff volunteering time, also facilities and equipment.

Employee-led support

The company's website states: 'Our employees support a huge range of national charities and those close to their hearts from Children in Need, Comic Relief, Marie Curie Cancer to Macmillan.' During the last year head office employees have donated time to a local primary school to help children with reading.

Corporate social responsibility

CSR committee: There were no details found of CSR committee presence. There is a Risk Management committee which oversees responsible business operation and disseminates educational material on business practices to partners and pubs' staff.

CSR information: Statement taken from the company's website:

> Corporate Social Responsibility (CSR) has been embedded across many elements of our business, from corporate fundraising to responsible retailing. Our CSR strategy seeks to involve our employees and partners in making our business, and in turn, their businesses more ethical and environmentally friendly.

CSR report: None published. Charitable activities are briefly discussed in the accounts and feature on the website's CSR section.

Applications

In writing to the correspondent. Jackie Burn is responsible for the group's volunteer and charitable programme.

QinetiQ Group plc

Defence, aerospace, marine, security services, telecommunications

Correspondent: Group Head of CR and Sustainibility, Cody Technology Park, Ively Road, Farnborough, Hampshire GU14 0LX (tel: 01252 392000; website: www.qinetiq.com)

Directors: Leo Quinn, Chief Executive Officer; David Mellors, Chief Financial Officer; Mark Elliott, Chair; Admiral Sir James Burnell-Nugent; Michael Harper; Ian Mason; Jon Messent; Paul Murray; Susan Searle (women: 1; men: 8)

Year end	31/03/2014
Turnover	£1,191,400,000
Pre-tax profit	£4,100,000

Nature of business: The group's principal activity is the global supply of scientific and technical solutions and services for business, defence and security.

Company registration number: 4586941

Subsidiary undertakings include: Analex Corporation; Apogen Technologies Inc; Foster-Miller Inc; Westar Aerospace and Defence Group Inc.

Main locations: Farnborough

Total employees: 9,134

Focus of giving: Education, health, ill health, science technology, children, young people.

Cash donations undeclared	✓
Charity of the Year	✓
Market-led giving	✓
Matched funding	✓
Overseas giving	✓
Payroll giving	✓

Charitable donations

Cash UK (latest available):	2014	£144,000
	2010	£114,100
	2009	£133,500
	2008	£184,000
	2007	£19,000
Cash worldwide:	2014	£144,000

Community involvement

The group supports a number of charities chosen by its employees. Individual company's sites are also supporting in their local community projects. Note that the group receives a large number of requests for support from charities.

QinetiQ has signed the Armed Forces Corporate Covenant declaring its intentions to support the Armed Forces both through its business operations, community involvement and charitable work.

Corporate giving

We could not identify the amount given in charitable contributions in from the annual report and accounts for 2013/14. We estimate that around £144,000 is given in cash support in the UK, based on figures from the three previous years, known to us.

Beneficiaries include: Cancer Research UK; Help for Heroes; RNLI.

In-kind support

Staff volunteering their time and professional skills, for example, through the UK Employee Volunteering Scheme.

Employee-led support

Employees are encouraged to volunteer by participating in the company's programmes, support the three corporate charities, or help organisations of their choice through the payroll scheme. In 2013/14 the UK Volunteer of the Year award has been introduced to an employee who 'has made an outstanding contribution in the community through the Employee Volunteering Scheme'.

Payroll giving

Payroll giving scheme is available.

Matched funding

Employee fundraising activities are matched by the company to support the three corporate charities (Cancer Research UK, Help for Heroes and RNLI).

Commercially led support

The CSR section on the group's website notes: 'As a significant employer of scientists and engineers, we have a vested interest in engaging with young people to encourage them to consider careers in science and engineering.' This is achieved through Science Technology Engineering and Maths (STEM) outreach programmes, supported through employee volunteering scheme. In the UK the programme has organised events for schoolchildren, including the annual powerboat and roboolympics challenges and Cyber Security Challenge UK.

The 5% Club

An initiative has also been launched aimed at investing in the young generation and creation of apprenticeships and employment opportunities. Its current target is for 5% of the UK workforce to be on apprenticeship or graduate programmes by March 2015.

Corporate social responsibility

CSR committee: The group's website states that its CR programmes 'are led by the Group Head of Corporate Responsibility and Sustainability' and 'further embedded in the business through domain experts from key business functions, such as health and safety, environment, human resources, learning and development, and procurement'. The implementation of the policies is overseen by the Group Risk and Corporate Social Responsibility Committee, which meets on a regular basis and reviews reports and briefings on all material CR topics, including business ethics, environment, health and safety, diversity and human rights.

CSR information: The group's CR strategy is based around four themes: people, community, environment, and business ethics. It is emphasised that the group's vision looks beyond financial success and 'managing risk, protecting its reputation and operating responsibly and safely are also key priorities'.

CSR report: A Corporate Responsibility and Sustainability review is contained within the annual report and accounts.

Exclusions

Political donations to parties are not made. The group notes that a 'number of normal business activities that would not commonly be perceived to be political donations, such as sponsorship of events' may be eligible.

Applications

In writing to the correspondent. Community appeals should be addressed to the Community Liaison Officer at a local branch.

The Rank Group plc

Leisure

Correspondent: Frances Bingham, Company Secretary, Statesman House, Stafferton Way, Maidenhead, West Berkshire SL6 1AY (tel: 01628 604000; fax: 01628 504042; website: www.rank.com)

Directors: Ian Burke, Chair; Henry Birch, Chief Executive Officer; Clive Jennings, Finance Director; Lord Kilmorey; Owen O'Donnell; Tim Scoble; Shaa Wasmund; Frances Bingham, Company Secretary (women: 2; men: 6)

Year end	30/06/2014
Turnover	£678,500,000
Pre-tax profit	£14,400,000

Nature of business: The Rank Group is an international leisure and entertainment company and providing services, including casinos, bingo clubs, pub restaurants and holiday resorts.

Company registration number: 3140769

Subsidiary undertakings include: Grosvenor Casinos Ltd; Mecca Bingo Ltd; Rank Digital Services (Gibraltar) Ltd; Rank Leisure Holdings Ltd; Rank Overseas Holdings Ltd; and The Gaming Group Ltd. A full list of subsidiary undertakings can be obtained from Companies House.

Brands include: Enracha; Grosvenor Casinos; and Mecca.

Main locations: London

Total employees: 10,900

Focus of giving: Education, health, ill health, marginalised people, unpopular causes, community/social welfare.

Cash donations undeclared	✓
Gifts in kind	✓
Market-led giving	✓

Charitable donations

Cash UK (latest available):	2014	£313,000
	2010	£360,000
	2009	£315,000
	2008	£264,000
	2007	£236,000
Total UK (cash and in kind):	2014	£315,000
Cash worldwide:	2014	£315,000
Total worldwide (cash and in kind):	2014	£315,000

Community involvement

The annual report and accounts for 2013/14 state that 'Rank and its brands have a long history of community involvement and charitable fundraising'.

Rank Cares

In 2014 this programme was launched to support the Carers Trust. The group had a target of raising £500,000 for the charity. 'The funds are distributed within the communities in which they are raised, via a series of grant panels. In addition, Rank Cares provides a framework for team members to volunteer their time to help the Carers Trust.'

The following funds have been set up:

- Essentials Fund, which provides basic household equipment to carers who are experiencing financial hardship
- Inspire to Be Fund, which enables carers to gain new skills
- Take a Break Fund, which gives carers time out from their caring role to relax and recharge their batteries

Responsible Gambling Trust

A total of £296,000 was contributed to the trust which was spent to fund counselling and treatment providers.

Keep it Fun programme

The group runs a programme to encourage healthy consumer attitudes towards gambling. During the year about £50,000 was invested in the programme, which was also assisted by the British Columbia Lottery Corporation's GameSense team, 'who have generously shared insights and ideas'.

During the year support was also given to the Dame Kelly Holmes Trust and Marie Curie Cancer Care.

Corporate giving

We could not find details of the annual total of charitable donations, as the group no longer declares this information in the annual report and accounts. We know that £296,000 was given to the Responsible Gambling Trust and that further initiatives would constitute considerable expenses to the group. Based on the figures from the three previous years known to us, we estimate that about £315,000 was given in cash in the UK.

Beneficiaries included: Carers Trust; the Dame Kelly Holmes Trust; Marie Curie Cancer Care; and Responsible Gambling Trust.

In-kind support

Employees' time and efforts, also provision of venues for community events.

Employee-led support

The group invites the staff members to contribute to good causes through volunteering and fundraising initiatives.

Commercially led support

Rank – University of Salford research project

The group is involved in furthering the understanding of gambling problems. In 2013/14 it worked with the University of Salford and the Responsible Gambling Trust to understand better the behaviour of problem gamblers and donated data processing equipment and data sets from the Grosvenor Casinos' Play Points rewards card programme.

In furtherance of the research on gambling issues through the GamePlan programme the group maintains relationships with other organisations, such as the Gambling Commission, GamCare, the British Columbia Lottery Corporation and the Campaign for Fairer Gambling. There is also involvement with The National Centre for Social Research.

Corporate social responsibility

CSR committee: There were no details found.

CSR information: The information taken from the website states:

> At Rank, our aim is to make an overwhelmingly positive contribution to the quality of life in the communities we serve, by bringing people together, creating fun experiences and making people happy. We understand that our success as a business is dependent upon society's view of our effectiveness in doing this – and that the value that we generate from our operations is a measure of the value that we add to people's lives.

CSR report: None published. Some CSR related details are available within the accounts under 'Operating Responsibly' section and throughout sections elsewhere.

Applications

In writing to the correspondent.

Rathbone Brothers plc

Financial services

Correspondent: The Social and Environmental Committee, 1 Curzon Street, Mayfair, London W1J 5HD (tel: 020 7399 0000; email: marketing@rathbones.com; website: www.rathbones.com)

Directors: Paul Stockton, Finance Director; Mark Nicholls, Chair; Paul Chavasse; David Harrel; Kathryn Matthews; Philip Howell, Chief Executive Officer; Jame Dean (women: 1; men: 6)

Year end	31/12/2013
Turnover	£176,409,000
Pre-tax profit	£44,204,000

Nature of business: The group is an independent provider of investment and wealth management services for private investors, charities and trustees. It operates in the UK and Jersey.

Company registration number: 1000403

Subsidiary undertakings include: Rathbone Investment Management Ltd; Rathbone Pension and Advisory Services Ltd; Rathbone Unit Trust Management Ltd. Other subsidiary undertakings are available from the group's accounts and a full list from Companies House.

Total employees: 833

Focus of giving: Education, enterprise/training, health, ill health, arts, culture, children, young people, community/social welfare.

Charity of the Year	✓
Gifts in kind	✓
Matched funding	✓
Payroll giving	✓
Sponsorship	✓

Charitable donations

Cash UK (latest available):	2013	£234,000
	2012	£206,000
	2011	£196,000
	2009	£174,000
Total UK (cash and in kind):	2013	£234,000
Cash worldwide:	2013	£234,000
Total worldwide (cash and in kind):	2013	£234,000

Community involvement

The group's CR report notes: 'Our corporate responsibility programme has increased extensively during 2013 and now includes several initiatives that focus on youth development.'

The Rathbones Financial Awareness Programme

This free scheme, aimed at 16- to 24-year-olds, forms a significant part of the youth development initiatives. It involves investment managers delivering presentations within the company's offices and at schools around the UK on financial matters, career routes and interview techniques in order to 'equip young people with the necessary information to understand their options and take ownership of their finances at a young age'. To date the group records that over 1,000 young people have benefited and relationships with over 20 public and private schools have been established.

The group's co-operation with schools includes support to sports through partnerships with English Lacrosse and Lacrosse Scotland. Additional initiatives are introduced to encourage participation in the sport at community level.

Charity partnership

A partnership with Brathay Trust (Cumbria) has been announced whereby a number of events and initiatives will be supported over the next three years, including the sponsorship of the trust's Aspiring Leaders Innovation Fund; another three-year commitment has been established to co-operate with the Chalke Valley History Festival for Schools.

The group's website concludes the following: 'We continue to review community activities, both on a national and a local scale, and support our employees' participation in a wide range of activities involving both local and international charities.'

Corporate giving

In 2013 the group spent a total of £234,000 (2012: 206,000) in charitable donations, including an award to the newly created Rathbone Charitable Foundation (we were not able to identify the specific amount given). Matched funding form the company totalled £128,000.

Beneficiaries have included: Anthony Nolan Trust; Children with Cancer UK; Claire House; Rathbone Charitable Foundation; and The Oliver King Foundation.

Revenue: The figure we used for the group's annual turnover is referred to as 'operating income' in the consolidated statement of comprehensive income, in the accounts.

See the corporate charity entry on p. 423 for more information.

In-kind support

Employee skills and time donated through the educational initiatives, for example, Financial Awareness Programme.

Employee-led support

Payroll giving

Employees can support charities through the Give As You Earn (GAYE) scheme. In 2013 employees donated £230,000 (2012: £167,000) through this scheme, administered by the Charities Aid Foundation.

Matched funding

The group will match staff donations of up to £200 per month made through Give As You Earn. In 2013 a total of £128,000 was given to increase staff donations to their chosen causes.

Charity of the Year

The CR Report states that 'in addition to corporate and payroll giving, for many years Rathbones has selected charities by employee ballot with funds being raised by a number of events'. In 2012 and 2013 employees chose to support the Claire House Hospice for children in the North West and The Oliver King Foundation with £22,000 being raised for these charities.

Commercially led support

Sponsorships

The report states that support of education includes sponsorship of events, such as the Education Business Awards. 'The development of this focused programme is an exciting progression for Rathbones and is something that we plan to build on throughout 2014 and beyond.' As part of the youth development programme the group also sponsors a freestyle skier Anna Vincenti.

Corporate social responsibility

CSR committee: The CR report for 2013 states:

> The Social and Environmental Committee (SEC) is responsible for ensuring that Rathbones effectively manages its sustainability issues. It is formed by members of staff from key functions, such as facilities management, personnel, marketing, IT and investment management. It meets on a quarterly basis and reports directly to the group executive committee of the board.

CSR information: Information taken from the 2013 CR report specifies that Rathbones' corporate responsibility strategy operates within the following areas:

- Environment – managing the group's environmental impact, reducing the carbon footprint by the efficient use of resources
- Clients and investments – maintaining and developing the relationships with clients, treating them fairly and continuing to meet their needs; considering corporate responsibility and governance issues in the companies in which the group invests on behalf of its clients
- Employees – motivating and rewarding appropriately, encouraging their development
- Communities – engaging in the communities in which the group operates

The group's website summarises its policies as follows: 'Our social and environmental policy aims to ensure that social, environmental and ethical considerations are taken into account in all aspects of our business activities.'

CSR report: Annual corporate responsibility report of the SEC is contained within the annual report and accounts.

Corporate charity: The Rathbone Brothers Foundation (Charity Commission no. 1150432).

Applications

Applications to the company and the foundation should be made in writing to the correspondent.

Ravensale Ltd

Property

Correspondent: Bruce Jarvis, Trustee, The Joron Charitable Trust, 115 Wembley Commercial Centre, East Lane, North Wembley, Middlesex HA9 7UR (tel: 020 8908 4655; email: ravensale100@btconnect.com)

Directors: Bruce Jarvis; Joseph Jarvis (women: 0; men: 2)

Year end	30/06/2013

Nature of business: The principal activity of Ravensale Ltd is property development and investment, and the design and manufacture of ballpoint pen components.

The number of employees is not known.

Company registration number: 1476675

Subsidiary undertakings include: Copartnership Developments Ltd; and JGR Enterprises, Ltd (USA).

Focus of giving: General charitable purposes, environment, health, ill health, medical research, children, young people, disability.

Charitable donations

Cash UK (latest available):	2013	£175,000

Charitable donations

Cash UK (latest available):	2013	£200,000
	2012	£324,000
	2011	£2,104,500
	2010	£1,500,000
Total UK (cash and in kind):	2013	£175,000
Cash worldwide:	2013	£175,000
Total worldwide (cash and in kind):	2013	£175,000

Community involvement

The Joron Charitable Trust (Charity Commission no. 1062547)

The company directs all its charitable giving through the Joron Charitable Trust, of which the directors are trustees. The trust was established in 1997 and derives almost all of its income from Ravensale Ltd. It aims to support general charitable purposes and makes grants to registered charities in various fields where it can be demonstrated that the grants will be used effectively.

We were unable to find a website for this company.

Corporate giving

The company's accounts for 2012/13 (the latest available at the time of writing) provided limited information, due to an exemption. The latest accounts of The Joron Charitable Trust note that during 2013/14 the trust received a donation of £175,000 (2012/13: £200,000) from the company. The trust states that it 'expects to receive the majority of its future grants from this source'. However, it would appear that support from the company has decreased over recent years. In the past donations to the trust have totalled: £324,000 (2011/12); £2.7 million (2010/11); £1.5 million (2009/10); and £1.1 million (2008/09). We have no other figures therefore use the donation to the charity as the company's total cash contributions.

During 2013/14 seven (2012/13: three) grants were made by the trust totalling £219,000 (2012/13: 304,000).

The trust's beneficiaries included: The Wilderness Foundation (£185,000); Carers Trust (£25,000); ACVV PE Central (£4,500); and Cancer Research UK, Devon Air Ambulance, Jamie Proctor Foundation and Maggie Keswick Jenks (£1,000 each).

See the corporate charity entry on p. 411 for more information.

Corporate social responsibility

CSR committee: We found no indications of a CSR committee.

CSR information: None published.

CSR report: None published. However, the company's charitable donation and its application are detailed in The Joron Charitable Trust's accounts.

Corporate charity: The Joron Charitable Trust (Charity Commission no. 1062547).

Exclusions

No support is given for political organisations.

Applications

There is no formal grant application procedure. Apply in writing to the correspondent.

Reckitt Benckiser Group plc

Healthcare, household, personal care products, pharmaceuticals

Correspondent: The Corporate Communications Department, 103–105 Bath Road, Slough, Berkshire SL1 3UH (tel: 01753 217800; email: sustainability@rb.com; website: www.rb.com)

Directors: Adrian Bellamy, Chair; Peter Harf; Rakesh Kapoor, Chief Executive Officer; André Lacroix; Judith Sprieser; Warren Tucker; Jaspal Bindra; Nicandro Durante; Adrian Hennah, Chief Financial Officer; Sue Shim; Doug Tough; Kenneth Hydon (women: 2; men: 8)

Year end	31/12/2013
Turnover	£10,043,000,000
Pre-tax profit	£2,314,000,000

Nature of business: Principal activities of the group are the manufacture and sale of household and healthcare products.

Company registration number: 527217

Subsidiary undertakings include: Reckitt Benckiser LLC; Reckitt Benckiser Pharmaceuticals Inc.; Schiff Nutrition International, Inc. A full list of principal subsidiary undertakings is available in the group's annual accounts and a full list of all subsidiaries from Companies House.

Brands include: Air Wick; Calgon; Durex; Finish; Harpic; Nurofen; Strepsils; Vanish; Veet; Woolite.

Main locations: Derby, Hull, Slough, Windsor, Swindon

Total employees: 37,100

Focus of giving: Education, health, ill health, children, young people, community/social welfare, disasters.

Cash donations undeclared	✓
Charity of the Year	✓
FTSE 100	✓
Gifts in kind	✓
Humanitarian aid: overseas	✓
Matched funding	✓
Overseas giving	✓
Payroll giving	✓

Charitable donations

Cash UK (latest available):	2013	£636,000
	2009	£568,000
	2008	£704,000
Total UK (cash and in kind):	2013	£636,000
Cash worldwide:	2013	£636,000
Total worldwide (cash and in kind):	2013	£5,500,000

Community involvement

Charity partnership

The group (RB) was Save the Children's first corporate partner in the Children's Emergency Fund (in 2007); support to the fund has continued in 2013. £1 million was given to help with the merger of Save the Children and Merlin charity, £500,000 to help the charity address natural disasters, and £50,000 in support after Typhoon Haiyan. RB is also supporting the charity's programme Save a Child Every Minute which aims to prevent deaths from diarrhoea in children under five. RB notes in its Sustainability Report 2013:

> A healthy lifestyle is still out of reach for billions of people – 1.2 billion experience water scarcity and 2.5 billion live without basic sanitation. Our ambition matches this huge challenge.... We will do this through innovation in close partnership with our brands, community mobilisation and education.

Through the partnership with Save the Children, RB is running a global Healthier Kids, Happier Homes programme to support the lives of vulnerable children and families.

Corporate giving

In 2013 RB committed £5.5 million to Save the Children, which includes 'a substantial portion coming from employees' fundraising' efforts, events, brand initiatives and corporate donations. By the end of 2015 the group has pledged to contribute £23.5 million. We could not determine with certainty a specific breakdown of the support in the sustainability report or the annual report and accounts to determine UK cash donations. We estimate that about £636,000 was given in cash donations in the UK, based on figures from two previous years, known to us.

Beneficiaries: Save the Children.

In-kind support

The group donates products (such as handwashing bags, soaps and liquids), educational material on health safety and hygiene, also organises health-related awareness campaigns (for example, health camps and planting of trees naturally repelling insects in India) and staff volunteering help.

Employee-led support

The staff of the group are engaged in fundraising activities and events. To mark the Universal Children's Day 45 offices collectively raised more than £100,000. As part of the Global Challenge 60 volunteers from 29 countries raised more than £315,000 in Indonesia for Save the Children.

Payroll giving

Payroll giving scheme operates.

Matched funding

In the past the employees' fundraising efforts could be match funded by the company, we found no indications that such means of support are no longer available.

Commercially led support

The sustainability report for 2013 states:

> Our contribution to human health comes from consumer education as well as product innovation. We introduced a new goal this year: to reach more than 200 million people by 2020, to improve their health and hygiene behaviour ... through social innovation led by our brands, working in partnership with suppliers, NGOs, governments and other key stakeholders.

Corporate social responsibility

CSR committee: The sustainability report for 2013 specifies that 'the board is responsible for the overall stewardship of the group, including sustainability and corporate responsibility'. The Chief Executive Officer is the board member with specific responsibility for the group's sustainability policies and performance. Senior management reports to the CEO regularly on sustainability matters.

The group's Senior Vice President of Corporate Communications and Affairs is responsible for the group's strategic charitable giving.

CSR information: Information taken from the group's website states:

> Our betterbusiness strategy responds to key global shifts and we're focusing on where we can make the biggest difference including: the need for better health and hygiene behaviour and the growing scarcity of water. We focus on reducing our environmental impacts across the value chain and maximising our positive impacts on health and hygiene behaviour through education and innovation.

The group's three main priority areas are: healthier communities, better and more sustainable design, and better production management. Its business is 'inspired by a vision of a world where people are healthier and live better'.

CSR report: A Sustainability Report is published annually.

Exclusions

Our research suggests that generally grants are not available for animal welfare charities, the arts, elderly people, political or religious appeals, science/technology, disability or sport causes.

Applications

In writing to the correspondent, referenced 'Sustainability'. The Corporate Communications and Affairs Department is concerned with charitable giving.

Redrow Group plc

Building/construction, property

Correspondent: The Corporate Responsibility Committee, Redrow House, St David's Park, Ewloe, Flintshire CH5 3RX (tel: 01244 520044; fax: 01244 520580; email: groupservices@redrow.co.uk; website: www.redrowplc.co.uk)

Directors: Steve Morgan, Chair; John Tutte, Group Chief Executive Officer; Barbara Richmond, Group Finance Director; Graham Cope; Liz Peace; Debbie Hewitt; Nick Hewson (women: 3; men: 4)

Year end	30/06/2014
Turnover	£864,500,000
Pre-tax profit	£132,600,000

Nature of business: The principal activity of the group is residential, commercial and mixed use development. Redrow plc is a public listed company, listed on the London Stock Exchange and domiciled in the UK.

Company registration number: 2877315

Subsidiary undertakings include: The principal subsidiary company is Redrow Homes Ltd. The annual report and accounts notes the following: 'The company has taken advantage of the exemption in Section 410 of the Companies Act 2006 which allows only principal subsidiaries to be disclosed. A full list of subsidiary undertakings as at 30 June 2014 will be appended to the Company's next annual return.'

Main locations: Barnsley, Bexhill on Sea, Liverpool, Flintshire, Leek, Falkirk, Aberdare, Preston Brook, High Wycombe, Leigh, Cardiff, Launceston

UK employees: 1,345

Total employees: 1,345

Focus of giving: Economic generation, education, health, ill health, arts, culture, sport, recreation, children, young people, community/social welfare.

Charity of the Year ✓

Charitable donations

Cash UK (latest available):	2014	£706,000
	2011	£568,000
	2009	£178,000
	2008	£281,000
	2007	£334,000
Total UK (cash and in kind):	2014	£113,000,000
Cash worldwide:	2014	£706,000
Total worldwide (cash and in kind):	2014	£113,000,000

Community involvement

The CSR report notes the group being involved in a number of community initiatives throughout the country. These include:

- Woodford Aerodrome Community Engagement – public consultation on re-development of former Woodford Aerodrome into a mixed purpose site
- Transport – development of sustainable transport practices by providing houses with a public transport node, access to car clubs or cycle stores and awarding homeowners with one-year free MetroCards
- Redrow Green Book Project – engaging with schools to educate children on the dangers of construction sites and sustainability issues; delivering a book on biodiversity to primary school pupils across West Midlands
- Graduate Community Project – as a part of the group's 15-month Graduate Training programme, trainees are involved in business-to-community projects, in 2014 the engagement being three-day accommodation refurbishment at Cardiff's University Hospital for the LATCH Welsh children's cancer charity
- Undergraduate and Technical Trainees Community Project – in 2014 the trainees worked with Ykids to help transform an abandoned site in Merseyside into a garden
- Preserving History at Lucas Green – working with Pre-Construct

Archaeology Ltd to uncover and begin the preservation of a rare WWII defensive installation in Lancashire

There is the Redrow Foundation (Charity Commission no. 1113073).

Corporate giving

In 2013/14 the group committed £133 million 'to fund the improvement of local communities', which can be broken down as follows:

Social or affordable housing	£96 million
Education	£7 million
Highway/transport	£4 million
Leisure	£2 million
Environmental	£1 million
Healthcare	£1 million
Sport	£1 million
Other	£1 million

The annual report and accounts for 2013/14 states that a total of £706,000 was paid in charitable donations. A donation of £654,000 was made to the Morgan Foundation, a UK-registered charity of which Steve Morgan, the Chair of the group, is also a trustee.

In-kind support

Books on environmental topics to schoolchildren; MetroCards.

Employee-led support

In its CSR report the group states:

> The company and its employees are actively involved in fundraising activities for specific charities and in the year of its 40th anniversary the Divisions, Group Services and Harrow Estates are undertaking the 'Redrow Charity Challenge' to raise as much money for charitable good causes as possible.

By the time the report was published, a total of £184,000 had already been raised. Charities chosen by the staff include: British Heart Foundation; CLIC Sargent; Dementia Concern and Heart of Kent Hospice; Hope House Children's Hospices; Lupus North Wales; Naomi House Children's Hospice.

Corporate social responsibility

CSR committee: The Corporate Responsibility Committee is responsible for management and performance monitoring of the CR activities. The overall CR responsibility lies with the Group Chair. The Research and Sustainability Director is accountable for sustainability issues – coordination and implementation of the CR strategy across the company, and also advising the CR Committee. The group directors also hold specific responsibilities regarding the CR strategy and have an obligation to regularly review these matters.

CSR information: The group's website states that its:

> Vision for a sustainable business is to ensure that each year it improves in all aspects of sustainability. It is an ongoing process of continuous improvement that, over time, will transform the business, keep customers satisfied and help to build local communities in a sustainable way.

The group has developed a Redrow Aspirations 2018 Action Plan, which outlines targets set to maintain responsible and sustainable business operation.

There are five key pillars of focus: people, environment, community, customers and design.

CSR report: Published annually.

Exclusions

Support is generally not given for circular appeals, advertising in charity brochures, purely denominational (religious) appeals, large national appeals, overseas projects or local appeals not in areas of company presence.

Applications

In writing to the correspondent, referencing 'The Corporate Responsibility Committee'. Our research suggests that it is helpful to state how you intend to match or increase any donation you may receive in your application.

Rentokil Initial plc

Business services

Correspondent: Paul Griffiths, Company Secretary, Riverbank, Meadows Business Park, Blackwater, Camberley GU17 9AB (tel: 020 7592 2700; website: www.rentokil-initial.com)

Directors: John McAdam, Chair; Andy Ransom, Chief Executive Officer; Peter Bamford; Richard Burrows; Alan Giles; Peter Long; Angela Seymour-Jackson; Jeremy Townsend, Chief Financial Officer; Julie Southern (women: 2; men: 7)

Year end	31/12/2013
Turnover	£2,327,100,000
Pre-tax profit	£122,600,000

Nature of business: International company providing services to businesses, including: workwear; plants and landscaping; hygiene services; medical services; pest control; package delivery; catering; electronic security; cleaning.

Company registration number: 5393279

UK subsidiaries include: Dudley Industries Ltd; Knightsbridge Guarding Ltd; Modus FM Ltd; Rentokil Insurance Ltd. A full list of UK and worldwide subsidiaries is available in the accounts.

Brands include: Rentokil; Initial; Ambius.

Main locations: East Grinstead, Orpington

Total employees: 53,508

Focus of giving: Education, environment, health, ill health, community/social welfare, disasters.

Membership: BITC

Gifts in kind	✓
Humanitarian aid: overseas	✓
Matched funding	✓
Overseas giving	✓

Charitable donations

Cash UK (latest available):	2013	£87,000
	2011	£58,000
	2009	£61,000
	2008	£142,000
	2007	£107,000
Total UK (cash and in kind):	2013	£87,000
Cash worldwide:	2013	£101,000
Total worldwide (cash and in kind):	2013	£101,000

Community involvement

The group's website states that Rentokil Initial 'actively supports charities both locally and internationally with the aim to inspire others and support colleagues, customers and suppliers in their own efforts to share time, skills and resources in their community support programmes'. The community involvement strategy involves four aspects:

- Local community and charity support – both in-kind and cash contributions
- Local community investment – likely to combine financial (often significant) and business support (e.g. cause-related marketing or employee volunteering)
- Global community and charity support – help to specific charities and the company's new global community health programme
- Global response to national disasters – in communities where the group operates

The group's global focus is on health education and hygiene promotion. Further assistance is provided in cases of natural disasters and partnerships are established with organisations, such as Red Cross.

Corporate giving

In 2013 a total of £101,000 (2012: £87,000) was awarded in charitable cash donations, including the matched donations via Helping Hands. In addition co-ordinated support was offered to Malaria No More and WaterAid, including in-kind support and provision of management time. We could not identify the sum awarded in cash contributions in the UK, therefore we estimate it was around £87,000, based on the figures from three previous years known to us.

Group's beneficiaries have included: Make a Wish Foundation (UK); Rainforest Rescue (Australia); Save the Children (Europe); The Zenzeleni Trust (South Africa).

UK beneficiaries of matched giving scheme: Acorns Children's Hospice; Barnardo's; Cancer Research UK; Dementia UK; Francis House; Red Nose Day; St Clare's Hospice; WheelPower; Zoe's Place Trust.

In-kind support

Staff volunteering time, management support, training and professional services, plants, also hygiene kits, food, clothing and toys to families in natural disaster affected areas.

Employee-led support

The group's Community Involvement policy paper states that one of its principles is to 'facilitate employees' involvement where possible in the cultural and educational development of their communities and adopt a permissive approach to employee's participation in community and civic affairs'. The group encourages charitable giving and involvement in local initiatives. In the UK employees volunteered for London's Science Museum during the Cockroach Tour to provide the public with information about pests and pest control.

Matched funding

A Helping Hands scheme operates to allow Rentokil Initial match any amount up to £1,000 raised by employees for charitable causes with an annual budget approved by the group board.

Commercially led support

The CSR report notes that in 2013 Community Orientated Health Education Programme (COHEP) was launched to provide health education in local communities suffering from a lack of hygiene, 'through branch colleagues, using material, and expertise from within the company, and using a structured delivery framework and coordinating group. The target is to roll out this programme globally by the end of 2015'.

Corporate social responsibility

CSR committee: The group's Chief Executive Officer is responsible for CR with the Executive Leadership Team reviewing all aspects of the strategy.

Specific corporate responsibility matters are also reviewed by the board regularly and broader consideration is performed at least once a year. There is a Safety Health and Environment (SHE) committee which produces quarterly reports to the board.

CSR information: Taken from the company's website:

> At the heart of Rentokil Initial's approach to corporate responsibility is a focus on doing what's right for colleagues and customers, and the vision and values which underpin the company. It emphasises local action to match the needs of individual businesses, while ensuring compliance with group-wide policies in areas such as health and safety, conduct, environment and product management.

The group's CR policy encompasses areas of responsible governance, workplace safety, customer care, supply chain management, environment and community involvement. National branches can choose areas of particular focus in their own markets.

The CSR report for 2013 notes that 2014 'will see a significant rollout of new training and skills development programmes'. The group:

> Will continue to enter new markets and is actively looking for opportunities in parts of Latin America, Africa and the Middle East. As part of the due diligence process, the social, economic and political environment of any country in which it enters for the first time will be analysed and taken into account in its decision making.

CSR report: Published annually.

Exclusions

Generally consideration will not be given to any charity or sponsorship related proposal from any organisation unless a company employee or employees are involved.

No payments are made to political organisations.

Applications

In writing to the correspondent.

Rexam plc

Industrial products/services, manufacturing, print/paper/ packaging

Correspondent: John Revess, Director of Group Sustainability, 4 Millbank, London SW1P 3XR (tel: 020 7227 4100; fax: 020 7227 4109; email: john.revess@rexam.com; website: www.rexam.com)

Directors: Stuart Chambers, Chair; John Langston; Leo Oosterveer; Ros Rivaz; Johanna Waterous; Graham Chipchase, Chief Executive Officer; David Robbie, Finance Director; Carl-Peter Forster (women: 2; men: 6)

Year end	31/12/2013
Turnover	£3,943,000,000
Pre-tax profit	£339,000,000

Nature of business: Rexam plc is an international beverage can maker and plastic packaging for health and personal care products provider.

Company registration number: 191285

Subsidiary undertakings include: Rexam European Holdings Ltd; Rexam Group Holdings Ltd; Rexam Inc; Rexam Overseas Holdings Ltd. A full list of subsidiaries can be obtained from Companies House.

Brands include: Rexam is producing beverage containers for companies, including Carlsberg Group, Coca-Cola, Heineken, Kirin, Monster, and Red Bull.

Main locations: Stevenage, Wakefield, Milton Keynes, Deeside, Luton, London, Tonbridge

Total employees: 8,000

Focus of giving: Education, enterprise/ training, environment, health, ill health, children, young people, community/ social welfare, disability, disasters.

Cash donations undeclared	✓
Gifts in kind	✓
Humanitarian aid: overseas	✓
Overseas giving	✓

Charitable donations

Cash UK (latest available):	2013	£94,000
	2012	£52,000
	2011	£55,000
	2009	£38,000
	2008	£61,000
Cash worldwide:	2013	£762,000
Total worldwide (cash and in kind):	2013	£856,029

Community involvement

The group aims to 'support markets with low recycling rates, establishing and enhancing collection mechanisms and foster a recycling culture among consumers'. It notes being 'an ambassador for recycling, dedicating a large amount of effort in promoting and encouraging it within the communities'.

An example of recycling initiatives by the group in Europe is the 'Community Can Challenge' fundraiser involving 12 Rexam plants across nine European countries with employees promoting recycling and collecting cans to maintain metal recycling. In Brazil it sponsors and supports can collection activities. The group 'will seek to find beneficial recycling options for its waste from operations within local communities'.

Part of the community support agenda is support for organisations 'whose aim is to enhance the lives of people, whether through education or improved life opportunities'. In the UK Rexam invests 'in tutoring, mentoring, and learning opportunities and educational materials to help motivated students from disadvantaged backgrounds to achieve university entrance or encourage them to aspire to a career in science or manufacturing'. Organisations working on scientific research into solutions for people who have had life-changing injuries are particularly supported.

Relationships are established with various local schools, charities and non-profit organisations in communities where the group operates. The sustainability report notes there being some long-term programmes across the globe and funds being raised to help in cases of natural disasters, for example, after floods in Rio de Janeiro in 2011.

Charity partnership

The group is a corporate partner of Forum for the Future, a non-profit UK organisation promoting sustainable development.

Corporate giving

In 2013 the group spent a total of £856,000 in charitable contributions, including cash and in-kind donations (in the previous years the total amount excluded employees' fundraising efforts). At the time of writing the latest corporate sustainability report available was for 2011/12. The report specified that the group's charitable contributions totalled £497,000, out of which cash donations amounted to £458,000, consisting of £55,000 in the UK and £403,000 elsewhere in the world. Based on the previous years' giving proportions we estimate that about £94,000 was donated in cash in the UK during 2013.

Revenue: The financial figure we used for the group's annual turnover is classified as 'sales' in the accounts.

In-kind support

Non-cash support may include facilities, products, also staff volunteering time.

Employee-led support

The group employees can donate their time and expertise as well as fundraise 'to support organisations, programmes and local agencies that benefit the local communities and beyond'. As a part of the Rexam Academy leadership training programme employees are involved in a leadership challenge, which in the past has hosted a charity dinner for UNICEF's East Africa Children's Crisis Appeal. Employees were also contributing to the fund.

Corporate social responsibility

CSR committee: The main responsibility for sustainability management rests with the group's executive leadership team. At the start of 2012 a Director of Group Sustainability was appointed 'to coordinate and structure our activities across the business and ensure [the group] gives this area the attention it deserves'.

CSR information: The group's sustainability report for 2011/12 (the latest available at the time of writing) states that the group's commitment is driven 'by the belief that running the business in a responsible and sustainable manner is fundamental to near term success and long-term prosperity' and 'also consistent with good economics'.

Rexam seeks 'to be recognised as a committed partner in the communities in which it operates' through promoting waste collection and recycling practices and through charitable and volunteering initiatives with local schools, charities and other groups.

The website also notes:

> We realise that our commitments need to go beyond traditional economic benefits such as jobs, security and local taxes. Our aim is to support organisations that align with and are central to our business strategy and company values and, in doing so, to have a positive and joined-up impact on the environment and communities in which we operate.

Attention is placed on three areas in particular: recycling, education/health, and local engagement. The strategies are implemented on regional and local basis focusing on products, operations and people.

CSR report: A sustainability report is published annually. Also some details are contained within the annual report and accounts.

Exclusions

The group does not make political donations.

Applications

In writing to the correspondent.

Ricardo-AEA

Information management and communication, information technology

Correspondent: Patricia Ryan, Company Secretary, Marble Arch Tower, 55 Bryanston Street, London W1H 7AA (tel: 01235 753000; fax: 01235 753001; website: www.ricardo-aea.com)

Directors: David Shemmans, Chief Executive Officer; Michael Harper, Chair; Peter Gilchrist; Ian Lee; Hans-Joachim Schöpf; David Hall; Ian Gibson, Chief Financial Officer; Mark Garrett; Terry Morgan (women: 0; men: 9)

Year end	31/03/2014
Turnover	£236,200,000
Pre-tax profit	£24,600,000

Nature of business: Ricardo is a global strategic, technical and environmental consultancy. It is also a specialist niche manufacturer of high performance products. The company employs over 2,000 professional engineers, consultants, scientists and support staff. Activities cover a range of market sectors including passenger cars, commercial vehicles, rail, defence, motorsport, motorcycles, off-highway, marine, clean energy and power generation, and government and environmental.

On 8 November 2012 the group acquired the business and certain operating assets of AEA Technology plc (in administration) for total cash consideration of £18 million.

Company registration number: 3095862

Subsidiary undertakings include: Ricardo UK Ltd; Ricardo-AEA Ltd; Ricardo, Inc.; Ricardo Deutschland GmbH; Ricardo Strategic Consulting GmbH; Ricardo Prague S.R.O.; Ricardo Shanghai Company Ltd; Ricardo Japan K.K.; Ricardo India Private Ltd; Ricardo Asia Ltd.

Main locations: Derby, Harlow, Harwell, Glengarnock, Risley, London, Winfrith, Barnsley

Total employees: 2,057

Focus of giving: Education, science technology, children, young people.

Membership: BITC

FTSE 100	✓
Gifts in kind	✓
Matched funding	✓

Charitable donations

Cash UK (latest available):	2014	£17,800
	2013	£25,300
	2009	£38,300
	2008	£8,957
	2007	£25,483
Total UK (cash and in kind):	2014	£17,800
Cash worldwide:	2014	£17,800
Total worldwide (cash and in kind):	2014	£17,800

Community involvement

The company's focus is education, particularly raising awareness of the business and the engineering profession, in areas local to its main sites. Activities are often used as development opportunities for staff and examples of this in-kind giving includes the company providing work experience placements for local schools; and active engagement in STEM events across the education age range, promoting engineering and Ricardo at careers fairs.

The company's Shoreham Technical Centre in partnership with Business in the Community (BITC), works with a local academy and undertakes community engagement projects as part of their Give and Gain programme.

Corporate giving

In 2013/14 the company gave £17,800 in charitable donations.

In-kind support

The company 'occasionally' matches staff donations to charitable activities, particularly where there is active staff participation in events.

Employee-led support

Staff are involved with fundraising events for example, several sites have engaged in the Movember campaign raising funds for prostate cancer. Some members of staff act as school and academy governors.

Corporate social responsibility

CSR committee: No evidence of a separate CSR Committee. The board as a whole reviews the key elements of corporate social responsibility on an annual basis.

CSR information: This information was available from the company's 2014 annual report:

> Ricardo has a proactive and engaged approach to Corporate Social Responsibility. The environment is a key driver for our strategy and is seen in many of our delivery streams where excellence through innovation and technology provides the missions to all of our teams. It is embedded in what we do and the solutions we deliver.

CSR report: There is a CSR report contained within the annual report and accounts.

Exclusions

Previously no support has been given for advertising in charity brochures, animal welfare, appeals from individuals, elderly people, fundraising events, medical research, overseas projects, political appeals, religious appeals, sickness/disability, social welfare or sport.

Applications

In writing to the correspondent referenced 'CSR in the Community'.

Richer Sounds plc

Retail – electrical

Correspondent: Teresa Chapman, PA to Julian Richer, Unit 3/4, Richer House, Gallery Court, Hankey Place, London SE1 4BB (tel: 2075515343; email: teresac@richersounds.com; website: www.richersounds.com)

Directors: Julian Richer; David Robinson, Chair; John Currier (women: 0; men: 3)

Year end	03/05/2014
Turnover	£143,371,000
Pre-tax profit	£5,756,000

Nature of business: Retailer and e-tailer of hi-fi, home cinema and flat screen TV and related equipment.

Company registration number: 1402643

Subsidiary undertakings include: Ariston Acoustics Ltd; Hi-fi Direct Ltd; R S Holland BV; and Richer Sounds International Ltd. The company holds more than 20% of the above companies.

Main locations: London

UK employees: 494

Total employees: 494

Focus of giving: Human rights, animal welfare, health, ill health, housing, homelessness, older people, poverty and social exclusion, safety and crime prevention, children, young people, disability.

Gifts in kind	✓
Market-led giving	✓
Matched funding	✓
Payroll giving	✓

Charitable donations

Cash UK (latest available):	2014	£887,000
	2013	£742,000
	2012	£779,000
	2011	£818,000
	2009	£515,000
Total UK (cash and in kind):	2014	£887,000
Cash worldwide:	2014	£887,000
Total worldwide (cash and in kind):	2014	£887,000

Community involvement

The Persula Foundation (Charity Commission no. 1044174)

The foundation was established in 1994 as an independent grant-making foundation. It states that it is currently interested in supporting initiatives in the following areas:

- Human rights and welfare
- Animal rights and welfare

Activities which supported these areas included supporting counsellors for the City and East Long Bereavement Service; activity weekends through the Douglas Bader Foundation for children with disabilities; and Stonewall's primary school DVD project.

The website notes the company being concerned with environmental impact of the business, recycling and sustainable waste management, and participating in Distributor Take Back Scheme. Through the scheme Richer Sounds has 'paid towards the provision and improvement of recycling facilities throughout the UK so that the customers can conveniently recycle their old TVs and Hi-Fi equipment free of charge'.

Corporate giving

The company is an unlisted plc 100% owned by Julian Richer, the founder and managing director of the company. Support for charitable causes is routed through The Persula Foundation which was initiated by Julian. During 2013/14 the company gave a total of £887,000 to various charities.

The latest accounts of the foundation at the time of writing were from 2012/13. During that year the foundation had an income of £760,000 (the donation from the company amounting for over £742,000) and spent £737,000 in charitable activities.

'Friends' of the company

The company's website states that the following are charities 'which it supports and which it would like others to support in turn' – Action Medical Research; Acts 435; ASB Help; Hope and Homes For Children; Kidscape; National Missing Persons Helpline; Oxfam; RNID; The Mayor of London's Fund for Young Musicians (Mayor's Music Fund).

The foundation's beneficiaries have included: Parent Circle Families Forum (£30,000); Amnesty International UK (£25,000), Tapesense scheme (£15,500); Douglas Bader Foundation; Chernobyl Children's Project; Hillside Animal Sanctuary; and Stonewall's primary school DVD project.

See the corporate charity entry on p. 423 for more information.

In-kind support

The company may provide staff time and expertise, office space and other facilities, for example, server. The Persula Foundation also has access to many resources from the company, such as marketing, design and strategic consultation. The foundation prefers to use these resources to provide an added value aspect to its collaboration with organisations.

Employee-led support

The company has let us know that it no longer offers office paid leave for volunteers.

Matched funding

There is a scheme in place to match employees' fundraising. We have been informed by the correspondent that 'Richer Sounds gives £100 to any colleague who is fundraising.'

Commercially led support

Through the foundation the company operates Tapesense scheme supplying blind and visually impaired people with subsidised audio products and accessories, such as audio cassettes, hi-fi accessories, interconnect cables, universal remote controls, headphones, microphones and digital (DAB) radios.

Corporate social responsibility

CSR committee: There were no details of CSR committee presence found.

CSR information: No information on specific CSR policies found. The company pays attention to environmental issues, recycling and sustainable waste management, and supports a range of organisations in the UK.

CSR report: No report found.

Corporate charity: The Persula Foundation (Charity Commission no. 1044174).

Exclusions

Grants cannot be given for buildings, individuals or core funding.

Applications

The Persula Foundation (Charity Commission no. 1044174) considers applications for funding from a variety of charitable organisations. Applications are reviewed and levels of grants payable are decided by the trustees.

Applications and queries regarding the Tapesense scheme should also be addressed to the correspondent.

Ridgesave Ltd

Property

Correspondent: Zelda Weiss, Secretary, 141B Upper Clapton Road, London E5 9DB (tel: 020 8806 4271; email: mail@cohenarnold.com)

Directors: Joseph Weiss, Chair; E. Englander; Zelda Weiss (women: 1; men: 2)

Year end	31/03/2013
Turnover	£406,093

Nature of business: Property investment and trading.

Ridgesave Ltd is a registered charity with two non-charitable operating subsidiaries: Bullion Properties Ltd and Doxit Company Ltd.

Company registration number: 1745720

Non-charitable subsidiaries are: Bullion Properties Ltd and Doxit Company Ltd.

Focus of giving: General charitable purposes, education, poverty and social exclusion, religion.

Overseas giving ✓

Charitable donations

Cash UK (latest available):	2011	£1,343,700
	2009	£1,900,000
	2008	£1,700,000
	2007	£1,100,000
	2006	£944,000
Cash worldwide:	2013	£2,300,000
Total worldwide (cash and in kind):	2013	£2,300,000

Community involvement

This is a somewhat unusual entry in the context of our research into company giving. Ridgesave, although registered as a company limited by guarantee, is also a registered charity (Charity Commission no. 288020). The charity concentrates its giving to assist institutions teaching the principles of traditional Judaism, and to provide philanthropic aid to those in need.

We have decided to include it here because it has two non-charitable operating subsidiaries – Bullion Properties Ltd (property trading) and Doxit Co. Limited (property investment). In addition, the bulk of the charity's income is derived from other companies of which some of the trustees of the charity are also directors. These companies include: Islehurst Ltd; Safeview Ltd; Shirestates Ltd; Urbanhold Ltd; and previously Halastar Ltd.

We were unable to find a website for this company.

Corporate giving

During 2013/14 the charitable company continued its charitable activities and supported organisations engaged in areas of education, advancement of religion, and provision of philanthropic aid. The income of the company was about £406,000, while grants and donations totalled over £2.3 million (2012/13: £2.1 million). The accounts did not provide a breakdown of charitable donations.

See the corporate charity entry on p. 424 for more information.

Corporate social responsibility

Corporate charity: Ridgesave Ltd (Charity Commission no. 288020).

Applications

In writing to the correspondent. The day-to-day management of the company affairs is undertaken by the directors who are also trustees.

Rio Tinto plc

Mining

Correspondent: The Community Relations Team, Legal and External Affairs, 2 Eastbourne Terrace, London W2 6LG (tel: 020 7781 2000; fax: 020 7781 1800; website: www.riotinto.com)

Directors: Sam Walsh, Chief Executive Officer; Jan du Plessis, Chair; Christopher Lynch, Chief Financial Officer; Robert Brown; Michael Fitzpatrick; Ann Godbehere; Richard Goodmanson; Lord Kerr of Kinlochard; Anne Lauvergeon; Michael L'Estrange; Paul Tellier; Simon Thompson; John Varley; Megan Clark (women: 3; men: 11)

Year end	31/12/2013
Turnover	£31,910,235,912
Pre-tax profit	£2,185,718,021

Nature of business: Rio Tinto is one of the world's largest mining companies. Based in the UK, Rio Tinto has substantial worldwide interests in metals and industrial minerals with major assets in Australia, South America, Asia, Europe and Southern Africa.

Company registration number: 719885

Principal subsidiaries include: Argyle Diamond Ltd; Alcan Alumina Ltda.; Iron Ore Company of Canada Inc.; Richards Bay Mining (Proprietary) Ltd; Riversdale Mining Ltd; Simfer Jersey Ltd; and U.S. Borax Inc. Note: 'The group's principal subsidiaries are mostly held by intermediate holding companies and not directly by Rio Tinto plc or Rio Tinto Ltd.' More information on subsidiary undertakings can be found in the accounts, which also state: 'The group comprises a large number of companies and it is not practical to include all of them in this list. The list therefore only includes companies that have a more significant impact on the profit or assets of the group.'

Main locations: London

Total employees: 66,331

Focus of giving: Human rights, education, enterprise/training, environment, equal opportunities, health, ill health, heritage, arts, culture, overseas projects, women's issues, community/social welfare.

Cash donations undeclared	✓
FTSE 100	✓
Overseas giving	✓
Sponsorship	✓

Charitable donations

Cash UK (latest available):	2013	£797,000
	2011	£400,000
	2009	£1,800,000
	2008	£1,900,000
	2007	£1,800,000
Total UK (cash and in kind):	2013	£797,000
Cash worldwide:	2013	£123,800,000
Total worldwide (cash and in kind):	2013	£206,400,000

Community involvement

The group's approach to working with communities aims to encompass three areas:

- Building knowledge – identifying and understanding key features of the community and assessing business impact
- Engaging – creating partnerships with government agencies, community and non-government organisations, academics and other bodies
- Developing – programmes covering educational, health or livelihood initiatives, which build long-term local skills and knowledge; and providing employment opportunities

Rio Tinto plc aims to 'work from a common communities and social performance framework of building knowledge, engaging with communities and developing programmes', which will vary according to the local context. Nevertheless some common themes include: preservation of cultural heritage, fostering community agreement and gender equality.

Support can be given through community contributions, sponsorships and donations, and seeks to: promote employment and local small businesses, facilitate long-term development, address community priorities (education, health, livelihoods, environmental protection, cultural maintenance, good governance, and so on), benefit community as a whole, and not substitute statutory provisions.

The company states:

> Our relationships with communities involve consultation to open new facilities, to run existing ones and to close them at

> the end of their productive lives. In doing so, we support community based projects that can make a difference in a sustainable way without creating dependency. We also assist regional development, training and employment and small business opportunities. In developing countries, we are often asked to support health, education and agricultural programs and, in collaboration with others, we help where practical.

It is stated that Rio Tinto works in partnership with bodies, such as:

> Leading universities, non-government organisations and industry suppliers who possess expertise to help it resolve some of the challenges faced in the group's business – including biodiversity loss, climate change and its impact on water and energy, and poverty and corruption.

Examples of community involvement, given in the sustainable development report often refer to activities undertaken as part of employee and working conditions development or wider reconciliation, participation and partnership with indigenous people agreements, such as: Argyle Diamonds seeking to grow the number of indigenous enterprises throughout the East Kimberley region and partnering with Gelganyem Trust and Many Rivers Microfinance Ltd over three years to establish an Indigenous Business Hub; and Rio Tinto Minerals Peru (RTMP), in partnership with an NGO and via agreement with the local village governments, supporting the formation and training of community-based committees to monitor the environmental impacts of La Granja copper project activities.

It is worth noting that some of the activities undertaken by the group we would not consider to be 'community/charitable contributions', such as 'agreement with the local village governments, supporting the formation and training of community-based committees to monitor the environmental impacts of La Granja copper project activities', where we would consider the balance of benefit to be more in the company's favour.

Education partnerships

The group creates partnerships with universities and colleges and supports institutions that are important to the industries and communities in which it operates; it also sponsors research activities and curriculum development. At the moment there are three global long-term partners: Imperial College London, University of Queensland and University of Western Australia. In the UK the Imperial College London partnership programme includes Rio Tinto Sports Innovation Challenge sponsoring the college's 'engineering students to design and prototype sporting equipment enabling people with disabilities to take part in sports'.

Corporate giving

In 2013 the group states having spent US$331 million (over £206.4 million) in 'community contributions'. The Sustainable Development Report for 2013 further specifies that of this sum 31% went directly to community programmes, 60% were 'direct payments into benefits-receiving trusts associated with community agreements', and 9% covered management costs. During the year 'just under 2,200 socio-economic programmes' were supported. Programmes covered a range of activities, including: education (29.5%); environment, culture and 'other' causes (11.9% each); business development (11.6%); health (8.8%); transport (5.2%); agricultural development (4.1%); recreation (3.6%); housing (1.4%); and HIV/AIDS (0.2%), and benefited the group, its employees and broader community in which they operate.

Based on the above specifications we estimate that direct cash contributions to charities worldwide totalled about £123.8 million and direct support to community programmes was £63.9 million.

The support was given in the following regions: Australia and New Zealand (37%); North America (25%); Europe/Africa (14%); Asia (14%); and South America (10%). We could not identify the amount awarded in the UK, therefore we estimate cash donations to have totalled around £797,000, based on the figures from the three previous years known to us.

Corporate social responsibility

CSR committee: There is a Sustainability Committee. The group states that its global code of business conduct *The Way We Work*, supported by corporate policies and strategies, is the foundation of its communities and social performance work. The management and governance systems are designed to ensure these standards are implemented throughout the group.

CSR information: The following is taken from the company's website:

> Good community relations are as necessary for our business success as the effective management of our operations. This belief is at the heart of our overall approach to communities work and is why we build good quality relationships with the people in the areas where we operate. We seek to understand the social, environmental and economic implications of our activities so we can optimise benefits and reduce negative impacts, both for local communities and for regional and national economies. We accept that we cannot meet everybody's concerns and expectations, but wherever we operate we seek to do so with broad-based community support.

The group's sustainable development strategies focus on four areas: social issues, environment, economic issues, and governance.

CSR report: There is an annual Sustainable Development Report on the company's website but no reference is made to UK charitable giving.

Exclusions

No support is given, directly or indirectly, to any sectarian, religious or political activity. No funding is provided for building projects or general running costs, nor for advertising in charity brochures. Support is not given to individuals, animal welfare or any sporting events.

Applications

In writing to the correspondent.

RM plc

Computer software, information management and communication

Correspondent: The Group HR Director, 140 Eastern Avenue, Milton Park, Abingdon, Oxfordshire OX14 4SB (tel: 0845 070 0300; fax: 0845 070 0400; website: www.rm.com)

Directors: Iain McIntosh, Chief Financial Officer; John Poulter, Chair; Lord Adonis; Patrick Martell; David Brooks, Chief Executive Officer; Deena Mattar (women: 1; men: 5)

Year end	30/11/2013
Turnover	£261,759,000
Pre-tax profit	£9,435,000

Nature of business: The principal activities of the group are the supply of educational products and services to schools, colleges and universities, local and central government departments and agencies.

Company registration number: 1749877

Subsidiary undertakings include: RM Books Ltd; RM Education Ltd; SpaceKraft Ltd; and TTS Group Ltd. A full list is available from the group's accounts.

Main locations: Glasgow, Cheadle, Otley, Sheffield, Leeds, Wrexham, Abingdon

Total employees: 2,148

Focus of giving: Education, health, ill health, children, young people.

Gifts in kind	✓
Market-led giving	✓
Matched funding	✓
Overseas giving	✓

Charitable donations

Cash UK (latest available):	2013	£14,500
	2011	£88,000
	2010	£23,000
	2009	£112,000
	2008	£98,000
Total UK (cash and in kind):	2013	£14,500
Cash worldwide:	2013	£14,500
Total worldwide (cash and in kind):	2013	£14,500

Community involvement

The RM Education section on the website notes the company's commitment to the environment and attempts to minimise the adverse impact on it. The 'Green RM team is a group of committed employees who are fully supported to drive green initiatives in RM Education – making a big impact by keeping the environment firmly on everyone's agenda.' It appears that environmental initiatives are limited within the company – there have been 'recycling facilities, car-sharing schemes and improved facilities for cyclists' introduced, and work is being done 'to reduce the amount of food packaging used onsite'.

The group has informed us that it does support employee fundraising for their chosen causes.

Corporate giving

In 2012/13 the group made charitable donations totalling about £14,500 (2012: £80,000). We could not find more specific information regarding the group's charitable giving or UK donations, but it appears that giving is concentrated on the UK charities.

In-kind support

Staff volunteering time and expert skills, advice services.

Employee-led support

All RM employees are given the opportunity to volunteer their time and efforts to help charitable organisations.

Matched funding

The group has informed us that it will support employee fundraising.

Commercially led support

In the past RM Education has run an incentive on the company's Customer Experience Survey. Every response to the survey generated a £1 donation from the company and an additional 33% to the total amount from the RM Charitable Foundation (now defunct). The initiative has collected over £1,000 donated to Ace Centre, Children in Touch, and Save the Children.

Corporate social responsibility

CSR committee: There were no details found.

CSR report: We found no indications of a CSR report being available.

Applications

In writing to the correspondent.

Rolls–Royce Holdings plc

Engineering, industrial products/services

Correspondent: The Corporate Sustainability Team, 65 Buckingham Gate, London SW1E 6AT (tel: 020 7222 9020; fax: 020 7222 9170; website: www.rolls-royce.com)

Directors: Ian Davis, Chair; John Rishton, Chief Executive Officer; Lewis Booth; Dame Helen Alexander; Ruth Cairnie; Sir Frank Chapman; Warren East; Lee Hsien Yang; Dr John McAdam; John Neill; Jasmin Staiblin; James Guyette; David Smith, Chief Financial Officer; Colin Smith; Pamela Coles, Company Secretary (women: 4; men: 11)

Year end	31/12/2013
Turnover	£15,513,000,000
Pre-tax profit	£1,870,000,000

Nature of business: Rolls-Royce is a global company providing power (gas turbines and reciprocating engines) on land, sea and air.

Company registration number: 1003142

Subsidiary undertakings include: Rolls-Royce Group plc (holding company); Rolls-Royce plc (principal trading company); Rolls-Royce Power Development; Rolls-Royce Marine India Private Ltd; Rolls-Royce Marine North America Inc.; and Rolls-Royce Singapore Pte. Limited. A full list of subsidiary undertakings is available in the group's annual report and accounts.

Main locations: Bristol, Derby, Dounreay, East Kilbride, Hucknall, Hillington, Newcastle, London, Sunderland, Barnoldswick, Ansty

UK employees: 24,800

Total employees: 55,200

Focus of giving: Economic generation, education, enterprise/training, environment, equal opportunities, STEM (science, technology, engineering and mathematics), overseas projects, science technology, sponsorship, children, young people, community/social welfare.

Membership: BITC, LBG

Cash donations undeclared	✓
FTSE 100	✓
Gifts in kind	✓
Payroll giving	✓
Sponsorship	✓

Charitable donations

Cash UK (latest available):	2013	£1,500,000
	2011	£2,100,000
	2009	£1,500,000
	2007	£1,100,000
	2006	£728,000
Total UK (cash and in kind):	2013	£1,500,000
Total worldwide (cash and in kind):	2013	£8,000,000

Community involvement

Rolls-Royce states it is 'committed to conducting business to the highest standards and building positive relationships within the communities where the group operates', and 'actively works with schools and universities to increase interest and encourage diversity amongst those taking STEM [science, technology, engineering and mathematics] subjects, to broaden the career aspirations of individuals from under-represented groups'.

Community investment

The website states that alongside STEM the community support is particularly focused on: education and skills; environmental activities; social investment, 'with the intention of making a positive contribution wherever we are in the world; and arts, culture and heritage'.

STEM programmes

There are a number of STEM outreach programmes aimed at pupils and students. The programmes: support educational influencers, including teachers, parents and youth leaders; engage a diverse audience in STEM subjects under-represented groups, including women; promote STEM subjects and their application in the world of work; and offer information on career options for young people. As part of the programme work-related learning experiences, such as work experience, internships, apprenticeships and graduate development programmes, for students in the group's key geographical areas are offered.

Rolls-Royce is a partner in a unique STEM education project with a strong engineering focus for primary schools based on Cirque du Soleil's annual show at the Royal Albert Hall:

> The project specifically targets disadvantaged schools, with about 500 children and 30 teachers from 15 schools taking part. The majority of children come from minority ethnic or socially disadvantaged backgrounds. Two of the schools are for children with special educational needs.

Rolls-Royce is a supporter of the UK Big Bang Fair and has partnerships with girl guides and boy scouts in the UK.

Charity partnerships

The group's co-operation includes a partnership with Mercy Ships and supports the operation of Africa Mercy – 'the largest non-governmental hospital ship in the world'.

Corporate giving

In 2013 the group's 'total contributions' amounted to £8 million. Unlike previously, the 2013 Sustainability Report did not offer a breakdown of community support. The website states that community contributions totalled £8.1 million, including charitable contributions, sponsorships, and over 80,000 hours in employee time. We could not determine the amount given in cash in the UK, therefore we estimate the figure to be around £1.5 million, based on the data from the three previous years, known to us.

In-kind support

According to our research, the group can offer support in-kind to local initiatives, including in-house training programmes, surplus computers, equipment and furniture, loans of engines and components, technical support, and free use of meeting rooms and premises.

Employee-led support

The group's Global Code of Conduct states that in most cases employees will be able to get support to work for voluntary organisations (for example, school communities or community groups). In 2013 employee donated time totalled 80,000 hours. The group states that it 'also supports its employees in making tax-free donations to their chosen charities in the UK and North Americas'.

Payroll giving

In the past the group operated a Payroll Giving Scheme for UK employees, enabling them to make tax-free donations to their chosen charities. We could find no mention of the scheme in the 2013 report.

Commercially led support

Sponsorship

In 2013 Rolls-Royce sponsored the UK Female Undergraduate of the Year 2013 awards with the winner taken on the group's Customer Management Graduate Programme.

Rolls Royce Science Prize

Established in 2004, the Rolls-Royce Science Prize is part of the company's commitment to promote science and engineering in schools by rewarding inspirational teaching. There is a total of £120,000 in prizes to be won each year. From 2014 the programme involves mathematics. This new element is undertaken in partnership with the Institute of Mathematics and its Applications (IMA) and The National Centre for Excellence in the Teaching of Mathematics (NCETM).

Corporate social responsibility

CSR committee: Charitable and community giving is detailed within the group's Sustainability Report. The annual report for 2013 states that the data on STEM education programmes and activities is:

> Subject to verification at both a business level (at the point of submission) and quarterly by the Corporate Community Investment and Education Outreach team on behalf of the Executive Leadership Team, via the Group Charitable Contributions and Sponsorships Committee.

There are also ethics, risk and safety committees, each overseeing elements of the sustainability issues.

CSR information: The group's sustainability focus is based around 'better power', 'better future' and 'better business', and seeks to cover areas including: community investment, employee development, health and safety, equal opportunities, and environment.

The statement taken from the 2013 Sustainability Report notes that the group is 'committed to conducting business to the highest standards and building positive relationships within the communities where it operates'.

The group's Global Code of Conduct notes that the community investment principles underpin the following:

- Contribution to the economic development and social well-being of the communities in which it operates
- Community investment being an intrinsic part of the way it conducts its business support being directed 'within the areas of education and skills, in particular STEM, the environment, social investment, arts, culture and heritage'
- Encouragement of community investment activities
- Making sure that company's charitable contributions are appropriate and proportionate

Note: In September 2011 the group issued a response to the Davies Report on women on boards committing to 'support the development of a diverse workforce' and stating that it 'expected to make demonstrable progress in this area by 2015'.

CSR report: A Sustainability Report is contained within the annual report and accounts.

Exclusions

Our research suggests support is not given for advertising in charity brochures, religious or local appeals not in areas of company presence.

Rolls-Royce does not 'make corporate contributions or donations to political parties or to any organisations, think-tanks, academic institutions or charities closely associated to a political party or cause'.

Applications

In writing to the correspondent, referenced 'Corporate Sustainability Team'.

N. M. Rothschild & Sons Ltd

Banking

Correspondent: Annette Shepherd, Secretary to the Charities Committee, New Court, St Swithin's Lane, London EC4P 4DU (tel: 020 7280 5968; website: www.rothschild.com/about_rothschild/community_and_environment)

Directors: Peter Smith, Chair; Anthony Alt, Deputy Chair; Peter Barbour; Andrew Didham; Anthony Salz; Daniel Bouton (women: 0; men: 9)

Year end	31/03/2014
Turnover	£392,802,000
Pre-tax profit	£54,620,000

Nature of business: The company and its subsidiaries carry on the business of merchants and bankers. It is the main UK operating entity of the wider Rothschild Group which is consolidated under Paris Orleans, the French listed parent company.

Company registration number: 925279

Principal subsidiary undertakings include: Five Arrows Leasing Group Ltd; Five Arrows Leasing Ltd; Five Arrows Business Finance plc; Specialist Fleet Services Finance Ltd; City Business Finance Ltd; Rothschilds Continuation Finance plc

Main locations: London, Manchester, Leeds, Birmingham

Total employees: 1,097

Focus of giving: Education, enterprise/training, environment, health, ill health, heritage, medical research, older people, arts, culture, children, young people, community/social welfare, disability.

Membership: BITC, LBG

Charity of the Year	✓
Gifts in kind	✓
Humanitarian aid: overseas	✓
Humanitarian aid: UK	✓
Matched funding	✓
Overseas giving	✓
Payroll giving	✓

Charitable donations

Cash UK (latest available):	2014	£247,500
	2013	£288,000
	2011	£546,000
	2009	£439,000
	2008	£624,000
Total UK (cash and in kind):	2014	£465,500
Cash worldwide:	2014	£250,000
Total worldwide (cash and in kind):	2014	£468,000

Community involvement

The group supports charities both in the areas in which it operates and those in the wider community. The company's subsidiaries around the world support causes in their areas of operation.

The Charities Committee

The Charities Committee was established in 1975 to consider the requests received every year from charities seeking financial support.

Typical beneficiaries continue to include organisations concerned with elderly people, healthcare, social welfare and education. Requests for support from staff in respect of charitable causes with which they are associated, or have an involvement, are actively encouraged. Applications from small, local charities are particularly welcomed.

Rothschild in the Community

Through its community initiative, Rothschild in the Community, UK staff are able to volunteer in their local communities on projects 'that have the potential to change people's lives'. In 2013/14, as part of the initiative's education programme, students at three partner schools in the disadvantaged areas of Kings Cross and Bow were supported to improve their educational attainment levels and self-development. The educational charities Teach First and Future First were also supported, as were organisations working to combat deprivation in the areas surrounding the partner schools.

Corporate giving

In 2013/14 £250,000 was paid out to charities. A total of 329 donations were made by the London Committee, and another 49 were made by the Northern Committee. We have taken this cash total to include a £2,500 payment given in support of a rebuilding project at the Calape Elementary School in the Philippines following the Philippines Typhoon.

The percentage of donations (by value) for particular charitable purposes were distributed as follows: Social welfare (39%); Medical (21%); Young people (20%); Cultural (8%); Armed forced (5%); Education (4%); 'Miscellaneous' (3%)

Macmillan Cancer Support received £575 through a collection of unwanted foreign coins and notes.

The group invested a further £218,000 in supporting local communities through the Rothschild in the Community programme, which we have taken to include staff time given to the value of £184,000, as well as other resources.

Core charities: Aside from supporting individual, unsolicited requests, the Charity Committee also supported the following group of 'core charities': Association of Jewish Ex-Service Men and Women (AJEX); City Gateway; Help for Heroes; London's Air Ambulance; London Symphony Orchestra; Maytree Respite Centre; Rehabilitation for Addicted Prisoners Trust (RAPT); St Mungo's Broadway; Spitalfields Music – Learning and Participation Schools Programme; Stepney City Farm; Wednesday's Child; World Jewish Relief

'Adopted charity' 2013/14: The Brain Tumour Charity received £15,500 from Rothschild during the year.

'Adopted charity' 2014/15: Headway – the Brain Injury Association

The figure for charitable gifts as declared in the Chair's report for the year ending 31 March 2014 (£355,000) differs from the figure reported in the Charities Report covering the same period. We have taken our figures from the Charities Report.

In-kind support

Staff time

Through Rothschild in the Community, the group committed 3,357 hours of staff volunteering time in 2013/14. More information on the group's community initiatives is available from the Rothschild in the Community 2014 review on the group's website.

Employee-led support

Matched funding

The following information is taken from the Charities Review 2014:

> Staff are encouraged to recommend charitable causes with which they are associated, or have an involvement, for support. The Charities Committee will consider favourably requests for a donation where the donation is being matched by the member of staff. By matching the Committee mean giving an appropriate sum of money relative to the amount of the donation requested or undertaking an event such as running a marathon to raise money generally for the charity concerned.

Employee volunteering

Apart from making financial donations, the group is committed to engaging in long-term relationships with local schools, charities and community organisations through community partnerships via the Rothschild in the Community programme. Through the Rothschild Gifted and Talented Mentoring Programme employees are volunteering to help 50 students learn about the benefits of higher education.

Requests for support from staff in respect of charitable causes with which they are associated, or have an involvement, are actively encouraged.

Payroll giving

The Give As You Earn scheme is in operation.

Nominated charities

Staff are balloted to nominate a new 'Adopted Charity' and, during the year, this received a 'very broad response'. Donations were made to charities including: Approximately 250 charities were supported during the 2013/14 financial year including: Action on Hearing Loss; Aid to the Church in Need; Arthritis Research UK; Alzheimer's Research UK; Basildon Special Care Baby Unit; The Big Issue Foundation. A full list of beneficiaries is available from the Charities Review 2014 (www.rothschild.com/about_rothschild/charitable_support).

Corporate social responsibility

CSR committee: In the UK the Rothschild Charities Committee meets quarterly to consider applications.

CSR information: This information was obtained from the group's Charities Report 2014:

> Rothschild remains committed to supporting charities both in the areas in which it operates and those which are active in the wider community.
>
> The Charities Committee was established in 1975 to consider the many requests every year from charities seeking financial support.
>
> Typical beneficiaries continue to include organisations concerned with elderly people, healthcare, social welfare and education.

CSR report: There is a CSR report included in the annual report and accounts and reviews on community partnerships and charities are published on the website.

Exclusions

Our research tells us that there will be no response to circular appeals, and that no grants are given for advertising in charity brochures; animal welfare; appeals from individuals; fundraising events; overseas projects; political appeals; religious appeals or sport.

Applications

In writing to the Secretary to the Charities Committee.

The following information is taken from the Charities Review 2014:

> It should be noted that the donation from the Committee will not normally exceed £500. The Committee thanks those concerned for suggestions received this year and notes that approximately 20 per cent of the donations made in the year under review were in response to appeals from staff.

Rotork plc

Engineering, industrial products/services

Correspondent: Stephen Jones, Company Secretary, Brassmill Lane, Bath BA1 3JQ (tel: 01225 733200; fax: 01225 333467; email: mail@rotork.co.uk; website: www.rotork.com)

Directors: Graham Ogden; John Nicholas; Peter France, Chief Executive; Roger Lockwood, Chair; Jonathan Davis, Finance Director; Bob Arnold; Gary Bullard; Stephen Jones; Lucinda Bell; Sally James; Martin Lamb (women: 2; men: 9)

Year end	31/12/2013
Turnover	£578,440,000
Pre-tax profit	£137,997,000

Nature of business: The company's activities include design and manufacture of actuators and flow control equipment.

Company registration number: 578327

Principal subsidiaries include: Rotork BV; Rotork Germany Holdings GmbH; Rotork Inc (intermediate holding company); Rotork Japan Co. Ltd; Rotork Overseas Ltd (intermediate holding company); and Rotork Sweden AB. A full list of subsidiary undertakings is attached to the annual return.

UK employees: 607

Total employees: 2,892

Focus of giving: Education, enterprise/ training, health, ill health, children, young people, community/social welfare, disability, disasters.

Charity of the Year	✓
Gifts in kind	✓
Humanitarian aid: overseas	✓
Matched funding	✓
Overseas giving	✓

Charitable donations

Cash UK (latest available):	2013	£83,000
	2011	£90,000
	2009	£87,000
	2008	£71,000
Total UK (cash and in kind):	2013	£83,000
Cash worldwide:	2013	£122,000
Total worldwide (cash and in kind):	2013	£122,000

Community involvement

There are local charity committees at each site providing donations to charitable causes. Local community activities throughout the group included:

- Visiting and donating in-kind gifts to As-Solihin Orphanage in Malaysia
- Running educational programmes, such as apprenticeships, work placements and internship programmes
- Co-operating with the Mexican Red Cross to provide food and personal hygiene items to storm victims
- Donation to a local school for children with disabilities in Sweden to organise a trip to the UK to meet pupils from similar schools
- Providing practice interview training at a local high school in Germany
- Giving a special donation to 'One bike, a thousand hopes 2013' campaign, in memory of the brother of an employee, based in Italy

Charity partnership

WaterAid remains the group's chosen global charity awarded £55,000 by the company, with a further contribution of £6,600 from employee fundraising, in 2013. In 2014 WaterAid's Metu-Hurum Woreda WASH Project is supported.

Rotork is the industry member of the Bath Education Trust and a member of an initiative of the Engineering Development Trust, helping 11- to 21-year-olds to develop their skills.

During the year City of Bath College became the group's partner to offer engineering apprenticeships.

Corporate giving

The group aims to donate 0.1% of its profits. In 2013 the CSR report identifies £122,000 being donated to charities. We found no specific information on UK contributions, therefore we estimate about £83,000 to be donated in cash in the UK, based on the average from the three previous years known to us.

Beneficiaries included: The Institute of Cancer Research (£57,000); WaterAid (£55,000); Mauro Talini and Father Kolbe International no-profit Association (£10,000).

In-kind support

Staff volunteering time, provision of expertise and specialist skills, food and clothing items, toys, other products.

Employee-led support

Staff fundraising efforts collected £6,600 to help WaterAid. In the USA employees donated Christmas gifts of toys and clothing to local children.

Matched funding

Our research suggests that the charity committee will normally match monies raised by employees who undertake charitable events personally.

Commercially led support

In 2013 City of Bath College partnered with the group to offer engineering apprenticeships.

Corporate social responsibility

CSR committee: Information taken from the annual report and accounts for 2013 states that the group's 'CSR objectives are monitored by four separate committees covering health and safety, environment, ethics and social issues which report to the CSR Committee chaired by the Chief Executive.' The CEO reports the progress to the board.

CSR policies and strategies are communicated throughout the group and implemented regionally. Each of the group's locations has its own charity committee which focuses on its local community needs.

CSR information: The group's mission statement claims that it will: '...be a good corporate citizen, supporting the local community, acting with integrity and honesty whilst always considering ways of improving our operational impact on the environment.'

The website states that the CSR is focused around four main themes: the environment; ethics and values; health and safety; and community involvement.

CSR report: Contained within the annual report and accounts.

Applications

In writing to the local charity committee.

The Royal Bank of Scotland Group plc

Financial services, insurance, banking

Correspondent: Group Sustainability Team, 36 St Andrew Square, Edinburgh EH2 2YB (tel: 01315 568555; email: group.sustainability@rbs.org.uk; website: www.rbs.com/community)

Directors: Ewen Stevenson, Chief Finance Director; Sir Sandy Crombie; Penny Hughes; Sir Philip Hampton, Chair; Ross McEwan, Chief Executive; Alison Davis; Brendan Nelson; Baroness Noakes; Morten Friis; Robert Gillespie; Aileen Taylor (women: 4; men: 7)

Year end	31/12/2013
Turnover	£16,740,000,000
Pre-tax profit	(£8,243,000,000)

Nature of business: RBS is a UK-based banking and financial services company. Headquartered in Edinburgh, RBS operates in the United Kingdom, Europe, the Middle East, the Americas and Asia, serving over 24 million customers worldwide.

Company registration number: SC045551

Subsidiary undertakings include: The Royal Bank of Scotland plc; National Westminster Bank plc; Citizens Financial Group, Inc.; Coutts and Company; RBS Securities Inc.; Direct Line Insurance Group plc; Ulster Bank Ltd; RBS Holdings N.V.

Brands include: NatWest; Coutts & Co.; Direct Line; Citizens Bank.

Main locations: Edinburgh

Total employees: 115,000

Focus of giving: Education, enterprise/training, health, ill health, arts, culture, poverty and social exclusion, community/social welfare.

Membership: BITC, LBG

Charity of the Year	✓
FTSE 100	✓
Gifts in kind	✓
Matched funding	✓
Overseas giving	✓
Payroll giving	✓

Charitable donations

Cash UK (latest available):	2013	£2,800,000
	2009	£34,700,000
	2008	£24,800,000
	2007	£32,173,000
	2006	£25,411,000
Total UK (cash and in kind):	2013	£2,800,000
Cash worldwide:	2013	£23,300,000
Total worldwide (cash and in kind):	2013	£50,618,915

Community involvement

Through its charitable giving programmes RBS seeks to help projects and causes in its communities that require support and which matter most to employees.

Community Grants programme

The RBS Community Grants programme was launched in 2013, to provide financial and volunteer support to communities across the UK. In the first year, £718,000 was distributed in grants to 69 charities in Great Britain and hosted clients at six charity balls and events including Barnardo's, Breast Cancer Care, Marie Curie and Edinburgh Zoo.

Anyone at RBS can nominate a charity or community group to get funding up to £10,000, as well as volunteer support. Registered charities whose programmes and services align with the group's aims and mirror the interests of staff and the communities in which they operate can apply. Grants are for the benefit of local disadvantaged people and fall under the following broad categories:

- Children and young people (under 18) e.g. Scouts
- Health and illness e.g. projects to support hospitals and health trusts
- Social welfare e.g. organisations addressing issues such as homelessness
- Environment e.g. conservation organisations

For grants over £10,000 charitable organisations apply via an application form and regional boards for Scotland, England and Wales, and London, evaluate the applications and provide a sounding board to link the applications with their local knowledge. 20 grants over £10,000 were made in 2013.

In November 2013, the bank launched its first ever international donation campaign, where employees could make a one-off donation straight from their salary. Since its launch in October 2012, a total of £876,000 has been donated to help nearly 50,000 children in 22 countries have the chance of a better future.

Partner charities for this campaign are:

- Barnardo's
- Oxfam
- Plan International (UK)
- Room to Read
- World Association of Girl Guides and Girl Scouts

Investing in the employment and advancement of girls and young women

In 2012, RBS launched its first ever global employee engagement campaign to unite colleagues from across the group to support a single charitable cause – fighting poverty by investing in girls. In 2012, over 22,000 colleagues from across all RBS signed a pledge in support of the campaign and RBS donated £20 for each signature received.

The Coutts Foundation Charity Commission no. (see separate entry for Coutts & Co.) provides a single focus for charitable disbursements. While an independent entity, it provides opportunities for staff in all locations to engage with local causes and give their time and financial support towards its objective of providing sustainable solutions to the causes and consequences of poverty in the markets in which Coutts operates.

The RBS Foundation India supports 76,000 families in 16 states in India. These projects focus on tackling a number of local issues in the community. For example targeting the poorest tribal households; promoting women's enterprise; facilitating financial literacy and financial inclusion; and tacking environmental issues. RBS employees volunteer their time and skills in these ongoing projects.

Corporate giving

In 2013 the group published the following table detailing its community giving.

Community investment by type	2012	2013
Cash support	£25.8 million	£23.3 million
Total value of staff time	£4.8 million	£5.1 million
In-kind contributions	£2.9 million	£3.8 million
Management costs	£2.9 million	£3.8 million
Total	£57.25 million	£54.46 million

Although there may be a percentage of giving declared in the group's totals that we would not normally include, (for example, the education/training of social entrepreneurs in market-led initiatives), we consider that it is best, because the amounts are substantial, to use the declared figure rather than estimate or use none at all. Unfortunately we could find no specific UK-only figures; however, we know from the declared amounts for matched funding, that it was UK employees who contributed £3.5 million and this was matched by the group with £2.1 million. We are therefore using this figure of £2.1 million and the amount of £718,000 given in grants (see community involvement section), as the group's total UK cash contribution although it would appear to be considerably more. We are unable to determine the UK-only in-kind contributions. The total worldwide contribution does not include the management costs of £3.8 million which, when known, it is our practice to exclude.

In-kind support

As can be seen from the section on employee-led support, the group is very involved with employees' contributions to their communities and as well as matching employee donations and fundraising, the bank also supports with a dedicated volunteering and giving programme.

Employee-led support

There is a well-established employee volunteering and giving programme at RBS. In 2013, there were 40,102 employees who volunteered almost 170,000 hours of work time to charitable causes.

Awards

Community Stars

The group's Community Stars programme gives employees the opportunity to nominate their colleagues for a Community Star for doing great work for their community and for local causes. Winners receive between £250 and £3,750 for their chosen charity or local community group. In 2013, RBS donated £48,500 to community causes with 119 Community Star award-winners.

Third Sector Business Awards

In 2013, the RBS graduate volunteering project Pilotlight was recognised at the prestigious Third Sector Business Charity Awards. The annual six-month project is a partnership between RBS Markets and International Banking graduates, and Pilotlight, a charity which enables charities and social enterprises through business coaching and mentoring support. The initiative was developed to benefit small charities by addressing their specific challenges and commercial needs, by tapping in to the skills and talent of future leaders.

Matched funding
The group continues to reward those who have volunteered in their community through 'Community Cashback' by giving their charity £250 when they have volunteered over 80 hours in the year in their own time or have fundraised more than £250.

In 2013, the group's Markets and International Banking colleagues, as a global team, helped to transform the lives of disadvantaged young people in the bank's local communities. In the UK, 'Team RBS' volunteers partnered with Islington Council to regenerate twelve adventure playgrounds giving more than 3,500 children free, safe, open access places to play.

Payroll giving
RBS runs a payroll giving scheme in the UK which allows employees to make a tax-free donation to charity direct from their salary. RBS matches payroll giving charitable donations with every £1 donated by an employee matched with a further £1 contribution from RBS up to a cap of £600 per annum. In 2013, an average of 19,144 UK employees contributed a total of £3.5 million and with the £2.1 million match from RBS this generated £5.8 million for charities in total.

In Australia, Hong Kong, India, the Netherlands, Republic of Ireland, Singapore and the US, the group matched employee donations totalling £933,000.

Commercially led support

The following information is taken from the company's website:

> *Sponsorship*
> RBS sponsors a number of reputable programmes and events worldwide. In 2011 we made a commitment to place a meaningful community programme at the heart of our major sponsorships. This practice continues today [2015].
>
> *From strength to strength with RugbyForce*
> Now in its fourth year, RBS RugbyForce is an initiative that helps rugby clubs across the country open their doors to the local community and show what they have to offer to potential new players, supporters, volunteers, members and sponsors. RugbyForce underpins RBS's sponsorship of the RBS Six Nations Championship, allowing us to support grassroots clubs and the communities they serve. The underlying goal of RugbyForce is to make local rugby clubs become sustainable small businesses and to cement their position as hubs in their communities.
>
> Rugby clubs across the UK and Ireland welcomed an army of volunteers from their local communities as part of RugbyForce weekends. Clubs called for local people to donate their time to help improve facilities through painting and general DIY. Each participating club was given £250 from RBS to pay for equipment and refreshments for the day. In 2013 there were 793 clubs that registered for RugbyForce.

Corporate social responsibility

CSR committee: The Group Sustainability Committee is responsible for reviewing the group's overall sustainability strategy, values and policies and aligning the group's approach to ethical, social and environmental issues. In addition to ongoing engagement which the company states takes place across its business each day, this board level committee runs a pro-active engagement programme whereby external stakeholders are invited to meet with, and challenge, the most senior decision-makers in RBS. In 2013 the committee met with 26 such advocacy groups, including Amnesty International UK, the New Economics Foundation, Federation of Small Business, Royal National Institute for the Blind and Unite.

CSR information: The following statement is taken from the website:

> *Supporting communities*
> We aim to make a positive social impact on the communities we operate in, through partnerships, local initiatives and supporting the charitable efforts of our employees. Our sponsorship approach also focuses on benefitting the local community.

CSR report: There is a sustainability report published each year which includes some information on community/charitable giving. The website is helpful and informative containing detailed information on the various ways in which RBS and its staff give both in the UK and overseas.

Exclusions

Previous research found the following information:

Sponsorship
Before completing the online sponsorship application form, be aware that in line with current strategic policy, RBS Group cannot consider new sponsorship applications to support the following:

- Motorsports
- Extreme danger/combat sports
- Political or religious groups/events
- Individual clubs or teams
- Funding for individuals (e.g. training, equipment or travel expenses), out-with the RBS Ambassadors programme or a wider national or international initiative
- Local or regional events (e.g. community festivals) without a wider national or international programme

Applications

Charitable requests should be directed to the Sustainability Team who manages RBS group's relationships with charitable organisations.

The Royal London Mutual Insurance Society Ltd

Insurance

Correspondent: The Corporate Responsibility Team, Royal London House, Alderley Road, Wilmslow SK9 1PF (tel: 0845 050 2020; website: www.royallondon.com)

Directors: Phil Loney, Group Chief Executive; Tim Harris, Group Finance Director; Andy Carter; Rupert Pennant-Rea, Chair; Jon Macdonald; Duncan Ferguson; Andrew Palmer; Tracey Graham; Kathryn Matthews; David Weymouth (women: 2; men: 8)

Year end	31/12/2013
Turnover	£1,092,000,000
Pre-tax profit	£449,000,000

Nature of business: Principal activities of the group's businesses are provision of pensions, life assurance, savings and investment products, protection insurance and investment management services.

The Group comprises The Royal London Mutual Insurance Society Ltd and its subsidiaries.

Company registration number: 99064

Subsidiary undertakings include: RLUM (CIS) Ltd; Royal London Asset Management Ltd; Royal London Pooled Pensions Company Ltd; Royal London Savings Ltd; and Wrap IFA Services Ltd. A full list of subsidiary undertakings can be obtained from Companies House.

Main locations: Wilmslow, Edinburgh, Douglas

Total employees: 3,050

Focus of giving: General charitable purposes, education, enterprise/training, environment, fundraising events, health, ill health, medical research, older people, arts, culture, sponsorship, sport, recreation, children, young people, disability.

Cash donations undeclared	✓
Charity of the Year	✓
Gifts in kind	✓
Sponsorship	✓

Charitable donations

Cash UK (latest available):	2013	£66,000
	2011	£67,000
	2009	£65,000
	2008	£65,000
	2007	£65,000
Total UK (cash and in kind):	2013	£66,000
Cash worldwide:	2013	£66,000
Total worldwide (cash and in kind):	2013	£66,000

Community involvement

The annual report and accounts for 2013 state: 'At Royal London, we believe social responsibility is at the centre of making mutuality meaningful. Phil Loney, Group CEO, leads by example and annually donates a quarter of his STIP and LTIS to charity.'

The Royal London Foundation

The foundation was launched in 2011 in honour of the founders Henry Ridge and Joseph Degge and the principles with which they set up Royal London. The foundation 'helps members create a better place to live by providing donations to charities and projects in their communities'. Grants of £1,000, £3,000, £5,000 or £10,000 for the duration of one year can be given to causes nominated by members. Support can be given to 'not-for-profit voluntary sector groups which are registered charities or those that can clearly demonstrate that they are working towards a charitable cause' and have a turnover of under £150,000 per year.

The foundation states that the focus is on the following areas:

- Education – causes that support education for people of any age, including skills to help those seeking employment
- Elderly – causes that help older generations who require assistance in their daily lives
- Health – causes that provide health and fitness related activities for those who might not otherwise have access to such facilities.

In the past there was the Degge and Ridge Award of £25,000 given each year to one deserving cause under one of the three themes (we found no information on whether the award is still given).

Charity partnership

The group has a set target of £100,000 to be raised over two years for its national charity partner – Leukaemia and Lymphoma Research.

Corporate giving

It appears that the group no longer declares its charitable contributions in the annual report and accounts. Our records suggest that the group's charitable giving is quite consistent. We estimate that about £66,000 was given during the year, based on the figures from the three previous years known to us.

In-kind support

According to our research, where possible the group can provide resources and facilities to charities and community organisations based in the locality of its offices.

Employee-led support

The annual report and accounts for 2013 state: that the group 'we also support our people in providing practical and financial support to the local communities in which we operate'. The group's employees fundraise in support of its national charity partner.

Stepforward

The group's employee volunteering programme allows employees to take up to two days each year of work time to volunteer in their communities.

Payroll giving

There are Give As You Earn schemes operating which 'have contributed significant donations to charity'.

Matched funding

Our research suggests that in the past Royal London has matched funds raised by an individual up to £250 and by a team up to £1,000.

Commercially led support

Sponsorship

Royal London has partnered with the England and Wales Cricket Board (ECB) to help them develop one-day cricket at an international and domestic level. Sponsorship covers: One-Day Internationals (men's); Women's One-Day Internationals; One-Day Cup; National Club Championship; and Junior County Cups.

Corporate social responsibility

CSR committee: We found no indications of a separate CSR committee.

CSR information: The group's Corporate Responsibility focuses on: environment; workplace; community; and marketplace.

The Community Strategy aims 'to engage employees and members with the local communities that [the group] supports' and its core themes are:

- Charitable giving
- Community investment
- Employer supported volunteering
- Commercial initiatives

CSR report: A brief CR section can be found within the annual report and accounts.

Exclusions

Support is not given for:

- Charities working with beneficiaries NOT living in the UK
- Profit making organisations
- Individuals
- Political causes
- Religious organisations or those promoting religious beliefs
- Any organisation which has received a grant from The Royal London Foundation in the previous 12 months
- Charities or organisations with a turnover of over £150,000

The group will not normally assist advertising in charity brochures, animal welfare or environment/heritage.

Applications

The foundation: Applications are accepted from Royal London members on behalf of organisations. Nominations can be made on the group's website.

Other enquiries should be made in writing to the correspondent.

Royal Mail plc

Miscellaneous

Correspondent: The Corporate Responsibility Team, 100 Victoria Embankment, London EC4Y 0HQ (tel: 03457740740(generalenquiries); email: community@royalmail.com or corporateresponsibility@royalmail.com; website: www.royalmailgroup.com)

Directors: Donald Brydon, Chair; Moya Greene, Chief Executive Officer; Orna Ni-Chionna; Matthew Lester, Chief Financial Officer; John Allan; Nick Horler; Cath Keers; Paul Murray; Les Owen (women: 3; men: 6)

Year end	30/03/2014
Turnover	£9,456,000,000
Pre-tax profit	£1,666,000,000

Nature of business: Royal Mail plc is the ultimate parent company of the Royal Mail Group, which operates through two core divisions UK Parcels, International and Letters (UKPIL) and GLS (operating in continental Europe and Ireland). The group's main activities include letter and parcel services, and design and manufacture of UK stamps and philatelic products.

Company registration number: 8680755

Subsidiary undertakings include: General Logistics Systems B.V.; Romec Ltd; Royal Mail Estates Ltd; Royal Mail Group Ltd; and Royal Mail Investments Ltd. More details of the group's principal subsidiaries can be seen within the accounts and a full list of subsidiary undertakings can be found within the annual return.

Brands include: General Logistics Systems (GLS); Parcelforce Worldwide, Royal Mail.

Main locations: London

UK employees: 149,172

Total employees: 166,813

Focus of giving: Education, health, ill health, heritage, housing, homelessness, older people, arts, culture, poverty and social exclusion, children, young people, community/social welfare, disability, disasters.

Membership: BITC, LBG

Charity of the Year	✓
FTSE 100	✓
Gifts in kind	✓
Market-led giving	✓
Matched funding	✓

Overseas giving ✓
Payroll giving ✓

Charitable donations

Cash UK (latest available):	2014	£3,130,000
	2012	£5,200,000
	2011	£2,100,000
	2010	£1,700,000
	2009	£2,000,000
Total UK (cash and in kind):	2014	£9,400,000
Cash worldwide:	2014	£3,130,000
Total worldwide (cash and in kind):	2014	£9,400,000

Community involvement

The group's website states that 'each year it invests around £10 million directly in UK communities, including support for the colleagues' fundraising and volunteering activities'.

Charity of the Year

The group launched a new Charity of the Year programme in 2012 introducing penny-for-penny matched funding (with an upper limit of £1 million each year) and an 'everyone's a winner' approach for the shortlisted charities. The first charity partner under the programme was Prostate Cancer UK. In 2013/14 a total of £2 million was raised for Prostate Cancer UK, the company matching employee donations 'penny-for-penny'. The donation was a result of a number of campaigns, for example, Movember, the Graduate and Apprentice Fundraising Challenge, Give a Quid Day and a newly introduced text-to-donate service. The CR Report estimates that the money will fund 'at least 34 specialist prostate cancer nurses in areas of need across the UK'. The partnership also included raising awareness of the condition through specially designed postmarks and the staff efforts. Once the £2 million target was reached the 'penny-for-penny' scheme was opened to the Alzheimer's Society and Whizz-Kidz UK (shortlisted charities). The group pledged to 'match funds raised for all three charities by Royal Mail employees up to a further £1 million in total'. The total group's contribution helped Whizz-Kidz UK acquire 31 wheelchairs for young people with mobility impairments and allowed the Alzheimer's Society to provide almost 3,100 hours of dementia support.

For the 2013/14 period (beginning in September) a new charity partner has been voted in March 2014. The Stroke Association has succeeded, with Age UK and Diabetes UK being shortlisted. The charity will use the money to provide 'grants of up to £300 to support 10,000 stroke survivors who do not qualify for government or other types of help' to fund essential home improvements (for instance, handrails and specialist kitchen equipment) also various activities leading to a more fulfiling life. 'The partnership will also aim to raise awareness of the condition and as well as steps people can take to reduce their stroke risk.' Age UK and Diabetes UK will each receive a donation of £50,000 each and once the £2 million target for Stroke Association is reached, 'funds raised for all three charities will be eligible for penny-for-penny matched giving from Royal Mail'.

Charity partnerships

Disability charity Remploy has been the group's partner since 2008. During the year about 300 people with disabilities started working at Royal Mail and by April 2014 employment had been provided to a total of 2,000 as a result of the partnership.

The Rowland Hill Fund

The fund (Charity Commission no. 207479) 'supports current and former Royal Mail employees who fall on hard times, helping those dealing with sudden illness or long-term sickness, redundancy and disability, or serious financial problems'. Royal Mail Group makes an annual donation to the fund.

Keep Me Posted

The group supports the Keep Me Posted campaign which began in 2013 and 'aims to ensure that consumers are always given the choice of receiving important information, such as utility bills and bank statements, in paper form' to help 'protecting vulnerable consumers, such as those without digital skills, those that do not have access to broadband internet connections and the elderly'. The campaign is supported by 50 charities, consumer organisations, businesses and trades unions.

Articles for the Blind

The service provides free postage for blind and partially-sighted Royal Mail workers with the Royal National Institute of Blind People (RNIB) and other charities for the blind to make sure the services meet their needs. The group has also helped RNIB deliver the new talking book USB service and update its previous audio CDs.

Communications Workers Union Humanitarian Aid

The union's national charity helps vulnerable children in the UK and overseas. Royal Mail staff have been directly involved in the projects and the transport convoys have delivered the aid to orphanages, foster and adoption centres, hospitals and families in Africa and Eastern Europe regions.

Sports Foundation

The foundation was set up in 2012 and 'offers grants to [Royal Mail] people to provide equipment, trophies and training to local clubs'. In 2013/14 a total of 51 sports clubs received support, with an estimated 1,500 people benefiting. Grants are up to a maximum of £500 and available to the group's employees.

Christmas giving

The group states that Christmas is a 'key focus of its direct charitable giving programme'. Before 2013 holidays a total of £50,000 was donated to three charities: Abbeyfields Society, FareShare and Together for Short Lives. The awards helped the charities work with vulnerable groups in the community at what is often a difficult time of the year: Together for Short Lives grants paid for Christmas lunches in hospices to families caring for a seriously ill child across the UK; Abbeyfields Society used the money to help 580 sheltered houses and care homes invite elderly people who would otherwise celebrate alone. FareShare support contributed to transportation of surplus food to a network of charities caring for the vulnerable, such as children, homeless people and elderly people.

Schools

The group is interested in supporting 'literacy levels amongst young people, encouraging confidence in reading, writing and creativity and promoting knowledge about the postal system's rich heritage and how it has shaped the modern world'. Support is offered to school teachers through provision of educational resource packs (for more details see www.teacherspost.co.uk). The resources are aligned with the National Curriculum and include adapted resources for teaching children with disabilities. Royal Mail employees are supported with resources for school visits, to cover subjects like letter writing, the history of Royal Mail and the importance of mail addressing.

In 2013/14 the group's 'mail centre in Medway launched a pilot programme ... working with the education authority and local schools to assess whether the available resources and school visit agendas meet teacher requirements with regards to the national curriculum'. The feedback will help the development of the Teachers Post online resources to support schools, teachers and children.

As part of a school engagement programme, run through Royal Mail Stamps and Collectibles, the group 'delivered lesson planning content inspired by Sporting Dreams, Dinosaurs, Doctor Who and classic children's TV stamps', provided 13,450 packs to schools across the UK and almost 55,000 resources were downloaded online.

GSL activities

This Royal Mail division has provided help in areas of need across Europe in 2013/14:

- Used its networks to collect and deliver aid supplies in Sassari, Italy, following

the devastation of Cyclone Cleopatra in November 2013
- Delivered organic breakfast boxes to pupils in Frankfurt
- Collected Christmas presents to be distributed through Caritas organisation for refugee children in Austria
- Helped the German Children Hospice Association make St Nicholas' Day special for terminally-ill children by delivering gifts, such as clothes, toiletries and toys, free of charge to participating children hospices and families all over Germany

The group's priorities for 2014/15 include: launch of a new Charity of the Year programme; raising awareness of the work of the Rowland Hill Benevolent Foundation; and continuing support for the schools programme.

Corporate giving

In 2013/14 Royal Mail gave £9.79 million 'directly to charities, good causes and schemes for disadvantaged groups', this figure includes the mandated commitments to Articles for the Blind and BPMA totalling £6.1 million. The company employees raised a further £3.25 million charities and good causes across the UK. Note that we deduct the figure for administration expenses from the group's overall contribution. We know that in-kind support is also provided through the GSL division in mainland Europe; however, main charitable support is focused on the UK. The CR Report provides the following breakdown:

Voluntary Contributions	
Cash – Royal Mail	£2.66 million
Cash – employee fundraising	£3.25 million
Time	£400,000
Administration	£370,000
In-kind	£240,000
Mandated Contributions	
In-kind	£5.64 million
Cash	£470,000

Beneficiaries included: Abbeyfields Society; Alzheimer's Society; Barnardo's; British Postal Museum and Archive; Communications Workers Union Humanitarian Aid; County Air Ambulance Trust; Dolly Parton's Imagination Library; FareShare; Help the Hospices; Prostate Cancer UK; Remploy; Royal National Institute of Blind People (RNIB); Royal Voluntary Service (RVS); The Stroke Association; The Rowland Hill Benevolent Fund; Together for Short Live; Whizz-Kidz UK.

In-kind support

The group provides in-kind educational resource packs and lesson planning content for school teachers, offers employee volunteering time and expert skills.

Articles for the Blind

The group's Articles for the Blind service provides about 4.8 million free of charge items to blind and partially-sighted people at a cost of about £5.6 million to the group.

Employee-led support

The group seeks to encourage the employees' community interests 'through the provision of grants, volunteering and fundraising support, helping them to contribute to a range of worthy causes'.

Staff are encouraged to volunteer and the group offers paid time off for employees supporting communities, and grants of up to £400 to cover volunteering costs. In 2013/14 over 2,000 days of paid leave for volunteering activities and almost 9,100 days of unpaid volunteering leave were provided. An example of staff volunteering included the group's HR Services Recruitment Field Team for the north of the UK working with 12 managers of Royal Voluntary Service (RVS) in Doncaster, providing a 'recruitment and interview techniques course to help them recruit volunteers for their 'Good Neighbour' project to support elderly people in communities'. Volunteers also helped to regenerate a garden for people suffering from dementia.

Payroll giving

According to the CR Report for 2013 the payroll giving scheme has been operated for 25 years and over this time £50 million has been donated to more than 975 charities. The report specifies that over 40,000 current and retired employees take part. In 2013/14 payroll giving scheme contributed over £2.5 million.

The biggest beneficiaries of the scheme have included: Barnardo's; County Air Ambulance Trust; Help the Hospices; Prostate Cancer UK; and the Rowland Hill Benevolent Fund.

Matched funding

The group will match funds raised by the staff up to £200 for each employee in a year, as part of the Community Matched Giving Scheme. A grant of up to £200 a year can also be obtained to cover the cost of fundraising activities. In 2013/14 Royal Mail provided £136,000 to match donations by employees to around 344 charities and causes.

It also matched staff donations to the Charity of the Year – Prostate Cancer UK (for more details see Charity of the Year details in the 'Community involvement' section). Funds raised by employees for the Charity of the Year can be matched up to £2,500 per individual a year.

The website specifies that one of the more remarkable actions was support of the Movember campaign in 2012, with over 2,500 employees taking part and over £525,000 being raised (including the matched funding from the group).

Commercially led support

Apprenticeship and graduate programmes

The programmes 'help young people into work and provide a route to gaining qualifications whilst earning a salary'. The Ready for Work programme provides opportunities for people in long-term unemployment. Royal Mail also works with Remploy to support people with disabilities gain and maintain employment. Work experience placements are also provided.

British Postal Museum and Archive (BPMA)

Royal Mail supports the heritage of the British postal system and looks after the Royal Mail Archive and the museum collection covering 500 years of postal history. Currently the creation of The Postal Museum is supported with 'a long-term funding and assistance for capital costs as well as a 999-year lease for the museum site'. The project was due to commence at the end of 2014. A plan is also developed 'to open up a section of the old subterranean mail railway ... [to] form a permanent exhibition space explaining the hidden history of moving the mail'. The day-to-day running of the BPMA, its educational programmes and exhibitions are also supported by the group with £1.4 million donated in cash and in-kind gifts during 2013/14. The new development will be an educational platform to the public.

Corporate social responsibility

CSR committee: The overall corporate responsibility strategy is led by the Managing Director of Strategy and Communications who reports to the Chief Executive Officer. The Senior Management Team has further responsibilities to ensure the implementation of individual strands of the CR programme.

All major CR policies and key performance indicators are reviewed by the Chief Executive Committee at least once a year. The CR strategy is designed and any issues considered by the Communications Action Group, chaired by the CEO. The Corporate Responsibility Team is accountable for implementing the strategy, supporting CR across the group and reporting on the progress.

CSR information: The group's Corporate Responsibility Policy states:

> Royal Mail Group is committed to making a positive contribution to the communities that we serve. We connect millions of customers, businesses, organisations and communities, including those in the most remote rural areas. Our objective is to

ensure a sound and sustainable Universal Service for the benefit of everyone in the UK.

The policy is designed to help 'responsibly manage relationships with, and impacts on, people, communities, customers and environment' and focuses on the following:

- Securing the sustainability of the Universal Service to deliver economic and social benefit to the UK
- Making commerce happen: linking customers, companies and communities for the same price across the UK
- Delivering the modernisation programme in a way which ... drives environmental efficiencies
- Communicating openly and transparently with stakeholders about our performance, our contribution to the UK and our future plans.

The group 'seeks new ways to leverage its business and assets to better support communities' and its strategy to connect and contribute to communities includes:

- Connecting through business – making an economic contribution to the UK
- Connecting through employees – providing the UK workforce with opportunities to get involved in their communities and help good causes
- Connecting with tomorrow – promoting education and literacy in the communities, supporting their future social and economic well-being

CSR report: A detailed annual CSR report is published.

Exclusions

The company does not normally consider circulars, political or general appeals, or applications from religious groups or individuals.

Applications

In writing to the correspondent. It appears that local organisations can also apply directly to their regional office for support.

The website provides more specific contact details of Lily Heinemann, Head of CR and Community Investment (lily.heinemann@royalmail.com), and Gary Grange, Community Investment Manager (gary.grange@royalmail.com). These people can be contacted regarding community investment while the CR Team can help with general corporate responsibility enquiries.

RPS Group plc

Consultancy, marine, oil and gas/fuel, water

Correspondent: The Corporate Governance Committee, Centurion Court, 85 Milton Park, Abingdon, Oxfordshire OX14 4RY (tel: 01235 438000; fax: 01235 384698; email: rpsmp@rpsgroup.com; website: www.rpsgroup.com/Group/About-Us/Corporate-Social-Responsibility.aspx)

Directors: Brook Land, Chair; Dr Alan Heame, Chief Executive; Gary Young, Finance Director; Dr Phil Williams; John Bennett; Louise Charlton; Robert Miller-Bakewell; Tracey Graham; Andrew Page; Nicholas Rowe, Company Secretary (women: 2; men: 8)

Year end	31/12/2013
Turnover	£567,614,000
Pre-tax profit	£43,607,000

Nature of business: RPS in the UK provides multi-disciplinary consultancies advising on all aspects of: built and natural environment; oil, gas and other natural resources; renewable energy; and energy infrastructure.

Company registration number: 2087786

Principal operating subsidiaries include: RPS Environmental Management Ltd; RPS bv; The Energy Ltd; and The Environmental Consultancy Ltd. A full list of subsidiary undertakings is available from the group's accounts.

Total employees: 4,306

Focus of giving: Education, environment, overseas projects, poverty and social exclusion, community/social welfare.

Cash donations undeclared	✓
Gifts in kind	✓
Overseas giving	✓

Charitable donations

Cash UK (latest available):	2013	£483,000
	2009	£480,000
Total UK (cash and in kind):	2013	£483,000
Cash worldwide:	2013	£483,000
Total worldwide (cash and in kind):	2013	£483,000

Community involvement

Charity partnership

Tree Aid (Charity Commission no. 1135156)

The group is a corporate sponsor of 'Tree Aid and its programme of education, tree planting and woodland conservation programmes to assist some of the poorest communities in sub-Saharan Africa.' In 2013 a total of £116,000 was contributed towards projects in Ghana and Mali. Besides the financial support RPS 'continues to harness the skills of its employees in providing important technical support for Tree Aid's work', which in 2013 included GIS mapping, a biodiversity study, a topographical survey and training for Tree Aid employees. The website specifies that in 2012 and 2013 the group supported projects up to the value of £2 million. Part of the Tree Aid's engagements is the Bongo River Trees project aiming 'to break the cycle of environmental decline and poverty in one of the poorest traditional communities in Africa'. RPS 'has pledged the budgeted funding for the project and is providing advice and support on erosion risk mapping, land cover and land use mapping using remote sensing and biodiversity baseline mapping and monitoring'.

RPS is also concerned with the environmental impact and can 'make a greater contribution to the environment through its own expertise and many of the projects with which it is involved'. The group provides advice to international bodies, governments, local authorities and companies on the improvement of environmental performance.

Education

RPS group also provides funding for academic bursaries and educational initiatives. In 2013 this totalled £233,000.

Corporate giving

In 2013 the group 'supported a range of community and charitable initiatives with gifts in kind and financial contributions... mostly at office level'. The annual report notes that a total of £973,000 (2012: £965,000) was awarded, which includes both the group and staff contributions and an additional £233,000 (2012: £168,000) spent on academic bursaries and educational initiatives. The Tree Aid annual report and accounts for 2012/2013 specify that RPS Group plc were providing £250,000 to the Ghana River Trees Restoration Project. We were unable to separate the money donated by the company from the employee contributions nor determine the amount awarded in cash in the UK. We use the £233,000 figure and the grant to the Tree Aid's Ghana River Trees Restoration Project to estimate that the group contributions totalled at least around £483,000.

Beneficiaries include: Tree Aid.

In-kind support

Staff volunteering time and expert advice and services.

Employee-led support

The group employees contribute to charitable causes supported by the group, through cash contributions and volunteering time.

Corporate social responsibility

CSR committee: There is a Corporate Governance Committee, which 'exercises general oversight in relation to environmental, social and governance matters although in the normal course of business the Board and the Executive Committee assess the risks and opportunities to which such issues give rise'.

CSR information: The Corporate Responsibility section in the annual report and accounts from 2013 states the following:

> The Group's corporate governance policies ... provide a framework within which it can look to achieve attractive levels of return for its shareholders whilst striking a balance between this objective and recognition of its obligations to its employees, clients and society in general.

The group focuses on environmental issues, education and poverty.

CSR report: Information on CSR is contained within the annual report and accounts.

Exclusions

Political donations are not made.

Applications

In writing to the correspondent, referenced 'Community Involvement'.

RSA Insurance Group plc

Insurance

Correspondent: Natalie Tickle, Corporate Responsibility Manager, 20 Fenchurch Street, London EC3M 3AU (tel: 020 7337 5337; email: natalie.tickle@uk.rsagroup.com; website: www.rsagroup.com)

Directors: Martin Scicluna, Chair; Stephen Hester, Group Chief Executive; Richard Houghton, Group Chief Financial Officer; Adrian Brown, Chief Executive; Kath Cates; Edward Lea; Alastair Barbour; Hugh Mitchell; Malcolm Le May; Joseph Streppel; Johanna Waterous (women: 2; men: 9)

Year end	31/12/2013
Turnover	£9,258,000,000
Pre-tax profit	(£244,000,000)

Nature of business: The group's principal activity is the transaction of personal and commercial general insurance business.

Company registration number: 2339826

Subsidiary undertakings include: Royal & Sun Alliance Reinsurance Ltd; British Aviation Insurance Company Ltd; Canadian Northern Shield Insurance Company; RSA Overseas Holdings BV; Codan A/S; Sun Alliance Insurance (China) Ltd. A full list of subsidiaries is provided in the annual report and accounts.

Brands include: Answer; Codan; Link4; More Th>n; RSA; Trygg Hansa.

Main locations: Belfast, Birmingham, Glasgow, Horsham, Leeds, Bristol, Manchester, Liverpool, London

UK employees: 9,585

Total employees: 23,872

Focus of giving: Education, children, young people, community/social welfare, disasters.

Membership: BITC, LBG

FTSE 100	✓
Gifts in kind	✓
Humanitarian aid: UK	✓
Market-led giving	✓
Matched funding	✓
Payroll giving	✓

Charitable donations

Cash UK (latest available):	2013	£722,000
	2011	£700,000
	2009	£1,500,000
	2008	£2,200,000
	2007	£2,278,660
Total UK (cash and in kind):	2013	£1,000,000
Cash worldwide:	2013	£1,860,000
Total worldwide (cash and in kind):	2013	£1,860,000

Community involvement

The group's CR report for 2013 specifies that its focus areas comprise: education and improvement of road safety practices; environmental issues, particularly related to natural disasters; and community support, including areas of unemployment and social inclusion. Local charitable committees engage with communities to identify partners and channel support. The group collaborates with Climate Wise, WWF and various social and environmental initiatives.

Charity partnership

The group works with WWF and in 2013 it also entered a three-year partnership with the Dame Kelly Holmes Legacy Trust helping disadvantaged young people (RSA provides access to the Learning Zone – an online learning portal and offers personal development and work experience opportunities).

Corporate giving

In 2013 the group made charitable donations of £1.86 million (2012: £2.6 million) worldwide, including donations matching the amount raised by the employees. The company has informed us that the total sum awarded in the UK totalled over £1 million, out of which cash donations amounted to £722,000.

In-kind support

Non-cash support includes staff volunteering, gifts in kind, work experience and training schemes, business skills, expertise and use of resources (facilities and equipment). An example of the group's in-kind giving was a distribution of over 245,000 reflectors, high-visibility vests, belts and back-pack covers.

Employee-led support

In 2013 employees of the group raised £344,000 for their chosen causes and donated 7,986 hours of their time. A Toy Appeal was launched and donated over 900 toys and books for children at Christmas.

Payroll giving

Where systems permit payroll schemes can operate allowing matched funding by the company.

Matched funding

The company matches employee donations to registered charities at a capped level, set nationally. In the past up to a maximum of £250 for individuals and up to £1,000 for teams of three or more people was available.

Commercially led support

The group runs partnerships with World Wildlife Fund (WWF) and Global Action Plan focusing on the insurance risks of environmental change. Previously RSA has supported conservation projects relevant to its business, such as a flood defence project in the UK, a marine protection project in Canada to help safeguard the long-term future of the fishing industry and a renewable energy project in China.

In the UK the group has provided emergency response vehicles offering help and advice to those affected by floods. The corporate responsibility report for 2013 notes that support is given to 'research and development of resilient flood-prevention measures including sustainable drainage systems'.

Corporate social responsibility

CSR committee: The CR strategy is managed by the CR Steering Committee led by senior executives, implemented through a Group CR team and local managers, and overseen by the Group CEO. The Steering Committee meets three to four times a year to oversee development, implementation and progress of the CR strategy and monitor compliance with its global CR, environmental, human rights and community policies. It provides a common reference point for regional businesses, where CR managers or co-ordinators are in place in all operating countries. Country and site-based community and environment committees determine and respond to local priorities.

CSR information: CSR information taken from the 2013 CR report specifies 'safe, secure world', 'thriving communities', and 'sustainable future' as three focus areas of the CR strategy. The policies apply to all operations, including wholly or majority-owned subsidiaries and associated companies where RSA has management control. The group aims to address issues of road safety, support communities and young entrepreneurs, and respond to natural and human generated environmental problems.

RSA aims to support registered charities in those communities where the group operates and also to encourage employees to volunteer and fundraise. Activities are particularly supported in the areas of education, employability and entrepreneurship.

CSR report: The group provides a corporate responsibility report covering its activities in the three focus areas.

Exclusions

The Group Charity Policy Statement notes that it is 'unable to support any organisation which supports one specific religious faith, political parties, sports (unless compelling community justification), arts (unless supporting disadvantaged groups) or individual sponsorships'. Our research indicates that requests received by circular are normally not actioned.

Donations are not made to political parties; however, the annual report for 2013 notes that the political expenditure of up to £100,000 (for each donation) can be authorised for 'funding of seminars, functions and charitable donations that may be regarded as political in nature'. During the year no such payments were made.

Applications

Generally applications should be made in writing to the correspondent.

Saga plc

Financial services, insurance, legal, leisure

Correspondent: John Billingham, Manager, or Sarah Jenner, Trust Executive, Enbrook Park, Sandgate, Folkestone, Kent CT20 3SE (tel: 01303 774421 or 01303 774069; email: On an online form; website: www.saga.co.uk/saga-charitable-foundation.aspx)

Directors: Andrew Goodsell, Chair; Lance Bathcelor, Chief Executive Officer; Stuart Howard, Group Finance Director; Phillip Green; James Arnell; Pev Hooper; Ray King; Orna Ni-Chionna; Charles Sherwood; Gareth Williams (women: 1; men: 9)

Year end	31/01/2013

Nature of business: The group provides travel, financial, insurance, health and lifestyle products and services for people aged 50 and over.

Company registration number: 8804263

Brands include: Allied Healthcare; Claimfast; Metromail; Nestor; Saga; and Titan Travel.

Focus of giving: Education, health, ill health, individuals, older people, overseas projects, children, young people, community/social welfare, disability.

Membership: BITC

Overseas giving	✓

Charitable donations

Cash UK (latest available):	2013	£256,000
	2011	£280,600
	2008	£274,000
	2007	£143,000
Total UK (cash and in kind):	2013	£256,000
Cash worldwide:	2013	£256,000
Total worldwide (cash and in kind):	2013	£256,000

Community involvement

Saga Charitable Trust (Charity Commission no. 291991)

The charity is founded by Saga holidays and seeks 'to benefit underprivileged communities at destinations in developing countries that host Saga holidaymakers'. The group's website invites donations to the charity and promises to cover 'all the UK overheads and administrative costs so that every penny donated goes to support projects overseas'.

Saga Respite for Carers Trust (Charity Commission no. 1124709)

The charity 'provides holidays for unpaid carers aged over 50, giving them a break away from their caring responsibilities', and pays for respite care while the carer is away.

Saga Charitable Foundation (Charity Commission no. 1147124)

The foundation set up in 2012 is 'the principal umbrella for all of Saga's charitable activities'. The charity raises funds for the two above trusts, commissions and undertakes research into the lives of people over the age of 50 and helps, advises and informs older people on a variety of public policy matters.

Corporate giving

At the time of writing the full year's accounts of the group were not yet available from Companies House, following its re-registration.

As the group appears to be channelling its charitable giving through the corporate charities, we estimate the amount contributed by the group to equal the amount donated to the three charities. The latest accounts for the corporate charities available to view at the time of writing were for 2012/13. In that year The Saga Charitable Trust received a donation of £128,000 from the group and a further £95,000 from Saga customers and staff donations; The Saga Respite for Carers Trust had a donation of almost £128,000 from the group. Based on these figures we estimate that the amount contributed by the group was £256,000.

See the corporate charity entry on p. 424 for more information.

Employee-led support

Donations from Saga staff and customers to the Saga Charitable Trust totalled £123,000 in 2013/14. Although the latest company accounts available were for 2012/13, the Saga Charitable Trust accounts for 2013/14 were published on the Charity Commission website.

Corporate social responsibility

CSR committee: We found no indication of a presence of a CSR committee.

CSR information: No CSR information found.

CSR report: No CSR report is available but there is a 'SAGA Charities' website page.

Corporate charity: The Saga Charitable Trust (Charity Commission no. 291991).

Exclusions

Our research indicates that support is not normally given for advertising in charity brochures, animal welfare, the arts, enterprise/training, fundraising events, medical research, political or religious appeals, science/technology; or sport.

Applications

Further information can be obtained by writing to the correspondent.

The Saga Charitable Trust (Charity Commission no. 291991)

In writing to the correspondent. Applications are accepted at any time throughout the year. Grants are decided at regular meetings by the trustees where applications are considered for various types of funding.

Funding proposals should include the following information: outline and objectives of the project; who will benefit and how; resources required and timeframe; management and sustainability of the project; how funds will be managed and accounted for; and three years of the organisation's financial accounts.

J Sainsbury plc

Retail – supermarkets

Correspondent: Corporate Responsibility and Sustainability, 33 Holborn, London EC1N 2HT (tel: 020 7695 6000; fax: 020 7695 7610; email: 20x20@sainsburys.co.uk; website: j-sainsbury.co.uk/responsibility)

Directors: David Tyler, Chair; Mike Coupe, Chief Executive; John Rogers, Chief Financial Officer; Matt Brittin; Mary Harris; Gary Hughes; John McAdam; Jean Tomlin; Susan Rice (women: 3; men: 6)

Year end	15/03/2014
Turnover	£23,949,000,000
Pre-tax profit	£898,000,000

Nature of business: A general merchandise and clothing retailer with UK-based supermarkets, convenience stores and an online presence. Banking and financial services products are offered through the wholly owned subsidiary, Sainsbury's Bank, and the group has a number of joint ventures, including property development.

Company registration number: 185647

Main locations: London

Total employees: 161,000

Focus of giving: Health, ill health, housing, homelessness, sport, recreation, children, young people, community/ social welfare, disability.

Membership: BITC, LBG

Cash donations undeclared	✓
Charity of the Year	✓
FTSE 100	✓
Gifts in kind	✓
Market-led giving	✓
Matched funding	✓
Payroll giving	✓
Sponsorship	✓

Charitable donations

Cash UK (latest available):	2010	£1,900,000
	2009	£5,700,000
	2005	£2,340,000
	2004	£1,600,000
Total UK (cash and in kind):	2014	£3,800,000
Total worldwide (cash and in kind):	2014	£3,800,000

Community involvement

Sainsbury's community involvement is supported at a local level by a 'national framework'. At a local level, charities and community groups are supported by individual Sainsbury's stores and nominated charities are supported. At a national level, through its community schemes such as Active Kids, Sainsbury's aims to make a positive contribution across the country.

Charity partners: Carers UK; Comic Relief; Royal British Legion

Sainsbury Family Charitable Trusts

The Sainsbury Family Charitable Trusts is the operating office of a group of 18 grant-making charities affiliated with the Sainsbury family. Each trust is operated independently with separate boards of trustees each led by a member of the family.

Corporate giving

The annual report and accounts for 2013/14 did not declare a figure for charitable donations from the group and so, we were unable to determine a total value for the cash and in-kind support given during the year. Though we know that at least £100,000 was donated through the 'Local Heroes' employee volunteering scheme, in previous years total charitable contributions have amounted to millions of pounds. The average of combined cash and in-kind donations based on the three most recent years for which we have figures was £3.8 million, and we have taken this as an estimate for such contributions in 2013/14.

Beneficiaries included: Betel of Britain; FareShare

Employee, customer and supplier contributions

The annual report and accounts for 2013/14 state that 'Over £40 million invested in good causes by us, our colleagues, customers and suppliers this year.'

During the year, more than £620,000 was donated to local non-profit causes through the Community Budget, which was part-funded by sales of the Bag for Life.

Other customer, employee and supplier contributions included:

- £100,000 raise by employees through volunteering activities
- £4.5 million raised for the Royal British Legion, bringing the total raised since 2008 to an estimated £19 million
- £6.7 million raised for Sport Relief in 2014
- £2 million raise by customers and employees for local charities and community groups

Employees and customers also continued to raise funds for Comic Relief, bringing the total raised since the partnership began in 1999 to £84 million, and through the Local Charity scheme, which has raised more than £6 million for local charities in the past five years.

Active Youth

Through the programme, which is part of Sainsbury's 20x20 Sustainability Plan, the group has given itself the target of encouraging 20 million children to enjoy physical activity. Active Youth encompasses a number of sports-based initiatives and to date:

- £150 million worth of sports and cooking equipment and experiences has been donated, with the help of customers, via the Active Kids scheme since 2005
- £10 million has been pledged to Sainsbury's School Games over three years
- More than 3,100 teachers have been trained and 73,000 young people have benefited from the £1 million Paralympic legacy programme, Active Kids for All. The programme works to include 500,000 children with disabilities in mainstream school sports
- 6.7 million children have participated in the 2014 Sainsbury's School Games

In-kind support

Gifts in kind

Surplus food fit for human consumption is donated from more than 300 local Sainsbury's stores to charities. In 2013/14 611 tonnes (more than 1.2 million meals) of surplus food from the chilled supply chain was donated to FareShare and Betel of Britain.

Employee-led support

Employee fundraising

Sainsbury's employees fundraise for various partner charities and causes. Though the Local Charity scheme, employees fundraise for a customer-nominated charity and also take part in national appeals such as Comic Relief. Activities have included dressing-up and running marathons.

Matched funding

Through the Local Heroes scheme, employees who volunteer in their own time for their community are acknowledged and rewarded. Sainsbury's donate £5 per hour spent volunteering to the employee's chosen charity or community group, up to a value of £200 per employee.

Payroll giving

Our research indicates that the Give As You Earn scheme is in operation.

Commercially led support

Customer support

Sainsbury's customers, along with employees and suppliers are involved with numerous fundraising initiatives. Examples include:

Active Kids – Customers are able to collect vouchers to donate to their local school. Schools can then use the vouchers to apply for sports and cooking equipment and related experiences to help support children to eat, exercise and live well.

Charity partners – Sainsbury's customers have helped to raise millions for charity partners including Comic Relief and the Royal British Legion through product sales (including poppies and red noses) and by taking part in fundraising initiatives.

Bag for Life – Sales of the Bag for Life part-fund the Community Budget scheme, which sees individual stores and depots manage their own budgets, which are used to support local charities and community groups.

Local charity scheme – Sainsbury's stores partner a local charity, as nominated in May or June each year by customers. From the nominations, one charity is selected and receives fundraising and volunteering support from the store for the following 12 months.

Sponsorship

Sainsbury's sponsored the British Paralympic Association to help support athletes competing at the Sochi Winter Games and, in line with its efforts to promote healthy living, also sponsored the Sainsbury's Summer Series and the Sainsbury's School Games in partnership with British Athletics.

Corporate social responsibility

CSR committee: The plc Board Corporate Responsibility and Sustainability Committee meets twice a year and is chaired by non-executive director, Jean Tomlin. The group's Chief Executive Mike Coupe is also a member.

It provides an oversight into the activities of the Operating Board's Corporate Responsibility and Sustainability Steering Group, which is chaired by the Chief Executive, meets twice a year and is made up of members of the Operating Board, each responsible for one of its five values.

The programme of work for each value is managed through a cross-functional Value Steering Group, which meets quarterly and is chaired by the accountable member of the Operating Board. Delivery against the group's 20x20 agenda is included in individual objectives.

CSR information: Sainsbury's strategy for growth is based around five principal values:

- Best for food and health
- Sourcing with integrity
- Respect for our environment
- Making a positive difference to our community
- A great place to work

Guided by these values, Sainsbury's has devised the 20x20 Sustainability Plan, a series of 20 commitments the group aims to deliver.

CSR report: Annual updates on the 20x20 Sustainability Plan are published on the website, as are quarterly 'Corporate Responsibility and Society' updates.

Exclusions

Our research indicates that no response is given to circulars and no support is given for: advertising in charity brochures; individuals; enterprise/training; environment/heritage; medical research; science/technology; social welfare; restoration/fabric of buildings; National Health projects; overseas projects; local appeals not in areas of company presence; political or religious causes; core or pump priming.

Applications

Support from J Sainsbury plc

Charities: All requests for local sponsorship and support are managed by the local Sainsbury's store, which are allocated budgets to support their local community. Contact your local store directly and, where possible, they will try to accommodate your request.

Local charity scheme: Nominations are initially made through an online nomination form. Each store then creates a shortlist of three local charities, which are then invited to present to the store. One is then selected to receive fundraising and volunteering support over the next 12 months.

Sponsorship: Sponsorship enquiries should be emailed to sponsorship.enquiries@sainsburys.co.uk.

Support from the Sainsbury Family Charitable Trusts

The trusts vary in their approach to grant-making and applications. Some have their own application forms, whereas others do not accept unsolicited proposals. More details are available from the Sainsbury Family Charitable Trusts website: www.sfct.org.uk.

Samsung Electronics (UK) Ltd

Electronics/computers

Correspondent: J. H. Hong, Company Secretary, Samsung House, 1000 Hillswood Drive, Chertsey, Surrey KT16 0PS (tel: 01932 455000; website: www.samsung.com/uk)

Directors: G. C. Song; A. R. Griffiths; J. Y. Kim; J. H. Hong

Year end	31/12/2013
Turnover	£3,423,500,000
Pre-tax profit	£59,412,000

Nature of business: Samsung Electronics (UK) Ltd's principal activities include: import and distribution of electronic and electrical goods; purchase and sale of components and capital equipment; provision of research and development services to the ultimate parent company; and import and distribution of telecommunications systems.

The accounts for 2013 state that 'all operations are UK-based with the exception of two small research and development facilities in Israel and Finland and a branch office in Ireland'.

The company's ultimate holding company is Samsung Electronics Co. Limited.

Company registration number: 3086621

Subsidiary undertakings include: Samsung Semiconductor Europe Ltd; Samsung Telecoms (UK) Ltd.

Main locations: Yateley, London, Telford, Chertsey, Wynard

Total employees: 1,244

Focus of giving: Education, environment, inner cities, STEM (science, technology, engineering and mathematics), arts, culture, sport, recreation, community/social welfare.

Membership: BITC

Cash donations undeclared	✓
Gifts in kind	✓

Charitable donations

Cash UK (latest available):	2013	£21,000
	2011	£29,400
	2009	£26,000
	2008	£7,300
Total UK (cash and in kind):	2013	£21,000
Cash worldwide:	2013	£21,000
Total worldwide (cash and in kind):	2013	£21,000

Community involvement

The company's business principles include the following statement: 'We keep an eye on developing a healthy society through public interest activities, such as intellectual and artistic study, culture, sport activities, etc. We actively participate in social service activities like volunteer work, disaster relief, etc.'

The Corporate Citizenship section on the website notes that 'with its domestic and international reach, Samsung is dedicated to being a respected company and contributing to the development of the communities it operates in'. The following UK initiatives undertaken by the company are specified on the website:

Digital Classrooms

The scheme provides schools with a suite of Samsung technology, teacher training, connectivity and maintenance support aimed at facilitating 'a creative teacher–led learning [and] peer-to-peer interaction through device mobility'. The company describes the project as creating 'an engaging and collaborative educational environment for nurturing the talent of the future'.

Digital Academies

The programme is aimed at 'vocational training and qualifications in technology for young people' and seeks to generate 'opportunities for employment'. There are two academies:

- In partnership with Newsham College, which 'features three new training classrooms for practical and vocational training' and will support up to 150 students a year, both through the 'state-of-the-art facility fully equipped with Samsung's latest devices' and through 'scholarships and start-up funds to outstanding students'
- Birmingham Metropolitan College receiving 'programmes designed to help learners gain technical knowledge and practical qualifications and provide them with a greater understanding of the latest smart device technologies'

Supporting STEM

The company supports Science, Technology, Engineering and Mathematics through its charity partnerships with Apps for Good and Code Club (see below).

Charity partnerships

Apps for Good – as part of the relationships with this charity which 'inspires children to build apps to help the community', Samsung supports ten schools in need of devices for researching and app testing and sponsors the 'learning category' of Apps for Good's annual app competition for schools.

Code Club – Samsung provides technology to Code Club volunteers lead coding sessions in schools and community centres across the UK.

Kids Company – the company is 'building new learning environments to provide educational support for vulnerable inner-city children in London and Bristol'.

Prince's Trust – the charity receives supports for its Fairbridge programme aimed at 'young people at risk of underachievement or exclusion from school and helping young adults back into education, training or employment', for xl clubs in schools and also had a Digital Classroom built and equipped in one of its centres.

Royal Albert Hall – Samsung opened a Digital Classroom in 2014 to enable young people to learn the principles of maths and science through music. The partnership is part of the Royal Albert Hall's education and outreach programme.

The British Museum – through the partnership established in 2009, the company provides the Samsung Digital Discovery Centre to schools, families and young people, which helps them 'to discover the Museum's collections in creative and educational ways'.

Corporate giving

We could not identify the amount donated for charitable causes within the company's annual report and accounts for 2013. Based on figures from the three previous years known to us, we estimate that the company spends around £21,000 in cash donations in the UK.

Globally the group provides support in line with its Corporate Citizenship Strategy in the communities in which it operates.

In-kind support

It appears that most of the company's giving is provided in kind – through Samsung technology devices, other equipment and maintenance.

Employee-led support

Payroll giving

The group's Corporate Sustainability Report for 2013 notes that Samsung Electronics employees 'have the opportunity to donate a portion of their salary each month to charitable causes'. We found no reference to payroll or matched giving opportunities relating to the UK company.

Commercially led support

It seems that most of the support is given through the provision of Samsung technology devices to be used for educational purposes. For more details on the programmes see the 'Community involvement' section in this entry.

Corporate social responsibility

CSR committee: No committee details relevant to the UK.

CSR information: The Global Corporate Citizenship strategy focuses on education and training, employment and community, environment and health.

We were unable to determine the ratio of women to men on the board.

CSR report: There is a group Sustainability Report. No reference to UK report found.

Applications

In writing to the correspondent.

Santander UK plc

Building society, banking

Correspondent: Sharon Squire, Head of CSR, 2 Triton Square, Regent's Place, London NW1 3AN (tel: 0870 607 6000; email: community@santander.co.uk; website: www.santander.co.uk/uk/about-santander-uk/csr)

Directors: Lord Burns, Chair; Ana Botin, Chief Executive Officer; José María Nus; Steve Pateman; Stephen Jones, Chief Financial Officer; Juan Rodríguez Inciarte; José María Carballo; José María Fuster; Antonio Escámez; Manuel Soto; Mike Amato; Roy Brown; Bruce Carnegie-Brown; Alain Dromer; Rosemary Thorne; Scott Wheway (women: 2; men: 14)

Year end	31/12/2013
Turnover	£4,029,000,000
Pre-tax profit	£1,139,000,000

Nature of business: Provision of personal and corporate financial products and services.

Santander UK plc is an autonomous unit and forms part of the Banco Santander group, which operates internationally with headquarters in Spain.

Company registration number: 2294747

Subsidiary undertakings include: Abbey National International Ltd (Jersey); Abbey National North America LLC (United States – held indirectly through subsidiary companies); Abbey National Treasury Services plc; Cater Allen Ltd (held indirectly through subsidiary companies); and Abbey National Treasury Services Overseas Holdings. A full list of subsidiary undertakings can be obtained from Companies House.

Main locations: Glasgow, Milton Keynes, London, Sheffield, Bradford, Leicester, Bootle, Teesside, Belfast

Total employees: 20,064

Focus of giving: Economic generation, education, enterprise/training, health, ill health, financial education, poverty and social exclusion, sponsorship, children, young people, community/social welfare.

Membership: BITC, LBG

Charity of the Year	✓
Gifts in kind	✓
Market-led giving	✓
Matched funding	✓
Payroll giving	✓
Sponsorship	✓

Charitable donations

Cash UK (latest available):	2013	£17,000,000
	2011	£14,000,000
	2009	£3,626,000
	2008	£3,047,000
	2007	£1,950,000
Total UK (cash and in kind):	2013	£21,600,000
Cash worldwide:	2013	£17,000,000
Total worldwide (cash and in kind):	2013	£21,600,000

Community involvement

The company 'aims to prioritise its support to society on education, enterprise and employment'. Three main 'flagship initiatives' of the company are The Santander Foundation, Santander Universities and Santander Breakthrough.

The Santander UK Foundation Ltd

(Charity Commission no. 803655)

The foundation was originally set up with a donation from the then Abbey National plc of £5 million following the sale of shares unclaimed since the company's flotation.

The foundation is the main channel of the company's corporate donations and provides grants to UK-registered charities helping 'disadvantaged people, usually in communities where Santander branches and business centres are based and locations where the bank has a significant presence, such as a main office or call centre'.

The accounts for 2013 stated that 'the charitable priorities for 2013 were to support local communities and disadvantaged people through: financial advice which helps them manage their money; and education and training'.

The foundation has three grants programmes: Community Plus (grants of up to £5,000); Learn and Grow (grants of up to £10,000); and Money Skills (grants of up to £10,000).

Santander Universities

This global programme is part of the company's commitment to higher education and forms 'a long-term, strategic alliance with universities that is beneficial to students and staff and the communities where [the company] present'. Since its inception in 1997 the programme has provided over £500 million via scholarships, travel grants, support for special projects, academic and non-academic awards. In the UK partnerships began in 2007 and offer scholarships available for students in the UK and abroad, mobility awards, research grants, funding for professors or staff and other assistance. Currently, over 1,000 universities around the world are part of the Santander Universities network and over 70 UK universities participate, including: Durham University; Cass Business School; Nottingham Trent University; University of Bath; University of Bristol; University of Chester; University of Liverpool; and Oxford Brookes University (a full list is available online).

In addition the company assists universities with their fundraising activities – it encourages its university branch staff to participate in fundraising activity held at the partner universities and matches any donations up to a maximum of £3,500 (depending on the number of staff involved).

There also is the Santander Universities Enterprise Portal 'designed to support entrepreneurs and the university, start-up and small business communities'.

In 2013 a total of £8.45 million was given in funding to higher education, including 980 scholarships for international students to study in the UK, 918 mobility awards for UK students/academics to study abroad, 148 entrepreneurship and enterprise awards; 273 special projects (for example, business incubators and international symposiums); and 1,460 internships to work in SMEs.

Charity partnerships

The company has a long-term partnership with British Heart Foundation, supporting the charity's cycling events and half marathons programme to encourage people to improve their health and raise funds for vital research into heart disease.

Charity of the Year

In 2013 employees chose CLIC Sargent to be the Charity of the Year. A total of £1.4 million was raised by the staff and customers which allowed the charity to fund Homes from Home centres for young children undergoing cancer treatment and their families. The 2014 charity has been selected to be National Society for the Prevention of Cruelty to Children (NSPCC).

The website notes: 'We have a long list of national charities that meet our criteria for Charity of the Year and we write to them each year inviting them to apply.' Charities wishing to be considered must be a large registered UK charity able to provide a dedicated account manager to work with Santander to deliver fundraising campaigns across its network of all branches and head office sites across the UK.

Previous charity partners have included: Great Ormond Street Hospital; Marie Curie Cancer Care; and The Alzheimer's Society.

Corporate giving

In 2013 Santander UK plc spent about £21.6 million in community investment, 'predominantly supporting projects related to education, enterprise and employment'. The three flagship initiatives provided above £15 million: The Santander Foundation gave £5.8 million in 2,556 grants, the principal source of funding source was £5.3 million from Santander UK plc; Santander Universities spent £8.4 million; and Santander Breakthrough and SEDA funding amounted to £4.4 million (it has not been possible to distinguish the amount given to non-charitable social enterprises). A further £2.9 million was spent to support other employment, education and community projects. Staff volunteering time value was estimated at £108,000. We would not normally consider the Breakthrough initiative as a strictly charitable activity, therefore we estimate that the company's cash contributions totalled at least £17 million with potentially more given to charitable bodies.

The CSR report for 2013 gives the following breakdown of support:

Education	£9.8 million	46%
Communities	£4.6 million	21%
Enterprise	£4.6 million	21%
Employment	£1.4 million	7%
Other	£1 million	5%

Beneficiaries have included: British Heart Foundation; CLIC Sargent; Great Ormond Street Hospital; Marie Curie Cancer Care; NSPCC; and The Alzheimer's Society.

Revenue: The figure we use as the company's turnover is defined as 'Total operating income' in the accounts.

See the corporate charity entry on p. 425 for more information.

In-kind support

In the past gifts in kind have been donated to the Santander Foundation. Other forms of non-cash support provided by the company include staff volunteering time and expert skills.

Employee-led support

Staff volunteering

In 2013 more than 1,700 staff volunteers donated their time supporting good causes, including local schools and Santander WorkWise financial education programme providing money management workshops to 14- to 16-year-olds. There is a matched time scheme which allows up to 35 hours of paid work time per year for volunteering purposes. In 2013 British Heart Foundation's programme of cycling events and half marathons was supported 'with over 100 Santander staff taking part in the event'.

Community Days

Staff are also able to leave the office for a day to volunteer for a local cause. In 2013 over 1,500 employees provided 7,000 hours to help 118 community projects, such as 'gardening, decorating and organising activities for community groups and day care centres'.

Matched funding

Santander employees raise significant amounts of money for charities across the UK which are matched by the company through the Santander Foundation Matched Donation Scheme. In 2013 the company provided about £2 million to increase the amount raised by the staff.

The company employees also choose and fundraise for the Charity of the Year partner (see Charity of the Year information in the 'Community involvement' section).

Payroll giving

Santander also participates in the Payroll Giving scheme to enable employees to make a monthly donation to charity directly from their salary.

Commercially led support

Santander Breakthrough

Launched in 2011 Santander Breakthrough programme 'seeks to identify the best entrepreneurial companies in the UK and help them achieve their full potential'. It is aimed at fast-growing small and medium-sized enterprises and aims to help them boost economic recovery and the creation of local employment. The company's website states:

> Over the next few years, we aim to make £200 million available for investment in businesses that we see as 'Growth Champions'. We will also ensure that any company selected for the programme will have access to some of the best advice and talent available, including businesspeople who have already established their own companies as market leaders on a national and global stage.

The scheme offers 'traditional debt facilities and mezzanine finance . . . offered through Breakthrough Growth Capital' and is available to high growth SMEs in the UK with a turnover of between £500,000 and £50 million per annum while posting growth of 20% or more in turnover, profit or employment. For more information see the company's website.

The company's accounts note that 'during 2013, more than 390 businesses benefited from the Breakthrough programme through overseas trade missions, roundtable events, masterclasses and internships'.

SEDA

In addition to supporting mainstream SMEs, Santander has created the Social Enterprise Development Awards (SEDA) to provide finance and support to growing social businesses. SEDA were set up in 2012 and are available to 'social enterprises and charities with trading activities looking to grow their business and improve their local community'. The company provides an annual award of £10,000 to 'social ventures that have ambitions to develop their organisation but need a financial boost to help them realise their potential'based on 'the strength of their business plan for growth'. To date over 170 social enterprises have been helped.

Sponsorships

The group's website notes that 'supporting sports is part of [Santander's] commitment to society, and identifies it with the values of teamwork, innovation, and leadership'. Santander sponsors a number of sports ambassadors, including Formula 1 Scuderia Ferrari and the McLaren Mercedes team drivers.

Corporate social responsibility

CSR committee: There is a CSR Committee chaired by the Chief Executive Officer. The committee 'considers and approves CSR strategic plans, corporate policies and reports for onward approval by the Executive Committee and the board, where appropriate'. The CSR team 'has responsibility for defining the content for the report and it works with representatives from around the business in order to prepare the material'. The head of CSR is Sharon Squire – see 'Contacts'.

CSR information: The company's website states: 'We recognise that our communities, customers, employees, suppliers and the environment are all fundamental in our business and it is our priority to make sure we act responsibly and make a positive contribution to society.'

Santander UK plc community model focuses on:

- Close support for the communities in which it operates, with branches and teams undertaking their own local charity activities
- Breakthrough programme supporting 'the fast-growth companies that create new jobs and enable economic growth'
- Supporting people in education, particularly through Santander Universities

CSR report: A detailed and informative CSR report is published annually.

Corporate charity: Santander UK Foundation Ltd (Charity Commission no. 803655).

Exclusions

The foundation will not fund the following:

- Individuals – including trips, overseas volunteering, gap year activity, medical treatment, bursary schemes, grants for studying or research
- Fundraising activities
- Unregistered charities, not-for-profit groups, Community Amateur Sports Clubs
- Community Interest Companies
- Charities which restrict their beneficiaries to a single religious or single ethnic group
- Events, conferences or sponsorship
- Party political activity

Applications

The company

The Head of CSR at Santander UK is Sharon Squire and community investment enquiries, other than those relating to the foundation, should be addressed to her at the address given under 'Contact'.

The Santander UK Foundation Ltd (Charity Commission no. 803655)

The correspondent of the foundation is: Alan Eagle, Santander UK Foundation Manager, Santander Foundation, 201 Grafton Gate East, Milton Keynes MK9 1AN (tel: 01908 343224; email: alan.eagle@santander.co.uk). The best way to contact the foundation if you still have a question is by email to grants@santander.co.uk.

Schroders plc

Financial services

Correspondent: Graham Staples, Company Secretary, 31 Gresham Street, London EC2V 7QA (tel: 020 7658 6000; fax: 020 7658 3977; email: cr@schroders.com; website: www.schroders.com)

Directors: Michael Dobson, Chief Executive; Peter Harrison; Richard Keers, Chief Financial Officer; Phillip Mallinckrodt; Massimo Tosato; Andrew Beeson, Chair; Ashley Almanza; Luc Bertrand; Robin Buchanan; Lord Howard of Penrith; Nichola Pease; Bruno Schroder (women: 1; men: 11)

Year end	31/12/2013
Turnover	£1,809,100,000
Pre-tax profit	£447,500,000

Nature of business: Schroders plc is an international asset management provider.

The group is organised into three principal operating divisions on a worldwide basis: Institutional, Retail/ Unit Trusts and Private Banking.

Company registration number: 3909886

Subsidiary undertakings include: Schroder Investment Company Ltd; Schroder Investment Management GmbH; Schroder Pension Management Ltd; Schroders (Bermuda) Ltd; and Schroder Property Managers (Jersey) Ltd. More subsidiaries are available from the company's accounts and a full list can be obtained from Companies House.

Total employees: 3,304

Focus of giving: Education, health, ill health, sponsorship, children, young people, community/social welfare.

Membership: BITC, LBG

FTSE 100	✓
Gifts in kind	✓
Matched funding	✓
Overseas giving	✓
Payroll giving	✓
Sponsorship	✓

Charitable donations

Cash UK (latest available):	2013	£967,000
	2011	£1,200,000
	2009	£600,000
	2008	£1,100,000
	2007	£1,252,090
Total UK (cash and in kind):	2013	£967,000
Cash worldwide:	2013	£1,000,000
Total worldwide (cash and in kind):	2013	£1,000,000

Community involvement

The group states that its 'approach to charitable giving focuses on employee choice and it supports and encourages employees to raise money for the charities that matter most to them'.

East London Business Alliance (ELBA)

In 2013 Schroders started working with the ELBA Graduate Local Employment Scheme (EaGLES). The scheme 'aims to address the high level of unemployment and underemployment in East London'. Successful candidates of the project receive a six-month paid placement at a company located in Canary Wharf or the City of London. The scheme benefits the participating companies (one of which is Schroders) which 'can add value to their CR programmes and local recruitment strategies by employing a trainee with sound knowledge of the charity and community needs in East London',as well as the graduates who are supported throughout their placement 'in enhancing their employability by learning new skills and being exposed to a wealth of knowledge and experience in their placement companies'.

Corporate giving

In 2013 the group made charitable donations of £1 million (2012: £1.2 million) around the world, 'much of which was donated through matching of employee donations and sponsorship', and 'which included discretionary donations of £300,000 to charities involved with social welfare'. We could not determine the amount awarded in cash donations in the UK, therefore we estimate it to be around £967,000, based on the figures from the previous three years known to us.

Beneficiaries included: Children with Cancer UK; Comic Relief; MagicMe; Mayor's Fund for London; Royal British Legion; and Royal Marsden Cancer Charity.

In-kind support

Staff volunteering efforts.

Employee-led support

Employee volunteering

Employees are encouraged to volunteer, with financial rewards being given to the charity they are involved with. The CSR report for 2013 notes that 'in many of [the group's] offices, employees are able to take up to 15 hours of paid leave per year, to offer their services to the charities which matter the most to them'. If the staff wish to volunteer outside working hours, 'volunteer time matching' can be claimed to secure a donation for the charity they work with.

Examples of employee volunteering include:

MagicMe
The charity runs Cocktails in Care Homes programme where volunteers from the group visit local care homes and interact with residents.

Mayor's Fund for London
The fund runs the Magic Breakfast Scheme which places employees in primary schools with over 40% free school meal rates where they play educational numeracy games with the children, while they have a free breakfast.

Comic Relief
Staff took part in Red Nose Day to raise money for the charity, including participating in home clothes day, bake sales and a 5k fun run.

Royal British Legion
As part of the annual Poppy Appeal the group employees were selling poppies at London underground stations to raise money for the charity.

Royal Marsden Cancer Charity
A London employee completed a swim across-Channel to raise money.

Children with Cancer UK
Three employees took part in the 2013 Scotland Coast to Coast challenge raising money for the children.

More examples of employee involvement, including international initiatives, can be found within the CSR report.

Matched funding

The group matches employee fundraising and employee giving up to a maximum of £2,400 per person per year.

Payroll giving

Payroll giving schemes are operated in a number of offices. In the UK 25% of employees chose to give in this way. The group contributed £311,000 (2012: £280,000) to increase the support.

Corporate social responsibility

CSR committee: CR matters are overseen by the Executive Director Philip Mallinckrodt. According to the CSR report, there are 'policies in place to ensure that Schroders behaves in a socially responsible way in its day-to-day activities'. The company also 'monitors the activities of the companies in which it invests and uses its influence as a shareholder to encourage these businesses to act responsibly'.

CSR information: The group's CSR report states:

> At Schroders, we have a long-term focus and have recognised the importance of sustainability for many years; not only where our clients are concerned, but also in respect of our employees, and the wider community. Integrity and appropriate conduct are integral to Schroders' culture.
>
> We support the communities in which we operate and encourage employees globally to take a proactive approach to corporate responsibility by participating in community or environmental schemes, fundraising or volunteering.

Schroders' focus is concentrated on four pillars – marketplace, people, environment and community.

CSR report: A CSR report is available from the group's website.

Exclusions

Our research suggests that support is not normally available for advertising in charity brochures, animal welfare, appeals from individuals, the arts, elderly people, environment, heritage, medical research, political and religious appeals, science/technology or sport.

Applications for Charity of the Year status are not considered.

Applications

In writing to the correspondent.

The group can provide policy guidelines to those seeking support.

Scott Bader Company Ltd

Chemicals and plastics

Correspondent: Sue Carter, Commonwealth Secretary, Wollaston Hall, Wollaston, Wellingborough, Northamptonshire NN29 7RL (tel: 01933 666755; fax: 01933 666139; email: commonwealth_office@scottbader.com; website: www.scottbader.com/sustainability/31/commonwealth-global-charity-fund)

Directors: Agne Bengtsson; Philip Bruce; Dean Bugg; Andrew Forrester, Group Finance Director; Peter Hartill; Calvin O'Connor; Malcolm Forsyth (women: 0; men: 7)

Year end	31/12/2013
Turnover	£198,688,000
Pre-tax profit	£2,073,000

Nature of business: The company is an internationally operating manufacturer and distributor of synthetic resins and chemical intermediates.

The annual report and accounts for 2013 state:

> Scott Bader Company Ltd is wholly owned as a financial and social investment by The Scott Bader

> Commonwealth Ltd, a company limited by guarantee and a registered charity. . . . Everyone working for Scott Bader may become a member of The Commonwealth and, by this mean, become a trustee holding, in common with other members, the shares of Scott Bader Company Ltd.

Company registration number: 189141

Subsidiary undertakings include: Synthetic Resins Ltd; Scott Bader UK Ltd; Scott Bader SA; Scott Bader Community Fund Trustee Ltd; and ATC Formulated Polymers Inc. These details were obtained from The Scott Bader Commonwealth Ltd annual report and accounts for 2013. **The Scott Bader Group Companies include:** Scott Bader-ATC; Scott Bader Company Ltd; Scott Bader Eastern Europe; Scott Bader France; Scott Bader Germany; Scott Bader Ireland; Scott Bader Scandinavia AB; and Scott Bader Spain. More details on the group components can be found in the accounts or from Companies House.

Brands include: Crestabond; Crestapol; Crystic Roof; FireGuard 75PA Excel; and Satyen.

Main locations: Fareham, Brierley Hill, Leeds, Stockport, Plymouth, Wollaston

Focus of giving: General charitable purposes, education, enterprise/training, environment, health, ill health, older people, overseas projects, science technology, children, young people, community/social welfare, disability, disasters.

Gifts in kind	✓
Humanitarian aid: overseas	✓
Matched funding	✓
Overseas giving	✓

Charitable donations

Cash UK (latest available):	2013	£16,000
	2011	£203,500
	2009	£30,600
	2008	£134,000
	2007	£123,000
Total UK (cash and in kind):	2013	£16,000
Cash worldwide:	2013	£205,000
Total worldwide (cash and in kind):	2013	£205,000

Community involvement

The company channels its charitable giving through **The Scott Bader Commonwealth Ltd** (Charity Commission no. 206391) which is both a charity and a parent company of Scott Bader Company Ltd.

The Group Charity Report 2013 says that 'there is an increase in the number of projects supported in [education/ training] category from the UK fund.'

There is a UK Nominations Scheme under which each Commonwealth Member in the UK has an allocation of £120 to nominate a chosen charity (or charities). In 2013 a total of 144 organisations were supported with donations ranging from £30 to £900 and the remainder of the money was used to help homelessness, educational and disability projects. Seven charities received awards from £500 to £5,000.

In 2013 grants were made totalling £155,000 of which £33,000 was given in the UK. £14,900 of the UK grant total was given through the nomination scheme whereby staff of Scott Bader can nominate a charity of their choice.

The remainder of the UK grant total was used to support local projects including: The Prince's Trust, Northampton (£5,000); Livability (£3,000); Family Support Link, Wellingborough (£2,500); Tall Ships Youth Trust (£1,800); Beanstalk (£700); and the Children's Aid Team, Northamptonshire (£500).

Corporate giving

The annual report for 2013 states that a substantial proportion of Scott Bader's profits each year are devoted to charitable and community work, administered by The Scott Bader Commonwealth. During the year a donation of £178,000 (2012: £176,000) was allocated to The Commonwealth. 'In addition to the donation to the charity the company also provided' £20,000 under the Matched Funding Scheme and £7,500 given to the chair of the company to help charities 'of specific interest to him'.

The website states that the company must donate at least 1% of the group salary bill to its Commonwealth Global Charity each year. The Group Charity Report 2013 specifies that £16,000 was given from the UK fund. We take this figure to represent UK giving; however, the amount could potentially be higher.

Beneficiaries of employee volunteering included: SERVE; Wellingborough Dog Welfare; Macmillan Cancer Support; Northampton Hope Centre; Victoria Centre; Nene Valley Community Action; and Beds and Northants Wildlife Trust.

See the corporate charity entry on p. 425 for more information.

In-kind support

As part of its community support Scott Bader offers the company facilities to be used by the local community. The company's employees volunteer their time and skills for good causes.

Employee-led support

Employee volunteering

The website notes that following a new group policy from 1 May 2014 everyone working at Scott Bader is given an additional one day's paid leave to use for volunteering purposes to help a non-profit/charitable organisation.

In the UK Volunteering Road Show was held to enable seven local charities (SERVE; Wellingborough Dog Welfare; Macmillan Cancer Support; Northampton Hope Centre; Wellingborough Victoria Centre; Nene Valley Community Action; and Beds and Northants Wildlife Trust) to share their volunteering opportunities with staff at the company's Head Office site in Wollaston.

Employees' volunteering activities included:

- Helping to repair a kissing gate, repair fences and clear paths for the Wildlife Trust
- Acting as steward a Wellingborough Dog Welfare event
- Assisting Wollaston Scout Group in taking young scouts on a four mile walk
- Becoming reader helpers at the local primary school
- Helping at the Pensioner's Christmas Tea Party
- Helping at the Chemistry at Work event
- Assisting at the Scott Bader sponsored fun fair

The Group Charity Report 2013 states that in the UK about £13,000 was raised by individuals taking part in a range of activities for their favourite charities.

Matched funding

The company offers to match employee fundraising up to £1,000 per person per year. At the end of June 2014 the Commonwealth Members across the group had raised over £4,900 under the scheme which was matched by company with further £4,100. The money benefited 11 charities: 2nd Wollaston Scout Group; Cancer Research UK; CANSA (South Africa); Helen House; Irchester Gala; Macmillan Cancer Support; Muscular Dystrophy Campaign; RSPCA; Sport Relief Mile; Turkey Patch Foundation; and Wollaston Association of Youth.

Corporate social responsibility

CSR committee: Scott Bader Commonwealth Ltd is a registered charity administered and managed by trustees. This charity is responsible for the company's charitable contribution in the UK and worldwide.

The Commonwealth Board is accountable for achieving the charitable objects, the company being run in accordance with the Commonwealth Principles, making sure the Commonwealth Charity is operating properly and ensuring that Commonwealth Members worldwide are involved.

CSR information: The following information is taken from the company's website:

> Scott Bader has a long-standing reputation for ethical, social and environmental concern and responsibility.

This has been facilitated by our unique and progressive history and company structure.

Scott Bader was founded in 1921 by Ernest Bader. He wanted to create a company whose well-being is entrusted to those who work in it, by championing democratic involvement inside the organisation. Accordingly, in 1951, the company was gifted to the workers. Shares of the chemical manufacturing company were transferred to Scott Bader Commonwealth Ltd, a company limited by guarantee and a registered charity, thereby incorporating Scott Bader into the local and wider community.

The company's annual report for 2013 notes that the way it conducts business is driven by the principles of its constitution, which in practice encompass: the way the company relates to the wider community; the service it offers to its customers; the ethical standards by which it trades; its concern for the environmental impact of the manufacturing activities and products; the effectiveness with which the company works together; and the extent to which democratic participation in the company's affairs is ensured.

CSR report: The company's website gives information on charitable activities undertaken. The company's annual report and accounts also provide information on charitable giving. The Commonwealth Charity accounts are available from the Charity Commission.

Corporate charity: The Scott Bader Commonwealth Ltd (Charity Commission no. 206391).

Exclusions

Charitable giving is not normally provided for:

- Charities concerned with animals
- Individual sponsorships
- Travel and adventure schemes
- Arts projects
- Any form of advertising
- Medical research and equipment
- Sports clubs
- General charitable appeals
- Construction/renovation/maintenance of buildings

Applications

The Scott Bader Commonwealth Ltd

Assessment criteria are available to download from the website. Application forms are available on request by post or email. Deadlines for the large project funding are available on the website. Applications for the Small International fund are accepted all year round. Applications for local funds should be made to the local office.

General enquiries regarding the group's giving or charitable policies can be addressed to the company at: enquiries@scottbader.com.

Scottish and Southern Energy plc

Electricity, oil and gas/fuel, telecommunications

Correspondent: The Community Investment Team, Inveralmond House, 200 Dunkeld Road, Perth PH1 3AQ (tel: 01738 456000; email: info@sse.com; website: www.scottish-southern.co.uk)

Directors: Alistair Phillips-Davies, Chief Executive Officer; Richard Gillingwater; Gregor Alexander, Finance Director; Jeremy Beeton; Katie Bickerstaffe; Lord Smith Of Kelvin, Chair; Richard Gillingwater; Sue Bruce; Peter Lynas (women: 2; men: 7)

Year end	31/03/2014
Turnover	£30,585,000,000
Pre-tax profit	£575,300,000

Nature of business: The group's main business is: generation, transmission, distribution and supply of electricity to industrial, commercial and domestic customers; electrical and utility contracting; and gas marketing.

The group operates in the UK in Ireland.

Company registration number: SC117119

Subsidiary undertakings include: Keadby Generation Ltd; Medway Power Ltd; Neos Networks Ltd; SSE Hornsea Ltd; SSE Renewables Holdings (UK) Ltd; and SSE Services plc. A full list of subsidiary undertakings can be found within the group's accounts.

Main locations: Perth

Total employees: 19,890

Focus of giving: Education, enterprise/training, animal welfare, heritage, local groups, arts, culture, sponsorship, sport, recreation, children, young people, community/social welfare.

Gifts in kind	✓
Market-led giving	✓
Matched funding	✓
Sponsorship	✓

Charitable donations

Cash UK (latest available):	2014	£4,500,000
	2012	£6,100,000
	2010	£1,410,000
	2009	£1,001,000
	2008	£873,000
Total UK (cash and in kind):	2014	£4,500,000
Cash worldwide:	2014	£4,500,000
Total worldwide (cash and in kind):	2014	£4,500,000

Community involvement

According to the company's 2014 annual report: 'In order to meet its objective of being a responsible member of the community, SSE continues to establish close working relationships with local community groups, organisations and charities in the regions in which it operates.'

The group estimates there to be about £130 million of funding to be awarded in the next two decades.

Local Community Funds

According to the company's website, funding is available 'to enable communities to develop sustainably by funding charitable and community initiatives available near each of SSE renewable energy developments.' In the past 13 years over 1,000 projects have been supported with over £13 million being spent. Local and regional community funds are set up for each new onshore wind farm. Community members panels review applications and decide which projects to support Each of the funds is listed in the Scottish Government's Community Benefit Register and more details on the programme can be found on the group's website. During 2013/14 over £5 million was provided to community projects in the UK and Ireland through these funds.

Sustainable Development Funds

The new programme was launched 'to support strategic, long-term projects delivering transformational social, economic and/or environmental changes in the community and develop sustainable ventures for the future' within any local authority where an SSE wind farm was constructed after 1 January 2012. The website further specifies that the fund could be worth more than £50 million over the next 25 years. The first example opened in 2014 was the Highland Sustainable Development Fund and an independent panel will grant over £1 million to regional community projects.

More information on the funds is available on the website along with an 'Expression of Interest Form'. You can also contact Graeme Keddie, Head of Community Investment (tel: 01738 512636; email: graeme.keddie@sse.com) or Ciara Wilson, Community Investment Advisor (tel: 01412 247191; email: ciara.wilson@sse.com).

The Scottish Hydro-Electric Community Trust (OSCR no. SC027243)

The Scottish Hydro Electric Community Trust established in 1998, is an independent charitable trust. Through it the group offers help to customers faced with high charges for an electricity connection (normally in excess of £3,000) within the Scottish Hydro Electric Power Distribution area, particularly those in rural areas.

Education

Investment from SSE funds towards projects for education and youth development was about £400,000.

Support included around £230,000 for improving and building new play parks and £33,000 awarded towards youth clubs and organisations, providing safe spaces for young people to meet and socialise.

Education resources

The group's website provides downloadable educational resources for teachers, parent, group leader or young people providing information on 'dangers of electricity, to learn about how electricity is made and what can be done to lead a more sustainable, greener life'.

Culture and heritage

More than £1.1 million was invested. A grant of £620,000 (the largest ever from the funds) was given to Biggar Museum Trust to establish a new state-of-the-art museum. About 30 festivals and cultural events were also supported, such as a whisky festival and a Gaelic Mod.

SSE Heritage Collection

During the year SSE continued:

> Cataloguing, maintaining and preparing for display [the collection], currently based in Dorset, developing a new £3m visitor centre at its Pitlochry hydro electric scheme and launching a Perthshire renewables trail guide, in order to make the built and natural heritage of SSE's hydro plant and wind farms more accessible to the public.

Sports

About £230,000 was invested in the area with over 40 sports clubs receiving funding towards equipment and facilities. The group also provides sponsorships (see 'Commercially led support' section in this entry).

Environment and conservation

During the year more than £490,000 was provided, including help to local communities by developing community owned turbines and hydro-electric schemes. While £325,000 was invested in community owned renewable projects, other energy efficiency measures for community buildings and preservation of local habitats and wildlife were also supported.

Charity partnerships

The group supports its 'key partner charities', such as Mission Christmas ('for which £9,000 was raised in cash and a further 1,000 Christmas gifts were donated by employees') and Sport Relief (for which more than £50,000 was raised). All staff raised funds were matched by the group.

Corporate giving

In 2013/14 the group made charitable contributions totalling £4.5 million to local communities. Support is given in the UK and Ireland. The Community Benefit Report for the year provides the following breakdown:

Culture, heritage and tourism	26%
Community facilities and services	24%
Skills and employment	23%
Environment and conservation	14%
Education and youth development	8%
Sport and recreation	5%

The report also notes that a total of 336 projects were supported form 22 active funds with an average grant being about £12,500.

Further breakdowns of support by the areas are available from the Community Benefit Report.

Beneficiaries included: Biggar Museum Trust (£620,000); South Lancashire Energy Academy (£267,000); Bonar Bridge Post Office (£43,000); Ridgeside Playparks Group (£32,000); Aberfeldy and District Rotary Club (£24,000); Heartland FM (£24,000); Tayside Mountain Rescue Team (£20,000); Royal School of Dunkeld Parent Partnership Group (£14,100); Biggar Rugby Football Club (£10,000); A&D Lockhart Joiners and Decorators (£5,600); Tummel and Tay Festival and Wiston Lodge (£5,000 each); Cumbria Primary School Parent Council (£3,000); Age UK; Citizens Advice; Mission Christmas; and Sport Relief.

In-kind support

Non-cash contributions include staff volunteering and skills and educational materials. The group's visitors' centres are normally free to schools organising visits.

Employee-led support

Employee volunteering

The group has an programme through which staff members are able to donate one day of their time and efforts to 'individually or in teams work on projects ranging from DIY, gardening, administrative tasks as well as supporting third sector organisations to deliver school talks or provide IT support'. Help is available 'in and around the areas where the group's sites and employees are located'. In addition staff volunteers regularly visit schools and deliver educational packages on electrical safety and sustainability.

Organisations wishing to receive volunteering help should complete a Volunteer Request Form, available to download from the website, which should then be scanned and emailed to the group at volunteering@sse.com or posted to SSE, Be the difference, Corporate Affairs, 55 Vastern Road, Reading RG1 8BU. More information can also be obtained from the website or by calling Be the difference team at 01189 534156.

In 2013/14 about 8,000 days were donated to 740 projects in the UK and Ireland with over 40% of employees participating in employee volunteering programme.

SSE staff also raise money for good causes, for example, Sport Relief.

Matched funding

The group can match employee fundraising efforts.

Commercially led support

Sponsorship

The group's sponsorship strategy is to support community based initiatives in the areas it serves. A number of initiatives are sponsored, including:

- Glasgow 2014 Commonwealth Games
- The SSE Arena, Wembley
- Sport Relief
- Sports Aid – 50 young athletes each year are sponsored across Scotland, England, Wales, Northern Ireland and Ireland

The company's website states: 'We have a full programme of sponsorship at present so are not seeking further opportunities. If you wish to make an enquiry about future sponsorship, please email us at **sponsorship@sse.com** and we'll be in touch if a suitable opportunity arises.'

Community energy

SSE is committed to supporting communities to mitigate climate change and – following a successful creation of a financial model providing a £1 million commercial loan over 15 years to help communities invest in solar projects in Bath – the group is looking for similar communities to work with again.

Furthermore, 'SSE has developed a community co-investment scheme with a pilot being developed with Melness & Tongue Community Development Trust where they are seeking to co-invest in SSE's proposed Strathy South wind farm development in North Sutherland.'

Sales Guarantee fund

The group shared a total of £2.5 million amongst eight UK charities (including Energy Action Scotland, Citizens Advice, Age UK, Save the Children and Macmillan Cancer Support) for projects aimed at improving the lives of people living in fuel poverty. Examples include training for local energy champions, energy awards for cancer sufferers and a grant scheme for energy efficiency measures:

> The money was made possible by the creation of a retrospective Sales Guarantee Fund from January 2008 to August 2013, which reimbursed any household customers who switched their energy supply to SSE after being given inaccurate or misleading information and were disadvantaged as a result. SSE pledged to donate any balance of the fund to charities.

Education and employment
The group also supported 328 work and training placements to a value of over £500,000. Over £1 million from the group's funds was used to facilitate a wide variety of employment initiatives in the community.

Corporate social responsibility

CSR committee: There were no details of a dedicated CSR committee found.

CSR information: The information given on the group's website not the group's core values being: Safety; Service; Efficiency; Sustainability; Excellence; Teamwork. The core purpose of SSE is 'providing the energy people need in a reliable and sustainable way' and in order to maintain this the group aims to:

- Achieve the highest standards of health and safety performance
- Provide opportunities for employees to be shareholders in the company
- Complying with or exceed all statutory and regulatory environmental requirements
- Maintain high environmental performance across all activities
- Working to ensure that the quality of service delivered to customers is sector-leading
- Respond effectively to any customer concerns about products and services
- Ensure that the communities which it operates have a safe and reliable supply of electricity
- Encourage employees to be good citizens in the communities in which they live and work

Sustainability is the guiding value defined as, the group's 'actions and decisions [being] ethical, responsible and balanced, helping to achieve environmental, social and economic well-being for current and future generations'.

CSR report: CSR achievements are outlined in the Community Investment Review.

Exclusions

The company does not normally support individuals, teams or organisations which have political affiliations. It also excludes advertising in charity brochures, research projects, including medical research, overseas projects and religious appeals.

Applications

In writing to the correspondent. To apply for Sustainable Development funds use the contacts given in the 'Community involvement' section.

Application forms for The Scottish Hydro-Electric Community Trust can be downloaded from the group's website.

ScottishPower UK plc

Electricity

Correspondent: The CSR and Reputation Committee in the UK, 1 Atlantic Quay, Glasgow G2 8SP (tel: 01412 488200; website: www.scottishpower.com)

Directors: Ignacio Sánchez Galán, Chair; José Miguel Alcolea; José Sáinz Armada; Juan Carlos Rebollo; Lord Macdonald of Tradeston; Lord Kerr of Kinlochard; Tom Farmer; Susan Deacon; Keith Anderson, Chief Corporate Officer (women: 1; men: 9)

Year end	31/12/2013
Turnover	£8,230,700,000
Pre-tax profit	£553,500,000

Nature of business: In 1995 Manweb and ScottishPower merged, and combined they provide 2.5 million homes in the UK with power.

ScottishPower has been part of the Iberdrola Group since April 2007, and is one of the UK's largest energy companies employing more than eight thousand people across Generation; Transmission; Distribution and Retail sectors.

Company registration number: SC117120

Subsidiary undertakings include: Coldham Windfarm Ltd; East Anglia Offshore Wind Ltd; ScottishPower Generation Ltd; SP Manweb plc; and SPD Finance UK plc. A full list of subsidiary undertakings can be found in the group's accounts.

Main locations: Warrington, Glasgow, Rhostylien

UK employees: 7,122

Total employees: 7,122

Focus of giving: Enterprise/training, environment, heritage, non-registered charities, STEM (science, technology, engineering and mathematics), arts, culture, science technology, sponsorship, community/social welfare.

Membership: BITC, LBG

Gifts in kind	✓
Market-led giving	✓
Matched funding	✓
Payroll giving	✓
Sponsorship	✓

Charitable donations

Cash UK (latest available):	2013	£3,300,000
	2011	£1,300,000
	2006	£2,610,000
Total UK (cash and in kind):	2013	£6,500,000
Cash worldwide:	2013	£3,300,000
Total worldwide (cash and in kind):	2013	£6,500,000

Community involvement

The company's website states: 'We have a long track record of supporting our local communities and helping causes that are close to people's hearts.' Support is given to various programmes 'that enhance education and employability, the environment, public safety and health'. Both national and local charities are supported.

Charity partnerships

Cancer Research UK
In 2012 the company launched a three-year partnership with the charity with the aim to raise £5 million. The amount has already been achieved and further funds are being raised.

Environment and safety

Countryside and Wildlife Rangers
In association with local authorities and the Scottish Wildlife Trust, ScottishPower continues to promote biodiversity and education of community groups through co-sponsorship of countryside rangers at its sites. These include: Loch Doon, close to the Lanark Hydro-electric Scheme; and at the Musselburgh Lagoons next to Cockenzie Power Station.

Crucial Crews
The company takes part in this national programme 'where children take part in a range of fast-paced scenarios designed to raise awareness of the dangers of electricity and other common hazards'. Staff members from the company's Networks business support the programmes events.

Safety education centres
Support is given to two safety education centres within ScottishPower's network areas – DangerPoint in Talacre (North Wales) and the Risk Factory in Edinburgh. The centres 'are designed to educate and raise awareness of accidents, injury prevention and personal safety, in a safe and controlled environment'.

Visitor centres
The company has visitor centres at several power stations which provide educational information on the station, power generation, safety and environmental issues.

The ScottishPower Energy People Trust Fund (OSCR no. SC0036980)
The trust was established in 2005 to help registered charities supporting people whose lives are affected by fuel poverty. Since its inception over £12.6 million has been provided to various projects. The fund is maintained through contributions from ScottishPower and voluntary donations from independent supporters. Decisions on funding are made independently of ScottishPower. Support is given in three funding areas: income maximisation, energy efficiency and fuel debt assistance.

The ScottishPower Foundation (OSCR no. SC043862)
The foundation was established in 2013 to provide help to registered charities in areas of: education; environmental protection; the arts, heritage, culture or science; disability; ill health; prevention or relief of poverty; and community development. Similarly to the above fund, decisions to award funding are made independently of ScottishPower. As part of its education focus, the foundation runs a scholarship programme for Masters Studies.

The Iberdrola Group has its foundation (Fundación IBERDROLA); ScottishPower Foundation appears to be a UK equivalent of which.

The ScottishPower Green Energy Trust (OSCR no. SC030104)
The trust was established in 1998 as an independent charity and is funded by ScottishPower Green tariff customers who make an annual donation to the trust. It aims to supports the development of new renewable sources in the UK, helping to reduce our reliance on fossil fuels and combat climate change.

Note: 'In response to regulatory changes, ScottishPower is not currently offering a Green Tariff and therefore the Trust cannot consider any new project applications at this time. The website will be updated in due course should this situation change.'

Corporate giving

The annual report and accounts for 2013 states:

> During the year ended 31 December 2013, ScottishPower contributed £6.5 million in community support activity of which £3.3 million was contributed to registered charitable organisations. The £6.5 million total incorporated £0.1 million categorised as charitable gifts, £4.0 million categorised as community investment and £2.4 million categorised as commercial initiatives; given in cash, through staff time and in-kind donations.

The group follows the LBG model to evaluate its community investment activity. We take the figure of £3.3 million contributed to registered charitable organisations to represent the company's cash giving. This sum would appear to include 'commercial initiatives' as well as 'charitable gifts'.

Political donations: During the year, the company made political contributions totalling £20,000 (The Conservative Party and The Labour Party (£7,000 each) and The Scottish National Party (£6,000)).

See the corporate charity entries on p. 426 for more information.

In-kind support

Employee volunteering time and skills. Educational information provision is available through the visitor centres. The company has also produced Powerwise – 'an educational website from ScottishPower that teaches children and young adults all about electricity and how to stay safe around it – inside and outside the home'.

Employee-led support

The company's employees participated in a number of volunteering and fundraising initiatives around the year, particularly in support of the partner charity. Our research suggests that in the past employee support has also been aimed at charities supporting community causes and national charities, such as Help for Heroes and Children in Need.

STEM Ambassadors
The company has its STEM Ambassadors – employee volunteers 'helping to encourage young people to study Science, Technology, Engineering and Mathematics' through their work with schools in the communities served by ScottishPower.

Iberdrola International Volunteering Day
The initiative was launched in 2010 and joins forces of employees in Spain, the US, Brazil, Mexico and the UK who join to complete a variety of projects across the five countries on the same day.

International volunteering holidays
In collaboration with Fundación Deporte Integra, Iberdrola employees are given the opportunity to take part in an international volunteering project in Sao Paulo (Brazil) each year. Volunteers work with 12- to 16-year-olds training them 'in computing and presentation skills to help them develop new skills and gain confidence to change their lives and aspire for a better future. On their return home, the volunteers then continue to provide on-line support to the students for a year'.

Matched funding
Staff fundraising efforts are matched up to a maximum of £200 per application.

Payroll giving
The company operates the Give As You Earn scheme in the UK.

Commercially led support

Sponsorships

Cycling
In 2013 ScottishPower became the official partner of Scottish Cycling:

> The sponsorship focuses on supporting a national series of youth racing opportunities across all cycling disciplines in Scotland. Through the ScottishPower National Youth Racing Series a dedicated events development officer provides support to volunteers and clubs to help them deliver these cycling opportunities across the country.

The events included ScottishPower Youth Tour of Scotland, road racing, BMX racing, track racing and Mini Downhill racing.

Arts and culture
ScottishPower has a long tradition of supporting the arts within and for local communities. Examples of sponsorships include:

- ScottishPower Piper Band – the company's award winning pipe band has been sponsored since 1989
- Edinburgh International Book Festival – in addition to sponsoring the festival ScottishPower runs Story Swap Shop; a competition (primary schoolchildren read, pass on their books to others and raise money for the Aberlour Children's Trust with the winning school receiving a visit from a well-known children's author); and Story Generator (to encourage creative writing with the winning school receiving a prize of books and the pupil receiving a Kindle)
- Llangollen International Eisteddfod – the company sponsors the International Children's Day at this major cultural event in Wales hosting choirs, dance groups, musicians, and vocal soloists

Previous sponsorships have also included: sponsorship of the venue for events for schools and creative communities through Transform project, organised by National Theatre of Scotland; and a three-year sponsorship of Scotland's international traditional music festival Celtic Connections.

Our research suggests that, the company also undertakes good cause sponsorship.

Cancer Research UK
As part of the partnership ScottishPower has developed Help Beat Cancer Discounted Energy tariff 'ScottishPower will make a donation to Cancer Research UK for every month [the customer] remains on the tariff, up to a maximum of £5 per fuel per annum, until the end of the tariff term' and are also distributing health information and advice to the customers.

Education and training
The company works closely 'with industry, academia, schools, colleges and universities throughout the UK to promote engineering as a desirable career choice, and also to attract more young women into engineering and other power sector professions'. There are a number of employability programmes, apprenticeships and graduate placements.

National Skills Academy for Power
The body was established by the Government and the company is represented on its board as well as contributing to an online source of information on careers in the UK power industry (www.thinkpowersector.co.uk).

The Institution of Engineering and Technology (IET) Power Academy
The company is a partner and a member of the Executive to this industry and academia partnership 'which seeks to address the looming skills shortage in the power-engineering sector, through a combination of financial support and work placements for students'.

Powerskills Programme
The programme was designed by ScottishPower in association with the Personal Development Partnership (which involves (Prince's Trust Scotland, Fairbridge, Venture Scotland and the Venture Trust) to encourage 'disadvantaged young people into engineering and help them to develop the skills needed to progress within the industry'. The project receives funding from The Scottish Government's Cashback for Communities initiative.

Corporate social responsibility

CSR committee: The website notes:

> ScottishPower is represented on the Iberdrola CSR and Reputation Committee, which identifies and implements the most appropriate actions at group and geographic levels to meet the needs and expectations of our stakeholders. We also operate the ScottishPower CSR & Reputation Committee in the UK, bringing together senior management from across the company to coherently monitor and manage these actions.

CSR information: Information taken from the company's website states:

> We are committed to doing business responsibly. The General Corporate Responsibility Policy sets out the basic principles and general framework of action for managing Corporate Social Responsibility practices undertaken by the company and the group. The policy is further developed and supplemented by various Social Responsibility Policies addressing the specific needs and expectations of stakeholders.

The company is committed to:

- Continuing to be a UK leader in renewable energy solutions
- Helping customers become more energy efficient
- Being socially aware and engaged in the community
- Helping customers find the best deal for them
- Listening and making improvements to its service

The group's CSR strategy focuses on economic, environmental and social sustainability.

CSR report: An annual Sustainability Report of Iberdrola Group is published online. In addition each year ScottishPower Sustainability Summary is produced to complement the Sustainability Report. The summary focuses on the issues that stakeholders have stated as important to them.

Corporate charity: The Scottish Power Energy People Trust (OSCR number SC036980); the Scottish Power Foundation (OSCR number SC043862).

Exclusions

Our research suggests that support is not generally given to appeals from individuals, expeditions, military organisations, circular appeals, advertising in charity brochures, animal welfare charities, religious appeals, local appeals not in areas of company presence or overseas projects.

Sponsorship for sporting events and advertisements in publications, etc., will normally only be considered commercially, in terms of potential advertising benefits.

Applications

The company: General enquiries regarding the company giving can be directed to the correspondent or for local requests – addressed to regional offices.

The charities: Applications to the foundation, the Energy People Trust Fund or the Green Energy Trust can be made online (see the company's website for links).

Email enquiries can be directed:

- The foundation: scottishpowerfoundation@scottishpower.com
- The Green Energy Trust: greenenergytrust@scottishpower.com
- The Energy People Trust: SPEnergyPeopleTrust@ScottishPower.com

SDL plc

Consultancy, information management and communication, information technology, professional support services

Correspondent: The Corporate Social Responsibility Team, Globe House, Clivemont Road, Maidenhead, Berkshire SL6 7DY (tel: 01628 410100; fax: 01628 410150; email: sdlfoundation@sdl.com; website: www.sdl.com)

Directors: David Clayton; Mark Lancaster, Chief Executive Officer; Dominic Lavelle, Chief Financial Officer; Joe Campbell; Alan McWalter; Mandy Gradden, Chair; Glen Collinson (women: 1; men: 6)

Year end	31/12/2013
Turnover	£266,100,000
Pre-tax profit	(£24,400,000)

Nature of business: Provision of technology products and language, consulting and education services to allow companies to trade effectively in global markets.

Company registration number: 2675207

Subsidiary undertakings include: Automated Language Processing Services Ltd; Language Weaver Inc; SDL Sheffield Ltd; SDL Tridion Ltd; and Tridion AB. A full list of subsidiary undertakings can be found within the group's accounts.

Total employees: 3,177

Focus of giving: General charitable purposes, economic generation, education, enterprise/training, health, ill health, housing, homelessness, women's issues, children, young people, community/social welfare.

Gifts in kind	✓
Overseas giving	✓

Charitable donations

Cash UK (latest available):	2013	£80,000
	2011	£262,000
	2009	£250,000
Total UK (cash and in kind):	2013	£80,000
Cash worldwide:	2013	£87,000
Total worldwide (cash and in kind):	2013	£87,000

Community involvement

SDL Foundation (Charity Commission no. 1127138)
The group channels most of its charitable support through the foundation, operating since 2008. Its aims are 'to provide support for sustainable, structural development that improves the quality of life for disadvantaged communities around the globe'. It seeks to 'build physical and economic infrastructures, assist community advancements and promote self-sufficiency'.

Corporate giving

In 2013 the group made donations totalling over £87,000, out of which £80,000 was given to the SDL Foundation and £7,100 to other charities. We maintain that at least £80,000 was given in the UK in cash contributions. The foundation's annual report and accounts say that a total of £260,000 was received as a donation from SDL plc. In this entry we use the figure provided by the group in its annual report and accounts.

Beneficiaries include: Thames Valley Adventure Playground (£5,000); MicroLoan Foundation; St Wilfrid's Centre; and The Prince's Trust.

See the corporate charity entry on p. 427 for more information.

In-kind support

Employee volunteering efforts.

Employee-led support

The group's staff can volunteer to help good causes in their local communities and choose the charities to be supported by the SDL Foundation. Additional days off are available to participate in helping the society. Some global examples given in the annual report include:

- Employees helping at a shelter for the homeless in Seattle
- Staff from Sheffield, Bristol and Maidenhead delivering CV workshops to young people for The Prince's Trust
- One SDL member spending time at Rejoice (Thailand) – a charity providing medical, social and educational support to communities affected by HIV/AIDS
- Employees from nine office worldwide co-ordinating fundraising efforts for BeadforLife through the sale of jewellery manufactured by the charity from recovered materials

Globally employees also engage in fundraising activities to support the foundation's work.

Commercially led support

According to the annual report, the group 'actively collaborates with universities and research centres to promote research, solutions and assist with recruitment for the technology areas of the business'. For instance, 'SDL Amsterdam was the industrial partner to a dozen European universities and research centres as part of the EU FP7 project HATS.'

Corporate social responsibility

CSR committee: Information taken from the annual report for 2013 states: 'The board has overall ownership of the Corporate Social Responsibility strategies and takes very seriously its broader responsibility to society and takes a progressive approach in ensuring it meets its broader social obligations.'

There were no details of a separate CSR committee found.

CSR information: The 2013 annual report notes that 'SDL is committed to being a good corporate citizen in the communities in which it operates, conducting business in a socially and ethically responsible manner.'

The group's social responsibility framework continues to target three primary areas:

- Supporting communities through the SDL Foundation, which aims to promote sustainable development
- Promoting and facilitating employee involvement in charitable endeavours
- Reducing its environmental impact

CSR report: CSR information is contained within the annual report.

Corporate charity: The SDL Foundation (Charity Commission no. 1127138).

Exclusions

The foundation will not give to causes where trustees or SDL employees would directly benefit. The foundation will also not support political or discriminatory activities; or those appeals that are recognised as being large or well-known.

Applications

Information taken from the website states:

> SDL employees create regional groups in SDL's worldwide offices to provide support for the SDL Foundation. Regional foundation groups provide: regular forum for brainstorming; focus and momentum; and supply of applications. All projects supported by the SDL Foundation have been presented by an SDL employee sponsor who is actively involved in the charitable cause and who is responsible, along with an SDL executive sponsor, for the success of the initiative.

Only causes supported and sponsored by SDL employees will be considered by the SDL Foundation.

For more details on the foundation you can contact the foundation directly via email: SDLFoundation@sdl.com.

Senior plc

Aerospace, industrial products/services, manufacturing

Correspondent: Andrew Bodenham, Group Company Secretary, 59–61 High Street, Rickmansworth, Hertfordshire WD3 1RH (tel: 01923 775547; fax: 01923 775583; email: companysecretary@seniorplc.com; website: www.seniorplc.com)

Directors: Charles Berry, Chair; Andy Hamment; Mark Rollins, Group Chief Executive; Celia Baxter; Derek Harding, Group Finance Director; Mark Vernon; Giles Kerr (women: 1; men: 6)

Year end	31/12/2013
Turnover	£775,100,000
Pre-tax profit	£83,800,000

Nature of business: Senior is an international manufacturing group with operations in 11 countries. The group designs, manufactures and markets high technology components and systems for the principal original equipment producers in the worldwide aerospace, defence, land vehicle and energy markets.

Company registration number: 282772

Subsidiary undertakings include: Senior Aerospace GmbH, Senior Flexonics GmbH; Senior Operations LLC; and Senior UK Ltd. A full list of all subsidiary undertakings can be obtained from Companies House.

Total employees: 6,362

Focus of giving: Education, enterprise/training, general appeals, STEM (science, technology, engineering and mathematics), community/social welfare.

Cash donations undeclared ✓

Charitable donations

Cash UK (latest available):	2013	£64,000
	2011	£113,000
	2009	£43,000
	2008	£35,000
Total UK (cash and in kind):	2013	£64,000
Cash worldwide:	2013	£64,000
Total worldwide (cash and in kind):	2013	£64,000

Community involvement

Education

The group is interested in promoting education, training and skills development, particularly in science, technology, engineering and mathematics (STEM). According to the Senior plc 2013 annual report: 'Several Senior businesses focus their community activities on educational outreach programmes supporting local schools, technical colleges and universities.' Examples include: Senior Aerospace BWT working on STEM initiatives with several local schools; and two BWT employees working as National STEM Ambassadors, 'supporting STEM clubs in local schools, mentoring and supporting students with Career Academies, and helping students gain invaluable work experience through paid work placements'.

Corporate giving

We could not identify the amount given towards charitable causes within the annual report and accounts for 2013. Based on the figures from three previous years known to us, we estimate that the group could have given about £64,000 in cash in the UK.

Employee-led support

The group's 2013 annual report states:

> The group's operations are encouraged to involve themselves in their local communities and to support local charities. These relationships are normally managed at a local level, where the employees typically select non-profit-making organisations and charitable interests active within their community. These are often long-standing relationships and involve employees volunteering their time, making financial donations and raising funds to help those in need of support within their local communities.

Corporate social responsibility

CSR committee: There is a Health, Safety and Environment Committee. No indications of CSR committee found.

CSR information: As stated in the annual report for 2013:

> The group has five core priorities to its corporate responsibility programme:
> - Developing People – attracting and retaining the best employees
> - Community Engagement – investing in the communities where it operates
> - Operating with Integrity – conducting senior's business responsibly and ethically
> - Environment – reducing the group's energy usage and environmental impact
> - Health and Safety – maintaining a safe and healthy workplace

CSR report: Contained within the annual report and accounts.

Exclusions

Political donations are not made.

Applications

In writing to the correspondent.

Severn Trent plc

Waste management, water

Correspondent: The Corporate Responsibility Team, Seven Trent Centre, PO Box 5309, Coventry CV3 9FH (tel: 02477 715000; email: corporate.responsibility@severntrent.co.uk; website: www.severn-trent.com)

Directors: Tony Ballance; Michael McKeon, Chief Financial Officer; Andy Smith; Martin Kane; Liv Garfield, Chief Executive Officer; John Coghlan; Richard Davey; Andrew Duff, Chair; Gordon Fryett; Martin Lamb; Phillip Remnant; Angela Strank (women: 2; men: 10)

Year end	31/03/2013
Turnover	£1,831,600,000
Pre-tax profit	£215,200,000

Nature of business: The group's principal activities are the supply of water and sewerage services, waste management and the provision of environmental services in the UK and internationally.

Company registration number: 2366619

Subsidiary undertakings include: Derwent Insurance Ltd (Gibraltar); Severn Trent Costain Water Ltd; and Severn Trent Water Ltd. A full list of subsidiaries can be obtained from Companies House.

Main locations: Birmingham

Total employees: 8,221

Focus of giving: Education, environment, STEM (science, technology, engineering and mathematics), poverty and social exclusion, children, young people.

Membership: LBG

FTSE 100	✓
Gifts in kind	✓
Market-led giving	✓
Matched funding	✓

Charitable donations

Cash UK (latest available):	2013	£3,000,000
	2012	£3,607,000
	2010	£2,326,000
	2009	£2,352,000
	2008	£413,000
Total UK (cash and in kind):	2013	£3,000,000
Cash worldwide:	2013	£3,098,000
Total worldwide (cash and in kind):	2013	£3,098,000

Community involvement

The group's website notes the following:

> We are dependent upon our relationships with local people, and the wider community as a whole. . . . We want our work to bring value to the community, not distress. . . . We care about the concerns of local communities and know how important it is for people to feel they are being heard. . . . We seek to play a positive and beneficial role in the wider community through charitable partnerships and by encouraging and supporting our employees to participate in community affairs.

The annual report and accounts for 2012/13 specify that 'donations are given to charities whose projects align closely with [the group's] aim to promote the responsible use of water resources and waste water services which provide the opportunity for longer term partnerships'. Support is also given to organisations nominated by employees (through matched funding and health and safety reward schemes).

Charity partnerships

WaterAid

The group has chosen the charity as its principal beneficiary. It is a one of the founding members of WaterAid and has committed five years 'to helping bring safe water and effective sanitation to people all over the world'.

WatersideCare

The partnership with Keep Britain Tidy, the Environment Agency and the Canal and River Trust aims 'to encourage and support communities to improve their local waterways'. 'The current network of volunteers have already contributed over 9688 hours of their time to improve their local environment.'

Big Bang

For the second year Severn Trent Water sponsored Big Bang 2014, giving young people hands-on experiences and activities in STEM (science, technology, engineering and maths).

The Severn Trent Trust Fund (Charity Commission no. 1108278)

The main charitable contributions are made through this avenue. The fund provides help to customers struggling to pay their water bills. It has also entered a partnership with the Citizens Advice to help people get skills to manage their finances 'at a deeper level'. A donation of £3 million was given to the fund by the group in 2012/13.

Corporate giving

In 2012/13 the group awarded a total of almost £98,000 (2011/12: 107,000). Additionally, each year the company donates to The Severn Trent Trust Fund, with £3 million being given during 2013. A further breakdown could not be found; however, we maintain that UK cash contributions totalled at least £3 million (given to the UK registered fund).

Beneficiaries included: The Severn Trent Trust Fund; WaterAid; and Water for People.

In-kind support

The website states that Severn Trent 'provides recreational facilities at [its] public access sites'. Staff volunteering time and fundraising efforts are available.

Girlguiding Midlands: Severn Trent Water supports the organisation with 'waste, water and me' badge. 'This free resource can be used to create fun and engaging activities with all age groups to learn about waste, water, WaterAid and the environment.'

Employee-led support

Employee Volunteering

A new employee volunteering initiative – Water Champions – has been launched in order to 'inform, inspire, and engage people of all ages to think, feel and act differently about water'. Staff members can contribute to the community by creating water efficient gardens in primary schools across the Severn Trent Water region. 'In Severn Trent Services we recognise it is not always as easy for employees to take time out to volunteer when working on third party contracts. However, we take the opportunities that suit our employees and their work patterns.'

According to the group's website, in 2012/13 'the Severn Trent WaterAid committee helped to raise over £331,000 for WaterAid through various fund raising events and projects'.

Matched funding

A scheme operates allowing the group to match employees' contributions.

Commercially led support

Customers who have trouble paying their bills are offered a range of flexible tariffs and schemes, such as matched payments, capping bills for people with low incomes who need large amounts of water for medical or family reasons, or arranging payments to be made directly from the benefits.

Corporate social responsibility

CSR committee: The CSR Committee provides an oversight of performance, including strategy, risk, policies and supporting measures and targets in conjunction with the Severn Trent Executive Committee. It provides guidance and direction to the group's Corporate Responsibility Programme, reviews the group's key non-financial risks and opportunities and monitors general progress. The terms of reference for the committee can be found on the company's website and are also available from the Company Secretary.

CSR information: The group's Corporate Responsibility Policy (reviewed in 2013) states:

> In Severn Trent our strategy is for sustainable growth through a focus on waste and water operations in the UK and internationally. To achieve this we are committed to operating in a responsible way across our business activities for the benefit of our customers, shareholders, employees and other stakeholders. This includes the delivery of essential services to customers and building supplier relationships, whilst demonstrating social responsibility, environmental sustainability and delivering value for all our stakeholders. We recognise that a responsible approach to running our business enables us to manage risk, drive improvement in our performance, safeguard our reputation and maintain pride and motivation across our workforce. We are also mindful that our current operations must make a positive contribution to the future and therefore fully embrace the concept of sustainability.

CSR report: Information regarding CSR achievements is published on the company's website. Some details are contained within the annual report and accounts.

Exclusions

Generally support is not available for advertising in charity brochures, appeals from individuals, local appeals not in areas of company presence, medical research, fundraising events, religious appeals, expeditions, study tours and cultural exchanges or third party organisations fundraising on behalf of national charities.

Severn Trent does not generally make any donations for political purposes in the UK to EU political parties or incur EU political expenditure. There was an authority to make political donations or incur political expenditure in the EU (which would not ordinarily be regarded as political donations) up to £50,000, given by the shareholders in 2012. This authority was sought to be renewed in the subsequent years.

Applications

In writing to the correspondent. Your application to the group should include:

- A summary of the aims and objectives of your charity
- A summary of the project for which the donation is required
- An explanation of how the money will be spent
- A copy of your latest annual report and accounts

Applications to The Severn Trent Trust Fund should be made via the fund, not the group. For further details also visit the website (www.sttf.org.uk).

Shaftesbury plc

Property

Correspondent: Penny Thomas, Company Secretary, Pegasus House, 37–43 Sackville Street, London W1S 3DL (tel: 020 7333 8118; fax: 020 7333 0660; email: penny.thomas@shaftesbury.co.uk; website: www.shaftesbury.co.uk)

Directors: Brian Bickell, Chief Executive Officer; Simon Qualye; Thomas Welton; Chritopher Ward, Finance Director; Jonathan Lane, Chair; Jill Little; Oliver Marriott; Hilary Riva; Dermot Mathias; Sally Walden (women: 3; men: 7)

Year end	30/09/2013
Turnover	£89,600,000
Pre-tax profit	£241,700,000

Nature of business: Property investors and developers. Shaftesbury owns a portfolio properties in London's West End (Carnaby, Charlotte Street, Chinatown, Covent Garden, Soho).

Company registration number: 1999238

Subsidiary undertakings include: Shaftesbury Carnaby Ltd; Shaftesbury Chinatown Ltd; and Shaftesbury Soho Ltd. Further subsidiary undertakings can be found within the group's annual report and accounts and a full list obtained from Companies House.

UK employees: 22

Total employees: 22

Focus of giving: Economic generation, education, enterprise/training, arts, culture, sponsorship, children, young people, community/social welfare.

Membership: LBG

Cash donations undeclared	✓
Payroll giving	✓
Sponsorship	✓

Charitable donations

Cash UK (latest available):	2013	£84,000
	2011	£48,000
	2009	£97,000
	2008	£108,000
Total UK (cash and in kind):	2013	£531,000
Cash worldwide:	2013	£84,000
Total worldwide (cash and in kind):	2013	£531,000

Community involvement

Community investment initiatives are concentrated in the areas where the group's villages are situated. Shaftesbury 'aligns its charitable giving and community involvement to organisations which focus their activities in the West End, including those which support the arts, bodies which encourage sustainability, as well as community groups, schools and charities'. In some cases the group can help them 'to be located in the areas in which they operate but would otherwise be unable to afford at market rents'.

The group also invites local groups and charities (as well as representatives of local authorities) to visit Shaftesbury to grasp a better understanding of its business and corporate responsibility objectives.

Sustainable Restaurant Association
The group 'continued promoting' the membership association which provides sustainability advice and support to restaurants. Subsidised membership is offered for two years to enable the restaurants to evaluate the membership value.

Arts, theatre and leisure
Work is undertaken with the English National Opera (the community choir of which is sponsored, also other arts organisations, theatres and galleries. Accommodation on flexible terms can be provided to organisations, for example Association of British Orchestras, Chinatown Arts Space, London Chinatown Association, National Campaign for the Arts, Stage One and Yellow Earth Theatre Company. The group also has sponsored an Opera Squad day, which introduced opera to local Westminster schools.

Charitable, community and educational purposes
Shaftesbury 'provides space in vacant units for periods of time to enable charitable, community and educational events to take place'. Partners include: House of St Barnabas; Make Justice Work; The Connection at St-Martins-in-the-Fields; and South Westminster Drug and Alcohol Service. Other groups working to address social challenges in the local community are eligible for help. Currently a pilot scheme (supported by Westminster City Council and other West End landlords) is tried in order to encourage employment of Westminster residents in the group's tenants' businesses by providing a free recruitment service.

Environmental Justice Foundation
Work with the foundation has been in place since 2009 the group donating space for temporary stores in its villages.

Local authorities
The group co-operates with Westminster City Council and the London Borough of Camden (within whose jurisdictions the properties are located) and seeks to help 'improve the public realm in and around [its] villages through contributions to street improvements, pedestrianisation and street lighting schemes'.

Scholarships
There are bursary schemes with the London College of Fashion for tailoring students and with Westminster Kingsway College for trainees in catering and hospitality.

Corporate giving
In 2012/13 the group measured its total charitable contributions at the value of £531,000 (2012: £404,000). The group measures its community investment in line with the London Benchmarking Group guidance. As the amount awarded in cash could not be determined, we estimated that a total of about £84,000 was given, based on figures from the three previous years known to us.

Employee-led support
The CSR Policy 2014 paper states that 'Shaftesbury's employees [are encouraged] to be involved in the work of ... charities and identify any additional assistance that the group may be able to provide or procure.' We could not identify more particular details of employee involvement.

Payroll giving
A scheme operates to allow payroll contributions.

Commercially led support
The group has provided sponsorships to arts organisations and events (see 'Community involvement' section in this entry).

Corporate social responsibility
CSR committee: No indication of a separate CSR committee found in the latest reports.

The annual report for 2012/13 notes the following: 'Whilst the board has ultimate responsibility for sustainability, its ethos is embedded in the day-to-day operations of our business.'

CSR information: The group's website notes: 'Our approach to corporate responsibility reflects how we operate, our impact on the environment and how we engage with our stakeholders.'

The following comprises Shaftesbury's overall environmental and corporate responsibility priorities:

- Operate in an environmentally sustainable manner and minimise the environmental impact of its operations
- Extend the economic useful lives of its buildings
- Comply with or exceed all legal and regulatory requirements,
- Establish annual targets and encourage continual improvement in its performance
- Engage with advisors, suppliers, tenants and stakeholders to disseminate the group's CSR policies and requirements
- Invest in its local community
- Conduct our business with integrity and in an open and ethical manner
- Invest in the welfare and development of its employees

CSR report: Reporting on CSR is published on the group's website.

Exclusions
According to the annual report for 2012/13, 'the group does not have affiliation to any political party nor is it the group's policy to make political donations'.

Applications
In writing to the correspondent. Community engagement matters are managed by Fiona Daly.

Shanks Group plc

Waste management

Correspondent: The CSR Team, Dunedin House, Auckland Park, Mount Farm, Milton Keynes, Buckinghamshire MK1 1BU (tel: 01908 650580; fax: 01908 650651; email: info@shanksplc.co.uk; website: www.shanksplc.co.uk)

Directors: Adrian Auer, Chair; Peter Dilnot, Chief Executive Officer; Toby Woolrych, Finance Director; Eric van Amerongen; Jacques Petry; Stephen Riley; Marina Wyatt (women: 1; men: 6)

Year end	31/03/2014
Turnover	£636,400,000
Pre-tax profit	£7,700,000

Nature of business: The group's activities involve management of solid, hazardous, organic and municipal waste. It operates in the UK, Canada and Belgium and Netherlands.

Note: the UK employee number relates to the UK Municipal division only.

Company registration number: SC077438

Subsidiary undertakings include: Icova B.V.; Orgaworld Canada Ltd; Shanks Argyll and Bute Ltd; Shanks Hainaut s.a.; Shanks Waste Management Ltd; and Wakefield Waste PFI Ltd. More subsidiary undertakings can be found in the accounts and a full list is available from Companies House.

UK employees: 545

Total employees: 3,741

Focus of giving: Environment, heritage, community/social welfare.

Membership: BITC

Cash donations undeclared ✓

Charitable donations

Cash UK (latest available):	2014	£18,300
	2011	£19,000
	2010	£552,000
Total UK (cash and in kind):	2014	£18,300
Cash worldwide:	2014	£18,300
Total worldwide (cash and in kind):	2014	£18,300

Community involvement
The CSR report mentions an education centre being included within the new South Kirkby treatment facility, where local children will be taught what Shanks do with the things thrown away.

Put Your Money Where Your Mouth Is Community (PYMWYMIC)
In 2013 the group was approached by PYMWYMIC for support for The Landfill Harmonic Orchestra – a group of young people from Paraguay playing musical instruments made from waste. The funding from Shanks allowed several of those people to travel to Amsterdam to participate at a concert.

Corporate giving
Charitable contributions could not be identified within the annual report and accounts for 2013/14 or the CSR report for 2014. In the past three years charitable giving has totalled on average about £18,300 annually with £15,000 being given to the Prince's Trust each year, as part of the three-year commitment (from 2011/12).

Corporate social responsibility
CSR committee: The group's Corporate Responsibility, Health and Safety, and Risk committees monitor the sustainability strategy and its implementation throughout business activities. The committees are comprised of senior sector and technical specialists (whose role is to drive improvements in these areas) and report to the group Executive Committee.

CSR information: The group's CSR report notes:

> Although our activities have significant advantages for society in terms of carbon avoidance and resource use, the advanced technologies and processes we operate are relatively new and we must, therefore, engage, inform and educate those living closest to our facilities. ... We believe that we have a responsibility to the communities where we operate, but excellent community relations are also critical to our business. ... We work closely with our local communities and strive to be transparent, flexible and a good neighbour.

The CSR strategy is largely focused on environment, health and safety and sustainable management of the business.

CSR report: An annual Corporate Responsibility Report is published.

Applications
In writing to the correspondent.

Shell (UK Ltd)

Oil and gas/fuel

Correspondent: Sarah Hughes, Head of Shell UK Social Investment, Shell Centre, York Road, Waterloo, London SE1 7NA (tel: 020 7934 1234; website: www.shell.co.uk)

Directors: Erik Bonino; Glen Cayley; Trui Hebbelinck; David Moss; Nigel Hobson; Michael Coates (women: 1; men: 5)

Year end	31/12/2013
Turnover	£15,318,000,000
Pre-tax profit	£296,000,000

Nature of business: Shell is a global group of energy and petrochemicals companies. Its activities in the UK correspond to those of the group and include exploration, production and sale of oil and natural gas and marketing of petroleum products. Shell activities also include: generating electricity (including wind power); providing oil products for industrial uses; producing petrochemicals used for plastics, coatings and detergents; and developing technology for hydrogen vehicles.

Shell UK Ltd forms part of the Shell Group controlled by Royal Dutch Shell plc.

Company registration number: 140141

Subsidiary undertakings include: Enterprise Oil Ltd; Murphy Schiehallion Ltd; Shell Service Station Properties Ltd; Shell UK North Atlantic Ltd; and Woodlea Ltd. A full list can be obtained from Companies House.

Main locations: Aberdeen, Fife, Ellesmere Port, London, Lowestoft, Stanlow (Merseyside), Wythenshawe

UK employees: 2,345

Total employees: 2,345

Focus of giving: Advertising in charity brochures, education, enterprise/training, environment, fundraising events, health, ill health, heritage, individuals, STEM (science, technology, engineering and mathematics), older people, arts, culture, science technology, sponsorship, children, young people, community/social welfare, disability, disasters.

Membership: BITC, LBG

Cash donations undeclared	✓
Charity of the Year	✓
FTSE 100	✓
Gifts in kind	✓
Humanitarian aid: overseas	✓
Market-led giving	✓
Matched funding	✓
Payroll giving	✓
Sponsorship	✓

Charitable donations

Cash UK (latest available):	2013	£11,785,000
	2011	£6,829,000
	2009	£15,525,000
	2007	£13,000,000
	2005	£7,730,000
Total UK (cash and in kind):	2013	£11,785,000

Community involvement
The UK website states:

> Social Investment is our voluntary contribution of funding, skills and resources to sustainable programmes that deliver wider benefits to our local communities and society. Nationally our principal focus is on supporting Enterprise Development and encouraging more young people to pursue STEM (Science, Technology, Engineering and Maths) education.

The website notes that Shell 'aims to encourage economic and social development while reducing any negative impact of [its] operations'; these may include 'relocating and resettling communities', 'affecting the health of local communities', 'disrupting local traditions, cultures and values' or 'pushing up the costs of housing and services and threaten traditional livelihoods, such as farming'.

Community development
Projects are supported directly and indirectly through the independent Shell Foundation (see below). Shell states the following on the 'Social investment' section of its global website:

> Our aim is to work with communities to understand local needs and address social or economic issues relevant to our business, such as access to energy, enterprise development and road safety. Many of the programmes we support aim to be self-sustaining, for example by helping young people to set up businesses or providing training for jobs.

According to the 'Communities' section of the UK website, Shell:

> May extend [its] social investments beyond [the] core areas of STEM (Science, Technology, Engineering and Maths) and Enterprise Development to include initiatives that address social, health and other local concerns. Preference is given to social investment projects that provide measurable societal benefits and are financially and operationally sustainable.

STEM
Various initiatives are undertaken in support of science education.

Shell Education Service

According to the UK website: 'SES delivers fun, interactive, investigative science workshops to thousands of children and teachers in primary schools across the UK every year. SES is a partnership between Shell and Sphere Science Ltd.'

Tomorrow's Engineers

Shell has invested more than £1 million in the national programme run by EngineeringUK. It seeks 'to give every 11–14 year old a first-hand engineering experience with local employers, and helps students connect what they learn in the classroom with the world around them and the opportunities of a career in engineering'. The priority of the project is to increase the number of girls studying STEM subjects and going into engineering.

STEM Education Scotland

Activities in Scotland include:

- Shell Engineering Scheme – training programme run in partnership with North East Scotland College (NECS)
- Girls in Energy programme – a one year course, delivered by the North East Scotland College (NESC)
- Young Engineers and Science Clubs Scotland – aimed at primary and secondary school pupils, the support includes educational resource kits provided to the clubs
- GeoBus – an educational outreach programme (sponsored by Shell, Centrica Energy, Dana Petroleum, Maersk Oil, Premier Oil, The University of St Andrews and the Natural Environmental Research Council) supports Earth Science teaching in secondary schools by providing resources that are not readily available to educators
- Techfest – co-sponsorship of this annual festival of STEM

Charity of the Year
Our research suggests that UK plants and offices can select their own Charity of the Year.

The Shell Foundation (Charity Commission no. 1080999)
The foundation was established with a $250 million (£156 million) endowment from Shell Group and is registered in the UK but operates overseas in South America, Africa, India, Mauritius, Mexico, Netherlands, Pakistan, Turkey and the United States. The foundation's annual grant programmes are funded by distributions from its endowment fund. The Shell Foundation's annual report and accounts for 2013 states that:

> Shell Group made unrestricted donations of $6 million (£3.7 million) in 2013, approved a similar donation for 2014, and agreed 'in principle' to funding in 2015 and 2016 in the event that the endowment does not generate sufficient income for the charity to achieve its objectives and maintain impact.

The foundation works with a small number of entrepreneurial partners by providing grant funding, extensive business support and access to networks. Through its foundation, Shell seeks to introduce a business approach to major social and environmental issues that are linked to the energy sector. It uses a mix of financial and non-financial resources and makes use of the private sector.

The Shell Centenary Scholarship Fund (Charity Commission no. 1071178)

The fund provides money for Shell Centenary Scholarships to support educational development and provide opportunities for graduate students from overseas to study in the UK. It provides at least 65 full cost scholarships (to cover tuition, accommodation, maintenance costs and return airfare) to international students on one year taught postgraduate courses at seven universities (Cambridge, Durham, Edinburgh, Imperial College London, Oxford and University College London).

The Shell Group has various worldwide initiatives, detailed examples of which can be found on the website or the global Sustainability Report.

Disaster relief

Globally Shell Group supports disaster appeals, including 2013 typhoon Haiyan in the Philippines. In the past help has been given to the appeals following earthquakes in China, hurricanes in the USA and floods in Thailand.

HIV/AIDS programmes

Worldwide Shell runs a programme with the aim of helping global and local partners to fight the HIV/AIDS. Partners include Niger Delta AIDS Response (NiDAR) and UNAIDS.

Corporate giving

The 2013 Sustainability Report, which covers all Shell Group's companies and subsidiaries, reports that in that year almost $159 million (£99.1 million) was spent on community investment projects ('voluntary social investment') around the world. We were unable to find any further breakdown of the investment or determine the amount given in the UK solely. The UK company did not seem to declare charitable donations, therefore we are estimating that UK cash donations totalled around £11.7 million, based on the figures from the three previous years known to us.

Revenue: We have used the figure defined as 'Sales proceeds' in the company's accounts as its annual turnover.

In-kind support

According to our research, Shell in the UK offers its facilities at key UK plants and offices to community organisations by prior arrangement. Contact your nearest local community relations team to discuss this.

Employee-led support

Shell Employee Action Grants Programme

Shell employees and pensioners in the UK are active in their local communities and get involved in local activities through initiatives run by local Shell sites. Through the programme grants are provided to support not-for-profit organisations where Shell people regularly volunteer. Examples of such activities include help to parent-teacher associations, mentoring schemes for the local homeless and planting gardens in local parks. Grants of £350 are given to Shell people who volunteer at least 20 hours a year within a UK community group or charity.

Project Better World

Through partnership with Earthwatch, international two-week-long volunteering trips overseas are also possible.

Payroll giving

Our research indicates that there has been the Give As You Earn scheme operating.

Matched funding

Shell matches employee fundraising up to a maximum of £350 for individuals and £500 for groups (three or more staff or pensioners).

Commercially led support

Shell Springboard

The initiative 'provides a financial boost to UK enterprises with innovative and commercially viable business ideas that contribute to the low-carbon economy'. Every year Shell awards £330,000 'to innovative and commercially viable business ideas that aim to reduce greenhouse gas emissions'.

Shell LiveWIRE

Through the website 'Shell helps thousands of young people to start-up their businesses, develop their skills, and boost their contacts.' The initiative also provides the Young Entrepreneur of the Year Award of £10,000 and four £1,000 Grand Ideas Awards 'every month to the most innovative or unusual ideas submitted by young entrepreneurs in their first 12 months of trading'.

Sponsorship

Science Museum

Shell has provided a three-year sponsorship to the museum. It helped to create Launchpad Gallery, space for visitors to learn about climate science and research and development of Launchbox classroom resource.

Techfest in September

The annual festival is sponsored by Shell and BP and 'aims to promote STEM subjects to young people and to the wider community'.

GeoBus

The programme is sponsored by Shell, Centrica Energy, Dana Petroleum, Maersk Oil, Premier Oil, The University of St Andrews and the Natural Environmental Research Council. It supports Earth Science teaching in secondary schools.

Arts

Shell has been a corporate sponsor to a number of arts and culture organisations, including British Film Institute, British Museum, National Theatre, National Maritime Museum, National Gallery, Natural History Museum and Southbank Centre.

Corporate social responsibility

CSR committee: The Group CEO and Executive Committee are accountable for sustainable development. There is a group level Corporate and Social Responsibility Committee, made up of four Non-executive Directors. According to the global website, the purpose of the committee is to:

> Assist the Board of Directors of the Company in reviewing the policies and conduct of the Shell Group of Companies with respect to the Shell General Business Principles (including Sustainable Development and the Health, Safety and Environment Policy), the Shell Code of Conduct and to major issues of public concern.
>
> The committee also carries out certain oversight functions on behalf of the board.

CSR information: Statements taken from the company's website note:

> Contributing to sustainable development is integral to the way we do business. As we work to help meet the world's growing energy needs, we aim to share benefits with local communities and reduce impacts of our operations, including managing carbon dioxide emissions.
>
> Shell contributes to sustainable development by helping to meet the world's growing energy needs in economically, environmentally and socially responsible ways. We work with partners, communities, governments and others to deliver energy for the future.

Environment seems to form the greatest part of the sustainability agenda.

CSR report: The Shell group publishes an annual Sustainability Report, available on the website.

Exclusions

Shell is unable to support individuals or third parties (for example, Cash for Kids, Help for Heroes, etc.). Our research suggests that animal welfare appeals are not likely to succeed either. Community grants are not given outside the company's operation area.

Applications

An application form for the UK Community Grants and sponsorship application form are available online. Otherwise enquiries about local support should be directed at the community relations teams at Shell plants or offices.

Shell does not award grants outside neighbourhoods surrounding Shell plants and offices, but if you have an enquiry not appropriate for local sites, you should address it to the UK Social Investment Department at the company's address.

Note: Unsolicited applications for community grants outside the communities in which Shell operates (Aberdeen, Bacton, Mossmorran and St Fergus) are not supported.

The foundation: The principal contact person for the foundation is Dr Chris West (tel: 020 7934 5496; email: shell-foundation@shell.com) at the company's address.

Shepherd Building Group Ltd

Building/construction

Correspondent: Philip Clarke, Company Secretary, Huntington House, Jockey Lane, Huntington, York YO32 9XW (tel: 01904 650700; fax: 01904 650701; email: information@shepherd-group.com; website: www.shepherd-group.com)

Directors: Alan Fletcher; Patrick Shepherd; Mark Perkins; Stephen Price; Alastair Shepherd; David Williams, Chair; Derek Carter; Kevin Parker (women: 0; men: 8)

Year end	30/06/2014
Turnover	£686,000,000
Pre-tax profit	£11,400,000

Nature of business: Shepherd Building Group Ltd is a holding company with subsidiaries engaged in building and ancillary activities, such as construction and engineering and residential property development.

Company registration number: 653663

Subsidiary undertakings include: Access Park Selby Ltd; Emersons Green Ltd; Portakabin Ltd; Portasilo Ltd; Rushden Properties Ltd; Shepherd Homes Ltd; and Zone F Ltd. A full list of subsidiaries can be obtained from the group's accounts.

Main locations: York, Manchester, London, Northampton, Langley, Leeds, Darlington, Birmingham

UK employees: 3,235

Total employees: 3,235

Focus of giving: General charitable purposes, education, enterprise/training, health, ill health, large national appeals, non-registered charities, small groups, local groups, armed forces personnel, arts, culture, sponsorship, sport, recreation, children, young people, community/social welfare.

Gifts in kind	✓
Sponsorship	✓

Charitable donations

Cash UK (latest available):	2014	£22,000
	2011	£87,000
	2009	£134,000
	2008	£157,000
	2007	£195,000
Total UK (cash and in kind):	2014	£22,000
Cash worldwide:	2014	£22,000
Total worldwide (cash and in kind):	2014	£22,000

Community involvement

According to the CSR report for 2013/14, the group's flexible Community Support Policy aims to help support people and organisations in the areas where it operates. Support is mainly given in the York area but initiatives elsewhere, relating to the group's operations and staff, are also considered. Priority is given to charities and non-profit organisations.

The budget for support forms part of the parent company budget. The group also reminds that it receives more requests than available resources can accommodate. Causes relating to education and training, backing local businesses, inward investment and employment, healthcare, the arts, sports and facilitating employee involvement are usually assisted.

Community support donations

The group's companies can make donations of £100 from their own budgets without referring to the group. Larger grants (£100–£500) require the group's advice (via Group Corporate Relations Manager) and grants of above £500 will need the group's approval.

During 2013/14 support has been given to Shepherd's Brass Band, York Early Music Festival, York Rotary Dragon Boat Challenge and York Students in Communities and York Students in Schools programmes.

Corporate giving

In 2013/14 a total of 91 requests have been approved and 34 rejected. The CSR report gives a following breakdown:

Area	2013/14	2012/13
Music and Arts	41%	40%
Education	26%	25%
Health	19%	19%
Local Business	10%	12%
Sport	4%	4%

The report states that 'there were 11 donations/sponsorships of £2,000.'

Since we were unable to identify any other figures, we use the £22,000 amount to represent the group's charitable giving.

Beneficiaries in 2013/14 included: Arboretum Trust; David Nolan; Diabetes UK; Guide Dogs; Outreach; Selby Abbey Appeal; The Royal British Legion – Poppy Appeal; York Civic Trust; and York Women's Counselling. An extensive list of all beneficiaries supported can be found within the CSR report for 2013 available online.

In-kind support

Employee time and skills.

Employee-led support

Staff are encouraged to get involved in various events organised by organisations supported by the group, for example, the annual Dragon Boat Challenge organised by the Rotary Club of York.

Commercially led support

Sponsorship

The group has been a sponsor of the York Rotary Dragon Boat Challenge since the beginning of the event. To date in aid of local charities a total of £700,000 has been generated.

Corporate social responsibility

CSR committee: We found no details of a separate CSR Committee. The Board of Directors is responsible for matters concerning charitable donations.

CSR information: The report on CSR, contained within the company's annual report and accounts, state that Shepherd Group's CSR programme 'is designed to ensure our operations are carried out with the highest regard for our people, customers, business partners, suppliers and the local communities where we undertake our work'.

Commitments are made to:

- Ensuring a healthy and safe work environment
- Building a sustainable future
- Being a good neighbour
- Taking care of our people

CSR report: The group publishes a publication with CSR updates on its website. A CSR report is available within the annual report and accounts.

Exclusions

No support is given for political appeals.

Applications

In writing to the correspondent.

Shire Pharmaceuticals Group

Pharmaceuticals

Correspondent: Brooke Clarke, Communications and Public Affairs, Hampshire International Business Park, Chineham, Basingstoke, Hampshire RG24 8EP (tel: 01256 894000; fax: 01256 894708; email: shirecorporateresponsibility@shire.com; website: www.shire.com)

Directors: Timothy Martel; Amanda Miller (women: 1; men: 1)

Year end	31/12/2013
Turnover	£100,196,931
Pre-tax profit	(£3,179,736)

Nature of business: The company is a provider of speciality biopharmaceutical products. Shire Pharmaceuticals Group is a wholly owned subsidiary within the Shire plc group.

The company's immediate parent company is Shire Biopharmaceuticals Holdings and the ultimate parent company and controlling party is Shire plc, incorporated in Jersey.

Company registration number: 2883758

Subsidiary undertakings include: Shire Europe Ltd; Shire Holdings UK Ltd; Shire Pharmaceutical Development Ltd; and Shire Pharmaceutical Services Ltd. A full list of subsidiary undertakings can be obtained from Companies House.

Main locations: Basingstoke

Total employees: 148

Focus of giving: Education, fundraising events, health, ill health, medical research, local groups, older people, overseas projects, sponsorship, children, young people, disability.

Membership: BITC

Cash donations undeclared	✓
Charity of the Year	✓
FTSE 100	✓
Gifts in kind	✓
Humanitarian aid: overseas	✓
Market-led giving	✓
Matched funding	✓
Overseas giving	✓
Payroll giving	✓
Sponsorship	✓

Charitable donations

Cash UK (latest available):	2013	£1,275,000
	2011	£496,000
	2009	£1,300,000
	2007	£243,000
	2006	£303,000
Total UK (cash and in kind):	2013	£1,275,000
Cash worldwide:	2013	£1,275,000
Total worldwide (cash and in kind):	2013	£1,275,000

Community involvement

The UK website states:

> Shire UK is proud of its commitment to help the local community and of the support we give to a variety of charitable events held each year. ... Through the commitment of our employees, we are aiming to make a difference to patients, their families and carers, as well as to the medical community.

Charity partnership

According to the website, Shire UK has established a partnership with a local voluntary service The Link. The organisation collects books, CDs, clothing, household equipment, small items of furniture, as well as unwanted office supplies and passes them on to worthy causes, including refuges, children's home, scout groups, local archaeological society, nurses' quarters and the children's wards at the local hospital. Some items are also passed on to Eastern Europe or Africa via Feed the Children to benefit those in need outside the UK.

The group's worldwide community engagement approach focuses on 'communities in the neighbourhoods where [it] operates as well as therapeutic communities, such as the groups that represent patients and their families'. Shire also recognises the following as its key community stakeholders: patient groups; medical/healthcare education bodies; and not-for-profit organisations that are linked with the group's therapy areas of focus and related research bodies.

The global website specifies the following components of the Shire Giving Program:

- Corporate donations – cash and in-kind support to local, national or international organisations 'that support Shire's community and/or disease in its therapeutic focus area'
- Employee-led giving – volunteering, fundraising and payroll contributions
- Corporate fundraising campaigns – at both global and local levels

Charity of the Year

The Shire group says that it 'does not send seasonal greetings cards to customers or suppliers, instead, a group of employees at each site nominates a not-for-profit beneficiary and a one-off donation is made'.

One of the main activities undertaken by the group worldwide is developing access to treatment for rare and specialist conditions through three strands:

- Availability – working on innovative treatments and therapies
- Accessibility – working with NGOs, government bodies and other organisations to remove the barriers that prevent medicines being delivered to patients (for example, lack of transport or medical infrastructure as well as absence of trained personnel)
- Affordability – through patient assistance programs in the US, Named Patient Program outside the US and Charitable Access Program (administered by Direct Relief in conjunction with an independent Medical Expert Committee) in countries where Shire has no commercial presence

According to the global website almost 50,000 patients around the world received charitable drug donations in 2013.

As part of its aim to develop knowledge and research into diseases Shire assists awareness raising campaigns and medical education. During the year a total $7 million (£4.3 million) was spent on educational grants worldwide.

Humanitarian aid

Shire group contributes to humanitarian and disaster relief worldwide. For instance, during the year medical products were donated to Project Hope to help Syrian refugees and provided financial support to people affected by Typhoon Haiyan.

Direct Relief

In 2013 Shire collaborated with this humanitarian medical aid organisation to help patients in countries where Shire has no commercial presence.

Corporate giving

Shire UK

The annual report and accounts of Shire Pharmaceuticals Group (registered number 02883758) did not seem to declare charitable donations. The annual report and accounts of Shire plc (registered number 99854) no longer gives the figure for charitable donations, which previously has also stated the amount given in the UK solely.

The correspondent has provided a helpful *Shire UK Disclosure Report for 2013* which notes the following figures (total of almost £1.3 million):

- MEGS (Medical Education Goods and Services) payments – include donations, grants and benefits in-kind and totalled £453,000
- Sponsorship of individuals to third party meetings – awards include registration fees, accommodations in and outside the UK and travel outside the UK and totalled £109,000 to 236 recipients
- Fees paid to healthcare professionals as consultants – £400,000 to 204 recipients
- Patient organisations – donations included financial assistance and 'significant non-financial support' and totalled £313,000 (contracted services constituted £41,000)

Although the 'disclosure report' gives full amounts of all contributions made, we cannot determine with certainty the amount given in cash *only* as the recipients benefited from both direct financial support and through in-kind assistance or services. It would appear that the vast majority of support is given in some type of grant or funding provision, therefore we use the full figure of almost £1.3 million to account for cash contributions. In practice the amount handed out in direct payments may be lower – see the report to get a deeper understanding on how the support is distributed.

Beneficiaries included: University College London (£69,000); Kidney Research UK and Queen Elizabeth Hospital (£30,000 each); Fabry International Network (£20,000); International Society of Nephrology (£18,000); The Academy of Medical Sciences (£5,000); University Hospitals Coventry and Warwickshire Trusts (£500); Oxford Health NHS Foundation Trust (£400); and Cambridge University Hospitals (£120).

The group

The following information is taken from the global website and refers to the *whole* of the Shire group operations. It says that the 'total of Shire donations to charitable groups and patient organisations in 2013' was of $27.5 million (£17.1 million). It is further noted that almost $100 million (£62.3 million) was spent on access and affordability programmes in 2013 (based on the cost of goods), $7 million (£4.3 million) on educational grants. The value of in-kind contributions was not separately specified.

Note: The annual reports and accounts provide figures in US dollars; we have converted the amounts using the exchange rate applicable at the time of writing. We have used the amounts given in the 'disclosure report', as these refer to the UK. Shire gives considerably more worldwide.

In-kind support

Medical products are donated as part of humanitarian aid as well as on ordinary basis. Globally the group has also donated manufacturing and laboratory equipment to educational institutions.

Employee-led support

Volunteering

Employee volunteering is the second main channel (the first being corporate contributions) of support and engagement with local communities. Shire provides one fully paid day off per year for every employee for volunteering purposes in support of non-profit organisation. The following activities have been undertaken by the staff:

- Volunteers serving Christmas lunch to the elderly residents at the Basingstoke Alzheimer's Society
- Support to charity events, including the Macmillan Big Coffee Morning appeal, Comic Relief, Wear it Pink Cancer Relief and the annual Jeans for Genes fundraising day where Shire matches employees' donations
- Volunteer days helping local schools and charities, for instance, accompanying children with disabilities on an outing with the local Rotary Club or creating garden space where children can learn to grow their own vegetables
- Donation of Christmas presents handed out to the elderly residents in the communities, identified by Age Concern

Matched funding

In support of corporate fundraising campaigns employees are invited to make personal one-off donations to a single high profile cause and Shire may match the total donation made by the staff. Shire UK also supports employees by making a donation towards their own fundraising activities.

Payroll giving

Give As You Earn Scheme is operating which allows regular deductions from salaries.

Commercially led support

Sponsorships

In the past Shire UK has sponsored long-term projects with: Kids Company to sponsor research at Great Ormond Street Hospital; and the Royal Society of Chemistry to encourage project to encourage young people to choose a career in science.

Education

Globally Shire also provides educational grants in furtherance of research into the diseases and treatments of conditions that Shire is working on.

Corporate social responsibility

CSR committee: The website states that Shire's:

> Community strategy and plan of activities are led and implemented by Shire's Corporate Communications Department in conjunction with HR Business Partners, Country or Site Managers and local groups of employees where relevant. Employee volunteering activities are agreed and arranged with line managers in consultation with Human Resources.

There also are 'a number of senior leaders each serving as sponsors for one area of responsibility'. The internal 'sponsors' set the goals to support the overall group's strategy and ensure their implementation and performance.

Shire group has a Responsibility Steering and Communications Group which 'facilitates the activities of the working groups, oversees communications and works with sponsors'.

CSR information: Information given on the group's website states:

> At Shire, the patient is at the heart of everything we do. In practical terms, this means we focus on areas of high medical need – in particular, on rare diseases and specialist conditions for which treatments are not readily available elsewhere. The specialist focus of our business directly informs our approach to responsibility. . . . Through conversations with our stakeholders, we have identified two core areas of responsibility where we know we can deliver the greatest value and make the biggest difference to patients: access to medicines and disease awareness.

Although patient-related areas receive special attention, there are 'four pillars of responsibility' – patients, people, planet and partners.

The Responsibility Policy (updated March 2014) notes:

> Connecting with our communities in meaningful and tangible ways is at the core of who we are at Shire. We recognise and value that the impact we as individuals and as a company can have on the lives of others is significant. We focus our connections in several areas but primarily neighbourhoods where we have a significant presence and therapeutic areas where we discover and develop medicines that help patients and their families.

CSR report: There are global reports available from the Shire's website – Responsibility Matters, corporate brochure Hand in Hand and also policy documents.

Exclusions

No support is given for political appeals.

Applications

In writing to the correspondent. Our research indicates that the use of charitable contribution funds is generally unrestricted, which means Shire does not control the recipient's use of the funds – the use is at the sole discretion of the recipient.

Shoe Zone Ltd

Retail – clothing and footwear

Correspondent: Michael Smith, Trustee of the Shoe Zone Trust, Haramead Business Centre, Humberstone Road, Leicester LE1 2LH (tel: 01162 223000; fax: 01162 223001; email: info@shoezone.com; website: www.shoezone.com)

Directors: Michael Smith; Anthony Smith; Clare Howes; Nick Davis; Naomi Shefford; Charlie Bloor; John Smith (women: 2; men: 5)

Year end	05/10/2013
Turnover	£193,882,000
Pre-tax profit	£9,529,000

Nature of business: The company is a footwear retailer in the UK and Ireland. It is a wholly owned subsidiary of Shoe Zone Group Ltd.

Company registration number: 148038

Total employees: 4,560

Focus of giving: Education, health, ill health, poverty and social exclusion, children, young people, disability.

Gifts in kind ✓

Charitable donations

Cash UK (latest available):	2013	£20,000
	2012	£100,000
	2010	£150,000
	2009	£70,000
	2008	£0
Total UK (cash and in kind):	2013	£20,000
Cash worldwide:	2013	£20,000
Total worldwide (cash and in kind):	2013	£20,000

Community involvement

The group's website notes that support is given to various causes, 'locally and further afield, directly and via the Shoe Zone Trust. Since 2001 Shoe Zone stores and Head Office have raised over £210,000 for nominated charities and the Shoe Zone Trust alone has donated over £420,000 since its start in 2005'.

The Shoe Zone Trust (Charity Commission no. 1112972)

The company has a corporate charity, through which charitable support is channelled. The trust supports organisations towards projects helping to relieve poverty or advance education (mainly of children and young people under the age of 18), particularly in Leicestershire and Rutland and for specific charities in Philippines and elsewhere abroad.

Corporate giving

In 2012/13 the company made a charitable donation of £20,000 (2011/12: £100,000) to its corporate charity – The Shoe Zone Trust, of which the trustees include Michael Smith, the company's Chair and Anthony Smith, its CEO. Further £100,000 had been committed to be paid in 2014. Employee donations contributed further £17,000. The Shoe Zone Trust's annual report for 2013 state that a total of £100,000 was received as a donation from Shoe Zone plc. In this entry we use the figure provided by the group in its annual report and accounts.

The trust states that beneficiaries for 2013 included: Shepherd of the Hills, Philippines (£49,000); Ministries Without Borders (£25,000); Mango Tree and Toyhouse (£6,500 each); 500 Miles and Amantani Boarding Houses (£5,000 each); Kids in Need of Education (£1,000); and Marie Curie Cancer Care (£400).

See the corporate charity entry on p. 428 for more information.

In-kind support

The company's Head Office employees have participated in community activities donating their time.

Employee-led support

Shoe Zone employees from Head Office volunteer in various activities in the local communities, including painting and decorating playground and a club for young people. The group's staff also raise money to their chosen charities. The annual report and accounts for 2012/13 says that employees raised a total of £17,000 (2011/12: £46,000) to various charities.

Commercially led support

The group's website notes Sherrardswood and Birchwood Rangers football club being sponsored as well as a sponsorship to a local boy on his trip to the World Karate Championships. The support, however, appears to be given through the Shoe Zone Trust.

Corporate social responsibility

CSR committee: No indications of a CSR committee.

CSR information: The following statement is published within the 2012/13 accounts: 'The company is committed to responsible growth. By putting customers first and through its relationship with its employees, the company has developed effective ways of making positive contributions to society and the environment.'

CSR report: No report published.

Corporate charity: The Shoe Zone Trust (Charity Commission no. 1112972).

Applications

The Shoe Zone Trust

Applications to the trust should be made in writing to the correspondent. Further enquiries can also be directed via telephone on 01162 223007.

Shop Direct Holdings Ltd (formerly Littlewoods Shop Direct Group Ltd)

Retail – department and variety stores

Correspondent: The Company Secretary, Skyways House, Speke Road, Speke, Liverpool L70 1AB (website: www.shopdirect.com/corporate-responsibility-page)

Directors: A. S. Barclay; H. M. Barclay; M. Seal; P. L. Peters

Year end	30/06/2013
Turnover	£1,712,800,000
Pre-tax profit	£17,600,000

Nature of business: The principal activities of the group are online and home shopping retail and financial services, customer relationship management solutions and property management.

Company registration number: 5059352

Subsidiary undertakings include: A full list of subsidiary companies is given in the accounts.

Main locations: Preston, Liverpool, Oldham, Sunderland

Total employees: 5,242

Focus of giving: Health, ill health, local groups, children, young people, community/social welfare.

Charity of the Year	✓
Gifts in kind	✓
Matched funding	✓
Payroll giving	✓

Charitable donations

Cash UK (latest available):	2013	£100,000
	2012	£100,000
	2011	£100,000
	2009	£300,000
	2008	£6,000,000
Total UK (cash and in kind):	2013	£100,000
Cash worldwide:	2013	£100,000
Total worldwide (cash and in kind):	2013	£100,000

Community involvement

Shop Direct looks to contribute positively to the communities in which it has a presence through its sustainability community investment and charity programme. The majority of charitable donations are made to organisations supporting children and young people in the North West, and particularly those on Merseyside and in Greater Manchester, through **The Shop Direct Charitable Foundation.** The foundation also works with grass-roots organisations 'to build capacity and help ensure their future sustainability' and is administered by Community Foundation for Merseyside. The group also supports a small group of long-term partner charities. Employees of the group actively support charitable causes through volunteering, fundraising and payroll giving.

Corporate giving

In 2012/13 the group made charitable donations of £100,000.

We could not determine a value for the in-kind support given by the group.

Partner charities: Alder Hey Children's Hospital; Baby Lifeline; Fashion and Textile Children's Trust; Retail Trust; Parklands High School

In-kind support

Pro bono

As part of the group's volunteering commitments, eight senior leaders have embarked on a volunteering programme through which they lend their 'insight, skills and expertise to local charities'. The team is working with four selected charities with the aim of delivering greater sustainability.

Employee-led support

Employee volunteering

Employees across the group are given opportunities to volunteer for local charities and community groups. Some teams of employees undertake work at the organisations supported by the Shop Direct Foundation and activities typically include gardening, improving facilities or providing themed activity days.

Employee fundraising
Employees take part in various fundraising activities, which have included cake sales, sporting challenges and fun days.

Matched funding
The group tops-up funds raised by employees through its Helping Hand scheme. In the last three years, more than £500,000 has been jointly contributed through the scheme.

Payroll giving
Employees are able to donate through the payroll giving facility.

Corporate social responsibility

CSR committee: There is a dedicated Corporate Responsibility Board chaired by the group CEO.

CSR information: The following information was taken from the group's website:

> At Shop Direct, we're determined to behave in a responsible way with strong ethical and environmental standards, and to be the best possible citizen we can in the communities where we operate.
>
> To help manage our corporate social responsibilities effectively, we divide our CSR stakeholders into five key groups:
> - Our customers
> - Our community
> - Our suppliers
> - Our people
> - The environment

We were unable to determine the ratio of women to men on the board.

CSR report: A CSR report is published annually. At the time of writing (January 2015) the latest CSR report available was for 2012.

Exclusions

Our research indicates that no support is given for advertising in charity brochures, animal welfare, appeals from individuals, children/youth, elderly people, fundraising events, medical research, overseas projects, political appeals, religious appeals, science/technology, sickness/disability, social welfare or sport.

Applications

For details of the Shop Direct Charitable Foundation, visit Community Foundation for Merseyside's website: www.cfmerseyside.org.uk.

Siemens plc

Electronics/computers, transport and communications

Correspondent: Claire Jarvis, Director of Communications, Sir William Siemens Square, Frimley, Camberley, Surrey GU16 8QD (tel: 01276 696000; website: www.siemens.co.uk)

Directors: Juergen Maier, Chief Executive; Andrew Hall, Chief Financial Officer; Helen Carless (women: 1; men: 2)

Year end	30/09/2013
Turnover	£2,664,590,000
Pre-tax profit	£235,585,000

Nature of business: Siemen's principal activities in the UK cover manufacture and sale of products in the areas of: electricity generation and distribution, transportation systems, industrial and building automation, metallurgical engineering and healthcare equipment and services. The company are also provides IT and other business infrastructure services.

The company is a subsidiary of the Siemens Group AG.

Company registration number: 727817

Subsidiary undertakings include: A full list of subsidiary undertakings can be found within the parent company's (Siemens AG) consolidated accounts.

Main locations: Birmingham, Banbury, Basildon, Frimley, Swindon, Telford, Wellingborough, Worcester, Congelton, Cirencester, Manchester, London, Newcastle, Milton Keynes, Nottingham, Oxford, Reading, Poole, Harrogate, Harrow, Ipswich, Hayes, Langley, Hitchin, Hinckley, Lincoln, Crawley, Staines, Ramsey, Walton on Thames

Total employees: 8,339

Focus of giving: Education, environment, STEM (science, technology, engineering and mathematics), children, young people, community/social welfare, disasters.

Membership: BITC, LBG

Cash donations undeclared	✓
Gifts in kind	✓
Payroll giving	✓
Sponsorship	✓

Charitable donations

Cash UK (latest available):	2013	£132,000
	2011	£270,000
	2009	£62,516
	2007	£62,516
	2006	£90,970
Total UK (cash and in kind):	2013	£132,000
Cash worldwide:	2013	£1,700,000
Total worldwide (cash and in kind):	2013	£1,700,000

Community involvement

The company focuses on activities that will 'improve education, help the development of young and vulnerable people, improve local environments and assist in disaster relief'.

The corporate citizenship is aimed to cover three areas: scientific, technical and engineering education; social and community assistance; and environmental protection and conservation. Help can be given to organisations, including charities, schools and environmental groups, also other local groups.

Greenpower
This educational trust is supported to inspire more young people to become engineers through encouraging schools to build and compete in regional and national events with electric cars.

Siemens Education
The company offers an interactive portal where pupils, teachers, parents and employees can find out information about STEM (science, technology, engineering, maths) related opportunities.

OCR
Siemens Education and the qualification body OCR (Oxford Cambridge and RSA) partnered to bring to provide educational resources for 14- to 16-year-olds.

Corporate giving

The UK website provides a table of 2013 sustainability performance. It states that 'Investment in improving society' totalled £1.7 million, 'Volunteering days (education)' totalled 1,205 days and 'Volunteering days (community)' totalled 666 days. The Sustainability at Siemens UK 2013 paper says that 'Siemens invested £2 million supporting employee volunteering and social programmes in the UK during 2013.' We have taken the lower figure to represent the company's total community contributions. We could not determine the amount awarded in cash in the UK; based on the figures from previous three years known to us we estimate that about £132,000 was given.

In-kind support

Staff volunteering efforts.

Employee-led support

The website notes that 'all employees are encouraged and supported through their local businesses to do voluntary work in the community'. In 2013 staff donated a total of 1,871 days of volunteering.

Payroll giving
A payroll giving scheme operates with 10% of employees participating in 2013.

Commercially led support

Sponsorships

- Big Bang Fair – for the fifth year Siemens was a major sponsor of the Big Bang Fair
- Museum of Science and Industry – Siemens supports activities, including Manchester Science Festival, STEMNET and the Saturday Science programme
- The Hallé – having supported the Hallé for a number of years Siemens is now a major sponsor and assists the organisations on their education programme and other initiatives
- The Curiosity Project – through this three-year engagement programme Siemens will sponsor major science related festivals throughout the UK (five in 2014)
- Infiniti Red Bull Racing – 'Infiniti Red Bull Racing develops and manufactures its championship winning car at the UK headquarters in Milton Keynes relying on a broad selection of Siemens PLM Software technologies.' In addition technical and business support is provided by the Siemens PLM professional services team

Corporate social responsibility

CSR committee: The company's website states the following:

> Siemens global sustainability organisation is led by Chief Sustainability Officer and Global Board Director. In the UK, sustainability responsibility sits with the Chief Executive Officer and the Executive Management Board. Co-ordination of UK operations is the responsibility of Head of Sustainability.

CSR information: Information taken from the UK website states: 'For Siemens, sustainability means acting in the best interest of coming generations – with respect to the environment, our business and society.'

CSR report: There is an Annual Sustainability Report and Update. Some details on community involvement are available online.

Exclusions

Political donations are not made. The company will not consider sponsorships for sports events or teams.

Applications

In writing to the correspondent.

SIG plc

Building materials, distribution

Correspondent: The Charities Committee, Corporate office, Signet House, 17 Europa View, Sheffield Business Park, Sheffield S9 1XH (tel: 01142 856300; fax: 01142 856385; email: info@sigplc.co.uk; website: www.sigplc.co.uk)

Directors: Leslie Van de Walle, Chair; Chris Geoghegan; Jonathan Nicholls; Janet Ashdown; Stuart Michell, Chief Executive Officer; Doug Robertson, Finance Director; Mel Ewell (women: 1; men: 6)

Year end	31/12/2013
Turnover	£2,719,800,000
Pre-tax profit	£2,100,000

Nature of business: The principal activity of the group is the supply of specialist products to construction and related markets in the UK, Ireland and Mainland Europe. The main products distributed are Insulation and Energy Management, Exteriors and Interiors.

Note: The figure for UK employees includes The Republic of Ireland.

Company registration number: 998314

Subsidiary undertakings include: Insulation Distributors Ltd; SIG Energy Management Ltd; SIG Nederland B.V.; SIG Trading Ltd; and WeGo Systembaustoffe GmbH.

Main locations: Sheffield, Southampton, Barking, Littleborough, Leominster, Leicester, London, Maidstone, Crawley, Cardiff, Wednesbury, Hyde, St Ives

UK employees: 5,070

Total employees: 9,335

Focus of giving: Education, children, young people, community/social welfare.

Membership: BITC

Market-led giving	✓
Matched funding	✓
Payroll giving	✓
Sponsorship	✓

Charitable donations

Cash UK (latest available):	2013	£109,000
	2011	£145,000
	2009	£138,000
	2008	£169,000
	2007	£162,000
Total UK (cash and in kind):	2013	£109,000
Cash worldwide:	2013	£109,000
Total worldwide (cash and in kind):	2013	£109,000

Community involvement

The group supports charities and community projects mainly in the areas where it operates. According to the SIG Ethics Policy, which can be found on the website: 'Each business unit is encouraged to develop programmes, which address the needs of their local community.'

The information quoted in the rest of this entry is taken from the Corporate Responsibility Report for 2013.

The group's main focus is on charities and community projects that:

- Enhance its engagement in the community
- Assist in managing the sustainability of the local environment
- Educate young people
- Assist disadvantaged groups

In 2013 SIG Energy Management in Leeds helped an inner city primary school by recycling materials from an ECO project to transform the school grounds.

According to the SIG 2013 CSR report, to support employees' fundraising efforts 'SIG also continued support of the Sheffield Children's Hospital through replacing Christmas cards with an additional donation to the hospital.'

Business in the Community

The group has been a co-operating member and has also enrolled on the Community's Business Class Programme to partner with local UK secondary schools for a period of three years, principally in in the most deprived communities. Starting in 2014 'the head teacher of the local school will drive the agenda with SIG working closely with the school across several key areas: leadership and governance, enterprise and employability, the curriculum and wider issues'.

Charitable activities are also undertaken in Mainland Europe, an example of such activities is as stated on the group's website:

> The sponsorship provided by WeGo Systembaustoffe GmbH to the seventh Hanau Soapbox Derby – a local initiative that promotes community involvement, team working, creativity and inter-generational involvement. The proceeds from the derby will be used to build a child-friendly outdoor play area at a local after-school care centre.

Corporate giving

In 2013 the group made donations totalling £109,000 (2012: £124,000).

Beneficiaries have included: Cancer Research UK; Comic Relief; Dementia UK; Leeds Children's Hospital; Motor Neurone Disease Association; and The British Heart Foundation.

Employee-led support

The group's employees participate in in a range of initiatives to support local communities, such as taking part in the Sheffield Half Marathon, football matches or fundraising in branches. For example, SIG Insulation Leeds staff raised £10,000 and SIG's Graduates completed a three dams challenge, held donut sales and organised a raffle to raise £5,000 for Sheffield Children's Hospital which will be used towards creating an Ante Room.

According to the SIG 2013 CSR report: 'The group actively encourages its UK employees to help charities through a dedicated intranet forum for employees to highlight their fundraising efforts and receive support from their colleagues.'

Charities supported by employees include: Cancer Research UK; Dementia UK; Leeds Children's Hospital; and The British Heart Foundation.

Payroll giving

The scheme allows UK employees to donate to their chosen charities. During the year £20,000 was given.

Matched funding

There is a matched funding initiative allowing employees to apply for a donation of up to £500 to match their fundraising efforts. In 2013 a total of £34,000 was raised through the programme and benefited charities, including: African Child Foundation (Kenya); Cancer Research UK; Comic Relief; Leeds Children's Hospital; Mama Cash (Netherlands); Motor Neurone Disease Association; and Roparun Foundation (Netherlands).

Commercially led support

The group has been the main sponsor of the Sheffield Half Marathon event for six years.

Education and training

The Apprenticeship Programme, launched in 2012, continues 'to attract talented individuals to the organisation, as well as supporting people looking to gain qualifications and work experience'. The Apprenticeship Development Programme has also been established and is 'bringing [the] apprentices together and building on key skills to support their career development'. There are also Graduate and Placement Programmes available.

Corporate social responsibility

CSR committee: The CR Committee, established in 2009, regularly accounts to the Executive Board on the significance of social, environmental and ethical matters to the business:

> The committee has a rolling three year plan which informs the CR objectives and target actions of the group and drives continual improvement of its CR performance. The Group Chief Executive has lead responsibility for policy implementation within the group and this policy is signed by the CEO to demonstrate the board's commitment.

The group's Human Resources Director is responsible for community issues and reports to the Chief Executive, who is accountable for community issues at the Executive Board level.

The Charities Committee approves applications (from employees) for matched donations and ensures that they are in line with SIG's Charitable Donations Policy.

CSR information: The Corporate Responsibility Report for 2013 states: 'SIG has a clear approach to business integrity and ethics which underlines the group's core values of openness, collaboration, mutual dependency, sustainability, profitable growth and innovation.'

The website maintains that:

> SIG continues to progressively integrate corporate responsibility across the group. It believes that the inclusion of broader social and environmental issues into its decision making will support the group in achieving its business goals as well as growing shareholder value.

The group's Corporate Responsibility Strategy focuses on workplace, environment, marketplace and community.

CSR report: Contained within the annual report and accounts.

Exclusions

The group has a policy not to support:

- Political parties
- Books, research papers or articles in professional journals
- Faith related causes, organisations or activities
- Anything that conflicts with its Ethics Policy

Applications

In writing to the correspondent.

Simmons & Simmons LLP

Legal

Correspondent: The Employee Relations and CR Team, CityPoint, One Ropemaker Street, London EC2Y 9SS (tel: 020 7825 3814; fax: 020 7628 2070; email: corporate.responsibility@simmons-simmons.com; website: www.simmons-simmons.com)

Directors: Colin Passmore, Chair; Jeremy Hoyland; Alex Brown; Fiona Loughrey; Alyson Lockett; Peter Meyer; Leo Verhoeff; Patrick Wallace; Rodger Hughes; David McLaughlin, Finance Director; David Staiano; Michael Woodford (women: 2; men: 10)

Year end	30/04/2014
Turnover	£265,953,000
Pre-tax profit	£75,344,000

Nature of business: Simmons & Simmons LLP is a limited liability partnership providing legal services and international tax advice.

Company registration number: OC352713

Subsidiary undertakings include: Beaufield Ltd; SimmLaw Services Ltd; Simmons & Simmons East Asia LLP; and Simmons & Simmons CIS LLP. A full list of subsidiaries can be found in the firm's accounts.

Main locations: London

Total employees: 1,262

Focus of giving: Human rights, education, environment, equal opportunities, health, ill health, arts, culture, sponsorship, women's issues, children, young people, community/social welfare, disability.

Cash donations undeclared	✓
Gifts in kind	✓
Market-led giving	✓
Overseas giving	✓
Sponsorship	✓

Charitable donations

Cash UK (latest available):	2014	£80,000
	2011	£80,000
	2010	£80,000
Total UK (cash and in kind):	2014	£5,000,000
Cash worldwide:	2014	£80,000
Total worldwide (cash and in kind):	2014	£5,000,000

Community involvement

Simmons & Simmons Charitable Foundation

The foundation was established in 2009 to support 'access to justice, work and opportunities' and prefers 'smaller charities where the funding can be shown to make a sustainable impact' or organisations 'in which the firm's staff can have an active involvement and address social inclusion'.

The Twist Partnership

The firm is in a partnership with the programme to support a youth inclusion programme Step Up which, according to the CR section on the firm's website:

> Aims to empower young people from Tower Hamlets who are at risk of offending or exclusion from school by giving them the responsibility to organise and execute a large project, supported by members of the firm, and the opportunity of work experience placements across the business services departments.

The Young Talent Programme

Through this secondary school programme the firm works in partnership with Frederick Bremer School in Walthamstow (London), supports the Social Mobility Business Compact, assists PRIME and works with the Twist Partnership. The programme is aimed at Year 10 students and offers a series of interventions and mentoring, including work experience, presentations, workshops and paid internships. Students are supported for up to seven years – while at school and college – and, an ongoing mentoring as well as an opportunity to apply for a bursary from the firm's charitable foundation once in university. At the end of 2013/14 financial year 36 people had been selected onto the programme. The firm notes in its 2013/14 CR review:

> Through ongoing development of the programme, we have strengthened our relationship with the school and its teaching staff and identified additional opportunities for collaboration and support involving our staff network groups. We have also partnered with our clients and suppliers and are delighted that they have volunteered their time to deliver challenging and thought provoking skills based sessions to the students. Our onsite suppliers have also offered work shadowing opportunities.

Moreland Primary School Mentoring Scheme

London office has been sending volunteers to Moreland Primary School in Islington to provide reading support once a week to children. The scheme is the firm's longest running social inclusion scheme. In 2013/14 a partnership was initiated with Create to further develop work with the school. 'Create used a donation from the Simmons & Simmons Charitable Foundation to take its 'A Wealth Of Stages' (AWOS) programme to two classes of children at [the school]'in order to provide an opportunity for 'children from the most deprived boroughs of London to develop financial literacy and literacy through non classroom-based creative activities led by professional drama artists'.

Access 2 Law

The scheme 'helps students from disadvantaged backgrounds to realise opportunities in commercial law' and 'has supported students from Tower Hamlets College and Crossways College in London from AS levels through to training contracts with mentoring and soft skills training'. The firm provides annual contributions towards university fees and legal work experience placements through the Charitable Foundation sponsorship scheme.

Visionpath

The Visionpath SKILL! Programme is funded through the charitable foundation and offers workshops on enterprise to engage young Londoners and provide them with essential skills to gain employment. The firm's staff work with the participants in order to increase their understanding of the communication and presentation skills.

Tsolmon – Ireedui Foundation (Hong Kong)

Advice has been provided on establishing the foundation, which aims to support poor and orphaned children in Mongolia. The Hong Kong office also donates items for the charity's winter clothing collections to children in Ulan Bator.

Arts and culture

The 2013/14 CR review states that:

> Through sponsorship and pro bono work the firm is committed to providing access to opportunities to engage with some of the most interesting aspects of contemporary art and culture. The firm been an associate sponsor of the Donmar Warehouse theatre since April 2010 and has longstanding pro bono relationships with Frieze London and English National Ballet.

Lawyers Volunteering for the Arts

The firm is a participant of the Lawyers Volunteering for the Arts scheme which provides legal advice to arts community organisations. A partnership with Frieze is established with the firm donating pro bono assistance to both Frieze Foundation and the art fair and magazine.

The Simmons & Simmons Contemporary Art Collection

The collection 'was designed to support young artists early in their careers and to develop a showcase for their work outside the traditional gallery environment'. In 2013 the first Artist in Residence was accepted to the London office and was given an opportunity to collaborate with both members of the firm and pupils and staff from the community partner Frederick Bremer School.

Centre for Recent Drawing

The centre is a museum space in Islington 'dedicated to the promotion of drawing in all its forms'. The firm assists in 'areas of IP, tax and property to enable this charity to use all its fund-raised money towards its objectives'.

Pro bono

Pro bono activities are provided globally and constitute the main form of support offered of by the firm. Some examples given in the CR Review for 2013/14 are as follows:

In the UK:

LawWorks

Recognising 'the impact of the legal aid cuts made in England and Wales from April 2013 on the most vulnerable in the community'the firm 'has increased its commitment and support provided to both individuals and community groups via LawWorks'. During the year eight community group projects and four cases or mediations for individuals have been taken on.

Legal advice clinics

The firm provides a weekly clinic at the Battersea branch of South West London Law Centres (SWLLC), which is the longest running pro bono scheme (the firm's involvement spanning over 27 years).

A monthly advice clinic at Queen Mary University of London 'Supporting Those Who Serve' is also available for members of the armed services and ex-services members 'for whom the clinic has plugged a gap identified in the provision of legal services'.

Staff from London IP team attend monthly clinics at the University of the Arts for Own-It (an advice centre offering intellectual property advice to creative businesses).

National Society for the Protection of Cruelty to Children (NSPCC)

The organisation has been assisted on various IP matters, including the filing and registration of trade marks.

The Big Issue Foundation

Simmons & Simmons LLP for six years has been participating in the Big Issue Vendor Development Programme allowing a vendor raise their revenue by selling copies of the magazine in the London office. Every six months a vendor is invited to join the firm to sell copies of the magazine and complete a personalised training programme.

The Big Issue Foundation is also provided with free legal advice, including:

> Negotiating contracts with commercial partners for TBIF's fundraising activities, advising on a project to provide all Big Issue vendors with free SIM cards for their mobile phones, and advising TBIF on various litigation matters, such as intellectual property rights.

London's Air Ambulance

The charity has been advised on employment law and HR issues through support on any day-to-day as well as more complex aspects.

Western Front Association

For two years the firm has represented this educational charity with branches in the UK and abroad 'committed to preserving the history and heritage of the Great War 1914–18'. The firm maintains that support to the organisation included: 'protection of the WFA's logo and name, raising money for the upkeep of the Welsh Memorial on the Somme by threatening to sue companies that were making replica statuettes without permission, and defending the Association against legal action from a publisher'. It is further noted: 'Our involvement in this area has been well received by clients and we now join with Barclays each year on Poppy Day in the City to raise money for veterans.'

The Gender Equality Project
Legal advice was given to the project regarding the registration of the foundation's certification mark and licensing agreement between the foundation and certified companies.

Schools OUT
Assistance was given to this organisation 'dealing with issues of homophobia and the visibility and safety of LGBT people in the education system', regarding its application to register as a Charitable Incorporated Organisation.

Royal National Institute for Blind People (RNIB)
Legal help, including drafting and negotiating an IT services contract and advising on the licensing issues.

Kids Company
The firm's Bristol Real Estate department advised the KidsCo in relation to their new Bristol office premises, replicating their model for youth work outside Greater London.

Internationally:

Dubai Caledonian Society
The firm's UAE offices assisted this organisation which raises funds for charities both in Scotland and the UAE. Advice was given on key constitution changes and the legal and practical consequences for the society and help with drafting of sponsorship contracts.

Voices for Families Scheme
The firm joined forces with the scheme, which seeks to assist children and young people with life-limiting or life-threatening conditions, and their families. Twelve volunteers undertook training to provide support to families under this scheme.

De Clinic
In Amsterdam the firm supports De Clinic: 'a law clinic run by students of Amsterdam universities providing free of charge legal advice to private individuals and start up enterprises in the fields of technology, media and telecommunications'. Apart from the advice provided to students in various legal issues, the firm might help court proceedings, in discrete cases.

Tablée des Chefs
The firm's Paris office has supported the Canadian NGO 'which sets up partnerships with restaurants and catering services to recover leftover goods and distribute them to food banks, as well as organising events and fundraisers relating to nutrition awareness and food autonomy'. The organisation received advice on its development in France.

Teach for China Inc
The organisation (which is Teach for All's only partner in China and follows the model of Teach for America) works to eliminate educational inequity in China by 'recruiting talented young people with excellent educational backgrounds from both China and the US and sending them to teach children in remote areas of China where there is a severe deficiency of educational resource'. It has been advised on legal matters, including employment, corporate and immigration issues in China.

Christian Aid
Advice services have been provided to Christian Aid on matters involving land rights in Colombia, complaints procedures, human rights and strategies for improving consultation with local indigenous communities. The firm states that there is a 'growing pro bono expertise connected to human rights and to Colombia'.

NGONET
There is an ongoing pro bono legal support for the Maasai people in Tanzania, which helped to retain a portion of proposed hunting ground land in favour of the local villages in 2013.This case is one of three in which the firm is working with the organisation.

Oxfam Hong Kong
Local teams have been advising the organisation which works on poverty alleviation and emergency relief in China focusing on 'rural community development, livelihood improvement, emergency relief, gender equity, advocacy, basic education, small-scale infrastructure, healthcare improvement and NGO development' on employment issues, intellectual property, general commercial legal advice and contract reviews.

Acumen Fund
The organisation was given advice on the development of the Acumen Safaa Giving Program, a Shariah informed philanthropic giving initiative. Acumen 'uses entrepreneurial approaches to change the way the world tackles poverty by investing in companies, leaders, and ideas' and 'helps to build financially sustainable businesses that provide affordable goods and services to improve the lives of the poor'.

Audaces Foundation
The firm's Italian offices assisted the foundation which 'highlights and advance leading models of sustainable social innovation', on the requirements to establish a UK Charitable Incorporated Organisation and the establishment of a charitable institution in Belgium.

Corporate giving

The amount awarded in cash contributions could not be determined. The firm estimates the pro bono work undertaken by its fee earners to have a value of over £5 million in 2013/14. It is also noted that 25% of donations from the charitable foundation were to projects outside the UK.

The Simmons & Simmons Charitable Foundation
The foundation's 2012/13 accounts state that the company gave it a £120,000 donation. Grants were made to over 17 organisations totalling £173,000. Grants were broken down as follows:

International	£62,000
Social inclusion	£52,000
Pro bono	£43,000
Other	£16,000

See the corporate charity entry on p. 428 for more information.

In-kind support

Pro bono
The firm provides pro bono services in the UK and internationally. Currently over 140 pro bono clients and 400 projects are supported on projects in jurisdictions in developing markets. In the past year particular focus was placed on Colombia and Africa focused NGOs and charities. New projects are taken on through: Advocates for International Development (A4ID); LawWorks; Lawyers Volunteering for the Arts; PURE Leapfrog; The International Senior Lawyers Project – UK; and TrustLaw (the Thomson Reuters Foundation's global pro bono service).

The CR Review values the pro bono work undertaken by its fee earners at over £5 million with 14,957 pro bono hours given in 2013/14. For more examples of projects supported see the 'Community involvement' section in this entry.

Employee-led support

There are employee fundraising, volunteering activities and initiatives globally, such as:

Sunshine Action
Hong Kong office organised a number of charitable events to raise funds for this organisation, which provides health and welfare support to low-income families and individuals living in Hong Kong.

Debate Mate
Helping this international educational charity associates and trainees from the London office attended and mentored the organisation's weekly sessions at the Central Foundation Boys School.

Staff Networks
There are a number of networks run by the firm's employees, such as The Number One Club (Women's Network),

which organises various events. Some examples of the network's initiatives, as listed in the company's 2013/14 CR review, include:

- Smart Works Professional Development Day – coinciding with International Women's Day 'the network hosted a professional development day with the charity Smart Works' which 'helps women on low incomes to find employment and become financially independent'
- In conjunction with the above the London office had a 'clothes drive' collecting work clothing for Smart Works and for the charity Suited and Booted (for men)
- BAFTA film screening – the network hosted an event organised by Women for Women International (a pro bono client of the firm)

Payroll giving

In the past there has been a payroll scheme operating; however, we did not find details of such scheme in the latest CR Review.

Commercially led support

UNICEF

Simmons & Simmons LLP has been in an ongoing legal partnership with UNICEF Netherlands since 2006, with the firm providing a range of legal advice, including tax and employment matters, at a significantly reduced rate. The firm sponsors the UNICEF Chair in Children's Rights Studies at Leiden University in the Netherlands.

Macmillan and the Alzheimer's Society

The firm's London Employment team is partners with Macmillan Cancer Support and provides employment advice on a wide range of Human Resource issues for a minimum agreed fee. Similar arrangements are present with the Alzheimer's Society where support includes conducting HR training sessions.

Corporate social responsibility

CSR committee: In the past a CSR Committee was present.

CSR information: The firm's annual report and accounts for 2013/14 specifies its CSR strategy being 'focused on social inclusion, pro bono, diversity, gender balance and environment. This provides an inclusive and supportive working environment for all members of the firm and enables staff to engage with the local community and key clients from across the network'.

The CR Review for 2013/14 states that the main theme of the CR Strategy is 'Access'. More specifically the following four strands:

- Supporting young people in education to access work and opportunities
- Making the world of work, and the legal profession in particular, more accessible to people from a diverse range of backgrounds and circumstances
- Making legal services and funding more accessible through pro bono legal work and donations from the Simmons & Simmons Charitable Foundation
- Supporting environmental issues and minimising the impact the firm has on the environment

The impact of the above is assessed within the local communities, the workplace and the environment, 'ensuring that at all times the business maintains its ethical standards'.

CSR report: A CSR report is available from the company's website.

Corporate charity: The Simmons & Simmons Charitable Foundation (Charity Commission no. 1129643).

Applications

Application forms for the foundation are available from the firm's website. Other queries regarding the firm's charitable activities can be directed to the correspondent.

Slaughter and May (Trust Ltd)

Legal

Correspondent: Kate Hursthouse, The Slaughter and May Charitable Trust, One Bunhill Row, London EC1Y 8YY (tel: 020 7600 1200 or 020 7090 3433 (Charitable Trust); fax: 020 7090 5000; email: corporateresponsibility@slaughterandmay.com; website: www.slaughterandmay.com)

Directors: Chris Saul; Paul Olney; Mark Bennett; Rebecca Cousin; John Nevin; Sandeep Maudgil; Richard Clark; Nick Gray (women: 1; men: 7)

Year end	30/04/2013

Nature of business: Slaughter and May is a law firm, regulated by the Solicitors Regulation Authority. We have used the information of the non-charitable Slaughter and May Trust Ltd company for the main company details. All the shares in the company are beneficially owned by the partners of Slaughter and May.

Company registration number: 335458

Main locations: London

Total employees: 1,140

Focus of giving: Education, enterprise/training, environment, inner cities, local groups, poverty and social exclusion, children, young people, community/social welfare.

Charity of the Year	✓
Gifts in kind	✓
Matched funding	✓
Overseas giving	✓
Payroll giving	✓
Sponsorship	✓

Charitable donations

Cash UK (latest available):	2013	£283,000
	2011	£351,400
	2009	£461,000
	2008	£333,000
Cash worldwide:	2013	£283,000

Community involvement

The Slaughter and May Charitable Trust (Charity Commission no. 1082765)

The firm's charitable donations are made through the corporate charity. The trust's annual report for 2013/14 states that it is 'reliant on its key donors, the partners of Slaughter and May' with all administrative and other office support being provided by the firm.

In the London borough of Islington there are partnerships with local schools and charities – 12 local community partners are supported and direct work is undertaken with around 400 beneficiaries.

Legal Social Mobility Partnership

The programme was developed following a joint initiative between Slaughter and May and ITV whereby students spent 'a week at the firm working on a mock legal task for ITV followed by two days with ITV's in-house legal team'. It co-operates with more than ten organisations to provide work experience opportunities and insight into the legal profession. In 2014 six students from Central Foundation Boys' School spent a day at ITV, Harlequins Rugby, Microsoft, MTV and Yahoo! following a week's work experience with the firm and further 14 people from three other London schools were meant to participate later.

City Solicitors' Educational Trust

The firm is a founding member of the trust funded by 'City law firms working together for the benefit of the wider legal profession' and helps it with financial sponsorship and in-kind support.

Pro bono

Pro bono services are offered to charities and individuals through two channels:

- Law Centre volunteering – according to the firm's website, every week the firm provides 'a team of volunteer advisers to staff an evening advice clinic at Islington Law Centre and an additional team of qualified litigators serve as Honorary Legal Advisers at the RCJ Advice Bureau'
- Charity clients – the firm supports its charity partners and 'actively seeks ways in which legal expertise might be used to support their causes'

The website also states that it has 'a network of partners in each of our practice areas who act as 'pro bono champions', encouraging pro bono work in their practice area' and that 'there is a strong appetite for international pro bono work among lawyers and we seek to use the breadth of our legal expertise to help NGOs and charities working in developing countries'.

The firm is a member of pro bono referral organisations, for example, LawWorks A4ID and TrustLaw (a global centre for free legal assistance run by the Thomson Reuters Foundation). International activities included:

- Provision of ongoing legal advice to African Revival – a charity working in Zambia, Uganda and South Sudan to provide children with a quality education
- Advising on the establishment of Lawyers for Justice in Libya
- Supporting the Capital Cases Charitable Trust providing 'pro bono representation to prisoners in the Caribbean sentenced to capital and non-capital terms in their appeals to the Judicial Committee of the Privy Council'

The Citizens Advice at the Royal Courts of Justice

Together with several other firms Slaughter and May provides Honorary Legal Advisers (volunteer lawyers), to work alongside the Citizens Advice's staff and advisers. The volunteers also contribute through annual donations and one of the firm's partners is a trustee of the organisation.

University House Legal Advice Centre (Bethnal Green)

The charity has been assisted for more than 15 years through pro bono and financial support.

Schools

Partnerships are undertaken with local primary and secondary schools, such as St Luke's Primary School, Moreland School and Central Foundation Boys' School. Staff volunteers work with young people on literacy, employability and enterprise projects.

Central Foundation Boys' School

In partnership with educational charity The Access Project the Key Project at Central Foundation was introduced in 2012 to help students achieve places at top universities through guidance on UCAS applications, career insight sessions and career networking events.

Slaughter and May is a founding member of PRIME initiative which aims to provide fair access to quality work experience. The social mobility project (see above) is part of the commitment to PRIME.

Primary Partners programme

The programme has facilitated partnerships with local primary schools for over ten years. According to the firm's website, the programme includes:

- Reading partners – volunteers offer much-needed reading support to primary school children. This is the longest running non-legal volunteering project, typically involving 40 volunteers at any one time
- Sports partners – volunteers coach pupils in football, cricket and other sporting activities over lunchtimes. The local primary school football league is also sponsored
- Green partners – volunteers spend one lunchtime a week at Moreland School's eco garden, planting vegetables and plants
- Sponsorship of the National Literacy Trust's Young Readers' Programme – this enables children to learn the excitement of owning their own books

Charities

The information quoted in this section is taken from the firm's website. Slaughter and May focuses 'on a small number of charities to ensure that each receives the level of support it needs', including 'legal and strategic expertise, volunteer participation, annual donations and in-kind assistance, such as hosting meetings and events'.

The Corporate Responsibility Brochure notes the firm working with: ACDiversity; BLD Foundation; Blind in Business; Business Disability Forum; Capital Cases Charitable Trust; Citizenship Foundation; InterLaw Diversity Forum for LGBT Networks; London Symphony Orchestra's Youth Choir; Opportunity Now and Race for Opportunity; Pure Potential; Rare; and Stonewall.

Charity partnerships

There are two key charity partnerships made since 2008: The National Literacy Trust and Carers Trust. Aside from pro bono activities in both organisations, the firm has provided financial support, maintains a legal toolkit sent out to all Carers Trust Network Partners, sponsors the National Literacy Trust's Young Readers' Programme 'designed to help children in disadvantaged areas develop a love of reading' and funds the National Literacy Trust's 'annual omnibus survey looking into literacy in young people aged 8–16 in the UK'.

CoRe (Community Resourcing) programme.

The firm collaborates with its client Macquarie and the Cripplegate Foundation on the programme as part of the focus on Islington and support of the BIG Alliance (Businesses for Islington Giving). 'The initiative puts volunteers into local Islington charities to provide strategic support and help them become more sustainable.' In 2013 a total of 33 volunteers were matched with six local charities donating over 1,500 hours of their time.

St Luke's Community Centre

Since 2008 the firm has worked closely with the centre 'to develop bespoke projects, tailored to the needs of the local community'. The collaboration included:

- Firm Futures project helping local unemployed people become self-employed – volunteers acted as business mentors and the firm provided cash bursaries to help the beneficiaries set up their own businesses
- PC Pals project aiming 'to support older local residents as they develop computer literacy skills and learn how to use the internet' with a number of employees volunteering
- Job Club with 'groups of volunteers attending weekly sessions to work directly with the long-term unemployed to support them with job applications'

Corporate giving

Charitable donations are, in the main, channelled through The Slaughter and May Charitable Trust. The trust's accounts for 2013/14 state that the trust received donations from partners of Slaughter and May totalling £267,000 and 'an advance from Slaughter and May of £67,000 that was outstanding at the year end, all of which was pending receipt of the tax recoverable from HMRC'.

The trust's accounts for 2013/14 say:

> The Slaughter and May Charitable Trust is funded principally by donations and gifted services (including the audit fee) from the partners of Slaughter and May. The directors of Slaughter and May Trust Ltd are all partners of Slaughter and May, the charity's main donors.

Beneficiaries have included: the Access Project, National Literacy Trust, Carers Trust, Islington Law Centre, St Luke's Parochial Trust, Legal Advice Centre Bethnal Green, BIG Alliance for the CORE Programme and London Symphony Orchestra.

Note: although the company's accounts were only available for 2012/13, the trust's accounts were available for 2013/14.

See the corporate charity entry on p. 429 for more information.

In-kind support

Pro bono work, staff volunteering time and expertise.

Employee-led support

The firm's website notes that half of its employees are participating in the community and pro bono work and it 'supports the philanthropy of employees through a number of initiatives, including Payroll Giving and Funds for Fundraisers scheme, as well as employee-led charity fundraising initiatives'.

There is the Employee Charity Committee where 'staff vote for their favourite UK charities and a committee of volunteers takes responsibility for planning and organising fundraising initiatives throughout the year'.

In December each year the firm's 'employees generously purchase presents from a list of items which are given out to the local residents at a special Christmas lunch', as part of the St Luke's Community Centre partnership (see 'Community involvement' section in this entry).

Furthermore, every year, volunteers collect money at a local underground station for the Royal British Legion for Poppy Day and take part in the annual London Legal Walk to raise money for the London Legal Support Trust.

Payroll giving

The firm operates payroll giving scheme and covers the administration costs.

Matched funding

Funds for Fundraisers scheme allows 'support of £500 to employees who fundraise in their own time for charities and schools'. Future trainees are also eligible to apply for the contribution.

Employees participate in a wide range of pro bono activities, organised by the firm. It constitutes a significant part of Slaughter and May support and further details of particular projects can be found in the 'Community involvement' section in this entry.

Commercially led support

The firm sponsors the National Pro Bono Centre.

Corporate social responsibility

CSR committee: There is a CSR Committee, chaired by Mark Bennett.

CSR information: The firm's website states:

> We are committed to acting responsibly and work hard to make a positive impact on the world around us. We provide long-term strategic support to a number of charities and local schools and are committed to reducing our carbon emissions.
>
> We aim to be an example of best practice in all of our community and environment activities - the full backing of the firm's partnership enables us to achieve this.

CSR report: No specific report was available but information on corporate responsibility is given online. The charitable trust's accounts are available from the Charity Commission website.

Corporate charity: The Slaughter and May Charitable Trust (Charity Commission no. 1082765).

Applications

The firm's CSR Committee meets regularly to review its policies and activities.

Note: Although the firm is proactive in supporting charitable groups, unfortunately it is unable to accept unsolicited funding applications from schools, charities or individuals.

The trust's 2013/14 annual report states that it 'makes annual grants at its discretion to a small number of specific charitable causes and does not generally accept unsolicited funding applications'.

DS Smith Holdings plc

Print/paper/packaging

Correspondent: Charities and Communities Team, 7th Floor, 350 Euston Road, Regent's Place, London NW1 3AX (tel: 020 7756 1800; website: www.dssmith.uk.com)

Directors: Gareth Davies, Chair; Miles Roberts, Group Chief Executive; Adrian Marsh, Group Finance Director; Chris Britton; Sian Griffiths; Jonathan Nicholls; Kathleen O'Donovan; Louise Smalley; Matt Jowett (women: 3; men: 6)

Year end	30/04/2014
Turnover	£4,035,000,000
Pre-tax profit	£167,000,000

Nature of business: Production of corrugated and plastic packaging, primarily from recycled waste, and the distribution of office products.

Company registration number: 1377658

Subsidiary undertakings include: DS Smith Holdings Ltd; DS Smith Packaging Ltd; DS Smith Paper Ltd; DS Smith Logistics Ltd; DS Smith Recycling UK Ltd; DS Smith Kaysersberg S.A.S.; DS Smith Packaging France S.A.S.; DS Smith Packaging Netherlands B.V.; DS Smith Packaging Deutschland Stiftung and Co.; DS Smith Recycling Deutschland GmbH; DS Smith Polska sp. z o.o; Toscana Ondulati SpA; DS Smith Packaging Italia SpA; DS Smith Plastics Ltd UK; DS Smith Cartón Plástico s.a.; D.W. Plastics NV; DS Smith Ducaplast S.A.S.

Main locations: London

UK employees: 5,256

Total employees: 21,464

Focus of giving: Education, enterprise/ training, environment, poverty and social exclusion, sport, recreation, children, young people, community/ social welfare.

Cash donations undeclared	✓
Charity of the Year	✓
Gifts in kind	✓

Charitable donations

Cash UK (latest available):	2014	£37,000
	2011	£76,000
	2009	£78,000
	2008	£72,000
	2007	£71,000
Total UK (cash and in kind):	2014	£37,000
Cash worldwide:	2014	£37,000
Total worldwide (cash and in kind):	2014	£37,000

Community involvement

The company's charitable giving appears to be channelled mainly through its associated charity, **The DS Smith Charitable Foundation** (Charity Commission no. 1142817). Established in 2011 the foundation supports charities that help advance environmental protection, advance education and alleviate poverty, with a strong preference for the environment and the education of young people. According to the 2013/14 annual report of the foundation, the trustees meet annually to agree strategy and the processing and handling of applications is carried out by the relevant subcommittee. The key element to the foundation's strategy is the forming of long-term partnerships with well-established charities in the areas of environmental protection and advancing education. These partnerships generally run for three or more years and would involve both financial support and in-kind support through a programme run by the company DS Smith who state: 'As a large employer with a responsibility to the communities in which we operate, the charitable foundation also supports charities which help train young people and assist them into work'.

Partner charities

The company establishes partnerships which are intended to run for three or more years.

Corporate giving

The group has not declared its cash and community contributions in its annual report (as it has done in the past) and the only figure we have is that donated by the company to the foundation. We have therefore taken the £37,000 paid into the foundation as the UK cash contribution although we know that the actual figure is probably more than this. In-kind giving has not been costed and so unfortunately, we have no information to base an estimate on.

See the corporate charity entry on p. 429 for more information.

In-kind support

The company has a dedicated programme to encourage the giving of time and talents of employees. In addition the businesses work closely with local schools and colleges providing training, mentoring, work experience placements and other opportunities for pupils to learn about industry and business. The group is involved in a wide range of other local community activities including sponsorship of community projects or sports teams and provision of adult skills training.

Employee-led support

DS Smith supports its employees in a range of charitable fundraising activities. For example, in September 2014 a group of fundraising cyclists from DS Smith cycled more than 900 miles over 11 days across the UK in order to raise money for Heart Research UK and Cancer Research UK. The team exceeded their fundraising goal of £100,000 and raised £102,000.

Corporate social responsibility

CSR committee: We could not find details of the structure or members of a separate CSR committee.

CSR information: The following statement is taken from the company's website:

> Our core business is the design and manufacture of recycled packaging for consumer goods. We recognise that our operations have both direct and indirect impacts. Those are upstream through our sourcing activities and downstream through the ways our customers use and dispose of our products.
>
> At DS Smith we are committed to conducting our business in a responsible and sustainable manner. All of our activities are directed towards delighting our customers, creating value for our shareholders and providing our employees with a safe and productive work place.

There is an associated charitable foundation.

CSR report: The group's performance on the key areas of corporate responsibility are described in the KPI's, sustainability and environment pages in the group's annual report.

Corporate charity: The DS Smith Charitable Foundation (Charity Commission no. 1142817).

Exclusions

No support is given for advertising in charity brochures, animal welfare, appeals from individuals, the arts, fundraising events, overseas projects, political or religious appeals.

Applications

In writing to the correspondent for company giving and volunteers, pro bono work and other gifts in kind. For grants from the foundation, contact: Rachel Stephens, Trustee of the DS Charitable Foundation at the company's Euston Road address, or email: charitablefoundation@dssmith.com

An application form for the charitable foundation is available from the company's website in the sustainability section.

WH Smith plc

Retail – miscellaneous

Correspondent: The Corporate Responsibility Team, Greenbridge Road, Swindon, Wiltshire SN3 3RX (tel: 01793 616161; email: corporate.responsibility@whsmith.co.uk; website: www.whsmithplc.co.uk)

Directors: Robert Moorhead, Chief Financial Officer; Steve Clarke, Chief Executive Officer; Drummond Hall; Henry Staunton, Chair; Ian Houghton; Susan Baxter; Annemarie Durbin (women: 2; men: 5)

Year end	31/08/2014
Turnover	£1,161,000,000
Pre-tax profit	£112,000,000

Nature of business: The group's principal activities are the retail, publishing and news distribution.

WH Smith currently operates stores in 18 countries outside the UK. The website states that 'some 14,000 people in the UK' are employed by the group, therefore we take this figure to represent the number of UK employees.

Company registration number: 5202036

Subsidiary undertakings include: Spilt Ink Studio Ltd; WH Smith Australia Ltd; WH Smith High Street Holdings Ltd; WH Smith Hospitals Ltd; WH Smith Ireland Ltd; and WH Smith Travel Ltd. A full list of subsidiaries can be obtained from Companies House.

UK employees: 14,000

Total employees: 14,391

Focus of giving: Education, environment, fundraising events, health, ill health, large national appeals, medical research, non-registered charities, small groups, local groups, armed forces personnel, children, young people, community/social welfare.

Membership: BITC

Gifts in kind	✓
Market-led giving	✓
Matched funding	✓

Charitable donations

Cash UK (latest available):	2014	£817,000
	2011	£313,000
	2009	£343,800
	2008	£399,250
	2007	£600,300
Total UK (cash and in kind):	2014	£943,000
Cash worldwide:	2014	£817,000
Total worldwide (cash and in kind):	2014	£943,000

Community involvement

The group states in its Community Engagement Policy that it in line with its business it will 'focus many of [its] community investment projects on supporting literacy and promoting a love of reading'. Part of WH Smith's commitment is to 'invest pre-tax profits in support of schools and charities, primarily in the local communities where [it] operates'. The targets for the 2020 decade include investing £10 million in local communities through donations of cash, employee time and gifts in kind; working in partnership with the WH Smith Trust to help over 20,000 children discover the joy of reading; and raising over £1.25 million to support partner charities through staff and customer fundraising initiatives.

The WH Smith Group Charitable Trust (Charity Commission no. 1013782)

According to the Community Engagement Policy, the trust 'raises and distributes funds to charitable organisations in which members of staff are involved, and also supports projects to promote literacy'. It also 'actively supports employees who volunteer for or raise funds for charitable organisations or schools in their local community'.

Support to schools is also available through: grants to employees who are on the PTA or Board of Governors; schools being nominated by staff members; and a monthly prize draw which any school is eligible to enter.

World Book Day

WH Smith continues to take a leading role in the overall organisation of the UK's World Book Day initiative, designated by UNESCO and marked in over 100 countries around the globe. According to the WH Smith website, the event 'is sponsored by National Book Tokens, with a group of publishers, booksellers and interested parties all working together to promote the enjoyment of reading'.

Charity partnerships

National Literacy Trust

The group and the trust have been working in partnership with National Literacy Trust since 2005 on projects to promote reading for pleasure and recently a new three-year partnership has been confirmed in 2013/14. The website states that partnership 'should see over 20 schools and around 7,500 children aged 6 to 9 taking part in the National Literacy Trust's Young Readers Programme, which gives children the opportunity to discover the pleasure of reading and choose their own books to keep'. Participating schools are partnered with their local WH Smith store, enabling children to learn about bookshops and the wider world of work and participate in a range of educational or creative activities.

The Woodland Trust

The group's donations from sales of reusable carrier bags have funded the planting of over 157,000 trees since 2010.

International activities

The website states that throughout its 138 international stores WH Smith is equally 'keen to promote literacy and a love of reading in these locations as well as at home'. The initiatives have included a 'partnership with Maktaba local literature group promoting the reading of Arabic and English to children, who took over the books corner space in our flagship store in Doha to hold a reading event'.

Corporate giving

The group's website and CSR report for 2013/14 provide a helpful breakdown of charitable giving:

Cash donated	£817,000
Gifts in kind	£82,000
Management costs	£64,000
Staff time donated	£44,000

We take the figure of £943,000 (excluding management costs) to represent the group's total community contributions. It would appear that charitable giving is mainly concentrated in the UK.

Note: WH Smith uses the London Benchmarking Group's reporting model to calculate community contributions.

Beneficiaries have included: Alzheimer's Society; Battersea Cats and Dogs; Bonners Primary School; Brake; Cancer Research UK; Help for Heroes; Macmillan Cancer Support; National Literacy Trust; The WH Smith Group Charitable Trust; and The Woodland Trust.

In-kind support

Around 70% of WH Smith stores regularly support local schools and charities through donations of depreciated stock. WH Smith stores also help fundraise for other good causes (for example, selling poppies for the Royal British Legion) and the head offices regularly host charity fundraising events (usually driven by groups of employees).

Hospitals

For over three years, working through the WH Smith Trust, thousands of books and craft kits were donated to over 30 hospitals across the UK, the latest example (according to the website) being Birmingham Children's Hospital receiving a donation of over 500 books from the local WH Smith.

Schools giveaway

For over five years, working with the WH Smith Trust, High Street stores can 'nominate themselves to receive a share of the £20,000 in WHSmith vouchers available to give to local schools'. Example include WH Smith's Princes Nottingham store inviting local schoolchildren to visit the store and collect their vouchers and WH Smith Uckfield presenting vouchers and raffle prizes to Bonners Primary School.

Employee-led support

The website claims: 'Our store teams are active members in their communities, with many store managers and staff giving their time to support local councils, town centre management and high street security groups to promote a thriving business environment.'

Fundraising

Annually the group's employees and customers are invited to participate in various fundraising activities, in support of charity partners. The WH Smith Trust being one of the main beneficiaries – customers provide support for the trust by donating their spare change into the collection tins in High Street and Travel stores, while staff give their help through sporting challenges (like the London Marathon, Great North Run or Sport Relief Mile) and support for the WH Smith Trust shop in the Swindon head office. Further examples have included a ballroom dancing show to raise money for Prospect Hospice, and staff wearing Christmas jumpers to raise money for Macmillan Cancer Support.

Matched funding

Employee fundraising efforts and volunteering can be match funded through the WH Smith Trust. A total of 47 grants worth over £38,000 were made during 2013/2014. Such beneficiaries have included Alzheimer's Society, Brake, Cancer Research UK, Macmillan Cancer Support, also scout groups, music groups, hospices and air ambulances.

Commercially led support

Through the sale of products, such as Christmas cards, the group continues to support a various charities 'ranging from Cancer Research UK to Battersea Cats and Dogs to Help for Heroes'. The group's exclusive Children in Need Christmas card continues to be a key part of the overall range with 100% of profits going to support BBC Children in Need fundraising. The card range also includes cards with images from the National Trust, the Woodland Trust and the RSPB.

Apprenticeship programmes

There are schemes 'designed to support the employment and upskilling of young people'. Apprentices are employed in Birmingham and Swindon distribution centres with 'the opportunity to apply for suitable permanent vacancies as they arise'. According to the group's website, 'in order to create the right environment to promote diversity among employees, flexible working schemes are designed to support working parents and carers'.

Corporate social responsibility

CSR committee: There was no evidence of a separate CSR Committee. The Community Engagement Policy is reviewed on an annual basis and:

> Its implementation is the responsibility of the Group Human Resources Director, Anthony Lawrence. Group Chief Executive, Stephen Clarke, is specifically tasked with keeping the board advised on compliance with the policy and ensuring that suitable support is available to the businesses.

The CSR report states:

> Our programme is comprised of four key areas of CR: Environmental management, Responsibility in the marketplace, Workplace practice and Community impact. Accountability for each area rests with named members of our board, who, in turn, are supported by senior executives responsible for delivering our objectives. In this way we ensure our CR work is embedded across our organisation. Our CR strategy is underpinned by our four corporate values, accountability, drive for results, customer focus and value our people, and developed taking into account the expectations of our key stakeholder groups.

CSR information: The following information was obtained from the company's website:

> WHSmith is a valued member of communities across the UK, and we are committed to making a positive impact wherever we operate our stores. Through our work to champion literacy and support good causes, our community programme enables us to contribute to local areas. We also want to provide customers with an opportunity to support their favourite charities through the products we sell.

The group's CR concentrates around environmental management, responsibility in the marketplace, workplace practice and community impact. According to the annual report and accounts for 2013/14, 'good corporate responsibility remains a key focal point for the business and [WH Smith is] making good progress towards [the] 2020 sustainability targets'.

CSR report: An annual CSR report is available from the company's website.

Exclusions

Unsolicited requests are not generally supported. No support is normally given for advertising in charity brochures, animal welfare, appeals from individuals, the arts, older people, enterprise/training, environment/heritage, fundraising events, medical research, overseas projects, political appeals, religious appeals, science/technology, sickness/disability, social welfare or sport.

Applications

Our research suggests that the group is proactive in identifying potential partners for its community programme. Unsolicited requests, therefore, are not generally considered. Requests for information on other means of support should be directed to the correspondent.

Smiths Group plc

Aerospace, engineering, information management and communication

Correspondent: The Corporate Responsibility Team, 2nd Floor, Cardinal Place, 80 Victoria Street, London SW1E 5JL (tel: 020 7808 5500; fax: 020 7808 5544; email: cr@smiths.com; website: www.smiths-group.com)

Directors: George Buckley, Chair; Philip Browman, Chief Executive Officer; Peter Turner, Finance Director; Bruno Angelici; David Challen; Tanya Fratto; Anne Quinn; Bill Seeger; Kevin Tebbit (women: 2; men: 7)

Year end	31/07/2014
Turnover	£2,951,600,000
Pre-tax profit	£302,000,000

Nature of business: The group has five division which are involved in the medical, industrial, energy, aerospace, communication, engineered components and threat and contraband detection markets. Its customers include governments, hospitals, petrochemical companies, equipment manufacturers and service providers in other sectors.

Company registration number: 137013

Subsidiary undertakings include: John Crane UK Ltd; Smiths Detection (Asia-Pacific) Pte Ltd (Singapore); Smiths Detection – Watford Ltd; Smiths Heimann GmbH (Germany); and Power Distribution, Inc. (US); More subsidiary undertakings can be found within the group's accounts and a full list is available from Companies House.

Brands include: There are five divisions – John Crane, Smiths Medical, Smiths Detection, Smiths Interconnect and Flex-Tek.

Main locations: Birmingham, Dundee, Eastleigh, Gloucester, Hounslow, Burnley, Crawley, Tewkesbury, Watford, Croydon, Glasgow, Wolverhampton, Hythe, Ilford, Orpington, Nelson, Onchan, Newmarket, Newbury, Manchester, Luton, Slough, Southampton, Christchurch

Total employees: 23,200

Focus of giving: Education, environment, health, ill health, medical research, non-registered charities, community/social welfare.

FTSE 100	✓
Gifts in kind	✓
Payroll giving	✓

Charitable donations

Cash UK (latest available):	2014	£119,000
	2011	£300,000
	2009	£504,000
	2007	£389,000
	2005	£625,000
Total UK (cash and in kind):	2014	£192,000
Cash worldwide:	2014	£119,000
Total worldwide (cash and in kind):	2014	£192,000

Community involvement

The Corporate Responsibility Report 2014 states:

> Building strong links with the communities in which we operate, through local engagement, charitable giving and education initiatives in order to contribute to local prosperity, enhance our reputation, foster employee engagement and attract new employees.
>
> Given the diversity of our business and our decentralised structure, our community relationships and charitable programmes are primarily managed at a local level to allow our businesses to focus on the needs of their markets and communities.

Support is generally given to organisations in or around London.

Charities and non-profit organisations working for health, education and well-being or environmental causes are assisted. Organisations have to demonstrate how the support 'will enhance the well-being of people through improved education, health and welfare, or environment' and should have connections to the industries in which the group operates. Your organisation does not need to be a registered charity, but it should be charitable.

Some global examples of community support given in the CR Report 2014 and the website include employee contributions (given in the 'Employee-led support' section in this entry) and also:

- Supporting employability (Czech Republic) – the HR department held four sessions to teach CV writing, job hunting, and interviewing skills, building skills in the community and enhancing employee engagement in support of the charity Association D, which aims to prepare teens for adult responsibilities
- Smiths Medical (South Africa) – provided and fitted a tracheostomy tube, specially designed for infants, for a boy with a serious lung condition

Corporate giving

In 2013/14 the group made charitable donations totalling £192,000. The donations are generally under £1,000. We could not determine the amount awarded in cash in the UK; based on the ratio of UK and worldwide giving in the past we estimate that about £119,000 was awarded in the UK during the year.

In-kind support

Staff volunteering time and expert knowledge.

Payroll giving

In the past there were a number of schemes operated by the company. We could not identify any references to payroll giving in the latest CR Report or accounts.

Employee-led support

The group's employees participate in fundraising initiatives, including:

- Smiths Day (Singapore)- employees donated blood and fundraised for the Red Cross
- Smiths Medical (Mexico) – employees helped the local food bank collecting a kilometre of food over two weeks
- Flex-Tek (US) – a team spent an afternoon creating a garden at a nearby nursing home; another group fundraised for a local shelter for victims of domestic abuse
- Food Bank Assistance (US) – employees helped raise funds, held food drives and donated time to support local food banks

Corporate social responsibility

CSR committee: There is a charitable donations committee.

The board has the ultimate responsibility for general stewardship of the business, including the CSR. 'The Chief Executive and the executive team are responsible for delivering the strategic objectives, upholding the Code [Code of Business Ethics], implementing its supporting policies and delivering both the overall business strategy and specific CR strategies.'

CSR information: The following information is taken from Chief Executive's statement from the 2014 Corporate Responsibility Report:

> Conducting our business with integrity, honesty, fairness and transparency is not just important to Smiths; it is one of our core values and a key element of our business strategy. By behaving ethically, working safely, reducing our environmental impact, attracting and developing our people and contributing to our communities, we help create long-term value for our shareholders and our wider stakeholders.

The CR strategy is informed by the Code of Business Ethics which applies to all Smiths businesses and employees worldwide. The strategy is made up of five core areas:

- Ethics – the highest standards of business behaviour
- Health and safety – safe workplace
- Environment – energy efficiency, cutting emissions and water consumption and generating less waste
- People – staff development
- Community – community engagement, charitable giving, and education initiatives contributing to local causes

CSR report: There is an annual CR Report published.

Exclusions

Support is generally not given for:

- Advertising in charity brochures
- Animal welfare
- The arts
- Overseas projects (except initiatives supported through the central group fund)
- Political and religious appeals
- Sports
- Individuals who are looking for sponsorship for fundraising activities
- Initiatives that involve people participating in dangerous activities (for example, bungee jumping or parachuting)
- Any initiative that is outside the eligibility criteria

Applications

If your organisation and proposed funding initiative fit the criteria complete the application form available from the website and email it to cr@smiths.com. Postal applications will not be responded to.

Each division is responsible for agreeing and administering its own charitable donations budget and requests should be addressed to the appropriate division directly.

Sodexo Ltd

Catering services, food services

Correspondent: Thomas Jelley, Corporate Citizenship Manager, Corporate Citizenship, Sodexo, One Southampton Row, London WC1B 5HA (tel: 020 7404 0110; email: corporate.citizenship@sodexo.com; website: uk.sodexo.com)

Directors: Jane Bristow; Stuart Carter; Sean Haley; Phil Hooper; Chris John; Andrew Leach; Tony Leach; Lynn Mawdsley, Chief Financial Officer; Neil Murray; Simon Scrivens; Debbie White, Chief Executive Officer; Angela Williams (women: 4; men: 8)

Year end	31/08/2014
Turnover	£1,062,925,000
Pre-tax profit	£48,156,000

Nature of business: The company provides catering, facilities, vending, health and fitness support and management services to clients in commercial, industrial, educational, healthcare and other establishments.

Sodexo Ltd operates in the UK and Ireland as a wholly owned subsidiary of Sodexo Holdings Ltd. The company's ultimate parent company is Sodexo S.A., a French company.

Note: the figure of UK employees includes Ireland.

Company registration number: 842846

Subsidiary undertakings include: Sodexo Education Services Ltd; Sodexo Land Technology Ltd; Sodexo Netherlands BV; Sodexo Prestige Ltd; Sodexo Property Solutions Ltd; and Vendability Ltd. A full list of subsidiary undertakings can be found in the company's accounts.

Main locations: Hitchin, Abertillery, Aberdeen, Alperton, Aldershot

UK employees: 30,650

Total employees: 30,650

Focus of giving: Education, health, ill health, individuals, unpopular causes, armed forces personnel, poverty and social exclusion, safety and crime prevention, sport, recreation, children, young people, community/social welfare.

Membership: BITC

Gifts in kind	✓
Payroll giving	✓

Charitable donations

Cash UK (latest available):	2014	£93,000
	2011	£89,000
	2009	£23,500
	2008	£16,500
	2007	£34,000
Total UK (cash and in kind):	2014	£93,000
Cash worldwide:	2014	£93,000
Total worldwide (cash and in kind):	2014	£93,000

Community involvement

The company states:

> We support local community development by making a positive impact in areas, such as employment, skills and training. We channel our social impact through a range of actions, including volunteering, financial support, employment, pro bono work, commercial contracts and in-kind donations.

The Sodexo Foundation (Charity Commission no. 1110266)

The foundation is the main platform for the company's charitable giving and focuses on education and relief of hardship in relation to health, nutrition and well-being. Sodexo Ltd operates and supports (through financial and human resources) the foundation's STOP Hunger campaign which helps organisations promoting healthy eating lifestyles, providing food to those in need and offering training in basic life skills.

The company states that it supports communities by tackling hunger and malnutrition, promoting employability skills, supporting smaller businesses and sourcing fair trade produce.

STOP Hunger

This is a global Sodexo initiative active in more than 40 countries worldwide which aims to tackle hunger and malnutrition, promote healthy eating and deliver basic life skills training, such as cooking in the communities where the group operates. The programme has been in the UK and Ireland since 2005 and is managed by The Sodexo Foundation (in Ireland the initiative is administered by the Community Foundation of Ireland).

FareShare

The company donates both financial support and employees' time and expertise to help tackle hunger and malnutrition. More recently a partnership has been established with the FareShare depot at Dale Barracks in Liverpool. Volunteers help FareShare collect, sort and distribute food to local charities.

The Scout Association

Through the foundation Sodexo created resources, games and activities for new UK Cub and Scout Chef Activity badges. The 2013 Corporate Citizen report states that a downloadable pack for Cub and Scout leaders which covers a variety of cooking skills and knowledge has been produced and 'once each badge's requirements are met, Cubs and Scouts receive a certificate and Sodexo Chef Activity badge'. It was hoped to extend this to Cubs and Scouts in Ireland.

The Outward Bound Trust

Three years in a row the Sodexo Foundation and Sodexo teams co-operated with the Outward Bound Trust to offer a programme to teenagers. The Sodexo website states: 'The challenge promotes healthy lifestyle choices and educates young people from disadvantaged areas about the benefits of healthy eating and an active lifestyle.' During the year 140 teenagers from seven schools in Edinburgh, Glasgow and Salford heard talks on health and nutrition from the company's employees and had an activity day of teambuilding and mountain biking. A third of the participants went on to participate in residential courses at Loch Tay in Scotland and Aberdovey in Wales developing their self-confidence, understanding of a balanced diet and healthy meal cooking skills.

Big Dig

The initiative encouraging people to get involved in community food-growing projects across England was attended by Sodexo employees who spent a day at Sutton Community Farm in Wallington (Greater London) removing weeds, preparing plant beds and planting various vegetable and flower plants.

Rocket Gardens

The company partnered with this organic farm in Cornwall which produces plants for gardeners to plant and grow. Funding was given through the foundation and Sodexo Education gave 295 schools the opportunity to plant fruit and vegetable gardens.

HMP Peterborough

People who have offended contributed to Sodexo's Coffee Grounds for Growth initiative and gained a qualification in the process. 'The initiative involves recovering used coffee grounds from Sodexo sites and donating them to customers as a natural garden fertiliser.' The prisoners from the carpentry workshop helped making boxes for the coffee grounds which formed a part of a six-week carpentry course leading to a National Certificate of Further Education (NCFE) awarded by Peterborough Regional College. The initiative was set up as a social enterprise and supplier to the wider Sodexo business. By the autumn of 2012, ten prisoners had participated in the carpentry course and received their diploma.

Corporate giving

In 2013/14 charitable donations from the company totalled £93,000 (2013: 29,000) and were all distributed through the Sodexo Foundation. Additionally, £425,000 was raised by employees. At the time of writing the latest accounts of The Sodexo Foundation were for 2012/13. In that year the donation from the company totalled almost £49,000 and further £447,000 was raised by the employees.

Beneficiaries of Sodexo Foundation included: FareShare (£90,000); SSAFA Forces Help (£80,000); Breast Cancer Haven (£30,000); Edinburgh Cyrenians (£11,000); Kids' Cookery School (£10,000); Barnardo's Ireland (£7,900); Emmaus Bristol (£5,500);The Haven (Wolverhampton); Centrepoint (£4,700); Aberlour Child Care Trust (£4,100); and BrendonCare (£1,800).

See the corporate charity entry on p. 429 for more information.

In-kind support

Volunteer time and expertise.

Employee-led support

Sodexo's employees participate in collective and individual fundraising activities while the company helps to co-ordinate some of those efforts in community involvement and charitable work. The staff are actively involved in many activities supported through the foundation, details of particular projects can be found in the 'Community involvement' section in this entry.

The Corporate Citizenship Report for 2013 also notes that a total of £425,000 was raised for STOP Hunger in the UK and Ireland.

Payroll giving

In the past the company has operated a giving scheme.

Corporate social responsibility

CSR committee: There is a Corporate Citizen Team.

Sodexo's board-level Corporate Affairs Director has formal responsibility for the UK and Ireland corporate citizenship strategy, policies and performance. He is supported by the Corporate Citizenship Manager and the Corporate Citizenship and Engagement Advisor.

CSR information: The company's Corporate Citizenship Report 2013/14 states:

> Our mission is to improve the quality of life of all the people we serve, and contribute to the economic, social and environmental development of the communities, regions and countries where we operate. To us, corporate citizenship is more than doing the right thing; it's embedded in our mission.

Sodexo group's sustainability strategy up till 2020 is informed by The Better Tomorrow Plan, which encompasses clients, consumers, employees, institutions and suppliers and aims to:

- Be a responsible employer
- Promote nutrition, health and well-being
- Support the development of local communities
- Ensure the sustainability of the group's supply chain
- Protect the environment

CSR report: There is a Corporate Citizenship Report published annually.

Corporate charity: Sodexo Foundation (Charity Commission no. 1110266).

Applications

The company: queries about Corporate Citizenship can be directed to the correspondent.

The foundation: enquiries about the activities of the foundation should be made Edwina Hughes (email: stophunger@sodexo.com) at the company's address. Application forms for the STOP Hunger initiative are also available online.

Note: In addition to supporting FareShare and a number of smaller charities that meet the STOP Hunger objectives, the trustees receive from time to time requests from employees to support a local cause. Such requests are usually met by Sodexo outside the Sodexo Foundation.

Sony Europe Ltd

Electronics/computers

Correspondent: The CSR Committee, UK Technology Centre, Pencoed, Bridgend CF35 5HZ (tel: 01656 860666 (reception); email: CSRPCD@eu.sony.com; website: www.sonypencoed.co.uk)

Directors: Masaru Tamagawa; Gildas Pelliet; Ricky Londema; Atsushi Kobayashi (women: 0; men: 4)

Year end	31/03/2014
Turnover	£4,492,200,000
Pre-tax profit	(£304,900,000)

Nature of business: The company is the distributor of Sony branded products. These are mainly electronic goods, such as video and audio system, computer systems and media peripheral and semiconductor products, for the domestic, leisure, business and professional markets throughout Europe. Broadcast camera and digital cinema equipment is also distributed.

The ultimate parent undertaking and controlling party of the company is Sony Corporation, incorporated in Japan. The company's' immediate parent undertaking is Sony Overseas Holding BV, incorporated in the Netherlands.

Note that UK employees figure includes the UK and Ireland.

Company registration number: 2422874

Subsidiary undertakings include: Ecophihas Lda; Hawk-Eye (Holdings) Ltd; Pulse Innovations Ltd; Sony Austria GmbH; and Sony (UK) Pension Trust Ltd. A full list of subsidiary undertakings can be found within the company's accounts.

Main locations: Bridgend, Thatcham, Pencoed, Weybridge, Basingstoke

UK employees: 1,274

Total employees: 3,944

Focus of giving: Education, health, ill health, local groups, STEM (science, technology, engineering and mathematics), sport, recreation, children, young people, community/social welfare.

Cash donations undeclared	✓
Charity of the Year	✓
Gifts in kind	✓
Humanitarian aid: overseas	✓
Market-led giving	✓
Matched funding	✓
Overseas giving	✓

Charitable donations

Cash UK (latest available):	2014	£123,000
	2011	£122,000
	2009	£125,000
	2008	£121,000
	2007	£84,000
Total UK (cash and in kind):	2014	£123,000

Community involvement

In the UK charitable activities are undertaken by the Sony UK Technology Centre and aimed at local charities, local community organisations and other youth groups. The website states:

> As part of our corporate social responsibility policy, Sony UK Technology Centre, Pencoed selects one organisation as our annual adopted charity that our main funding efforts are geared towards. We may also support local organisations with donations which are usually in the form of a modest product to help with fundraising and/or raffles.

Charity partnership

In 2014 Sony UK Technology Centre announced a partnership with The Children's Ward at the Princess of Wales Hospital in Bridgend and organised a range of activities fundraising for the cause. Previously the company supported NSPCC Cymru (2012).

Sony Corporation

Globally Sony operates six foundations in Japan (two), USA, Australia, Canada and Pan-Europe. Disaster relief undertaken by the corporation has taken place in Asian countries and the USA.

The global CSR report notes:

> In addition to Sony's global program, which is spearheaded by its headquarters in Tokyo, Sony Group companies worldwide, as well as six foundations, promote initiatives tailored to local needs in accordance with the Sony Group's community engagement policy, cooperating with various international organisations including NGOs.

Corporate giving

The company's annual report and accounts for 2013/14 did not seem to declare charitable donations. Based on the figures from the three previous years known to us we estimate that about £123,000 could have been given in cash in the UK. In the previous years the company has stated that charitable giving has been concentrated on Community (76%) and Sport (24%).

Global giving

The global CSR report for 2013/14 notes that the Sony group allocates most of its 'community activity expenditure' on education support (64%). The remainder is given to: local community contributions (12%); arts and culture (7%); health/welfare and other causes (5% each); emergency relief (4%); environment (2%); and sports-related activities (1%). Bear in mind that these figures relate to worldwide activities and could be allocated differently in the UK. The report does not single out the UK market; however it is noted that only 2% of the overall amount is given in Europe (most support is concentrated in Japan (43%) and USA (34%)). The overall expenditure is used for: program expenses (63%); monetary donations/membership fees (25%); advertisement/sponsorships (10%); and donated products (2%).

In-kind support

Sony can provide product donations, generally to help with fundraising and/or raffles. Volunteer support from the group employees as well as donations are given in areas affected by natural disasters

South Africa Mobile Library Project

The project, run by South Africa Primary Education Support Initiative (SAPESI), provides free and easy access to the books for children, especially in remote areas. Companies in English-speaking countries (Australia, Canada, Hong Kong, Malaysia, New Zealand, Singapore, South Africa, United Kingdom and United States) invited employees to donate English children's books to support the initiative. The total number of books donated by global employees is about 125,000 (since 2008).

Employee-led support

Charity Golf Day

At the Sony UK Technology Centre an annual Charity Golf Day raises money for good causes.

Someone Needs You

Employee volunteering forms part of the Sony's community contributions and is provided through a global Someone Needs You scheme. The scheme aims to encourage employee involvement in efforts to help local communities. Sony companies create their own volunteer programmes tailored to local needs and enables staff participation in community matters. According to the global CSR report, in 2013 a total of 70,000 Sony group employees participated in volunteer activities (including fundraising).

The global CSR report for 2013/14 says the following:

> To support employee participation in volunteer activity initiatives, Sony Corporation has an employee volunteer support system, making it easier for employees to participate in volunteer activities by allowing them to use accumulated holidays for initiatives requiring extended leaves of absence.

Matched funding

Many of the Sony worldwide companies have 'matching gifts programmes', 'whereby Sony matches charitable donations made by employees up to established limits to encourage employees' fundraising efforts'. We found no information on whether such schemes are participated in by the UK divisions.

The global website states:

> Sony believes that employee participation is crucial to ensuring its community engagement activities are truly meaningful. Accordingly, Sony encourages employees to be aware of social issues, strive constantly to deepen their understanding and then to participate in fundraising initiatives, community projects and/or other activities. Sony also encourages employees to act as instructors for workshops organized for children and students and in other capacities that capitalize on their specialized skills.

Commercially led support

Sony Science Program

Through the global program, which is one of the main community engagement initiatives, Sony provides support for science education for children and young people. Particular attention is paid to science education. Sony Corporation also organises exhibitions of various kinds, including at educational museums 'that are designed to stimulate interest in media, science, technology and entertainment'.

Apprenticeship and graduate schemes

There are schemes, run at the UK Technology Centre, 'aimed to develop the next generation of Sony engineers, innovators and business leaders'.

Corporate social responsibility

CSR committee: The UK Technology Centre has a CSR Committee.

According to Sony's website, globally, there is:

> An office for CSR that is responsible for formulating policies concerning Sony's social responsibilities, implementing these policies throughout the group and communicating with third parties through, among others, the sharing of information.
>
> The relevant departments promote CSR activities throughout the group by ensuring policies and initiatives thus incorporated are conveyed to group companies.

CSR information: The UK Technology Centre concentrates its CSR policy on environment and helping local causes. Its website notes:

> The Sony UK Technology Centre is a socially aware business that seeks to minimise its impact on the environment, supports its local community through charity work and sponsorship, and has the welfare of its staff at the heart of its operation.

The global website states:

> Sony's corporate social responsibility (CSR) activities reflect its philosophy of implementing sound business practices;

innovating to realize products, services and content that inspire and excite; assisting the communities in which we operate; and helping to shape a better, more sustainable society. Sony believes that these activities both benefit society and enhance corporate value.

CSR report: A global CSR report is available from the Sony Corporation's website. Activities of the UK Technology Centre are given on the centre's website.

Exclusions

Sony states that the following are not considered for support:

- Promotion of religious ideas
- Sexist or racist groups
- Political groups, private or secret societies
- Profit making bodies

Applications

Application forms for the support from Sony UK Technology Centre can be found on the website and should be addressed to the correspondent (by post or email).

Other enquiries should be addressed to the Company Secretary at the Sony Europe Ltd registered office (The Heights, Brooklands, Weybridge, Surrey KT13 0XW).

The Southern Co-operative Ltd

Retail – miscellaneous, retail – supermarkets

Correspondent: Silena Dominy, Company Secretary, 1000 Lakeside, Western Road, Portsmouth, Hampshire PO6 3FE (tel: 02392 222500; fax: 02392 222650; website: www.thesouthernco-operative.co.uk)

Directors: Pauline Lympany; Amber Vincent-Prior; Fran Hobson; Tom Blair; Neil Blanchard; Mike Hastilow, Chair; Diane Knight; John Harrington; Kelly Emmence; Silena Dominy, Company Secretary (women: 6; men: 4)

Year end	25/01/2014
Turnover	£326,716,000
Pre-tax profit	£11,790,000

Nature of business: Independent consumer co-operative society. It operates over 187 community stores and over 44 funeral homes in Berkshire, Bristol, Devon, Dorset, Hampshire, Isle of Wight, Kent, Somerset, Surrey, Sussex and Wiltshire. In addition to that the co-operative operates a home shopping business supplying aids to daily living and a portfolio of rental properties.

Company registration number: IP01591R

Subsidiary undertakings include: Caring Lady Funeral Directors Ltd; J Edwards and Son (Funeral Directors) Ltd; Mutual Associates Ltd; Mutual Services (Portsmouth) Ltd; SCL (Members) Trustee Ltd; and Sussex Woodlands Ltd. A full list of subsidiary undertakings can be found within the society's accounts.

UK employees: 3,982

Total employees: 3,982

Focus of giving: Education, enterprise/training, environment, small groups, local groups, poverty and social exclusion, community/social welfare, disability.

Charity of the Year	✓
Gifts in kind	✓
Market-led giving	✓

Charitable donations

Cash UK (latest available):	2014	£474,000
	2009	£119,000
	2008	£69,000
	2007	£77,000
Total UK (cash and in kind):	2014	£589,000
Cash worldwide:	2014	£474,000
Total worldwide (cash and in kind):	2014	£589,000

Community involvement

Support for community environmental projects

The following information in this section is taken from the co-operative's website.

In 2013 The Southern Co-operative continued supporting EYE (Eco, Young and Engaged), 'which brings school children from West Sussex together for annual eco summits', and Tuppenny Barn, 'which is building a sustainable education centre to host organic food workshops for local children and other courses and events'. In Bristol funding has been given to Youth Moves project 'to engage school children in growing vegetables at their dedicated allotment' and there were plans for 2014 to help the organisation build a community space.

Food banks

In addition to providing a platform for collecting donations and fundraising platform, money was donated 'to each of the food banks to enable them to continue operating when stock levels are low'. On the IOW this was match-funded by the local council.

ProxyWatch

The Southern Co-operative has been involved in an initiative with Portsmouth City Council delivering 'a 24-hour hotline for members of the public and shop staff to report incidences of proxy-purchasing' and raising awareness of the issue among retailers.

Bereavement Centre

Through the centre's support and education service people can find: 'educational study days and bereavement workshops; local support, friendship and social groups; one-to-one bereavement support; memorial services held throughout the year; and major bereavement seminars and conferences'. The centre is open to everyone.

Charity partnerships

Hampshire and Isle of Wight, Sussex and Dorset Wildlife Trusts

Dorset Wildlife Trust's Urbanlink project 'creating an urban 'living landscape' across south-east Dorset' and Sussex Wildlife Trust's Forest Rangers project were supported. The society is 'involved in supporting and judging the Community and Voluntary category in CPRE (Campaign to Protect Rural England) Hampshire's Countryside awards'.

The Southern Co-operative's key priorities for 2014 include:

> To invest a minimum of 6% of pre-tax, pre-dividend profits in the communities; create more opportunities for colleagues to volunteer and increase the hours volunteered by 10% each year; continue to tackle the issues that matter most to [the] communities, like food poverty, rolling out food collection points to areas of greatest need across [the] trading area.

Canine Partners

Due to the popularity with both customers and colleagues alike, the charity was retained as a charity partner for a second year and ended in 2014. Colleagues raised over £268,000 during 2013 in support of the organisation.

Whizz-Kidz

The charity helping children with disabilities is a new partner with The Southern Co-operative.

Corporate giving

According to the Sustainability Report for 2013, a total of £474,000 (2012: £554,000) was provided in 'Investment in Community and Co-operative Initiatives'. In addition to that working hours donated to community projects totalled £115,000 (2012: £118,000). We take the figure of £474,000 to represent the society's cash contributions, which is reported to have amounted to 4% of the pre-tax profits.

Most recently beneficiaries have included: Hayling Islands play parks (£25,000); Freshwater community and Wickham community (£20,000 each); Emsworth community and Riding for the Disabled (£15,000 each); Mere guiding and scouting groups and Lanbourne community (£10,000 each); and Selsey Community Nursery (£1,000). There is a list and further details of the causes supported on the website's 'News' section.

In-kind support

Vouchers for refreshments can be supplied.

Food banks

During the year The Southern Co-operative helped local food banks by introducing 'food collection points in six stores in Portsmouth, four stores in Chichester and 11 stores on IOW (with donations accepted in our IOW funeral homes too) alongside smaller schemes in other locations'.

Employee-led support

The society's colleagues contribute to good causes through fundraising activities and community involvement. In 2013 more than £268,000 was raised for Canine Partners. In addition the Sustainability Report states: 'In 2013 our communities benefited from individual contributions totalling more than £100,000.' We take the figure of £368,000 to represent staff contributions.

Employee volunteering

According to the 2013/14 annual report: 'TSC actively encourages colleagues working at all levels of the business to volunteer in work time and as a result, this has contributed to over 4,800 hours of volunteering during 2013.' For example, staff volunteering efforts helped the partners – Hampshire and Isle of Wight, Sussex and Dorset Wildlife Trusts – and over the Christmas period a meal was cooked for the Royal Voluntary Service lunch club.

Commercially led support

Education and training

The society has programmes of work experience placements for young people at schools and colleagues. The Learning and Development Teams also organise initiatives to enhance the skills of young job seekers in local communities, for example, running workshops as part of the nationwide Skills for Work month (promoted by the Institute of Grocery Distribution and Jobcentre Plus) and similar sessions for other local youth groups.

Community Support Card (CSC)

The CSC helps to provide support for local charities and organisations through the backing of customers. The Southern Co-operative makes a donation to the community support fund every time a member has their card (issued free in the store) swiped. According to the 2013/14 annual report: 'The recipients [of grants] are chosen by a panel made up of co-operative members and the store team.' In 2013 cheques totalling £250,000 were presented to local good causes (of this £135,700 will be added to the 2014 contributions and paid to the recipients when their schemes complete during the year).

Corporate social responsibility

CSR committee: We found no indication of a CSR committee.

CSR information: The Sustainability Report for 2013/14 (within the annual report) states:

> The Southern Co-operative (TSC) has always had a purpose beyond profit and a desire to create a different kind of business. Our long established values and principles continue to guide us today in developing and managing our business in a responsible and sustainable manner.

In 2013 The Southern Co-operative developed a Sustainability Plan 'Making a Difference' which has three main pillars – protect, share and support. It encompasses the environment, leading a responsible business and engagement with local communities:

- *Protect* our environment by: reducing carbon emissions; saving energy and water; preventing waste; championing local wildlife and countryside
- *Share* our success with others by: engaging members and others in our business; supporting young people into work; helping our colleagues to realise their potential; promoting local food and drink; trading responsibly
- *Support* our communities by: getting actively involved in our local communities; helping to tackle important community issues; extending the reach of our bereavement education and support service; making healthy and sustainable living easier

CSR report: An annual report is available from the website and the Sustainability Report is contained within.

Applications

Applications for support for community based initiatives can be addressed to local stores. Otherwise, enquiries can be made in writing to the correspondent.

Spar (UK) Ltd

Retail – supermarkets

Correspondent: Phillip Marchant, Company Secretary and Trustee of the Fund, Mezzanine Floor, Hygeia Building, 66–68 College Road, Harrow, Middlesex HA3 1BE (tel: 020 8426 3700; fax: 020 8426 3701; website: www.spar.co.uk)

Directors: Susan Darbyshire; Richard Hill; Mark Keeley; Christopher Lewis; Deborah Robinson; Phillip Marchant (women: 2; men: 4)

Year end	27/04/2013
Turnover	£64,805,994
Pre-tax profit	£317,000

Nature of business: The entity is a voluntary, independently-owned trading group operating stores under the SPAR banner throughout the UK.

The company's accounts state: 'Spar (UK) Ltd is the Central Office of the Spar retail organisation owned 100% by Spar Food Distributors Ltd whose shareholders are five regional distribution companies.' The companies are: A F Blakemore and Son Ltd Wales/ Midlands/Eastern England); Appleby Westward Group Ltd (South West/ Southern England); C J Lang and Son Ltd (Scotland); Henderson Wholesale Ltd (Northern Ireland); and James Hall and Company (Holdings) Ltd (Northern England).

Company registration number: 634226

Subsidiary undertakings include: Buying International Group B V; B V Intergroup Trading (IGT) (Netherlands); and Inter-Spar (UK) Ltd.

UK employees: 62

Total employees: 62

Focus of giving: Health, ill health, individuals, children, young people.

Cash donations undeclared	✓
Market-led giving	✓

Charitable donations

Cash UK (latest available):	2013	£53,000
	2011	£55,500
	2009	£90,500
Total UK (cash and in kind):	2013	£53,000
Cash worldwide:	2013	£53,000
Total worldwide (cash and in kind):	2013	£53,000

Community involvement

The Spar Charitable Fund (Charity Commission no. 236252)

Information taken from the fund's annual report and accounts for 2012/13 states:

> The Spar Charitable fund with the support and assistance of the Spar Benevolent Fund seeks to provide charitable assistance to independent Spar retailers who face adverse problems and difficulties with health, bereavement, and social issues. The charitable fund also supports retail industry charitable organisations.

The main objective for the fund is 'to provide a vehicle to enable the Spar organisation through its 2600 stores across the UK to engage with the public to raise awareness of public charitable needs and raise funding in a wide variety of ways'.

Charity partnership

Branches of the NSPCC local to Spar stores. For more details, see 'Commercially led giving' section in this entry.

Corporate giving

In 2013/14 The Spar Charitable Fund had a total income of £49,000, of which £32,000 was generated from investments and £10,000 was a donation from the Spar Benevolent Fund and £7,000 constituted 'funds raised on behalf of NSPCC'. Grants were made totalling £90,000.

Revenue: for the company's turnover we used the figure defined as 'turnover as principal' in the annual accounts.

See the corporate charity entry on p. 430 for more information.

Commercially led support

National Society for the Prevention of Cruelty to Children (NSPCC) and ChildLine

NSPCC has been Spar's chosen charity for the past seven years with the last two years support being given to the charity's ChildLine programme. During the partnership over £3.5 million has been raised for the charity.

ChildLine Schools Service

The company's website notes Spar helping the NSPCC to establish the ChildLine Schools Service through raising funds and awareness. 'The ChildLine Schools Service is a pioneering service which visits primary schools in every region of the UK to help children understand abuse and give them the confidence to seek help if they need it.'

Corporate social responsibility

CSR committee: None found.

CSR information: No specific CSR details found. The accounts state that 'the company operates in a way to be as environmentally friendly as possible complying with all relevant laws and regulations'.

CSR report: No indications of a CSR report found.

Corporate charity: Spar Charitable Fund (Charity Commission no. 236252).

Exclusions

Support is not given for political or religious causes.

Applications

The company: enquiries regarding local initiatives should be addressed to the local store manager.

The Spar Charitable Fund (Charity Commission no. 236252): queries should be directed to Phillip Marchant (email: philip.marchant@spar.co.uk), trustee of the fund, at the company's address.

Spectris plc

Engineering, industrial products/services

Correspondent: The Corporate Responsibility Team, Church Road, Egham, Surrey TW20 9QD (tel: 01784 470470; fax: 01784 470848; email: info@spectris.com; website: www.spectris.com)

Directors: John Hughes, Chair; John O'Higgins, Chief Executive Officer; Clive Watson, Group Finance Director; Peter Chambré; John Warren; Roger Stephens; Martha Wyrsch; Lisa Davis; Russell King (women: 2; men: 7)

Year end	31/12/2013
Turnover	£1,202,000,000
Pre-tax profit	£271,700,000

Nature of business: Develops and markets productivity enhancing instrumentation and controls.

Company registration number: 2025003

Subsidiary undertakings include: Beta LaserMike Inc (US); Hottinger Baldwin Messtechnik GmbH; Malvern Instruments Ltd; Red Lion Controls Inc (US); PANalytical BV (Netherlands); and Servomex Group Ltd. A full list of subsidiary undertakings can be found within the group's accounts.

Total employees: 7,344

Focus of giving: Education, enterprise/training, local groups, STEM (science, technology, engineering and mathematics), arts, culture, overseas projects, sport, recreation, children, young people, community/social welfare, disasters.

Cash donations undeclared	✓
Gifts in kind	✓
Humanitarian aid: overseas	✓
Market-led giving	✓
Overseas giving	✓
Sponsorship	✓

Charitable donations

Cash UK (latest available):	2013	£13,000
	2011	£11,000
	2009	£6,000
	2008	£22,400
Total UK (cash and in kind):	2013	£13,000

Community involvement

The group 'participates in a range of local activities and educational initiatives in support of the local communities' and makes donations to charities and community causes. Support also includes provision of apprenticeships and work placements for students, working with local schools and colleges on science projects, and sponsoring scientists attending key scientific conferences.

Corporate giving

The latest figures provided on the group's website relate to 2011 charitable giving, when donations to charities and community causes totalled almost £77,000, with about £11,000 being given in the UK. We could not identify charitable donations made in 2013 in the latest annual report, therefore we estimate that about £13,000 was given in cash in the UK, based on the data from the three previous years known to us.

In-kind support

There are indications of in-kind support being available; however, further details were not specified.

Commercially led support

The group provides apprenticeship opportunities and work placements to students and can also sponsor scientist to attend conferences.

Corporate social responsibility

CSR committee: According to the Spectrics plc website:

> Overall responsibility for developing corporate policies on environmental, social, ethical and health and safety matters, and for reviewing their effectiveness, lies with the Spectris board of directors, and, in particular, the Chief Executive. These policies are mandated across all business units and applied within each particular business, taking account of local legislation and regulation. All policies are reviewed periodically and any updates are communicated to the operating companies.

CSR information: The group's Corporate Responsibility section within the annual report and accounts for 2013 states:

> Corporate responsibility encompasses all aspects of business decision-making and, as such, is fully integrated into our strategy, policies and processes in order that Spectris can continue to deliver shareholder value in a sustainable manner.

The CSR strategy aims to address those areas 'which are considered to be material by [the group's] customers, shareholders and employees', and include:

- Developing products which help customers to be more sustainable
- Engaging and retaining the employees
- Human rights
- Ethics
- Minimising the group's impact on the environment

The report confirms that 'community involvement and decisions on charitable donations and sponsorship are undertaken by local management teams, and may vary from one company to another, depending on business and regional priorities'.

The Code of Business Ethics forms the standards of behaviour for all employees.

CSR report: Published annually and contained within the annual report and accounts.

Exclusions

Donations or provision of support in-kind to political parties or campaigns is not available.

Applications

In writing to the correspondent.

Speedy 1 Ltd (holding company of Kwik Fit Group Ltd)

Motors and accessories

Correspondent: Company Secretary, ETEL House, Avenue One, Letchworth Garden City, Hertfordshire SG6 2HU (website: www.kwik-fit.com)

Directors: K. Murai; S. C. Parker; M. Slade

Year end	31/03/2014
Pre-tax profit	£149,046,000

Nature of business: Holding company of Kwik-Fit Group Ltd (which specialises in automotive parts repair including tyres, brakes, exhausts, MOT testing, car servicing, and air conditioning recharge) and other subsidiary companies.

Company registration number: 5452193

Subsidiary undertakings include: Kwik-Fit Group Ltd

Main locations: Broxburn, Uddingston

Focus of giving: General charitable purposes, enterprise/training, safety and crime prevention, children, young people, community/social welfare.

Cash donations undeclared	✓
Gifts in kind	✓
Sponsorship	✓

Charitable donations

Cash UK (latest available):	2014	£100,000
	2010	£100,000
	2009	£200,000
	2008	£100,000
	2007	£100,000
Total UK (cash and in kind):	2014	£100,000
Cash worldwide:	2014	£100,000
Total worldwide (cash and in kind):	2014	£100,000

Community involvement

We have previously been advised that the company's subsidiaries and their employees continue to support, financially and in kind, a wide range of charitable activities. In particular, there is an emphasis on initiatives that support children and young people, community development and road safety. We cannot find any information demonstrating that this has changed.

Corporate giving

The annual report and accounts for 2013/14 did not declare a figure for charitable donations during the financial year. The last recorded figure we have obtained for such contributions was £100,000, and we have taken this as an estimate for charitable donations in 2013/14.

Commercially led support

Sponsorship

Previous research indicates that the company undertakes good cause sponsorship of local community events and competitions for local schoolchildren.

Corporate social responsibility

CSR information: We found no specific CSR information. There was, however, information on the environment and recycling on the website.

We were unable to determine the ratio of women to men on the board.

Exclusions

Our research indicates that no response is given to circular appeals, and no grants are given for advertising in charity brochures or appeals from individuals.

Applications

Previous research indicates: 'It would appear that any unsolicited applications the company receives are unlikely to be successful and we would therefore advise you not to write.'

Spirax Sarco Engineering plc

Engineering, industrial products/services

Correspondent: A. J. Robson, General Counsel and Company Secretary, Charlton House, Cirencester Road, Cheltenham, Gloucestershire GL53 8ER (tel: 01242 521361; fax: 01242 581470; email: company.secretary@uk.spiraxsarco.com; website: www.spiraxsarcoengineering.com)

Directors: Bill Whiteley, Chair; Neil Daws; Krishnamurthy Rajagopal; Clive Watson; Nick Anderson; Jamie Pike; David Meredith; Trudy Schoolenberg; Jay Whalen (women: 1; men: 8)

Year end	31/12/2013
Turnover	£689,388,000
Pre-tax profit	£145,714,000

Nature of business: The supply of engineered solutions for the efficient design, maintenance and operation of industrial and commercial steam systems.

Company registration number: 596337

Subsidiary undertakings include: Bio Pure technology Ltd; Watson-Marlow Bredel BV (Netherlands; Watson-Marlow Ltd; Watson-Marlow Pty Ltd (Australia); and W-M Alitea A B (Sweden). A full list of subsidiary undertakings can be found within the group's annual report and accounts.

UK employees: 1,315

Total employees: 4,725

Focus of giving: Disasters, education, enterprise/training, health, ill health, medical research, sponsorship, children, young people, community/social welfare, disability.

Gifts in kind	✓
Humanitarian aid: overseas	✓
Market-led giving	✓
Overseas giving	✓
Sponsorship	✓

Charitable donations

Cash UK (latest available):	2013	£200,000
	2011	£132,000
	2009	£86,000
	2008	£81,000
	2007	£72,000
Total UK (cash and in kind):	2013	£200,000
Cash worldwide:	2013	£200,000
Total worldwide (cash and in kind):	2013	£200,000

Community involvement

According to the group's website, Spirax Sarco group is 'committed to improving the social and economic conditions of the communities in which it operates'. While recognising 'that the most effective way of doing this is through managing the business effectively to ensure its on-going success and providing employment that fairly remunerates people for the work that they do, it' will also 'seek to positively engage in our local communities, particularly through improving educational access and helping disadvantaged children'.

The group may also contribute to the employee initiated giving, for example 'Jo Club' (Korea) – see 'Employee-led support' section in this entry.

Charity partnership

For more than five years the group has been supporting the National Star College (NSC) in Cheltenham. As stated in the group's 2013 annual report the college 'provides specialist further education, training and personal development for young people aged 16 to 25 with complex physical, educational and emotional needs'. In 2013 Spirax Sarco employee group raised over £1,600 in sponsorship for the NSC.

The Spirax Sarco Group Charitable Trust

The Charity Commission's records note that the trust was removed from the register (Charity Commission no. 1082534) in 2010 due to not operating; however, it appears that the group maintains its charitable giving through the trust. The website and the latest annual report and accounts make references to the charity stating that it:

> Meets regularly throughout the year to determine its donations to registered charities in the UK and worldwide, focusing on social services (for the less advantaged, disabled or abused), education, healthcare, arts and the environment, as well as natural disaster recovery efforts.

Corporate giving

In 2013 the group made charitable 49 donations (ranging from £1,000 to £15,000) totalling £136,000 (2012: 132,000) through the corporate charity (The Spirax Sarco Group Charitable Trust) and gave a further £64,000 (2012: £40,000) through the operating companies.

Beneficiaries of the trust included: Cobalt and Open Door (£15,000 each); and Philippines Typhoon Disaster Appeal (£10,000).

In-kind support

Donations of old office equipment or facilities. For example, computers were donated to a local school and building space was offered for training activities of a local fire department by the German company of the group.

Employee-led support

Staff members throughout the group are involved in charitable activities and 'encouraged by the group to contribute their time and resources towards improving the quality of life in the communities in which they live and work'. An international example, given in the Sustainability Report, talks about the Korean 'Jo Club', members of which were donating money to local charities, visiting and helping at a centre for people with disabilities and volunteering in a soup kitchen. The members also delivered coal, bread and rice to the elderly. The club is financed by donations from the Spirax Sarco as well as from the members' contributions and fundraising efforts.

During the year UK employees raised over £1,600 to support the group's chosen National Star College (NSC) in Cheltenham.

Commercially led support

The group is an annual sponsor of the Cheltenham Science Festival, where it holds a stand, managed by its employees, and engages local people and, in particular, schoolchildren in the science of steam and its modern applications.

Internationally the group also has offered work experience placements to schoolchildren, internships to local students and apprenticeship opportunities.

Corporate social responsibility

CSR committee: There was no evidence of a separate CSR Committee.

The annual report states:

> The Group Chief Executive has overall responsibility for the company's sustainability strategy and is fully supported by the board of directors. We have a senior Group Health, Safety and Environment executive who ensures that appropriate policies, systems and reporting metrics are in place to achieve the group's sustainability objectives. Regional and general managers have responsibility for ensuring that the group's sustainability policies are upheld and implemented by our operating companies, and at a local level individuals and groups are organised to oversee and report on key aspects of sustainability within their workplaces.

CSR information: The group's Sustainability Report for 2013 notes the following:

> We are committed to increasing the sustainability of our business and that of our customers, and recognise our responsibilities towards the environment, the communities in which we operate and the people in our workplaces.

The CSR strategy concentrates on:

- Business – using the group's expertise to provide innovative solutions to meet its customers' needs and to ensure increasing shareholder value
- Environment - leading as an accountable company working with its customers and suppliers to minimise the impact on the environment
- Communities – being a positive influence in the communities in which the group operates
- Workplaces – maintaining a professionally challenging, respectful and safe workplace for all Spirax Sarco Engineering associates and business partners

CSR report: CSR report is contained within the annual report and accounts.

Exclusions

Our research suggests that the group does not respond to circular appeals and gives no grants for advertising in charity brochures, religious appeals, local appeals not in areas of company presence or large national appeals. Political donations are not made.

Applications

In writing to the correspondent.

Sportech plc

Gaming

Correspondent: Richard Boardley, Director of Corporate Affairs, 101 Wigmore Street, London W1U 1QU (tel: 020 7268 2400; email: cr@sportechplc.com; website: www.sportechplc.com)

Directors: Roger Withers, Chair; Ian Penrose, Chief Executive Officer; Cliff Baty, Chief Finance Officer; Rich Roberts; Peter Williams; David McKeith (women: 0; men: 6)

Year end	31/12/2013
Turnover	£1,103,000,000
Pre-tax profit	£5,200,000

Nature of business: The principal activities of the group are sports betting entertainment and provision of wagering technology solutions.

Company registration number: SC69140

Subsidiary undertakings include: Sportech Alderney Ltd; Sportech Gaming Ltd; Sportech Racing GmbH; Sportech Venues Inc. (US); and UK Lottery Management Ltd. More subsidiary undertakings can be found within the company's accounts and a full list is available from Companies House.

Brands include: MyWinners; Runnerz; Sportshero; The Football Pools;

Main locations: Liverpool, London

Total employees: 795

Focus of giving: Health, ill health, arts, culture, sport, recreation, community/social welfare, disability.

Cash donations undeclared ✓

Charitable donations

Cash UK (latest available):	2013	£930,000
	2011	£800,000
	2009	£1,000,000
	2008	£1,000,000
	2007	£1,300,000
Total UK (cash and in kind):	2013	£930,000
Cash worldwide:	2013	£930,000
Total worldwide (cash and in kind):	2013	£930,000

Community involvement

The group's website states:

> At Sportech we partner official sporting bodies and have donated over £1.1 billion to sports, the arts and good causes, leaving a lasting legacy by putting money back into funding grass roots sporting initiatives that make a real difference in the community.

Assistance is given towards sports, the arts and other charitable causes.

GamCare

The group promotes the activities of the charity, which supports people suffering from gambling addictions, and has provided about £500,000 to the major funders of the charity throughout the years.

Carers Trust
The CSR report mentions the trust receiving a total of £20,000, as part of the initiative with Preston North End FC.

Football
The report notes that in recent years support has focused on football. Over £600,000 (over unspecified time) has been donated to schemes in partnership with the English and Scottish Football Leagues, for example through the SPL's Football Fans in Training programme, promoting fitness and weight loss. The website notes that charitable contributions to British football totalled £530,000 over the years.

Charity partnership
StreetGames
In 2013 the group arranged a two-year funding agreement with StreetGames worth £1.7 million to create a new football programme 'StreetGames Football Pools Fives' which will work with young people in disadvantaged areas across the UK. Former England player Gareth Southgate became an ambassador for the programme in 2013.

Past initiatives
Some of the projects supported in the past include:

Every Player Counts
The group has partnered with The Football League Trust to support a three-year scheme developing football opportunities for people with disabilities. A total of over £2.5 million has been given.

Premier League Health
The Football Pools gave £1.63 million to this three-year initiative, which ended in 2012.

Fit For Football, Fit for Life
The Football Pools donated £1 million to the scheme in partnership with The Scottish Football League to help tackle serious health issues for young people across 30 Scottish Football League Clubs.

Foundation for Sport and the Arts
For a number of years the group was the sole funder of the foundation, which closed in 2012.

Corporate giving

The annual CSR report for 2013 states that about '£500,000 is generated annually for charitable causes through the management and operation of society lottery products within its Football Pools business activities.' We could not determine specific figures relating to that year, even though the report gives some examples of previous or ongoing projects. The group's website notes that 'today Sportech generates nearly £1 million per annum for charitable causes'. Based on the figures from the three previous years known to us, we estimate that UK cash contributions totalled about £930,000.

Beneficiaries include: Carers Trust; GamCare; and StreetGames.

Employee-led support

Our research indicates that employees are encouraged to fundraise for local charities and will support those efforts where appropriate.

Corporate social responsibility

CSR committee: No specific details found.

CSR information: The group's CSR strategy encompasses its responsibility to customers, society, environment and employees.

The website states: 'At Sportech we always strive to ensure we not only offer the best products and services to our customers, but to ensure we continue to operate with the highest levels of responsibility and integrity in all that we do.'

CSR report: An annual CSR report is published and available from the group's website (also contained within the annual report and accounts). Examples of charitable activities are given on the website.

Applications

Any enquiries should be made in writing to the correspondent.

Sportingbet Ltd (formerly Sportingbet plc)

Gaming

Correspondent: The Company Secretary, 3rd Floor, 45 Moorfields, London EC2Y 9AE (tel: 0800 028 0348; website: www.sportingbetplc.com)

Directors: Richard Cooper; Kenneth Alexander (women: 0; men: 2)

Year end	31/12/2013
Turnover	£0
Pre-tax profit	£276,982,000

Nature of business: Sportingbet is an online gaming company. Sportingbet plc annual report and accounts for 2013 state that the principal activity of the company is 'the provision of administrative services to GVC Holdings plc and its subsidiary undertakings'.

In March 2013 Sportingbet was acquired by GVC Holdings plc (headquartered in the Isle of Man) in conjunction with William Hill. Sportingbet is now part of the GVC group, which holds offices in Dublin, Malta, Tel Aviv, Guernsey, Alderney, Manila, Barbados and London.

In 2014 Sportingbet plc changed its name to Sportingbet Ltd

Company registration number: 3534726

Subsidiary undertakings include: Interactive Sports (C.I.) Ltd; Spread Your Wings Ltd; Sportingbet Holdings Ltd; and Sportingbet (IT) Services Ltd. A full list of subsidiary undertakings can be obtained from Companies House.

Total employees: 5

Focus of giving: Animal welfare, unpopular causes, sponsorship, sport, recreation.

Cash donations undeclared	✓
Market-led giving	✓
Sponsorship	✓

Charitable donations

Cash UK (latest available):	2011	£240,000
	2010	£229,600

Community involvement

Responsible Gambling
In order to mitigate potentially negative aspects of its business activities the company's website links customers to various organisations helping people with gambling problems. We know that Sportingbet/GVC Holdings plc has been supporting the Responsible Gambling Trust.

In the past Sportingbet has said (in its 2009/10 annual report) – 'in order to encourage a socially-integrated work environment, we place an emphasis on investing in the local communities in which we operate'.

Homing Ex-Racehorses Organisation Scheme (HEROS)
Sportingbet has supported the organisation 'throughout the years'.

Corporate giving

The annual report and accounts for 2013 did not give any information regarding the company's charitable giving. It is possible that charitable giving policies have been altered following the acquisition. In the past Sportingbet has given about £235,000 a year in the UK (we estimate the amount based on the figures from the two previous years known to us).

Note: We have used the latest accounts of Sportingbet plc, compiled prior to the change of the name.

Commercially led support

Sponsorship
In the past Sportingbet has sponsored various sports events, including Wolverhampton Wanderers football team (until 2013) and racing in Chester, and also individuals. In 2015 Sportingbet sponsors Lingfield Winter Derby.

Corporate social responsibility

CSR committee: We found no indications of a separate CSR committee for the company.

CSR information: We found no details regarding community contributions or CSR strategy. The company appears to concentrate on the promotion of responsible gambling.

CSR report: None found.

Applications

In writing to the correspondent.

St James's Place plc

Financial services

Correspondent: Hugh Gladman, Company Secretary and Foundation Director, St James's Place House, 1 Tetbury Road, Cirencester, Gloucestershire GL7 1FP (tel: 01285 640302 or 0800 013 8137; email: hugh.gladman@sjp.co.uk; website: www1.sjp.co.uk)

Directors: David Bellamy, Chief Executive Officer; Andrew Croft, Chief Financial Officer; David Lamb; Ian Gascoigne; Sarah Bates, Chair; Iain Cornish; Roger Yates; Simon Jeffreys; Baroness Wheatcroft; Mark Weinberg; Mike Wilson (women: 2; men: 9)

Year end	31/12/2013
Pre-tax profit	£461,200,000

Nature of business: St James's Place plc is a financial services group involved in the provision of wealth management services.

Company registration number: 3183415

Subsidiary undertakings include: St James's Place Acquisition Services Ltd; St James's Place UK plc; St James's Place Unit Trust Group Ltd; and St James's Place Wealth Management Group plc. A full list of subsidiary undertakings can be obtained from Companies House.

Main locations: London

UK employees: 985

Total employees: 985

Focus of giving: Health, ill health, marginalised people, poverty and social exclusion, sponsorship, sport, recreation, children, young people, disability, disasters.

Membership: BITC

FTSE 100	✓
Gifts in kind	✓
Market-led giving	✓
Matched funding	✓
Sponsorship	✓

Charitable donations

Cash UK (latest available):	2013	£1,900,000
	2011	£1,500,000
	2009	£1,333,000
	2008	£1,041,000
	2007	£1,200,000
Total UK (cash and in kind):	2013	£1,900,000
Cash worldwide:	2013	£1,900,000
Total worldwide (cash and in kind):	2013	£1,900,000

Community involvement

Schools and colleges

The group states that focus on schools and colleges remains the central strand of activity in local communities with two key initiatives.

Cirencester College – SJP supports the Academies Programme designed for students who aspire to work in a particular market sector and operated in co-operation with Career Academies UK. The company offers paid summer internships to students and extensive personal mentoring and business coaching as well as sponsoring awards.

Financial Education – partnerships are established with local schools in partnership with The Money Charity in order to help young people learn to manage their finances better. Staff members help deliver financial education sessions. During the year work has also began with teachers 'to support them in the development of the financial education curriculum in their own schools', assisted by SJP volunteers.

St James's Place Foundation (Charity Commission no. 1144606)

The group channels its charitable contributions through the corporate foundation (established in 1992) some of the trustees of which are also the group directors. All administrative and management costs are met by St James's Place Management Services Ltd. The foundation is a grant-making charity which relies on the support it receives from the entire SJP community, including employees, partners, suppliers, fund managers and other third parties connected to the group. Over 80% of all the partners and employees make regular monthly donations out of their income or salary to the foundation and also help to raise funds from events and sponsored activities. The website also notes that to date the foundation has raised more than £34 million supporting special schools and registered small/medium size charities in three areas – helping children, fighting cancer and assisting hospices. Support is usually given in the communities local to the group's offices.

Disaster appeals from UK-registered charities can also be supported, at the trustees' discretion.

Corporate giving

According to the group's annual report and accounts for 2013 SJP community raised £2.6 million, matched by a further £1.9 million, all donated to the St James's Place Foundation.

The foundation's accounts for 2013 state that covenant and Gift Aid contributions totalled £1.1 million, the SJP matched funding totalled more than £2.4 million and audit fee, staff and support services costs (amounting to £255,000) were donated by the group. Fundraising events amounted to £1.4 million of the income total. It is further specified that a total of £466,000 went to hospices, £282,000 to support charities helping people with cancer and £3.1 million to causes focusing on disadvantaged young people or those with disabilities.

We take the figure of over £1.9 million (given as matched funding and adding the administration support costs), to represent the group's direct contribution.

Beneficiaries of the foundation included: Smile, Support and Care (£1 million); Paul's Cancer Support Centre (£10,000); Chicks; Education for Children; Help the Hospices; and Onside.

See the corporate charity entry on p. 430 for more information.

In-kind support

Staff volunteering efforts.

Employee-led support

In 2013 a new initiative was launched to recognise and support employees who volunteer. It allows staff members to apply for a small grant of up to £250 to be used for the benefit of their supported sports club or association. The group had plans to repeat and extend this initiative in 2014.

The CSR report confirms that 40% of SJP employees are actively engaged in volunteering in their local communities. The group notes that 'this is an important part of our culture and is an area we are seeking to develop'.

Matched funding

Many of the partners and employees give both by covenant and engage in other fundraising activities. Such funds are then matched by the group 'pound by pound'.

Commercially led support

Sponsorships

The group is sponsor of the Loughborough University Swimming Programme. The relationship with the university has been extended until 2016. According to the SJP's website 'the support provided by St James's Place safeguards and secures the existing swimming development programme, allowing the squad to maintain its current highly effective performance programme'. Help includes various support to swimmers, scholarships, specialist sessions, subsidised accommodation and so on.

Corporate social responsibility

CSR committee: The following statement is taken from the CSR report for 2013:

> Responsible management is central to our culture, and the task of maintaining this culture (including our CSR ambitions) is a key focus of the Executive Committee of the Board, comprising the four Executive Directors. Oversight of this key aspect of our business is provided by the full board. The Executive Committee of the Board is supported in this objective (as in all of their work) by a number of sub-committees, which are chaired by the directors and which involve other members of senior management. Responsibility for specific areas has been further delegated to a number of specialist sub-committees.

CSR information: Information provided in the CSR report for 2013 states:

> St James's Place is committed to growing the business in a way that considers the economic, social and environmental impacts of what we do. We understand that responsible management is increasingly important to all our stakeholders – shareholders, clients, partners, employees, suppliers and the communities in which we operate.

CSR report: An informative and detailed CSR report is published within the annual report and accounts.

Corporate charity: St James's Place Foundation (Charity Commission no. 1144606).

Exclusions

Our research indicates that the following are not generally eligible:

- Charities with reserves of over 50% of income
- Administrative costs
- Activities primarily the responsibility of statutory agencies
- Replacement of lost statutory funding
- Research
- Events
- Advertising
- Holidays
- Sponsorship
- Contributions to large capital appeals
- Single faith charities
- Charities that are raising funds on behalf of another charity

Applications

St James's Place Foundation (Charity Commission no. 1144606): applicants who believe that they fit the criteria are welcome to apply at any time via the foundation's website. The application procedure for all of the programmes can take between four to six months. The following information is given on the foundation's website: 'applications for a small grant will normally receive a visit from a representative of the foundation, who will subsequently report to the trustees. Following the trustees' decision, successful applicants will be notified'.

Further details can be found on the website or by contacting the Foundation Manager, Mark Longbottom (tel: 01285 878562; email: mark.longbottom@sjp.co.uk) at the group's address.

The SJP: enquiries about general giving by the group should be directed to the correspondent.

St Modwen Properties plc

Property

Correspondent: The Corporate Social Responsibility Team, Park Point, 17 High Street, Longbridge, Birmingham B31 2UQ (tel: 01212 229400; fax: 01212 229401; email: info@stmodwen.co.uk; website: www.stmodwen.co.uk)

Directors: Bill Shannon, Chair; Bill Oliver, Chief Executive; Michael Dunn, Group Finance Director; Steve Burke; Lesley James; John Salmon; Simon Clarke; Richard Mully; Kay Chaldecott; Ian Bull (women: 2; men: 8)

Year end	30/11/2013
Turnover	£161,100,000
Pre-tax profit	£80,500,000

Nature of business: Residential and commercial property development. The group has four specialisations: town centre regeneration; partnering industry in its restructuring; brownfield land renewal; and heritage restoration.

Company registration number: 349201

Subsidiary undertakings include: Festival Waters Ltd; St Modwen Developments (Chorley) Ltd; and St Modwen Developments (Wythenshawe) Ltd; A full list of subsidiary undertakings can be obtained from Companies House.

UK employees: 255

Total employees: 255

Focus of giving: Enterprise/training, health, ill health, safety and crime prevention, sport, recreation, children, young people, community/social welfare, disability.

Cash donations undeclared	✓
Gifts in kind	✓
Market-led giving	✓

Charitable donations

Cash UK (latest available):	2013	£10,700
	2011	£11,000
	2009	£14,000
	2008	£7,000
Total UK (cash and in kind):	2013	£10,700
Cash worldwide:	2013	£10,700
Total worldwide (cash and in kind):	2013	£10,700

Community involvement

According to the group's website, support is given to local charities and community groups. Some examples of community engagement include:

- St Columba's Catholic Primary School (Longbridge) – pupils receiving a lesson in site safety, organised by St Modwen Homes. Children visited the site, were given personal protective equipment and learned about the dangers of entering a live building site. Following the visit a poster competition was launched with the winning artist receiving a voucher for Toys R Us
- Art competition – organised by St Modwen Homes with community groups from Brent and surrounding area. 'The Mayor announced the winner at a special presentation event hosted at Wembley Central, where winners and runners-up were presented with prizes including cheques for £250 and £150 to be spent on resources for the groups'
- ArtStart – St Modwen co-operated with local Edmonton Green arts charity ArtStart. The charity, which 'helps local children express themselves through art rather than 'hanging out' on the streets'. Workshops were held in the centre where children designed a mural representing what they loved about Edmonton Green
- Oasis Children's Venture (London) – *through the St Modwen Environmental Trust* £6,400 was awarded to the organisation. The support will benefit local deprived children and young people by 'combining innovative play facilities with the promotion of environmental education'. The donation funded, among other things, an outdoor puppet theatre, a storytelling space and enhancements to the outdoor classroom

The St Modwen Environmental Trust

According to the CSR report for 2013, 'established in 2008, the trust has funded over £250,000 of community projects and in 2013, it reached the end of its lifecycle'. The trust was funded through the group and by the Landfill Communities Fund and supported environmental schemes, historic buildings and public amenities. The group is now working to renew its strategy for charitable support which will be aligned with the business strategy and have both local and national focus.

Corporate giving

We could not identify the amount donated to charitable causes in 2012/13. We estimate the amount to have totalled about £10,700, based on the figures form the three previous years known to us.

In-kind support

Employee involvement and expertise.

Employee-led support

Staff members participate in community engagement initiatives by the group.

Commercially led support

Enfield borough council

According to the company's website, the group works in partnership with Enfield borough council promoting the 'Jobsnet' via St Modwen's Edmonton Green Shopping Centre. The initiative for over five years has been helping unemployed local residents get back into work through provision of 'CV advice and printing, application form completion and interview techniques, signposting to relevant free training schemes and a job search facility.'

Apprenticeships

The website notes that apprenticeships are encouraged across all sites. There are partnerships with two colleges (Warwickshire College and Bournville College) 'to appoint a number of local students to work on [the group's] sites, learn important skills, gain site experience and ultimately employment opportunities'.

Corporate social responsibility

CSR committee: There is a CSR Team.

CSR information: The group's website states the following:

> Acquiring brownfield sites, remediating and transforming them into cleaner, greener and brighter environments where businesses and communities can thrive: this is the essence of what we do. In turn, it promotes positive social, economic and environmental change.

Accordingly, the CSR strategy focuses on economic, social, sustainability and health and safety impact.

CSR report: The company's CSR report is contained within the annual report and accounts.

Exclusions

Political donations are not made.

Applications

In writing to the correspondent.

Stagecoach Group plc

Transport and communications

Correspondent: Steven Stewart, Director of Corporate Communications, 10 Dunkeld Road, Perth PH1 5TW (tel: 01738 442111; fax: 01738 443076; email: charity@stagecoachgroup.com or steven.stewart@stagecoachgroup.com; website: www.stagecoachgroup.com)

Directors: Brian Souter, Chair; Martin Griffiths, Chief Executive Officer; Ross Paterson, Finance Director; Gregor Alexander; Helen Mahy; Garry Watts; Phill White; Will Whitehom; Ann Gloag; Ewan Brown (women: 2; men: 8)

Year end	30/04/2014
Turnover	£2,930,000,000
Pre-tax profit	£158,000,000

Nature of business: Principal activity of the group is the provision of public transport services in the UK and North America.

Company registration number: SC100764

Subsidiary undertakings include: East Midland Motor Services Ltd; Stagecoach Bus Holdings Ltd; Stagecoach South Western Trains Ltd; Thames Transit Ltd; and The Yorkshire Traction Company Ltd. A full list of subsidiary undertakings can be found in the annual report and accounts.

Main locations: Ilford, Chichester, Isle of Wight, Exeter, Gwent, Northampton, Perth, Sheffield, Rugby, Sunderland, Oxford, Manchester, London, Liverpool, Cowdenbeath, Cambridge, Chesterfield, Carlisle, Gloucester, Ayr

UK employees: 30,000

Total employees: 35,000

Focus of giving: Education, enterprise/training, health, ill health, large national appeals, local groups, overseas projects, sponsorship, children, young people, community/social welfare, disasters.

Charity of the Year	✓
Gifts in kind	✓
Humanitarian aid: overseas	✓
Market-led giving	✓
Matched funding	✓
Overseas giving	✓
Sponsorship	✓

Charitable donations

Cash UK (latest available):	2014	£700,000
	2012	£500,000
	2011	£600,000
	2009	£700,000
	2008	£700,000
Total UK (cash and in kind):	2014	£700,000
Cash worldwide:	2014	£700,000
Total worldwide (cash and in kind):	2014	£700,000

Community involvement

Stagecoach Group Community Fund

Charitable support is channelled through the fund, supporting 'a range of good causes, community projects and individual initiatives every year'.

The group's CSR report for 2013/14 states:

> We share our success with local people and communities by funding the vital work of local, national and international charities. For many years, Stagecoach Group has invested between 0.5% and 1% of the profits from our transport operations in the UK and North America in good causes and community projects.

Over the past six years about £3.8 million has been given to support good causes.

Many of the companies 'have adopted specific good causes as their charities of the year and focus for local fundraising'.

National Literacy Trust

The group has recently released a children's book, written by an employee. 'At least £1.50 from the sale of each book will be donated to the National Literacy Trust, which works to improve the reading, writing, speaking and listening skills in the UK's most disadvantaged communities.'

Air Ambulances

In 2013 a total of £100,000 (over the following five years) was committed to Scotland's Charity Air Ambulance and there was a previous agreement to donate £100,000 (over four years) to the London Air Ambulance service.

Sunday Mail Centenary Fund

The fund was given £10,000 towards its work supporting charities in Scotland and the rest of the UK.

Philippines Typhoon Appeal

A total of £10,000 was donated to the appeal and the group also agreed to match the fundraising of employees across the group up to £40,000.

Charity partnerships

Mencap

The CSR report notes that the group has 'partnered with Mencap and taken part in a number of work experience programmes for people with learning difficulties'.

Guide Dogs for the Blind

The partnership allows the dog trainers free travel on the group's buses and trains.

Transaid

This international development charity is helped through 'the secondment of Stagecoach driving instructors to help improve driving standards, and reduce road accidents, in sub-Saharan Africa'. Two vehicles to be used in driver training in Zambia and Tanzania have also been donated.

Charity of the Year

A number of companies have a selected Charity of the Year.

Initiatives include:

- Stagecoach Merseyside and South Lancashire working with a local Travelsafe scheme and partnering Your Choice scheme, 'which educates young children of the danger of misbehaving around buses'
- South West Trains-Network Rail Alliance donating 'thousands of pounds to local charities every year as well as a similar value in complimentary train tickets across the network'
- East Midlands Trains and South West Trains-Network Rail Alliance taking part in several train naming events to help local organisations
- Stagecoach Yorkshire raising £3,000 for Sheffield Children's Hospital by producing and selling a 'Calendar Girls' style calendar
- Stagecoach London helping to raise £3,000 for a local hospice by donating a vehicle for a bus pull event
- East Midlands Trains being involved in a range of community rail initiatives (through three community rail partnerships) – events are held at stations include community days, fundraising events, community arts and gardening days
- Stagecoach Cumbria and North Lancashire supporting Carlisle Youth Zone – 'an after-school initiative to keep children engaged in safe, educational and healthy activity' – with £30,000 over the past three years

Assistance is also given to bus and rail industry charities and events.

Corporate giving

In 2013/14 the group made charitable contributions totalling £700,000 (2012/13: £700,000) 'to help a number of charities and to support fundraising events and vital services'. We could not determine a breakdown of support provided; however, the correspondent has confirmed that the amount awarded in cash in the UK only was £700,000.

Beneficiaries include: Carlisle Youth Zone; Children in Need; Comic Relief; National Literacy Trust; Sheffield Children's Hospital; Sport Relief; and Transaid.

In-kind support

Non-cash support includes: provision of buses and coaches for various local and national events as well as vehicles to assist with emergency services exercises; free travel, for example, for on-duty police officers or tickets for raffles and charity events; secondment of staff to good causes overseas,; and provision of management support and employee time. During the London Olympic and Paralympic Games the group handed out free ice lollies to spectators.

Employee-led support

Stagecoach employees help good causes overseas through the group's secondment and take part in a number of local or national fundraising events (such as Children in Need, Comic Relief, Sport Relief or Movember campaign).

Matched funding

Employees participate in fundraising activities in their spare time and such efforts are matched by the group's contributions.

Commercially led support

Sponsorship

According to the group's website, it provides sponsorship of 'charity occasions'.

Jobcentre Plus

The group supported the government's back to work initiative in co-operation with Jobcentre Plus offices to recruit and train potential new drivers.

The website provides an example of Stagecoach East supporting Cancer Research UK 'by operating pink buses in Bedford, Cambridge and Peterborough in an awareness raising drive'.

Corporate social responsibility

CSR committee: No specific details found.

CSR information: The CSR report for 2013/14 states:

> Every day, our business and our employees touch people's lives and we make a significant contribution to society. Like all businesses, we want to grow, but we want to do that responsibly.
>
> Supporting the community. Working with the community. Part of the community. That is embedded in our business philosophy.

The group's CSR approach is concentrated on: its people and customers; safety and security; accessibility and affordability; environmental stewardship and performance; building community relationships; and corporate governance.

There are separate documents outlining Stagecoach Group's approach to CSR, which can be found on the website. A major part of the group's focus is environment and sustainability issues.

CSR report: There is a Sustainability Report, which mainly relates to environmental initiatives and reduction of carbon emission, is published annually and available from the website. CSR is reported on within the Financial Review of the annual report and accounts. More details of charitable activities are also available online.

Applications

Applications for Stagecoach Group Community Fund can be downloaded from the group's website. Once completed, they should be emailed to: charity@stagecoachgroup.com.

Further enquiries should be directed to the correspondent.

Stansted Airport Ltd

Airport operators

Correspondent: Community Relations Office, Enterprise House, Bassingbourn Road, Essex CM24 1QW (email: stn_communityrelations@stanstedairport.com; website: www.stanstedairport.com)

Year end	31/03/2014

Nature of business: Airport operator. Stansted airport is now owned by M.A.G plc. This entry concentrates on the subsidiary company Stansted Airport Ltd.

The Manchester Airports Group plc (M.A.G) is the country's largest UK-owned airport operator. M.A.G owns and operates Manchester, Stansted, East Midlands and Bournemouth airports. Its property and facilities management arm, M.A.G Developments, is responsible for the group's estate and also the development of Manchester's Airport City.

M.A.G is privately managed on behalf of its shareholders, the local authorities of Greater Manchester and Industry Funds Management. M.A.G is a private company, with shareholdings held by Council of the City of Manchester (35.5%), Industry Funds Management (35.5%) and the nine remaining Greater Manchester local authorities (29%).

Focus of giving: General charitable purposes, environment, animal welfare, community/social welfare.

Charity of the Year	✓
Sponsorship	✓

Community involvement

Stansted airport works with the community in schools, education, sport, employment, skills training and other projects. The recently formed 'Stansted Airport Community Network' provides links and advice to neighbouring businesses about how they can join forces with the airport and participate in a range of education, employment and volunteering projects 'to help make the local community a more vibrant place to live and work'.

Local community projects and initiatives are supported through three categories of funding:

- Stansted Airport Passenger Community Fund
- Stansted Airport Community Trust

▸ Stansted Community Fund

Charity partner
Each year staff at Stansted Airport vote to select a nominated charity partner, giving a clear focus for the airport's fundraising activities, offering staff volunteering opportunities and supporting the role the airport plays in helping good causes in the local community. In 2013 the chosen partner was Essex and Herts Air Ambulance Trust.

Corporate giving

Stansted Airport Community Trust is funded by the airport and fines from aircraft which infringe noise level regulations. In 2013/14 a total of £112,000 was donated to 102 local charities. Beneficiaries included: Age Concern Harlow and Barnston Village Hall (£2,000 each).

The separate **Stansted Airport Passenger Community Fund** also donates money to local causes within a 20-mile radius of Stansted airport. The money is raised from unwanted foreign currency which is collected in the terminal – £26,000 was collected from January to December 2013. The fund is used to support local sports clubs, preschool nurseries as well as the elderly and animal charities.

The information in this entry is limited as Stansted airport is now owned by M.A.G plc. Figures relating to charitable giving and information on the company's activities relate to the Stansted airport site. M.A.G plc also owns the airports at Bristol, Bournemouth and East Midlands – see separate entries. We have not recorded the amount spent by the Stansted Airport Community Trust in 'Cash donations' as the trust is ultimately funded by M.A.G. and this would have meant recording the group's giving figures twice.

In-kind support

Staff volunteer and raise funds for local community groups and for the airport's Charity partner.

Employee-led support

At London Stansted Airport, a total of 500 hours were recorded on various volunteer schemes. These included a dedicated team of employee volunteers who co-ordinated and sat on the London Stansted Airport Passenger Fund committee, others who supported the Panathlon Challenge, as well as those who regularly volunteer as mentors.

Applications

In writing to the correspondent address.

Steria Ltd

Consultancy, computer software, professional support services

Correspondent: P. A. Cashmore, Company Secretary, Three Cherry Trees Lane, Hemel Hempstead, Hertfordshire HP2 7AH (tel: 0845 601 8877; fax: 01442 884335; website: www.steria.co.uk)

Directors: John Torrie, Chief Executive Officer (UK. and Asia); D. S. Ahluwaha; Laurent Lemaire; J. J. Moran; S. C. M. Dangu (women: 1; men: 4)

Year end	31/12/2013
Turnover	£442,662,000
Pre-tax profit	£24,193,000

Nature of business: The principal activities of the company are the provision of computing, consultancy and business processing outsourcing services to private and public sector organisations.

The company's immediate parent company is Steria Services Ltd and ultimate parent company – Groupe Steria SCA (Steria Group), registered in France.

Company registration number: 4077975

Subsidiary undertakings include: NHS Shared Business Services Ltd; Shared Services Connected Ltd; and Steria Recruitment Ltd.

Main locations: Bedford, Manchester, Northampton, Southampton, Reading, Edinburgh, Holborn

UK employees: 3,206

Total employees: 3,206

Focus of giving: Education, enterprise/training, science technology, children, young people, community/social welfare, disability.

Cash donations undeclared ✓
Gifts in kind ✓

Charitable donations

Cash UK (latest available):	2013	£78,000
	2011	£86,000
	2009	£74,000
	2007	£74,000
	2006	£683,000
Total UK (cash and in kind):	2013	£78,000
Cash worldwide:	2013	£78,000
Total worldwide (cash and in kind):	2013	£78,000

Community involvement

Our research indicates that the company has supported community and social welfare, children and young people, computing and educational causes. Assistance is particularly given to activities and training programmes promoting employability, also IT related programmes and education. Its past charity partner was Scope.

According to the company's website, the global strategy, which we believe informs group-wide policies, puts emphasis on:

> Strengthening community links through education and employment … Our volunteer-driven community programmes exist to give people in the communities where we operate the access they need to education, IT and jobs. Within this framework, Steria operations in different countries are free to support and work in partnership with their neighbouring communities in the ways that make the most sense for all concerned.

The following information is taken from the global CR Report for 2014:

> In the UK, we work with the local Chamber of Commerce and the University both in Hertfordshire near our HQ to develop a 'Smart County in the UK' as part of the Environment Forum of the Chamber.

Corporate giving

Charitable donations made in 2013 could not be determined. Based on the figures from the past three years known to us, we estimate that about £78,000 is given in cash contributions in the UK.

In-kind support

Employee volunteering.

Employee-led support

The global CR Report for 2014 states that Steria's 'employees, largely on a volunteer basis, participate in community activities in the countries in which the group operates'.

One Day Challenge
The group-wide initiative invites employees, clients and partners to contribute generously to charitable causes. During 2013 UK employees raised about £27,000 to charities, including Action for Children, Cancer Research and Children in Need. A total of 141 activities were organised for the benefit of 77 charities with the support of 188 volunteers and 29 clients and partners. Some activities were jointly undertaken with Cleveland Police and Co-operative Banking Group helping Catcote Academy and Ronald McDonald House (linked to the Manchester Children's Hospital).

Fish and Chip Babies
Steria UK staff supported the initiative and engaged in knitting jumpers and hats to new born babies in Africa.

Matched funding
Our research notes there being matched funding opportunities in the past; however, we could not find any information on whether the scheme is still operating.

Corporate social responsibility

CSR committee: There were no details found.

CSR information: We did not find any specific policy for Steria Ltd. Globally the group focuses on seven corporate responsibility areas – human rights, living green, people, business ethics, community, governance and clients.

The website states:

> We have put corporate responsibility at the heart of our strategy. The principles of corporate responsibility and ethics have been integral to our culture for over 40 years. They shape the way in which we fulfil our responsibilities to all Steria stakeholders, from our shareholders and clients to the communities in which we operate and our employees – past, present and prospective.

CSR report: No report is published for the UK company. The group's CR Report is available from the group's website.

Applications

In writing to the correspondent.

J Stobart and Sons Ltd

Transport and communications

Correspondent: Ronnie Stobart, Trustee, Newlands Mill, Hesket Newmarket, Wigton, Cumbria CA7 8HP (tel: 01697 478261)

Directors: R. J. Stobart; R. A. Stobart; P. J. Stobart; L. E. Rigg (women: 1; men: 3)

Year end	31/12/2013
Turnover	£20,553,300
Pre-tax profit	(£40,037)

Nature of business: The manufacture and retail of animal feedstuffs.

Company registration number: 783738

Main locations: Carlisle

UK employees: 20

Total employees: 20

Focus of giving: General charitable purposes, overseas projects, religion.

Charitable donations

Cash UK (latest available):	2013	£1,520,000
	2012	£1,900,000
	2010	£625,000
	2008	£890,000
	2007	£785,000
Total UK (cash and in kind):	2013	£1,520,000
Cash worldwide:	2013	£1,520,000
Total worldwide (cash and in kind):	2013	£1,520,000

Community involvement

J Stobart and Sons channels its support through **The Stobart Newlands Charitable Trust** (Charity Commission no. 328464), which makes grants, mainly to Christian and missionary organisations.

We were unable to find a website for this company.

Corporate giving

In 2013 the company made donations of more than £1.5 million to **The Stobart Newlands Charitable Trust**.

See the corporate charity entry on p. 431 for more information.

Corporate social responsibility

CSR information: We found no details on CSR.

Corporate charity: The Stobart Newlands Charitable Trust (Charity Commission no. 328464).

Exclusions

Grants are not made to individuals.

Applications

In writing to: Mr Ronnie Stobart, The Stobart Newlands Charitable Trust, Mill Croft, Newlands, Hesket Newmarket, Wigton, Cumbria CA7 8HP. Note, however, that unsolicited requests are unlikely to succeed.

Stobart Group

Logistics, professional support services

Correspondent: The Community Team, Stretton Green Distribution Park, Langford Way, Appleton Thorn, Warrington WA4 4TZ (tel: 01925 605400; email: charity@stobartgroup.com; website: www.stobartgroup.co.uk)

Directors: Andrew Tinkler, Chief Executive Officer; Ben Whawell, Chief Financial Officer; Richard Butcher; Andrew Wood; Iain Ferguson; John Coombs; John Garbutt (women: 0; men: 7)

Year end	28/02/2014
Turnover	£99,179,000
Pre-tax profit	(£10,187,000)

Nature of business: Stobart Group is an infrastructure development and support services business 'operating in the biomass energy, railway maintenance and aviation sectors as well as having investments in a national property and logistics portfolio'.

There are four main areas: Stobart Energy; Stobart Rail; Stobart Aviation; and Stobart Investments.

Company registration number: 39117

Subsidiary undertakings include: London Southend Airport Company Ltd; Stobart Holdings Ltd; Stobart Rail Ltd; O'Connor Container Transport Ltd; and Westlink Group Ltd. A full list of subsidiaries can be found within the group's accounts.

Focus of giving: Health, ill health, sponsorship, children, young people, community/social welfare.

Charity of the Year	✓
Market-led giving	✓
Sponsorship	✓

Charitable donations

Cash UK (latest available):	2014	£188,000
	2012	£223,000
	2010	£30,000
Total UK (cash and in kind):	2014	£188,000
Cash worldwide:	2014	£188,000
Total worldwide (cash and in kind):	2014	£188,000

Community involvement

The group's website states that its Charitable Donations and Sponsorship Policy is currently under review – 'We aim to release an update as soon as possible so please check our website periodically for updates.'

According to the CSR Policy paper Stobart supports charities and initiatives in the communities in which it operates. 'Each business unit is encouraged to develop schemes which will support the requirements of the community in the local area alongside the donations that the group makes annually to its chosen charity partners.'

Charity partnerships

Carlisle Youth Zone

The group added almost £38,000 to employee donations to support the initiative through. The youth club is aimed at young people of the area and allows them undertake activities when the schools are closed.

Roald Dahl's Marvellous Children's Charity

The year witnessed the launch of a three year relationship between Steady Eddie and the charity in order to help seriously ill children and young people in the UK.

Charity of the Year

Cancer Research UK has been supported for a number of years and in 2013/14 received a donation of £150,000.

Corporate giving

We take it that in 2013/14 the company's contributions to charitable causes totalled almost £188,000, based on examples given in the latest CSR report for 2013/14. Further amounts were donated by the group's employees through the donation scheme (totalling almost £15,000) and donations to specific causes through individual employees' efforts were of about £60,000 – Alfi Walk (£21,000) and The Starlight Ladies' Walk (£39,000).

Beneficiaries included: Cancer Research UK (£150,000) and Carlisle Youth Zone (£37,500).

In-kind support

Our research indicates that in the past the group has provided in-kind support

Employee-led support

During the year Stobart piloted Get Involved – an employee engagement initiative which seeks to encourage employees to get more hands-on within their local community.

Employee Donation Scheme
The scheme allows staff members to get a grant of £50 to donate to a charity or a good cause of their choice. The group has 'actively encouraged employee team pooling of donations to increase targeted engagement and provide greater positive impact'.

The CSR report for 2013/14 notes that employee donations totalled almost £5,600 with ad hoc donations totalling a further £9,300.

Examples of employee engagement, given in the report, are:

The Children's Brain Tumour Research Centre – Walk for Alfi
The Bardon team raised donations from local businesses and held a special 'Alfi Day'. According to the report, the initiative 'proved very popular with the local community and seems set to become an annual event'. Other Stobart employees were also asked to allocate their £50 employee donation (almost £3,200 was raised) and in total almost £21,000 was collected. There is now an official Site Charity Committee established with plans for the year ahead.

St Rocco's Hospice – The Starlight Ladies' Walk
An employee participated in the walk to raise money for this Warrington hospice. Some colleagues contributed their £50 employee donation adding £900 to the total of over £39,000.

Other initiatives undertaken by the staff included: food bank donations; Movember campaign raising over £8,000; and fancy dress cycling and uniform free days in support of Children in Need.

Commercially led support

Professional Jockeys Association
There is a long standing relationship with the association with the group providing Career Ending Insurance scheme. According to the CSR report:

> Without Stobart's partnership with the PJA they simply would not be able to offer jockeys this valued support scheme. As part of the agreement, jockeys wear Stobart branded breaches and Stobart Group becomes headline sponsor of The Lesters which serve to recognise jockey achievements.

Corporate social responsibility

CSR committee: The CSR Committee, appointed in 2012, comprises a number of Senior Executives from across the group, each of which 'has a specific area of expertise and clearly defined responsibilities, ensuring that each operating Division and every employee is represented and considered'. The committee is chaired by Chief Financial Officer and meets on a regular basis to ensure 'the implementation of the CSR work programme and the delivery of the Stobart Group's CSR strategy'.

CSR information: The CSR report for 2013/14 states: 'Positive engagement with the local community is at the heart of our business aims to minimise our local impact and ensure we act as a 'responsible neighbour.'

The group's CSR Strategy concentrates on four areas: environmental responsibility; business integrity; Stobart people; and community.

The CSR Policy paper states that Stobart 'aims to achieve its business objectives in a responsible manner, recognising the economic, social and environmental impacts of our activities' and provides the following commitments:

- Minimising environmental impacts as a result of its activities
- Ensuring that the business is managed in all areas according to the highest ethical and professional standards
- Continuing the annual charitable donations and to encourage staff and business units to support and develop initiatives within the communities in which it operates
- Providing a safe and structured platform to enable all staff to grow and develop within the business . . . and treating all of its employees in a fair and equitable way

CSR report: An annual CSR report is published within the annual report and accounts.

Exclusions

Our research suggests that support is not ordinarily given to the following:

- Requests from external parties
- Funding for overseas visits or trips
- Funding for arts/media projects (such as student films, exhibitions and so on)
- Projects that only benefit one person

Applications

Sponsorship and charitable donations enquiries: In writing to the correspondent. Our research indicates that due to the volume of applications the group receives staff will only respond to successful applications.

Corporate social responsibility enquiries: Enquiries can be directed to the CSR Committee (email: csr@stobartgroup.com). The group asks: 'For enquiries relating to Environmental Responsibility, Business Integrity and Employee Engagement please refer to our CSR Policy before making an enquiry.'

STV Group plc

Media

Correspondent: Jane E. A. Tames, Secretary, Pacific Quay, Glasgow G51 1PQ (tel: 01413 003000 (main switchboard); email: jane.tames@stv.tv; website: www.stvplc.tv)

Directors: Margaret Ford, Chair; Rob Woodward, Chief Executive Officer; George Watt, Chief Financial Officer; David Shearer; Jamie Matheson; Michael Jackson; Genevieve Shore; Christian Woolfenden; Anne Cannon (women: 3; men: 6)

Year end	31/12/2013
Turnover	£112,100,000
Pre-tax profit	£14,300,000

Nature of business: STV Group plc is a Scottish media company.

Company registration number: SC042391

Subsidiary undertakings include: Ginger Television Productions Ltd; STV Central Ltd; STV North Ltd; and STV Productions Ltd. A full list of subsidiary undertakings can be obtained from Companies House.

Main locations: Glasgow

UK employees: 396

Total employees: 396

Focus of giving: Education, enterprise/ training, poverty and social exclusion, children, young people, community/ social welfare.

Cash donations undeclared	✓
Gifts in kind	✓

Charitable donations

Cash UK (latest available):	2011	£93,000
	2009	£19,000
	2008	£15,000
	2007	£29,000

Community involvement

STV Appeal Charity (OSCR no. SC042429)
The group's major initiative is the STV Appeal, mainly funded by individual donations from STV viewers and fundraising from corporate partners. In 2013 the charity raised £2.5 million with all overheads being met by STV and the Hunter Foundation. Some of the executive directors are trustees of the charity. For more details see 'In-kind support' section in this entry.

Charity partnership
In 2013 the STV Appeal became an official charity partner of the freshnlo Pedal for Scotland (Glasgow to Edinburgh) cycle. Over £100,000 was raised, including fundraising from employees and 'supporters'.

Education

According to the group's 2013 annual report, STV has relationships with colleges and universities 'to support the development of future talent to the industry and work to develop relationships with educational institutions across Scotland'. Two formal partnerships have been established with Glasgow Caledonian University and Napier University in Edinburgh. 'Through these partnerships students will be able to develop skills in a live broadcast and production environment and they will be provided opportunities to showcase content they develop.'

Corporate giving

During 2013 the STV Appeal raised a total of £2.5 million. While running the initiative will involve substantial expenses for the group, the £2.5 million was collected through viewers' or staff contributions and donations from corporate partners, rather than STV itself. Unfortunately, we were unable to determine the cash contributions or community support costs spent by the group.

In-kind support

STV Appeal 2013

The appeal was launched in 2011 in partnership with The Hunter Foundation and aims to address the child poverty Scotland. It is funded through individual donations from STV viewers and fundraising from corporate partners. The group's employees take part through fundraising and volunteering. In 2013 the charity raised £2.5 million with all overheads being met by STV and the foundation. The Scottish Government for the three years of the appeal's existence has provided matched funding for the first £1 million raised. The same arrangement was confirmed for 2014 as well. The appeal works closely with six charities and also smaller community based projects.

> The STV Appeal endeavours to work beyond reactive grant-making, to identify and target key areas of unmet need. Investment is made in innovative and effective projects that will make a sustainable difference to Scotland's most disadvantaged children and young people, and support long-term social change.

The money raised goes towards the provision of food and clothing, opportunities for training and employability, also practical, social and emotional support. Since its inception, the appeal has made 172 big and small grants to projects across all 32 local authority areas in Scotland, helping 27,000 children. The CSR report further specifies that of the 2013 support 28% has been allocated to projects that help build stronger communities and 25% to projects supporting employability.

The CSR report states: 'STV is in a privileged position using our unparalleled convening power to raise awareness of child poverty and make a positive difference and this commitment will continue in the year ahead.'

We classify the appeal as in-kind support, as the group provides a platform for charitable donations.

Employee-led support

The group's employees contribute their time and fundraising efforts to the STV Appeal.

Commercially led support

Employment

Work placements and internships are offered across all areas of the business for pupils in secondary education and further and higher education. In 2013 a total of 70 placements were provided.

Get Ready for Work

STV continues to support the government's programme, which provides mentored training programmes for young people not in education, employment or training (NEET).

Corporate social responsibility

CSR committee: There was no evidence of a separate CSR Committee.

CSR information: The group's CSR report for 2013 states: 'As a company with deep connections with consumers, communities and a strong public service content ethos, we recognise the need to give something back and make a positive difference.'

CSR report: A CSR report is contained within the annual report and accounts.

Exclusions

Our research indicates that sponsorships are not undertaken and help is not given for fundraising events, advertising in charity brochures, religious) appeals or overseas projects. Political donations are not made.

Applications

In writing to the correspondent.

Swann-Morton Ltd

Manufacturing

Correspondent: Michael Hurst, Company Secretary, Owlerton Green, Sheffield S6 2BJ (tel: 01142 344231; fax: 01142 314966; website: www.swann-morton.com)

Directors: Michael Hirst; Richard Whiteley; Christopher Taylor (women: 0; men: 3)

Year end	31/10/2013
Turnover	£20,369,331
Pre-tax profit	£1,466,565

Nature of business: The company's main activity is the manufacture of fine edge blades for both surgical and industrial purposes.

The company is a wholly owned subsidiary of WR Swann and Co. Limited.

The Swann Morton Group consists of Swann Morton Ltd, Swann Morton (Services) Ltd and Swann Morton (Microbiological Laboratory Services) Ltd.

Company registration number: 696744

Main locations: Sheffield

Total employees: 315

Focus of giving: Education, health, ill health, medical research, older people, disability.

Gifts in kind ✓

Charitable donations

Cash UK (latest available):	2013	£6,500
	2011	£4,300
	2009	£45,000
	2008	£45,800
	2007	£53,600
Total UK (cash and in kind):	2013	£6,500
Cash worldwide:	2013	£6,500
Total worldwide (cash and in kind):	2013	£6,500

Community involvement

The company channels its charitable giving through a corporate charity.

The Swann-Morton Foundation (Charity Commission no. 271925)

The foundation was established in 1976 and helps in the areas of education, study and research of surgery and medicine, health causes and disability. It supports both organisations and individuals (mainly medicine students through scholarships). The company secretary and one of the directors is the trustee of the charity. The charity's audit costs are met by Swann-Morton Ltd.

Corporate giving

According to the company's annual report and accounts for 2012/13 a total of £6,500 was given in charitable donations.

The Swann Morton Foundation's annual report for 2013/14 states that the foundation had an income of £55,000, which was obtained from Gift Aid donations of £55,000 received from Swann-Morton (Microbiological Laboratory Services) Ltd. Grants were made totalling £44,000.

Beneficiaries included: Sheffield Children's Hospital and St Luke's Hospice (£3,500 each); and Royal College of Surgeons and Whirlow Farm Trust (£1,000 each).

Note: although the latest set of company accounts available were from 2012/13, the foundation's accounts were available for 2013/14.

See the corporate charity entry on p. 431 for more information.

In-kind support

Our research suggests that medical instruments or equipment for people who are infirm may be available.

Corporate social responsibility

CSR committee: We found no indication of a CSR committee.

CSR information: The website contains Environmental Policy Key Statements. No other policies regarding CSR could be identified.

CSR report: None published.

Corporate charity: The Swann-Morton Foundation (Charity Commission no. 271925).

Applications

In writing to the correspondent.

John Swire & Sons Ltd

Marine, aviation, property

Correspondent: The Administrator, The Swire Charitable Trust, Swire House, 59 Buckingham Gate, London SW1E 6AJ (tel: 020 7834 7717; email: Sarah.Irving@jssldn.co.uk; website: www.swire.com/en/sustainability)

Directors: Baroness Dunn; N. A. H. Fenwick; J. E. Hughes-Hallett; B. N. Swire; J. S. Swire; M. B. Swire; W. J. Wemyss; R. B. Woods

Year end	31/12/2013
Turnover	£6,253,000,000
Pre-tax profit	£1,110,000,000

Nature of business: Principal activities: marine including ship-owning and operating, aviation (via Cathay Pacific Airways), cold storage and road transport, industrial and trading activities, plantations and property. The company owns a stake in the tea trader, James Finlay.

Company registration number: 133143

Subsidiary undertakings include: See the annual report and accounts for a full list of subsidiaries.

Main locations: London

Total employees: 82,752

Focus of giving: General charitable purposes, education, health, ill health, medical research.

Cash donations undeclared	✓
Gifts in kind	✓

Charitable donations

Cash UK (latest available):	2013	£1,100,000
	2010	£602,000
	2008	£805,000
	2007	£635,000
	2006	£634,000
Total UK (cash and in kind):	2013	£1,100,000
Cash worldwide:	2013	£1,100,000
Total worldwide (cash and in kind):	2013	£1,100,000

Community involvement

John Swire & Sons Ltd appears to direct its charitable contributions through several charities connected to the company. These include: **John Swire (1989) Charitable Trust** (Charity Commission no. 802142), the **Swire Educational Trust** (Charity Commission no. 328366) and the **Swire Charitable Trust** (Charity Commission no. 270726). Support is also given to local communities by employees who volunteer their time and skills.

Corporate giving

Although there are several trusts with connections to the company – **John Swire (1989) Charitable Trust** (whose income was wholly derived from investments), the **Swire Educational Trust** and the **Swire Charitable Trust** – it is the latter that receives almost all of its income from the company and it is to this that we refer.

The 2013 annual report and accounts for the Swire Charitable Trust state: 'The charity received donations from John Swire & Sons Ltd totalling £1.1 million.'

See the corporate charity entries on pp. 431 for more information.

Employee-led support

Employee volunteering

The annual report for 2013 states that staff are supported in sharing their time and skills to help their communities.

Corporate social responsibility

CSR committee: The Swire Group website states the following: 'Given the wide diversity of the group's business portfolio, implementation of the policy is handled on a company-by-company basis and is overseen by the Directors appointed to the company by Swire; this is a core responsibility of each company's management team.'

CSR information: The following information is taken from the group's website:

> The Swire Group's Sustainable Development Policy commits the group to working on the environmental, health and safety, employment, supply chain and community issues that our operations affect, and to working with other parties to promote sustainable development in the industries in which we operate.
>
> It would appear that much of the company's community contribution is aimed at minimising the impact of the company's operations.

We were unable to determine the ratio of women to men on the board.

CSR report: The major operating companies within the Swire group annually publish their own sustainable development reports. Details can be found on the group's website.

Corporate charity: The John Swire (1989) Charitable Trust (Charity Commission no. 802142); the Swire Charitable Trust (Charity Commission no. 270726).

Applications

In writing to the correspondent saying how the funds could be used and what would be achieved.

Synergy Health plc

Health/beauty products, healthcare

Correspondent: The CSR Team, Ground Floor Stella, Windmill Hill Business Park, Whitehill Way, Swindon, Wiltshire SN5 6NX (tel: 01793 891891; fax: 01793 891892; email: csr@synergyhealthplc.com; website: www.synergyhealthplc.com)

Directors: Richard Steeves, Group Chief Executive; Adrian Coward; Gavin Hill, Group Finance Director; Duncan Nichol, Chair; Constance Baroudel; Jeff Harris; Bruce Edwards (women: 1; men: 6)

Year end	30/03/2014
Turnover	£380,453,000
Pre-tax profit	£42,893,000

Nature of business: Synergy Health is an international provider of specialist outsourced services and products in areas of healthcare and management.

Company registration number: 3355631

Subsidiary undertakings include: Gammaster Sweden AB; Shiloh Mobility Ltd; Synergy Health US Holdings Ltd; and Synergy Health Westport Ltd. A full list of the group's subsidiaries is contained within the annual report and accounts.

Total employees: 5,107

Focus of giving: Education, health, ill health, medical research, overseas projects, sponsorship, children, young people, disasters.

Gifts in kind	✓
Humanitarian aid: overseas	✓
Market-led giving	✓
Overseas giving	✓
Sponsorship	✓

Charitable donations

Cash UK (latest available):	2014	£39,000
	2013	£5,000
	2011	£17,000
	2010	£5,000
	2009	£8,000
Total UK (cash and in kind):	2014	£39,000
Cash worldwide:	2014	£88,000
Total worldwide (cash and in kind):	2014	£88,000

Community involvement

The website states that Synergy Health is committed to extending its work in the community. An example of community involvement includes and education day which featured a tour of the Gamma site at Elgin and the South Marston laboratory and presentations given to Sixth grade students in Swindon.

The group looks 'to build strategic partnerships with healthcare organisations to promote continuous development in the industry'. Globally it has been involved in a number of exhibitions, training and educational events.

There are some ongoing partnerships with various charities. For further examples, see the 'In-kind support' section in this entry.

Corporate giving

In 2013/14 the group awarded a total of £88,000 (2012/13: £5,000) in charitable donations. There was no breakdown provided, therefore we estimate that cash donations in the UK totalled about £39,000, based on the figures form the three previous years known to us.

Beneficiaries included: Age UK East London; Facing Africa; Heart Your Smile; Love Underdogs; and The Royal College of Surgeons.

In-kind support

Non-cash contributions include employee volunteering time and medical products. For example, during the in 2013/14 period the group:

- Donated over 120,000 bottles of ASSURE hand sanitisers to Healthcare4Africa (UK-based charity) to be distributed in Ghana
- Gave over 10,000 bottles ASSURE hand sanitisers to its long-supported organisation Matthew 25: Ministries, operating across the US and worldwide
- Provided surgical swabs to Facing Africa (Charity Commission no. 1129170) to fight Noma
- Donated the hand sanitisers to Love Underdogs, a UK charity helping vulnerable animals
- Provided single use instrument packs to The Royal College of Surgeons
- Partnered with Age UK East London to give a year's supply of hand sanitisers

Employee-led support

The group's employees actively engage in fundraising activities to support charitable causes. The website notes Synergy Health having its own JustGiving page 'to promote charitable activity internally, helping employees reach charitable fundraising targets'.

Our research further indicates that there were plans to implement a scheme to allow employees choose a company charity. However, we could not find any references to the initiative within the latest reports or information given on the website.

Commercially led support

Heart Your Smile

This UK-based charity for dental professionals was sponsored through donations of 10p for every sale of AZO branded products.

MRSA Action UK

The group has sponsored the charity through giving 5p for each UK purchase of the ASSURE hand sanitiser.

Corporate social responsibility

CSR committee: There is a CSR Team leading group-wide CSR activities. Regional teams incorporate CSR within their roles and responsibilities.

CSR information: Information taken from the company's CSR report for 2013/14 states the following:

> At Synergy Health, we recognise the importance of CSR, and understand that we have an obligation to run our business in a responsible and sustainable way for all our stakeholders. We are committed to upholding the highest professional and ethical standards and we encourage and support all our people in having a positive impact in everything they do, whether it is in the workplace or the local community. We recognise the importance of managing day-to-day activities in a responsible way, being accountable for the impact of all operational activities on the environment and on those around us, and creating a working environment in which our colleagues can flourish.

The CSR strategy focuses on three areas: caring for people; caring for tomorrow; caring for community; and caring for stakeholders.

CSR report: The CSR report is contained within the annual report and accounts.

Applications

Enquiries regarding charitable or community partnerships should be directed to the correspondent via email.

Synthomer plc (formerly Yule Catto and Co.)

Building/construction, chemicals and plastics, pharmaceuticals

Correspondent: Richard Atkinson, Company Secretary, Central Road, Temple Fields, Harlow, Essex CM20 2BH (tel: 01279 436211; fax: 01279 444025; email: info.uk@synthomer.com; website: www.synthomer.com)

Directors: A. M. Whitfield, Chief Executive Officer; D. C. Blackwood, Chief Financial Officer; N. A. Johnson, Chair; A. G. Catto; J. Chen; BWD. Connolly; Dr J. Jansz; Dato' Lee Hau Hian; J. K. Maiden (women: 0; men: 9)

Year end	11/12/2013
Turnover	£992,700,000
Pre-tax profit	£59,100,000

Nature of business: The group is involved in development and marketing of polymers for industries around the world to be used in production of everyday consumer products.

Company registration number: 98381

Subsidiaries and joint ventures include: Arkem (Pty) Ltd; Revertex (Malaysia) Sdn Bhd; Synthomer GmbH; Synthomer sae; Synthomer (UK) Ltd; and William Blythe Ltd. Further subsidiary undertakings can be found within the group's accounts.

Brands include: Alcotex; Emultex; Lipaton; Lithene; M Grade; Methyl; Plextol; and Reversol.

Main locations: Harlow

Total employees: 2,030

Focus of giving: Health, ill health, medical research, older people, children, young people, disability.

Cash donations undeclared ✓

Charitable donations

Cash UK (latest available):	2013	£54,000
	2011	£54,000
	2009	£56,000
	2008	£51,500
	2007	£54,000
Total UK (cash and in kind):	2013	£54,000
Cash worldwide:	2013	£54,000
Total worldwide (cash and in kind):	2013	£54,000

Community involvement

Our research indicates that the group supports an established list of charities, mainly in the fields of children and youth, elderly people, medical research, and sickness/disability charities. Both local and national charities are supported. We know that in the past support has been given to Age Concern

– England, Barnardo's, Community Trust, Help the Aged, and St Clare Hospice Care Trust.

Corporate giving

We were unable to determine the amount awarded in 2013. Based on the figures from the three previous years known to us, we estimate that about £54,000 was given in the UK.

Corporate social responsibility

CSR committee: There was no evidence of a separate CSR Committee.

CSR information: The company's website notes that Synthomer 'is committed to approaching its business in an ethical and environmentally sound manner' and 'encourages continuous improvement in safety health, and environmental (SHE) performance and transparency to stakeholders'.

The main concern of the CSR policy is environmental issues, sustainability and health and safety.

CSR report: A CSR report is available from the website; however, it mostly concentrates on environmental issues.

Exclusions

No support is given for overseas projects, political appeals, or religious appeals.

Applications

In writing to the correspondent, but note that as the company has charities which it supports regularly, unsolicited applications are unlikely to be successful.

Tata Steel Europe Ltd

Manufacturing, metals

Correspondent: See 'Applications', 30 Millbank, London SW1P 4WY (tel: 020 7717 4444; fax: 020 7717 4455; email: See 'Applications'; website: www.tatasteeleurope.com)

Directors: Koushik Chatterjee; Ishaat Hussain; Dr Karl Köhler, Managing Director and Chief Executive Officer; Jacques Schraven; Andrew Robb, Chair; Narendra Misra; Thachat Narendran (women: 0; men: 7)

Year end	31/03/2014
Turnover	£8,556,000,000
Pre-tax profit	(£562,000,000)

Nature of business: Tata Steel is involved in the manufacture and sale of steel products.

The company is a wholly owned subsidiary of Tata Steel Global Holdings Pte Ltd, an unlisted company based in Singapore. The ultimate parent company is Tata Steel Ltd, incorporated in India.

Company registration number: 5957565

Subsidiary undertakings include: Corus Group Ltd; Tata Steel UK Ltd; Tata Steel UK Holdings Ltd; and The Steel Company of Ireland Ltd. A full list of subsidiary undertakings is published in the annual report and accounts.

Main locations: York, Wolverhampton, Rotherham, Port Talbot, Newport

Total employees: 31,400

Focus of giving: Education, enterprise/training, environment, health, ill health, heritage, STEM (science, technology, engineering and mathematics), sponsorship, sport, recreation, children, young people, community/social welfare.

Cash donations undeclared	✓
Gifts in kind	✓
Market-led giving	✓
Sponsorship	✓

Charitable donations

Cash UK (latest available):	2014	£550,000
	2012	£550,000
Total UK (cash and in kind):	2014	£550,000
Cash worldwide:	2014	£550,000
Total worldwide (cash and in kind):	2014	£550,000

Community involvement

The following information is taken from the Sustainability section of the company's website.

Community partnership programme

The programme focuses on the communities in which the company operates. Current theme – Future Generations – has been chosen for the period from 2013 to April 2016. The areas of education, environment and health and well-being are targeted.

In addition to collaborative projects, the company 'provides proactive investment in local community initiatives' through donations to charitable and non-profit organisations. Priority is given to 'applications that demonstrate evidence of bringing sustainable and measurable benefits to large groups of individuals'.

Education

Tata Steel proactively supports learning and education with programmes in the UK and Netherlands, particularly in the areas of science and technology. For example, in Wales the company runs interactive sessions with primary and secondary schools and offers advice on careers and skills development. More than 2,600 schoolchildren benefit from Tata Steel's education and learning initiatives annually. In Teesside the company organise an annual Industrial Cadet programme attended by around 75 teenagers. The programme provides 'hands on business experience, information about careers in manufacturing and engineering, and the chance to gain a nationally recognised qualification'.

UK Steel Enterprise

UK Steel Enterprise is the subsidiary of Tata Steel. It aims to 'help the economic regeneration of communities affected by changes in the steel industry' through supporting small and medium sized businesses with finance and business premises.

Corporate giving

It appears that the company did not declare its charitable contributions in the annual report and accounts for 2013/14. We know that in the past the company has contributed about £550,000 in charitable donations in the UK, including helping the Queen Elizabeth Prize for Engineering Foundation, therefore we use this figure as the company's cash donations in the UK.

In-kind support

In-kind donations are available. An example includes, artificial reefs made from steel products to help preserve the marine environment (given in Thailand).

Employee-led support

The company's employees volunteer their time and expert skills. Our research suggests that individual fundraising activities are also encouraged. In the past employee efforts have benefited Macmillan and Marie Curie cancer charities.

Commercially led support

Sponsorship

Tata Steel has a small number of corporate sponsorships. Since 2006 it has sponsored the British Triathlon Federation. In 2007 Tata Kids of Steel children's triathlon series were launched for children aged 8 to 13. According to the website, 'by working in partnership with the British Triathlon Federation, schools, and the local communities in which [the company] operates, Tata Kids of Steel series has introduced nearly 70,000 youngsters to the sport'. There is also a long-running sponsorship of the Tata Steel Chess Tournament in the Netherlands.

Education and training

The company offers graduate placements and it is stated on the website that 'after completing a placement with Tata Steel [students] will have the opportunity to apply for [its] sponsorship scheme', dependent on meeting placement objectives, success in the sponsorship interview and acceptable university reports. There are apprenticeship schemes available with Tata Steel providing bursary or salary throughout the training period.

Corporate social responsibility

CSR committee: There were no details relevant to the UK.

CSR information: Information given on the company's website states:

> Sustainability is at the very heart of what we do. As one of the world's leading steel producers, we are dedicated to both managing our operations responsibly and to continuous improvement. ... Above all we operate in a way that is safe for our people and respectful to the environment. We behave responsibly and with care towards the communities surrounding and impacted by our operations.

As part of its CSR approach Tata Steel focuses on ethical business behaviour, environmental issues, employee well-being and communities in which it operates.

The website also notes:

> Our philosophy is based on that of the founder of the Tata Group, Jamsetji Tata, who believed passionately that a company should play a significant and beneficial role within the local community and society in general. Tata Steel is committed to working in partnership with its local communities to support their social and economic well-being.

CSR report: An annual Corporate Citizenship Report is published online. The latest available at the time of writing was for 2010/11.

Exclusions

Our research suggests that no support is given for purely denominational appeals, small purely local appeals not in areas of company presence, appeals from individuals, fundraising events or circulars. Political donations are not made.

The website states: 'Tata Steel is not able to offer support to commercial or profit-making organisations. The company is not able to offer donations to individuals, or to cover participation fees, expeditions or trips performed by individuals in the context of fundraising.'

Applications

Tata Steel invites applicants to complete an online questionnaire, available on the company's website in the 'Communities' section.

The website notes:

> Applications are assessed by a panel of representatives from Tata Steel and the communities in which we operate. If you need more information about the Community Partnership Programme or donations from Tata Steel please email your local contact from the below list:
>
> - Scotland and North of England – Kendra Stonehouse at kendra.stonehouse@tatasteel.com
> - Wales – Nia Singleton at nia.singleton@tatasteel.com
> - Netherlands – Myrna Kleinen at Myrna.kleinen@tatasteel.com
> - All other areas – Rachel Lawrence at rachel.lawrence@tatasteel.com

Note: 'Tata Steel is not currently accepting new requests for corporate sponsorship.'

Tate & Lyle plc

Food manufacture, sugar refiners

Correspondent: The Corporate Responsibility Manager, 1 Kingsway, London WC2B 6AT (tel: 020 7257 2100; fax: 020 7257 2200; email: tateandlyle@tate-lyle.co.uk; website: www.tateandlyle.com)

Directors: Peter Gershon, Chair; Javed Ahmed, Chief Executive Officer; Nick Hampton, Chief Financial Officer; Liz Alrey; William Camp; Douglas Hurt; Dr Ajai Puri; Robert Walker; Virginia Kamsky; Anne Minto; Paul Forman (women: 3; men: 8)

Year end	31/03/2014
Turnover	£3,147,000,000
Pre-tax profit	£290,000,000

Nature of business: The group is a global provider of ingredients and solutions for the food, beverage and other industries. The company's UK sugar refinery is in London.

Company registration number: 76535

Subsidiaries, joint ventures and associates include: G.C. Hahn and Company Ltd; Tate & Lyle Industries Ltd; Tate & Lyle Investments Ltd; and Tate & Lyle LLC. A full list of subsidiary undertakings can be found in the company's annual report and accounts.

Brands include: Tate & Lyle and Lyle's.

Total employees: 4,467

Focus of giving: Education, environment, health, ill health, heritage, housing, homelessness, STEM (science, technology, engineering and mathematics), arts, culture, poverty and social exclusion, children, young people, community/social welfare.

Gifts in kind	✓
Humanitarian aid: overseas	✓
Matched funding	✓
Overseas giving	✓
Payroll giving	✓

Charitable donations

Cash UK (latest available):	2014	£10,000
	2012	£6,000
	2009	£699,000
	2008	£642,000
	2007	£687,000
Total UK (cash and in kind):	2014	£10,000
Cash worldwide:	2014	£501,000
Total worldwide (cash and in kind):	2014	£501,000

Community involvement

The CR Report for 2013/14 (from which the information in this section is gathered) states that the group has 'a strong history of community involvement' and during the year support to communities was given both globally and locally. The group seeks to support causes in the areas where it operates. The staff members can choose to support their preferred projects and develop chosen partnerships.

Tate & Lyle aims to establish a lasting relationship with the community, particularly on three areas (see below).

Well-being – 'providing practical assistance in the area ... from health issues, including nutrition, to general welfare, such as supporting food banks'. For example, through the group's e-Christmas card support was given to a homeless people charity Crisis at Christmas.

Education – 'to develop young people's knowledge and understanding of science, technology, engineering and mathematics (STEM subjects), and their preparedness for a career in a STEM-based discipline, either academically or vocationally'. During the year schools, colleges and universities were helped with new equipment, road safety events for pupils and provision of scholarship funds for higher education.

Environment – 'to promote environmental sustainability and good environmental management, addressing issues of climate change, natural resources and conservation'. Examples included improvement works to local park and conservation areas and tree planting.

Charity partnerships

Tate & Lyle Sugars is represented on the Newham Education Business Partnership Board (NEBP). The board runs programmes helping young people in Newham schools and colleges develop the skills and qualities needed for employment.

Support has also been given to Richard House Children's Hospice for about 15 years and financial assistance and in-kind support is provided to Community Food Enterprise.

Global partnerships

Throughout the year relationships were held with the Global Alliance for Improved Nutrition (GAIN) and support was provided to the Red Cross to help the Philippines typhoon victims. The group is also a corporate partner of the environmental research and engagement charity Earthwatch.

Corporate giving

In 2013/14 Tate & Lyle gave a total of £501,000 (2013: £376,000). The group states that it 'aims to increase its investment in community involvement each year, in line with the growth of its business'. The CSR report for 2013/14 further specifies that 39% of the support went to well-being, 34% – to education, 18% – to environment and 9% to other causes. Further breakdown by regions was not available, therefore we were unable to determine the amount given in the UK. Based on the proportions of charitable giving in the previous year known to us, we estimate that cash donations in the UK were about £10,000, although the amount may be higher.

Beneficiaries included: Crisis at Christmas; Community Food Enterprise; Community Links; Richard House Children's Hospice.

In-kind support

Examples of non-cash support has included: Tate & Lyle Sugars providing space at its refinery site for the use of the Metropolitan Police's Junior Citizens Programme for primary school pupils; provision of secure overnight bus parking space for Community Links; and provision of office and warehouse accommodation.

Employee-led support

The Tate & Lyle website states that it 'gives all employees the opportunity to get involved in volunteering, either as individuals or as part of a team, and sees it as an important development opportunity to further enhance their skills'.

Volunteer in the Community (VitC) Scheme

Through the scheme employees can take up to three days of paid leave per year to participate in their chosen activity in the local communities and are given a £250 donation to their preferred organisation.

Matched funding

Employee donations to main community partners are 100% matched up to a maximum of £3,000. For other charities donations are matched by 50% up to a maximum of £250 (certain charities are excluded).

Payroll giving

The Give As You Earn (GAYE) scheme allows staff members to make tax-efficient donations to charity.

Corporate social responsibility

CSR committee: There is a Corporate Responsibility Committee, which also oversees health and safety matters and reports to the board. The CEO is the director with specific responsibility for CR matters. The group's annual report states that 'CR matters are integrated into the group's enterprise-wide risk management and reporting process.'

CSR information: The annual report for 2013/14 states: 'It is important that we act responsibly and consider carefully the impact our activities have on all stakeholders, including employees, customers and the communities in which we operate.'

The CSR strategy focuses on workplace safety, environmental impact, ethical business conduct and community involvement.

The highest priority for the group is said to be health and safety.

CSR report: A CSR report is published within the annual report and accounts.

Exclusions

Support is not generally given to circular appeals, advertising in charity brochures, individuals, purely denominational (religious) appeals, local appeals not in areas of company presence, animal welfare, sport or large national appeals. Political donations are only made outside the EU.

Applications

In writing to the correspondent.

Taylor Wimpey plc

Building/construction

Correspondent: The Charity Committee, Gate House, Turnpike Road, High Wycombe, Buckinghamshire HP12 3NR (tel: 01494 558323; fax: 01494 885663; email: twplc@taylorwimpey.com; website: www.taylorwimpey.co.uk/corporate)

Directors: Kevin Beeston, Chair; Pete Redfern, Chief Executive Officer; Ryan Mangold, Group Finance Director; James Jordan; Robert Rowley; Mike Hussey; Kate Barker; Margaret Ford (women: 2; men: 6)

Year end	12/12/2013
Turnover	£2,995,500,000
Pre-tax profit	£306,200,000

Nature of business: The group is a residential developer operating at a local level from 24 regional businesses across the UK with further operations undertaken in Spain.

Taylor Wimpey was formed through the merger of George Wimpey and Taylor Woodrow on 3 July 2007. Both businesses have a history dating 80 years or more with George Wimpey dating back to the 1880's and Taylor Woodrow to the 1920's.

Company registration number: 296805

Subsidiary undertakings include: George Wimpey Ltd; Taylor Wimpey de España S.A.U.; Taylor Wimpey Developments Ltd; Taylor Wimpey Holdings Ltd; and Taylor Wimpey UK Ltd.

UK employees: 3,629

Total employees: 3,700

Focus of giving: Children, young people, education, enterprise/training, housing, homelessness, sponsorship, sport, recreation, community/social welfare.

Charity of the Year	✓
Gifts in kind	✓
Market-led giving	✓
Sponsorship	✓

Charitable donations

Cash UK (latest available):	2013	£280,000
	2011	£211,000
	2009	£55,000
	2008	£132,000
	2007	£13,000
Total UK (cash and in kind):	2013	£280,000
Cash worldwide:	2013	£280,000
Total worldwide (cash and in kind):	2013	£280,000

Community involvement

The group focuses its charitable giving on the areas linked to its business and the communities where it operates. Main assistance is delivered through the network of homelessness charities, led by the group's national charity Centrepoint and supported by smaller regional charities across the UK (each of the 24 regional units is paired with a local charity). The group states that it often funds community buildings and other facilities for local residents and the wider community.

Education

Education is regularly supported in the areas where building takes place. The group works with local schools to educate pupils about building sites safety through talks and other engaging efforts. The new Berryfields Church of England Primary School was co-founded by the group.

St Edmunds Society

In partnership with the society, which provides training and education for vulnerable young people in Norwich, presentations and an opportunity to spend the afternoon at Middleton Park development were given to students.

Charity of the Year

There is the Taylor Wimpey UK National Charity Scheme which supports the charity, chosen by employees annually.

CRASH

Taylor Wimpey is a patron of this construction and property industry's homelessness charity.

Corporate giving

The following information is taken from the CSR report for 2013. In 2013 the group donated a total of £327,000 (2012: £247,000) to charitable causes and employees contributed £88,000 to the charities supported by the group. This sum included a donation of £210,000 (2012: £149,000) to Centrepoint and the network of homelessness charities. The amount given to Centrepoint consisted of £163,000 cash contribution made by the Company and £47,000 raised by employees. We take the figure of £280,000 to represent the company's contributions.

Beneficiaries included: Centrepoint (£103,000); St Edmunds Society (£41,000); Crisis (£23,000); The Rock Trust (£8,800); St Basil's (£8,400); Crash (£8,200); Keyhouse and Amber (£6,100 each); and Llamau (£5,000).

In-kind support

Non-cash contributions include staff volunteering time and expert skills. Our research suggests that materials may also be available.

Employee-led support

The group's donations policy notes that the group will 'encourage teams to volunteer their services in support of suitable causes from the communities in which it operates or seeks to do so'.

For example, a team from Briars Chase development in Ilkeston helped to clear a courtyard area at Bennerley Fields Specialist Speech and Language College so that the college could afford to install a sensory garden for their pupils.

The Youth Adventure Trust

In 2014 over 40 teams from the group raised more than £126,000 to the charity.

Macmillan Cancer Support

The group participates in the annual House of Lords versus House of Commons Tug of War. In 2013 more than £128,000 was raised to support Macmillan and for the first time ladies' team joined the event.

Centrepoint

Staff members took place in Sleep Out raising £17,000 for the charity and the network.

Commercially led support

Apprenticeships and work placements

In 2013 the group introduced a new site management apprenticeship scheme to tackle a skills shortage in the industry. During the year six apprenticeships were recruited (it is aimed to have around 100 apprentices by the end of 2015) and 405 days of work experience was available for students and schoolchildren.

Sponsorships

During the year the sponsoring partnership with Government-funded Buckinghamshire University Technical College (UTC) was continued. The college specialises in construction and IT and is helped by Taylor Wimpey to shape the construction course curriculum and provide valuable work experience to the students, 'who, unlike any other students, wear Taylor Wimpey branded personal protective equipment (PPE) as part of their dress code when working in the college workshops'.

Sponsorship is available to sports teams and events.

Corporate social responsibility

CSR committee: There is a Charity Committee responsible to the CSR Committee. CSR and Health and Safety matters are overseen by the CEO and the Sustainability Steering Group (SSG) co-ordinates sustainability activities at the operational level.

CSR information: The website states:

> We seek to be a responsible organisation and strive to make a positive difference to the communities in which we operate. We are committed to delivering high-quality homes that are energy-effcient and address a wide range of environmental and social issues through the design of our developments.

The CSR focus is in two categories:

'Our homes and communities' – this encompasses five key areas and looks at different aspects of how the group goes about creating sustainable communities

'The way we work' – this focuses on management systems and the group's approach to the key areas of employees, health, safety and environment and supply chain management.

The group aims to deliver sustainable developments 'by balancing the environmental, economic and social aspects of communities'.

Corporate Responsibility, Donations and Community policies are available online.

CSR report: There is an annual CSR report available from the website.

Exclusions

No help for appeals from individuals, fundraising events or religious appeals. Support will not be generally given 'to national charities or major events that are able to attract large corporate donors or elicit a national response', with an exception of those that are closely linked to the group's business and concerned with housing, homelessness or charitable projects requiring building work. Political donations are not made.

Applications

In writing to the correspondent.

The website notes that requests for national sponsorship enquiry should be directed at TayWeb.Info@taylorwimpey.com; and for regional sponsorships you should approach your nearest regional office.

Any feedback or comments on the group's approach to corporate responsibility are welcomed at crreport@taylorwimpey.com.

TelecityGroup

Information management and communication

Correspondent: The CSR Team, Exchange Tower, 4th Floor, 2 Harbour Exchange Square, London E14 9GE (tel: 020 7001 0000; fax: 020 7001 0001; website: www.telecitygroup.com)

Directors: John Hughes, Chair; Eric Hageman, Chief Financial Officer; Claudia Arney; Simon Batey; Mauritzio Carli; Nancy Cruickshank; John O'Reilly; Michael Tobin, Chief Executive Officer (women: 2; men: 6)

Year end	31/12/2013
Turnover	£325,550,000
Pre-tax profit	£88,440,000

Nature of business: The group is European-wide operator of network independent data centres.

Company registration number: 5603875

Subsidiary undertakings include: Data Electronics Group Ltd; TelecityGroup International Ltd; TelecityGroup Netherlands B.V.; and TelecityGroup UK Ltd. A full list of subsidiary undertakings is available from Companies House.

Total employees: 691

Focus of giving: Education, children, young people, community/social welfare.

Cash donations undeclared	✓
Gifts in kind	✓

Charitable donations

Cash UK (latest available):	2013	£67,000
	2009	£81,000
	2008	£52,000
Total UK (cash and in kind):	2013	£67,000
Cash worldwide:	2013	£67,000
Total worldwide (cash and in kind):	2013	£67,000

Community involvement

The group notes:

> Community investment and charitable partnerships continue to play an important role within our business and we strive to support the local communities in which the business operates. We believe the group can have most impact by focusing on initiatives that promote education and opportunities for disadvantaged children and young people.

Particular attention is also paid to social welfare causes.

Charity partnerships

The Prince's Trust

TelecityGroup is a patron of The Prince's Trust Technology Leadership Group.

FILMCLUB

As a partner of the educational charity, TelecityGroup helps to offer 'tailored opportunities' to students in schools surrounding offices in Tower Hamlets and Manchester.

The Loomba Foundation (Charity Commission no. 1064988)
Close relationship is developed with the charity which helps educate disadvantaged children in India and Africa.

Corporate giving

The amount awarded in charitable donations in 2013 could not be determined. Based on the figures from the two previous years known to us, we estimate that cash donations in the UK totalled about £67,000.

Beneficiaries have included: Action for Children; Alzheimer's Society; Cancer Charity Trust; Great Ormond Street Hospital; Help for Heroes; Make-A-Wish Foundation; NSPCC; The Children's Society; WaterAid; and Worshipful Company of IT.

In-kind support

Non-cash contributions include employee time and expert skills as well as other in-kind support. In the past the group has provided fleeces and travel bags for the Byte Night sleepers.

Employee-led support

The group's employees participate in fundraising and volunteering activities. For example: the London office is involved with Trident organisation helping young people develop their employability skills and participates in Byte Night annual sleep out raising money for Action for Children; teams also take part in other fundraising initiatives, such as Red Nose Day and Jeans for Genes.

Corporate social responsibility

CSR committee: There is a board level CSR Committee, which 'assists the board in the discharge of its corporate social responsibilities by overseeing the group's activities in the areas of environmental affairs, marketplace, workplace and community' and normally meets at least twice a year.

CSR information: The group's website states:

> We are committed to driving our business, and expanding our capacity pipeline, in a way that is responsible, ensures our own business sustainability and therefore meets the expectations of our stakeholders... We have identified our material issues to be:
> - Carbon efficiency
> - Customer satisfaction
> - Employee engagement
> - Accreditation on robust management systems
> - Business integrity

There are set targets for the group in all of these areas which are monitored, managed and improved on a regular basis.

CSR report: Information given in the 2011 annual report and accounts had noted:

> The shift towards reporting on business-critical corporate responsibility issues means that, in future annual reports, data on some of the group's activities, such as community investment and charitable partnerships, will only feature in the corporate responsibility section of the group website at www.telecity.com.

The CSR report for 2013 gives little or no details on community contributions.

Applications

In writing to the correspondent.

Telefónica UK Ltd

Telecommunications

Correspondent: See 'Applications', 260 Bath Road, Slough, Berkshire SL1 4DX (tel: 01132 722000 (main switchboard); website: www.o2.com)

Directors: Ronan Dunne; Mark Evans (women: 0; men: 2)

Year end	31/12/2013
Turnover	£5,535,000,000
Pre-tax profit	£609,000,000

Nature of business: The principal activities of the company are the operation of a cellular communications network, and the sale of fixed and mobile, voice and data services.

The company is a wholly owned subsidiary of Telefónica Europe plc (incorporated in England and Wales) and its ultimate parent company is Telefónica S.A. (incorporated in Spain).

Company registration number: 1743099

Subsidiary undertakings include: giffgaff Ltd; O2 Third Generation; O2 Unify Ltd; Telefónica Financial Services UK Ltd; and Weve Ltd. A full list of subsidiary undertakings can be found within the company's accounts.

Brands include: O2

Main locations: Braddan, Bury, Hammersmith, Douglas, Leeds, Runcorn, Slough

UK employees: 8,692

Total employees: 8,692

Focus of giving: Economic generation, education, enterprise/training, environment, health, ill health, individuals, non-registered charities, financial education, older people, arts, culture, safety and crime prevention, sponsorship, sport, recreation, children, young people, community/social welfare, disability, disasters.

Membership: BITC

Cash donations undeclared	✓
Gifts in kind	✓
Market-led giving	✓
Sponsorship	✓

Charitable donations

Cash UK (latest available):	2013	£953,000
	2011	£1,435,000
	2009	£750,000
	2007	£675,000
	2006	£264,000
Total UK (cash and in kind):	2013	£953,000

Community involvement

Think Big

Information gathered throughout our previous research notes that:

> The Think Big programme was launched in Europe during 2010 to support young people in their transition to an independent and responsible adult life. Think Big was set up with backing from Fundación Telefónica. Its aim is to provide financial support and training so that young people can demonstrate their talent to the wider community, make a positive impact and drive forward their role as agents of social change, inspiring and celebrating their successes as they take the lead in their own projects.

There is a group-wide Telefónica Volunteers network which contributes to the support provided by the group and a number of schemes are undertaken in partnership with various NGOs. Telefónica Foundation (O2) funds the Think Big programme, National Youth Agency manages the programme and UK Youth offers training and support for Think Bigger.

In accordance with the global guidelines, in the UK Think Big mainly focuses on education, children and young people, also environmental impact. Support given includes assistance through the following schemes:

Think Big Youth Programme
Aimed at people between the ages of 13 and 25 to help them 'lead positive change in their communities'. The company provides funding, training and other support, including volunteer mentoring. According to the website £5 million is being invested to the programme over three years. Examples of projects supported include: 'a project to help disabled young people go kayaking in Halifax; refurbishment of a senior citizens' garden by young people in Carlisle; and a youth dance centre in Plymouth'. O2 also supported Lives Not Knives campaign against knife crimes, led by Eliza Rebeiro, which provides special booklets (funded by the company) to primary schoolchildren and invites them talk about their experiences of knife crime through art, poetry and storytelling.

O2 Learn
Secondary school teachers are enabled to share their showcase summary lessons on the company's free website, this way

contributing to an educational video library. Students are able to rate the lessons with the authors of the teaching material being awarded. According to the website, 'to date O2 Learn has awarded over £300,000 directly to teachers and schools in the UK.'

Partners of the O2 Learn include: Child Exploitation and Online Protection Centre (CEOP); Family Lives; National Union of Teachers (NUT); School Governors' One-Stop Shop; Teach First; Teaching Leaders; The Specialist Schools and Academies Trust (SSAT); and The Training and Development Agency for Schools.

Motimator
In 2014 a new employability app was launched in partnership with digital charity YouthNet.

Child Protection
The company gives attention to child safety using modern technologies. There are partnerships with organisations, such as the Child Exploitation and Online Protection Centre or the UK Council of Child Internet Safety, with support provided to a range of other child protection groups. Together with Telefónica group and other industry partners an online teacher resource has been developed to provide 'valuable information and advice on the positive, responsible and safe use of new technologies'.

The company's website notes that as part of its commitments it aims to: back 5,000 young people leading community projects across the UK; connect volunteers to local community initiatives and social action programmes; improve the lives of over 600,000 young people through the development of local community initiatives, inspired and led by young people; deliver 2 million extra secondary school lessons through O2 Learn; support 4,000 young people to gain work skills and experience to help them get a job or start an enterprise; and, through apprenticeships, support young people to get into work through training on the job (all by 2015).

Social enterprise
O2 works with social enterprises to provide them with useful information and help develop their activities. For more information see o2socialenterprise.co.uk/support.

Global support
The group's community support activities include helping people with disabilities, health causes, disaster appeals, digital education and entrepreneurship. For more details on global community involvement see the group's online Sustainability Report.

Corporate giving
We could not determine the amount donated in charitable contributions in 2013. Based on the figures from the past three years known to us, we estimate that about £953,000 was given in the UK.

In-kind support
Non-cash contributions include staff volunteering time and efforts, also various digital platforms for learning provided as a part of Think Big initiatives.

Employee-led support
Volunteers at Telefónica
Fundación Telefónica runs a multicultural network of volunteers from Telefónica group, which supports social and collaborative projects by employees. The volunteers undertake charity work either as part of Fundación Telefónica's own programmes or in partnership with other foundations. Support given includes mentoring for the Think Big youth projects. The group's Sustainability Report notes that in 2013, there were 26,614 active Telefónica volunteers, who gave a total of 195,906 hours throughout the group.

Commercially led support
The group states that it contributes to the society 'by sponsoring, above all, sporting, cultural and social activities'.

Sponsorships
For the past ten years the company has sponsored the annual Nordoff-Robins Silver Clef Awards, which raise money for the charity. It also sponsors The O2 Arena in London O2 Academy venues and the England rugby team.

Our research indicates that the group's global policy is not to consider commercial sponsorships for funding unless the key objective is to address a charitable or social cause. The marketing teams within the Telefónica Europe operating businesses deal with commercial sponsorships.

Employability
O2 supports youth employability and skills development and provides work experience opportunities (through GoThinkBig website) to young job-seekers. The company states – 'we want to support young people to gain work skills and experience and help them get jobs or start enterprises'. Work with suppliers is also undertaken to help young people get into work.

Access for All
The company's website offers accessible customer care and services to people with disabilities, for example bills in Braille and accessibility features for mobile phones. It is also noted that O2 aims to help other vulnerable or older people enjoy a more independent, safer life through the digital services.

Corporate social responsibility
CSR committee: Our research indicates that globally the:

> Overall corporate responsibility activities, policies, practices and strategic objectives, are overseen by the board. Reviews are carried out both through an annual conference and at regular board meetings.
>
> Individual directors [including the UK company] take responsibility for different aspects of [the CSR] programme and act as champions for the business, led by the Chief Executive who has responsibility for all aspects of the social, environmental and ethical activities.

CSR information: The company's website notes:

> Our activities have a social impact. We want to make sure it's a positive one. We want to bring the benefits of mobile communications and the internet to as many people as possible. Without ignoring the associated privacy risks and the possibility of social exclusion. And although we want to provide best value, we take social and environmental factors into account when working with our suppliers. And we want to give something back to the wider community.

CSR report: There is an annual Corporate Sustainability Report covering Telefónica's global CSR activities available online (on the group's website). Some details of the UK CSR and outline of community activities are given online.

Exclusions
According to o2thinkbig.co.uk the Think Big programme does not support the following:

- Businesses or any projects that will make a profit
- Fundraising projects for charities
- Projects that are just for equipment or trips out
- Professional fees (for example, web developer to build a website)
- Projects that aim to convert people to a religion
- Applications relating to something an individuals does for a living
- Promotion of political parties or religious activity
- Anything dangerous or illegal

Please note you cannot apply directly for £2,500, you must do your £300 project first, and only if everything is going really well might you get invited to apply for more.

Applications
The company's website states: 'we receive a great number of requests for support from individuals and charities. Sadly there are too many for us to be able to support them all, so we focus all our funding into our flagship programme, Think Big'.

Full details of how to apply for Think Big are available at: www.o2thinkbig.co.uk/(tel: 0800 902 0250; email: hello@o2thinkbig.co.uk). The application round is open from January, 2015.

Sponsorship requests – applications for commercial sponsorship from O2 should be sent to: sponsorshiprequests@o2.com.

Telegraph Media Group Ltd

Media

Correspondent: Rigel Mowatt, Director and Company Secretary, 111 Buckingham Palace Road, London SW1W 0DT (tel: 020 7931 5000; website: www.telegraph.co.uk)

Directors: Aidan Barclay, Chair; Murdoch MacLennan, Chief Executive Officer; Finbarr Ronayne, Chief Financial Officer; Howard Barclay; Rigel Mowatt; Philip Peters; Michael Seal; Lorraine Twohill (women: 1; men: 7)

Year end	29/12/2013
Turnover	£352,200,000
Pre-tax profit	£57,000,000

Nature of business: The company is a multi-platform publisher of national newspapers (The Daily Telegraph, The Sunday Telegraph and The Telegraph).

The company's immediate parent company is Press Acquisitions Ltd (PAL), ultimately controlled by David and Frederick Barclay's Family Settlements.

Company registration number: 451593

Subsidiary undertakings include: The Sunday Telegraph Ltd; The Evening Post Ltd; The Morning Post Ltd; Telegraph Publishing Ltd; Telegraph Secretarial Services Ltd; and VOS Media Ltd (all dormant companies except the last one).

Main locations: London

UK employees: 1,034

Total employees: 1,034

Focus of giving: Health, ill health, older people, community/social welfare.

Charity of the Year	✓
Gifts in kind	✓
Market-led giving	✓
Payroll giving	✓

Charitable donations

Cash UK (latest available):	2013	£1,000,000
	2012	£1,000,000
	2011	£126,000
	2009	£58,000
	2008	£52,000
Total UK (cash and in kind):	2013	£1,000,000
Cash worldwide:	2013	£0
Total worldwide (cash and in kind):	2013	£0

Community involvement

The company supports The Barclay Foundation (Charity Commission no. 803696), of which two company directors are trustees. Some support is given to charities associated with the newspapers and their employees.

Corporate giving

In 2012/13 the company donated a total of over £1 million (2011/12: more than £1 million) to charities. Out of that sum £14,300 (2011/12: 56,000) went to charities associated with the newspapers and their employees and £1 million (2011/12: £1 million) was awarded to The Barclay Foundation (Charity Commission no. 803696), which used the whole amount to support the Great Ormond Street Hospital Children's Charity (Charity Commission no. 235825).

Beneficiaries included: The Barclay Foundation (£1 million).

In-kind support

Telegraph Christmas Appeal

Every year the company selects three charities from dozens of applications for the readers to support. In 2014 the 25th appeal raised money for Masanga Mentor Initiative, Medical Detection Dogs and The Abbeyfield Society. We class the appeal as in-kind support, as the company provides the fundraising platform.

Employee-led support

Payroll giving

In the past the company has been operating Give As You Earn (GAYE) scheme.

Commercially led support

Work experience

Internships and other work experience opportunities are available to students.

Corporate social responsibility

CSR committee: No information identified.

CSR information: No CSR details found.

CSR report: None present.

Applications

We would suggest that applications should be made in writing to the correspondent although it should be noted that support for organisations unconnected with the newspaper industry appears to be very limited.

Tesco plc

Retail – supermarkets

Correspondent: Laurence Webb, Group Corporate Responsibility, New Tesco House, Delamare Road, Cheshunt, Hertfordshire EN8 9SL (tel: 01992 632222 (main switchboard); email: charity.enquiries@uk.tesco.com; website: www.tescoplc.com)

Directors: Richard Broadbent, Chair; Dave Lewis, Group Chief Executive; Alan Stewart, Chief Financial Officer; Patrick Cescau; Mark Armour; Gareth Bullock; Stuart Chambers; Richard Cousins; Olivia Garfield; Ken Hanna; Mikael Ohlsson; Deanna Oppenheimer; Jacqueline Tammenoms Bakker; Jonathan Lloyd, Company Secretary (women: 3; men: 11)

Year end	22/02/2014
Turnover	£63,557,000,000
Pre-tax profit	£2,259,000,000

Nature of business: The principal activity of the group is retailing and associated activities in the UK and around the world, including China, the Czech Republic, Hungary, the Republic of Ireland, India, Japan, Malaysia, Poland, Slovakia, South Korea, Thailand and Turkey. The group also provides retail banking and insurance services through its subsidiary, Tesco Bank, mobile services through Tesco Mobile, and petrol station services.

Company registration number: 445790

Subsidiary undertakings include: blinkbox Entertainment Ltd; Fresh and Easy Neighborhood Market Inc.; Tesco Corporate Treasury Services plc; Tesco-Global Stores Privately Held Co. Limited; Tesco International Sourcing Ltd; Tesco Ireland Ltd; Tesco Personal Finance Group Ltd (trading as Tesco Bank); and Tesco Stores Ltd. See the group's annual report and accounts for a full list of subsidiaries.

Brands include: Everyday Value and Finest*.

Main locations: Cheshunt

UK employees: 317,847

Total employees: 510,444

Focus of giving: Education, fundraising events, health, ill health, armed forces personnel, older people, poverty and social exclusion, sponsorship, sport, recreation, children, young people, community/social welfare, disability, disasters.

Membership: BITC

Charity of the Year	✓
FTSE 100	✓
Gifts in kind	✓
Humanitarian aid: overseas	✓
Humanitarian aid: UK	✓
Market-led giving	✓

Overseas giving	✓
Payroll giving	✓
Sponsorship	✓

Charitable donations

Cash UK (latest available):	2014	£25,400,000
	2012	£25,600,000
	2009	£28,200,000
	2008	£22,600,000
	2007	£17,698,393
Total UK (cash and in kind):	2014	£25,400,000
Cash worldwide:	2014	£25,400,000
Total worldwide (cash and in kind):	2014	£53,000,000

Community involvement

The group provides assistance to large national appeals and local causes. Each UK store has a community donation budget to help local organisations with their fundraising events.

Eat Happy Project

According to the Our Community section of ourtesco.com, this project is aimed at children and seeks to help them 'have a better relationship with food through field trips, live video chats, hands-on cooking and much more'. Tesco offers an online Resource Hub, online field trips, free cookery courses at 50 UK stores in partnership with the Children's Food Trust, and Farm to Fork Trails which allow children to visit Tesco suppliers or receive a visit to the school. The project also works in partnership with FACE and Magic Breakfast.

Charity partnerships

The following information is taken from the Tesco and Society section of tescoplc.com. During the year Diabetes UK was chosen as a national charity partner with more than £10 million being donated by employees and customers (including sale of certain products). In 2014/15 charity partners are Diabetes UK and Cancer Research UK. As part of the support, Tesco offers a free diabetes screening service, provide in-store healthy eating messages and Tesco pharmacies distribute support packs (produced by Diabetes UK).

Across Europe Tesco co-operates with food poverty charities (see 'Commercially led support' for more details). In Scotland Tesco Bank has a partnership with The Reading Agency which runs an annual summer reading challenge 'to get thousands of children across Scotland reading through their summer holidays'. International partnerships also include a three-year programme with the Turkish Education Volunteers Foundation 'to provide over 100,000 children with personal development, healthy nutrition, physical activity and sports training'.

Disaster relief

Tesco responded to the February 2014 UK flooding through transportation of more than 1,500 bales of hay to affected farms and helping move 2,500 tonnes of sand to disaster areas. A clean-up operation was launched to help the communities and included 5,000 hours of employee time, 30 new home starter kits donated to Somerset County Council, delivering four lorry loads of furniture and collection of £100,000 through fundraising events.

In 2013 flood relief was also provided in Malaysia through employee volunteering and customer contributions.

At the end of 2014 Tesco has become a founding member of the British Red Cross Disaster Relief Alliance which, according to tescoplc.com, is a 'new initiative which aims to unite the British Red Cross with the private sector in order to provide financial support before crises occur'. The group provided £50,000 to the Ebola Outbreak Appeal in 2014.

Tesco Charity Trust (Charity Commission no. 297126)

The trust was set up on 1 June 1987 to support national, local and international community charities, and to add a 20% top up to staff fundraising. It is the group's main channel of charitable giving, run by a board of trustees recommended by the main board of Tesco plc. The trust supports charitable activities on a local, national and international basis and its main income comes from donations made by Tesco plc, Tesco Stores Ltd and staff fundraising. Donations under the company's Give As You Earn scheme are managed by the trust. The Tesco Charity Trust runs the Community Awards scheme.

According to the Tesco Charity Trust's annual report and accounts for 2013/14, 'Tesco Stores Ltd permits national collections on behalf of RSPCA and Scottish SPCA, Cancer Research UK, Food Bank, Help for Heroes, Diabetes UK and the Royal British Legion Poppy Appeal.'

In 2014 Tesco signed the Ministry of Defence's Armed Forces Corporate Covenant and committed 'to do more to support serving personnel, veterans and reservists'.

Community Champions

The group has over 300 Community Champions working the stores who identify initiatives and causes (such as charity events or career fairs) in the local community which could be supported.

Corporate giving

Tesco has a set target of at least 1% of pre-tax profit to be donated to charities through various means, including direct cash contributions and cause-related marketing.

The group's annual report states that in 2013/14 a total of £53 million of pre-tax profit was donated to charities and good causes, 'through direct donations, cause-related marketing, gifts in kind, colleague time and management costs'. The figure is £13 million lower than in 2012/13 (excluding the contribution of £66 million from Fresh and Easy in the US), which the group largely attributes to 'the transition from Tesco for Schools and Clubs to [the] Eat Happy initiative'. It is further stated that a total of £22.7 million was raised by customers and colleagues, including £4.5 million raised through food collections in the UK and £10 million raised for Diabetes UK (as confirmed by the company).

We were unable to obtain a detailed breakdown of the support given, as the group does not differentiate between cash donations and other types of support, such as cause-related marketing. The Group Corporate Responsibility Department has informed us that the £53 million figure does not include the £22.7 million that were raised by colleagues and customers. Unfortunately, the correspondent was 'unable to disclose more details about the £53 million figure'. Based on the figures from the three previous years known to us, we estimate that about £25.4 million was given in cash in the UK.

The annual report and accounts of the Tesco Charity Trust state that in 2013/14 donations totalling £2 million (2012/13: £2 million) were received from Tesco Stores Ltd. Grants were made during the year totalling £8.6 million.

The three largest beneficiaries were Diabetes UK (£6 million); Cancer Research UK (£1 million); and Barking Badgers (£40,000). Other grant allocations were broken down as follows:

Disabilities and health	£406,000
Children and youth	£268,000
Education	£197,000
Older people	£177,000
20% top up of colleague fundraising	£175,000
Other	£330,000

Grant amounts were not available but other beneficiaries included: Age Concern Neath Port Talbot, the Brain Injury Foundation, Hammersmith and Fulham Mencap, Leeds Powerchair Football Club, Multiple Sclerosis UK, Starbeck School, the Stuart Low Trust and Trinity Community Centre.

See the corporate charity entry on p. 432 for more information.

In-kind support

The group facilitates and organises various events and campaigns to collect money for good causes, this way providing a fundraising platform. As part of the Neighbourhood Food Collection programme, surplus food is distributed to support FareShare.

Separate stores (excluding Express stores) allow and manage their own bag packing bookings.

Employee-led support

Tesco employees volunteer their time and efforts as well as contribute to the good causes. An example of employee involvement is the BAFTA Young Game Designers Competition. Tesco people have been mentoring four teams preparing their entries for the competition.

Payroll giving

Information taken from the Tesco Charity Trust annual report and accounts for 2013/14 notes that 'Tesco Stores Ltd operates a Give As You Earn scheme for all Tesco colleagues.' Throughout the year 170,000 (2012/13: 130,000) donations totalled over £737,000 (2012/13: £733,000).

The website states:

> *20% Top-Up*
> All Tesco colleagues may apply to the Tesco Charity Trust for 20% top-up on their personal fundraising. We automatically top-up colleague fundraising for our National Charity Partner and Cancer Research UK's Race for Life.

Note that the top-up is made by the corporate charity.

Commercially led support

Sponsorship

For over 13 years Tesco has been a sponsor of Cancer Research UK's Race for Life and has supported similar events abroad. The website, however, notes that Tesco plc is 'unable to sponsor events or individuals'.

Tesco Youth Academy

The programme aims to help unemployed young people through work placements and retail training across the business. Tesco works with its suppliers and supports Movement to Work. Vocational training programmes are available with a prospect of future employment.

Cause-related marketing

There are various events and activities facilitated by the group in order to raise funds for good causes. Donations from customers and employees across the group totalled £22.7 million during the year.

Through Buy One, Give One programme uniforms are provided by F&F to children in the area in which the clothing is made. For every product purchased by a Tesco costumer from the F&F Back to School uniform range a full uniform is given. Since 2009 over 20,000 school uniforms have been donated to children in Kenya, Sri Lanka and Bangladesh by F&F.

Throughout Europe partnerships are established with food poverty charities to help feed people in need. In the UK in 2013 Tesco partnered with The Trussell Trust and FareShare to hold two Neighbourhood Food Collections (in July and in the run-up to Christmas). Tesco customers are invited to donate non-perishable food items. The group 'tops up' customers' donations by 30%.

During the year Tesco also committed to donate profits from an increase in sales of ice, due to the trend of the ice bucket challenge. At least £20,000 has been donated to the Motor Neurone Disease Association.

Corporate social responsibility

CSR committee: The Corporate Responsibility Committee, chaired by Jacqueline Tammenoms Bakker, is accountable for defining the group's CSR policies and overseeing their implementation.

There is also a dedicated team dealing with charity issues.

CSR information: The annual Corporate Responsibility Report for 2013/14 states that in 2013 the group set out a new CSR strategy which aims to address food waste, health and youth unemployment, and also seeks to strengthen Tesco's work in 'trading responsibly, reducing [the] impact on the environment, being a great employer and supporting local communities'.

The new group's value is 'using its scale for good' – making a wider contribution to the society by drawing on its operational skills and its scale. In the annual report for 2013/14 it is further noted:

> Through our scale for good strategy we are addressing some of the key challenges that societies are facing which are closely aligned to specific human rights as defined by the UN. For example:
> - Right to education – we are working to provide opportunities for millions of young people
> - Right to be free from hunger – we are building close relationships with food banks and food surplus charities who are helping to feed people in need
> - Right to the enjoyment of the highest attainable standards of physical and mental health – we are helping our colleagues and customers to lead healthier lives

The CR Report states:

> It is essential that every community we operate in can thrive and be successful. We know that our business can only be vibrant if those communities are vibrant – and we work hard to support local communities in a variety of ways. Significantly, what matters about our approach is that alongside the support we provide to local and national charities, we also use our skills and scale in order to help tackle local problems and address urgent challenges.

CSR report: An annual Corporate Responsibility Report is published.

Corporate charity: Tesco Charity Trust (Charity Commission no. 297126).

Exclusions

No grants to political organisations, individuals or towards new buildings. The trust will not make donations to other trusts or charities for onward transmission to other charitable organisations.

Applications

The company: In writing to the correspondent. There is also a dedicated team dealing with charity issues which should be contacted at: charity.enquiries@uk.tesco.com.

The trust: the principal contact is Michelle Cornish (tel: 01992 644598; email: charity.enquiries@uk.tesco.com) at 25 Furlong Way, Great Amwell, Near Ware, Hertfordshire SG12 9TE.

Further comments or questions on the group's CSR can also be directed at: cr.enquiries@uk.tesco.com.

Other information: The Tesco Retired Staff Association maintains links with retired employees and can offer support and assistance to those in retirement who need it. More information is available at: 01992647089; or rsa.admin@uk.tesco.com.

Thales UK Ltd

Defence, aerospace, engineering, manufacturing, transport and communications

Correspondent: Mike Seabrook, Thales Charitable Trust, 2 Dashwood Lang Road, The Bourne Business Park, Addlestone, Surrey KT15 2NX (tel: 01932 824800; email: mike.seabrook@thalesgroup.com; website: www.thalesgroup.co.uk)

Directors: Victor Chavez; Kathryn Jenkins; Marion Broughton; Edward Lowe; Dean Mason; Alistair McPhee; Philip Naybour; Alvin Wilby; Evan McCrorie; Paul Watson; Peter Hitchcock; Guy Baruchel; Peter Rowley; Justin Walker; Dr Paul Gosling; Ben Olivier (women: 2; men: 14)

Year end	31/12/2013
Turnover	£346,166,000
Pre-tax profit	£146,113,000

Nature of business: The company is involved in the fields of aerospace, defence, security and transportation. Its activities involve design, manufacture and sale of defence electronic products, encompassing electronic warfare, radar, displays, defence radio and command information systems.

The company's immediate parent company is Thales Holdings UK plc and the ultimate parent company is Thales SA, incorporated in France.

Company registration number: 868273

Subsidiary undertakings include: nCipher Ltd; Quintec Associates Ltd; Thales Air Defence Ltd; Thales ATM Ltd; Thales e-Security Ltd; and XPI Stimulation Ltd. A full list of subsidiary undertakings can be obtained from Companies House.

Main locations: Belfast, Birmingham, Bury St Edmunds, Glasgow, Doncaster, Stockport, Addlestone

UK employees: 1,664

Total employees: 1,664

Focus of giving: Education, health, ill health, STEM (science, technology, engineering and mathematics), science technology, children, young people, community/social welfare.

Membership: BITC

Cash donations undeclared	✓
Humanitarian aid: UK	✓
Market-led giving	✓

Charitable donations

Cash UK (latest available):	2013	£150,000
	2011	£150,000
	2010	£150,000
	2008	£150,000
	2007	£166,000
Total UK (cash and in kind):	2013	£150,000
Cash worldwide:	2013	£150,000
Total worldwide (cash and in kind):	2013	£150,000

Community involvement

Thales Charitable Trust (Charity Commission no. 1000162)

The trust mainly helps organisations operating on a national basis, working with children and young people, supporting technology and education and assisting health causes, particularly care for permanent or terminal conditions. An example of the trust's activities in 2013 is a donation to the UK Electronics Skills Foundation to establish a residential summer school for students preparing to enrol at university.

Details given in the group's Corporate Responsibility Report for 2013 inform that:

> In the United Kingdom, Community Investment lies at the heart of Thales's initiatives in respect of employees, customers, investors and suppliers. These initiatives include working with schools and higher education institutions to give children and young people a better idea of the career prospects offered by studying engineering.

Charity partnership

The company has a continuing partnership with Railway Children, which provides shelter, clothes and meals to homeless children.

Corporate giving

The Thales Charitable Trust's accounts for 2013 note that a total of £150,000 was received in donations and 43 organisations were supported, including seven main charities (Alzheimer's Society, Arkwright Scholars, Combat Stress, Engineering UK, Railway Children, RUSI and UK Electronics Skills Foundation) and 36 other organisations (such as Benevolent Funds and a number of educational charities). It appears that the company does not declare its charitable donations in the annual report and accounts, therefore we take the sum of £150,000 to represent the company's charitable giving.

The trust's beneficiaries included: Alzheimer's Society; Arkwright Scholars; Children's Heart Federation; Combat Stress; Engineering UK; Imagineering UK; QED Foundation; Map Action; Railway Children; RUSI; Shaftesbury Young People; and UK Electronics Skills Foundation.

See the corporate charity entry on p. 432 for more information.

In-kind support

Staff volunteering time and fundraising efforts.

Employee-led support

Staff members are invited to contribute to good causes through volunteering efforts. In 2014 employees' assistance has been called to help the flood relief.

We found examples of Thales people undertaking various fundraising activities in support of good causes, such as: the Great Wall of China challenge to help Marie Curie Cancer Care; Three Peaks Challenge for three charities (British Heart Foundation, Macmillan Cancer Support and Ty Hafan); and various Ironman and endurance events in supporting Marie Curie, Help for Heroes and the Royal Navy and Royal Marines.

Payroll giving

The Give As You Earn scheme was set up in 2012 and allows employees 'to give a percentage of their gross salary to a charity of their choice, with only part of it deducted from their net salary (the rest is covered by Thales)'. During the financial year contributions from staff and Thales provided a cheque for £170,000 to the Alzheimer's Society, chosen by employees as a key charity partner.

Commercially led support

Sponsorship

Thames UK has been a corporate sponsor of a The Big Bang Fair 2014 and Thales Research and Technology (TRT UK) provided a sponsorship of the University Research Group of the Year award, 'which focuses on university research groups that demonstrate excellent liaison and partnership with industry'.

Women into Science and Engineering

During the year the company supported the competition which aims to encourage young women to pursue careers in science.

Arkwright Scholarships programme

Thales UK supported ten scholarships for science students through the programme.

Apprenticeships

In 2013 a new Apprentice Training Centre was opened at the Glasgow site.

Corporate social responsibility

CSR committee: The group has an Ethics and Corporate Responsibility Committee. Email: ethics.cr@thalesgroup.com

CSR information: Information given on the company's website states that Thales UK **CR principles** focus on four pillars: Business; People; Communities ('we are dedicated to supporting local and national causes particularly for causes related to youth, technology and education'); and Environment.

The company's **CR Mission** is 'to be committed to a better future for our people, our communities, our environment and our business'. Its **CR Policy** is to create a better future for our people, communities, environment and business by acting in a corporately responsible manner, in all our activities and relationships and in doing so achieve business growth.

The Thales Group's CR Report for 2013 states that the group:

> Invests in communities by establishing educational partnerships, donating to health and educational charities and, on a more local level, supporting veterans and military families, among other efforts. Any financial support granted anywhere is provided in compliance with the rules defined in the Thales Code of Ethics.

CSR report: The Group's CSR report is published annually.

Corporate charity: The Thales Charitable Trust (Charity Commission no. 1000162).

Exclusions

Political donations are not normally made.

Applications

Enquiries should be addressed to the correspondent who is the trust's administrator and Thales Ethics and Corporate Responsibility Committee member representing UK stakeholders' interests.

Thomas Cook Group plc

Leisure

Correspondent: The Health Safety and Environment Committee, 3rd Floor, South Building, 200 Aldersgate, London EC1A 4HD (tel: 020 7557 6400; fax: 020 7557 6401; email: Group.communications@thomascook.com; website: www.thomascookgroup.com)

Directors: Michael Healey, Group Chief Financial Officer; Peter Fankhauser, Group Chief Executive Officer; Dawn Airey; Frank Meysman, Chair; Carl Symon; Warren Tucker; Martine Verluyten; Emre Berkin; Annet Aris; Harriet Green (women: 4; men: 6)

Year end	30/09/2013
Turnover	£9,314,500,000
Pre-tax profit	(£158,100,000)

Nature of business: Thomas Cook Group is a global leisure travel provider. The group also offers airline and online accommodation booking services.

Company registration number: 742748

Subsidiary undertakings include: Condor Berlin GmbH; TCCT Retail Ltd; Thomas Cook AG; Thomas Cook Austria AG; Thomas Cook Finance plc; Thomas Cook Tour Operations Ltd; and Thomas Cook UK Ltd. A full list can be obtained from Companies House.

Brands include: Airtours; Cresta; escapades; Flexible Trips Hotels4u; Netflights; and The Co-operative Travel.

Main locations: Rochdale

UK employees: 12,941

Total employees: 26,448

Focus of giving: Environment, animal welfare, health, ill health, children, young people.

Membership: BITC, LBG

Gifts in kind	✓
Market-led giving	✓
Overseas giving	✓

Charitable donations

Cash UK (latest available):	2013	£36,000
	2011	£36,300
	2009	£0
	2005	£15,000
Total UK (cash and in kind):	2013	£238,000
Total worldwide (cash and in kind):	2013	£309,000

Community involvement

The group's Sustainability Report for 2014 states:

> Thomas Cook has a strong tradition of charitable giving and community investment, dating back to our founder who was a passionate philanthropist. We continue to support charities and community development across the destinations in which we operate and work through fundraising, corporate giving, staff time and resource, volunteering and in-kind donations. We also contribute to disaster and emergency relief efforts.

The Thomas Cook Children's Charity (Charity Commission no. 1091673)

The charity was established in 2009 with the aim to improve the lives of children. According to the charity's website, since the inception over £5 million has been raised. The charity operates separately from the company and is funded through the contributions by customers and employees. Funds collected are spent on Making Dreams Come True initiative which helps sick and disadvantaged children (aged 0–18) by improving educational and well-being and health care facilities and through working with charity partners in the areas of environment and clear water supply. There are two strands of support available: **national charity partnerships** (undertaking for various periods of time); and **community grants programme** (supporting local causes nominated by the customers and employees). The charity invites requests for support and/or partnership agreements from organisations.

The charity's correspondent has informed us that currently Thomas UK and Ireland does not provide any direct funding to the charity; however, it covers the cost of annual Christmas flights (see below)

Flight of Dreams

The scheme has been run for the past six years and gifts children in communities around the group's airport basis a flight experience. The charity's correspondent let us know that 'Thomas Cook Airlines donate the staff time, the aircraft and the associated costs (airport fees) at a total of [about] £8,500 per flight.' In 2014 there were three flights so the in-kind donation was at a cost of £25,500 for Thomas Cook Airlines.

Employees volunteer in these flights together with Father Christmas who gives children presents. The cost is roughly estimated at around £20,000; however, it varies annually.

Group-wide initiatives

Thomas Cook UK works with ABTA and industry colleagues to highlight the issues of animal welfare within the supply chain and was instrumental in the creation of the ABTA Animal Welfare Committee. The group also supported and endorsed the Society for the Protection of Animals Abroad (SPANA) campaign.

In 2014, working with The Travel Foundation, donations of Thomas Cook UK customers and employees helped to set up a co-operative to conserve the Melipona bees and improve local livelihoods for the Mayan women in Mexico.

Thomas Cook Central Europe has donated €100,000 (about £79,000) to finance the construction of schools in Northern Sri Lanka.

Disaster relief activities include a £52,000 donation 'to a number of charities', including Save the Children, Haiyan 2020 and Help without Frontiers, following the Typhoon Haiyan in 2013.

Charity partnerships

The Thomas Cook Group develops partnerships with a number of tourism industry organisations and initiatives, sustainability reporting organisations, and charities, including: animal charities (Born Free Foundation, Greek Animal Welfare Fund, SPANA, The Brooke and Zante Animal Welfare Fund); Charities Aid Foundation; Help Alliance; The Code; The Travel Foundation; and Wings of Help.

Corporate giving

The group's Sustainability Report for 2014 gives the following information on total community investment:

Cash contributions	£1.6 million
In-kind contributions	£300,000
Employee volunteering	£8,800
Total value	**£1.9 million**

Note that the value of 'cash contributions' contains employee, customer and corporate donations (in 2013 this figure consisted of employee and customer contributions only). We take the sum of at least £309,000 to represent the group's contributions (consisting of in-kind support and employee volunteering), as we have no means of breaking down the cash contributions figure and it would appear from that the majority of it is given by employees and customers. The breakdown of UK and worldwide donations was not available, unlike previously. Based on the ratio from the past giving we estimate that total contributions in the UK could have totalled about £238,000 and cash in the UK about £36,000.

In-kind support

Non-cash contributions are available. Thomas Cook Airlines donate the staff time, the aircraft and the associated costs (airport fees) through the Flight of Dreams initiative.

The charity's correspondent has informed us that Thomas Cook UK and Ireland enables customer donations of £2 to be made in support of The Thomas Cook Children's Charity making bookings online or in-store. Moreover, all company's flights returning to UK collect passenger donations, often in the form of foreign change, to be given to the charity. We would consider such support as a provision of a fundraising platform.

Employee-led support

The Sustainability Report for 2014 states:

> We facilitate and support employees who wish to undertake voluntary work within the community or for charitable institutions. In 2014 we enabled 101 volunteers to spend 123 hours of volunteering time. Our employees have a wide range of skills and knowledge which, when shared, can have a big impact on the organisations they wish to support, while also increasing individual engagement and motivation.

Each employee of the group is entitled to one day per year for volunteering purposes to help their chosen cause. The charity's correspondent said that UK and Ireland staff volunteering is being reviewed in order to achieve greater employee engagement and provide better community engagement opportunities on local level.

Staff members participate in a number of fundraising activities which in the UK and Ireland each year generate about £1 million in support of The Thomas Cook Children's Charity.

An example of fundraising efforts, given in the Sustainability Report for 2014, notes a team of employees raising over £100,000 split equally split between the Thomas Cook Children's Charity and Whizz-Kidz.

Payroll giving

There is a scheme operating which allows employees to contribute to the corporate charity.

Commercially led support

The German company of the group, Condor, has offered a percentage of flight ticket sales and the revenue of numerous special promotions to support the campaign of BILD hilft e.V. Ein Herz für Kinder.

Apprenticeships

Thomas Cook is a supporter of apprenticeship programmes and offers training for new entrants to the travel industry, across its shop, airline and travel businesses, in the UK and Germany in particular.

Corporate social responsibility

CSR committee: There is the Sustainability Steering Committee which reviews the policies and performance. According to the Sustainability section of the group's website 'The board is responsible for the long-term success and sustainability of the group and holds responsibility for overseeing the development and approval of strategy being delegated to the Health, Safety and Environmental Committee.'

Across the group policies are communicated through intranet, emails, employee magazines and newsletters. There also are networks of sustainability champions, leading the sustainability focus of their businesses.

CSR information: In 2013 the group created a new framework (outlined in its Sustainability Report 2013) which:

> Has four major pillars, with the customer at the heart of everything it does. It drives the high tech, high touch delivery of trusted personalised products, supported by an efficient, lean and innovative system that is overseen with relentless performance management.

In the same report, the group states:

> Sustainability is fundamental to the success of our business. Not only is it at the heart of how we behave, it's a principle that we work hard to embed at each stage of our customers' experience with us. From planning their holiday through to booking, arriving home and sharing their experience with friends, sustainability plays a key role in how we operate on a daily basis.

CSR report: There is an Annual Sustainability Report published.

Applications

The company: In writing to the correspondent.

The charity: The contact person is Aoife McDonogh (Thomas Cook Ltd, Unit 15–30, The Thomas Cook Business Park, Conningsby Road, Bretton PE3 8SB; tel: 01733 417436; email: thomascook.childrenscharity@thomascook.com; website: www.thomascookchildrenscharity.com)

Nominations for charities or charitable projects are welcomed from both customers and staff.

Thomson Reuters (Reuters Ltd)

Media

Correspondent: The Corporate Responsibility Team, The Thomson Reuters Building, 30 South Colonnade, Canary Wharf, London E14 5EP (tel: 020 7542 7015 (general enquiries) or 020 7542 4148 (foundation); email: foundation@thomsonreuters.com; website: www.thomsonreuters.com)

Directors: Priscilla Hughes; Peter Moss; Helen Campbell; David Mitchley; Giray Erol (women: 2; men: 3)

Year end	31/12/2013
Turnover	£1,582,000,000
Pre-tax profit	£118,000,000

Nature of business: The company 'supplies the global business community and news media with a wide range of products, including real-time financial data, information management systems, access to numeric and textual databases, news and news pictures'. The majority of operations are located in the UK but also in Continental Europe, Africa, Asia and Latin America.

Reuters Ltd immediate parent company is Reuters Holdings Ltd. The company's ultimate parent company and controlling party is Thomson Investments Ltd. The latter, as well as the Thomson Reuters Corporation, is incorporated in Canada.

Company registration number: 145516

Subsidiary undertakings include: Blaxmill Ltd; Lipper Ltd; Thompson Reuters Group Overseas Holdings UK Ltd; and Thompson Reuters India Private Ltd. A full list of subsidiary undertakings can be obtained from Companies House.

Brands include: 3E; ProView; Sweet and Maxwell; and Westlaw UK.

Main locations: London, Edinburgh

Total employees: 4,594

Focus of giving: Human rights, education, enterprise/training, environment, equal opportunities, heritage, unpopular causes, overseas projects, sponsorship, sport, recreation, women's issues, community/social welfare.

Gifts in kind	✓
Market-led giving	✓
Matched funding	✓
Overseas giving	✓
Payroll giving	✓
Sponsorship	✓

Charitable donations

Cash UK (latest available):	2013	£4,000,000
	2011	£4,260,000
	2009	£3,330,000
	2008	£1,100,000
Cash worldwide:	2013	£4,000,000

Community involvement

Thomson Reuters Foundation (Charity Commission no. 1082139)

The Charity Commission's summary of the foundation's activities states that it was established in 2000 with the aim of:

> Leveraging the skills, values and expertise to run programmes that trigger change and empower people across the world: free legal assistance, media development, and in-depth coverage of the world's under-reported stories. [It] stands for Human Rights, women's empowerment, anti-corruption and for the rule of law.

The income comes primarily from Thomson Reuters; accordingly, 'the work of the foundation reflects the values and concerns of the company and its employees'.

During the year the foundation particularly engaged in supporting independent journalism (47% of the funds), covering under-reported issues (27% of the funds), providing free legal assistance to NGOs and social enterprises (14% of the funds) and running Trust Women Conference and promoting women's rights (12% of the funds).

The following information is given in the company's annual report and accounts for 2013:

> In 2010 the company entered into an agreement with Thomson Reuters Foundation to undertake to grant not less than £1.1 million to the foundation by way of funding each of the calendar years 2011, 2012 and 2013. If the foundation, as a direct result of the company no longer funding it, becomes unable to pay its debts, the company guarantees to meet the liabilities of the foundation in respect of money due to the University of Oxford for the Reuters Institute for the Study of Journalism and the cost of foundation staff redundancies up to a maximum cumulative amount of £1.5 million.

Greenhouse 101

The global CSR report for 2013 informs that there is a partnership with this organisation which 'seeks to empower young people in London's most disadvantaged communities to realise their potential through sports programs, delivered by inspirational coaches'. Thomson Reuters sponsors the charity's annual dodgeball tournament and in addition during the year 62 customers, technology partners and staff cycled from Paris to London over three days, raising US $101,000 (about £63,000) for the charity.

Practical Law

In 2013 Thomson Reuters acquired the Practical Law business which maintains its long-term partnerships in the London Borough of Southwark. The partnership includes a scholarship program offering grants for children of low-income families to study law at undergraduate level.

Save the Children – International Financing Review (IFR) Awards

The following information is taken from the IFR Awards website:

> Thomson Reuters is Save the Children's longest-serving corporate partner, with the IFR Awards Dinner being the charity's largest annual fundraising event. 2015 marks the 20th year of our association and, over this time, we have raised over £22 million thanks to the generosity of the global investment banking community. [In 2014 over £1 million was raised for the cause.]
>
> The IFR Awards are part of the Thomson Reuters Awards for Excellence, recognising corporate and individual success in the global financial industry.

The Save the Children website notes that:

> Funds raised through the Thomson Reuters IFR Awards have supported a wide range of projects, including providing pregnant women and children in Mozambique with vital healthcare, giving street children in Bangladesh a safe place to play and learn, and giving the most marginalised girls in Mozambique a chance to have access to quality, life-changing education.

Corporate giving

During 2013 the company made charitable contributions totalling £4 million (2012: £4 million). This amount primarily consists of support to the corporate charity – Thomson Reuters Foundation.

The foundation's annual report and accounts for 2013 state that 'an annual grant from Reuters Ltd, a wholly owned subsidiary of Thomson Reuters... was £3.7 million (2012: £3.8 million) and an additional £38,000 (2012: £0) [was given] to fund projects in South Africa'. The foundation received gifts in kind from Thomson Reuters of £2.3 million (2012: £2.88 million). During the year the foundation spent a total of about £8.7 million in directly undertaken activities and grant funding (£410,000 to Oxford University).

We do not know other details of the £4 million figure.

Beneficiaries of the foundation included: Oxford University (£410,000); Hagio Prize awards (£5,000) to individuals.

Note: We have used the accounts of Reuters Ltd (registered company no. 145516), a company registered in the UK.

See the corporate charity entry on p. 433 for more information.

In-kind support

In-kind donations is given to the Thomas Reuters Foundation, including office space, communications, computer equipment, also marketing services, licences, staff time and trainers, lending of tools, advertising platform and legal collateral. The foundation's annual report and accounts note that 'donated staff time totalled £571,000 (2012: £550,000)'.

The London office runs an annual Toy Appeal (see 'Employee-led support').

Employee-led support

The following information is taken from the global Thomas Reuters CSR Report for 2013 and appears to be implemented across all businesses.

Community Champion Awards

The annual Community Champion Awards program celebrates the personal volunteer commitments of employees. Winners receive a substantial donation for the cause of their choice. In 2013 the scheme celebrated its 12th year and a total of 43 grants were awarded to the value of US $100,000 (about £62,000 – two top awards were of US $10,000 (about £6,200) each). 'Projects supported included the provision of early childhood education for special needs and high-risk children, together with housing and healthcare services for the homeless and elderly population.' Since its beginning the scheme has provided over US $1 million (about £624,000) to charities across the globe.

Matched funding

Employees' charitable donations to registered charities are matched up to US$1,000 (about £624) a year. Our research suggests that the Executive Committee members and their direct staff also have access to a bespoke matching programme with an annual limit of US$10,000 (about £6,200) and US$5,000 (about £3,100) respectively. In 2013 a total of 3,616 employees made use of the programme, raising more than US $1.5 million (over £935,000) of donations for charities across the globe, which were matched by the group. The Matching Gifts programme can be accessed via the My Community platform.

Payroll giving

In 2014 a new My Giving system was launched on the My Community platform. The system incorporates US-based Employee Giving Campaign, along with schemes in the UK and India.

Volunteering

Staff are encouraged to volunteer and offered two days a year with pay if volunteering for a registered charity. In 2013 a total of 91,326 were spent volunteering across the group, and in the UK the number of hours volunteered totalled 6,685.

Dollars for Doers

This programme, open to all regular employees, makes a donation of US $500 (about £312) to a charity for every 20 hours volunteered (both inside and outside working hours) by a staff member, and US $1,000 (about £624) for 40 volunteering hours. In 2013 the scheme resulted in grants totalling US $434,500 (about £271,000) to 444 organisations.

Toy Appeal

Every year during the winter holiday season the UK office in London runs a Toy Appeal to collect toys for community organisations – employees are invited to donate funds or purchase a suitable gift for a child up to the age of 16. In 2013 a total of 646 gifts were donated and included games, books, puzzles and cuddly toys.

Commercially led support

Sponsorship

The CSR report for 2013 states: that: 'Sponsorship represents a key opportunity to reinforce our brand values and corporate responsibility commitments for an external audience.'

Globally, Thomson Reuters has partnerships with Aspen Ideas Festival (Washington), Ideas Forum28 and World Economic Forum. It also sponsors the National Ballet of Canada and Williams F1 Team. As part of the latter, in 2013 an engineering student was given the opportunity to work with the team in a two-week placement at the team's Head Office in The Grove (Oxford). The company also provides an ongoing supply of professional trading equipment for Cass Business School in London.

Social enterprise

Thomson Reuters' CSR report states:

> Investing in social enterprises is something we're proud of, and our partnership with the Social Business Trust is now in its fourth year. The relationship enables us to provide financial capital alongside professional support to help grow inspiring social enterprises and invest in a diversified local economy. Working alongside a network of six other founding companies, our experienced business leaders take charge of projects for the social enterprises, providing expertise to meet agreed objectives.

Corporate social responsibility

CSR committee: Globally, Thompson Reuters has a Governance Roundtable which is made up of representatives from across the business and headed by the Global Head of CR. The roundtable, which meets three times a year, has oversight of key charitable activities and is updated on the latest projects and initiatives for feedback throughout the year.

CSR information: The CR section of the Thomson Reuters website states:

> At Thomson Reuters, we all have a shared responsibility to do business in ways that respect, protect and benefit our customers, our employees, our communities and our environment. This responsibility informs everything we do, both as a company and as individuals. Our commitments as a responsible business are guided by our Trust Principles and are core to our purpose and values, our policies and flagship programs are focused on the following areas: Citizenship; Marketplace; and Workplace.
>
> ... We have updated our CR strategy, integrating what we previously called 'Community' into our new Citizenship program. We feel this repositioning reflects more accurately our role as an ethical business, or good 'corporate citizen'.

CSR report: A global CSR report is published annually.

Corporate charity: Thomson Reuters Foundation (Charity Commission no. 1082139).

Applications

Thomson Reuters Foundation does not consider unsolicited requests for support. The foundation's annual report and accounts for 2013 (obtained from the Charity Commission) state:

> Thomson Reuters Foundation does not accept applications for cash grants but focuses on using the skills, values and expertise of Thomson Reuters to run its global programmes. Grants are rarely made and only where they are in line with the foundation's programme objectives or meet the conditions of restricted funds.

Other enquiries relating to the company should be directed to the CSR Team.

Daniel Thwaites plc

Brewers/distillers

Correspondent: Susan Woodward, Company Secretary, Penny Street, Star Brewery, Blackburn, Lancashire BB1 6HL (tel: 01254 686868; fax: 01254 681439; website: www.thwaites.co.uk)

Directors: Richard Bailey, Chief Executive Officer; Ann Yerburgh, Chair; Kevin Wood, Group Finance Director; Peter Boddy; John Barnes; Arabella Yerburgh (women: 2; men: 4)

Year end	31/03/2014
Turnover	£138,700,000
Pre-tax profit	£7,800,000

Nature of business: The principal activities of Daniel Thwaites plc are the brewing and canning of beer, the distribution of wines and spirits and the operation of hotels and public houses.

Company registration number: 51702

Main locations: Blackburn

UK employees: 1,459

Total employees: 1,459

Focus of giving: Health, ill health, children, young people, community/ social welfare, disability.

Charity of the Year	✓
Gifts in kind	✓

Charitable donations

Cash UK (latest available):	2014	£25,000
	2009	£29,200
	2008	£16,600
	2006	£27,000
	2005	£28,000
Total UK (cash and in kind):	2014	£25,000
Cash worldwide:	2014	£25,000
Total worldwide (cash and in kind):	2014	£25,000

Community involvement

We have no information on this company's community and charitable initiatives, apart from the cash donations declared in its annual report (one small donation to one charity), and the existence of **The Daniel Thwaites Charitable Trust** (Charity Commission no. 1038097) which has previously benefited from the company's annual charitable donation.

Established in 1994, 'emphasis is placed on giving tangible, physical help, be that wheelchairs, computers, musical instruments, beds or other specialist equipment for helping improve interaction, or items such as bingo machines and televisions that improve the quality of life for groups of people'. Support is given across the UK, although there is a preference for appeals from within a 50-mile radius of Blackburn.

The trust has had no income since 2009 and looked as though it might be dormant when the Charity Commission's webpage showed that in 2013 there had been a total expenditure of £750. Whilst this isn't a great deal of money, it does mean that the trust is still in existence and operating. It would appear though that the company has stopped paying money into it on an annual basis.

Charity partner

British Heart Foundation

Corporate giving

In 2013/14 the company gave £25,000 in one charitable donation awarded to Blackburn Youth Zone.

See the corporate charity entry on p. 433 for more information.

Employee-led support

The group encourages pub staff to be part of their local communities and supports their work in sponsoring local events. In the last financial year, through raffles, auctions and other fundraising activities, money was raised by staff and customers for a variety of charitable causes. Staff raised £8,000 for the charity partner British Heart Foundation.

Corporate social responsibility

CSR committee: There was no evidence of a CSR committee.

CSR information: The following statements appear on the group's website:

> Our commitment to corporate social responsibility is underpinned through our core values and our commitment to quality, integrity and care. Our directors ensure that each of our businesses works to improve performance across a wide range of CSR activities.
>
> Every year we will identify key CSR issues arising in the company, agree actions for improvement as well as measuring how we have got on with the previous year's objectives.

CSR report: We could not find a CSR publication.

Corporate charity: The Daniel Thwaites Charitable Trust (Charity Commission no. 1038097).

Applications

We would advise contacting your local Thwaites pub in the first instance for further advice.

Time Inc. (UK) Ltd (formerly IPC Media Ltd)

Media

Correspondent: Jane Mortimore, Corporate Responsibility Manager, Blue Fin Building, 110 Southwark Street, London SE1 0SU (tel: 020 3148 5404; email: jane.mortimore@timeinc.com; website: www.timeincuk.com/about/responsibility)

Directors: F. A. Dent; S. Hirst; C. L. Meredith; J. A. Newcombe; N. S. Robinson; P. R. Williams; J. J. Bairstow; A. C. Davies; M. A. Rich

Year end	31/12/2013
Turnover	£292,701,000
Pre-tax profit	£21,514,000

Nature of business: The publication of magazines.

Company registration number: 53626

Brands include: Country Life, InStyle, Look, NME, Now, TV and Satellite Week,

UK employees: 1,676

Total employees: 1,676

Focus of giving: General charitable purposes, education, health, ill health, arts, culture, children, young people.

Charity of the Year	✓
Gifts in kind	✓
Market-led giving	✓
Payroll giving	✓

Charitable donations

Cash UK (latest available):	2013	£31,000
	2012	£4,500
	2011	£5,120
	2008	£22,000
	2007	£24,000
Total UK (cash and in kind):	2013	£31,000
Cash worldwide:	2013	£31,000
Total worldwide (cash and in kind):	2013	£31,000

Community involvement

Time Inc. (UK) Ltd looks to support communities in the area surrounding its main office, which it does through:

- Building relationships with local schools
- Selecting a charity partner on a two year basis, for which employees fundraise, lend their skills and which benefits from the company's editorial and advertising expertise
- Supporting its brands that have selected their own charity partner (an example of this is *Woman and Home* magazine, which has opted to support Breast Cancer Care, mainly through events involving its readership)

Charity of the Year

Time Inc. (UK) Ltd opted to support CALM – The Campaign Against Living Miserably as its partner in 2013–14. The charity, whose aim is to prevent male suicides in the UK, benefitted from in-kind support in the form of editorial coverage, advertising, and pro bono support. It was also the focus of individual and collective staff fundraising efforts during the two years of partnership.

The website states:

> We also provide ad hoc support to other charities, either via a financial or an in-kind donation. Support is typically given to organisations that are local to our offices and whose work is aligned with our key community priorities (young people, arts, education and literacy).

Corporate giving

In 2013 the company made charitable donations of £31,000. A list of specific beneficiaries was not available.

We were unable to determine a value for the in-kind support given by the company.

In-kind support

Pro bono

Staff are able to contribute their skills and expertise to local causes, partner charities, as well as through the company's own educational initiatives. Employees can request up to two days' paid time per year for volunteering purposes.

Employee-led support

Employee volunteering

Staff are given opportunities to contribute to their communities from 'skilled' volunteering, which uses their media skills and expertise, to 'more general' activities such as primary school reading activities or by taking part in a 'team challenge'. Employees are also able to source their own volunteering opportunities.

Employee fundraising

Employees have contributed to charitable fundraising through their participation in sponsored events.

Payroll giving

Employees are able to donate to charities through a payroll giving scheme.

Commercially led support

At the time of writing, the company is developing a new educational initiative aimed at students in Year 10 at schools located close to its offices. The programme will replace the long-running 'Schools' Design Programme' and has the aims of educating young people about careers in the media; improving employability skills; promoting Time Inc. UK as a media company; and involving Time employees in the programme.

Time Inc. UK also regularly hosts visits by students from educational establishments, which provide them with the opportunity of learning about the company and the media industry through interaction with 'editors, designers and other senior employees'.

Corporate social responsibility

CSR committee: We found no evidence of there being a CSR committee.

CSR information: The website states the following: 'Time Inc. UK's corporate responsibility agenda comprises three priority areas: community and educational initiatives; the input and involvement of our employees; and the environment.'

We were unable to determine the ratio of men to women on the board.

CSR report: No CSR report was published; however, there is an informative section on CSR on the company's website.

Applications

In writing to the correspondent.

TJX UK (formerly TK Maxx)

Retail – clothing and footwear

Correspondent: The Marketing Department, 50 Clarendon Road, Watford, Hertfordshire WD17 1TX (tel: 01923 473000 (main switchboard); website: www.tkmaxx.com)

Directors: Mary Blier Reynolds; Michael Macmillan; David Averill; Scott Goldenberg (women: 1; men: 4)

Year end	01/02/2014
Turnover	£1,995,000,000
Pre-tax profit	£91,500,000

Nature of business: A nationwide chain of stores and selling clothing, gifts and homeware below recommended retail prices. Online sales are also made.

TJX UK owns and operates TK Maxx and HomeSense. It is a subsidiary of The TJX Companies Inc.

Company registration number: 3094828

Subsidiary undertakings include: TJX Ireland; TJX Europe Buying Group Ltd; TJX European Distribution; and TJX Distribution GmbH. Further details of subsidiary undertakings can be obtained from Companies House.

Brands include: TK Maxx and HomeSense.

Main locations: Watford

Total employees: 15,659

Focus of giving: Education, environment, fundraising events, health, ill health, overseas projects, children, young people.

Cash donations undeclared ✓
Gifts in kind ✓
Market-led giving ✓
Overseas giving ✓

Charitable donations

Cash UK (latest available):	2014	£903,000
	2011	£879,000
	2009	£931,000
	2007	£897,520
	2006	£750,824
Total UK (cash and in kind):	2014	£2,300,000
Cash worldwide:	2014	£903,000
Total worldwide (cash and in kind):	2014	£2,300,000

Community involvement

Although a name change took place in 2007, the company still trades under the TK Maxx brand. The information contained in this entry relates to the UK company TJX UK.

Community Fund

The majority of the company's giving is to support its partner charities but it also supports local charities, in the areas where the company operates or sources its goods. The website notes that in 2013 over 250 local charities have benefitted from donations. The fund supports 'smaller charities that matter to our employees and customers – either through personal experiences or due to the support they deliver in local communities'.

Examples have included:

- Bury Hospice, which works to provide end of life and palliative care to people who have been diagnosed with a life limiting disease
- CHICKS, which provides free respite breaks for vulnerable children aged between 8–15 who may be in care, poverty or suffering due to illness or bereavement
- The Brain Research Trust, which funds vital basic and clinical research into the causes, treatments, prevention and cure of neurological diseases
- Julia's House Children's Hospice, which is based in Dorset, and cares for children with life limiting illnesses, the majority of which won't live past the age of 16

Corporate giving

In 2013/14 TJX UK:

> Supported six major charities by raising funds for Action for Children, Cancer Research UK, Comic Relief, Prince's Trust, The Woodland Trust and the Uganda Community Project (working with Save the Children). All charity initiatives within the business were directed towards work for these organisations. Smaller charities that are important to company employees and customers were supported through the Company's Community Fund.

The administration of the programme and company donations totalled £2.3 million (2012/13: £600,000). In addition to this sum a total of £1.7 million was generated through fundraising activities. The accounts did not provide a further breakdown, therefore we estimate that about £903,000 was given in cash in the UK, based on figures from the three previous years known to us.

Beneficiaries included: Action for Children, Cancer Research UK, Comic Relief, Enable Ireland The Woodland Trust and Uganda Classroom Fund (Save the Children).

In-kind support

Give Up Clothes for Good

Cancer Research UK

Relationship with the charity began in 2004. Part of the partnership is the Give Up Clothes for Good campaign, which:

> Encourages people to donate their high-quality used clothes, accessories and homeware to Cancer Research UK, by dropping them off at nearby T.K. Maxx and HomeSense locations. Most of the donated items are then sold through Cancer Research U.K.'s nearly 600 charity shops, with the proceeds dedicated to research into beating children's cancers.

Enable Ireland

Through Give Up Clothes For Good scheme, operating on the same principle as in the UK, customers and associates raised over €100,000 (about £79,000) worth of donations to support children with disabilities and their families in local communities in Ireland.

We would consider the above to be a type of in-kind support, whereby the company provides a fundraising platform for the charities.

Employee-led support

According to the global CSR report for 2013, the company's employees are encouraged to volunteer and raise funds for the charitable causes they personally care about. Through the Community Fund, grants for members of staff teams are available to support local causes. The fund has helped over 300 projects, 'from supporting children with multiple sclerosis to providing art and music workshops for socially disadvantaged children'.

Significant fundraising is carried out by the company's employees and customers. For example, since 2005 customers and employees have raised over £13.4 million for Comic Relief's Red Nose Day campaigns (£3.7 million raised in 2013), including profit from the sales of exclusive t-shirts. The money raised is distributed between the projects in Africa (60%) and the UK (40%).

Commercially led support

Charity partnerships

The company has six main charity partners supported through various fundraising campaigns and commercially led initiatives: Action for Children, Cancer Research UK, Comic Relief, Enable Ireland The Woodland Trust and Uganda Classroom Fund (working with Save the Children).

Sport Relief

Two limited edition aprons have been created for Sport Relief 2014 by British pottery maker Emma Bridgewater, available to purchase exclusively from TK Maxx UK stores and TKmaxx.com. 'The money raised from the apron will be used to help transform the lives of some of the poorest and most disadvantaged people – both on your doorstep in the UK and around the world.'

Comic Relief

TK Maxx stores across the country sell Christmas cards and chocolate coins to help raise money for children's charities: Action for Children, Cancer Research UK, Comic Relief and Enable Ireland. The company donates £1.50/€1.40 from the sale of every pack of cards and turns chocolate coins into real money by donating 65pence/55cents from every bag of treats sold.

Woodland Trust

The company is donating the money raised through the sale of single use carrier bags to the trust. Donations are made through the Welsh Assembly's will help plant 22,242 trees at community planting events. According to the website, to date more than £700,000 has been raised for the trust.

Action for Children

The global CSR report 2013 notes that 'through awareness campaigns, merchandise sales and raising funds, HomeSense stores support Action for Children, a group that serves disadvantaged and vulnerable children in approximately 50 local programs in our stores' communities'.

Uganda Community Project

According to the website this Save the Children project, supported by the company since 2008, seeks to improve 'access to a quality basic education that empowers children and their communities' that have been severely affected by years of war. Funds are generated by customers and employees and have helped to 'build classrooms and toilet blocks, provided textbooks and solar lamps, helped recruit teachers, to name just a few activities'. In addition, materials, teacher training, community engagement and trading opportunities are supported. In 2012 the company ran 'an associate book and stationery collection campaign ... to form libraries and stationery cupboards in our 12 school communities'. According to the global CSR report, 'TJX Europe has extended its support to sourcing products from these communities with the aim of helping to support long-term social and economic improvement.'

Corporate social responsibility

CSR committee: There were no details found of a separate UK committee.

CSR information: The company's website states:

> We're passionate about being a responsible retailer. Globally, we have an amazing history of giving back and it's at the heart of how we do business. We have four commitments: to the communities where we live and work; to our current and future associates; to our vendors and business partners in our supply chain; and to the environment, which we have a responsibility to preserve and protect for future generations.

CSR report: An annual CSR report covers the group's global programme.

Exclusions

Political contributions are not generally made.

Applications

In writing to the correspondent.

TNT UK Ltd

Logistics, transport and shipping services

Correspondent: The Managing Director, TNT Express Services UK and Ireland, PO Box 99, Stubbins Vale Mill, Stubbins Vale Road, Ramsbottom, Bury, Lancashire BL8 9BF (tel: 01827 303030; website: www.tnt.co.uk)

Directors: Jonathan Downing; Susan Barnes; Simon Harper; Daniel Vines; Stuart Stobie (women: 1; men: 4)

Year end	31/12/2013
Turnover	£742,880,000
Pre-tax profit	(£6,413,000)

Nature of business: TNT UK Ltd provides transportation, logistics and international mail services, warehousing, record storage and facility management.

The immediate parent undertaking of the company is TNT Transport Ltd and the ultimate parent undertaking and controlling party is TNT Express NV, incorporated in Netherlands.

Company registration number: 1628530

Subsidiary undertakings include: Equity Credit Services Ltd; TNT Fashion Group France SAS; TNT Offshore Islands Express Ltd TNT Transport (NI) Ltd; and Sayer and Company (Transport – IOM) Ltd. A full list of subsidiary undertakings can be found in the accounts.

Main locations: Atherstone, Bury, Stubbins

UK employees: 9,484

Total employees: 9,484

Focus of giving: Human rights, education, environment, fundraising events, health, ill health, overseas projects, sponsorship, sport, recreation, children, young people, community/ social welfare, disability, disasters.

Charity of the Year	✓
Gifts in kind	✓
Humanitarian aid: overseas	✓
Market-led giving	✓
Sponsorship	✓

Charitable donations

Cash UK (latest available):	2013	£14,000
	2012	£9,000
	2011	£35,000
	2009	£529,000
	2007	£529,000
Total UK (cash and in kind):	2013	£14,000
Cash worldwide:	2013	£14,000
Total worldwide (cash and in kind):	2013	£14,000

Community involvement

The company's website notes that TNT's 'strategy is to develop mutually beneficial partnerships with charitable organisations that focus on the personal development of young people and those whose success depends on efficient transport networks'. Support is given in the areas of children and young people, education, disability, disadvantaged people and community causes.

Charity partnership

The company's principal charity is Wooden Spoon. Funds for the charity are generated by the company's employees and so far have reached over £3 million (since 1997). According to the website, 98% of all funds raised are 'going directly to frontline projects to benefit the disabled, sick and disadvantaged children'.

Global humanitarian partnerships

Across the group initiatives are undertaken to form partnerships with a range of organisations. TNT will often help deliver relief supplied to disaster affected areas and until 2013 worked with the United Nations' World Food Programme through 'Moving the World' partnership. The group's annual report and accounts for 2013 say – 'to ensure maximum impact for local partners and engagement of employees, TNT Express will continue to provide logistics supply chain solutions at the local level'.

Fleet Forum

TNT participates in the Fleet Forum – an 'independent knowledge centre within the international aid and development community that is focused on issues surrounding humanitarian fleets' founded in 2003. The forum is managed by the Red Cross and Red Crescent Societies, UN World Food Programme, World Vision International, Care and TNT.

Corporate giving

The company's annual report and accounts for 2013 say that during the year there were 'numerous small charitable donations amounting to £14,000 (2012: £9,000) to national and local charities'. The latest CSR report from TNT Express Services UK and Ireland is for 2011.

Beneficiaries include: BBC Children in Need; Breast Cancer Campaign; Comic Relief; Sport Relief; and Wooden Spoon.

In-kind support

Globally TNT has provided transportation services in aid of disaster appeals.

Employee-led support

TNT employees engage in various activities to raise funds in support of the charities. For example, the Virgin London Marathon, End2End Challenge, the River Deep Mountain High Challenge and the TNT Great British Bike Ride.

Employees support both the principal charity Wooden Spoon and other selected charities, such as Comic Relief, Sport Relief and BBC Children in Need, as well as a range of local causes. The CR Report for 2011 (the latest available at the time of writing) states that 'every year TNT transforms one of its customer contact centres into a Children in Need call centre where employees from throughout the country give up their time to man the phones'. According to the report at least one day every year is a Wear it Pink Day to support Breast Cancer Campaign.

Seeing is Believing

The programme allows employees to take time out of their working day to visit children at Wooden Spoon supported projects or receive 'Spoon on Site' visits. This initiative has been running since 2003 with over 2,600 staff members having participated.

Commercially led support

Sponsorship

The company sponsors the TNT Great British Bike Ride, is the main sponsor of Nuneaton Rugby Union Football Club and supports a number junior and school sports clubs.

Corporate social responsibility

CSR committee: The company's Corporate Responsibility Report for 2011 (the latest available at the time of writing) says that the Managing Director of TNT Express Services UK and Ireland 'is responsible for implementing TNT's corporate responsibility policies and the CR performance of the UK & Ireland business unit'.

On a global level CSR agenda is in the hands of the Executive Board. The central CR Steering Committee, chaired by the CEO, advises and assists the board:

> In developing, executing and monitoring the performance of TNT Express' CR strategy and its associated policies and procedures. . . . The corporate CR department facilitates the committee and coordinates global CR activities and performance in cooperation with the business units and networks. Annually, the Supervisory Board evaluates the company's CR approach and performance.

CSR information: The company's website states: 'TNT is committed to managing its business in a socially responsible manner – one that seeks to make a positive contribution to the communities in which it works and yet has a minimum impact on the environment in which it operates.'

The four key strands of CR activity are: 'Care for employees; Care for the environment; Care for our customers; and Care for the society in which we all live and work – nationally and globally.'

The following statements are taken from the global TNT website:

> At TNT Express, we have a long-standing commitment both to protecting the environment, promoting social values and to conducting our operations with integrity and with respect for the interests of all our stakeholders.
>
> Corporate responsibility (CR) is an integral part of TNT Express' business strategy and embedded in its business and operational activities. Given TNT Express' business and operational profile, health & safety and the environment are given priority on TNT Express' strategic CR agenda.

Other items on TNT's social agenda include promotion of human rights and provision of expertise and capacity to several humanitarian partners.

CSR report: A global CSR report is published within the group's annual report and accounts, which covers group-wide activities. There is a UK and Ireland CR Report, and details referring to UK community activities can also be found on the company's website.

Exclusions

No support is generally given for political and religious appeals.

Applications

In writing to the correspondent. Corporate responsibility enquiries can also be made using an online form on the global website – www.tnt.com/corporate/en/site/contact.html.

Toshiba Information Systems (UK) Ltd

Electronics/computers, retail – electrical, telecommunications

Correspondent: Patrick Whelan, Company Secretary, Toshiba Court, Weybridge Business Park, Addlestone Road, Weybridge, Surrey KT15 2UL (tel: 01932 841600; fax: 01932 852455; website: www.toshiba.co.uk)

Directors: Damian Jaume; Patrick Whelan; Kiyofumi Kakudo (women: 0; men: 3)

Year end	31/03/2014
Turnover	£381,440,520
Pre-tax profit	£7,023,931

Nature of business: The principal activities of the company include sale, marketing and distribution of computers and telephone systems, consumer electrical products and mobile phones, all obtained or manufactured by other Toshiba group companies.

The ultimate parent company is Toshiba Corporation, incorporated in Japan.

Company registration number: 918861

Subsidiary undertakings include: None given in the accounts.

Main locations: Weybridge

Total employees: 233

Focus of giving: Education, enterprise/training, health, ill health, sponsorship, sport, recreation, children, young people, community/social welfare, disability.

Gifts in kind	✓
Market-led giving	✓
Sponsorship	✓

Charitable donations

Cash UK (latest available):	2014	£6,100
	2013	£7,700
	2012	£18,850
	2009	£21,600
	2008	£47,000
Total UK (cash and in kind):	2014	£6,100
Cash worldwide:	2014	£6,100
Total worldwide (cash and in kind):	2014	£6,100

Community involvement

The global website states:

> Toshiba Group contributes to the development of local communities and solution to issues imposed on them through not only our business activities, but also our worldwide corporate citizenship activities. . . . We have also contributed to the development of social infrastructure in developing and emerging countries in addition to the development of products that meet the needs of local communities.

Globally Toshiba group supports a range of causes in developing countries and helps in disaster appeals, often in Asia.

Corporate giving

The annual report and accounts for 2013/14 note that a total of £6,100 (2012/13: £7,700) was given in charitable contributions, including a number of small donations to local charities. Note that this information relates to Toshiba Information Systems (UK) Ltd and not the Toshiba Corporation, which gives mainly to organisations in developing countries.

We were unable to find details of the beneficiaries.

In-kind support

We found indications of Toshiba providing a £13,000 worth piece of equipment to Bowel Cancer UK in the past.

Employee-led support

Information taken from Toshiba Corporation global website states:

> Toshiba Corporation and its worldwide group of companies are celebrating December as CSR month, a series of events that underline the global Toshiba group's commitment to management grounded in corporate social responsibility, recognise achievements in the last year, and encourage participation in voluntary activities by all of the group's 200,000 employees.

The CSR month has been celebrated since 2006 and includes the International Volunteer Day (the 5th of December). Worldwide companies are also planning their own activities during the month.

The company's employees engage in fundraising activities, for instance, in support of Alzheimer's Society.

Commercially led support

Sponsorships

Toshiba has sponsored sports events and music in the UK. For example: Mencap's 'Little Noises Sessions'; the Toshiba Windsor Triathlon (in partnership with Human Race); and Glasgow 2014 Commonwealth Games. Globally the group sponsors sports activities.

Corporate social responsibility

CSR committee: We found no indications of a committee relevant to the UK.

CSR information: The global website notes the following:

> We endeavour to serve the needs of all people, especially our customers, shareholders, and employees, by implementing forward-looking corporate strategies while carrying out responsible and responsive business activities. As good corporate citizens, we actively contribute to further the goals of society.
>
> By continually developing innovative technologies centering on the fields of Electronics and Energy, we strive to create products and services that enhance human life, and which lead to a thriving, healthy society. We constantly

> seek new approaches that help realize the goals of the world community, including ways to improve the global environment.

The Corporation's CSR community investment does not include the UK.

CSR report: There is an annual global CSR report published on the website but has no information regarding UK community giving.

Applications

In writing to the correspondent.

Toyota Motor Manufacturing (UK) Ltd

Motors and accessories

Correspondent: Julie Langley, Corporate Planning and External Affairs, Burnaston, Derbyshire, East Midlands DE1 9TA (tel: 01332 283611; email: external.affairs@toyotauk.com; website: www.toyotauk.com)

Directors: Takeshi Numa; Shigeru Teramoto; Anthony Walker; James Crosbie; Timothy Freeman; Eiji Takeichi; Takao Gonno (women: 0; men: 7)

Year end	31/03/2014
Turnover	£2,378,751,000
Pre-tax profit	(£87,931,000)

Nature of business: The principal activity of the company is car and engine manufacture.

The immediate parent company of Toyota Motor Manufacturing (UK) Ltd is Toyota Motor Europe SA/NV, incorporated in Belgium. The ultimate parent undertaking and controlling party is Toyota Motor Corporation, incorporated in Japan.

Company registration number: 2352348

Subsidiary undertakings include: None given in the annual report and accounts.

Brands include: Auris; Auris Hybrid; Avensis; Aygo; Corolla; Urban Cruiser; and Yaris.

Main locations: Burnaston, Deeside

Total employees: 3,144

Focus of giving: Education, enterprise/ training, environment, health, ill health, medical research, non-registered charities, small groups, local groups, STEM (science, technology, engineering and mathematics), safety and crime prevention, sponsorship, children, young people.

Membership: BITC

Charity of the Year	✓
Gifts in kind	✓
Market-led giving	✓
Matched funding	✓
Payroll giving	✓
Sponsorship	✓

Charitable donations

Cash UK (latest available):	2014	£750,000
	2011	£645,000
	2009	£541,000
	2008	£350,000
	2007	£257,000
Total UK (cash and in kind):	2014	£750,000
Cash worldwide:	2014	£750,000
Total worldwide (cash and in kind):	2014	£750,000

Community involvement

Toyota Manufacturing UK Charitable Trust (Charity Commission no. 1124678)

The trust was established in 2008 and relies on funds are raised by members of the company. During 2013/14 a total of £151,000 (2012/13: £175,000) was donated to local charities within the Burnaston and Deeside areas.

Community Grants

Awards of up to £1,000 for successful projects in the fields of the environment, children, education and health are available to organisations or charities that are local to Toyota's Burnaston and Deeside facilities. The website states that 'these grants are intended for the purchase of long-term tangible equipment and resources up to the value of £1,000 (covering the total cost of the intended purchase)'.

The website furthermore states:

> Since the start of production in 1992, we have contributed to a variety of local and national community causes. Through the social contributions programme, over £4.5 million has been donated to charities and organisations. Our focus of support is based around our main focus areas – environment, children, education, and health.

Charity of the Year

The company's website states that each year two charities are chosen by employees to be supported over a three-year period. In 2013 these were the National Society for the Prevention of Cruelty to Children (NSPCC) and the British Heart Foundation. According to the information given on the website, in 2006 Toyota committed to raise £1 million for the NSPCC and since then has given over £975,000 to local NSPCC projects. Partnership with the British Heart Foundation began in 2009 with over £166,000 being donated. In 2014 Macmillan Cancer Support was chosen to benefit from fundraising activities and in 2015 Toyota has announced a target of £1 million to be raised in support of Comic Relief – Toyota GB will be an official partner of the annual Red Nose Day event and the events around it.

The website states:

> Fundraising activities throughout 2013 enabled the trust to make valued donations through our End of Year Awards, not only to our two nominated charities who each received cheques for over £45,000, but to a number of local charities.

About 30% of the funds raised were available to local charities.

Lucy Prince Community Grant Award

The award was initiated to commemorate an employee who passed away. The annual award provides an annual one-off grant of £5,000 to an organisation which 'aims to support and bring about improvements in family life, specifically targeting families within the Derbyshire area'. Past recipients have included: Cruse Bereavement Care (2013); Alfreton Park Community Special School (2012); The Arena Food bank, Ilkeston (2011); and The Derbyshire Children's Holiday Centre (2010).

Derbyshire Wildlife Trust

The company is a corporate member of the trust and works together on a number of projects. For example, it signed up to the trust's Transforming the Trent Valley initiative, which according to the company's website 'aims to encourage businesses and landowners to commit to preserving or restoring wildlife habitats on their land' and 'was recognised for the hard work involved in setting up [its] own wildlife site'.

Education

The Education section of the website states that Toyota 'is committed to supporting education within [its] local communities and welcomes initiatives aimed at engaging with young people and encouraging and inspiring them to be the next generation of engineers'.

Europe

On a global level there is the Toyota Fund for Europe (outlined on the toyotafund.eu website) 'which operates at a pan-European level and supports projects that operate across a number of different European countries or regions'. The fund 'supports projects in the fields where Toyota can join the force with our stakeholders to tackle the issues using our best competence: the environment, road safety and technical education'.

Toyota believes that 'financial support is just part of the solution'. The website states:

> At both the European and local levels we try to utilise the skills and resources of Toyota and our staff to make a real difference to your project. This involvement can take many forms but may include training, knowledge transfer, materials or even human resources. We are always looking for new projects to support.

Corporate giving

In 2013/14 the company donated £901,000 for charitable purposes

(2012/13: £832,000). These donations comprised:

- £34,000 (2012/13: £59,000) to charities involved in conserving the environment and promoting environmental preservation and awareness
- £72,000 (2012/13: £88,000) to charities involved in medical research
- £795,000 (2012/13: 685,000) to local charities involved in a range of activities in the communities surrounding Burnaston and Deeside

The amount given through the Toyota Manufacturing UK Charitable Trust (£151,000 raised by members of the company) is included in the above, therefore we deduct this amount and take the sum of £750,000 to be the company's cash donations.

The latest accounts of the trust were not available to view at the time of writing.

Beneficiaries included: Burton-on-Trent Sea Cadets; Claymills Pumping Engines Trust; Derbyshire and Cheshire Fire and Rescue Services; Derbyshire Disabled Cricket Club; Family Support Group for Visually Impaired Children in Derbyshire; Flintshire Foodbank; Green Valley Trust Ltd; Inland Waterways Association; North Wales Wildlife Trust; South Derbyshire District Scouts; South Derbyshire Mental Health Association; Staffordshire Fire and Rescue Service; The British Red Cross; and The Laura Centre (Derby).

See the corporate charity entry on p. 434 for more information.

In-kind support

Local charitable events are regularly supported through the donation of raffle prizes. Occasionally local schools and colleges are provided parts and components to be used as training aids.

Ex-trial vehicles are also donated to educational establishments and emergency services (note that there are certain criteria in place). In 2013 a total of 63 vehicles were donated, and 40 of these went to Derbyshire and Cheshire Fire and Rescue Services. The cars are used for training purposes. For example, according to the Community section of the company's website, in 2011 the service used a donated car to make a 'Transformer' vehicle, with the training being visited by neighbouring Nottinghamshire and South Yorkshire services; and Staffordshire Fire and Rescue Service, 'have worked with students from Burton and South Derbyshire College, to produce 'The Consequence Car' which is used to educate both firefighters and young drivers on the roads in Staffordshire'.

The company's employees provide their time and expert skills through programmes, such as the Young Engineers Club (see 'Commercially led support' section). For two years the company has also worked with young people from the YMCA 'to provide them with skills and experience to get into work or further education', including improving their literacy, numeracy, CV writing and interview skills.

Employee-led support

Employee involvement in the community is encouraged and, where suitable, financial support is given. The company is a member of the Business in the Community and participates in its Give and Gain programme – a nationwide day of volunteering. In 2013 and 2014 Toyota Manufacturing UK joined the initiative by teaming up with the Education Team at Rosliston Forestry Centre in South Derbyshire. Volunteers supported the centre by completing various projects within the forest.

Staff members get involved in fundraising opportunities to support the corporate charity. Activities include mountain climbing, cycling, Christmas jumper day and so on.

Matched funding

Employee fundraising efforts are matched by the company, previously up to a maximum of £250 per activity. According to the Community and Social Report for 2012/13 (the latest available at the time of writing), in that year matched funding from the company totalled £9,600.

Payroll giving

A payroll giving scheme has been in operation.

Lottery donations

Twice a year there is a lottery for employees to win vehicles and other prizes. A total of 5% of the income is available for application by employees who are involved in community organisations, societies and charities. In 2012/13 the lottery fund donated £6,800.

Commercially led support

Sponsorship

Since 1992 the company has been a corporate sponsor of Derby County Football Club. Currently the West Stand at the Pride Park Stadium is sponsored where Toyota has an executive box, the walls of which are decorated with details of the company's key environmental achievements.

The Toyota Technology Challenge (TTC)

The initiative was developed in 2003, in partnership with educational supplier Rapid Electronics Ltd. It 'aims to stimulate the interest of young students in technology and engineering, whilst encouraging pupils to consider the environment and the potential use of recycled materials'.

Public visit programme

The programme 'allows members of the local community, businesses, education groups and customers to visit [the] Burnaston plant and learn more about [Toyota's] UK operations, company culture and the Toyota Production System'. The company notes that the 'programme typically runs between April and October each year, however, due to production restrictions in 2015, the programme will not commence until July'. The website reminds: 'we do, however, receive more requests for visits than we have places available so it is, therefore, necessary for us to prioritise each request against set criteria'. Application forms for public visits scheme at Burnaston site have to be made online, using the 'Register Your Interest' section. Further details on public visits at Deeside site can be directed to Martin Fry (tel: 01244282498; email: martin.fry@toyotauk.com).

Educational plant visits are also available and are targeted specifically at students who are particularly interested in manufacturing, production or engineering subjects at local universities, colleges and schools. Individual requests are not accepted. For more details see the company's website or contact the above correspondent.

See Inside Manufacturing

Toyota participates in the initiative between the Government and the UK motor industry 'calling on the budding young designers and engineers of tomorrow to see how they can play a role in developing or producing some of the world's most admired and ground-breaking products'. It is open to all young people in the UK and allows them to get behind the scenes of automotive facilities to learn about modern manufacturing and the range of jobs available in the sector.

Young Engineers

The educational charity aims to inspire young people to develop an interest in engineering. The company joined the charity's Young Engineer Clubs scheme in 2000 and now supports clubs at three local schools – John Port School, Etwall, Derbyshire, Littleover Community School, Littleover, Derbyshire, and Flint High School, Flintshire, North Wales. Each has its own Toyota engineer who supports the club on a weekly basis by providing professional guidance and technical advice as well as an overall co-ordinating engineer who provides extra knowledge and support when necessary.

Apprenticeships

There are two apprenticeship programmes (maintenance and

production) operated in partnership with Burton and South Derbyshire College.

Corporate social responsibility

CSR committee: We found no indications of a separate CSR committee. There is Community Liaison Committee, made up of representatives from the parish councils, local authorities and agencies. Meeting are held twice a year 'to keep the local community informed of relevant activities and the issues that affect the company and the local community'.

CSR information: The Company Information and Background Sheet, dated January 2015, has the following noted regarding 'community relations philosophy':

> On a global basis, Toyota wishes to be a good corporate citizen in every respect and Toyota Manufacturing UK follows this philosophy. We are closely involved with 'our' community on a local, regional and national level. Over £5 million has been donated to charities and foundations. Our focus of support is in 4 main areas: Environment; Children; Education; and Health.

The company's Community and Social Report covers four sectors – Marketplace, Environment, Workplace and Community.

CSR report: There is a Community and Social Report available online. Update on environment policy is published within the annual report and accounts. Details on community involvement are provided online and in the 'Together' brochure. Toyota Europe sustainability report is also available, which appear to focus on environment and responsible business operations.

Corporate charity: Toyota Manufacturing UK Charitable Trust (Charity Commission no. 1124678).

Exclusions

Our research suggests that support is not given for advertising in charity brochures, animal welfare, appeals from individuals, the arts, fundraising events, overseas projects, political or religious appeals, science/technology, social welfare, sport, or local appeals not in areas of company presence. No response to circular appeals.

Applications

The company: A self-screening eligibility form and an application form for the community grants programme are posted on the company's website. If your organisation meets the eligibility criteria, forward your completed application form to the correspondent.

At the time of writing the criteria for evaluation was under review and applicants were advised that they may be contacted by the company in order to request additional information. Applications are fully assessed on a quarterly basis, usually in March, June, September and December.

The company politely comments: 'Please bear in mind that we receive many more requests than we are able to satisfy, so ultimately, we must make difficult choices. We do wish you every success should you decide to apply.'

The trust: The contact person for trust related enquiries is Laura Kristiansen (tel: 01332 283608; email: charitabletrust@toyotauk.com) at 3 Bretby Fairways, Bretby, Burton-on-Trent, Staffordshire DE15 0QY.

Travis Perkins plc

Building materials, building/construction

Correspondent: The Internal Communications Manager, Corporate Communications, Lodge Way House, Harlestone Road, Northampton NN5 7UG (tel: 01604 752424; fax: 01604 758718; email: communications@travisperkins.co.uk; website: www.travisperkinsplc.co.uk)

Directors: Robert Walker, Chair; John Carter, Chief Executive Officer; Tony Buffin, Group Finance Director; Carol Kavanagh; Deborah Grimason, Company Secretary and General Counsel; Norman Bell; Martin Meech; Robin Proctor; Ian Preedy; Arthur Davidson; Frank Elkins; Paul Tallentire; Ruth Anderson; John Coleman; Andrew Simon; Christopher Rogers (women: 3; men: 13)

Year end	31/12/2013
Turnover	£5,148,700,000
Pre-tax profit	£312,600,000

Nature of business: Travis Perkins group is involved in marketing and distribution of timber, building and plumbing materials and the hiring of tools to the building trade and industry generally.

Company registration number: 824821

Subsidiary undertakings include: City Plumbing Supplies Holdings Ltd; Keyline Builders Merchants Ltd; PTS Group Ltd; Solfex Energy Systems Ltd; Travis Perkins Trading Company Ltd; and Wickes Building Supplies Ltd. A full list is available in the group's accounts.

Brands include: Benchmarx; BSS Industrial; City Plumbing Supplies; City Heating Spares; Keyline; Primaflow and Solfex.

Main locations: Northampton

UK employees: 21,937

Total employees: 21,937

Focus of giving: Fundraising events, health, ill health, older people, children, young people, disability.

Cash donations undeclared	✓
FTSE 100	✓
Gifts in kind	✓
Market-led giving	✓
Payroll giving	✓
Sponsorship	✓

Charitable donations

Cash UK (latest available):	2013	£142,000
	2011	£146,000
	2009	£211,000
	2008	£211,000
	2007	£154,000
Total UK (cash and in kind):	2013	£142,000
Cash worldwide:	2013	£142,000
Total worldwide (cash and in kind):	2013	£142,000

Community involvement

Support is given in local communities where the group operates. Each of the 17 businesses as well as the central functions has a partnership with a number of British charities, each of which is selected by employees.

Charity partnerships

Assistance has been given to: Age UK; Alzheimer's Society; Breast Cancer Campaign; Keech Hospice Care for Children; Mind and Cruse Bereavement Care; Parkinson's UK; RNLI; Together for Short Lives; and Warwickshire and Northamptonshire Air Ambulance (WNAA).

The latest annual report and accounts for 2013 give an example of City Plumbing Supplies fundraising to support its new partner Teenage Cancer Trust and the website also lists the following beneficiaries: Clic Sargent; Derian House Children's Hospice; Help for Hospices; Leukaemia and Lymphoma Research; Mind and Cruse Bereavement Care; Pancreatic Cancer; and Prostate Cancer UK.

The group is a supporter of road safety charity Brake and has planned to start a 'no speeding' initiative.

Corporate giving

In 2013 a total of £142,000 (2012: £166,000) was donated directly by the company. The 2013 annual report and accounts state that, taking into account employee fundraising efforts and donation schemes, 'the group is pleased to have donated more than £1.9 million (2012: £2.1 million) through group activities ... to worthwhile causes in the fields of cancer research, support for children and young people, and the hospice movement, to name a few'.

We have taken the figure of £142,000 as the group's UK charitable contribution as we have no way of estimating any expenses to the company incurred through volunteering or fundraising time, gifts in kind and so on.

Beneficiaries have included: Age UK; Alzheimer's Society; Breast Cancer

Campaign; Clic Sargent; Derian House Children's Hospice; Help for Hospices; Keech Hospice Care for Children; Leukaemia and Lymphoma Research; Mind and Cruse Bereavement Care; Parkinson's UK; Pancreatic Cancer; Prostate Cancer UK; RNLI; Teenage Cancer Trust; Together for Short Lives; and Warwickshire and Northamptonshire Air Ambulance (WNAA).

In-kind support

In support of the Breast Cancer Campaign, Travis Perkins has adopted a pink theme and re-sprayed some of its delivery trucks bright pink to be used in the local area when fundraising takes place. Material donations and pro bono services are also offered. For instance, according to the Community section of the Travis Perkins website, materials were donated to Live Train – 'a London-based training scheme which equips unemployed people with the skills and experience to start a sustainable career in the construction industry'; and part of the group's branch in Vauxhall was given to house a new Live Train training centre.

Employee-led support

The Charity Support section of the website states that 'Travis Perkins Group greatly appreciates the efforts and kind donations made by its employees, customers and suppliers.' Employee fundraising efforts have included parachute jumps, marathons and fun runs, auctions, charity balls, '3 Peaks' and 'Beat the Moon' challenges, car washes, bake sales and so on.

Staff members from Wickes joined 40 tradespeople and 270 young people to renovate four community spaces across London in support of VIY 'Volunteer It Yourself' project, which combines volunteering and DIY by challenging 14- to 17-year-olds to learn trade and building skills.

Payroll giving

A scheme operates allowing employees to support charities directly through their salaries. The group matches any donations made. The Charity Support section also notes that: 'Travis Perkins also runs a colleague lottery and salary sacrifice scheme called 'Small Change, Big Difference', where employees donate the 'spare' pennies from their monthly salary to the company's nominated charities.'

Commercially led support

Sponsorships

The group is a corporate sponsor of sport teams and events. Examples have included:

- The Travis Perkins Masters and similar golf events
- The Northampton Rugby Club (until at least 2016)

Corporate social responsibility

CSR committee: There were no details of a specific CSR committee. There is a charity committee which helps to steer a variety of fundraising activities at branches nationwide and the head office throughout the year.

CSR information: The CR Statement for 2013 states:

> Travis Perkins understands that as a major UK plc it has a responsibility to conduct its business in a way that recognises its obligations to all its stakeholders as well as to society as a whole. As such it actively seeks to embed the principles of good corporate responsibility in its day-to-day activities throughout the group.

The CR focuses on health and safety, environment, community engagement, colleague engagement, ethical policies and equal opportunities and diversity.

The group's website notes: 'We believe in being a good neighbour, operating responsibly, being sympathetic to the local environment, supporting the local communities in which we operate and supporting British sport.'

CSR report: The Corporate Responsibility Statement is available within the annual report and accounts. Further details are given in various sections of the report and the website.

Exclusions

Support is not generally given for: advertising in charity brochures; animal welfare; appeals from individuals; the arts; heritage; overseas projects; political or religious appeals; local appeals not in areas of company presence; or large national appeals.

Applications

In writing to the correspondent. Travis Perkins reviews its supported charities every two years. Contact the Internal Communications Manager at 01604 752424 to request help or enquire about charitable support.

Note the following polite message from the group: 'We receive many applications for help and assistance, and while we do our best to support as many as we can, it is not always possible.'

Trinity Mirror plc

Media

Correspondent: Paul Vickers, Group Secretary and Legal Director, One Canada Square, Canary Wharf, London E14 5AP (tel: 020 7293 3000; fax: 020 7510 3405; email: paul.vickers@trinitymirror.com; website: www.trinitymirror.com)

Directors: David Grigson, Chair; Simon Fox, Chief Executive Officer; Mark Hollinshead; Vijay Vaghela, Group Finance Director; Jane Lighting; Donal Smith; Helen Stevenson; Dr David Kelly; Lee Ginsberg (women: 2; men: 7)

Year end	29/12/2013
Turnover	£663,800,000
Pre-tax profit	(£160,800,000)

Nature of business: The main activity of the group is the publication of newspapers, websites and digital products as well as provision of printing services in the UK.

Company registration number: 82548

Subsidiary undertakings include: AMRA Ltd; Gazette Media Company Ltd; Media Wales Ltd; MEN Media Ltd; Rippleffect Studio Ltd; Trinity Mirror Group Ltd; and Trinity Mirror Merseyside Ltd; A full list of subsidiaries is available in the group's accounts.

Brands include: Liverpool Echo; The Daily Mirror; The Manchester Evening News; The Newcastle Chronicle; The People; The Sunday Mail; The Sunday Mirror; and The Western Mail.

UK employees: 5,033

Total employees: 5,033

Focus of giving: Advertising in charity brochures, health, ill health, housing, homelessness, medical research, armed forces personnel, older people, children, young people, community/social welfare, disability.

Cash donations undeclared	✓
Charity of the Year	✓
Gifts in kind	✓
Market-led giving	✓

Charitable donations

Cash UK (latest available):	2013	£81,000
	2011	£75,000
	2009	£84,000
	2008	£84,000
	2007	£80,000
Total UK (cash and in kind):	2013	£81,000
Cash worldwide:	2013	£81,000
Total worldwide (cash and in kind):	2013	£81,000

Community involvement

The CSR report for 2012/13 notes that Trinity Mirror will make direct cash donations to charities in certain limited circumstances:

- At a group level assistance can be given to charities connected with or associated with the newspaper, printing or advertising industries. 'The national titles of the Daily Mirror, Sunday Mirror and Sunday People are most unlikely to make direct cash donations. They will do so only where they are asked to make a payment to a charity in lieu of a fee for an interview or some form of support'

- At local level direct cash support is available to charities operating in the communities immediately surrounding the group's offices and print sites. Each of the regional newspaper companies have a small budget to make direct cash donations to charities working in the community in which the newspaper is based (Scottish Daily Record and Sunday Mail Ltd can help charities based in Scotland). Preference is given to smaller community-based charities where a modest donation will make a big impact

There is also 'a limited general pool of funds out of which donations can be made to legitimate and supportable causes that fall outside the above two criteria'. Each case would need to demonstrate business or commercial reason why such support should be given.

Awards

The group runs a number of award ceremonies both nationally and at regional level, including:

Daily Mirror Pride of Britain Awards – since 1999 the annual awards honour the UK's 'unsung heroes' – 'members of the emergency services and armed forces, exemplary teachers, care workers, charity fundraisers and courageous people who have overcome huge challenges to help others'.

Sunday Mail Young Scot Awards – 'recognises and publicises the good work that young people carry out and works closely with Young Scot, the national youth information and citizenship charity for Scotland'. A total of 20% of the event's contribution goes to the charity together with the proceeds from the charity raffle.

Inspire Wales Awards and Welsh Business Awards – organised in partnership with the Institute of Welsh Affairs.

Campaigns

Campaigning on behalf of the readers is considered 'a vital part of a newspaper's role' and includes 'awareness-raising over local issues, holding authorities to account or in helping to generate funds for a local charity or worthy cause'. During 2013 the group highlighted, amongst other things, bedroom tax issues and the role of the food banks.

Charity initiatives

The CSR report says that the group's titles regularly choose a charity to support over the year or set up their own.

For example, *The Sunday Mail* Centenary Fund was launched in 2014, which hoped to raise £1 million for 17 charities in that year and also use the paper's editorial resources to showcase the charities' work. Support available covers medical research, homeless people, vulnerable children and war veterans, to name a few.

The *Coventry Telegraph*'s Snowball Charity was launched in 1985 and 'helps sick and disabled youngsters across Coventry and Warwickshire with equipment to make their lives easier'. It works in partnership with local radio station Free Radio, to collect funds 'from the efforts of big-hearted individuals and organisations who help the newspaper's appeal raise funds'. According to the website, the charity has provided over £250,000 in grants in the past ten years. In 2012 a donation of £20,000 was made to a Coleshill special needs school towards a new minibus.

Corporate giving

We could not determine the amount awarded in charitable contributions in 2012/13 as the group seems to no longer declare the figure in the annual report and accounts. Based on figures from the three previous years known to us, we estimate that about £81,000 was given in cash in the UK.

In-kind support

Office facilities are available for use by charitable organisations as well as used computer equipment, furniture, books and so on. Staff volunteering time and expert skills are also offered.

Employee-led support

The group's employees contribute to good causes through fundraising initiatives and participate in volunteering activities and mentoring programmes through the group's community involvement programmes.

Tŷ Gobaith

Staff members at the Daily Post and North Wales Weeklies undertake various activities, including a 220-mile cycle from Cardiff to Conwy in 2013, as part of an ongoing fundraising for Tŷ Gobaith – the only children's hospice in North Wales. 'Tŷ Gobaith's fundraising arm also shares the Daily Post's office, at no cost.'

Commercially led support

Wish Campaign

According to the website, during 2012 a total of £285,000 was donated to charitable organisations through this scheme. 'Created by the Teesside Gazette over seven years ago, Wish now runs across 11 newspapers within England, Scotland and Wales and over 2,000 schools, charities and community groups registered their interest online.' The scheme allows the readers to collect tokens in return for cash for their chosen charitable or non-profit organisation. For six years Zoe's Place has been a regular beneficiary of the scheme.

Corporate social responsibility

CSR committee: There was no evidence of a separate CSR Committee.

CSR information: The CSR report for 2012/13 states:

> Trinity Mirror believes that it can best support charities through the pages of its newspapers. This support will either be through appeals to readers for donations or through editorial content, describing the aims and activities of various charities. In every case the decision as to whether or not to support a charity appeal or whether to run editorial comment will be one for the editor of each newspaper.

Trinity Mirror's 'continues to care for the communities in which [it] publishes and where the businesses operate'. Its values concentrate on environment and community.

CSR report: The CSR report is contained within the annual report and accounts.

Exclusions

Support is not generally given for local appeals not in areas of company presence. Political donations are not normally made.

Applications

At group level: Eligible applicants should approach the correspondent in writing.

At regional level: Enquiries should be addressed to the editor or manager of the newspaper/print site based in your community. Prior agreement of the relevant managing director will be required before a donation can be made.

The CSR report further notes:

- Any corporate donations requested from the national titles are likely to be redirected to the group headquarters
- All group donations need the prior agreement of the Secretary and Group Legal Director
- Any local business donations require the prior agreement of the relevant managing director

Tullis Russell Group Ltd

Print/paper/packaging, professional support services

Correspondent: Geoffrey Miller, Company Secretary, Rothersfield, Markinch, Glenrothes, Fife KY7 6PB (tel: 01592 753311; fax: 01592 755872; website: www.trg.co.uk)

Directors: Frederick Bowden; Barrie Jackson; Geoffrey Miller; Christopher Parr; Michael Arrowsmith (women: 0; men: 5)

Year end	31/03/2014
Turnover	£158,585,000
Pre-tax profit	(£2,980,000)

Nature of business: Tullis Russell Group Ltd 'is an employee-owned industrial holding company, providing management services'. The principal subsidiary companies are involved in the manufacture of papers, boards and other paper products for clients world-wide.

Company registration number: SC150075

Subsidiary undertakings include: Tullis Russell Coaters Ltd; Tullis Russell France SARL; Tullis Russell Iberia SL; Tullis Russell Inc.; and Tullis Russell Papermakers Ltd. A full list of subsidiary undertakings can be obtained from Companies House.

Main locations: Bollington, Hanley, Glenrothes

Total employees: 692

Focus of giving: Education, environment, health, ill health, heritage, small groups, local groups, arts, culture, sponsorship, sport, recreation, children, young people, community/social welfare.

Sponsorship ✓

Charitable donations

Cash UK (latest available):	2014	£1,000
	2013	£1,000
	2011	£349,000
	2009	£39,000
	2008	£17,000
Total UK (cash and in kind):	2014	£1,000
Cash worldwide:	2014	£1,000
Total worldwide (cash and in kind):	2014	£1,000

Community involvement

The 2013/14 annual report and accounts state that 'donations were all made to local charitable organisations in order to support the community'.

The Russell Trust (OSCR no. SC004424)

The trust was established in 1947 in memory of Captain Pat Russell for a range of charitable purposes, including education, health, civic responsibility or community development, arts, heritage, culture, or science, public participation in sport, environmental protection and improvement, also relief in need. The trust is funded mainly from its ownership of about a quarter of the otherwise employee-owned Tullis Russell group and will generally support Scottish charities working for the benefit of children and education, or local organisations. The group's website states:

> Every year [the trust] donates significant amounts to hundreds of different charities and educational institutions. It operates under a guiding philosophy to keep Tullis Russell independent and by so doing keep it flexible and responsive to its customers. Decisions are based on the best interests of our customers, our suppliers and above all, our employees.

Tullis Russell Environmental Education Ltd (OSCR number SC044222) – T.R.E.E.

The T.R.E.E. centre aims to advance education, environmental protection and improvement, heritage and science, citizenship and community development, and to provide recreational facilities and organise recreational activities. The group's website states:

> The centre has attracted significant funding from the Climate Challenge Fund, The Russell Trust and Tullis Russell itself, without which the centre could not have been built. With learning at its core, The T.R.E.E. Centre aims to motivate the local community to take action to help secure a more sustainable future. Through a wide base of highly stimulating resources and activity that builds a solid understanding of the environmental issues that face our world, we hope to inspire young and old to take practical steps in their daily lives to reduce their own environmental impact.

Some activities delivered through the centre include a Paper Angels competition for primary schools with prizes including a complimentary class educational session at the centre. Note that a school visits programme has been launched in the centre; however, there seems to be a charge.

Corporate giving

During 2013/14 the group made donations to charitable and public organisations totalling £1,000 (2012/13: £1,000). We were unable to view the accounts of the two trusts to determine any contributions from the group.

See the corporate charity entry on p. 424 for more information.

Employee-led support

The group members engage in fundraising activities in support of good causes. For example, in celebration of 'Employee Ownership Day', funds were raised for Maggie's charity and Ansan Ferry Disaster Appeal. Other beneficiaries of employee fundraising have also included The Cottage Family Centre in Kirkcaldy (£700 raised).

Commercially led support

Sponsorship

In 2014 the group sponsored the four-annual Bollington Festival which 'aims to promote community involvement and inclusivity'.

Since 2007 Tullis Russell has also sponsored the national teams at European and World Championship level. Now it is 'looking to support Scotland's future generation of curlers by providing all the paper requirements for the Curling's Cool programme literature, distributed to over 5000 young participants'. The Curling's Cool programme is implemented by the Royal Caledonian Curling Club with qualified coaches providing sessions to teach children the basics of the game.

Scholarships

Through The Russell Trust (OSCR number SC004424) scholarships are given. At the University of St Andrews the David Russell Scholarships were established and resources for the library computer clusters, MUSA and underwater archaeological research provided. In addition, staff awards, postgraduate support and accommodation bursaries are also offered via the charity.

Corporate social responsibility

CSR committee: We found no indication of a CSR committee.

CSR information: No CSR information found. A subsidiary of the group Tullis Russell Coaters Ltd is a member of the BITC.

CSR report: None found.

Corporate charity: The Russell Trust (OSCR number SC004424).

Exclusions

Our research suggests that grants are not given for local appeals not in areas of company presence, large national appeals, enterprise/training, medical research, overseas projects, political appeals, science/technology or sport.

Applications

The company: In writing to the correspondent.

The trust: Both trusts are based at the company's address.

UIA (Insurance) Ltd

Insurance

Correspondent: Jackie White, Foundation Administrator, Kings Court, London Road, Stevenage, Hertfordshire SG1 2TP (tel: 01438 761761 (main switchboard); fax: 01438 761762; email: charitable.foundation@uia.co.uk; website: www.uia.co.uk)

Directors: Ian Cracknell, Chief Executive Officer; Ben Terrett, Finance Director; Mike Hayes, Chair; Peter Dodd; Marion Saunders; Andrew Wainwright-Brown; Eleanor Smith; Bob Abberley; Lucia McKeever (women: 3; men: 6)

Year end	31/12/2013
Turnover	£26,482,000
Pre-tax profit	£6,397,000

Nature of business: UIA is a mutual insurance company primarily serving members of selected trade unions and other not-for-profit organisations, but also offering services to general public.

Company registration number: AC000532

Wholly owned subsidiaries include: UIA (Call Centres) Ltd; UIA Lottery Management Services Ltd; UIA (Trustees) Ltd; and Uniservice Ltd. Further details can be obtained from Companies House.

Main locations: Stevenage

UK employees: 136

Total employees: 136

Focus of giving: Human rights, equal opportunities, health, ill health, housing, homelessness, small groups, marginalised people, unpopular causes, older people, overseas projects, poverty and social exclusion, sponsorship, sport, recreation, women's issues, children, young people, community/social welfare, disability, disasters.

Market-led giving	✓
Overseas giving	✓
Sponsorship	✓

Charitable donations

Cash UK (latest available):	2013	£36,000
	2012	£28,000
	2011	£50,000
	2009	£48,600
	2008	£12,500
Total UK (cash and in kind):	2013	£36,000
Cash worldwide:	2013	£36,000
Total worldwide (cash and in kind):	2013	£36,000

Community involvement

The annual report and accounts for 2013 state the following:

> In 2013 we reviewed the guidelines for the UIA Charitable Foundation to focus on engagement with charities on particular projects where our funding could make a positive difference to the work of grant recipients over a period of time. We have been particularly interested in supporting causes that are of specific interest to our members, our trade union partners and our staff.

UIA Charitable Foundation (Charity Commission no. 1079982)

The foundation was set up in 1999 and is funded entirely by the donations from the company. It is managed by UIA (Trustees) Ltd. Support is given to small organisations or groups where a modest grant (generally under £1,000) will make a real difference and which deal with:

- Victims of domestic abuse
- Victims of drug and alcohol addiction
- Rehabilitation of offenders
- Third World poverty
- Third World human rights

Note that the list is not exhaustive and can be amended. In 2014 the focus on tackling problems faced by disadvantaged and minority groups and activities that are potentially difficult to finance through conventional fundraising.

There are two main categories:

- **The Community Support Programme** – aimed primarily at local communities in the UK (but may support smaller charitable projects internationally) and seeking to tackle homelessness, help victims of domestic abuse, rehabilitation of offenders, support the elderly and young people
- **The World Programme** – supporting projects that tackle causes of poverty and improve human rights throughout the world

The company's website states:

> In both areas, we are interested in working with charities who can demonstrate a strategy for change over a specific timeframe, supported through the achievement of project objectives that can be monitored and evaluated. We will consider projects that empower individuals and communities to improve their lives and the prospects of the community.

Since its inception the foundation has provided over £450,000 to projects based in the UK and abroad.

Corporate giving

According to the company's annual report and accounts during 2013 a total of £51,000 was either paid or approved in grants by the foundation. The foundation's annual report and accounts for 2013 note that a donation of over £36,000 (2012: 28,000) was received from the company and grants totalling almost £36,000 were made in 46 grants.

Beneficiaries of the foundation included: Theatre Workshop Scotland (£2,500); Breakthrough Foundation, Building Hope, Kaloko Trust UK, Kirklees Rape and Sexual Abuse Counselling Centre and Prisoners Advice Service (£1,000 each); Project Colt (£950); Border Arts 2000 (£800); Street Kids Rescue (£700); and The Counselling Centre (£500).

Revenue: We used the figure defined as 'Gross premiums written' as the company's annual turnover.

See the corporate charity entry on p. 435 for more information.

Commercially led support

Sponsorship

The company continues sponsorship of Amy Marren – a Paralympic swimmer in her preparation for the preparation of Rio 2016.

Corporate social responsibility

CSR committee: We found no evidence of a separate CSR Committee.

CSR information: The company's guiding principles encompass: excellence in service and products; working with responsible partners and suppliers; staff well-being and development; community involvement; and conducting a transparent and responsible business.

The company's community support programme is directed through a charitable foundation funded entirely by donations from UIA (Insurance) Ltd.

CSR report: There was no evidence of a separate CSR report.

Corporate charity: UIA Charitable Foundation (Charity Commission no. 1079982).

Exclusions

The foundation's website states that it will not fund the following:

- Work which it believes to be publicly funded
- Retrospective projects
- Organisations that have an annual turnover in excess of £500,000 unless the organisation is acting as a conduit for a partner that fulfils the criteria and may find it difficult to obtain access to funding through independent channels
- Organisations whose combined grant related support costs and governance costs are greater than 10% of their turnover

Applications

In writing to the correspondent. Further information on application process can be obtained via email.

The company's website states – 'UIA and its key partners, members and staff proactively seek and nominate good causes all year round for consideration at trustee meetings.' The meetings are currently held twice a year, in February and September and applications should be received in advance (note that receipt of an application does not guarantee that it will be considered at the next meeting). Our research also suggests that the trustees operate on a first come first served basis and require copies of annual accounts with the application.

UK Asset Resolution

Acquisitions

Correspondent: Community Investment Team, Croft Road, Crossflatts, Bingley, West Yorkshire BD16 2UA (tel: 01274 555555; website: www.ukar.co.uk)

Directors: Richard Pym, Chair; Michael Buckley; Richard Banks, Chief Executive Officer; John Tattersall; Sue Langley; Ian Hares, Finance and Investment Director; Keith Morgan; David Lunn (women: 1; men: 7)

Year end	31/03/2014
Turnover	£1,374,300,000
Pre-tax profit	£1,523,200,000

Nature of business: UKAR has been established to facilitate the orderly management of the closed mortgage books of both B&B and NRAM to maximise value for taxpayers.

The Executive team of UKAR manages both organisations focusing on this common objective, whilst ensuring that both companies continue to treat customers fairly, deliver consistently high levels of service and support those customers who are facing financial difficulty.

In addition, from 8 October 2013, UKAR Corporate Services became responsible for the day to day administration of the Government's Help To Buy Mortgage Guarantee Scheme on behalf of HM Treasury.

Company registration number: 7301961

Subsidiary undertakings include: Bradford & Bingley plc; NRAM plc; UKAR Corporate Services Ltd; and indirectly: Mortgage Express.

UK employees: 2,111

Total employees: 2,111

Focus of giving: General charitable purposes, health, ill health.

Charity of the Year	✓
Gifts in kind	✓
Matched funding	✓
Payroll giving	✓

Charitable donations

Cash UK (latest available):	2014	£55,000
Total UK (cash and in kind):	2014	£55,000
Cash worldwide:	2014	£55,000
Total worldwide (cash and in kind):	2014	£55,000

Community involvement

In 2014/15 the company's community investment approach will focus on using the skills of the business to support youth education in its communities and to 'address health as a social issue which affects our business and the communities we operate in'.

At each site support is given to a local charity chosen by employees. These are Martin House Children's Hospice in Crossflatts (West Yorkshire), and Daft as a Brush Cancer Patient Care in Doxford (Sunderland).

Charity partners

The company's focus in 2013/14 was to support Heart Research UK. UKAR's corporate charity in 2014/15 is Mind.

Local offices will continue to support: Crossflatts Martin House Children's Hospice and Doxford Daft as a Brush Cancer Patient Care.

Corporate giving

During 2013/14, in total, UKAR matched employee fundraising to the total of £36,000 and payroll giving totalled £19,000, UK cash contributions therefore totalled £55,000.

In-kind support

UKAR supports employees' charitable fundraising activities by adding up to £250 to funds raised per employee and by matching employee donations to charity through a payroll giving programme. Wherever possible surplus furniture and equipment is donated to charitable organisations or is recycled in other ways.

Employee-led support

The following amounts were raised by employees for these charities in 2013/14:

Heart Research UK	£18,000
Yorkshire Air Ambulance	£15,000
Grace House Children's Hospice	£11,000
Other charities	£6,000

UKAR works with Young Enterprise to give colleagues the opportunity to have a positive impact on young people in the local communities by volunteering to deliver their programmes in local schools. Young Enterprise is a charity set up to work with schools to inspire young people with the confidence, ability and ambition to succeed in a challenging and changing economy.

During 2013/14, a total of 543 employees took part in volunteering events.

Corporate social responsibility

CSR committee: There was no evidence of a CSR committee.

CSR information: The following statement is taken from the company's website:

> UKAR aims to conduct its business in a socially responsible manner in respect of our customers, the environment, the communities we operate in and the workplace.
>
> *Community*
>
> We are committed to:
>
> - Using the skills of the business to support education in our communities
> - Building the skills of our colleagues through community engagement
> - Supporting colleagues with their own community and charity initiatives

CSR report: There is a CSR report within the annual report of the company.

Applications

The company's contact details are scant. The website has an email facility which states:

> The information you provide will only be used in response to your enquiry. Make sure you include a summary of your query and include your contact details so we can get back to you. Please also advise us of any deadlines if you require an urgent response within a specific timescale.

We would recommend that you telephone before sending an application or correspondence.

Unipart Group of Companies Ltd

Acquisitions, instrumentation, motors and accessories, professional support services

Correspondent: Frank Nigriello, Director of Corporate Affairs, Unipart House, Garsington Road, Cowley, Oxford OX4 2PG (tel: 01865 778966; website: www.unipart.co.uk)

Directors: John Neill, Chair and Group Chief Executive; Anthony Mourgue, Group Finance Director; John Clayton; Frank Burns; Fred Vinton; Steve Johnson; Bryan Jackson (women: 0; men: 7)

Year end	31/12/2013
Turnover	£1,056,300,000
Pre-tax profit	(£14,800,000)

Nature of business: Unipart Group provides manufacturing, logistics and consultancy services in a range of markets including railway industry, automotive technology, retail and consumer industries.

NB 'Unipart Group sold control of Unipart Automotive in 2011 and exercised no control over its operations since then.'

Company registration number: 1994997

Subsidiary undertakings include: E W (Holdings) Ltd; Gresty Road 2005 Ltd; Kautex Unipart Ltd; Serck Services (Bahrain) EC; and Van Wezel GmbH. For a full list of subsidiary undertakings see the accounts.

Total employees: 6,931

Focus of giving: Economic generation, education, environment, health, ill health, heritage, STEM (science, technology, engineering and mathematics), arts, culture, poverty and social exclusion, sponsorship, sport, recreation, children, young people, community/social welfare.

Membership: BITC

Gifts in kind	✓
Market-led giving	✓
Overseas giving	✓
Sponsorship	✓

Charitable donations

Cash UK (latest available):	2013	£53,000
	2010	£23,200
	2009	£15,900
	2008	£19,200
Total UK (cash and in kind):	2013	£275,000
Cash worldwide:	2013	£53,000
Total worldwide (cash and in kind):	2013	£275,000

Community involvement

The group's community investment targets include:

- Investing 1% of pre-tax profit in community activities through cash donations, staff time, and gifts in kind
- Having divisional cash donations level at £15,000 per division
- Making above 75% of community investment in areas of education, employability, health environment and economic development
- Having at least one community partner per site

Education

The group has worked in partnership with Foyer Foundation, Nuffield Bursary Scheme and Engineering Education scheme. There are STEM ambassadors who work in local schools and Unipart also runs entrepreneurial events, such as the Unipart Challenge.

The Talent Factory

Support is given to the programme alongside Oxford United Football Club. The initiative aims to find and develop talent in young people by combining top level sport with challenging work experience and works with a number of schools.

Life in the Fast Lane

Links have been established with Holbrook Primary School, adjacent to the factory. For the third consecutive year Unipart 'has helped to deliver the year 6, Creative Curriculum topic In the fast lane the outcome of which is to design, manufacture, test, evaluate a powered vehicle then to present their findings to [the] senior managers'.

University of Huddersfield

In 2013 Unipart Rail concluded a Collaboration Agreement with the university supporting the new Centre for Innovation in Rail (CIR). 'This new facility will utilise the world-class product design and R&D capability of the project partners, to provide industry and academia with training, research and expert services to develop and improve critical engineering interfaces in the rail industry.'

Partnerships in India

Unipart's community strategy and partnership approach is not limited to the UK but applies across the global sites. In India three major sites – in Pune, Sanand and Bangalore – have all identified local schools to partner with. Support activities have included:

> Provision of drinking water facilities on-campus, provision of computers and training of teaching staff in their use, cleaning up outside play areas and planting trees, drawing competitions for younger children, basic computer training and maths tricks for older children.

Corporate giving

The group's CSR report for 2013 values its total community investment (excluding fundraising) at under £275,000. The report says that:

> Over 75% of investment has been in form of time, reinforcing [the group's] belief that community activity and volunteering enhance employee engagement, and the value [it] can add through donating time and skills has more long-term value to [its] community partners than cash.

The support was given as follows:

Employee time	£214,000
Company donations	£53,000
Gifts in kind	£7,600
Total	**£275,000**

Health and education causes received most support. For the past three years community cash contributions have been totalling just over £50,000 each year.

Beneficiaries have included: BBC Children in Need; Great Ormond Street Hospital; High Sheriff Challenge; Macmillan Cancer Support; Maggie's; Movember campaign; Nuneaton Foodbank; and West Midlands Air Ambulance.

In-kind support

In-kind donations are available.

Employee-led support

Volunteering

The CSR report says:

> In addition to the time that our employees spend during their working day, a significant number of our employees dedicate their personal time to supporting our community and charity activities. In 2013 the proportion of total time spent on community activity which was personal time was 17% – equating to over 1,100 hours!

For example, Burton site employees took part in a 'sleepout' with the local community to raise money for Burton YMCA; and Unipart Technology Logistics worked with Warwick Education Business Partnership as part of the Unipart Challenge – 'students from Nuneaton and Rugby schools were given £50 and a UTL mentor to set up their own business'. The programme also raised about £5,000 for local hospices.

Employee activities also include:

- Expert Practitioners going into local schools to work with the leadership teams and share their expertise on developing and delivering strategy and objectives through policy deployment
- Team members teaching problem solving skills to young people in schools and colleges
- Using expertise in supply chain and logistics to help local charity shops better manage their warehousing and delivery
- Human Resources teams delivering employability workshops to students, school leavers and job seekers to improve their employment outcomes

Fundraising

Each site also has a Community Champion and many have a committee or team focused on fundraising. According to the website, in addition to group's contributions, 'employees raised over £70,000 for charities – through activities such as dress down days, cake bakes, sponsored sporting endeavours, among other things'. The group continues by saying – 'it is worth noting that many of these charities have reciprocated by attending our sites to raise awareness of various health and well-being matters'.

Commercially led support

Sponsorships

The group has sponsored education and sports events, such as Novus programme, Grand Prix racing and rugby.

Education and training

Apprenticeships

There is a formal apprenticeship scheme operating as well as graduate schemes. Work experience placements are also offered.

Unipart Inspires

The group started a programme 'aimed at equipping young job seekers with skills for work at Unipart House in Oxford'. The three-week programme 'combines work experience with training in job hunting skills such as interview practice, CV writing and using social media to search for jobs'.

Academy

In 2013 the group has worked with Job Centre Plus helping to establish an academy 'to equip people with the skills required for a career in the Logistics Industry'. The first academy was hosted in Cowley Distribution Centre. 'The majority of the participants in the Academy were subsequently offered roles with the agency and many were ultimately offered placements with Unipart.'

Corporate social responsibility

CSR committee: Each division has a CR Team responsible for developing its own CR programmes following the group's framework and values. Each site also has a Community Champion and many have a committee or team focused on fundraising – 'on some sites it may be a dedicated charity committee, on others this may be covered by the CSR Committee and on some smaller sites it might be the Staff Forum'.

CSR information: The CSR report for 2013 states the following:

> Corporate Responsibility at Unipart is engrained in our culture and is woven into the philosophy and values that are at the heart of our organisation and underpin everything that we do.

The groups CSR strategy aims to maintain responsible operation of business, address environmental issues, provide community support and ensure employee well-being.

The group's Community Strategy encompasses:

- Understanding local and national issues
- Considering how the core skills and capabilities of the site can be deployed to help solve those issues
- Linking volunteering and community activity to personal development plans
- Identifying local community partners and drawing up meaningful partnership agreements
- Measuring inputs and outputs

CSR report: An annual CSR report is published and available online. There is a CSR section within the annual report and accounts.

Exclusions

Unipart will not support an activity whose purpose is to benefit a political or morally corrupt cause.

Applications

In writing to the correspondent. Local sites can be approached directly.

Unisys Ltd

Electronics/computers, professional support services, services

Correspondent: The Human Resources Department, Hertford House, Hertford Place, Denham Way, Maple Cross, Rickmansworth, Hertfordshire WD3 9AB (tel: 01895 237137; fax: 01895 862093; website: www.unisys.co.uk)

Directors: Matthew Piercy; Franco Mallia; Martin Godfrey; Nicholas Fraser; Martin Walker (women: 0; men: 5)

Year end	31/12/2013
Turnover	£153,398,000
Pre-tax profit	£29,345,000

Nature of business: The development, manufacture, supply and maintenance of information technology systems and related services and supplies.

The company is a wholly owned subsidiary of Unisys Corporation, incorporated in the US. The immediate parent company of Unisys Ltd is BMX Information Systems (UK) Ltd.

Company registration number: 103709

Subsidiary undertakings include: Intelligent Processing Solutions Ltd; Unisys European Services Ltd; Unisys Payment Services Ltd; and Unisys Treasury Services Ltd.

Main locations: Altrincham, Birmingham, Bristol, Glasgow, Leeds, Slough, Milton Keynes, Liverpool, Uxbridge

UK employees: 684

Total employees: 684

Focus of giving: Education, equal opportunities, health, ill health, arts, culture, science technology, sponsorship, sport, recreation, community/social welfare.

Cash donations undeclared	✓
Matched funding	✓
Sponsorship	✓

Charitable donations

Cash UK (latest available):	2013	£29,000
	2010	£16,000
	2008	£22,000
	2007	£48,000
	2006	£32,400
Total UK (cash and in kind):	2013	£29,000
Cash worldwide:	2013	£29,000
Total worldwide (cash and in kind):	2013	£29,000

Community involvement

In the past we have been advised that the company no longer makes cash donations directly to charitable organisations. Instead, it channels financial help towards supporting employee initiatives with a preference to invest in those communities in which it has a presence. The investments take the form of:

- Technology and business education
- Health and human services
- Arts, cultural and civic organisations
- Global diversity

Corporate giving

The annual report and accounts for 2013 did not appear to declare charitable donations. Based on the figures from the three previous years known to us, we estimate that about £29,000 was given in charitable contributions.

Employee-led support

Matched funding

The company provides support to charitable organisations through supporting employee initiatives.

Commercially led support

Sponsorship

We found indications of Unisys sponsoring the arts, sports and industry-related events in the past. For example, Management Today Service Excellence Awards, The Ryder Cup and the London Marathon.

Corporate social responsibility

CSR committee: There were no details found.

CSR information: The company's website states:

> Unisys is committed to operating our business in an ethical, socially responsible, and sustainable manner. We believe that corporate citizenship is good business. Through our commitment to ethics, diversity, and environmental responsibility, we build long-term relationships with our clients, partners, and communities and contribute to their mission critical initiatives.

CSR report: None found.

Exclusions

Charitable causes operating outside community focused employee-led initiatives are not generally assisted.

Applications

In writing to the correspondent. However, our research suggests that in view of support being directed towards matching employee fundraising initiatives, unsolicited applications are unlikely to be successful.

UNITE Group plc

Property

Correspondent: Jenny Shaw, Trustee of The UNITE Foundation, The Core, 40 St Thomas Street, Bristol BS1 6JX (tel: 01173 027067 or 01173 027000 (main switchboard); fax: 01173 027400; email: info@unite-group.co.uk; website: www.unite-group.co.uk)

Directors: Phil White, Chair; Mark Allan, Chief Executive Officer; Joe Lister, Chief Financial Officer; Richard Simpson; Richard Smith; Manjit Wolstenholme; Professor Tim Wilson; Andrew Jones; Liz McMeikan (women: 2; men: 7)

Year end	31/12/2013
Turnover	£101,600,000
Pre-tax profit	£77,100,000

Nature of business: The group is involved in developing and co-managing student accommodation.

Company registration number: 3199160

Subsidiary undertakings include: LDC (Holdings) plc; OCB UNITE Property Holdings (Jersey) Ltd.; UNITE Finance One (Property) Ltd; UNITE Holdings plc; USAF Jersey Investments Ltd; and USAF LP Ltd. A full list of subsidiaries is available from Companies House.

UK employees: 890

Total employees: 890

Focus of giving: Education, enterprise/training, equal opportunities, health, ill health, housing, homelessness, individuals, marginalised people, children, young people, community/social welfare, disability.

Membership: BITC

Cash donations undeclared	✓
Gifts in kind	✓
Market-led giving	✓

Charitable donations

Cash UK (latest available):	2013	£82,000
	2012	£195,000
	2011	£21,000
	2009	£30,000
	2008	£20,000
Total UK (cash and in kind):	2013	£82,000
Cash worldwide:	2013	£82,000
Total worldwide (cash and in kind):	2013	£82,000

Community involvement

The UNITE Foundation (Charity Commission no. 1147344/SC043324)

The foundation was created in 2012 and focuses on causes which have the most resonance for the sector in which the group operates. In 2013 further expansions of the UNITE Foundation Scholarship programme took place and 56 students from disadvantaged backgrounds were being supported through partnerships with seven universities. Targeted awards are also made to established charities, including an annual donation to IntoUniversity (a charity supporting young people from disadvantaged backgrounds to enter higher or further education) and support to Enactus and LandAid.

The foundation seeks to widen access to higher education, integrate students within local communities and promote employability. It is currently funded by the group and supported by annual donations from UNITE Students.

Speaker's Parliamentary Placements Scheme

The UNITE Foundation partners with the Social Mobility Foundation to support the scheme which offers a paid internship to spend more than nine months working with a Member of Parliament in Westminster.

The group maintains relationships with local councils, organisations and emergency services:

- The North London team piloted a scheme with Islington Council which helps adults with learning difficulties find employment and so far has provided one permanent role
- The Bath team co-operated with local Police and a Communities Together group to host meetings in the company's common rooms
- The Liverpool team partnered with Student Grub and Liverpool John Moores University to provide every flat in one of the group's properties with a box of healthy food
- The Nottingham team set up relationships with the University Volunteering scheme, the University Tutor scheme and IntoUniversity to involve customers in volunteering and encourage students to become involved in the local community
- The Newcastle team partnered with a local café (which is run as a social enterprise, training and employing homeless people) by using it for meetings and team events, ordering its catering and allowing the café to use UNITE's common room for events

The group's website states: 'Our teams work with a variety of charitable organisations and the NUS to promote environmental awareness and help our students develop new skills and gain experience, while having fun.'

Corporate giving

We could not determine the amount awarded in charitable contributions in 2013, as the group appears to have stopped declaring the figures in its annual report. The latest annual report and accounts for the foundation were for 2012, when UNITE plc awarded £195,000 (being the sole donor to the foundation in its first period) and planned to increase its level of donations to up to £1 million a year within five years of the establishment of the charity. Based on the figures from the three previous years known to us, we estimate that the group has contributed at least about £82,000. Bear in mind, however, that this figure is likely to be much higher – the data available from the Charity Commission at the time of writing states that the foundation had an income of £500,000 in 2013, which is likely to have been provided by UNITE plc.

Beneficiaries have included: Enactus; IntoUniversity; LandAid; and SIFE.

See the corporate charity entry on p. 435 for more information.

In-kind support

Office facilities and employee time and skills.

Employee-led support

The group's employees and customers are given opportunities to volunteer to support good causes. For example, in 2013 IntoUniversity was helped to prepare a new centre for opening in Nottingham, and a Christmas party was organised for children from the Bristol centre with students living with UNITE also volunteering as mentors to the children.

Matched funding

In the past a charity match scheme has operated; however, we could find no references to this in the latest annual report and accounts.

Commercially led support

The group offers subsidised accommodation to interns from the Speaker's Parliamentary Placements Scheme and Upreach so that they can take up employment opportunities away from home.

Corporate social responsibility

CSR committee: No identifications of a separate CSR committee.

CSR information: UNITE's annual report and accounts state:

> We recognise that all businesses have a responsibility to manage their operations in a way which has a positive impact on all stakeholders and communities. We take this responsibility very seriously and believe that forming stronger relationships with local communities, charities, businesses, universities, our staff and the students who live with us, creates additional value for wider society.

The CSR report covers the areas of: environment; communities; business; and people.

CSR report: Published within the annual report and accounts.

Corporate charity: The UNITE Foundation (Charity Commission no. 1147344).

Applications

In writing to the correspondent.

United Utilities Group plc

Electricity, oil and gas/fuel, water

Correspondent: Corporate Responsibility Committee, Haweswater House, Lingley Mere Business Park, Lingey Green Avenue, Great Sankey, Warrington WA5 3LP (tel: 01925 237000; fax: 0845 070 2058; email: sustainability@uuplc.co.uk; website: www.unitedutilities.com)

Directors: Dr John McAdam, Chair; Steve Mogford, Chief Executive Officer; Russ Houlden, Chief Financial Officer; Dr Catherine Bell; Stephen Carter; Mark Clare; Brian May; Sara Weller (women: 2; men: 6)

Year end	31/03/2014
Turnover	£1,704,500,000
Pre-tax profit	£544,700,000

Nature of business: United Utilities Group plc is the intermediate holding company of the UK's largest listed water business. The group owns and manages the regulated water and wastewater network in the North West of England, through its subsidiary United Utilities Water plc (UUW), which constitutes the vast majority of the group's assets and profit. The group also applies its utility skills to manage and operate other utility infrastructure.

Company registration number: 6559020

Subsidiary undertakings include: AS Tallinna Vesi (Tallinn Water); United Utilities Energy Ltd; United Utilities Operational Services Ltd; United Utilities Property Services Ltd; and United

Utilities Water plc. A full list of subsidiary undertakings is available from Companies House.

Main locations: Warrington

UK employees: 5,329

Total employees: 5,329

Focus of giving: Education, enterprise/training, environment, STEM (science, technology, engineering and mathematics), poverty and social exclusion.

Membership: BITC, LBG

Charity of the Year	✓
FTSE 100	✓
Gifts in kind	✓
Market-led giving	✓
Matched funding	✓
Payroll giving	✓

Charitable donations

Cash UK (latest available):	2014	£2,300,000
	2011	£3,200,000
	2010	£5,000,000
	2009	£3,670,000
	2008	£3,790,569
Total UK (cash and in kind):	2014	£2,800,000
Cash worldwide:	2014	£2,300,000
Total worldwide (cash and in kind):	2014	£2,800,000

Community involvement

Community partnerships

The group's Community Fund offers grants between £500 and £1,000 to voluntary organisations and charities in selected communities where United Utilities is carrying out engineering work. According to the CSR Report for 2014 in 2013/14 a total of 101 grants have been awarded to a wide range of organisations 'from church groups to hospices, sports clubs to Morris Dancing troupes, with investment taking place across the region'.

The following organisations have been included amongst the group's partners:

- Groundwork UK (the key United Futures project)
- Royal Society for the Protection of Birds (RSPB)
- Cumbria Woodlands
- Moors for the Future
- Young Enterprise
- Street League
- UTV Media
- BeachCare
- Catchment Wise
- Canal and Rivers Trust

The website states: 'We continually look for new opportunities for partnerships that offer mutual benefit. We believe that working in this way gives something back to the community while meeting a business objective, ranging from operational performance through to employee engagement.'

For further details on particular projects undertaken, see the CSR information on the group's website.

Rivington Heritage Trust (Charity Commission no. 1064700)

The trust was set up by United Utilities to preserve and take care of Rivington Terraced Gardens. the website notes that 'several United Utilities employees sit on the trust, with other members including Chorley and Bolton Borough Councils, Lancashire County Council and several independent trustees'. Judging from the Charity Commission's records, in the past four years there has been no expenditure. According to the website, in 2013 the trust received a development grant of £60,000; however this figure did not seem to be reflected in the financial information for 2013/14 given by the Charity Commission.

Charity of the Year

A charity partner is chosen with the help of employees and most recently, according to the website, North West Air Ambulance has been selected (in 2011). Employee fundraising efforts and a matched funding scheme provided a total of £150,000 'to date' (as stated on the website).

Education

In order to contribute to educational causes United Utilities:

- Runs an educational programme tailored for primary and secondary schoolchildren
- Provides various workshops on environmental efficiency
- As part of the involvement in the STEM (science, technology, engineering and maths) programme, gives career advice
- Partners with the Future Tech Studio college (as part of the partnership United Utilities will offer work experience opportunities for the students)
- Works with UTV Media to run an annual schools campaign allowing students the chance to create a radio advertisement

Recreation

The group owns and manages land around its reservoirs and has initiated the following activities to encourage and develop public access:

- Produced an interactive map
- Resurfaced bridleways and footpaths in Macclesfield Forest
- Together with the Youth Hostel Association and other bodies supported the £325,000 redevelopment of the Black Sail Youth Hostel on the Ennerdale catchment
- Runs an ongoing campaign to educate people of the dangers of swimming in reservoirs

Corporate giving

The web CSR report for 2014 provides the figure of £2.8 million as the amount spent in 'investing in community partnerships for mutual benefit with particular focus on current social issues' and 'encouraging our employees to get involved and make a positive contribution to local communities', measured by the LGB method. The group has informed us that the amount given in cash totalled £2.3 million.

Beneficiaries have included: BeachCare; Canal and Rivers Trust; Catchment Wise; Cumbria Woodlands; Groundwork UK; Moors for the Future; Royal Society for the Protection of Birds (RSPB); Street League; UTV Media; and Young Enterprise.

See the corporate charity entry on p. 436 for more information.

In-kind support

Staff volunteering time and efforts.

Employee-led support

The group's employees are allowed three days to volunteer in the local community. In 2013/14 more than 1,000 employees gave over 15,000 hours of voluntary work within company time (which is calculated as the equivalent to a £300,000 investment). Activities included: delivering talks and workshops in schools; running customer road shows in shops and county shows; and participating in various environmental projects (such as tree planting and canal-side improvements). During special volunteering days staff members work with the group's partners.

The CSR report for 2014 states: 'Our volunteering activities were an essential part of a wider programme of community investment in 2013/14, which totalled £2.8 million.'

Employees participate in a number of fundraising events, such as:

- *UU Does Strictly* – an annual dance contest. Most recent event, according to the website, generated over £48,000 for the North West Air Ambulance and Claire House Children's Hospice; since the beginning of the event over £200,000 has been donated
- *Total Warrior* – an obstacle race, which raised more than £6,000 for the North West Air Ambulance.

Matched funding

United Utilities match employees' fundraising efforts on behalf of charitable organisations (in the past the maximum amount was £250 per application).

Payroll giving

The company operates a payroll giving scheme.

Commercially led support

United Utilities Trust Fund (Charity Commission no. 1108296)

The grant-making trust was established in 2005 to help people out of poverty and debt and is funded partly by United Utilities and partly by the contribution from customers through their water bills. It 'has an annual budget to allocate of £5 million – swelled to £7 million in 2013/14 through an extra £2 million contribution by United Utilities'. As with similar trusts established by other utility companies, it primarily assists customers who are unable to pay their water bills. According to the trust's website it 'is also able to make grants available to organisations to support debt and money advice work'.

The Arrears Allowance Scheme

The scheme allows customers to clear their water bill debts more quickly by receiving matched funding from the company – £1 contribution for every £1 paid (for the first six months), and afterwards £2 for every £1 paid, until the arrears are cleared. Currently over 8,800 customers are using the scheme.

The Support Tariff

This 'means-tested tariff promoted in conjunction with debt advice agencies in the region' is currently on a trial basis, with the participation of almost 4,000 customers who are in receipt of a means tested benefit, in arrears and live in rented accommodation.

WaterSure

This financial support scheme is designed for customers with water meters who receive benefits and have a family member with a medical condition that requires the use of large amounts of water. More than 6,000 customers are currently on this tariff.

Local Authority Discount Tariff

There are collection agreements with local authorities and housing associations in the region which allow a £10 reduction in the annual bills of tenants who pay their bills via this method (to reflect the lower administration costs).

PayPlan Referral (pilot scheme)

In collaboration with PayPlan (free money advice providers) customers are assisted to get help for all their debts by introducing them to the support mechanisms that PayPlan provide.

Education and training

There are apprenticeship and graduate schemes operating. The group is also 'leading the Energy Efficiency Industrial Partnership, a cross utility company initiative targeting those not in education, employment and training into utility related training programmes'.

Corporate social responsibility

CSR committee: There is a board-level Corporate Responsibility Committee, chaired by Catherine Bell. The committee meets twice a year and is responsible for 'developing and overseeing the company's corporate responsibility strategy'.

CSR information: The annual CSR report specifies the following as the five key areas for the group:

- Providing a great service to our customers
- Protecting and enhancing our environment
- Actively supporting our local communities
- Supporting our employees to achieve their full potential in a safe workplace
- Delivering good value to stakeholders and managing our supply chain fairly

The group's website states: 'We work at the heart of local communities, and are always keen to support worthwhile grass roots initiatives, when our budgets and time commitments allow.'

CSR report: An annual CSR report is published.

Corporate charity: United Utilities Trust Fund (Charity Commission no. 1108296).

Exclusions

No support is normally given for individual or religious appeals.

The group 'does not support any political party and does not make what are commonly regarded as donations to any political party or other political organisations'.

Applications

The group: In writing to the correspondent.

The Trust: Enquiries regarding the United Utilities Trust Fund should be addressed to the Secretary (tel: 0845 179 1791; email: contact@uutf.org.uk) at Emmanuel Court, 12–14 Mill Street, Sutton Coldfield B72 1TJ. For more details see www.uutf.org.uk.

Unum Ltd

Insurance

Correspondent: Susan Sanderson, CSR Manager, Charitable Donations Committee, Milton Court, Dorking, Surrey RH4 3LZ (tel: 01306 887766; fax: 01306 881394; email: susan.sanderson@unum.co.uk; website: www.unum.co.uk)

Directors: Richard McKenney, Chair; Stephen Harry, Chief Financial Officer; Peter O'Donnell, Chief Executive Officer; Thomas Watjen, Chair; Peter Hales; Edward Langston; Malcolm McCaig; Ian Owen (women: 0; men: 8)

Year end	31/12/2013
Turnover	£436,919,000
Pre-tax profit	£61,596,000

Nature of business: The company provides income protection insurance products, including income protection, life insurance and critical illness cover.

Its immediate parent company is Unum European Holding Company Ltd (UEHCL), through UEHCL's ownership of the Company's class A share capital. Unum Group, incorporated in the USA, is the ultimate parent company and controlling party.

Unum Ltd is a member of the Unum Group of Companies.

Company registration number: 983768

Subsidiary undertakings include: Claims Services International Ltd. More information can be obtained from Companies House.

Main locations: Dorking

UK employees: 900

Total employees: 900

Focus of giving: Education, environment, health, ill health, heritage, older people, arts, culture, community/social welfare, disability.

Cash donations undeclared	✓
Charity of the Year	✓
Gifts in kind	✓
Matched funding	✓
Payroll giving	✓

Charitable donations

Cash UK (latest available):	2009	£168,000
	2008	£578,000
	2007	£921,400
	2006	£704,700
	2005	£400,000
Total UK (cash and in kind):	2013	£358,000
Total worldwide (cash and in kind):	2013	£358,000

Community involvement

The Charitable Donations Committee can provide grants of up to £10,000 in the areas of education, arts and culture and health and well-being.

Charity partnerships

Charity of the Year

Each year the employees choose charities to be helped. In 2014 the company formally supported the following four organisations:

- National charity: Cardiac Risk in the Young (CRY)
- Dorking: St Catherine's Hospice, Crawley
- Basingstoke: Sebastian's Action Trust
- Bristol: Wallace and Gromit's Grand Appeal for Bristol Children's Hospital

Maggie's

Unum is partnering with Maggie's charity offering 'free emotional, practical and social support to people with cancer and their families and friends'. The partnership has commissioned a research (through Oxford Economics) to better understand the issue of barriers to work for people with cancer. In 2013 educational events were run and resources created 'to help employers and employees address the challenges they both face as a result of cancer in the workplace'.

Corporate giving

The company's annual report and accounts for 2013 state that a total of £358,000 (2012: 276,000) was given in charitable donations, including volunteering time. The website informs that in 2013 more than £140,000 was raised for Unum partner charities (Alzheimer's Society (£77,000), Naomi House and Jacksplace, The Grange and Wallace and Gromit's Grand Appeal). No further breakdown of the support given could be found, therefore we are unable to determine the amount given in cash by the company itself.

Beneficiaries have included: Alzheimer's Society (£77,000); Cardiac Risk in the Young; Maggie's; Naomi House and Jacksplace; Sebastian's Action Trust; St Catherine's Hospice; The Grange; and Wallace and Gromit's Grand Appeal.

Revenue: We have used the figure defined as 'Direct insurance' to represent the company's turnover.

In-kind support

Employee volunteering time and expert skills.

Employee-led support

Volunteering

Annually 'every Unum employee is allowed 2 working days to carry out volunteering duties for a charity or local community project'. During 2013 staff members volunteered more than 6,800 hours (947 working days) on projects, including painting, decorating, landscaping and conservation team challenges. Employees also use their business skills to help organisations with their websites, marketing materials, accounting and auditing, and social media and PR work.

Payroll giving

A scheme allowing payroll contributions is in place. The company's website notes that at least 10% of its employees donate regularly to charities through the payroll.

Matched funding

Through its Matching Gifts Programme the company matches employee donations to charities that are aligned with its 'pillars of giving' (see 'CSR information').

Corporate social responsibility

CSR committee: There is a Charitable Donations Committee which regulates the company's charitable giving.

CSR information: The company notes the following as its three key pillars of CSR activities in the UK:

- Education – efforts 'to include corporate giving and volunteer support for school programmes', and 'education and mentoring relationships with young people in local communities'
- Health and well-being (including disability) – charitable donations and other activities to support the health of children and adults in local communities. As a provider of disability benefits, the company claims to 'have a strong understanding of the complex challenges created by disabilities' and is 'committed to aiding young people and families who are confronting those challenges through charitable donations and volunteering opportunities'
- Arts and Culture – support to 'organisations that embrace creative expression in our local communities, from displaying public art in our offices to sponsoring local festivals and other cultural programmes that enhance the community'

CSR report: There is no published report but there is a dedicated page on the company's website.

Exclusions

Support is not normally given for advertising in charity brochures, animal welfare, appeals from individuals, enterprise/training, local appeals outside areas of company presence, medical research, overseas projects, political/religious appeals, or science/technology.

The application form further reminds that 'Unum does not provide charitable donations for administrative, staffing or other general running costs.'

Applications

The application form can be found online or requested from the correspondent. Once completed it should be returned via post or email.

Also note that: 'Only one request per charitable organisation will be considered during a 12 month period. Many of our employees volunteer and/or participate on boards, and special consideration is given to these organisations to recognise our employees' commitments.'

UPS (Ltd)

Logistics, transportation

Correspondent: The Sustainability Team, UPS House, Forest Road, Feltham, Middlesex TW13 7DY (tel: 0845 787 7877; email: custsvcgben@ups.com; website: www.ups.com)

Directors: Cindy Miller; Hans Mensing; Peter Dunstan; George Willis (women: 1; men: 3)

Year end	31/12/2013
Turnover	£758,021,000
Pre-tax profit	£39,575,000

Nature of business: Domestic and international carrier and package delivery services, specialist transportation, logistics, capital and e-commerce services.

UPS Ltd is a subsidiary of UPS (UK Holding) Ltd which itself is a subsidiary of United Parcel Service Inc.

Company registration number: 1933173

Main locations: Feltham

UK employees: 5,114

Total employees: 5,114

Focus of giving: Education, environment, health, ill health, marginalised people, poverty and social exclusion, children, young people, community/social welfare, disability, disasters.

Gifts in kind	✓
Humanitarian aid: overseas	✓
Market-led giving	✓
Sponsorship	✓

Charitable donations

Cash UK (latest available):	2013	£154,000
	2011	£150,000
	2009	£150,000
	2008	£150,000
	2007	£148,500
Total UK (cash and in kind):	2013	£154,000
Cash worldwide:	2013	£154,000
Total worldwide (cash and in kind):	2013	£154,000

Community involvement

The UPS Foundation

The foundation is UPS's global charitable arm and is responsible for facilitating community involvement on a local, national, and global level. Its global philanthropy program was launched in 2004 which extended charitable giving beyond the USA.

The UPS Foundation directs its giving through four global giving strategies: diversity; volunteerism; community safety; and environment.

Our research indicates that grants in the UK are made through the US-based UPS Foundation (Federal Tax ID No. 13–6099176). Previous beneficiaries have included: 1st Bury St Edmunds Scout Troop; Business Dynamics; Children's Adventure Farm Trust; RNIB; and RNID. The donations are normally initiated by the company proactively seeking potential beneficiaries whose work ties in with the interests of the foundation. National and local charities UK-wide can be supported.

According to the website, the foundation has partnered with relief agencies to provide in-kind shipments of the highest priority items needed for recovery. The global network comprises channels in over 220 countries and territories. The group provided $7.5 (£4.6 million) million in humanitarian relief funding and $2 million (£1.2 million) in the form of in-kind services in 2013, including in support of typhoon Haiyan in the Philippines.

Corporate giving

The annual report and accounts of the company state that a total of £4,000 (2012: £2,200) was paid in charitable donations in 2013. Our research indicates that generally about £150,000 is provided in the UK through the global foundation, therefore we take the figure of £154,000 to represent UPS's charitable giving in the UK.

During that year the global foundation provided grants to British Paralympic Association, Elford Hall Garden Project, FIA Foundation – Road Safety Fund, Friends of Newark and Sherwood Museum Service, Landgate Special School for Learners – Students with Autism and Communication Disorders, Southampton Society for the Blind, UK Youth, World Association of Girl Guides and Girl Scouts and Zoe's Place Trust.

In-kind support

Globally in-kind contributions are available, including materials and employee volunteering time and expertise. We found no further details specifically relating to the UK.

Employee-led support

Volunteering

The UPS employees are encouraged to contribute to their local communities. The group has 'recently pledged to complete 20 million hours of global volunteerism and community service by the end of 2020'. Throughout the group, UPS people with their friends and family donated a total of 1.8 million hours of volunteer service in 2013 (we could not find a separate UK figure). October is known as UPS Global Volunteer Month when various opportunities are organised for employees. 'Community service also plays an integral role in [the group's] immersive Community Internship Program and The UPS Foundation Local Grants Program.' On a group level employee volunteering efforts are supported by the Neighbor to Neighbor internal online system which helps UPS employees find organisations and community service opportunities.

Commercially led support

Sponsorships

The group is an official partner of The Open Championship and The Masters golf championships. It sponsors Ferrari in Formula 1 racing, supports the Olympic Games, including 2012 London Olympics, and is the official logistics partner of the NCAA.

Corporate social responsibility

CSR committee: There is a Sustainability Steering Committee at a group level.

CSR information: The group's CSR policies comprise four sustainability pillars: environmental responsibility; employee well-being and development; community causes; and economic enhancement.

The global website states:

> UPS has a legacy of connecting and improving communities around the world. We collaborate with partners to help people plan and prepare for unexpected events. We also bring relief when it matters most, offering logistics expertise, funds and in-kind assistance to support those impacted by disasters.

CSR report: An up-to-date group Sustainability Report is available on the website.

Exclusions

Support is not generally awarded to individuals, religious organisations, theological functions, or church-sponsored programmes limited to church members, capital campaigns, endowments or operating expenses. Political donations are not made.

Applications

The UPS Foundation does not accept or respond to unsolicited proposals.

Information available: UPS's sustainability report can be accessed at: www.sustainability.ups.com. Further information about its community support programme is available at: www.community.ups.com.

Valero Energy UK Ltd (formerly Valero Energy Ltd)

Oil and gas/fuel

Correspondent: The Company Secretary, Westferry Circus, Canary Wharf, London E14 4HA (tel: 020 7513 3737; website: texaco.co.uk)

Directors: Martin Loeber; Eric Fisher; Nicholas Roberts (women: 0; men: 3)

Year end	31/12/2013
Turnover	£161,000,000
Pre-tax profit	£101,300,000

Nature of business: The principal activities of the company are the refining, distribution, transport and marketing of petroleum products (under the Texaco brand in the UK and Ireland).

In August 2011 Valero Energy Corporation, through Valero Energy Ltd, acquired the network of more than 1,000 Texaco branded wholesale sites (the largest branded network in the UK) from Chevron Ltd. Valero has continued with the Texaco brand in the market.

The company's ultimate parent undertaking and controlling party is Valero Energy Corporation, incorporated in the US. Previous names of the company have included Chevron Ltd and Texaco Ltd.

Company registration number: 145197

Subsidiary undertakings include: Mainline Pipelines Ltd; Valero Energy (Ireland) Ltd; and Valero Equity Services. A full list of undertakings, including associates and significant holdings, can be found in the accounts.

Brands include: Texaco.

Main locations: Pembroke, Aberdeen

UK employees: 788

Total employees: 788

Focus of giving: Education, environment, medical research, local groups, arts, culture, sponsorship, sport, recreation, children, young people, community/social welfare.

Membership: BITC

Cash donations undeclared	✓
Charity of the Year	✓
Gifts in kind	✓
Market-led giving	✓
Matched funding	✓
Sponsorship	✓

Charitable donations

Cash UK (latest available):	2013	£329,000
	2011	£163,500
	2009	£422,000
	2006	£400,000
	2005	£300,000
Total UK (cash and in kind):	2013	£329,000
Cash worldwide:	2013	£329,000
Total worldwide (cash and in kind):	2013	£329,000

Community involvement

The website states:

> Since its inception in 1980, Valero has been a part of the life and spirit of the communities in which we live and work. It is our policy to play an active role in these communities by investing in projects that will make a positive difference to the quality of life. We support a number of national charities and charities local to our operations in London and Pembroke.

In the past donations were given to local charities in the areas of music, arts, extra-curricular education, environmental and community projects, sports, youth services and other charitable causes. The Pembroke refinery has a history of more than 45 years of community engagement in rural Pembrokeshire in southwest Wales. Examples include:

- *Action For Children* – through employee fundraising and matched funding over £1.1 million has been raised
- *Pembroke Dock Sunderland Trust* – the charity has been supported to undertake an upgrade of its IT equipment

- *Pembrokeshire County Council* – in sports development partnership with the county council's primary schoolchildren have been supported

Charity partnerships

The company has a fundraising partnership with Macmillan Cancer Support, which is now in its third decade.

Charity of the Year

The Pembroke Refinery chooses a Charity of the Year. In the past this has been the Wales Air Ambulance (2011).

Information taken from Texaco website notes that Valero supports a number of national charities. It is further stated: 'Unfortunately, as our budget is allocated in advance, we are only able to support a small number of additional requests through the Valero Volunteer Programme.'

Corporate giving

The company's annual report and accounts for 2013 did not seem to declare the amount given in charitable donations. Based on the figures from the three previous years known to us we estimate that about £329,000 was given in cash in the UK.

In-kind support

Staff volunteering time is available.

Employee-led support

Volunteering

According to the website, 'Valero has an active volunteering culture and in 2013 completed almost 4,000 voluntary hours for local and national charities in the UK.'

Valero employees globally engage in a range community projects. According to the global website in 2013 a total of 131,000 hours have been donated and included mentoring students, participating in fundraising and clean-up events, volunteering at youth centres and so on.

Matched funding

The company operates a scheme to match employee fundraising.

Commercially led support

Sponsorships

The company is a Gold Associate Supporter of the Duke of Edinburgh Awards in Wales, a member of the Welsh National Opera sponsors' group and sponsored the 2013 Tour of Pembrokeshire (supported by the Pembrokeshire Coast National Park).

In the US Valero provides sports sponsorships and scholarships in educational establishments.

Corporate social responsibility

CSR committee: We found no indication of a CSR committee relating to the UK company.

CSR information: We were unable to find CSR information relating specifically to the company. Globally, Valero focuses on environment and provides community support, especially for children and young people.

CSR report: A global Valero CSR report is available online, which appears to be focused on the US solely.

Exclusions

Support is not generally given for circular appeals, individuals, local appeals not in areas of company presence, large national appeals or overseas projects.

Applications

In writing to the correspondent. Our research suggests that normally decisions are not discussed over the telephone.

Applications local to the Pembroke Refinery may be directed to the site at Pembroke, Wales SA71 5SJ (tel: 01646 641331).

Virgin Atlantic Two Ltd (formerly Virgin Atlantic Ltd)

Leisure, aviation

Correspondent: Jenny Brigden, Community Investment Manager, The Office, Manor Roay, Crawley, West Sussex RH10 9NU (tel: 01293 562345 or 0844 811 0000 (main switchboard); email: community.investment@fly.virgin.com)

Directors: Richard Branson, President; Peter Norris, Chair; Craig Kreeger; Shai Weiss; Gordon McCallum; Edward Bastian; Glen Hauenstein; Perry Cantarutti; Wayne Aaron; Ian Woods (women: 0; men: 10)

Year end	31/12/2013
Turnover	£2,570,600,000
Pre-tax profit	(£48,000,000)

Nature of business: Virgin is an international investment group. Conceived in 1970 by Richard Branson, the Virgin Group has gone on to grow successful businesses in sectors ranging from mobile telephony, travel, financial services, leisure, music, holidays and health and wellness.

Virgin Atlantic Two Ltd group comprises three main operations:

- A UK international scheduled airline (Virgin Atlantic Airways Ltd)
- A tour operator providing inclusive package holidays and flights from the UK (Virgin Holidays Ltd)
- Brand licensing entities managing the use of the Virgin name in the airline and tourism industries

At the end of the financial year the company's ultimate parent company was Virgin Group Holdings Ltd, whose principal shareholders are Richard Branson and certain trusts, none of which individually has a controlling interest in Virgin Group Holdings Ltd. Virgin Group Holdings Ltd is registered in the British Virgin Islands.

Company registration number: 3552500

Subsidiary undertakings include: Bales Worldwide Ltd; Campden Securities Ltd; Junopart Ltd; Speed 5024 Ltd; Threesixty Aerospace Ltd; Virgin Atlantic Airways Ltd; Virgin Holidays Ltd; and Virgin Travel Group Ltd; A full list of subsidiary undertakings can be obtained from Companies House.

Total employees: 9,529

Focus of giving: Economic generation, enterprise/training, environment, health, ill health, overseas projects, poverty and social exclusion, women's issues, children, young people, community/social welfare, disability, disasters.

Gifts in kind	✓
Humanitarian aid: overseas	✓
Market-led giving	✓
Overseas giving	✓
Payroll giving	✓

Charitable donations

Cash UK (latest available):	2013	£6,000,000
	2011	£5,842,000
Total UK (cash and in kind):	2013	£6,000,000
Cash worldwide:	2013	£5,500,000
Total worldwide (cash and in kind):	2013	£6,000,000

Community involvement

The Virgin Group includes a number of companies which engage in various charitable activities, normally in the areas of the company's presence. For instance, information taken from the Virgin Atlantic website states that 'Virgin Atlantic **only** supports projects in the United Kingdom and in the destinations in which it operates.' Furthermore: 'At Virgin Atlantic we're passionate about supporting local communities both in the UK and in our global destinations. We tackle difficult social challenges by using all the global resources we have available to us.'

In the past over £1 million a year has been given to help children and young people who face extreme neglect, abuse, poverty, violence and social exclusion. According to the website this support has benefitted a number of global organisations including Muscular Dystrophy (£90,000) and Children with Aids Charity (£88,000) in the UK.

There are two UK-registered charities linked to Virgin:

The Virgin Foundation (known as Virgin Unite) (Charity Commission no. 297540)

According to the Charity Commission entry, the foundation 'was established by Richard Branson and staff across the Virgin Group to deliver entrepreneurial approaches to social and environmental issues'. It began its life in 1987 and works with all the Virgin companies across the globe as well as creating partnerships with social entrepreneurs. Virgin Unite's work encompasses leadership and advocacy, business innovation, entrepreneurship and working with the company's global community. The charity seeks to implement programmes and campaigns around issues such as health, economic empowerment, conservation and climate change. The foundation's overheads are covered by Richard Branson and the Virgin Group.

Virgin Atlantic Foundation (Charity Commission no. 1097580)

The foundation was set up in 2003 'to support the welfare of children and young people, using funds raised through Virgin Atlantic's Community Investment programme'. All Change for Children collections (see 'Commercially led support') and staff fundraising efforts go to the foundation and are used by Free The Children to support projects in the UK and overseas. It aims to support charities that alleviate sickness, poverty and distress affecting children in the UK and around the world and 'gives special consideration to less well known charities for whom funding is not always forthcoming compared to well-known charities'. The foundation is funded through donations made by individuals either directly to the charitable company or via the Virgin Money Giving website and collection boxes in Travelex shops.

Free The Children

In 2010 Virgin partnered with Free The Children and since then employees, partners and customers have raised over £3 million for projects in the UK and overseas. The charity remains one of the main charitable partners of Virgin. Free The Children was founded in Canada in 1995 by 12-year-old Craig Kielburger who read about child labour in financially developing countries and was so moved he decided to take action. The organisation has since grown into the worldwide network of children helping children through education, with more than one million young people involved in their innovative education and development programmes.

UK schools' programme

In the UK Virgin Atlantic Foundation funds the programme 'aimed at children aged between 7 and 18, it has three guiding principles: educate, engage and empower'. The programme incorporates educational resources and staff support to enhance the existing school curriculum. The programme has three parts:

- A motivational speech given during a school assembly to the entire school
- A Leadership and Entrepreneurship training workshop for around 30 students selected by the school, who 'receive ongoing support, mentoring and skills training in campaigning and making a difference' and 'debate social and environmental issues and discuss entrepreneurship
- Youth in Action groups are formed, bringing together exceptional students along with their teachers to learn how to bring change to their local and global communities

Scholarship programme

Students from the Free The Children's UK schools' programme are given 'the opportunity to compete for a place on Virgin Atlantic's annual international scholarship trip to one of the international funded villages'. In 2013 a total of 30 students went to India for an 18-day experience.

We Day

The annual event is organised by Free The Children. Students cannot buy the tickets but earn them by taking social action. The event holds inspirational speeches from global leaders, activists, and performances from entertainers and celebrities. In the UK the first We Day was organised in March 2014 with 12,000 students and teachers participating.

International development

International development projects undertaken by Virgin with Free The Children 'focus on delivering real, long-term improvements on social and environmental issues'. Eight communities in Africa, India and China are assisted through the Adopt a Village model which comprises five pillars: education; clean water and sanitation; health; alternative income; and agriculture and food security.

> Free The Children works closely with local government to make sure that community members are empowered and hold ownership over each and every project...
>
> Success is achieved when someone doesn't need charity again. We believe that the 'Adopt a Village' model can accomplish this. Building a healthy community through the 'Adopt a Village' model is like building the framework of a house. Each pillar provides crucial support, without which we'd not be able to support an entire community and its long-term development. Alongside the 'Adopt a Village' projects, Virgin Atlantic is proud to be funding a variety of innovative environment projects, supporting communities facing the harsh effects of climate change and other environmental impacts on a daily basis.
>
> Please note, Change for Children is supporting Free the Children until December 2015 so we are unable to take any other applications at this time.

Other charity partnerships

In addition to the relationship with Free the Children Virgin has worldwide partnerships. In the UK these include: working with Crawley Council and a local secondary school to help raise the aspirations of pupils in the local area, which is known for high teen pregnancy rates and a disproportionate number of NEETS (not in education, employment or training); and providing an annual donation of holidays to Dreams Come True – a charity which provides 'once of a lifetime' experiences for terminally ill children and their families.

Virgin also seeks to invest in 'destination initiatives that help make it easier for [its] suppliers to do the right thing'. For example, Virgin Holidays, Oxfam and the Travel Foundation had a joint project 'to help Caribbean farmers grow more product and encourage local hotels to buy it, rather than relying on imported goods'.

Support to the communities in which Virgin operates is also channelled through the Helping You Shine programme with various projects aimed at creating life changing opportunities for young people. These projects mainly take place at the Virgin Holiday destinations (including in the Caribbean, Africa and Asia).

Emergency relief

Through Virgin Unite the company responds to major humanitarian emergencies by both financial and cargo support. The company works with international organisations, such as Save the Children and UNICEF to help them provide humanitarian assistance.

Corporate giving

Because of the very many companies registered under the Virgin brand name, we have used the financial information declared in the annual report and accounts for Virgin Atlantic Two Ltd (registered company no. 3552500; formerly Virgin Atlantic Ltd). We have also used the company's latest Sustainability Report – *Change is in the Air 2014* – and focused on Virgin Atlantic's community and charitable involvement, as we believe it represents the philosophy behind the Virgin brand and offers good examples of activities undertaken by staff and the involvement of the company's customers.

The annual report and accounts of the company state that 'in 2013 almost £1.2 million was given in time, flights, baggage allowance and money'. The

Sustainability Report provides the following breakdown of the figure which was given through Virgin Atlantic Foundation:

Change for Children on board donations	£587,000
Flights and miscellaneous items	£361,000
Staff fundraising	£217,000
Volunteer staff time	£109,000
Total	**£1.2 million**

Virgin Unite accounts for 2012/13 state that 'the principal funding sources during the year were the Virgin Group and Sir Richard Branson in relation to his speaking fees at various events throughout the year, which he kindly donated to the charity'. Richard Branson's speaking fee donations were £2.7 million (2011/12: £3.3 million) and donations received from the Virgin Group totalled £2.8 million (2011/12: £3.3 million). In-kind donations to the charity from Virgin Management Ltd, Virgin Atlantic and Virgin Mobile totalled £470,000 (2011/12: £152,000) and included taxation and human resources services, flights and mobile phone costs.

We use the amount of in-kind donations and staff volunteering time, both totalling about £470,000 and also know that a total of £5.5 million was given in speaking fee donations and Virgin Group contributions to Virgin Unite, a charity registered in the UK. We count these speaking fee donations as cash contributions. Although we have used the figure of almost £6 million to represent the company's giving, Virgin has probably given substantially more both in cash and in kind throughout the range of companies under the Virgin name.

Virgin Unite

In 2012/13 the foundation made grants totalling £2.7 million, which included £361,000 as part of the UK 'Entrepreneurial Incubator' and £30,000 to King's College London.

Virgin Atlantic Foundation

The foundation's annual report and accounts for 2012/13 (the latest available at the time of writing) note that during the year a total of over £800,000 was donated. Practically this entire sum went to Free The Children, except for a special one-off collection for Caudwell Children (£110). The report states that Free the Children will continue as the main beneficiary of support at least until the end of 2015.

See the corporate charity entry on p. 436 for more information.

In-kind support

The website states: 'Each year, we're able to offer a small number of discounted flights to people who genuinely need our help. We receive thousands of requests and consider applications based on our funding criteria and on the individual merits of the applicant(s).'

A small number of flights are also donated for children who need medical treatment in a destination in which Virgin Atlantic operates (all taxes need to be paid by the beneficiary).

In aid of emergency appeals Virgin provides cargo space to charities, including ShelterBox, Save the Children and UNICEF. Help has been given in support of disaster relief in Asia and Africa, most recently after Haiyan Typhoon in 2013. In addition free on-board space can be offered for charitable shipments that meet the criteria and help children and young people across the Virgin network.

In 2013 a total of 195 flight tickets were donated to good causes. 'Tickets were auctioned to raise valuable funds for charities like CLIC Sargent, Action for Children, children's hospices, and others.' Every month the company also holds a flight prize draw for staff with a pair of tickets available for their chosen charity.

Employee-led support

Virgin employees contribute to good causes through fundraising efforts, which include annual events (for example, Virgineers golf day and Facilities race night) and also one-off activities (such as cake sales, quiz nights, raffles and staff sales where old merchandise is sold to Virgin people).

50:50

In 2013 a new initiative was launched which 'enables staff members to support charities close to their own hearts as well as Free The Children, by splitting donations 50:50'.

During the year staff fundraising resulted in £85,000 for Free The Children and £62,000 for other charities, including Caudwell Children, Chestnut Tree House, Footsteps for Oliver, Great Ormond Street, Macmillan, Prostrate Cancer, St Catherine's Hospice and The Variety Club.

Payroll giving

There is a Pennies scheme operating which allows staff to donate the pennies from their salaries on a monthly basis.

Volunteering

Staff members get involved in community activities, including through volunteering holidays. In 2013 more than 200 Virgin employees used their own holiday time to travel to Ghana, India and Kenya to get to know the communities the company supports. Volunteering is also undertaken through Free The Children's UK Schools' Programme with employees being given opportunities to work with local schools – for example, providing first aid workshops, supporting schools' fundraising events, and teaming up with schools to support Free The Children's We Scare Hunger initiative to help food banks in Crawley, Heathrow and Manchester.

Commercially led support

On-board charity appeals

Each month there is a different on-board charity collection. At the time of writing funds were being raised for Queen Elizabeth Hospital's Perinatal Intensive Care Unit (PICU) in Barbados.

Change for Children

This appeal is administered by the Virgin Atlantic Foundation and involves collecting change in various currencies from passengers travelling on Virgin Atlantic Airways Ltd. Donations are processed by Travelex Foreign Coin Services Ltd which deducts a handling fee but also collect donations through donation boxes in its shops. The donations are contributed to Free The Children funds.

Flying Club

Between 2011 and 2013 Virgin passengers donated more than 9 million Flying Club miles to Free The Children, which allowed young people from the UK and US to participate in international volunteer trips to China, India and Ghana as well as helping the founders of Free The Children attend events as keynote speakers.

Corporate social responsibility

CSR committee: There is a Sustainable Development Team which 'advises and facilitates action around the business, as well as incubating and managing specific initiatives until they become part of everyday business'.

CSR information: The following statement is taken from the Sustainability Report 2014:

> In April 2014 we updated our Sustainability Policy. It states our vision: To be the leading airline on sustainability, driving innovative solutions for the whole industry. We want to offer our customers clarity and peace of mind about our commitment to sustainability. We care about our impact on the environment. We actively and creatively address it. And we support communities in the destinations we fly to. Like safety and security, these commitments are fundamental to our long-term business strategy.

In addition the website states:

> At Virgin Atlantic, sustainability means change. Changing how we engage with the communities where we operate, how we fly our planes, how we work with our suppliers, how we get our staff and customers involved and, most of all, changing how we fly in a lower carbon world. Sustainability is at the core of what we do as a business.

CSR report: There is an annual Sustainability Report published online.

Corporate charity: Virgin Atlantic Foundation (Charity Commission no. 1097580).

Exclusions

The Virgin Atlantic website provides the following exceptions:

- Cash donations – 'Virgin Atlantic is unable to offer any cash donations; our contribution is always via tickets or discounts.'
- Individual charity sponsorship 'for flights to destinations where a fundraising activity is taking place or to make a donation to a charity other than those which Virgin staff choose each year' is also unavailable
- Sponsorship of charity events – Virgin Atlantic does not sponsor charity events and makes its contribution through tax payable or discounted tickets. 'Our sponsorship strategy is focused on reinforcing our product through partnership opportunities instead of branding opportunities.' Eligible sponsorship proposals can, however, be emailed to: sponsorship@fly.virgin.com
- Excess baggage – 'in the face of extremely high fuel prices, we've had to make the tough decision to discontinue our policy of waiving the cost of excess baggage for charities'
- Virgin Atlantic-branded items for charity events – due to the high amount of requests Virgin is not providing any current branded items for charitable causes
- Staff sponsorship – 'Virgin Atlantic is unable to make any financial contributions to staff seeking sponsorship'

Applications

Note: The Virgin Group operates a number of companies, therefore there is not one source to which applications for funding can be made. Applicants should refer to Virgin's individual companies' websites. The company states: 'For business proposals, sponsorship, charity, or enquiries regarding specific Virgin companies, please see our Contact Virgin Companies section [www.virgin.com/contact-us].'

Virgin Atlantic: The website states that projects matching the funding criteria should apply via email at community.investment@fly.virgin.com.

The company politely notes – 'We try our best to respond to all requests within 2 weeks. We receive thousands of requests each month and it takes time to thoroughly review and assess them, so please be patient if this takes a little longer than expected!'

The Virgin Foundation (known as Virgin Unite): Contact the correspondent – Rosanne Gray (email: contact@virginunite.co.uk) at 179 Harrow Road, London W2 6BN.

Virgin Atlantic Foundation: Contact the correspondent – Ian de Sousa, Foundation Trustee (tel: 01293 747128) at the company's address.

Vodafone Group plc

Telecommunications

Correspondent: The Sustainability Team, Vodafone House, The Connection, Newbury, Berkshire RG14 2FN (tel: 01635 33251; fax: 01635 238080; email: sustainability@vodafone.com; website: www.vodafone.com)

Directors: Gerard Kleisterlee, Chair; Vittorio Colao, Chief Executive Officer; Nick Read, Chief Financial Officer; Crispin Davis; Clara Furse; Val Gooding; Renee James; Samuel Jonah; Nick Land; Stephen Pusey; Luc Vandevelde; Philip Yea (women: 3; men: 9)

Year end	31/03/2014
Turnover	£38,346,000,000
Pre-tax profit	(£5,270,000,000)

Nature of business: The group is a mobile telecommunications provider operating worldwide.

The annual report and accounts for 2014 specify that 16% of employees are UK-based. Based on this we estimated the average number of UK employees to be about 14,850.

Company registration number: 1833679

Subsidiary undertakings include: Vodafone 6 UK; Vodafone Europe B.V.; Vodafone GmbH; Vodacom Group Ltd; Vodafone India Ltd; Vodafone Ireland Ltd; Vodafone Malta Ltd; and Vodafone Sales and Services Ltd. For the full list see the company's annual report and accounts.

Main locations: Banbury, Gloucester, Warrington, Welwyn Garden City, Theale, Trowbridge, Croydon, Newbury, Abingdon

UK employees: 14,850

Total employees: 92,812

Focus of giving: Education, enterprise/training, environment, health, ill health, heritage, older people, women's issues, children, young people, community/social welfare, disasters.

FTSE 100	✓
Gifts in kind	✓
Humanitarian aid: overseas	✓
Humanitarian aid: UK	✓
Market-led giving	✓
Matched funding	✓
Overseas giving	✓
Payroll giving	✓

Charitable donations

Cash UK (latest available):	2014	£1,600,000
	2011	£21,000,000
	2010	£2,838,440
	2008	£6,743,199
	2006	£5,390,000
Total UK (cash and in kind):	2014	£1,800,000
Cash worldwide:	2014	£45,000,000
Total worldwide (cash and in kind):	2014	£50,900,000

Community involvement

Vodafone supports good causes nationally, globally and in the communities around its offices. Its support in the UK is mainly given through the Vodafone Foundation.

The Vodafone Foundation (Charity Commission no. 1089625)

The foundation supports a wide range of causes. The group has 28 local foundations across the globe. The UK registered Vodafone Foundation encompasses both UK and wider activities.

Information taken from the website notes that in the UK the following initiatives are undertaken and managed through the foundation:

- JustTextGiving – the free text donation service (forming part of the Vodafone Foundation Mobile for Good programme) allows individuals and charities collect donations via text, using a unique code with the total amount going to the charity. Vodafone UK invested £5 million in creating JustTextGiving and bears all the running costs. The group states that 'over 20,600 charities have signed up to JustTextGiving with over 160,000 individual fundraisers using the service'
- TecSOS – a specialised handset for the victims of domestic violence, originally developed by the Vodafone Spain Foundation in collaboration with the Spanish Red Cross and the TecSOS Foundation, was introduced to the UK in 2010. It 'enables a user to push a central button and activate immediate contact with the police, provide instant details of location and enable an immediate recording of all activity in the vicinity of the handset'. According to Vodafone, 'as of June 2014 TecSOS had been implemented in over 50% of UK Police forces and over 7,000 victims in the UK have benefitted from the handset'.
- Take a Chance – the programme, run since 2007 and managed by the Education Business Partnership West Berkshire, 'aims to increase the confidence and motivation of students aged 14–15 in West Berkshire and enables them to broaden their skills and horizons by providing personal development opportunities within a business context. This is achieved

through coaching/mentoring by trained Vodafone staff in a series of workshops and mentoring sessions based at Vodafone HQ'

Corporate giving

The 2013/14 annual report and accounts of the group note that the total amount of donations made to the Vodafone Foundations in 2013 was £50.9 million, which included £5.9 million towards operating costs. According to the report, 'since its inception, Vodafone has donated over £475 million to the charitable programmes led by [the] foundations'.

The latest accounts available for the foundation were from 2013/14, when a total of £19 million was donated by the group, plus £1.5 million from Vodafone UK, and donated services and facilities provided the Vodafone group companies, including governance costs totalled over 902,000. Donated services and facilities represent the estimated financial cost borne by Vodafone Group plc in providing seconded staff and other management and administrative services. In 2013/14 the foundation awarded £19.6 million in grants.

We use the figure of £50.9 million to represent the group's total worldwide contribution and the figure of £1.6 to represent cash donations in the UK. We estimate the UK total contributions to be around £1.8 million (which comprises cash donations and part (1/28th) of the operational costs donated by the group). It would appear that charitable contributions are distributed about equally amongst the 28 funds.

Note: The group's website states:

> In countries in which Vodafone operates, our social investment is delivered by a unique footprint of 28 Vodafone Foundations and social investment programmes. These programmes are directed and chosen by the foundation trustees and receive funding from the Vodafone Foundation in the UK as well as their local Vodafone company.

The information available suggests that the trustees of the Vodafone Foundation (registered in the UK) administer the funds for use across the 28 locations. A separate Vodafone UK Foundation has been removed from the Charity Commission's records in February 2009 due to the transfer of funds.

See the corporate charity entry on p. 437 for more information.

In-kind support

The group offers staff volunteering time and specialist skills. The group also provides its foundations with management and administration support. In 2013/14 such support totalled £5.9 million.

Employee-led support

Volunteering

Staff members can use their time and skills to help the local community (Vodafone UK gives employees 24 hours' paid volunteering leave every year). The Vodafone Foundation will also offer up to £1,000 to volunteer teams for the purchase of materials or equipment hire.

JustTextGiving challenges

Various fundraising initiatives are offered to the employees as well, such as marathons, cake bakes, blanket knitting, a sponsored zip wire ride across the Vodafone HQ in Newbury and Big Bike and Big Bold bike ride challenges.

Take a chance

Newbury headquarters' staff participated in this programme mentoring young people from West Berkshire schools in 2013/14.

Payroll giving

Vodafone employees in the UK are able to donate through this method. The administration charge for this is paid by Vodafone.

Matched funding

The Vodafone Foundation gives financial support to UK-based Vodafone employees or teams who fundraise in their own time. Employees can claim up to £350 each financial quarter in matched funding. According to the Vodafone UK website, in 2013/14 its employees raised £940,000 for charity with an extra £320,000 given by the company in matched funding.

Commercially led support

Accessibility

The group pays attention to accessibility issues and seeks to provide solutions to people with disabilities, elderly people and other individuals who may have trouble using technologies. The group claims that they 'partner with accessibility organisations to understand the needs of people with severe disabilities and work with handset manufacturers to develop specialist assistive products and services'. A big part of this work is led by Vodafone Spain and its local foundation. There are specialist products and accessibility apps as well as initiatives to help older people overcome loneliness.

Child safety

There are digital parenting resources and guidance to parents and grandparents on protecting kids from inappropriate online content. In the UK 400,000 copies of a specially printed magazine were provided for distribution in schools across the country. In 2013/14 Vodafone 'also launched Web Super Skills – free internet safety cards designed with the creators of Moshi Monsters – to help parents teach young children good habits to ensure they stay safe online'.

Health

Globally the group uses its:

> Mobile health solutions to help governments and healthcare providers respond to global health challenges in four key areas:
>
> - Access to healthcare (helping patients in emerging markets access treatment, medicines and vaccines, by facilitating them to travel to hospitals, supporting the management of drug stock levels and improving the effectiveness of vaccination programmes)
> - Remote care (enabling doctors to treat patients remotely and improving quality of life for people with chronic diseases, by enabling them to monitor and manage their conditions at home)
> - Assisted living (using mobile technology to support assisted living, helping elderly people to live independently, in their own homes, for longer
> - Smart working (enabling healthcare workers to access patient records and hospital systems remotely to improve quality of care, reduce administration time and increase the time they can spend with patients, as well as helping to keep lone healthcare workers safer)

For example, in the UK Vodafone works with Baxter healthcare to provide a mobile system enabling patients with immune deficiencies in three cities in the UK to receive long-term treatment at home rather than travelling to hospital and clinicians to monitor patients' treatment process remotely. The group's website claims that Vodafone's smart working solutions enabled the NHS in Cumbria to help staff access clinical information and update patient records on the go and cut administration time.

Mobile education

During 2013/14 the group 'partnered with specialist education organisations to expand new learning solutions and address illiteracy in several emerging markets' (in India and Egypt).

See the group's website for more details on the above topics.

Apprenticeship scheme

The group offers apprenticeship schemes for 12 to 24 months with a potential for future employment.

Corporate social responsibility

CSR committee: The board has an ultimate responsibility of supervising the sustainability performance and is informed annually by the Executive Committee. The committee is accountable for the sustainability policy, implementation and review of performance. There is a dedicated Group Sustainability Team which formulates and maintains sustainability policies and initiatives and makes sure these are applied across the group. Each locally operating company has its own sustainability management structure while being overseen by the group. CSR is also integrated into risk management processes, such as the formal annual confirmation provided by each local operating company detailing the operation of their controls system.

CSR information: The group's website notes:

> Operating responsibly is essential to our licence to operate and delivers commercial advantages to the business, helping to turn potential risks into opportunities and enhancing the contribution of our products and services to sustainable living. By acting with honesty and integrity we can secure the trust of our customers, which is integral to the long-term success of our business.
>
> . . . we aim to help consumers, governments and businesses tackle some of the significant challenges they face – from food shortages and ageing populations, to lack of access to communications, healthcare and financial services.

Vodafone Group's sustainability agenda focuses on customer security and privacy, supply chain management, the environment, health and safety, child safety, human rights, ethical business management and accessibility.

Vodafone UK has the following to say on its website: 'Our commitment to society and the communities where we work goes beyond providing a great network and great products and services. We believe in the principle of giving something back.'

CSR report: There is a CSR report published annually.

Corporate charity: The Vodafone Foundation (Charity Commission no. 1089625).

Exclusions

The company does not normally support political appeals, religious causes, individuals, advertising in charity brochures, local appeals not in the company's areas of operation, or non-registered charities.

Applications

The group: In writing to the correspondent.

The foundation: Further details can be found on The Vodafone Foundation's website (www.vodafonefoundation.org). Alternatively, you can email Andrew Dunnett at groupfoundation@ vodafone.co.uk.

Waitrose Ltd

Retail – supermarkets

Correspondent: The Waitrose Community Matters Team, Doncastle Road, Southern Industrial Area, Bracknell, Berkshire RG12 8YA (tel: 01344 424680; website: www.waitrose.com)

Directors: Charlie Mayfield, Chair; Tom Athron; Nigel Keen; Mark Price; Helen Weir; Mark Williamson; Margaret Casely-Hayford, Company Secretary and Director of Legal Services (women: 2; men: 5)

Year end	25/01/2014
Turnover	£5,640,900,000
Pre-tax profit	£109,100,000

Nature of business: The company operates supermarkets and convenience stores, Leckford Farm, online sales and business to business contracts.

The immediate parent undertaking of Waitrose Ltd is John Lewis plc and John Lewis Partnership plc is the company's ultimate parent company. Ultimate control rests with John Lewis Partnership Trust Ltd, which holds the equity of John Lewis Partnership plc Trust for the benefit of the employees.

Company registration number: 99405

Subsidiary undertakings include: Waitrose (Guernsey) Ltd; and Waitrose (Jersey) Ltd.

UK employees: 54,335

Total employees: 54,335

Focus of giving: Economic generation, education, enterprise/training, environment, health, ill health, housing, homelessness, older people, poverty and social exclusion, sponsorship, children, young people, community/social welfare.

Membership: BITC, LBG

Cash donations undeclared	✓
Gifts in kind	✓
Market-led giving	✓
Sponsorship	✓

Community involvement

Grow and Sell Seed Kits

The programme aims to encourage 7- to 11-year-olds in local schools to grow their own produce and sell it outside Waitrose stores to its customers. Every branch has the opportunity 'to work with local schools, encouraging children to eat well and gain wider variety in their food choices'.

The annual report and accounts of the Partnership for 2013/14 note that Waitrose also 'teamed up with Start – a charitable initiative set up by HRH The Prince of Wales to inspire and encourage people to live more sustainably'.

Note that we classified Waitrose Ltd as a member of Business in the Community and the LBG, as it is a constituent part of the Partnership, which is a member of both.

Corporate giving

We could not determine the amount donated solely by Waitrose Ltd. The annual report and accounts do not seem to specify the figure and John Lewis Partnership Sustainability Review for 2014 gives the information relating to *the whole of the Partnership*, which was as follows:

Total value of cash contributions	£9.8 million
Total value of time contributions	£2.4 million
Total value of management costs	£1.3 million
Total value of in-kind contributions	£615,000

Due to the entry being new we have no previous figures to make an informed estimate. It is known that at least £25,000 has been given through the Community Matters programme from September 2014 to November 2014; and since 2008 a total of £14 million has been provided to good causes, which indicates that charitable giving could be considerable, although we would consider a lot of it to be consumer-driven.

Beneficiaries have included: Neuroblastoma Children's Cancer Alliance UK (£12,000); Missing people (£7,700); Keep Britain Tidy (£5,300); Age UK; Great Ormond Street Hospital; and Network Foodbank.

In-kind support

Community Matters Partner Volunteering

The scheme was launched in 2012 and allows local causes to bid for 'partner time'. Waitrose has allocated 75,000 hours to be invested in volunteering and also advertises vacancies in the stores where it supports causes under Community Matters.

Employee-led support

Partners of the group are invited to support charities and community groups. According to the John Lewis Partnership Sustainability Review for 2014:

> Among a number of volunteering initiatives across the country, Waitrose shops took part in Business in the Community's Give and Gain global volunteering day in May spending the day in local primary schools running activities that included fun tastings of healthy food and quizzes about healthy eating. Children were also invited to tour [the] shops to taste some delicious fresh produce and learn about the importance of healthy eating.

The Bridge Project

Volunteers from Waitrose pay monthly visits to the Bridge Project to teach its members – adults with learning disabilities – how to cook.

Commercially led support

The Waitrose Foundation

The Waitrose website states that the foundation:

> Is a partnership created in 2005 to help improve the lives of the farm workers and smallholders who grow our produce in South Africa, Kenya and Ghana.
>
> Instead of funding through a price premium, Waitrose – in conjunction with growers, importers and exporters, passes a percentage of profits into a trust to pay for projects. These include educational, social and healthcare projects, and are chosen by farm workers and smallholder committees. Money raised by the sale of Waitrose Foundation produce is therefore spent on projects that are chosen by and directly benefit the farm workers and smallholders.

The John Lewis Partnership Sustainability Review for 2014 also informs that the project was match-funded by the Department for International Development and is aimed to 'increase employment prospects for 500 unemployed and seasonally employed 18–28 year olds in the South African agricultural sector through dedicated theoretical and practical training'.

The Woodland Trust

In partnership with the trust, Waitrose 'links the planting of trees in the UK to the activity of its home delivery vehicles'. According to the company's website, every Waitrose.com delivery helps plant new trees.

Community matters

The company facilitates fundraising opportunities in support of good causes whereby shoppers can receive tokens to be used to support a chosen charity (the more tokens a cause gets, the bigger the donation it receives). Each month every Waitrose branch donates £1,000 (£500 in convenience shops) between three local good causes chosen by customers. The website notes that since the launch of Community Matters scheme in 2008, a total of £14 million has been donated. Similarly, a donation of £25,000 is also shared between three national causes, chosen by online shoppers. Most recently (at the time of writing) Age UK, Great Ormond Street Hospital, Keep Britain Tidy, Neuroblastoma Children's Cancer Alliance UK, Network Foodbank, and Missing People have been supported.

Some of the projects supported through the scheme include: a weekly lunch club for elderly people in Hampshire, where they are collected in a minibus and served a free two-course home-cooked meal; and The MK Soup Run in Milton Keynes – which is 'a group of volunteers who travel around the town distributing tea, coffee and soup to over 50 homeless people a night'.

Sponsorship

Waitrose is the official team sponsor of England Cricket. It is further noted on the company's website that in partnership with the ECB Club, Waitrose will be supporting over 1,000 cricket clubs to host open days; £100 of products are being provided by Waitrose to each event. Five clubs will be selected to host a Showcase Club Open Day with professional players running special masterclasses.

> As well as providing food and volunteers for these events, Waitrose will donate £100 to the England Cricket Board's Charitable Trust for every 4 or 6 scored in an international England match this summer. The Waitrose Small Grants Scheme will see the money distributed to cricket clubs in the UK for improvements and refurbishments of facilities.

Corporate social responsibility

CSR committee: There is no evidence of a CSR committee specific to the company.

CSR information: The latest annual report and accounts of the company state that:

> We encourage our partners to actively forge links and become involved in the local communities in which they live and work. We work with organisations like Business in the Community to continually improve the impact we have as a business on society.

The information given on the Partnership's website would also apply to Waitrose activities and notes the following:

> The Partnership is at the heart of the many communities we serve, and we believe that it makes sense to act locally wherever we do business. We support a diverse range of community initiatives and we constantly appraise and prioritise how we can best serve our communities to maximise the positive impact we can have.

CSR report: There is no separate CSR report for the company; however, one is available for the Partnership.

Applications

The company's website informs that UK-registered national charities who wish to be considered for the Community Matters Online initiative should post their applications on headed paper for consideration to the correspondent. The application should include a brief outline (no more than one side of A4) of the work your charity does along with details of any current projects that you are seeking funding for. The response will only be given if your application is successful or if the Community Matters Team requires further details.

Warburtons Ltd

Food manufacture

Correspondent: Nichola Atkinson, Community and Communications Co-ordinator, Back o'th' Bank House, Hereford Street, Bolton, Lancashire BL1 8JB (tel: 01204 556600; website: www.warburtons.co.uk)

Directors: Jonathan Warburton, Chair; Brett Warburton; Ross Warburton; Angela Megson; Nigel Dunlop (women: 1; men: 4)

Year end	28/09/2013
Turnover	£562,139,000
Pre-tax profit	£36,327,000

Nature of business: Warburtons is a family-owned bakery producer and distributer. The ultimate parent company of Warburtons Ltd is Warburtons 1876 Ltd.

Company registration number: 178711

Wholly owned subsidiaries include: Alliedtropic Ltd; Burneys Ltd; RBJ Foods Ltd; Warburton Asset Management Ltd; and Warburton Foods Ltd. Further details of subsidiary undertakings can be obtained from Companies House.

Main locations: Wakefield, Bolton, Enfield, North London

UK employees: 4,534

Total employees: 4,534

Focus of giving: Education, enterprise/training, health, ill health, financial education, poverty and social exclusion, community/social welfare.

Membership: BITC

Gifts in kind	✓
Matched funding	✓
Payroll giving	✓

Charitable donations

Cash UK (latest available):	2013	£192,000
	2011	£254,000
	2009	£183,000
	2008	£219,000
	2007	£191,000
Total UK (cash and in kind):	2013	£225,000
Cash worldwide:	2013	£192,000
Total worldwide (cash and in kind):	2013	£225,000

Community involvement

The company provides support in a number of ways, including grants, a national school visitors programme, product donation, volunteering matched funding, fundraising and payroll giving.

Families Matter

During the year a new national community investment strategy was launched, which works in partnership with the Charities Aid Foundation and the British Nutrition Foundation. The programme seeks to address the key difficulties faced by families on a daily basis, which, according to Warburtons'

National Community Policy, it considers to include:

- Health – help families lead healthier lifestyles
- Financial Stability – help families manage their finances
- Worklessness – help families recognise the economic and social benefits of employment

Financial giving is aimed at charitable organisations and projects which will benefit families and seek to solve significant social issues. The following help is available:

- Community Grants – applications from across England, Wales and Scotland can be made online for awards of up to £250. The awards are allocated to and considered by the local bakeries and depot sites
- Bakery Hub Project Grants – suitable organisations are contacted directly and invited to apply. The website reminds – 'organisations invited to apply for project grants are considered on an annual basis through an independent review by our partner, the Charities Aid Foundation. Unfortunately, as a result, there are no opportunities to put forward a request seeking support for your own organisation.' Awards range from £1,000 to £10,000 and are given to projects located within 15 miles of the company's bakeries or depot sites
- Centre Project Grants – are provided throughout England, Wales and Scotland, but are administered through a closed process

Warburtons works in collaboration with the Waste and Resources Action Programme (WRAP) and the World Wildlife Fund (WWF).

Bolton at Home

In the Community Investment Report for 2012/13, the local housing association is given as an example of organisations supported through the Families Matter Scheme. Warburtons, in partnership with Citizens Advice, MoneySkills, Hoot Credit Union and Bolton at Home Income Management Team, delivered the project, which supported 347 family members affected by debt. Help included one-to-one tailored debt, welfare and financial advice.

Corporate giving

The annual report and accounts for 2012/13 state that during the year Warburtons contributed £225,000 to its community and charitable grants programme. The Community Investment Report for 2012/13 states that a total of £192,000 was 'distributed to charities and community groups supporting local community activity'.

In-kind support

Product donations

Bakery sites can support local communities through the provision of products for various events. In 2012/13 a total of 937 organisations benefited from 103,871 products supplied.

School visits

The National School Visitor Programme has been running for over 20 years. It enables the company's School Visitors who deliver the programme to pay annual visits to primary schools to introduce pupils to bread making, food and healthy eating. Children are also provided an educational booklet to complete and necessary tools and ingredients. In 2012/13 there were 934 visits.

Employee-led support

The company's employees fundraise for good causes and participate in volunteering activities, including through local contacts, Business in the Community and Community Service Volunteers. The website notes that Warburtons 'is currently reviewing [its] approach to volunteering to create further impact'. Updates on volunteering activities will be available online. In 2012/13 a total of 484 hours were donated.

Payroll giving

A payroll giving scheme operates to enable monthly deductions from salaries in support of charitable causes. During 2012/13 over 750 staff members gave almost £52,000 to charity.

Matched funding

The company matches employee fundraising efforts. In 2012/13 funds raised totalled almost £33,000. The programme is currently being updated – see the company's website for any updates.

Commercially led support

Tickled Pink

A total of £75,000 was donated to the breast cancer campaign in 2012/13. Asda was selling special edition Warburton crumpets promoting breast cancer awareness with a percentage from all sales going to charity.

Corporate social responsibility

CSR committee: There is a Community Investment Committee and Michael McDermott acts as the Community and Corporate Responsibility Manager. Every Warburtons bakery has a Community Champion who represents the community giving programme, managing funds and exploring local needs.

CSR information: The CSR section within the annual report and accounts for 2012/13 states: 'The company takes its responsibilities to wider society seriously and supports the development of a sustainable and socially responsible business model, underpinned by a set of values that guide our behaviours.'

The website notes:

> We take pride in making sure that we look after our people, support our communities and work closely with our suppliers.
>
> We firmly believe that a sustainable business is a better business and have set out a number of commitments to improve our impact on the environment and to build a better society in the communities in which we operate. Our community investment and charitable giving has been at the heart of Warburtons from the earliest days of our business.

The CSR focus is placed on the following key areas: carbon and waste management; sustainable supply; employee well-being; and community investment.

CSR report: There is a Corporate Responsibility section on the website and within the annual report and accounts. A Community Investment Report is also published.

Exclusions

According to Warburtons' Financial Giving Policy financial support cannot be given for:

- Political parties
- Animal causes
- Anything outside England, Wales or Scotland
- Organisations that discriminate by race, creed, gender, sexual orientation, age, religion or national origin
- Individuals (in contrast to groups, teams or communities)
- Individuals or organisations seeking educational bursaries (assistance to individuals for school research projects, travel costs or college and university fees)
- Organisations which are not charitable and do not operate on a not-for-profit basis
- Applications that solely seek support for salaries (however [the company] will consider funding a proportion of a salary or sessional worker fees where these are directly linked to project delivery)
- Part funding
- Activities with a negative impact on the environment
- Organisations with which association can be potentially harmful to the Warburtons business
- Third party fundraising (e.g. sponsoring an individual to complete a challenge)
- Sponsorship, advertising and promotion alone, which primarily generate commercial returns
- Raffle prizes, but please note it is possible to provide a donation for a raffle prize or a cause, but [Warburtons] cannot provide goods [itself]
- Requests that solely seek to purchase something (except Community Grants)

(e.g. the buying of a building or other significant purchase)

The policy notes the following exception:

In limited cases, the Community and CR Manager can authorise support for Bakery Hub projects outside the 15 mile radius with agreement with the Chair of the Community Investment Committee. Such projects will require benefits for both the community and the business as a result of making this exception.

Applications

Applications for small grants and product donations should be made via the online form.

School visits can be arranged by contacting the Warburtons Customer Care Team (tel: 0800 243 684) at the company's address.

Note: There is a limited amount of money for grant funding and not all applications can be supported. The application process takes approximately eight weeks. Where a financial donation is being applied for, the company requests that the money is used to fund a specific need or project. Financial support will not be awarded to assist ongoing fundraising activity.

If you are requesting a product donation, remember that the company will need at least two weeks' notice of the date of your event.

Wates Group Ltd

Building/construction

Correspondent: Louise Hyde, Group Community Investment Manager, Wates House, Station Approach, Leatherhead, Surrey KT22 7SW (tel: 01372 861000 (main switchboard); fax: 01372 861182; email: info@wates.co.uk; website: www.wates.co.uk)

Directors: James Wates, Chair; Andrew Davies, Chief Executive Officer; Huw Davies, Chief Financial Officer and Company Secretary; David Smith; Timothy Wates; Jonathan Wates; Andrew Wates; Charles Wates; Deena Mattar; Graeme McFaull; David Barclay (women: 1; men: 10)

Year end	31/12/2013
Turnover	£931,171,000
Pre-tax profit	£22,340,000

Nature of business: The Wates Group is a provider of construction services and residential development.

It has been wholly owned by the Wates family since its inception in 1897 and currently has over 2,000 employees and 16 offices across the UK.

Company registration number: 1824828

Subsidiary undertakings include: Needspace? Ltd; and Wates Developments Ltd. More details of subsidiary undertakings of the group can be obtained from Companies House.

UK employees: 2,074

Total employees: 2,074

Focus of giving: Economic generation, education, enterprise/training, environment, health, ill health, housing, homelessness, local groups, poverty and social exclusion, sponsorship, sport, recreation, children, young people, community/social welfare.

Membership: BITC

Charity of the Year	✓
Gifts in kind	✓
Market-led giving	✓
Matched funding	✓
Payroll giving	✓
Sponsorship	✓

Charitable donations

Cash UK (latest available):	2013	£1,300,000
	2011	£1,400,000
	2009	£45,000
	2007	£58,000
Total UK (cash and in kind):	2013	£1,300,000
Cash worldwide:	2013	£1,300,000
Total worldwide (cash and in kind):	2013	£1,300,000

Community involvement

The Wates Family Enterprise Trust (Charity Commission no. 1126007)

The trust was set up in 2008 by the Wates family with the aim 'to empower initiatives that make a real difference to society'. In 2013 a total of £1.3 million was given to local community projects.

Wates Giving

The charitable programme supports the company's Reshaping Tomorrow initiatives. Its priority is local projects that can bring long-term benefits for the community. Wates Giving is run and funded by The Wates Family Enterprise Trust.

- Major Awards – since 2008 Wates Giving programme has invested over £8 million in local initiatives through the following themes: education; employment and training; social enterprise; sustainability; thought leadership; and community building. Wates Giving also makes annual donations to the community organisations and groups supported during the Community Week
- Employee Sponsored Awards – 'Through Wates Giving, the Wates Family owners also back the causes that our people support with their own time and resources. ... Wates Giving has boosted the almost £300,000 raised for charities by Wates employee fundraising activities with an additional £100,000'
- Other Awards – these awards support the personal causes of the Wates Family

Reshaping Tomorrow

The Reshaping Tomorrow policy booklet 2014 outlines the following commitments to:

- Align [the company's] commitments with [its] business activities so that [it] makes best use of [its] skills and expertise
- Work in partnership with organisations who share [Wates's] values and who bring additional expertise, including non-governmental Organisations (NGOs), charities and not-for-profit organisations
- Measure the impact of [its] work in the community and share this with [its] people, customers, supply chain and wider stakeholders
- Support and encourage other organisations to invest time and resources into their local communities
- Encourage individuals in their personal charitable activities through fundraising and volunteering
- Support the community projects of [the company's] employees, customers and partners through Wates Giving, the charitable arm of the Wates Family

Charity partnerships

Prince's Trust

According to the group's website, the latest two-year partnership was launched in June 2014. As part of the partnership, Wates 'will be supporting the TEAM programme through volunteering on these 12 week personal development courses and fundraising £50,000 per annum'.

Past partnerships were with Barnardo's (the three-year partnership from 2011 to 2014 saw Wates employees raising over a quarter of a million pounds for the charity) and Shelter (the two-year partnership ran from 2009 until 2011 and provided staff fundraising and volunteering to support the charity's activities with almost £167,000 being raised).

Trafford Housing Trust

According to the group's *Communities Count* report, since 2006 Wates Living Space has been working with the trust and has delivered innovative programmes, including the Building Futures programme. Wates has also 'given grants to young people to fund social enterprise ideas and donated time and resources to turn a previously dilapidated Scout Hut into a nursery to provide childcare for local residents'.

The Wates Foundation (Charity Commission no. 247941)

The Wates Group also runs an independent grant-making family trust supporting the charitable and voluntary sector. It has been established in 1966 and since then has made grants totalling over £100 million. The charity's objectives mirror the group's values with family being at the heart of their grant-making aims. Its interests are categorised into five themes: building family values; community health; life transitions; safer communities; and strengthening the voluntary sector. Wates family members seek out charities to support through 'family committees', frequently within their own community, which often results in greater family engagement with the beneficiaries supported. All awards are sponsored by a Wates family member who will lead a grant assessment visit. The foundation's website informs that it is 'conducting a reduced grant making programme until March 2015 when a new pro-active strategy will be launched'.

Corporate giving

In 2013 Wates Giving invested about £1.3 million in 'charitable awards'. This sum was given to the corporate charity. In addition £69,000 was raised by employees for a charity partner.

The trust's annual report and accounts for 2013 state: 'The trust's income arises from a formal agreement with the Wates Group in accordance with the wishes of the Wates Family owners and shareholders of the Wates businesses.'

Beneficiaries of the trust have included: Alexander Devine Children's Hospice; Breast Cancer Care; Changing Paths Charitable Trust; Derby and District RSPCA; Friends of Heyswood; Langlands and Nottage Social Club; Marie Curie; National Trust; Prisoners Education Trust; and Walton Centre NHS Foundation Trust.

See the corporate charity entry on p. 437 for more information.

In-kind support

Business Class

The website notes that during the year work has been undertaken with over 8,500 young people through Wates's schools programme Business Class which provides CV workshops, careers fairs and mentoring.

Employee-led support

Wates people volunteer their time and participate in fundraising activities in support of various charities. For example, an expedition to the Everest Base Camp raised over £69,000 for Barnardo's in 2013.

Community Day

The annual Community Day brings together employees, customers and supply chain partners to carry out a wide range of projects. In 2013 employees donated 3,725 during the day across the UK.

Lend a Hand

This scheme enables staff to take two paid days of leave per year for volunteering activities.

Matched funding

In 2013 more than £30,000 was provided in matching employees' fundraising efforts.

Payroll giving

There is a Give As You Earn scheme which allows regular salary deductions to support good causes.

Commercially led support

Sponsorship

Wates Giving sponsors the company's people and their families who compete in sport at the highest level. In 2014 three scholarship holders took part at the Commonwealth Games.

Education and training

The company states – 'our aim is to help reshape communities by creating local employment and training opportunities'. Through the Wates Apprenticeship Training Agency, apprenticeship opportunities are provided, and through the Building Futures programme and involvement with the Prince's Trust Get into Construction initiative support to people facing barriers to employment is offered. In addition Wates provides work placements, mentoring, team building exercises, workshops and careers fairs.

Business Class

Through the Business in the Community's education programme Wates builds long-term partnerships with, currently, eight schools. According to the website, 'in the academic year 2012/13 [Wates] supported over 8,500 students and 450 of [its] employees and supply chain were involved in the programme.'

In support of educational initiatives the company partners with a number of organisations, including: Considerate Constructors Scheme (a non-profit-making, independent organisation founded by the industry); Ixion Holdings (a not-for-profit organisation that is part of Anglia Ruskin University); The Prince's Trust (which is also the Charity of the Year); Social Enterprise UK; and Supply Chain Sustainability School.

The Hazeley Academy

Wates has a three-year partnership with The Hazeley Academy in Milton Keynes 'to raise students' career aspirations and help them secure employment when they leave' which provides monthly mentoring sessions, literacy workshops and career guidance sessions and site visits.

The website notes: 'Wates engages with schools to encourage more young people to join the sector. Through work experience and site visits we promote the range of roles available to them. We are a proud supporter of the industry 'Born to Build' campaign.'

This campaign offers careers advice and information of apprenticeships, graduate recruitment schemes and jobs in the construction industry.

Social Enterprise Brokerage (SEB)

In 2013 Wates 'launched the industry's first national Social Enterprise Brokerage to help social enterprises trade with our projects across the country'. The initiative is run in partnership with Social Enterprise UK.

Corporate social responsibility

CSR committee: There is a Corporate Responsibility Committee, led by the CEO, which co-ordinates CSR and sustainability matters.

CSR information: The company's website states:

> 'Reshaping Tomorrow' is our framework for a sustainable future. ... [It] is a programme that prioritises those environmental and community issues where we can make a real difference and where we can strengthen our relationships with our customers, partners and the communities in which we work.
>
> Through our community investment activities we aim to raise aspirations of young people; and create local employment and training opportunities for those facing barriers to work. By integrating these principles throughout our projects, we can deliver more sustainable buildings for our customers and help to shape the communities around them.

The CSR policy encompasses areas of environment, education and employability.

It is also noted that 'with a long track record of philanthropy, the Wates family is pleased to support the corporate responsibility aims and community work of the group through their trusts and the Wates Foundation'.

CSR report: A Sustainability Report is contained within the annual report and accounts.

Corporate charity: Wates Family Enterprise Trust (Charity Commission no. 1126007).

Applications

The company: In writing to the correspondent or the Group Sustainability Team.

Note, however, that according to the Charity Commission record: 'The Wates Family Enterprise Trust does not accept unsolicited applications. All such applications will be rejected automatically.' All the proposals for Wates Giving awards come from employees or the Wates Family.

The Wates Foundation: A small number of applications are still considered by the Wates Family Grants Committees. However, these applications are sought by invitation only.

Weetabix Ltd

Food manufacture

Correspondent: Lyne Booth, Company Secretary, Weetabix Mills, Burton Latimer, Kettering, Northamptonshire NN15 5JR (tel: 01536 722181; website: www.weetabix.co.uk)

Directors: Giles Turrell, Chief Executive Officer; Xiaofeng Cao; Dominik Halstenberg; Li Lin; Richard Martin, Chief Financial Officer; Lili Wang; Yin Ye

Year end	28/12/2013
Turnover	£366,398,000
Pre-tax profit	£116,039,000

Nature of business: The principal activity of the company is the manufacture, marketing and sale of ready to eat cereal foods and breakfast drinks.

The website informs that Weetabix was a family controlled company until 2003:

> Weetabix Food Company is now 60% owned by Bright Food (Group) Co., Ltd, one of the largest Chinese international conglomerates in the food industry, with operations throughout the entire food industrial chain including agriculture, food processing, brand agency service and retail amongst others.

The remaining share capital is largely owned by Lion Capital.

The annual report and accounts for 2012/13 further specify that 'the company is a subsidiary undertaking of B.L. Marketing Ltd and a member of the Latimer Newco 2 Ltd group'.

Company registration number: 267687

Subsidiary undertakings include: Alpen Food Company South; Barbara's Bakery Inc; Ryecroft Foods Ltd; Vibixa Ltd; Weetabix GmbH; Weetabix Ireland Ltd; and Weetabix Mexico SA de CV. A full list of subsidiary undertakings can be obtained from Companies House.

Brands include: Alpen; Oatibix; Ready brek; Weetabix; and Weetos.

Main locations: Hastings, Corby

Total employees: 1,063

Focus of giving: Education, safety and crime prevention, sponsorship, sport, recreation, community/social welfare.

Cash donations undeclared	✓
Sponsorship	✓

Charitable donations

Cash UK (latest available):	2013	£116,000
	2010	£123,000
	2009	£130,000
	2008	£96,000
	2007	£87,000
Total UK (cash and in kind):	2013	£116,000
Cash worldwide:	2013	£116,000
Total worldwide (cash and in kind):	2013	£116,000

Community involvement

The Weetabix Charitable Trust (Charity Commission no. 1044949)

The trust was established in 1995 to support education and training, children and young people, disability causes and community development. Donations are principally made to schools and organisations involved with children and young people, usually within the local area. It is unclear whether the income is still received from or contributed to by the company.

Corporate giving

It would appear that the company no longer declares charitable donations in its annual report and accounts. Based on the figures from the three previous years known to us, we estimate that about £116,000 was given in cash in the UK.

The latest accounts of the trust were not required by the Charity Commission. We know that in 2012/13 the trust had an income of £43 and made no charitable donations, and the year before it had an income of £114 and an expenditure of £30. The trust's expenditure and income has gradually decreased since 2009, when income was £3,000 and the expenditure £46,000.

Our research suggests that in the past support has been mainly given to the National Grocers Benevolent Fund and local charities.

Commercially led support

Sponsorships

In the past the company was a long-term corporate sponsor of the Women's British Open and supported the Northamptonshire Police. A recent 12-month sponsorship campaign is with ITV's Lorraine breakfast show.

Ultimate Sports Day

According to the company's website, the campaign was run throughout spring and summer 2014 with the aim to 'inspire mums, children and teachers to recapture the excitement of London 2012'. Promotional packs of Weetabix, featuring Mo Farah, were available in stores. The campaign's competition (which could be entered via the pack or through schools) 'locked into the healthy living strand of the school curriculum with educational packs issued to Primary Schools in the UK'. The winners could win a school trip to the Ultimate Sports Day and compete with Mo Farah.

Corporate social responsibility

CSR committee: We found no details of a separate CSR committee.

CSR information: The CSR policy is confined to environmental and sustainability issues.

We were unable to determine the ratio of women to men on the board.

CSR report: There is a short dedicated section within the annual report and accounts and achievements (environment and sustainability) are listed within the CSR policy brochure, which is available on the website.

Exclusions

According to our research, local appeals not in areas of company presence or requests from individuals are not generally supported.

Applications

In writing to the correspondent, who is also the administrator of the trust.

Wessex Water Services Ltd

Water

Correspondent: Group Head of Public and Community Relations, Claverton Down Road, Claverton Down, Bath BA2 7WW (tel: 01225 526000; fax: 01225 528000; email: sustainability@wessexwater.co.uk; website: www.wessexwater.co.uk)

Directors: Francis Yeoh, Chair; Colin Skellett, Chief Executive Officer; Mark Watts, Director of Finance and Treasurer; David Barclay; Gillian Camm; Peter Costain; Fiona Reynolds; Hong Yeoh; Kathleen Chew; Mark Yeoh; Hann Yeoh; Huw Davies (women: 3; men: 9)

Year end	31/03/2013
Turnover	£492,100,000
Pre-tax profit	£138,500,000

Nature of business: The company is a regional water and sewage treatment business serving an area of the south west of England, covering 10,000 square kilometres including Dorset, Somerset, Bristol, most of Wiltshire and parts of Gloucestershire and Hampshire.

The ultimate parent company of Wessex Water Services Ltd is YTL Corporation Berhad (which is incorporated in Malaysia).

Company registration number: 2366648

Subsidiary undertakings include: Wessex Water Services Finance plc.

Main locations: Bath

UK employees: 1,741

Total employees: 1,741

Focus of giving: Education, environment, individuals, non-registered charities, financial education, older people, overseas projects, children, young people, community/social welfare.

Gifts in kind	✓
Market-led giving	✓
Payroll giving	✓

Charitable donations

Cash UK (latest available):	2013	£320,000
	2012	£350,000
	2011	£360,000
	2008	£150,000
	2007	£93,000
Total UK (cash and in kind):	2013	£320,000
Cash worldwide:	2013	£320,000
Total worldwide (cash and in kind):	2013	£320,000

Community involvement

Watermark awards

The scheme has been run for over 20 years and helps organisations and individuals with their environmental projects. It is organised by the Conservation Foundation. During the year 'thousands of pounds to nearly 50 environmental groups' have been given in awards from £150 to £1,500 and included funding for nature trails for a disabled access group, the restoration of a charity bus and a pond to protect great crested newt colonies.

For its 20th anniversary a special award for water conservation projects in the region was organised with the Sustainable Watermark providing grants of up to £2,000 for groups that work on water-saving projects in community halls, schools or other community buildings. The winners included Rainbow Gardens in Weymouth which installed rainwater harvesting equipment to enable its community garden to be self-sufficient in water during the summer. Every three months a special project receives the Wessex Watermark gold award worth £2,500.

Education

The company states in its 2013 annual report:

> Informing customers of all ages about what we do and encouraging them to use water wisely forms an important part of our work. In the past year our education officers have received an unprecedented number of requests from schools, colleges and community groups across our region.

The education services that Wessex Water offers include:

- Primary and secondary education packs
- Education advisers
- Visits to schools
- Tailor-made lessons (about the water cycle, river and pond studies, WaterAid and practical sessions)
- Education centres
- Site visits

Education officers deliver lessons about the company's water and sewage treatment, activities on environmental topics and water saving, and behind-the-scenes insight into how drinking water is supplied and sewage treated.

Partners Programme

The programme began in 2010 and welcomed seven new or continuing projects which were supported until 2015. Assistance was given to 'projects carried out by wildlife organisations to conserve and enhance biodiversity throughout [the] region, and it complemented [the company's] own work to help wildlife on [its] sites and protect the environment during construction'. Previous partners include the South West Farmland Bird Initiative (which includes Cranborne Chase and West Wiltshire Downs AONB, Natural England and the RSPB as partners). Funding contributed to core costs of the projects, such as: a new water supply to enable re-introduction of grazing on chalk grassland; scrub clearance to improve bird habitat in the Wylye Valley; new fencing to allow grazing of chalk grassland created from arable land; a research study into rare arable plant records to identify future target areas; and new tree sparrow nest boxes for farms with known breeding populations.

WaterAid

Since its creation Wessex Water has supported the international water and sanitation charity by organising fundraising events and raising money through customers and staff. In 2008 an ongoing campaign – Wessex for West Africa – began with contractors, consultants and suppliers helping to raise money over a one-year period by fundraising within their organisations.

Our research suggests that in addition to the above, local charities based within the region also receive support through the company's Community Involvement Committee which awards small grants every month.

Corporate giving

During the year 2012/13 a total of £320,000 (2012: £350,000) was given to UK charities, 'of which £255,000 was donated to local debt advice agencies to help provide debt and financial advice to customers in our area who are struggling to pay their water bills'.

In-kind support

The company's Sustainability Indicators paper states: 'We have an extensive free education service for schools, colleges and community groups cover the water cycle, environmental topics, water saving and our water and sewerage operations.'

Employee-led support

Employee volunteering

Speaker service

The volunteer speaker service gives staff the opportunity to meet groups to tell them more about Wessex Water. According to the website, several hundred community groups request talks every year.

Payroll giving

Our research indicates that the company has operated the Give As You Earn scheme.

Commercially led support

Apprenticeships

The website states that 'from time to time' apprenticeship opportunities are offered for young people.

WaterSave pack

Free WaterSave packs for the company's customers are provided to help them save water and lower their energy bills and include: a shower flow regulator to reduce the flow rate in power and mixer showers; a save a flush bag for use in cisterns, to save a litre every flush; a self-audit guide to help customers work out where the most water is used in the home and garden.

Customer Care Plus

This special programme is designed for customers with special needs, including those who are older and/or have disabilities. A register of such customers is held for the company to identify and respond to their requirements. Help includes: a text telephone service for people with impaired hearing; Braille or audio bills; a doorstep security password system; and advance warning of interruptions to water supply.

Financial education

The information in this section is mainly gathered from the company's 2013 annual report.

Money Matters awards scheme

The awards were launched 'to improve financial literacy and money management skills among young people across [the] region' and offers grants of up to £10,000 towards specific projects.

'tap'

During the year the company launched the programme 'tap' (tailored assistance programme) which offers 'tailored assistance helping more than 12,000 vulnerable customers to afford their ongoing water bills and repay their debt'. In partnership with Citizens Advice, Wessex Water Services expanded its social tariff scheme Assist by introducing WaterSure Plus. 'This year we have increased the funding to agencies in our region to acknowledge an increase in the demand for their independent services.'

According to the 2014 Sustainability Indicators, during 2013/14 work with organisations offering telephone and online advice, such as National Debtline and StepChange, increased.

Corporate social responsibility

CSR committee: In 2013 a Corporate Responsibility Committee was established:

> To make recommendations to the board about the company's corporate and social obligations to its employees and other stakeholders.
>
> The board also receives reports from its Sustainability Panel and four Liaison Panels as part of the company's commitment to wide stakeholder engagement.

CSR information: The website states that:

> Achieving our aim of becoming a truly sustainable company means more than just 'being green'. It is about excellent customer service, strong community engagement, meeting employee's needs, sound asset management, finance responsibility and good environmental practice – all at the same time.

Sustainability is based on the following categories:

- Customers and communities
- The environment
- Employees
- Infrastructure
- Finance

It would appear that the main CSR focus is on the environment and education.

CSR report: A Sustainability Indicators paper with a section devoted to community matters was available from the company's website.

Exclusions

Support is not generally given for national charities, advertising in charity brochures, animal welfare, the arts, enterprise/training, political appeals, religious appeals or science/technology.

Applications

In writing to the correspondent. The community involvement committee meets monthly.

The website notes that 'if you have any questions, would like to know more or have suggestions on how we could improve the information provided, please drop us an email'.

J. D. Wetherspoon plc

Leisure, retail – restaurants/ fast food

Correspondent: The Company Secretary, Wetherspoon House, Central Park, Reeds Crescent, Watford WD24 4QL (tel: 01923 477777; website: www.jdwetherspoon.co.uk/home/investors/csr)

Directors: Tim Martin, Chair; John Hutson, Chief Executive; Su Cacioppo; Elizabeth McMeikan; Debra van Gene; Sir Richard Beckett; Mark Reckitt (women: 3; men: 5)

Year end	27/07/2014
Turnover	£1,409,333,000
Pre-tax profit	£78,365,000

Nature of business: The development and management of public houses.

Company registration number: 1709784

UK employees: 34,417

Total employees: 34,417

Focus of giving: Health, ill health, children, young people, community/ social welfare.

Membership: BITC

Cash donations undeclared	✓
Charity of the Year	✓

Charitable donations

Cash UK (latest available):	2014	£0
	2013	£96,000
	2012	£0
	2011	£0
	2009	£69,000
Total UK (cash and in kind):	2014	£0
Cash worldwide:	2014	£0
Total worldwide (cash and in kind):	2014	£0

Community involvement

J. D. Wetherspoon employees and customers raise funds and awareness for CLIC Sargent, the children's cancer charity.

Beneficiaries: CLIC Sargent

Corporate giving

There was no evidence of corporate charitable contributions having been made during the 2013/14 financial year. However, the company continues to work in partnership with CLIC Sargent and stated the following in its annual report: 'In the last year, we raised approximately £1.7 million, bringing the total raised to over £9.2 million – more than any other corporate partner has raised for this charity.'

Based on figures from recent years, we believe the £96,000 contribution to Drinkaware in 2013 was a one-off charitable donation.

Corporate social responsibility

CSR committee: There was no evidence of a separate CSR committee.

CSR information: This information was obtained from the company's website:

> The Company aims to be an important part of the local communities in which it trades, managing its responsibilities from both corporate and social perspectives. The Company's corporate social responsibility plan identifies four areas: people; responsible retailing; community and charity; the environment.

CSR report: There was no evidence of a separate CSR report; however, there is a small section regarding CSR on the company's website.

Applications

In writing to the correspondent referenced 'Charitable donations'.

Whitbread plc

Hotels, leisure, retail – restaurants/fast food

Correspondent: The Corporate Responsibility Team, Whitbread Court, Houghton Hall Business Park, Porz Avenue, Dunstable LU5 5XE (tel: 01582 424200; website: www.whitbread.co.uk)

Directors: Patrick Dempsey; Christopher Rogers; Richard Baker, Chair; Andy Harrison, Chief Executive Officer; Stephen Williams; Wendy Becker; Ian Cheshire; Simon Melliss; Susan Taylor Martin; Nicholas Cadbury, Group Finance Director; Louise Smalley (women: 3; men: 8)

Year end	27/02/2014
Turnover	£2,294,300,000
Pre-tax profit	£347,000,000

Nature of business: The group's principal activities are the operation of hotels, restaurants and coffee shops.

Company registration number: 29423

Subsidiary undertakings include: Coffee Nation Ltd; Coffeheaven International Ltd; Costa Ltd; Premier Inn Hotels Ltd; and Whitbread Restaurants Ltd. Further details of the group's subsidiary undertakings can be obtained from Companies House.

Brands include: Beefeater Grill, Brewers Fayre, Costa, Hub, Premier Inn, Table Table, Taybarns and Whitbread.

Main locations: London

Total employees: 36,447

Focus of giving: Education, enterprise/ training, children, young people.

Membership: BITC, LBG

Cash donations undeclared	✓
FTSE 100	✓
Gifts in kind	✓
Market-led giving	✓
Matched funding	✓
Payroll giving	✓

Charitable donations

Cash UK (latest available):	2014	£484,000
	2012	£578,000
Total UK (cash and in kind):	2014	£484,000
Cash worldwide:	2014	£484,000
Total worldwide (cash and in kind):	2014	£484,000

Community involvement

Good Together

According to the company's website, this programme was launched in 2009 and, following a 2012 review, it seeks to achieve the following teams and community targets by 2017:

- £7.5 million raised for the Premier Inn Clinical Building at Great Ormond St Hospital
- Costa Foundation to educate 50,000 children and have 50+ school projects in coffee growing communities
- WHR [Whitbread Hotels and Restaurants] – 10,000 nationally recognised qualifications for team members including 3,000 apprenticeships
- WHR [Whitbread Hotels and Restaurants] – 4,500 school work experience placements
- Costa – 20,000 enhanced skills training and 5,000 management progression opportunities

An example of local charitable contributions given in the Corporate Responsibility Report for 2013/14 notes a Costa store in Ripon presenting local pre-school, Puddleducks, with £850 towards new outdoor play facilities.

The Costa Foundation (Charity Commission no. 1147400)
The foundation was established in 2007 (registered independently in 2012) and aims to relieve poverty, advance education and the health and environment of coffee-growing communities around the world. The foundation's work follows on from the support Costa has provided for many years via funds donated to the Charities Trust, also a registered charity. According to the group's annual report and accounts for 2013/14, since 2008 a total of 40 schools or school projects have been completed in Colombia, Costa Rica, Ethiopia, Guatemala, Peru, Uganda and Vietnam. In 2013/14 over £1.5 million was raised through dedicated fundraising and donations. The Corporate Responsibility Report further states that 'more than £600,000 of this came from the commitment and fundraising efforts of Costa team members in stores and support offices'.

Great Ormond Street Hospital Children's Charity
Since 2012 Whitbread Hotels and Restaurants has chosen the charity as a long-term charity partner with the aim of helping children suffering from rare, complex and life-threatening conditions. The annual report and accounts for 2013/14 state:

> In June 2013 we announced that Whitbread Hotels & Restaurants had pledged £7.5 million towards the construction of a new clinical building at Great Ormond Street Hospital which is to be called The Premier Inn Clinical Building. The building will provide much needed new in-patient wards, more operating theatres and a recovery unit. It will contain a new surgery centre, respiratory ward and a specialist ward for children with severe forms of arthritis, skin conditions or infectious diseases. ... At the date of this report we have raised over £2.2 million towards the £7.5 million target.

The Corporate Responsibility Report for 2014 provides the update that £3 million has been raised to date (with £1.48 million collected during in 2013/14).

The group's partners include: Believe in Young People; Springboard; and The Prince's Trust.

Corporate giving

The group's 2014 CSR report states that, in support of Great Ormond Street Hospital, its Raise and Match scheme brought in £16,000 and Whitbread's matched funding contribution totalled almost £172,000. In support of The Costa Foundation, Whitbread contributed matched funding and a donation from Costa's profits that totalled £296,000.

We take the figure of £484,000 (comprising matched funding and Costa profits donations) to represent the group's charitable giving, as no other figures could be used. It appears that charitable cash giving to the two charities is mainly contributed by customers, employees and suppliers as opposed to the company itself and the value of in-kind support and other costs to the group could not be determined.

Beneficiaries include: Great Ormond Street Hospital Children's Charity; and The Costa Foundation.

In-kind support

The annual report and accounts note that a total of 16,905 volunteering hours were given in 2013/14.

Costa in local communities
During 2013/14 Costa launched a UK-wide local community partnership initiative encouraging store teams to give support to local community projects and get involved in local causes that matter to their customers. This support can come in the form of giving funds, space and time. The website notes that 'during 2013/14 hundreds of Costa stores were utilised by local community groups during and after trading hours' and became 'the venue for groups needing a place to meet in a warm, friendly environment with all the facilities provided for an informal meeting'. The community programme has already supported more than 240 activities and over 1,500 hours have been volunteered by Costa teams.

Work Inclusion
According to the 2014 CR report, this Costa programme saw 'managers working closely with prisons in Milton Keynes and Aylesbury to develop employability skills in prisoners, and the experience required for making superb coffee'. The programme was co-ordinated by Milton Keynes College. There were plans 'to roll the model out with Costa, to support prisoners across England, Wales and Scotland'.

Costa for Schools
During the year a new website created by teachers has been launched to provide UK secondary school teachers with the resources to support the delivery of certain parts of the national curriculum in Geography.

Employee-led support

Payroll giving
Give and Match is Whitbread's payroll giving scheme which allows employees to donate to their chosen charity. Whitbread will 'double match' each team member's first month's donation and pay all of their future monthly administration fees. In 2013/14 14% of team members participated and donated £350,000 to charities.

Matched funding
The Raise and Match scheme supports staff members who are fundraising in their own personal time for charities and good causes based in the UK. The scheme offers pound-to-pound matched funding to employees who have worked for Whitbread for more than 12 months and raise £250 or more. Up to a maximum of £750 is available for an individual's fundraising efforts and £1,500 for group fundraising efforts. In 2013/14 matched funding totalled £115,000 and benefited 65 charities.

Commercially led support

Education and training

Apprenticeships
The programme was introduced in 2010. In 2013/14 a total of 557 apprenticeships have been awarded.

Work experience
Aimed at 11- to 18-year-olds the scheme seeks to introduce hospitality industry as a career choice.

Work placements
In partnership with the Prince's Trust individuals between 17 and 24 years old are referred to undertake a work placement with Costa or Premier Inn. Further activities are undertaken in partnership with Job Centre Plus.

WISE
The group runs a skills and employment programme called WISE (Whitbread Investing in Skills and Employment), which is funded by a £4.3 million Employer Ownership grant from the government.

The above and related initiatives, such as business-related skills academies, form a major part of the group's corporate responsibility agenda. Team and Career Development is one of the three purposes of the Good for Team and

Community heading. The company includes the development of its workforce and job opportunities under this heading.

Corporate social responsibility

CSR committee: We found no indication of a separate CSR committee. According to the website:

> Responsibility for driving the [CR] strategy forward and delivering against [the group's] targets is part of the remit of the Boards and Executive Management Teams. This embedment of corporate responsibility into the key decision-making functions has enabled [Whitbread] to integrate the Good Together principles and targets into [its] strategic business plans.

CSR information: The following outlines the Chief Executive's statement on Corporate Responsibility:

> At Whitbread, we believe that a business should not just be about making profits, but should also make a valuable contribution to society. We have a corporate responsibility programme which we call Good Together, and our goal is to be a force for good in all the communities in which we operate. ... Sustainability is all about strategy and leadership, a visionary approach has helped us to embed sustainability into our business operating models, to the extent that today, Good Together is part and parcel of the way we think and act across Whitbread.

The website states:

> We are fully committed to our corporate responsibility programme, Good Together. This is the way we work together with our team members, our customers and our suppliers to be a Force for Good. We want to make lives better for our teams and communities through industry leading training and community programmes. We know our customers care and we want to help by providing trusted products and informed choices. We reduce our impact on the environment and take care of our business by using less carbon and water and managing waste effectively.

The three strategic pillars of Good Together are:

- Team and Community
- Customer Wellbeing
- Environmental Management

CSR report: There is a CSR report published.

Exclusions

Political donations are not made.

Applications

In writing to the correspondent.

Wilko Retail Ltd (formerly Wilkinson Hardware Stores Ltd)

Household, retail – DIY/ furniture

Correspondent: The Charity Department, J. K. House, Roebuck Way, Manton Wood, Worksop, Nottinghamshire S80 3EG (tel: 0800 032 9329; website: www.wilko.com)

Directors: Lisa Wilkinson, Family Director; Sean Toal; Ian Ellis, Chief Financial Officer; Stephen Sinclair (women: 1; men: 3)

Year end	01/02/2014
Turnover	£1,462,843,000
Pre-tax profit	£27,612,000

Nature of business: The principal activity of the Wilko group is high street retailing of products for family and home.

The accounts note that 'the company is wholly controlled by the Wilkinson family via direct interests and through trusts in which they jointly or individually have interests'.

Company registration number: 365335

Subsidiary undertakings include: Wilkinson Asia Ltd; Wilkinson Hardware Stores (Leicester) Ltd; Wilkinson Property Ltd; Wilkinson Retail Ltd; and W'Innovate Ltd. A full list of subsidiary undertakings is available from the company's accounts.

Main locations: Worksop

Total employees: 21,648

Focus of giving: Education, health, ill health, individuals, armed forces personnel, sponsorship, sport, recreation, children, young people, community/social welfare, disability.

Membership: BITC

Charity of the Year	✓
Gifts in kind	✓
Market-led giving	✓
Sponsorship	✓

Charitable donations

Cash UK (latest available):	2014	£308,000
	2013	£316,000
	2011	£800,000
	2009	£462,000
	2008	£400,000
Total UK (cash and in kind):	2014	£308,000
Cash worldwide:	2014	£308,000
Total worldwide (cash and in kind):	2014	£308,000

Community involvement

The annual report and accounts for 2013/14 state that all of the company's stores 'embraced [Wilko's] 2013/14 charity programme which enables [them] to play an active role in the local community.'

Corporate partners

Each retail region, service centres and Head Office have chosen their own charity to support. Beneficiaries chosen for 2014/15 cycle include: Birmingham Children's Hospital; Cash for Kids; Children's Hospice Association Scotland; Cornwall Air Ambulance; Dreams and Wishes; Great Ormond Street Hospital; Macmillan Cancer Support; Parkinson's UK; RNLI; and Warwickshire and Northamptonshire Air Ambulance. For a full list, see the company's website.

Local support

Helping Hands

Local charities or community groups in need of a 'Helping Hand' are invited to visit their local store to pick up an application form – either at the customer service desk or by asking a Wilkinson's Team Member. Each store has a small budget allocated to help its local good causes. The company states on its website:

> We want our donations to improve the lives of as many local people as possible and can make a big difference to lots of good causes. Whether you need a small raffle prize or pot of paint or even something a little bigger, come along to your local Wilkinson store to see if we can help you.

It is further reminded to give as much notice as possible as the company 'receives lots of application forms and [its] team members will meet once a month to review your request and get in contact with you as quickly as they can'.

Corporate giving

According to the company's annual report and accounts for 2013/14 a total of 35 charities were supported locally. It is noted that £1.35 million was raised and staff members donated 4,100 hours of volunteering. During the year 'payments of a charitable nature' totalled £308,000 (2012/13: £316,000). We have no details of specific donations but there is a list of supported charities given on the company's website.

Beneficiaries include: BBC's Children in Need; Birmingham Children's Hospital; Cash for Kids; Children's Hospice Association Scotland; Comic Relief; Cornwall Air Ambulance; Dreams and Wishes; Great Ormond Street Hospital; Macmillan Cancer Support; Parkinson's UK; RNLI; The Royal British Legion; and Warwickshire and Northamptonshire Air Ambulance.

In-kind support

Staff volunteering and fundraising efforts.

Employee-led support

The company's employees engage in a range of fundraising activities to support local charities as well as national causes. Volunteering time is also provided by the staff, which totalled 4,100 hours in 2013/14. In addition to helping local causes and the company's partner charities, employees across the business also get involved in national charity campaigns including helping BBC's Children in Need, Comic Relief and the Royal British Legion.

Commercially led support

Sponsorship

Local Stars

Wilko can sponsor 'life's big achievers from right across the UK' to help them fulfil their dreams. The company states on its website:

> Whether they've got a special talent, have overcome personal difficulties or benefitted others in their community – they're all winners in our eyes. If you or someone you know deserves to be recognised, then we'd love to hear all about it.

Carrier Bag Charge in Wales

The company's website states:

> In line with our long-established charity-giving procedures, we obtained valuable feedback from each of our stores (including our distribution centre in Wales) about which charity they most wanted to benefit under the requirements of the Welsh Carrier Bag Charge. Our Charity Committee carefully reviewed the nominations and the following charities were selected to receive the money (net proceeds equally split) raised through the carrier bag charge scheme.
>
> The successful charities we will partner with are as follows:
>
> - Keep Wales Tidy
> - Ty-Hafen (cancer charity)
> - Welsh air ambulance
> - Pettifor Trust (animal welfare)
> - Age UK Cymru

In 2013/14 the charities were each set to receive about £13,500.

Corporate social responsibility

CSR committee: There is a Corporate Social Responsibility committee which meets quarterly.

CSR information: The following statement is taken from the company's website:

> It is so important for Wilkinson to support and to be part of the communities that we serve. We aim to help our communities by supporting local registered charities that share our family values, culture and business heritage. We want to build sustainable local relationships through supporting charity, community initiatives and volunteering our time.

Wilko's CSR policies cover:

- CSR best practice
- Environment
- Energy
- Sustainable procurement
- Ethical practice
- Communities
- Engagement
- Diversity

CSR report: We did not find one published but some information is contained within the annual report and accounts.

Exclusions

No support is given for local appeals not in areas of company presence.

Applications

The company asks for applications for small donations to be directed to your local Wilko store. The application forms can be picked up from the store or downloaded from the website. Once completed they should be returned to the store.

Application forms for the Local Stars scheme can be picked up from your local store or downloaded from the website. Once completed, they should be posted to the correspondent. The application will then be considered by the Charity Committee. Note that 'Only completed Local Stars application forms will be considered please do not write in separately to the Local Stars Scheme.'

Any other enquiries can be made in writing to the correspondent at the company's address.

Willmott Dixon Holdings plc

Building/construction

Correspondent: Andy Geldard, Head of Communications – Foundation, Spirella 2, Icknield Way, Letchworth Garden City, Hertfordshire SG6 4GY (tel: 01462 671852; fax: 01462 681852; website: www.willmottdixon.co.uk)

Directors: Colin Enticknap, Chair; Rick Willmott, Group Chief Executive; Andrew Telfer; Jonathan Porritt; Christopher Sheridan; Paul Smith (women: 0; men: 6)

Year end	31/12/2013
Turnover	£1,038,451,000
Pre-tax profit	£12,974,000

Nature of business: The group is organised into three activities: contracting, development and property support. It provides major capital works construction to non-housing clients, including building fabric maintenance and care, interior design and fit-out, plus sustainable consultancy.

Company registration number: 198032

Subsidiary undertakings include: Prime Place Developments Ltd; Willmott Dixon Capital Works Ltd; Willmott Dixon Housing Ltd; Willmott Dixon Partnerships Ltd; and Willmott Dixon Support Services Ltd. A full list of subsidiary undertakings can be found in the group's accounts.

Main locations: Letchworth

UK employees: 3,070

Total employees: 3,070

Focus of giving: General charitable purposes, economic generation, enterprise/training, poverty and social exclusion, health, ill health, housing, homelessness, non-registered charities, small groups, armed forces personnel, older people, overseas projects, children, young people, community/social welfare.

Membership: BITC, LBG

Gifts in kind	✓
Humanitarian aid: UK	✓
Market-led giving	✓
Overseas giving	✓

Charitable donations

Cash UK (latest available):	2013	£173,000
	2009	£23,000
	2008	£5,000
	2007	£23,000
	2006	£18,000
Total UK (cash and in kind):	2013	£1,248,000
Cash worldwide:	2013	£173,000
Total worldwide (cash and in kind):	2013	£1,248,000

Community involvement

Willmott Dixon seeks to tackle social exclusion, inspire young people and lead community transformation. The group states:

> In addition, we feel that we can maximise our contribution to society by focusing on a particular social issue. Our adopted theme of Social Exclusion and Anti-social behaviour is an area which is closely aligned to the core values of the group and to which we feel the company is well placed to make a contribution.

Local businesses and sites work with their clients and the local communities to identify their needs, while at national and regional levels work is done with charity partners. These include: Action for Children; Construction Youth Trust; Prince's Trust; The Future Melting Pot; and UK Youth.

The group is also a partner and member of a number of other organisations such as the Carbon Trust, Energy Saving Trust and Passivhaus Trust (see the website for a full list). There are strong links with Birmingham city and many initiatives are focused there.

The Willmott Dixon Foundation (Charity Commission no. 326530)

The foundation supports projects which advance the training of young people and the welfare of people with special needs. According to its annual report and accounts for 2013, the foundation 'is dependent on funding from Willmott Dixon Holdings Ltd and donations through JustGiving'.

Community investment

According to the company's website, typical activities include: providing work experience; organising school visits; providing local employment or training; supporting community festivals; rejuvenating gardens for community groups and hospices; repainting community halls; and supporting community cafes.

Opening Doors Programme

The scheme 'provides skills, training and work experience for local people', where Willmott Dixon provides maintenance services to tenants.

There are a number of community investment case studies given on the group's website, some of which include:

4Life Academy

The academy 'supports the development of Birmingham apprentices as well as benefitting the wider community, who can take courses on technical trade skills, emerging technologies, health and safety, supervisor skills and energy efficiency', and also sessions on employability, IT, CV writing and DIY.

Adult Learners' Week

The group supported the event co-ordinated by the National Institute of Adult Continuing Education which aims to 'inspire people to discover how learning can change their lives'.

Play Day

Willmott Dixon organised a series of outdoor events as part of its Community Day initiative, 'which pledges to offer support to community groups and organisations which operate in areas in which the company works'. Play Day is organised by Play England.

Boxing gyms

To help with issues of social exclusion and to support young people to gain self-respect, the company provides support to boxing gyms in Oldham and Sheffield. A club in Sheffield was given assistance totalling £20,000 in addition to in-kind contributions (see the 'In-kind support' section).

Corporate giving

The 'sustainability' section on the website notes that in 2013 the value of community investment through the foundation totalled £1.37 million (up by 20% on 2012), which included the 'gift of time and skills, donations and other 'in-kind' services'. We deduct the amount raised by employees from the company's total contributions. The Willmott Dixon Foundation Annual Review 2013 (available online) further details the support:

Staff time	£1.1 million
Cash donations	£173,000
Fundraising	£122,000
In-kind support	£78,000

The support given was distributed between the following areas:

Community transformation	£605,000
Young people	£562,000
Social exclusion	£209,000
Other charities	£108,000
Other	£33,000

Beneficiaries included: Age UK; Autism Plus; BEN; Demelza; Diabetes UK; Help for Heroes; MSA Trust; Papyrus; Save the Children; Tom's Trust; and WellChild. A full list and further examples are available in the review.

Note: The Willmott Dixon Foundation's annual report and accounts for 2013 note that Gift Aid donations from Willmott Dixon Holdings Ltd totalled over £81,000. The charity gave £83,000 in grants.

See the corporate charity entry on p. 439 for more information.

In-kind support

The website states that during the year the group also provided:

- Mentoring to nearly 1,500 young people
- Work experience to 350 young people
- 50 presentations in schools to over 5,500 pupils
- Site visits for 2,400 schoolchildren

Staff members donate their time and expert skills; for example, in support of boxing gyms the group donated 600 hours of staff time to renovate the Sheffield's club facilities. Other in-kind support to the club totalled £7,000.

A fair amount of support is given through construction and renovation work in schools, hospitals, charities and so on.

Food banks

Support given includes the provision of new premises to Hounslow Community FoodBox and the donation of 50 Christmas Hampers with food supplies to People in Crisis.

Disaster relief

During the year the group responded to the appeal to help the victims of North Wales and Somerset flooding by providing insulation for temporary accommodation. Further work was also undertaken by the group's subcontractors to rebuild and repair some of the affected properties.

Employee-led support

Staff members volunteer and fundraise for good causes, with over £122,000 being collected in 2013. Volunteering activities included (amongst other things) helping greater Manchester Police through the Give and Gain Day, a UK-wide walking and cycling challenge in help of Dekamile and FareShare, and fundraising and in-kind support to the Special Care Baby Unit at Rotherham Hospital.

Construction Ambassadors' Scheme

The group participates in this scheme with its employees visiting schools, colleges and career events to promote construction as a rewarding career.

Commercially led support

Apprenticeships

According to the group, providing apprenticeships has been an important way to support local communities for years. The scheme helps people learn life-long skills while studying for a qualification, supported by a mentor. Since 2013 apprentices are shared with other organisations and work is being undertaken with Construction Industry Training Board to increase the number of shared apprenticeships.

Corporate social responsibility

CSR committee: There were no details found.

CSR information: The website states the following:

> We believe that sustainable development is about much more than internal policies, procedures and plans. It's about the quality and energy efficiency of the buildings we construct and maintain. It's about the relationships we build and the impact we have on local communities. It's about how we raise standards across the industry, and influence the quality of the built environment nationally.

Willmott Dixon's sustainability agenda underpins four themes:

- Putting People First
- Climate Change and Energy Efficiency
- Smarter Use of Natural Resources
- Responsible Business

Putting People First

The group's ambitions are to:

> Leave a lasting legacy in communities, helping them to thrive and prosper by enabling and creating a sustainable built environment; have a workforce that is safe, healthy, challenged and contented; inspire young people, particularly those who are socially-excluded, by providing opportunities for them to improve their lives; and add social value to the communities in which it works that is aligned to local needs within the context of wider social environment.

CSR report: An annual Sustainability Review is published and can be found on the group's website.

Corporate charity: The Willmott Dixon Foundation (Charity Commission no. 326530).

Exclusions

General and unsolicited appeals are not normally considered. Grants are not generally given for local appeals not in areas of company presence.

Applications

In writing to the correspondent. The group channels its giving through the corporate foundation.

WPP plc

Advertising/marketing, information management and communication

Correspondent: Vanessa Edwards, Head of Sustainability, 27 Farm Street, London W1J 5RJ (tel: 020 7408 2204; fax: 020 7493 6819; email: vanessa.edwards@wpp.com or enquiries@wpp.com; website: www.wpp.com)

Directors: Philip Lader, Chair; Martin Sorrell, Chief Executive Officer; Paul Richardson, Finance Director; Mark Read; Roger Agnelli; Jacques Airgrain; Charlene Begley; Colin Day; Esther Dyson; Orit Gadiesh; Dr John Hood; Ruigang Li; Daniela Riccardi; Jeffrey Rosen; Nicole Seligman; Hugo Shong; Timothy Shriver; Sally Susman; Sol Trujillo (women: 5; men: 14)

Year end	31/12/2013
Turnover	£11,019,400,000
Pre-tax profit	£1,295,800,000

Nature of business: WPP Group is an international family of companies providing a wide range of communications, management, advertising and public relations services.

Note the following information, taken from the annual report and accounts for 2013:

> On 30 August 2012, the Group announced its intention to return its headquarters to the United Kingdom. In order to effect its return to the United Kingdom, the Group put in place a new United Kingdom tax resident parent company (WPP 2012 plc) by means of a scheme of arrangement… The new scheme became effective on 2 January 2013, with WPP 2012 plc becoming the new parent company of the WPP Group and being renamed WPP plc. At the same time, the existing parent company of the WPP Group, WPP plc, was renamed WPP 2012 Ltd and, shortly after the Scheme became effective, changed its status to a private company.

WPP plc is a company incorporated in Jersey.

Company registration number: 111714

Subsidiary undertakings include: Grey Global Group, Inc.; GroupM Worldwide, Inc.; J. Walter Thompson Company, Inc.; TNS Group Holdings Ltd; and Young and Rubicam, Inc. A full list of the group's companies and subsidiary undertakings can be found within the annual report and accounts.

Main locations: London

UK employees: 11,925

Total employees: 117,115

Focus of giving: Human rights, education, environment, health, ill health, arts, culture, sponsorship, children, young people, community/social welfare.

Membership: BITC

FTSE 100	✓
Gifts in kind	✓
Market-led giving	✓
Sponsorship	✓

Charitable donations

Cash UK (latest available):	2013	£4,900,000
	2011	£4,800,000
	2009	£4,100,000
	2007	£3,500,000
	2006	£3,900,000
Total UK (cash and in kind):	2013	£4,900,000
Cash worldwide:	2013	£4,900,000
Total worldwide (cash and in kind):	2013	£19,600,000

Community involvement

WPP's Sustainability Policy on social investment states that 'WPP companies are encouraged to undertake pro bono work for not-for-profit organisations involved in tackling social and environmental issues' and 'make appropriate financial and other donations to social and environmental organisations'.

The company's social investment includes pro bono work, in-kind and cash donations to charity and employee volunteering. Pro bono projects are agreed between WPP companies and the charities concerned. The companies often have long-standing relationships with their pro bono partners. WPP, the parent company, helps to co-ordinate pro bono projects involving multiple WPP companies or cross-group collaborations.

The Sustainability Report for 2013 gives the following information relating to the UK charitable giving:

> The parent company supports charities and non-profit organisations, with a particular focus on education, the arts and young people. Our support includes advice on strategy and communications as well as financial donations.

Corporate giving

The Group CEO's statement in the Sustainability Report for 2013/14 says:

> Our companies continue to share their creative talents to support charities and non-profits working on some of society's greatest challenges. Our pro bono work, charitable donations and the free media space negotiated by WPP agencies on behalf of clients was worth £39.4 million in 2013.

The report details the 'total social contribution' in 2013 as follows:

Value of free media space	£19.8 million
Total pro bono	£14.7 million
Total charitable donations	£4.9 million
Total	**£39.4 million**

It is further explained that 'the total social contribution includes the pro bono work and charitable donations made by [the group's] companies, as well as the free media space negotiated by [its] media agencies on behalf of charity clients'. The sum does not include the value of volunteering undertaken by employees.

The group's 'social investment' was valued at £19.6 million (2012: £16.2 million). This figure 'includes cash donations to charities of £4.9 million and £14.7 million worth of pro bono work based on fees the organisations would have paid for [the] work'. The report also informs that 'the value of pro bono work increased by 31% on the previous year, while charitable donations saw a small decrease of 2%'.

Charitable donations and pro bono work in 2013 were distributed between the following categories:

Category	Charitable contributions	Pro bono work
Human rights	30%	24%
Health	31%	31%
Local community	21%	20%
Education	20%	14%
Arts	6%	5%
Environment	2%	6%

We take the figure of 'social investment' to represent the group's total charitable contributions. There was no breakdown of UK support or assistance given worldwide. Although we do not know what proportion of cash contributions went to UK organisations, previous organisations supported have in the main been registered in the UK; we have used the £4.9 million figure as the UK cash contribution.

Recent beneficiaries have included: British Red Cross Typhoon Haiyan Appeal; Central Saint Martin's College of Art and Design; Coram; Education and Employers Task Force UK; FIA Road Safety Campaign; Gates Cambridge Scholarships; Henry Jackson Initiative; IESE Business School; NABS; National Citizen Service; National Equality Standard; Place2Be; Royal College of Music; St Gabriel College; The British Museum; The City UK; The National History Museum; The National Portrait Gallery; The Outward Bound Trust; The Prime Minister's Dementia Challenge; The Prince's Foundation; The Queen Elizabeth Diamond Jubilee Trust; The Royal Foundation; and Word Economic Forum Sustainability Board.

Note: We have used the accounts of a new parent company WPP plc, incorporated in Jersey.

In-kind support

The group states on its website: 'Our companies have a long tradition of pro bono work – providing creative services to charities at little or no cost. This work can be invaluable, helping raise money and awareness for hundreds of good causes every year.' Assistance to charitable causes may be given through gifts in kind, joint promotions, small one-off campaigns, pro bono marketing and communication support, as well as long-term partnerships. There is a separate document giving examples of pro bono campaigns assisted by WPP in 2013, available online.

Employee-led support

Employee volunteering time and expert skills are available. The initiatives undertaken vary between operating companies. The Sustainability Report states:

> As a large employer, we are members of the communities where our companies are based. Our companies operate volunteering schemes at many of our locations. Volunteering can support employee engagement, team building and professional development. Many of our executives support charities by providing advice and support or by serving as trustees.

Organisations supported by the advisors or trustees of WPP included: Ad Council; Advertising Education Foundation; CLIC Sargent; Down Syndrome Association; East London Business Alliance; Leonard Cheshire Disability and Development Programme; Stephen Sills Foundation; Street Child Africa; Working for Change; and WWF. For more examples see the Sustainability Report.

Commercially led support

Sponsorship
Our research indicates that arts and education sponsorships can be offered. For instance, WWP has sponsored Charles Edward Brooke Girls' School, which specialises in media arts, the Royal College of Art, supported the National Portrait Gallery in London and provided awards for D&AD, the professional association for design and advertising.

Education and training
Throughout the group, apprenticeship and internship schemes are operating. For example, The Futures Company – an 'apprenticeship through City Gateway, a charity that provides training and employment opportunities for disadvantaged youngsters'. Currently about 4,000 internship positions are offered across the group.

A big part of the support given by the group is the provision of pro bono services, which, the website stresses,:

> also benefits WPP by showcasing [its] creative skills and ability to create compelling communications on a wide range of social and environmental issues. [WPP] people gain a breadth of experience and the chance to contribute to their communities

.

Corporate social responsibility

CSR committee: According to the website, 'WPP has a Sustainability Committee that advises on policy, monitors significant corporate responsibility risks and opportunities, determines sustainability strategy and co-ordinates communication among group companies.' The committee is made up of senior representatives from the companies and group functions and is chaired by the WPP Group Finance Director who assesses and presents the sustainability risks and performance to the board annually. The committee meets on the Sustainability Strategy Day each September to review progress on a variety of sustainability issues.

CSR information: The group's website states:

> WPP aims to make a positive contribution to society and the environment. We work hard to reduce our impact on the environment, to manage any ethical issues associated with our work, to support and engage our people and to help good causes through our pro bono work.

CSR report: An annual Sustainability Report and a review of the group's pro bono work are available on the group's website.

Exclusions

According to the Sustainability Report for 2013, 'WPP does not make political contributions from corporate resources with the occasional exception of very small, lawful contributions to local candidates in the US.'

Applications

In writing to the correspondent.

Wragge Lawrence Graham & Co. LLP

Legal

Correspondent: Lorna Gavin, Head of CR, 55 Colmore Row, Birmingham B3 2AS (tel: 01219 031000; fax: 01219 041099; email: lorna.gavin@wragge-law.com; website: www.wragge.com)

Directors: Quentin Poole, Designated Member; Ian Metcalfe, Designated Member (women: 0; men: 2)

Year end	30/04/2013
Turnover	£120,543,000
Pre-tax profit	£40,154,000

Nature of business: Wragge Lawrence Graham & Co. LLP is an international legal firm headquartered in the UK. The current body was formed after the merger of Wragge & Co. LLP and Lawrence Graham in 2014.

Company registration number: OC304378

Subsidiary undertakings include: As at 30 April 2013, Wragge & Co. LLP and Group had investments in various entities, including Ingleby Services, Wragge & Co. Limited, and Wragge & Co. Middle East LLP. As at 30 April 2013, Wragge & Co. LLP had the power to exercise or actually exercise control over various entities, including Wragge & Co. Legal AARPI and Wragge & Co. Legal Consultants LLC.

Main locations: London, Birmingham

Total employees: 960

Focus of giving: Education, health, ill health, housing, homelessness, inner cities, medical research, armed forces personnel, older people, arts, culture, children, young people, community/social welfare, disability.

Membership: BITC, LBG

Cash donations undeclared	✓
Charity of the Year	✓
Gifts in kind	✓

Charitable donations

Cash UK (latest available):	2013	£63,000
	2011	£67,000
	2009	£20,000
	2007	£45,000
	2004	£64,000
Total UK (cash and in kind):	2013	£63,000
Cash worldwide:	2013	£63,000
Total worldwide (cash and in kind):	2013	£63,000

Community involvement

The Wragge & Co. Charitable Trust (Charity Commission no. 803009)
The trust was established in 1990 to support various charitable organisations and causes and appears to be the main channel of charitable support. Generally assistance is given in the fields of children and young people, elderly people, health and disability and disadvantaged individuals in the West Midlands area and nationally.

Charity of the Year
Each year Wragge Lawrence Graham & Co. people nominate a charity to be supported. The website informs that during 2013 Make-A-Wish received support from the company as its nominated UK Charity of the Year. It is further noted that 'following ... a fundraising year in 2014 in which [the company] raised more than £65,000, [it] will be supporting Dogs for the Disabled during 2015'.

Memberships
Domestic violence
The company is a member of the Corporate Alliance Against Domestic Violence (CAADV) – a group of companies working collectively to raise awareness of the impact of domestic violence and to provide assistance and resources for employees.

LGBT
Wragge Lawrence Graham & Co. joined Stonewall's Diversity Champions programme which promotes good

practice regarding sexual orientation in the workplace. Following this commitment the company promoted LGBT events (for example, Out of Office, InterLaw Diversity Forum and Pride and Halcyon) and formed an in-house LGBT network. The firm was invited to join The Human Dignity Trust's Litigation Steering Group and provide international pro bono services to help the organisation's work towards changing the laws criminalising an individual's sexuality.

Corporate giving

The company's annual report and accounts for 2012/13 does not appear to declare charitable contributions.

The information available from the Wragge & Co. Charitable Trust's annual report and accounts for 2013/14 notes that during the year the trust received a total of almost £63,000 as Gift Aid donations. Grants were made to 106 charitable organisations totalling £68,000.

Note: We have used the accounts of the company before the merger (Wragge & Co. LLP), as these were the latest accounts available from Companies House at the time of writing.

Beneficiaries of the trust have included: Alzheimer's Society (£5,000); University of Birmingham (£3,600); WaterAid (£1,300); Movember Europe (£1,200); The Royal British Legion, The White Ensign Association Ltd and Wolverhampton Amateur boxing club (£500 each); Shelter (£300); Penny Brohn Cancer Care and Transplant Support Network (£100 each).

See the corporate charity entry on p. 439 for more information.

In-kind support

Wragge Lawrence Graham & Co. provides expert services free of charge, such as legal advice for not-for-profit organisations and job coaching for homeless people (the assistance given includes drafting CVs, preparing for interviews and giving people practical work experience). Our research suggests that the firm's staff have been reading partners with primary schoolchildren in some of the more deprived areas of Birmingham and London and acted as mentors to law students in local universities. The company's website notes that a total of 4,500 pro bono hours were given 'last year' (which we understand refers to 2014).

Employee-led support

The company's employees participate in volunteering and fundraising activities in support of good causes. An example includes a team of cyclists completing a 450-mile bike ride and raising more than £13,800 for the company's 2013 Charity of the Year: Make-A-Wish Foundation UK.

There is a team of Charity Champions across Birmingham and London who contribute to planning fundraising events. Events for 2015 include dress down days, coffee mornings, the annual big quiz, and walking and cycling challenges.

Commercially led support

'Day in the life of a lawyer' programme

The programme is aimed year 12 students in the Midlands who are interested in a career in law and targets 'talented students from backgrounds traditionally underrepresented in the legal profession'. As part of the programme students are offered work placements, role models and mentoring. In addition, one partial university sponsorship has recently been made available.

Corporate social responsibility

CSR committee: We did not find any indications of a CSR committee in the latest annual report and accounts or online sources.

CSR information: The company's website explains:

> We take our responsibility to our people, our environment and our communities seriously. Trust and transparency are embedded in everything we do and impact every business decision we make.
>
> For us, corporate responsibility is all about making connections and making a difference. Not just to benefit the not-for-profits, individuals and suppliers we work with; but to strengthen relationships with our communities and clients and for the personal and professional development of our people.

The main areas the company wants to address are: 'homelessness, education and inner city needs; reducing [its] impact on the environment; and encouraging responsible business behaviour with [its] external partners'.

CSR report: An annual Corporate Responsibility Report is published online.

Corporate charity: The Wragge & Co. Charitable Trust (Charity Commission no. 803009).

Exclusions

Our research indicates that grants for individuals or for local appeals not in the area of company presence are not normally made. Note that the trust does not support animal welfare and does 'not usually make grants to individuals or organisations which are not themselves charities'.

Applications

The company: Enquiries can be directed to the correspondent.

The trust: Applications to the trust should be made in writing to the charity's trustee Lee Nuttall (tel: 01212 331000) at 2 Snowhill, Birmingham B4 6RW. Our research suggests that a copy of the most recent accounts should be enclosed.

The trust's annual report for 2013/14 states:

> The day to day management of the charity is carried on by Wragge & Co. LLP, solicitors, by whom all applications for grants are coordinated and presented to the trustees. The trustees meet at intervals during the year to consider applications.

WSP Group Ltd

Professional support services

Correspondent: Mike Sheehan, UK Director of Sustainability, WSP House, 70 Chancery Lane, London WC2A 1AF (tel: 020 7314 5000 or 01256 318756; fax: 020 7314 5111; email: mike.sheehan@wspgroup.com; website: www.wspgroup.com)

Directors: Paul Dollin; Andrew Noble (women: 0; men: 2)

Year end	31/12/2013
Turnover	£6,850,000
Pre-tax profit	£685,000

Nature of business: WSP group is an international business supplying specialist management and integrated services in the built and natural environment.

The company is an intermediate holding company of WSP Global Inc., incorporated in Canada. The annual report and accounts for 2013 state that 'the company's immediate parent undertaking is WSP Holding UK Ltd'.

The group's Sustainability Report for 2013 notes that a total of 2,700 employees are working in the UK.

Company registration number: 2136404

Subsidiary undertakings include: WSP Group Africa (Pty) Ltd; and WSP Group Holdings Ltd. The information on subsidiary undertakings can be obtained from Companies House.

Main locations: London

UK employees: 22

Total employees: 22

Focus of giving: Advertising in charity brochures, education, environment, safety and crime prevention, disasters.

Membership: BITC

Cash donations undeclared	✓
Gifts in kind	✓
Market-led giving	✓
Payroll giving	✓

Charitable donations

Cash UK (latest available):	2013	£22,100
	2011	£24,000
	2009	£7,029
	2008	£35,180
	2007	£26,902
Total UK (cash and in kind):	2013	£22,100
Cash worldwide:	2013	£22,100
Total worldwide (cash and in kind):	2013	£22,100

Community involvement

Our research suggests that donations can be made mainly to local charities and organisations serving the communities in which the group operates. Causes supported normally cover economic, social and sustainable development of the communities. Donations may also be made to support charities with which staff members are involved.

Corporate giving

The company's annual report and accounts for 2013 did not appear to declare charitable donations. We were unable to find any other figures, therefore we estimate that the group has donated about £22,100, based on the figures from the three previous years known to us.

In-kind support

In the past the group has offered pro bono environmental consultancy services to medium-sized charities.

Employee-led support

We found indications of employees being engaged in fundraising activities in support of good causes, for example the British Heart Foundation. Employee volunteering time and expert skills may be available.

Payroll giving

Our research suggests that a wider-reaching Give As You Earn scheme was launched in 2008.

Commercially led support

Apprenticeships and work placements

WSP UK has a three-year long apprenticeship program. 'WSP is one of the founder members of the industry led Technician Apprenticeship Consortium that develops apprenticeship frameworks and opportunities across the industry in civil engineering and building services.'

Summer and industrial placements are offered to university students to work on projects across all sectors, within the UK and abroad. The website indicates that some universities may have a WSP scholarship scheme operating.

Corporate social responsibility

CSR committee: The global Sustainability Report makes a reference to the Corporate Responsibility Committee; however, it is unclear whether it refers to global operations or the UK business. The report also says: 'The Executive Committee is informed about sustainability matters through the Chair of the Primary Network of Sustainability ... Members speak for their respective operational regions [including UK] and are usually also members of these regions' Management Committees.'

CSR information: The group's four key sustainability objectives are to:

- Use the growth of the sustainable economy as an opportunity to grow new markets and commercial opportunities
- [Have] all of [the group's] advice and designs ready for the future and help [the] clients reduce environmental impacts over the life cycle of their assets
- Actively manage [its] own environmental and social impacts, improving the positive, reducing the negative
- Be an active participant in the communities in which [it] operates

CSR report: There was no evidence of a separate CSR report for the UK business. A global Sustainability Report is available on the website, but it focuses on business activities.

Exclusions

Support is not generally provided for general or circular appeals, individuals, political or religious causes, or local appeals not in areas of company presence.

Applications

In writing to the correspondent.

Xerox (UK) Ltd

Print/paper/packaging

Correspondent: M. J. Barrett, Company Secretary, Bridge House, Oxford Road, Uxbridge UB8 1HS (tel: 01895 251133; website: www.xerox.com)

Directors: Francis Mooney; Mary O'Driscoll; Marion Richards; Darren Cassidy, Managing Director; Olivier Dehon (women: 2; men: 3)

Year end	31/12/2013
Turnover	£258,700,000
Pre-tax profit	£8,000,000

Nature of business: The principal activity of the group is marketing and financing of xerographic and electronic printing equipment, document managing systems and ancillary supplies in the UK.

The ultimate parent company of Xerox (UK) Ltd is Xerox Corporation, incorporated in the USA.

Company registration number: 330754

Subsidiary undertakings include: Bessemer Trust Ltd; and Xerox Finance Ltd.

Main locations: Mitcheldean, Cambridge, Welwyn Garden City

UK employees: 2,237

Total employees: 2,237

Focus of giving: General charitable purposes, economic generation, education, enterprise/training, animal welfare, health, ill health, older people, arts, culture, poverty and social exclusion, sport, recreation, children, young people, community/social welfare, disability.

Gifts in kind ✓

Charitable donations

Cash UK (latest available):	2013	£0
	2010	£30,000
	2009	£0
	2008	£60,000
Total UK (cash and in kind):	2013	£0
Cash worldwide:	2013	£0
Total worldwide (cash and in kind):	2013	£0

Community involvement

Normally the company provides support through its corporate charity.

The Xerox (UK) Trust (Charity Commission no. 284698)

The charity was established to support education, health, disability, arts and culture, sports, animals, economic generation, relieve poverty and assist other charitable causes.

Charity partnership

The annual report and accounts state:

> We are very proud to have become patron of the Prince's Trust during 2013. We look forward to our employees being involved in many team building events including sponsored marathons and bike rides which will raise funds for the trust. Xerox employees will be encouraged to work alongside the young people of the trust in volunteering opportunities and possible work placements.

Corporate giving

According to the annual report and accounts for 2013 no donations have been made to Xerox (UK) Trust (2012: £30,000), 'as the directors deemed there to be sufficient funds for charitable purposes in respect of the year'.

Past beneficiaries of the trust have included: Birmingham Youth Foundation; Clapton Common Boys Club; Holidays For Disabled People; Inspirations; Kids'n'Action; Mid Sussex Community Support Association; and The Sunrise Education Trust.

Beneficiaries of the company: Prince's Trust.

See the corporate charity entry on p. 440 for more information.

In-kind support

Staff volunteering time and expert skills.

Employee-led support

The company's employees are encouraged to participate in various activities to support organisations supported by the company.

Globally there are volunteer initiatives, such as the Community Involvement Program or Social Service Leave which allow employees to donate their time and efforts for good causes.

Corporate social responsibility

CSR committee: There is no evidence of a CSR committee for the UK company.

CSR information: The CSR section within the annual report and accounts notes the following: 'The company is committed to reducing its impact on the environment, and in line with group policy, continues to review and develop initiatives to reduce waste and minimise energy consumption.'

CSR report: We found no indications of a UK CSR report. There is a Global Report on Corporate Citizenship.

Corporate charity: The Xerox (UK) Trust (Charity Commission no. 284698).

Exclusions

Our research shows that strictly no support is given for non-registered charities or charities concerned with non-UK activities or causes.

Applications

The company: In writing to the correspondent.

The trust: The contact person for trust-related enquiries is Cheryl Walsh (tel: 01895251133) at the company's address.

Yattendon Group plc (formerly Yattendon Investment Trust)

Agriculture, leisure, media, print/paper/packaging, property

Correspondent: Catherine Fleming, Trustee of the Iliffe Family Charitable Trust, Barn Close, Burnt Hill, Yattendon, Newbury, Berkshire RG18 0UX (tel: 01635 203929; email: info@yattendongroup.co.uk; website: www.yattendongroup.co.uk)

Directors: Lord Iliffe, Chair; Francois Austin; David Fordham; Simon Gray; Edward Iliffe, Group Chief Executive; Michael Spencer; Stephen Sadler, Group Finance Director (women: 0; men: 7)

Year end	31/03/2014
Turnover	£74,450,000
Pre-tax profit	£7,008,000

Nature of business: Yattendon Group plc is a private company owned by the Iliffe family, which operates in the UK and North America through its subsidiaries. Principal business activities include marina operations, farming, printing and property development and renting. Previously the group operated a publishing business, which was sold in 2013 (Yattendon group has retained its state-of-the-art printing press in Cambridge).

Company registration number: 288238

Subsidiary undertakings include: MDL Developments Ltd; MDL Marinas Group Ltd; MK Web Ltd; Ocean Village Resorts Ltd; Sant Carles Marina SA; and Westminster Management Corporation. A full list of subsidiary undertakings can be obtained from Companies House.

Main locations: Thatcham

Total employees: 388

Focus of giving: Education, environment, animal welfare, health, ill health, heritage, medical research, older people, arts, culture, religion, children, young people, community/social welfare, disability.

Cash donations undeclared ✓

Charitable donations

Cash UK (latest available):	2014	£225,000
	2011	£350,000
	2010	£175,000
	2009	£150,000
	2008	£150,000
Total UK (cash and in kind):	2014	£225,000
Cash worldwide:	2014	£225,000
Total worldwide (cash and in kind):	2014	£225,000

Community involvement

The group gives through its corporate charity; two of the directors are the trustees of the trust.

The Iliffe Family Charitable Trust (Charity Commission no. 273437)

The trust was established in 1977 to support charitable organisations for 'such exclusively charitable objects and purposes in the United Kingdom or in any other part of the world as the trustees ... think fit'. In practice, the majority of donations are made to UK-registered charities in the areas of education, health and disability, welfare, religion, conservation and heritage, children and young people and the elderly.

Beneficiaries of the trust have included organisations such as: Alzheimer's Research UK; Afghan Connection; Ellen McArthur Cancer Trust; Macmillan Cancer Support; QUEST Scholarship; Red Squirrel Survival Trust; RNLI Crew Training; and Watermill Theatre.

Corporate giving

The group did not appear to declare its charitable donations in its annual report and accounts for 2013/14. Based on the figures from the three previous years known, we estimate that the group's cash contributions totalled about £225,000 in 2013/14.

The trust's annual report and accounts for 2012/13 (the latest available at the time of writing) note:

> The trustees have a policy to distribute all the income arising each year subject to funding applications received. The trust holds a restricted capital account of £608,219 which is made up of investments deriving from shares and securities settled to the trust by the Iliffe family which are held to generate funds to distribute to charitable purposes.

In 2012/13 there was no 'distribution from RPR and JD Iliffe 1982 Settlement'.

During the year the trust had an income of almost £31,000, all of which consisted of investment income. We found no indications of any Gift Aid donations from the company in 2012/13. In the previous years such donations have totalled £350,000 (2011), £175,000 (2010), £150,000 (2009) and £150,000 (2008) – averaging at about £206,000 per year. No other donations were made by the company in this financial year.

Corporate social responsibility

CSR committee: We found no indications of a CSR Committee.

CSR information: No CSR information available.

CSR report: None found.

Exclusions

No grants are given to individuals and rarely to non-registered charities. Political donations do not seem to be made.

Applications

Applications to the trust can be made in writing to the correspondent at the company's address. The trustees do not always apply to unsuccessful applicants for grants.

Yorkshire Building Society

Building society, financial services

Correspondent: Pauline Giroux, Corporate Responsibility Manager, Yorkshire House, Yorkshire Drive, Bradford BD5 8LJ (tel: 01274 472512; website: www.ybs.co.uk)

Directors: Ed Anderson, Chair; Lynne Charlesworth, Vice Chair; Philip Johnson; John Heaps, Chair Designate; Guy Parsons; Mark Pain; David Paige; Chris Pilling, Chief Executive Officer; Mike Regnier; Andy Caton; Ian Bullock; Robin Churchouse, Chief Operating Officer and Finance Director; Kate Barker (women: 2; men: 11)

Year end	31/12/2013
Turnover	£1,405,600,000
Pre-tax profit	£199,300,000

Nature of business: The Building Society provides financial services, including mortgages, insurance products and financial advice. Yorkshire Building Society is part of a bigger group that includes Barnsley Building Society, Chelsea Building Society and Norwich and Peterborough Building Society.

The number of employees given consists of both full-time (3,327) and part-time (891) staff members.

FSA registration number: 106085

Subsidiary undertakings include: Accord Mortgages Ltd; Chelsea Mortgage Services Ltd; Lynch Wood Services Ltd; Norwich and Peterborough Share Dealing Services Ltd; YBS Properties Ltd; and Yorkshire Guernsey Ltd. A full list of subsidiaries is published in the annual report and accounts.

UK employees: 4,218

Total employees: 4,218

Focus of giving: Fundraising events, animal welfare, health, ill health, housing, homelessness, small groups, local groups, older people, poverty and social exclusion, children, young people, community/social welfare, disability.

Charity of the Year	✓
Gifts in kind	✓
Payroll giving	✓

Charitable donations

Cash UK (latest available):	2013	£1,200,000
	2011	£45,250
	2009	£75,000
	2008	£75,000
	2007	£50,000
Total UK (cash and in kind):	2013	£1,200,000
Cash worldwide:	2013	£1,200,000
Total worldwide (cash and in kind):	2013	£1,200,000

Community involvement

Societies Together

According to the group's website, this community programme across the group of building societies 'aims to inspire people to make a difference by getting involved in community, charity and volunteering work'. Members of the society, local residents and people working in Yorkshire are all invited to participate. The programme has four main initiatives:

- Marie Curie Hour of Need Campaign (2014–16)
- Yorkshire Building Society Charitable Foundation
- Actionteering
- Community Involvement

Marie Curie Hour of Need Campaign (2014–16)

The campaign aims to raise £500,000 by December 2016. The website notes that 'throughout the campaign our colleagues, members and the general public will be involved in a variety of exciting fundraising activities and events. Our colleagues will also be volunteering their time and experience to Marie Curie'.

Yorkshire Building Society Charitable Foundation (Charity Commission no. 1069082)

The foundation supports registered charities that provide help to vulnerable individuals, particularly the elderly, children and people with disabilities, also animal causes, individuals with special needs and those suffering from hardship. It is run by five trustees, three of which are independent of the society. Assistance can be given in the areas where the society's members and staff reside. It is noted that 80% of causes are nominated by members. Preference is given on small donations for specific tangible items. Direct applications can receive grants of up to £500 and causes nominated by the members and staff can receive grants of up to £2,000. The foundation's 2013 annual report states that:

> The foundation receives donations from the society and other funding arranged by the society in connection with specific grant giving activities. This additional funding comes primarily from the Small Change Big Difference (SCBD) scheme which the society includes as an optional term in most of its savings and mortgage products [see 'Employee-led support'].

Community involvement

In addition to providing support to national projects through the foundation, the society helps local initiatives. Causes can be nominated by members at their local branches. The website states:

> Whether it's a small one-off monetary gift or a benefit-in-kind donation, it's another way that we're giving back to the communities our members and employees live and work in.

The Yorkshire Building Society annual report and accounts for 2013 state the following:

> It is important to us that our people across the branch network and within our Head Offices connect with their local communities. During 2013 we rolled out a branch revitalisation programme across the Yorkshire and Chelsea networks that put our branches even more at the heart of their communities. This includes our Charity Choices programme where members of the community elect which local charities their branch will support.

Charity partnership

The society was 'honoured to be made the Royal National Lifeboat Institution's (RNLI) Corporate Supporter of the Year'. The partnership continued for the second year (2012–13) and raised £154,000 in 2013.

Corporate giving

The annual report and accounts further note:

> In 2013 the group donated £1.2 million to charities, good causes and community groups across the UK ... In addition our Charity partnership with the Royal National Lifeboat Institution (RNLI) continued for a second year, raising £154,000 in 2013.

We understand that the latter sum was raised through various fundraising events by employees, members and the general public (similar to the Marie Curie campaign). A total of 2,800 good causes were supported across the UK. We have used the declared amount of £1.2 million as the society's total UK cash contribution.

The foundation's annual report and accounts for 2013 state: 'In so far as it is complementary to and supportive of the charity's objects, the charity works closely with the society.' The foundation's income was received from gifts and donations which also included:

Donations from SCBD	£382,000
Donations from Yorkshire Building Society	£80,000
Donations received from fundraising events	£8,700

See the corporate charity entry on p. 441 for more information.

In-kind support

In-kind gifts are available, including employee time and fundraising efforts. The society states – 'We know that time can be just as valuable a gift as money to charities and community groups.'

Employee-led support

Actionteering

In 2013 a total of 9,016 employee hours were spent supporting local community projects. Every employee is given two days paid leave each year to work on voluntary or charitable activities. According to the website, since the beginning of the programme in 2007, over 13,000 hours have been donated. Individually undertaken volunteering projects include::

> becoming student mentors; becoming business mentors; helping social enterprises to set up; assisting teachers with reading and number-partner activities at local schools; and offering friendship and support to the elderly with weekly phone calls

.

Managers across the society and employees from all parts of the group also get involved in team activities. For example, 'building outdoor classrooms and nature trails at local primary schools, creating sensory gardens for sight impaired children and redecorating and rejuvenating community centres'.

Small Change Big Difference
According to the foundation's 2013 annual report, the scheme works as follows:

> Holders of savings or loan accounts agree to the transfer to the charity an amount equivalent to the pence of interest received on a savings account, or, rounding up to the nearest pound, the pence of interest paid on a mortgage account (never exceeding 99p per year, per account). Members of the society can opt out of the SCBD scheme at any time.

The average donation is under 50p per year. Current number of participating accounts is over 800,000 and since its inception in 2000 the scheme has raised almost £3 million.

Make a Difference Week
This annual initiative invites members of the society to nominate charities and good causes to receive a small donation. The week is funded by members participating in the Small Change Big Difference (SCBD) scheme.

Corporate social responsibility

CSR committee: We found no details of a specific CSR committee. There is a 'dedicated team of experts' – the Societies Together Team – 'which co-ordinates wide range of activities ensuring they keep going from strength to strength'.

CSR information: The Corporate Responsibility Report for 2013 notes:

> Our contribution to society goes beyond providing great customer service and simple, straightforward products. Through our Societies Together programme we're also proud to play a key role in the local communities we're part of, supporting causes close to your hearts.

CSR report: A CSR report is contained within the annual report and accounts.

Corporate charity: Yorkshire Building Society Charitable Foundation (Charity Commission no. 1069082).

Exclusions

The society's website states:

> Please be aware, we are unable to support contributions towards large funds, expenses, fees, salaries, administration, research or sponsorship of individuals and events. We also can't support the advancement of religious or political activities (including specific sectors of the community), mainstream schools and other local or government funded bodies.

The foundation's guidelines provide the following examples where support could not be given:

- Applications for general on-going funding, running costs, research, sponsorship, payment of salaries or expenses
- Requests for any administration equipment, such as telephones, security systems or computers, for a charity's own use
- Causes serving only a specific sector of the community selected on the basis of ethnic, racial, political or religious grounds/advancement
- Overseas travel, expeditions or educational expenses, including causes that would otherwise qualify for support but require funds for activities outside the UK
- Support of activities in, or equipment for mainstream schools, sports clubs, scouts/guides groups, local/ government funded bodies (unless for special needs groups). However, scouts/guides groups may be considered on an individual application basis taking into consideration levels of deprivation, etc

Applications

The foundation: Applications to the foundation can be made online. The foundation's administrator is Nirmisha Popat (tel: 01274706606, email: charitable@ybs.co.uk) at the society's address. The society's members and staff can also nominate a cause to be supported by the foundation.

Local causes: Nominations for local initiatives to be supported are received from members of the society or through the society's branches or head office departments. Members can 'just speak to one of the team who can tell [them] more about how the process works and our possible support for [their] nomination'. This helps ensure support is given to local charities and good causes in areas important to members and staff.

Zurich Financial Services (UKISA) Ltd

Insurance, life assurance

Correspondent: Sophie Spink, Head of CR, Zurich House, 2 Gladiator Way, Farnborough, Hampshire GU14 6GB (tel: 01252 387779; email: sophie.spink@uk.zurich.com; website: www.zurich.co.uk)

Directors: Eugen Angehrn; Stephen Lewis; Oscar Tengtio; Paul Sutton; John Dyke; Neil Evans; Neil Freshwater; Gary Shaughnessy (women: 0; men: 8)

Year end	31/12/2013
Pre-tax profit	(£42,200,000)

Nature of business: Zurich Financial Services (UKISA) is a holding company and part of the Zurich Financial Services Group. The company comprises the group's operations in the UK, Ireland and South Africa and provides insurance services.

The annual report and accounts state that 'staff are not employed directly by the company'. The UK website notes the group having over 60,000 employees worldwide with 11,000 in the UK. We use these figures.

Company registration number: 1860680

Subsidiary undertakings include: Allied Dunbar Assurance plc; Eagle Star Holdings Ltd; Sterling ISA Managers Ltd; Zurich Employment Services Ltd; and Zurich Finance (UK) plc. A full list of subsidiary undertakings can be obtained from Companies House.

Main locations: Swindon

UK employees: 11,000

Total employees: 60,000

Focus of giving: General charitable purposes, education, health, ill health, housing, homelessness, older people, overseas projects, poverty and social exclusion, sponsorship, children, young people, community/social welfare, disability.

Membership: BITC, LBG

Cash donations undeclared	✓
Gifts in kind	✓
Matched funding	✓
Overseas giving	✓
Payroll giving	✓

Charitable donations

Cash UK (latest available):	2013	£2,260,000
	2011	£2,670,000
	2008	£2,655,000
	2007	£1,900,000
	2006	£1,900,000
Total UK (cash and in kind):	2013	£2,260,000
Cash worldwide:	2013	£2,260,000
Total worldwide (cash and in kind):	2013	£2,260,000

Community involvement

Zurich Community Trust (UK) Ltd (Charity Commission no. 266983)
According to the trust's 2013 annual report, the charity delivers support through grant-making and volunteer programmes in the UK and overseas which are aimed at 'helping disadvantaged people to move from dependence to independence'. The trust states: 'our long-term social transformation programmes tackle key social issues in innovative ways and seek to deliver long-term sustainable solutions'. It also, as stated on the 'Community trust' section of the Zurich website, supports 'Zurich's commitment to corporate responsibility with numerous other initiatives and by encouraging employees to dedicate both time and money.' The charity is funded by an annual donation from the Zurich UK businesses and by donations from Zurich UK employees.

Support is given through the following programmes:

UK Grant and Volunteer Programme
The programme supports three national partners, which currently are Alzheimer's

Society, CLIC Sargent and Mind, and helps local charities in the areas of the company's presence. 'Zurich employees are involved in the selection of [the three] national partnerships and provide input to the ongoing support of them.'

According to the trust's 2013 annual report and accounts, 'a wide range of local and overseas charities are supported each year through grant programmes with an emphasis on core funding and multi-year relationships'. The website states that grants given range from £100 to £5,000 (depending on location) and can fund 'a range of issues including supporting carers, special needs children, older people, people with disabilities, counselling, homeless people and many more'.

Zurich Cares
This fund is the employee engagement programme. It is supported by the trust and jointly funded through employee donations and matched funding from the Zurich business donation to the trust.

Overseas Grant Programme
This programme supports UK charities working overseas, particularly in the Middle East, Africa and Asia. According to the website, the annual budget for the fund is £70,000.

Social transformation programmes
According to the Zurich UK CR report 2012/13, these 'focus on key social issues that are often overlooked and where the trust can have the biggest impact' and seek to 'create sustainable change through long-term funding and active Zurich employee involvement'. Currently activities are aimed at addressing 'generational drug misuse in families, supporting isolated older people through a telephone befriending service and providing help to young people dealing with mental health issues'.

Openwork Foundation
The network is formed from over 780 financial advice firms backed by the worldwide Zurich group. The objective of the Openwork Foundation is to help disadvantaged children in the UK and overseas. The Zurich Community Trust (UK) Ltd supports the foundation as a subsidiary fund. The fund is supported by the trust and funded through donations from advisors and employees of Openwork Ltd. The trust's annual report and accounts state:

> [It] also provides in-kind support by covering most of the salary of the Openwork Foundation Manager currently seconded to the Zurich Community Trust Team. Zurich employees along with advisors and employees of Openwork are involved in supporting the delivery of the fundraising, volunteering and grant giving programmes under the guidance and responsibility of the team who work for the trust, in line with the delegation document from the board of trustees.

Currently the foundation's focus is Cares 4 Kids, 'which supports disadvantaged children and young people between 0 and 18 years of age in the UK and overseas who face social, physical or mental challenges'. Grants are provided to charities 'to deliver change that lasts, providing long-term solutions and support for these children.'

The network's partners have included: Carers Trust (2012–16); The Philippine Community Fund; and Together for Short Lives. Further grants have been awarded to various organisations (see the website for details).

Note: According to the Zurich Community Trust website: 'The Openwork Foundation only considers applications that have been nominated by a member of Openwork or employees ... The Foundation awards local grants of £3000 – £10,000 and covers both capital and revenue funding.'

India Programme
The Zurich UK CR report 2012/13 states that for over 18 years the programme has combined 'core funding with the sharing of skills through an assignment programme to help [its] NGO partners build their capacity'.

Group initiatives
According to the Zurich CR website, globally Zurich Group's CSR activities include flood resilience projects comprising 'flood research, community-based programs and risk expertise' and working in partnership with the International Federation of Red Cross and Red Crescent Societies (IFRC), Practical Action (a UK-based international NGO) and two research institutes.

There is a global Z Zurich Foundation which 'expresses [the company's] commitment to community involvement at the Zurich Group level'. Its aim is to help individuals and communities manage risk.

Corporate giving

We could not find the declaration of charitable donations in Zurich Financial Services (UKISA) Ltd's annual report and accounts. According to the trust's annual report and accounts in 2013 a total of £2.26 million (2012: £1.51 million) was donated by Zurich. In addition, more than £1 million (2012: over £1 million) was raised via Zurich employees and members of Openwork through regular giving and fundraising activities. We use the figure £2.26 to represent Zurich's charitable donations in the UK.

Beneficiaries have included: Addaction; Age UK; Alzheimer's Society; CLIC Sargent; Mind; Place2Be; and Prince's Trust.

Note: Although we have used the accounts for Zurich Financial Services (UKISA) Ltd (1860680), the trust's annual report and accounts state:

> Voluntary income includes the amount receivable under Gift Aid from Zurich Assurance Ltd, Zurich Management Services Ltd and Zurich Insurance Group Ltd group staff and members of Openwork. Also included are other voluntary donations received.

See the corporate charity entry on p. 442 for more information.

In-kind support

In-kind support is provided. This includes assistance from Zurich employees in supporting the Zurich Community Trust's activities. These also include:

- 'Business to charity mentoring' – internal and external mentoring schemes between a staff member and the CEO or senior manager of a local or national charity
- Skillshare projects – 'usually one-off projects designed to make a quick and valuable difference to a community organisation' can take between two and 20 hours with Zurich employees providing their expert skills

Employee-led support

Employee Involvement – Zurich Cares
The trust's annual report and accounts for 2013 state that it 'uses some of the financial donation from the Zurich UK businesses to match the financial donations from Zurich employees'. Business time is also provided 'to enable employees to volunteer in the community and get involved in organising and managing fundraising events, volunteering schemes and local grant programmes'. Staff members' personal time is also given through various programmes.

According to the website, 'over 40% of the Zurich UK workforce is engaged in sharing their skills with the community each year'. Volunteering activities may include: 'team challenge; lunchtime volunteering schemes; virtual volunteering; India assignments; telephone befriending older people; and one-off opportunities'. More details and examples can be found on the company's website.

Evolving programme
The new programme is 'aimed at supporting Zurich retirees by providing them with the opportunity to use the valuable skills and experience developed at work, and to learn new ones'.

Payroll giving
Staff can contribute to the Zurich Cares programme through a Give As You Earn

scheme. There is 'a monthly lottery and a scheme where employees can round up the pennies from their pay each month provides additional regular income'. The website notes that about 23% of all employees give regularly to the Zurich Cares programme through the scheme.

Matched funding

According to the CR Report for 2012/13 there is a matching programme which provides matching grants to charities that employees have raised funds for and a Trustee and Governor scheme which provides 'an annual grant of £200 to a charity or school where an employee volunteers as a Trustee or School Governor'. The website states that each donation through the payroll scheme is 100% matched by the trust.

Commercially led support

My Community Starter

According to www.mycommunitystarter.co.uk (created by Zurich), this free information resource is available to help 'people who want to get involved in organising smaller, straightforward community activities' to help people understand and overcome potential barriers to volunteering in the local community. The website will help the public to understand some of the legal, health and safety, planning issues and insurance considerations of whatever they are involved in. The website offers a free personalised starter pack.

Support for the voluntary sector

The information in this section is gathered from the 2012/13 CR report.

Risk Guides

Zurich has produced free risk guides aimed specifically at the voluntary sector. 'For example, 'Planning for and dealing with major incidents' contains guidance to help organisations prepare for a crisis and minimise the impact should the worst happen, minimising the impact on beneficiaries.'

Partnerzones

In collaboration with *The Guardian* newspaper, Zurich has set up a Teachers Partnerzone and a voluntary sector Partnerzone, where it shares its expertise on risk.

Arson Combated Together (ACT)

ACT is an initiative developed by the company together with the Fire and Rescue Services and other arson-related organisations. Its aim is to teach children about the risk and consequences of arson. In addition the company states that its lobbying was instrumental in persuading the government to ensure that all new school buildings include sprinkler systems.

Education

The 2012/13 CR report also provides the following information:

The School We'd Like

The competition, organised in conjunction with *The Guardian* newspaper, was 'designed to encourage students and teachers to work together to develop an idea that will improve the quality of life for their school community' for which a prize of £5,000 was given.

Fire safety

In 2013 working with the Department of Communities and Local Government Zurich 'provided fire safety advice to universities and their students, highlighting the risks of fire in halls of residence and suggesting preventative measures'. A free tool called the 'Risk Curriculum' was developed to provide schools 'with guidance and support across a broad spectrum of areas including Risk Management, Business Continuity, Health and Safety, Liability and Fire and Security Guidance'.

UK Flood Guide

This free guide provides advice on preparing for a flood, dealing with flood and beginning recovery and is available online. 'It builds on lessons learned from significant flooding in recent years, such as the UK-wide floods of 2012.' There is also a severe weather microsite maintained which offers 'before', 'during' and 'after' guidance to people coping with severe weather. The CR Report for 2012/13 states that 'the microsite continues to be a central information resource for those seeking advice and guidance on the range of issues associated with flooding and other severe weather events in the UK'.

Sponsorship

Our research suggests that arts and good-cause sponsorship may be undertaken.

Corporate social responsibility

CSR committee: There is a Corporate Responsibility Council in the UK. It 'acts as a steering group for all CR activity' and 'includes senior representatives from all areas of the business to ensure [the] objectives and activities are directly linked to the business strategy'.

CSR information: The following statement is taken from the Zurich UK website:

> At Zurich we embrace Corporate Responsibility (CR) and understand the need to set and maintain high standards of integrity towards our customers, employees, local communities, society and the environment. We are proud of a corporate community programme that contributes to both our global and local communities. In the UK, we demonstrate our commitment to Corporate Responsibility with numerous Zurich initiatives and the dedication of both time and money.

Zurich UK focuses on four priority areas which are: Workplace; Marketplace; Environment; and Communities.

CSR report: An annual CSR report is published and available from the company's website.

Corporate charity: Zurich Community Trust (UK) Ltd (Charity Commission no. 266983).

Exclusions

Our research suggests that no grants are given to:

- Individuals
- Medical research
- Advertising or sponsorship connected with charitable activities
- Fundraising events
- Animal welfare
- Conservation or environmental projects
- Emergency or disaster appeals
- Political, religious or mainstream educational institutions
- Statutory organisations
- Scouts, guides, cadets and other similar organisations
- Sports clubs, village halls, playgroups and mother and toddler groups

Funding may still be given to some of the above if the purpose will directly benefit people with disabilities or special needs groups.

Applications

The company: Enquiries regarding the company's Corporate Responsibility Programme can be directed at the correspondent.

The trust: The principal contact for trust related enquiries is Pam Webb (tel: 01793 502450; email: pam.webb@zct.org.uk) at PO BOX 1288, Swindon SN1 1FL. More details can be found online at www.zurich.co.uk/zurichcommunitytrust/home/home.htm.

Trust programmes: Note that potential partners are generally researched, identified and selected for participation by the trust. Applications for grants for local community organisations and overseas projects can be made online.

Corporate foundations

This edition of the guide provides a new source of information in the shape of corporate charities. All the 114 corporate charities included have a close association with the company to which they are linked, usually relying on those companies for a substantial part of their income.

Each entry provides an overview of charitable activities as well as details on grant-making such as the number of grants made, the total value of those grants, the beneficiaries and beneficial areas. This information can provide a useful starting point for any organisation considering applying to a corporate charity for funding.

Aberdeen Asset Management Charitable Foundation

Education, social welfare, children and young people

£682,000 (2012/13)

Beneficial area

UK and overseas where the company has a presence.

Correspondent: Anne Richards, Trustee, 10 Queen's Terrace, Aberdeen AB10 1YG (tel: 01224 631999; fax: 01224 647010; email: foundation.uk@aberdeen-asset.com; website: www.aberdeen-asset.com/aam.nsf/foundation/home)

Trustees: Anne Richards; Paul Aggett; Gary Marshall; Samantha Walker; Hugh Young

OSCR number: SC042597

Registered in 2011, this is the charitable foundation of Aberdeen Asset Management plc, a global investment management group, which manages assets for both institutional and retail clients from some 33 offices in 26 countries. The trustees include Anne Richards, Aberdeen's Chief Investment Officer and Head of Europe, Middle East and Africa, and other Aberdeen Asset Management directors.

The following information on the foundation's activities is taken from the company's website.

> The foundation seeks partnerships with smaller charities around the world, where funds can be seen to have a meaningful and measurable impact and we encourage employees to use their time and skills to support our charitable projects.
>
> To focus and unite our efforts as a global business, the foundation has adopted two key strategic themes:
>
> ***Emerging Markets***
>
> The foundation seeks to develop partnerships with charities working in emerging markets to tackle the educational needs of disadvantaged young people.
>
> Our people are central to our business and we see education and the promotion of opportunities as the natural target for our investment: as a business we value knowledge, learning and skills and we want to ensure that the communities in which we operate are able to offer young people those tools and opportunities which we see as being key, not only to us, but to wider social and economic development.
>
> Each year, the board selects a new emerging markets country and, through global employee participation, a new long-term charity partner in that country is chosen.
>
> Our first major emerging markets project is located in Brazil. The charity we chose to support for three years in 2012 is Action for Brazil's Children (the ABC Trust) which seeks to promote social change through projects targeting education, shelter, care and advice.
>
> In 2013, SeeBeyondBorders, another small and dynamic charity, was chosen by employees globally. The foundation's investment will help to provide over five thousand Cambodian children access to a better education and encourage best practice amongst local teachers through a programme of training and mentoring.
>
> [Due to the foundation's proactive approach under this theme it is unlikely that support will be given to unsolicited applications.]
>
> ***Local Communities***
>
> As a business we value the communities in which we operate and invest, recognising the benefits we gain from them as well as the potential impact we can have. The majority of our investment is therefore focused on the local communities in which Aberdeen employees live and work.
>
> Employees are empowered to develop their local approach to charitable giving within global guidelines, supporting causes that are relevant to their community and the local team.
>
> All charities applying for local community grants must meet the following criteria:
>
> - Clear connection to a community local to one of Aberdeen's offices
> - The investment should be capable of having a clear and meaningful impact, for example: small charities where the contribution amount is significant relative to the charity's size; larger charities with identifiable project opportunities that Aberdeen could put its name to; projects which include the opportunity for Aberdeen employee involvement through volunteering; and local organisations where Aberdeen can have a visible impact
> - A governance structure in place to allow Aberdeen to monitor the impact of the investment

In 2012/13, the year for which the most recent accounts were available at the time of writing (December 2014), the foundation had assets of £633,000 and an income of £557,500, most of which came from Aberdeen Asset Management. Grants were made totalling £682,000, which included £100,000 to emerging markets projects and £582,000 to local communities projects.

The foundation's 2012/13 accounts note that a commitment of £240,000 over four years has been made to SeeBeyondBorders, until 2017. The accounts also note the company's strategy when providing funding to the foundation:

> Each year a global budget [for the foundation] is approved by the board of Aberdeen Asset Management plc. This is divided between the emerging markets and the local communities' allocation.
>
> From the local communities' allocation, the budget is further split between the offices [of the company], with headcount used as the basis. Regional committees are responsible for this division of budget by office. Each individual office has the discretion to choose the projects it wishes to support in line with the overall strategy of supporting local communities.

Exclusions

The foundation does not support political causes or parties, or organisations or charities with a religious focus.

Applications

On an application form available to download from the foundation's page on the company's website. Completed application forms should be emailed to the foundation for consideration. The following further guidance and information is given by the foundation:

> All applicants will be notified within a three month period following application whether their application has been successful or not. If a grant is awarded, an annual impact assessment form will be required to be completed. Please ensure you attach a PDF copy of your latest annual review and please do not send DVDs or CDs.
>
> By submitting an application you are confirming that you have read and accept the following terms and conditions:
>
> *Grant fraud*
>
> Grant fraud is taken very seriously by the foundation. We appreciate your co-operation in ensuring that all grants made are used for their intended charitable purpose. In instances where we believe that grant fraud has taken place we will request repayment of the grant and will not accept future applications.
>
> *Data usage*
>
> The application process requires that the foundation collects data about your charity. This information may be used as part of the process of monitoring the use of our funding. On occasion, the foundation may share the information with other grant providers and auditors for the following purposes:
>
> - Determining, preventing or detecting crime
> - Ensuring that no one individual is receiving multiple grants
> - As part of our external auditing requirements
>
> Information will not be kept for longer than is required and, will be destroyed in accordance with local laws and regulations. By submitting an application you give your explicit consent for us to process data relating to your organisation for the purposes outlined here and to the transfer of this data outside your organisation's home country, and to such countries where the level of privacy protection may be less than provided under the laws of the European Unions.

The Accenture Foundation

Education, economic development and employment, children and young people

£1.8 million (2012/13)

Beneficial area

UK and overseas.

Correspondent: Anthony Richardson, Administrator, 1 Plantation Place, 30 Fenchurch Street, London EC3M 3BD (tel: 020 7844 4000; fax: 020 7844 4444; email: corporatecitizenship@accenture.com; website: www.accenture.com)

Trustees: Peter Webb; Camilla Drejer; Fiona Gibson; Gareth Newton; Tracy-Joy Harrison

CC number: 1057696

Registered in 1996, this is the charitable foundation of Accenture UK Ltd, a company that provides management consulting, technology and outsourcing services with more than 305,000 employees, and offices and operations in more than 200 cities in 56 countries.

The following information is given in the foundation's annual report and accounts:

> The Accenture Foundation runs a focused programme of long-term grants funded by the sponsoring company. Through establishment of long-term strategic partnerships the foundation continues to be able to make a real difference to our chosen charities, which include:
>
> *Global Giving Grant*
>
> - Leonard Cheshire Disability
> - Youth Business International
> - Voluntary Services Overseas
> - Save the Children
>
> *Local Giving Grant*
>
> - Global Action Plan
> - Onside Northwest Ltd
>
> In addition to grants to these charities, ad hoc grants were made to other charitable causes, via the Charities Aid Foundation, to support the sponsoring company's employee fundraising 'matching scheme' – allowing Accenture employees in the UK to apply for up to £100 of matching for funds raised for charitable causes each year.
>
> The foundation's grant making activities continued to centre on supporting charities with a focus on disadvantaged people and assisting them to break the cycle of deprivation and under achievement through upskilling and employability interventions.
>
> *Grant making policy*
>
> The trustees meet quarterly to review grant progress and to consider what grants they will make. Nominations for grants are elicited by formal means, primarily through the sponsoring company's UKI or Global Corporate Citizenship functions.
>
> Though the trustees may make some grants with no formal application, they would normally ask invited organisations to submit a formal application, applying the sponsoring company's standard application forms and criteria, saying how the funds would be used and what would be achieved. The trustees prefer to enter into long-term relationships with the main organisations to which they make grants; however, this is always subject to annual review and no guarantee of future funding is given.
>
> The Accenture Foundation trustees have agreed criteria under the theme of Skills to Succeed which covers the following areas of focus:
>
> - Employability – to equip people with critical skills for employment
> - Enterprise – to equip people with the skills required to establish and sustain enterprises
>
> In addition, the Accenture Foundation considers grants that:
>
> - Are conducive to Accenture employees' involvement (or potential for) e.g. through employee volunteering to enhance the overall impact of the grant
> - Have measurable impact in the UK or other key Accenture geographies (i.e. demonstrable impact)
> - Do not lead the supported organisation to become dependent/reliant on the Accenture Foundation or Accenture
>
> Additional robust due diligence and opportunity scoping criteria are applied by the sponsoring company's Global Giving Team as they shape global giving propositions for the consideration of the UK foundation trustees. For Local Giving proposition, the sponsoring company's UKI Corporate Citizenship Lead will apply the standard due diligence and opportunity scoping criteria before presenting Local Giving propositions to the UK foundation trustees for consideration.
>
> Potential grantees must be registered UK charities or equivalent.
>
> The foundation has a policy of not responding to any correspondence unless it relates to grants it has agreed to make or to the general management of the foundation. The trustees plan to continue with the current grant making strategy for the foreseeable future.

In 2012/13 the foundation had assets of £6.6 million and an income of £208,500, which included £56,000 from Accenture UK Ltd. Grants were made totalling £1.8 million.

Beneficiaries included: Prince of Wales Youth Business International (£592,000); Leonard Cheshire Disability (£486,500); Voluntary Services Overseas (£312,000); Save the Children (£165,000); Onside Northwest Ltd (£99,000); and Global Action Plan (£85,000). Smaller grants were made to other organisations totalling £53,000.

Exclusions

No grants to political or religious organisations, or to individuals are given.

Applications

The foundation's annual report and accounts states that:

> Proposals are generally invited by the trustees or initiated at their request or come via the sponsoring company's Global Giving function for whom the UK foundation manages grant disbursement. Unsolicited applications are discouraged and are unlikely to be successful, even if they fall within an area in which the trustees are interested.

The Addleshaw Goddard Charitable Trust

General, education and social welfare

£57,000 (2012/13)

Beneficial area

Greater London, Manchester and Leeds.

Correspondent: Christopher Noel, Trustee, Addleshaw Goddard LLP, 100 Barbirolli Square, Manchester M2 3AB (tel: 020 7788 5504; fax: 01619 346060; email: christopher.noel@ addleshawgoddard.com)

Trustees: Bruce Lightbody; Jonathan Cheney; Monica Burch; Lisa Rodgers; Pervinder Kaur; Christopher Noel

CC number: 286887

Registered in 1983, this is the charitable trust of Addleshaw Goddard LLP, a law firm with UK offices in London, Leeds and Manchester. The objects of the trust are as follows:

- To promote any charitable purpose for the benefit of the communities in the cities of London, Leeds and Manchester, and in particular the advancement of education, the furtherance of health and the relief of poverty, distress and sickness
- To promote any charitable object or purpose connected with the legal profession and in particular to assist the persons engaged in that profession and the wives, widows, children and other dependents of such persons being in conditions of need, hardship or distress
- To advance legal education in all its aspects insofar as such advancement may be charitable

In 2012/13 the trust had assets of £149,000 and an income of £64,000, which included £50,000 from Addleshaw Goddard LLP. Grants were made totalling £57,000 and were broken down as follows:

Manchester	£21,500
Leeds	£15,500
London	£15,000
National and other charities	£2,500
Matching Addleshaw Goddard staff fundraising	£2,500

The listed beneficiaries were: Francis House Children's Hospice – Manchester (£21,500); Leeds Community Foundation (£15,500); Maggie's Centres – London (£15,000); and Citizenship Foundation, Learning Partnerships, Bolton Lads' and Girls' Club, Outward Bound Trust and the Anthony Nolan Trust (£500 each).

Applications

In writing to the correspondent.

The Adnams Charity

General charitable purposes

£67,000 (2012/13)

Beneficial area

Within a 25-mile radius of St Edmund's Church, Southwold.

Correspondent: Rebecca Abrahall, Charity Administrator, Adnams plc, Sole Bay Brewery, East Green, Southwold, Suffolk IP18 6JW (tel: 01502 727200; email: charity@adnams.co.uk; website: www.adnams.co.uk/charity)

Trustees: Jonathan Adnams, Chair; Elizabeth Cantwell; Guy Heald; Emma Hibbert; Melvyn Horn; Simon Loftus; Andy Wood; Alison Kibble; Ann-Marie Cross

CC number: 1000203

The Adnams Charity was founded in 1990 to mark the centenary of the Adnams brewing company and is funded mainly by the annual donation from the profits of Adnams plc. It supports a wide variety of organisations within a 25-mile radius of Southwold, including those involved with health and social welfare, education, recreation, the arts, environment and conservation and historic buildings.

Applications from national charities which operate within a 25-mile area of Southwold may be considered if assurances can be given that the money will be used for a specific purpose within the area.

The charity prefers to make one-off grants for specific items which normally range from £100 to £2,500, and the trustees expect to see the result of their donations within 12 months.

Further information is given in the charity's accounts:

- The trustees prefer applications for specific items
- Grants are generally of a one-off nature
- Grants are not generally made in successive years
- The trustees are reluctant to give grants to cover on-going running costs, although in very exceptional circumstances they may do so
- The charity does not provide sponsorship of any kind
- The charity does not provide raffle prizes
- The charity does not give funds indirectly to charities, for example, by sponsoring the fundraising efforts of individuals
- The charity does not provide funding for any hardware associated with solar panels. However, consideration will be given to applications for educational equipment linked to 'green energy' and energy conservation
- The charity will only award grants of up to £500 towards the cost of computers

In 2012/13 the charity had an income of £36,000, most of which came from Adnams plc. During the year 68 grants were made totalling £67,000.

Beneficiaries included: Halesworth Millennium Green Trust (£2,300); Listening Books (£2,250); Pro Corda (£1,300); The Country Trust, Lowestoft Town Cricket Club and Yoxford Primary School (£1,000 each); Fressingfield Music Festival (£700); East Point Academy and Linstead Village Hall (£500 each); and the Children's Safety Education Foundation (£330).

Exclusions

The charity does not normally make grants to religious organisations or private clubs unless they can demonstrate that the purpose of the grant is for something of clear public benefit and is accessible to all. It does not provide raffle prizes or sponsorship of any kind. No grants are made to individuals; however, public bodies and charities may apply on behalf of individuals. Grants are not made in successive years.

Applications

Application forms are available on request to the Charity Administrator. Grants are considered at quarterly meetings, in January, April, July and October. Application deadlines usually fall in the previous month and are listed on the charity's website.

Allchurches Trust Ltd

Churches, general

£9.5 million (2013)

Beneficial area

UK.

Correspondent: Rachael Hall, Administrator, Beaufort House, Brunswick Road, Gloucester GL1 1JZ (tel: 01452 873189; email: atl@ecclesiastical.com; website: www.allchurches.co.uk)

Trustees: Michael Chamberlain; The Right Revd. Nigel Stock; Philip Mawer; Christopher Smith; Annette Cooper; Denise Wilson; David Christie; Laurence Magnus; Michael Arlington

CC number: 263960

Allchurches Trust Ltd was established in 1972. Its income is derived from its wholly owned subsidiary company Ecclesiastical Insurance Office plc. Its aims are to promote the Christian religion, to contribute to the funds of any charitable institutions or associations and to carry out any charitable purpose.

Grants will be considered in response to appeals in support of churches, church establishments, religious charities and charities preserving UK heritage.

The trust describes its grants strategy as:

- Supporting deployment of clergy at parish level, particularly within deprived areas
- Funding other staff to support the work of the clergy
- Funding new initiatives ranging from supporting parishes to educational work in schools
- Maintaining and repairing church and cathedral buildings
- Funding specific mission and outreach activities

Grantmaking in 2013

The trust described its activities during the year in its annual report as follows, including a list of sample beneficiaries:

Dioceses	123	£6.3 million
Parishes and other charities	933	£1.8 million
Cathedrals	164	£1.4 million

Dioceses and cathedrals

The majority of ATL's donations are used to support the dioceses and cathedrals of the Church of England. During the year, ATL allocated donations of £7.7 million (2012: £7.6 million) to those beneficiaries.

Anglican churches, churches of other denominations and the Christian community

ATL responds to requests for financial assistance from Anglican churches, churches of other denominations, the Christian community and other charitable organisations in accordance with its grant-making policy. In general, ATL supports appeals from churches for building and restoration projects, the repair of church fabric and church community initiatives, and from religious charities and charities preserving the UK heritage.

Special project fund

This fund was established in 1999. Its purpose is to support a small number of projects on a larger basis. During the year, ATL provided funds to support church growth initiatives such as 'Back to Church Sunday' and 'Leading your Church into Growth', work at the Arthur Rank Centre in respect of the rural church, and the training of senior church leaders.

Overseas projects fund

This fund was established in 2005. During the prior year ATL allocated funds amounting to £121,000 to support Christian causes overseas. In the current year, subsidiary companies operating in Australia and Canada donated £229,000 (2012: £357,000) to charitable causes in those countries.

Delivering public benefit

Some examples of recent grants are listed below, which highlight some of the charity's achievements and performance. The charity's beneficiaries provided much positive feedback on the value and impact of ATL's contributions.

In 2013 the trust had an income of £5.4 million including £4 million from Ecclesiastical Insurance plc. Grants were made totalling £9.5 million.

Beneficiaries included: Beachy Head Chaplaincy Team; Better Together Trust; Bingham Methodist Church, Nottingham; East Cheshire Area Quaker Meeting; First Comber Presbyterian Church, County Down; Guildford Cathedral; Holy Trinity Church – Nailsea; Totland Methodist Church; and Waen Congregational Chapel.

Exclusions

The trust is unable to support:

- Charities with a political association
- National charities
- Individuals
- Appeals for running costs and salaries
- An appeal from an applicant within 24 months of the date of a successful appeal
- Churches which are not members of Churches Together in England/Action of Churches Together in Scotland/ Cytun Churches Together in Wales/ the Irish Council of Churches

Applications

Applications should ideally be submitted online via the trust's website.

Where the total project cost exceeds £300,000, your most recent audited or independently examined accounts should be submitted.

For an application to be processed, considered by the trustees and for the decision to be communicated to you, allow up to three months for routine and/or smaller projects and up to six months for larger and/or more complex projects.

Alliance Trust Staff Foundation

General charitable purposes, children and young people

£29,000 (2014)

Beneficial area

Dundee, Edinburgh and City of London.

Correspondent: Jack Willis, Secretary, Alliance Trust plc, 8 West Marketgait, Dundee DD1 1QN (tel: 01382 321000; fax: 01382 321185; email: contact@alliancetrust.co.uk; website: investor.alliancetrust.co.uk/ati/investorrelations/staff-foundation)

Trustees: Ramsay Urquhart, Chair; Jack Willis; James Brown; Sinead Lennon; Ann McLeod; Stuart McMaster; Alvina Menzies; Kerry Moores; Kathryn Taylor

OSCR number: SC044113

Registered with the Scottish Charity Regulator in 2013, this is the charitable foundation of Alliance Trust plc, an investment, savings and wealth management company. The foundation's income derives from Alliance Trust employees' fundraising activities and matched funding from the company. The following information on the foundation's activities is given by the company on its website:

> The [foundation] was formed with the purpose of building partnerships between Alliance Trust and its local communities in Dundee, Edinburgh and London.
>
> Community engagement is more than just supporting charities and sponsoring events and the foundation aims to engage with local communities through funding specific charitable projects that will impact the local communities for the long-term.
>
> The foundation is run by a committee of Alliance Trust employees from across the business. It aims to engage staff through various initiatives such as dress down days and bakes sales to raise money for local charities, and with funds raised from larger events such as the Cateran Yomp, it donates to a select number of charities during the year.

In 2014 the foundation donated over £29,000 to local charities and community organisations.

According to the foundation's 2014 annual newsletter the following amounts were donated to these organisations: Streetwork – Edinburgh (£5,000); Baytree Centre, Dundee Disabled Children's Association, Links Park

Community Trust and Action for Children Scotland (£2,000 each).

Applications

In writing to the correspondent.

Anglo American Group Foundation

Support towards development initiatives both locally and globally; education, international development, health/HIV, environment, London-based community development causes are particularly welcomed

£1.6 million to organisations

(2013)

Beneficial area

United Kingdom and overseas (priority countries include Brazil, Peru, Chile, Colombia, China, UK, Zimbabwe, Botswana, Namibia and the Democratic Republic of Congo, amongst others).

Correspondent: Erica Shinnie, Administrator, Anglo American plc, 20 Carlton House Terrace, London SW1Y 5AN (tel: 020 7968 8727; email: aagf@angloamerican.com; website: www.angloamericangroupfoundation.org)

Trustees: Angela Bromfield; Ian Botha; Duncan Wanblad; Jonathan Samuel

CC number: 1111719

The foundation was established in 2005 by Anglo American plc, a large multinational mining company. The trust supports development initiatives directed towards the global and local community and a diversified group of socio-economic programmes. The trust prefers providing funding to a selected range of projects on a sustained basis rather than having a high turnover of partners. In this way, it can help the charities with long-term budget planning. It welcomes applications from charitable organisations associated with the following areas:

- Education
- International development
- Health/HIV
- Environment
- London-based community development

In 2013 the trust had assets of £367,000 and an income of £1.4 million. A total of £1.6 million was distributed in grants, broken down as follows:

Education and training	£452,000
Community Development – other	£288,000
Health and welfare	£276,000
Community development, enterprise development and micro-credit	£270,000
Community development – housing	£102,000
Water and sanitation	£84,000
Employee matched funding	£78,000
Other social investment or charitable giving	£60,000

Beneficiaries which were given more than £20,000 included: Pro Mujer Inc. (£167,000); Leonard Cheshire Disability (£155,000); the Royal Academy of Engineering (£150,000); Engineers Without Borders (£125,000); the Terrence Higgins Trust (£104,000); the Cambridge Foundation (£100,000); WaterAid (£84,000); the Prince's Trust (£71,000); Care International (£60,000); the Connection at St Martin's (£51,000); Diamond Development Initiative International, Institute for Human Rights and Business (£50,000 each); International Women's Health Coalition (£46,000); the London Community Foundation (£43,000); Body and Soul (£40,000); Keeping Kids Company (£35,000); Engineering Development Trust (£31,000); Sentebale (£30,000); Kriel Orphanage (£29,000); Action for Brazil Children, the National AIDS Trust, and St Andrews Club (£25,000 each); and the Samaritans (£23,000).

Exclusions

The foundation only funds registered charities and does not support:

- Animal charities
- Armed forces charities
- Community interest companies
- Educational fees
- Expeditions overseas
- General health charities
- Hospital trusts
- Individuals
- Music festivals and choirs
- Political or quasi-political bodies
- Religious organisations (other than community outreach)
- Trade unions

Applications

Applications should be made in writing to the correspondent. The trustees meet quarterly.

The Apax Foundation

Relief in need, education

£953,000 (2013/14)

Beneficial area

UK, USA, Asia, Africa, Europe.

Correspondent: David Marks, Trustee, Apax Partners, 33 Jermyn Street, London SW1Y 6DN (tel: 020 7872 6300; email: foundation@apax.com; website: www.apax.com/responsibility/apax-foundation)

Trustees: Sir Ronald Cohen, Chair; Peter Englander; Martin Halusa; David Marks; John Megrue; Michael Phillips; Simon Cresswell; Mitch Truwit; Shashank Singh

CC number: 1112845

The following information is taken from the foundation's annual report:

> The Apax Foundation is the formal channel for Apax Partners' charitable giving and receives a percentage of the firm's profits and carried interest.
>
> The charity's objects are:
>
> - The relief of financial hardship, either generally or individually, of people living in socially and economically deprived areas in the UK and overseas through the provision of grants, goods or services
> - The advancement of education
> - To further such other purposes which are charitable in accordance with the law of England and Wales as the trustees think fit

In 2013/14 the foundation had assets of £17.8 million and an income of £567,000. Grants were made totalling £953,000.

Beneficiaries included: Impetus – Private Equity Foundation (£215,000); Schwab Foundation for Social Enterprise (£102,000); Emmaus Norwich, and INSEAD (£100,000 each); Mosaic (£86,000); Trickle Up (£50,000); Finanzierungsagentur fur Social Entrepreneurship (£42,000); Bridges Ventures USA (£32,000); Shivia Finance (£25,000); Pilotlight (£18,000); and Crisis UK (£13,500).

Donations given to organisations of £10,000 or less totalled £169,000.

Applications

In writing to the correspondent. The following information is provided by the foundation in its 2013/14 accounts:

> To ensure that the charity reaches out as widely as possible in fulfilment of its objectives, the Apex Foundation's grant application process is open to all charities operating in all countries. The sole restriction is that the work of those organisations must be focused in the charity's primary fields of education or the relief of poverty through the stimulation of entrepreneurship.
>
> The Apax Foundation's trustees review grant applications received from all charities which meet these criteria and grants are awarded on the basis of the trustees' evaluation of: the charity's effectiveness in achieving its aims, the number of beneficiaries reached, the sustainability of the charity's programmes, the strength and stability of its management team and internal processes, and the long-term public benefits that would flow from the deployment of a grant from the Apax Foundation.

The Ove Arup Foundation

Construction – education and research

£120,000 (2013/14)

Beneficial area

UK and overseas.

Correspondent: John Ward, Administrator, Ove Arup and Partners, 13 Fitzroy Street, London W1T 4BQ (tel: 020 7636 1531; email: ovarfound@arup.com; website: www.theovearupfoundation.com)

Trustees: Caroline Cole; Richard Haryott; Duncan Michael; Andrew Chan; Joanna Kennedy; Gregory Hodkinson; Terry Hill

CC number: 328138

The trust was established in 1989 with the principal objective of supporting education in matters associated with the built environment, including construction-related academic research. The trustees are appointed by the board of the Ove Arup Partnership. The trust gives grants for research and projects, including start-up and feasibility costs.

In 2013/14 the foundation had assets of £3.5 million which includes an endowment of £2.7 million and an income of £242,000. Grants were made totalling £120,000.

Beneficiaries included: the University of Edinburgh (£57,000); Useful Simple Projects Ltd (£25,000); BCAA, MADE, and the University of Queensland (£10,000 each); University College London (£6,000); and the Anglo Danish Society (£2,000).

Exclusions

No grants are given to individuals, including students.

Applications

Applications can be made on a form which is available to download from the foundation's website.

The Asda Foundation

Sport and recreation, community development, general charitable purposes

£7.9 million to organisations (2013)

Beneficial area

England and Wales.

Correspondent: Julie Ward, Foundation Manager, Asda Stores Ltd, Asda House, Great Wilson Street, Leeds LS11 5AD (tel: 01132 435435; website: www.asdafoundation.org)

Trustees: David Wickert; Ann Marie Rocks; John Cookman; Jim Jefcoate; Helen Milford; Dominic Birch; Alison Seabrook; Munazah Dar; Lisa Smith; Gerald Oppenheim; Lorraine Jackson; Lynne Tooms

CC number: 1124268

The Asda Foundation is Asda's charitable trust. It supplements the good causes that colleagues support locally, as well as a number of bigger ad-hoc projects in local communities. It also manages all funds raised for national charities and monies raised in Asda House.

The foundation funds a wide range of causes that Asda colleagues are involved in, including everything from local charities and playgroups to football teams.

> The Asda Foundation is set up to assist any charity in the UK as well as people and projects who require financial assistance.
>
> Asda Foundation's main objective is to make donations to the local good causes that our colleagues support. Colleagues raise funds for their local charities/communities and apply to ASDA Foundation for further funding where the following guidelines are applied for a minimum of two trustees to approve:
>
> - Teams of colleagues raising money for a good cause – ASDA Foundation will make a reasonable donation depending on the number of colleagues involved, local good cause and amount raised
> - One colleague raising money for a good cause – £100 max
> - Colleague teams raising money for an individual – £200 max
> - Charity expeditions e.g., white water rafting, marathons – £50 per colleague
> - Sponsored activity e.g., London Marathon – £50 per colleague
> - Colleague teams raising money for close immediate family – £500 max

In 2013 the foundation had an income of £8.7 million and a total expenditure of £8.1 million. Grants totalled £7.9 million, with £5.5 million going to the foundation's national campaigns: Breast Cancer Care (£2.8 million); Orchid (£806,000); BBC Children in Need (£742,000); Fields in Trust (£384,000); Text Santa (£315,000); Tommy's (£292,000); Pedal Power (£141,000); and Sporting Chance (£1,800).

A further £2.4 million was donated to other organisations.

Beneficiaries included: Run For All (£110,000); the Trussell Trust (£80,000); FareShare (£40,000); Age UK – Community Project (£20,000); Community Development Fund (£15,000); Leeds Rugby (£9,000); Yorkshire Cancer Centre (£7,500); the Freedom Centre – Community Project (£4,900); Playful Leeds (£2,000); and All Saints Landmark Centre (£1,000).

Exclusions

Asda Foundation does not fund expeditions or sponsor charitable activities by people other than Asda colleagues.

Applications

In the first instance, contact your local store or depot with your proposal/application. This will then be passed on to the trustees who will make a final decision. There is an eligibility tool and store locator on the website.

> The Asda Foundation receives many requests for support each year so unfortunately we can't support each cause that applies. We will look at each application based on criteria and merit – this is why you should provide as much information as possible on the application on how this will benefit the local community.

The Ashmore Foundation

Community and economic development, education and training, health

£846,000 to organisations (2013)

Beneficial area

Worldwide.

Correspondent: The Trustees, Ashmore Group, 5th Floor, 61 Aldwych, London WC2B 4AE (tel: 020 3077 6153; email: foundation@ashmoregroup.org; website: www.ashmorefoundation.org)

Trustees: Mark Coombs; James Carleton; Marlon Balroop; Samuel Rickard; Robert Rainey; Nadine Cottrell; Helen Mackay; Samantha Pope; Mythili Orton; Christoph Hofman

CC number: 1122351

Established in 2008, the Ashmore Foundation is the charity of the Ashmore Group, an emerging markets investment management company. The foundation's website states:

> The Ashmore Foundation's application and assessment process is designed to identify particularly high impact organisations which are well managed and accountable. Grants are currently provided through two schemes – a small grants scheme and a partnership grants scheme. The small grants scheme is designed to support a wide range of eligible charities with grants of up to £5,000 of flexible funding. Under this scheme, smaller charities and employee recommendations are prioritised. The

> Partnership Grants scheme aims to fund particularly strong organisations with larger grants, potentially over a number of years, in order to achieve a defined set of goals.
>
> The features we look for in our grantees and partners include:
>
> - Transparency: we expect the organisation's activities to be well documented with clearly evidenced results
> - Efficiency: well-managed grantees with a strong focus on results and an understanding and evidence of what activities will have the most impact on their beneficiaries
> - Connected: these organisations have a strong understanding of what the pressing social issues are, what is already being done to address these issues and where the gaps and critical points of leverage are. They show success in implementing interventions that make a positive change
>
> The foundation sources new partners through recommendations from experts, existing partners, suggestions from Ashmore staff and detailed research by the foundation team. Organisations need to be operating in the emerging markets as a registered non-profit organisation, working in the areas of health, education and/or livelihoods, benefiting disadvantaged groups, with an independent website and externally audited financial accounts available for review, their own bank account and a minimum annual income equivalent to £50,000.

In 2013 the foundation had an income of £240,000 and expenditure of £925,000. Grants made to organisations totalled £846,000.

Beneficiaries include: STARS Foundation (£499,000); Manav Seva Sansthan (£65,000); Save the Children, IDEP Foundation (£50,000 each); CASA (£45,000); KEDV (£35,000); Lend a Hand India (£30,000); ABC Trust (£20,000); United Way India (£10,000); and Afghan Action (£1,000).

Applications

The foundation does not accept unsolicited applications. The trustees source new partners through recommendations from experts, existing partners, suggestions from Ashmore staff and detailed research by the foundation team.

The Balfour Beatty Charitable Trust

Children and young people

£360,000 (2013)

Beneficial area

UK.

Correspondent: The Trustees, Company Secretarial Department, Balfour Beatty Ltd, 130 Wilton Road, London SW1V 1LQ (tel: 020 7216 6800; email: bbfutures@balfourbeatty.com; website: www.balfourbeatty.com)

Trustees: Mark Peters; Paul Raby

CC number: 1127453

Balfour Beatty plc is a multinational infrastructure group with capabilities in construction services, support services and infrastructure investments. The trust was founded by the company to support its corporate and social responsibility provision and to act as a focus for employee fundraising as well as to develop into a significant grant funder. Since its inception in 2009 the trust has donated £2 million to help over 20,000 young people suffering from disadvantage across the UK.

The objectives of the trust are:

- To advance in life and relieve the needs of young people suffering disadvantage by assisting with the provision of advice, training and education and other activities as a means of encouraging and helping them to develop their skills, capacities and capabilities
- To enable young people to enter and participate in society as independent, mature and responsible individuals
- To advance the education of children and young people through such means as the trustees think fit in accordance with the charity law

In 2013 the trust had assets of £79,000 and an income of £247,000. Grants to four organisations totalled £360,000.

Beneficiaries included: Barnardo's and the Prince's Trust (£100,000 each); and Action for Children and the Thomas Coram Foundation (£80,000 each).

Applications

The trustees work together with the Balfour Beatty Community Engagement Working Group (CEWG) to identify suitable charities to support.

BC Partners Foundation

General

£404,000 (2013)

Beneficial area

UK.

Correspondent: The Trustees, BC Partners Ltd, 40 Portman Square, London W1H 6DA (tel: 020 7009 4800; email: bcpfoundation@bcpartners.com; website: www.bcpartners.com/about-us/bcp-foundation.aspx)

Trustees: Nikos Stathopolous; Joseph Cronly; Lorna Parker; Michael Pritchard; Richard Kunzer; Cedric Dubourdieu

CC number: 1136956

Established in 2010 for general charitable purposes, this is the foundation of private equity firm BC Partners.

The foundation's annual report states:

> The foundation's goal is to support a wide range of organisations that positively affect the advancement of the communities where BC Partners and its employees and alumni are active. Its mandate is intentionally broad so that it can support giving to charities of all kinds.
>
> The foundation's main charitable activity focuses on providing employee matching grants and supporting charities proposed by the employees of BC Partners or trustees of the BC Partners Foundation. The foundation is not restricted in relation to the beneficiaries of its charitable giving, but focuses on the following areas:
>
> - Community development including infrastructure advancements, development aid, health care improvements
> - Conservation of the environment including endeavours related to pollution reduction, natural preservation, clean technologies
> - Arts and education including support for educational, scholastic, or artistic programs

In 2013 the foundation had assets of £372,000 and an income of £612,000. Grants were made to organisations totalling £404,000.

The largest grant was made to the Private Equity Foundation (£104,000), of which Nikos Stathopolous is also a trustee. There were also grants for Over the Wall (£31,000) of which Joseph Cronly is a trustee and Burghley Road Under 5s (£1,000) of which Michael Pritchard is a trustee.

Other beneficiaries included: BCPF Inc. (£67,000); the Latymer Foundation (£40,000); Vocal Futures (£16,000); the Samson Centre (£10,000); Great Ormond Street Hospital (£8,000); Royal Opera House (£6,000); Music as Therapy (£5,000); Macmillan, and C-R-Y (£1,900 each); and the Shakespeare Globe Trust (£1,000).

Applications

The foundation does not accept unsolicited applications.

The Berkeley Charitable Foundation

General charitable purposes, education, health, social welfare, the environment, community development

Around £2 million (2013/14)

Beneficial area

England and Wales.

Correspondent: Charmaine Young, Trustee, The Berkeley Group plc, Berkeley House, 19 Portsmouth Road, Cobham, Surrey KT11 1JG (tel: 020 7720 2600; email: info@berkeleyfoundation.org.uk; website: www.berkeleyfoundation.org.uk)

Trustees: Anthony Pidgley; Charmaine Young; Robert Perrins; Wendy Pritchard

CC number: 1152596

The Berkeley Charitable Foundation was established in 2011 and registered with the Charity Commission in June 2013. The foundation was established by Anthony Pidgley, founder and chair of the Berkeley Group, a British house building company based in Surrey.

This is a grant-making charity operating throughout England and Wales. According to its Charity Commission entry, The Berkeley Foundation's charitable objectives are:

- Education amongst young and unemployed people
- Urban regeneration
- Provision of recreational facilities for the public, in particular those who are young, elderly or disabled
- Advancement of health
- Promotion of conservation
- Promotion of sustainable development
- Relief of those in need due to poverty, age, ill health or disability

The foundation's website highlights its partnership with Shelter and its work within the community. Examples of previous beneficiaries, taken from the foundation's website, are: The Mayor's Fund for London, The Centre for Social Justice and No Second Night Out (NSNO). The foundation has also established a partnership with Crisis.

In 2013/14 the foundation had an income of £3.3 million and a total expenditure of £2.3 million. The foundation's 2013/14 annual review contains full details of its fundraising activities and the projects it supports.

Applications

The foundation has stated that it very rarely makes unsolicited donations; however, organisations can write to the correspondent if they believe there is a partnership that could be explored.

The Bestway Foundation

Education and training, social welfare, health, medical

£272,000 to UK organisations (2012/13)

Beneficial area

UK and overseas.

Correspondent: M. Y. Sheikh, Trustee, Bestway (Holdings) Ltd, Abbey Road, London NW10 7BW (tel: 020 8453 1234; email: zulfikaur.wajid-hasan@bestway.co.uk; website: www.bestwaygroup.co.uk/responsibility/bestway-foundation)

Trustees: Younus Sheikh; Abdul Khalique Bhatti; Adalat Khan Chaudhary; Sir Anwar Pervez; Zameer Choudrey; Dawood Pervez; Rizwan Pervez; Arshad Chaudhary

CC number: 297178

Registered with the Charity Commission in 1987, the Bestway Foundation is the corporate charity of Bestway (Holdings) Ltd, an independent food wholesale group in the UK with 63 Bestway and Batleys branches across England, Scotland and Wales. All of the charity's trustees are directors and shareholders of Bestway (Holdings) Ltd.

The Bestway Foundation's website states that its mission statement is as follows:

- The advancement of education for public benefit in both the UK and overseas by providing assistance through promotion of local schools; provision of scholarships to university students; supporting education initiatives and endowing universities
- The relief of sickness and the preservation of health for public benefit in both the UK and overseas by way of grants and endowments to existing hospitals, clinics, medical research establishments; and by establishing new health facilities
- The provision of financial and material support to victims of natural disasters
- To have a significant impact on poverty reduction in Pakistan through strategic investments in affordable financial and social services catering to the poor
- The development of technical skills within the local communities in which we operate through structured apprenticeship and training programmes

Donations on behalf of students are made directly to academic institutions.

In 2012/13 the trust had assets of over £6.7 million and an income of £737,000, of which almost £440,000 was a donation from Bestway (Holdings) Ltd. Grants were made totalling £272,000 and were given to charities based in the UK. In addition to this, £154,000 was awarded to foreign charities and individuals, making a total of £426,000 in grants. The foundation awarded 18 grants to organisations and 48 grants to individuals.

Beneficiaries included: the Royal Marsden Cancer Charity (£60,000); University of Bradford (£50,000); British Pakistan Foundation (£34,000); Ancient India and Iran Trust and British Asian Trust (£20,000 each); Duke of Edinburgh's Award (£16,000); Grocery Aid and Real Medicine Foundation (£10,000 each); the Graham Layton Trust and Pan Asian Women's Association (£5,000 each); Helen and Douglas House and Wines and Spirits Trades Benevolent Society (£1,000 each); and Springboard (£500).

Applications

Applications should be made in writing to the correspondent, enclosing an sae.

BHP Billiton Sustainable Communities

General

Beneficial area

UK.

Correspondent: The Trustees, BHP Billiton plc, Neathouse Place, London SW1V 1LH (tel: 020 7802 4000; email: hsec@bhpbilliton.com)

Trustees: Ian Wood; Melinda Buckland; Robert McDonald; Fiona Wild; Christine Barnesby

CC number: 1131066

BHP Billiton is a large international mining company. The group gives generously worldwide in areas where it has operational sites. It no longer has a site in the UK but the registered office is still in London and in-kind giving by staff may be available from there, (such as volunteering or fundraising). The future of the UK-registered charity BHP Billiton Sustainable Communities is to be considered in view of the company's decision that it is more effective to contribute to its other recently established corporate charity in the US, BHP Billiton Foundation. It is thought that the UK charity will continue for at least the next five years. It is not clear if UK charities can still benefit from grants and contact should be made to the correspondent before making application. In view of the company divesting its operating assets in the UK, contributions can no longer be made to the BHP Billiton Sustainable Communities charity from the company.

Applications

It is not clear if UK charities can still benefit from grants and so contact should be made to the correspondent before making an application.

Birmingham International Airport Community Trust

Community, environment, heritage conservation, sport and recreation, preservation of wildlife

£68,500 (2013/14)

Beneficial area

The areas affected by the airport's operation (East Birmingham, Solihull and parts of north Warwickshire).

Correspondent: Andrew Holding, Trustee, Birmingham International Airport Ltd, Diamond House, Birmingham B26 3QJ (tel: 01217 677448; email: community@birminghamairport.co.uk; website: www.birminghamairport.co.uk)

Trustees: Cllr Michael Wood; Cllr Michael Robinson; Cllr Martin Hewings; Paul Orton; Andrew Holding; Edward Richards; Margaret Kennett; James Dunlop Williams; Cllr Majid Mahmood

CC number: 1071176

Established in 1998, the trust aims to compensate those communities most affected by Birmingham International Airport. The airport company donates £75,000 each year to the trust, which is topped up by fines imposed on airlines for exceeding the airport's noise violation levels (this usually amounts to very modest amounts). Geographically, the trust supports a very defined area that, broadly speaking, is that bounded by Grove End, Berkswell, Honiley and Washwood Heath. Projects outside this region cannot be funded, even if the communities feel they are affected by the disruption caused by the airport.

The trust acts independently of the airport management, with nine representatives of the following bodies making up the trustees: The Airport Consultative Committee (3), Birmingham City Council (2), Birmingham International Airport (2) and Solihull Council (2).

Areas of work the trust supports are:

- Environment improvement and heritage conservation
- Bringing the community closer together through facilities for sport, recreation and other leisure-time activities
- Improving awareness of environmental issues or environmental education and training activities
- Encouraging and protecting wildlife

It describes the types of projects it wishes to support as including community centres, community groups, sports, playgroups, schools, youth clubs, scouts, gardens/parks, environment, music and churches. Work should benefit a substantial section of the community rather than less inclusive groups, although work with older people or people with special needs is positively encouraged.

The maximum grant made is for £3,000, and grants tend to go to community groups with low incomes; organisations with large turnovers are rarely supported. Grants may be for capital or revenue projects, although the trust will not commit to recurrent or running costs, such as salaries.

In 2013/14 the trust had an income of just over £75,000 and made grants totalling £68,500.

Previous beneficiaries have included: 298th Birmingham Brownies/Rangers Pack, Age Concern – Castle Bromwich, Blakenhale Infant School, Chelmsley Town Football Club, Coleshill Bell Ringers, Coleshill Town Football Club, George Fentham Endowed School, Hatchford Brook Youth and Community Centre, and Land Lane Baptist Free Church.

Exclusions

The following are not eligible for grants:

- Individuals
- Projects which have already been carried out or paid for
- Organisations which have statutory responsibilities such as hospitals, surgeries, clinics, schools, etc. unless the project is clearly not a statutory responsibility

Applications

The trust gives the following information:

> To apply, you must contact us to receive an application form. This allows us to discuss with you whether or not your proposal meets the trust fund criteria and how to maximise your chances of making a successful application. Please be aware that the trustees meet twice a year in April and October and that there are deadlines in February and August respectively for the receipt of completed applications. Late applications cannot be considered.

Full guidelines are available from the trust's page on the company's website, along with specific deadline dates, which are usually towards the end of the months stated.

The BlackRock (UK) Charitable Trust

General charitable purposes

£1,300 (2013)

Beneficial area

UK.

Correspondent: Agnieszka Caban, Administrator, BlackRock, 12 Throgmorton Avenue, London EC2N 2DL (tel: 020 7743 3000)

Trustees: Richard Royds; Andrew Johnston; Elizabeth Tracey; Peter Walker; BlackRock Group Ltd

CC number: 1065447

BlackRock is an international investment management company that set up a charitable trust in 1999.

In 2013 the trust had an income of £1,200 and an expenditure of £1,300. No further information was available.

Previous beneficiaries have included: BlackRock Community Action Team, British Red Cross, Changing Faces, Eating Disorders Association and Cross, Ovarian Cancer Action and Women in Prison.

Applications

The trust states that 'the trustees invite staff, clients and business associates of BlackRock Investment Management (UK) Ltd to submit applications for grants to a registered charity of their choice'. Other appeals would usually be declined.

The Body Shop Foundation

Animal protection, human rights, environmental protection

£816,000 (2013/14)

Beneficial area

UK and overseas.

Correspondent: Lisa Jackson, Administrator, The Body Shop, Watersmead Business Park, Littlehampton, West Sussex BN17 6LS (tel: 01903 844039; email: bodyshopfoundation@thebodyshop.com; website: thebodyshopfoundation.org)

Trustees: Andrew Radford; Bhupendra Mistry; Paul Sanderson, R. Godfrey; Andrew Wade; Jason Matthews; Mark Davies; Jill Cochrane; Guy Culquhoun; Paolo Sala

CC number: 802757

Founded in 1989, the Body Shop Foundation is a charitable company, limited by guarantee, which operates closely with The Body Shop International. It gives money to innovative, global projects working for social and environmental change. The foundation's website states:

> The Body Shop Foundation is funded through the sale of a charity product – Dragon Fruit Lip Butter – sold globally in the stores of the Body Shop and through various fundraising activities. This allows us to run three different grants programmes – addressing issues about animal protection, human rights and environmental protection around the world.

The Body Shop runs a variety of grant programmes, details of which can be viewed on the foundation's website.

In 2013/14 the foundation had assets of £645,000 and an income of £1.5 million. Grants to 206 organisations totalled £816,000.

Beneficiaries included: Foundation for Australia's Most Endangered Species Ltd, Australia (£62,000); Orangutan Foundation, Indonesia (£42,000); 1001 Fontaines Pour Demain, Cambodia (£30,000); International Gender Studies Centre (£23,000); Environmental Investigation Agency (£15,000); Book-Cycle, UK (£6,400); The Worthing Foodbank (£5,000); Centro Canino, Spain (£4,800); Seeds of Diversity, Canada (£3,800); Look Good, Feel Better, New Zealand (£3,700 each).

Exclusions

As the majority of applications come from projects nominated by staff, the foundation does not ask for public applications or nominations. Nor does it:

- Sponsor individuals
- Fund sporting activities or the arts
- Sponsor or support fundraising events, receptions or conferences

Applications

The foundation does not accept unsolicited applications. The trustees research projects which meet their funding criteria and only then invite organisations to make an application.

The Boodle & Dunthorne Charitable Trust

General charitable purposes

£121,000 (2012/13)

Beneficial area

UK.

Correspondent: Nicholas Wainwright, Administrator, Boodle & Dunthorne, 35 Lord Street, Liverpool L2 9SQ (tel: 01512 240580)

Trustees: Nicholas Wainwright; Michael Wainwright

CC number: 1077748

Established in 1999, this is the charitable trust of Boodles, a family jewellers based in North West England.

In 2012/13 the trust had assets of £372,000 and an income of £204,000. Grants totalling £121,000 were made to 19 organisations.

Beneficiaries included: Shining Faces in India (£50,000); Rainbow Trust (£14,000); the Household Cavalry and Great Ormond Street Children's Charity (£10,000 each); the Outward Bound Trust and Lt Dougie Dalzell MC Memorial Trust (£5,000 each); Emmanuel Baptist Church and the Aspinall Foundation (£2,500 each); Ventureco Worldwide (£500); and Northfield Church (£250).

Applications

In writing to the correspondent.

Boots Charitable Trust

Health, social welfare, education and training, community development

£250,000 (2013/14)

Beneficial area

Nottingham and Nottinghamshire.

Correspondent: Caroline Ward, Trustee, Boots UK Ltd, 1698 Melton Road, Rearsby, Leicester LE7 4YR (tel: 01159 591285; email: Julie.Lawrence@boots.co.uk; website: www.boots-uk.com/corporate_social_responsibility/community/boots-charitable-trust.aspx)

Trustees: Oonagh Turnbull; Judith Lyons; Kay Croot; Richard Burbidge

CC number: 1045927

Registered with the Charity Commission in 1995, Boots Charitable Trust is wholly funded by Boots UK Ltd. Boots UK is part of the Retail Pharmacy International Division of Walgreens Boots Alliance, Inc. Boots became a subsidiary of the new company, Walgreens Boots Alliance, on 31 December 2014. The trust is administered by members within the corporate social responsibility team, including Head of CSR, Oonagh Turnbull.

The trust gives to charities and voluntary organisations that benefit Nottingham and Nottinghamshire. The website states that grants are given in the following areas:

- **Health:** both community healthcare such as homecare or support for sufferers of medical conditions as well as health education and prevention
- **Lifelong learning:** for example literacy and numeracy projects
- **Community development:** such as supporting councils in providing voluntary services
- **Social care:** be it personal, social or community activities or schemes

In 2013/14 the trust had assets of £270, an income of £273,000, of which £250,000 was a donation from the company and £23,000 was donated services. It gave 40 grants totalling £250,000 during the year, broken down as follows:

Health	15	£93,000
Social care	11	£74,000
Lifelong learning	7	£48,000
Community development	7	£36,000

Beneficiaries included: Groundwork Greater Nottingham (£15,000); Base 51 and Newark, Notts Child Bereavement and Loss Centre and Survivors Helping Each Other (£10,000 each); Home Start Newark (£8,200); Age UK Nottinghamshire and Pintsize Theatre Ltd (£7,000 each); Bassetlaw CVS (£6,300); and Malt Cross Trust Company, Spring Nottingham and St Ann's Allotments (£5,000 each).

Grants under £5,000 totalled £29,000.

Note: the company also has another charity, **Boots Benevolent Fund** (Charity Commission no. 1046559), which provides financial help and support to serving and retired colleagues who are unexpectedly experiencing financial hardship.

Exclusions

The trust does not provide funding for:

- Projects benefiting people outside Nottinghamshire
- Individuals
- Organisations which are not registered charities and which have income or expenditure of more than £5,000 per year
- Charities seeking funds to redistribute to other charities
- Projects for which there is a legal statutory obligation or which replace statutory funding

Applications

On a form available, with guidelines, from the website or by post. Completed forms should be sent to the correspondent with the latest annual report and accounts.

For applications for amounts greater than £2,000 the deadlines are on 7th of February, April, June, August, October and December. These applications take between two and four months to process.

There is no deadline for applications under £2,000, and these applications take between one and two months to be processed.

The Bruntwood Charity

General, social welfare

£90,000 (2012/13)

Beneficial area

UK.

Correspondent: Sally Hill, Trustee, Bruntwood Ltd, City Tower, Piccadilly Plaza, Manchester M1 4BT (tel: 01612 373883)

Trustees: Katharine Vokes; Andy Allan; Rob Yates; Sally Hill; Kathryn Graham; Jane Williams

CC number: 1135777

The charity was established in 2010 for general charitable purposes. It is the charity of Bruntwood Ltd, a company which owns and manages commercial property and office space in Birmingham, Leeds, Manchester and Liverpool. The founder of Bruntwood is Michael Oglesby of the Oglesby Charitable Trust.

The charity focuses on fundraising for five charities: Claire House Children's Hospice (Liverpool); Onside and the Factory Youth Zone (Manchester); St Gemma's Hospice (Leeds); and Whizz-Kidz (Birmingham).

In 2012/13 the charity had assets of £26,000 and an income of £95,000. Grants were made totalling £90,000.

Beneficiaries include: Onside (£40,000); Factory Youth Zone (£30,000); Clare House (£8,000); Prince's Trust (£6,000); Whizz-Kidz (£4,000); and St Martens House (£2,300).

Applications

In writing to the correspondent, although potential applicants should be aware that the relationships with the nominated charities may continue.

The Cadbury Foundation

Education and enterprise, poverty and homelessness, the environment and international development

£435,000 (2013)

Beneficial area

UK and Africa, particularly in areas where the company has operations.

Correspondent: Louise Ayling, Administrator, Mondelez UK, Unit 3, Sanderson Road, Uxbridge Business Park, Uxbridge UB8 1DH (tel: 01895 615000; email: louise.ayling@mdlz.com)

Trustees: Jonathan Horrell; Diane Tomlinson; Neil Chapman; David Oliver; Vinzenz Gruber; Michael Huggins; Sonia Farrell; Mary Barnard; Eoin Kellet

CC number: 1050482

The Cadbury Foundation was set up in 1935 in recognition of the company founders George and Richard Cadbury and their investment in the welfare of their employees and wider communities. In 2010 Kraft Foods Inc. gained control of Cadbury plc. In 2012 Kraft Foods Inc. was split into Kraft Food Group plc and Mondelez which now funds the Cadbury Foundation. The following information was taken from the foundation's 2013/14 accounts:

> The Cadbury Foundation contributes to communities near the company's operations so that where possible donations can be backed up with employee volunteering work and gifts in kind.
>
> From 2013 grants are made by the trustees whose current focus is on the four pillars:
>
> - **Skills Development** – giving an awareness of the world of work and enhancing the ability of young people and disadvantaged adults to gain and sustain employment
> - **Olympic and Paralympic Legacy** – to build stronger, healthier communities through sport
> - **Source Projects** – supporting the development of sustainable cocoa growing communities where Mondelez International sources its cocoa and coffee beans
> - **Employee Passions** – some funds are reserved for employee-related grants and cash match where company volunteers can either have their fundraising efforts matched, or where they can bid for a grant to support the work of a chosen charity

In 2013 the foundation had assets of £193,000 and an income of £784,000 which included £750,000 from Mondelez UK Holdings and Services Ltd. Grants to 11 organisations totalled £435,000.

Beneficiaries included: Charities Aid Foundation (£105,000); British Paralympic Association (£100,000); National Grocer Benevolent Fund (£75,000); Northside Partnership (£50,000); Tembisa Child Welfare (£30,000); the Achimota Trust (£25,000); Groundworth South Trust (£15,000); Mondelez UK Holdings and Services – Ghana Wells, Trinity Homeless Project, Disaster Emergency Committee (£10,000 each); and Bournville Village Trust (£5,000).

Applications

The foundation actively seeks out projects to support and therefore cannot accept any unsolicited requests for funding.

The Cadogan Charity

General charitable purposes, in particular, social welfare, medical research, service charities, animal welfare, education, and conservation and the environment

£2.7 million (2013/14)

Beneficial area

Worldwide. In practice, UK with a preference for London and Scotland.

Correspondent: Paul Loutit, Secretary, The Cadogan Group, 18 Cadogan Gardens, London SW3 2RP (tel: 020 7730 4567)

Trustees: Earl Cadogan; Countess Cadogan; Viscount Chelsea; Lady Anna Thomson; The Hon. William Cadogan

CC number: 247773

The trust was established in 1966 for general charitable purposes and operates two funds, namely, the general fund and the rectors' fund. The rectors' fund was created with a gift from Cadogan Holdings Company in 1985 to pay an annual amount to one or any of the rectors of Holy Trinity Church – Sloane Street, St Luke's Church and Chelsea Old Church. The general fund provides support for registered charities in a wide range of areas (see below).

In 2013/14 the trust had assets of £48.5 million and an income of £2.3 million. The trust made 88 grants totalling almost £2.7 million and they were categorised as follows:

Social welfare in the community	39	£1.9 million
Military charities	8	£248,000
Medical research	24	£208,000
Education	6	£170,000
Animal welfare	9	£68,000
Conservation and the environment	2	£20,000

Beneficiaries included: St Georges Cathedral, Perth (£445,000); Culford School (£100,000); Battle of Britain Memorial Trust (£50,000); Alzheimer's Research Trust (£37,000); Home of Horse Racing Trust (£25,000); Samaritans (£20,000); Royal Ballet School and Scotland Uplands Appeal (£10,000 each) Guard's Museum and Animal Health Trust (£5,000 each); World Sight Foundation (£4,000); Epilepsy Research Foundation and Family Holiday Association (£1,000 each).

Exclusions

No grants to individuals.

Applications

In writing to the correspondent. However, note that we have received information stating that the trust's funds are fully committed until 2016.

The CIBC World Markets Children's Miracle Foundation

General

£851,000 (2013/14)

Beneficial area

UK and the Netherlands.

Correspondent: Howard Redgwell, Trustee, Canadian Imperial Bank of Commerce, 150 Cheapside, London EC2V 6ET (tel: 020 7234 6000; email: ukchildrensmiracle@cibc.co.uk; website: www.cibc.com/ca/miracleday/international/childrens-foundation.html)

Trustees: Mark Beels; Howard Redgwell; Helen Hayes; Martin Autotte; Andrew Ryde; Paul Weidemann

CC number: 1105094

CIBC World Markets is the investment banking subsidiary of the Canadian Imperial Bank of Commerce. The CIBC Children's Foundation was established in 1984 to raise funds for children's charities around the world. Since its inception, £138 million has been raised to improve the quality of life of thousands of children affected by disability, illness, social deprivation or life-limiting conditions. The following information was taken from the foundation's website:

> The majority of fundraising takes place on CIBC Miracle Day, which takes place annually on the first Wednesday in December. On this day, participating CIBC wholesale banking employees donate their fees and commissions to the CIBC Children's Foundation.
>
> In London, funds are also raised through a number of staff and client fundraising events held throughout the year. This ensures Miracle Day has become an integral part of our business. CIBC's wholesale banking European operation has donated over £4.5 million to numerous children's charities across the United Kingdom and Europe since it became involved in 1994. In July 2004, the CIBC Children's Foundation became a registered charity in England and Wales, having also Dutch charitable status since 1 April 2012.
>
> The objectives of the foundation are:
>
> - To raise the quality of life for children in the communities served by CIBC London
> - To demonstrate our dedication in helping to prepare children for future success
> - To encourage volunteerism and foster community involvement for future success
>
> ***Eligibility Guidelines***
>
> Please note that our charities' work must fall under all of the following criteria to qualify:
>
> - UK/European registered charities that are well administered, with a record of achievement or potential for success in line with our overall goals
> - UK/European registered charities with an annual income of less than £5 million pounds
> - Projects or programs that provide a tangible benefit to European children and the communities where they live; which may also have potential for CIBC to donate time and resources in a non-financial capacity

In 2013/14 the foundation had assets of £703,000 and an income of £526,000, including £83,000 from CIBC World Markets. Grants to 12 organisations totalled £851,000.

Beneficiaries include: CHICKS (£380,000); the PACE Centre (£250,000); Haven House Children's Hospice, Rainbow Trust Children's Charity and Rays of Sunshine (£63,000 each); Honeypot (£28,000); and Homestart Greenwich, Roald Dahl's Marvellous Children's Charity, the Sick Children's Trust, Tommy's and WellChild (£1,000 each).

Exclusions

The following categories of requests would typically not be considered for foundation funding:

- Donations to individuals; political or advocacy groups; private schools and groups that limit their activities to benefiting persons of a designated ethnic or religious affiliation
- Endowments: funds given permanently to a foundation so it may produce its own income for grant-making purposes
- Multi-year projects or commitments
- Charities with an annual income over £5 million

Applications

In the past the foundation has chosen its charities for the year through funding requests that are accepted only in January. The foundation's website provides the following details at the time of writing, but it is worth checking the website for the latest details.

> All applications should be made by email. If this is not possible please contact Howard Redgwell.
>
> All applicants should read the eligibility guidelines and must also send:
>
> - A brief presentation/document detailing the charity's background and activities
> - Last year's accounts filed with the Charity Commission
> - A very short memo (up to one A4 page) detailing how the funds raised by CIBC will be used, and the potential need for non-financial assistance from CIBC and its staff
>
> Once all of the applications have been received, the trustees for the CIBC Children's Foundation in Europe will decide which charity or charities will be chosen for the year. Charities may be invited to make presentations to the trustees.

The Congregational & General Charitable Trust

Protestant churches, in particular those of the United Reformed and Congregational denominations

£142,000 (2013)

Beneficial area

UK.

Correspondent: Robert Wade, Congregational & General Insurance, Currer House, Currer Street, Bradford BD1 5BA (tel: 01274 700700; email: trust@congregational.co.uk; website: www.congregational.co.uk)

Trustees: Revd Arnold Harrison; Robert Wade; Margaret Atkinson; Robert Copleton; Revd William Adams; Revd Pamela Ward; Stephen Wood; Stuart Young; Gordon Pullan

CC number: 297013

According to the trust's website:

> The aim of the Congregational & General Charitable Trust is to make grants for building maintenance and towards the capital costs of community projects to support Protestant churches, in particular those of the United Reformed and Congregational denominations.
>
> Established in 1956 as the charitable arm of the Congregational & General Insurance Company and reformed in 1987 as a separate entity, the trust receives a contribution from the insurance company. This has been wholly owned by the trust since 1994.
>
> A council of management is responsible for the administration and management of

the trust and all grants made are based on the trust's objectives.

Trust Objectives

- To make grants for the overall care, upkeep and extension of churches
- To make grants towards the capital costs of church community projects
- To promote the Christian religion and, in particular, the United Reformed Church, Congregational Denominations and other churches which are of the Protestant tradition

The amount of money given to the trust from the company is dependent on profits made and varies from year to year.

In 2013 the trust had an income of £963,000 and made grants totalling £142,000.

Applications

On a form which can be downloaded from the trust's website. 'When sending your application please attach any supporting documentation – such as your church's or organisation's accounts, the project's accounts, appeal leaflets or project literature – along with your signed application form.'

Grants are awarded by the Congregational & General Charitable Trust twice a year to churches and charitable causes. The closing dates for applications to be considered are 31 January and 31 July each year.

Note that as the trust does not have any full-time employees it is unable to take any queries or applications by telephone. If you wish to email, you may do so at: trust@congregational.co.uk.

Co-operative Community Investment Foundation

General charitable purposes, environmental, community development, young people

£4.6 million (2013)

Beneficial area

UK.

Correspondent: Clare Oakley, Administrator, The Co-operative Group, 1 Angel Square, Manchester M60 0AG (tel: 01618 341212; website: www.co-operative.coop/our-ethics/our-plan/keeping-communities-thriving/funds-and-foundations)

Trustees: Robert Haber; Jennifer Barnes; Herbert Daybell; David Pownall; Andrew Donkin; David Smith; David Morrow

CC number: 1093028

Established in 2000 the Co-operative Community Investment Foundation is administered by the Co-operative Group and funded by its members who have agreed to donate some of their profit share to the foundation. The foundation operates three grant schemes: the Community Fund, Truth about Youth and the Environment Fund.

The following information is taken from the annual report and accounts:

> **Truth about Youth.** The Truth about Youth programme aims to challenge and change negative perceptions of young people. The objectives are:
>
> - To support young people to deal positively with the challenge of growing up in a culture, which has a widespread negative perception of youth
> - To increase levels of interaction between young people and adults to develop projects in which they all have an interest and for those projects to have a lasting benefit
> - To engage young people in identifying and setting up their own co-operative projects which address their needs and demonstrate young people's value to society
> - To successfully communicate the outputs and outcomes of the projects to as wide an audience as possible
>
> During the year ended 31 December 2013, the foundation has awarded 6 grants totalling £1.54 million in relation to the 'Truth about Youth' programme.
>
> **Environment Fund.** The objective of the fund is to support one or two environmental projects each year in the North of England and Northern Ireland. Projects should bring benefits to significant numbers of people, leave a lasting legacy, be innovative and provide clear cut environmental benefits. In 2013 one grant was awarded a grant to Buglife (£25,000).
>
> **The Community Fund.** The fund invites applications for funding of projects through advertising in the Co-operative Group retail outlets, via the Co-operative Group's website and through active promotion in areas in which the Co-operative Group trades. Voluntary, self-help, or not-for-profit organisations are invited to submit a summary of their proposals in a specific format. The applications are reviewed against specific criteria to be successful.
>
> A group must carry out positive work in the community and a project must:
>
> - Address a community issue
> - Provide a good long-term benefit to the community
> - Support co-operative values and principles
> - Ideally be innovative in its approach
>
> In 2013 the Co-operative Membership Community Fund awarded 2,429 grants, totalling £3 million, to community, self-help and voluntary groups in the UK. Community was the main issue addressed with 29% of awards being made in this category. This included projects that helped bring local communities together and offer opportunities such as community homework clubs, gardening clubs and events. 15% of grants were awarded to projects relating to sports including junior sporting teams, gymnastics, martial arts and sporting events throughout the UK.

A list of beneficiaries was not available for the Community Fund. The fund made grants to the following regions during the year:

South and West	462	£593,000
North	457	£534,000
Central and Eastern	396	£513,000
North West and North Midlands	380	£497,000
South East	314	£430,000
Scotland and Northern Ireland	246	£315, 000
Wales and Borders	174	£156,000

In 2013 the foundation had assets of £14 million and an income of £3.4 million. Grants were made to 2,436 organisations totalling £4.6 million. Only the beneficiaries which received the largest amounts were noted in the accounts. Beneficiaries included: British Film Academy (£350,000); Oval House, Princes Trust, Prince's Trust Cymru, Royal Exchange (£280,000 each); and Envision (£73,000).

Exclusions

The Co-operative Membership Community Fund generally excludes:

- Groups other than community, self-help and voluntary
- The core activities of auxiliary groups
- Non-charitable purposes (although a group does not have to be a registered charity)
- Overseas activities
- Grant or loan schemes
- Religious worship
- Core activities of statutory services
- Improvements to property not owned by the applicant
- Party political activity
- Individual sponsorship
- Cadets

Applications

Applications can usually be made online; however, the following was taken from the foundation website:

> Unfortunately, we are not accepting applications to The Community Fund for the time being. The charity's trustees are currently looking at the best way to develop the scheme and to continue to support local communities in the future.
>
> Please accept our apologies for any inconvenience this has caused you, but watch this space for updates and future funding opportunities.
>
> If you have already submitted an application and have received a confirmation email with a case number, your application will be considered before 31 December 2014 and we will email you with an outcome as soon as possible.
>
> If you have any questions, please contact either the helpline team on **0844 262 4001**, or email **community.fund@co-operative.coop**.

Coutts Charitable Foundation

Relief of poverty, general charitable purposes

£197,000 (2013/14)

Beneficial area

UK and overseas.

Correspondent: Kay Boland, Administrator, Coutts & Co., Strand, 440 London WC2R 0QS (tel: 020 7957 2822; email: coutts.foundation@coutts.com; website: www.coutts.com/foundation)

Trustees: Christopher Geidt; Ian Ewart; William Arthur Waldegrave; Nicholas Tapner; Alexander Classen; Leslie Gent; Shirley Tang; Michael Morley; Shivaashish Gupta; Andrew Sumner; Dr Linda Yueh

CC number: 1150784

Coutts & Co. is a private bank and wealth manager. It is one of the world's oldest banks (founded in 1692) and is wholly owned by the Royal Bank of Scotland Group. Headquartered in London, Coutts is the wealth division of Royal Bank of Scotland Group, with clients from over 40 offices in financial centres in the UK, Switzerland, the Middle East and Asia.

The Coutts Charitable Foundation was established in February 2013 and registered with the Charity Commission within the same month. The following information is taken from the Coutts website:

> The Coutts Foundation, established in 2013, is an independent charity registered in England and Wales. Our mission is to support sustainable approaches to tackle the causes and consequences of poverty, focusing on the communities where Coutts has a presence (the UK, Switzerland, Middle East, Asia and Russia/CIS). The foundation board, chaired by Rory Tapner, includes a number of Coutts staff and other highly experienced individuals who strongly identify with the foundation's mission and approach.
>
> The foundation currently focuses its support on a small number of organisations that are delivering sustainable solutions to ensure basic human needs are met (including energy, water, access to education). Building the resilience of vulnerable communities so they are better able to tackle current and future challenges is key.

In 2013/14 the foundation had assets of £445,000 and income of £642,000 from Coutts and Company. Grants to five organisations totalled £197,000.

Beneficiaries include: Lien Aid (£95,000); Ranthambhore Foundation (£45,000); Ashden Trust (£30,000); Connection at St Martins (£17,000); and City Gateway (£10,000).

Applications

The following information is taken from the company's website:

> The Coutts Foundation takes a proactive approach to identifying its grantees. We prefer to fund organisations where our funding can be catalytic – either testing a new idea or helping scale a tested programme.
>
> The Foundation does not accept unsolicited proposals for funding. However, we welcome information about organisations that fit our funding priorities and approach.

There is an information submission form on the website which can be emailed or posted to the foundation.

Coventry Building Society Charitable Foundation

General

£129,000 (2013)

Beneficial area

The Midlands.

Correspondent: Alison Readman, Administrator, Coventry Building Society, Oak Tree Court, Binley Business Park, Binley, Coventry CV3 2UN (tel: 02476 435231; email: alison.readman@thecoventry.co.uk; website: www.coventrybuildingsociety.co.uk/your-society/community.aspx#tabs-3)

Trustees: Emma Brodie; Anna Cuskin

CC number: 1072244

The foundation was launched in 1998. It is a separate entity managed by a board of trustees who determine the policies and decide on the grants to be made. Although some of the trustees are appointed by Coventry Building Society (its main source of income), the majority are independent.

The foundation supports a wide range of causes based, or active, in the Midlands, with a preference for smaller local charities.

It makes donations only to registered charities that are based or active within the region covered by Coventry Building Society's branch network.

Its priority is to give to groups, or activities, aimed at improving the quality of life and opportunity among groups who are disadvantaged or deprived, the consequence of which may lead to social exclusion.

Applications that focus on the following will be welcomed:

- Young people, particularly those who are disadvantaged
- Vulnerable groups such as frail and elderly people, people with a physical disability, people with learning difficulties or those who are mentally ill
- Small neighbourhood groups in areas where they are experiencing the greatest disadvantage
- Supporting communities and voluntary organisations through assisting them in the achievement of social and community development

In 2013 the foundation had assets of £5,000 and an income of £106,000. The foundation made 37 grants totalling £129,000.

Beneficiaries include: Heart of England Community Foundation (£35,000); Gloucestershire Community Foundation (£13,000); Quartet Community Foundation (£7,200); Volunteer Centre Daventry (£2,000); Wales Community Foundation (£1,700); Doorway (£1,500); Orbit Charitable Trust and Coventry Artspace Ltd (£1,000 each); Mobility Trust (£850); and National Coalition Building Institution (£600).

Exclusions

No grants can be given outside the Midlands area. The following are not eligible for support:

- Large charities which enjoy national coverage
- Charities with no base within the branch area
- Charities with an annual donated income in excess of £250,000
- Charities with assets over £500,000
- Projects requiring ongoing commitment
- Large capital projects
- Maintenance or building works for buildings, gardens or playgrounds
- Major fundraising
- Projects which are normally the responsibility of other organisations such as the NHS and local authorities
- Sponsorship of individuals
- Requests from individuals
- Replacing funds which were the responsibility of another body
- Educational institutions, unless for the relief of disadvantage
- Promotion of religious, political or military causes
- Sporting clubs or organisations, unless for the relief of disadvantage
- Medical research or equipment
- More than one donation to the same organisation in a year – further applications will be considered after a period of three years
- Animal welfare

Applications

Applications can be made online through the community foundation for your area. In order to do this, choose the area closest to where your charity operates from the table at the bottom of the Coventry Building Society Charitable Foundation website and click on the relevant link. This will take you to the community foundation website for your area. From here, you will be able to find out more about your local community foundation and all of the information that you'll need to apply for a grant.

Debenhams Foundation

Health, social welfare, breast cancer, children's charities

£368,000 (2013)

Beneficial area

UK.

Correspondent: Kate Thomas, Administrator, Debenhams plc, 10 Brock Street, Regent's Place, London NW1 3FG (tel: 020 3549 6418; email: kate.thomas@debenhams.com; website: www.debenhams.com)

Trustees: Keith Markham; Nicola Zamblera; Patricia Skinner

CC number: 1147682

Established in 2012, this is the charitable foundation of Debenhams Retail plc, a large chain of department stores.

The following information was taken from the foundation's annual report:

> The objects of the charity are to preserve and protect health and to relieve financial hardship, primarily, but not exclusively by in making grants of money, or to pursue other purposes which are exclusively charitable and for public benefit. Following feedback from a survey of Debenhams customers in 2012, 'breast cancer' and 'children' were identified as the most important causes to Debenhams customers. The charity strategy is therefore mainly focused on these two areas. Through a mixture of product sales and fundraising in Debenhams stores money is raised for children's charities and Think Pink, Debenhams own breast cancer initiative. Debenhams stores also participant in fundraising events to support their local charities. The trustees confirm that they have referred to the guidance contained in the Charity Commission's general guidance on public benefit when reviewing the charitable company's aims and objectives and in planning its activities.
>
> The charity receives funding both from Debenhams Retail plc and Debenhams Retail (Ireland) Ltd (in accordance with the respective funding agreements) and also from Debenhams customers and employees. Some projects are supported over a number of years and are monitored on a regular basis. Other projects are funded on a one-off basis at the discretion of the trustees.

In 2013 the foundation had assets of £301,000 and an income of £673,000. It made 30 grants totalling £368,000.

Beneficiaries include: Debenhams Retirement Association (£74,000); BBC Children in Need (£72,000); Breakthrough Breast Cancer, Breast Cancer Campaign (£60,000 each); Pink Ribbon Foundation (£24,000); Retail Trust North (£19,000); NSPCC (£13,000); Marie Curie Cancer Care (£9,000); Wessex Cancer Trust (£500); and Children 1st Scotland (£100).

Applications

In writing to the correspondent for grant-giving or to the local store for community projects.

The Desmond Foundation (formerly known as the RD Crusaders Foundation)

General charitable purposes, especially for the relief of poverty and sickness amongst children and Jewish causes

£780,000 (2013)

Beneficial area

Worldwide.

Correspondent: Allison Racher, Administrator, Northern & Shell Media Group Ltd, The Northern & Shell Building, 10 Lower Thames Street, London EC3R 6EN (tel: 020 8612 7760; email: allison.racher@express.co.uk)

Trustees: Richard Desmond; Northern & Shell Services Ltd; Northern & Shell Media Group Ltd

CC number: 1014352

Registered with the Charity Commission in 1992, the RD Crusaders Foundation was renamed the Desmond Foundation in 2013. The trustees of the charity are Richard Desmond, the owner of Express Newspapers and founder of Northern & Shell, Northern & Shell Services Ltd and Northern & Shell Media Group Ltd. The accounts for 2013 state that 'RD Crusaders Ltd, a company wholly owned by [Richard] Desmond, was incorporated in December 2007 with the purpose of fundraising on behalf of the charity'.

The foundation gives grants for general charitable purposes, especially for the relief of poverty and sickness amongst children and Jewish causes.

In 2013 the foundation had assets of £58,000 and an income of £770,000. Cash totalling £1.1 million was received during the year, of which £350,000 was related to pledges made in prior years. £870,000 was donated by Richard Desmond and £15,000 was donated by ITN – a subsidiary of Northern & Shell Media Group Ltd. There were 64 grants made totalling £780,000 during the year.

Beneficiaries include: Norwood (£250,000); World Jewish Relief (£137,000); UJIA (£100,000); Fight for Sight (£50,000); Variety, the Children's Charity (£21,000); Presidents Club Charitable Trust (£17,500); Well Being of Women (£15,000); Clinton Foundation, Holocaust Education Trust and RNIB (£10,000 each); Chai Cancer Care, the Disability Foundation and Duchenne Children's Trust (£5,000 each); and Lawnfest and Walk the Walk (£1,000 each).

There were 28 grants of less than £1,000 which totalled £9,800.

Applications

In writing to the correspondent. All grant requests are considered and awards made are based on the merits of each proposal.

The Laduma Dhamecha Charitable Trust

General

£258,000 (2013/14)

Beneficial area

UK and overseas.

Correspondent: Pradip Dhamecha, Trustee, The Dhamecha Group, 2 Hathaway Close, Stanmore, Middlesex HA7 3NR (tel: 020 8903 8181; email: info@dhamecha.com)

Trustees: K. R. Dhamecha; S. R. Dhamecha; P. K. Dhamecha

CC number: 328678

The trust was founded by the Dhamecha family who founded and operate the Dhamecha Cash & Carry group based in Greater London. The trust supports a wide range of organisations in the UK and overseas. The aims of the trust are listed in the annual report as being:

- To provide relief of sickness by the provision of medical equipment and the establishing or improvement of facilities at hospitals
- To provide for the advancement of education and/or an educational establishment in rural areas to make children self-sufficient in the long term
- Other general charitable purposes

In 2013/14 the trust had assets of £1.75 million and an income of £349,000 including £300,000 from Dhamecha Foods Ltd. Grants totalled £258,000. No information was available on the size or number of beneficiaries during this year.

Applications

In writing to the correspondent.

The Diageo Foundation

General charitable purposes, education and training, disaster relief, community development

£1.3 million (2012/13)

Beneficial area

Worldwide.

Correspondent: Lynne Smethurst, Administrator, Diageo plc, Lakeside Drive, Park Royal, London NW10 7HQ (tel: 020 8978 6000; email: diageofoundation@diageo.com; website: www.diageo.com)

Trustees: William Bullard; Geoffrey Thomas Bush; James Crampton; Georgie Passalaris

CC number: 1014681

Diageo plc is an international manufacturer and distributor of premium drinks. The company produces and markets a wide range of premium brands, including Johnnie Walker, Crown Royal, J&B, Windsor, Buchanan's and Bushmills whiskies, Smirnoff, Ciroc and Ketel One vodkas, Baileys, Captain Morgan, Jose Cuervo, Tanqueray and Guinness.

The foundation is a registered charity funded entirely by Diageo. It makes grants in support of projects or causes proposed by Diageo businesses and externally.

The following information was taken from the foundation's website:

> The foundation provides focus for our community investment programme by defining areas where we can make the most difference.
>
> Targeting developing countries in Africa, Latin America, Asia and Eastern Europe, as well as awarding grants, the Foundation acts as a catalyst for:
>
> - Encouraging contributions from Diageo businesses and external sources
> - Engaging Diageo employees in fundraising, giving and volunteering
> - Developing partnerships with NGOs and other external bodies
> - Providing expertise and support for establishing and managing effective projects
>
> To be eligible for funding from the Diageo Foundation, projects must fall within one of the four key focus areas: Skills for Life, Water of Life, Local Communities or Disaster Relief. They must also demonstrate the following:
>
> - Addressing a community/social need, in particular excluded and disadvantaged people who, with support, can help themselves to transform their own lives
> - Building partnerships with community groups and NGOs helping build the skills-base of individuals or communities
> - Maximising grants to make them as effective as possible building the economic prosperity of a community
> - Planning a clear exit strategy and appropriate mechanisms to ensure that the benefits derived from the project are sustainable
> - Having clear, well-defined objectives in place, including planned outcomes, desired impact, measurement and evaluation
> - Enhancing the project, if appropriate, by working in partnership with a local Diageo business

In 2012/13 the foundation had assets of £1.7 million and an income of £1.1 million. Grants were made totalling £1.3 million.

Beneficiaries include: Desnoes and Geddes Foundation (£139,000); Water In Africa (Ghana) (£74,000); African Medical and Research (£52,000); Care International (Nepal) (£48,000); Fundación Arrayanes (£19,000); Family Action (£12,000); Christian Aid (£10,000); Ayrshire Cancer Support (£9,000); Islay and Jura Palliative Care Fund (£5,000); Sports for Special Needs (£3,000); and Cancer Research UK and Prostate Scotland (£2,000 each).

Applications

In writing to the correspondent.

The Doughty Hanson Charitable Foundation

General charitable purposes

£272,000 (2013)

Beneficial area

UK and overseas.

Correspondent: Julie Foreman, Secretary, PO Box 31064, London SW1Y 5ZP

Trustees: Richard Hanson; Stephen Marquardt; Richard Lund; Graeme Stening

CC number: 1080755

Established in May 2000, this foundation is the charitable giving arm of Doughty Hanson & Co., an independent private equity fund manager. The objects of the foundation are to relieve poverty distress and suffering, to advance the education and appreciation of the public in the arts and science, and to further religious work and other charitable purposes in any part of the world.

The foundation supports individuals and smaller organisations and prefers to identify specific projects where its contribution can be seen.

In 2013 the foundation had an income of £266,000, all of which came from the company. Grants were made to 43 organisations totalling £272,000.

Beneficiaries included: MediCinema (£20,000); the Snowdon Award Scheme (£15,500); Elizabeth Finn Care (£14,000); the Sick Children's Trust, Brainwave and Canine Partners (£10,000 each); Cancer Research UK (£6,500); Prostate Cancer UK, Brake and the Parkinson's Disease Society (£5,000 each); Listening Books (£3,000); Children's Heart Federation (£2,500); and Coeliac UK (£1,000).

Applications

In writing to the correspondent, although note that the trustees have a preference for personally identifying projects to support.

The James Dyson Foundation

Science, engineering, medical research and education

£944,000 (2014)

Beneficial area

Mainly UK, local community around the Dyson company's UK headquarters, in Malmesbury, Wiltshire.

Correspondent: Kevin Walker, Administrator, Dyson Group plc, Tetbury Hill, Malmesbury, Wiltshire SN16 0RP (tel: 01666 828416; email: jamesdysonfoundation@dyson.com; website: www.jamesdysonfoundation.com)

Trustees: Sir James Dyson; Lady Deirdre Dyson; Valerie West; Prof. Sir Christopher Frayling

CC number: 1099709

This company foundation was set up in 2002 to promote charitable giving, especially to charities working in the fields of science, engineering, medicine and education.

The annual trustees' report states:

> The objects of the foundation, as stated in its governing document, are as follows:
>
> - To advance education and training, particularly in the fields of design and technology – this work can take a number of forms including the free provision of support resources for teachers of design and technology in schools, the running of design engineering workshops and lectures in schools and universities, as well as bursary schemes and collaborative projects
> - To support medical and scientific research
> - To support charitable and educational projects in the region in which the foundation operates

Each year, the foundation donates a number of Dyson vacuum cleaners (for raffle prizes) to charitable causes which fall within its objectives. The cost of these is included in the total grants figure. Small grants may also be made to charitable projects that share the philosophies and objectives of the foundation.

In 2013, the foundation's had assets of £627,000 and an income of £1.1 million. Grants totalled £944,000 and were distributed in three categories as follows:

Education and training	£899,000
Science and medical research	£40,000
Social and community welfare	£4,300

Beneficiaries included: US Education Programme (£211,000); James Dyson Award (£106,000); Royal College of Art (£100,000); D&T Association CPD Project (£70,500); Malmesbury Schools Project (£24,000); Malaysia/Singapore Education Programme (£23,000); Japan Education Programme (£16,000); and Local Community and Education Fund (£11,000).

Applications

Organisations can apply through the 'get in touch' section of the foundation's website.

The Economist Charitable Trust

General charitable purposes, education and training

£98,000 (2013/14)

Beneficial area

UK.

Correspondent: Matthew Hanratty, Administrator, The Economist Group, 25 St James's Street, London SW1A 1HG (tel: 020 7576 8546; email: mathewhanratty@economist.com; website: www.economist.com)

Trustees: Ada Simkins; Kiran Malik; Daniel Franklin; Cecelia Block

CC number: 293709

The Economist Newspaper Ltd is a multinational media company specialising in international business and world affairs. Its principal activities are newspapers, magazines, conferences and market intelligence.

The primary activity of the trust is the disbursement of monies received from the Economist Newspaper Ltd to various charities. Of the trust's donations 50–60% go to charities in the fields of communication, education, literacy and re-training for individuals and groups who are disadvantaged in some way. Approximately 30–40% of funds are used to match donations made by employees of the Economist Group. Remaining funds are utilised to make small donations to small and local charities.

In 2013/14 the trust had assets of £61,000. It had an income of £119,000 from the Economist Newspaper Ltd, £16,000 of which was funds relating to donations made to the Kennedy Memorial Trust. Grants were made totalling £98,000. Details of the beneficiaries were not available.

Applications

In writing to the correspondent. A simple letter plus your latest report and accounts is preferred – a telephone call to clarify specific queries is welcomed (contact number: 020 7576 8546). Applications can be made at any time.

EDF Energy Trust (EDFET)

Grants to individuals to cover the payment of energy bills and other essential household bills or costs and voluntary organisations working in the field of money advice, debt counselling or energy efficiency advice

About £400,000 to organisations (2013)

Beneficial area

UK.

Correspondent: The Trustees, Freepost RLXG-RBYJ-USXE, EDF Energy, PO Box 42, Peterborough PE3 8XH (tel: 01733 421021; fax: 01733 421020; email: edfet@charisgrants.com; website: www.edfenergytrust.org.uk)

Trustees: Denice Fennell; Vic Szewczyk; Tim Cole; Brian Cole; Bob Richardson; Richard Sykes; David Hawkes

CC number: 1099446

The EDF Energy Trust was established in October 2003 to assist individuals who are in debt with their electricity and gas bills. According to the trust's website:

> Our aim is to help people take control of their finances by reducing the burden of their debts and helping them meet their future bills. We hope that the awarding of grants and the provision of money advice and energy efficiency advice will enable people to make a fresh start.

The trust offers two types of grants:

- **Individual grants:** to cover the payment of gas and electricity debts and other essential household debts or costs (applicants must be EDF Energy account holders)
- **Organisational grants:** for organisations working in the field of money advice, debt counselling or energy efficiency advice

The trust periodically agrees an allocation of funding for organisational grants and a set of criteria. Previously, grants have related to raising awareness of the trust and helping vulnerable customers of EDF Energy apply for help from the trust.

Future grant rounds will be announced on the trust's website and in its newsletter.

In 2013 the trust had an income of £3 million and a total expenditure of £2.4 million. Grants were made totalling about £1.9 million, of which around £1.5 million was given to individuals and around £400,000 to organisations.

Previous beneficiaries include: Bristol Debt Advice Centre and East London Financial Inclusion (£20,000 each); Brixton Advice Centre (£18,300); and Brighton and Hove Citizens Advice (£13,800).

Exclusions

No grants are given for: fines for criminal offences; educational or training needs; debts to central government departments; medical equipment, aids and adaptations; holidays; business debts; catalogues; credit cards; personal loans; deposits for secure accommodation; or overpayment of benefits.

Applications

Individual grants: the easiest way to apply for a grant is via the trust's online application form. Alternatively you can print an application form to complete by hand which can be sent to the trust's freepost address or request one from the trust. Forms may also be available from some advice centres such as Citizens Advice.

Organisational grants: it is advisable to contact the foundation for further information on future grant programmes and deadlines.

The ERM Foundation

Environment, sustainable development

£32,000 (2013/14)

Beneficial area

UK and overseas.

Correspondent: Shona King, ERM Group Holdings Ltd, Exchequer Court, 33 St Mary Axe, London EC3A 8AA (email: shona.king@erm.com; website: www.erm.com/foundation)

Trustees: Tassilo Metternich-Sandor; Robin Bidwell; John Simonson; Ian Bailey; Sabine Hoefnagel

CC number: 1113415

Registered in 2006, this is the charitable foundation of Environmental Resources Management Ltd, a global provider of environmental, health, safety, risk and 'social' consulting services. The foundation's annual report states that its objectives are 'to provide human resources and/or financial assistance to projects around the world that contribute to the improvement of the earth's environment, quality of life and sustainable development', and that 'this is done through appropriate charitable, educational and technical endeavours'.

The foundation's annual report also provides details on its relationship with the company and how it operates:

> The ERM Foundation selects projects to support that adhere to one or more of the following criteria: reducing carbon emissions, environmental education, biodiversity and conservation and clean water and sanitation. The foundation works with a wide range of partners to achieve its goals. In addition to ERM [the company], it works with other not-for-profit, private and public sector organisations, both overseas and in the UK.
>
> The foundation seeks, through its programmes and partnerships, to provide financial resources and volunteering or pro-bono support in a way that results in a better global environment achieved through sustainable and equitable development. ERM has provided generous support through making available technical, administrative and management support on an as-needed basis.
>
> The foundation aims to be a responsive and learning organisation that is knowledgeable about the development, aspirations, needs, culture and environment of its partners. It is committed to encouraging diversity, professionalism and contestability of ideas among all its members, staff and volunteers.
>
> The foundation raises money from employees of ERM and other donors. ERM provides matching funds where those donations are raised by employees specifically for charitable purposes. For example, during 2013/14, employees raised funds for a cycle charity in Oxford. The foundation also raised significant funds for its regional flagship project (the Ruvuma Elephant Conservation project in Tanzania). The foundation is advised by a committee of specialists from ERM's current staff and alumni. The foundation also coordinates a variety of activities whereby ERM staff provide professional and volunteering support to environmental initiatives of benefit to local communities. Examples of such activities include providing ecology surveys for a wildlife trust in the UK, technical support for the foundation's elephant conservation flagship project in Tanzania and developing environmental education materials for school children in the UK.
>
> A key programme of the foundation is the Low Carbon Enterprise Fund (LCEF), which supports enterprises in the developing world where the entrepreneurs are seeking to build a low carbon business. The LCEF provides financial support (low interest loans and equity stakes) to these small businesses and also provides pro-bono management and technical support for a wide range of low carbon enterprises.

In 2013/14 the foundation had assets of around £790,000 ($1.2 million) and an income of £272,000 ($413,000), which included funds from the company and the value of donated services. Grants were made totalling around £32,000, with further charitable expenditure focused on support services through the LCEF.

Applications

In writing to the correspondent.

Esh Foundation

Social welfare, environment, education and health, children and young people

£91,500 (2013)

Beneficial area

Cumbria, Durham, North Yorkshire and Northumberland.

Correspondent: Andrew Radcliffe, Administrator, Esh Holdings Ltd, Esh House, Bowburn North Industrial Estate, Bowburn, Durham DH6 5PF (tel: 07976 077621; email: enquiries@esh.uk.com)

Trustees: Brian Walker; Michael Hogan; Austin Donohoe; Karen Humble; Eric Morgan; John Flynn; Jack Lumsden; Dougie Emmerson; Ron Batty; Tony Carroll; Brian Manning

CC number: 1112040

Registered in 2005, this is the charitable foundation of the Esh Group, a civil engineering, construction and house building company based in County Durham. The company has committed to provide the foundation with £1 million over five years until 2017, subject to profits.

The foundation's annual report states that its funding is given in the following areas:

> *Children and young people*
> Groups and projects that help children and young people access activities and services
>
> *Vulnerable people*
> Groups and projects working with disadvantaged and isolated people, in particular providing increased access to services and facilities for people with disabilities, the homeless and the elderly.
>
> *Environmental community regeneration*
> Groups and projects looking to improve local facilities for community use including refurbishment of community buildings and greening and opening up access to the local physical environment
>
> *Education, capacity and skills development*
> Group and community based training and education programmes, particularly for those who have had no previous access to training opportunities, or for the long-term unemployed.
>
> *Health*
> Groups and community based projects providing access to healthy eating, increased physical activity and self-help services, which aim to improve the health and well-being of local people.

In 2013 the foundation had an income of almost £142,000, which included £100,000 from the company and £42,000 from individuals and other local businesses. There were 52 grants made totalling £91,500.

Grants of £1,000 or more were made to: County Durham Community Foundation and Eagles Community Foundation (£20,000 each); NUFC Foundation (£6,500); SAFC Foundation (£6,000); St Cuthbert's Hospice, Butterwick Hospice, Esh Winning AFC and Durham County Cricket Club (£5,000 each); and Avalunch Community Services and Artichoke Trust (£1,000 each).

Applications

In writing to the correspondent. The trustees meet regularly to review applications and further support with the process is provided by the County Durham Community Foundation.

Euro Charity Trust

Relief of poverty, education

£2.4 million (2013)

Beneficial area

Worldwide, mainly India, Africa, Bangladesh and the UK.

Correspondent: Nasir Awan, Trustee, Euro Packaging plc, 4 Woodbourne Road, Edgbaston, Birmingham B15 3HQ (email: info@eurocharity.org.uk)

Trustees: Nasir Awan; Abdul Malik; Abdul Alimahomed

CC number: 1058460

The trust receives the majority of its income from Euro Packaging Holdings Ltd. Donations are made to both organisations and individuals worldwide. Euro Packaging has grown from a small paper bag merchants into a large diversified packaging group. Paper bag production commenced in 1984 and today the firm is the UK's largest manufacturer. It has its own facilities for polythene bag manufacture, and also recycles both plastic and paper products.

According to the 2013 annual report and accounts, the trust's objects are as follows:

- The relief of poverty
- The relief of the elderly, the vulnerable (such as young children or anyone with special needs) or hardship, including orphans and widows
- The provision of basic necessities and amenities to those in need wheresoever such as water, electricity and medical facilities
- The advancement of education
- [general charitable purposes]

In 2013 the trust had assets of £327,000 and an income of £2.1 million. Grants were made totalling £2.5 million. Over two thirds of the trust's grant-making is concentrated in India. It is also likely that grants are made to organisations in the local area around Euro Packaging sites (in the UK in Birmingham and in Malaysia) and Malawi, where the settlor is originally from. Grants were broken down as follows:

	Amount*
Welfare including the provision of food, water, clothing and healthcare	£733,000
Education and sponsorship	£1.33 million
Construction and land	£654,000
Medical provision	£30,000
Other activities	£7,000

*this includes £31,000 to individuals.

Beneficiaries included: Nathani Charitable Trust (£1.26 million); Maulana Hussain Ahmed Madani Charitable Society and Charitable Trust (£440,000); Anfar Foundation (£279,000); Anjuman-i-Islam (£219,000) Imadul Muslimeen (£204,000); and Mehboob Memorial Centre (£135,000).

Applications

In writing to the correspondent.

The Fidelity UK Foundation

General, primarily in the fields of arts and culture, community development, education and health

£4.8 million (2013)

Beneficial area

Particular preference is given to projects in Kent, Surrey, London and continental Europe.

Correspondent: Sian Parry, Administrator, Oakhill House, 130 Tonbridge Road, Hildenborough, Tonbridge, Kent TN11 9DZ (tel: 01732 777364; website: www.fidelityuk foundation.org)

Trustees: Edward Johnson; Barry Bateman; Anthony Bolton; Richard Millar; John Owen; Sally Walden

CC number: 327899

This foundation was established in 1988 to strengthen not-for-profit organisations primarily in regions surrounding Fidelity International's major corporate locations. Particular preference is given to projects in Kent, Surrey and London. Grants from the foundation are made only for charitable purposes and are designed to encourage the highest standards of management and long-term self-reliance in non-profit organisations. Taking an investment approach to grant-making, it funds organisations where it can add lasting, measurable value. The aim is to support major initiatives that charitable organisations undertake to reach new levels of achievement.

The foundation's charitable giving is mainly in the areas of:

- Arts and culture
- Community development
- Education
- Health

The following information is provided by the foundation on its website:

> Investment is typically directed to specific projects in the following categories:
>
> - **Capital improvements** such as new construction, renovations, expansions and equipment which are central to sustainability and the strategic vision of the organisation
> - High impact **information technology upgrades** which substantially increase an organisation's efficiency, effectiveness and sustainability
> - **Organisational development** projects which seek to establish a new, transformational strategic path. This can include helping charities to investigate and proceed with mergers
> - **Planning initiatives**, including those that use expert/external consultants
>
> Grants will not normally cover the entire cost of a project. We see an organisation's ability to attract support from a broad range of funders as a key sign of its strength and sustainability. Applicants should have significant funding in place prior to application. The foundation typically invests when the majority of required funding has been raised from other sources.
>
> Grants for applicants in London, Kent and Surrey are normally made towards projects with a total budget in excess of £50,000. Applications from Birmingham and Manchester will only be considered for substantial projects. Applicants must normally have annual revenue in excess of £1 million and be applying for a grant of £150,000 or more.
>
> *How we assess an applicant*
>
> Beyond our basic grant guidelines, we review the organisation to determine whether our investment can add value. Among the factors we consider are the organisation's financial health, the strength of its management team and board, and the quality of its strategic and operational plans.
>
> We also look at the size and scope of the organisation, evaluating its position within the context of its market and the needs of the people and stakeholders it serves. We look for leverage and wider impact. This analysis helps us evaluate if a grant has the realistic potential to measurably improve a charity's impact in its sector, and its sector's potential to bring about fundamental, lasting change.
>
> *How we assess a project*
>
> We view each project in the context of the organisation's strategy and long-term goals. Funded projects tend to be those which transform the organisation's ability to achieve its mission.
>
> As an investor, we ultimately seek to understand a project's potential social return. We want to understand if it will work and what it will achieve. In evaluating its potential for success, we seek evidence of:
>
> - The extent and nature of the need
> - A realistic, transformational uplift in quantitative and qualitative outcomes
> - A costed project budget which demonstrates value for money
> - A thorough implementation plan, including a plan for performance measurement and evaluation
> - Growth in value to the organisation and the community it serves
> - Significant support from other funders

Some international grants are made outside the UK by the FIL Foundation, which shares some administration with the Fidelity Foundation. The priorities and restrictions are similar and grants are made to established charities which serve beneficiaries in Continental Europe, Australia, Japan, China, Hong Kong, Korea and Taiwan.

Grantmaking in 2013

During the year the foundation had an income of £9.1 million and assets of £154.2 million which includes a permanent endowment of £151.1 million. Grants totalled £4.8 million which were broken down into the following areas:

Arts, Culture and Heritage	12	£2.1 million
Community development	15	£1.4 million
Education	13	£1.1 million
Health9	9	£515,000

Beneficiaries included: Tate Foundation and The National Trust for Places of Historic Interest or Natural Beauty: Knol (£315,000 each); Kent Community Foundation (£300,000); Young Epilepsy (£250,000); Cancer Research Trust UK (£176,000); Scottish Opera Theatre Royal Ltd (£170,000); Livability (£50,000); Rainbow Trust Children's Society (£34,000); Bow Arts Trust (£27,000); Hospice in the Weald (£23,000).

The foundation also gives a helpful breakdown of the type of grants awarded:

Building acquisition/ development/restoration	19	£2.6 million
Information technology	16	£1.3 million
Programme costs	5	£745,000
Equipment	5	£383,000
Organisational development/ planning	4	£95,000

Exclusions

Grants are not generally made to:
- Charities that have been in existence for less than three years
- Sectarian or political organisations
- Schools, colleges, universities or playgroups
- Individuals
- Community centres
- Sports clubs
- General appeals and circulars

Grants are not made for:
- Salaries or general running/core costs
- Training projects
- The replacement of dated or out-of-warranty IT equipment
- Marketing costs
- The promotion of religion
- Sponsorships or benefit events
- University/college fees, research projects or gap year expeditions

Grants will not normally:
- Cover the entire cost of a project
- Be awarded to an organisation in successive years
- Cover costs incurred prior to application and/or the grant being awarded.

Grants are given for one-off investments and planned expenditure.

Applications

In writing to the correspondent. Applicants should enclose a summary form (the form can be downloaded from the foundation's website) as well as a separate document outlining (as advised on the foundation's website):

The organisation:
- A brief history and key achievements
- An overview of the forward strategy and key objectives

Project details including:
- An indication and evidence of the need for the project that requires funding
- An outline of the proposed project, and how it fits into the wider strategic plan
- The project's objectives and forecast outcomes
- An indication of how the project's success will be monitored and evaluated
- An implementation plan/timeline
- An itemised budget
- The fundraising plan, including a list of other actual/potential funders and the status of each request
- An indication of what a grant would allow your organisation to achieve, and how a grant will change or improve the long-term potential and sustainability of your organisation

Please also supply the following supplementary documentation:
- A list of the directors and trustees with their backgrounds
- The most recently audited annual financial statements
- The most recent monthly management accounts

There are no deadlines for submitting grant proposals. All applications will normally receive an initial response within three months. The review process can take up to six months, so it is worth factoring this into your funding plan. The foundation may request additional information or a site visit to better familiarise themselves with the organisation, its management team and the project. The foundation welcomes informal phone calls prior to the submission of a formal application.

Applicants for international grants should not use the application form. Instead you should post a brief outline of your organisation and funding proposal. If the trustees would like to take your application further they will respond and advise you whether you should make a full application.

Ford Britain Trust

Community service, education, environment, disability, schools, special needs education, young people

£119,000 (2013/14)

Beneficial area

Local to the areas in close proximity to Ford Motor Company Ltd's locations in the UK. These are Essex (including East London), Bridgend, Southampton and Daventry.

Correspondent: Gary Smith, Administrator, Room 1/445, c/o Ford Motor Company Ltd, Eagle Way, Brentwood, Essex CM13 3BW (tel: 01268 404831; email: fbtrust@ford.com; website: www.ford.co.uk/fbtrust)

Trustees: Michael Callaghan; David Russell; Michael Brophy; Dr June-Alison Sealy; Wendy James; Jane Skerry; Paul Bailey; Lara Nicoll

CC number: 269410

The Ford Britain Trust serves the communities in which Ford Motor Company Ltd and its employees are located. The trust provides grants mainly to registered charities and schools that are in support of youth development; schools and education that have a particular emphasis on special educational needs; people with disabilities; and community-related services.

The trust particularly encourages applications from Ford employees, but is open to all, provided that applicants meet the selection criteria.

Grants are typically one-off, provided for specific capital projects or parts of a project, and fall into two categories:
- Small grants – for amounts up to £250, available four times a year
- Large grants – for amounts over £250 and usually up to £3,000, available twice a year

Applications for new Ford vehicles are considered when two-thirds of the purchase price is available from other sources. These grants are not usually more than £2,000, but registered charities may be able to arrange a reduction from the recommended retail price. Grants are not available for second-hand vehicles.

In 2013/14 the trust had assets of £338,000 and an income of £161,000. Grants totalled £119,000, broken down as follows:

Community service	42	£34,000
Schools/education	24	£33,000
Youth	26	£32,000
Disability	13	£18,000
Special needs education	3	£2,800

Beneficiaries included: Malayalee Association of the UK (£3,100); Ashlawn School, Nantymoel Primary School and Pavilion Pirates Preschool (£3,000 each); Belchamps Scout Activity Centre and Havering Citizens Advice (£2,700 each); Oldcastle Primary School, Thames Tennants and Residents Association (£2,500 each); SNAP (£2,400); and Ian Mikardo Primary School (£2,300).

Grants of £2,000 each or less totalled £74,000.

Exclusions

Ford Britain Trust does not make grants for the following purposes:
- Major building works
- Sponsorship or advertising
- Research
- Overseas projects
- Travel
- Religious projects
- Political projects
- Purchase of second-hand vehicles
- Third party fundraising initiatives (exceptions may be made for fundraising initiatives by Ford Motor Company Ltd employees and retirees)

Applications

Applications can be made in three ways:
- Download the PDF version from the website to print out, complete and return by post to the correspondence address
- Save the Word version to your computer, complete it electronically and return it by email to fbtrust@ford.com

- Request a paper copy on 01277 252551 to complete and return by post to the correspondence address

Applications for large grants should include a copy of the organisation's most recent report and accounts.

Small grant applications are considered in March, June, September and November and should be submitted by the 1st of each month. Applications for large grants are considered in March and September.

The Goldman Sachs Charitable Gift Fund (UK)

Education, arts and culture, social welfare, medical

£1.6 million (2012/13)

Beneficial area

USA, UK, Canada, France and Hong Kong.

Correspondent: Mike Housden, Trustee, Goldman Sachs International, Peterborough Court, 133 Fleet Street, London EC4A 2BB (tel: 020 7774 1000)

Trustees: Robert Katz; Mike Housden; Peter Fahey

CC number: 1120148

This fund was established by Goldman Sachs International in 2007 as one of the vehicles for its charitable giving. The fund states that it makes grants in the USA and the UK, and well as Canada, France and Hong Kong, although in practice organisations are supported worldwide. It is also connected to Goldman Sachs Gives (which is outlined in the next entry).

The fund's annual report provides information on its operational activities, a summary of which is given here:

> The objects of the fund are to promote for the public benefit the advancement of education, the relief of poverty and any other charitable purposes in both English and American law.
>
> The on-going strategy of the fund is to make grants pursuant to its objects from donated funds solicited from the Goldman Sachs Group, Inc. and its predecessors, subsidiaries, affiliates and successors, current and former employees, partners and managing directors of Goldman Sachs. The fund, including its Hong Kong branch, operates as a donor advised fund whereby the directors establish donor accounts for individual donors to make recommendations, although the ultimate decision for the distribution of funds rests solely with the directors [trustees] of the fund. Consequently, the directors consider that it is appropriate to disclose the funds as unrestricted. The directors pursue a broad strategy of ensuring proper due diligence in the assessment of grant applications with regard, among other things, to:
>
> - Proper identification of grant recipients
> - Establishing that grant purposes are charitable in both English and American law; and
> - Ensuring the legality of making grants to the recipients
>
> The fund has established its grant making policy to achieve its objects for the public benefit. The fund ensures that proper due diligence is undertaken to establish that proposed projects are charitable. In addition, the fund's grants are made on terms either requiring reporting or entitling the Fund to require reporting at its discretion, and in all cases restrict private benefit to donors to the Fund (and those connected with them).

In 2012/13 the fund had assets of £9.2 million ($14 million) and an income of £1.7 million ($2.6 million). There were 69 grants made during the year totalling around £1.6 million ($2.4 million), broken down as follows (with figures converted from $US):

Education	£1.2 million
Arts and culture	£164,500
Community	£145,500
Humanitarian	£87,000
Other	£28,000
Medical	£2,300

The largest donations, listed in the fund's accounts, were largely made to organisations in the USA. They were: Pacific Ridge School (£658,000); American Associates of the Royal National Theatre Inc. (£164,500); Yale University (£131,500); Trustees of Columbia University (£72,500); EMpower – Emerging Markets Foundation (a UK-registered charity) (£51,500); and Cornell University (£50,000).

It is unknown where the remaining £472,000 in grants was awarded, although it is likely that this was given to further US organisations as well as those in the UK and elsewhere.

Applications

In writing to the correspondent.

Goldman Sachs Gives (UK)

Education, arts and culture, social welfare, medical

£14.5 million (2012/13)

Beneficial area

Worldwide.

Correspondent: Mike Housden, Trustee, Goldman Sachs International, Peterborough Court, 133 Fleet Street, London EC4A 2BB (tel: 020 7774 1000)

Trustees: Jennifer Evans; Robert Katz; Mike Housden; Peter Fahey; Sally Ann Boyle

CC number: 1123956

This fund was established by Goldman Sachs International in 2008 as one of the vehicles for its charitable giving. It is also connected to the Goldman Sachs Charitable Gift Fund.

The fund's annual report provides information on its operational activities, which is identical to the quoted section listed in the previous entry, Goldman Sachs Charitable Gift Fund, and so has the same objects and strategy.

In 2012/13 the fund had assets of £77.9 million and an income of £19.1 million, including £17.8 million from the company. There were 419 grants made during the year totalling just over £14.5 million, broken down as follows:

Education	£4.55 million
Medical	£4 million
Community	£3.2 million
Arts and culture	£1.28 million
Humanitarian	£1.21 million
Other	£384,500

The largest donations, listed in the fund's accounts, were made to: Cancer Research UK (£2 million); The Rector and Scholars of Exeter College, University of Oxford (£1.1 million, largely for scholarships); St Jude India ChildCare Centres UK (£843,000); Room to Read UK Ltd (£603,500); Foundation HEC (£496,000); Stanford Trust (£432,000); and the Royal British Society of Sculptors (£400,000).

Applications

In writing to the correspondent.

The Greggs Foundation (formerly Greggs Trust)

Social welfare. Projects in the fields of the arts, the environment, conservation, education and health will be considered so long as they have a social welfare focus and/or are located in areas of deprivation

£1.54 million (2013)

Beneficial area

UK, with a preference for the north east of England, and in the regional divisions of Greggs plc.

Correspondent: David Carnaffan, Grants Manager, Greggs plc, Fernwood House, Clayton Road, Jesmond, Newcastle upon Tyne NE2 1TL (tel: 01912 127626; email: greggsfoundation@greggs.co.uk; website: www.greggsfoundation.org.uk)

Trustees: Andrew Davison; Kate Welch; Anne Marie Norman; Fiona Nicholson; Richard Hutton; Tony Rowson; Nigel

Murray; Roisin Currie; Karen Wilkinson-Bell

CC number: 296590

Registered with the Charity Commission in 1987, the Greggs Foundation is the corporate charity of Greggs plc, whose principal activity is the retailing of sandwiches, savouries and other bakery-related products with a particular focus on takeaway food and catering. Greggs plc donates at least 1% of its pre-tax profit annually to the foundation. In addition to cash donations, Greggs plc also provides office accommodation and finance and administrative support via part-time secondment of qualified staff.

The accounts for 2013 state that 'Ian Gregg (former chairman of Greggs plc) set up the foundation as a registered charity in 1987 with the aim of giving something back to the communities where Greggs plc trades, and where customers and employees live.'

The trust makes grants to organisations with charitable objectives in the north east of England with the aim of improving the lives of disadvantaged people and enhancing the quality of life in local communities. Divisional Charity Committees based within the regional divisions of Greggs plc also make grants on behalf of the trust and are located in Newcastle upon Tyne, Glasgow, Manchester, Birmingham, Treforest, Enfield and Twickenham.

The foundation's accounts for 2013 state that it currently runs the following four grant programmes:

- **Major Grants** offer financial support to help sustain and increase the capacity of organisations that are based in and support people who live in the north east of England
- **Hardship Fund** makes grants to individuals and families who live in extreme financial hardship. The grants are used to provide household goods such as cookers, clothing, beds and bedding
- **Regional Grants** are administered by seven regional charity committees based throughout the UK. Each regional grants aims to make a difference to people in need in our local areas. Grants of up to £2,000 are offered on a one-off basis
- **Breakfast Clubs** provide healthy breakfasts for pupils at primary schools in disadvantaged areas to help them get a great start to their day.

In 2013 the foundation had assets of £11.2 million and an income of over £1.8 million, of which £650,000 was donated by Greggs plc. Employees also donated £40,000 to the foundation through the Give As You Earn Scheme. Grants totalled £1.54 million during the year.

Beneficiaries include: Benwell Young People's Development Group and North East Special Needs Network (£45,000 each); the Hextol Foundation (£31,000); Eastlea Community Centre (£28,000); Forward Assist and Lynemouth Trust (£25,000 each); Making A Difference (£21,000); Resource Project and Shiney Advice (£15,000 each); Redesign 4 U Ltd (£10,000); Safe@Last (£9,000); Teesside Homeless Action Group (£5,000); St Andrew's Hospice and Survivors in Transition (£4,000 each); St Andrew's Hospice (£3,000); the Gladiator Programme, RDA Glasgow and Woodlands Community Development Trust (£2,000 each); the Phoenix Detached Youth Project and Sunderland Gateway (£1,500 each); Ashington Joint Welfare Scheme, Baby Buttercup Community Interest Company and Southlands School (£1,000 each).

Exclusions

Major grants are not made to:

- Animal charities
- Friends of associations
- Branches or federations of national charities
- Larger organisations with a greater capacity to fundraise
- Uniformed groups such as scouts, guides and sea cadets
- Sports clubs and associations

They are also not made for:

- Overseas travel
- Curricular activities that take place during the school day
- Religious promotion
- Research grants
- Repayment of loans
- Purchase of vehicles
- Unspecified running costs
- Equipment for hospitals
- Major capital projects

Hardship fund grants are not made for:

- Unspecified costs
- Repayment of loans
- Bankruptcy petition fees
- Holidays
- Funeral expenses
- Medical equipment
- Computer equipment

Regional grants are not made for:

- Ongoing running costs
- Contributions towards larger projects/ fundraising appeals
- Animal charities
- Friends of associations
- Uniformed groups such as scouts, guides and sea cadets
- Sports clubs and associations
- Overseas travel
- Curricular activities that take place during the school day
- Religious promotion
- Research grants
- Repayment of loans
- Purchase of vehicles
- Medical equipment
- Major capital projects
- Sponsorship of events or activities

Applications

Each grant programme has its own criteria, guidelines and application process, all of which are available to view on the website.

The H. J. Heinz Company Ltd Charitable Trust

Social welfare, Children and young adults

Around £25,000 (2013)

Beneficial area

UK.

Correspondent: Kelly Barker, Trustee, H. J. Heinz Manufacturing UK Ltd, Hayes Park South Building, Hayes End Road, Hayes, Middlesex UB4 8AL (tel: 020 8848 2346; email: charitable.trust@uk.hjheinz.com; website: www.heinz.co.uk/en/Our-Company/Sustainability/Economic-Sustainability)

Trustees: Drue Heinz; Simon Cowdroy; Nigel Dickie; Chris Humphries; Kelly Barker; P. Jones; S. Digby; C. Winter

CC number: 326254

The Heinz Charitable Trust has long been committed to providing support to promote the quality of life among the communities in which they are present. The trust is overseen by a group of appointed trustees, drawn from all areas of the company. The majority of the trust's income comes form H J Heinz Manufacturing UK Ltd.

The trust's guidelines state that the charities it supports should be from one of the following areas:

Nutrition – promoting improvements in and a better understanding of good nutrition, and contributing to the health and well-being of people and communities.

Healthy Children and Families – improving the overall well-being of people by ensuring children and families have the resources and services necessary to help them live healthy and happy lives.

In 2013 the trust had an income of £4,000 and an expenditure of £26,000. We estimate that around £25,000 was made in grants.

Previous beneficiaries include: Foundation for the Study of Infant Deaths, Children's Sunshine Home, Community Albums, Wigan Stars Nelson's Journey and Hope House Children's Hospice (£5,000 each).

Exclusions

Generally, the foundation does not make loans and does not provide grants for individuals, equipment, conferences, travel, general scholarships, religious purposes, political campaigns, and unsolicited research projects.

Applications

In writing to the correspondent.

UK bodies are more likely to be favoured than local groups unless local applicants operate in the immediate vicinity of the company's main operating locations.

The Hoover Foundation

Social welfare, health, education

£74,000 (2012/13)

Beneficial area

UK, but with a special interest in South Wales, Glasgow and Bolton.

Correspondent: Susan Whetter, Administrator, Hoover Candy Group, Pentrebach, Merthyr Tydfil, Mid Glamorgan CF48 4TU (tel: 01685 725530; email: susan.whetter@hoovercandy.com)

Trustees: David Lunt; Alberto Bertali; Robert Mudie; Matthew Given

CC number: 200274

The objectives of the foundation are primarily to support educational, environmental and charitable work in and around the areas of Hoover Ltd locations throughout the UK namely South Wales, Glasgow and Bolton.

In 2012/13 the foundation had assets of £3.1 million and an income of £87,000. Grants were made totalling £74,000.

Beneficiaries include: Prostate Cancer UK and Genesis Breast Cancer Prevention (£30,000 each); Welsh Young Consumer of the Year Award (£3,000); and Bolton Brass Fund (£2,500).

Grants of less than £1,000 totalled £8,500 and were awarded to organisations that were not listed in the accounts.

Exclusions

The trustees do not make grants to individuals, including students.

Applications

In writing to the correspondent.

The Hudson Foundation

Older people, general

£96,500 (2012/13)

Beneficial area

UK, with a preference for the Wisbech area.

Correspondent: David Ball, Trustee, 1–3 York Row, Wisbech, Cambridgeshire PE13 1EA (tel: 01945 461456; email: davidwball@hotmail.co.uk)

Trustees: David Ball; Stephen Layton; Edward Newling; Stephen Hutchinson

CC number: 280332

Registered in 1980, this foundation wholly owns Alan Hudson Ltd, a fruit and vegetable producing company, from which it receives its income. The object of the foundation is the relief of infirm and/or older people, in particular the establishment and maintenance of residential accommodation for relief of infirm and/or older people and to make donations to other charitable purposes with a preference for the Wisbech area. The accounts state that 'whilst the trustees do make contributions to revenue expenditure of charitable organisations, they prefer to assist in the funding of capital projects for the advancement of the community of Wisbech and district'.

In 2012/13 the foundation had assets of just over £2.1 million and an income of £1.2 million, most of which was trading income from the company. Grants were made to 12 organisations totalling £96,500.

The beneficiaries were: Wisbech Grammar School (£26,500); Wisbech St Mary PCC (£15,000); Wisbech St Mary Playing Fields Association (£12,500); Methodist Homes for the Aged (£10,500); Wisbech Swimming Club (£10,000); Wisbech Angles Theatre (£6,000); Help for Heroes (£5,000); Age is Just a Number (£3,500); Listening Books (£3,000); Wisbech Sea Cadets (£2,000); Mobility Trust (£1,800); and Motability UK (£1,000).

Applications

In writing to the correspondent. The trustees meet quarterly.

IBM United Kingdom Trust

Education and training in ICT

£1.7 million (2013)

Beneficial area

UK, Europe, Middle East and Africa.

Correspondent: Mark Wakefield, Trust Manager, IBM United Kingdom Ltd, 76/78 Upper Ground, South Bank, London SE1 9PZ (tel: 020 7202 3608; email: wakefim@uk.ibm.com)

Trustees: Brendan Dineen; Prof. Derek Bell; Jonathan Batty; Anne Wolfe; Naomi Hill

CC number: 290462

The focus areas for IBM's community investment are the strategic and innovative use of information and communication technology (ICT) in education and training and the promotion of digital inclusion, with the broad objective of raising standards of achievement. Most activity is within the compulsory education phase. The vast majority of IBM's community investment is delivered through specific programmes initiated and developed by IBM in partnership with organisations with appropriate professional expertise. The trust gives preference to organisations concerned with people disadvantaged by poverty and/or at risk of digital exclusion. Preference is given to supporting projects and organisations in areas in which the company is based and/or where there is employee involvement.

The trust's annual report gives the following information on its objects and activities:

- The advancement of education, particularly through the use and understanding of information technology
- The advancement of research, with emphasis (though not exclusively) on information technology
- Improving the condition of life for the disadvantaged or disabled through the use of information technology
- Encouraging the use and understanding of information technology in the charitable sector
- Through the provision of information technology and related services, or otherwise, supporting the relief of poverty, the health of the community and the preservation of the environment

Based on the above objects, and with consideration for public benefit, the trust has the following focuses:

- Increasing the scope, usage and understanding of information technology
- Enabling the disadvantaged to acquire skills, particularly through the use of information technology

- Providing aid in the form of technology and technical support for disaster relief

The trust primarily achieves its aims by supporting the development and delivery of IBM's own community programmes, where these meet the charitable objects of the trust. The support is delivered through the provision of grants of equipment, technical support and cash. The support is provided for IBM's community involvement programmes in the United Kingdom, and across Europe, the Middle East and Africa (EMEA).

The trust's approach to grant making falls into three key areas:

- The provision of grants that advance both the aims of the trust and support IBM programmes
- The provision of small grants in support of charitable organisations in the communities surrounding IBM sites
- The provision of grants that support and encourage employee volunteering by IBM staff

In this way the trust seeks to achieve its aims, not only through key longer term programmes but also through support for smaller scale initiatives by providing direct contributions and encouraging ongoing links between charitable and educational organisations and IBM.

In 2013 the trust had assets of £3.8 million and an income of £1.9 million, which included £1.6 million from IBM International Foundation and £277,000 for IBM subsidiaries. Grants were made totalling just over £1.7 million, broken down as follows:

Increasing use of technology in education	£1.47 million
Provision of IT and other services	£264,000
Disaster relief	£49,000
Support for research	£6,000
Miscellaneous	£1,000

There was also £62,000 towards promoting volunteering, although this cost had been accrued for during the previous year. Specific details of beneficiaries are not listed in the accounts, although information is given there on the IBM programmes and initiatives which the trust supports.

Exclusions

The trust does not provide core funding or contribute to appeals for building projects, religious or sectarian organisations, animal charities, individuals (including students), overseas activities or expeditions, recreational and sports clubs, appeals by third parties on behalf of charities or individuals. The company does not currently offer full-time secondments of employees to voluntary organisations.

Applications

Very few unsolicited requests are considered. If requests are submitted then these should be by email or in writing and include a brief résumé of the aims of the organisation and a detail of what assistance is required. Those considering making an application are advised to telephone first for advice.

Impetus – Private Equity Foundation (Impetus-PEF)

Children and young people, education and training, economic and community development, crime prevention

Around 3.2 million (2013)

Beneficial area

UK.

Correspondent: The Trustees, 138 Eversholt Street, London NW1 1BU (tel: 020 3474 1000; email: info@impetus-pef.org.uk; website: impetus-pef.org.uk)

Trustees: Louise Elson; Johannes Huth; Lionel Assant; Marc Boughton; Stephen Dawson; Craig Dearden-Phillips; Charles Green; Carl Parker; Karl Petersen; Nathaniel Sloane; Hanneke Smits; Nikos Stathopoulos; Prof. Becky Francis; Caroline Mason

CC number: 1152262

Registered with the Charity Commission in 2013, Impetus – Private Equity Foundation was formed from the merger of the Impetus Trust and Private Equity Foundation, bringing together 16 years of experience supporting charity sustainability, effectiveness and growth through its venture philanthropy model.

The foundation's website states that it is:

> Committed to transforming the lives of 11–24 year olds from disadvantaged backgrounds by ensuring they get the support they need to succeed in education, find and keep jobs, and achieve their potential.
>
> We find the most promising charities and social enterprises that work with these children and young people. We help them become highly effective organisations that transform lives; then we help them expand significantly so as to dramatically increase the number of young people they serve.

Packages of support are built upon a venture philanthropy approach which consists of funding, management support from the investment team and specialist expertise from pro bono professionals. Funding is not given for specific items or projects, the packages of support are designed to develop and grow organisations that have ambitions to build their capacity. Organisations must be able to demonstrate clear outcomes and have ambitious growth plans.

The foundation calls the organisations it supports 'the portfolio'. It provides support for those organisations that fall under the following themes:

- Educational attainment
- Work readiness
- Reducing reoffending
- Early years

In 2013 the foundation had assets of £14.7 million and an income of over £15.5 million, of which £3.9 million was cash donations from individuals and companies. Charitable expenditure, which is listed in the accounts as 'supporting charities and capacity building', totalled £8.9 million during the year. Grants paid to portfolio charities in the year totalled £3.2 million and grants to research organisations totalled £72,000.

Beneficiaries included: Place2Be (£516,000); Tomorrow's People (£418,000); Skill Force (£282,000); WorkingRite (£240,000); Street League (£179,000); Blue Sky (£129,000); Prison Radio Association, Resurgo and Ripplez (£100,000 each); Unitas (£50,000); Education Endowment Fund (£42,000); Oxpip (£25,000); Social Economy Alliance (£15,000); Millennium Kids (£6,500); FRC Group and Kainos Community (£5,000 each).

Applications

The foundation's website states that it does not accept unsolicited applications and instead works through referrals from trusted partners who know its investment model. Once a potential charity has been identified, it will undergo a screening process to determine eligibility for the portfolio.

The Johnson Wax Ltd Charitable Trust

Social welfare, education and training, the environment, health, the arts, local community

Around £220,000 (2012/13)

Beneficial area

Areas surrounding S. C. Johnson's sites.

Correspondent: Faye Gilbert, Trustee, S. C. Johnson Ltd, Frimley Green Road, Frimley, Camberley, Surrey GU16 7AJ (email: givinguk@scj.com)

Trustees: Faye Gilbert; Trevor Jessett

CC number: 200332

Registered with the Charity Commission in 1961, Johnson Wax Ltd Charitable Trust is the corporate charity of S. C. Johnson Ltd, a manufacturer of cleaning products for the consumer and industrial markets. The trust receives an annual donation from S. C. Johnson Ltd.

The company's accounts for 2012/13 stated that the company donated a total of £132,000 to the Johnson Wax Charitable Trust. Each year about 2.5% of pre-tax profit from S. C. Johnson goes to the trust.

The trust states that it has the following objectives for the areas where the company operates:

- Promote general charitable purposes for the benefit of the local communities surrounding the sites of S. C. Johnson Ltd
- Provide relief from financial hardship or economic disadvantage
- Advance the education of its residents of all ages, especially young people and schools close to the sites of S. C. Johnson by providing facilities that are not provided by the local education authority
- Develop the capacity and skills of socially and economically disadvantaged people
- Relieve financial hardship, sickness and poor health of elderly people
- Promote the arts
- Provide recreation facilities for young people and people with disabilities
- Promote urban or rural regeneration through conservation, the provision of public amenities and the relief of unemployment

In 2012/13 the trust had an income of £154,000 and a total expenditure of £240,000. Grants for the year are estimated to have totalled around £220,000.

Unfortunately no further information was available at the time of writing (February 2015) as the trust's latest accounts were overdue at the Charity Commission.

Exclusions

No grants to individuals.

Applications

In writing to the correspondent detailing the amount requested and what it is needed for, details of how the grant will benefit a broad cross-section of the Frimley Green community and how a clear social need will be met within it.

The Joron Charitable Trust

Jewish, education, medical research, general

£219,000 (2013/14)

Beneficial area

UK.

Correspondent: Bruce Jarvis, Trustee, Ravensale Ltd, 115 Wembley Commercial Centre, East Lane, North Wembley, Middlesex HA9 7UR (tel: 020 8908 4655; email: ravensale100@btconnect.com)

Trustees: Bruce Jarvis; Joseph Jarvis; Sandra Jarvis; Juliet Jarvis

CC number: 1062547

Established in 1997 the trust receives the majority of its funding from Ravensale Ltd. The company is owned by the Jarvis family and is involved in property investment and development as well as the manufacture of ballpoint pens. Both the company's directors Bruce Jarvis and Joseph Jarvis are also trustees of the trust.

The trust's policy is to make grants to registered charities in the fields of education and medical research and other charities which can demonstrate that the grants will be used effectively.

In 2013/14 the trust had assets of £44,000 and an income of £175,000 received in donations from Ravensale Ltd. Grants to seven organisations totalled £219,000.

The beneficiaries were: The Wilderness Foundation (£185,000); Carers Trust (£25,000); ACVV Central (£4,500); Cancer Research UK, Devon Air Ambulance, Jamie Proctor Foundation and Maggie Keswick Jenks (£1,000 each).

Applications

In writing to the correspondent. The 2013/14 accounts state that: 'There is no formal grants application procedure. The trustees retain the services of a charitable grants advisor and take account of the advice when deciding on grants.'

Ladbrokes in the Community Charitable Trust

General, health, education, community projects

£422,000 (2013)

Beneficial area

UK (communities in which the shops and businesses of Ladbrokes Betting and Gaming Ltd or Ladbrokes eGaming Ltd operate).

Correspondent: Michael O'Kane, Trustee, Ladbrokes plc, Imperial House, Imperial Drive, Harrow, Middlesex HA2 7JW (tel: 020 8515 5611; email: claire.simpkin@ladbrokes.co.uk)

Trustees: Michael O'Kane; Susan Trill; Jan Kunicki; Lucy Capon

CC number: 1101804

Ladbrokes in the Community Charitable Trust was established in 2003. Funding comes not from the Ladbrokes company, but via the fundraising efforts of head office and shop staff, customers and 'Event Days'.

The three areas for which grants are most commonly awarded are:

Health – principally research/treatment, hospice services and disability support

Education – to support people with disabilities and disadvantaged people

Community – focusing on projects for homeless and elderly people or social activity projects for those at risk

In 2013 the trust had an income of £515,000 from fundraising activities. Grants were made totalling £422,000 and were broken down as follows:

Medical	£188,000
Social welfare	£137,000
Hospitals and hospices	£53,000
Others	£27,300
Youth support	£7,700
Environment and animals	£7,600

Beneficiaries include: Barnardo's; Bobby Moore Fund; Cancer Research UK; Child Victims of Crime; Haven House Children's Hospice; NSPCC, Prostate Cancer UK and the Responsible Gambling Trust.

Applications

In the first instance, the support of a local shop should be secured in raising funds on behalf of a cause. The grants committee meets monthly to consider applications.

Leeds Building Society Charitable Foundation

General charitable purposes, with a preference for social welfare

£122,000 to organisations (2013)

Beneficial area

Areas where the society's branches are located.

Correspondent: Sally Smith, Reward Manager, Leeds Building Society, 105 Albion Street, Leeds, West Yorkshire LS1 5AS (tel: 01132 167296; website: www.leedsbuildingsociety.co.uk/foundation)

Trustees: Peter Chadwick; Ann Shelton; Robert Wade; Gary Brook; Martin Richardson; Michael Garnett; Gary Hetherington

CC number: 1074429

Registered with the Charity Commission in 1999, Leeds Building Society Charitable Foundation is closely associated with Leeds Building Society.

The accounts for 2013 state that the foundation will 'consider applications and grant donations to UK-registered charities which are working to relieve suffering, hardship, poverty and the associated direct consequences'.

It aims to benefit as many people in need who either live or work in the areas in which the company's branches operate in the UK. Grants range between £200 and £1,000 and must be for capital expenditure only.

The foundation's website lists some of the areas it supports:

- Homeless people
- Adults and children with physical and mental disabilities
- Older people
- Underprivileged families
- Deaf, blind and partially sighted people
- Community projects benefiting local residents
- Victims of natural and civil disasters in the UK
- Scout, guide and play groups

In 2013 the foundation had assets of £2,200 and an income of £120,000. During the year 164 grants were made totalling £122,000. No grants were given for amounts over £1,500, apart from one grant given to Mencap (£3,300).

A list of beneficiaries was unavailable at the time of writing (February 2015).

Exclusions

The foundation is unlikely to support:

- The restoration or upgrading of building, including churches
- Environmental charities (unless there is a benefit to a disadvantaged community)
- Administration equipment such as IT equipment
- Projects with religious, political or military purposes
- Individuals, including sponsorship of individuals
- Animal welfare projects
- Medical research

Applications

In writing to the correspondent, including the following information: the name of the organisation; the name of the project, and brief information about its work; a contact name, address and phone number; the registered charity number; details of what the donation would be used for; who would benefit from the donation; and the nearest Leeds Building Society branch.

Criteria is available to view on the website. The trustees meet four times a year in March, June, September and November. Following the meeting the foundation will write to each applicant to inform them as to whether their application has been successful.

The trust is unable to consider applications if support has been provided in the last two years.

The foundation operates independently of Leeds Building Society and so local branch staff are unable to answer questions about the foundation. For further information the foundation can be contacted directly.

LHR Airport Communities Trust

Supporting projects which benefit the local community in the areas of education, environment and economic regeneration/employment

£1 million (2012)

Beneficial area

Communities local to Heathrow Airport Holdings Group's four UK airports; Aberdeen, Glasgow, Heathrow and Southampton.

Correspondent: Caroline Nicholls, Director, LHR Airports Ltd, The Compass Centre, Nelson Road, Hounslow, Middlesex TW6 2GW (tel: 07836 342495; email: communitiestrust@heathrow.com; website: www.baacommunitiestrust.com)

Trustees: Mary Francis; Alison Moore; Alan Coates; Matthew Gorman; Clare Harbord; Punham Karbanda; Steve Ronald; Christine Rawlings

CC number: 1058617

BAA plc established this trust, formerly the BAA 21st Century Communities Trust, in 1996 and is the main funder, donating 0.15% of pre-tax profits per annum.

The trust was set up as a grant-making charity to support and strengthen local communities close to the airports at Aberdeen, Glasgow, Heathrow and Southampton. It focuses on education, environment and economic regeneration/employment.

The trust has set a vision to work with communities, to create significant and positive social change.

Its objectives are:

- To create learning opportunities for young people and so raise their aspirations
- To break down barriers to employment through skills development
- To help protect the environment
- To support staff active in the community.

The trust's activities include:

- Funding projects in the communities local to the Heathrow Airport Holdings Group's four UK airports: Aberdeen, Glasgow, Heathrow and Southampton. The local community fund panels seek and review grant applications for projects and is focused mainly on education, youth development and the environment
- Supporting projects and charitable initiatives put forward by staff
- Local community projects delivered through international and national programmes; this includes partnerships with the youth volunteering charity vInspired and The Challenge Network, providing a public benefit through integration with the local community and the grant-making undertaken as a result.

Grantmaking policy

Grant applicants must demonstrate that at least one of the following objectives is met:

- Create learning opportunities for young people and so raise their aspirations
- Help protect the environment
- Break down barriers to employment through skills development
- Support staff active in the community

In 2013 the trust had assets of £1.3 million and an income of £931,000. There were 243 grants made totalling £1 million.

Beneficiaries included: the Groundwork South Trust Ltd (£147,000) Eastleigh Youth Trust (£50,000); Kibbleworks (£38,000); the Challenge Network (£25,000); Volunteer Centre Hounslow (£12,600); Friends of the River Crane (£6,400); Houston Playpark Improvement Group (£2,500); the Conservation Volunteers (£2,000); Hamble Sea Scouts and Mackie Academy School Fund (£1,000 each); Tonic Music for Mental Health and Woodlands Primary School (£500 each).

Exclusions

Applications which benefit individuals only, whether or not they meet the other criteria, will fail. No support is given for religious or political projects. Grants will not be made to nationally based organisations unless the direct benefit will be felt locally and the other criteria are satisfied. The trust does not support general running costs or staff costs.

Applications

Each airport runs its own community fund. Application forms, criteria and guidelines, for the four funds, are available to download on the website. Before making a formal grant application, email a summary of your proposal to your local community fund representative, or the correspondent, so that they can give guidance. The trustees meet four times a year to assess applications over £5,000. Each local panel meets at least three times a year to consider applications under £5,000.

Lloyd's Charities Trust

General charitable purposes
£619,000 (2013)

Beneficial area

UK, with particular interest in East London.

Correspondent: Suzanna Nagle, Secretary, Lloyd's of London, Lloyd's Building, 1 Lime Street, London EC3M 7HA (tel: 020 7327 6144; email: suzanna.nagle@lloyds.com; website: www.lloyds.com/lct)

Trustees: John Spencer; Lawrence Holder; Iain Wilson; Rupert Atkin; Graham Clarke; Chris Harman; Vicky Mirfin; Neil Smith; Victoria Carter

CC number: 207232

The charity was set up in 1953, and is the charitable arm of Lloyd's insurance market in London. There are three separate funds that are used to administer grants. Through these, the trust looks to support London-based charities in the fields of education, employability, enterprise and sport. It also seeks to support emergency appeals.

The following information on the funds was available on the trust's website:

> *General fund*
> Lloyd's Charities Trust's current funding priorities aim to maximise the impact of the Trust's charitable giving, by focusing on three key areas:
> - Making a great city greater: at home in London, we give to tackle disadvantage and foster opportunity
> - Responding to disasters and emergencies: around the world, we give to relieve suffering and rebuild lives
> - Preparing for the future: we give to equip individuals and communities with the resources and skills they need to meet the challenges of a rapidly changing world
>
> *Lloyd's Community Programme*
> Lloyd's Community Programme (LCP) is a sub-fund of the Trust. The Lloyds Community Programme aims to improve the opportunities and environment of the people of Tower Hamlets and neighbouring East London boroughs by mobilising the support and involvement of individuals and companies in the Lloyd's market, primarily through volunteering.
>
> *Lloyd's Education Fund (previously the Cuthbert Heath Centenary Fund)*
> Following the 2009 review of Lloyd's Charities Trust's charitable giving strategy, it was agreed that the income of the Cuthbert Heath Centenary Fund, which had previously been providing bursaries at nine public schools, should be used to benefit a greater number of young people with a particular focus on London communities.

In 2013 the trust had assets of £2.6 million and an income of £517,000. Grants were made in the form of donations and bursaries totalling £619,000.

Previous beneficiaries include: the Prince's Trust (£75,000); and Bromley By Bow Centre (£50,000).

Exclusions

The trust's website states that:

> Lloyd's Charities Trust will not fund the following:
> - Organisations that are not registered charities or non-UK-registered charities (except at the occasional discretion of trustees)
> - Political parties or lobbying organisations
> - Local charities outside London, unless there is significant involvement from a person currently working in the Lloyd's market, in which case the application must come from that individual (see 'Lloyd's Market Charity Awards')
> - Mainstream schools, PTAs and educational establishments unless there is significant involvement from a person currently working in the Lloyd's market, in which case the application must come from that individual (see 'Lloyd's Market Charity Awards')
> - Grant-making bodies to make grants on our behalf
> - Animal welfare causes, zoos, animal rescue
> - The promotion of religion or other beliefs
> - Individuals, including student grants, bursaries, medical costs or financial assistance
> - Sponsorship of events or individuals including taking tables at gala dinners
> - Advertising including in brochures for charitable events
> - Costs associated with expeditions
> - Retrospective funding for work that has already taken place
>
> Lloyd's Charities Trust will typically not fund the following:
> - Military causes (see 'Lloyd's Patriotic Fund' for support for military welfare charities)
> - Arts, culture or heritage charities
> - Outward bound courses and adventure experiences
> - Conferences, cultural festivals, exhibitions and events
> - Churches, cathedrals and other historic buildings

For more information on the sections referred to, see the trust's website.

Applications

Lloyd's Charities Trust will be supporting our partner charities for the next three years and are therefore not inviting new proposals for funding.

Lloyds Bank Foundation for England and Wales

Social and community needs
£21 million (2013)

Beneficial area

UK.

Correspondent: Mr Paul Streets, Administrator, Pentagon House, 52–54 Southwark Street, London SE1 1UN (tel: 020 7378 4601; email: enquiries@lloydstsbfoundations.org.uk; website: www.lloydstsbfoundations.org.uk)

Trustees: Paul Farmer; Dame Denise Platt; Prof. Ian Diamond; Rob Devey; Hilary Armstrong; Carolyn Fairbairn; Sir Clive Booth; Philip Grant; Mohammad Naeem; Prof. Patricia Broadfoot; Helen Edwards; Catherine Kehoe

CC number: 327114

The foundation receives the majority of its income from Lloyds Bank plc. There is an agreement with Lloyds Bank that until 2020 the foundation will receive 0.3616% of the group's adjusted pre-tax profits/loss, averaged over three years.

The foundation's Community Programme has recently been replaced with the Invest and Enable programmes in order to create a more flexible and responsive approach to grant-making.

The following information on the programmes was available on the trust's website:

> **Invest** – A flexible, long-term core funding programme for organisations delivering clear, targeted outcomes for disadvantaged people. Grants range from £10,000 to £25,000 for two to six years.
>
> **Enable** – A smaller and shorter grants programme for organisations that have identified clear development needs. Grants are up to £15,000 for one to two years.
>
> **Enhance** – A programme working alongside the Invest or Enable programme providing an option of tailored in-kind support to strengthen and develop charities' effectiveness.
>
> In order to obtain funding you must work with people aged 17 and over who are experiencing at least one of the following:
> - Have been abused or are at risk of abuse
> - Are victims of sexual exploitation
> - Are ex-offenders or those at risk of offending
> - Are long-term unemployed
> - Are leaving care
> - Are homeless
> - Have learning disabilities
> - Have mental health and well-being issues
> - Have addictions
> - Are isolated and vulnerable

- Have severe financial difficulty as a compounding disadvantage

The only exceptions are people aged under 17 that are:

- Young parents
- Looked after children and disabled young people moving into independent living

It is expected that organisations that receive funding would normally work with people experiencing multiple disadvantage at one of the critical points in their life – transition points. A detailed list of transition points can be found on the foundation's website.

Grantmaking in 2013

In 2013 the foundation had assets of £45.5 million, an income of £26.8 million including £25.2 million received under deed of covenant from Lloyds Bank plc. There were 841 grants made totalling £21 million.

The following summary analysis of grant-making is taken from the foundation's 2013 annual report, the full version of which is available from the foundation's website:

London	119	£3.5 million
North West	132	£2.9 million
Yorkshire and the Humber	90	£2.2 million
West Midlands	73	£2.2 million
East of England	47	£1.3 million
South East	63	£1.8 million
South West	95	£1.5 million
East Midlands	72	£1.4 million
Wales	76	£1 million
North East	65	£1 million

During 2013, our top funded issues across all geographies in the Community Programme were:

Children and young people	136	£3.1 million
People with disabilities	127	£2.9 million
Community support	104	£2.4 million
Health including mental health	82	£1.8 million
Advice and advocacy	70	£1.7 million
Relationships including caring	63	£1.4 million
Victim support	47	£1.1 million
Training employment and learning	46	£1.1 million
Support for older people	40	£835,000
Homelessness	38	£922,000

Previous beneficiaries include: Hackney CVS (£250,000); Age Concern in Cornwall and The Isles of Scilly (£188,000); Working With Men (WWM) (£38,000); Norfolk Community Law Service and Sexual Abuse and Rape Advice Centre (£30,000 each); Rainbow Services and Greenwich Mencap (£28,000 each); CVS Tamworth (£27,000); Burnley and Pendle Citizens Advice (£22,000); Mind in West Cumbria (£20,000); Hodan Somali Community (£19,000); Broxlow Youth Homelessness (£18,000); Pakistan Association Liverpool (£15,000); Down's Syndrome Association (£12,000); Halton Disability Advice and Appeals Centre (£14,000); and Children and Families in Grief (£8,000).

Exclusions

The foundation does not fund the following types of organisations and work:

Organisations

- Organisations that are **not** registered charities
- Second- or third-tier organisations (unless there is evidence of direct benefit to disadvantaged people)
- Charities that mainly work overseas
- Charities that mainly give funds to other charities, individuals or other organisations
- Hospitals, hospices or medical centres
- Rescue services
- Schools, colleges and universities

Types of work

- Activities which a statutory body is responsible for
- Capital projects or refurbishments
- Environmental work, expeditions and overseas travel
- Funding to promote religion
- Holidays or trips
- Loans or business finance
- Medical research, funding for medical equipment or medical treatments
- Sponsorship or funding towards a marketing appeal or fundraising activities
- Work with animals or to promote animal welfare

Applications

For more information on applications, see the 'how to apply' guide on the website:

Step 1 – Review our funding criteria – check what we do and do not fund

Step 2 – Complete the charity eligibility questionnaire – fill in the short on-line questionnaire which has 3 parts

Step 3 – If your charity is eligible – we will call to discuss if your work is eligible

If the project is eligible the local grants manager will contact the applicant to discuss the best way to make an application and make the form available. A grants manager will visit the charity for any eligible applications for more than £5,000.

We receive applications on an on-going basis. We do not publish formal deadlines or decision dates as these vary between programmes. When you submit your application form we will let you know when to expect our decision but it's normally from three to six months depending on the size of the grant.

Common reasons for unsuccessful applications

The foundation cannot fund all eligible applications even if they are of a high quality because each year the total amount requested by charities exceeds the money that we have available. Other reasons for the foundation not being able to make a grant include:

- Charities' core work not being sufficiently focused on our mission
- Applications not falling within our guidelines
- Charities not filling in the application form properly
- Charities not having up to date annual returns or accounts filed with the Charities Commission or other relevant regulatory bodies

When can I re-apply?

If you receive a grant, you will not be eligible to apply for another grant from the Community Programme for another two years from receipt of the grant (or from receipt of the final payment if it has been two or three-year funding). If your application is unsuccessful, you must wait for a year before you apply again.

Lloyds Bank Foundation for Northern Ireland

Social and community need, education and training

£2.2 million (2013)

Beneficial area

Northern Ireland.

Correspondent: Sandara Kelso-Robb, Executive Director, Lloyds Bank, 2nd Floor, 14 Cromac Place, Gasworks, Belfast BT7 2JB (tel: 02890 323000; email: info@lloydstsbfoundationni.org; website: www.lloydstsbfoundationni.org)

Trustees: Tony Reynolds; Paddy Bailie; Angela Colhoun; Brian Scott; Hugh Donnelly; Carmel McGukian; Lord Leitch; Janet Leckey; Jim McCooe; Janine Donnelly; Robert Agnew; Sandara Kelso-Robb

IR number: XN72216

The overall aim of the foundation is to support underfunded, grassroots charities that enable people, especially disadvantaged people and people with disabilities, to play a fuller role in society. The two main target areas of the foundation are social and community needs and education and training.

Most donations are said to be one-off, with a small number of commitments made over two or more years. The trustees say that they prefer to make donations towards specific items rather than contributions to large appeals, though the trust will consider core funding for small local charities. Applications which help to develop voluntary sector infrastructure are encouraged.

The foundation has in the past run The Community Grant Programme, The Creating Change Programme, The International Programme, The

Partnership Programme, Collaborative Programmes, The Social Enterprise Programme and The Matched Giving Scheme. At the time of writing (February 2015) only the Community Grant Programme and the Matched Giving Scheme are still running.

Matched Giving Scheme

In 2013 there were 145 approved claims made and the average claim was for £364. Thanks to the energy and commitment of the staff of Lloyds Banking Group £52,748 was given to a wide range of organisations working throughout Northern Ireland including Lloyds Banking Group Charity of the Year, Alzheimer's Society.

The following information on the foundation's programmes is taken from the foundation's website:

> *The Community Grant Programme*
>
> The Community Grant Programme remains the main focus of the foundation, and focuses on social and community welfare and education and training.
>
> There are four closing dates per year, usually the second Friday of January, April, July and October. The dates for 2015 are listed [on the Lloyds TSB foundation website]. The board meet to consider applications, normally during the first week of March, June, September and December, making the waiting time for a decision around 10 weeks from the closing date. You should be notified of the result of your application no more than 2 weeks after the board have met.
>
> The average grant is currently between £3,000–4,000.
>
> In order for organisations to be eligible to apply, they must have an income of less than £1 million in the previous 12 months. For registered charities with a headquarters based outside Northern Ireland, the income of their Northern Ireland operation will be the figure used to assess eligibility.
>
> The trustees have taken this decision as there have been an increasing number of applications to the Foundation which makes the decision process more difficult. Also the trustees are keen to ensure they stay in line with the overall aim of the foundation, 'to support *underfunded* charities that enable people, especially disadvantaged or people with special needs, to play a fuller role in the community.' This new eligibility will stay in place for the foreseeable future.

Guidelines for applicants

The guidelines for applicants, detailed on the foundation's website, read as follows:

> The overall policy of the charity is to support underfunded charities which enable people, especially disadvantaged or disabled people, to play a fuller role in the community.
>
> The foundation has two main target areas to which it seeks to allocate funds:
>
> - Social and community needs
> - Education and training
>
> *Social and Community Needs*
>
> A wide range of activities are supported and the following are meant as a guide only.
>
> - **community services**: family centres, women's centres, youth and older people's clubs, after school clubs, play schemes, help groups, childcare provision
> - **advice services:** homelessness, addictions, bereavement, family guidance, money advice, helplines
> - **disabled people:** residences, day centres, transport, carers, information and advice, advocacy
> - **promotion of health**: information and advice, mental health, hospices, day care, home nursing, independent living for older people
> - **civic responsibility**: juveniles at risk, crime prevention, promotion of volunteering, victim support, mediation, rehabilitation of offenders
> - **cultural enrichment:** improving participation in and access to the arts and national heritage for disadvantaged and disabled people
>
> *Education and Training*
>
> The objective is to enhance educational opportunities for disadvantaged people and those with special needs.
>
> - Projects which help socially excluded people develop their potential and secure employment.
> - Employment training (for disadvantaged people and those with special needs)
> - Promotion of life skills, independent living skills for people with special needs
> - Enhancing education for disabled pre-school children and young people (where no other support is available).

Grantmaking in 2013

In 2013 the foundation had assets of £2.1 million and an income of £1.9 million. There were 527 grants given totalling £2.2 million. Most of the grants made were for social and community welfare.

Grants were distributed across various programmes:

The Community Grant Programme	339	£1.2 million
The Creating Change Programme	16	£156,000
The International Programme	14	£95,000
The Partnership Programme	1	£73,000
Matched Giving	145	£53,000
Social Enterprise Programme	9	£27,000
Age NI and CFNI	2	£18,000
Special Initiatives Programme	2	£18,000

Grants were broken down geographically as follows:

Belfast	160
County Antrim	76
UK Based	67
County Tyrone	54
County Down	50
County Armagh	30
Derry/Londonderry	29
International	14
Co. Fermanagh	12

Grants approved by programme area in the Community Grants Programme were as follows:

Community	180
Disability	37
Promotion of health	31
Cultural enrichment	28
Civic responsibility	22
Education and training	21
Advice	20

Beneficiaries included: Aisling Centre (£5,000); Arts for All (£4,500); Age Concern Causeway (£4,000); Belfast Interface Project (£3,000); Hillstown Rural Community Group (£2,500); Newtown Butler Playgroup and the Oxygen Therapy Centre (£1,500 each); Meigh Community Pre-School (£1,000); the Open Door Centre (£600); and Green Elves Playgroup (£500).

Exclusions

Grants are not usually given for: organisations which have an income of more than £1 million in the previous year's accounts; organisations which are insolvent; organisations which have over 12 months reserves would not be seen as a priority; individuals, including students; animal welfare; the environment; hospitals and medical centres; schools, universities and colleges (except for projects specifically to benefit pupils with special needs); sponsorship or fundraising events either for your own organisation or another; promotion of religion; endowment funds; organisations which do not charge a nominal fee for activities; activities that are normally the responsibility of central or local government or some other responsible body; loans and business finance; travel or activities outside Northern Ireland; capital build (except in the case of disability access); salary or training costs for the pre-school sector.

Applications

All applications to the Community Grant Programme must be made online. Supporting documents to help you complete the form are also available once you register or can be downloaded from the Community Grant Programme section of the website. These include: Guidelines for Applicants, Advice on Completing the Form, Monitoring and Evaluation Factsheet and Supporting Document Checklist. There are four closing dates per year, usually the second Friday of January, April, July and

October. Check the website for exact dates. The board meets to consider applications normally during the first week of March, June, September and December, making the waiting time for a decision around ten weeks from the closing date. You should be notified of the result of your application no more than two weeks after the board have met.

Lloyds Bank Foundation for the Channel Islands

General

£881,000 (2013).

Beneficial area

The Channel Islands.

Correspondent: John Hutchins, Executive Director, Lloyds Bank, PO Box 160, 25 New Street, St Helier Jersey JE4 8RG (tel: 01534 845889; email: John.Hutchins@lloydsbankfoundation.org.uk; website: www.lloydsbankfoundationci.org.uk)

Trustees: John Bootham; Dr John Ferguson; Patricia Tumelty; Sarah Bamford; Simon Howitt; Andrew Dann; Michael Starkey; Timothy Cooke; Kathryn Le Quesne

CC number: 327113

The foundation was set up by Lloyds Bank in 1986 and its mission is to 'support charitable organisations which help people, especially those who are disadvantaged or disabled, to play a fuller role in communities throughout the Channel Islands'.

The overall policy of the trustees is to support underfunded charities which enable people, especially disadvantaged people or people with disabilities, to play a fuller role in the community. The trustees are keen to support organisations which contribute to local community life at the grass-roots level. The trustees are also keen to encourage the infrastructure of the voluntary sector and encourage applications for operational costs. This includes salary costs, which may be funded over two or three years, and training and education for managers and staff.

Donations for one-off projects are generally in the region of £2,500 to £25,000, but there is no minimum amount set by the trustees. Applications for larger amounts will be considered where there is a wider benefit. The trustees generally make donations towards specific items rather than making contributions to large appeals, such as building costs. The majority of donations are made on a one-off basis. Successful applicants are advised to leave at least one year before reapplying.

The foundation provides the following information on its website:

> *Social Partnership Initiative*
>
> In 2001 we launched the Social Partnership Initiative, designed to encourage real working partnerships to be set up between the voluntary sector and the relevant States departments' in the Islands, to stimulate the voluntary sector into seeking out opportunities to develop new services, increase knowledge and key skills.
>
> Our funding goes mainly to charities working in Social and Community Needs and Education and Training. The Trustees regularly review changing social needs and identify specific areas they wish to focus on within their overall objectives. Current priorities are:
>
> - **Creating Positive Opportunities for Disabled People** – enabling people with either learning or physical disabilities to live independently
> - **Family Support** – including the development of relationship skills for young people, and encouraging good relationships between generations
> - **Homelessness** – in particular helping homeless people back into mainstream society, including support after temporary or permanent accommodation has been secured
> - **Promoting Effectiveness in the Voluntary Sector** – supporting the training of trustees, managers, staff and volunteers and encouraging the sector to communicate and work together
> - **Prevention of Substance Misuse** – including both education and rehabilitation
> - **The Needs of Carers** – for example, information and support services, and the provision of respite care
> - **Challenging Disadvantage and Discrimination** – promoting understanding and encouraging solutions which address disadvantage, discrimination or stigma.

In 2013 the foundation had assets of £1.8 million and an income of £1.1 million including £1,074,500 under Deed of Covenant from Lloyds Bank. Grants to 30 organisations totalled £881,000 (not including matched giving).

Guernsey	13	£465,000
Jersey	16	£403,000
Channel Islands wide and UK	1	£5,000
Staff matched giving	N/A	£37,000

Beneficiaries included: Drug Concern (£105,000); Shelter Trust Jersey (£75,000); Autism Jersey (£73,000); Guernsey Youth LBG (£66,000); the Antoine Trust (£40,000); Creative Learning in Prison (£25,000); St Breland Youth Project (£10,000); Jubilee Sailing Trust Jersey (£7,000); Music in Hospitals (£5,000); and Helping Wings Guernsey (£1,000).

Exclusions

No grants are given for:

- Organisations which are not recognised charities
- Activities which are primarily the responsibility of the Insular Authorities in the Islands or some other responsible body
- Activities which collect funds to give to other charities, individuals or other organisations
- Animal welfare
- Corporate subscription or membership of a charity
- Endowment funds
- Environment – conserving and protecting plants and animals, geography and scenery
- Expeditions or overseas travel
- Fabric appeals for places of worship
- Fundraising events or activities
- Hospitals and medical centres (except for projects which are clearly additional to statutory responsibilities)
- Individuals, including students
- Loans or business finance
- Promotion of religion
- Schools and colleges (except for projects that will benefit students with disabilities and are clearly additional to statutory responsibilities)
- Sponsorship or marketing appeals
- International appeals – trustees may from time to time consider a limited number of applications from UK-registered charities working abroad

Applications

Applications are only accepted on the foundation's own form which should be submitted with:

- An income tax letter of exemption
- Your latest audited accounts and a copy of bank statement
- A job description (if salary funding is requested)

The form and guidelines are available from the foundation's website or from its office in Jersey and can be returned at any time. Applications must be returned by post as the foundation does not accept forms that have been emailed or faxed.

All applications are reviewed on a continual basis. The trustees meet three times a year to approve donations in March, July and November and deadlines are usually the middle of the preceding month. Decision-making processes can therefore take up to four months. Applications for up to £5,000 are normally assessed within one month and all applicants are informed of the outcome of their application.

Applicants are encouraged to discuss their project with one of the foundation's staff before completing an application form. This will help ensure that your project is within its criteria and that you are applying for an appropriate amount. You will also be informed of when you should hear a decision.

Man Group plc Charitable Trust

General

£1.1 million (2013)

Beneficial area

UK, with some preference for London.

Correspondent: Lisa Clarke, Trust Manager, Man Group plc, Riverbank House, 2 Swan Lane, London EC4R 3AD (tel: 020 7144 1000; email: charitable.trust@man.com; website: www.man.com/GB/man-charitable-trust)

Trustees: Murray Steel; Jasveer Singh; David Kingsley; Colin Bettison

CC number: 275386

Most charitable donations by the company Man Group plc are made through this trust, which was established in 1978. The trust is funded by a percentage of Man Group plc by 2.5% of performance fee income and 0.25% of management fee income. The following information was taken from the trust's website:

> The charity prefers to concentrate its support on smaller charities where its donations make a material difference and where it can work in partnership with charities that are less likely to obtain support from the general public. The trust likes to focus on activities that offer assistance directly to individuals, families and communities as well as those that increase the capacity of organisations and individuals.

In 2013 the trust had assets of £2.3 million and an income of £56,000. There were 24 grants made totalling £1.1 million.

Grants were allocated as follows:

Disadvantaged youth – promoting inclusion	£314,000
Literacy and numeracy	£185,000
Ongoing support	£143,000
Disadvantaged youth – education	£112,000
Vulnerable populations – domestic violence	£100,000
Vulnerable populations – homeless	£75,000
Disaster relief	£50,000
Vulnerable populations – mental health	£40,000
Employee sponsorship matching	£23,000
Employee Give As You Earn matching	£17,000
Employee volunteering	£3,200

Beneficiaries included: Eaves (£100,000); MapAction, National Numeracy Trust, the Passage, School-Home Support, XLP (£50,000 each); Changing Faces (£40,000); Inspire! (£30,000); Community Links and 999 Club (£25,000 each); Ocean Youth Trust South (£15,000); and City of London School (£6,500).

Exclusions

The trust does not normally support:

- Large national charities
- Charities that use outside fundraising organisations
- Charities whose administration costs are thought to be excessive
- Animal charities
- Applicants who have applied within the previous 12 months
- Requests that directly replace statutory funding
- Individuals (unless under a sponsorship scheme)
- Endowment funds
- Charities where the main purpose is to promote religious beliefs

Applications

Grants are provided on an invitation to bid basis or through negotiated partnerships with selected charities. The trust has stated that it cannot commit to responding to organisations that make unsolicited applications. See the trust's website for criteria.

Manchester Airport Community Trust Fund

Environment, social welfare, community and economic development

£140,000 (2013/14).

Beneficial area

The area which is most affected by Manchester Airport. This covers an approximate ten-mile radius of the airport, concentrating on the areas most exposed to aircraft noise.

Correspondent: Ruth Flatman, Administrator, Manchester Airport plc, 5 Rutland Drive, Weaverham, Northwich, Cheshire CW8 3JF (tel: 01614 895833; email: trust.fund@manairport.co.uk; website: www.manchesterairport.co.uk)

Trustees: Cllr Paul Andrews; Cllr John Pantall; Cllr Don Stockton; Cllr Malcolm Byram; Michael Whetton; Wendy Sinfield; John Twigg; Bill Fairfoull

CC number: 1071703

Registered with the Charity Commission in 1998, the Manchester Airport Community Trust Fund is the corporate charity of Manchester Airport plc. Trustees are employees of Manchester Airport plc, as well as trustees appointed by the Manchester Airport Consultative Committee from the council areas of Stockport, Manchester, Trafford, Tameside, Cheshire East and Cheshire West and Chester.

According to the accounts for 2013/14 the trust aims to support projects which:

> - Promote, enhance, improve, protect and conserve the natural and built environment by projects of tree planting, afforestation and landscaping and other works of environmental improvement and heritage conservation
> - Enable within those areas facilities in the interests of social welfare for recreation, sport and leisure time occupation with the object of improving the conditions of life for those living or working in or visitors to those areas
> - Promote and provide for the benefit of the public a better appreciation of the natural and urban environment and ways of better serving, protecting and improving the same and education and training in all matters relating to the natural, physical environment and its interaction with the economic well-being of the community
>
> Grants will be awarded only for tangible items, which give enduring benefit, but excluding applications that involve the purchase of land and buildings.

Charitable organisations must be community, socially or environmentally focused.

In 2013/14 the trust held assets of £76,000 and had an income of £164,000, of which £100,000 was a monetary donation and £15,000 an in-kind donation from Manchester Airport plc. Grants to 71 charitable organisations were made totalling £140,000.

Beneficiaries included: Henbury Millennium Green Trust (£3,300); Community Spirit, Mersey Valley Sports Club and Toft Cricket Club (£3,000 each); Chorlton Arts Festival (£2,800); 162 (Stockport) Squadron ATC (£2,500); Agricultural and Rural Centre CIC and Knutsford Cricket Club (£2,000 each); High Legh Bowling Club and Peel Hall Moatwatch (£1,000 each); Penny Lane Party and Trafford Basketball Club (£800 each); Bowling Green Hotel Bowling Club (£400); Goostrey Parish Archive (£250); and Inspire (£120).

Exclusions

Grants are not made to individuals.

Applications

In writing to the correspondent via an application form which must be submitted online and can be found on the fund's website.

Successful applicants are encouraged to promote their grant through the local media, and in their own newsletters and publications.

D. G. Marshall of Cambridge Trust

Education and training, social welfare, aviation, disability, health, children and young people

£65,000 (2013/14)

Beneficial area

UK with a preference for Cambridgeshire.

Correspondent: Sarah Moynihan, Trustee, Marshall of Cambridge (Holdings) Ltd, Control Building, The Airport, Newmarket Road, Cambridgeshire CB5 8RY (tel: 01223 373273; email: sjm@marcamb.co.uk)

Trustees: Jonathan Barker; Bill Dastur; Michael Marshall; Robert Marshall

CC number: 286468

Registered with the Charity Commission in 1983, the D. G. Marshall of Cambridge Trust is closely associated with Marshall of Cambridge (Holdings) Ltd, which conducts its activities through its four business sectors: aerospace and defence; motor retail and leasing; property; and fleet solutions. Trustees are all employees of the company and include the Chair, Michael Marshall, and the Chief Executive, Robert Marshall.

The trust's accounts for 2013/14 state that its objects are to support:

- Needy and deserving cases arising anywhere but in particular among employees or ex-employees or their relatives or dependants of the company or any subsidiary or associated company
- Local charities
- Local educational institutions as are charitable in nature

The trust supports community projects and local appeals as well as UK charities.

In 2013/14 the trust had assets of almost £1.7 million and an income of £218,000, of which £150,000 was donated from Marshall of Cambridge (Holdings) Ltd. 40 grants were made totalling £65,000. These were broken down as follows:

Education	£17,000
Aviation	£17,000
Children's charities	£13,000
Disability, health and life-threatening illnesses	£8,000
Hospitals and related organisations	£6,700
Local community	£2,700
Churches	£500

Beneficiaries included: SOS Children (£10,000); American Air Museum and Arthur Rank Hospice Charity (£5,000 each); Arkwright Scholarship Trust (£4,000); Battle of Britain Memorial Trust (£2,500); the Avenues Youth Project and Ely Cathedral Restoration Trust (£1,500 each); CLIC Sargent and East Anglian Children's Hospice (£1,000 each); Institute of Economic Affairs and Teversham Baptist Church (£500 each); and Rainbows Children's Hospice and Sheffield Children's Hospital (£250 each).

Applications

The charity will consider all applications, providing they are consistent with the objectives of the charity.

Mazars Charitable Trust

General charitable purposes

£283,000 (2013/14)

Beneficial area

UK and Ireland.

Correspondent: Bryan Rogers, Administrator, 1 Cranleigh Gardens, South Croydon, Surrey CR2 9LD (tel: 020 7063 4000; website: www.mazars.co.uk/Home/About-us/Corporate-Responsibility/Charities)

Trustees: Bob Neate; David Evans; Phil Verity; Alan Edwards

CC number: 1150459

The firm Mazars specialises in audit, tax and advisory services across a range of markets and sectors. This associated charitable trust was registered with the Commission in January 2013 and makes grants to charitable organisations in the UK and Ireland. In 2013/14 the majority of the trust's income was received from Mazars LLP. It does not respond to unsolicited applications; however, applications can be made through a team member of Mazars LLP.

The company has a commitment to corporate social responsibility and states on its website that:

> In addition to our Mazars Community Days, individuals or teams in particular offices also undertake a number of self-organised charity initiatives such as participation in marathons or parachute jumps. These are often supported by many team members and may also be eligible for a discretionary contribution from the Mazars Charitable Trust.

In 2013/14 the trust had assets of £276,000 and an income of £525,000. The trust made 216 grants totalling £283,000.

Beneficiaries included: The Prince's Trust (£26,000); Viva (£15,000); The Heal Project (£12,500); Swindon Christian Community Projects (£10,000); Kids Company (£7,500); St Andrew's Hospice (£5,200); CCHF All About Kids (£3,000); RealLondon Mentoring CIC (£2,000); Diabetes UK (£1,600); and the British Heart Foundation (£1,300).

Applications

Charities cannot apply directly for funding but, rather, are nominated by Mazars partners and employees. Unsolicited applications will receive no response.

The Robert McAlpine Foundation

General charitable purposes, medical research, social welfare, disabled children, older people

£728,000 (2013/14)

Beneficial area

UK.

Correspondent: Brian Arter, Administrator, Sir Robert McAlpine Ltd, Eaton Court, Maylands Avenue, Hemel Hempstead, Hertfordshire HP2 7TR (tel: 01442 233444; email: b.arter@sir-robert-mcalpine.com)

Trustees: Adrian McAlpine; Cullum McAlpine; The Hon David McAlpine; Kenneth McAlpine

CC number: 226646

Sir Robert McAlpine Ltd is a family-owned UK construction and civil engineering company. Its most recent projects have included the O2 Arena, Emirates Stadium, the Eden Project and the Olympic Stadium. The Robert McAlpine Foundation was registered with the Charity Commission in 1964 and its current trustees are all members of the McAlpine family; two of which are directors of the company.

Its 2013/14 accounts stated that 'the foundation operates virtually exclusively by making identified benefit grants to carefully selected charitable organisations working in the sectors which the foundation particularly wishes to support'.

The foundation generally supports causes concerned with children with disabilities, older people, medical research and social welfare and charities with an income of less than £1 million. The annual report for 2013/14 also states that: 'the policy of the trustees is to make grants to charitable institutions of amounts from £2,500 upwards in the specific categories of objectives which they support'.

In 2013/14 the trust had assets of £15.5 million and had an income of £862,000, which included a £500,000 donation from Sir Robert McAlpine Ltd. Grants paid during the year totalled £728,000.

A list of beneficiaries was unavailable at the time of writing (January 2015).

Previous beneficiaries have included: Age Concern, Community Self Build Agency, DENS Action Against Homelessness, Downside Fisher Youth Club, Ewing Foundation, the Golden Oldies, Grateful Society, James Hopkins Trust, Merchants Academy Withywood, National Benevolent Fund for the Aged, National Eye Research Centre, Prostate UK, Royal Marsden NHS Trust, St John's Youth Centre and the Towers School and Sixth Form Centre.

Exclusions

The trust does not fund overheads or give grants to individuals.

Applications

In writing to the correspondent at any time. Applications are considered annually, normally in November.

The Mersey Docks and Harbour Company Charitable Fund

Seafaring and seafarers, social welfare

£39,000 (2013)

Beneficial area

Merseyside.

Correspondent: Caroline Gill, Secretary, The Mersey Docks and Harbour Company Ltd, Maritime Centre, Port of Liverpool, Liverpool L21 1LA (tel: 01519 496349)

Trustees: Gary Hodgson; Mark Whitworth; Ian Charnock

CC number: 206913

Registered with the Charity Commission in 1963, The Mersey Docks and Harbour Company Charitable Fund is the corporate charity of the Mersey Docks and Harbour Company Ltd.

The 2013 accounts state that the charity has the following objectives:

- To reward people that help to save the life of the crew of any ship wrecked in the port of Liverpool, preserve the ship or cargo, or try to save people from drowning
- For the relief of people who are sick, disabled and retired in the dock service or the families of those who were killed in service
- To benefit charities in the town or port of Liverpool

In 2013 the trust had assets of £13,500 and an income of £40,000, which was wholly donated by The Mersey Docks and Harbour Company Ltd. Grants totalled £39,000 during the year.

Beneficiaries included: Community Foundation for Merseyside (£15,500); Liverpool Seafarer's Centre (£10,500); RNLI (£5,000); Plaza Community Cinema (£3,000); Farm Africa and North West Air Ambulance (£1,000 each); Brain Tumour Research (£500); and North West Cancer Research (£100).

Applications

In writing to the correspondent.

Morgan Stanley International Foundation

Education and training, children's health, social welfare, disadvantaged communities and young people

£1.7 million (2013)

Beneficial area

London boroughs of Tower Hamlets and Newham; Glasgow and overseas.

Correspondent: Anish Shah, Vice President, Morgan Stanley and Co. International plc, 20 Bank Street, London E14 4AD (tel: 020 7425 1302; email: communityaffairslondon@morganstanley.com; website: www.morganstanley.com/globalcitizen/msif_guidelines.html)

Trustees: Clare Woodman; Hanns Seibold; Maryann McMahon; Stephen Souchon; Malcolm Bryant; Stephen Mavin; Fergus O'Sullivan; Sue Watts; Oliver Stuart; Kamal Jabre; Gordon Fraser; Matthew Ostrower

CC number: 1042671

The Morgan Stanley International Foundation (MSIF) was registered with the Charity Commission in 1994 and is the corporate charity of Morgan Stanley and Co. International plc, the financial services corporation. The foundation's trustees are all present employees of the company. The foundation focuses on supporting organisations in the London boroughs of Tower Hamlets and Newham, Glasgow and overseas.

The foundation's 2013 accounts state that:

> The principal objective of the foundation is to make a sustainable impact to children's welfare in disadvantaged communities across Europe, the Middle East and Africa (EMEA). Focusing primarily on child health and education, the foundation works in partnership with charitable organisations to direct funding and utilise expertise of Morgan Stanley employees to benefit the communities in which the firm operates.
>
> The foundation gives grants through two different channels: direct charitable grants and employee matching grants. Applications are invited for funding of projects in the EMEA region, and are reviewed at quarterly trustees' meetings against specific grant objectives. Multi-year grants are monitored on an annual basis to ensure the grant criteria continue to be met.

The foundation matches any contribution, either monetary or through volunteering, by employees to a maximum of £500 per employee in one given year.

The website states that its activities are primarily concerned with the following:

> ***Children's Health***
>
> The foundation looks to invest in innovation and development in children's healthcare. Working with charitable organisations, hospitals and community based initiatives; MSIF focuses on supporting young people from ages 0–18. MSIF strives to ensure that more children have acces , to quality healthcare to enable th n to have a more meaningful life.
>
> ***Education***
>
> The MSIF aims to work with registered charities and state-funded schools which provide benefit to communities across EMEA. The foundation works with organisations that can increase access and opportunity for young people aged 4 to 21. Supported programmes that are predominantly based in schools, specifically address academic achievement and employability skills, by inspiring talent but underserved young people.

In 2013 the foundation had assets of almost £1.5 million and an income of £1.34 million, of which £900,000 was a donation from Morgan Stanley and Co. International plc. Grants totalling £1.7 million were made during the year.

The largest beneficiary was the Prince's Trust, which received £802,000.

Other beneficiaries included: Kids Company (£116,000); Great Ormond Street Hospital (£78,000); Community Links and East End Community Foundation (£52,000 each); Action For Children (£40,000); UK Career Academy Foundation (£32,000); Pilotlight (£28,000); Tower Hamlets Summer University (£25,000); Gyermekétkeztetési Alapítvány (£24,000); Tower Hamlets Education Business Partnership (£20,000); Reliable Cancer Therapies (£14,000); Movember Europe (£12,700); Envision (£10,000); Refuge (£4,000); and the Kiltwalk and Wildhearts (£2,500 each).

Exclusions

The website states that:

> The foundation does not make contributions to organisations that fall within the following criteria:
>
> - Organisations which are not registered as a non-profit organisation with the appropriate regulatory agencies in their country (unless a state funded school)
> - National or international charities which do not operate in the regions we are located

- Political or religious organisations, 'pressure groups' or individuals outside the firm who are seeking sponsorship either for themselves (e.g. to help pay for education) or for onward transmission to a charitable organisation
- Programmes that do not include opportunities for employee volunteer engagement

Applications

The foundation's website gives the following details on making an initial approach for funding:

> Morgan Stanley International Foundation takes a proactive approach to grant making and therefore does not accept unsolicited proposals. If you think your organisation is a match for the criteria ... please send an email to: communityaffairslondon@morganstanley.com. You will then be sent the guidelines and if your organisation is successful in the first stage of application, you will be invited to complete a full proposal.
>
> Grant applications are considered quarterly and the trustees are senior representatives from across the firm's divisions.

Mothercare Group Foundation

Health and well-being of children and their mothers

Beneficial area

UK and worldwide.

Correspondent: Lynne Medini, Trustee, Mothercare plc, Cherry Tree Road, Watford, Hertfordshire WD24 6SH (tel: 01923 206186; website: www.mothercareplc.com/charity)

Trustees: Lynne Medini; Tim Ashby

CC number: 1104386

The Mothercare Group Foundation was registered with the Charity Commission in June 2004 and has ties with Mothercare plc, a British retailer that specialises in products for expectant mothers and merchandise for children.

The 2013/14 accounts state that:

> Mothercare plc, a related party, has in the past, made donations to the foundation from its annual pre-tax profits. For the year ended 31 March 2014 no donations have been received from its annual pre-tax profits. Funds also flow in from proceeds from the staff shop, ad hoc donations and staff fundraising.
>
> The Mothercare Group Foundation aims to help parents in the UK and worldwide to meet the needs and aspirations for their children and to give their children the very best chance of good health, education, well-being and a secure start in life.
>
> Specifically, the foundation considers registered charities and research organisations associated with the following criteria:
>
> - Ensuring the good health and well-being of mums-to-be, new mums and their children
> - Special baby-care needs and premature births
> - Other parenting initiatives relating to family well-being

In 2013/14 the foundation had assets of £69,000 and an income of £45,000, of which £44,000 was raised from donated stock sold in the staff shop. There were no grants made during the year.

Although grants have diminished greatly in the past few years, the foundation's accounts do state that 'The trustees will continue to consider donations to charities whose objectives are aligned with the foundation's own giving structure.'

Previous beneficiaries have included: Anthony Nolan Trust, the Healing Foundation, KIDS, Meningitis Research Foundation, PHG Foundation, Wellbeing of Women, WellChild and University of Bristol.

Exclusions

No response is given to circular appeals. Support is not given to: animal welfare; appeals from individuals; the arts; elderly people; environment/heritage; religious appeals; political appeals; or sport.

Applications

The website states that 'the foundation is not accepting funding applications at present, although this situation may change in the future'.

The National Express Foundation

General, social welfare, education, sport, children and young people

£65,000 (2013)

Beneficial area

West Midlands and South Essex or East London within five miles of the c2c rail line.

Correspondent: The Trustees, National Express Group plc, National Express House, Digbeth, Birmingham B5 6DD (tel: 01214 608423; email: foundation@nationalexpress.com; website: nationalexpressgroup.com/foundation)

Trustees: Anthony Vigor; Denise Rossiter; John Fraser; Lesley Dorrington; Madi Pilgrim; Shabana Mahmood MP

CC number: 1148231

Registered with the Charity Commission in July 2012, the charitable foundation is a key part of the National Express Group's community support in the UK. Trustees include directors of the National Express Group. The group's employees play a central role in its community involvement through volunteering, fundraising activities and a payroll giving scheme.

The National Express Foundation's objectives are to promote education, including awarding scholarships, maintenance allowances or grants to those in higher or further education, as well as to provide grants for recreational activities for disaffected and disadvantaged young people, which will in turn develop their skills and harness their potential. Preference is given to areas where the National Express Group operates services – mainly the West Midlands, but also south Essex and East London.

The following information is taken from the company's website:

> The public order disturbances in July 2011 highlighted the issues facing young people living in inner-city areas in the UK. The disturbances involved a disproportionate number of people in the 15–24 year age group. Unemployment, boredom and lack of motivation among this group were all cited as factors.
>
> The foundation aims to tackle these issues in two ways:
>
> - Support for students with challenging personal and financial circumstances to enable them to advance their further and higher education
> - The provision of grants to charitable and community groups for projects which support children and young people and promote cross-community cohesion and understanding
>
> *Students*
>
> We have identified that a lack of funds may be a deterrent to young people attending and completing courses of higher and further education.
>
> To assist more students from the communities we serve to advance their education, the foundation plans to offer funding to educational institutions which can be used to provide individual financial support.
>
> Universities and colleges are far better placed to understand the student population and use their expertise to direct funds to those who are in the greatest need. They have well established systems in place for administering grants and bursaries, and we want to make use of these rather then set up an application process of our own.
>
> *Community groups*
>
> An immense amount of work to tackle these issues is also being carried out by local community groups. The foundation aims to support some of these initiatives by providing funding via a programme of community grants.
>
> The grants will enable the successful applicants to run projects which foster cross-community cohesion and understanding.

In 2013 the foundation had an income of £200,000 and an expenditure of £175,000. The foundation made grants of £35,000 to ten community groups and annual instalments totalling £30,000 to three educational institutions.

Beneficiaries included: Newman University (£30,000 over three years); South Essex College of Further and Higher Education and Walsall College (£20,000 each over two years); Disability Resource Centre (Birmingham), Olio Youth Hub, and Theatre Royal Stratford East (£5,000 each); Changing Our Lives, Sport 4 Life and Voluntary Action Coventry (£2,500 each).

Applications

The foundation states in its guidance notes, which are available on the website, that applicants are required to provide the following information:

- Background to the organisation, membership and funding
- Evidence of constitution and independent bank account
- Description of what the funding would be used for
- Explanation of how the proposed project would benefit the community
- Timescale and process for delivering the project
- Proposals for promoting the link with the foundation
- Plans to evaluate and quantify the benefits

> Applicants should indicate the size of grant that they are applying for: £2,500 or £5,000, and explain what they would deliver for the level of grant applied for.
>
> While we do not propose to set restrictions on how the funding would be applied, we will be seeking evidence of innovation in how the projects will be delivered. We will also want to ensure the successful project benefits the maximum number of children and young people in the community it serves.

The Nationwide Foundation

Community development, housing, legal assistance and social welfare

£957,000 (2013/14)

Beneficial area

UK.

Correspondent: Lorna Mackie, Grants Officer, Nationwide Building Society, Nationwide House, Pipers Way, Swindon SN38 2SN (tel: 01793 655113; email: enquiries@nationwidefoundation.org.uk; website: www.nationwidefoundation.org.uk)

Trustees: Michael Coppack; Benedict Stimson; Christopher Rhodes; Fiona Ellis; Graeme Hughes; Juliet Cockram; Sarah Mitchell; Bryce Glover; John Taylor; Antonia Bance

CC number: 1065552

Registered with the Charity Commission in 1997, the Nationwide Foundation is principally funded by Nationwide Building Society, which donates 1% of its pre-tax profit. Its aims and objectives are to create decent affordable housing for people in need, as well as to create conditions which increase the number of decent affordable homes.

The foundation's accounts for 2013/14 state that the:

> Increasing supply of and access to truly affordable and decent homes will primarily lead to the relief of financial hardship. Other health benefits include better health conditions with improved living standards, community regeneration and engagement, stability and security.

Its website states that:

> The foundation makes grants and programme related (social) investments in the following areas:
>
> - Bringing empty properties back into use as homes for people in need
> - Improving the living conditions of tenants in private rented sector homes
> - Supporting the development of alternative, scalable housing models to provide more affordable housing

Grants will be given towards the costs of refurbishment and can include a fair contribution towards organisational core costs. Funds will also be considered towards legal and other such costs associated with obtaining empty homes.

In 2013/14 the foundation had assets of £1.65 million and an income of £727,000, with a £608,000 donation from Nationwide Building Society. In addition the society donated services to the foundation totalling £83,000, which represented the provision of office space, technology, legal and accountancy support. Grants were made totalling £957,000 during the year.

Beneficiaries included: Generation Rent (£198,000); GIPSIL (£140,000); Changing Lives (£128,000); Freebridge Community Housing (£96,000); LATCH and Canopy Housing (£56,000 each); Big Issue Invest (£39,000); National CLT Network (£28,000); Sliced Bread (£6,900); and DAH Added Value (£1,300).

The foundation also made social investments totalling £183,000 during the year to Community Land Trust Fund II (£113,000) and Highlands Small Communities Housing Trust (£70,000).

Exclusions

The foundation will not consider funding for the following:

- Charities with 'unrestricted reserves' which exceed 50% of annual expenditure, as shown in their accounts
- Charities which are in significant debt as shown in their accounts
- The promotion of religion or politics
- Charities which have been declined by the foundation within the last 12 months
- Applications which do not comply with the foundation's funding criteria/guidelines

Applications

The foundation's website states that 'funding is only available for projects where alternative scalable models can provide more affordable homes, however there is not an open grant programme. If you think you have a project that might fit with our strategy, please contact us to discuss further.'

The NFU Mutual Charitable Trust

Community development, education, the relief of poverty, social welfare and research focusing on initiatives that will have a significant impact on rural communities

£249,000 (2013)

Beneficial area

UK, with a preference for rural areas.

Correspondent: James Creechan, Secretary to the Trustees, The National Farmers Union Mutual Insurance Society Ltd, Tiddington Road, Stratford-upon-Avon, Warwickshire CV37 7BJ (tel: 01789 204211; email: nfu_mutual_charitable_trust@nfumutual.co.uk; website: www.nfumutual.co.uk/company-information/charitable-trust)

Trustees: Lord Curry of Kirkharle; Stephen James; Lindsay Sinclair; Sir Ian Grant; Richard Percy; Richard Butler; Nigel Miller; Ian Marshall; Meurig Raymond

CC number: 1073064

Registered with the Charity Commission in 1998, the NFU Mutual Charitable Trust is the corporate charity of the National Farmers Union Mutual Insurance Society Ltd (NFU Mutual), one of the UK's leading insurers. Notable trustees include Richard Percy, Chair of NFU Mutual, and Lindsay Sinclair, its Chief Executive.

The website states that:

> The objectives of the NFU Mutual Charitable Trust are to promote, facilitate and support such purposes as are exclusively charitable according to the laws of England and Wales in the areas of agriculture, rural development and insurance in the United Kingdom and in particular to:

- Advance the education of the public by means of research and dissemination of information in relation to agriculture
- Advance the education of young people within rural areas
- Relieve poverty within rural areas
- Promote the benefit and social welfare of inhabitants or rural communities by associating together with the inhabitants and local authorities, voluntary and other organisations to advance education and leisure
- Promote research into agriculture associated activities
- Advance the education of the public by means of research and dissemination of information in relation to insurance.

The trust continues to support the NFU Mutual Charitable Trust Centenary Award, which gives annual bursaries of up to 75% of the course fees for selected postgraduate students in agriculture. Three bursaries were awarded in 2013.

In 2013 the trust had assets of £264,000 and an income of £258,000, of which £250,000 was a donation from NFU Mutual. Grants totalled £249,000 and were made to 21 charitable organisations.

Beneficiaries included: Farming and Countryside Education, FACE (£47,000); the National Federation of Young Farmers Clubs (£30,000); Addington Fund and Royal Agricultural Benevolent Institution (£20,000 each); Royal Highland Education Trust (£15,500); Rural Support (£12,500); Farming Community Network and Shakespeare Hospice at Home Service (£10,000 each); Henry Plumb Foundation, Isle of Man Agricultural Benevolent Trust and Ulster Open Farm Weekend (£5,000 each); Yorkshire Rural Support Network (£2,000); and Children's Country Holiday Fund and Isle of Man Federation of Young Farmers Club (£1,000 each).

Applications

In writing to the correspondent either via post or email. The trustees meet twice a year to consider applications received. These meetings are currently held in June and December. According to the website, applications should include details of:

> The project, initiative or organisation for which funding is sought; an indication of the amount of the donation requested; any business plans; details of any other funding sought and/or obtained; any recognition which would be given to the trust in recognition of its support; and confirmation of whether or not the applicant is a registered charity.

Ambika Paul Foundation

Education, young people

£50,000 (2012/13)

Beneficial area

Mainly UK and India.

Correspondent: Lord Paul of Marylebone, Trustee, Caparo Group, Caparo House, 103 Baker Street, London W1U 6LN (tel: 020 7486 1417; email: georgina.mason@caparo.com)

Trustees: Lord Paul of Marylebone; Lady Aruna Paul; Hon. Angad Paul; Hon. Anjli Paul; Hon. Ambar Paul; Hon. Akash Paul

CC number: 276127

The foundation was set up in 1978 in memory of Lord Paul's daughter Ambika who died of leukaemia aged four. A large proportion of its income comes from the Caparo Group which is wholly owned by the Paul family. Many of the family also act as trustees for the foundation.

The foundation supports large organisations, registered charities, colleges and universities that benefit children, young adults and students mostly in the UK and India. Main areas of interest are to do with young people and education. The foundation receives the majority of its income from Caparo Group Ltd with five of the six trustees sitting on its board. Grants usually range from £100 to £3,000.

In 2012/13 the foundation had no income and an expenditure of £51,000. We estimate that around £50,000 was made in grants. No further information was available.

Previous beneficiaries include: Loreto College, India (£76,000); Zoological Society of London (£15,000); Shri Venkateswara (£11,000); Indian Orthopaedic Society (£10,000); Lamu Dispensary (£5,000); Anglican Communion Ministries (£2,600); Bharatiya Vidya Bhavan (£1,500); and Sindi Nari Sabha and CST (Protecting our Jewish Community) (£500 each).

Exclusions

Applications from individuals, including students, are mainly ineligible. Funding for scholarships is made directly to colleges/universities, not to individuals. No expeditions. The foundation will not offer support for political appeals or fundraising events.

Applications

In writing to the trustees at the correspondence address. Acknowledgements are sent if an sae is enclosed. However, the trust has no paid employees and the enormous number of requests it receives creates administrative difficulties.

The Personal Assurance Charitable Trust

General charitable purposes, social welfare, health

£73,000 (2013)

Beneficial area

Mainly UK with a preference for the Milton Keynes area, overseas considered.

Correspondent: Sarah Mace, Trustee, Personal Group Holdings plc, John Ormond House, 899 Silbury Boulevard, Milton Keynes MK9 3XL (email: sarah.mace@personal-group.com)

Trustees: Michael Dugdale; Philip Yates; Sarah Mace

CC number: 1023274

The Personal Assurance Charitable Trust (PACT) was registered with the Charity Commission in 1993. It is the corporate charity of Personal Group Holdings plc, a provider of employee benefits and financial services. The trust's annual report states that:

> There are no geographical or other restrictions on the type of donations that can be made. However preference will be given to recommendations made by policyholders of Personal Assurance Plc, their employers, and employees of Personal Group Holdings Plc and its subsidiary undertakings. In addition the trustees prefer to make donations that benefit the wider community rather than individual causes.

In 2013 the trust had assets of £155,000 and an income of £101,000, of which £100,000 was received as a donation from Personal Assurance Group Holdings plc. Grants were made totalling almost £73,000.

Beneficiaries included: St John Ambulance School Competition (£24,000); Movember and the Retail Trust (£5,000 each); MK Christmas Day Party for the Elderly (£4,500); Little Lives Appeal and Transaid (£3,600 each); Unite the Union (£3,000); British Heart Foundation and Hospitality Action Charity (£2,200 each); and TNT Wooden Spoon, Tree of Hope and Shelf Pre-School (£1,000 each).

Donations under £1,000 totalled £11,000.

Exclusions

Grants are rarely made to individuals.

Applications

In writing to the correspondent.

The Persula Foundation

General charitable purposes, including people who are homeless, people with disabilities, human rights and animal welfare

£845,000 (2013/14)

Beneficial area

Worldwide.

Correspondent: Teresa Chapman, Secretary to the Trustees, Richer Sounds plc, Gallery Court, Hankey Place, London SE1 4BB (tel: 020 7551 5343; email: info@persula.org)

Trustees: Hanna Oppenheim; Julian Richer; David Robinson; Rosie Richer; Robert Rosenthal; Jonathan Levy

CC number: 1044174

The Persula Foundation was established in 1994 by Richer Sounds plc, the UK home entertainment retailer. It is an independent grant-making foundation and supports any cause which the trustees feel strongly about. Trustees include Julian Richer, founder of the company and David Robinson, the Managing Director.

The foundation states that it is currently interested in supporting initiatives in the following areas:

- Human rights and welfare
- Animal rights and welfare

Activities which supported these areas included supporting the work of Fair Trials International, helping with Freshfield Animal Sanctuary's cat neutering project and working with Mission Rabies in Nepal.

The Persula Foundation also continued with some of its existing projects, including Storytelling Tour, which gave over 100 free sessions of storytelling and music to visually impaired and older people and children and adults with disabilities. The foundation has also supported a new project called ACTS 435, which is a website that allows people to give money directly to those who are struggling financially.

In 2013/14 the foundation had assets of £81,000 and an income of £882,000, of which the principal funding source was a £871,000 donation from Richer Sounds plc. Grants totalled around £845,000 and were broken down as follows:

Human welfare	£530,000
Animal welfare	£228,000
People with disabilities	£48,000
Human rights	£29,000
Storytelling	£10,000

Beneficiaries were: ACTS 435 (£65,000); Compassion in World Farming (£40,000); Animal Aid (£30,000); RSPCA (£27,000); and League Against Cruel Sports (£25,000).

Exclusions

Grants cannot be given for buildings, individuals or core funding.

Applications

In writing to the correspondent. The charity considers applications from a variety of charitable organisations for funding. Applications are reviewed and levels of grants payable are decided upon by the trustees.

The PwC Foundation

Sustainable development, social inclusion, education and training, healthcare, the environment

£933,000 (2012/13)

Beneficial area

UK.

Correspondent: David Adair, Trustee, PricewaterhouseCoopers LLP, 1 Embankment Place, London WC2N 6RH (tel: 020 7212 7140; website: www.pwc.co.uk/corporate-sustainability/the-pwc-foundation.jhtml)

Trustees: Neil Sherlock; Gaenor Bagley; Kevin Ellis; David Adair

CC number: 1144124

The PwC Foundation was established in 2011 and is the corporate charity of PricewaterhouseCoopers LLP (PwC), which was formed by a merger between Coopers and Lybrand and Price Waterhouse in 1998. The foundation consists of a board of trustees, all of whom are current members of PWC.

The objectives of the PWC Foundation are to promote sustainable development and social inclusion for the public benefit. The foundation's 2012/13 annual report states that it 'also provides the vehicle for providing the matched funding given by PwC for charitable work undertaken across the charitable sector ... This funding is provided to a maximum of £250 per individual per financial year'.

In 2012/13 the foundation had assets of £76,000 and an income of £1 million, of which £985,000 was donated from the company. It made grants totalling £933,000, which were broken down as follows:

Employability	£367,000
PwC Matched Giving Programme	£234,000
Education	£209,000
Healthcare	£58,000
Environment	£37,000
Other	£28,000

Beneficiaries included: Wellbeing of Women (£100,000); Teach First (£90,000); School for Social Entrepreneurs (£77,000); Beyond Food Foundation and Private Equity Foundation (£50,000 each); the Shakespeare Globe Trust (£45,000); Business in the Community (£28,000); the Connection at St Martin's and Tomorrow's People (£17,000 each); and Enabling Enterprise and Tomorrow's Company (£10,000 each).

Exclusions

The foundation will not fund political organisations, lobbying groups, animal rights groups or religious bodies.

Applications

The following was taken from the PwC Foundation's website: 'the distribution of funds donated to the foundation are decided by the foundation trustees taking into account the voting preferences of our people'.

The Rathbone Brothers Foundation

General charitable purposes

£20,000 (2013)

Beneficial area

UK.

Correspondent: Joanna Gostling, Administrator, 1 Curzon Street, London W1J 5FB (tel: 020 7399 0000; email: rathbonefoundation@rathbones.com)

Trustees: Geoffrey Powell; Richard Lanyon; Paul Stockton; Rathbone Trust Company Ltd

CC number: 1150432

This foundation was established in November 2012 for general charitable purposes and registered with the Charity Commission in January 2013. It is the associated charitable foundation of Rathbone Brothers plc, a company which is one of the UK's leading providers of investment management services for private clients, charities and professional advisers.

In 2013 the foundation had assets of £136,000 and an income of £151,000. One grant of £20,000 was made during the year.

Beneficiaries include: Arts Insight (£20,000).

Applications

In writing to the correspondent. The following statement is taken from the Commission's website: 'The trustees consider applications for funding as and when received.'

Ridgesave Ltd

Jewish, education and training and social welfare

£2.3 million (2013/14)

Beneficial area

UK and overseas.

Correspondent: Hannah Zelda Weiss, Trustee, Ridgesave Ltd, 141b Upper Clapton Road, London E5 9DB (email: mail@cohenarnold.com)

Trustees: Hannah Zelda Weiss; Joseph Weiss; E. Englander

CC number: 288020

Ridgesave Ltd was registered with the Charity Commission in 1983 and is also a company limited by guarantee. The charity has two non-charitable operating subsidiaries: Bullion Properties Ltd and Doxit Company Ltd. The trustees are all directors of Bullion Properties Ltd.

The charity is largely focused on supporting organisations, both in the UK and abroad, engaged in activities that promote the teaching principles of traditional Judaism and the giving of philanthropic aid to the needy.

In 2013/14 the charity had assets of £322,000 and an income of £406,000. It received most of its income from investments (£187,000) and voluntary income related to the trustees (£195,000). Grants were made totalling almost £2.3 million. Information on recent beneficiaries was not available.

Previous beneficiaries have included: All in Together Girls, Ateres Yeshua Charitable Trust, British Friends of Rinat Aharon, Chanoch Lenaar, My Dream Time, Square Foundation Ltd and Side by Side.

Applications

In writing to the correspondent. All requests are considered and donations are made based on the level of funds available.

The Russell Trust

General charitable purposes

£150,000 (2013/14)

Beneficial area

UK, especially Scotland.

Correspondent: Iona Russell, Trustee, Markinch, Glenrothes, Fife KY7 6PB (tel: 01592 753311; email: russelltrust@trg.co.uk)

Trustees: Fred Bowden; Cecilia Croal; Graeme Crombie; David Erdal; Don Munro; Iona Russell; Alan Scott; C. A. G. Parr

OSCR number: SC004424

This family trust was established in 1947 in memory of Capt. J P O Russell who was killed in Italy during the Second World War. The trust is a shareholder in Tullis Russell Group Ltd. The trustees prefer to make grants to pump-prime new projects, rather than giving on an ongoing basis. Grants of up to £10,000 can be distributed; however, generally the amounts given are for between £250 and £2,000. Three or four larger grants of up to £20,000 may be awarded annually.

In 2013/14 the trust had an unusually low income of £6,000 (£268,000 in 2012/13) and a total expenditure of £162,500. Grants were made totalling around £150,000. No grants list was available, but donations are generally broken down into the following categories:

- Youth work
- Health and welfare
- Education
- Local
- Music and the arts
- Church
- Preservation/conservation
- Archaeology
- St Andrew's University

Exclusions

Only registered charities or organisations with charitable status are supported.

Applications

On a form available from the correspondent. A statement of accounts must be supplied. Trustees meet quarterly, although decisions on the allocation of grants are made more regularly.

The Saga Charitable Trust

Community projects in developing countries that provide education, training, healthcare and income generation

£106,000 (2013/14)

Beneficial area

Developing countries.

Correspondent: John Billingham, Trust Manager, Saga plc, Enbrook Park, Sandgate High Street, Sandgate, Folkestone CT20 3SE (tel: 01303 774421; email: contact@sagacharitabletrust.org; website: www.sagacharitabletrust.org)

Trustees: Makala Thomas; James Duguid; Andrew Stringer; Helen Adamson; Timothy Pethick

CC number: 291991

Saga plc is a UK company which focuses on serving the needs of those aged 50 and over through insurance, travel, financial services and healthcare. The Saga Charitable Trust was registered with the Charity Commission in June 1985 and is funded by the Saga plc, Saga customers and staff.

The prime objective of its charitable work is to benefit worthy community projects at destinations in developing countries that host Saga holidaymakers. It focuses on education, training, healthcare and income generation projects. The trust aims not just to donate money, but to invest in projects that will 'empower and support' local communities, provide practical help to those in need, and offer increased opportunities for disadvantaged groups to benefit from tourism.

Projects have included an educational programme in Kenya; housing and education to over 40 blind and physically disabled children in Vietnam; and the construction of 14 water treatment plants in the Amazon region of Peru.

In 2013/14 the trust had assets of £460,000, an income of £130,000, of which £123,000 was donations from Saga customers and staff donations. Grants were made totalling £106,000.

Beneficiaries include: Swim Vietnam (£21,000); the Butterfly Tree, Zambia (£15,000); Kalela Primary School, Kenya and Mikoroshoni Primary School, Kenya (£12,000 each); Centre for Early Childhood Development, South Africa and the Civil Association for Conservation of the Peruvian Amazon Environment, Peru (£9,300 each); This Life Cambodia, Cambodia (£6,100); Philippines Community Fund, the Philippines and Tears of Hope, Namibia (£4,200 each); and Himaljyoti Community School, Nepal (£1,700).

Exclusions

No grants are given to individuals.

Applications

In writing to the correspondent. Applications are accepted at any time throughout the year. Grants are decided at regular meetings by the trustees where applications are considered for various types of funding.

Funding proposals should include the following information: outline and objectives of the project; who will benefit and how; resources required and timeframe; management and sustainability of the project; how funds will be managed and accounted for; and three years of the organisation's financial accounts.

Santander UK Foundation Ltd

Social welfare, education and training, money advice

£5.8 million (2013)

Beneficial area

UK.

Correspondent: Alan Eagle, Foundation Manager, Santander UK plc, Santander House, 201 Grafton Gate East, Milton Keynes MK9 1AN (tel: 01908 343224; email: grants@santander.co.uk; website: www.santanderfoundation.org.uk)

Trustees: Lord Terence Burns; Steven Williams; Simon Lloyd; Jennifer Scardino; Angela Wakelin; Sue Wills; Keith Moore

CC number: 803655

The Santander UK Foundation was established in 1990 by Santander UK plc, the UK bank, and changed its name from the Abbey National Charitable Trust in 2010. The trustees are all directors and employees of Santander.

The foundation is the main channel of the company's corporate donations and provides grants to UK-registered charities that help 'disadvantaged people, usually in communities where Santander branches and business centres are based and locations where the bank has a significant presence, such as a main office or call centre'.

The accounts for 2013 stated that 'the charitable priorities for 2013 were to support local communities and disadvantaged people through: financial advice which helps them manage their money; and education and training'.

The following information was taken from the foundation's website:

> The Santander Foundation has three grants programmes to help disadvantaged people in the UK:
>
> *Community Plus* offers grants of up to £5,000. The scheme is open to small local UK charities or local projects of national charities with funding available to cover salaries, equipment or materials.
>
> *Learn and Grow* offers grants of up to £10,000 to fund activities which help disadvantaged people to improve skills, build confidence or employability.
>
> *Money Skills* offers grants of up to £10,000 to charities and credit unions who want to help disadvantaged people to understand and manage their money.

For further details of each funding programme see the foundation's website.

In 2013 the foundation had assets of £13 million and an income of £5.8 million. The principal source of income was £5.3 million from Santander UK plc which included matched funding for staff donations and investment income of £368,000. Grants were made to almost 2,600 organisations and totalled £5.8 million.

Grants made were broken down into the following categories:

Relief of suffering	£2.9 million	1,666
Education and training	£1.1 million	305
Financial capability	£682,000	77
Other	£1.1 million	508

Beneficiaries included: Teens and Toddlers (£25,000); Action for Blind People, Association of Charitable Foundations, BASIC, Disability Resource Centre, Family Tree Wirral, Manchester Carers Centre, Norfolk Rural Community Council, Shine Project, Sign Health and Stop Abuse For Everyone (£10,000 each).

Exclusions

The foundation will not fund the following:

- Individuals – including trips, overseas volunteering, gap year activity, medical treatment, bursary schemes, grants for studying or research
- Fundraising activities
- Unregistered charities, not-for-profit groups, Community Amateur Sports Clubs
- Community Interest Companies or social enterprises
- Charities which restrict their beneficiaries to a single religious or single ethnic group
- Events, conferences or sponsorship
- Party political activity

Applications

For Community Plus, a completed nomination form should be submitted to the nearest branch of Santander. For Learn and Grow or Money Skills, an email including a completed initial proposal form downloaded from the foundation's website should be sent directly to the foundation.

Applicants are welcome to apply for all grants programmes, but a grant from one programme will prevent applicants from getting a grant from another.

The Scott Bader Commonwealth Ltd

Social welfare, education and training, overseas aid, conservation, children and young people, socially excluded and disadvantaged people, women, and minority communities

£33,000 to organisations in the UK (2013)

Beneficial area

UK, as well as locations close to where the company operates.

Correspondent: Sue Carter, Commonwealth Secretary, Scott Bader Company Ltd, Wollaston Hall, Wollaston, Nr Wellingborough, Northants NN29 7RL (tel: 01933 666755; email: commonwealth_office@scottbader.com; website: www.scottbader.com)

Trustees: Andrew Radford; Syed Hayat; Julie Rogers; Anne Atkinson-Clark; Les Norwood; Jacquie Findlay; Barry Mansfield; Christian Caulier; Karl Funke

CC number: 206391

The Scott Bader Commonwealth Ltd was established in 1967. It is a registered charity and a company limited by guarantee, which owns the share capital of the global chemical company, Scott Bader Company Ltd and receives 1% of the annual staff salary cost of the group.

The charity is a membership organisation and everyone employed by the Scott Bader Commonwealth Ltd or any of its subsidiaries may become a member of the charity. There are around 640 people employed worldwide, of which more than 500 are members of the charity.

The charity fulfils its objectives by making grants to charitable organisations around the world whose purposes are to help young or disadvantaged people, especially anyone suffering deprivation and discrimination, such as poor, homeless and vulnerable women and children, and minority communities, particularly where people are affected by poverty, a lack of education, malnutrition and disease.

Funds are divided into two categories:

Local Funds: funds are made available to all the companies in the Scott Bader Group for them to submit applications to the Commonwealth for charities they wish to support. Each supports the work of charities associated with them or situated nearby.

Central Fund:

- £50,000 is allocated to annually support two large, community-based environmental or educational projects to the value of £25,000 each, which can be located anywhere in the world
- £10,000 was allocated in 2013 to a Small International Fund to provide small grants of £500–£2,000 to support international projects that do not fit the local fund or large fund criteria
- £5,000 is made available for distribution to charities chosen by the Life President, Godric Bader

In 2013 the charity had assets of £42 million and an income of £199,000, primarily in donations from the Scott Bader Company. Grants were made totalling £155,000 of which £33,000 was given in the UK. £14,900 of the UK grant total was given through the nomination scheme whereby staff of Scott Bader can nominate a charity of their choice.

The remainder of the UK grant total was used to support local projects including: The Prince's Trust, Northampton (£5,000); Livability (£3,000); Family Support Link, Wellingborough (£2,500); Tall Ships Youth Trust (£1,800); Beanstalk (£700); and the Children's Aid Team, Northamptonshire (£500).

Exclusions

No support is given for charities concerned with animals; individual sponsorships; travel and adventure schemes; arts projects; any form of advertising; medical research and equipment; sports clubs; general charitable appeals; and construction/ renovation/maintenance of buildings.

Applications

Assessment criteria are available to download from the website. Application forms are available on request by post or email. Deadlines for the large project funding are available on the website. Applications for the Small International fund are accepted all year round. Applications for local funds should be made to the local office.

The Scottish Power Energy People Trust

Fuel poverty, social welfare, energy efficiency

£1 million (2013)

Beneficial area

UK.

Correspondent: Kirsteen Lappin, Account Manager, Scottish Power Energy Retail Ltd, Cathcart Business Park, 44 Spean Street, Glasgow G44 4BE (tel: 01416 144480; email: SPEnergyPeopleTrust@ScottishPower.com; website: www.energypeopletrust.com)

Trustees: Ann Loughrey, Secretary; Norman Kerr, Chair; Douglas McLaren; Joan Fraser; Neil Hartwell; Dr Bill Sheldrick; Alan Hughes; Peter Sumby

OSCR number: SC036980

Established by Scottish Power in 2005, the trust has distributed over £12.6 million to projects run by grass-roots organisations that help people who are on low incomes, live in poor housing or suffer ill health.

The trust is funded primarily by donations from Scottish Power; however, funding decisions are made by the independent trustee board. The following projects are eligible for funding (taken from the trust's website).

> Registered charities can apply for funding to support projects in the following categories:
>
> - Energy Efficiency Advice – it is a condition of funding that all projects include the provision of energy efficiency advice. Energy advisors should be trained to City and Guilds standard or equivalent
> - Energy Efficiency Measures – improving home energy efficiency through draught proofing, insulating and or other practical measures
> - Income Maximisation – providing funding to front line charities who carry out benefits advice to households missing out on financial help that they are entitled to through welfare benefits and tax credits
> - Fuel Debt Assistance – providing assistance, or funding the provision by other persons of assistance, to reduce or cancel debts for household electricity or gas supply, where such assistance is provided as part of a package of measures aimed at providing customers with long-term relief from fuel poverty
>
> Or any combination of the above. Priority will be given to projects aimed at helping families with young children and young people.
>
> Please note that all projects must address fuel poverty explicitly and as the primary purpose (not just as an add on).
>
> The trust will award funding at levels appropriate to the type of project and the number of people to be helped, from small sums up to a maximum of £50,000.
>
> Projects may be funded for a maximum of one year, but the maximum amount of £50,000 applies, regardless of the timescale of the project.
>
> We provide funding on the condition that overheads or administration costs associated with a project do not exceed 12.5% of the total funding requested. However, the trustees may make an exception to this condition in special circumstances, where a valid reason is provided.

In 2013 the trust had an income of £453,000 and a total expenditure of almost £1.2 million. Grants are estimated to have totalled about £1 million.

Beneficiaries included: Heely City Farm (£40,000); LESS (£39,500); Doorway (£38,500); Action for Children – Perthshire Families Service partnership project (£30,500); Quarries Homeless Energy Action Project (£23,500); Family Link Stockport (£22,000); and Northern Oak Credit Union (£20,000).

Exclusions

Grants are not made to individuals.

Applications

On an online application on the trust's website. Trustees meet to consider applications three times a year, in March, July and November. Applications should be submitted at least seven weeks prior to the date of the meeting (exact dates are available on the trust's website). However, early applications are advised as only 30 applications will be considered at each meeting, with additional applications received being carried over to the next meeting.

The following guidelines are available on the trust's website:

> All projects must address fuel poverty explicitly. Tackling fuel poverty must be the primary purpose of the project (not just as an add on).
>
> Project applications must identify how the outcomes and outputs of a project will reduce fuel poverty and how a project will meet the trust objectives.
>
> Each application should demonstrate how many people will be helped as a direct result of the project.
>
> Please note that we will only accept one application per organisation at each trustee meeting.
>
> All applicants should create a link to their organisation's latest annual audited accounts and confirm any previous applications to the trust. This information should be updated in the **Project Controls** section of the application.
>
> Charity registration number must be included in application, if not it will be rejected.

The trust also cautions that funding is made on the condition that overheads or administration costs associated with a project do not exceed 12.5% of the total funding requested. In special circumstances the trustees may make an exception to this condition provided a valid reason is supplied. Applicants will be notified within two weeks of the trustee meeting and unsuccessful applicants may re-apply only after six months. Successful applicants may re-apply for further funding either six months after the initial funding has expired, or on completion of the project – whichever happens first.

Grants are usually made in annual instalments with 10% of the annual total retained by the trust pending receipt of a satisfactory annual report on the progress or completion of the project which the trust says is to 'encourage transparency and responsible reporting'. More details on reporting requirements are available on the trust's website.

The Scottish Power Foundation

General charitable purposes

Around £60,000 (2013).

Beneficial area

UK.

Correspondent: María Elena Sanz Arcas, Administrator, 1 Atlantic Quay, Robertson Street, Glasgow G2 8SP (tel: 0800 027 0072; email: scottishpowerfoundation@scottishpower.com; website: www.scottishpower.com/pages/the_scottishpower_foundation.asp)

Trustees: Mike Thornton; Elaine Bowker; Sarah Mistry; Mike Thornton; Keith Anderson; Ann Loughrey

OSCR number: SC043862

Scottish Power is part of the Iberdrola Group, a global energy company and world leader in wind energy with operations focused in the UK, US, Brazil, Mexico and Spain. The foundation was set up in 2013 in order to reinforce the company's commitment to supporting charitable work throughout Britain.

The following information was taken from the foundation's website:

> The ScottishPower Foundation will consider applications from registered charities and non-profit organisations under the following categories:
> - The advancement of education
> - The advancement of environmental protection or improvement, in particular the promotion, dissemination and support of knowledge, research and culture in their most varied forms, with a special focus on the development of and progress toward a sustainable energy model that respects the environment and biodiversity
> - The advancement of the arts, heritage, culture or science, in particular:
>   - Cultural initiatives for the promotion and support of scientific, technological dissemination and environmental protection activities, encouraging, in particular, the development of studies of all kinds in the areas of energy, biodiversity and environmental impact in general
>   - In the areas of restoration, development and conservation of the cultural heritage, as well as the development of projects and activities to promote and disseminate art and culture, and to technically and financially support cultural and artistic activities carried out by public and private institutions
> - The prevention or relief of poverty and the relief of those in need by reason of disability or other disadvantage, in particular, the development of initiatives to support social action in the areas of cooperation and solidarity in order to actively contribute to the improvement of the quality of life of the most underprivileged groups, through initiatives for the development of infrastructure and services that provide for their full social and labour integration, as well as professional training, insertion into the work force and the generation of employment opportunities for disadvantaged persons that allows for the creation of jobs for them, and ultimately, for the integration into the labour market;
> - The advancement of citizenship and community development

In 2013 the foundation had an income of £192,000 and an expenditure of £60,000. We estimate that around £60,000 was made in grants.

Previous beneficiaries include: Action for Achievement; Children's University Scotland; Clwyd Theatre Cymru; Duke of Edinburgh's Award; Loch Lomond and The Trossachs Countryside Trust; National Theatre for Scotland; Northern Lights; O Ddrws i Ddrws; Outward Bound; and the Scottish Youth Hostels Association.

Exclusions

- Organisations that are not registered charities or non-profit general appeals and circulars including contributions to endowment funds
- Local charities whose work takes place outside the United Kingdom
- Medical research
- Individuals or support organisations for travel or for expeditions, whether in the United Kingdom or abroad
- Projects which are primarily or exclusively intended to promote political or religious beliefs
- Second or third tier organisations (unless there is evidence of direct benefit to disadvantaged people)
- Sponsorship or funding towards a marketing appeal or fundraising activities

Applications

The foundation will be inviting applications for projects commencing in 2016 in the summer of 2015. Check the website for the latest information.

Applications should be made using the application form which will be available to download from the website during the next application period. Applications should be submitted via email along with:

- A copy of your most recent annual report and accounts (note that these should have been independently examined or audited)
- An initial high level project plan with key milestones

The SDL Foundation

Social welfare, community and economic development, education and training

£160,000 (2013)

Beneficial area

Worldwide.

Correspondent: Alastair Gordon, Trustee, SDL plc, 64 Castelnau, London SW13 9EX (email: SDLFoundation@sdl.com; website: www.sdl.com/about/corporate-citizenship/foundation)

Trustees: Mark Lancaster; Alastair Gordon; Dominic Kinnon; Michelle Wilson

CC number: 1127138

Established in 2008, this is the corporate charity of SDL plc. The company provides interpretation and translation services, and content and software development. It is one of the largest language services companies in the world, working in over 30 countries. The global nature of the company's business is reflected in the activities and aspirations of the foundation. The foundation's trustees are all present or former employees of SDL International plc, most notably Mark Lancaster who is the CEO and founder of the company.

The objects of the SDL Foundation are to promote sustainable development in order to relieve poverty and improve the lives of disadvantaged communities; and to promote sustainable means of achieving economic growth and regeneration.

The following information is taken from the company's website:

> ***SDL Foundation Mission***
>
> The SDL Foundation is committed to supporting charities and projects across the world which work with disadvantaged

communities. It aims to provide sutatinable aid through financial grants and educational and voactional training to help people become self-sufficient. It also encourages and enables SDL employees to get involved in charitable activities in their local communities.

SDL Foundation Projects SDL Foundation Endorsements

UK Charity

The SDL Foundation is a UK charity . . . and is managed by an independent Trustee committee, chaired by ex SDL CFO, Alastair Gordon. To show its commitment to the SDL Foundation, the SDL Board has resolved to donate a percentage of the Group's pre tax profits to the SDL Foundation each year.

Employee involvement

As an international organization working in over 30 countries worldwide, SDL strives to make a significant and positive impact in the countries where it operates and supports the efforts of their employees in their own charitable activities. All SDL employees are actively encouraged to nominate and sponsor deserving causes in their local communities.

All projects supported by the SDL Foundation have been presented by an SDL Employee sponsor who is actively involved in the charitable cause and who is responsible, along with an SDL Executive sponsor, for the success of the initiative. SDL Employees create regional groups in SDL's worldwide offices to provide support for the SDL Foundation.

Regional Foundation groups provide:

- Regular forum for brainstorming
- Focus and momentum
- Supply of applications

In 2013 the foundation had assets of £332,000 and an income of £261,000, £260,000 of which was received as a donation from SDL plc. Grants totalled £160,000 during the year.

Beneficiaries included: Gua Africa, Sudan (£43,000); Village Water, Zambia (£25,000); Hatua Likoni, Kenya (£20,000); Bead For Life, Uganda (£13,000); Able Children Africa, Kenya Food for the Hungry UK, Kenya and St Wilfrid's, UK (£10,000 each); Stichting Miramundo, Honduras (£8,700); PRIDE, Ethiopia (£6,400); Niall Mellon Township Fund, Kenya (£3,400); Translators Without Borders (£1,600); and Operation Sack Lunch, USA (£350).

Exclusions

No grants will be given to causes where trustees or SDL employees would directly benefit. The foundation will also not support political or discriminatory activities; or those appeals that are recognised as being large or well-known.

Applications

Only causes supported and sponsored by SDL employees will be considered by the SDL Foundation. Contact the foundation by email for further information on how to request the support of staff and application procedures.

The Shoe Zone Trust

Education and training, social welfare, children and young people

£107,000 (2013)

Beneficial area

Preference for Leicestershire and Rutland and for certain charities operating in the Philippines and other countries.

Correspondent: Michael Smith, Trustee, Shoe Zone Retail Ltd, Haramead Business Centre, Humberstone Road, Leicester LE1 2LH (tel: 01162 223007; website: www.shoezone.net/sztrust.html)

Trustees: Michael Smith; Anthony Smith; John Smith

CC number: 1112972

Registered with the Charity Commission in 2006, The Shoe Zone Trust is the corporate charity of Shoe Zone Retail Ltd, a UK footwear retailer. Trustees include Michael Smith, the company's Chair and Anthony Smith, its CEO.

The trust's 2013 annual report states that it aims 'to make grants to charities that relieve financial hardship and poverty and/or advance education, mainly for children and young people in Leicestershire and Rutland and for certain charities operating in the Philippines and other countries.'

In 2013 the trust had assets of £79,000 and an income of £163,000, £100,000 of which was a direct donation from Shoe Zone Retail Ltd and £38,000 of which was due to carrier bag sales donated by the company. Grants totalled £107,000 during the year.

Beneficiaries included: Shepherd of the Hills, Philippines (£49,000); Ministries Without Borders (£25,000); Mango Tree and Toyhouse (£6,500 each); 500 Miles and Amantani Boarding Houses (£5,000 each); Kids in Need of Education (£1,000); and Marie Curie Cancer Care (£400).

Donations of £250 and under totalled £2,300.

Applications

In writing to the correspondent.

The Simmons & Simmons Charitable Foundation

Social welfare, education and training, access to justice and legal aid

£173,000 (2012/13)

Beneficial area

Worldwide, with a preference for the City of London and Tower Hamlets.

Correspondent: The Trustees, Simmons & Simmons LLP, CityPoint, 1 Ropemaker Street, London EC2Y 9SS (tel: 020 7628 2020; email: corporate.responsibility@simmons-simmons.com; website: www.simmons-simmons.com)

Trustees: Richard Dyton; Fiona Loughrey; Colin Passmore; Michele Anahory

CC number: 1129643

The foundation was established in 2009 by the law firm Simmons & Simmons LLP. Its four trustees are all partners in the firm: Richard Dyton (CR and Pro Bono Partner), Fiona Loughrey (Partner Hong Kong), Colin Passmore (Senior Partner) and Michele Anahory (Partner Paris).

The following information was taken from the foundation's 2012/13 accounts:

> The foundation seeks to support smaller charitable organisations which are local to the offices of Simmons & Simmons and which seek to address social exclusion. The foundation also seeks to provide access to justice, work and opportunities to those less privileged or fortunate, for example by providing direct grants to talented individuals from low income backgrounds.

In 2012/13 the foundation had assets of £174,000 and an income of £170,000, which included a donation of £120,000 from Simmons & Simmons. Grants were made to over 17 organisations totalling £173,000. Grants were broken down as follows:

International	£62,000
Social inclusion	£52,000
Pro bono	£43,000
Other	£16,000

Beneficiaries included: UNICEF (£42,000); Battersea Legal Advice Centre (£36,000); Five Talents UK (£15,000); Spitalfields Music (£10,000); Create (£8,000); Envision, Fair Trials, Room to Read and Working Families (£5,000 each); and Ivy Street Family Centre (£2,500).

Smaller grants totalled £6,000.

Applications

On an application form available to download from the company's website. Completed forms should then be emailed for consideration. Applicants must explain how they meet one of the following objectives:

- Social inclusion (increasing access to education and/or work)
- Governance (supporting the rule of law and access to justice)

They must also explain how they will provide support to communities local to where Simmons & Simmons have offices.

The Slaughter and May Charitable Trust

Legal advice, education and training, health, social welfare, children and young people and older people

£337,000 (2013/14)

Beneficial area

Mainly local to the Slaughter and May offices in Islington and close to Tower Hamlets and Hackney.

Correspondent: Kate Hursthouse, Corporate Responsibility Manager, Slaughter and May (Trust Ltd), 1 Bunhill Row, London EC1Y 8YY (tel: 020 7090 3433; email: corporateresponsibility@slaughterandmay.com; website: www.slaughterandmay.com)

Trustee: Slaughter and May Trust Ltd

CC number: 1082765

Established in 1991 and registered with the Charity Commission in 2000, this trust is the corporate charity of the legal firm Slaughter and May. The trust's annual report for 2013/14 states that it is 'reliant on its key donors, the partners of Slaughter and May' with all administrative and other office support being provided by the firm. 'The trustee of the charity is Slaughter and May Trust Ltd, a company whose directors are all partners in Slaughter and May.'

The trust supports a range of legal, educational, health and community projects, with a particular interest in children and young people and older people.

In 2013/14 the trust had assets of -£37,000 and an income of £342,000, of which £337,000 was donated by the partners of Slaughter and May. Grants totalled £337,000.

Beneficiaries included: National Literacy Trust (£53,000); the Access Project (£49,000); Islington Law Centre (£35,000); Legal Advice Centre Bethnal Green and Seeing is Believing (£15,000 each); London Symphony Orchestra (£10,000); CLEFT and RCJ Advice Bureau (£5,000 each); Marie Curie Cancer Care (£2,000); and Royal National Institute for the Blind and Unicef (£1,000 each).

Note:

> the charity's intention is to distribute all donations received in the year. Any net surplus or deficit (other than the initial £10 capital sum) is due to short-term timing differences. The deficit in 2014 of £36,745 (under the initial capital sum) is comprised of grants which the charity is committed to paying but which are not payable until subsequent years (e.g. three year commitments).

Applications

The trust's 2013/14 annual report states that it 'makes annual grants at its discretion to a small number of specific charitable causes and does not generally accept unsolicited funding applications'.

The DS Smith Charitable Foundation

Education and training, conservation

£149,000 (2013/14)

Beneficial area

England and Wales.

Correspondent: Rachel Stevens, Trustee, 7th Floor, 350 Euston Road, London NW1 3AX (tel: 020 7756 1823; email: charitablefoundation@dssmith.com; website: www.dssmith.com/company/sustainability/social-responsibility/charitable-trust)

Trustees: Anne Steele; Rachel Stevens; Nicholas Feaviour; Mark Greenwood

CC number: 1142817

DS Smith was started by the Smith brothers in 1940. The company provides corrugated packaging in Europe and plastic packaging worldwide. It operates across 25 countries and employs around 21,500 people.

Registered in 2011, the foundation supports charities engaged in conservation of the environment and provides training and educational opportunities.

The foundation is a supporter of the Arkwright Engineering Scholarships. The following was taken from the foundation's website:

> Arkwright Engineering Scholarships are awarded to high-calibre students in year 11 (England and Wales), S4 (Scotland), year 12 (Northern Ireland). The Engineering Scholarships support students through their A Levels or Scottish Highers and encourage students to pursue engineering or related areas of design at university or through a higher-level apprenticeship and to take up careers in the field. The scholarships consist of an annual financial award to each Scholar and to his/her school, and a range of enrichment activities, such as mentoring and industry visits, that enhance a Scholar's experience of engineering in a real-world context.

In 2013/14 the foundation had assets of £2.7 million and an income of £83,000. Around £149,000 was made in grants to institutions.

Beneficiaries included: D'Artgens (£42,000); Arkwright Scholarship Trust and In Kind Direct (£30,000 each); Heart Research UK (£8,400); Royal Institution (£5,000); and CHAS and IT Schools Africa (£3,200 each).

Applications

On an application form available from the foundation's website.

Sodexo Foundation

Education and training, health, community and economic development, social welfare

£418,000 (2012/13)

Beneficial area

UK and Ireland.

Correspondent: Edwina Hughes, Corporate Responsibility Manager, Sodexo Ltd, 1 Southampton Row, London WC1B 5HA (email: stophunger@sodexo.com; website: uk.sodexo.com/uken/corporate-responsibility/local-communities/local-communities.aspx)

Trustees: Phil Hooper; Harbhajan Singh Brar; Rebecca Symon; David Mulcahy; Gareth John; Margot Slattery; Debra White

CC number: 1110266

Registered with the Charity Commission in June 2005, the Sodexo Foundation is the corporate charity of the food services and facilities management company, Sodexo Ltd. The trustees are all Sodexo Ltd employees, most notably CEO Debra White.

The foundation's 2012/13 annual report states that the principal objectives of the foundation 'focus on either advancing the education of the general public in relation to health nutrition and well-being or providing relief from financial hardship and the improvement of the quality of life in socially and/or economically disadvantaged communities.'

The foundation's STOP Hunger campaign was launched in 2005. It aims to tackle poor nutrition in local communities, promote good nutrition and healthy lifestyles and offers training in basic life skills. The campaign provides a central focus for Sodexo's charitable and community interests.

The trustees continue to work particularly closely with FareShare as it was felt that a stronger alliance with the charity would more clearly meet the objectives of the Sodexo Foundation. In addition to supporting FareShare and a number of smaller charities that meet the STOP Hunger objectives, the trustees receive from time to time requests from employees to support a local cause. Such requests are usually met by Sodexo outside the Sodexo Foundation.

In 2012/13 the foundation had assets of £131,000 and an income of £495,000, of which £49,000 was income from Sodexo Ltd and £446,000 raised by Sodexo employees. Grants totalled £418,000 and were given to 14 organisations.

Beneficiaries included: FareShare (£120,000); Breast Cancer Haven (£60,000); Outward Bound Trust (£53,000); Scouts Association (£48,000); Coram Life (£41,000); SSAFA (£31,000); Council for Homelessness, NI (£20,000); Action for Kids (£5,000); Club Hampshire (£2,100); and schools receiving Rocket Gardens (£150).

Applications

In writing to the correspondent. Application forms can be downloaded from the foundation's website.

Spar Charitable Fund

General, with a preference for children and young people

£90,000 (2013/14)

Beneficial area

UK.

Correspondent: Philip Marchant, Trustee, Spar (UK) Ltd, Hygeia Building, 66 – 68 College Road, Harrow, Middlesex HA1 1BE (tel: 020 8426 3700; email: philip.marchant@spar.co.uk)

Trustees: Kevin Hunt; Martin Agnew; Peter Dodding; Philip Marchant; Claire Bolton; Colin Landsburgh; Mark Gillett; Patrick Doody; Christopher Sharrinton; Dominic Hall; Bryan Walters

CC number: 236252

Registered with the Charity Commission in 1970, the Spar Charitable Fund is the corporate charity of the retail chain, Spar (UK) Ltd.

Its 2013/14 accounts state that:

> The Spar Charitable Fund with the support and assistance of the Spar Benevolent Fund seeks to provide charitable assistance to independent Spar retailers who face adverse problems and difficulties with health, bereavement and social issues. The charitable fund also supports retail industry charitable organisations.
>
> One major objective of the Spar Charitable Fund is to provide a vehicle to enable the Spar organisation through its 2,323 stores across the UK to engage with the public to raise awareness of public charitable needs and raise funding in a wide variety of ways.

In 2013/14 it had assets of £872,000 and an income of £49,000, of which £32,000 was generated from investments, £10,000 was a donation from the Spar Benevolent Fund and £7,000 constituted 'funds raised on behalf of NSPCC'. Grants were made totalling £90,000.

As in previous years, NSPCC was a beneficiary, which received £8,500. Spar Benevolent Fund received a donation of £65,000, £10,000 was granted to the Philippines Appeal and another £6,600 to Retail Industry.

Applications

In writing to the correspondent.

St James's Place Foundation

Social welfare, education and training, children and young people (up to the age of 25) with mental or physical conditions, life threatening or degenerative illnesses, young carers

£4.9 million (2013)

Beneficial area

UK.

Correspondent: Mark Longbottom, Foundation Manager, St James's Place plc, St James's Place House, 1 Tetbury Road, Cirencester GL7 1FP (tel: 01285 878562; email: mark.longbottom@sjp.co.uk; website: www.sjpfoundation.co.uk)

Trustees: David Bellamy; Ian Gascoigne; Malcolm Cooper-Smith; Hugh Gladman; Andrew Croft; David Lamb; Michael Wilson

CC number: 1144606

The St James's Place Foundation was originally established in 1992, when it was known as the J. Rothschild Assurance Foundation. Following a strategic review, the foundation was wound up in 2012 and re-registered with the Charity Commission with a new registered charity number. The foundation is the corporate charity of St James's Place Wealth Management, a leading UK wealth management company.

The foundation's grant-making is guided by three themes which are updated every three years. The current themes are as follows:

Cherishing Children
Cherishing Children is aimed at supporting young people under the age of 25 with physical or mental health difficulties or life threatening or degenerative conditions, young carers and those who are socially or economically disadvantaged. Grants are given for small capital items, support for staff working directly with beneficiaries and support for projects of direct benefit to beneficiaries.

Combating Cancer
Grants are given for capital items of direct benefit to cancer patients, support towards the salary of staff working directly with cancer patients and grants and support projects aimed at increasing the quality of life for cancer patients. Small grants of up to £10,000 are available to UK charities with an annual income of up to £750,000 supporting individuals of all ages suffering from cancer and their families.

Supporting Hospices
The foundation is currently working with Help the Hospices who will distribute funds to hospices on the foundation's behalf.

Grant Programmes

- **Small Grants Programme:** grants of up to £10,000 are available to UK charities with an annual income of up to £750,000
- **Major Grants Programme:** this programme is not currently open to unsolicited applications; instead charities are invited to apply
- **Major Projects:** projects are funded from the company's matched funding of money raised by partners and staff. The foundation's trustees and management committee will select a cause and then a charity working within that field will be approached by the foundation
- **Local Office Allowance:** £20,000 is available for each of the St James's Place locations. Grants of up to £2,500 can be given to any local charity

In 2013 the foundation had assets of £427,000 and an income of £5.4 million, of which £1.9 million was a donation from St James's Place plc. Audit fees were detailed as donated services by PwC (PricewaterhouseCoopers). Grants during the year totalled £4.9 million.

A list of beneficiaries was not available in the 2013 accounts; however, the most recent beneficiaries for 2014 were listed on the foundation's website.

Beneficiaries were: National Star College (£162,000); Brainwave and Leeds Rugby Foundation (£99,000 each); Worldwide Volunteering (£90,000); Winston's Wish (£85,000); the Rose Road Association (£84,000); the Ear Foundation (£74,000); AfriKids (£66,000); British Association for Adoption and Fostering (£65,000); Action for Kids (£50,000); Action for Brazil's Children Trust (£46,000); Jamie's Farm (£45,000); East London

Advanced Technology Training (£34,000); Impact Initiatives (£23,000); Castlehaven Community (£10,000); Vauxhall City Farm Riding Therapy Centre (£9,900); and Gaddum Centre (£2,500).

Exclusions

The foundation does not provide support for:

- Charities with reserves of over 50% of income
- Administrative costs
- Activities primarily the responsibility of statutory agencies
- Replacement of lost statutory funding
- Research
- Events
- Advertising
- Holidays
- Sponsorship
- Contributions to large capital appeals
- Single faith charities
- Charities that are raising funds on behalf of another charity

Applications

Applicants who believe that they fit the criteria are welcome to apply at any time via the foundation's website. The application procedure for all of the programmes can take between four to six months. The following information is given on the foundation's website: 'applications for a small grant will normally receive a visit from a representative of the foundation, who will subsequently report to the trustees. Following the trustees' decision, successful applicants will be notified.'

Consult the foundation's website for further details.

The Stobart Newlands Charitable Trust

Christian, religious and missionary causes

£1.6 million (2013)

Beneficial area

Worldwide.

Correspondent: Ronnie Stobart, Trustee, J. Stobart and Sons Ltd, Mill Croft, Newlands, Hesket Newmarket, Wigton CA7 8HP (tel: 01697 478631)

Trustees: Ronnie Stobart; Linda Rigg; Peter Stobart; Richard Stobart

CC number: 328464

Registered in 1989 with the Charity Commission, the Stobart Newlands Charitable Trust is the corporate charity of J Stobart and Sons Ltd, a manufacturer and retailer of animal feedstuffs. The trustees are directors and shareholders of J Stobart and Sons Ltd, which is the source of almost all of the trust's income. This family trust makes up to 60 grants a year, nearly all on a recurring basis to Christian religious and missionary bodies.

In 2013 the trust had assets of £453,000 and an income of almost £1.8 million, of which £1.5 million was donated by the company and £236,000 was made in individual gifts by the trustees under the Gift Aid scheme. Grants were made totalling £1.6 million.

Beneficiaries included: World Vision (£360,000); Mission Aviation Fellowship (£280,000); Operation Mobilisation (£175,000); Caring for Life (£155,000); Moorlands (£80,000); Bible Society and Tear Fund (£35,000 each); Christian Medical Fellowship and CUMNISCU (£20,000 each); Biblica Europe, Trans World Radio and Torch Trust (£10,000 each).

Grants for less than £10,000 totalled £120,000.

Exclusions

No grants for individuals.

Applications

Unsolicited applications are most unlikely to be successful.

The Swann-Morton Foundation

Medical research, education and training, health, disability, social welfare, animal welfare

£44,000 to organisations and individuals (2013/14)

Beneficial area

UK, with a preference for South Yorkshire.

Correspondent: Michael Hirst, Director, Swann-Morton Ltd, Owlerton Green, Sheffield S6 2BJ (tel: 01142 344231)

Trustees: Judith Gilmour; Michael McGinley; George Rodgers

CC number: 271925

Registered with the Charity Commission in 1976, the Swann-Morton Foundation is the corporate charity of Swann Morton Ltd, a British manufacturer of scalpel handles, blades and surgical equipment.

According to the foundation's 2013/14 annual report, the aims of the foundation are as follows:

- The purchase of medical instruments or equipment for the use by or for patients with infirmity
- The promotion of education and research in medicine and surgery aimed at the relief of suffering or handicap
- For the encouragement of scholarship at schools, colleges and universities

In 2013/14 the foundation had assets of £112,000 and an income of £55,000, which was obtained from Gift Aid donations received from Swann-Morton (Microbiological Laboratory Services) Ltd. Grants were made totalling £44,000.

Beneficiaries included: Sheffield Children's Hospital and St Luke's Hospice (£3,500 each); and Royal College of Surgeons and Whirlow Farm Trust (£1,000 each).

Other donations totalled £22,000 and student grants and electives totalled £10,000.

Exclusions

No grants are given for gap years.

Applications

In writing to the correspondent. The foundation's annual report for 2013/14 states that it:

> Invites applications for funding of projects from hospitals, charities and students. Applicants are invited to submit a summary of their proposals in a specific format. The applications are reviewed against specific criteria and research objectives which are set by the trustees.

The John Swire (1989) Charitable Trust

General charitable purposes, especially arts, welfare, education, sports, medicine and research

£1.6 million (2013)

Beneficial area

UK, with some preference for Kent.

Correspondent: Michael Todhunter, Administrator, John Swire & Sons Ltd, Swire House, 59 Buckingham Gate, London SW1E 6AJ (tel: 020 7834 7717; email: Sarah.Irving@jssldn.co.uk)

Trustees: B. Swire; J. Swire; Lady Moira Swire; Michael Cradock Robinson; Sir John Swire

CC number: 802142

Established in 1989 by Sir John Swire of John Swire & Sons Ltd, merchants and ship owners, the trust supports a wide range of organisations, especially in the areas of arts, welfare, health, sports, education, medicine and research.

In 2013 the trust had assets of almost £32.3 million and an income of £1.2 million, which was wholly derived from investments. Grants were made totalling almost £1.6 million.

Beneficiaries included: St John of Jerusalem Eye Hospital Group (£1.1 million); Riding for the Disabled, Cobbes Meadow (£103,000); Kent Wildlife Trust (£50,000); Catching Lives and Faversham Buildings Preservation

Trust (£20,000 each); Carers First and Prior's Court Foundation (£15,000 each); Parkinson's UK, School Home Support Service UK and Stour Music (£5,000 each); Artists' General Benevolent Institution and Pilsdon at Malling Community (£4,000 each); GB Women's Rafting Team, Pilgrims Hospices, RNLI and Mission to Seafarers (£2,500 each); the Alternative Theatre Company Ltd, Canterbury Choral Society, Chatham Historic Dockyard Trust and Essex Wildlife Trust (£1,000 each).

Grants of less than £1,000 amounted to a total of £20,000.

Applications

In writing to the correspondent explaining how the funds would be used and what would be achieved.

The Swire Charitable Trust

General charitable purposes, including the armed forces, health, medical research, social welfare, the environment and animal welfare

£863,500 (2013)

Beneficial area

Worldwide.

Correspondent: Sarah Irving, Administrator, John Swire & Sons Ltd, Swire House, 59 Buckingham Gate, London SW1E 6AJ (tel: 020 7834 7717; email: Sarah.Irving@jssldn.co.uk)

Trustees: B. Swire; J. Swire; Sir Adrian Swire; Sir John Swire; Merlin Swire; James Hughes-Hallett

CC number: 270726

Established in 1976 by Sir John Swire of John Swire & Sons Ltd, merchants and ship owners, the trust supports a wide range of organisations and has general charitable purposes.

In 2013 the trust had assets of £193,000 and an income of £1.1 million, which was almost entirely from donations received from John Swire & Sons Ltd. Grants to over 145 organisations totalled £863,000.

Beneficiaries included: Marine Society and Sea Cadets (£50,000); the Air League Trust (£27,000); Bentley Priory, Oracle Cancer Trust and the Norman Trust (£25,000 each); Cancer Vaccine Institute and Monte San Martino Trust (£15,000 each); National Maritime Museum, the Stroke Association and Sightsavers International (£10,000 each); British Lung Foundation, Diabetes UK, English Heritage and Missing People (£5,000 each); Buttle UK, Care for Casualties, Prospect Burma and Target Ovarian Cancer (£2,500 each); and International Fund for Animal Welfare and Westminster Tree Trust (£1,000 each).

Grants of less than £1,000 each totalled almost £320.

Applications

In writing to the correspondent. Applications are considered throughout the year. The annual report for 2013 states that 'although the trustees make some grants with no formal applications, they normally require organisations to submit a request explaining how the funds could be used and what would be achieved'.

Tesco Charity Trust

Education and training, social welfare, health, people with disabilities, children and young people, older people

£8.6 million (2013/14)

Beneficial area

Worldwide.

Correspondent: Michelle Cornish, Corporate Responsibility Executive, Tesco plc, 25 Furlong Way, Great Amwell, Near Ware, Hertfordshire SG12 9TE (tel: 01992 644598; email: charity.enquiries@uk.tesco.com; website: www.tescoplc.com/tescocharitytrust)

Trustees: Paul Smythe; Juliet Crisp; Christophe Roussel; Rebecca Shelley; John Scouler; Damian Leeson

CC number: 297126

Registered with the Charity Commission in June 1987, the Tesco Charity Trust is the corporate charity of Tesco plc, the grocery and general merchandise retailer. The trust is dependent on donations made by Tesco plc, Tesco Stores Ltd and colleague fundraising. It is run by a board of trustees who are all employees or directors of the company and were recommended by the main board of Tesco plc.

According to Tesco's website, the 'Tesco Charity Trust aims to help Tesco support the local communities in which we operate, supporting both national and local community charities, and adding a 20% top up to colleague fundraising.'

The accounts for 2013/14 stated that 'Tesco Stores Ltd permits national collections on behalf of RSPCA and Scottish SPCA, Cancer Research UK, Food Bank, Help for Heroes, Diabetes UK and the Royal British Legion Poppy Appeal.'

The trust supports projects concerned with promotion the welfare and education of children, older people, people with disabilities and health related causes through its Community Award Scheme. This scheme aims to distribute around £600,000 each year to charities in areas where Tesco has stores. Grants range between £500 and £4,000.

Donations under the company's Give As You Earn scheme are managed by the trust and totalled £737,000 in 2013/14. The trust also recycled inkjet cartridges, money from which totalled £153,000.

In 2013/14 the trust had assets of £807,000 and an income of almost £9.2 million, of which £2 million was a donation made by Tesco Stores Ltd. Grants were made during the year totalling £8.6 million.

The three largest beneficiaries were Diabetes UK (£6 million); Cancer Research UK (£1 million); and Barking Badgers (£40,000). Other grant allocations were broken down as follows:

Disabilities and health	£406,000
Children and youth	£268,000
Education	£197,000
Older people	£177,000
20% top up of colleague fundraising	£175,000
Other	£330,000

Grant amounts were not available but other beneficiaries included: Age Concern Neath Port Talbot, the Brain Injury Foundation, Hammersmith and Fulham Mencap, Leeds Powerchair Football Club, Multiple Sclerosis UK, Starbeck School, the Stuart Low Trust and Trinity Community Centre.

Exclusions

No grants to political organisations, individuals or towards new buildings. The trust will not make donations to charities for onward transmission to other charitable organisations.

Applications

Applications should be made via the trust's website.

The Thales Charitable Trust

General charitable purposes, education, technology, children and young people, health, people with disabilities

£224,000 (2013)

Beneficial area

UK.

Correspondent: Michael Seabrook, Trustee, Thales Corporate Services Ltd, 2 Dashwood Lang Road, Bourne Business Park, Addlestone, Surrey KT15 2NX (tel: 01932 824800; email: mike.seabrook@thalesgroup.com)

Trustees: John Howe; Michael Seabrook; Marion Broughton; Markus Leutert

CC number: 1000162

Registered in 1990 with the Charity Commission, the Thales Charitable Trust is the corporate charity of Thales Corporate Services Ltd, a major electronic systems company acting in areas such as defence, airlines security and safety, information technology and transportation.

The trust has general charitable purposes but principally supports charitable organisations in the fields of youth, technology, education and training and the care for those with terminal illnesses. From time to time the trustees use their discretion to meet requests from other causes as they determine appropriate.

In 2013 the trust had assets of £61,000 and an income of £150,000 and was wholly received from donations. Grants totalled £224,000.

The trust has stated in its Summary Information Return (SIR) for 2013 that it gave grants to seven main organisations and also gave a further 36 grants to other organisations.

The seven main organisations during the year were:

Alzheimer's Society, Arkwright Solicitors, Combat Stress, Engineering UK, Railway Children, RUSI and UK Electronics Skills Foundation.

Other beneficiaries included: Children in Need, Hope UK, Jubilee Sailing Trust, QED Foundation and Shaftesbury Young People.

Applications

In writing to the correspondent. The trust does not generally solicit requests unless for major donations.

Thomson Reuters Foundation

General charitable purposes, education and training, humanitarian causes, free speech, women's rights

£410,000 to one organisation (2013)

Beneficial area

Worldwide.

Correspondent: The Trustees, Thomson Reuters (Reuters Ltd), Thomson Reuters Building, 30 South Colonnade, Canary Wharf, London E14 5EP (tel: 020 7542 4148; email: foundation@reuters.com; website: www.trust.org)

Trustees: Sir Crispin Tickell; Ken Olisa; Geert Linnebank; Lawton Fitt; David Craig; David Binet; Peter Warwick; Eileen Lynch; Stephen Adler; Susan Martin

CC number: 1082139

Registered with the Charity Commission in 2000, the Thomson Reuters Foundation is the corporate charity of Thomson Reuters Ltd, the major multinational mass media and information firm. Its 2013 accounts stated that:

> The foundation is primarily funded by Thomson Reuters, the global news and information group, and the work of the foundation reflects the values and concerns of the company and its employees. It focuses in particular on areas where the company's skills and expertise in information gathering and communications can be put to use in ways which will benefit the communities in which it works worldwide.

The foundation's website states that it:

> Stands for free, independent journalism, human rights, women's empowerment and the rule of the law. We expose corruption worldwide and play a leading role in the global fight against human trafficking. We use the skills, values and expertise of Thomson Reuters to run programmes that trigger real change and empower people around the world, including free legal assistance, journalism and media training, coverage of the world's under-reported stories and the Trust Women Conference. We tackle global issues and achieve lasting impact.

Legal assistance

The foundation offers TrustLaw, which is a programme designed to give free legal assistance to NGOs and social enterprises. It connects charitable organisations with law firms worldwide to provide pro bono work.

Journalism and media training

The Thomson Reuters Foundation provides a number of different initiatives, which are designed to support journalism worldwide. These are the Reuters Institute for the Study of Journalism, devoted to innovative and comparative international research; journalism training worldwide; and the creation of news platforms for independent media.

Under-reported stories

The trust.org website covers under-reported stories concerning aid development, human rights, climate change, corruption and social innovation.

Trust Women Conference

The Trust Women Conference was launched in 2012 and has become one of the leading forums to discuss human trafficking and slavery, as well as many other issues concerning women's economic and social empowerment.

In 2013 the foundation had assets of £1.9 million and an income of £8.37 million, with a donation of £3.7 million from Reuters Ltd, a wholly owned subsidiary of Thomson Reuters. An additional £38,000 was granted to fund projects in South Africa. Total charitable activities amounted to £8.7 million and were broken down as follows:

Supporting independent journalism	£4.07 million
Under-reported stories	£2.33 million
Free legal assistance	£1.22 million
Trust Women conference	£1.08 million

The foundation also made one organisational grant to Oxford University, which totalled £410,000.

Applications

The foundation's annual report for 2013 states that:

> Thomson Reuters Foundation does not accept applications for cash grants but focuses on using the skills, values and expertise of Thomson Reuters to run its global programmes. Grants are rarely made and only where they are in line with the foundation's programme objectives or meet the conditions of restricted funds.

The Daniel Thwaites Charitable Trust

General charitable purposes

£0 (2013/14)

Beneficial area

Blackburn.

Correspondent: Susan Woodward, Trustee, Daniel Thwaites plc, PO Box 50, Blackburn BB1 5BU (tel: 01254 686868; email: samwalker@thwaites.co.uk; website: www.thwaites.co.uk)

Trustees: Julie Telford; Joan Halse; Susan Woodward; Julian Markham; Charles Beardmore

CC number: 1038097

Registered with the Charity Commission in 1994, the Daniel Thwaites Charitable Trust is the corporate charity of Daniel Thwaites plc, the Blackburn based brewery. The trustees are all past or present members of the company.

The object of the trust is to support charitable organisations whose primary purpose is to improve the conditions of life for the residents, and visitors, within a 50 mile area of the Blackburn brewery.

In 2013/14 the trust had both an income and total expenditure of £0. No grants will be awarded until at least 2015.

Previous beneficiaries have included: Audiotec-Trinity Community Partnership – towards audio equipment; Cardiac Risk in Young – towards a monitor; Green Lane Community Association – towards a digital camera; HARV Outreach Domestic Violence

Team – towards a projector; Motability – towards a wheelchair hoist; MS Regional Therapy and Support – towards aromatic oil; Pendle Riding for the Disabled – towards a visit to MEN arena; Read United Reformed Church – towards range style cookware; RNID – towards flashing doorbells; and The Women's Centre – towards refurbishment of its training room.

Exclusions

Organisations or activities not usually considered by the trust:

- National appeals
- Appeals for large projects where the trust's contributions would not be permanently recognisable (i.e. contributions to building projects or vehicle acquisitions)
- Activities which are primarily the responsibility of central or local government or some other responsible or statutory body
- Activities which collect funds for subsequent redistribution to other charities or individuals
- Animal welfare
- Advertising or membership of other bodies
- Expeditions or overseas travel
- Student support or sponsorship
- Schools, universities and colleges
- Sponsorship or marketing appeals

Applications

The trust has stated that it is not accepting applications until at least 2015.

TONI&GUY Charitable Foundation Ltd

General charitable purposes, children and young people, health, disability, social welfare, accommodation and housing

£50,000 (2012/13)

Beneficial area

Worldwide.

Correspondent: Michela Lodovichi, Charity and Fundraising Co-ordinator, TONI&GUY Academy, 58–60 Stamford Street, London SE1 9LX (email: charitablefoundation@mascolo.co.uk; website: www.toniandguyfoundation.org.uk)

Trustees: Toni Mascolo; Pauline Mascolo; Richard Freeman; James McDonnell; Rupert Berrow; Paul Jukes; Simon Melhuish-Hancock; Brenda Mail

CC number: 1095285

The TONI&GUY Foundation was established in 2003 and is the official charity of the UK-based hairdressing and training company, TONI&GUY, which was set up by brothers Giuseppe (Toni) and Gaetano (Guy) Mascolo in 1963. Mascolo Ltd is the parent company of the TONI&GUY salons. The trustees include Toni Mascolo, co-founder/CEO of TONI&GUY, as well as company directors and franchisees.

Strength in Style

Strength in Style is the TONI&GUY Foundation's collaboration with Macmillan Cancer Support, which was set up in 2009 and looks to help those affected by cancer with a specialised training scheme for hairdressers. New staff are trained through courses which are held four times a year in London and Manchester. There are currently 150 trained consultants in salons across the UK who have been trained as part of the Strength in Style scheme.

Previously, the foundation has supported the renovation of the TONI&GUY children's ward at King's College Hospital by donating £700,000 to The Variety Club Children's Charity. Following the completion of the ward, the foundation now supports the ward's maintenance and upkeep.

In 2012/13 the foundation had assets totalling £14,200 and an income of £83,000, which was made up primarily of donated goods and services from Mascolo Ltd (£19,000), general donations (£18,000) and from specific fundraising by staff, customers and business partners (£46,000).

Grants made totalled £50,000. There were three beneficiaries during the year, which were: The Variety Club – The TONI&GUY Ward (£25,000); Macmillan (£21,500); and the Stroke Association (£3,500).

In June 2014 the foundation sponsored the Stroke Association Life After Stroke Awards.

Exclusions

No grants for individuals.

Applications

In writing to the correspondent.

Toyota Manufacturing UK Charitable Trust

Children and young people, education, health and the environment

£160,000 (2013)

Beneficial area

Burnaston (Derbyshire) and Deeside (North Wales).

Correspondent: Laura Kristiansen, Administrator, 3 Bretby Fairways, Bretby, Burton-on-Trent, Staffordshire DE15 0QY (tel: 01332 283608; email: charitabletrust@toyotauk.com; website: www.toyotauk.com/the-toyota-charitable-trust/charitable-trust-overview)

Trustees: Michael Mitchell; Anthony Walker

CC number: 1124678

Registered in 2008, this is the charitable trust of Toyota Motor Manufacturing (UK) Ltd. Income is largely derived from company employees through fundraising activities. The trust makes donations to local organisations in the Burnaston (Derbyshire) and Deeside (North Wales) areas with a focus on the environment, children and young people, education and health.

According to the latest available annual report via the Charity Commission, the trust makes five types of award:

Nominated charities
Appointed for a minimum three year period and decided through company and employee discussion, supports the work of the charity in the local area.

Community Grant Programme
Supports the work of local good causes and charities.

Member match funding
Supports the charitable work undertaken by TMUK employees matching their fundraising efforts.

One-off grants
To support projects which benefit the local community.

Annual grants
Available once per year for larger projects and activity.

In 2013 the trust had an income of £316,500 and a total expenditure of £178,000. Grants were made totalling around £160,000.

The latest accounts were not available to view at the Charity Commission at the time of writing (January 2015), although previous accounts show numerous local organisations benefited as well two larger national charities nominated by company employees.

Applications

In writing to the correspondent.

UIA Charitable Foundation

Developing countries, human rights, social welfare, rehabilitation for offenders, victims of domestic abuse, victims of drug and alcohol addiction

£36,000 (2013)

Beneficial area

Worldwide.

Correspondent: Jackie White, Administrator, UIA (Insurance) Ltd, Kings Court, London Road, Stevenage, Hertfordshire SG1 2TP (tel: 01438 761761; fax: 01438 761762; email: charitable.foundation@uia.co.uk; website: www.uia.co.uk/About-Us/Charitable-foundation)

Trustee: UIA. Trustees Ltd

CC number: 1079982

The UIA Charitable Foundation is a grant-making body established to provide financial support to formally constituted voluntary organisations and small registered charities that help people in need. It is funded entirely by donations from UIA (Insurance) Ltd, a mutual insurance company, that is provider of insurances to members of UNISON, UNITE and other trade unions.

The objectives are to support the relief of poverty, sickness, disability and suffering, the advancement of education and the promotion of other purposes that are beneficial to the community.

The foundation's aim is to support charities that help people in need to improve the quality of their lives. The preferred areas for the provision of funding to good causes in 2013 were those that dealt with:

- Human rights in developing countries
- Poverty in developing countries
- Rehabilitation of offenders
- Victims of domestic abuse
- Victims of drug and alcohol addiction

In 2013 the foundation had an income of £36,000, which was wholly a donation from UIA (Insurance) Ltd. 46 grants were made and totalled almost £36,000, and were broken down as follows:

Poverty in developing countries	£11,200
Victims of drug and alcohol addiction	£10,600
Victims of domestic abuse	£6,800
Rehabilitation of offenders	£4,600

Beneficiaries included: Broxtowe Women's Project, Genesis Trust, Hebron Trust, International Development Partnerships, Kaloko Trust UK and Prisoners' Advice Service (£1,000 each); Body of Christ Charity and Border Arts 2000 (£800 each); and the Counselling Centre (£500).

Exclusions

The foundation's website states that it will not fund the following:

- Work which it believes to be publicly funded
- Retrospective projects
- Organisations that have an annual turnover in excess of £500,000 unless the organisation is acting as a conduit for a partner that fulfils the criteria and may find it difficult to obtain access to funding through independent channels
- Organisations whose combined grant related support costs and governance costs are greater than 10% of their turnover

Applications

The foundation is not accepting new applications for funding. The website states that:

> The UIA Charitable Foundation is not accepting new applications for funding at this time. UIA and its key partners, members and staff proactively seek and nominate good causes all year round for consideration at trustee meetings. At present, trustee meetings are held twice a year in February and September. Receipt of a nomination does not guarantee that it will be considered at the next meeting. You will be informed of the decision in writing as soon as possible after the meeting.

Check the foundation's website for further information.

The UNITE Foundation

Education and training, student scholarships

£90,500 to organisations (2013)

Beneficial area

UK.

Correspondent: Jenny Shaw, Trustee, The Core, 40 St Thomas Street, Bristol BS1 6JX (tel: 01173 027073; email: info@unitefoundation.co.uk; website: www.unitefoundation.co.uk)

Trustees: Sally Quigg; Prof. Stuart Cooper Billingham; Jenny Shaw; Richard Smith; Nicholas Miller; Joe Lister

CC number: 1147344

This is the charitable foundation of the UNITE Group plc, a manager and developer of student accommodation in the UK. Registered in 2012, the foundation has three aims:

- To enable access to higher education for young people facing serious disadvantage and/or challenging circumstances
- To help young people develop employability skills
- To integrate students into local communities

The company was the sole donor to the foundation during 2013, and it plans to donate up to £1 million each year by 2017. The foundation now also seeks other corporate donors in an effort to diversify its income streams to avoid over-reliance on the UNITE Group.

The foundation's annual report provides further detail on its activities:

> The foundation supports three organisations that support its objectives with sizeable donations and partnership work:
>
> - IntoUniverslty – this charity provides local learning centres where young people from Britain's poorest backgrounds are inspired to achieve and gain the skills which will help them to attain either a university place or another chosen aspiration
> - Enactus – a global non-profit organisation that works with business and higher education leaders to mobilise students around the world to make a difference to their communities while developing the skills they need to become social responsible business leaders
> - Land Aid which uses the collective resources, expertise and influence of the property industry to help the young and disadvantaged in the UK access the buildings, skills and opportunities they need to achieve their potential
>
> The other major activity of the foundation is a scholarship scheme. The scholarships consist of up to £4,000 towards living expenses and free accommodation for every year of study up to a maximum of 3 years (4 in Scotland). Student recipients of the scholarships are agreed between the Unite Foundation trustees and the partnership universities. Many of these students have lived in local authority care – the most under represented group in UK Higher Education.
>
> *Grants policy*
>
> The trustees take a decision about grants to be awarded on an annual basis during a trustees meeting, normally during the period August-October. This will include: a decision about the level of grant to be awarded to long-term charity partners; inclusion of additional charity partners; a decision about the number of scholarships to be awarded through the existing Scholarship Scheme partners, and the number of additional partners to be added.
>
> During years in which the Scholarship Scheme is to be extended to additional partners, the trustees will agree a shortlist of potential higher education partners to be approached. This shortlist is selected on the basis of their known commitment to widening participation in higher education. They will normally be within reasonable travelling distance of a Unite property, so that the free accommodation aspect of the scheme may be offered.

> Shortlisted institutions are invited to complete a pro forma detailing their approach to selecting and awarding scheme recipients, fit with the Unite Foundation's three strategic objectives and fit with their own widening participation strategy. Pro formas are assessed by trustees and partners are selected on this basis. Once confirmed as a partner, budget is set aside to offer scholarships to a specified number of students within that institution.

For universities and other organisations looking to work with the foundation, its website states:

> The Unite Foundation does more than offer free accommodation and a generous scholarship to young people from the most challenging backgrounds. We also want to promote better understanding of the issues that affect our scholars, and would be interested in collaborating with universities and other organisations on research and communications. We would be very interested in getting the message about the Unite Foundation Scholarships, including positive case studies, out to young people from care, estranged or homeless backgrounds. Even if they do not apply for a scholarship, we hope this will help them to aspire to a university education.

In 2013 the foundation had an income of £500,000 from the company (£195,000 in 2012). Grants were made totalling £495,500, and were broken down as follows:

Student rental payments	£243,000
Student bursaries	£162,000
Donations	£90,500

Further details are given in the foundation's annual report:

> In 2013, working in partnership with four universities, the foundation awarded 33 further scholarships to students from the University of Edinburgh, Sheffield Hallam University, the University of Bristol, King's College London, Queen Mary University of London and Liverpool John Moores University. Two of these were on an 'accommodation only' basis to backfill for existing scholars who had left their accommodation but continued to receive the cash scholarship. Of the 19 students awarded a scholarship in 2012, 18 continued their studies and were supported into their second year of study during 2013.

Applications

Contact the foundation via its website to discuss how you might work with the foundation.

United Utilities Trust Fund

Money advice, debt counselling and financial literacy

£330,000 to organisations (2013/14)

Beneficial area

The area supplied by United Utilities Water plc (predominantly the north west of England).

Correspondent: The Secretary (Auriga Services Ltd), United Utilities (tel: 0845 179 1791; email: contact@uutf.org.uk; website: www.uutf.org.uk)

Trustees: Deborah Moreton; Alastair Richards; Simon Dewsnip; Allen Mackie; Carl Smith

CC number: 1108296

United Utilities Trust Fund is an independent grant-making trust established in early 2005. Grants are mainly awarded to individuals in financial hardship 'who have a liability to pay water charges to United Utilities Water (directly or indirectly) and who are unable to pay'.

Grants are also given to organisations who can deliver money advice and financial literacy services.

In 2013/14 the trust had assets of £404,000 and an income of £7 million, all of which came from United Utilities. Grants were made totalling over £6.2 million, with £330,000 of this awarded to organisations.

Beneficiaries included: Sefton Citizens Advice (£30,000); Salford Mental Health Services (£29,000); Blackburn with Darwen Citizens Advice (£26,500); Fylde Coast Women's Aid (£23,000); and Advocacy in Wirral (£22,000).

Exclusions

The trust will not fund:

- Existing projects
- Charities which appear to us to have sufficient unrestricted or free reserves, or are in serious deficit
- Projects outside the geographical area
- National charities that do not have the facility to accept the funding on a regional basis
- Grant-making bodies seeking to distribute grants on UUTF's behalf
- General appeals, sponsorship and marketing appeals
- Replacement of existing programmes or statutory funding

Applications

On an application form available from the correspondent or the trust's website. At the time of writing (February 2015) the trust was closed to applications from organisations – check the trust's website for current information.

Virgin Atlantic Foundation

Health, social welfare, general

£800,500 (2012/13)

Beneficial area

UK and overseas.

Correspondent: Ian de Sousa, Trustee, Virgin Atlantic Airways Ltd, The Office, Manor Royal, Crawley, West Sussex RH10 9NU (tel: 01293 747128)

Trustees: Ian de Sousa; Jillian Brady; Thomas Maher; Maria Sebastian; Craig Kreeger; Meigan Terry

CC number: 1097580

Registered in 2003, the foundation's objects are general charitable purposes with an emphasis on health, social welfare and the relief of poverty. The foundation states that it supports organisations in the UK as well as organisations working in India, China and Kenya, although in practice just one organisation working in China and Kenya received almost all of the foundation's donations in 2012/13.

The foundation's annual report gives details on how its income is generated:

> The charitable company administers the 'Change for Children' Appeal which involves collecting change in various currencies from passengers travelling on Virgin Atlantic Airways Ltd. Donations in various currencies are collected by the cabin crew employees of Virgin Atlantic Airways Ltd and monies are processed by Travelex Foreign Coin Services Ltd who pass on a sterling amount to the charitable company after deducting a handling fee. Travelex also collect donations through donation boxes in their shops.
>
> From January 2011 onwards Virgin Atlantic Foundation has also started receiving funds raised through Virgin Atlantic Airways staff fundraising – this includes cash and cheques banked directly, monies raised through the Virgin Money Giving website and amounts donated by employees through the 'Pennies from Heaven' scheme run by Virgin Atlantic Airways Ltd.
>
> From October 2012 onwards Virgin Atlantic Foundation has included the option of Gift Aid on the onboard donation envelopes.
>
> [In the future] the trustees intend to continue to raise funds principally to support charities that alleviate sickness, poverty and distress affecting children in the United Kingdom and around the world.

In 2012/13 the foundation had an income of £824,000, although it appears that none of this came directly from the company's profits. Grants were made totalling £800,500, with almost all of this given to Free the Children, 'to help support the eradication of poverty and sustainable community developments for marginalised children and their families in China and Kenya'. (Caudwell Children received £110.)

The company and the foundation are connected to Virgin Unite (the Virgin Foundation), through which the Virgin Group of companies direct other charitable giving.

Applications

In writing to the correspondent, although potential applicant should be aware that currently the foundation's sole charity partner is Feed the Children.

The Vodafone Foundation

General charitable purposes, with a preference for technology, disadvantaged communities, humanitarian crises and disasters

Beneficial area

UK and overseas (where Vodafone operates).

Correspondent: Andrew Dunnett, Director, Vodafone Group plc, 1 Kingdom Street, London W2 6BY (email: groupfoundation@vodafone.com; website: www.vodafone.com/content/index/about/foundation.html)

Trustees: Nick Land; Margherita Della Valle; Hatem Dowidar; Elizabeth Filkin; Lord Hastings of Scarisbrick; Jeroen Hoencamp; Matthew Kirk; Francisco Roman; Ronald Schellekens; Helen Lamprell; Mwamvita Makamba; Andrew Dunnett

CC number: 1089625

The Vodafone Foundation was established in 2001. Its annual report for 2013/14 states that the foundation has a 'funding partnership with Vodafone's local foundations to provide public benefit by investing in programmes that support communities in which Vodafone has commercial roots'. It also gives financial support through matched funding to UK-based employees or teams that fundraise in their own time. The group has 28 local foundations across the globe. The UK registered Vodafone Foundation encompasses both UK and geographically wider activities.

The foundation's annual report for 2013/14 states that it will fund projects that fall under four major themes:

- Mobile for Good: through use of mobile communication technologies, we fund projects that address some of the world's most pressing humanitarian challenges
- Disaster relief: through our instant network programme we aim to deploy Vodafone volunteers and technology in emergencies to provide free communications and technical support to aid agencies and victims and develop new technologies to support the humanitarian community, Vodafone continues to enable customers to donate to charity via our network and through the Vodafone foundation's mobile giving programme
- In-country Grants: through the 28 local Vodafone foundations, we give financial support to good causes that benefit local communities in significant and timely ways

The foundation directs its grants to countries where Vodafone Group companies operate. It has a strong belief in the social benefits offered by mobile telecommunications technology. It makes two types of grants:

- Direct grants are made to not-for-profit external partners who usually have a global or multinational focus
- Grants to the local foundation established by local Vodafone companies

The Vodafone Foundation is responsible for Vodafone UK's social investment activities. The foundation's website states that the programmes include:

> ***JustTextGiving***
>
> JustTextGiving by Vodafone lets individuals and charities collect donations via text. Our partnership with JustGiving means individuals and charities of any size can use the power of text messaging to raise money for charity.
>
> ***TecSOS***
>
> This specialised handset has been developed for use by victims of domestic violence.
>
> The handset enables a user to push a central button and activate immediate contact with the police, provide instant details of location and enable an immediate recording of all activity in the vicinity of the handset.
>
> ***Take a Chance***
>
> The programme aims to increase the confidence and motivation of students aged 14–15 in West Berkshire and enables them to broaden their skills and horizons by providing personal development opportunities within a business context.

In 2013/14 the foundation had assets of nearly £7.4 million and an income of £22 million, of which £19 million was donated by Vodafone Group plc and £1.5 million was donated by Vodafone UK. 'Donated services and facilities' were also provided by the Vodafone group companies, including governance costs and totalled over £902,000. During the year, the foundation made grants worldwide totalling £19.6 million, which included over £14.5 million worth of grants to local Vodafone Foundations.

Beneficiaries of 'direct grants' included: Télécoms Sans Frontières (£400,000); Moyo Tanzania (£398,000); UN World Food Programme (£264,000); Keeping Kids Company (£200,000); Democratic Republic of Congo Charitable Fund (£167,000); Tanzania Charitable Fund (£144,000);Text Santa (£101,000); Vidavo SA (£109,000); DEC Philippines Typhoon Appeal (£93,000); Naomi House (£51,000); Dream Foundation (£4,000); and RSPB (£200).

Applications

Contact the foundation or see the website for details of all application processes for different grant programmes.

Wates Family Enterprise Trust

Education, employment and training, community projects

£661,000 (2013)

Beneficial area

UK.

Correspondent: Brian Wheelwright, Director, Wates House, Station Approach, Leatherhead, Surrey KT22 7SW (tel: 01372 861373; email: director@watesfoundation.org.uk; website: watesgiving.org.uk)

Trustees: Andrew Wates, Chair; James Wates; Paul Wates; Tim Wates; Andy Wates; Michael Wates; Charles Wates; Jonathan Wates

CC number: 1126007

Registered in 2008, the trust is the vehicle for the philanthropic and charitable activities of the Wates family, owners of the Wates Group. The following information is taken from the trust's 2013 report and financial statements:

> The purpose of Wates Family Enterprise Trust Ltd is to provide a means for the Wates family to be engaged stewards of the family business, blending wealth creation with social responsibility, to deliver impact on social need for the public benefit through an effective charitable programme – Wates Giving. Over a five to ten-year period, the objective set for the trust is to connect the family's motivation as its patrons to the resources, enthusiasm, leadership and knowledge intrinsic to its enterprises; and in doing so to create opportunities for business to play a responsible philanthropic role in the communities in which the family business and its employees live, work and build.
>
> The trust makes its awards in six areas or themes as follows:
>
> - Education

- Employment and training
- Community building
- Social enterprise
- Sustainability
- Thought leadership

Funding is allocated to bids originating from initiatives of the Wates Group and its business units, the Wates family and employees of the Wates businesses acting in a personal capacity. This includes: fundraising for local charitable and community causes; Give As You Earn donations through payroll; engagement with community organisations as volunteers, trustees, governors or similar roles; participation in sport at national and international levels; and major sponsorship events for a Charity of the Year.

In 2013 the trust had an income of just over £1.3 million, almost all of which came from the Wates Group. Charitable expenditure totalled almost £661,000 and was broken down as follows:

Major projects	£432,000
Family projects	£117,500
Community projects	£58,500
Matched funding	£20,000
Give As You Earn	£18,500
Gold award	£5,000
Supply chain fund	£4,000
Sports sponsorship (individuals)	£5,500

The trust's accounts provide more detail on how this expenditure was spent:

The trust made 100 new Wates Giving awards in the year, valued at £739,500. Thirty major awards totalling £503,500 were made to projects across England, Wales and Scotland.

Wates Giving supported 23 community projects sponsored by the employees of Wates businesses valued at £42,500. Match funding of £12,000 was added to £32,000 raised by individual Wates employees for their charities of choice. Since inception of this scheme in 2009 to the end of December 2013, Wates Giving has added over £85,000 to individuals' fundraising of £259,000 for a grand total over the period of £344,000.

Six match funding awards were also made to Wates teams raising money for Barnardo's, Alzheimer's UK, Marie Curie Cancer Care, Brain Tumour UK, Shelter, the Royal Marsden Hospital, the North London Hospice and the Alder Hey Rocking Horse Appeal.

Other awards provided match funding to Give As You Earn commitments and monetary donations in addition to the 3,500 hours of time contributed by 700 Wates employees to 64 community projects, as part of the Wates Group's Community Week 2013.

Seven awards valued at £4,000 were made to support the charitable sponsorships of companies in the Wates Group's supply chain under a programme started in 2011. The trust also made 26 awards worth £120,000 to projects with public benefit initiated by members of the Wates family. During the year, the trustees gave further support to their sports sponsorship programme that was started in 2009 with four new awards worth £10,500. Recipients of these awards routinely compete at national team level and in international events.

Beneficiaries of major awards included: Business Class 4 (£64,000); Royal Institute off British Architects (£55,500); Campaign for Youth Social Action (£40,000); Dollywood Imagination Library (£25,000); Barlow Moor Community Centre (£20,000); Walsall Enterprise Hub (£16,000); Institute for Family Business Research Foundation (£15,000); Reform (£10,000); Surrey Fire and Rescue Service (£7,500); and Shackleford Cricket Club (£5,000).

Applications

Unsolicited applications are not considered.

The Westminster Foundation

Social welfare, with an emphasis on homelessness

£2.1 million (2013)

Beneficial area

Unrestricted, in practice mainly UK. Local interests in central London (SW1 and W1 and immediate environs), North West England, especially rural Lancashire and the Chester area, and the Sutherland area of Scotland.

Correspondent: Jane Sandars, Director, 70 Grosvenor Street, London W1K 3JP (tel: 020 7408 0988; fax: 020 7312 6244; email: westminster.foundation@grosvenor.com; website: www.westminsterfoundation.org.uk)

Trustees: The Duke of Westminster, Chair; Jeremy Newsum; Mark Loveday; Mark Preston

CC number: 267618

The foundation was established in 1974 for general charitable purposes by the fifth Duke of Westminster and continues to make grants to a wide range of charitable causes. In 1987 the Grosvenor Foundation, a separately registered charity, transferred all its assets to the Westminster Foundation. This is assumed to be a largely 'personal' charity, created by the present duke. He is well known in the charity world for his active personal involvement in many organisations, and no doubt a significant number of the regular beneficiaries are organisations with which he has developed a personal connection that goes beyond grant-making. The foundation's annual reports state:

The foundation receives regular donations from Grosvenor Group Ltd and its operating companies, and, on occasion, from members of the Grosvenor Family. Grosvenor Group Ltd is an international property development and investment group, largely owned by trusts for the benefit of current and future members of the Grosvenor Family, which is headed by the Duke of Westminster.

The following information is taken from the foundation's website:

Our current grant-making strategy is focused on the issues around poverty in the UK.

Research we commissioned in 2012 highlighted several ways in which we could address some of these issues.

For 2014, the trustees have chosen to focus on two key themes:

- Youth homelessness
- Supporting communities

[For 2015 and beyond, check the foundation's website for any revised themes.]

What do we mean by youth homelessness?

Homelessness amongst young people is an increasingly significant issue, both in London and across the UK.

In this programme, we are working with charitable organisations to prevent homelessness amongst young adults (in the age range 16 to 30). We are focusing on solutions that strengthen their self-sufficiency, improve well-being and assist with access to accommodation. Our Youth Homelessness Programme has two sub-themes: building self-sufficiency – equipping young people who are homeless, or at risk of becoming homeless, with the skills and support they need to obtain long-term economic stability and personal independence; supporting access to accommodation – this might include the provision of emergency shelters, hostels and support into longer-term accommodation to give people a chance to become independent young adults in society. Examples may include: emergency night shelters, housing advice services and innovative long-term approaches to breaking the cycle of homelessness in young people.

What do we mean by supporting communities?

Our Supporting Communities Programme targets issues of isolation, in both rural and urban contexts. We are working with charities and other voluntary organisations in our key locations: identifying the needs of residents in these communities and supporting local providers in addressing these needs.

Small Grants

- This fund is for one-off requests of up to £5,000
- Appeals are reviewed and decided on by our Small Grants Panel, which meets approximately every eight weeks

Major Grants

- £5,000 upwards
- This is our primary grant fund and the trustees distribute significant sums, often over more than one year
- Our Major Grants aim to address issues in a more targeted way and help bring about long-term change

In 2013 the foundation had assets of £41.9 million and an income of £2.6 million, which included £1.9 million from Grosvenor Group Ltd. There were 160 grants made totalling £2.1 million, with the average grant being £13,500.

Beneficiaries of larger grants included: Cardinal Hume Centre (£153,500), over three years towards the costs of an employment and training officer, a support worker for new move-on accommodation, and training for hostel staff; ABF The Soldiers' Charity (£60,000), towards rent; Cheshire Community Foundation (£50,000), towards core funding; RAIS Fundación, Madrid (£50,000), towards the costs of a kitchen in a hostel; Crisis UK (£33,000), support for the Christmas Card Campaign 2013; The Zacchaeus 2000 Trust (£25,000), for the salary of a Tenancy Support Officer in south Westminster; Hong Kong Cancer Fund (£20,500), sponsorship of a fundraising event; Debt Advice Network (£20,500), towards core funding to expand services in Cheshire West and Chester. According to the foundation's Grant Application Guidelines:

> The Westminster Foundation only considers applications for funding that will benefit people living in the UK. Outside the UK, the foundation only funds projects that have been nominated by the local Grosvenor teams in Continental Europe and Asia. It is not possible to apply for international or overseas funding.

Exclusions

The Grant Application Guidelines also state that the foundation does not consider:

- General appeals or letters requesting non-specific donations (i.e. an application that is not specifically tailored to one of our funding programmes)
- Organisations that do not have charitable aims (e.g. commercial companies and companies limited by shares)
- Overtly political projects (including party-political and campaigning projects)
- Individuals (or organisations applying on behalf of an individual)
- Student fees/bursaries
- Projects taking place or benefiting people outside the UK
- Projects benefiting people outside our specific geographical criteria
- Holidays/trips
- Projects where the main focus is website development or maintenance
- Start up costs
- Organisations that have applied to us unsuccessfully within the previous 12 months

Applications

The foundation provides the following information on its website:

> Before reading our guidelines in full and making an application for funding to the Westminster Foundation, we recommend you check your organisation against this brief eligibility test to ensure you do not spend time preparing an application that does not fit within our grant-making criteria. In order to apply to the Westminster Foundation:
>
> - Your organisation needs to be a charity registered with the Charity Commission, or with exclusively charitable objectives (organisations that have exempt or excepted status such as educational establishments and churches may qualify under these criteria)
> - Your funding request needs to benefit people within the UK, and specifically within: Westminster (parts of the old Metropolitan Borough of Westminster); Cheshire West and Chester; rural Lancashire (near the Forest of Bowland); North West Sutherland
> - Your funding request cannot be for an individual person, trips or holidays, an animal charity or a medical research charity
> - Your appeal should fall within one of our poverty-related funding programmes

Applications should be made via the foundation's website.

The Willmott Dixon Foundation

Young people, people with disabilities

£83,000 (2012/13)

Beneficial area

UK.

Correspondent: Laurence Holdcroft, Administrator, Willmott Dixon Holdings plc, Spirella 2, Icknield Way, Letchworth Garden City, Hertfordshire SG6 4GY (tel: 01462 671852; email: laurence.holdcroft@willmottdixon.co.uk; website: www.willmottdixongroup.co.uk/being-unique/willmott-dixon-foundation)

Trustees: Colin Enticknap; Richard Willmott; Andrew Telfer

CC number: 326530

Willmott Dixon Group is a privately owned construction, housing and property development business. The Willmott Dixon Foundation was set up in 1984 and is chaired by the Group Chief Executive, Rick Willmott. The current focus of the foundation is tackling social exclusion, inspiring young people and community transformation.

The following information was taken from the foundation's website:

> The aims and objectives of the foundation are: to strategically channel our skills, experience and know-how to make a positive impact in local communities and, more widely, society to maximise the impact of the time and money we invest in social causes to use our local teams to improve the communities in which we work to help Willmott Dixon build strong partnerships with customers through a focused approach to social investment to provide transparency and public reporting of Willmott Dixon's social investment and the outcomes.

The local businesses and sites work with their clients and the local communities to identify their needs and aspirations. At the same time the company also works at regional and national level with charity partners to develop programmes of activity to maximise the impact it can have.

In 2012/13 the foundation had assets of £8,000 and an income of £83,000 including £81,000 from Willmott Dixon Holdings Ltd. Grants were made totalling £83,000. A list of beneficiaries was not available.

Applications

In writing to the correspondent. Note that the foundation tends to work with a small number of partner charities.

The Wragge & Co. Charitable Trust

General charitable purposes with an interest in health and social welfare

£68,000 (2013/14)

Beneficial area

Mainly West Midlands.

Correspondent: Lee Nuttall, Trustee, Wragge Lawrence Graham & Co. LLP, 2 Snowhill, Birmingham B4 6WR (tel: 01212 331000)

Trustees: Lee Nuttall; Quentin Poole; Philip Clissitt

CC number: 803009

Registered in 1990, the Wragge & Co. Charitable Trust is the corporate charity of Wragge Lawrence Graham & Co. LLP, the UK-based international law firm.

The trust's accounts for 2013/14 state that 'the trustees have no fixed policy on grant making and support a wide range of local and national charities. ... However, they do not usually make grants to individuals or organisations which are not themselves charities'.

Generally assistance is given in the fields of children and young people, elderly people, health and disability and disadvantaged individuals in the West Midlands area and nationally.

In 2013/14 the trust had assets of £42,000 and an income of £63,000, which was wholly made from Gift Aid donations. Grants were made to 106 charitable organisations totalling £68,000.

Beneficiaries include: SIFA Fireside (£6,000); Make a Wish (£4,200); University of Birmingham (£3,600); Movember Europe (£2,600); Deptford Action Group for the Elderly (£1,300); Birmingham LGBT and Free@last (£1,000 each); Birmingham Children's Hospital Charity (£900); Ackers Adventure, Asthma Relief and Birmingham City Mission (£500 each); Heart of England Community Foundation (£350); Acorns Children's Hospice, Bag Books and Buttle UK (£250 each); and Rainbow Children's Hospice and Walk the Walk Worldwide (£100 each).

Exclusions

No grants to individuals or to organisations which are not charities.

Applications

In writing to the correspondent.

The Xerox (UK) Trust

Education, social welfare and general charitable purposes

£5,000 (2013)

Beneficial area

UK.

Correspondent: Cheryl Walsh, Trust Secretary, Xerox Ltd, Bridge House, Oxford Road, Uxbridge UB8 1HS (tel: 01895 251133)

Trustees: Francis Mooney; John Edwards; John Hopwood

CC number: 284698

Xerox is a multinational company that produces printers, photocopiers, printing presses and printing supplies. This trust supports local or mid-sized organisations working towards the advancement of equality of opportunities; particularly amongst people who are young, have disabilities, disadvantaged or terminally ill.

In 2013 the trust had an income of £65,000 and an expenditure of £5,000. We estimate that around £5,000 was made in grants.

Previous beneficiaries include: Gobo Theatre Foundation (£2,500); Hertfordshire Multiple Sclerosis Therapy Centre (£2,000); Clapton Common Boys Club (£1,600); Holidays for Disabled People and Special Needs Adventure Playground (£1,000 each); the Respite Association (£600) and Birmingham Youth Foundation, Deptford Action Group for the Elderly, Mid Sussex Community Support Association and Cerebral Palsy Plus (£500 each).

Exclusions

No grants to individuals, religious or political organisations or national bodies.

Applications

In writing to the correspondent. Priority is given to charities with strong links to Xerox (UK) Ltd employees.

Yorkshire and Clydesdale Bank Foundation

Health, education, community development, social welfare, sports, the environment, arts and culture, equality and diversity, animal welfare, young people, older people, people with disabilities, disadvantaged people and communities

£826,000 (2012/13)

Beneficial area

UK.

Correspondent: Graeme Duncan, Assistant Company Secretary, Ground Floor Mezzanine, 30 St Vincent Place, Glasgow G1 2HL (website: www.cbonline.co.uk/about-clydesdale-bank/community)

Trustees: Douglas Campbell; Lorna Macmillan; David Thorburn

OSCR number: SC039747

The Yorkshire and Clydesdale Bank Foundation was established in 2008 with the Office of the Scottish Charity Register. It is the corporate charity of the Clydesdale Bank, a commercial bank formed in Glasgow in 1838. The bank itself has a long tradition of providing funds that help make life easier, healthier and better for the communities in which it works.

The foundation's 2012/13 accounts state that it looks to support registered charities, not-for-profit organisations and community and other voluntary organisations under the following categories:

- Prevention and relief of poverty
- Advancement of education
- Advancement of health
- Advancement of citizenship or community development
- Advancement of the arts, heritage, culture or science
- Advancement of public participation in sport
- Promotion of equality and diversity
- Advancement of environmental protection or improvement
- Relief of those in need by reason of age, ill health, disability, financial hardship or disadvantage
- Advancement of animal welfare
- Saving of lives

The foundation also offers grants through its Spirit of the Community Awards. Its guidelines state that awards will be considered for projects in one of the following three categories:

- Financial education: this category will focus on initiatives that advance financial education including initiatives that promote accessibility to both financial education and financial services
- Employability: this category will focus on initiatives that build on and develop skills in individuals to equip them for the workplace and help them become ready for work
- Environment: this category will focus on projects seeking to protect or improve the environment

In 2012/13 the foundation had assets of £302,000 and an income of £714,000, of which it is estimated that £700,000 was a donation from Clydesdale Bank. Grants made totalled £826,000, were made to 486 organisations and were broken down as follows:

Health	£257,000
Education	£222,000
Citizenship or community development	£91,000
Relief of those in need by reason of age, ill health, disability, financial hardship or other disadvantage	£83,000
Sports	£72,000
Environmental protection or improvement	£70,000
Arts, heritage, culture or science	£27,000
Equality and diversity	£3,000
Prevention or relief of poverty	£1,800
Animal welfare	£1,000
Saving of lives	£500

Beneficiaries included: Help the Hospices (£252,000); Spirit of the Community Awards (£250,000); Money Advice Trust (£50,000); Business in the Community (£26,000); The Chartered Institute of Bankers in Scotland (£12,000); Charities Aid Foundation (£7,000); and Bank Workers Charity and Yorkshire Business in the Arts (£2,000 each).

Donations under £2,000 totalled £201,000.

Applications

Application forms and guidelines can be found on the foundation's website. Applicants will be expected to demonstrate:

- The need/demand for the project and how the project will effectively respond to/meet the need
- An innovative approach to addressing the issue which should be unique in the community
- Positive and practical benefits for the wider community

- Evidence of how the project will be managed and monitored
- A practical vision for the longer term sustainability of the work of the project

Yorkshire Building Society Charitable Foundation

General charitable purposes including education and training, health, animal welfare, people with disabilities, children and young people, older people

£529,000 (2013)

Beneficial area

UK, with a preference for grant-making in branch localities.

Correspondent: Nirmisha Popat, Company Secretary, Yorkshire Building Society, Yorkshire House, Yorkshire Drive, Bradford, West Yorkshire BD5 8LJ (tel: 01274 706606; email: charitable@ybs.co.uk; website: www.ybs.co.uk/your-society/charity/charitable-foundation/apply.html)

Trustees: Christopher Parrish; Andy Caton; Christopher Faulkner; Richard Brown; Linda Oakes

CC number: 1069082

Registered with the Charity Commission in 1998, the Yorkshire Building Society Charitable Foundation is the channel of giving of Yorkshire Building Society. Its purpose is to support good causes where the society's members and staff live and work, helping to demonstrate the value and support that it provides to local communities throughout the UK.

The foundation's income is acquired from Yorkshire Building Society and SCBD, a scheme promoted by Yorkshire Building Society under which the holders of savings or loan accounts agree to transfer an amount equivalent to the pence of interest received on savings accounts, or rounding up to the nearest pound, the pence of interest paid on a mortgage account.

The accounts for 2013 state that the foundation supports:

> Registered charities or good causes involving anyone who is vulnerable (particularly children, the elderly or those with physical/mental/communication disabilities). The trustees also extend these priorities to registered charities working to relieve suffering in animals, and will consider other locally based charities and good causes.

The foundation has also stated that it prefers to assist with specific tangible items rather than donating to general funds or expenses:

> The following list provides some examples of activities likely to fall within our main areas of focus:
>
> - Sensory toys and equipment for children with special needs
> - Items to care for isolated and/or vulnerable elderly peoples
> - Support of specially adapted equipment to be used by people with physical/mental/communication disabilities
> - Items and equipment for causes that care for the seriously ill
> - Apparatus for children with special needs in schools/community groups
> - Equipment for charitable sectors of the NHS
> - Items or equipment to aid the recovery of, or ease the suffering of animals (animal homes/sanctuaries)
> - Items or tangible social activities for Community Centres providing a benefit to many in the local community
> - Provision of tangible and social interaction activities for the vulnerable and/or isolated

In 2013 the foundation has assets of £139,000 and an income of £524,000, which included an £80,000 donation from Yorkshire Building Society and a £382,000 donation from SCBD. Grants totalling £529,000 were made to 2,266 'charities and good causes'. 79% of the 2,266 grants made to good causes that were supported in the financial year were nominated by the society's staff and members, with the remainder of causes being requests received directly by the charity.

Beneficiaries included: Age UK (£6,300); RSPCA (£5,900); Norfolk Community Foundation (£5,200); Butterwick Hospice (£4,600); One In A Million (£3,600); Cancer Research UK and Marie Curie Cancer Care (£3,100 each); Hospiscare and Trinity Hospice (£3,000 each); East Anglia Children's Hospice (£2,700); Multiple Sclerosis Society (£2,200); and Five Lamps, Loxwood House and Teesside Homeless (£2,000 each).

Donations under £2,000 totalled £424,000.

Exclusions

The society's website states:

> Please be aware, we are unable to support contributions towards large funds, expenses, fees, salaries, administration, research or sponsorship of individuals and events. We also can't support the advancement of religious or political activities (including specific sectors of the community), mainstream schools and other local or government funded bodies.

The foundation does not support the following:

- Contributions towards large funds
- Expenses
- Fees
- Salaries
- Administration
- Research
- Sponsorship of individuals or events
- Religious or political activities
- Mainstream schools, sports clubs, scouts/guides groups
- Local or government funded bodies
- Overseas travel, expeditions or educational expenses

Applications

Application forms can be downloaded, together with guidelines and criteria, from the society's website. Alternatively, you can apply in your local branch of Yorkshire Building Society.

The foundation's accounts for 2013 state the following:

> Applications for support are usually made through the submission of a form (which members can obtain from society branches, agencies and online). In addition, requests are received direct from external applicants. All nominations and requests are reviewed by the administrative personnel of the society who are charged with undertaking support for the charity under the framework agreement as referred to above.

The Zochonis Charitable Trust

General, particularly youth education and welfare

£2.5 million (2012/13)

Beneficial area

UK, particularly Greater Manchester, and overseas, particularly Africa.

Correspondent: Marie Gallagher, Administrator, Manchester Business Park, 3500 Aviator Way, Manchester M22 5TG (tel: 01614 351005; email: enquiries@zochonischaritabletrust.com)

Trustees: Christopher Green; Archibald Calder; Paul Milner

CC number: 274769

Registered in 1978, the trust was established by the late Sir John Zochonis, former head of P Z Cussons plc, the soap and toiletries manufacturer, with shares in the company. It has general charitable objectives but tends to favour local charities with a particular emphasis on education and the welfare of children. Grants do not appear to be ongoing, but local charities with an established relationship with the trust are supported intermittently, if not regularly, over many years.

In 2012/13 the trust had assets of £195 million and an income of over £4.5 million, with £1.1 million of this in the form of P Z Cussons shares. Grants were made to 145 organisations totalling £2.5 million.

Beneficiaries included: Cancer Research UK (£300,000); University of Manchester – MAP Scholarship Fund (£75,000); Manchester High School for Girls (£60,000); British Red Cross and Oxfam (£50,000 each); Francis House Family Trust (£45,000); Bolton School (£40,000); Breakthrough Breast Cancer (£25,000); After Adoption and Child Victims of Crime (£10,000 each); Asthma Relief at Work in Manchester (£4,000); National Talking Newspapers and Magazines (£2,500); and West Coast Crash Wheelchair Rugby (£2,000).

Exclusions

No grants for individuals.

Applications

In writing to the correspondent.

Zurich Community Trust (UK) Ltd

Social welfare, community and economic development, helping disadvantaged people move from dependence to independence

About £2.1 million (2013)

Beneficial area

UK and overseas, with priority given to locations where the company has offices.

Correspondent: Pam Webb, Head of Zurich Community Trust (UK) Ltd, Zurich Financial Services (UKISA) Ltd, PO Box 1288, Swindon SN1 1FL (tel: 01793 502450; email: pam.webb@zct.org.uk; website: www.zurich.co.uk/zurichcommunitytrust/home/home.htm)

CC number: 266983

Registered with the Charity Commission in 1974, the Zurich Community Trust (UK) Ltd is the corporate charity of Zurich Financial Services (UKISA) Ltd, a holding company and part of the Zurich Financial Services Group, which comprises the group's operations in the UK, Ireland and South Africa and provides insurance services.

Its main purpose is helping disadvantaged people move from dependence to independence by giving time, money and skills donated by Zurich and its employees. It focuses on issues that are often overlooked and where the charity can have the biggest impact.

Grant programmes

According to the 2013 accounts it fulfils its objectives through:

- Long-term transformation programmes focusing on particular areas of social need

  Long-term transformation programmes are delivered over a minimum five year period. During 2013 grants totalling £578,000 were made through transformational programmes. These were made to: Breaking the Cycle (Addaction), (£319,000); Young People's Mental Health (£92,000); Call in Time (Age UK), (£90,000); and India Programme, (£77,000)
- Charity partnerships and grant programmes through the Zurich Cares programme

  Charity partnerships through the Zurich Cares programme are currently with CLIC Sargent, Alzheimer's Society and Mind. During 2013 a total of £1.17 million was committed through these partnerships, which brokered 6,423 volunteering days and enabled 271 team challenges with charities to be completed. Grant allocations were as follows: CLIC Sargent, Alzheimer's Society and Mind (£50,000 each)
- Charity partnerships and grant programmes through the Openwork Foundation

  The objective of the Openwork Foundation is to help disadvantaged children under a theme of Cares 4 Kids. In 2013 the foundation focused on supporting the national charity partner, the Carers Trust, in supporting a project to identify hidden young carers and provide respite for existing young carers. Grant allocations were as follows: the Carers Trust (£52,000)
- An employee volunteering programme through the Zurich Cares programme.

It also supports other charities working with disadvantaged children through a regional grant programme, via sponsored applications and a small grant programme where advisors and employees of Openwork can recommend charities to support.

Local communities

Zurich Community Trust (UK) Ltd also gives to local community organisations that are located close to where the company operates. Local budgets are delegated to staff committees to award local grants and usually range from between £250 to £1,000. The following locations are eligible:

- Birmingham (within a 15-mile radius of the Zurich office)
- Bristol
- Cardiff
- Cheltenham
- Fareham
- Farnborough
- Glasgow
- Leeds (within a 15-mile radius of the Zurich office)
- London
- Manchester
- Swindon

Overseas communities

It also considers applications for overseas projects provided that there is a UK partner organisation to administer the grant. The trust's annual overseas budget is £70,000. The website states that the trust is looking for projects which show some or all of the following:

- High degree of training and skills transfer
- Innovation
- Holistic approach to development
- Cost effective and effective solutions
- Clear objectives and outcomes which can be measured and evaluated within a reasonable timescale

In 2013 the trust had assets of £4.3 million and an income of £3.7 million, of which nearly £2.7 million was a donation from Zurich UK businesses. Grants were made across all programmes totalling around £2.1 million.

A list of local and overseas grants was not available at the time of writing (February 2015).

Exclusions

No grants made for: individuals; medical research; statutory organisations including mainstream schools and hospitals, unless exclusively for a special needs group; animal welfare; conservation or environmental projects, unless involving disadvantaged people; political or military organisations; religious organisations; sports clubs, village halls, playgroups and mother and toddler groups, unless for a special needs group; scouts, girl guides, cadets and other similar organisations, unless specifically supporting disadvantaged children; fundraising events including appeals or events for national charities; and advertising or sponsorship connected with charitable activities.

For overseas projects the trust will not fund: disaster relief or emergency work; proposals which show any racial, political or religious bias; individuals; expeditions or study exchanges; medical research; and fundraising events or appeals.

Applications

In the first instance, visit the trust's website and follow the links to check eligibility and download the guidelines and application forms.

Business in the Community

Business in the Community (BITC) aims to make community involvement a natural part of successful business practice, and to increase the quality and extent of business activity in the community. It exists to work with companies to mobilise resources (skills, expertise, influence, products and profits) to promote social and economic regeneration. ProHelp (see page 455) is an initiative of BITC.

In 2011 Arts & Business merged with BITC combining their expertise in the arts with the wider function of Business in the Community. This year Arts & Business membership will be phased out and integrated into Business in the Community. All Arts & Business members have therefore been integrated with the BITC list in order to reflect the upcoming changes.

Contacts

Business in the Community Head Office (covering London and South East)

137 Shepherdess Walk
London
N1 7RQ

Tel: 020 7566 8650
Email: information@bitc.org.uk
Web: www.bitc.org.uk

Northern Ireland

Belfast

Bridge House
Paulett Avenue
Belfast
BT5 4HD

Tel: 02890 460606
Email: info@bitcni.org.uk

Northern Ireland

North West

BEAM Social Enterprise Centre
Invista House
Maydown Works
Derry/Londonderry
BT47 6TH

Tel: 02871 861550
Email info@bitcni.org.uk

Wales

Cardiff

2nd Floor, Riverside House
31 Cathedral Road
Cardiff
CF11 9HB

Tel: 02920 780050
Email: wales@bitc.org.uk

England

North East

c/o The Sage Group
North Park
Newcastle upon Tyne
NE13 9AA

Tel: 01912 946033
Email: northeast@bitc.org.uk

North West

Manchester

2nd Floor
Amazon House
3 Brazil Street
Manchester
M1 3PJ

Tel: 01612 337750
Email: northwest@bitc.org.uk

North West

Merseyside

Suite 117
Municipal Buildings
Dale Street
Liverpool
L2 2DH

Yorkshire and Humberside

Leeds

West 44
44–60 Richardshaw Lane
Pudsey
Leeds
West Yorkshire
LS28 7UR

Tel: 01132 058200
Email: yorkshire@bitc.org.uk

Sheffield

SOAR Works Enterprise Centre
Knutton Road
Parson Cross
Sheffield
S5 9NU
Tel: 01142 134691

Hull

c/o Arco Ltd
Henry Boot Way
Hull
HU4 7DY

Tel: 01482 351609

East Midlands

3rd Floor
30–34 Hounds Gate
Nottingham
NG1 7AB

Tel: 01159 247400
Email: eastmidlands@bitc.org.uk

West Midlands
83 Bournville Lane
Birmingham
B30 2HP

Tel: 01214 512227
Email: westmidlands@bitc.org.uk

West Midlands
Black Country
c/o Blakemore Wholesale
Wolverhampton Science Park
Coxwell Avenue
Wolverhampton
WV10 9RT

Tel: 01902 717491
Email: westmidlands@bitc.org.uk

West Midlands
Coventry and Warwickshire
c/o Jaguar Cars Limited
B/7/006 Browns Lane
Coventry
CV5 9DR

Tel: 02476 401056
Email: westmidlands@bitc.org.uk

South East
Langstone Technology Park
Building 6000
Langstone Road
Havant
Hampshire
PO9 1SA

South West
Bristol
Portwall Place
Portwall Lane
Bristol
BS99 7UD

Tel: 01179 309380

South West
Plymouth
c/o Shekinah Mission
Bath Street
Plymouth
PL1 3LT

Tel: 01752 203484

Members (as of December 2014)

* Denotes former members of Arts & Business.

12/8 Group
1st Solutions Employment and Training Services Ltd
2 Sisters Food Group
3fivetwo Healthcare*
3M UK
ABB Ltd
Abbey Bond Lovis*
Abbot House Heritage Centre*
Aberdeen and Grampian Chamber of Commerce*
Aberdeen Asset Management
Aberdeen City Council*
Aberdeen International Youth Festival
Accenture Scotland*
Accenture
Acorn Environment Services
ACT Training
Addleshaw Goddard
ADI Group
Admiral Group*
Adnams plc
AES*
AESSEAL plc
AF Blakemore and Son Ltd
Affinity Sutton Group
Affinity Water
Afton Chemical Limited
Aircelle Ltd
Alliance Boots
Allianz*
Alstom UK
American Express Services Europe
Amey
Amicus Horizon
Ancre Hill Vineyard*
Andras House Ltd*
Anglian Water Group
Anglo American
Anglo Beef Processors
Anna's Welsh Zoo*
Anthesis Consulting Group plc
API Laminates Ltd
APS Group
Aramark
Arbuthnot Museum*
Archant
Arches, The*
Arco
Ardmore Group
Art in Healthcare*
Arthur Cox*
Arts Centre and Theatre Aberdeen*
Arup*
Asda Stores Ltd
Ashleybank Investments*
Aspall
Asra Housing Group
Associated British Foods
ATLAS Arts*
Avensure
Avios
Aviva plc
AVOX
AWE
Axis Europe

Bain & Company
Baker Tilly
Baker Tilly Mooney Moore*
Bangor University*
Bank of America Merrill Lynch
Banks Group
Barclays Corporate Banking*
Barques Design
Bartholomew Hawkins
Blackhorse*
BaxterStorey
BBC
BBI Solutions
BCSC
Beacon Arts Centre*
Belfast City Airport*
Belfast Harbour Commissioners*
Belfast Media Group*
Bentley Motors Limited
Bettys and Taylors Group Ltd
Bevan Brittan LLP
BHP Billiton
Bird and Bird LLP
Birmingham Airport
Birmingham City University
Birmingham Metropolitan College
Black Hearted Press*
Black Light*
BlackBerry
Bloody Scotland – The Caledonian Crime*
Bloomberg
Bluestone Resorts Limited
BNL Productions*
BNP Paribas
BNY Mellon
Bolton at Home
Bombardier Transportation UK
boohoo.com
Bordeaux Quay
Bouygues Energies and Services FM
Bouygues UK
Bowmer and Kirkland
BP
Brakes
Bray Leino
Bristol Zoo Gardens
British Airways
British American Tobacco

British Horseracing Authority
British Land Company
Britvic Soft Drinks
Broadridge Financial Solutions Ltd
Broomfield and Alexander*
Brother Industries UK (Wales)
BSkyB
BT
BT Ireland*
Bupa
Burges Salmon
Burke Shipping Group*
Business First*
Business in the Community

C Spencer Limited
Cadwyn Housing Association
Cairn Energy plc*
Calderdale Council
Calico Housing
Callcredit Information Group
Calor Gas Ltd
Cambridge University Press
Camelot Group plc
Canary Wharf Group
Capgemini
Capital One
Cappella Nova*
Cardiff Airport*
Cardiff Harbour Authority*
Cardiff School of Art and Design*
Caretech
Carillion plc
Carlson-Rezidor
Carmarthenshire County Council*
Carnegie Dunfermline Trust*
Carrick Creative*
Carson McDowell*
Cartrefi Conwy*
Castell Howell Foods
Castle Leisure
Castleoak Holdings
Cathy Law Communications*
Catlin Group
CB Richard Ellis (CBRE) Ltd*
CBI Wales*
CBRE
CDL
Ceidiog Communication*
Central England Co-operative
Centre for Contemporary Arts*
Centre for the Moving Image*
Centrestage Music Theatre CIC*
Centrica
Certas Energy UK Limited
CH2M Hill
Chapelfield Shopping Centre
Charles Rennie Mackintosh Society*
Chevron Upstream Europe*
Chime Communications
Christeyns UK Ltd
Circle Housing
Cisco
Citi
Citizens' Theatre*
Citrix Systems
City and Guilds
City of Bradford Metropolitan District Council
City of London
CityWest Homes
Clearview Traffic Group
Cleaver, Fulton and Rankin*
Cleone Foods
Clugston Construction
Cluttons
Clydesdale Bank plc*
Coastal Housing Group Ltd*
Cobham
Coca-Cola HBC Northern Ireland*
Coca-Cola
Colas
Companies House
Compass Group
Confused.com*
Conti's of Lampeter*
Conwy County Borough Council*
Corporate Culture
Costain Group
Cowan and Partners*
Craft Scotland*
Creative Edinburgh*
Creative Scotland*
Creative Therapies*
Croda International plc
Cryptic*
Crystal Collections Ltd
Culture Republic*
CultureNL (North Lanarkshire Council)*
Cumbernauld Theatre*
Cunningham Coates Stockbrokers*
Cushman and Wakefield

DAC Beachcroft LLP
DAHER Aerospace Ltd
Daily Post*
Dairy Crest Group
Dalehead Foods
Danks Cockburn Communications Ltd
Danone Nutricia Early Life Nutrition
Danske Bank*
Darlington Building Society
Darwin Gray*
David Huges Dance Scotland*
Days Contract Hire
DCD Property Ltd
Deloitte LLP
Department for Transport
DePuy UK
Derby College
Derwentside Homes
DFS Trading Ltd
DHL
Diageo
DIAGEO Northern Ireland*
Diamond Corrugated*
Diamond Resorts International
Direct Line Group
Dolmans Solicitors
Domino's Pizza Group plc
Donnelly Neary and Donnelly*
Doosan Babcock Ltd
Drake Music Scotland*
Drax Power
DTZ
Duchy of Cornwall
Dundee and Angus Chamber of Commerce*
Dundee City Council/Leisure and Culture Dundee*
Dundee Contemporary Arts*
Dundee Rep Theatre*
Dunhills (Pontefract) plc
DWF LLP
Dŵr Cymru Welsh Water*

E. H. Booth and Co
e2v technologies (UK)
East Coast Main Line Company Ltd
East Lothian Council*
East of England Co-operative Society
East Renfrewshire Council*
East Thames Group
Ecclesiastical Insurance Group
Edelman
Eden Court Theatre*
EDF Energy
Edinburgh College of Art*
Edinburgh Festival Fringe Society*
Edinburgh International Book Festival*
Edinburgh International Festival*
Edinburgh International Science Festival*
Edinburgh Iranian Festival*
Edinburgh Sculpture Workshop*
Edinburgh UNESCO City of Literature Trust*
Edinburgh World Heritage Trust*
Edwards and Co.*
EE
Electricity North West Ltd
Elior UK
EMCOR (UK)
EMIS Group plc
Energy Saving Trust
Enterprise Music Scotland*
Enterprise Rent-A-Car
Environment Agency
ERIKS UK
Erith Contractors Ltd
Escape Boutique*
Esh Group
Eurovia UK Ltd

Evander Glazing and Locks Ltd
EventMen Ltd
Everglades*
Eversheds*
Experian
EY

Fairmont Hotels and Resorts
Farrows
Fasset
FBC Manby Bowdler
Ferrovial Agroman
Finance Wales plc
First Ark Group
First Choice Homes Oldham
First ScotRail*
FirstGroup
Ford
Four Seasons Hotels and Resorts
Frank Roberts and Sons Limited
Freight Design*
Freixenet Ltd
Freshfields Bruckhaus Deringer
Freshwater PR and Marketing*
Friends Life
Front Page*
Fujitsu
Fulcrum Direct*

GW Consulting*
G4S
Gala Coral Group
Gamlins Law Ltd*
Gateshead College
General Electric
Genesis Housing Association
Gentle Dental Care*
Gentoo Group
Gi Group Recruitment Ltd
Glasgow Caledonian University
Glasgow Chamber of Commerce*
Glasgow Life/Glasgow City Council*
GlaxoSmithKline
Gleeds
GoCompare.com
Goldman Sachs International
Golley Slater*
Google
Graham and Brown Ltd
Grant Thornton
Grayling
Great Circle Communications*
Greggs
Grundfos Manufacturing Limited
GTR (Govia Thameslink Railway)

Hadley Group
Hafod Housing Association
Halfords Ltd
Hallmark Cards
Harbinson Mulholland*
Harper Adams University
Harrison Photography*
Heathrow Airport Limited
Heathrow Express
Heineken UK*
Henzteeth*
Herbert Smith Freehills*
Hewlett-Packard
hibu plc
Higgs and Sons Solicitors
High Speed 2 Limited
Hill Business Growth Consultants Ltd*
Hilton Hotel Cardiff*
Hilton Worldwide
Hippo Waste Management
Hitachi Europe
Hitex International Group
HLN Group
Hogan Lovells International LLP
Hogg Robinson Group plc
Home Retail Group
Hospital Innovations*
Housing 21
HR Connections Wales*
HSBC Bank
Hugh James Solicitors*
Hull University Business School
Hyatt Hotels Corporation

IBM UK
Image Zoo*
Impact International
Impax Asset Management
Imperial Tobacco Group
Imtech UK Ltd
Incommunities Group Limited
Institute of Directors Scotland*
Intellectual Property Office
InterContinental Hotels Group
International Nuclear Services
Interserve plc
Intertek Group
Intu Properties plc
Inverness Chamber of Commerce*
Ipsos MORI
Ipswich Building Society
Irwin Mitchell
Irwin Donaghey Stockman LLP*
ISG
Isos Housing Ltd
ISS UK
ITV

J. D. Wetherspoon
J Sainsbury
J. Thomson Colour Printers*
Jaguar Land Rover
James Law*
James Street South*
JN Bentley
Jobsite UK
John Laing
John Lewis Partnership/Waitrose
John Lewis*
Johnson Matthey plc
Jones Bros*
Jones Lang LaSalle
JTI
JTI*
Jumeirah Group
Just Retirement

KBC Bank*
KC
Keegan and Pennykid*
Keele University
Keepmoat
Kelda Group
Kellogg Company of Great Britain
Kempiniski Hotels
Kier
Kingfisher plc
Kingspan Group
Kirsten Gallagher Consultancy*
Knauf Insulation Ltd
Knight Frank
KP Snacks
KPMG*
Kynesis*

L&Q Group
Laing O'Rourke
Lancaster University
Land Registry
Land Securities
Landmarc Support Services Limited
LAS Claims Management
Leaseplan
Leeds Building Society
Leeds City College
Leeds City Council
Legal & General Group plc*
Lend Lease
Leo Burnett
Liddell Thomson*
Linbrooke Services Ltd
Lincolnshire Co-operative
Linklaters
Livin Housing Ltd
Lloyds Banking Group*
Lloyd's of London
LSI Architects LLP
Lubrizol Ltd

Mabey Bridge Limited
Maersk Oil North Sea UK*
Magnox Limited
Mainstream Renewable Power Ltd
Malcom Cannon*
Manchester Airport Group
Manorhaus*
Manufacturing Technology Centre
Marks and Spencer
Marriott International

Mars UK
Marsh
Marshalls
Marston Group
Matchtech Group
Material Marketing and Communications*
Mayborn Group
Mazars
Maze Long Kesh Corporation*
McCain Foods (GB) Ltd
McDonald's Restaurants
McFadden Associates*
McKinsey and Co UK
McKinty and Wright Solicitors*
McLaren Group
Media Wales
Merseytravel
Met Office
Metro Bank
MFS
Midland Heart
Millar McCall Wylie Solicitors*
Miller Construction
Mills and Reeve Solicitors
MITIE Group
Moat
Mondelēz International
Mondi Group plc
Morgan Lovell
Morgan Sindall plc
Morgan Stanley
Morrison Utility Services
Morston Assets
MotoNovo Finance
Moy Park
MPCT*
Murray Beith Murray*
MWH Ltd

National Grid
National House Building Council
Nationwide
NATS
Navigator Blue*
NBC Bird and Pest Solutions
Nestle Holdings UK
Network Rail
New Charter Housing Trust Group
Newcastle Building Society
Newport City Council*
Next
nFocus Testing ltd
NFU Mutual Insurance Co
NG Bailey
NH Hotels
Nicholson and Bass*
Noble Foods
Nominet
Norse Commercial Services
North Midland Construction plc
North Wales Housing
Northern Gas Networks
Northern Powergrid
Northern Rail Ltd
Northumbrian Water Group
Norton Rose Fulbright
Nottingham City Council
Nottingham Trent University
Nottingham University Business School
Novacroft
Novus Property Solutions
npower
NPS Group Property Consultants
NPTC Group of Colleges
NSG Group
Nutricia

Oakland International
OCR–Oxford Cambridge and RSA Examinations
Office for National Statistics
Oracle Corporation UK
Orbit Group Ltd
Ordnance Survey
Osborne King*

P&A Group
Park Plaza Cardiff*
PD Ports
Peabody
Pearn Kandola
Pearson
Peel Holdings (Management) Ltd
Pendine Park Care Homes*
Pennine Healthcare
Perrett Laver
Pertemps Ltd
Perth and Kinross Council*
Petrofac Services
Phoenix Group
PHS Group
Pinsent Masons LLP*
PKF Cooper Parry Group Limited
Places for People
Pobol*
Port of Milford Haven*
Port of Tyne
Portakabin Group
Post Office
Principality Building Society*
Procter & Gamble UK
Provident Financial
Prudential*
PwC*
PZ Cussons (UK) Ltd

Quality Scotland*
Quilter Cheviot

R. G. Carter Construction LTD
RCT Homes
Real Radio
Reed Elsevier
Reed Smith
Refreshing Law*
Regular Cleaning Services
Remploy LTD
Rempower Limited
Rentokil Initial
Research Institute for Arts and Humanities at Swansea University*
reusemypc Ltd
Rhondda Housing Association
Ricardo
Ricoh UK
Ridgeons
Right Management
Riverside Group
RKCR/Y&R
Rockwool
Rogers Jones Auctioneers and Valuers*
Rolls-Royce
Rothschild
Royal Bank of Scotland
Royal Institution of Chartered Surveyors*
Royal Mail Group
Royal Oak Hotel*
RR Donnelley
RSA Insurance Group

S4C*
Saga Group
Sage (UK) Limited
Saint-Gobain Limited
Salisbury Accountants*
Samsung Electronics UK
Samworth Brothers (Holdings)
Santander UK
Santia
Schroders
Scottish Business in the Community*
Scottish Council for Development and Industry*
Scottish Friendly Assurance*
Scottish Government*
Scottish Retail Consortium*
ScottishPower*
Seddon Construction Ltd
SEGRO
Seiont Research Ltd*
Serco
Sers Ltd
SGH Martineau LLP
Shakespeares Legal LLP
Shanks Group
Sheffield Business School
Shell UK*
Shields Environmental
Shoosmiths
Siemens plc
SIG plc
SiteVisibility

Skanska UK
Skipton Building Society
Skypark Unit Trust*
Smarts Communicate*
Smurfit Kappa Group
Société Générale
Society
Sodexo
Solo Cup Europe
Soneva
South West Wales Media Ltd
South West Water
Southampton Solent University
Southern Co-operatives Limited
Southern Water
Space Engineering Services Ltd
Speedy Hire
Spicerhaart
Spindogs*
Squire Patton Boggs (UK) LLP
SRK Consulting*
St James's Place
Stadco Ltd
Staffordshire University
Standard Utilities (SU)*
Starbucks Coffee Company
Starwood Hotels and Resorts
State Street
Statoil Fuel and Retail ASA
Steelite International plc
Story Homes
Stratagem*
Studio Norse*
Styles and Wood Ltd
Swayne Johnson Solicitors*
Symantec

Talisman Energy (UK)*
Tangerine Confectionery Limited
TAQA Bratani*
Tata Consultancy Services
TD Direct Investing
Telefónica O2 UK
telent Ltd
TEN Group
Tesco
TESCO Bank*
Teva UK Limited
Thales Group
Thames Tideway Ltd
Thames Water
The Clancy Group plc (Clancy Docwra Limited)
The Community Housing Group
The Concerto Group
The Cook Foundation
The Co-operative
The Creative Work Place*
The Crown Estate
The Hongkong and Shanghai Hotels, Ltd
The Hyde Group
The List*
The Marketing Network*
The Midcounties Co-operative
The OUTLET*
The Real Good Food Company plc
The Town House Company*
The Wilkes Partnership LLP
Thermo Fisher Scientific (Newport)
Thirteen Group
Thomas Cook Group
Thomas Carroll Group
Threadneedle Investments
Tidal Lagoon Swansea Bay*
Titanic Quarter*
Tolent Construction
Total E&P UK*
Totem Learning Limited
Towers Watson
Toyota Motor Manufacturing (UK)
Trafford Housing Trust
Translink*
Tughans*
Tulip Ltd
Tullis Russell Coaters Ltd
Turcan Connell*

U105*
UBS
UES Energy
UK Container Maintenance Limited
UK Power Networks
UKAR
Ulster Bank*
Unilever
Unipart Group
Unite Students
United Biscuits
United Utilities
University of Bradford
University of Central Lancashire
University of Derby
University of Manchester
University of Portsmouth
University of Sheffield Management School
University of South Wales*
University of Sunderland
University of Ulster*
University of Wales*
University of Warwick
University of Winchester
UPP
Utilitywise plc

Valero*
Vauxhall
Veolia
Victrex plc
Virgin Money
Virgin Trains
Viridor Waste Management
Visa Europe
Vista (previously Logistik)
VocaLink
Volvo Construction Equipment

Wakefield and District Housing
Wakefield Council
Wales and West Housing
Wales and West Utilities*
Walker Morris
Walt Disney Company
Wandle Housing Association Ltd
Warburtons
Waterstones Homes*
Wates Group
Watts Truck and Van
We are Duo Ltd*
Wesleyan Assurance Society
West Coast Energy*
Western Power Distribution*
Westmorland
Whitbread
Whitenoise*
Whitespace*
WH Smith Retail
Wilko Retail Ltd
William Grant and Sons Distillers*
Willmott Dixon
WJR Consulting*
Wm Morrison Supermarkets plc
Wolffe*
Woodford Investment Management LLP
Working Links
Workspace Group
World Pay
WPP Group
Wragge Lawrence Graham & Co LLP
Writing Festival*
WSP Group
WWRD United Kingdom Ltd
Wyndham Worldwide
Wythenshawe Community Housing Group

Your Housing Group

Zenith Intelligent Vehicle Solutions
Zolfo Cooper
Zurich

Scottish Business in the Community

Scottish Business in the Community (SBC) acts as a broker between business and communities, providing support and advice as well as channelling resources to deliver sustainable community investment. The SBC website states regarding its activities:

> *We form a vital bridge to help make the right difference in communities all over the country by:*
>
> - *Helping to tackle poverty and getting vulnerable, disadvantaged people into work – and back on their feet*
> - *Working with children and young people to gain skills and have aspirations that can change the course of their lives*
> - *Making workplaces fairer, more productive and more sustainable*
> - *Improving our civic spaces through harnessing the effort, expertise and commitment of Scotland's workforce*
>
> *We have members of all sizes in a wide range of sectors who represent over ten per cent of the working population in Scotland. We are the industry experts in socially responsible business in Scotland and, with our members, provide the thought leadership that will help transform our businesses and communities here and beyond.*

SBC promotes CSR as a mark of sound business practice. This is achieved through an integrated mix of national programmes and contributions, to genuine effective local partnerships.

SBC's programmes and activities are designed to offer companies a practical means of engaging in community investment.

Scottish Business in the Community
Livingstone House
First Floor (East)
43a Discovery Terrace
Heriott-Watt Research Park
Edinburgh
EH14 4AP
Tel: 01314 511100
Email: info@sbcscot.com
Web: www.sbcscot.com

Members (as of December 2014)

Aberdeen City Council
Aberdeen Harbour Board
Action Provocateurs
Advance Social Marketing
A-Haven Townhouse
Alliance Boots
Amey
Anderson Strathern
Arts & Business Scotland
ASA Recruitment
Asda

Baker Tilly
BEAR Scotland
Blackadders
BP plc
BT Scotland
Buro Happold Ltd

Capability Scotland
Chartermarque
City of Edinburgh Council
CMS Cameron McKenna

DC Thomson and Co Ltd
Diageo plc
DWF

Enable Scotland
Enterprise Rent-A-Car
Escrivo Internet Consulting

Ferrovial Agroman
The Firefly Group
FirstGroup plc
Forss House

Glasgow Caledonian Business School
Glenmorangie Company
GMP Print Solutions Ltd

Haven Products Ltd
Hewlett Packard
Highlands and Islands Airports Limited

IH Aberdeen

John Lewis Partnership
Johnson and Johnson Medical Ltd
Johnston Carmichael
Johnstons of Elgin

K. A. Javid and Co.
Kingdom Shopping Centre

LifeScan Scotland
Lloyds Banking Group
Lothian Buses plc

Marks and Spencer plc
Marshalls plc
Maxxium UK Ltd
Mercat Tours Ltd
Michael Page International
Michelin Tyre plc
Mitie
Morrisons
MY Adventure

National Australia Group (Clydesdale Bank)
National Express
Network Rail
North Highland Initiative

Ocean Terminal
OPITO

People's Postcode Lottery
Prudential Corporation plc
PwC

Quality Scotland

Rabbie's Trail Burners Ltd
Recruit With Conviction
Royal Bank of Scotland
Royal Edinburgh Military Tattoo
Royal Mail
Royal Society of Edinburgh

Scottish Enterprise
Scottish Gas
ScottishPower
Scottish Water
Sew Good Curtains and Blinds
Shoosmiths LLP
Skills Development Scotland
Social Bite
SQA
SSE plc
Standard Life
State Street

TAQA Bratani Limited
The Caves
The Crown Estate
Total E&PUK Limited
Town House Collection

Virgin Money

Wates Scotland
Wheatley Group
Wolffe
Wood Group plc

Zero Waste Scotland

Business in the Community's CommunityMark

Business in the Community (BITC) aims to make community involvement a natural part of successful business practice, and to increase the quality and extent of business activity in the community. BITC states on its website that:

> *CommunityMark companies take a holistic approach to community investment, which means they are good from the inside, out. The CommunityMark is not an award – it is an independent, 360-degree, rigorous assessment process that defines innovators and leaders in community investment.*
>
> *Open to companies in the UK of all sizes and sectors, this national standard has been developed by Business in the Community in consultation with the private, public and voluntary sector bodies. The CommunityMark challenges companies to minimise their negative and maximise their positive impact on society through an assessment process that recognises milestones to achieving long term sustainable benefits to both business and the community.*

There are 52 companies that have achieved the CommunityMark since its launch. Of these, 40 are currently recognised as upholding this standard of excellence, and are listed below.

Axis
Barclays (Global holder)
Boots UK
Brentford Football Club
British Gas
Capgemini
Capital One
Contract Scotland
Deloitte
East Midlands Airport
Ecclesiastical Insurance
Ernst & Young
Heineken UK
Hogan Lovells
Jaguar Land Rover
John Laing plc
KPMG
Lend Lease
Linklaters LLP
Liverpool Football Club
Lloyds Banking Group
LSI Architects
Manchester Airport
Marks and Spencer
Nationwide Building Society
Octink
Prudential
PwC
RWE npower
Sainsbury's
Siemens Automation and Drive
TD Direct Investing
The Midcounties Co-operative
Thinktastic
UBS
Wates Group
Willmott Dixon
Workspace Group
Zurich UK

Institute of Corporate Responsibility and Sustainability

The Institute of Corporate Responsibility and Sustainability (ICRS) is the new institute dedicated to helping corporate responsibility and sustainability professionals to excel at all stages of their careers. ICRS's organisational membership was historically known as CRG (Corporate Responsibility Group), which was established in 1987 by a small group of senior corporate affairs professionals. In January 2015, the CRG members became a part of the ICRS brand as organisational members.

The role of the ICRS is to:

- Recognise professional achievements through assessment
- Reward accomplished professionals through granting post-nominal letters
- Support professionals through continuing professional development
- Listen to and represent the corporate responsibility and sustainability profession

Members (as of February 2015)

Accenture
Alliance Boots
AstraZeneca
Axa
BAE Systems
BBC
British American Tobacco
Camelot
Centrica
City of London
City and Guilds
Clifford Chance
CMS
Coca-Cola Enterprises Ltd
Credit Suisse
CSC
Deloitte
Diageo
EE
Financial Conduct Authority
Flag
GlaxoSmithKline
Herbert Smith Freehills
Hogan Lovells
IBM
Imperial Tobacco
ISG
John Lewis Partnership
KPMG
Marks and Spencer
Linklaters
Lloyd's
MBDA
National Grid
Nestle
Npower
Northern Trust
O2
Olswang
Pearson
PwC
QuinetiQ
Reed Elsevier
ReedSmith
Res
Santander
Scottish Power
Shell
Société Générale
Tata Consultancy Services
Telereal Trillium
The Crown Estate
Tesco
Thomson Reuters
Wates
White and Case
Wragge Lawrence Graham & Co
Zurich

London Benchmarking Group

The London Benchmarking Group (LBG) is a group of over 120 companies working together to measure Corporate Community Investment (CCI). It is a member-driven organisation where companies have been working collectively since 1994 to:

- Continue development of a global measurement standard – the LBG model
- Benchmark and share best practice
- Develop and refine measurement tools
- Improve management and implementation of CCI projects
- Better communicate CCI results to stakeholders with LBG centres

The challenge facing the founding members of the LBG was how to effectively report their community activities to demonstrate that they are indeed responsible corporate citizens. Effective reporting is best based on solid measures of performance, but in the 'soft' area of social reporting hard measures are still in their infancy.

Their solution was to devise a tool with which to manage, measure and compare their relationship with the community – the London Benchmarking Model. The model is used by hundreds of leading businesses around the world and LBG has centres in a number of key world markets including Australia, Canada, the Czech Republic, Germany and the United States. Members include multinationals such as McDonalds, KPMG and Unilever, as well as major UK companies such as Marks and Spencer and BSkyB.

All members recognise that companies are expected to get involved in the community and are often judged on the amount they contribute. This involvement often goes beyond straightforward donations to charity. The LBG model provides a comprehensive and consistent set of measures for CCI professionals to determine their company's contribution to the community, including cash, time and in-kind donations, as well as management costs. The model also captures the outputs and longer-term impacts of CCI projects on society and the business itself.

Further information about the group and its benchmarking model may be found at www.lbg-online.net

Members (as at December 2014)

3M
Abbott
AbbVie
Accenture
Access Bank
Aegis
AgustaWestland
AkzoNobel Decorative Paints UK
Alcatel Lucent
Allianz Group
Arab African International Bank
ARM
Asda
Astra Zeneca
Aviva
AXA UK
Bacardi
BAE Systems
BAM Construct UK
Bank of America Merrill Lynch
Barclays
Boots UK
British Airways
British American Tobacco
British Land
Britvic
BskyB
BT
Intel Corporation
Capital One
Carillion
Centrica
Citi
Clarks
Coca-Cola Enterprises
Coca-Cola Hellenic
Deliotte and Touche
Deutsche Bank AG London
Deutsche Post DHL
Diageo
East Midlands Airport
EDP
Electricity North West
Experian
First Group
Freshfields Bruckhaus Deringer
Friends Life
Galp Energia
GlaxoSmithKline
Go Ahead
Hammerson
Heineken International B.V.
Hibu
Home Retail Group
ING
Intesa San Paolo
Intu Properties plc
Investec plc
IPF
ISS UK
Jaguar Land Rover

Jeronimo-Martins
JLL UK
John Lewis Partnership
Johnson Matthey
JTI
KPMG
L&Q Housing Group
Land Securities
Lend Lease
Liberty Global Europe
Linklaters
L'Occitane
L'Oréal
M&S
McDonalds
Michelin
Mondelēz
National Grid
Nationwide
Novo Banco S.A.
Old Mutual Group
Olswang
Pearson
Philip Morris International Management
Pinsent Masons LLP
Port of Tyne
Portugal Telecom
ST Microelectronis
Deutsche Telekom AG
Procter & Gamble UK
Provident Financial
Prudential
PwC
RBS
Reed Elsevier
Ricoh UK
Rolls-Royce
Rothschild
Royal Mail
RSA Group
RWE npower
SABMiller
Sainsbury's
Sanctuary Housing Group
Santander UK
Schroders
Scotia Gas Networks
ScottishPower
Severn Trent
Shaftesbury
Shell UK
Siemens
Standard Chartered
Standard Life
Terna
Thames Water
The Co-operative Group
The Crown Estate
Thomas Cook
UBS
UniCredit
Unilever
United Utilities
Whitbread
Willmott Dixon
Wood Group
Wragge Lawrence Graham & Co LLP
Zurich

ProHelp

What is ProHelp?

A Business in the Community (BITC) initiative, ProHelp is a national network of over 400 professional firms committed to making a difference in their local community by providing free advice and professional support. Collectively, ProHelp is the largest national provider of pro bono support in England, Wales and Northern Ireland.

Participating professional firms include lawyers, accountants, IT consultants, architects, surveyors, marketing specialists and engineers. Community groups that receive support from ProHelp are non-profit-making, locally based and cannot afford to pay for professional services. Firms can contribute towards a single project or give longer-term strategic support such as becoming a trustee.

What help can it provide?

The professional firms undertake short assignments which include feasibility studies, structural surveys, marketing and business plans, legal and accountancy advice and property valuations.

Will my project be eligible?

You must be a community-based not-for-profit organisation working for the social and economic regeneration of your local area and fit within the following criteria:

- You must have a track record of working successfully with the local community
- You must not have the funding for the specific piece of work to be done nor be retaining paid advisors to do the work
- If your organisation is a branch of a national organisation, it must be locally constituted and prove that neither the expertise nor the funding to pay for the work is available centrally
- Your project must be realistic and viable
- Your governing body must authorise the involvement of ProHelp

When will a project not qualify?

- Applications for assistance with litigation will not be considered
- Help is generally not given to animal welfare organisations, nor to those whose primary focus is overseas aid
- Assistance to religious groups will only be offered if the project benefits the wider community

What do I do now?

If you have a project in mind which could benefit from support from ProHelp, please get in touch with the relevant regional contact listed on the BITC website listed below.

What happens next?

Your completed application form will be checked by the local ProHelp Manager once it is received. They will contact you if they have any questions or need to discuss the application. Sometimes it may be necessary for you to meet with a representative from ProHelp to develop a fuller brief for the project assignment.

A summary of your request will then be taken to ProHelp members to consider and where possible match. If a firm is able to help, a meeting will then be arranged with you to take things further.

BITC is not always able to help with every project request but will always communicate this to you and where possible make alternative suggestions for organisations that may be able to help.

It can take a couple of weeks or often much longer to match a project; the local ProHelp Manager will give you an indication of timescales.

What will happen then?

If your project is appropriate, you will be asked to fill in a standard questionnaire. It may also be necessary for you to meet with a representative from ProHelp to develop a fuller brief for the assignment. A summary of your project will then be taken to a group who will decide whether or not your project meets the eligibility criteria and if there is a firm available to do the work. A meeting will then be arranged between you and the interested professional firm.

For more information, see the ProHelp website: www.bitc.org.uk/programmes/prohelp

Geographical listing of head offices

This geographical index is based on the head office address given at the start of each company entry. While it is generally the case that companies give some preference to charities local to their operating sites, including the head office, this is not always so. Once this index has been used to produce a preliminary list of potential companies to approach, the individual entries for each company should be read carefully to determine whether or not your particular project falls within the company's criteria.

England

Bedfordshire

Baxter Healthcare Limited
General Motors UK Ltd (Vauxhall Motors)
Kier Group plc
Whitbread plc

Berkshire

3M United Kingdom plc
Bayer plc
BMW UK Ltd
HP Enterprise Services UK Limited
Keysight Technologies UK Limited (formerly Agilent Technologies UK Limited)
Logica Ltd (formerly Logica plc)
Micro Focus International plc
Microsoft Ltd
Morgan Advanced Materials plc
The Rank Group plc
Reckitt Benckiser Group plc
SDL plc
Telefónica UK Limited
Vodafone Group plc
Waitrose Ltd
Yattendon Group plc (formerly Yattendon Investment Trust)

Bristol

Bristol Airport Limited
Imperial Tobacco Group plc
MITIE Group plc
PPL WW Holdings Limited (Western Power Distribution)
UNITE Group plc

Buckinghamshire

GE Healthcare Limited
Personal Group Holdings plc
Shanks Group plc
Taylor Wimpey plc

Cambridgeshire

Anglian Water
Aveva Group plc
British Sugar plc
Domino Printing Sciences plc
Alan Hudson Limited
Marshall of Cambridge (Holdings) Ltd

Cheshire

BASF plc
Bodycote plc
Findel plc
Johnson Service Group plc
Moneysupermarket.com Group plc
The Royal London Mutual Insurance Society Limited
Stobart Group
United Utilities Group plc

County Durham

The Banks Group Limited
Esh Group
Northumbrian Water Group Ltd (formerly Northumbrian Water Group plc)

Cumbria

J. Stobart and Sons Ltd

Derbyshire

East Midlands Airport
Toyota Motor Manufacturing (UK) Limited

Devon

Pennon Group plc

Dorset

Bournemouth International Airport Ltd
Cobham plc
Liverpool Victoria
Lush Cosmetics Limited
Meggitt plc
Organix Brands Ltd

East Sussex

Family Assurance Friendly Society Limited

East Yorkshire

Fenner plc

Essex

Ford Motor Company Ltd
Stansted Airport Limited
Synthomer plc (formerly Yule Catto and Co.)

Gloucestershire

Ecclesiastical Insurance Group plc
Spirax Sarco Engineering plc
St James's Place plc

Greater Manchester
adidas (UK) Limited
N. Brown Group plc
Bruntwood Group Limited
Co-operative Group Limited
P. Z. Cussons plc
Manchester Airport Group plc
Manchester Airport plc

Hampshire
Ageas (UK) Limited
Game Digital plc (formerly The Game Group plc)
IBM United Kingdom Ltd
Psion Holdings Limited (Motorola Solutions)
QinetiQ Group plc
Shire Pharmaceuticals Group
The Southern Co-operative Limited
Zurich Financial Services (UKISA) Limited

Hertfordshire
Britvic Soft Drinks plc
Camelot UK Lotteries Limited
Computacenter plc
EE Limited (formerly T-Mobile (UK) Ltd)
Imagination Technologies Group plc
Sir Robert McAlpine Ltd
Merck Sharp & Dohme Ltd
Mothercare plc
Ocado Group Ltd
Premier Foods plc
Senior plc
Speedy 1 Ltd (holding company of Kwik Fit Group Ltd)
Steria Limited
Tesco plc
TJX UK (formerly TK Maxx)
UIA (Insurance) Ltd
Unisys Ltd
J. D. Wetherspoon plc
Willmott Dixon Holdings plc

Kent
Coca-Cola Holdings (United Kingdom) Limited
FIL Holdings (UK) Ltd (formerly Fidelity Investment Management Limited)
Pfizer Limited
Saga plc

Lancashire
JD Sports Fashion plc
Lofthouse of Fleetwood Ltd
Daniel Thwaites plc
TNT UK Limited
Warburtons Limited

Leicestershire
Aggregate Industries Ltd
Dunelm Group plc
Next plc
Shoe Zone Ltd

London
3i Group plc
Abbott Mead Vickers – BBDO Ltd
Accenture UK Ltd
Addleshaw Goddard LLP
Amec Foster Wheeler plc (formerly Amec plc)
Amlin plc
Anglo American plc
Apax Partners LLP
Arup Group Ltd
Ashmore Group plc
Associated British Ports Holdings Ltd and Subsidiaries
AstraZeneca
Aviva plc
AXA UK plc
Babcock International Group plc
BAE Systems plc
Balfour Beatty plc
Bank of England
Bank of Ireland UK (plc)
Barclays plc
A. G. Barr plc
Barratt Developments plc
BBA Aviation plc
BC Partners Limited
Beazley plc
Bestway (Holdings) Limited
Betfair Group Ltd
BHP Billiton
BlackRock Investment Management (UK) Limited
Bloomsbury Publishing plc
BP plc
British Airways plc
British American Tobacco plc
British Land Company plc
British Sky Broadcasting Group plc
BT Group plc
BTG plc
Bunzl plc
Bupa Ltd
Cadogan Group Ltd
Caledonia Investments
Canary Wharf Group plc
Caparo Group Ltd
Channel 4 Television Corporation
CIBC World Markets plc
Close Brothers Group plc
Coutts & Co
Cummins Ltd
DDB UK Ltd
Debenhams plc
Deutsche Bank
Dhamecha Holdings Ltd
Diageo plc
Doughty Hanson & Co Managers Ltd
Dow Chemical Company Ltd
Duchy Originals Ltd
Economist Newspaper Ltd
EDF Energy plc
Elementis plc
ERM Group Holdings Ltd
Freshfields Bruuckhaus Deringer LLP
Fujitsu Services Holdings plc
GAP (UK Holdings) Ltd
GlaxoSmithKline plc
The Go Ahead Group plc
Goldman Sachs International
Grainger plc
Great Portland Estates plc
Grosvenor Group
Guardian Media Group plc
Hammerson plc
Hasbro UK Limited
Heathrow Airport Holdings Limited (formerly BAA Limited)
H. J. Heinz Manufacturing UK Ltd (formerly H J Heinz Company Ltd)
Helical bar plc
Henderson Group plc
Hikma Pharmaceuticals plc
William Hill plc
HSBC Holdings plc
ICAP plc
Impetus – Private Equity Foundation
Inchcape plc
Informa plc
intu Properties plc (formerly Capital Shopping Centres Group plc)
Jardine Lloyd Thompson Group plc
Johnson Matthey plc
KPMG LLP
Ladbrokes plc
Leeds Building Society
Legal & General Group plc
John Lewis Partnership
Lloyds Banking Group
Man Group plc
Marks and Spencer Group plc
Marsh Ltd
Mascolo Ltd
Mazars LLP
McDonalds Restaurants Ltd
Mondelēz UK Ltd (formerly Kraft Foods UK Ltd)
Morgan Stanley International Limited
National Magazine Co Ltd
Network Rail Infrastructure Limited
Northern Shell & Media Group Ltd (entry formerly titled Northern & Shell Network Limited)
Novae Group plc
Piranha Trading Limited
Premier Farnell plc

PricewaterhouseCoopers LLP
Prudential plc
Rathbone Brothers plc
Ravensale Limited
Rexam plc
Ricardo-AEA
Richer Sounds plc
Ridgesave Limited
Rio Tinto plc
Rolls-Royce Holdings plc
N. M. Rothschild & Sons Ltd
Royal Mail plc
RSA Insurance Group plc
J. Sainsbury plc
Schroders plc
Shaftesbury plc
Shell (UK Limited)
Simmons & Simmons LLP
Slaughter and May (Trust Limited)
DS Smith Holdings plc
Smiths Group plc
Sodexo Ltd
Spar (UK) Ltd
Sportech plc
Sportingbet Limited (formerly Sportingbet plc)
John Swire & Sons Ltd
Tata Steel Europe Limited
Tate & Lyle plc
TelecityGroup
Telegraph Media Group Ltd
Thomas Cook Group plc
Thomson Reuters (Reuters Limited)
Time Inc. (UK) Ltd (formerly IPC Media Limited)
Trinity Mirror plc
UPS (Limited)
Valero Energy UK Limited (formerly Valero Energy Ltd)
WPP plc
WSP Group Limited
Xerox (UK) Ltd

Merseyside

Boodle & Dunthorne Ltd
The Mersey Docks and Harbour Company Limited
T. J. Morris Limited
Shop Direct Holdings Ltd (formerly Littlewoods Shop Direct Group Ltd)

Norfolk

Archant
Bernard Matthews Ltd

North Yorkshire

Broadland Properties Ltd
Costcutter Supermarkets Group Ltd
Drax Group plc
McCain Foods (GB) Ltd
Persimmon plc
Shepherd Building Group Limited

Northamptonshire

Avon Cosmetics Ltd
Booker Group plc
Scott Bader Company Ltd
Travis Perkins plc
Weetabix Ltd

Nottinghamshire

Alliance Boots Holdings Limited
Capital One (Europe) plc
Center Parcs Ltd
Nottingham Building Society
Wilko Retail Limited (formerly Wilkinson Hardware Stores Ltd)

Oxfordshire

Amey UK plc
Electrocomponents plc
RM plc
RPS Group plc
Unipart Group of Companies Ltd
Shropshire
Müller UK and Ireland Group LLP (the entry formerly related to Robert Wiseman Dairies Limited)

Somerset

Future plc
Rotork plc
Wessex Water Services Ltd

South Yorkshire

Keepmoat Ltd
SIG plc
Swann-Morton Limited

Staffordshire

Central England Co-operative
Michelin Tyre plc
Punch Taverns plc

Suffolk

Adnams plc
Greene King plc

Surrey

Air Products Group Ltd

Allianz Insurance plc

Berkeley Group plc
Biwater Holdings Ltd
Cargill plc
CEMEX UK Operations Limited
Colgate-Palmolive UK Ltd
Dairy Crest Group plc
Fidessa Group plc
Friends Life Group plc (formerly Friends Provident plc)
S. C. Johnson Ltd
Philips Electronics UK Ltd
Procter & Gamble UK
Rentokil Initial plc
Samsung Electronics (UK) Ltd
Santander UK plc
Siemens plc
Spectris plc
Thales UK Limited
Toshiba Information Systems (UK) Limited
Unum Limited
Wates Group Ltd

Tyne and Wear

Arriva plc
Bellway plc
Fenwick Ltd
Greggs plc
Newcastle Building Society
Northern Powergrid Holdings Company (formerly C E Electric UK Funding Company)

Warwickshire

Calor Gas Ltd
CEF Holdings Ltd
The Midcounties Co-operative
The National Farmers Union Mutual Insurance Society Limited
National Grid plc

West Midlands

Birmingham International Airport Ltd
Carillion plc
Citroen UK Ltd
Coventry Building Society
Euro Packaging UK Limited
Genting UK plc (formerly Genting Stanley plc)
IMI plc
Jaguar Land Rover Ltd
Lafarge Aggregates Ltd
Marston's plc
Mitchells & Butlers plc
National Express Group plc
Paragon Group of Companies plc
Severn Trent plc
St Modwen Properties plc
Wragge Lawrence Graham & Co LLP

West Sussex

The Body Shop International plc
G4S plc
Nestlé Holdings (UK) plc
Virgin Atlantic Two Limited (formerly Virgin Atlantic Limited)

West Yorkshire

Arla Foods Ltd
Asda Stores Ltd
Bradford & Bingley plc
Congregational & General Insurance plc
Evans Property Group Limited
Filtronic plc

HESCO Bastion Limited
International Personal Finance
ITV plc
Wm Morrison Supermarkets plc
Northern Foods Limited
NRAM plc (formerly Northern Rock (Asset Management) plc)
Provident Financial plc
UK Asset Resolution
Yorkshire Building Society

Wiltshire

Dyson Limited
Honda of the UK Manufacturing Limited
Nationwide Building Society
WH Smith plc
Synergy Health plc

Worcestershire

GKN plc
Halfords Group plc

Scotland

Aberdeen

Aberdeen Asset Management plc
FirstGroup plc

Edinburgh

Aegon (Scottish Equitable plc)
Forth Ports plc
John Menzies plc
Miller Group Limited
The Royal Bank of Scotland Group plc
Dundee Alliance Trust plc

Fife

Avant Homes Group Ltd (formerly Gladedale Group Holdings Ltd)
Deep Sea Leisure plc
Muir Group plc
Tullis Russell Group Limited

Glasgow

Aggreko plc
Clydesdale Bank plc
Highland Group Holdings Ltd (entry formerly House of Fraser (Stores) Ltd)
ScottishPower UK plc
STV Group plc

Moray

Baxters Food Group Limited

Perth

Scottish and Southern Energy plc
Stagecoach Group plc

Wales

Caerphilly

Celtic Energy Ltd

Cardiff

Admiral Group plc
Principality Building Society

Flintshire

Redrow Group plc
Mid Glamorgan
Dŵr Cymru Welsh Water
Hoover Ltd
Sony Europe Limited

Vale of Glamorgan

Dow Corning Ltd

Overseas

Gibraltar

bwin.party

Useful contacts

In this section we list national agencies which may be helpful in the context of company giving, under the general headings: employees/ professional advice, sponsorship, enterprise and training, education, donations, promoting good practice, media and general company information.

Employees/ professional advice

Business in the Community

137 Shepherdess Walk
London
N1 7RQ

Tel: 020 7566 8650
Email: info@bitc.org.uk
Web: www.bitc.org.uk

Chartered Surveyors Voluntary Service

Most large towns and rural areas in the UK are covered by CSVS (Charity Commission no. 1043479). If you feel that the CSVS could benefit you they can be contacted through your Citizens Advice (Citizens Advice) and other advice agencies.

Tel: 0870 333 1600
Email: csvs@rics.org
Web: www.ricsfirms.co.uk

Community Service Volunteers (CSV)

18–24 Lower Clapton Road
London
E5 0PD
Tel: 020 3780 5870
Web: www.csv.org.uk

Life Academy

Beechwood House
Christchurch Road
Newport
NP19 8AJ

Tel: 01633 548026
Email: info@life-academy.co.uk
Web: www.life-academy.co.uk

ProHelp

c/o Business in the Community
137 Shepherdess Walk
London
N1 7RQ

Tel: 020 7566 8650
Web: www.bitc.org.uk

REACH (Retired Executives Action Clearing House)

89 Albert Embankment
London
SE1 7TP

Tel: 020 7582 6543
Web: www.reachskills.org.uk

Volunteering England (Part of NCVO)

Society Building
8 All Saints Street
London
N1 9RL

Tel: 020 7713 6161
Web: www.volunteering.org.uk

Sponsorship

Community Links

Canning Town Public Hall
105 Barking Road
Canning Town
London
E16 4HQ

Tel: 020 7473 2270
Web: www.community-links.org

Groundwork UK

Lockside
5 Scotland Street
Birmingham
B1 2RR

Tel: 01212 368565
Email: info@groundwork.org.uk
Web: www.groundwork.org.uk

Enterprise and training

Common Purpose UK

Common Purpose
Discovery House
28–42 Banner Street
London
EC1Y 8QE

Tel: 020 7608 8118
Email:
enquiries@commonpurpose.org.uk
Web: www.commonpurpose.org.uk

There are regional offices throughout the UK.

Community Development Foundation (CDF)
Headquarters
Unit 5, Angel Gate
320–326 City Road
London
EC1V 2PT

Tel: 020 7833 1772
Email: admin@cdf.org.uk
Web: www.cdf.org.uk

National Enterprise Network
12 Stephenson Court
Fraser Road
Priory Business Park
Bedford
MK44 3WJ

Tel: 01234 831623
Email: enquiries@nationalenterprisenetwork.org
Web: www.nfea.com

Education

Confederation of British Industry (CBI)
Cannon Place
78 Cannon Street
London
EC4N 6HN

Tel: 020 7379 7400
Email: enquiries@cbi.org.uk
Web: www.cbi.org.uk

National Centre for Universities and Business
Studio 11
Tiger House
Burton Street
London
WC1H 9BY

Tel: 020 7383 7667
Email: ncub@ncub.co.uk
Web: www.ncub.co.uk

The Work Foundation
The Work Foundation
21 Palmer Street
London
SW1H 0AD

Tel: 020 7976 3509
Email: info@theworkfoundation.com
Web: www.theworkfoundation.com

Donations

CAF (Charities Aid Foundation)
25 Kings Hill Avenue
Kings Hill
West Malling
Kent
ME19 4TA

Tel: 03000 123 000
Web: www.cafonline.org

Charities Trust
Suite 20–22
Century Building
Brunswick Business Park
Tower Street
Liverpool
L3 4BJ

Tel: 01512 865129
Web: www.charitiestrust.org

Charity Commission
London
2nd Floor
One Drummond Gate
Victoria
London
SW1V 2QQ

Liverpool
Redgrave Court
Bootle
L20 7HS

Taunton
Woodfield House
Tangier
Taunton
Somerset
TA1 4BL

Newport
Room 1.364
Government Buildings
Cardiff Road
Newport
NP10 8XG

In Kind Direct
62–64 Cornhill
London
EC3V 3PL

Tel: 0300 30 20 200
Web: www.inkinddirect.org

ShareGift
17 Carlton House Terrace
London
SW1Y 5AH

Tel: 020 7930 3737
Web: www.sharegift.org

Workplace Giving UK
2nd Floor
Cavendish House
369 Burnt Oak Broadway
Edgware
Middlesex
HA8 5AW

Tel: 020 8731 5125
Web: www.workplacegiving-uk.co.uk

Promoting good practice

Business in the Community
137 Shepherdess Walk
London
N1 7RQ

Tel: 020 7566 8650
Web: www.bitc.org.uk

Scottish Business in the Community
Livingstone House
First Floor (East)
43a Discovery Terrace
Heriott-Watt Research Park
Edinburgh
EH14 4AP

Tel 01314 511100
Email: info@sbcscot.com
Web: www.sbcscot.com

Charities Tax Group (CTG)
Church House
Great Smith Street
London
SW1P 3AZ

Tel: 020 7222 1265
Email: info@charitytax.info
Web: www.ctrg.org.uk

Corporate Citizenship
Holborn Gate
26 Southampton Buildings
London
WC2A 1PQ

Tel: 020 7861 1616
Email: mail@corporate-citizenship.com
Web: www.corporate-citizenship.com

Institute of Corporate Responsibility and Sustainability
Durham House
Durham House Street
London
WC2N 6HG

Tel: 020 7839 0199
Email: info@icrs.info
Web: www.icrs.info

Directory of Social Change
London
Resource for London
356 Holloway Road
London
N7 6PA

Tel: 0845 077 7707

Liverpool
Suites 103–106
1 Old Hall Street
Liverpool
L3 9HG

Research: 0151 708 0117

International Business Leaders Forum (IBLF)
30 Hardcourt Street
London
W1H 4AA

Tel: 020 3355 5464
Web: www.iblfglobal.org

The London Benchmarking Group
c/o Corporate Citizenship
5th Floor Holborn Gate
330 High Holborn
London
WC1V 7QG

Tel: 020 7861 1616
Email: lbg@corporate-citizenship.com
Web: www.lbg-online.net

Media

BBC Charity Appeals Office
BC2 A1 Broadcast Centre
201 Wood Lane
London
W12 7TP

Tel: 020 8752 7044
Email: charityappeals@bbc.co.uk
Web: www.bbc.co.uk/charityappeals

Campaign for Press and Broadcasting Freedom
2nd Floor
Vi and Garner Smith House
23 Orford Road
Walthamstow
London
E17 9NL

Tel: 07729 846 146
Email: freepress@cpbf.org.uk
Web: www.cpbf.org.uk

Channel Four Television Company
Channel 4 Enquiries
PO Box 1058
Belfast
BT1 9DU

Tel: 0345 076 0191
Web: www.channel4.com

CSV Action Network
237 Pentonville Road
London
N1 9NJ

Tel: 020 7278 6601
Web: www.csv.org.uk/campaigns/csv-action-network

ITV Network Centre
200 Gray's Inn Road
London
WC1X 8HF

Tel: 020 7156 6000
Web: www.itv.com

Media Trust
Centre House
56 Wood Lane
London
W12 7SB

Tel: 020 7871 5600
Email: info@mediatrust.org
Web: www.mediatrust.org

General company information

Companies House
Crown Way
Maindy
Cardiff
CF14 3UZ

Tel: 0303 1234 500
Email: enquiries@companies house.gov.uk
Web: www.companieshouse.gov.uk

Co-operative and Community Finance
Brunswick Court
Brunswick Square
Bristol
BS2 8PE

Tel: 01179 166750
Web: www.coopfinance.coop

UK Regeneration
10 Mount Row
London
W1K 3SA

Email: info@ukregeneration.org.uk
Web: www.ukregeneration.org.uk

Trades Union Congress (TUC)
Congress House
Great Russell Street
London
WC1B 3LS

Tel: 020 7636 4030
Web: www.tuc.org.uk

URBED (Urbanism Environment Design)
The Building Centre
26 Store Street
London
WC1E 7BT

Tel: 01612 005500
Email: info@urbed.coop
Web: www.urbed.com

Young Enterprise UK
Peterley House
Peterley Road
Oxford
OX4 2TZ

Tel. 01865 776845
Email: info@y-e.org.uk
Web: www.young-enterprise.org.uk

Company activity listing

This section classifies the companies included in the guide according to their main activities. It should enable charities to target companies for specific appeals or services. Companies which fall into two or more categories are listed under each one, except in the more obvious cases. For example, building companies and property companies, where the categories have been cross-referenced. Retailers have been split into further categories due to the variety covered.

Accountants

Accenture UK Ltd
Caledonia Investments
KPMG LLP
Mazars LLP
PricewaterhouseCoopers LLP

Acquisitions

UK Asset Resolution
Unipart Group of Companies Ltd

Advertising/marketing

Abbott Mead Vickers – BBDO Ltd
DDB UK Ltd
WPP plc

Aerospace

BAE Systems plc
Cobham plc
QinetiQ Group plc
Senior plc
Smiths Group plc
Thales UK Ltd

Agriculture

Alan Hudson Ltd
Man Group plc
Pfizer Ltd
Yattendon Group plc (formerly Yattendon Investment Trust)

Airport Operators

Bournemouth International Airport Ltd
Bristol Airport Ltd
East Midlands Airport
Heathrow Airport Holdings Ltd (formerly BAA Ltd)
Manchester Airport Group plc
Stansted Airport Ltd

Aviation

British Airways plc
John Swire & Sons Ltd
Virgin Atlantic Two Ltd (formerly Virgin Atlantic Ltd)

Banking

Bank of England
Barclays PLC
CIBC World Markets plc
Close Brothers Group plc
Clydesdale Bank plc
Co-operative Group Ltd
Coutts & Co
Deutsche Bank
Goldman Sachs International
HSBC Holdings plc
Lloyds Banking Group
N. M. Rothschild & Sons Ltd
The Royal Bank of Scotland Group plc
Santander UK plc

Brewers/distillers

Adnams plc
Daniel Thwaites plc
Diageo plc
Greene King plc
Marston's plc

Building materials

Aggregate Industries Ltd
SIG plc
Travis Perkins plc

Building Society

Bradford & Bingley plc
Coventry Building Society
Leeds Building Society
Nationwide Building Society
Newcastle Building Society
Nottingham Building Society
Principality Building Society
Yorkshire Building Society

Building/construction

Amec Foster Wheeler plc (formerly Amec plc)
Avant Homes Group Ltd (formerly Gladedale Group Holdings Ltd)
Barratt Developments plc
Bellway plc
Berkeley Group plc
Carillion plc
CEMEX UK Operations Ltd
Esh Group
Keepmoat Ltd
Kier Group plc
Miller Group Ltd
Persimmon plc
Redrow Group plc
Shepherd Building Group Ltd
Sir Robert McAlpine Ltd
Synthomer plc (formerly Yule Catto and Co.)
Taylor Wimpey plc
Travis Perkins plc
Wates Group Ltd
Willmott Dixon Holdings plc

Business Services
Ashmore Group plc
Balfour Beatty plc
Domino Printing Sciences plc
Economist Newspaper Ltd
ERM Group Holdings Ltd
Fidessa Group plc
Informa plc
Logica Ltd (formerly Logica plc)
Micro Focus International plc
MITIE Group plc
Rentokil Initial plc

Cash 'n' Carry
Bestway (Holdings) Ltd
Booker Group plc
Dhamecha Holdings Ltd

Catalogue shopping
Findel plc
Mothercare plc

Catering Services
Punch Taverns
Sodexo Ltd

Chemicals and plastics
3M United Kingdom plc
BASF plc
Bayer plc
Dow Chemical Company Ltd
Dow Corning Ltd
Elementis plc
Fenner PLC
Pfizer Ltd
Scott Bader Company Ltd
Synthomer plc (formerly Yule Catto and Co.)

Clothing manufacture
GAP (UK Holdings) Ltd

Commodity traders
Cargill plc

Computer software
Game Digital plc (formerly The Game Group plc)
Microsoft Ltd
RM plc
Steria Ltd

Confectionery
Lofthouse of Fleetwood Ltd

Consultancy
ERM Group Holdings Ltd
RPS Group Plc
SDL plc
Steria Ltd

Consulting engineers
Amec Foster Wheeler plc (formerly Amec plc)
Arup Group Ltd
Babcock International Group plc

Dairy products
Dairy Crest Group plc
Müller UK and Ireland Group LLP (the entry formerly related to Robert Wiseman Dairies Ltd)

Defence
BAE Systems plc
HESCO Bastion Ltd
QinetiQ Group plc
Thales UK Ltd

Distribution
Bunzl plc
Cargill plc
Electrocomponents plc
John Menzies plc
SIG plc

Domestic appliances
Dyson Ltd
Hoover Ltd

Drinks Manufacture
A. G. Barr plc
Britvic Soft Drinks plc
Coca-Cola Holdings (United Kingdom) Ltd
Nestlé Holdings (UK) plc

Electricity
Drax Group plc
EDF Energy PLC
National Grid plc
Northern Powergrid Holdings Company (formerly C E Electric UK Funding Company)
PPL WW Holdings Ltd (Western Power Distribution)
Scottish and Southern Energy plc
ScottishPower UK plc
United Utilities Group PLC

Electronics/computers
CEF Holdings Ltd
Cobham plc
Filtronic plc
IBM United Kingdom Ltd
Philips Electronics UK Ltd
Premier Farnell plc
Samsung Electronics (UK) Ltd
Siemens plc
Sony Europe Ltd
Toshiba Information Systems (UK) Ltd
Unisys Ltd

Engineering
Aggreko plc
Amec Foster Wheeler plc (formerly Amec plc)
BBA Aviation plc
Biwater Holdings Ltd
Bodycote plc
Cummins Ltd
Dyson Ltd
GKN plc
IMI plc
Marshall of Cambridge (Holdings) Ltd
Meggitt PLC
Network Rail Infrastructure Ltd
Premier Farnell plc
Rolls-Royce Holdings plc
Rotork plc
Sir Robert McAlpine Ltd
Smiths Group plc
Spectris plc
Spirax Sarco Engineering plc
Thales UK Ltd

Financial services
3i Group plc
Aberdeen Asset Management plc
Alliance Trust PLC
Apax Partners LLP
Bank of Ireland UK (plc)
BC Partners Ltd
BlackRock Investment Management (UK) Ltd
The British Land Company plc
Caledonia Investments
Capital One (Europe) plc
Close Brothers Group plc
Doughty Hanson & Co. Managers Ltd
Family Assurance Friendly Society Ltd
FIL Holdings (UK) Ltd (formerly Fidelity Investment Management Ltd)
Henderson Group plc
HSBC Holdings plc
ICAP plc
Impetus – The Private Equity Foundation
International Personal Finance
intu Properties plc (formerly Capital Shopping Centres Group plc)
Legal & General Group plc
Liverpool Victoria
Lloyds Banking Group
Man Group plc
Marks and Spencer Group plc
The Midcounties Co-operative
Morgan Stanley International Ltd
NRAM plc (formerly Northern Rock (Asset Management) plc)
PricewaterhouseCoopers LLP
Principality Building Society
Provident Financial plc

Prudential plc
Rathbone Brothers Plc
The Royal Bank of Scotland Group plc
Saga plc
Schroders plc
St James's Place plc
Yorkshire Building Society

Food manufacture

Arla Foods Ltd
Baxters Food Group Ltd
Bernard Matthews Ltd
Diageo plc
Greggs plc
H. J. Heinz Manufacturing UK Ltd (formerly H J Heinz Company Ltd)
McCain Foods (GB) Ltd
Mondelez UK Ltd (formerly Kraft Foods UK Ltd)
Nestlé Holdings (UK) plc
Northern Foods Ltd
Organix Brands Ltd
Premier Foods plc
Tate & Lyle plc
Warburtons Ltd
Weetabix Ltd

Food services

Cargill plc
Duchy Originals Ltd
Ocado Group Ltd
Organix Brands Ltd
Punch Taverns plc
Sodexo Ltd

Furniture manufacture

Cadogan Group Ltd

Gaming

Betfair Group Ltd
bwin.party
Camelot UK Lotteries Ltd
Genting UK plc (formerly Genting Stanley plc)
Ladbrokes PLC
Sportech plc
Sportingbet Ltd (formerly Sportingbet plc)
William Hill plc

Health/beauty products

Avon Cosmetics Ltd
Lush Cosmetics Ltd
Mascolo Ltd
Procter & Gamble UK
Synergy Health plc

Healthcare

Alliance Boots Holdings Ltd
AXA UK plc
Baxter Healthcare Ltd
Bupa Ltd
GE Healthcare Ltd
GlaxoSmithKline plc
Pfizer Ltd
Procter & Gamble UK
Reckitt Benckiser Group plc
Synergy Health plc

Hotels

Adnams plc
Ladbrokes plc
Whitbread plc

Household

P. Z. Cussons plc
S. C. Johnson Ltd
Procter & Gamble UK
Reckitt Benckiser Group plc
Wilko Retail Ltd (formerly Wilkinson Hardware Stores Ltd)

Industrial products/services

Rexam plc
Rolls-Royce Holdings plc
Rotork plc
Senior plc
Spectris plc
Spirax Sarco Engineering plc

Information management and communication

Accenture UK Ltd
Informa plc
Ricardo-AEA
RM plc
SDL plc
Smiths Group plc
TelecityGroup
WPP plc

Information Technology

Aveva Group plc
Computacenter plc
Doughty Hanson & Co. Managers Ltd
Fujitsu Services Holdings PLC
HP Enterprise Services UK Ltd
Keysight Technologies UK Ltd (formerly Agilent Technologies UK Ltd)
Ricardo-AEA
SDL plc

Instrumentation

Unipart Group of Companies Ltd

Insurance

Admiral Group plc
Aegon (Scottish Equitable plc)
Ageas (UK) Ltd
Allianz Insurance plc
Amlin plc
Aviva plc
AXA UK plc
Beazley plc
Bupa Ltd
Congregational & General Insurance plc
Co-operative Group Ltd
Ecclesiastical Insurance Group plc
Friends Life Group plc (formerly Friends Provident plc)
Jardine Lloyd Thompson Group plc
Liverpool Victoria
Lloyd's
Marsh Ltd
The National Farmers Union Mutual Insurance Society Ltd
Novae Group plc
Personal Group Holdings plc
Prudential plc
The Royal Bank of Scotland Group plc
The Royal London Mutual Insurance Society Ltd
RSA Insurance Group plc
Saga plc
UIA (Insurance) Ltd
Unum Ltd
Zurich Financial Services (UKISA) Ltd

Legal

Addleshaw Goddard LLP
Co-operative Group Ltd
Freshfields Bruuckhaus Deringer LLP
Saga plc
Simmons & Simmons LLP
Slaughter and May (Trust Ltd)
Wragge Lawrence Graham & Co. LLP

Leisure

Caledonia Investments
Center Parcs Ltd
Deep Sea Leisure plc
Ladbrokes PLC
Saga plc
The Rank Group plc
Thomas Cook Group plc
Virgin Atlantic Two Ltd (formerly Virgin Atlantic Ltd)
J. D. Wetherspoon plc
Whitbread plc
William Hill plc
Yattendon Group plc (formerly Yattendon Investment Trust)

Life assurance

Zurich Financial Services (UKISA) Ltd

Logistics

John Menzies plc
Stobart Group
TNT UK Ltd
UPS (Ltd)

Manufacturing
Caparo Group Ltd
Euro Packaging UK Ltd
Imagination Technologies Group plc
Morgan Advanced Materials plc
Rexam plc
Senior plc
Swann-Morton Ltd
Tata Steel Europe Ltd
Thales UK Ltd

Marine
Babcock International Group plc
Forth Ports plc
John Swire & Sons Ltd
The Mersey Docks and Harbour Company Ltd
QinetiQ Group plc
RPS Group Plc

Media
Archant
Bloomsbury Publishing plc
British Sky Broadcasting Group plc
Economist Newspaper Ltd
Future plc
Guardian Media Group plc
ITV plc
National Magazine Co. Ltd
Northern Shell & Media Group Ltd (entry formerly titled Northern & Shell Network Ltd)
STV Group plc
Telegraph Media Group Ltd
Thomson Reuters (Reuters Ltd)
Time Inc. (UK) Ltd (formerly IPC Media Ltd)
Trinity Mirror plc
Yattendon Group plc (formerly Yattendon Investment Trust)

Metals
Johnson Matthey plc
Tata Steel Europe Ltd

Mining
Anglo American plc
The Banks Group Ltd
BHP Billiton
Celtic Energy Ltd
Rio Tinto plc

Miscellaneous
Amey UK plc
Johnson Service Group plc
The Midcounties Co-operative
Moneysupermarket.com Group plc
Royal Mail plc

Motors and accessories
Arriva plc
BMW UK Ltd
Citroen UK Ltd
Ford Motor Company Ltd
General Motors UK Ltd (Vauxhall Motors)
Honda of the UK Manufacturing Ltd
Inchcape plc
Jaguar Land Rover Ltd
Michelin Tyre plc
Speedy 1 Ltd (holding company of Kwik Fit Group Ltd)
Toyota Motor Manufacturing (UK) Ltd
Unipart Group of Companies Ltd

Oil and gas/fuel
Air Products Group Ltd
Amec Foster Wheeler plc (formerly Amec plc)
BP plc
Calor Gas Ltd
RPS Group Plc
Scottish and Southern Energy plc
Shell (UK Ltd)
United Utilities Group PLC
Valero Energy UK Ltd (formerly Valero Energy Ltd)

Personal care products
Colgate-Palmolive UK Ltd
Mascolo Ltd
Procter & Gamble UK
Reckitt Benckiser Group plc

Pharmaceuticals
Alliance Boots Holdings Ltd
AstraZeneca
BTG plc
Co-operative Group Ltd
P. Z. Cussons plc
GlaxoSmithKline plc
Hikma Pharmaceuticals PLC
Merck Sharp & Dohme Ltd
Reckitt Benckiser Group plc
Shire Pharmaceuticals Group
Synthomer plc (formerly Yule Catto and Co.)

Print/paper/packaging
Bunzl plc
Domino Printing Sciences plc
Rexam plc
D. S. Smith Holdings plc
Tullis Russell Group Ltd
Xerox (UK) Ltd
Yattendon Group plc (formerly Yattendon Investment Trust)

Professional support services
Accenture UK Ltd
Impetus – The Private Equity Foundation
SDL plc
Steria Ltd
Stobart Group
Tullis Russell Group Ltd
Unipart Group of Companies Ltd
Unisys Ltd
WSP Group Ltd

Property
Amec Foster Wheeler plc (formerly Amec plc)
Avant Homes Group Ltd (formerly Gladedale Group Holdings Ltd)
The Banks Group Ltd
Berkeley Group plc
The British Land Company plc
Broadland Properties Ltd
Bruntwood Group Ltd
Cadogan Group Ltd
Caledonia Investments
Canary Wharf Group plc
Dhamecha Holdings Ltd
Doughty Hanson & Co. Managers Ltd
Evans Property Group Ltd
Grainger plc
Great Portland Estates plc
Grosvenor Group
Hammerson plc
Helical bar plc
John Swire & Sons Ltd
Miller Group Ltd
Muir Group plc
Paragon Group of Companies plc
Ravensale Ltd
Redrow Group plc
Ridgesave Ltd
Shaftesbury plc
St Modwen Properties plc
UNITE Group plc
Yattendon Group plc (formerly Yattendon Investment Trust)

Quarrying
Aggregate Industries Ltd
Lafarge Aggregates Ltd

Retail – clothing and footwear
Dunelm Group plc
GAP (UK Holdings) Ltd
JD Sports Fashion plc
Marks and Spencer Group plc
Next plc
Shoe Zone Ltd
TJX UK (formerly TK Maxx)

Retail – Department and variety stores
Central England Co-operative
Co-operative Group Ltd
Debenhams plc
Dunelm Group plc
Fenwick Ltd
Highland Group Holdings Ltd (entry formerly House of Fraser (Stores) Ltd)

Index